Cisco CCNP ROUTE Simplified

Your Complete Guide to Passing the
CCNP ROUTE Exam

Paul Browning (LLB Hons) CCNP, MCSE
Farai Tafa dual CCIE

ISBN: 978-0-9557815-7-5

Published by:
Reality Press Ltd.
Midsummer Court
314 Midsummer Blvd.
Milton Keynes
MK9 2UB
help@reality-press.com

LEGAL NOTICE

The advice in this book is designed to help you achieve the standard of Cisco Certified Network Engineer which is Cisco's foundation internetworking examination. A CCNA is able to carry out basic router and switch installations and troubleshooting. Before you carry out more complex operations it is advisable to seek the advice of experts or Cisco Systems, Inc.

The practical scenarios in this book are meant to illustrate a technical point only and should be used on your privately owned equipment only and never on a live network.

INTRODUCTION

Thank you for purchasing *Cisco CCNP ROUTE Simplified.*

The ROUTE exam is acknowledged as one of Cisco's most difficult exams and many who start on the journey towards the coveted CCNP certification fall down at this first hurdle. Perhaps it is due to the overwhelming amount of information they need to digest and understand, or perhaps it is because what they are trying to learn never seems to sink in.

If you have ever struggled to retain what you have read or have struggled to apply your knowledge to a live network, then we know how you feel; we felt the same way, which is why we decided to develop our own learning materials. *Cisco CCNP ROUTE Simplified* has been written with the busy student in mind. We understand that many of you are studying around a full-time job, as well as family and other commitments. For this reason, we decided to strip out all of the usual 'fluff' you find in most Cisco manuals and give you the information you need to pass your ROUTE exam AND apply what you have learned to a live Cisco network.

Passing your ROUTE exams will give you a massive boost in confidence, as well as dramatically improve your ability as a Cisco network engineer. Once you understand the major routing concepts, you will find the other CCNP materials much easier to understand and apply. Passing the CCNP certification will also give you a very strong foundation for becoming an IT contractor, consultant, designer, or even a voice or security engineer.

In order to become a CCNP engineer, you will need to pass the following exams (preferably in this order):

    642-902 ROUTE—Implementing Cisco IP Routing
    642-813 SWITCH—Implementing Cisco IP Switched Networks
    642-832 TSHOOT—Troubleshooting and Maintaining Cisco IP Networks

We have broken down each chapter of this book to match exam requirements and have added more information when needed to give you a deeper understanding of the technologies introduced. Each chapter ends with a review and the book finishes with several hands-on labs for you to follow on our live racks (at http://racks.howtonetwork.net) or on your own home lab.

Aim to take your ROUTE exam after around 60 to 90 days of studying 2 to 3 hours per day. If you are a member of www.howtonetwork.net, then please ensure that you make use of the other study materials, including the flash cards and exams, as well as the CCIE-moderated forum.

Best of luck with your studies.

Paul Browning

Farai Tafa

ABOUT THE AUTHORS

Paul Browning

Paul Browning is the author of CCNA Simplified, which is one of the industry's leading CCNA study guides. Paul previously worked for Cisco TAC but left in 2002 to start his own Cisco training company in the UK. Paul has taught over 2,000 Cisco engineers with both his classroom-based courses and his online Cisco training site, www. howtonetwork.net. Paul lives in the UK with his wife and daughter.

Farai Tafa

Farai Tafa is a Dual CCIE in both Routing and Switching and Service Provider. Farai currently works for one of the world's largest telecoms companies as a network engineer. He has also written workbooks for the CCNA, CCNP, and Cisco Security exams. Farai lives in Washington, D.C. with his wife and daughter.

TABLE OF CONTENTS

PART 1

Theory

CHAPTER 1

Internet Protocol Routing Fundamentals

Welcome to the ROUTE course of the Cisco Certified Network Professional (CCNP) certification program. The focus of this guide is to pick up on IP routing concepts where the Cisco Certified Network Administrator (CCNA) certification program left off. In addition, this guide will introduce and explain, in detail, additional relevant concepts that are mandatory requirements of the current ROUTE certification exam.

The ROUTE certification exam focuses primarily on the implementation of IP routing protocols within the enterprise network. In addition, you are also expected to demonstrate a solid theoretical and practical understanding of routing solutions to support remote offices as well as mobile workers. These concepts will be covered in detail in this guide. This chapter lays the foundation for the core concepts that will be described throughout this guide. The Internet Protocol routing foundation topics that will be covered in this chapter include the following:

- Internet Protocol Routing Fundamentals
- Flat and Hierarchical Routing Algorithms
- IP Addressing and Address Summarization
- Administrative Distance
- Routing Protocol Metrics
- Prefix Matching
- Building the IP Routing Table or RIB
- Routing Protocol Classes
- The Objectives of Routing Protocols
- On-Demand Routing (ODR)

INTERNET PROTOCOL ROUTING FUNDAMENTALS

A routing protocol allows a router to learn dynamically how to reach other networks. A routing protocol also allows the router to exchange learned network information with other routers or hosts. Routing protocols may be used for connecting interior (internal) campus networks as well as for connecting different enterprises or routing domains. Different routing protocols use different means of determining the best or most optimal path to a network or network node.

Some types of routing protocols work best in static environments or environments with few or no changes, but they might take a long time to converge when changes to those environments are made. Other routing protocols, however, respond very quickly to changes in the network and can converge rapidly. Network convergence occurs when all routers in the network have the same view and agree on optimal routes. When convergence takes a long time to occur, intermittent packet loss and loss of connectivity may be experienced between remote networks. In addition to these problems, slow convergence can result in network routing loops and outright network outages. Convergence is determined by the routing protocol algorithm used.

Because routing protocols have different characteristics, they differ in their scalability and performance. Some routing protocols are suitable only for small networks, while others may be used in small, medium, and large networks. Therefore, in addition to understanding the intricacies of routing protocols, it is also important to have a solid understanding of when and in what situation one routing protocol would be used versus another.

FLAT AND HIERARCHICAL ROUTING ALGORITHMS

Routing protocol algorithms operate using either a flat routing system or a hierarchical routing system. A hierarchical routing system uses a layered approach wherein routers are placed in logical groupings referred to as domains, areas, or autonomous systems. This allows different routers within the network to perform specific tasks, optimizing the functionality performed at those layers. Some routers in the hierarchical system can communicate with other routers in other domains or areas, while other routers can communicate only with routers in the same domain or area. This reduces the amount of information that routers in the domain or area must process, which allows for faster convergence within the network.

A flat routing system has no hierarchy. In such systems, routers must typically be connected to every other router in the network and each router essentially has the same function. Such algorithms work well in very small networks, however, they are not scalable. In addition, as the network grows, troubleshooting becomes much more difficult because instead of just focusing your efforts on certain areas, for example, you now have to look at the entire network.

The primary advantage afforded by hierarchical routing systems is their scalability. Hierarchical routing systems also allow for easier changes to the network, in much the same way afforded by the traditional hierarchical design comprised of the Core, Distribution, and Access layers. In addition, hierarchical algorithms can be used to reduce routing update traffic as well as routing table size in certain areas of the network while still allowing full network connectivity.

IP ADDRESSING AND ADDRESS SUMMARIZATION

An IP address is divided into two parts. The first part designates the network address while the second part designates the host address. When designing a network, an IP addressing scheme is used to uniquely identify hosts and devices within the network. The IP addressing scheme should be hierarchical and should build on the traditional logical hierarchical model. This allows the addressing scheme to provide designated points in the network where effective route summarization can be performed.

Summarization reduces the amount of information that routers must process, which allows for faster convergence within the network. Summarization also restricts the size of the area that is affected by network changes by hiding detailed topology information from certain areas within the network. This concept is illustrated in Figure 1-1 below:

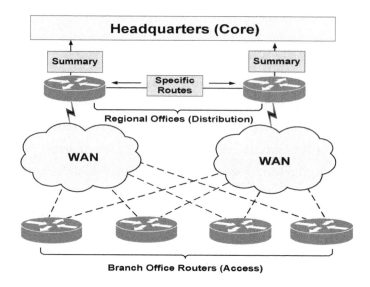

Fig. 1-1. Route Summarization

Referencing Figure 1-1, the branch offices (Access layer) are dual-homed to the regional office routers (Distribution layer). Using a hierarchical addressing scheme allows the Distribution layer routers to advertise a summary route for the branch office subnets to the Core layer. This protects the Core layer from the effects of any route flapping between the Distribution and the Access layer routers because a summary route will not flap until every last one of the more specific prefixes from which it is derived is removed from the routing table. This increases stability within the area. In addition, the routing table size at the Core layer is further reduced.

ADMINISTRATIVE DISTANCE

Administrative distance is used to determine the reliability of one source of routing information from another. Some sources are considered more reliable than others are; therefore, administrative distance can be used to determine the best or preferred path to a destination network or network node when there are two or more different paths to the same destination from two or more different routing protocols.

In Cisco IOS software, all sources of routing information are assigned a default administrative distance value. This default value is an integer between 0 and 255, with a value of 0 assigned to the most reliable source of information and a value of 255 being assigned to the least reliable source of information. Any routes that are assigned an administrative distance value of 255 are considered untrusted and will not be placed into the routing table.

The administrative distance is a locally significant value that affects only the local router. This value is not propagated throughout the routing domain. Therefore, manually adjusting the default administrative distance for a routing source or routing sources on a router affects the preference of routing information sources only on that router. Table 1-1 below shows the default administrative values used in Cisco IOS software:

Table 1-1. Administrative Distance Values

Route Source	AD
Connected Interfaces	0
Static Routes	1
Enhanced Interior Gateway Routing Protocol (EIGRP) Summary Routes	5
External Border Gateway Protocol (eBGP) Routes	20
Internal Enhanced Interior Gateway Routing Protocol (EIGRP) Routes	90
Open Shortest Path First (OSPF) Internal and External Routes	110
Intermediate System-Intermediate System (IS-IS) Internal and External Routes	115
Routing Information Protocol (RIP) Routes	120
Exterior Gateway Protocol (EGP) Routes	140
On-Demand Routing (ODR) Routes	160
External Enhanced Interior Gateway Routing Protocol (EIGRP) Routes	170
Internal Border Gateway Protocol (iBGP) Routes	200
Unreachable or Unknown Routes	255

The default route source administrative distance is displayed in the output of the `show ip protocols` command. This is illustrated in the following output:

```
R1#show ip protocols
Routing Protocol is "isis"
  Invalid after 0 seconds, hold down 0, flushed after 0
  Outgoing update filter list for all interfaces is not set
  Incoming update filter list for all interfaces is not set
  Redistributing: isis
  Address Summarization:
    None
  Maximum path: 4
  Routing for Networks:
    Serial0/0
```

```
Routing Information Sources:
  Gateway          Distance     Last Update
  10.0.0.2            115        00:06:53
Distance: (default is 115)
```

The administrative distance value assigned to an individual route is viewed in the output of the show ip route [prefix] command. This is illustrated in the following output:

```
R1#show ip route 150.1.1.0
Routing entry for 150.1.1.0/28
  Known via "isis", distance 115, metric 20, type level-2
  Redistributing via isis
  Last update from 10.0.0.2 on Serial0/0, 00:00:11 ago
  Routing Descriptor Blocks:
  * 10.0.0.2, from 150.1.1.2, via Serial0/0
      Route metric is 20, traffic share count is 1
```

In addition to allowing administrators to change the default administrative distance values of individual routing protocols, Cisco IOS software also allows administrators to adjust the administrative distance of individual prefixes learned via a dynamic routing protocol. This will be described in detail later in this guide.

ROUTING PROTOCOL METRICS

Routing protocol algorithms use metrics, which are numerical values that are associated with specific routes. These values are used to prioritize or prefer routes learned by the routing protocol from the most preferred to the least preferred. In essence, the lower the route metric, the more preferred the route by the routing protocol. The route with the lowest metric is typically the route with the least cost or the best route to the destination network. This route will be placed into the routing table and be used to forward packets to the destination network.

Different routing algorithms use different variables to compute the route metric. Some routing algorithms use only a single variable, while other advanced routing protocols may use more than one variable to determine the metric for a particular route. In most cases, the metrics that are computed by one routing protocol are incompatible with those used by other routing protocols. The different routing protocol metrics may be based on one or more of the following:

- Bandwidth
- Cost
- Delay
- Load
- Path Length
- Reliability

Bandwidth

The term bandwidth refers to the amount of data that can be carried from one point to another in a given time period. Routing algorithms may use bandwidth to determine which link type is preferred over another. For example, a routing algorithm might prefer a GigabitEthernet link over a FastEthernet link because of the increased capacity of the GigabitEthernet link over the FastEthernet link.

In Cisco IOS software, the `bandwidth` interface configuration command can be used to adjust the default bandwidth value for an interface, effectively manipulating the selection of one interface against another by a routing algorithm. For example, if the FastEthernet interface was configured with the `bandwidth 1000000` interface configuration command, both the FastEthernet and the GigabitEthernet links would appear to have the same capacity to the routing algorithm and would be assigned the same metric value. The fact that one of the links is actually a FastEthernet interface while the other is actually a GigabitEthernet link is irrelevant to the routing protocol.

From a network administrator's point of view, it is important to understand that the bandwidth command does not affect the physical capability of the interface. In other words, configuring the higher bandwidth on the FastEthernet interface does not mean that it is capable of supporting GigabitEthernet speeds. OSPF and EIGRP use bandwidth in metric calculation.

Cost

The cost, as it pertains to routing algorithms, refers to communication cost. The cost may be used when, for example, a company prefers to route across private links rather than public links that include monetary charges for sending data across them or for the usage time. Intermediate System-to-Intermediate System supports an optional expense metric that measures the monetary cost of link utilization. IS-IS is beyond the scope of the ROUTE exam requirements and will not be described in this guide.

Delay

There are many types of delay, all of which affect different types of traffic. In general, delay refers to the length of time required to move a packet from source to destination through the internetwork. In Cisco IOS software, the interface delay value is in microseconds (µs).

The interface value is configured using the `delay` interface configuration command. When you configure the interface delay value, it is important to remember that this does not affect traffic. For example, configuring a delay value of 5000 does not mean that traffic sent out of that interface will have an additional delay of 5000. Table 1-2 below shows the default delay values for common interfaces in Cisco IOS software:

Table1-2. Interface Delay Values

Interface Type	Delay (μs)
10 Mbps Ethernet	1000
FastEthernet	100
GigabitEthernet	10
T1 Serial	20000

Enhanced Interior Gateway Routing Protocol uses the interface delay value as part of its metric calculation. Manually adjusting the interface delay value results in the re-computation of the EIGRP metric.

Load

The term load means different things to different people. For example, in general computing terminology, load refers to the amount of work a resource, such as the CPU, is performing. Load, as it applies in this context, refers to the degree of use for a particular router interface. The load on the interface is a fraction of 255. For example, a load of 255/255 indicates that the interface is completely saturated, while a load of 128/255 indicates that the interface is 50% saturated. By default, the load is calculated as an average over a period of five minutes. The interface load value can be used by EIGRP in its metric calculation.

Path Length

The path length metric is the total length of the path that is traversed from the local router to the destination network. Different routing algorithms represent this in different forms. For example, Routing Information Protocol (RIP) counts all intermediate routers (hops) between the local router and the destination network and uses the hop count as the metric, while Border Gateway Protocol (BGP) counts the number of traversed autonomous systems between the local router and the destination network and uses the autonomous system count to select the best path.

Reliability

Like load, the term reliability means different things depending on the context in which it is used. In this guide, unless stated otherwise, it should always be assumed that reliability refers to the dependability of network links or interfaces. In Cisco IOS software, the reliability of a link or interface is represented as a fraction of 255. For example, a reliability value of 255/255 indicates the interface is 100% reliable. Similar to the interface load, by default the reliability of an interface is calculated as an average over a period of five minutes.

PREFIX MATCHING

Cisco routers use the longest prefix match rule when determining which of the routes placed into the routing table should be used to forward traffic to a destination network or node. Longer, or more specific routing table entries are preferred over less specific entries, such as summary addresses, when determining which entry to use to route traffic to the intended destination network or node.

The longest prefix or the most specific route will be used to route traffic to the destination network or node regardless of the administrative distance of the route source, or even the routing protocol metric assigned to the prefix if multiple overlapping prefixes are learned via the same routing protocol. Table 1-3 below illustrates the order of route selection on a router sending packets to the address 1.1.1.1. This order is based on the longest prefix match lookup.

Table1-3. Matching the Longest Prefix

Routing Table Entry	Order Used
1.1.1.1/32	1st
1.1.1.0/24	2nd
1.1.0.0/16	3rd
1.0.0.0/8	4th
0.0.0.0/0	5th

NOTE: Although the default route is listed last in the route selection order in Table 1-3, keep in mind that a default route is not always present in the routing table. If that is the case and no other entries to the address 1.1.1.1 exist, packets to that destination are simply discarded by the router. In most cases, the router will send the source host an ICMP message indicting that the destination is unreachable.

BUILDING THE IP ROUTING TABLE OR RIB

Without a populated routing table or Routing Information Base (RIB) that contains entries for remote networks, routers will not be able to forward packets to those remote networks. The routing table may include specific network entries or simply a single default route. The information in the routing table is used by the forwarding process to forward traffic to the destination network or host. The routing table itself does not actually forward traffic.

Cisco routers use the administrative distance, routing protocol metric, and the prefix length to determine which routes will actually be placed into the routing table, which allows the router to build the routing table. The routing table is built via the following general steps:

1. If the route entry does not currently exist in the routing table, add it to the routing table.
2. If the route entry is more specific than an existing route, add it to the routing table. It should also be noted that the less specific entry is still also retained in the routing table.
3. If the route entry is the same as an existing one, but is received from a more preferred route source, replace the old entry with the new entry.
4. If the route entry is the same as an existing one, and is received from the same protocol:
    e) Discard the new route if the metric is higher than the existing route; or
    f) Replace the existing route if the metric of the new route is lower; or
    g) If the metric for both routes is the same, use both routes for load-balancing.

When building the RIB by default, the routing protocol with the lowest administrative distance value will always win when the router is determining which routes to place into the routing table. For example, if a router receives the 10.0.0.0/8 prefix via external EIGRP, OSPF, and internal BGP, the OSPF route will be placed into the routing table. If that route is removed or is no longer received, the external EIGRP route will be placed into the routing table. Finally, if both the OSPF and the external EIGRP routes are no longer present, the internal BGP route is used.

Once routes have been placed into the routing table, by default the most specific or longest match prefix will always be preferred over less specific routes. This is illustrated in the following example, which shows a routing table that contains entries for the 80.0.0.0/8, 80.1.0.0/16, and the 80.1.1.0/24 prefixes. These three route prefixes are received via the EIGRP, OSPF, and RIP routing protocols, respectively.

```
R1#show ip route
Codes: C - connected, S - static, R - RIP, M - mobile, B - BGP
       D - EIGRP, EX - EIGRP external, O - OSPF, IA - OSPF inter area
       N1 - OSPF NSSA external type 1, N2 - OSPF NSSA external type 2
       E1 - OSPF external type 1, E2 - OSPF external type 2
       i - IS-IS, L1 - IS-IS level-1, L2 - IS-IS level-2, ia - IS-IS inter
       area
       * - candidate default, U - per-user static route, o - ODR
       P - periodic downloaded static route

Gateway of last resort is not set

R       80.1.1.0/24 [120/1] via 10.1.1.2, 00:00:04, Ethernet0/0.1
D       80.0.0.0/8 [90/281600] via 10.1.1.2, 00:02:02, Ethernet0/0.1
O E2    80.1.0.0/16 [110/20] via 10.1.1.2, 00:00:14, Ethernet0/0.1
```

Referencing the output shown above, the first route is the 80.1.1.0/24 route. This route is learned via RIP and therefore has a default administrative distance value of 120. The second route is the 80.0.0.0/8 route. This route is learned via internal EIGRP and therefore has a default administrative distance value of 90. The third route is the 80.1.0.0/16 route. This route is learned via OSPF and is an external OSPF route that has an administrative distance of 110.

NOTE: Because the routing protocol metrics are different, they are a non-factor in determining the best route to use when routes from multiple protocols are installed into the routing table. The following section will describe how Cisco IOS routers build the routing table.

Based on the contents of this routing table, if the router received a packet destined to 80.1.1.1, it would use the RIP route because this is the most specific entry, even though both EIGRP and OSPF have better administrative distance values and are therefore more preferred route sources. The show ip route 80.1.1.1 command illustrated below can be used to verify this statement:

```
R1#show ip route 80.1.1.1
Routing entry for 80.1.1.0/24
  Known via "rip", distance 120, metric 1
  Redistributing via rip
  Last update from 10.1.1.2 on Ethernet0/0.1, 00:00:15 ago
  Routing Descriptor Blocks:
  * 10.1.1.2, from 10.1.1.2, 00:00:15 ago, via Ethernet0/0.1
      Route metric is 1, traffic share count is 1
```

ROUTING PROTOCOL CLASSES

There are two major classes of routing protocols. These two classes are the Distance Vector and the Link State routing protocol classifications. Distance Vector routing protocols traditionally use a one-dimensional vector when determining the most optimal path(s) through the network, while Link State routing protocols use the Shortest Path First (SPF) when determining the most optimal path(s) through the network. Before delving into the specifics of these two classes of routing protocol, we will first take a look at vectors, as well as at the elusive SPF algorithm.

Understanding Vectors

A one-dimensional vector is a directed quantity. It is simply a quantity (number) in a particular direction or course. The vector concept is illustrated in Figure 1-2 below:

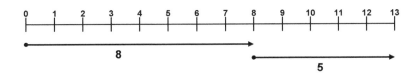

Fig. 1-2. Understanding Vectors

Referencing Figure 1-2, the first line starts at 0 and ends at 8, and the second line begins at 8 and ends at 13. The vector for the first line is 8, while the vector for the second line is 5. Using basic math, we know that 8 + 5 = 13. The starting and ending points of the vector are not relevant. Instead, the only thing that actually matters is how long the vector is and how far it travels.

NOTE: Vectors can also travel in the opposite direction (negative numbers).

The Shortest Path First Algorithm

The SPF algorithm creates a shortest-path tree to all hosts in an area or in the network backbone, with the router that is performing the calculation at the root of that tree. In order for the SPF algorithm to work in the correct manner, all routers in the area should have the same database information. In OSPF, this is performed via the database exchange process, which will be described in detail later in this guide. The SPF calculation is performed in iterations using three sets, as follows:

1. Unknown
2. Tentative (TENT)
3. PATH

When the SPF algorithm initializes, all nodes, except for the root, which is also referred to as 'self,' are placed in the Unknown set or list. The root is the router performing the SPF calculation. As SPF continues to run, nodes in the Unknown set are moved to the Tentative set beginning with the nodes directly connected to the root. The Tentative set is also commonly referred to simply as the TENT set or list.

As the router goes through the SPF calculation, the node in the TENT set or list that is closest to the root is moved to the PATH or PATHS list or set. This process is repeated until all nodes are in the PATH set and the shortest-path tree is built. Once the tree has been completely built, routes are then derived from the tree. This concept is illustrated referencing the basic network topology in Figure 1-3 below:

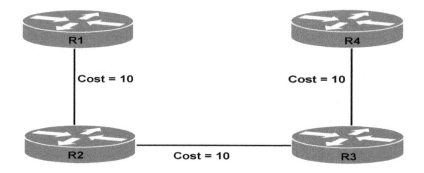

Fig. 1-3. Shortest Path First Algorithm

Referencing Figure 1-3, it is assumed that R1 is the router performing the SPF calculation. The following are the sequence of steps taken by this router:

R1 places itself in the PATH list with a next-hop of itself and a cost of 0. When R1 places itself in the PATH list, R1 is also referred to as the PATH node, in addition to being the SPF root. All other nodes or routers are temporarily placed in the Unknown set and have their cost presently set to infinity.

R1 examines the neighbors of the PATH node (itself) and because its only neighbor is R2, R1 adds R2 to the TENT list. Open Shortest Path First is able to do so by looking at the Link State Advertisement (LSA) packets that are exchanged during the database exchange and the synchronization process.

R1 calculates the cost to R2 from the PATH node. This is performed by adding the cost to the PATH node and the cost from the PATH node to the TENT node. In this example, the cost from R1 to the PATH node (itself) is 0, and the cost from the PATH node (R1) to the TENT node (R2) is 10. The total path cost to reach R2 from R1 is 0 + 10 = 10.

Because the cost of 10 is less than the cost of infinity that was initially assigned, the infinity value is overwritten with the cost value of 10. R2 is then moved to the PATH list.

Once R2 is placed in the PATH list, it becomes the newest PATH node and the second SPF iteration begins on R1. Remember, SPF stops when all nodes are in the PATH set.

1. R1 examines the neighbors of the new PATH node (R2), which are R3 and itself. Because R1 is already added to the PATH list (in step 1) it is ignored. R3, however, is moved from the Unknown set to the TENT set.
2. R1 calculates the cost to R3 by adding the cost to the PATH node (R2) and the cost from the PATH node (R2) to the TENT node (R3). The cost from R1 to the PATH node (R2) is 10, and the cost from the PATH node to the TENT node (R2) is 10. The total path cost to reach R3 from R1 is 10 + 10 = 20.
3. Because the cost of 20 is less than the cost of infinity that was initially assigned, the infinity value is overwritten with the cost value of 20. R3 is then moved to the PATH list.

This process is repeated until there are no more routers in the TENT list on any of the routers participating in OSPF. Figure 1-4 below shows the SPF tree as it would appear on routers R1 and R2:

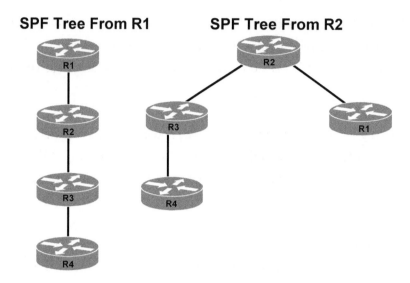

Fig. 1-4. SPF Tree on R1 and R2

Referencing the diagram in Figure 1-4, notice that the tree is built on the perspective of the root, which is the local router itself. Figure 1-5 below shows the SPF tree as it would appear on R3 and R4:

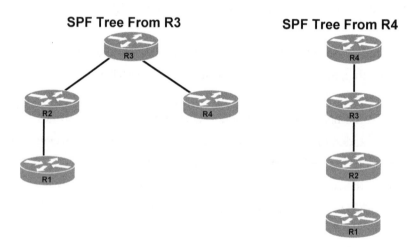

Fig. 1-5. SPF Tree on R3 and R4

Distance Vector Routing Protocols

A Distance Vector protocol is a routing protocol that uses distance or hop count as its primary metric for determining the best forwarding path. Distance Vector protocols are primarily based on the Bellman-Ford algorithm. Distance Vector routing protocols periodically send their neighbor routers copies of their entire routing tables to keep them up to date on the state of the network. While this may be acceptable in a small network, it increases the amount of traffic that is sent across networks as the size of the network grows. All Distance Vector routing protocols share the following characteristics:

- Counting to Infinity
- Split Horizon
- Poison Reverse
- Hold-Down Timers

Utilizing the counting to infinity characteristic, if a destination network is more than the maximum number of hops allowed for that routing protocol, it would be considered unreachable. The network entry would therefore not be installed into the IP routing table.

Split horizon mandates that routing information cannot be sent back out of the same interface through which it was received. This prevents the re-advertising of information back to the source from which it was learned. While this characteristic is a great loop prevention mechanism, it is also a significant drawback, especially in hub-and-spoke networks.

Poison reverse (or route poisoning) expands on split horizon. When used in conjunction with split horizon, poison reverse allows the networks to be advertised back out of the same interface on which they were received. However, poison reverse causes the router to advertise these networks back to the sending router with a metric of unreachable so that the router that receives those entries will not add them back into its routing table.

Hold-down timers are used to prevent networks that were previously advertised as down from being placed back into the routing table. When a router receives an update that a network is down, it begins its hold-down timer. This timer tells the router to wait for a specific amount of time before accepting any changes to the status of that network.

During the hold-down period, the router suppresses the network and prevents advertising false information. The router also does not route to the unreachable network, even if it receives information from another router (that may not have received the triggered update) that the network is reachable. This mechanism is designed to prevent black-holing traffic.

The two most common Distance Vector routing protocols are RIP and IGRP. Enhanced Interior Gateway Routing Protocol, which uses both Distance Vector and Link State features, is an advanced Distance Vector routing protocol.

Link State Routing Protocols

Link State routing protocols are hierarchical routing protocols that use the concept of areas to logically group routers within a network. This allows Link State protocols to scale better and operate in a more efficient manner than Distance Vector routing protocols. Routers running Link State routing protocols create a database that comprises the complete topology of the network. This allows all routers within the same area to have the same view of the network.

Because all routers in the network have the same view of the network, the most optimal paths are used for forwarding packets between networks and the possibility of routing loops is eliminated. Therefore, techniques such as split horizon and route poisoning do not apply to Link State routing protocols as they do to Distance Vector routing protocols.

Link State routing protocols operate by sending Link State Advertisements or Link State Packets to all other routers within the same area. These packets include information on attached interfaces, metrics, and other variables. As the routers accumulate this information, they run the SPF algorithm and calculate the shortest (best) path to each router and destination network.

Using the received Link State information, routers build the Link State Database (LSDB). When the LSDBs of two neighboring routers are synchronized, the routers are said to be adjacent.

Unlike Distance Vector routing protocols, which send their neighbors their entire routing table, Link State routing protocols send incremental updates when a change in the network topology is detected, which makes them more efficient in larger networks. The use of incremental updates also allows Link State routing protocols to respond much faster to network changes and thus converge in a shorter amount of time than Distance Vector routing protocols. Table 1-4 below lists the different Interior Gateway Protocols (IGPs) and their classification:

Table 1-4. IGP Classification

Protocol Name	Classful / Classless	Protocol Classification
RIP (version 1)	Classful	Distance Vector
IGRP	Classful	Distance Vector
RIP (version 2)	Classless	Distance Vector
EIGRP	Classless	Advanced Distance Vector
IS-IS	Classless	Link State
OSPF	Classless	Link State

NOTE: Although the Border Gateway Protocol (BGP) uses the autonomous system path or AS PATH to determine the best path to a destination network, it is not considered a Distance Vector routing protocol. BGP is referred to as a Path Vector protocol, which is a derivative of Distance Vector routing protocols. Unlike RIP, for example, the BGP path selection process is complex and detailed and is not entirely based on the AS PATH. Border Gateway Protocol is a core ROUTE requirement. This protocol will therefore be described in detail later in this guide.

THE OBJECTIVES OF ROUTING PROTOCOLS

Routing algorithms, while different in nature, all have the same basic objectives. While some algorithms are better than others are, all routing protocols have their advantages and disadvantages. Routing algorithms are designed with the following objectives and goals:

- Optimal Routing
- Stability
- Ease of Use
- Flexibility
- Rapid Convergence

Optimal Routing

One of the primary goals of all routing protocols is to select the most optimal path through the network from the source subnet or host to the destination subnet or host. The most optimal route depends on the metrics used by the routing protocols. A route that may be considered the best by one protocol may not necessarily be the most optimal route from the perspective of another protocol. For example, RIP might consider a path that is only two hops long as the most optimal path to a destination network, even though the links were 64Kbps links, while advanced protocols such as OSPF and EIGRP might determine that the most optimal path to that same destination is the one traversing four routers but using 10Gbps links.

Stability

Network stability, or a lack thereof, is another major objective for routing algorithms. Routing algorithms should be stable enough to accommodate unforeseen network events, such as hardware failures and even incorrect implementations. While this is typically a characteristic of all routing algorithms, the manner and time in which they respond to such events makes some better than others and thus more preferred in modern-day networks.

Ease of Use

Routing algorithms are designed to be as simple as possible. In addition to also providing the capability to support complex internetwork deployments, routing protocols should take into consideration the resources required to run the algorithm. Some routing algorithms require more hardware or software resources (e.g., CPU and memory) to run than others; however, they are capable of providing more functionality than alternative simple algorithms.

Flexibility

In addition to providing routing functionality, routing algorithms should also be feature-rich, allowing them to support the different requirements encountered in different networks. It should be noted that this capability typically comes at the expense of other features, such as convergence, which is described next.

Rapid Convergence

Rapid convergence is another primary objective of all routing algorithms. As stated earlier in this chapter, convergence occurs when all routers in the network have the same view and agree on optimal routes. When convergence takes a long time to occur, intermittent packet loss and loss of connectivity may be experienced between remote networks. In addition to these problems, slow convergence can result in network routing loops and outright network outages.

ON-DEMAND ROUTING (ODR)

In addition to understanding how to implement routing protocols in Cisco IOS software, as a Cisco network engineer, it is also important to understand how to leverage one of the most common Cisco protocols, which is the Cisco Discovery Protocol, when designing and implementing large, scalable networks. This section describes On-Demand Routing (ODR).

The Cisco Discovery Protocol (CDP) is a Cisco proprietary protocol that, among other things, is used to discover other Cisco devices on either broadcast or non-broadcast media. CDP provides administrators with information that includes the IP address, software version, and the capabilities of the neighbor device. ODR is an enhancement to CDP that advertises the connected IP prefix or prefixes of a stub router via CDP. ODR also supports VLSM, which means that it can be used in just about any network.

It is important to know that ODR is not a routing protocol. Instead, it is simply an enhancement to CDP that is used to dynamically propagate routing information at Layer 2. The primary reason ODR is often incorrectly referred to as a routing protocol is because it allows routers to dynamically exchange routing information. The secondary reason is because ODR is enabled using the `router odr` global configuration command.

The primary benefit of using ODR is that it is not CPU-intensive and it consumes very little bandwidth. Consider a network using the topology illustrated in Figure 1-6 below, for example:

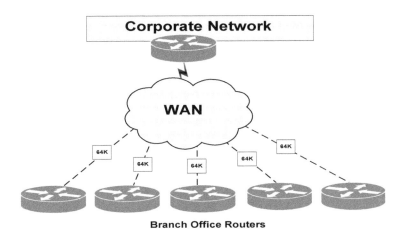

Fig. 1-6. A Hub-and-Spoke Network

Figure 1-6 illustrates a typical hub-and-spoke network. The branch office routers (spokes) are connected to the hub (headquarters) using low-speed WAN links. While a dynamic routing protocol such as EIGRP or OSPF could be used to exchange dynamically the routing information between the hub and the spoke routers, the amount of bandwidth consumed by the routing protocol updates becomes a great concern, especially on the low-speed WAN links.

Another alternative would be to use static routing. However, the administrative overhead that is required to manually configure static routing, especially as the network grows, quickly becomes a cumbersome and negative factor, despite the low overhead afforded by static routing. ODR can be used in such cases due to its low bandwidth consumption and resource requirements. This is because ODR only requires an additional five bytes, which can contain the IP address of the connected subnet plus 1 byte for the subnet mask, in comparison to OSPF, which sends Hello packets that are comprised of 20 bytes of IP header, 24 bytes of OSPF header, 20 bytes of hello parameters, and 4 bytes for each neighbor seen, for example.

At the hub router, the prefixes received via ODR can then be redistributed into another routing protocol, such as OSPF, and propagated to the rest of the network. This allows the network to scale while taking into consideration the bandwidth limitations at the spokes.

Configuring ODR

In order to use ODR, CDP must be enabled on the router. If disabled, CDP can be enabled on the router using the cdp enable global configuration command. There is no explicit configuration required to enable ODR on the spoke routers. However, it is important to ensure that there are no other routing protocols running on the spoke routers. If Cisco IOS detects that a dynamic routing protocol is configured, ODR will not be used to exchange routing information with the hub router(s). This is a common configuration mistake when using ODR.

On the hub router, ODR is enabled using the `router odr` global configuration command. Unlike the spoke router(s), a routing protocol can be enabled on the hub router. The ODR routes can then be redistributed into the dynamic routing protocol and propagated throughout the routing domain. The ODR configuration example in this section will be based on the network topology illustrated in Figure 1-7 below:

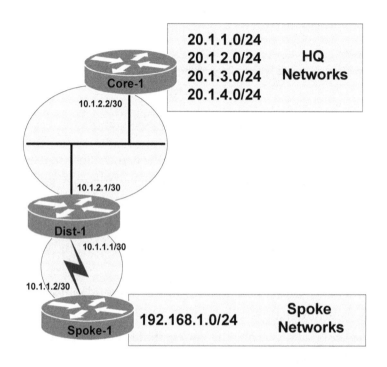

Fig. 1-7. Implementing ODR in a Hub-and-Spoke Network

It is assumed that in the network illustrated in Figure 1-7, the OSPF routing protocol is enabled between the Distribution router and the Core router. The HQ networks are being advertised to the Distribution router via OSPF by the Core router. ODR will then be enabled between the Distribution router and the spoke (Access). However, prior to the implementation of ODR, OSPF routing between the Core and the Distribution routers is verified as illustrated in the following output:

```
Dist-1#show ip route ospf
     20.0.0.0/24 is subnetted, 4 subnets
O IA    20.1.4.0 [110/2] via 10.1.2.2, 00:02:29, FastEthernet0/0
O IA    20.1.1.0 [110/2] via 10.1.2.2, 00:02:29, FastEthernet0/0
O IA    20.1.3.0 [110/2] via 10.1.2.2, 00:02:29, FastEthernet0/0
O IA    20.1.2.0 [110/2] via 10.1.2.2, 00:02:29, FastEthernet0/0
```

In addition to verifying OSPF between the Core and the Distribution routers, it is also important to verify and ensure that CDP is running between the Distribution and the Access routers as illustrated in the following outputs:

```
Dist-1#show cdp neighbors
Capability Codes: R - Router, T - Trans Bridge, B - Source Route Bridge
                  S - Switch, H - Host, I - IGMP, r - Repeater


Device ID       Local Intrfce    Holdtme    Capability  Platform  Port ID
Spoke-1         Ser 0/0          176            R        2621      Ser 0/0

Spoke-1#show cdp neighbors
Capability Codes: R - Router, T - Trans Bridge, B - Source Route Bridge
                  S - Switch, H - Host, I - IGMP, r - Repeater


Device ID       Local Intrfce    Holdtme    Capability  Platform  Port ID
Dist-1          Ser 0/0          171           R S I     2650XM    Ser 0/0
```

Finally, it is important to ensure that there are no routing protocols enabled on the spoke router. If any routing protocol is configured, it must be removed using the no router [protocol] global configuration command. This is mandatory on the spokes when implementing ODR. You can verify configured routing protocols using the show ip protocols summary command as illustrated in the following output:

```
Spoke-1#show ip protocols summary
Index Process Name
0     connected
1     static
```

As previously stated, no explicit configuration is required on the spoke router. The only single configuration command required on the hub router is the router odr global configuration command. This is implemented on the Distribution router as illustrated in the following output:

```
Dist-1#conf t
Enter configuration commands, one per line.  End with CNTL/Z.
Dist-1(config)#router odr
Dist-1(config-router)#exit
Dist-1(config)#exit
```

When ODR is enabled on the hub router, the following two things automatically occur:

The spoke router dynamically advertises connected prefixes to the hub router.
The hub router dynamically advertises a default route to the spoke router.

Referencing the first point made above, the hub router receives the 192.168.1.0/24 prefix from the spoke router dynamically. This is present in the routing table as illustrated below:

```
Dist-1#show ip route odr
o    192.168.1.0/24 [160/1] via 10.1.1.2, 00:00:15, Serial0/0
```

Referencing the second point made above, the spoke router receives a default route from the hub router. This is performed because it is assumed that the spoke router has a single ingress and egress point, which is the hub router. Advertising a single default route to the spoke reduces the routing table size on the router, which keeps resource (e.g., CPU and memory) utilization to a minimum while allowing the spoke router access to the rest of the networks. This is illustrated in the following output:

```
Spoke-1#show ip route
Codes: C - connected, S - static, R - RIP, M - mobile, B - BGP
       D - EIGRP, EX - EIGRP external, O - OSPF, IA - OSPF inter area
       N1 - OSPF NSSA external type 1, N2 - OSPF NSSA external type 2
       E1 - OSPF external type 1, E2 - OSPF external type 2
       i - IS-IS, su - IS-IS summary, L1 - IS-IS level-1, L2 - IS-IS level-2
       ia - IS-IS inter area, * - candidate default, U - per-user static route
       o - ODR, P - periodic downloaded static route

Gateway of last resort is 10.1.1.1 to network 0.0.0.0

     10.0.0.0/30 is subnetted, 1 subnets
C       10.1.1.0 is directly connected, Serial0/0
C    192.168.1.0/24 is directly connected, FastEthernet0/0
o*   0.0.0.0/0 [160/1] via 10.1.1.1, 00:00:37, Serial0/0
```

A more detailed look at the default route received by the spoke reveals the following:

```
Spoke-1#show ip route 0.0.0.0
Routing entry for 0.0.0.0/0, supernet
  Known via "odr", distance 160, metric 1, candidate default path
  Last update from 10.1.1.1 on Serial0/0, 00:00:10 ago
  Routing Descriptor Blocks:
  * 10.1.1.1, from 10.1.1.1, 00:00:10 ago, via Serial0/0
      Route metric is 1, traffic share count is 1
```

In order to allow the spoke routers to reach all other routers in the network, the received ODR routes must be redistributed into OSPF on the Distribution router. When redistributing on the Distribution router, the subnet space for the links between the Distribution and the Access routers should also be included to allow for complete connectivity to all devices. The route redistribution configuration is omitted in this section for brevity and because redistribution is a core requirement for the ROUTE exam and as such is covered in detail later in this guide. Assuming the correct configuration, the spoke router and the Core router now have full IP reachability between their respective subnets as illustrated in the following outputs:

```
Core-1#ping 192.168.1.1

Type escape sequence to abort.
```

```
Sending 5, 100-byte ICMP Echos to 192.168.1.1, timeout is 2 seconds:
!!!!!
Success rate is 100 percent (5/5), round-trip min/avg/max = 4/4/4 ms
Spoke-1#ping 20.1.1.1

Type escape sequence to abort.
Sending 5, 100-byte ICMP Echos to 20.1.1.1, timeout is 2 seconds:
!!!!!
Success rate is 100 percent (5/5), round-trip min/avg/max = 1/3/4 ms
```

While ODR is not a routing protocol, the configuration logic of ODR parameters, such as timers, is similar to routing protocol configuration and is performed in router configuration mode following the issuing of the router odr global configuration command. ODR configuration options are illustrated in the following output:

```
Dist-1(config)#router odr
Dist-1(config-router)#?
Router configuration commands:
  default            Set a command to its defaults
  default-metric     Set metric of redistributed routes
  distance           Define an administrative distance
  distribute-list    Filter networks in routing updates
  exit               Exit from routing protocol configuration mode
  help               Description of the interactive help system
  maximum-paths      Forward packets over multiple paths
  neighbor           Specify a neighbor router
  network            Enable routing on an IP network
  no                 Negate a command or set its defaults
  passive-interface  Suppress routing updates on an interface
  redistribute       Redistribute information from another routing protocol
  timers             Adjust routing timers
  traffic-share      How to compute traffic share over alternate paths
```

NOTE: You are not required to go into any advanced ODR configuration in the ROUTE exam. The options presented above will therefore not be described in further detail in this guide.

CHAPTER SUMMARY

The following section is a summary of the major points you should be aware of in this chapter.

Internet Protocol Routing Protocol Fundamentals

- A routing protocol allows a router to dynamically learn how to reach other networks
- Routing protocols may be used to connect internal and external networks
- Different types of routing protocols use different means of determining the best path
- All routing protocols will differ in their scalability and performance

Flat and Hierarchical Routing

- Routing protocol algorithms operate using either a flat or hierarchical routing system
- A hierarchical routing system uses a layered approach
- Hierarchical routing systems reduce the information routers in the area must process
- A flat routing system has no hierarchy
- In a flat routing system, routers must typically be connected to every other router
- In a flat routing system, each router essentially has the same function
- The primary advantage afforded by hierarchical routing systems is their scalability
- Flat routing systems are not scalable and are difficult to troubleshoot

IP Addressing and Address Summarization

- An IP address is divided into two parts: the network address and the host address
- The IP addressing scheme should be hierarchical
- A hierarchical addressing scheme provides points in the network for summarization
- Summarization reduces the amount of information that routers must process
- Summarization allows for faster convergence in different areas of the internetwork
- Summarization restricts the size of the area that is affected by network changes

Administrative Distance

- The administrative distance is used to determine the reliability of different routing sources
- This default administrative distance value is in an integer between 0 and 255
- Routes with an administrative value of 255 are untrusted and are not placed into the RIB
- The administrative distance is a locally significant value that affects only the local router
- The default administrative distance values are listed in t he following table:

Route Source	AD
Connected Interfaces	0
Static Routes	1
Enhanced Interior Gateway Routing Protocol (EIGRP) Summary Routes	5
External Border Gateway Protocol (eBGP) Routes	20
Internal Enhanced Interior Gateway Routing Protocol (EIGRP) Routes	90
Open Shortest Path First (OSPF) Internal and External Routes	110
Intermediate System-Intermediate System (IS-IS) Internal and External Routes	115
Routing Information Protocol (RIP) Routes	120
Exterior Gateway Protocol (EGP) Routes	140
On Demand Routing (ODR) Routes	160
External Enhanced Interior Gateway Routing Protocol (EIGRP) Routes	170
Internal Border Gateway Protocol (iBGP) Routes	200
Unreachable or Unknown Routes	255

Routing Protocol Metrics

- All routing protocol algorithms use route metrics for network route preference selection
- The lower the route metric, the more preferred the route by the routing protocol
- The lowest cost route is placed into the routing table and is used to reach the destination
- Different routing algorithms use different variables to compute the route metric
- In most cases, the metrics used by one routing protocol are incompatible with another's
- The different routing protocol metrics may be based on one or more of the following:
    1. Bandwidth
    2. Cost
    3. Delay
    4. Load
    5. Path Length
    6. Reliability

Prefix Matching

- Cisco routers use the longest prefix match rule when determining which route to use
- Longer, or more specific routing table entries are preferred over less specific entries

Building the Routing Table

- The routing table may include specific network entries or simply a single default route
- The routing table itself does not actually forward traffic
- The routing table is built using the following general steps:
    1. If the route entry does not currently exist in the routing table, add it to the routing table
    2. If the route entry is more specific than an existing route, add it to the routing table. It should also be noted that the less specific entry is still also retained in the routing table
    3. If the route entry is the same as an existing one, but is received from a more preferred route source, replace the old entry with the new entry
    4. If the route entry is the same as an existing one, and is received from the same protocol:
        a) Discard the new route if the metric is higher than the existing route
        b) Replace the existing route if the metric of the new route is lower
        c) If the metric for both routes is the same, use both routes for load-balancing

Routing Protocol Classes

- There are two major classes of routing protocols: Distance Vector and Link State
- A one-dimensional vector is a directed quantity
- SPF creates a shortest-path tree to all hosts in an area or within the backbone
- The three sets that are used in the SPF calculation are:
    1. Unknown

2. Tentative (TENT)
3. PATH

- A Distance Vector routing protocol uses either distance or hop count as its primary metric
- Distance Vector protocols are primarily based on the Bellman-Ford algorithm
- Distance Vector protocols periodically send neighbors copies of their entire routing tables
- All Distance Vector routing protocols share the following characteristics:
  1. Counting To Infinity
  2. Split Horizon
  3. Poison Reverse
  4. Hold Down timers

- Link State routing protocols are hierarchical routing protocols that use logical network areas
- Routing running Link State routing protocols create a database of the network topology
- Link State routing protocols send either Link State Advertisements or Link State Packets
- Link State routing protocols send incremental updates when changes in the network occur
- BGP is not a Distance Vector routing protocol; instead it is a Path Vector routing protocol

The Objectives of Routing Protocols

- Routing algorithms, while different in nature, all have the same basic objectives and goals
- All routing algorithms are designed with the following objectives and goals:
  1. Optimal Routing
  2. Stability
  3. Ease of Use
  4. Flexibility
  5. Rapid Convergence

On-Demand Routing (ODR)

- CDP is a Cisco proprietary protocol that works on both broadcast and non-broadcast media
- ODR is an enhancement to CDP that advertises the connected prefixes of stub routers
- ODR also supports VLSM, which means that it can be used in modern-day internetworks
- On Demand Routing is not a routing protocol
- ODR is not CPU intensive and it consumes very little bandwidth
- When used in internetworks, ODR only requires an additional five bytes
- ODR can be redistributed into other routing protocols

CHAPTER 2

Enhanced Interior Gateway Routing Protocol

Enhanced Interior Gateway Routing Protocol is a proprietary Interior Gateway Protocol that was developed by Cisco. Enhanced Interior Gateway Routing Protocol (EIGRP) includes traditional Distance Vector characteristics, such as split horizon, as well as characteristics that are similar to those used by Link State routing protocols, such as incremental updates.

Although EIGRP has Link State routing protocol characteristics, EIGRP falls under the Distance Vector routing protocol classification and is referred to as an advanced Distance Vector routing protocol instead. EIGRP runs directly over IP using protocol number 88. The ROUTE exam objective covered in this chapter is as follows:

- Implement an EIGRP-based solution, given a network design and a set of requirements.

This chapter contains the following sections:

- Cisco EIGRP Overview and Fundamentals
- EIGRP Configuration Fundamentals
- EIGRP Messages
- EIGRP Neighbor Discovery and Maintenance
- Metrics, DUAL, and the Topology Table
- Equal Cost and Unequal Cost Load Sharing
- Default Routing Using EIGRP
- Split Horizon in EIGRP Networks
- EIGRP Stub Routing
- Securing EIGRP Protocol Messages
- EIGRP Route Summarization
- Understanding Passive Interfaces
- Understanding the Use of the EIGRP Router ID
- EIGRP Logging and Reporting

CISCO EIGRP OVERVIEW AND FUNDAMENTALS

Cisco developed Enhanced IGRP to overcome some of the limitations of its proprietary Distance Vector routing protocol, Interior Gateway Routing Protocol (IGRP). IGRP offered improvements over Routing Information Protocol (RIP), such as support for an increased number of hops; however, IGRP still succumbed to the traditional Distance Vector routing protocol limitations, which included the following:

- Sending full periodic routing updates
- A hop limitation
- The lack of VLSM support
- Slow convergence
- The lack of loop prevention mechanisms

Unlike the traditional Distance Vector routing protocols, which send their neighbors periodic routing updates that contain all routing information, EIGRP sends non-periodic incremental routing updates to distribute routing information throughout the routing domain. The EIGRP incremental updates are sent when there is a change in the network topology.

By default, RIP has a hop-count limitation of up to 15 hops, which makes RIP suitable only for smaller networks. EIGRP has a default hop-count limitation of 100; however, this value can be manually adjusted by the administrator using the `metric maximum-hops <1-255>` router configuration command when configuring EIGRP. This allows EIGRP to support networks that contain hundreds of routers, making it more scalable and better suited for larger networks.

Enhanced IGRP uses two unique Type/Length/Value (TLV) triplets to carry route entries. These TLVs are the Internal EIGRP Route TLV and the External EIGRP Route TLV, which are used for internal and external EIGRP routes, respectively. Both TLVs include an 8-bit Prefix Length field that specifies the number of bits used for the subnet mask of the destination network. The information that is contained in this field allows EIGRP to support variably subnetted networks.

Enhanced IGRP converges much faster than the traditional Distance Vector routing protocols. Instead of relying solely on timers, EIGRP uses information contained in its Topology Table to locate alternate paths. EIGRP can also query neighboring routers for information if an alternate path is not located in the local router's Topology Table. The EIGRP Topology Table will be described in detail later in this chapter.

In order to ensure that there are loop-free paths through the network, EIGRP uses the Diffusing Update Algorithm (DUAL), which is used to track all routes advertised by neighbors and then select the best, loop-free path to the destination network. DUAL is a core EIGRP concept that will be described in detail later in this chapter.

Protocol-Dependent Modules

Enhanced IGRP Protocol-Dependent Modules (PDMs) are responsible for Network Layer (Layer 3) protocol-specific requirements, such as IP, IPX, and AppleTalk. This means that if you are running IP EIGRP, IPX EIGRP, and AppleTalk EIGRP, there will be three different EIGRP Neighbor Tables for the following:
- IP EIGRP neighbors
- IPX EIGRP neighbors
- AppleTalk EIGRP neighbors

Because IPX and AppleTalk are beyond the scope of the ROUTE exam requirements, it should be assumed that all references to the Neighbor Table are regarding IP neighbors.

Using the IP PDM, IP EIGRP asks DUAL to make routing decisions. IP EIGRP is responsible for redistributing routes learned by other IP routing protocols. This information is then stored in the EIGRP Topology Table. Both the EIGRP DUAL and the Topology Table are core components of EIGRP that will be described in detail later in this chapter.

EIGRP CONFIGURATION FUNDAMENTALS

Enhanced IGRP is enabled in Cisco IOS software using the router eigrp [ASN] global configuration command. The [ASN] designates the EIGRP autonomous system number. This is a 32-bit integer between 1 and 65535. In addition to other factors, which will be described later in this chapter, routers running EIGRP must reside within the same autonomous system to form a neighbor relationship successfully. Following the configuration of the router eigrp [ASN] global configuration command, the router transitions to EIGRP router configuration mode wherein you can configure parameters pertaining to EIGRP. The configured autonomous system number can be verified in the output of the show ip protocols command as follows:

```
R1#show ip protocols
Routing Protocol is "eigrp 150"
  Outgoing update filter list for all interfaces is not set
  Incoming update filter list for all interfaces is not set
  Default networks flagged in outgoing updates
  Default networks accepted from incoming updates
  EIGRP metric weight K1=1, K2=0, K3=1, K4=0, K5=0
  EIGRP maximum hopcount 100
  EIGRP maximum metric variance 1
...
```

In addition to the show ip protocols command, the show ip eigrp neighbors command prints information on all known EIGRP neighbors and their respective autonomous systems. This command, and its available options, will be described in detail later in this chapter. On routers running multiple instances of EIGRP, the show ip eigrp [ASN] command can be used to view information pertaining only to the autonomous system that is specified in this command. The use of this command is illustrated in the following output:

```
R1#show ip eigrp 150 ?
  interfaces   IP-EIGRP interfaces
  neighbors    IP-EIGRP neighbors
  topology     IP-EIGRP Topology Table
  traffic      IP-EIGRP Traffic Statistics
```

In the output above, 150 is the autonomous system number. The default in Cisco IOS software is to print information on all EIGRP instances if an autonomous system is not specified with any show ip eigrp commands.

Once in router configuration mode, the network command is used to specify the network(s) for which EIGRP routing will be enabled. When the network command is used and a major Classful network is specified, the following actions are performed on the EIGRP-enabled router:
  • EIGRP is enabled for networks that fall within the specified Classful network range
  • The Topology Table is populated with these directly connected subnets
  • EIGRP Hello packets are sent out of the interfaces associated with these subnets
  • EIGRP advertises the network(s) to EIGRP neighbors in Update messages
  • Based on the exchange of messages, EIGRP routes are then added to the IP routing table

For example, assume that the router has the following Loopback interfaces configured:
  • Loopback 0—IP Address 10.0.0.1/24
  • Loopback 1—IP Address 10.1.1.1/24
  • Loopback 2—IP Address 10.2.2.1/24
  • Loopback 3—IP Address 10.3.3.1/24

If EIGRP is enabled for use and the major Classful 10.0.0.0/8 network is used in conjunction with the network router configuration command, all four Loopback interfaces are enabled for EIGRP routing. This is illustrated in the following output:

```
R1#show ip eigrp interfaces
IP-EIGRP interfaces for process 150

                      Xmit Queue   Mean   Pacing Time   Multicast    Pending
Interface     Peers Un/Reliable   SRTT   Un/Reliable   Flow Timer   Routes
Lo0             0       0/0         0        0/10          0            0
Lo1             0       0/0         0        0/10          0            0
Lo2             0       0/0         0        0/10          0            0
Lo3             0       0/0         0        0/10          0            0
```

You can use the show ip protocols command to verify that EIGRP is enabled for the major Classful 10.0.0.0/8 network. The output of this command is illustrated below:

```
R1#show ip protocols
Routing Protocol is "eigrp 150"
  Outgoing update filter list for all interfaces is not set
  Incoming update filter list for all interfaces is not set
  Default networks flagged in outgoing updates
  Default networks accepted from incoming updates
  EIGRP metric weight K1=1, K2=0, K3=1, K4=0, K5=0
```

```
EIGRP maximum hopcount 100
EIGRP maximum metric variance 1
Redistributing: eigrp 150
EIGRP NSF-aware route hold timer is 240s
Automatic network summarization is in effect
Maximum path: 4
Routing for Networks:
  10.0.0.0
Routing Information Sources:
  Gateway          Distance      Last Update
Distance: internal 90 external 170
```

The EIGRP Topology Table can be viewed using the show ip eigrp topology command. The output of this command is illustrated below:

```
R1#show ip eigrp topology
IP-EIGRP Topology Table for AS(150)/ID(10.3.3.1)

Codes: P - Passive, A - Active, U - Update, Q - Query, R - Reply,
       r - reply Status, s - sia Status

P 10.3.3.0/24, 1 successors, FD is 128256
        via Connected, Loopback3
P 10.2.2.0/24, 1 successors, FD is 128256
        via Connected, Loopback2
P 10.1.1.0/24, 1 successors, FD is 128256
        via Connected, Loopback1
P 10.0.0.0/24, 1 successors, FD is 128256
        via Connected, Loopback0
```

NOTE: The Topology Table, EIGRP Hello packets, and Update messages are described in detail later in this chapter. The focus of this section is restricted to EIGRP configuration implementation.

Using the network command to specify a major Classful network allows multiple subnets that fall within the Classful network range to be advertised at the same time with minimal configuration. However, there may be situations where administrators may not want all of the subnets within a Classful network to be enabled for EIGRP routing. For example, referencing the Loopback interfaces configured on R1 in the previous example, assume that you want EIGRP routing enabled only for the 10.1.1.0/24 and 10.3.3.0/24 subnets, and not for the 10.0.0.0/24 and 10.2.2.0/24 subnets. While it appears that this would be possible if one specified the networks (i.e., 10.1.1.0 and 10.3.3.0) when using the network command, Cisco IOS software still converts these statements to the major Classful 10.0.0.0/8 network as illustrated below:

```
R1(config)#router eigrp 150
R1(config-router)#network 10.1.1.0
R1(config-router)#network 10.3.3.0
R1(config-router)#exit
```

Despite the configuration above, the show ip protocols command reveals the following:

```
R1#show ip protocols
Routing Protocol is "eigrp 150"
  Outgoing update filter list for all interfaces is not set
  Incoming update filter list for all interfaces is not set
  Default networks flagged in outgoing updates
  Default networks accepted from incoming updates
  EIGRP metric weight K1=1, K2=0, K3=1, K4=0, K5=0
  EIGRP maximum hopcount 100
  EIGRP maximum metric variance 1
  Redistributing: eigrp 150
  EIGRP NSF-aware route hold timer is 240s
  Automatic network summarization is in effect
  Maximum path: 4
  Routing for Networks:
    10.0.0.0
  Routing Information Sources:
    Gateway         Distance      Last Update
  Distance: internal 90 external 170
```

NOTE: A common misconception is that disabling the EIGRP automatic summarization feature addresses this issue; however, this has nothing to do with the auto-summary command. For example, assume we issued the no auto-summary command to the configuration used in the previous example as follows:

```
R1(config)#router eigrp 150
R1(config-router)#network 10.1.1.0
R1(config-router)#network 10.3.3.0
R1(config-router)#no auto-summary
R1(config-router)#exit
```

The show ip protocols command still shows that EIGRP is enabled for network 10.0.0.0/8 as illustrated below:

```
R1#show ip protocols
Routing Protocol is "eigrp 150"
  Outgoing update filter list for all interfaces is not set
  Incoming update filter list for all interfaces is not set
  Default networks flagged in outgoing updates
  Default networks accepted from incoming updates
  EIGRP metric weight K1=1, K2=0, K3=1, K4=0, K5=0
  EIGRP maximum hopcount 100
  EIGRP maximum metric variance 1
```

```
Redistributing: eigrp 150
EIGRP NSF-aware route hold timer is 240s
Automatic network summarization is not in effect
Maximum path: 4
Routing for Networks:
  10.0.0.0
Routing Information Sources:
  Gateway          Distance      Last Update
Distance: internal 90 external 170
```

In order to provide more granular control of the networks that are enabled for EIGRP routing, Cisco IOS software supports the use of wildcard masks in conjunction with the network statement when configuring EIGRP. The wildcard mask operates in a manner similar to the wildcard mask used in ACLs and is independent of the subnet mask for the network.

As an example, the command network 10.1.1.0 0.0.0.255 would match the 10.1.1.0/24 network, the 10.1.1.0/26 network, and the 10.1.1.0/30 network. Referencing the Loopback interfaces configured in the previous output, R1 would be configured as follows to enable EIGRP routing for the 10.1.1.0/24 and 10.3.3.0/24 subnets, and not for the 10.0.0.0/24 subnet or the 10.2.2.0/24 subnet:

```
R1(config)#router eigrp 150
R1(config-router)#network 10.1.1.0 0.0.0.255
R1(config-router)#network 10.3.3.0 0.0.0.255
R1(config-router)#exit
```

This configuration can be validated using the show ip protocols command as follows:

```
R1#show ip protocols
Routing Protocol is "eigrp 150"
  Outgoing update filter list for all interfaces is not set
  Incoming update filter list for all interfaces is not set
  Default networks flagged in outgoing updates
  Default networks accepted from incoming updates
  EIGRP metric weight K1=1, K2=0, K3=1, K4=0, K5=0
  EIGRP maximum hopcount 100
  EIGRP maximum metric variance 1
  Redistributing: eigrp 150
  EIGRP NSF-aware route hold timer is 240s
  Automatic network summarization is in effect
  Maximum path: 4
  Routing for Networks:
    10.1.1.0/24
    10.3.3.0/24
  Routing Information Sources:
    Gateway          Distance      Last Update
  Distance: internal 90 external 170
```

Additionally, the show ip eigrp interfaces command can be used to validate that EIGRP routing has been enabled only for Loopback 1 and Loopback 3:

```
R1#show ip eigrp interfaces
IP-EIGRP interfaces for process 150

                  Xmit Queue   Mean   Pacing Time   Multicast    Pending
Interface  Peers  Un/Reliable  SRTT   Un/Reliable   Flow Timer   Routes
Lo1        0      0/0          0      0/10          0            0
Lo3        0      0/0          0      0/10          0            0
```

As illustrated in the output above, EIGRP routing is enabled only for Loopback 1 and Loopback 3 because of the wildcard mask configuration.

It is important to remember that the network command can be configured using the subnet mask, rather than the wildcard mask. When this is the case, Cisco IOS software inverts the subnet mask and the command is saved using the wildcard mask. For example, referencing the same Loopback interfaces on the router, R1 could also be configured as follows:

```
R1(config-router)#router eigrp 150
R1(config-router)#network 10.1.1.0 255.255.255.0
R1(config-router)#network 10.3.3.0 255.255.255.0
R1(config-router)#exit
```

Based on this configuration, the following is entered in the running configuration:

```
R1#show running-config | begin router eigrp
router eigrp 150
 network 10.1.1.0 0.0.0.255
 network 10.3.3.0 0.0.0.255
 auto-summary
```

If a specific address on the network is used, in conjunction with the wildcard mask, Cisco IOS software performs a logical AND operation to determine the network that will be enabled for EIGRP. For example, if the network 10.1.1.15 0.0.0.255 command is issued, Cisco IOS software performs the following actions:

- Inverts the wildcard mask to the subnet mask value of 255.255.255.0
- Performs a logical AND operation
- Adds the network 10.1.1.0 0.0.0.255 command to the configuration

The network configuration used in this example is illustrated in the following output:

```
R1(config)#router eigrp 150
R1(config-router)#network 10.1.1.15 0.0.0.255
R1(config-router)#exit
```

Based on this, the running configuration on the router displays the following:

```
R1#show running-config | begin router eigrp
router eigrp 150
 network 10.1.1.0 0.0.0.255
 auto-summary
```

If a specific address on the network is used in conjunction with the subnet mask, the router performs the same logical AND operation and adds the network command to the running configuration using the wildcard mask format. This is illustrated in the configuration below:

```
R1(config)#router eigrp 150
R1(config-router)#network 10.1.1.15 255.255.255.0
R1(config-router)#exit
```

Based on this configuration, the following is added to the current configuration on the router:

```
R1#show running-config | begin router eigrp
router eigrp 150
 network 10.1.1.0 0.0.0.255
 auto-summary
```

As illustrated in the configuration above, the use of either the wildcard mask or the subnet mask results in the same operation and network statement configuration in Cisco IOS software.

 REAL WORLD IMPLEMENTATION

When configuring EIGRP in production networks, it is common practice to use a wildcard mask of all zeros or a subnet mask of all 1s. For example, the network 10.1.1.1 0.0.0.0 and network 10.1.1.1 255.255.255.255 commands perform the same actions. Using all zeros in the wildcard mask or all ones in the subnet mask configures Cisco IOS software to match an exact interface address, regardless of the subnet mask configured on the interface itself. Either one of these commands would match interfaces configured with the 10.1.1.1/8, 10.1.1.1/16, 10.1.1.1/24, and 10.1.1.1/30 address, for example. The use of these commands is illustrated in the following output:

```
R1(config)#router eigrp 150
R1(config-router)#network 10.0.0.1 0.0.0.0
R1(config-router)#network 10.1.1.1 255.255.255.255
R1(config-router)#exit
```

The show ip protocols command verifies that the configuration of both network statements is treated in a similar manner on the router as illustrated below:

```
R1#show ip protocols
Routing Protocol is "eigrp 150"
  Outgoing update filter list for all interfaces is not set
  Incoming update filter list for all interfaces is not set
  Default networks flagged in outgoing updates
  Default networks accepted from incoming updates
  EIGRP metric weight K1=1, K2=0, K3=1, K4=0, K5=0
  EIGRP maximum hopcount 100
  EIGRP maximum metric variance 1
  Redistributing: eigrp 150
  EIGRP NSF-aware route hold timer is 240s
  Automatic network summarization is in effect
  Maximum path: 4
  Routing for Networks:
     10.0.0.1/32
     10.1.1.1/32
  Routing Information Sources:
    Gateway         Distance      Last Update
  Distance: internal 90 external 170
```

When a subnet mask with all ones or a wildcard mask with all zeros is used, EIGRP is enabled for the specified (matched) interface and the network the interface resides on is advertised. In other words, EIGRP will not advertise the /32 address in the output above but, instead, the actual network based on the subnet mask configured on the matched interface. The use of this configuration is independent of the subnet mask configured on the actual interface matched.

EIGRP MESSAGES

This section describes the different types of messages used by EIGRP. However, before delving into the specifics of the different message types, it is important to have a solid understanding of the EIGRP packet header, wherein these messages are contained.

EIGRP Packet Header

Although going into specifics on the EIGRP packet formats is beyond the scope of the ROUTE exam requirements, a fundamental understanding of the EIGRP packet header is important in order to understand completely the overall operation of the EIGRP routing protocol. Figure 2-1 below illustrates the format of the EIGRP packet header:

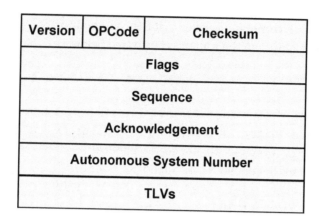

Fig. 2-1. EIGRP Packet Header Fields

Within the EIGRP packet header, the 4-bit Version field is used to indicate the protocol version. Current Cisco IOS images support EIGRP version 1.x. The 4-bit OPCode specifies the EIGRP packet or message type. The different EIGRP packet types are each assigned a unique OPCode value, which allows them to be differentiated from other packet types. These messages will be described in detail later in this chapter.

The 24-bit Checksum field is used to run a sanity check on the EIGRP packet. This field is based on the entire EIGRP packet, excluding the IP header. The 32-bit Flags field is used to indicate an INIT either for a new EIGRP neighbor or for the Conditional Receive (CR) for EIGRP Reliable Transport Protocol (RTP). RTP and CR will be described in detail later in this chapter.

The 32-bit Sequence field specifies the sequence number used by EIGRP RTP to ensure orderly delivery of reliable packets. The 32-bit Acknowledgment field is used to acknowledge the receipt of an EIGRP reliable packet.

The 32-bit Autonomous System Number field specifies the Autonomous System Number of the EIGRP domain. Finally, the 32-bit Type/Length/Value (TLV) triplet field is used to carry route entries as well as provide EIGRP DUAL information. EIGRP supports several different types of TLVs, with the most common being the following:
- The Parameters TLV, which has the parameters to establish neighbor relationships
- The Sequence TLV, which is used by RTP
- The Next Multicast Sequence TLV, which is used by RTP
- The EIGRP internal route TLV, which is used for internal EIGRP routes
- The EIGRP external route TLV, which is used for external EIGRP routes

NOTE: You are not required to go into detail on the different EIGRP TLVs.

Figure 2-2 below illustrates the different fields as they appear in a wire capture of an EIGRP packet:

```
Cisco EIGRP
  Version    = 2
  Opcode = 5 (Hello)
  Checksum   = 0xee36
  Flags      = 0x00000000
  Sequence   = 0
  Acknowledge = 0
  Autonomous System  : 150
  EIGRP Parameters
  Software Version: IOS=12.4, EIGRP=1.2
```

Fig. 2-2. EIGRP Packet Header Capture

Within the EIGRP packet header, the 4-bit OPCode field is used to specify the EIGRP packet type or message. EIGRP uses different message or packet types, which are Hello packets, Acknowledgement packets, Update packets, Query packets, Reply packets, and Request packets. These packet types are described in detail in the following sections.

Hello Packets

Enhanced IGRP sends Hello packets once it has been enabled on a router for a particular network. These messages are used to identify neighbors and, once identified, serve or function as a keepalive mechanism between neighbors. EIGRP neighbor discovery and maintenance is described in detail later in this chapter.

Enhanced IGRP Hello packets are sent to the link local Multicast group address 224.0.0.10. Hello packets sent by EIGRP do not require an Acknowledgment to be sent confirming that they were received. Because they require no explicit acknowledgment, Hello packets are classified as unreliable EIGRP packets. EIGRP Hello packets have an OPCode of 5.

Acknowledgement Packets

An EIGRP Acknowledgment (ACK) packet is simply an EIGRP Hello packet that contains no data. Acknowledgement packets are used by EIGRP to confirm reliable delivery of EIGRP packets. The ACK packets are always sent to a Unicast address, which is the source address of the sender of the reliable packet, and not to the EIGRP Multicast group address. In addition, ACK packets will always contain a non-zero acknowledgment number. The ACK packet uses the same OPCode as the Hello packet because it is essentially a Hello packet that contains no information. The OPCode is 5.

Update Packets

Enhanced IGRP Update packets are used to convey reachability of destinations. In other words, Update packets contain EIGRP routing updates. When a new neighbor is discovered, Update packets are sent via Unicast so the neighbor can build up its EIGRP Topology Table. In other cases, such as a link cost change, updates are sent via Multicast. It is important to know that Update packets are always transmitted reliably and always require explicit acknowledgement. Update packets are assigned an OPCode of 1. An EIGRP Update packet is illustrated in Figure 2-3 below:

```
Cisco EIGRP
  Version    = 2
  Opcode = 1 (Update)
  Checksum   = 0x1629
  Flags      = 0x00000008
  Sequence   = 7
  Acknowledge = 10
  Autonomous System  : 150
  IP internal route  =   1.0.0.0/8
  Type = 0x0102 (IP internal route)
  Size = 26 bytes
  Next Hop    = 0.0.0.0
  Delay       = 128000
  Bandwidth   = 256
  MTU         = 1514
  Hop Count   = 0
  Reliability = 255
  Load        = 1
  Reserved
  Prefix Length = 8
  Destination = 1.0.0.0
```

Fig. 2-3. EIGRP Update Packet

NOTE: You are not required to go into detail on the information contained in EIGRP packets.

Query Packets

Enhanced IGRP Query packets are Multicast and are used to request reliably routing information. EIGRP Query packets are sent to neighbors when a route is not available and the router needs to ask about the status of the route for fast convergence. If the router that sends out a Query does not receive a response from any of its neighbors, it resends the Query as a Unicast packet to the non-responsive neighbor(s). If no response is received in 16 attempts, the EIGRP neighbor relationship is reset. This concept will be described in further detail later in this chapter. EIGRP Query packets are assigned an OPCode of 3.

Reply Packets

Enhanced IGRP Reply packets are sent in response to Query packets. The Reply packets are used to respond reliably to a Query packet. Reply packets are Unicast to the originator of the Query. The EIGRP Reply packets are assigned an OPCode of 4.

Request Packets

Enhanced IGRP Request packets are used to get specific information from one or more neighbors and are used in route server applications. These packet types can be sent via either Multicast or Unicast but are always transmitted unreliably. In other words, they do not require an explicit acknowledgment.

NOTE: While EIGRP Hello and ACK packets have been described as two individual packet types, it is important to remember that in some texts, EIGRP Hello and ACK packets are considered the same type of packet. This is because, as was stated earlier in this section, an ACK packet is simply an EIGRP Hello packet that contains no data.

The debug eigrp packets command may be used to print real-time debugging information on the different EIGRP packets described in this section. Keep in mind that this command also includes additional packets that are not described, as they are beyond the scope of the current ROUTE exam requirements. The following output illustrates the use of this command:

```
R1#debug eigrp packets ?
  SIAquery  EIGRP SIA-Query packets
  SIAreply  EIGRP SIA-Reply packets
  ack       EIGRP ack packets
  hello     EIGRP hello packets
  ipxsap    EIGRP ipxsap packets
  probe     EIGRP probe packets
  query     EIGRP query packets
  reply     EIGRP reply packets
  request   EIGRP request packets
  retry     EIGRP retransmissions
  stub      EIGRP stub packets
  terse     Display all EIGRP packets except Hellos
  update    EIGRP update packets
  verbose   Display all EIGRP packets
  <cr>
```

The show ip eigrp traffic command is used to view the number of EIGRP packets sent and received by the local router. This command is also a powerful troubleshooting tool. For example, if the routing is sending out Hello packets but is not receiving any back, this could indicate that the intended neighbor is not configured, or even that an ACK may be blocking EIGRP packets. These concepts are expanded on in the TSHOOT study guide. The following output illustrates this command:

```
R2#show ip eigrp traffic
IP-EIGRP Traffic Statistics for AS 150
  Hellos sent/received: 21918/21922
  Updates sent/received: 10/6
  Queries sent/received: 1/0
  Replies sent/received: 0/1
  Acks sent/received: 6/10
  SIA-Queries sent/received: 0/0
  SIA-Replies sent/received: 0/0
  Hello Process ID: 178
  PDM Process ID: 154
  IP Socket queue:  0/2000/2/0 (current/max/highest/drops)
  Eigrp input queue: 0/2000/2/0 (current/max/highest/drops)
```

Table 2-1 summarizes the EIGRP packets described in this section and whether they are sent unreliably or reliably:

Table 2-1. EIGRP Packet Summary

Message Type	Description	Sent
Hello	Used for neighbor discovery, maintenance, and keepalives	Unreliably
Acknowledgement	Used to acknowledge receipt of information	Unreliably
Update	Used to convey routing information	Reliably
Query	Used to request specific routing information	Reliably
Reply	Used to respond to a Query	Reliably
Request	Used to request information in route server applications	Unreliably

EIGRP NEIGHBOR DISCOVERY AND MAINTENANCE

Enhanced IGRP may be configured to discover neighboring routers dynamically (default) or via manual administrator configuration. Both methods, as well as other EIGRP neighbor-related topics, will be described in the following sections.

Dynamic Neighbor Discovery

Dynamic neighbor discovery is performed by sending EIGRP Hello packets to the destination Multicast group address 224.0.0.10. This is performed as soon as the network command is used when configuring EIGRP on the router. In addition, as stated earlier in this guide, EIGRP packets are sent directly over IP using protocol number 88. Figure 2-4 below illustrates the basic EIGRP neighbor discovery and route exchange process:

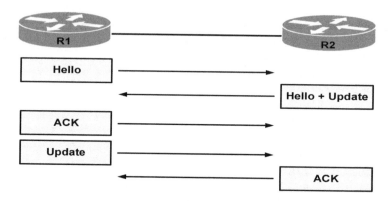

Fig. 2-4. EIGRP Neighbor Discovery and Route Exchange

Referencing Figure 2-4, upon initialization, the EIGRP neighbors send Hello packets to discover other neighbors. The neighbors then exchange their full routing tables via full Updates. These Updates contain information about all known routes. Because Update packets are sent reliably, they must be explicitly acknowledged by the recipient.

After the neighbors have exchanged their routing information, they continue to exchange Hello packets to maintain the neighbor relationship. Additionally, the EIGRP neighbor routers will only send incremental updates to advise neighbors of status or routing changes. They will no longer send full Updates to neighbor routers.

It is important to understand that simply enabling EIGRP between two or more routers does not guarantee that a neighbor relationship will be established. Instead, some parameters must match in order for the routers to become neighbors. The EIGRP neighbor relationship may not establish due to any of the following circumstances:

- Mismatched EIGRP Authentication Parameters (if configured)
- Mismatched EIGRP K Values
- Mismatched EIGRP Autonomous System (AS) Number
- Using secondary addresses for EIGRP neighbor relationships
- The neighbors are not on a common subnet

While the `show ip eigrp neighbors` command does not differentiate between dynamically and statically configured neighbors, the `show ip eigrp interfaces detail <name>` command can be used to verify that the router interface is sending out Multicast packets to discover and maintain neighbor relationships. The output of this command on a router enabled for dynamic neighbor discovery is illustrated below:

```
R2#show ip eigrp interfaces detail FastEthernet0/0
IP-EIGRP interfaces for process 150
                     Xmit Queue   Mean   Pacing Time   Multicast    Pending
Interface     Peers  Un/Reliable  SRTT   Un/Reliable   Flow Timer   Routes
Fa0/0           1       0/0        1         0/1           50           0
   Hello interval is 5 sec
   Next xmit serial <none>
   Un/reliable mcasts: 0/2  Un/reliable ucasts: 2/2
   Mcast exceptions: 0  CR packets: 0  ACKs suppressed: 0
   Retransmissions sent: 1  Out-of-sequence rcvd: 0
   Authentication mode is not set
   Use multicast
```

NOTE: The `show ip eigrp neighbors` command is described in detail later in this section. When looking at the output of the show `ip eigrp interfaces detail <name>` command, keep in mind that because EIGRP uses both Multicast and Unicast packets, the command counters will include values for both types of packets as shown in the output above.

Static Neighbor Discovery

Unlike the dynamic EIGRP neighbor discovery process, static EIGRP neighbor relationships require manual neighbor configuration on the router. When static EIGRP neighbors are configured, the local router uses the Unicast neighbor address to send packets to these routers.

Static neighbor relationships are seldom used in EIGRP networks. The primary reason for this is manual configuration of neighbors does not scale well in large networks. However, it is important to understand why this option is available in Cisco IOS software and the situations in which this feature can be utilized. A prime example of when static neighbor configuration could be used would be in a situation where EIGRP is being deployed across media that does not natively support Broadcast or Multicast packets, such as Frame Relay.

A second example would be to prevent sending unnecessary EIGRP packets on multi-access networks, such as Ethernet, when only a few EIGRP-enabled routers exist. In addition to basic EIGRP configuration, the neighbor command must be configured on the local router for all static EIGRP neighbors. EIGRP-enabled routers will not establish an adjacency if one router is configured to use Unicast (static) while another uses Multicast (dynamic).

In Cisco IOS software, static EIGRP neighbors are configured using the `neighbor <address>` `<interface>` router configuration command. Keep in mind that this is simply in addition to the basic EIGRP configuration. The simple network topology that is illustrated in Figure 2-5 below will be used both to demonstrate and to verify the configuration of static EIGRP neighbors:

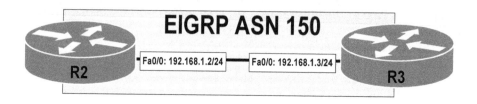

Fig. 2-5. Configuring Static EIGRP Neighbors

Referencing the topology illustrated in Figure 2-5, router R2 is configured as follows:

```
R2(config)#router eigrp 150
R2(config-router)#network 192.168.1.0 0.0.0.255
R2(config-router)#neighbor 192.168.1.3 FastEthernet0/0
R2(config-router)#no auto-summary
R2(config-router)#exit
```

The configuration implemented on router R3 is as follows:

```
R3(config)#router eigrp 150
R3(config-router)#network 192.168.1.0 0.0.0.255
R3(config-router)#neighbor 192.168.1.2 FastEthernet0/0
R3(config-router)#no auto-summary
R3(config-router)#exit
```

The show ip eigrp interfaces detail <name> command can be used to determine whether the router interface is sending Multicast (dynamic) or Unicast (static) packets for neighbor discovery and maintenance. This is illustrated in the following output:

```
R2#show ip eigrp interfaces detail FastEthernet0/0
IP-EIGRP interfaces for process 150
                      Xmit Queue   Mean   Pacing Time   Multicast    Pending
Interface      Peers  Un/Reliable  SRTT   Un/Reliable   Flow Timer   Routes
Fa0/0            1       0/0         2       0/1            50           0
   Hello interval is 5 sec
   Next xmit serial <none>
   Un/reliable mcasts: 0/1  Un/reliable ucasts: 3/8
   Mcast exceptions: 1  CR packets: 1  ACKs suppressed: 2
   Retransmissions sent: 1  Out-of-sequence rcvd: 0
   Authentication mode is not set
   Use unicast
```

Additionally, the show ip eigrp neighbors [detail] command can be used to determine the type of EIGRP neighbor. This command is described in detail later in this chapter.

EIGRP Hello and Hold Timers

Enhanced IGRP uses different Hello and Hold timers for different types of media. Hello timers are used to determine the interval rate EIGRP Hello packets are sent. The Hold timer is used to determine the time that will elapse before a router considers an EIGRP neighbor as down. By default, the Hold time is three times the Hello interval.

Enhanced IGRP sends Hello packets every 5 seconds on Broadcast, point-to-point serial, point-to-point subinterfaces, and multipoint circuits greater than T1 speed. The default Hold Time is 15 seconds. EIGRP sends Hello packets every 60 seconds on other link types. These include low-bandwidth WAN links less than T1 speed. The default Hold time for neighbor relationships across these links is also three times the Hello interval and therefore defaults to 180 seconds.

Enhanced IGRP timer values do not have to be the same on neighboring routers in order for a neighbor relationship to be established. In addition, there is no mandatory requirement that the

Hold time be three times the Hello interval. This is only a recommended guideline, which can be manually adjusted in Cisco IOS software. The EIGRP Hello time can be adjusted using the `ip hello-interval eigrp <ASN> <secs>` interface configuration command, while the EIGRP Hold time can be adjusted using the `ip hold-time eigrp <ASN> <secs>` interface configuration command.

It is important to understand the use of both Hello timers and Hold timers as they pertain to EIGRP. The Hold time value is advertised in the EIGRP Hello packet, while the Hello time value tells the local router how often to send its neighbor(s) Hello packets. The Hold time, on the other hand, tells the neighbor router(s) of the local router how long to wait before declaring the local router 'dead'. The EIGRP Hello packet and the Hold Time field is illustrated in Figure 2-6 below:

```
Cisco EIGRP
 Version     = 2
 Opcode = 5 (Hello)
 Checksum    = 0xee36
 Flags       = 0x00000000
 Sequence    = 0
 Acknowledge = 0
 Autonomous System  : 150
 EIGRP Parameters
  Type = 0x0001 (EIGRP Parameters)
  Size = 12 bytes
  K1 = 1
  K2 = 0
  K3 = 1
  K4 = 0
  K5 = 0
  Reserved
  Hold Time = 15
 Software Version: IOS=12.4, EIGRP=1.2
```

Fig. 2-6. EIGRP Hold Time in the EIGRP Hello Packet

Referencing Figure 2-6, the EIGRP Hello packet (OPCode 5) contains, among other things, the configured Hold time value. The value of 15 illustrated in Figure 2-6 is a non-default configured value implemented using the `ip hold-time eigrp <ASN> <secs>` interface configuration command. It is important to remember that the actual Hello time interval is not included. However, the configured Hello time can be viewed using the `show ip eigrp interfaces detail <name>` command. The information printed by this command is illustrated below:

```
R2#show ip eigrp interfaces detail FastEthernet0/0
IP-EIGRP interfaces for process 150
                    Xmit Queue   Mean  Pacing Time   Multicast   Pending
Interface    Peers  Un/Reliable  SRTT  Un/Reliable   Flow Timer  Routes
Fa0/0          1       0/0        7       0/1           50          0
   Hello interval is 5 sec
   Next xmit serial <none>
   Un/reliable mcasts: 0/1  Un/reliable ucasts: 2/5
```

```
Mcast exceptions: 1  CR packets: 1  ACKs suppressed: 0
Retransmissions sent: 1  Out-of-sequence rcvd: 0
Authentication mode is not set
Use multicast
```

The most common reason for adjusting the default EIGRP timer values is to speed up routing protocol convergence. For example, on a low-speed WAN link, a Hold time of 180 seconds might be a long time to wait before EIGRP declares a neighbor router down. Inversely, in some situations, it may be necessary to increase the EIGRP timer values on high-speed links in order to ensure a stable routing topology. This is common when implementing a solution for Stuck-In-Active (SIA) routes. SIA will be described in detail later in this chapter.

EIGRP Neighbor Table

The EIGRP Neighbor Table is used by routers running EIGRP to maintain state information about EIGRP neighbors. When newly discovered neighbors are learned, the address and interface of the neighbor is recorded. This is applicable to both dynamically discovered neighbors and statically defined neighbors. There is a single EIGRP Neighbor Table for each Protocol-Dependent Module (PDM).

When an EIGRP neighbor sends a Hello packet, it advertises a Hold time, which is the amount of time a router treats a neighbor as reachable and operational. After a router receives a Hello packet, the Hold time value begins to decrement and count down to zero. When another Hello packet is received, the Hold time value restarts from the beginning and the process is continually repeated. If a Hello packet is not received within the Hold time, then the Hold time expires (goes to 0). When the Hold time expires, DUAL is informed of the topology change and the neighbor is declared down by EIGRP. A message similar to the following is then printed and logged by the router:

```
%DUAL-5-NBRCHANGE: IP-EIGRP(0) 1: Neighbor 10.1.1.2 (Serial0/0) is down:
holding time expired
```

The EIGRP Neighbor Table entry also includes information required by the Reliable Transport Protocol (RTP). RTP is the protocol that is used by EIGRP to ensure that Update, Query, and Reply packets are sent reliably. In addition, sequence numbers are also used to match acknowledgments with data packets. The last sequence number received from the neighbor is recorded in order to detect out-of-order packets. This ensures reliable packet delivery.

NOTE: RTP is described in detail later in this chapter.

The Neighbor Table includes a transmission list that is used to queue packets for possible retransmission on a per neighbor basis. Additionally, round-trip timers are kept in the neighbor data structure to estimate an optimal retransmission interval. All of this information is printed in the output of the `show ip eigrp neighbors` command as illustrated below:

```
R2#show ip eigrp neighbors
IP-EIGRP neighbors for process 150
H   Address              Interface      Hold Uptime    SRTT   RTO  Q  Seq
                                        (sec)          (ms)        Cnt Num
0   192.168.1.3          Fa0/0          14 00:43:08       2   200  0  12
```

It is important to understand the information printed by this command, both as a basis for demonstrating competency on a core EIGRP component and for troubleshooting EIGRP issues. Table 2-2 below lists and describes the fields contained in the output of this command:

Table 2-2. EIGRP Neighbor Table Fields

Field	Description
H	The list of neighbors in the order they are learned, starting at 0
Address	The IP address of the neighbor
Interface	The interface via which the neighbor is learned
Hold	The Hold timer for the neighbor; if it gets to 0, the neighbor is down
Uptime	Timer for how long the neighbor relationship has been up
SRTT	Smooth Round-Trip Time, which is the time it takes to send and receive a reliable EIGRP packet
RTO	Round-Trip Timeout, which is the amount of time the router will wait to retransmit the EIGRP reliable packet if an ACK is not received
Q Cnt	The number of EIGRP packets (Update, Query, and Reply) that the software is waiting to send
Sequence Number	The sequence number of the last EIGRP reliable packets being received from the neighbor to ensure that packets received from the neighbor are in order

While the `show ip eigrp neighbors` command prints out information on known EIGRP neighbors, it does not differentiate between dynamically discovered and manually configured neighbors. For example, the output of the `show ip eigrp neighbors` command on R2 indicates that the router has two EIGRP neighbor relationships. Based on this configuration, one is a statically configured neighbor, while the other is dynamically discovered. As we can see, it is not possible to determine which is which based on the following output:

```
R2#show ip eigrp neighbors
IP-EIGRP neighbors for process 150
H   Address              Interface      Hold Uptime    SRTT   RTO  Q  Seq
                                        (sec)          (ms)        Cnt Num
```

```
1    150.2.2.2              Se0/0              13 00:00:48  153   918 0  4
0    192.168.1.3           Fa0/0              10 08:33:23   1    200 0  20
```

In environments where the router has both dynamically discovered and manually configured neighbor relationships, the show ip eigrp neighbors detail command can be used to determine which neighbor is statically configured and which is dynamically discovered as illustrated below:

```
R2#show ip eigrp neighbors detail
IP-EIGRP neighbors for process 150
H   Address                 Interface       Hold Uptime   SRTT   RTO  Q  Seq
                                            (sec)         (ms)      Cnt Num
1   150.2.2.2               Se0/0             11 00:04:22  153   918 0  4
    Version 12.3/1.2, Retrans: 0, Retries: 0, Prefixes: 1
0   192.168.1.3             Fa0/0             10 08:36:58   1    200 0  20
    Static neighbor
    Version 12.4/1.2, Retrans: 0, Retries: 0, Prefixes: 1
```

Referencing the output above, neighbor 192.168.1.3 is a manually configured neighbor and neighbor 150.2.2.2 is a dynamically discovered neighbor. The static neighbors can also be viewed using the show ip eigrp neighbors static <interface> command as illustrated below:

```
R2#show ip eigrp neighbors static FastEthernet0/0
IP-EIGRP neighbors for process 150
Static Address              Interface
192.168.1.3                 FastEthernet0/0
```

Reliable Transport Protocol

Enhanced IGRP needs its own transport protocol to ensure the reliable delivery of packets. RTP is the protocol that is used by EIGRP to ensure that Update, Query, and Reply packets are sent reliably. The use of sequence numbers also ensures that the EIGRP packets are received in the correct order.

When reliable EIGRP packets are sent to a neighbor, the sending router expects an ACK from the receiving routers stating that the packet has been received. Using RTP, EIGRP maintains a transport window of one unacknowledged packet, which means that every single reliable packet that is sent out must be acknowledged before the next reliable packet can be sent. The sending router will retransmit the unacknowledged reliable packet until it receives an ACK.

It is important to note, however, that the unacknowledged packet will be retransmitted only up to 16 times. If there is still no acknowledgment after 16 retransmissions, EIGRP will reset the neighbor relationship. RTP uses both Multicast and Unicast packets. On Broadcast multi-access networks such as Ethernet, EIGRP uses Multicast packets instead of sending an individual packet (Unicast) to each router on the segment. However, packets may also be sent using Unicast if a response is not received from one or more of the neighbors on the multi-access segment. This is described referencing the diagram in Figure 2-7 below:

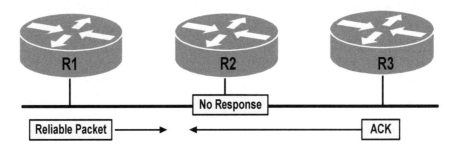

Fig. 2-7. EIGRP RTP Operation

In Figure 2-7, routers R1, R2, and R3 reside on a common subnet on the multi-access segment. Given the media, EIGRP will use Multicast to send reliable packets between the routers. Assume, for example, that R1 sends out a packet that requires acknowledgment to routers R2 and R3. R1 then waits for acknowledgement from R2 and R3 confirming receipt of this packet.

Assume that R3 responds but R2 is unable to respond to this packet. Given that EIGRP maintains a transport window of one unacknowledged packet, which means that every individual reliable packet that is sent out must be acknowledged explicitly by the neighbor router(s) before the next reliable packet can be sent, this presents a possible issue on the multi-access segment because R1 will not be able to send out packets until it has received the acknowledgment from R2. R3 is therefore indirectly affected by the issues on R2.

To avoid this potential pitfall, R1 will wait for the Multicast Flow Timer (MFT) on the Ethernet interface connected to the multi-access segment to expire. The MFT, or simply the Flow Timer, is the maximum amount of time that the sending router will wait for an ACK packet from a group member. When the timer expires, R1 will Multicast a special EIGRP packet called a Sequence TLV. This packet lists R2 (the offender) and indicates an out-of-sequence Multicast packet. Because R3 is not listed in this packet, it enters Conditional Receive (CR) mode and continues listening to Multicast packets. R1 uses Unicast to retransmit the packet to R2. The Round-Trip Timeout (RTO) indicates the time that the router waits for an acknowledgement of that Unicast packet. If after 16 total attempts there is still no response from R2, then EIGRP will reset the neighbor.

NOTE: You are not required to go into any further detail on MFT or RTO in the ROUTE exam.

METRICS, DUAL, AND THE TOPOLOGY TABLE

When implementing EIGRP, it is important to understand the various aspects used within and by the protocol before routes are actually placed into the IP routing table. In this section, we will learn about the EIGRP composite metric and how it is calculated. We will also learn about the different ways to influence metric calculation, as well as to adjust the calculated metric.

Following that, we will learn about the Diffusing Update Algorithm (DUAL) and the EIGRP Topology Table and conclude by discussing how the information covered in this section meshes when it comes to populating the IP routing table on a router running EIGRP.

EIGRP Composite Metric Calculation

Enhanced IGRP uses a composite metric, which includes different variables referred to as the K values. The K values are constants that are used to distribute weight to different path aspects, which may be included in the composite EIGRP metric. The default values for the K values are K1 = K3 = 1 and K2 = K4 = K5 = 0. In other words, K1 and K3 are set to a default value of 1, while K2, K4, and K5 are set to a default value of 0.

Assuming the default K value settings, the complete EIGRP metric can be calculated using the following mathematical formula:

[K1 * bandwidth + (K2 * bandwidth) / (256 - load) + K3 * delay] * [K5 / (reliability + K4)]

However, given that only K1 and K3 have any positive values by default, the default EIGRP metric calculation is performed using the following mathematical formula:

$[(10^7/\text{least bandwidth on path}) + (\text{sum of all delays})] \times 256$

This essentially means that, by default, EIGRP uses the minimum bandwidth on the path to a destination network and the total delay to compute routing metrics. However, Cisco IOS software allows administrators to set other K values to non-zero values to incorporate other variables into the composite metric. This may be performed using the `metric weights [tos] k1 k2 k3 k4 k5` router configuration command.

When using the `metric weights` command, `[tos]` stands for Type of Service. Although the Cisco IOS software shows that any value between 0 and 8 may be used, as of the time of the writing of this guide, this field can currently be set only to zero. The K values can be set to any value between 0 and 255. The default EIGRP K values can be viewed by issuing the `show ip protocols` command. This is illustrated in the following output:

```
R2#show ip protocols
Routing Protocol is "eigrp 150"
  Outgoing update filter list for all interfaces is not set
  Incoming update filter list for all interfaces is not set
  Default networks flagged in outgoing updates
  Default networks accepted from incoming updates
  EIGRP metric weight K1=1, K2=0, K3=1, K4=0, K5=0
  EIGRP maximum hopcount 100
  EIGRP maximum metric variance 1
  Redistributing: eigrp 150
  EIGRP NSF-aware route hold timer is 240s
  Automatic network summarization is not in effect
  Maximum path: 4
  Routing for Networks:
    192.168.1.0
  Routing Information Sources:
    Gateway          Distance      Last Update
    192.168.1.3            90      00:00:15
  Distance: internal 90 external 170
```

When adjusting the EIGRP K values, it is important to remember that the same values must be configured on all routers within the EIGRP domain. If the K values are mismatched, EIGRP neighbor relationships will not be established.

> **NOTE:** Adjusting the default K value settings is not recommended. It should be done only with the assistance of seasoned senior-level engineers who have a solid understanding of the implications of such actions within the network or based upon the recommendation of the Cisco Technical Assistance Center (TAC).

Using Interface Bandwidth to Influence EIGRP Metric Calculation

Enhanced IGRP metric calculation can be directly influenced by adjusting the default bandwidth values assigned to individual interfaces using the bandwidth command. The bandwidth values specified by this command are in Kilobits. The bandwidth used in EIGRP metric calculation is also in Kilobits. Figure 2-8 below illustrates a network comprised of two routers connected via two Serial (T1) links that have a bandwidth value of 1544Kbps:

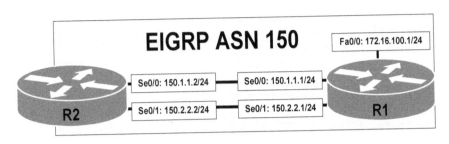

Fig. 2-8. EIGRP Metric Bandwidth Manipulation

Referencing the diagram in Figure 2-8, because of the equal bandwidth (and delay) values of the links between R1 and R2, the same EIGRP metric will be derived for both paths from R2 to the 172.16.100.0/24 subnet. EIGRP will load-share traffic between the two Serial links as illustrated in the following output on R2:

```
R2#show ip route 172.16.100.0 255.255.255.0
Routing entry for 172.16.100.0/24
  Known via "eigrp 150", distance 90, metric 2172416, type internal
  Redistributing via eigrp 150
  Last update from 150.2.2.1 on Serial0/1, 00:48:09 ago
  Routing Descriptor Blocks:
    150.2.2.1, from 150.2.2.1, 00:48:09 ago, via Serial0/1
      Route metric is 2172416, traffic share count is 1
      Total delay is 20100 microseconds, minimum bandwidth is 1544 Kbit
      Reliability 255/255, minimum MTU 1500 bytes
      Loading 1/255, Hops 1
  * 150.1.1.1, from 150.1.1.1, 00:48:09 ago, via Serial0/0
      Route metric is 2172416, traffic share count is 1
      Total delay is 20100 microseconds, minimum bandwidth is 1544 Kbit
      Reliability 255/255, minimum MTU 1500 bytes
      Loading 1/255, Hops 1
```

Adjusting the default bandwidth value on either interface will directly influence EIGRP metric calculation for the path to the destination network. Such actions can be used for path control within larger networks (i.e., controlling the path that traffic takes based on administrator-defined values and configurations). For example, if it was preferred that EIGRP use Serial0/0 as the primary path to the destination network and Serial0/1 as the backup path to the destination, one of two actions could be taken.

The first is that the bandwidth value on Serial0/0 could be incremented, resulting in a better (lower) metric for this path. The second is that the bandwidth value on Serial0/1 could be decremented, resulting in a worse (higher) metric for this path. Either option is acceptable and will achieve the desired result. The following illustrates how to decrement the default bandwidth value on Serial0/1, effectively ensuring that Serial0/0 is used as the primary path between R2 and the 172.16.100.0/24 network:

```
R2(config)#interface Serial 0/1
R2(config-if)#bandwidth 1024
R2(config-if)#exit
```

NOTE: As stated in Chapter 1, this configuration does not mean that Serial0/1 is now capable of only 1024Kbps of throughput through this interface.

The result of this configuration is that Serial0/0 is the primary path used by R2 to get to the 172.16.100.0/24 destination network. This is illustrated in the following output:

```
R2#show ip route 172.16.100.0 255.255.255.0
Routing entry for 172.16.100.0/24
  Known via "eigrp 150", distance 90, metric 2172416, type internal
  Redistributing via eigrp 150
  Last update from 150.1.1.1 on Serial0/0, 00:01:55 ago
  Routing Descriptor Blocks:
  * 150.1.1.1, from 150.1.1.1, 00:01:55 ago, via Serial0/0
      Route metric is 2172416, traffic share count is 1
      Total delay is 20100 microseconds, minimum bandwidth is 1544 Kbit
      Reliability 255/255, minimum MTU 1500 bytes
      Loading 1/255, Hops 1
```

NOTE: The asterisk (*) points to the interface over which the next packet is sent. In the event that there are multiple equal-cost routes in the routing table, the position of the * rotates among the equal-cost paths.

Although the path via the Serial0/1 interface is not installed into the routing table, when using EIGRP as the routing protocol, it is important to remember that this path is not completely ignored, however. Instead, this path is stored in the EIGRP Topology Table, which contains the primary and alternate (backup) paths to remote destination networks. The EIGRP Topology Table will be described in detail later in this chapter.

While adjusting the default bandwidth value on the interface can be used for path control, it is important to understand that the bandwidth value can also affect other configurations on the router. A primary example would be certain Quality of Service (QoS) implementations that use the interface bandwidth value to determine the bit rate afforded to each traffic class. For example, referencing the network in Figure 2-8 above, assume that voice engineers have implemented a QoS policy that allocates 30% of the available link bandwidth to voice bearer traffic. The policy is applied to both the Serial0/0 and Serial0/1 interfaces, which are both T1 speed. Prior to any changes on R2, the policy shows the following bandwidth allocation for Serial0/0:

```
R2#show policy-map interface Serial0/0 output class Voice-Bearer-Traffic
Serial0/0

  Service-policy output: QoS-Implementation

    Class-map: Voice-Bearer-Traffic (match-all)
      0 packets, 0 bytes
      5 minute offered rate 0 bps, drop rate 0 bps
      Match: ip dscp ef (46)
      Queueing
        Strict Priority
        Output Queue: Conversation 264
        Bandwidth 30 (%)
        Bandwidth 463 (kbps) Burst 11575 (Bytes)
        (pkts matched/bytes matched) 0/0
        (total drops/bytes drops) 0/0
```

The same QoS bandwidth allocation is also reflected for the Serial0/1 interface as illustrated below:

```
R2#show policy-map interface Serial 0/1 output class Voice-Bearer-Traffic
Serial0/1

  Service-policy output: QoS-Implementation

    Class-map: Voice-Bearer-Traffic (match-all)
      0 packets, 0 bytes
      5 minute offered rate 0 bps, drop rate 0 bps
      Match: ip dscp ef (46)
      Queueing
        Strict Priority
        Output Queue: Conversation 264
        Bandwidth 30 (%)
        Bandwidth 463 (kbps) Burst 11575 (Bytes)
        (pkts matched/bytes matched) 0/0
        (total drops/bytes drops) 0/0
```

As illustrated in the two outputs above, the bandwidth allocations for both links is identical and 30% (463Kbps) is afforded to voice traffic based on the calculations of the voice engineers. By adjusting the default interface bandwidth to influence EIGRP path selection, you will also affect the configuration implemented by the voice engineers.

For example, referencing the same bandwidth configuration as shown in the previous example, changing the interface bandwidth value on Serial0/1 to 1024Kbps results in the following change to the QoS configuration that is implemented on the Serial0/1 interface:

```
R2#show policy-map interface Serial 0/1 output class Voice-Bearer-Traffic
  Serial0/1

  Service-policy output: QoS-Implementation

    Class-map: Voice-Bearer-Traffic (match-all)
      0 packets, 0 bytes
      5 minute offered rate 0 bps, drop rate 0 bps
      Match: ip dscp ef (46)
      Queueing
        Strict Priority
        Output Queue: Conversation 264
        Bandwidth 30 (%)
        Bandwidth 307 (kbps) Burst 7675 (Bytes)
        (pkts matched/bytes matched) 0/0
        (total drops/bytes drops) 0/0
```

Now, the 30% allocation is approximately 307Kbps, instead of 463Kbps. Therefore, although the bandwidth change achieves the desired objective from a routing perspective, it affects other configurations on the router. In addition, adjusting the bandwidth value could also affect other things, such as interface statistics, SNMP reporting, or even TCP-based applications.

NOTE: By default, when EIGRP is enabled, it can use up to 50% of the interface bandwidth to send EIGRP packets. EIGRP determines the bandwidth amount based on the `bandwidth` interface configuration command. Therefore, when adjusting interface bandwidth values, it is important to keep this fact in mind. This default setting can be adjusted by using the `ip bandwidth-percent eigrp [ASN] [percentage]` interface configuration command.

In summation, when using the bandwidth command to influence EIGRP metric calculation, it is important to remember that EIGRP uses the minimum bandwidth on the path to a destination network, along with the cumulative delay, to compute routing metrics. It is important to have a solid understanding of the network topology to best determine where to use the bandwidth command to influence EIGRP metric calculation.

Using Interface Delay to Influence EIGRP Metric Calculation

The interface delay value is presented in microseconds. The delay value used in EIGRP metric calculation is in tens of microseconds. Therefore, the delay value on the interface must be divided by

10 in order to compute the EIGRP metric. Table 2-3 below shows the default interface bandwidth and delay values used in Cisco IOS software:

Table 2-3. Default Interface Bandwidth and Delay Values

Interface	Bandwidth (Kilobits)	Delay (Microseconds)
Ethernet	10000	1000
FastEthernet	100000	100
GigabitEthernet	1000000	10
Ten GigabitEthernet	10000000	10
Serial (T1)	1544	20000
Serial (E1)	2048	20000
Serial (T3)	44736	200
Serial (E3)	34010	200

When working with the interface bandwidth and delay values, it is very important to remember that adjusting the interface bandwidth value does not automatically adjust the interface delay value, and vice-versa. The two values are independent of each other. As an example, the output that follows shows the default bandwidth and delay values for a FastEthernet interface:

```
R2#show interfaces FastEthernet0/0
FastEthernet0/0 is up, line protocol is up
  Hardware is AmdFE, address is 0013.1986.0a20 (bia 0013.1986.0a20)
  Internet address is 192.168.1.2/24
  MTU 1500 bytes, BW 100000 Kbit/sec, DLY 100 usec,
    reliability 255/255, txload 1/255, rxload 1/255
...
```

To reinforce this concept, the bandwidth value on the FastEthernet interface is adjusted to 1544Kbps using the bandwidth interface configuration command as follows:

```
R2(config)#interface FastEthernet0/0
R2(config-if)#bandwidth 1544
R2(config-if)#exit
```

While the bandwidth value now displayed in the output of the show interfaces command reflects the implemented configuration, the default interface delay value remains the same as illustrated below:

```
R2#show interfaces FastEthernet0/0
FastEthernet0/0 is up, line protocol is up
  Hardware is AmdFE, address is 0013.1986.0a20 (bia 0013.1986.0a20)
  Internet address is 192.168.1.2/24
```

```
MTU 1500 bytes, BW 1544 Kbit/sec, DLY 100 usec,
     reliability 255/255, txload 1/255, rxload 1/255
...
```

The cumulative delay used by EIGRP is the sum of all interface delays between the source and the destination network. Changing any of the delay values in the path influences EIGRP metric calculation. The interface delay value is adjusted using the delay interface configuration command. This value is then divided by 10 when used in EIGRP metric calculation. Figure 2-9 below illustrates a network comprised of two routers connected via two Serial (T1) links that have a bandwidth value of 1544Kbps and a default delay of 20000 microseconds. In addition, the 172.16.100.0/24 network is directly connected to a FastEthernet interface, which has a default bandwidth of 100000Kbps and a default delay value of 100 microseconds:

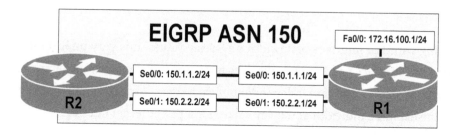

Fig. 2-9. EIGRP Metric Delay Manipulation

The EIGRP metric from R2 to the 172.16.100.0/24 network is calculated as follows:

Metric = [(10^7/least bandwidth on path) + (sum of all delays)] × 256
Metric = [(10000000/1544) + (2000+10)] × 256

NOTE: Remember to divide the interface delay values by 10 for EIGRP metric calculation.

Metric = [(10000000/1544) + (2000+10)] × 256

NOTE: The calculated value should always be rounded down to the nearest integer.

Metric = [6476 + 2010] × 256
Metric = 8486 × 256
Metric = 2172416

NOTE: For the purposes of the ROUTE exam, ensure that you are familiar with the way in which the EIGRP metric is calculated, assuming that the relevant variables have been provided.

This calculation can be verified in the output of the show ip route command as follows:

```
R2#show ip route 172.16.100.0 255.255.255.0
Routing entry for 172.16.100.0/24
  Known via "eigrp 150", distance 90, metric 2172416, type internal
  Redistributing via eigrp 150
  Last update from 150.2.2.1 on Serial0/1, 00:03:28 ago
  Routing Descriptor Blocks:
    150.2.2.1, from 150.2.2.1, 00:03:28 ago, via Serial0/1
      Route metric is 2172416, traffic share count is 1
      Total delay is 20100 microseconds, minimum bandwidth is 1544 Kbit
      Reliability 255/255, minimum MTU 1500 bytes
      Loading 1/255, Hops 1
  * 150.1.1.1, from 150.1.1.1, 00:03:28 ago, via Serial0/0
      Route metric is 2172416, traffic share count is 1
      Total delay is 20100 microseconds, minimum bandwidth is 1544 Kbit
      Reliability 255/255, minimum MTU 1500 bytes
      Loading 1/255, Hops 1
```

As with the bandwidth command, you can either increment or decrement the interface delay value using the delay command to influence EIGRP metric calculation. For example, to configure R2 to use the Serial0/0 link to get to the 172.16.100.0/24 network, with Serial0/1 being used as a backup link only, the delay value on Serial0/0 could be decremented as follows:

```
R2(config)#int s 0/0
R2(config-if)#delay 100
R2(config-if)#exit
```

This configuration adjusts the EIGRP metric for the path via Serial0/0 as illustrated below:

```
R2#show ip route 172.16.100.0 255.255.255.0
Routing entry for 172.16.100.0/24
  Known via "eigrp 150", distance 90, metric 1686016, type internal
  Redistributing via eigrp 150
  Last update from 150.1.1.1 on Serial0/0, 00:01:09 ago
  Routing Descriptor Blocks:
  * 150.1.1.1, from 150.1.1.1, 00:01:09 ago, via Serial0/0
      Route metric is 1686016, traffic share count is 1
      Total delay is 1100 microseconds, minimum bandwidth is 1544 Kbit
      Reliability 255/255, minimum MTU 1500 bytes
      Loading 1/255, Hops 1
```

The path via Serial0/1 is retained in the Topology Table as an alternate path to the network.

Adjusting the Calculated EIGRP Metric Using Offset Lists

Cisco IOS software allows network administrators to use a feature called an offset list to adjust the calculated EIGRP metric. Unlike the bandwidth and delay, the offset list does not directly influence the calculation of the EIGRP metric. Instead, it is used to adjust the computed metric by the value specified in the offset list configuration.

An EIGRP offset list is configured via the offset-list [0-99 | 1300-1399] [in|out] [off-set] [interface name|CR] router configuration command. If an offset list is configured using 0 (e.g., offset-list 0 in), then the offset list configuration will be applied to all networks. However, if any other value is specified in the offset list configuration, the configuration is applied to the prefixes that match the ACL number. The offset is a numerical value between 0 and 2147483647; however, this may be different depending on the Cisco IOS software version. You can use the question mark to validate the range supported in your image.

Figure 2-10 below illustrates a network comprised of two routers connected via two Serial links. The 172.16.100.0/24 and 172.16.200.0/24 networks are directly connected to R1:

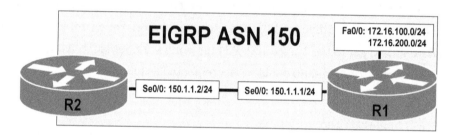

Fig. 2-10. Using EIGRP Offset Lists

For EIGRP routes placed into the routing table, offset lists adjust the EIGRP route metric in the output of the show ip route command by the value specified in the offset list. The EIGRP metric for both of the routes before the implementation of an offset list is illustrated in the show ip route command as follows:

```
R2#show ip route eigrp
      172.16.0.0/24 is subnetted, 2 subnets
D        172.16.200.0 [90/2172416] via 150.1.1.1, 00:00:06, Serial0/0
D        172.16.100.0 [90/2172416] via 150.1.1.1, 00:00:06, Serial0/0
```

In the EIGRP Topology Table, the offset list adjusts the Feasible Distance (FD), which is the minimum metric toward the destination and is the same as the route metric in the routing table, as well as the Reported Distance (RD), which is the metric toward a destination network as advertised by an upstream neighbor. These values are printed in the output of the show ip eigrp topology [prefix] [mask] command. Both terms are described in detail in the following section on the Diffusing Update Algorithm. These values for the 172.16.100.0/24 prefix are illustrated below:

```
R2#show ip eigrp topology 172.16.100.0 255.255.255.0
IP-EIGRP (AS 150): Topology entry for 172.16.100.0/24
  State is Passive, Query origin flag is 1, 1 Successor(s), FD is 2172416
  Routing Descriptor Blocks:
  150.1.1.1 (Serial0/0), from 150.1.1.1, Send flag is 0x0
      Composite metric is (2172416/28160), Route is Internal
      Vector metric:
        Minimum bandwidth is 1544 Kbit
        Total delay is 20100 microseconds
        Reliability is 255/255
        Load is 1/255
        Minimum MTU is 1500
        Hop count is 1
```

NOTE: Because the values will be the same for 172.16.200.0, the output is omitted for brevity.

To increment the route metric in the inbound direction for both prefixes by 1000, for example, we can use the offset-list 0 in 1000 router configuration command or the offset-list 0 in 1000 Serial0/0 router configuration command. Either one is acceptable.

NOTE: In situations where the router has multiple EIGRP neighbor relationships via multiple interfaces, and is receiving routing information from these different neighbors, it is always best practice to add the interface to the end of this command. This restricts the offset list configuration to routes received or sent via that interface and only to the known neighbors of those interfaces. In the event that the interface is not specified, the offset list configuration applies to all prefixes received and sent on all interfaces.

Following best practices, the offset list is configured as follows on R1:

```
R1(config)#router eigrp 150
R1(config-router)#offset-list 0 in 1000 Serial0/0
R1(config-router)#exit
```

Based on this configuration, the route metric for both received prefixes on R2 is incremented by 1000, from 2172416 to 2173416, as illustrated in the following output:

```
R2#show ip route eigrp
     172.16.0.0/24 is subnetted, 2 subnets
D       172.16.200.0 [90/2173416] via 150.1.1.1, 00:00:27, Serial0/0
D       172.16.100.0 [90/2173416] via 150.1.1.1, 00:00:27, Serial0/0
```

In the EIGRP Topology Table, the Feasible Distance and Reported Distance (FD/RD) values are also incremented by 1000, from 2172416/28160 to 2173416/29160, as illustrated below:

```
R2#show ip eigrp topology 172.16.200.0 255.255.255.0
IP-EIGRP (AS 150): Topology entry for 172.16.200.0/24
  State is Passive, Query origin flag is 1, 1 Successor(s), FD is 2173416
  Routing Descriptor Blocks:
  150.1.1.1 (Serial0/0), from 150.1.1.1, Send flag is 0x0
      Composite metric is (2173416/29160), Route is Internal
      Vector metric:
        Minimum bandwidth is 1544 Kbit
        Total delay is 20139 microseconds
        Reliability is 255/255
        Load is 1/255
        Minimum MTU is 1500
        Hop count is 1
```

NOTE: The same metric manipulation is also applicable to the 172.16.100.0/24 subnet.

For more granular control, an ACL can be used in conjunction with the offset list. Referencing the network in Figure 2-10 above, the routing table on R2 shows the following:

```
R2#show ip route eigrp
      172.16.0.0/24 is subnetted, 2 subnets
D        172.16.200.0 [90/2172416] via 150.1.1.1, 00:00:12, Serial0/0
D        172.16.100.0 [90/2172416] via 150.1.1.1, 00:00:12, Serial0/0
```

The FD and the RD values for both prefixes are the same in the EIGRP Topology Table. For brevity, illustrated below are the values for the 172.16.100.0/24 prefix only:

```
R2#show ip eigrp topology 172.16.100.0 255.255.255.0
IP-EIGRP (AS 150): Topology entry for 172.16.100.0/24
  State is Passive, Query origin flag is 1, 1 Successor(s), FD is 2172416
  Routing Descriptor Blocks:
  150.1.1.1 (Serial0/0), from 150.1.1.1, Send flag is 0x0
      Composite metric is (2172416/28160), Route is Internal
      Vector metric:
        Minimum bandwidth is 1544 Kbit
        Total delay is 20100 microseconds
        Reliability is 255/255
        Load is 1/255
        Minimum MTU is 1500
        Hop count is 1
```

To demonstrate the use of offset lists in the outbound direction, as well as in conjunction with ACLs, an offset list will be configured on R1 to increment by 5000 the route metric for outbound updates for the 172.16.100.0/24 prefix only. This is implemented on R1 as illustrated below:

```
R1(config)#access-list 1 remark 'Offset Metric For 172.16.100.0/24 Only'
R1(config)#access-list 1 permit host 172.16.100.0
R1(config)#router eigrp 150
R1(config-router)#offset-list 1 out 5000 Serial0/0
R1(config-router)#exit
```

Based on this configuration, the routing table entries for the two prefixes on R2 are illustrated as follows:

```
R2#show ip route eigrp
      172.16.0.0/24 is subnetted, 2 subnets
D        172.16.200.0 [90/2172416] via 150.1.1.1, 00:00:22, Serial0/0
D        172.16.100.0 [90/2177416] via 150.1.1.1, 00:00:22, Serial0/0
```

Notice that the metric for the 172.16.100.0/24 prefix is higher than that of the 172.16.200.0/24 prefix by 5000. This change is also reflected in the following EIGRP Topology Table for the 172.16.100.0/24 prefix:

```
R2#show ip eigrp topology 172.16.100.0 255.255.255.0
IP-EIGRP (AS 150): Topology entry for 172.16.100.0/24
  State is Passive, Query origin flag is 1, 1 Successor(s), FD is 2177416
  Routing Descriptor Blocks:
  150.1.1.1 (Serial0/0), from 150.1.1.1, Send flag is 0x0
     Composite metric is (2177416/33160), Route is Internal
     Vector metric:
        Minimum bandwidth is 1544 Kbit
        Total delay is 20295 microseconds
        Reliability is 255/255
        Load is 1/255
        Minimum MTU is 1500
        Hop count is 1
```

NOTE: When applying or removing offset lists, EIGRP will reset the neighbor relationships of the specified interface (if specified) or for all neighbors (if no interface is specified). This is illustrated in the following output in which an offset list is applied to a router with three EIGRP neighbors of three different interfaces:

```
R2#show ip eigrp neighbors
IP-EIGRP neighbors for process 150
H   Address              Interface       Hold Uptime   SRTT   RTO  Q  Seq
```

```
                                          (sec)        (ms)      Cnt Num
2    150.2.2.1           Se0/1           14 00:02:23   74   444  0   58
1    192.168.1.3         Fa0/0           10 00:05:54    1   200  0   13
0    150.1.1.1           Se0/0           11 00:22:32   31   200  0   59
R2#
R2#conf t
Enter configuration commands, one per line.  End with CNTL/Z.
R2(config)#router eigrp 150
R2(config-router)#offset-list 0 in 55555
R2(config-router)#exit
R2(config)#
*Mar  1 09:06:33.520: %DUAL-5-NBRCHANGE: IP-EIGRP(0) 150: Neighbor 150.1.1.1
(Serial0/0) is resync: route configuration changed
*Mar  1 09:06:33.520: %DUAL-5-NBRCHANGE: IP-EIGRP(0) 150: Neighbor 150.2.2.1
(Serial0/1) is resync: route configuration changed
```

The Diffusing Update Algorithm (DUAL)

The Diffusing Update Algorithm is at the crux of the EIGRP routing protocol. DUAL looks at all routes received from neighbor routers, compares them, and then selects the lowest metric (best), loop-free path to the destination network, which is the Feasible Distance (FD), resulting in the Successor route. The Feasible Distance includes both the metric of a network as advertised by the connected neighbor plus the cost of reaching that particular neighbor.

The metric that is advertised by the neighbor router is referred to as the Reported Distance (RD) or as the Advertised Distance (AD) to the destination network. Therefore, the Feasible Distance includes the Reported Distance plus the cost of reaching that particular neighbor. The next hop router for the Successor route is referred to as the Successor. The Successor route is placed into the IP routing table and the EIGRP Topology Table and points to the Successor.

Any other routes to the same destination network that have a lower Reported Distance than the Feasible Distance of the Successor path are guaranteed to be loop-free and are referred to as Feasible Successor (FS) routes. These routes are not placed into the IP routing table; however, they are still placed into the EIGRP Topology Table, along with the Successor routes.

In order for a route to become a Feasible Successor route, it must meet the Feasibility Condition (FC), which occurs only when the Reported Distance to the destination network is less than the Feasible Distance. In the event that the Reported Distance is more than the Feasible Distance, the route is not selected as a Feasible Successor. This is used by EIGRP to prevent the possibility of loops. The network topology illustrated in Figure 2-11 below will be used to clarify the terminology referred to in this section:

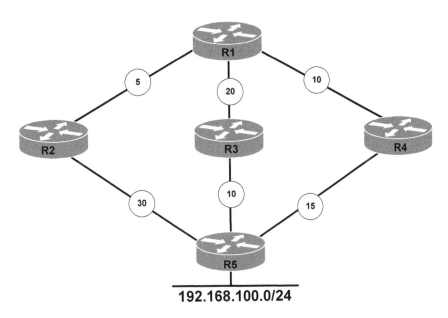

Fig. 2-11. Understanding the Diffusing Update Algorithm

Referencing Figure 2-11, Table 2-4 below shows the Feasible Distance and the Reported Distance values as seen on R1 for the 192.168.100.0/24 network:

Table 2-4. R1 Paths and Distances

Network Path	R1 Neighbor	Neighbor Metric (RD)	R1 Feasible Distance
R1—R2—R5	R2	30	35
R1—R3—R5	R3	10	30
R1—R4—R5	R4	15	25

Based on the information in Table 2-4, R1 will select the path through R4 as the Successor route based on the Feasible Distance for the route, which is 25. This route will be placed into the IP routing table as well as the EIGRP Topology Table. R1 then looks at alternate paths to the 192.168.100.0/24 network. The metric for neighbor R3 to the 192.168.100.0/24 network, also referred to as the Reported Distance or Advertised Distance, is 10. This is less than the Feasible Distance and so this route meets the Feasibility Condition and is placed into the EIGRP Topology Table. The metric for neighbor R2 to the 192.168.100.0/24 network is 30. This value is higher than the Feasible Distance of 25. This route does not meet the Feasibility Condition and is not considered a Feasible Successor. The route, however, is still placed into the EIGRP Topology Table. This is illustrated in the section on the EIGRP Topology Table that follows.

When a neighbor changes a metric, or when a topology change occurs, and the Successor route is removed or changes, DUAL checks for Feasible Successors for the route and if one is found, then

DUAL uses it to avoid re-computing the route unnecessarily. This is referred to as local computation. Performing a local computation saves CPU power because the Feasible Successor has been chosen and already exists before the Successor or primary route fails.

When no Feasible Successor for the destination network exists, the local router will send a Query to neighboring routers asking if they have information on the destination network. If the information is available and another neighbor does have a route to the destination network, then the router performs a diffusing computation to determine a new Successor.

The EIGRP Topology Table

The EIGRP Topology Table is populated by EIGRP PDMs acted upon by the DUAL Finite State Machine. All known destination networks and subnets that are advertised by neighboring EIGRP routers are stored in the EIGRP Topology Table. This includes Successor routes, Feasible Successor routes, and even routes that have not met the Feasibility Condition.

The Topology Table allows all EIGRP routers to have a consistent view of the entire network. It also allows for rapid convergence in EIGRP networks. Each individual entry in the Topology Table contains the destination network and the neighbor(s) that have advertised the destination network. Both the Feasible Distance and the Reported Distance are stored in the Topology Table. The EIGRP Topology Table contains the information needed to build a set of distances and vectors to each reachable network, including the following:

* The lowest bandwidth on the path to the destination network
* The total or cumulative delay to the destination network
* The reliability of the path to the destination network
* The loading of the path to the destination network
* The minimum Maximum Transmission Unit (MTU) to the destination network
* The Feasible Distance to the destination network
* The Reported Distance by the neighbor router to the destination network
* The route source (only external routes) of the destination network

NOTE: While the MTU is included in the Topology Table, EIGRP does not use this value in actual metric computation. Instead, the MTU is simply tracked to determine the minimum value to the destination network. The interface MTU specifies the largest size of datagram that can be transferred across a certain link without the need for fragmentation, or breaking the datagram or packet into smaller pieces.

The contents of the EIGRP Topology Table are viewed using the `show ip eigrp topology` command. The options that are available with this command are illustrated below:

```
R2#show ip eigrp topology ?
  <1-65535>        AS Number
  A.B.C.D          IP prefix <network>/<length>, e.g., 192.168.0.0/16
  A.B.C.D          Network to display information about
  active           Show only active entries
  all-links        Show all links in topology table
  detail-links     Show all links in topology table
  pending          Show only entries pending transmission
  summary          Show a summary of the topology table
  zero-successors  Show only zero successor entries
  |                Output modifiers
  <cr>
```

The show ip eigrp topology command with no options prints only the Successor and Feasible Successor information for routes in the Topology Table and for all of the EIGRP instances enabled on the router. The output printed by this command is illustrated below:

```
R2#show ip eigrp topology
IP-EIGRP Topology Table for AS(150)/ID(2.2.2.2)
Codes: P - Passive, A - Active, U - Update, Q - Query, R - Reply,
       r - reply Status, s - sia Status

P 150.2.2.0/24, 1 successors, FD is 20512000
        via Connected, Serial0/1
        via 150.1.1.1 (2195456/2169856), Serial0/0
P 150.1.1.0/24, 1 successors, FD is 1683456
        via Connected, Serial0/0
P 172.16.100.0/24, 1 successors, FD is 1686016
        via 150.1.1.1 (1686016/28160), Serial0/0
```

The show ip eigrp topology [network]/[prefix] and show ip eigrp topology [network] [mask] commands print Successor routes, Feasible Successor routes, and routes that have not met the Feasibility Condition for the route specified in either command. The following illustrates the use of the show ip eigrp topology [network]/[prefix]command:

```
R2#show ip eigrp topology 172.16.100.0/24
IP-EIGRP (AS 150): Topology entry for 172.16.100.0/24
  State is Passive, Query origin flag is 1, 1 Successor(s), FD is 1686016
  Routing Descriptor Blocks:
  150.1.1.1 (Serial0/0), from 150.1.1.1, Send flag is 0x0
      Composite metric is (1686016/28160), Route is Internal
      Vector metric:
        Minimum bandwidth is 1544 Kbit
```

```
        Total delay is 1100 microseconds
        Reliability is 255/255
        Load is 1/255
        Minimum MTU is 1500
        Hop count is 1
   150.2.2.1 (Serial0/1), from 150.2.2.1, Send flag is 0x0
       Composite metric is (2167998207/2147511807), Route is Internal
       Vector metric:
        Minimum bandwidth is 128 Kbit
        Total delay is 83906179 microseconds
        Reliability is 255/255
        Load is 1/255
        Minimum MTU is 1500
        Hop count is 1
```

In the output above, we can determine that the path via Serial0/1 does not meet the Feasibility Condition because the Reported Distance exceeds the Feasible Distance. This is why the path is not printed in the output of the show ip eigrp topology command. Instead of viewing each prefix on an individual basis to determine Successor routes, Feasible Successor routes, and routes that did not meet the Feasibility Condition, you can use the show ip eigrp topology command to view all possible routes for all of the prefixes in the EIGRP Topology Table. The output of this command is illustrated below:

```
R2#show ip eigrp topology all-links
IP-EIGRP Topology Table for AS(150)/ID(2.2.2.2)
Codes: P - Passive, A - Active, U - Update, Q - Query, R - Reply,
       r - reply Status, s - sia Status

P 150.2.2.0/24, 1 successors, FD is 20512000, serno 42
        via Connected, Serial0/1
        via 150.1.1.1 (2195456/2169856), Serial0/0
P 150.1.1.0/24, 1 successors, FD is 1683456, serno 32
        via Connected, Serial0/0
        via 150.2.2.1 (21024000/2169856), Serial0/1
P 172.16.100.0/24, 1 successors, FD is 1686016, serno 47
        via 150.1.1.1 (1686016/28160), Serial0/0
        via 150.2.2.1 (2167998207/2147511807), Serial0/1
```

Within the EIGRP Topology Table, entries may be marked either as Passive (P) or as Active (A). A route in the Passive state indicates that EIGRP has completed actively computing the metric for the route and traffic can be forwarded to the destination network using the Successor. This is the preferred state for all routes in the Topology Table.

Enhanced IGRP routes are in an Active state when the Successor has been lost and the router sends out a Query packet to determine a Feasible Successor. Usually, a Feasible Successor is present and EIGRP promotes that to the Successor. This way, the router converges without involving other routers in the network. This process is referred to as a local computation.

However, if the Successor has been lost or removed, and there is no Feasible Successor, then the router will begin diffused computation. In diffused computation, EIGRP will send a Query out to all neighbors and out of all interfaces, except for the interface to the Successor. When an EIGRP neighbor receives a Query for a route, and if that neighbor's EIGRP Topology Table does not contain an entry for the route, then the neighbor immediately replies to the Query with an unreachable message, stating that there is no path for this route through this neighbor.

If the EIGRP Topology Table on the neighbor lists the router sending the Query as the Successor for that route, and a Feasible Successor exists, then the Feasible Successor is installed and the router replies to the neighbor Query that it has a route to the lost destination network.

However, if the EIGRP Topology Table lists the router sending the Query as the Successor for this route and there is no Feasible Successor, then the router queries all of its EIGRP neighbors, except those that sent out the same interface as its former Successor. The router will not reply to the Query until it has received a Reply to all Queries that it originated for this route.

Finally, if the Query was received from a neighbor that is not the Successor for this destination, then the router replies with its own Successor information. If the neighboring routers do not have the lost route information, then Queries are sent from those neighboring routers to their neighboring routers until the Query boundary is reached. The Query boundary is either the end of the network, the distribute list boundary, or the summarization boundary.

Once the Query has been sent, the EIGRP router must wait for all replies to be received before it calculates the Successor. If any neighbor has not replied within three minutes, the route is said to be Stuck-in-Active (SIA). When a route is SIA, the neighbor relationship of the router(s) that did not respond to the Query will be reset. In such cases, you will see a message logged by the router similar to the following:

```
%DUAL-5-NBRCHANGE: IP-EIGRP 150:
    Neighbor 150.1.1.1(Serial0/0) is down: stuck in active
%DUAL-3-SIA:
    Route 172.16.100.0/24 stuck-in-active state in IP-EIGRP 150.
Cleaning up
```

There are several reasons why the EIGRP neighbor router(s) may not respond to the Query, which include the following:

- The neighbor router's CPU is overloaded and it cannot respond in time
- The neighbor router itself has no information about the lost route
- Quality issues on the circuit are causing packets to be lost
- Low-bandwidth links are congested and packets are being delayed

To prevent SIA issues due to delayed responses from other EIGRP neighbors, the local router can be configured to wait for longer than the default of three minutes to receive responses back to its Query packets using the `timers active-time` command in router configuration mode.

> **NOTE:** It is important to note that if you change this default parameter on one EIGRP router in your network, you must change it on all the other routers within your EIGRP routing domain.

Troubleshooting SIA, and other EIGRP issues, is incorporated in the TSHOOT exam. You can refer to the TSHOOT study guide available online for more information on SIA routes.

EQUAL COST AND UNEQUAL COST LOAD SHARING

Cisco IOS software supports equal cost load sharing for a default of up to four paths for all routing protocols. This is illustrated below in the output of the `show ip protocols` command:

```
R2#show ip protocols
Routing Protocol is "eigrp 150"
  Outgoing update filter list for all interfaces is not set
  Incoming update filter list for all interfaces is not set
  Default networks flagged in outgoing updates
  Default networks accepted from incoming updates
  EIGRP metric weight K1=1, K2=0, K3=1, K4=0, K5=0
  EIGRP maximum hopcount 100
  EIGRP maximum metric variance 1
  Redistributing: eigrp 150
  EIGRP NSF-aware route hold timer is 240s
  Automatic network summarization is not in effect
  Maximum path: 4
  Routing for Networks:
    150.1.1.2/32
    150.2.2.2/32
  Routing Information Sources:
    Gateway         Distance      Last Update
    Gateway         Distance      Last Update
```

```
   150.2.2.1                90      00:00:52
   150.1.1.1                90      00:00:52
Distance: internal 90 external 170
```

The `maximum-paths <1-6>` router configuration command can be used to change the default value of four maximum paths up to a maximum of six equal cost paths. When performing equal cost load balancing, the router distributes the load evenly among all paths. The traffic share count identifies the number of outgoing packets on each path. When performing equal cost load balancing, one packet is sent on each individual path as illustrated in the following output:

```
R2#show ip route 172.16.100.0 255.255.255.0
Routing entry for 172.16.100.0/24
   Known via "eigrp 150", distance 90, metric 2172416, type internal
   Redistributing via eigrp 150
   Last update from 150.2.2.1 on Serial0/1, 00:04:00 ago
   Routing Descriptor Blocks:
      150.2.2.1, from 150.2.2.1, 00:04:00 ago, via Serial0/1
         Route metric is 2172416, traffic share count is 1
         Total delay is 20100 microseconds, minimum bandwidth is 1544 Kbit
         Reliability 255/255, minimum MTU 1500 bytes
         Loading 1/255, Hops 1
    * 150.1.1.1, from 150.1.1.1, 00:04:00 ago, via Serial0/0
         Route metric is 2172416, traffic share count is 1
         Total delay is 20100 microseconds, minimum bandwidth is 1544 Kbit
         Reliability 255/255, minimum MTU 1500 bytes
         Loading 1/255, Hops 1
```

In addition to equal cost load balancing capabilities, EIGRP is also able to perform unequal cost load sharing. This unique ability allows EIGRP to use unequal cost paths to send outgoing packets to the destination network based on weighted traffic share values. Unequal cost load sharing is enabled using the `variance <multiplier>` router configuration command.

The multiplier is an integer between 1 and 128. A multiplier of 1, which is the default, implies that no unequal cost load sharing is being performed. This default setting is illustrated below in the output of the `show ip protocols` command:

```
R2#show ip protocols
Routing Protocol is "eigrp 150"
   Outgoing update filter list for all interfaces is not set
   Incoming update filter list for all interfaces is not set
   Default networks flagged in outgoing updates
   Default networks accepted from incoming updates
```

```
EIGRP metric weight K1=1, K2=0, K3=1, K4=0, K5=0
EIGRP maximum hopcount 100
EIGRP maximum metric variance 1
Redistributing: eigrp 150
EIGRP NSF-aware route hold timer is 240s
Automatic network summarization is not in effect
Maximum path: 4
Routing for Networks:
   150.1.1.2/32
   150.2.2.2/32
Routing Information Sources:
   Gateway         Distance       Last Update
   Gateway         Distance       Last Update
   150.2.2.1             90        00:00:52
   150.1.1.1             90        00:00:52
Distance: internal 90 external 170
```

The multiplier is a variable integer that tells the router to load share across routes that have a metric that is less than the minimum metric multiplied by the multiplier. For example, specifying a variance of 5 instructs the router to load share across routes whose metric is less than 5 times the minimum metric. The default variance of 1 tells the router to perform equal cost load balancing. When the variance command is used and a value other than 1 is specified as the multiplier, the router will distribute traffic among the routes proportionately, with respect to the metric of each individual route. In other words, the router will send more traffic using those paths with lower metric values than those with higher metric values.

Figure 2-12 below illustrates a basic network running EIGRP. R1 and R2 are connected via back-to-back Serial links. The 150.1.1.0/24 link between the two routers has a bandwidth of 1024Kbps. The 150.2.2.0/24 link between the routers has a bandwidth of 768Kbps. R1 is advertising the 172.16.100.0/24 prefix via EIGRP to R2:

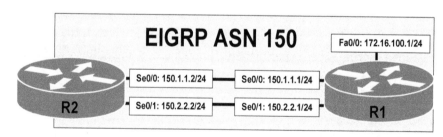

Fig. 2-12. Understanding EIGRP Variance

Based on the topology illustrated in Figure 2-12, the routing table on R2 for the 172.16.100.0/24 prefix is shown in the following output:

```
R2#show ip route 172.16.100.0 255.255.255.0
Routing entry for 172.16.100.0/24
  Known via "eigrp 150", distance 90, metric 3014400, type internal
  Redistributing via eigrp 150
  Last update from 150.1.1.1 on Serial0/0, 00:00:11 ago
  Routing Descriptor Blocks:
  * 150.1.1.1, from 150.1.1.1, 00:00:11 ago, via Serial0/0
      Route metric is 3014400, traffic share count is 1
      Total delay is 20100 microseconds, minimum bandwidth is 1024 Kbit
      Reliability 255/255, minimum MTU 1500 bytes
      Loading 1/255, Hops 1
```

The following EIGRP Topology Table shows both the Successor and the Feasible Successor routes:

```
R2#show ip eigrp topology 172.16.100.0 255.255.255.0
IP-EIGRP (AS 150): Topology entry for 172.16.100.0/24
  State is Passive, Query origin flag is 1, 1 Successor(s), FD is 3014400
  Routing Descriptor Blocks:
  150.1.1.1 (Serial0/0), from 150.1.1.1, Send flag is 0x0
      Composite metric is (3014400/28160), Route is Internal
      Vector metric:
        Minimum bandwidth is 1024 Kbit
        Total delay is 20100 microseconds
        Reliability is 255/255
        Load is 1/255
        Minimum MTU is 1500
        Hop count is 1
  150.2.2.1 (Serial0/1), from 150.2.2.1, Send flag is 0x0
      Composite metric is (3847680/28160), Route is Internal
      Vector metric:
        Minimum bandwidth is 768 Kbit
        Total delay is 20100 microseconds
        Reliability is 255/255
        Load is 1/255
        Minimum MTU is 1500
        Hop count is 1
```

To determine the variance value to configure on the router, we can use the following formula:

Variance = Highest metric for the paths being considered / Metric for the best route

Using this formula, we can calculate the variance value to configure on R2 as follows:

Variance = Highest metric for the paths being considered / Metric for the best route

Variance   =   3847680/ 3014400
Variance   =   1.28

This value must then be rounded up to the nearest whole integer, which in this case is 2. Given this, R2 can be configured to perform unequal cost load sharing by implementing the following configuration in router configuration mode:

```
R2(config)#router eigrp 150
R2(config-router)#variance 2
R2(config-router)#exit
```

Following this configuration, the routing table entry for 172.16.100.0/24 is illustrated below:

```
R2#show ip route 172.16.100.0 255.255.255.0
Routing entry for 172.16.100.0/24
  Known via "eigrp 150", distance 90, metric 3014400, type internal
  Redistributing via eigrp 150
  Last update from 150.2.2.1 on Serial0/1, 00:00:36 ago
  Routing Descriptor Blocks:
    150.2.2.1, from 150.2.2.1, 00:00:36 ago, via Serial0/1
      Route metric is 3847680, traffic share count is 47
      Total delay is 20100 microseconds, minimum bandwidth is 768 Kbit
      Reliability 255/255, minimum MTU 1500 bytes
      Loading 1/255, Hops 1
  * 150.1.1.1, from 150.1.1.1, 00:00:36 ago, via Serial0/0
      Route metric is 3014400, traffic share count is 60
      Total delay is 20100 microseconds, minimum bandwidth is 1024 Kbit
      Reliability 255/255, minimum MTU 1500 bytes
      Loading 1/255, Hops 1
```

The traffic share count indicates that for every 60 packets forwarded via Serial0/0, the router will forward 47 packets via Serial0/1. This is performed proportionally in respect to the route metric of either path. This is the default behavior when the variance command is implemented. This intelligent traffic sharing functionality is enabled via the traffic-share balanced router configuration command, which requires no explicit configuration.

NOTE: The traffic-share balanced command is enabled by default and does not appear in the running configuration, even if manually configured. This is illustrated below:

```
R2(config)#router eigrp 150
R2(config-router)#vari 2
R2(config-router)#traffic-share balanced
R2(config-router)#exit
```

```
R2(config)#do show run | begin router
router eigrp 150
 variance 2
 network 150.1.1.2 0.0.0.0
 network 150.2.2.2 0.0.0.0
 no auto-summary
```

As stated previously in this section, when the variance command is used, all paths that meet both the Feasibility Condition and have a metric that is less than the minimum metric multiplied by the multiplier will be installed into the routing table. The router will then use all paths and load share traffic proportionally based on the route metric.

In some cases, you may want to allow alternate routes, such as the Feasible Successor route, to be placed into the routing table but not be used unless the Successor route is removed. Such actions are typically performed to reduce convergence times in EIGRP-enabled networks. To understand this concept, recall that, by default, the router only places the Successor route into the IP routing table. In the event that the Successor route is no longer available, the Feasible Successor is promoted to the Successor. This route is then installed into the routing table as the primary path to the destination network.

The traffic-share min across-interfaces router configuration command can be used in conjunction with the variance command to install all routes that have a metric less than the minimum metric multiplied by the multiplier into the routing table, but use only the route with the minimum (best) metric to forward packets until that route becomes unavailable. The primary objective of this configuration is that in the event that the primary route is lost, the alternative route is already in the routing table and can be used immediately.

The following configuration example uses the topology illustrated in Figure 2-12 above to illustrate how to configure the router to place routes with a metric less than two times the minimum metric into the routing table, but use only the route with the lowest metric to actually forward packets:

```
R2(config)#router eigrp 150
R2(config-router)#vari 2
R2(config-router)#traffic-share min across-interfaces
R2(config-router)#exit
```

This configuration results in the following output for 172.16.100.0/24 in the routing table:

```
R2#show ip route 172.16.100.0 255.255.255.0
Routing entry for 172.16.100.0/24
```

```
Known via "eigrp 150", distance 90, metric 3014400, type internal
Redistributing via eigrp 150
Last update from 150.2.2.1 on Serial0/1, 00:09:01 ago
Routing Descriptor Blocks:
   150.2.2.1, from 150.2.2.1, 00:09:01 ago, via Serial0/1
      Route metric is 3847680, traffic share count is 0
      Total delay is 20100 microseconds, minimum bandwidth is 768 Kbit
      Reliability 255/255, minimum MTU 1500 bytes
      Loading 1/255, Hops 1
 * 150.1.1.1, from 150.1.1.1, 00:09:01 ago, via Serial0/0
      Route metric is 3014400, traffic share count is 1
      Total delay is 20100 microseconds, minimum bandwidth is 1024 Kbit
      Reliability 255/255, minimum MTU 1500 bytes
      Loading 1/255, Hops 1
```

As is illustrated in the output above, the two different metric routes have been installed into the routing table based on the variance configuration. However, notice the traffic share count for the route via Serial0/1 is 0 while the traffic share count for the route via Serial0/0 is 1. This means that the router will not send any packets to 172.16.100.0/24 via Serial0/1, even though the route entry is installed into the routing table, until the path via Serial0/0 is no longer available.

DEFAULT ROUTING USING EIGRP

Enhanced IGRP supports numerous ways to advertise dynamically the gateway or network of last resort to other routers within the routing domain. These methods are as follows:

- Using the ip default-network command
- Using the network command to advertise network 0.0.0.0/0
- Redistributing the default static route
- Using the ip summary-address eigrp [asn] [network] [mask] command

The use of the ip default-network command is considered a legacy method of advertising the default route dynamically using EIGRP. However, because it is still supported in current IOS software versions, it is worth mentioning.

The ip default-network configuration command flags a network as the default network by inserting an asterisk (*) next to the network in the routing table. Traffic for destinations to which there is no specific routing table entry is then forwarded by the router to this network. The implementation of this feature is illustrated referencing the EIGRP topology in Figure 2-13 below:

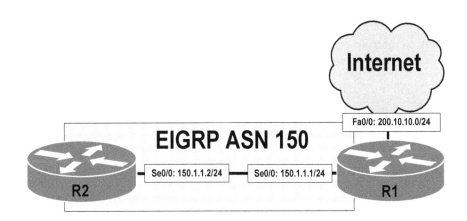

Fig. 2-13. EIGRP Default Routing

Referencing Figure 2-13, assume that the 200.10.10.0/24 subnet is connected to the Internet. This subnet resides off the FastEthernet0/0 interface of R1. R1 and R2 are in turn connected via a back-to-back Serial connection. Both routers reside in EIGRP AS 150. To flag the 200.10.10.0/24 network as the network of last resort, the following configuration is implemented on R1:

```
R1(config)#router eigrp 150
R1(config-router)#network 200.10.10.0 0.0.0.255
R1(config-router)#exit
R1(config)#ip default-network 200.10.10.0
R1(config)#exit
```

Based on this configuration, R2 receives 200.10.10.0/24 as the network of last resort as follows:

```
R2#show ip route
Codes: C - connected, S - static, R - RIP, M - mobile, B - BGP
       D - EIGRP, EX - EIGRP external, O - OSPF, IA - OSPF inter area
       N1 - OSPF NSSA external type 1, N2 - OSPF NSSA external type 2
       E1 - OSPF external type 1, E2 - OSPF external type 2
       i - IS-IS, su - IS-IS summary, L1 - IS-IS level-1, L2 - IS-IS level-2
       ia - IS-IS inter area, * - candidate default, U - per-user static
route
       o - ODR, P - periodic downloaded static route

Gateway of last resort is 150.2.2.1 to network 200.10.10.0

D*    200.10.10.0/24 [90/2172416] via 150.2.2.1, 00:01:03, Serial0/0
      150.1.0.0/24 is subnetted, 1 subnets
C        150.1.1.0 is directly connected, Serial0/0
```

The network command can be used to advertise an existing static default route point to either a physical or a logical interface, typically the Null0 interface.

> **NOTE:** The Null0 interface is a virtual interface on the router that discards all traffic that is routed to it. If you have a static route pointing to Null0, all traffic destined for the network specified in the static route is simply discarded. Think of the Null0 interface as a black hole: packets enter, but none ever leaves. It is essentially a bit-bucket on the router.

Referencing the diagram in Figure 2-13 above, the use of the network command in conjunction with an existing default static route is illustrated in the following configuration on R1:

```
R1(config)#ip route 0.0.0.0 0.0.0.0 FastEthernet0/0
R1(config)#router eigrp 150
R1(config-router)#network 0.0.0.0
R1(config-router)#exit
```

Based on this configuration, the IP routing table on R2 is illustrated in the following output:

```
R2#show ip route
Codes: C - connected, S - static, R - RIP, M - mobile, B - BGP
       D - EIGRP, EX - EIGRP external, O - OSPF, IA - OSPF inter area
       N1 - OSPF NSSA external type 1, N2 - OSPF NSSA external type 2
       E1 - OSPF external type 1, E2 - OSPF external type 2
       i - IS-IS, su - IS-IS summary, L1 - IS-IS level-1, L2 - IS-IS level-2
       ia - IS-IS inter area, * - candidate default, U - per-user static
route
       o - ODR, P - periodic downloaded static route

Gateway of last resort is 150.1.1.1 to network 0.0.0.0

D    200.10.10.0/24 [90/2172416] via 150.1.1.1, 00:01:11, Serial0/0
     150.1.0.0/24 is subnetted, 1 subnets
C       150.1.1.0 is directly connected, Serial0/0
D*   0.0.0.0/0 [90/2172416] via 150.1.1.1, 00:00:43, Serial0/0
```

Although route redistribution will be covered in detail later in this guide, the third method of advertising a default route via EIGRP is to redistribute the existing static default route into EIGRP using the redistribute static metric [bandwidth] [delay] [reliability] [load] [MTU] router configuration command. The same network topology used in the previous outputs in this section will be used to illustrate the implementation of this method as illustrated in Figure 2-14 below:

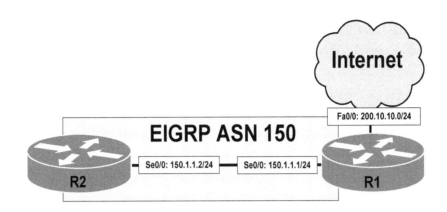

Fig. 2-14. EIGRP Default Routing Continued

Referencing Figure 2-14, which is the same as Figure 2-13, the following is performed on R1:

```
R1(config)#ip route 0.0.0.0 0.0.0.0 FastEthernet0/0
R1(config)#router eigrp 150
R1(config-router)#redistribute static metric 100000 100 255 1 1500
R1(config-router)#exit
```

NOTE: The values used in the metric can be derived from the interface or you can specify any values that you want when using this command.

Based on this configuration, the routing table on R2 is illustrated below:

```
R2#show ip route
Codes: C - connected, S - static, R - RIP, M - mobile, B - BGP
       D - EIGRP, EX - EIGRP external, O - OSPF, IA - OSPF inter area
       N1 - OSPF NSSA external type 1, N2 - OSPF NSSA external type 2
       E1 - OSPF external type 1, E2 - OSPF external type 2
       i - IS-IS, su - IS-IS summary, L1 - IS-IS level-1, L2 - IS-IS level-2
       ia - IS-IS inter area, * - candidate default, U - per-user static
route
       o - ODR, P - periodic downloaded static route

Gateway of last resort is 150.1.1.1 to network 0.0.0.0

     150.1.0.0/24 is subnetted, 1 subnets
C       150.1.1.0 is directly connected, Serial0/0
D*EX 0.0.0.0/0 [170/2195456] via 150.1.1.1, 00:01:16, Serial0/0
```

Because the route was redistributed into EIGRP on R1, it is an external EIGRP route as reflected in the output above. For external routes, the EIGRP Topology Table includes information such as the router that originated the route, the protocol the route was received for, and the metric of the external route, for example. This is illustrated in the following output:

```
R2#show ip eigrp topology 0.0.0.0/0
IP-EIGRP (AS 150): Topology entry for 0.0.0.0/0
  State is Passive, Query origin flag is 1, 1 Successor(s), FD is 2195456
  Routing Descriptor Blocks:
  150.1.1.1 (Serial0/0), from 150.1.1.1, Send flag is 0x0
      Composite metric is (2195456/51200), Route is External
      Vector metric:
        Minimum bandwidth is 1544 Kbit
        Total delay is 21000 microseconds
        Reliability is 255/255
        Load is 1/255
        Minimum MTU is 1500
        Hop count is 1
      External data:
        Originating router is 1.1.1.1
        AS number of route is 0
        External protocol is Static, external metric is 0
        Administrator tag is 0 (0x00000000)
        Exterior flag is set
```

From the information in bold, we can determine that the default route is a static route that was re-distributed into EIGRP on R1. This route has a metric of 0. In addition, we can also determine that the EIGRP Router ID (RID) of R1 is 1.1.1.1.

The final method of advertising the default route is by using the `ip summary-address eigrp [asn] [network] [mask]` interface configuration command. EIGRP route summarization will be described in detail later in this chapter. For the moment, concentrate on the use of this command to advertise the default route when using EIGRP.

Referencing the network topology diagram illustrated in Figure 2-14 above, R1 is configured with the `ip summary-address eigrp [asn] [network] [mask]` interface configuration command to advertise the default route to R2 as follows:

```
R1(config)#interface Serial0/0
R1(config-if)#description 'Back-to-Back Serial Connection To R2 Serial0/0'
R1(config-if)#ip summary-address eigrp 150 0.0.0.0 0.0.0.0
R1(config-if)#exit
```

The primary advantage to using this command is that a default route or network does not need to exist in the routing table in order for EIGRP to advertise network 0.0.0.0/0 to its neighbor routers. When this command is issued, the local router generates a summary route to the Null0 interface and flags the entry as the candidate default route. This is illustrated below:

```
R1#show ip route
Codes: C - connected, S - static, R - RIP, M - mobile, B - BGP
       D - EIGRP, EX - EIGRP external, O - OSPF, IA - OSPF inter area
       N1 - OSPF NSSA external type 1, N2 - OSPF NSSA external type 2
       E1 - OSPF external type 1, E2 - OSPF external type 2
       i - IS-IS, su - IS-IS summary, L1 - IS-IS level-1, L2 - IS-IS level-2
       ia - IS-IS inter area, * - candidate default, U - per-user static
route
       o - ODR, P - periodic downloaded static route

Gateway of last resort is 0.0.0.0 to network 0.0.0.0

     150.1.0.0/24 is subnetted, 1 subnets
C       150.1.1.0 is directly connected, Serial0/0
D*   0.0.0.0/0 is a summary, 00:02:26, Null0
```

The summary route is received as an internal EIGRP route on R2 as illustrated below:

```
R2#show ip route
Codes: C - connected, S - static, R - RIP, M - mobile, B - BGP
       D - EIGRP, EX - EIGRP external, O - OSPF, IA - OSPF inter area
       N1 - OSPF NSSA external type 1, N2 - OSPF NSSA external type 2
       E1 - OSPF external type 1, E2 - OSPF external type 2
       i - IS-IS, su - IS-IS summary, L1 - IS-IS level-1, L2 - IS-IS level-2
       ia - IS-IS inter area, * - candidate default, U - per-user static
route
       o - ODR, P - periodic downloaded static route

Gateway of last resort is 150.1.1.1 to network 0.0.0.0

     150.1.0.0/24 is subnetted, 1 subnets
C       150.1.1.0 is directly connected, Serial0/0
D*   0.0.0.0/0 [90/2297856] via 150.1.1.1, 00:03:07, Serial0/0
```

SPLIT HORIZON IN EIGRP NETWORKS

In Chapter 1, we learned that split horizon is a Distance Vector protocol feature mandating that routing information cannot be sent back out of the same interface through which it was received. This prevents the re-advertising of information back to the source from which it was learned. While this characteristic is a great loop prevention mechanism, it is also a significant drawback, especially in hub-and-spoke networks. To better understand the drawbacks of this feature, we will refer to the EIGRP hub-and-spoke network in Figure 2-15 below:

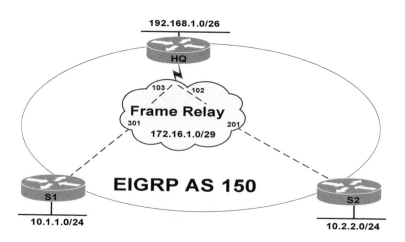

Fig. 2-15. EIGRP Split Horizon

The topology in Figure 2-15 illustrates a classic hub and spoke network, with router HQ as the hub router and routers S1 and S2 as the two spoke routers. On the Frame Relay WAN, each spoke router has a single DLCI provisioned between itself and the HQ router in a partial mesh topology. The Frame Relay configuration on the routers is verified as follows:

```
HQ#show frame-relay map
Serial0/0 (up): ip 172.16.1.2 dlci 102(0x66,0x1860), static,
               broadcast,
               CISCO, status defined, active
Serial0/0 (up): ip 172.16.1.1 dlci 103(0x67,0x1870), static,
               broadcast,
               CISCO, status defined, active

S1#show frame-relay map
Serial0/0 (up): ip 172.16.1.2 dlci 301(0x12D,0x48D0), static,
               broadcast,
               CISCO, status defined, active
Serial0/0 (up): ip 172.16.1.3 dlci 301(0x12D,0x48D0), static,
               broadcast,
               CISCO, status defined, active
S2#show frame-relay map
Serial0/0 (up): ip 172.16.1.1 dlci 201(0xC9,0x3090), static,
```

```
                    broadcast,
                    CISCO, status defined, active
    Serial0/0 (up): ip 172.16.1.3 dlci 201(0xC9,0x3090), static,
                    broadcast,
                    CISCO, status defined, active
```

NOTE: You are not expected to perform any Frame Relay configuration in the ROUTE exam. This output is provided for clarity.

Enhanced IGRP has been enabled on all three routers, using AS 150. The following output illustrates the EIGRP neighbor relationships between the HQ router and the spoke routers:

```
HQ#show ip eigrp neighbors
IP-EIGRP neighbors for process 150
H   Address            Interface      Hold Uptime    SRTT   RTO  Q  Seq
                                      (sec)          (ms)        Cnt Num
1   172.16.1.1         Se0/0          165 00:01:07    24   200  0  2
0   172.16.1.2         Se0/0          153 00:01:25   124   744  0  2
```

The following output illustrates the EIGRP neighbor relationship between the first spoke router, S1, and the HQ router:

```
S1#show ip eigrp neighbors
IP-EIGRP neighbors for process 150
H   Address            Interface      Hold Uptime    SRTT   RTO  Q  Seq
                                      (sec)          (ms)        Cnt Num
0   172.16.1.3         Se0/0          128 00:00:53   911  5000  0  4
```

The following output illustrates the EIGRP neighbor relationship between the second spoke router, S2, and the HQ router:

```
S2#show ip eigrp neighbors
IP-EIGRP neighbors for process 150
H   Address            Interface      Hold Uptime    SRTT   RTO  Q  Seq
                                      (sec)          (ms)        Cnt Num
0   172.16.1.3         Se0/0          156 00:02:20     8   200  0  4
```

By default, EIGRP split horizon is enabled for WAN interfaces connected to packet-switched networks, such as Frame Relay. This means that the HQ router will not advertise routing information learned on Serial0/0 out of the same interface. The effect of this default behavior is that the HQ router will not advertise the 10.1.1.0/24 prefix received from S1 to S2 because the route is received via the Serial0/0 interface and the split horizon feature prevents the router from advertising information learned on that interface back out onto the same interface. The same is also applicable for the 10.2.2.0/24 prefix the HQ router receives from S2.

This default behavior means that while the HQ router is aware of both prefixes, the spoke routers have only partial routing tables. The routing table on the HQ router is as follows:

```
HQ#show ip route eigrp
     10.0.0.0/8 is variably subnetted, 2 subnets, 2 masks
D       10.1.1.0/24 [90/2195456] via 172.16.1.1, 00:12:04, Serial0/0
D       10.2.2.0/24 [90/2195456] via 172.16.1.2, 00:12:06, Serial0/0
```

The routing table on spoke S1 is as follows:

```
S1#show ip route eigrp
     192.168.1.0/26 is subnetted, 1 subnets
D       192.168.1.0 [90/2195456] via 172.16.1.3, 00:10:53, Serial0/0
```

The routing table on spoke S2 is as follows:

```
S2#show ip route eigrp
     192.168.1.0/26 is subnetted, 1 subnets
D       192.168.1.0 [90/2195456] via 172.16.1.3, 00:10:55, Serial0/0
```

The result of this default behavior is that while the HQ router will be able to reach both of the spoke router networks, neither spoke router will be able to reach the network of the other. There are several ways such a situation can be addressed and they are as follows:

•   Disabling split horizon on the HQ (hub) router
•   Advertising a default route from the HQ router to the spoke routers
•   Manually configuring EIGRP neighbors on the routers

Disabling split horizon is performed at the interface level using the no ip split-horizon eigrp [AS] interface configuration command on the hub router. Referencing the network topology illustrated in Figure 2-15 above, this interface configuration command would be applied to the Serial0/0 interface on the HQ router. This is performed as follows:

```
HQ(config)#interface Serial0/0
HQ(config-if)#no ip split-horizon eigrp 150
```

After split horizon is disabled, the HQ router can advertise information back out onto the same interface on which it was received. For example, the routing table on spoke S2 now shows a routing entry for the 10.1.1.0/24 prefix advertised by spoke S1 to the HQ router:

```
S2#show ip route eigrp
     10.0.0.0/8 is variably subnetted, 2 subnets, 2 masks
D       10.1.1.0/24 [90/2707456] via 172.16.1.3, 00:00:47, Serial0/0
     192.168.1.0/26 is subnetted, 1 subnets
D       192.168.1.0 [90/2195456] via 172.16.1.3, 00:00:47, Serial0/0
```

A simple ping test from spoke S2 to the 10.1.1.0/24 subnet can be used to verify connectivity as illustrated below:

```
S2#ping 10.1.1.2

Type escape sequence to abort.
Sending 5, 100-byte ICMP Echos to 10.1.1.2, timeout is 2 seconds:
!!!!!
Success rate is 100 percent (5/5), round-trip min/avg/max = 24/27/32 ms
```

The second method to disabling split horizon is simply to advertise a default route from the HQ router to the spoke routers. In this situation, the `ip summary-address eigrp 150 0.0.0.0 0.0.0.0` interface configuration command could be applied to the Serial0/0 interface of the HQ router. This would allow the spoke routers to reach each other through the HQ router, which contains the full routing table negating the need to disable split horizon.

The final alternative method to disabling split horizon is to configure manually EIGRP neighbor statements on all routers using the `neighbor` router configuration command. Because updates between neighbors are Unicast when this configuration is used, the split horizon limitation is removed. This option works well in small networks; however, as the network grows and the number of spoke routers increases, so does the configuration overhead.

Given that the configuration of both EIGRP default routing and static neighbors was described in detail in earlier sections in this chapter, the configuration of these features is omitted for brevity. EIGRP stub routing is a core ROUTE requirement that is described in the section below.

EIGRP STUB ROUTING

Stub routing is an EIGRP feature primarily designed to conserve local router resources, such as memory and CPU, and improve network stability. The stub routing feature is most commonly used in hub-and-spoke networks. This feature is configured only on the spoke routers. When configured on the spoke router, the router announces its stub router status using a new TLV in the EIGRP Hello messages. When the hub router receives the Hello packet from the spoke router, one of two things happens:

1. If the hub router is running a newer version of software, upon receiving the Hello packet with the new TLV, the router will not query the stub router about the status of any prefixes. This is the default mode of operation in current Cisco IOS software versions.

2. If the hub router is running a version of software less than 12.0(7)T, upon receiving the Hello with the new TLV, the router will ignore this field because it does not understand it. The router will send Query packets to the stub router if it needs information about a route or routes. However, the stub router will respond with a message of inaccessible to any queries received from the hub router. This method allows for backward compatibility with older versions of software while retaining stub routing functionality.

When the stub routing feature is enabled on the spoke router, the router advertises only specified routes to the hub router. The router will not advertise routes received from other EIGRP neighbors to the hub router. Cisco IOS software allows administrators to select the type of routes that the stub router should advertise to the hub router. These options are described in the configuration examples later in this section. The EIGRP stub routing feature provides four advantages when implemented in hub-and-spoke networks and they are as follows:

- It prevents sub-optimal routing from occurring within hub-and-spoke EIGRP networks
- It prevents stub routers with low-speed links from being used as transit routers
- It eliminates EIGRP Query storms, allowing the EIGRP network to convergence faster
- It reduces the required amount of configuration commands on the stub routers

The stub routing feature prevents sub-optimal routing in typical hub-and-spoke networks by preventing stub routers from being used as transit routers. This is illustrated in Figure 2-16 below:

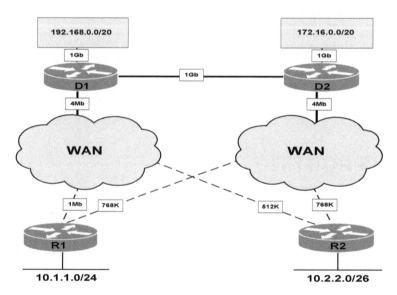

Fig. 2-16. A Redundant Hub-and-Spoke Network

Figure 2-16 illustrates a redundant hub-and-spoke network. The two branch office routers, R1 and R2, are connected to regional routers, D1 and D2, across a Frame Relay WAN. The two regional routers are each connected to a different /20 subnet as well as to each other via a high-speed 1Gbps link. The spoke routers are connected to the WAN using low-speed links. Assume, for example, that the high-speed connection between the regional D1 and D2 routers fails. Because there is no longer a direct path between the 192.168.0.0/20 and 172.16.0.0/20 subnets, traffic between these two subnets must now be routed via one of the spoke routers.

Given the low-speed WAN links on the spoke routers, such a situation leads to congestion, which affects both spoke-router users in addition to the users in the 192.168.0.0/20 and 172.16.0.0/20 subnets. This is illustrated in Figure 2-17 below:

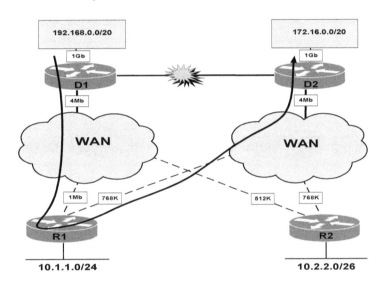

Fig. 2-17. Sub-Optimal Routing in Hub-and-Spoke Networks

Referencing the network topology illustrated in Figure 2-17, after the failure of the high-speed link between the two regional routers, traffic between the datacenters must now transit the lower-end spoke routers. Even a relatively small traffic stream between the datacenters, such as a 5Mb stream, will result in degraded performance for both the regional and the spoke routers.

By preventing the hub router from querying the spoke router and preventing the stub router from advertising routes from other EIGRP neighbors, the EIGRP stub-routing feature would effectively ensure that there was no alternate path between the 192.168.0.0/20 and the 172.16.0.0/20 subnets through any of the spoke routers.

As you may recall, earlier in this chapter we learned that when a neighbor changes a metric, or when a topology change occurs, and the Successor route is removed or changes, DUAL checks for Feasible Successors for the route and if one is found, then DUAL uses it to avoid re-computing the route unnecessarily. However, if no Feasible Successor for the destination network exists, the router will send a Query to neighboring routers asking if they have information on the destination network. In hub-and-spoke networks, this may lead to a Query storm. This concept is illustrated in Figure 2-18 below:

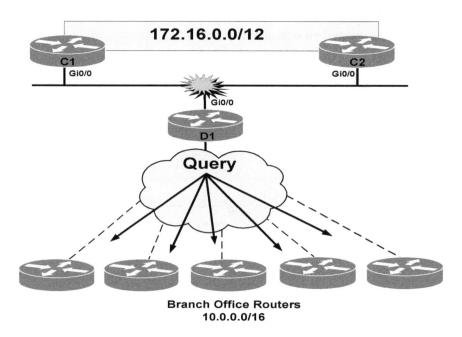

Fig. 2-18. A Non-Redundant Hub-and-Spoke Network

Referencing the network topology illustrated in Figure 2-18, the five branch office routers are connected to the hub router across a Frame Relay WAN using point-to-point Frame Relay connections. The hub is in turn connected to the core routers, C1 and C2, via a GigabitEthernet LAN connection. The core routers are connected to the 172.16.0.0/12 subnet. Router D1 has EIGRP neighbor relationships with both the core and the branch office routers. D1 has all the routes for the 172.16.0.0/12 and the 10.0.0.0/16 subnets.

Assume that the GigabitEthernet0/0 connection on D1 fails. This results in the loss of the router's EIGRP neighbor relationships with the core routers. The router also loses all routes within the 172.16.0.0/12 address space. Based on this network topology, we know that there is no Feasible Successor for any prefixes within the 172.16.0.0/12 address space. Router D1 therefore begins a diffused computation and sends out a Query to all of its neighbors asking if they have routing information for those prefixes.

The Query is sent out to the five branch office routers. While the network illustrated in Figure 2-18 above is relatively small, to really understand this point, assume that there were 50 or even

100 branch office routers, for example. In that case, given that each neighbor resides on its own point-to-point subnet, we quickly can see why this would be referred to as a Query storm because of the sheer amount of packets that would be sent to the neighbors. Sending the packets would be a waste of bandwidth and processing resources because all spoke routers would simply respond with an unreachable message, stating that there is no path for this route through this neighbor. The unnecessary Query storm can be prevented by using the EIGRP stub routing feature, which prevents the hub router from querying the spoke router(s).

Stub routing is enabled using the `eigrp stub [receive-only] [leak-map <name>] [connected] [static] [summary] [redistributed]` router configuration command. The `receive-only` keyword configures the router as a receive-only router. In other words, when this keyword is used, the stub router does not advertise any prefixes. Instead, it only receives, or accepts, prefixes advertised to it by its neighbor(s). This keyword cannot be used in conjunction with any other keywords when configuring stub routing.

The `leak-map <name>` keyword configures the EIGRP stub router to advertise those routes that have not been previously advertised based on the default operation of the stub routing feature. The leak map references a route map that matches one or more ACLs that permit the matched subnets or addresses to be leaked. While the configuration of leak maps with stub routing is beyond the scope of the ROUTE exam requirements, leak map configuration will be illustrated in the section on EIGRP manual route summarization.

The `connected` keyword configures the stub router to advertise connected subnets. These are subnets on any interface directly connected to the router. The `static` keyword configures the stub router to advertise static routes. The `summary` keyword configures the stub router to advertise summary routes. The `redistributed` keyword configures the stub router to advertise routes that have been redistributed in EIGRP from other route sources, such as OSPF.

The network topology in Figure 2-19 below illustrates stub router configuration:

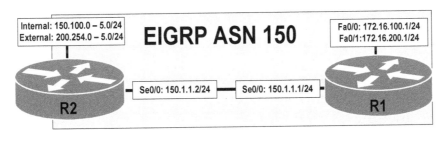

Fig. 2-19. Enabling EIGRP Stub Routing

Referencing the network illustrated in Figure 2-19, R1 and R2 are connected via a back-to-back Serial connection. R2 (the hub) is advertising the 150.100.0.0/24—150.100.5.0/24 internal networks as well as the 200.254.0.0/24—200.254.5.0/24 external networks via EIGRP to R1. R1 has two subnets, 172.16.100.0/24 and 172.16.200.0/24, which are advertised to R2.

Before delving into the configuration of the stub routing feature, we will begin by verifying the neighbor relationship status and routing tables on both routers. Router R2 shows the following neighbor relationship status for R1:

```
R2#show ip eigrp neighbors detail
IP-EIGRP neighbors for process 150
H   Address              Interface      Hold Uptime   SRTT    RTO   Q   Seq
                                        (sec)         (ms)          Cnt Num
0   150.1.1.1            Se0/0            11 00:00:04  589    3534   0   8
     Version 12.3/1.2, Retrans: 0, Retries: 0, Prefixes: 2
```

The IP routing table on R2 shows the following:

```
R2#show ip route eigrp
     172.16.0.0/24 is subnetted, 2 subnets
D       172.16.200.0 [90/2172416] via 150.1.1.1, 00:00:32, Serial0/0
D       172.16.100.0 [90/2172416] via 150.1.1.1, 00:00:32, Serial0/0
```

Router R1 shows the following neighbor relationship status for R2:

```
R1#show ip eigrp neighbors detail
IP-EIGRP neighbors for process 150
H   Address              Interface      Hold Uptime   SRTT    RTO   Q   Seq
                                        (sec)         (ms)          Cnt Num
0   150.1.1.2            Se0/0            13 00:01:11    4     200   0   3
     Version 12.4/1.2, Retrans: 1, Retries: 0
```

The IP routing table on R1 shows the following:

```
R1#show ip route eigrp
D EX 200.254.4.0/24 [170/7289856] via 150.1.1.2, 00:02:03, Serial0/0
D EX 200.254.5.0/24 [170/7289856] via 150.1.1.2, 00:02:03, Serial0/0
D EX 200.254.0.0/24 [170/7289856] via 150.1.1.2, 00:02:03, Serial0/0
D EX 200.254.1.0/24 [170/7289856] via 150.1.1.2, 00:02:03, Serial0/0
D EX 200.254.2.0/24 [170/7289856] via 150.1.1.2, 00:02:03, Serial0/0
D EX 200.254.3.0/24 [170/7289856] via 150.1.1.2, 00:02:03, Serial0/0
     150.100.0.0/24 is subnetted, 6 subnets
```

```
D        150.100.2.0 [90/2169856] via 150.1.1.2, 00:02:03, Serial0/0
D        150.100.3.0 [90/2169856] via 150.1.1.2, 00:02:03, Serial0/0
D        150.100.0.0 [90/2169856] via 150.1.1.2, 00:02:03, Serial0/0
D        150.100.1.0 [90/2169856] via 150.1.1.2, 00:02:03, Serial0/0
D        150.100.4.0 [90/2169856] via 150.1.1.2, 00:02:03, Serial0/0
D        150.100.5.0 [90/2169856] via 150.1.1.2, 00:02:03, Serial0/0
```

EIGRP stub functionality is enabled by issuing the `eigrp stub` router configuration command on the stub (spoke) router. This is illustrated in the following output:

```
R1(config)#router eigrp 150
R1(config-router)#eigrp stub
R1(config-router)#exit
```

By default, when this command is enabled, the following is true on the stub router:

- The stub router advertises all connected subnets
- The stub router advertises all summary routes

NOTE: It is important to remember that EIGRP must be enabled for the networks before they are advertised by the router.

Upon receiving the new TLV, the hub router immediately suppresses queries to the spoke router. This can be validated by issuing the `show ip eigrp neighbors detail` command and viewing the status of the neighbor relationship on the hub (R1) as illustrated below:

```
R2#show ip eigrp neighbors detail
IP-EIGRP neighbors for process 150
H   Address              Interface       Hold Uptime    SRTT   RTO  Q  Seq
                                         (sec)          (ms)        Cnt Num
0   150.1.1.1            Se0/0            13 00:00:06   793   4758  0  10
    Version 12.3/1.2, Retrans: 0, Retries: 0, Prefixes: 2
    Stub Peer Advertising ( CONNECTED SUMMARY ) Routes
    Suppressing queries
```

When the stub router feature is enabled, the EIGRP neighbor relationship is reset. This allows the spoke router to send the Hello packet(s) with the new TLV. Another important point pertaining to the stub router feature is that while it prevents the router from being queried by neighbor routers, this feature does not prevent the hub router from advertising its complete routing table to the spoke router. Instead, this must be configured manually on the hub router using either of the following solutions:

- Advertising a default route to the spoke router and filtering all other specific routes
- Summarizing the routes advertised to the spoke router

The hub router can be configured to advertise the default route to the spoke router(s) and then filter all other specific route entries, effectively reducing the routing table on the spoke to a single default route entry. EIGRP supports the use of distribute lists to filter both incoming and outgoing route updates. Distribute lists are described in detail later in this guide.

Route summarization, which will be described in detail later in this chapter, may also be used to advertise aggregate route entries for multiple prefixes to the spoke routers. However, it is important to remember that route summarization is dependent on the IP addressing scheme, as is described in Chapter 1, and is not always feasible in all networks.

To provide an additional example of the stub routing feature, the following static routes are added to router R1:

- Network 10.1.1.0/24 via Null0
- Network 10.1.2.0/24 via Null0

This configuration is implemented as follows:

```
R1(config)#ip route 10.1.1.0 255.255.255.0 null 0
R1(config)#ip route 10.1.2.0 255.255.255.0 null 0
```

As was stated earlier in this section, the eigrp stub [receive-only] [leak-map <name>] [connected] [static] [summary] [redistributed] router configuration command allows any combination of the supported keywords, with the exception of the receive-only keyword, which can be used only on its own. This particular example has been chosen to highlight the important fact that, by default, simply issuing the eigrp stub static command, for example, does not automatically mean that the stub router will advertise static routes. As was illustrated in the first example when the network command was still used prior to using the eigrp stub command, static routes must be known to EIGRP before the stub routing feature will advertise them. This may be performed in one of two ways:

1. Using the network command to enable EIGRP routing for the configured static routes
2. Redistributing the static routes into EIGRP using the redistribute command

If the eigrp stub connected static command was issued on R1 and neither one of the options specified above was used, then EIGRP would not advertise the static routes, even though the neighbor router would show that the stub router was configured to advertise both connected and summary routes. This is illustrated below on R2:

```
R2#show ip eigrp neighbors detail
IP-EIGRP neighbors for process 150
```

```
H   Address             Interface        Hold Uptime   SRTT   RTO  Q  Seq
                                         (sec)         (ms)       Cnt Num
0   150.1.1.1           Se0/0             13 00:11:47  313   1878  0  16
      Version 12.3/1.2, Retrans: 0, Retries: 0, Prefixes: 2
      Stub Peer Advertising ( CONNECTED STATIC ) Routes
      Suppressing queries
```

As illustrated below, while R2 does reflect the correct configuration implemented on R1, the static routes configured on R1 are not received on the router:

```
R2#show ip route eigrp
      172.16.0.0/24 is subnetted, 2 subnets
D        172.16.200.0 [90/2172416] via 150.1.1.1, 00:12:35, Serial0/0
D        172.16.100.0 [90/2172416] via 150.1.1.1, 00:12:35, Serial0/0
```

Using the network command, R1 can be configured to advertise the static routes as follows:

```
R1(config)#router eigrp 150
R1(config-router)#network 10.1.1.0 0.0.0.255
R1(config-router)#network 10.1.2.0 0.0.0.255
R1(config-router)#exit
```

EIGRP will now advertise the static routes included in stub router configuration. This can be verified using the show ip protocols command on R1 as illustrated below:

```
R1#show ip protocols
Routing Protocol is "eigrp 150"
  Outgoing update filter list for all interfaces is not set
  Incoming update filter list for all interfaces is not set
  Default networks flagged in outgoing updates
  Default networks accepted from incoming updates
  EIGRP metric weight K1=1, K2=0, K3=1, K4=0, K5=0
  EIGRP maximum hopcount 100
  EIGRP maximum metric variance 1
  EIGRP stub, connected, static
  Redistributing: eigrp 150
  EIGRP NSF-aware route hold timer is 240s
  Automatic network summarization is not in effect
  Maximum path: 4
  Routing for Networks:
    10.1.1.0/24
    10.1.2.0/24
    150.1.1.0/24
    172.16.100.0/24
    172.16.200.0/24
```

```
     Routing Information Sources:
       Gateway        Distance      Last Update
       150.1.1.2           90       00:03:19
     Distance: internal 90 external 170
```

The same is also reflected on R2, which now shows the received route entries as follows:

```
R2#show ip route eigrp
      172.16.0.0/24 is subnetted, 2 subnets
D         172.16.200.0 [90/2172416] via 150.1.1.1, 00:16:00, Serial0/0
D         172.16.100.0 [90/2172416] via 150.1.1.1, 00:16:00, Serial0/0
      10.0.0.0/24 is subnetted, 2 subnets
D         10.1.2.0 [90/2169856] via 150.1.1.1, 00:02:27, Serial0/0
D         10.1.1.0 [90/2169856] via 150.1.1.1, 00:02:32, Serial0/0
```

The second method, using the redistribute command, would be implemented as follows:

```
R1(config)#router eigrp 150
R1(config-router)#redistribute static metric 1544 20000 255 1 1500
R1(config-router)#exit
```

Again, the show ip protocols command on R1 can be used to validate this configuration as illustrated below:

```
R1#show ip protocols
Routing Protocol is "eigrp 150"
  Outgoing update filter list for all interfaces is not set
  Incoming update filter list for all interfaces is not set
  Default networks flagged in outgoing updates
  Default networks accepted from incoming updates
  EIGRP metric weight K1=1, K2=0, K3=1, K4=0, K5=0
  EIGRP maximum hopcount 100
  EIGRP maximum metric variance 1
  EIGRP stub, connected, static
  Redistributing: static, eigrp 150
  EIGRP NSF-aware route hold timer is 240s
  Automatic network summarization is not in effect
  Maximum path: 4
  Routing for Networks:
    150.1.1.0/24
    172.16.100.0/24
    172.16.200.0/24
  Routing Information Sources:
    Gateway        Distance      Last Update
    150.1.1.2           90       00:01:10
  Distance: internal 90 external 170
```

The routes are advertised to R2; however, one important point to note is that because of the route redistribution, the same routes are advertised as external EIGRP routes instead as illustrated below:

```
R2#show ip route eigrp
      172.16.0.0/24 is subnetted, 2 subnets
D        172.16.200.0 [90/2172416] via 150.1.1.1, 00:20:09, Serial0/0
D        172.16.100.0 [90/2172416] via 150.1.1.1, 00:20:09, Serial0/0
      10.0.0.0/24 is subnetted, 2 subnets
D EX     10.1.2.0 [170/7289856] via 150.1.1.1, 00:02:13, Serial0/0
D EX     10.1.1.0 [170/7289856] via 150.1.1.1, 00:02:13, Serial0/0
```

In conclusion, remember that the stub routing feature provides great flexibility by allowing you to use any combination of keywords, with the exception of the receive-only keyword. However, this does not necessarily mean that two or more keywords must be used. Instead, any one of the keywords may be used on its own, with the most common configuration on the stub router being simply the eigrp stub connected command on all the spoke routers.

SECURING EIGRP PROTOCOL MESSAGES

Enhanced IGRP supports Message Digest 5 (MD5) hashing to ensure the integrity of EIGRP messages and to prevent the injection of false routing information into the EIGRP domain. Message Digest (MD) algorithms are a series of byte-oriented cryptographic hash functions that take variable-length data and produce a mathematically computed 128-bit fixed-length hash value. This hash is commonly referred to as the fingerprint, message digest, or simply just the digest. One significant advantage to hashing plaintext is that the original message cannot be reconstituted, even with knowledge of the hash algorithm.

NOTE: This is not a security-related exam and you are not required to demonstrate detailed knowledge of hashing algorithms; however, ensure that you have a basic understanding of this concept.

Enhanced IGRP message authentication consists of several steps, which are as follows:
- Configuring a key chain name in global configuration mode
- Configuring one or more keys within the key chain
- Configuring a key string for the key
- Configuring EIGRP to use Message Digest 5 (MD5) authentication
- Configuring EIGRP to use the key chain and key(s)

The key chain is configured using the key chain [name] global configuration command and is used to identify a group of authentication keys. The key chain can be assigned any name and this name does not have to be the same on all routers. A key chain must have at least one key and can have up to 2147483647 keys.

Following the configuration of the key chain, one or more keys must be configured using the `key <1-2147483647>` key chain configuration command. Although multiple keys are supported within a single key chain, the recommended practice when configuring key chains for EIGRP message authentication is to configure a single key per key chain. The key numbers should be the same on all routers.

Following the configuration of the key, the key string must be specified. The key string is used to specify the authentication string that will be used to derive the MD5 hash, which is used to ensure the integrity of the EIGRP messages. The key string is case-sensitive and should be configured the same on all routers. This is configured using the `key-string [string]` key configuration command.

Enhanced IGRP is configured to use MD5 authentication via the `ip authentication mode eigrp [ASN] md5` interface command. MD5 authentication is the only authentication type that is supported by EIGRP.

Enhanced IGRP is configured to use the key chain via the `ip authentication key-chain eigrp [ASN] [key-chain-name]` interface command. This command references the key chain that was previously configured in the first configuration step.

By default, when a key chain is configured, all keys within that key chain are automatically enabled and may be used immediately. In addition, all keys have an infinite lifetime, meaning they never expire. This default behavior, however, can be adjusted using the `accept-lifetime start-time [infinite | end-time | duration <seconds>]` and the `send-lifetime start-time [infinite | end-time | duration <seconds>]` key configuration commands. The use of both of these commands will be described and illustrated later in this section. For now, concentrate on basic EIGRP message authentication based on the topology illustrated in Figure 2-20 below:

Fig. 2-20. Enabling EIGRP MD5 Authentication

Figure 2-20 illustrates a basic EIGRP network comprised of two routers. R1 is advertising two networks, 172.16.100.0/24 and 172.16.200.0/24, to R2. It should be assumed that an EIGRP neighbor relationship is established between routers R1 and R2. This is illustrated in the following output:

```
R1#show ip eigrp neighbors
IP-EIGRP neighbors for process 150
H   Address              Interface     Hold Uptime    SRTT   RTO   Q  Seq
                                       (sec)          (ms)         Cnt Num
0   150.1.1.2            Se0/0          13 00:09:14     8    200   0  7
R2#show ip eigrp neighbors
IP-EIGRP neighbors for process 150
H   Address              Interface     Hold Uptime    SRTT   RTO   Q  Seq
                                       (sec)          (ms)         Cnt Num
0   150.1.1.1            Se0/0          14 00:09:28     4    200   0  1
```

Following the sequence of configuration steps that were listed and described earlier in this section, the authentication for R1 is configured as follows:

```
R1(config)#key chain R1-EIGRP-AUTH
R1(config-keychain)#key 1
R1(config-keychain-key)#key-string ROUTE
R1(config-keychain-key)#exit
R1(config-keychain)#exit
R1(config)#interface Serial0/0
R1(config-if)#ip authentication mode eigrp 150 md5
R1(config-if)#ip authentication key-chain eigrp 150 R1-EIGRP-AUTH
R1(config-if)#exit
```

The key chain configuration can be validated using the show key chain command as follows:

```
R1#show key chain
Key-chain R1-EIGRP-AUTH:
    key 1 -- text "ROUTE"
        accept lifetime (always valid) - (always valid) [valid now]
        send lifetime (always valid) - (always valid) [valid now]
```

The show key chain command shows the key chain name, the key (or keys), and the key string associated with the key (or keys). As stated earlier, by default, the key is valid immediately and has an infinite lifetime.

The show ip eigrp interfaces detail [name] command can be used to validate the key chain applied to a particular interface. This is illustrated in the following output:

```
R1#show ip eigrp interfaces detail Serial0/0
IP-EIGRP interfaces for process 150

                          Xmit Queue   Mean   Pacing Time   Multicast
Pending
Interface      Peers   Un/Reliable  SRTT   Un/Reliable   Flow Timer
Routes
Se0/0              0       0/0        0       0/15          0           0
   Hello interval is 5 sec
   Next xmit serial <none>
   Un/reliable mcasts: 0/0  Un/reliable ucasts: 2/1
   Mcast exceptions: 0  CR packets: 0  ACKs suppressed: 0
   Retransmissions sent: 0  Out-of-sequence rcvd: 0
   Authentication mode is md5,  key-chain is "R1-EIGRP-AUTH"
```

When the key chain is applied to the interface, the neighbor relationship is reset. If the neighbor router is not configured for authentication, the neighbor relationship will not be re-established. This can be validated using the debug eigrp packets command as follows:

```
R1#debug eigrp packets
EIGRP Packets debugging is on
    (UPDATE, REQUEST, QUERY, REPLY, HELLO, IPXSAP, PROBE, ACK, STUB,
SIAQUERY, SIAREPLY)
R1#
*Mar  1 03:52:24.959: EIGRP: Serial0/0: ignored packet from 150.1.1.2,
opcode = 5 (missing authentication)
*Mar  1 03:52:26.915: EIGRP: Sending HELLO on FastEthernet0/0
*Mar  1 03:52:26.915:   AS 150, Flags 0x0, Seq 0/0 idbQ 0/0 iidbQ un/rely
0/0
*Mar  1 03:52:28.491: EIGRP: Sending HELLO on Serial0/0
*Mar  1 03:52:28.491:   AS 150, Flags 0x0, Seq 0/0 idbQ 0/0 iidbQ un/rely
0/0
*Mar  1 03:52:29.655: EIGRP: Serial0/0: ignored packet from 150.1.1.2,
opcode = 5 (missing authentication)
*Mar  1 03:52:31.879: EIGRP: Sending HELLO on FastEthernet0/0
*Mar  1 03:52:31.879:   AS 150, Flags 0x0, Seq 0/0 idbQ 0/0 iidbQ un/rely
0/0
R1#
*Mar  1 03:52:32.959: EIGRP: Sending HELLO on Serial0/0
*Mar  1 03:52:32.959:   AS 150, Flags 0x0, Seq 0/0 idbQ 0/0 iidbQ un/rely
0/0u all
*Mar  1 03:52:34.351: EIGRP: Serial0/0: ignored packet from 150.1.1.2,
opcode = 5 (missing authentication)
```

In the output above, the Hello packets (OPCode 5) from R2 are being ignored because R2 has yet to be configured for authentication. The same command on R2 is illustrated as follows:

```
R2#debug eigrp packets
EIGRP Packets debugging is on
    (UPDATE, REQUEST, QUERY, REPLY, HELLO, IPXSAP, PROBE, ACK, STUB,
SIAQUERY, SIAREPLY)
R2#
*Mar  1 16:20:36.085: EIGRP: Sending HELLO on Serial0/0
*Mar  1 16:20:36.085:   AS 150, Flags 0x0, Seq 0/0 idbQ 0/0 iidbQ un/rely
0/0
*Mar  1 16:20:39.619: EIGRP: ddb not configured on FastEthernet0/0
*Mar  1 16:20:39.703: EIGRP: Serial0/0: ignored packet from 150.1.1.1,
opcode = 5 (authentication off or key-chain missing)
*Mar  1 16:20:41.053: EIGRP: Sending HELLO on Serial0/0
*Mar  1 16:20:41.053:   AS 150, Flags 0x0, Seq 0/0 idbQ 0/0 iidbQ un/rely
0/0
*Mar  1 16:20:44.062: EIGRP: ddb not configured on FastEthernet0/0
*Mar  1 16:20:44.335: EIGRP: Serial0/0: ignored packet from 150.1.1.1,
opcode = 5 (authentication off or key-chain missing)
*Mar  1 16:20:45.657: EIGRP: Sending HELLO on Serial0/0
*Mar  1 16:20:45.657:   AS 150, Flags 0x0, Seq 0/0 idbQ 0/0 iidbQ un/rely
0/0
*Mar  1 16:20:48.774: EIGRP: ddb not configured on FastEthernet0/0
*Mar  1 16:20:49.183: EIGRP: Serial0/0: ignored packet from 150.1.1.1,
opcode = 5 (authentication off or key-chain missing)
```

In the output above, R2 is ignoring the Hello packets from R1 because it is not configured for authentication. The EIGRP authentication configuration status of the interface can be verified using the show ip eigrp interfaces detail [name] command as illustrated below:

```
R2#show ip eigrp interfaces detail Serial0/0
IP-EIGRP interfaces for process 150
                        Xmit Queue   Mean   Pacing Time   Multicast
Pending
Interface      Peers   Un/Reliable   SRTT   Un/Reliable   Flow Timer
Routes
Se0/0            0         0/0         0        0/15          50          0
   Hello interval is 5 sec
   Next xmit serial <none>
   Un/reliable mcasts: 0/0  Un/reliable ucasts: 0/10
   Mcast exceptions: 0  CR packets: 0  ACKs suppressed: 2
   Retransmissions sent: 3  Out-of-sequence rcvd: 0
   Authentication mode is not set
   Use unicast
```

To allow the neighbor relationship to be re-established and to secure the message exchange between R1 and R2, R2 is also configured for authentication as follows:

```
R2(config)#key chain R2-EIGRP-AUTH
R2(config-keychain)#key 1
R2(config-keychain-key)#key-string ROUTE
R2(config-keychain-key)#exit
R2(config-keychain)#exit
R2(config)#interface Serial0/0
R2(config-if)#ip authentication mode eigrp 150 md5
R2(config-if)#ip authentication key-chain eigrp 150 R2-EIGRP-AUTH
R2(config-if)#exit
```

Following this configuration on R2, the neighbor relationship is re-established as illustrated below:

```
R2#show ip eigrp neighbors
IP-EIGRP neighbors for process 150
H   Address              Interface       Hold Uptime    SRTT  RTO  Q  Seq
                                         (sec)          (ms)       Cnt Num
0   150.1.1.1            Se0/0            12 00:00:58    4     200  0  2
```

The `debug eigrp packets` command now shows that EIGRP messages between the two routers are being authenticated using key 1 as illustrated below:

```
R2#debug eigrp packets
EIGRP Packets debugging is on
    (UPDATE, REQUEST, QUERY, REPLY, HELLO, IPXSAP, PROBE, ACK, STUB,
SIAQUERY, SIAREPLY)
R2#
*Mar  1 16:28:09.148: EIGRP: Sending HELLO on Serial0/0
*Mar  1 16:28:09.148:   AS 150, Flags 0x0, Seq 0/0 idbQ 0/0 iidbQ un/rely
0/0
*Mar  1 16:28:09.941: EIGRP: ddb not configured on FastEthernet0/0
*Mar  1 16:28:11.059: EIGRP: received packet with MD5 authentication, key id
= 1
*Mar  1 16:28:11.059: EIGRP: Received HELLO on Serial0/0 nbr 150.1.1.1
*Mar  1 16:28:11.059:   AS 150, Flags 0x0, Seq 0/0 idbQ 0/0 iidbQ un/rely
0/0 peerQ un/rely 0/0
*Mar  1 16:28:13.663: EIGRP: Sending HELLO on Serial0/0
*Mar  1 16:28:13.663:   AS 150, Flags 0x0, Seq 0/0 idbQ 0/0 iidbQ un/rely
0/0
*Mar  1 16:28:14.853: EIGRP: ddb not configured on FastEthernet0/0
*Mar  1 16:28:15.498: EIGRP: received packet with MD5 authentication, key id
= 1
*Mar  1 16:28:15.502: EIGRP: Received HELLO on Serial0/0 nbr 150.1.1.1
```

```
*Mar  1 16:28:15.502:   AS 150, Flags 0x0, Seq 0/0 idbQ 0/0 iidbQ un/rely
0/0 peerQ un/rely 0/0
*Mar  1 16:28:18.131: EIGRP: Sending HELLO on Serial0/0
*Mar  1 16:28:18.131:   AS 150, Flags 0x0, Seq 0/0 idbQ 0/0 iidbQ un/rely
0/0
*Mar  1 16:28:19.601: EIGRP: ddb not configured on FastEthernet0/0
*Mar  1 16:28:20.118: EIGRP: received packet with MD5 authentication, key id
= 1
*Mar  1 16:28:20.118: EIGRP: Received HELLO on Serial0/0 nbr 150.1.1.1
*Mar  1 16:28:20.118:   AS 150, Flags 0x0, Seq 0/0 idbQ 0/0 iidbQ un/rely
0/0 peerQ un/rely 0/0
*Mar  1 16:28:22.626: EIGRP: Sending HELLO on Serial0/0
*Mar  1 16:28:22.626:   AS 150, Flags 0x0, Seq 0/0 idbQ 0/0 iidbQ un/rely
0/0
*Mar  1 16:28:24.333: EIGRP: ddb not configured on FastEthernet0/0
*Mar  1 16:28:24.445: EIGRP: received packet with MD5 authentication, key id
= 1
*Mar  1 16:28:24.445: EIGRP: Received HELLO on Serial0/0 nbr 150.1.1.1
*Mar  1 16:28:24.445:   AS 150, Flags 0x0, Seq 0/0 idbQ 0/0 iidbQ un/rely
0/0 peerQ un/rely 0/0
```

Cisco IOS software allows administrators to specify when the key (or keys) configured in the key chain will and will not be valid using the accept-lifetime start-time [infinite | end-time | duration <seconds>] and the send-lifetime start-time [infinite | end-time | duration <seconds>] key configuration commands.

The send-lifetime command is used to specify the date and time the router should begin sending the particular key (i.e., when the key will be active) and how long that key will be active. The accept-lifetime command is used to specify the date and time the router should accept the key and how long the key will be considered valid. Before using either one of these commands, it is important to ensure that the router clocks are set to the correct time because the router will reference the dates and times used in either of these commands with its own clock. The router clocks may be synchronized in two different ways:

1. By manually setting the clock using the clock set privileged EXEC command
2. By synchronizing the router with a Network Time Protocol (NTP) source

Manually setting the system time using the clock set command is described in detail in the CCNA guide. This configuration will not be illustrated in this chapter. Configuring a router to synchronize with an NTP reference is beyond the scope of the ROUTE exam requirements; however, if configured, the show ntp status command should be used to ensure that the router is indeed synchronized with the NTP server. A sample output of this command is shown below:

```
R2#show ntp status
Clock is synchronized, stratum 9, reference is 172.16.1.1
nominal freq is 249.5901 Hz, actual freq is 249.5901 Hz, precision is 2**18
reference time is CD9F1EA4.3DCF06A0 (00:55:48.241 UTC Sat May 15 2010)
clock offset is 0.0407 msec, root delay is 5.95 msec
root dispersion is 0.09 msec, peer dispersion is 0.03 msec
```

In the output above, R2 is synchronized with NTP server 172.16.1.1. The current time is 12:55 AM on Saturday, May 15, 2010. Based on this time, the following configuration example illustrates how to configure R1 and R2 to send and accept key 1 using the key string ROUTE, beginning at 12:00 AM on May 15, 2010, and ending at 11:59 PM on May 14, 2011. Key 2, using the key string CCNP, will be sent and accepted by both routers beginning at 12:00 AM on May 15, 2011, and ending at 11:59 PM on May 14, 2012:

```
R2(config)#key chain R2-EIGRP-AUTH
R2(config-keychain)#key 1
R2(config-keychain-key)#key-string ROUTE
R2(config-keychain-key)#$lifetime 00:00:00 15 May 2010 11:59:59 14 May 2011
R2(config-keychain-key)#$lifetime 00:00:00 15 May 2010 11:59:59 14 May 2011
R2(config-keychain-key)#exit
R2(config-keychain)#key 2
R2(config-keychain-key)#key-string CCNP
R2(config-keychain-key)#$lifetime 00:00:00 15 May 2011 11:59:59 14 May 2012
R2(config-keychain-key)#$lifetime 00:00:00 15 May 2011 11:59:59 14 May 2012
R2(config-keychain-key)#exit
```

This configuration can be validated using the show key chain command as follows:

```
R2#show key chain
Key-chain R2-EIGRP-AUTH:
    key 1 -- text "ROUTE"
        accept lifetime (00:00:00 UTC May 15 2010) - (11:59:59 UTC May 14
2011) [valid now]
        send lifetime (00:00:00 UTC May 15 2010) - (11:59:59 UTC May 14
2011) [valid now]
    key 2 -- text "CCNP"
        accept lifetime (00:00:00 UTC May 15 2011) - (11:59:59 UTC May 14
2012)
        send lifetime (00:00:00 UTC May 15 2011) - (11:59:59 UTC May 14
2012)
```

In the output above, we can see that only key 1 is currently active based on the configuration. Key 2, which will be used starting in 2011, will not be used until that time.

EIGRP ROUTE SUMMARIZATION

As stated in Chapter 1, route summarization reduces the amount of information that routers must process, which allows for faster convergence within the network. Summarization also restricts the size of the area that is affected by network changes by hiding detailed topology information from certain areas within the network. Finally, as was stated earlier in this chapter, summarization is used to define a Query boundary for EIGRP, which supports two types of route summarization as follows:

1. Automatic route summarization
2. Manual route summarization

By default, automatic route summarization is in effect when EIGRP is enabled on the router. This is implemented using the `auto-summary` command. This command allows EIGRP to perform automatic route summarization at Classful boundaries. The operation of this default feature is illustrated referencing the network topology in Figure 2-21 below:

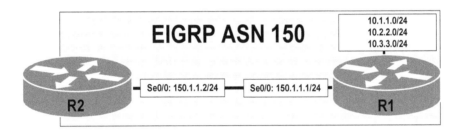

Fig. 2-21. EIGRP Automatic Route Summarization

Referencing the EIGRP network illustrated in Figure 2-21, R1 and R2 are running EIGRP and are using autonomous system 150. The 10.1.1.0/24, 10.2.2.0/24, and 10.3.3.0/24 subnets are directly connected to R1. R1 is advertising these routes to R2. R1 and R2 are connected using a back-to-back Serial connection on the 150.1.1.0/24 subnet. Based on the networks connected to these routers, by default, EIGRP will perform automatic summarization as follows:

- The 10.1.1.0/24, 10.2.2.0/24, and 10.3.3.0/24 subnets will be summarized to 10.0.0.0/8
- The 150.1.1.0/24 subnet will be summarized to 150.1.0.0/16

This default behavior can be validated by viewing the output of the `show ip protocols` command. The output of this command on R1 is illustrated below:

```
R1#show ip protocols
Routing Protocol is "eigrp 150"
   Outgoing update filter list for all interfaces is not set
   Incoming update filter list for all interfaces is not set
   Default networks flagged in outgoing updates
```

```
Default networks accepted from incoming updates
EIGRP metric weight K1=1, K2=0, K3=1, K4=0, K5=0
EIGRP maximum hopcount 100
EIGRP maximum metric variance 1
Redistributing: eigrp 150
EIGRP NSF-aware route hold timer is 240s
Automatic network summarization is in effect
Automatic address summarization:
  150.1.0.0/16 for Loopback1, Loopback2, Loopback3
    Summarizing with metric 2169856
  10.0.0.0/8 for Serial0/0
    Summarizing with metric 128256
Maximum path: 4
Routing for Networks:
  10.1.1.0/24
  10.2.2.0/24
  10.3.3.0/24
  150.1.1.0/24
Routing Information Sources:
  Gateway         Distance      Last Update
  (this router)         90      00:03:12
  150.1.1.2             90      00:03:12
Distance: internal 90 external 170
```

In the output above, the 10.1.1.0/24, 10.2.2.0/24, and 10.3.3.0/24 subnets have been automatically summarized to 10.0.0.0/8. This summary address is advertised out of Serial0/0. The 150.1.1.0/24 subnet has been summarized to 150.1.0.0/16. This summary address is advertised out of Loopback 1, Loopback 2, and Loopback 3. Remember, by default, EIGRP will send out updates on all interfaces for which EIGRP routing is enabled.

Referencing the output printed above, we know that sending updates on a Loopback interface is a waste of resources because a device cannot be connected physically to a router Loopback interface listening for such updates. This default behavior can be disabled by using the passive-interface router configuration command as follows:

```
R1(config)#router eigrp 150
R1(config-router)#passive-interface loopback 1
R1(config-router)#passive-interface loopback 2
R1(config-router)#passive-interface loopback 3
R1(config-router)#exit
```

The result of this configuration is that EIGRP packets are no longer sent out of the Loopback interfaces. Therefore, as illustrated below, the summary address is not advertised out of these interfaces:

```
R1#show ip protocols
Routing Protocol is "eigrp 150"
  Outgoing update filter list for all interfaces is not set
  Incoming update filter list for all interfaces is not set
  Default networks flagged in outgoing updates
  Default networks accepted from incoming updates
  EIGRP metric weight K1=1, K2=0, K3=1, K4=0, K5=0
  EIGRP maximum hopcount 100
  EIGRP maximum metric variance 1
  Redistributing: eigrp 150
  EIGRP NSF-aware route hold timer is 240s
  Automatic network summarization is in effect
  Automatic address summarization:
    10.0.0.0/8 for Serial0/0
      Summarizing with metric 128256
  Maximum path: 4
  Routing for Networks:
    10.0.0.0
    150.1.0.0
  Passive Interface(s):
    Loopback0
    Loopback1
    Loopback2
    Loopback3
  Routing Information Sources:
    Gateway         Distance      Last Update
    (this router)         90      00:03:07
    150.1.1.2             90      00:01:12
  Distance: internal 90 external 170
```

NOTE: The `passive-interface` command is described in detail later in this chapter.

Continuing with automatic summarization, following automatic summarization at the Classful boundary, EIGRP installs a route to the summary address into the EIGRP Topology Table and the IP routing table. The route is highlighted below in the EIGRP Topology Table, along with the more specific entries and their respective directly connected interfaces:

```
R1#show ip eigrp topology
IP-EIGRP Topology Table for AS(150)/ID(10.3.3.1)

Codes: P - Passive, A - Active, U - Update, Q - Query, R - Reply,
       r - reply Status, s - sia Status
```

```
P 10.0.0.0/8, 1 successors, FD is 128256
        via Summary (128256/0), Null0
P 10.3.3.0/24, 1 successors, FD is 128256
        via Connected, Loopback3
P 10.2.2.0/24, 1 successors, FD is 128256
        via Connected, Loopback2
P 10.1.1.0/24, 1 successors, FD is 128256
        via Connected, Loopback1
...
[Truncated Output]
...
```

In the routing table, the summary route is connected directly to the Null0 interface. The route has a default administrative distance value of 5. This is illustrated in the following output:

```
R1#show ip route 10.0.0.0 255.0.0.0
Routing entry for 10.0.0.0/8
  Known via "eigrp 150", distance 5, metric 128256, type internal
  Redistributing via eigrp 150
  Routing Descriptor Blocks:
  * directly connected, via Null0
      Route metric is 128256, traffic share count is 1
      Total delay is 5000 microseconds, minimum bandwidth is 10000000 Kbit
      Reliability 255/255, minimum MTU 1514 bytes
      Loading 1/255, Hops 0
```

When EIGRP performs automatic summarization, the router advertises the summary route and suppresses the more specific routes. In other words, while the summary route is advertised, the more specific prefixes are suppressed in updates to EIGRP neighbors. This can be validated by looking at the routing table on R2 as illustrated below:

```
R2#show ip route eigrp
D    10.0.0.0/8 [90/2298856] via 150.1.1.1, 00:29:05, Serial0/0
```

This default behavior works well in basic networks, such as the one illustrated in Figure 2-21 above. However, it can have an adverse impact in a discontiguous network, which comprises a major network that separates another major network, as illustrated in Figure 2-22 below:

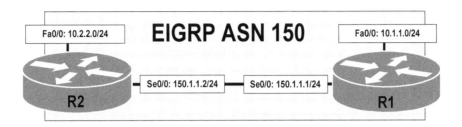

Fig. 2-22. Discontiguous Networks

Referencing the diagram illustrated in Figure 2-22, the major 150.1.0.0/16 network separates the two major 10.0.0.0/8 networks. When automatic summarization is enabled, both R1 and R2 will summarize the 10.1.1.0/24 and 10.2.2.0/24 subnets, respectively, to the 10.0.0.0/8 address. This summary route will be installed with a next hop interface of Null0. The Null0 interface is a 'bit-bucket.' Any packets sent to this interface are effectively discarded.

Because both routers advertise to each other only the summary addresses, neither router will be able to reach the 10.x.x.x/24 subnet of the other router. To understand the ramifications of automatic summarization in the network illustrated in Figure 2-22, let us go through the steps one at a time, beginning with the configuration on R1 and R2, which is as follows:

```
R1(config)#router eigrp 150
R1(config-router)#network 10.1.1.0 0.0.0.255
R1(config-router)#network 150.1.1.0 0.0.0.255
R1(config-router)#exit
R2(config)#router eigrp 150
R2(config-router)#network 10.2.2.0 0.0.0.255
R2(config-router)#network 150.1.1.0 0.0.0.255
R2(config-router)#exit
```

Because automatic summarization at the Classful boundary is enabled by default on both of the routers, they will both generate two summary addresses: one for 10.0.0.0/8 and another for 150.1.0.0/16. These summary addresses will both point to the Null0 interface and the routing table on R1 will display the following entries:

```
R1#show ip route eigrp
     10.0.0.0/8 is variably subnetted, 2 subnets, 2 masks
D       10.0.0.0/8 is a summary, 00:04:51, Null0
     150.1.0.0/16 is variably subnetted, 2 subnets, 2 masks
D       150.1.0.0/16 is a summary, 00:06:22, Null0
```

Similarly, the routing table on R2 also reflects the same as follows:

```
R2#show ip route eigrp
     10.0.0.0/8 is variably subnetted, 2 subnets, 2 masks
D       10.0.0.0/8 is a summary, 00:01:58, Null0
     150.1.0.0/16 is variably subnetted, 2 subnets, 2 masks
D       150.1.0.0/16 is a summary, 00:01:58, Null0
```

Even though a summary address of 150.1.0.0/16 has been installed into the IP routing table, R1 and R2 are still able to ping each other because the more route-specific entry (150.1.1.0/24) resides on a directly connected interface. The more specific entries in a summary route can be viewed by issuing the show ip route [address][mask] longer-prefixes command. The output of this command is illustrated below for the 150.1.0.0/16 summary:

```
R1#show ip route 150.1.0.0 255.255.0.0 longer-prefixes
Codes: C - connected, S - static, R - RIP, M - mobile, B - BGP
       D - EIGRP, EX - EIGRP external, O - OSPF, IA - OSPF inter area
       N1 - OSPF NSSA external type 1, N2 - OSPF NSSA external type 2
       E1 - OSPF external type 1, E2 - OSPF external type 2
       i - IS-IS, su - IS-IS summary, L1 - IS-IS level-1, L2 - IS-IS level-2
       ia - IS-IS inter area, * - candidate default, U - per-user static
route
       o - ODR, P - periodic downloaded static route

Gateway of last resort is not set

     150.1.0.0/16 is variably subnetted, 2 subnets, 2 masks
C       150.1.1.0/24 is directly connected, Serial0/0
D       150.1.0.0/16 is a summary, 00:10:29, Null0
```

Because the more specific 150.1.1.0/24 route entry exists, packets sent to the 150.1.1.2 address will be forwarded via the Serial0/0 interface. This allows connectivity between R1 and R2 as illustrated below:

```
R1#ping 150.1.1.2

Type escape sequence to abort.
Sending 5, 100-byte ICMP Echos to 150.1.1.2, timeout is 2 seconds:
!!!!!
Success rate is 100 percent (5/5), round-trip min/avg/max = 1/3/4 ms
```

However, packets to any other subnets of the major 150.1.0.0/16 will be sent to the Null0 interface because no specific route entries exist.

So far, everything appears to be in order. We have determined that due to the more specific route entry of the major 150.1.0.0/16 network, R1 and R2 are able to ping each other. The problem, however, is connectivity between the major 10.0.0.0/8 subnets on R1 and R2. Router R1 displays the following specific route entries for its generated 10.0.0.0/8 summary address:

```
R1#show ip route 10.0.0.0 255.0.0.0 longer-prefixes
Codes: C - connected, S - static, R - RIP, M - mobile, B - BGP
       D - EIGRP, EX - EIGRP external, O - OSPF, IA - OSPF inter area
       N1 - OSPF NSSA external type 1, N2 - OSPF NSSA external type 2
       E1 - OSPF external type 1, E2 - OSPF external type 2
       i - IS-IS, su - IS-IS summary, L1 - IS-IS level-1, L2 - IS-IS level-2
       ia - IS-IS inter area, * - candidate default, U - per-user static
route
       o - ODR, P - periodic downloaded static route

Gateway of last resort is not set

     10.0.0.0/8 is variably subnetted, 2 subnets, 2 masks
C       10.1.1.0/24 is directly connected, FastEthernet0/0
D       10.0.0.0/8 is a summary, 00:14:23, Null0
```

Similarly, router R2 displays the following specific entries for its generated 10.0.0.0/8 summary:

```
R2#show ip route 10.0.0.0 255.0.0.0 longer-prefixes
Codes: C - connected, S - static, R - RIP, M - mobile, B - BGP
       D - EIGRP, EX - EIGRP external, O - OSPF, IA - OSPF inter area
       N1 - OSPF NSSA external type 1, N2 - OSPF NSSA external type 2
       E1 - OSPF external type 1, E2 - OSPF external type 2
       i - IS-IS, su - IS-IS summary, L1 - IS-IS level-1, L2 - IS-IS level-2
       ia - IS-IS inter area, * - candidate default, U - per-user static
route
       o - ODR, P - periodic downloaded static route

Gateway of last resort is not set

     10.0.0.0/8 is variably subnetted, 2 subnets, 2 masks
C       10.2.2.0/24 is directly connected, FastEthernet0/0
D       10.0.0.0/8 is a summary, 00:15:11, Null0
```

Neither router has a route to the other router's 10.*x.x.x*/24 subnet. If, for example, R1 attempts to send packets to 10.2.2.0/24, the summary address will be used and the packets are forwarded to the Null0 interface. This is illustrated in the following output:

```
R1#show ip route 10.2.2.0
Routing entry for 10.0.0.0/8
  Known via "eigrp 150", distance 5, metric 28160, type internal
```

```
Redistributing via eigrp 150
Routing Descriptor Blocks:
* directly connected, via Null0
    Route metric is 28160, traffic share count is 1
    Total delay is 100 microseconds, minimum bandwidth is 100000 Kbit
    Reliability 255/255, minimum MTU 1500 bytes
    Loading 1/255, Hops 0
```

R1 will be unable to ping the 10.*x.x.x*/24 subnet on R2 and vice-versa as illustrated below:

```
R1#ping 10.2.2.2

Type escape sequence to abort.
Sending 5, 100-byte ICMP Echos to 10.2.2.2, timeout is 2 seconds:
.....
Success rate is 0 percent (0/5)
```

Two solutions to this issue are as follows:
1. Manually configure static routes for the 10.*x.x.x*/24 subnets on both routers
2. Disable EIGRP automatic Classful network summarization

The first option is very basic. However, static route configuration is not scalable and requires a great deal of configuration overhead in large networks. The second option, which is also the recommended option, is both scalable and requires less configuration overhead than the first. Automatic summarization is disabled by issuing the no auto-summary command as illustrated below:

```
R1(config)#router eigrp 150
R1(config-router)#no auto-summary
R1(config-router)#exit
R2(config)#router eigrp 150
R2(config-router)#no auto-summary
R2(config-router)#exit
```

The result of this configuration is that the specific subnets of the major network are advertised by both routers. A summary route is not generated as illustrated below:

```
R2#show ip route eigrp
     10.0.0.0/24 is subnetted, 2 subnets
D       10.1.1.0 [90/2172416] via 150.1.1.1, 00:01:17, Serial0/0
```

IP connectivity between the 10.*x.x.x*/24 subnets can be validated using a simple ping as illustrated below:

```
R2#ping 10.1.1.1 source 10.2.2.2 repeat 10

Type escape sequence to abort.
Sending 10, 100-byte ICMP Echos to 10.1.1.1, timeout is 2 seconds:
Packet sent with a source address of 10.2.2.2
!!!!!!!!!!
Success rate is 100 percent (10/10), round-trip min/avg/max = 1/3/4 ms
```

Before we go into the details pertaining to manual route summarization, it is important to know that EIGRP will not automatically summarize external networks unless there is an internal network that will be included in the summary. To better understand this concept, we will refer to Figure 2-23 below, which illustrates a basic EIGRP network:

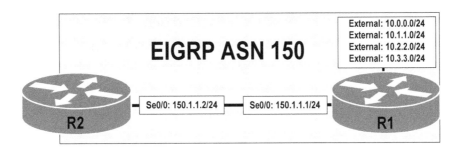

Fig. 2-23. Summarizing External Networks

Referencing Figure 2-23, R1 is redistributing and then advertising the 10.0.0.0/24, 10.1.1.0/24, 10.2.2.0/24, and 10.3.3.0/24 external networks via EIGRP. Automatic route summarization is enabled on R1. The initial configuration on R1 is as follows:

```
R1(config)#router eigrp 150
R1(config-router)#redistribute connected metric 8000000 5000 255 1 1514
R1(config-router)#network 150.1.1.1 0.0.0.0
R1(config-router)#exit
```

The show ip protocols command shows that EIGRP is enabled for Serial0/0 and is redistributing connected networks. Automatic summarization is also enabled as illustrated below.

```
R1#show ip protocols
Routing Protocol is "eigrp 150"
  Outgoing update filter list for all interfaces is not set
  Incoming update filter list for all interfaces is not set
  Default networks flagged in outgoing updates
  Default networks accepted from incoming updates
  EIGRP metric weight K1=1, K2=0, K3=1, K4=0, K5=0
```

```
EIGRP maximum hopcount 100
EIGRP maximum metric variance 1
Redistributing: connected, eigrp 150
EIGRP NSF-aware route hold timer is 240s
Automatic network summarization is in effect
Maximum path: 4
Routing for Networks:
  150.1.1.1/32
Routing Information Sources:
  Gateway          Distance      Last Update
  150.1.1.2              90       00:00:07
Distance: internal 90 external 170
```

Because the 10.*x.x.x*/24 prefixes are all external routes, EIGRP will not automatically summarize these prefixes as illustrated in the previous example. Therefore, EIGRP will not add a summary route to either the Topology Table or the IP routing table for these entries. This is illustrated in the following output:

```
R1#show ip eigrp topology
IP-EIGRP Topology Table for AS(150)/ID(10.3.3.1)

Codes: P - Passive, A - Active, U - Update, Q - Query, R - Reply,
       r - reply Status, s - sia Status

P 10.0.0.0/24, 1 successors, FD is 1280256
        via Rconnected (1280256/0)
P 10.1.1.0/24, 1 successors, FD is 1280256
        via Rconnected (1280256/0)
P 10.2.2.0/24, 1 successors, FD is 1280256
        via Rconnected (1280256/0)
P 10.3.3.0/24, 1 successors, FD is 1280256
        via Rconnected (1280256/0)
...
[Truncated Output]
...
```

The specific route entries are advertised to R2 as external EIGRP routes as illustrated below:

```
R2#show ip route eigrp
     10.0.0.0/24 is subnetted, 4 subnets
D EX    10.3.3.0 [170/3449856] via 150.1.1.1, 00:07:02, Serial0/0
D EX    10.2.2.0 [170/3449856] via 150.1.1.1, 00:07:02, Serial0/0
D EX    10.1.1.0 [170/3449856] via 150.1.1.1, 00:07:02, Serial0/0
D EX    10.0.0.0 [170/3449856] via 150.1.1.1, 00:07:02, Serial0/0
```

Now, assume that the 10.0.0.0/24 subnet is an internal network, while the 10.1.1.0/24, 10.2.2.0/24, and 10.3.3.0/24 subnets are external routes. Because one of the routes that will comprise the Classful summary address 10.0.0.0/8 is an internal route, EIGRP will create a summary address and include that in the EIGRP Topology Table and the IP routing table. The show ip protocols command shows that the 10.0.0.0/24 network is now an internal EIGRP network as illustrated below:

```
R1#show ip protocols
Routing Protocol is "eigrp 150"
  Outgoing update filter list for all interfaces is not set
  Incoming update filter list for all interfaces is not set
  Default networks flagged in outgoing updates
  Default networks accepted from incoming updates
  EIGRP metric weight K1=1, K2=0, K3=1, K4=0, K5=0
  EIGRP maximum hopcount 100
  EIGRP maximum metric variance 1
  Redistributing: connected, eigrp 150
  EIGRP NSF-aware route hold timer is 240s
  Automatic network summarization is in effect
  Automatic address summarization:
    150.1.0.0/16 for Loopback0
      Summarizing with metric 2169856
    10.0.0.0/8 for Serial0/0
      Summarizing with metric 128256
  Maximum path: 4
  Routing for Networks:
    10.0.0.1/32
    150.1.1.1/32
  Routing Information Sources:
    Gateway         Distance      Last Update
    (this router)         90      00:00:05
    Gateway         Distance      Last Update
    150.1.1.2             90      00:00:02
  Distance: internal 90 external 170
```

In the output above, EIGRP automatic summarization has generated a summary address for 10.0.0.0/8 because the 10.0.0.0/24 internal subnet is a part of the aggregate address. The EIGRP Topology Table displays the external and internal entries, as well as the summary address, as illustrated below:

```
R1#show ip eigrp topology
IP-EIGRP Topology Table for AS(150)/ID(10.3.3.1)

Codes: P - Passive, A - Active, U - Update, Q - Query, R - Reply,
```

```
        r - reply Status, s - sia Status

P 10.0.0.0/8, 1 successors, FD is 128256
        via Summary (128256/0), Null0
P 10.0.0.0/24, 1 successors, FD is 128256
        via Connected, Loopback0
P 10.1.1.0/24, 1 successors, FD is 1280256
        via Rconnected (1280256/0)
P 10.2.2.0/24, 1 successors, FD is 1280256
        via Rconnected (1280256/0)
P 10.3.3.0/24, 1 successors, FD is 1280256
        via Rconnected (1280256/0)
...
[Truncated Output]
...
```

This time, only a single route is advertised to R2 as illustrated in the following output:

```
R2#show ip route eigrp
D     10.0.0.0/8 [90/2297856] via 150.1.1.1, 00:04:05, Serial0/0
```

From the perspective of R2, this is simply an internal EIGRP route. In other words, the router does not have any knowledge that the summary address is also comprised on external routes as illustrated below:

```
R2#show ip route 10.0.0.0 255.0.0.0
Routing entry for 10.0.0.0/8
  Known via "eigrp 150", distance 90, metric 2297856, type internal
  Redistributing via eigrp 150
  Last update from 150.1.1.1 on Serial0/0, 00:05:34 ago
  Routing Descriptor Blocks:
  * 150.1.1.1, from 150.1.1.1, 00:05:34 ago, via Serial0/0
      Route metric is 2297856, traffic share count is 1
      Total delay is 25000 microseconds, minimum bandwidth is 1544 Kbit
      Reliability 255/255, minimum MTU 1500 bytes
      Loading 1/255, Hops 1
```

R2 is able to reach both the internal 10.0.0.0/24 network and the other external 10.*x.x.x*/24 networks via the received summary route as illustrated below:

```
R2#ping 10.0.0.1

Type escape sequence to abort.
```

```
Sending 5, 100-byte ICMP Echos to 10.0.0.1, timeout is 2 seconds:
!!!!!
Success rate is 100 percent (5/5), round-trip min/avg/max = 1/2/4 ms
R2#ping 10.3.3.1

Type escape sequence to abort.
Sending 5, 100-byte ICMP Echos to 10.3.3.1, timeout is 2 seconds:
!!!!!
Success rate is 100 percent (5/5), round-trip min/avg/max = 1/3/4 ms
```

Unlike EIGRP automatic summarization, EIGRP manual route summarization is configured and implemented at the interface level using the `ip summary-address eigrp [ASN] [network] [mask] [distance] [leak-map <name>]` interface configuration command. By default, an EIGRP summary address is assigned a default administrative distance value of 5. This default assignment can be changed by specifying the desired administrative distance value as specified by the distance keyword.

By default, when manual route summarization is configured, EIGRP will not advertise the more specific route entries that fall within the summarized network entry. The `leak-map <name>` keyword can be configured to allow EIGRP route leaking wherein EIGRP allows specified specific route entries to be advertised in conjunction with the summary address. Those entries that are not specified in the leak map are still suppressed.

When manually summarizing routes, it is important to be as specific as possible. Otherwise, the configuration might result in a black-holing of traffic in a manner similar to the example pertaining to discontiguous networks that was described earlier in this section. This concept is illustrated in Figure 2-24 below:

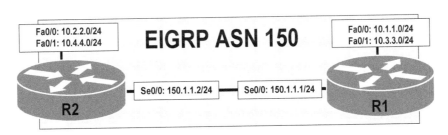

Fig. 2-24. Black-Holing Traffic with Poor Route Summarization

Referencing Figure 2-24, if a manual summary address of 10.0.0.0/8 is configured on both of the routers, then the more specific prefixes are suppressed. Because EIGRP also installs a route to the summary address into both the EIGRP Topology Table and the IP routing table with a next hop interface of Null0, the same issue experienced with automatic summarization in discontiguous networks is experienced in this network, and the respective subnets on either router will be unable to communicate with each other.

Additionally, it is also important to understand that if poorly implemented within the network, route summarization may result in sub-optimal routing within the network. This concept is illustrated in Figure 2-25 below:

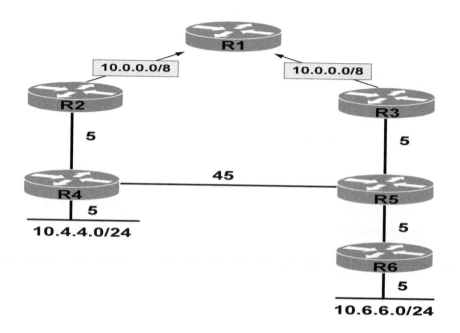

Fig. 2-25. Sub-Optimal Routing with Route Summarization

By default, when a summary route is created for EIGRP, the router advertises the summary address with a metric equal to the minimum of all the more specific routes. In other words, the summary address will have the same metric as the lowest most specific route included in the creation of the summary address.

Referencing the network topology illustrated in Figure 2-25, both R2 and R3 are advertising the summary address 10.0.0.0/8 to R1. This summary is comprised of the more specific 10.4.4.0/24 and 10.6.6.0/24 prefixes. The metric used by the summary address on both routers is calculated as illustrated below in Table 2-5:

Table 2-5. Summary Route Metric Calculation

Starting Point (Router)	Metric To 10.4.4.0/24	Metric to 10.6.6.0/24
R2	5 + 5 = 10	5 + 45 + 5 + 5 = 60
R3	5 + 45 + 5 = 55	5 + 5 + 5 = 15

Based on the metric calculation in Table 2-5, R2 clearly has the lowest metric path to 10.4.4.0/24 for traffic originating from R1, while R3 has the lowest metric path to 10.6.6.0/24 for traffic originating from R1. However, when the 10.0.0.0/8 summary address is advertised to R1, the summary address uses the lowest minimum metric of all routes of which the summary is comprised. Based on this example, R2 advertises the summary address to R1 with a metric of 10. R3 follows the same logic and advertises the summary route to R1 with a metric of 15.

When R1 receives the summary routes from R2 and R3, it uses the one with the lowest metric to forward traffic destined to subnets contained within the 10.0.0.0/8 major Classful network via R2. This is illustrated in Figure 2-26 below:

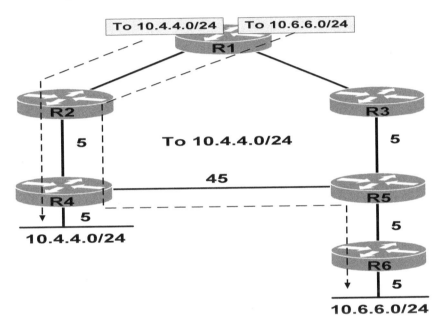

Fig. 2-26. Sub-Optimal Routing with Route Summarization

Referencing Figure 2-26, we can clearly see that while this is the optimal path for the 10.4.4.0/24 subnet, it is a suboptimal path for the 10.6.6.0/24 subnet. It is therefore very important to understand the network topology before implementing route summarization in the network.

Reverting back to the configuration of manual route summarization when using EIGRP, the network topology illustrated in Figure 2-27 below will be used to demonstrate manual route summarization and route leaking:

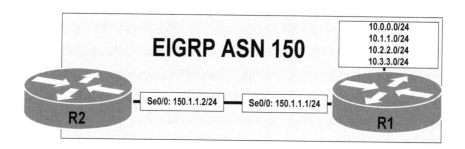

Fig. 2-27. Configuring EIGRP Route Summarization

Based on the interfaces configured on R1, the routing table on R2 displays the following entries:

```
R2#show ip route eigrp
     10.0.0.0/24 is subnetted, 4 subnets
D       10.3.3.0 [90/2297856] via 150.1.1.1, 00:00:14, Serial0/0
D       10.2.2.0 [90/2297856] via 150.1.1.1, 00:00:14, Serial0/0
D       10.1.1.0 [90/2297856] via 150.1.1.1, 00:00:14, Serial0/0
D       10.0.0.0 [90/2297856] via 150.1.1.1, 00:00:14, Serial0/0
```

To summarize these entries on R1 and to advertise a single specific route, the following configuration is applied to the Serial0/0 interface of R1:

```
R1(config)#interface Serial0/0
R1(config-if)#ip summary-address eigrp 150 10.0.0.0 255.252.0.0
R1(config-if)#exit
```

Following this configuration, the summary entry 10.0.0.0/14 is installed into the EIGRP Topology Table and the IP routing table on R1. The EIGRP Topology Table entry is as follows:

```
R1#show ip eigrp topology
IP-EIGRP Topology Table for AS(150)/ID(10.3.3.1)

Codes: P - Passive, A - Active, U - Update, Q - Query, R - Reply,
       r - reply Status, s - sia Status

P 10.0.0.0/14, 1 successors, FD is 128256
        via Summary (128256/0), Null0
P 10.3.3.0/24, 1 successors, FD is 128256
        via Connected, Loopback3
P 10.2.2.0/24, 1 successors, FD is 128256
        via Connected, Loopback2
P 10.0.0.0/24, 1 successors, FD is 128256
        via Connected, Loopback0
```

```
P 10.1.1.0/24, 1 successors, FD is 128256
        via Connected, Loopback1
...
[Truncated Output]
...
```

The routing table entry also reflects the summary route with a next hop interface of Null0 as illustrated below:

```
R1#show ip route
Codes: C - connected, S - static, R - RIP, M - mobile, B - BGP
       D - EIGRP, EX - EIGRP external, O - OSPF, IA - OSPF inter area
       N1 - OSPF NSSA external type 1, N2 - OSPF NSSA external type 2
       E1 - OSPF external type 1, E2 - OSPF external type 2
       i - IS-IS, su - IS-IS summary, L1 - IS-IS level-1, L2 - IS-IS level-2
       ia - IS-IS inter area, * - candidate default, U - per-user static
route
       o - ODR, P - periodic downloaded static route

Gateway of last resort is not set

     10.0.0.0/8 is variably subnetted, 5 subnets, 2 masks
C        10.3.3.0/24 is directly connected, Loopback3
C        10.2.2.0/24 is directly connected, Loopback2
C        10.1.1.0/24 is directly connected, Loopback1
C        10.0.0.0/24 is directly connected, Loopback0
D*       10.0.0.0/14 is a summary, 00:02:37, Null0
     150.1.0.0/24 is subnetted, 1 subnets
C        150.1.1.0 is directly connected, Serial0/0
     150.2.0.0/24 is subnetted, 1 subnets
C        150.2.2.0 is directly connected, Serial0/1
```

Again, the show ip route [address] [mask] longer-prefixes command can be used to view the specific route entries that comprise the aggregate or summary route as illustrated in the following output on R1:

```
R1#show ip route 10.0.0.0 255.252.0.0 longer-prefixes
Codes: C - connected, S - static, R - RIP, M - mobile, B - BGP
       D - EIGRP, EX - EIGRP external, O - OSPF, IA - OSPF inter area
       N1 - OSPF NSSA external type 1, N2 - OSPF NSSA external type 2
       E1 - OSPF external type 1, E2 - OSPF external type 2
       i - IS-IS, su - IS-IS summary, L1 - IS-IS level-1, L2 - IS-IS level-2
       ia - IS-IS inter area, * - candidate default, U - per-user static
route
       o - ODR, P - periodic downloaded static route
```

```
Gateway of last resort is not set

     10.0.0.0/8 is variably subnetted, 5 subnets, 2 masks
C       10.3.3.0/24 is directly connected, Loopback3
C       10.2.2.0/24 is directly connected, Loopback2
C       10.1.1.0/24 is directly connected, Loopback1
C       10.0.0.0/24 is directly connected, Loopback0
D       10.0.0.0/14 is a summary, 00:04:03, Null0
```

On R2, a single route entry for the 10.0.0.0/14 summary address is received as illustrated below:

```
R2#show ip route eigrp
     10.0.0.0/14 is subnetted, 1 subnets
D       10.0.0.0 [90/2297856] via 150.1.1.1, 00:06:22, Serial0/0
```

To reinforce the concept regarding the metric for the summary route, assume that the routes on R1 are all external EIGRP routes (i.e., they have been redistributed into EIGRP) with different metrics. The EIGRP Topology Table on R1 displays the following:

```
R1#show ip eigrp topology
IP-EIGRP Topology Table for AS(150)/ID(10.3.3.1)

Codes: P - Passive, A - Active, U - Update, Q - Query, R - Reply,
       r - reply Status, s - sia Status

P 10.0.0.0/24, 1 successors, FD is 10127872
        via Rconnected (10127872/0)
P 10.1.1.0/24, 1 successors, FD is 3461120
        via Rconnected (3461120/0)
P 10.2.2.0/24, 1 successors, FD is 2627840
        via Rconnected (2627840/0)
P 10.3.3.0/24, 1 successors, FD is 1377792
        via Rconnected (1377792/0)
...
[Truncated Output]
...
```

The same summary address configured on R1 in the previous example is configured again as follows:

```
R1(config)#int s 0/0
R1(config-if)#ip summary-address eigrp 150 10.0.0.0 255.252.0.0
R1(config-if)#exit
```

Based on this configuration, the summary route is placed into the EIGRP Topology Table and the IP routing table with a metric equal to the lowest metric of all routes that it encompasses. Based on the output of the show ip eigrp topology command shown previously, the summary address will be assigned the same metric assigned to the 10.3.3.0/24 prefix as illustrated below:

```
R1#show ip eigrp topology
IP-EIGRP Topology Table for AS(150)/ID(10.3.3.1)

Codes: P - Passive, A - Active, U - Update, Q - Query, R - Reply,
       r - reply Status, s - sia Status

P 10.0.0.0/14, 1 successors, FD is 1377792
        via Summary (1377792/0), Null0
P 10.0.0.0/24, 1 successors, FD is 10127872
        via Rconnected (10127872/0)
P 10.1.1.0/24, 1 successors, FD is 3461120
        via Rconnected (3461120/0)
P 10.2.2.0/24, 1 successors, FD is 2627840
        via Rconnected (2627840/0)
P 10.3.3.0/24, 1 successors, FD is 1377792
        via Rconnected (1377792/0)
P 150.1.1.0/24, 1 successors, FD is 2169856
        via Connected, Serial0/0
```

UNDERSTANDING PASSIVE INTERFACES

As stated earlier in this chapter, when EIGRP is enabled for a network, the router begins to send out Hello packets on all interfaces that fall within the specified network range. This allows EIGRP to discover neighbors dynamically and establish network relationships. This is desired on interfaces that are actually connected to physical media, such as Ethernet and Serial interfaces. However, this default behavior also results in an unnecessary waste of router resources on logical interfaces, such as Loopback interfaces, that will never have any other device connected to them with which the router could ever establish an EIGRP neighbor relationship.

Cisco IOS software allows administrators to use the passive-interface [name|default] router configuration command to specify the named interface as passive, or all interfaces as passive. EIGRP packets are not sent out on passive interfaces; therefore, no neighbor relationship will ever be established between passive interfaces. The following output illustrates how to configure two EIGRP-enabled interfaces as passive on a router:

```
R1(config)#interface loopback 0
R1(config-if)#ip address 10.0.0.1 255.255.255.0
```

```
R1(config-if)#exit
R1(config)#interface loopback 1
R1(config-if)#ip address 10.1.1.1 255.255.255.0
R1(config-if)#exit
R1(config)#interface Serial0/0
R1(config-if)#ip address 150.1.1.1 255.255.255.0
R1(config-if)#exit
R1(config)#router eigrp 150
R1(config-router)#no auto-summary
R1(config-router)#network 150.1.1.0 0.0.0.255
R1(config-router)#network 10.0.0.0 0.0.0.255
R1(config-router)#network 10.1.1.0 0.0.0.255
R1(config-router)#passive-interface loopback 0
R1(config-router)#passive-interface loopback 1
R1(config-router)#exit
```

Based on this configuration, Loopback 0 and Loopback 1 are enabled for EIGRP routing and the directly connected networks will be advertised to EIGRP neighbors. However, no EIGRP packets will be sent by R1 out of these interfaces. Serial0/0, on the other hand, is also configured for EIGRP routing but EIGRP is allowed to send packets on this interface because it is not a passive interface. All three network entries are installed in the EIGRP Topology Table as illustrated below:

```
R1#show ip eigrp topology
IP-EIGRP Topology Table for AS(150)/ID(10.3.3.1)

Codes: P - Passive, A - Active, U - Update, Q - Query, R - Reply,
       r - reply Status, s - sia Status

P 10.1.1.0/24, 1 successors, FD is 128256
        via Connected, Loopback1
P 10.0.0.0/24, 1 successors, FD is 128256
        via Connected, Loopback0
P 150.1.1.0/24, 1 successors, FD is 2169856
        via Connected, Serial0/0
```

However, the output of the show ip eigrp interfaces command shows that EIGRP routing is enabled only for the Serial0/0 interface as illustrated below:

```
R1#show ip eigrp interfaces
IP-EIGRP interfaces for process 150

                        Xmit Queue   Mean   Pacing Time   Multicast   Pending
```

```
Interface      Peers  Un/Reliable  SRTT  Un/Reliable  Flow Timer  Routes
Se0/0            1        0/0         0       0/15          0          0
```

You can also view the interfaces configured as passive in the output of the show ip protocols command as illustrated below:

```
R1#show ip protocols
Routing Protocol is "eigrp 150"
  Outgoing update filter list for all interfaces is not set
  Incoming update filter list for all interfaces is not set
  Default networks flagged in outgoing updates
  Default networks accepted from incoming updates
  EIGRP metric weight K1=1, K2=0, K3=1, K4=0, K5=0
  EIGRP maximum hopcount 100
  EIGRP maximum metric variance 1
  Redistributing: eigrp 150
  EIGRP NSF-aware route hold timer is 240s
  Automatic network summarization is not in effect
  Maximum path: 4
  Routing for Networks:
    10.0.0.0/24
    10.1.1.0/24
    150.1.1.0/24
  Passive Interface(s):
    Loopback0
    Loopback1
  Routing Information Sources:
    Gateway         Distance      Last Update
  Distance: internal 90 external 170
```

The default keyword makes all interfaces passive. Assume that a router is configured with 50 Loopback interfaces configured. If you wanted to make each Loopback interface passive, you would need to add 50 lines of code. The passive-interface default command can be used to make all interfaces passive. Those interfaces that you do want to send EIGRP packets to can then be configured with the no passive-interface [name] command. The following illustrates the use of the passive-interface default command:

```
R1(config)#interface loopback 0
R1(config-if)#ip address 10.0.0.1 255.255.255.0
R1(config-if)#exit
R1(config)#interface loopback 1
R1(config-if)#ip address 10.1.1.1 255.255.255.0
R1(config-if)#exit
```

```
R1(config)#interface loopback 3
R1(config-if)#ip address 10.3.3.1 255.255.255.0
R1(config-if)#exit
R1(config)#interface loopback 2
R1(config-if)#ip address 10.2.2.1 255.255.255.0
R1(config-if)#exit
R1(config)#interface Serial0/0
R1(config-if)#ip address 150.1.1.1 255.255.255.0
R1(config-if)#exit
R1(config)#router eigrp 150
R1(config-router)#network 10.0.0.1 255.255.255.0
R1(config-router)#network 10.1.1.1 255.255.255.0
R1(config-router)#network 10.3.3.1 255.255.255.0
R1(config-router)#network 10.2.2.1 255.255.255.0
R1(config-router)#network 150.1.1.1 255.255.255.0
R1(config-router)#passive-interface default
R1(config-router)#no passive-interface Serial0/0
R1(config-router)#exit
```

The show ip protocols can be used to view which interfaces are passive under EIGRP as illustrated below:

```
R1#show ip protocols
Routing Protocol is "eigrp 150"
  Outgoing update filter list for all interfaces is not set
  Incoming update filter list for all interfaces is not set
  Default networks flagged in outgoing updates
  Default networks accepted from incoming updates
  EIGRP metric weight K1=1, K2=0, K3=1, K4=0, K5=0
  EIGRP maximum hopcount 100
  EIGRP maximum metric variance 1
  Redistributing: eigrp 150
  EIGRP NSF-aware route hold timer is 240s
  Automatic network summarization is not in effect
  Maximum path: 4
  Routing for Networks:
    10.0.0.0/24
    10.1.1.0/24
    10.2.2.0/24
    10.3.3.0/24
    150.1.1.0/24
  Passive Interface(s):
    Loopback1
    Loopback2
```

```
    Loopback3
    Loopback4
  Routing Information Sources:
    Gateway          Distance     Last Update
    (this router)          90     00:02:52
  Distance: internal 90 external 170
```

By using the `passive-interface default` command, the configuration of multiple passive interfaces is simplified and reduced. Used in conjunction with the `no passive-interface Serial0/0` command, EIGRP packets are still sent out on Serial0/0, allowing EIGRP neighbor relationships to be established across that interface as illustrated below:

```
R1#show ip eigrp neighbors
IP-EIGRP neighbors for process 150
H   Address              Interface      Hold Uptime    SRTT   RTO  Q  Seq
                                        (sec)          (ms)       Cnt Num

0   150.1.1.2            Se0/0          12 00:02:47    1    3000  0  69
```

UNDERSTANDING THE USE OF THE EIGRP ROUTER ID

Unlike OSPF, which uses the Router ID (RID) to identify the OSPF neighbor, the primary use of the EIGRP RID is to prevent routing loops. The RID is used to identify the originating router for external routes. If an external route is received with the same RID as the local router, the route is discarded. This feature is designed to reduce the possibility of routing loops in networks where route redistribution is being performed on more than one ASBR.

> **NOTE:** Route redistribution is a core ROUTE topic that is described in detail later in this guide.

When determining the RID, EIGRP will select the highest IP address that is configured on the router. If Loopback interfaces are also configured on the router, those interfaces are preferred, since a Loopback interface is the most stable interface that can exist on a router. The RID will never change unless the EIGRP process is removed (i.e., if the RID is manually configured). The RID will always be listed in the EIGRP Topology Table as illustrated below:

```
R1#show ip eigrp topology
IP-EIGRP Topology Table for AS(150)/ID(10.3.3.1)

Codes: P - Passive, A - Active, U - Update, Q - Query, R - Reply,
       r - reply Status, s - sia Status
```

```
P 10.2.2.0/24, 1 successors, FD is 128256
        via Connected, Loopback2
P 10.3.3.0/24, 1 successors, FD is 128256
        via Connected, Loopback3
P 10.1.1.0/24, 1 successors, FD is 128256
        via Connected, Loopback1
P 10.0.0.0/24, 1 successors, FD is 128256
        via Connected, Loopback0
P 150.1.1.0/24, 1 successors, FD is 2169856
        via Connected, Serial0/0
```

NOTE: It is important to understand that the RID and the neighbor ID will typically be different, although this may not be the case in routers with a single interface, for example.

The EIGRP RID is configured using the `eigrp router-id [address]` router configuration command. When this command is entered, the RID is automatically updated with the new address in the EIGRP Topology Table. To demonstrate this point, let us begin by looking at the current RID on the router as stated in the Topology Table below:

```
R1#show ip eigrp topology
IP-EIGRP Topology Table for AS(150)/ID(10.3.3.1)

Codes: P - Passive, A - Active, U - Update, Q - Query, R - Reply,
       r - reply Status, s - sia Status
...
[Truncated Output]
...
```

A RID of 1.1.1.1 is now configured on the router as follows:

```
R1(config)#router eigrp 150
R1(config-router)#eigrp router-id 1.1.1.1
R1(config-router)#
*Mar  1 05:50:13.642: %DUAL-5-NBRCHANGE: IP-EIGRP(0) 150: Neighbor 150.1.1.2
(Serial0/0) is down: route configuration changed
*Mar  1 05:50:16.014: %DUAL-5-NBRCHANGE: IP-EIGRP(0) 150: Neighbor 150.1.1.2
(Serial0/0) is up: new adjacency
```

Following the change, the EIGRP neighbor relationship is reset and the new RID is reflected immediately in the EIGRP Topology Table as illustrated below:

```
R1#show ip eigrp topology
IP-EIGRP Topology Table for AS(150)/ID(1.1.1.1)

Codes: P - Passive, A - Active, U - Update, Q - Query, R - Reply,
       r - reply Status, s - sia Status
...
[Truncated Output]
...
```

When configuring the EIGRP RID, the following should be remembered:

- You cannot configure the RID as 0.0.0.0
- You cannot configure the RID as 255.255.255.255

All external routes that are originated by the router now contain the EIGRP RID. This can be verified in the following output of neighbor router R2:

```
R2#show ip eigrp topology 192.168.254.0/24
IP-EIGRP (AS 150): Topology entry for 192.168.254.0/24
  State is Passive, Query origin flag is 1, 1 Successor(s), FD is 7289856
  Routing Descriptor Blocks:
  150.1.1.1 (Serial0/0), from 150.1.1.1, Send flag is 0x0
      Composite metric is (7289856/6777856), Route is External
      Vector metric:
        Minimum bandwidth is 1544 Kbit
        Total delay is 220000 microseconds
        Reliability is 255/255
        Load is 1/255
        Minimum MTU is 1500
        Hop count is 1
      External data:
        Originating router is 1.1.1.1
        AS number of route is 0
        External protocol is Connected, external metric is 0
        Administrator tag is 0 (0x00000000)
```

The RID is not included for internal EIGRP routes as illustrated in the following output:

```
R2#show ip eigrp topology 10.3.3.0/24
IP-EIGRP (AS 150): Topology entry for 10.3.3.0/24
  State is Passive, Query origin flag is 1, 1 Successor(s), FD is 2297856
  Routing Descriptor Blocks:
  150.1.1.1 (Serial0/0), from 150.1.1.1, Send flag is 0x0
      Composite metric is (2297856/128256), Route is Internal
```

```
Vector metric:
   Minimum bandwidth is 1544 Kbit
   Total delay is 25000 microseconds
   Reliability is 255/255
   Load is 1/255
   Minimum MTU is 1500
   Hop count is 1
```

EIGRP LOGGING AND REPORTING

As a network engineer, it is important to ensure that you understand how to configure EIGRP to log and report events, such as neighbor relationship resets. EIGRP event logging configuration parameters are configured in router configuration mode. These options are illustrated in the following output:

```
R2(config)#router eigrp 150
R2(config-router)#eigrp ?
   event-log-size        Set EIGRP maximum event log entries
   event-logging         Log IP-EIGRP routing events
   log-neighbor-changes  Enable/Disable IP-EIGRP neighbor logging
   log-neighbor-warnings Enable/Disable IP-EIGRP neighbor warnings
   router-id             router-id for this EIGRP process
   stub                  Set IP-EIGRP as stubbed router
```

The eigrp event-logging router configuration command is enabled by default. This EIGRP command enables the router to store a log of EIGRP events, such as when a metric for a route changes and an Update message is sent to a neighbor or group of neighbors. The contents of the EIGRP log can be viewed by issuing the show ip eigrp events command as follows:

```
R2#show ip eigrp event
Event information for AS 150:
1    13:15:27.440 Change queue emptied, entries: 1
2    13:15:27.440 Route OBE net/refcount: 150.1.1.0/24 1
3    13:15:27.440 Metric set: 150.1.1.0/24 3011840
4    13:15:27.440 Update reason, delay: metric chg 512000
5    13:15:27.440 Update sent, RD: 150.1.1.0/24 2169856
6    13:15:27.440 FC sat rdbmet/succmet: 3011840 0
7    13:15:27.440 FC sat nh/ndbmet: 0.0.0.0 2169856
8    13:15:27.440 Find FS: 150.1.1.0/24 2169856
9    13:15:27.440 Rcv update met/succmet: 3011840 0
...
[Output Truncated]
...
```

The entries in the event log are listed with the most recent first. By default, the EIGRP event log stores up to 500 lines of events. This default behavior can be configured using the `event-log-size` `<0-443604>` router configuration command. The following output illustrates how to configure an event log size of five lines:

```
R2(config)#router eigrp 150
R2(config-router)#eigrp event-log-size 5
R2(config-router)#exit
```

The `eigrp log-neighbor-changes` router configuration command allows the router to log EIGRP neighbor relationship changes. This command is enabled by default. The `eigrp log-neighbor-warnings [seconds]` router configuration command is also enabled by default. This command logs EIGRP neighbor warning messages at 10-second intervals. This default interval can be configured to any value between 1 and 65535 seconds. The following output illustrates how to configure the router to log neighbor warnings in 5-second intervals:

```
R2(config)#router eigrp 150
R2(config-router)#eigrp log-neighbor-warnings 5
```

CHAPTER SUMMARY

The following section is a summary of the major points you should be aware of in this chapter.

*   EIGRP runs directly over Internet Protocol and uses IP protocol number 88
*   EIGRP sends non-periodic incremental routing updates
*   EIGRP has a default hop-count limitation of 100; this can be adjusted to 255
*   Enhanced IGRP uses two unique triplets to carry route entries
*   EIGRP converges much faster than the traditional Distance Vector routing protocols
*   EIGRP uses DUAL to ensure loop-free path to destination networks
*   EIGRP PDMs are responsible for Network Layer protocol-specific requirements
*   A separate Neighbor Table is maintained for each Network protocol

EIGRP Configuration Fundamentals

*   The EIGRP autonomous system number (ASN) is a 32-bit integer between 1 and 65535
*   When the network command is used with a major network, the following happens:
    1. EIGRP is enabled for networks that fall within the specified Classful network range
    2. The Topology Table is populated with these directly connected subnets
    3. EIGRP Hello packets are sent out of the interfaces associated with these subnets
    4. EIGRP advertises the network(s) to EIGRP neighbors in Update messages
    5. Based on the exchange of messages, EIGRP routes are then added to the IP routing table

- The EIGRP wildcard mask uses a Logical AND operation
- The EIGRP wildcard mask is independent of the subnet mask for the network

EIGRP Messages

- The EIGRP packet header contains the following fields and information:
    1. The 4-bit Version field is used to indicate the protocol version number
    2. The 4-bit OPCode specifies the EIGRP packet or message type
    3. The 24-bit Checksum field is used to run a sanity check on the EIGRP packet
    4. The 32-bit Flags field is used to indicate either an INIT or for the CR
    5. The 32-bit Sequence field specifies the sequence number used by EIGRP RTP
    6. The 32-bit Autonomous System Number field specifies the ASN
    7. The 32-bit TLV triplet field is used to carry route entries and DUAL information

- EIGRP Hello packets are sent to the link local Multicast group address 224.0.0.10
- Hello packets sent by EIGRP do not require an Acknowledgment
- An EIGRP ACK packet is simply an EIGRP Hello packet that contains no data
- EIGRP ACK packets are used by EIGRP to confirm reliable delivery of EIGRP packets
- EIGRP ACKs are always sent to a Unicast address
- EIGRP Update packets are used to convey reachability of destinations
- Update packets are sent using Unicast and Multicast
- Update packets are always transmitted reliably and require acknowledgement
- EIGRP Query packets are Multicast and are used to reliably request routing information
- If no Query response is received in 16 attempts, the relationship is reset
- EIGRP Reply packets are sent in response to Query packets
- Request packets are used to get specific information from one or more neighbors
- Request packets are used in route server applications

EIGRP Neighbor Discovery and Maintenance

- Upon initialization, the EIGRP neighbors send Hello packets to discover other neighbors
- Hello packets are also used to maintain the EIGRP neighbor relationship
- The EIGRP neighbor relationship may not establish due to any of the following:
    1. Mismatched EIGRP Authentication Parameters (if configured)
    2. Mismatched EIGRP K Values
    3. Mismatched EIGRP Autonomous System (AS) Number
    4. Using secondary addresses for EIGRP neighbor relationships
    5. The neighbors are not on a common subnet

- Static EIGRP neighbor relationships require manual neighbor configuration on the router

- Static neighbor routers do not Multicast updates; they use Unicast
- Both routers must be configured with `neighbor` statements when using static neighbors
- EIGRP uses different Hello and Hold timers for different types of media
- The Hold time is three (3) times the Hello interval
- Hellos are sent every 5 seconds on Broadcast, P2P, and multipoint circuits greater than T1
- Hellos are sent every 60 seconds on other link types
- EIGRP timer values do not have to be the same on neighboring routers
- The Neighbor Table is used to maintain state information about EIGRP neighbors
- There is a single EIGRP Neighbor Table for each Protocol Dependent Module
- The Neighbor Table includes information required by the Reliable Transport Protocol
- EIGRP uses RTP to ensure that packets are sent reliably
- Sequence numbers are used to ensure that packets are received in the right order
- RTP uses both Multicast and Unicast packets

Metrics, DUAL, and the Topology Table

- EIGRP uses a composite metric, which may be comprised of many different variables
- K values are constants that are used to distribute weight to different path aspects
- The default values for the K values are K1 = K3 = 1 and K2 = K4 = K5 = 0
- The default EIGRP metric is: $[(10^7/\text{least bandwidth on path}) + (\text{sum of all delays})] \times 256$
- The K values can be set to any value between 0 and 255
- EIGRP metric calculation can be directly influenced by adjusting interface bandwidths
- Adjusting the bandwidth value can affect other configurations, such as QoS
- By default, when EIGRP is enabled, it can use up to 50% of the interface bandwidth
- The interface delay value is presented in microseconds
- The delay value used in EIGRP metric calculation is in tens of microseconds
- EIGRP metric calculation can be directly influenced by adjusting interface delay values
- Offset lists can be used to adjust the calculated EIGRP metric
- Configuring an offset list of 0 applies the offset to all EIGRP routes
- In EIGRP, the best route, which is the route with the lowest FD called the successor route
- The FD includes the RD (AD) and the cost of reaching that neighbor
- The RD (AD) is the metric of the neighbor itself to the specified destination network
- The Feasibility Condition (FC) occurs only when the RD is less than the FD value
- A local computation is performed by EIGRP when a Feasible Successor exists
- A diffusing computation is performed by EIGRP when no Feasible Successor exists
- The EIGRP Topology Table is populated by EIGRP PDMs
- The EIGRP Topology Table contains the following information:
  1. The lowest bandwidth on the path to the destination network
  2. The total or cumulative delay to the destination network

3. The reliability of the path to the destination network

4. The loading of the path to the destination network

5. The minimum Maximum Transmission Unit (MTU) to the destination network

6. The Feasible Distance to the destination network

7. The Reported Distance by the neighbor router to the destination network

8. The route source (only external routes) of the destination network

- EIGRP routes are Active when the Successor is lost and another route must be found
- EIGRP routes are Passive when EIGRP has completed actively computing the route

Equal Cost and Unequal Cost Load Sharing

- EIGRP has aunique ability amongst routing protocols to support unequal-cost load sharing
- Unequal-cost load sharing is configured using the `variance <1-255>` command
- The default variance is 1, which implies equal cost load balancing

Default Routing Using EIGRP

- EIGRP supports the use of the following methods to dynamically advertise a default route:
    1. Using the `ip default-network` command
    2. Using the `network` command to advertise network 0.0.0.0/0
    3. Redistributing the default static route
    4. Using the `ip summary-address eigrp [asn] [network] [mask]` command

Split Horizon in EIGRP Networks

- Split horizon prevents information being advertised the same interface it was learned
- Split horizon is enabled by default for EIGRP WAN interfaces
- Workarounds to disabling split horizon for EIGRP on WAN interfaces include the following:
    1. Advertising a default route from the HQ router to the spoke routers
    2. Manually configuring EIGRP neighbors on the routers

EIGRP Stub Routing

- EIGRP stub routing conserves router resources and improves network stability
- Stub routing requires the use of a new TLV
- Stub routers respond to Query packets with a message of inaccessible
- EIGRP stub routing provides four advantages, which are as follows:
    1. It prevents sub-optimal routing from occurring within hub-and-spoke EIGRP networks
    2. It prevents stub routers with low-speed links from being used as transit routers
    3. It eliminates EIGRP Query storms, allowing the EIGRP network to convergence faster
    4. It reduces the required amount of configuration commands on the stub routers

- By default, when this command is enabled, the following is true on the stub router:
  1. The stub router advertises all connected subnets
  2. The stub router advertises all summary routes

Securing EIGRP Protocol Messages

- EIGRP supports MD5 hashing to ensure the integrity of EIGRP messages
- EIGRP message authentication consists of several steps. These steps are as follows:
  1. Configuring a key chain name in global configuration mode
  2. Configuring one or more keys within the key chain
  3. Configuring a key string for the key
  4. Configure EIGRP to use Message Digest 5 (MD5) authentication
  5. Configuring EIGRP to use the key chain and key(s)

- When using authentication, the router clocks may be synchronized in two different ways:
  1. By manually setting the clock using the `clock set` privileged EXEC command
  2. By synchronizing the router with an Network Time Protocol (NTP) source

EIGRP Route Summarization

- Summarization reduces the size of (number of entries in) the IP routing table
- Summarization restricts the size of the area affected by network topology changes
- Summarization also defines a Query boundary for EIGRP packets
- EIGRP supports two different types of route summarization (aggregation):
  1. Automatic route summarization
  2. Manual route summarization

- Automatic summarization is enabled by default in Cisco IOS software
- With automatic summarization, internal routes are summarized by default
- With automatic summarization, external routes are not summarized by default
- External routes are summarized if they include an internal network
- Manual summarization requires explicit administrator configuration

Understanding Passive Interfaces

- Passive interfaces will still be advertised if included by a `network` statement
- EIGRP packets will not be sent out of interfaces configured as passive
- Subnets for interfaces marked as passive are still entered into the Topology Table

Understanding the Use of the EIGRP Router ID

- The primary use of the EIGRP Router ID (RID) is to prevent routing loops
- The RID is used to identify the originating router for external routes
- If an external route with a RID of the local router is received, it is discarded
- EIGRP will select the highest IP address that is configured on the router as the RID
- If Loopback interfaces are configured, EIGRP will select the highest interface
- When configuring the EIGRP Router ID, the following should be remembered:
    1. You cannot configure the RID as 0.0.0.0
    2. You cannot configure the RID as 255.255.255.255

- The RID is not included for internal EIGRP routes

EIGRP Logging and Reporting

- EIGRP event logging functionality is enabled by default in Cisco IOS software
- The default size of the EIGRP event log is set to 500 lines
- EIGRP neighbor change logging is enabled by default in Cisco IOS software
- EIGRP neighbor warning logging is enabled by default in Cisco IOS software

CHAPTER 3

Open Shortest Path First

Open Shortest Path First (OSPF) is an open-standard Link State routing protocol. Link State routing protocols advertise the state of their links. When a Link State router begins operating on a network link, information associated with that logical network is added to its local Link State Database (LSDB). The local router then sends Hello messages on its operational links to determine whether other Link State routers are operating on the interfaces as well. OSPF runs directly over Internet Protocol using IP protocol number 89. The ROUTE exam objective covered in this chapter is as follows:

- Implement a multi-area OSPF network, given a network design and a set of requirements

This chapter contains the following sections:
- OSPF Overview and Fundamentals
- OSPF Configuration Fundamentals
- OSPF Packet Types
- Establishing Adjacencies
- OSPF LSAs and the Link State Database (LSDB)
- OSPF Areas
- Route Metrics and Best Route Selection
- OSPF Default Routing
- OSPF Virtual Links
- OSPF Route Summarization
- OSPF Passive Interfaces
- Securing OSPF Messages
- Configuring OSPF over Non-Broadcast Networks
- OSPF Logging and Reporting

OSPF OVERVIEW AND FUNDAMENTALS

Several Requests for Comments (RFCs) have been written for OSPF. In this section, we will learn about the history of OSPF based on some of the most common RFCs that pertain to OSPF. The OSPF working group was formed in 1987 and it has since released numerous RFCs. Some of the most common RFCs on OSPF are listed below:
- RFC 1131 - OSPF Specification
- RFC 1584 - Multicast Extensions to OSPF
- RFC 1587 - The OSPF NSSA Option
- RFC 1850 - OSPF Version 2 Management Information Base
- RFC 2328 - OSPF Version 2
- RFC 2740 - OSPF Version 3

RFC 1131 describes the first iteration of OSPF and it was used in initial tests to determine whether the protocol worked.

RFC 1584 provides extensions to OSPF for the support of IP Multicast traffic. This is commonly referred to as Multicast OSPF (MOSPF). However, this standard is seldom used and, most importantly, it is not supported by Cisco.

RFC 1587 describes the operation of an OSPF Not-So-Stubby Area (NSSA). An NSSA allows for the injection of external routing knowledge by an ASBR using an NSSA External LSA. NSSAs are described in detail later in this chapter.

RFC 1850 allows network management of OSPF using the Simple Network Management Protocol (SNMP). SNMP is used in network management systems to monitor network-attached devices for conditions that warrant administrative attention. The implementation of this standard is beyond the scope of the ROUTE exam requirements and is not described in this guide.

RFC 2328 details the latest update to OSPF version 2 (OSPFv2), which is the default version of OSPF in use today. OSPFv2 was initially described in RFC 1247, which addressed a number of issues discovered during the initial rollout of OSPF version 1 (OSPFv1) and modified the protocol to allow future modifications without generating backward-compatibility issues. Because of this, OSPFv2 is not compatible with OSPFv1.

Finally, RFC 2740 describes the modifications to OSPF to support version 6 of the Internet Protocol (IPv6). IPv6 is described in detail later in this guide. It should be assumed that all references to OSPF in this chapter are for OSPFv2.

Link State Fundamentals

When a Link State routing protocol is enabled for a particular link, information associated with that network is added to the local Link State Database (LSDB). The local router then sends Hello messages on its operational links to determine whether other Link State routers are operating on the interfaces as well. The Hello messages are used for neighbor discovery as well as to maintain adjacencies between neighbor routers. These messages are described in detail later in this chapter.

When a neighbor router is located, the local router attempts to establish an adjacency, assuming both routers share the same common subnet, are in the same area, and that other parameters, such as authentication and timers, are identical. This adjacency enables the two routers to advertise summary LSDB information to each other. This exchange is not the actual detailed database information but is instead a summary of the data.

Each individual router evaluates the summary information against its local LSDB to ensure that it has the most up-to-date information. If one side of the adjacency realizes that it requires an update, the router requests the new information from the adjacent router. The update from the neighbor includes the actual data contained in the LSDB. This exchange process continues until both routers have identical LSDBs. OSPF uses different types of messages to exchange the database information and to ensure that all routers have a consistent view of the network. These different packet types are described in detail later in this chapter.

Following the database exchange, the SPF algorithm runs and creates a shortest-path tree to all hosts in an area or in the network backbone, with the router that is performing the calculation at the root of that tree. The SPF algorithm is described in detail in Chapter 1.

OSPF Fundamentals

Unlike EIGRP, which can support multiple Network Layer protocols, OSPF can only support the Internet Protocol (IP), specifically IPv4 and IPv6. Like EIGRP, OSPF supports VLSM and authentication and utilizes IP Multicast when sending and receiving updates on multi-access networks, such as Ethernet.

OSPF is a hierarchical routing protocol that logically divides the network into sub-domains referred to as areas. This logical segmentation is used to limit the scope of Link State Advertisements (LSAs) flooding throughout the OSPF domain. LSAs are special types of packets sent by routers running OSPF. Different types of LSAs are used within an area and between areas. By restricting the propagation of certain types of LSAs between areas, the OSPF hierarchical implementation effectively reduces the amount of routing protocol traffic within the OSPF network.

NOTE: OSPF LSAs will be described in detail later in this chapter.

In a multi-area OSPF network, one area must be designated as the backbone area or Area 0. The OSPF backbone is the logical center of the OSPF network. All other non-backbone areas must be connected physically to the backbone. However, because it is not always possible or feasible to have a physical connection between a non-backbone area and the backbone, the OSPF standard allows the use of virtual connections to the backbone. These virtual connections are described in detail later in this chapter.

Routers within each area store detailed topology information for the area in which they reside. Within each area, one or more routers, referred to as Area Border Routers (ABRs), facilitate inter-area routing by advertising summarized routing information between the different areas. This functionality allows for the following within the OSPF network:

- Reduces the scope of LSAs flooding throughout the OSPF domain
- Hides detailed topology information between areas
- Allows for end-to-end connectivity within the OSPF domain
- Creates logical boundaries within the OSPF domain

The OSPF backbone area receives summarized routing information from the ABRs. The routing information is disseminated to all other non-backbone areas within the OSPF network. When a change to the network topology occurs, this information is disseminated throughout the entire OSPF domain, allowing all routers in all areas to have a consistent view of the network. The network topology illustrated in Figure 3-1 below is an example of a multi-area OSPF implementation:

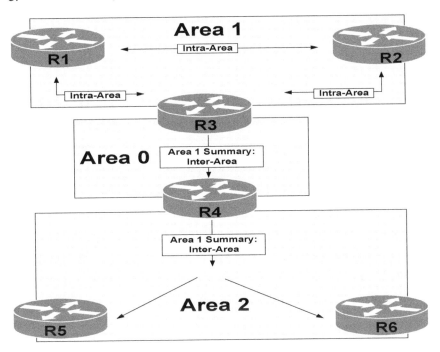

Fig. 3-1. A Multi-Area OSPF Network

Figure 3-1 illustrates a basic multi-area OSPF network. Areas 1 and 2 are connected to Area 0, the OSPF backbone. Within Area 1, routers R1, R2, and R3 exchange intra-area routing information and maintain detailed topology for that area. R3, the ABR, generates an inter-area summary route and advertises this to the OSPF backbone.

R4, the ABR for Area 2, receives the summary information from Area 0 and floods it into its adjacent area. This allows routers R5 and R6 to know of the routes that reside outside of their local area but within the OSPF domain. The same concept would also be applicable to the routing information within Area 2.

In summation, the ABRs maintain LSDB information for all the areas in which they are connected. All routers within each area have detailed topology information pertaining to that specific area. These routers exchange intra-area routing information. The ABRs advertise summary information from each of their connected areas to other OSPF areas, allowing for inter-area routing within the domain.

NOTE: OSPF ABRs and other OSPF router types are described in detail later in this chapter.

Network Types

OSPF uses different default network types for different media, which are as follows:

- Non-Broadcast
- Point-to-Point
- Broadcast
- Point-to-Multipoint

Non-Broadcast networks are network types that do not support natively Broadcast or Multicast traffic. The most common example of a non-Broadcast network type is Frame Relay. Non-Broadcast network types require additional configuration to allow for both Broadcast and Multicast support. On such networks, OSPF elects a Designated Router (DR) and/or a Backup Designated Router (BDR). These two routers are described later in this chapter.

In Cisco IOS software, OSPF-enabled routers send Hello packets every 30 seconds on non-Broadcast network types. If a Hello packet is not received in four times the Hello interval, or 120 seconds, the neighbor router is considered 'dead.' The following illustrates the output of the show ip ospf interface command on a Frame Relay Serial interface:

```
R2#show ip ospf interface Serial0/0
Serial0/0 is up, line protocol is up
  Internet Address 150.1.1.2/24, Area 0
  Process ID 2, Router ID 2.2.2.2, Network Type NON_BROADCAST, Cost: 64
  Transmit Delay is 1 sec, State DR, Priority 1
  Designated Router (ID) 2.2.2.2, Interface address 150.1.1.2
  Backup Designated router (ID) 1.1.1.1, Interface address 150.1.1.1
  Timer intervals configured, Hello 30, Dead 120, Wait 120, Retransmit 5
    oob-resync timeout 120
    Hello due in 00:00:00
  Supports Link-local Signaling (LLS)
  Index 2/2, flood queue length 0
  Next 0x0(0)/0x0(0)
  Last flood scan length is 2, maximum is 2
  Last flood scan time is 0 msec, maximum is 0 msec
  Neighbor Count is 1, Adjacent neighbor count is 1
    Adjacent with neighbor 1.1.1.1  (Backup Designated Router)
  Suppress Hello for 0 neighbor(s)
```

A point-to-point connection is simply a connection between two endpoints only. Examples of point-to-point connections include physical WAN interfaces using HDLC and PPP encapsulation, and Frame Relay and ATM point-to-point subinterfaces. No DR or BDR is elected on OSPF point-to-point network types. By default, OSPF sends Hello packets out every 10 seconds on point-to-point network types. The 'dead' interval on these network types is four times the Hello interval, which is 40 seconds. The following illustrates the output of the show ip ospf interface command on a P2P link:

```
R2#show ip ospf interface Serial0/0
Serial0/0 is up, line protocol is up
  Internet Address 150.1.1.2/24, Area 0
  Process ID 2, Router ID 2.2.2.2, Network Type POINT_TO_POINT, Cost: 64
  Transmit Delay is 1 sec, State POINT_TO_POINT
  Timer intervals configured, Hello 10, Dead 40, Wait 40, Retransmit 5
    oob-resync timeout 40
    Hello due in 00:00:03
  Supports Link-local Signaling (LLS)
  Index 2/2, flood queue length 0
  Next 0x0(0)/0x0(0)
  Last flood scan length is 1, maximum is 1
  Last flood scan time is 0 msec, maximum is 0 msec
  Neighbor Count is 1, Adjacent neighbor count is 1
    Adjacent with neighbor 1.1.1.1
  Suppress Hello for 0 neighbor(s)
```

Broadcast network types are those that natively support Broadcast and Multicast traffic, the most common example being Ethernet. As is the case with non-Broadcast networks, OSPF also elects a DR and/or a BDR on Broadcast networks. By default, OSPF sends Hello packets every 10 seconds on these network types and a neighbor is declared 'dead' if no Hello packets are received within four times the Hello interval, which is 40 seconds. The following illustrates the output of the show ip ospf interface command on a FastEthernet interface:

```
R2#show ip ospf interface FastEthernet0/0
FastEthernet0/0 is up, line protocol is up
  Internet Address 192.168.1.2/24, Area 0
  Process ID 2, Router ID 2.2.2.2, Network Type BROADCAST, Cost: 64
  Transmit Delay is 1 sec, State BDR, Priority 1
  Designated Router (ID) 192.168.1.3, Interface address 192.168.1.3
  Backup Designated router (ID) 2.2.2.2, Interface address 192.168.1.2
  Timer intervals configured, Hello 10, Dead 40, Wait 40, Retransmit 5
    oob-resync timeout 40
    Hello due in 00:00:04
  Supports Link-local Signaling (LLS)
  Index 1/1, flood queue length 0
  Next 0x0(0)/0x0(0)
  Last flood scan length is 1, maximum is 1
  Last flood scan time is 0 msec, maximum is 0 msec
  Neighbor Count is 1, Adjacent neighbor count is 1
```

```
    Adjacent with neighbor 192.168.1.3  (Designated Router)
    Suppress Hello for 0 neighbor(s)
```

Point-to-multipoint is a non-default OSPF network type. In other words, this network type must be configured manually using the `ip ospf network point-to-multipoint [non-broadcast]` interface configuration command. By default, the command defaults to a Broadcast point-to-multipoint network type. This default network type allows OSPF to use Multicast packets to discover dynamically its neighbor routers. In addition, there is no DR/BDR election held on Broadcast point-to-multipoint network types.

The `[non-broadcast]` keyword configures the point-to-multipoint network type as a non-Broadcast point-to-multipoint network. This requires static OSPF neighbor configuration, as OSPF will not use Multicast to discover dynamically its neighbor routers. Additionally, this network type does not require the election of a DR and/or a BDR router for the designated segment. The primary use of this network type is to allow neighbor costs to be assigned to neighbors instead of using the interface-assigned cost for routes received from all neighbors. This concept will be described in detail later in this chapter.

The point-to-multipoint network type is typically used in partial-mesh hub-and-spoke NBMA networks. However, this network type can also be specified for other network types, such as Broadcast Multi-Access networks (e.g., Ethernet). By default, OSPF sends Hello packets every 30 seconds on point-to-multipoint networks. The default dead interval is four times the Hello interval, which is 120 seconds.

The following illustrates the output of the `show ip ospf interface` command on a Frame Relay Serial interface that has been configured manually as a point-to-multipoint network:

```
R2#show ip ospf interface Serial0/0
Serial0/0 is up, line protocol is up
  Internet Address 150.1.1.2/24, Area 0
  Process ID 2, Router ID 2.2.2.2, Network Type POINT_TO_MULTIPOINT, Cost: 64
  Transmit Delay is 1 sec, State POINT_TO_MULTIPOINT
  Timer intervals configured, Hello 30, Dead 120, Wait 120, Retransmit 5
    oob-resync timeout 120
    Hello due in 00:00:04
  Supports Link-local Signaling (LLS)
  Index 2/2, flood queue length 0
  Next 0x0(0)/0x0(0)
  Last flood scan length is 1, maximum is 2
  Last flood scan time is 0 msec, maximum is 0 msec
  Neighbor Count is 1, Adjacent neighbor count is 1
    Adjacent with neighbor 1.1.1.1
  Suppress Hello for 0 neighbor(s)
```

The primary reason for the OSPF requirement that the network type be the same on both routers is because of the timer values. As illustrated in the outputs above, different network types use different Hello and Dead timer intervals. In order for an OSPF adjacency to be established successfully, these values must match on both routers.

Cisco IOS software allows the default OSPF Hello and Dead timers to be changed using the `ip ospf hello-interval <1-65535>` and the `ip ospf dead-interval [<1-65535>|minimal]` interface configuration commands. The `ip ospf hello-interval <1-65535>` command is used to specify the Hello interval in seconds. When issued, the software automatically configures the Dead interval to a value four times the configured Hello interval. For example, assume that a router was configured as follows:

```
R2(config)#interface Serial0/0
R2(config-if)#ip ospf hello-interval 1
R2(config-if)#exit
```

By setting the Hello interval to 1 on R2 above, Cisco IOS software automatically adjusts the default Dead timer to four times the Hello interval, which is 4 seconds. This is illustrated in the following output:

```
R2#show ip ospf interface Serial0/0
Serial0/0 is up, line protocol is up
  Internet Address 10.0.2.4/24, Area 2
  Process ID 4, Router ID 4.4.4.4, Network Type POINT_TO_POINT, Cost: 64
  Transmit Delay is 1 sec, State POINT_TO_POINT
  Timer intervals configured, Hello 1, Dead 4, Wait 4, Retransmit 5
    oob-resync timeout 40
    Hello due in 00:00:00
...

[Truncated Output]
```

While setting the Hello interval results in an automatic adjustment of the Dead timer, setting the Dead timer does not result in an automatic adjustment of the Hello interval. As an example, consider the following Dead timer configuration on the router:

```
R2(config)#interface Serial0/0
R2(config-if)#ip ospf dead-interval 60
R2(config-if)#exit
```

Despite this configuration, the Hello interval remains the same at 10 seconds (this is a P2P link) and is not affected by this configuration. This is illustrated in the following output:

```
R4#show ip ospf interface Serial0/0
Serial0/0 is up, line protocol is up
  Internet Address 10.0.2.4/24, Area 2
  Process ID 4, Router ID 4.4.4.4, Network Type POINT_TO_POINT, Cost: 64
  Transmit Delay is 1 sec, State POINT_TO_POINT
  Timer intervals configured, Hello 10, Dead 60, Wait 60, Retransmit 5
    oob-resync timeout 60
    Hello due in 00:00:09
...

[Truncated Output]
```

NOTE: If the Dead interval is changed on one side of the link, or one of the routers on a multi-access segment, the same value should be configured on all routers. Otherwise, OSPF adjacencies will not be established by the routers.

Going back to the OSPF network types, note that different network types can be configured on either side of the link as long as the timer values are the same. However, when doing so, ensure that you configure similar network types.

For example, you could adjust the OSPF timers to ensure that two routers, one configured with a Broadcast network type and the other with a non-Broadcast network type (because they both use DR and BDR routers), successfully establish an adjacency. The same could be applied to two routers, one configured with a point-to-point network type and the other configured with a point-to-multipoint network type, because neither type elects a DR or a BDR. The timers need to be changed only on one of the routers.

To establish an OSPF adjacency between point-to-point and point-to-multipoint network types, change the point-to-point Hello and Dead timer values to match those of the point-to-multipoint network type, or change those of the point-to-multipoint network type to match those of the point-to-point network type. Once the timers match, and assuming all other configuration is correct, the routers will establish an adjacency.

NOTE: While it is possible technically to establish an adjacency between dissimilar network types with the same timer values (e.g., between a Broadcast and a point-to-multipoint network type), for reasons beyond the scope of the ROUTE exam requirements, this is not recommended because it could result in unexpected behavior within the OSPF network.

In addition to adjusting timer values to allow adjacencies to be established on different network types, OSPF timers can also be adjusted to reduce protocol convergence time. However, be cautious when setting aggressive timers, as this may cause more problems than are addressed.

Designated and Backup Designated Routers

As stated in the previous section, OSPF elects a Designated Router and/or a Backup Designated Router on Broadcast and non-Broadcast network types. It is important to understand that the BDR is not a mandatory component on these network types. In fact, OSPF will work just as well when only a DR is elected and there is no BDR; however, there will be no redundancy if the DR fails and the OSPF routers will need to go through the election process again to elect a new DR.

On the segment, each individual non-DR/BDR router establishes an adjacency with the DR and, if one has also been elected, the BDR, but not with any other non-DR/BDR routers on the segment. The DR and BDR routers are fully adjacent with each other and all other routers on the segment. The non-DR/BDR routers send messages and updates to the AllDRRouters Multicast group address 224.0.0.6. Only the DR/BDR routers listen to Multicast messages sent to this group address. The DR then advertises messages to the AllSPFRouters Multicast group address 224.0.0.5. This allows all other OSPF routers on the segment to receive the updates.

It is important to understand the sequence of message exchanges when a DR and/or a BDR router have been elected. As an example, imagine a Broadcast network with four routers, which are R1, R2, R3, and R4. Assume that R4 has been elected DR, and R3 has been elected BDR. R2 and R1 are neither DR nor BDR and are therefore referred to as DROther routers in Cisco OSPF terminology. A configuration change is made on R1 and R1 then sends an update to the AllDRRouters Multicast group address 224.0.0.6. R4, the DR, receives this update and sends an acknowledgement back to the AllSPFRouters Multicast group address 224.0.0.5. R4 then sends this update to all other non-DR/BDR routers using the AllSPFRouters Multicast group address. This update is received by the other DROther router, R2, and R2 sends an acknowledgement to the AllDRRouters Multicast group 224.0.0.6. This is illustrated in Figure 3-2 below:

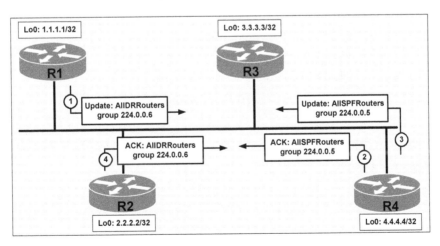

Fig. 3-2. OSPF DR and BDR Advertisements

NOTE: The BDR simply listens to the packets sent to both Multicast groups.

In order for a router to be the DR or the BDR for the segment, the router must be elected. This election is based on the following:

- The highest router priority value
- The highest router ID

By default, all routers have a default priority value of 1. This value can be adjusted using the `ip ospf priority <0-255>` interface configuration command. The higher the priority, the greater the likelihood the router will be elected DR for the segment. The router with the second highest priority will then be elected BDR. If a priority value of 0 is configured, the router will not participate in the DR/BDR election process.

When determining the OSPF router ID, Cisco IOS selects the highest IP address of configured Loopback interfaces. If no Loopback interfaces are configured, the software uses the highest IP address of all configured physical interfaces as the OSPF router ID. Cisco IOS software also allows administrators to specify the router ID manually using the `router-id [address]` router configuration command.

It is important to remember that with OSPF, once the DR and the BDR have been elected, they will remain as DR/BDR routers until a new election is held. For example, if a DR and a BDR exist on a multi-access network and a router with a higher priority or IP address is added to the same segment, the existing DR and BDR routers will not change. If the DR fails, the BDR will assume the role of the DR, not the new router with the higher priority or IP address. Instead, a new election will be held and that router will most likely be elected BDR. In order for that router to become the DR, the BDR must be removed or the OSPF process must be reset using the `clear ip ospf` command, forcing a new DR/BDR election. Once elected, OSPF uses the DR and the BDR routers as follows:

- To reduce the number of adjacencies required on the segment
- To advertise the routers on the multi-access segment
- To ensure that updates are sent to all routers on the segment

To better understand these fundamental concepts, reference the basic OSPF network topology illustrated in Figure 3-3 below:

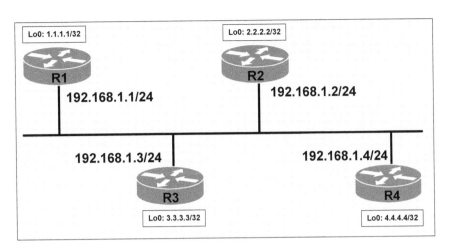

Fig. 3-3. OSPF DR and BDR Fundamentals

Referencing Figure 3-3, each router on the segment establishes an adjacency with the DR and the BDR but not with each other. In other words, non-DR/BDR routers do not establish an adjacency with each other. This prevents the routers on the segment from forming N(N-1) adjacencies with each other, which reduces excessive OSPF packet flooding on the segment.

For example, without the concept of a DR/BDR on the segment, each individual router would need to establish an adjacency with every other router on the segment. This would result in 4(4-1) or 12 adjacencies on the segment. However, with the DR/BDR, each individual router needs to establish an adjacency with only these two routers and no other non-DR and BDR routers. The DR and BDR also establish an adjacency between themselves. This reduces the number of adjacencies required on the segment and on each individual OSPF router, which in turn reduces resources consumption (e.g., memory and processor utilization) on the routers.

Regarding the second point, OSPF views a link as a connection between two routers or nodes. In multi-access networks, such as Ethernet, multiple routers can reside on the same segment, as illustrated in Figure 3-3. On such networks, OSPF uses the Network Link State Advertisement (Type 2 LSA) to advertise the routers on the multi-access segment. This LSA is generated by the DR and is flooded only within the area. Because the other non-DR/BDR routers do not establish adjacencies with each other, this LSA allows those routers to know about the other routers on the multi-access segment.

To further clarify this point, referencing Figure 3-3, assuming that all routers on the segment have the default OSPF priority value of 1, R4 is elected as the Designated Router for the segment because it has the highest router ID. R3 is elected as Backup Designated Router for the segment because it has the second highest router ID. Because R2 and R1 are neither the DR nor the BDR, they are referred to as DROther routers in Cisco terminology. This can be validated using the show ip ospf neighbor command on all routers as follows:

```
R1#show ip ospf neighbor

Neighbor ID   Pri   State          Dead Time   Address        Interface
2.2.2.2        1    2WAY/DROTHER   00:00:38    192.168.1.2    Ethernet0/0
3.3.3.3        1    FULL/BDR       00:00:39    192.168.1.3    Ethernet0/0
4.4.4.4        1    FULL/DR        00:00:38    192.168.1.4    Ethernet0/0


R2#show ip ospf neighbor

Neighbor ID   Pri   State          Dead Time   Address        Interface
1.1.1.1        1    2WAY/DROTHER   00:00:32    192.168.1.1    FastEthernet0/0
3.3.3.3        1    FULL/BDR       00:00:33    192.168.1.3    FastEthernet0/0
4.4.4.4        1    FULL/DR        00:00:32    192.168.1.4    FastEthernet0/0


R3#show ip ospf neighbor

Neighbor ID   Pri   State          Dead Time   Address        Interface
1.1.1.1        1    FULL/DROTHER   00:00:36    192.168.1.1    FastEthernet0/0
2.2.2.2        1    FULL/DROTHER   00:00:36    192.168.1.2    FastEthernet0/0
4.4.4.4        1    FULL/DR        00:00:35    192.168.1.4    FastEthernet0/0


R4#show ip ospf neighbor

Neighbor ID   Pri   State          Dead Time   Address        Interface
1.1.1.1        1    FULL/DROTHER   00:00:39    192.168.1.1    FastEthernet0/0
2.2.2.2        1    FULL/DROTHER   00:00:39    192.168.1.2    FastEthernet0/0
3.3.3.3        1    FULL/BDR       00:00:30    192.168.1.3    FastEthernet0/0
```

NOTE: The DROther routers remain in the 2WAY/DROTHER state because they exchange their databases only with the DR and the BDR routers. Therefore, because there is no full database exchange between the DROther routers, they will never reach the OSPF Full adjacency state.

Because R4 has been elected DR, it generates the Network LSA, which advertises the other routers on the multi-access segment. This LSA advertises the routers on the multi-access segment. This can be verified using the show ip ospf database network [link state ID] command on any router on the segment or the show ip ospf database network self-originate command on the DR only. The following illustrates the output of the show ip ospf database network self-originate command on the DR (R4):

```
R4#show ip ospf database network self-originate

        OSPF Router with ID (4.4.4.4) (Process ID 4)

        Net Link States (Area 0)
```

```
Routing Bit Set on this LSA
LS age: 429
Options: (No TOS-capability, DC)
LS Type: Network Links
Link State ID: 192.168.1.4 (address of Designated Router)
Advertising Router: 4.4.4.4
LS Seq Number: 80000006
Checksum: 0x7E08
Length: 40
Network Mask: /24
        Attached Router: 4.4.4.4
        Attached Router: 1.1.1.1
        Attached Router: 2.2.2.2
        Attached Router: 3.3.3.3
```

Referencing the output above, the DR (R4) originates the Type 2 (Network LSA) representing the 192.168.1.0/24 subnet. Because multiple routers exist on this subnet, this 192.168.1.0/24 subnet is referred to as a transit link in OSPF terminology. The Advertising Router field shows the router that originated this LSA. The Network Mask field shows the subnet mask of the transit network, which is 24-bit or 255.255.255.0.

The Attached Router fields list the router IDs of all routers that are on the network segment. This allows all of the routers on the segment to know what other routers also reside on the segment. The output of the `show ip ospf database network [link state ID]` command on R1, R2, and R3 reflects the same information as illustrated in the following outputs:

```
R2#show ip ospf database network

            OSPF Router with ID (2.2.2.2) (Process ID 2)

            Net Link States (Area 0)

Routing Bit Set on this LSA
LS age: 923
Options: (No TOS-capability, DC)
LS Type: Network Links
Link State ID: 192.168.1.4 (address of Designated Router)
Advertising Router: 4.4.4.4
LS Seq Number: 80000006
Checksum: 0x7E08
Length: 40
Network Mask: /24
        Attached Router: 4.4.4.4
        Attached Router: 1.1.1.1
        Attached Router: 2.2.2.2
        Attached Router: 3.3.3.3
```

```
R1#show ip ospf database network

              OSPF Router with ID (1.1.1.1) (Process ID 1)

                Net Link States (Area 0)

    Routing Bit Set on this LSA
    LS age: 951
    Options: (No TOS-capability, DC)
    LS Type: Network Links
    Link State ID: 192.168.1.4 (address of Designated Router)
    Advertising Router: 4.4.4.4
    LS Seq Number: 80000006
    Checksum: 0x7E08
    Length: 40
    Network Mask: /24
          Attached Router: 4.4.4.4
          Attached Router: 1.1.1.1
          Attached Router: 2.2.2.2
          Attached Router: 3.3.3.3

          OSPF Router with ID (4.4.4.4) (Process ID 4)

R3#show ip ospf database network

              OSPF Router with ID (3.3.3.3) (Process ID 3)

                Net Link States (Area 0)

    Routing Bit Set on this LSA
    LS age: 988
    Options: (No TOS-capability, DC)
    LS Type: Network Links
    Link State ID: 192.168.1.4 (address of Designated Router)
    Advertising Router: 4.4.4.4
    LS Seq Number: 80000006
    Checksum: 0x7E08
    Length: 40
    Network Mask: /24
          Attached Router: 4.4.4.4
          Attached Router: 1.1.1.1
          Attached Router: 2.2.2.2
          Attached Router: 3.3.3.3
```

The functionality of the Network LSA and how it is correlated to another LSA, specifically the Router LSA (Type 1), will be described in detail later in this chapter. For this section, primary emphasis should be placed on understanding that the DR generates and advertises the Network LSA on the multi-access segment to advertise other routers that reside on the same segment. This is because routers on the segment establish an adjacency only with the DR and the BDR routers and not with each other. Without an adjacency with each other, the routers would never know about other non-DR/BDR routers on the multi-access segment.

Finally, regarding the third point made on DR/BDR routers, the DR/BDR routers ensure that all routers on the segment have complete databases. Non-DR/BDR routers send updates to the Multicast group address 224.0.0.6 (AllDRRouters). The DR then advertises these updates to other non-DR/BDR routers by sending the update to the Multicast group address 224.0.0.5 (AllSPFRouters). Figure 3-4 below illustrates an update from R1 (a DROther) to the DR group address referencing the routers illustrated in Figure 3-3:

```
Internet Protocol, Src: 192.168.1.1 (192.168.1.1), Dst: 224.0.0.6 (224.0.0.6)
Open Shortest Path First
OSPF Header
LS Update Packet
 Number of LSAs: 1
 LS Type: Router-LSA
  LS Age: 1 seconds
  Do Not Age: False
  Options: 0x22 (DC, E)
  Link-State Advertisement Type: Router-LSA (1)
  Link State ID: 1.1.1.1
  Advertising Router: 1.1.1.1 (1.1.1.1)
  LS Sequence Number: 0x80000006
  LS Checksum: 0x5f95
  Length: 60
  Flags: 0x00 ()
  Number of Links: 3
  Type: Stub     ID: 10.10.10.10   Data: 255.255.255.255 Metric: 1
  Type: Stub     ID: 1.1.1.1       Data: 255.255.255.255 Metric: 1
  Type: Transit  ID: 192.168.1.4   Data: 192.168.1.1     Metric: 10
```

Fig. 3-4. DROther Update to DR/BDR Group Address

R4 (DR) receives this update and in turn sends the same to Multicast group address 224.0.0.5. This group address is used by all OSPF routers, ensuring that all other routers on the segment receive this update. This update from the DR (R4) is illustrated in Figure 3-5 below:

```
Internet Protocol, Src: 192.168.1.4 (192.168.1.4), Dst: 224.0.0.5 (224.0.0.5)
Open Shortest Path First
OSPF Header
LS Update Packet
 Number of LSAs: 1
 LS Type: Router-LSA
  LS Age: 2 seconds
  Do Not Age: False
  Options: 0x22 (DC, E)
  Link-State Advertisement Type: Router-LSA (1)
  Link State ID: 1.1.1.1
  Advertising Router: 1.1.1.1 (1.1.1.1)
  LS Sequence Number: 0x80000006
  LS Checksum: 0x5f95
  Length: 60
  Flags: 0x00 ()
  Number of Links: 3
  Type: Stub     ID: 10.10.10.10   Data: 255.255.255.255 Metric: 1
  Type: Stub     ID: 1.1.1.1       Data: 255.255.255.255 Metric: 1
  Type: Transit  ID: 192.168.1.4   Data: 192.168.1.1     Metric: 10
```

Fig. 3-5. DR Update to OSPF Group Address

NOTE: We can determine this is the Update from R1 because the Advertising Router field in both Figures 3-4 and 3-5 contains the router ID (RID) of R1, which is 1.1.1.1.

NOTE: The other LSAs used by OSPF will be described in detail later in this chapter.

Additional Router Types

In addition to the Designated Router and the Backup Designated Router on multi-access segments, OSPF routers are also described based on their location and function within the OSPF network. The additional router types that are commonly found within the OSPF network include the following:

- Area Border Routers
- Autonomous System Boundary Routers
- Internal Routers
- Backbone Routers

Figure 3-6 below illustrates a basic OSPF network comprised of two areas, the OSPF backbone area and an additional normal OSPF area (Area 2).R2 has an external BGP neighbor relationship with R1. This diagram will be used to describe the different OSPF router types within this network.

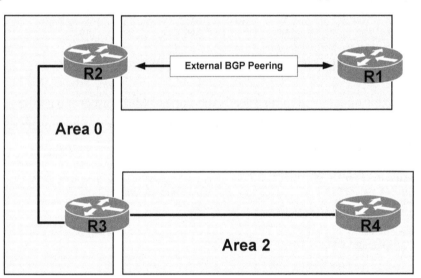

Fig. 3-6. Additional OSPF Router Types

An Area Border Router (ABR) is an OSPF router that connects one or more OSPF areas to the OSPF backbone. This means that it must have at least one interface in Area 0 and another interface, or interfaces, within a different OSPF area. ABRs are members of all areas to which they belong and keep a separate Link State Database for every area to which they belong. Referencing Figure 3-6, R3 would be considered an ABR, as it connects Area 2 to the OSPF backbone, or Area 0.

An Autonomous System Boundary Router (ASBR), in the traditional sense, resides at the edge of the routing domain and defines the boundary between the internal and the external networks. Referencing Figure 3-6, R2 would be considered an ASBR. In addition to injecting routing information from other protocols (e.g., BGP), a router can also be classified as an ASBR if it injects static routes or connected subnets into the OSPF domain.

Internal routers maintain all operational interfaces within a single OSPF area. Based on the network topology illustrated in Figure 3-6, R4 would be considered an internal router because its only interface resides within a single OSPF area.

Backbone routers are routers that have an interface in the OSPF backbone. Backbone routers can include routers that have interfaces only in the OSPF backbone area or routers that have an interface in the OSPF backbone area as well as interfaces in other areas (ABRs). Based on the topology illustrated in Figure 3-6, both R2 and R3 would be considered backbone routers.

NOTE: OSPF routers can have multiple roles. For example, R2 is both an ASBR and a backbone router, while R3 is both a backbone router and an ABR. Throughout this chapter, we will take a detailed look at these types of routers and their roles and functions within the OSPF domain.

OSPF CONFIGURATION FUNDAMENTALS

This section describes OSPF configuration fundamentals and builds upon the configuration of OSPF as described in the CCNA certification course.

Enabling OSPF in Cisco IOS Software

OSPF is enabled in Cisco IOS software by issuing the `router ospf [process id]` global configuration command. The `[process id]` is locally significant and does not need to be the same on all routers in the network in order to establish an adjacency. The use of the locally significant process ID allows you to configure multiple instances of OSPF on the same router.

The OSPF process ID is an integer between 1 and 65535. Each OSPF process maintains its own separate Link State Database; however, all routes are entered into the same IP routing table. In other words, there is no unique IP routing table for each individual OSPF process configured on the router. A separate routing table is used only when OSPF Virtual Routing and Forwarding or VPN Routing and Forwarding (VRF) configuration is implemented on the router. VRF will be described in detail later in this guide.

In earlier versions of Cisco IOS software, OSPF would not be enabled if the router did not have at least one interface configured with a valid IP address in the up/up state. This restriction has been removed in current versions of Cisco IOS software. In the event that the router has no interfaces configured with a valid IP address and in the up/up state, Cisco IOS will create a Proximity Database (PDB) and allow the process to be created. However, it is important to remember that the process will be inactive until a router ID is selected, which can be performed in the following two ways:

1. Configuring a valid IP address on an interface and bringing the interface up
2. Configuring the router ID manually using the router-id command

As an example, consider the following router, which has all interfaces disabled:

```
R3#show ip interface brief
Interface          IP-Address      OK? Method Status                  Protocol
FastEthernet0/0    unassigned      YES manual administratively down down
Serial0/0          unassigned      YES NVRAM  administratively down down
Serial0/1          unassigned      YES unset  administratively down down
```

Next, OSPF is enabled on the router using the router ospf [process id] global configuration command as illustrated in the following output:

```
R3(config)#router ospf 1
R3(config-router)#exit
```

Based on this configuration, Cisco IOS software assigns the process a default router ID of 0.0.0.0 as illustrated in the following output of the show ip protocols command:

```
R3#show ip protocols
Routing Protocol is "ospf 1"
  Outgoing update filter list for all interfaces is not set
  Incoming update filter list for all interfaces is not set
  Router ID 0.0.0.0
  Number of areas in this router is 0. 0 normal 0 stub 0 nssa
  Maximum path: 4
  Routing for Networks:
 Reference bandwidth unit is 100 mbps
  Routing Information Sources:
    Gateway         Distance      Last Update
  Distance: (default is 110)
```

However, the show ip ospf [process id] command reveals that the process is not actually active and indicates that a router ID needs to be configured as illustrated below:

```
R3#show ip ospf 1
%OSPF: Router process 1 is not running, please configure a router-id
```

Enabling OSPF Routing for Interfaces or Networks

After OSPF has been enabled, two actions can be performed to enable OSPF routing for one or more networks or interfaces on the router as follows:

1. Using the [network] [wildcard] area [area id] router configuration command
2. Using the ip ospf [process id] area [area id] interface configuration command

The network [network] [wildcard] area [area id] router configuration command is a legacy method (regarding the newer Cisco IOS versions) of enabling OSPF routing for one or more links. Unlike EIGRP, the wildcard mask is mandatory in OSPF and must be configured; however, as is the case with EIGRP, it serves the same function in that it matches interfaces within the range specified. As an example, the statement network 10.0.0.0 0.255.255.255 Area 0 would enable OSPF routing for interfaces with the IP address and subnet mask combination of 10.0.0.1/30, 10.5.5.1/24, and even 10.10.10.1/25. The interfaces would all be assigned to OSPF Area 0 based on the OSPF network configuration.

> **NOTE:** As was described in Chapter 2, the wildcard mask for OSPF can also be entered in the same format as a traditional subnet mask, for example, network 10.0.0.0 255.0.0.0 Area 0. In this case, Cisco IOS software will invert the subnet mask and the wildcard mask will be entered into the running configuration. In addition, it is important to remember that OSPF also supports the use of the all ones or all zeros wildcard mask to enable OSPF routing for a specific interface. This configuration enables OSPF on a particular interface but the router advertises the actual subnet mask configured on the interface itself.

After the network [network] [wildcard] area [area id] command has been issued, the router sends out Hello packets on interfaces matching the specified network and wildcard mask combination and attempts to discover neighbors. The connected subnet is then advertised to one or more neighbor routers during the OSPF database exchange, and, finally, this information is then added to the OSPF Link State Database of the OSPF routers.

When the network [network] [wildcard] area [area id] command is issued, the router matches the most specific entry in order to determine the area the interface will be assigned to. Consider the following OSPF network statement configurations, as an example:

- First configuration statement: network 10.0.0.0 0.255.255.255 Area 0
- Second configuration statement: network 10.1.0.0 0.0.255.255 Area 1
- Third configuration statement: network 10.1.1.0 0.0.0.255 Area 2
- Fourth configuration statement: network 10.1.1.1 0.0.0.0 Area 3
- Fifth configuration statement: network 0.0.0.0 255.255.255.255 Area 4

Following this configuration on the router, the Loopback interfaces shown in Table 3-1below are then configured on the same router:

Table 3-1. Assigning Interfaces to OSPF Areas

Interface	IP Address/Mask
Loopback 0	10.0.0.1/32
Loopback 1	10.0.1.1/32
Loopback 2	10.1.0.1/32
Loopback 3	10.1.1.1/32
Loopback 4	10.2.0.1/32

As was previously stated, when the network [network] [wildcard] area [area id] command is issued, the router matches the most specific entry in order to determine the area in which the interface will be assigned. Taking the network statement configuration and the Loopback interfaces configured on the router, the show ip ospf interface brief command would show that the interfaces were assigned to the following OSPF areas:

```
R1#show ip ospf interface brief
Interface    PID    Area        IP Address/Mask    Cost    State Nbrs F/C
Lo4          1      0           10.2.0.1/32        1       LOOP  0/0
Lo1          1      0           10.0.1.1/32        1       LOOP  0/0
Lo0          1      0           10.0.0.1/32        1       LOOP  0/0
Lo2          1      1           10.1.0.1/32        1       LOOP  0/0
Lo3          1      3           10.1.1.1/32        1       LOOP  0/0
```

NOTE: Regardless of the order in which the network statements are entered, within the running configuration, the most specific entries are listed first in the output of the show running-config command on the router.

The ip ospf [process id] area [area id] interface configuration command negates the need to use the network [network] [wildcard] area [area id] router configuration command. This command enables OSPF routing for the specified interface and assigns the interface to the specified OSPF area. These two commands perform the same basic function and may be used interchangeably.

Additionally, if, for example, two routers are connected back-to-back, with one router configured using the ip ospf [process id] area [area id] interface configuration command and the neighbor router configured using the network [network] [wildcard] area [area id] router configuration command, then, assuming the area IDs are the same, the routers will successfully establish an OSPF adjacency.

Using the OSPF Interface and Network Configuration Commands

There are several important reasons for using both the ip ospf [process id] area [area id] interface configuration command and the network [network] [wildcard] area [area id] router configuration command with which you should be familiar. These aspects are described in detail in the sections that follow.

The first important reason is that if an interface is already enabled for OSPF routing via the use of the network command, and the ip ospf interface configuration command is issued assigning the interface to a different OSPF process or area, then the explicit interface configuration will be used. Assume that a Cisco IOS router has the following Loopback interfaces configured on it:

```
R2#show ip interface brief | include Loopback
Loopback0              10.2.2.2         YES manual up up
Loopback1              20.2.2.2         YES manual up up
```

Next, an OSPF process ID of 1 is enabled on the router and both Loopback interfaces are assigned to Area 1 under this process as illustrated in the following output:

```
R2(config)#router ospf 1
R2(config-router)#network 10.2.2.2 0.0.0.0 Area 1
R2(config-router)#network 20.2.2.2 0.0.0.0 Area 1
R2(config-router)#exit
```

Based on this configuration, the Loopback interfaces are both assigned to Area 1 under an OSPF process ID of 1. This can be validated using the show ip ospf interface brief command as illustrated in the following output:

```
R2#show ip ospf interface brief
Interface    PID    Area         IP Address/Mask    Cost   State  Nbrs F/C
Lo0          1      1            10.2.2.2/32        1      LOOP   0/0
Lo1          1      1            20.2.2.2/32        1      LOOP   0/0
```

This same information can be validated by using the show ip ospf interface command as illustrated in the following output:

```
R2#show ip ospf interface Loopback0
Loopback0 is up, line protocol is up
  Internet Address 10.2.2.2/32, Area 1
  Process ID 1, Router ID 2.2.2.2, Network Type LOOPBACK, Cost: 1
  Loopback interface is treated as a stub Host
```

Now the `ip ospf` interface configuration command is issued under Loopback 0 using a local process ID of 2 and assigning this interface to Area 2 as follows:

```
R2(config)#interface Loopback0
R2(config-if)#ip ospf 2 Area 2
R2(config-if)#exit
```

Based on this configuration, the `ip ospf` interface-specific configuration takes precedence over the `network` configuration and the interface will be removed from process ID 1 and reattached to process ID 2. This is illustrated in the following output:

```
R2#show ip ospf interface brief
Interface   PID   Area        IP Address/Mask   Cost   State  Nbrs F/C
Lo1         1     1           20.2.2.2/32       1      LOOP   0/0
Lo0         2     2           10.2.2.2/32       1      LOOP   0/0
```

A detailed look at the interface reveals that it is configured using interface-specific configuration and not the `network` router configuration command as illustrated in the following output:

```
R2#show ip ospf interface Loopback0
Loopback0 is up, line protocol is up   ·
  Internet Address 10.2.2.2/32, Area 2
  Process ID 2, Router ID 2.2.2.3, Network Type LOOPBACK, Cost: 1
  Enabled by interface config, including secondary ip addresses
  Loopback interface is treated as a stub Host
```

By default, the `ip ospf` interface configuration command also enables OSPF routing for any secondary addresses configured on the interface as illustrated above. However, this default behavior can be disabled by issuing the `ip ospf [process id] area [area id] secondaries none` interface configuration command when enabling OSPF under the desired interface. This is illustrated in the following configuration output:

```
R2(config)#interface Loopback0
R2(config-if)#ip ospf 1 Area 1 secondaries none
R2(config-if)#exit
```

The `show ip ospf interface` command can be used to validate this configuration as illustrated in the following output:

```
R2#show ip ospf interface Loopback0
Loopback0 is up, line protocol is up
  Internet Address 10.2.2.2/32, Area 1
  Process ID 1, Router ID 10.2.2.2, Network Type LOOPBACK, Cost: 1
```

```
Enabled by interface config, excluding secondary ip addresses
Loopback interface is treated as a stub Host
```

In addition, also keep in mind that even though the ip ospf interface configuration command has been issued for the Loopback interface, the network configuration is not removed from the configuration. It must be removed manually from the router configuration.

The second important reason is that the ip ospf interface configuration command can be used even if the router ospf command has not been issued. In such cases, Cisco IOS software simply creates the OSPF process ID specified using the interface configuration command. This is performed transparently; that is, there is no warning or other message printed on the console indicating that a new OSPF process has been enabled based on the new interface configuration.

The third important reason is that if the interface is included for the same OSPF process ID and resides in the same area for both the network and the ip ospf interface configuration commands, then, again, the ip ospf interface configuration command takes precedence and the router will indicate that the interface has been configured using an interface-specific command, even though the network statement is retained. As an example, assume that Loopback 0 is enabled under a process ID of 1 and is assigned to Area 1 as illustrated in the following configuration:

```
R2(config)#router ospf 1
R2(config-router)#network 10.2.2.2 0.0.0.0 Area 1
R2(config-router)#exit
```

The output of the show ip ospf interface command reveals that the interface falls under the process ID of 1 configuration and is assigned to Area 1 as follows:

```
R2#show ip ospf interface Loopback0
Loopback0 is up, line protocol is up
  Internet Address 10.2.2.2/32, Area 1
  Process ID 1, Router ID 2.2.2.2, Network Type LOOPBACK, Cost: 1
  Loopback interface is treated as a stub Host
```

Next, the interface-specific configuration is applied using the same OSPF process ID and area allocation as illustrated in the following output:

```
R2(config)#interface Loopback0
R2(config-if)#ip ospf 1 Area 1
R2(config-if)#exit
```

The output of the show ip ospf interface command now displays the following:

```
R2#show ip ospf interface Loopback0
Loopback0 is up, line protocol is up
  Internet Address 10.2.2.2/32, Area 1
  Process ID 1, Router ID 2.2.2.2, Network Type LOOPBACK, Cost: 1
  Enabled by interface config, including secondary ip addresses
  Loopback interface is treated as a stub Host
```

NOTE: You can also use the show ip protocols command to determine which interfaces have interface-specific configuration applied to them as follows:

```
R2#show ip protocols
Routing Protocol is "ospf 1"
  Outgoing update filter list for all interfaces is not set
  Incoming update filter list for all interfaces is not set
  Router ID 2.2.2.2
  Number of areas in this router is 1. 1 normal 0 stub 0 nssa
  Maximum path: 4
  Routing for Networks:
    10.2.2.2 0.0.0.0 Area 1
    20.2.2.2 0.0.0.0 Area 1
  Routing on Interfaces Configured Explicitly (Area 1):
    Loopback0
 Reference bandwidth unit is 100 mbps
  Routing Information Sources:
    Gateway         Distance       Last Update
  Distance: (default is 110)
```

The fourth important reason is that if OSPF routing is enabled for an interface using ip ospf interface-specific configuration and the no router ospf [process id] command is issued on the router specifying the process ID configured on the interface, then the interface-specific configuration is removed along with all other configuration for that OSPF process.

However, if OSPF routing is enabled for an interface using the ip ospf interface-specific configuration, and the same process is also configured globally on the router with one or more network commands, then issuing the no ip ospf interface configuration command does not remove the global OSPF configuration on the router.

OSPF Area Fundamentals

The OSPF area ID may be configured either as an integer between 0 and 4294967295 or using dotted-decimal notation (i.e., using IP address format). Unlike the OSPF process ID, the OSPF area ID must match in order for adjacency to be established. Mismatched area IDs are analogous to mismatched EIGRP autonomous system numbers. The most common type of OSPF area configuration is using an integer to specify the OSPF area. However, ensure that you are familiar with both supported methods of area configuration.

OSPF PACKET TYPES

The different types of packets sent by OSPF routers are contained in the common 24-byte OSPF header. While delving into the specifics of the OSPF header is beyond the scope of the ROUTE exam requirements, it is still important to have a basic understanding of the fields contained within this header and what they are used for. Figure 3-7 below illustrates the common 24-octet OSPF header:

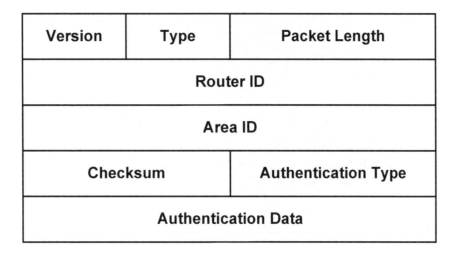

Fig. 3-7. The OSPF Packet Header

The 8-bit Version field specifies the OSPF version. The default value for this field is 2. However, when OSPFv3 is enabled, this field is also set to 3. OSPFv3 will be described in detail later in this guide.

The 8-bit Type field is used to specify the OSPF packet type. The five main OSPF packet types, which are described in detail later in this chapter, are as follows:

- Type 1 = Hello packet
- Type 2 = Database Description packet
- Type 3 = Link State Request packet
- Type 4 = Link State Update packet
- Type 5 = Link State Acknowledgement packet

The 16-bit Packet Length field is used to specify the length of the protocol packet. This length includes the standard OSPF header.

The 32-bit Router ID field is used to specify the IP address of the router from which the packet originated. On Cisco IOS devices, this field will contain the highest IP address of all physical interfaces configured on the device running OSPF. If Loopback interfaces are configured on the device, the field will contain the highest IP address of all configured Loopback interfaces. Alternatively, this field can also contain a manually configured router ID if one has been explicitly configured or specified by the administrator.

> **NOTE:** When the router ID has been selected, it will never change unless the router is reloaded, the interface that the IP address was derived from is shut down or removed, or the OSPF process is reset using the `clear ip ospf process` privileged EXEC command on the router.

The 32-bit Area ID field is used to identify the OSPF area of the packet. A packet can belong only to a single OSPF area. If the packet is received via a virtual link, then the Area ID will be the OSPF backbone, or Area 0. Virtual links are described in detail later in this chapter.

The Checksum field is 16-bits long and indicates the standard IP checksum of the entire contents of the packet, starting with the OSPF packet header but excluding the 64-bit Authentication Data field. If the packet's length is not an integral number of 16-bit words, the packet is padded with a byte of zero before being checksummed.

The 16-bit Authentication (Auth) Type field identifies the type of authentication used. This field is valid only for OSPFv2 and may contain one of the following three codes:
- Code 0—This means that there is null (no) authentication; this is the default
- Code 1—This means that the authentication type is plain text
- Code 2—This means that the authentication type is Message Digest 5 (MD5)

> **NOTE:** OSPF authentication is a core ROUTE exam requirement. It is described later in this chapter.

Finally, the 64-bit Authentication Data field is for the actual authentication information or data, if authentication has been enabled. It is important to remember that this field is valid only for OSPFv2. If plain text authentication is being used, this field contains the authentication key. However, if MD5 authentication is being used, this field is redefined into several other fields, which are beyond the scope of the ROUTE exam requirements. Figure 3-8 below shows the different fields as they appear in a wire capture of an OSPF packet:

```
Open Shortest Path First
 OSPF Header
  OSPF Version: 2
  Message Type: Hello Packet (1)
  Packet Length: 48
  Source OSPF Router: 3.3.3.3 (3.3.3.3)
  Area ID: 0.0.0.0 (Backbone)
  Packet Checksum: 0x4d3a [correct]
  Auth Type: Null
  Auth Data (none)
 OSPF Hello Packet
 OSPF LLS Data Block
```

Fig. 3-8. OSPF Packet Header Capture

Within the OSPF packet header, the 8-bit Type field is used to specify the OSPF packet type. Again, the five OSPF packet types are as follows:

- Type 1 = Hello packet
- Type 2 = Database Description packet
- Type 3 = Link State Request packet
- Type 4 = Link State Update packet
- Type 5 = Link State Acknowledgement packet

OSPF Hello Packets

Hello packets are used to discover other directly connected OSPF routers and to establish OSPF adjacencies between OSPF routers. OSPF uses Multicast to send Hello packets for Broadcast and point-to-point network types. These packets are addressed to the AllSPFRouters Multicast group address 224.0.0.5. For non-Broadcast links (e.g., Frame Relay), OSPF uses Unicast to send Hello packets directly to statically configured neighbors.

> **NOTE:** By default, all OSPF packets (i.e., Multicast and Unicast) are sent with an IP TTL of 1. This limits these packets to the local link. In other words, you cannot establish an OSPF adjacency with another router that is more than one hop away. This is also applicable to EIGRP.

OSPF Hello packets are also used on Broadcast links to elect a Designated Router (DR) and a Backup Designated (BDR) router. The DR listens specifically to the Multicast address 224.0.0.6 (AllDR-Routers). The DR and the BDR were described in detail previously in this chapter. Figure 3-9 below illustrates the fields contained within the OSPF Hello packet:

```
Open Shortest Path First
 OSPF Header
 OSPF Hello Packet
  Network Mask: 255.255.255.0
  Hello Interval: 10 seconds
  Options: 0x12 (L, E)
   0... .... = DN: DN-bit is NOT set
   .0.. .... = O: O-bit is NOT set
   ..0. .... = DC: Demand circuits are NOT supported
   ...1 .... = L: The packet contains LLS data block
   .... 0... = NP: Nssa is NOT supported
   .... .0.. = MC: NOT multicast capable
   .... ..1. = E: ExternalRoutingCapability
  Router Priority: 1
  Router Dead Interval: 40 seconds
  Designated Router: 192.168.1.3
  Backup Designated Router: 192.168.1.2
  Active Neighbor: 20.2.2.2
 OSPF LLS Data Block
```

Fig. 3-9. OSPF Hello Packet

The 4-byte Network Mask field contains the subnet mask of the advertising OSPF interface. The network mask is checked only on Broadcast media. Unnumbered point-to-point interfaces and virtual links, both of which will be described later in this chapter, set this value to 0.0.0.0.

The 2-byte Hello field displays the value of the Hello interval, which is the number of seconds between two Hello packets, requested by the advertising router. Possible values range from 1 to 255. By default, the Hello interval is 10 seconds on Broadcast and point-to-point media and 30 seconds on all other media.

The 1-byte Options field is used by the local router to advertise optional capabilities. Each bit in the Options field represents a different function. The various bit definitions are as follows:

- The DN bit is used for loop prevention in a Virtual Private Network environment. An OSPF router receiving an update with this bit set does not forward that update.
- The O bit indicates that the local router supports Opaque LSAs, mentioned in RFC 2370. Opaque LSAs are described later in this chapter.
- The DC bit indicates that the local router supports Demand Circuits, mentioned in RFC 1793. Demand Circuits are described later in this chapter.
- The L bit, which is set only in OSPF Hello and Database Description packets, indicates that the local router supports Link Local Signaling (LLS). When this bit is sent, OSPF routers add a special data block at the end of OSPF packets or right after the authentication data block when cryptographic authentication is used. LLS is beyond the scope of the ROUTE exam requirements and will not be described in any further detail in this guide.
- The NP bit describes the handling and support of Not-So-Stubby Area (NSSA) LSAs, mentioned in RFC 1587. NSSAs are described later in this chapter.
- The MC bit indicates that the local router supports Multicast OSPF LSAs. This is not supported in Cisco IOS software, as Cisco does not support Multicast OSPF.
- The E bit describes the handling and support of external LSAs.

The 1-byte Router Priority field contains the priority of the local router. By default, this field has a value of 1. The value is used in the election of the Designated Router and the Backup Designated Router. Possible values range from 0 to 255. The higher the priority, the higher the chances the local router will become the DR. A priority value of 0 means the local router will not participate in the DR or the BDR election.

The 4-byte Router Dead Interval field shows the value of the dead interval. The dead interval is the time (seconds) before a neighbor router is declared dead. This value is requested by the advertising router. The default value for the dead interval is four times the value of the Hello interval, which would be a default of 40 seconds on Broadcast and point-to-point interfaces and 120 seconds on all other types of media.

The 4-byte Designated Router field lists the IP address of the DR. A value of 0.0.0.0 is used when no designated router has been elected, for example, on a point-to-point link or when a router has been explicitly configured not to participate in this election.

The 4-byte Backup Designated Router field identifies the BDR and lists the interface address of the current BDR. A value of 0.0.0.0 is used when no BDR has been elected.

Finally, the (Active) Neighbor field is a variable length field that displays the router ID of all OSPF routers for which a Hello packet has been received on the network segment.

Database Description Packets

Database Description packets are used during the database exchange when each OSPF router advertises its local database information. These packets are commonly referred to as DBD packets or also as DD packets. The first DBD packet is used for the Master and Slave election for database exchange. The DBD packet also contains the initial sequence number selected by the Master. The router with the highest router ID becomes the Master and initiates database synchronization. This is the only router that can increment the sequence number. The Master router begins the database exchange and polls the Slave for information. The Master and Slave election is held on a per-neighbor basis.

It is important to understand that the Master and Slave election process is not the same as the DR and BDR election process. This is commonly incorrectly assumed. The Master and Slave election process is based solely on the router with the highest IP address; however, the DR/BDR election process may be determined using either the IP address or the priority value.

Assume, for example, two routers named R1 and R2 are beginning the adjacency establishment process. R1 has a RID of 1.1.1.1 while R2 has a RID of 2.2.2.2. The network administrator has configured R1 with an OSPF priority value of 255 to ensure that this router will be elected the DR. During the Master and Slave determination process, R2 will be elected master by virtue of the higher RID. However, the priority value configured on R1 results in R1 being elected the DR. In essence, the DR (R1) can be the Slave during the Master and Slave election process.

After the Master and Slave have been elected, DBD packets are used to summarize the local database by sending LSA headers to the remote router. The remote router analyzes these headers to determine whether it lacks any information within its own copy of the LSDB. The OSPF Database Description packet is illustrated in Figure 3-10 below:

```
Open Shortest Path First
 OSPF Header
 OSPF DB Description
  Interface MTU: 1500
 Options: 0x52 (O, L, E)
   0... .... = DN: DN-bit is NOT set
   .1.. .... = O: O-bit is SET
   ..0. .... = DC: Demand circuits are NOT supported
   ...1 .... = L: The packet contains LLS data block
   .... 0... = NP: Nssa is NOT supported
   .... .0.. = MC: NOT multicast capable
   .... ..1. = E: ExternalRoutingCapability
 DB Description: 0x02 (M)
   .... 0... = R: OOBResync bit is NOT set
   .... .0.. = I: Init bit is NOT set
   .... ..1. = M: More bit is SET
   .... ...0 = MS: Master/slave bit is NOT set
  DD Sequence: 5409
 LSA Header
 LSA Header
 OSPF LLS Data Block
```

Fig. 3-10. OSPF Database Description Packet

Within the DBD packet, the 2-byte Interface MTU field contains the MTU value, in octets, of the outgoing interface. In other words, this field contains the largest data size that can be sent through the associated interface (in bytes). When the interface is used on a virtual link, the field is set to a value of 0x0000. In order for an OSPF neighbor adjacency to be established successfully, the MTU must be the same on all routers. If you change this value on one router, you must configure the same value on all other routers on the same subnet.

NOTE: The interface MTU values for EIGRP do not have to be the same in order for an EIGRP neighbor relationship to be established successfully.

The 1-byte Options field contains the same options contained within the OSPF Hello packet. For brevity, these options will not be described again.

The Database Description or Flags field is a 1-byte field that provides an OSPF router with the capability to exchange multiple DBD packets with a neighbor during an adjacency formation. The various bit definitions contained within this field are as follows:

- The R bit indicates Out-Of-Band (OOB) LSDB resynchronization. All DBD packets sent during the OOB resynchronization procedure are sent with the R-bit set. Going into detail on this field is beyond the scope of the ROUTE exam requirements.
- The Initial (I) bit designates whether this DBD packet is the first in a series of packets. The first DBD packet has a value of 1, while subsequent packets have a value of 0.
- The More (M) bit informs the neighboring router whether the DBD packet is the last in a series. The last packet has a value of 0, while previous packets have a value of 1. In other words, if this field has a value of 1, it means more packets will follow.
- The Master/Slave (MS) bit is used to identify which OSPF router is in control of the actual database synchronization process. The Master router uses a value of 1 in this field, while the Slave uses a value of 0 in this field.

The 4-byte DBD Sequence Number field is used to guarantee that all DBD packets are received and processed during the synchronization process through use of a sequence number. The Master router initializes this field to a unique value in the first DBD packet, with each subsequent packet being incremented by 1. The sequence number is incremented only by the Master.

Finally, the variable length LSA Header field carries the LSA headers describing the local router's database information. Each header is 20 octets in length and uniquely identifies each LSA in the database. Each DBD packet may contain multiple LSA headers.

Link State Request Packets

Link State Request (LSR) packets are sent by OSPF routers to request missing or out-of-date database information. These packets contain identifiers that uniquely describe the requested Link State Advertisement. An individual LSR packet may contain a single set of identifiers or multiple sets of identifiers to request multiple Link State Advertisements. LSR packets are also used after database exchange to request LSAs that were seen during the database exchange that the local router does not have. Figure 3-11 below illustrates the format of the OSPF LSR packet:

```
Open Shortest Path First
 OSPF Header
 Link State Request
  Link-State Advertisement Type: Router-LSA (1)
  Link State ID: 3.3.3.3
  Advertising Router: 3.3.3.3 (3.3.3.3)
 Link State Request
  Link-State Advertisement Type: Network-LSA (2)
  Link State ID: 192.168.1.3
  Advertising Router: 3.3.3.3 (3.3.3.3)
```

Fig. 3-11. OSPF Link State Request Packet

The 4-byte Link State Advertisement Type field contains the type of LSA being requested. It may contain one of the following fields:

- Type 1 = Router Link State Advertisement
- Type 2 = Network Link State Advertisement
- Type 3 = Network Summary Link State Advertisement
- Type 4 = ASBR Summary Link State Advertisement
- Type 5 = AS External Link State Advertisement
- Type 6 = Multicast Link State Advertisement
- Type 7 = NSSA External Link State Advertisement
- Type 8 = External Attributes Link State Advertisement
- Type 9 = Opaque Link State Advertisement—Link Local
- Type 10 = Opaque Link State Advertisement—Area
- Type 11 = Opaque Link State Advertisement—Autonomous System

NOTE: The LSAs listed above are described in detail in the following section.

The 4-byte Link State ID field encodes information specific to the LSA. The information that is contained in this field depends on the type of LSA. Finally, the 4-byte Advertising Router field contains the RID of the router that first originated the LSA.

Link State Update Packets

Link State Update (LSU) packets are used by the router to advertise LSAs. LSU packets may be Unicast to an OSPF neighbor in response to a received Link State Request from that neighbor. Most commonly, however, they are reliably flooded throughout the network to the AllSPFRouters Multicast group address 224.0.0.5 until each router has a copy. The flooded updates are then acknowledged in the LSA Acknowledgement packet. If the LSA is not acknowledged, it will be retransmitted every five seconds, by default. Figure 3-12 below shows an LSU sent to a neighbor in response to an LSR:

```
Internet Protocol, Src: 192.168.1.3 (192.168.1.3), Dst: 192.168.1.2 (192.168.1.2)
Open Shortest Path First
OSPF Header
LS Update Packet
 Number of LSAs: 1
 LS Type: Summary-LSA (IP network)
  LS Age: 3600 seconds
  Do Not Age: False
 Options: 0x22 (DC, E)
  Link-State Advertisement Type: Summary-LSA (IP network) (3)
  Link State ID: 150.1.1.0
  Advertising Router: 20.2.2.2 (20.2.2.2)
  LS Sequence Number: 0x80000001
  LS Checksum: 0x70d9
  Length: 28
  Netmask: 255.255.255.0
  Metric: 64
```

Fig. 3-12. Unicast LSU Packet

Figure 3-13 below illustrates an LSU that is reliably flooded to the Multicast group address 224.0.0.5:

```
Internet Protocol, Src: 192.168.1.2 (192.168.1.2), Dst: 224.0.0.5 (224.0.0.5)
Open Shortest Path First
OSPF Header
LS Update Packet
 Number of LSAs: 1
 LS Type: Summary-LSA (IP network)
  LS Age: 1 seconds
  Do Not Age: False
  Options: 0x22 (DC, E)
  Link-State Advertisement Type: Summary-LSA (IP network) (3)
  Link State ID: 150.1.1.0
  Advertising Router: 20.2.2.2 (20.2.2.2)
  LS Sequence Number: 0x80000002
  LS Checksum: 0x6eda
  Length: 28
  Netmask: 255.255.255.0
  Metric: 64
```

Fig. 3-13. Multicast LSU Packet

The LSU is comprised of two parts. The first is the 4-byte Number of LSAs field. This field displays the number of LSAs carried within the LSU packet. The second part is one or more Link State Advertisements. This variable-length field contains the complete LSA. Each type of LSA has a common header format along with specific data fields to describe its information. An LSU packet may contain a single LSA or multiple LSAs.

Link State Acknowledgement Packets

The Link State Acknowledgement (LSAck) packet is used to acknowledge each LSA and is sent in response to LSU packets. By explicitly acknowledging packets with LSAcks, the flooding mechanism used by OSPF is considered reliable.

The LSAck contains the common OSPF header followed by a list of LSA headers. This variable-length field allows the local router to acknowledge multiple LSAs using a single packet. LSAcks are sent using Multicast. On multi-access networks, if the router sending the LSAck is a DR or a BDR router, then Link State Acknowledgements are sent to the Multicast group address 224.0.0.5 (AllSPFRouters). However, if the router sending the Link State Acknowledgements is not a DR or a BDR device, then LSAck packets are sent to the Multicast group address 224.0.0.6 (AllDRRouters). Figure 3-14 below illustrates the format of the LSAck:

```
Open Shortest Path First
 OSPF Header
  OSPF Version: 2
  Message Type: LS Acknowledge (5)
  Packet Length: 84
  Source OSPF Router: 20.2.2.2 (20.2.2.2)
  Area ID: 0.0.0.0 (Backbone)
  Packet Checksum: 0xca63 [correct]
  Auth Type: Null
  Auth Data (none)
 LSA Header
 LSA Header
 LSA Header
```

Fig. 3-14. Link State Acknowledgement Packet

In conclusion, it is important to remember the different OSPF packet types and what information they contain. This not only will benefit you in the exam but also will aid you to understand the overall operation of OSPF as a protocol.

In Cisco IOS software, you can use the show ip ospf traffic command to view OSPF packet statistics. This command shows the total count for the sent and received OSPF packets and then segments this further to the individual OSPF process and, finally, to the interfaces enabled for OSPF routing under that process. This command can also be used to troubleshoot OSPF adjacency establishment and is not as processor-intensive as debugging. The information printed by this command is illustrated in the following output:

```
R4#show ip ospf traffic

OSPF statistics:
  Rcvd: 702 total, 0 checksum errors
        682 hello, 3 database desc, 0 link state req
        12 link state updates, 5 link state acks

  Sent: 1378 total
        1364 hello, 2 database desc, 1 link state req
        5 link state updates, 6 link state acks

        OSPF Router with ID (4.4.4.4) (Process ID 4)

OSPF queue statistics for process ID 4:

                    InputQ      UpdateQ     OutputQ
  Limit             0           200         0
  Drops             0           0           0
  Max delay [msec]  4           0           0
  Max size          2           2           2
```

```
      Invalid        0          0          0
      Hello          0          0          1
      DB des         2          2          1
      LS req         0          0          0
      LS upd         0          0          0
      LS ack         0          0          0
 Current size        0          0          0
      Invalid        0          0          0
      Hello          0          0          0
      DB des         0          0          0
      LS req         0          0          0
      LS upd         0          0          0
      LS ack         0          0          0
```

Interface statistics:

    Interface Serial0/0

OSPF packets received/sent
    Invalid Hellos   DB-des   LS-req   LS-upd   LS-ack   Total
Rx: 0   683   3   0   12   5   703
Tx: 0   684   2   1   5   6   698

OSPF header errors
    Length 0, Auth Type 0, Checksum 0, Version 0,
    Bad Source 0, No Virtual Link 0, Area Mismatch 0,
    No Sham Link 0, Self Originated 0, Duplicate ID 0,
    Hello 0, MTU Mismatch 0, Nbr Ignored 0,
    LLS 0, Unknown Neighbor 0, Authentication 0,
    TTL Check Fail 0,

OSPF LSA errors
    Type 0, Length 0, Data 0, Checksum 0,

    Interface FastEthernet0/0

OSPF packets received/sent
    Invalid Hellos   DB-des   LS-req   LS-upd   LS-ack   Total
Rx: 0   0   0   0   0   0   0
Tx: 0   682   0   0   0   0   682

OSPF header errors
    Length 0, Auth Type 0, Checksum 0, Version 0,
    Bad Source 0, No Virtual Link 0, Area Mismatch 0,
    No Sham Link 0, Self Originated 0, Duplicate ID 0,

```
Hello 0, MTU Mismatch 0, Nbr Ignored 0,
LLS 0, Unknown Neighbor 0, Authentication 0,
TTL Check Fail 0,

OSPF LSA errors
  Type 0, Length 0, Data 0, Checksum 0,

Summary traffic statistics for process ID 4:

Rcvd: 703 total, 0 errors
      683 hello, 3 database desc, 0 link state req
      12 link state upds, 5 link state acks, 0 invalid
Sent: 1380 total
      1366 hello, 2 database desc, 1 link state req
      5 link state upds, 6 link state acks, 0 invalid
```

ESTABLISHING ADJACENCIES

Routers running OSPF transition through several states before establishing an adjacency. The routers exchange different types of packets during these states. This exchange of messages allows all routers that establish an adjacency to have a consistent view of the network. Additional changes to the current network are simply sent out as incremental updates. The different states are the Down, Attempt, Init, 2-Way, Exstart, Exchange, Loading, and Full states as described below:

- The Down state is the starting state for all OSPF routers. However, the local router may also show a neighbor in this state when no Hello packets have been received within the specified router dead interval for that interface.

- The Attempt state is valid only for OSPF neighbors on NBMA networks. In this state, a Hello has been sent but no information has been received from the statically configured neighbor; however, some effort is being made to establish an adjacency with this neighbor.

- The Init state is reached when an OSPF router receives a Hello packet from a neighbor but the local RID is not listed in the received Neighbor field. If OSPF Hello parameters, such as timer values, do not match, then OSPF routers will never progress beyond this state.

- The 2-Way state indicates bi-directional communication with the OSPF neighbor(s). In this state, the local router has received a Hello packet with its own RID in the Neighbor field and Hello packet parameters are identical on the two routers. On multi-access networks, the DR and BDR routers are elected during this phase.

- The Exstart state is used for the initialization of the database synchronization process. It is at this stage that the local router and its neighbor establish which router is in charge of the database synchronization process. The Master and Slave are elected in this state and the first sequence number for DBD exchange is decided by the Master in this stage.

- The Exchange state is where routers describe the contents of their databases using DBD packets. Each DBD sequence is explicitly acknowledged, and only one outstanding DBD is allowed at a time. During this phase, LSR packets are also sent to request a new instance of the LSA. The M (More) bit is used to request missing information during this stage. When both routers have exchanged their complete databases, they will both set the M bit to 0.

- In the Loading state, OSPF routers build an LSR and Link State Retransmission list. LSR packets are sent to request the more recent instance of an LSA that has not been received during the Exchange process. Updates that are sent during this phase are placed on the Link State Retransmission list until the local router receives an acknowledgement. If the local router also receives an LSR during this phase, it will respond with a Link State Update that contains the requested information.

- The Full state indicates that the OSPF neighbors have exchanged their entire databases and both agree (i.e., have the same view of the network). Both neighboring routers in this state add the adjacency to their local database and advertise the relationship in a Link State Update packet. At this point, the routing tables are calculated, or recalculated if the adjacency was reset.

In order for an OSPF adjacency to be established successfully, certain parameters on both routers must match. These parameters include the following:

- The interface MTU values
- The Hello and Dead Timers
- The Area ID
- The Authentication Type and Password
- The Stub Area flag

These parameters will be described as we progress through this chapter. If these parameters do not match, the OSPF adjacency will never fully establish. The different states that the router may show for the neighbor due to a mismatch of any one of the parameters above is beyond the scope of the ROUTE exam requirements; however, you will be expected to understand the implications of such mismatches in the TSHOOT exam. This information is included in that guide.

NOTE: In addition to mismatched parameters, it is also important to remember that on a multi-access network, if both routers are configured with a priority value of 0, then the adjacency will not be established. The DR must be present on such network types.

OSPF LSAS AND THE LINK STATE DATABASE (LSDB)

As stated in the previous section, OSPF uses several types of Link State Advertisements. Each LSA begins with a standard 20-byte LSA header. This header contains the following:

- Link State Age
- Options
- Link State Type
- Link State ID
- Advertising Router
- Link State Sequence Number
- Link State Checksum
- Length

The 2-byte Link State Age field states the time (in seconds) since the LSA was originated. The maximum age of the LSA is 3600 seconds, which means that if the age reaches 3600 seconds, the LSA is removed from the database. To avoid this, the LSA is refreshed every 1800 seconds.

The 1-byte Options field contains the same options as those in the OSPF Hello packet.

The 1-byte Link State Type field represents the types of LSAs. These different LSA packet types are described in detail in the following sections.

The 4-byte Link State ID field identifies the portion of the network that is being described by the LSA. The contents of this field depend on the advertisement's LS type.

The 4-byte Advertising Router field represents the router ID of the router originating the LSA.

The 1-byte Link State Sequence Number field detects old or duplicate Link State Advertisements. Successive instances of an LSA are given successive Link State Sequence Numbers. The first sequence number 0x80000000 is reserved; therefore, the first sequence number is always 0x80000001. This value is incremented as packets are sent. The maximum sequence number is 0x7FFFFFFF.

The 2-byte Link State Checksum field performs the Fletcher checksum of the complete contents of the LSA, including the LSA header. The Link State age field is not included in the checksum. The checksum is performed because Link State Advertisements can be corrupted while being stored in memory due to router software or hardware issues or during flooding due to Physical Layer errors, for example.

NOTE: The checksum is performed at the time the LSA is generated or is received. In addition, the checksum is performed at every CheckAge interval, which is 10 minutes. If this field has a value of 0, then it means that the checksum has not been performed.

The 2-byte Length field is the final field and includes the length (in bytes) of the LSA. This includes the 20-byte LSA header. Figure 3-15 below illustrates the LSA header:

```
Open Shortest Path First
 OSPF Header
 LSA Header
  LS Age: 3600 seconds
  Do Not Age: False
  Options: 0x22 (DC, E)
  Link-State Advertisement Type: Router-LSA (1)
  Link State ID: 20.2.2.2
  Advertising Router: 20.2.2.2 (20.2.2.2)
  LS Sequence Number: 0x80000005
  LS Checksum: 0xcb54
  Length: 36
 LSA Header
 LSA Header
```

Fig. 3-15. Link State Advertisement Header

While OSPF supports 11 different types of Link State Advertisements, only LSAs Type 1, 2, and 3, which are used to calculate internal routes, and LSAs Type 4, 5, and 7, which are used to calculate external routes, are within the scope of the ROUTE exam requirements. These LSAs will be described in detail in the following section. The basic network topology illustrated in Figure 3-16 below will be used to describe the different types of LSAs.

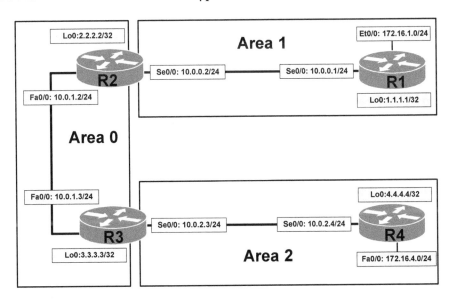

Fig. 3-16. Understanding OSPF LSAs

In Cisco IOS software, the show ip ospf database command is used to view the contents of the Link State Database. This command, when used without any keywords, prints out a summary of LSAs in all areas to which the router is connected. The command supports several keywords that provide greater granularity in allowing network administrators to restrict output only to specific types of LSAs, LSAs advertised by the local router, or even LSAs advertised by other routers within the OSPF domain.

While illustrating the output of the usage of each keyword is unrealistic, the following section describes the different LSAs and the common keywords used in conjunction with the show ip ospf database command to view detailed information on these LSAs. The keywords supported by this command are illustrated in the following output:

```
R3#show ip ospf database ?
  adv-router        Advertising Router link states
  asbr-summary      ASBR Summary link states
  database-summary  Summary of database
  external          External link states
  network           Network link states
  nssa-external     NSSA External link states
  opaque-area       Opaque Area link states
  opaque-as         Opaque AS link states
  opaque-link       Opaque Link-Local link states
  router            Router link states
  self-originate    Self-originated link states
  summary           Network Summary link states
  |                 Output modifiers
  <cr>
```

Router Link State Advertisements (Type 1)

Type 1 LSAs are generated by each router for each area to which it belongs. The Router LSA lists the originating router's router ID (RID). Each individual router will generate a Type 1 LSA for the area in which it resides. The Router LSAs are the first LSA types printed in the output of the show ip ospf database command. For example, referencing Figure 3-16 above, both R3 and R4 will generate a Type 1 LSA for Area 2 as illustrated in the following outputs:

```
R3#show ip ospf database

            OSPF Router with ID (3.3.3.3) (Process ID 3)

            Router Link States (Area 0)
```

```
Link ID          ADV Router       Age        Seq#        Checksum Link Count
2.2.2.2          2.2.2.2          704        0x80000005 0x0048A2 2
3.3.3.3          3.3.3.3          424        0x80000004 0x003AA4 2
...
[Truncated Output]


R4#show ip ospf database

              OSPF Router with ID (4.4.4.4) (Process ID 4)

              Router Link States (Area 2)

Link ID          ADV Router       Age        Seq#        Checksum Link Count
3.3.3.3          3.3.3.3          249        0x80000004 0x0082DA 2
4.4.4.4          4.4.4.4          62         0x80000005 0x00273E 4
...
[Truncated Output]
```

When a router is connected to more than one area, it generates a Type 1 LSA for each area to which it is connected. For example, in addition to generating a Type 1 LSA for Area 2, R3 will also generate a Type 1 LSA for Area 0, to which it is also connected. This is illustrated in the following output:

```
R3#show ip ospf database

              OSPF Router with ID (3.3.3.3) (Process ID 3)

              Router Link States (Area 0)

Link ID          ADV Router       Age        Seq#        Checksum Link Count
2.2.2.2          2.2.2.2          793        0x80000005 0x0048A2 2
3.3.3.3          3.3.3.3          513        0x80000004 0x003AA4 2
...
[Truncated Output]

              Router Link States (Area 2)

Link ID          ADV Router       Age        Seq#        Checksum Link Count
3.3.3.3          3.3.3.3          515        0x80000004 0x0082DA 2
4.4.4.4          4.4.4.4          329        0x80000005 0x00273E 4
...
[Truncated Output]
```

NOTE: The same would be applicable to R2, which is also connected to more than one area.

To view detailed information on the Router LSA, you can use the `show ip ospf database router` command. The options available with this command are listed in the output below:

```
R4#show ip ospf database router ?
  A.B.C.D          Link state ID (as an IP address)
  adv-router       Advertising Router link states
  internal         Internal LSA information
  self-originate   Self-originated link states
  |                Output modifiers
  <cr>
```

Within the output of this command, the Link ID identifies the link itself. This field will differ depending on the link type. The following link types are supported:

- Point-to-Point Link
- Link to Transit Network
- Link to Stub Network
- Virtual Link

For a point-to-point link type, the Link ID will always be the neighbor RID. For a link to a transit network, the Link ID will always be the IP address of the DR. This was illustrated earlier in this chapter and will be illustrated again when we discuss Type 2 LSAs. A Stub network simply refers to a link on which no DR/BDR has been elected, such as a point-to-point network type. Links to Stub networks are also links for which no neighbors have been discovered. For these link types, the Link ID will always be the network/subnet number. Finally, for a virtual link, the Link ID will always contain the neighbor ID. Virtual links will be described later in this chapter.

The Advertising Router field displays the IP address of the router advertising this information. This field will contain the RID of the advertising router. The Age field indicates the age of the LSA. By default, OSPF re-floods all LSAs every 30 minutes (1800 seconds) based on the Link State Age field. The Age is reset when a new LSA is received by the router. If a router wants to remove a particular LSA, it can flood the LSA with a MaxAge value of 3600 seconds.

Other routers that receive an LSA with this Age flush or purge the LSA from their databases. For example, if a router previously advertising an External LSA for a route was reconfigured and the route redistribution configuration was removed, then the router would flood the removed External LSAs with a MaxAge value of 3600 seconds and a maximum metric value throughout the domain, allowing other routers to flush or purge this LSA entry from their Link State Database as illustrated in the following output:

```
R4#show ip ospf database external

            OSPF Router with ID (4.4.4.4) (Process ID 4)

            Type-5 AS External Link States

  Delete flag is set for this LSA
  LS age: MAXAGE(3600)
  Options: (No TOS-capability, DC)
  LS Type: AS External Link
  Link State ID: 192.168.0.0 (External Network Number)
  Advertising Router: 4.4.4.4
  LS Seq Number: 80000003
  Checksum: 0x5E5E
  Length: 36
  Network Mask: /22
        Metric Type: 1 (Comparable directly to link state metric)
        TOS: 0
        Metric: 16777215
        Forward Address: 0.0.0.0
        External Route Tag: 0
```

It should be noted that it is also possible for the router to be removed before it can send out the flood update for the LSA with the MaxAge set. In such cases, the LSA is retained in the databases of other OSPF routers; however, the Age counter continues to increment and when it reaches 3600 seconds, the LSA is removed or purged.

NOTE: In Cisco IOS software, the `max-metric router-lsa [external-lsa <max-metric-value>] [include-stub] [on-startup <seconds> | wait-for-bgp] [summary-lsa <max-metric-value>]` OSPF router configuration command can be issued to configure the router to advertise a maximum metric so that other routers do not prefer the router as an intermediate hop in their shortest path first (SPF) calculations. This command may be applied in the following situations:

- When reloading a router, and you do not want other routers to attempt to forward traffic through that router, as it may result in a black-holing of network traffic
- When introducing a new router into the OSPF network and you do not want other routers to forward traffic through the new router for the time being
- When gracefully removing a router from the network, which allows other routers to select alternate paths before the router is actually removed from the network

The Sequence number is the Link State sequence number. This is used to detect old or duplicate LSAs. As stated at the beginning of this section, the first sequence number of 0x80000000 is reserved; therefore, LSAs will always begin with the sequence number 0x80000001. This value is incremented by the router that originates the LSA when it re-floods it every 30 minutes. This action also resets the Age of the LSA.

The Checksum field pertains to the Fletcher checksum of the complete contents of the LSA. Finally, the Link Count field indicates the number of interfaces detected for the router. For example, to view detailed Type 2 LSA information, the show ip ospf database router 4.4.4.4 command could be used on R4 as illustrated in the following output:

```
R4#show ip ospf database router 4.4.4.4

          OSPF Router with ID (4.4.4.4) (Process ID 4)

             Router Link States (Area 2)

  LS age: 870
  Options: (No TOS-capability, DC)
  LS Type: Router Links
  Link State ID: 4.4.4.4
  Advertising Router: 4.4.4.4
  LS Seq Number: 80000006
  Checksum: 0x253F
  Length: 72
  Number of Links: 4

    Link connected to: a Stub Network
     (Link ID) Network/subnet number: 4.4.4.4
     (Link Data) Network Mask: 255.255.255.255
      Number of TOS metrics: 0
       TOS 0 Metrics: 1

    Link connected to: a Stub Network
     (Link ID) Network/subnet number: 172.16.4.0
     (Link Data) Network Mask: 255.255.255.0
      Number of TOS metrics: 0
       TOS 0 Metrics: 1

    Link connected to: another Router (point-to-point)
     (Link ID) Neighboring Router ID: 3.3.3.3
     (Link Data) Router Interface address: 10.0.2.4
      Number of TOS metrics: 0
```

```
      TOS 0 Metrics: 64

  Link connected to: a Stub Network
   (Link ID) Network/subnet number: 10.0.2.0
   (Link Data) Network Mask: 255.255.255.0
    Number of TOS metrics: 0
     TOS 0 Metrics: 64
```

Take a moment to understand the output above. First, the Link State ID of R4's Type 1 LSA is printed above as 4.4.4.4. This is the RID assigned to R4.

Next, look at the number of links. We know that R4 has three interfaces: Loopback0, FastEthernet0/0 (connected to the 172.16.4.0/24 subnet), and Serial0/0 (connected to the 10.0.2.0/24 subnet, and a P2P link to R3). By default, all Loopback interfaces are considered Stub networks by OSPF. Therefore, the first link described as a link to a Stub network is that for the Loopback0 interface on R4.

The second link, also described as a link to a Stub network, is that for the FastEthernet0/0 172.16.4.0/24 subnet because, although the interface is not a Loopback interface, there are no other OSPF neighbors discovered off that particular link.

The third link, described as a link connected to another router, represents the Serial0/0 P2P link between R4 and R3. This is a point-to-point link type as shown in parenthesis (brackets). For these link types, the Link ID will always be the neighbor RID. Finally, because there is no DR/BDR election on the P2P link between R4 and R3, the link is also designated as connected to a Stub network. The link ID is therefore the network/subnet number and the subnet mask for the link is included in the Link Data field, as is the case for the other two links connected to Stub networks.

Because Type 1 LSAs are flooded within a single area and all routers within the area receive these LSAs from all other routers in the same area, the show ip ospf database router adv-router 3.3.3.3 command can be issued on R4 to view the Type 1 LSAs advertised by R3. The output of this command would be the same as the output of the show ip ospf database router 3.3.3.3 command on R3 itself. This is illustrated in the following output:

```
R4#show ip ospf data router adv-router 3.3.3.3

          OSPF Router with ID (4.4.4.4) (Process ID 4)

          Router Link States (Area 2)
```

```
Routing Bit Set on this LSA
LS age: 526
Options: (No TOS-capability, DC)
LS Type: Router Links
Link State ID: 3.3.3.3
Advertising Router: 3.3.3.3
LS Seq Number: 80000006
Checksum: 0x7EDC
Length: 48
Area Border Router
Number of Links: 2

   Link connected to: another Router (point-to-point)
   (Link ID) Neighboring Router ID: 4.4.4.4
   (Link Data) Router Interface address: 10.0.2.3
    Number of TOS metrics: 0
     TOS 0 Metrics: 64

   Link connected to: a Stub Network
   (Link ID) Network/subnet number: 10.0.2.0
   (Link Data) Network Mask: 255.255.255.0
    Number of TOS metrics: 0
     TOS 0 Metrics: 64
```

Referencing the output above, the Link State ID of R3's Type 1 LSA is printed as 3.3.3.3. This is the RID assigned to R3. Although R3 is connected to two different areas, the router will flood the Type 1 LSA into all areas to which it is connected. In other words, on R3, this same LSA would also be flooded into Area 0.

Unlike R4, R3 has only a single link in Area 2, which is the Serial0/0 interface. Loopback0 is configured as part of Area 0 as illustrated in Figure 3-16. Using the same logic, Serial0/0 is described as a link connected to another router because it is a point-to-point link type connecting R3 and R4. The same link is also described as being connected to a Stub network because there is no DR/BDR elected on that link.

Before we move on to Network LSAs (Type 2), we will look at the Type 1 LSAs on R3, which has connections in both Area 0 and Area 2 and is therefore an Area Border Router (ABR). This is illustrated in the following output:

```
R3#show ip ospf database router 3.3.3.3

          OSPF Router with ID (3.3.3.3) (Process ID 3)

             Router Link States (Area 0)
```

```
LS age: 386
Options: (No TOS-capability, DC)
LS Type: Router Links
Link State ID: 3.3.3.3
Advertising Router: 3.3.3.3
LS Seq Number: 8000000C
Checksum: 0x2AAC
Length: 48
Area Border Router
Number of Links: 2

   Link connected to: a Stub Network
    (Link ID) Network/subnet number: 3.3.3.3
    (Link Data) Network Mask: 255.255.255.255
     Number of TOS metrics: 0
      TOS 0 Metrics: 1

   Link connected to: a Transit Network
    (Link ID) Designated Router address: 10.0.1.2
    (Link Data) Router Interface address: 10.0.1.3
     Number of TOS metrics: 0
      TOS 0 Metrics: 1


                Router Link States (Area 2)


LS age: 387
Options: (No TOS-capability, DC)
LS Type: Router Links
Link State ID: 3.3.3.3
Advertising Router: 3.3.3.3
LS Seq Number: 8000000C
Checksum: 0x72E2
Length: 48
Area Border Router
Number of Links: 2

   Link connected to: another Router (point-to-point)
    (Link ID) Neighboring Router ID: 4.4.4.4
    (Link Data) Router Interface address: 10.0.2.3
     Number of TOS metrics: 0
      TOS 0 Metrics: 64

   Link connected to: a Stub Network
    (Link ID) Network/subnet number: 10.0.2.0
    (Link Data) Network Mask: 255.255.255.0
     Number of TOS metrics: 0
      TOS 0 Metrics: 64
```

From the output above, the Link State ID shows R3's Type 1 LSA into Area 0. This LSA contains the RID of R3, which is 3.3.3.3. Because R3 is connected to both Area 0 and Area 2, it is considered an Area Border Router (ABR). Within Area 0, the LSA shows two links. The first is for the Loopback0 interface, which is listed as a Stub network connection.

The second link is connected to a transit network. Recall earlier in this chapter we learned that multi-access links are referred to as transit networks in OSPF terminology. The Link ID for this LSA will always list the router ID of the Designated Router, while the Link Data field contains the actual IP address of the router interface. The same would also be reflected on R2 as illustrated in the following output:

```
R3#show ip ospf database router adv-router 2.2.2.2

            OSPF Router with ID (3.3.3.3) (Process ID 3)

              Router Link States (Area 0)

    Routing Bit Set on this LSA
    LS age: 1688
    Options: (No TOS-capability, DC)
    LS Type: Router Links
    Link State ID: 2.2.2.2
    Advertising Router: 2.2.2.2
    LS Seq Number: 8000000B
    Checksum: 0x3CA8
    Length: 48
    Area Border Router
    Number of Links: 2

      Link connected to: a Stub Network
       (Link ID) Network/subnet number: 2.2.2.2
       (Link Data) Network Mask: 255.255.255.255
        Number of TOS metrics: 0
         TOS 0 Metrics: 1

      Link connected to: a Transit Network
       (Link ID) Designated Router address: 10.0.1.2
       (Link Data) Router Interface address: 10.0.1.2
        Number of TOS metrics: 0
         TOS 0 Metrics: 1
```

From this output, we can determine that R2 is the elected DR. Additionally, we also know that a Type 2 LSA is generated to represent the routers attached to the segment. Type 2 LSAs are described in the following section.

Network Link State Advertisements (Type 2)

OSPF uses the Network Link State Advertisement (Type 2 LSA) to advertise the routers on the multi-access segment. This LSA is generated by the DR and is flooded only within the area. Because the other non-DR/BDR routers do not establish adjacencies with each other, the Network LSA allows those routers to know about the other routers on the multi-access segment.

To view information specific to the Network LSAs, the show ip ospf database network [options] commands should be used. As stated earlier, using the show ip ospf database command not only reduces the amount of information you have to parse through, it also indicates that you understand what you are looking for. The show ip ospf database network command on R3 is illustrated in the following output:

```
R3#show ip ospf database network

            OSPF Router with ID (3.3.3.3) (Process ID 3)

              Net Link States (Area 0)

  Routing Bit Set on this LSA
  LS age: 248
  Options: (No TOS-capability, DC)
  LS Type: Network Links
  Link State ID: 10.0.1.2 (address of Designated Router)
  Advertising Router: 2.2.2.2
  LS Seq Number: 80000008
  Checksum: 0x8E7B
  Length: 32
  Network Mask: /24
        Attached Router: 2.2.2.2
        Attached Router: 3.3.3.3
```

From the output above, the Link State ID prints the interface address of the DR. This is the same address that is printed in the (Link ID) Designated Router address field in the Type 1 LSA for the transit network, as was shown in the previous section. The Advertising Router field contains the RID for the DR. The Attached Router field lists the router IDs of all routers connected or attached to the same multi-access network segment.

> **NOTE:** The same information can be viewed using the show ip ospf database network adv-router 2.2.2.2 command, which lists the Network LSAs advertised by the DR (R2), or the show ip ospf database network 10.0.1.2 command, which lists the Link State ID and which is also the physical address of the router. This is illustrated in the following outputs:

```
R3#show ip ospf database network adv-router 2.2.2.2

            OSPF Router with ID (3.3.3.3) (Process ID 3)

            Net Link States (Area 0)

  Routing Bit Set on this LSA
  LS age: 728
  Options: (No TOS-capability, DC)
  LS Type: Network Links
  Link State ID: 10.0.1.2 (address of Designated Router)
  Advertising Router: 2.2.2.2
  LS Seq Number: 80000008
  Checksum: 0x8E7B
  Length: 32
  Network Mask: /24
        Attached Router: 2.2.2.2
        Attached Router: 3.3.3.3


R3#show ip ospf database network 10.0.1.2

            OSPF Router with ID (3.3.3.3) (Process ID 3)

            Net Link States (Area 0)

  Routing Bit Set on this LSA
  LS age: 755
  Options: (No TOS-capability, DC)
  LS Type: Network Links
  Link State ID: 10.0.1.2 (address of Designated Router)
  Advertising Router: 2.2.2.2
  LS Seq Number: 80000008
  Checksum: 0x8E7B
  Length: 32
  Network Mask: /24
        Attached Router: 2.2.2.2
        Attached Router: 3.3.3.3
```

Network Summary Link State Advertisements (Type 3)

The Network (Type 3) LSA is a summary of destinations outside of the local area but within the OSPF domain. In other words, this LSA advertises inter-area routing information. The Network LSA does not carry any topological information. Instead, the only information contained in the LSA is an IP prefix. Type 3 LSAs are generated by ABRs and are flooded to all adjacent areas. By default, each Type 3 LSA matches a single Router or Network LSA on a one-for-one basis. In other words, a Type 3 LSA exists for each individual Type 1 and Type 2 LSA. Special attention must be paid to how these LSAs are propagated in relation to the OSPF backbone. This propagation or flooding is performed as follows:

- Network Summary (Type 3) LSAs are advertised from a non-backbone area to the OSPF backbone for intra-area routes (i.e., for Type 1 and Type 2 LSAs)
- Network Summary (Type 3) LSAs are advertised from the OSPF backbone to other non-backbone areas for both intra-area (i.e., Area 0 Type 1 and Type 2 LSAs) and inter-area routes (i.e., for the Type 3 LSAs flooded into the backbone by other ABRs)

The same network topology used in previous LSA examples is again shown in Figure 3-17 below and will be used to reinforce the theoretical discussion pertaining to Type 3 LSAs in the network:

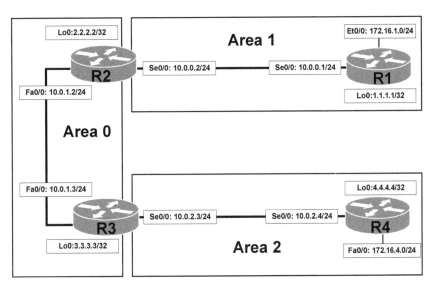

Fig. 3-17. Understanding OSPF LSAs

In Cisco IOS software, the `show ip ospf database summary [options]` command is used to view the Summary LSAs in the LSDB. If no options are specified, then the entire LSDB is printed as illustrated in the following output:

```
R4#show ip ospf database

        OSPF Router with ID (4.4.4.4) (Process ID 4)

        Router Link States (Area 2)

Link ID         ADV Router      Age        Seq#       Checksum Link Count
3.3.3.3         3.3.3.3         427        0x80000001 0x0088D7 2
4.4.4.4         4.4.4.4         426        0x80000002 0x0087E0 4
```

```
                Summary Net Link States (Area 2)

 Link ID          ADV Router         Age         Seq#        Checksum
 1.1.1.1          3.3.3.3            353         0x80000001 0x009753
 2.2.2.2          3.3.3.3            354         0x80000001 0x00E640
 3.3.3.3          3.3.3.3            412         0x80000001 0x00AE75
 10.0.0.0         3.3.3.3            28          0x80000003 0x0035AE
 10.0.1.0         3.3.3.3            427         0x80000001 0x00AB79
 172.16.1.0       3.3.3.3            353         0x80000001 0x008F98
```

In the output above, we can see that a Network Summary 3 LSA is included in the LSDB for all inter-area routes in the network. These LSAs are generated by the ABR, which is R3, and are then flooded into Area 2. The show ip ospf database summary command prints detailed information on each of the individual LSAs. In addition to other information, the show ip ospf database summary command prints the Link State ID for each LSA, the network mask, and the route metric, which is the ABR lowest-cost metric (best route) to the destination network, not the metric of the local router that receives the LSA. The output of this command is illustrated below:

```
R4#show ip ospf database summary

        OSPF Router with ID (4.4.4.4) (Process ID 4)

        Summary Net Link States (Area 2)

 Routing Bit Set on this LSA
 LS age: 1612
 Options: (No TOS-capability, DC, Upward)
 LS Type: Summary Links(Network)
 Link State ID: 1.1.1.1 (summary Network Number)
 Advertising Router: 3.3.3.3
 LS Seq Number: 80000001
 Checksum: 0x9753
 Length: 28
 Network Mask: /32
        TOS: 0  Metric: 66

 Routing Bit Set on this LSA
 LS age: 1612
 Options: (No TOS-capability, DC, Upward)
 LS Type: Summary Links(Network)
 Link State ID: 2.2.2.2 (summary Network Number)
 Advertising Router: 3.3.3.3
 LS Seq Number: 80000001
```

```
Checksum: 0xE640
Length: 28
Network Mask: /32
     TOS: 0  Metric: 2


Routing Bit Set on this LSA
LS age: 1677
Options: (No TOS-capability, DC, Upward)
LS Type: Summary Links(Network)
Link State ID: 3.3.3.3 (summary Network Number)
Advertising Router: 3.3.3.3
LS Seq Number: 80000001
Checksum: 0xAE75
Length: 28
Network Mask: /32
     TOS: 0  Metric: 1

Routing Bit Set on this LSA
  LS age: 1487
  Options: (No TOS-capability, DC, Upward)
  LS Type: Summary Links(Network)
  Link State ID: 10.0.0.0 (summary Network Number)
  Advertising Router: 3.3.3.3
  LS Seq Number: 80000003
  Checksum: 0x35AE
  Length: 28
  Network Mask: /24
       TOS: 0  Metric: 65
 ...


[Truncated Output]
```

NOTE: As can be seen in the output above, the metric for the 2.2.2.2 route, for example, is listed as 2. This is the metric to reach that subnet from R3, not from R4. R3 would calculate its metric to this same destination by adding that metric to the cost (metric) between itself and R4. Assuming a default OSPF cost of 64 for the link between R4 and R3, the route metric for the 2.2.2.2 route would be calculated by adding 64 and 2, resulting in a metric of 66 as illustrated below:

```
R4#show ip route 2.2.2.2 255.255.255.255
Routing entry for 2.2.2.2/32
  Known via "ospf 4", distance 110, metric 66, type inter area
  Last update from 10.0.2.3 on Serial0/0, 00:22:11 ago
  Routing Descriptor Blocks:
```

```
 * 10.0.2.3, from 3.3.3.3, 00:22:11 ago, via Serial0/0
     Route metric is 66, traffic share count is 1
```

The same would be applicable for the other entries in the LSDB. The route metric for 1.1.1.1 would be 64 + 66, which results in a metric of 130, while the route metric for 10.0.0.0 would be 64 + 65, which results in a metric of 129. This is reflected in the following outputs:

```
R4#show ip route 1.1.1.1 255.255.255.255
Routing entry for 1.1.1.1/32
  Known via "ospf 4", distance 110, metric 130, type inter area
  Last update from 10.0.2.3 on Serial0/0, 00:22:58 ago
  Routing Descriptor Blocks:
  * 10.0.2.3, from 3.3.3.3, 00:22:58 ago, via Serial0/0
      Route metric is 130, traffic share count is 1


R4#show ip route 10.0.0.0 255.255.255.0
Routing entry for 10.0.0.0/24
  Known via "ospf 4", distance 110, metric 129, type inter area
  Last update from 10.0.2.3 on Serial0/0, 00:24:24 ago
  Routing Descriptor Blocks:
  * 10.0.2.3, from 3.3.3.3, 00:24:24 ago, via Serial0/0
      Route metric is 129, traffic share count is 1
```

It is important to understand this concept when viewing the LSDB, as it is often a source of confusion. OSPF metric calculation will be described in detail later in this chapter.

In a large multi-area OSPF network, this command prints a great deal of information. Therefore, if you know exactly what you are looking for, information on specific Type 3 LSAs can be viewed by issuing the show ip ospf database summary [Link State ID] command as illustrated in the following output for the 172.16.1.0/24 link on router R1 as seen on router R4:

```
R4#show ip ospf database summary 172.16.1.0

            OSPF Router with ID (4.4.4.4) (Process ID 4)

            Summary Net Link States (Area 2)

  Routing Bit Set on this LSA
  LS age: 76
  Options: (No TOS-capability, DC, Upward)
  LS Type: Summary Links(Network)
  Link State ID: 172.16.1.0 (summary Network Number)
```

```
Advertising Router: 3.3.3.3
LS Seq Number: 80000002
Checksum: 0x8D99
Length: 28
Network Mask: /24
        TOS: 0  Metric: 75
```

The next three Link State Advertisements, Type 4, Type 5, and Type 7, are used in external route calculation. Type 4 and Type 5 LSAs are described in the following section. Type 7 LSAs will be described later in this chapter when we discuss the different types of OSPF areas.

Network Summary Link State Advertisements (Type 4)

The Type 4 LSA describes information regarding the Autonomous System Boundary Router (ASBR). This LSA contains the same packet format as the Type 3 LSA and performs the same basic functionality, with some notable differences. Like the Type 3 LSA, the Type 4 LSA is generated by the ABR. For both LSAs, the Advertising Router field contains the RID of the ABR that generated the summary LSA. However, the Type 4 LSA is created by the ABR for each ASBR reachable by a Router LSA. The ABR then injects the Type 4 LSA into the appropriate area. This LSA provides reachability information on the ASBR itself. The key differences between the Type 3 and Type 4 LSAs that you should be familiar with are listed below in Table 3-2:

Table 3-2. Type 3 and Type 4 Summary LSAs

Type 3 Summary LSA	Type 4 Summary LSA
Provides information about the network link	Provides information about the ASBR
The Network Mask field contains the subnet mask value of the network	The Network Mask field will always contain a value of 0.0.0.0 or simply just 0
The Link State ID field contains the actual network number	The Link State ID field contains the router ID of the ASBR

Based on the topology illustrated in Figure 3-17, the current LSBD on R4 shows the Type 1 and Type 3 LSAs as illustrated in the previous examples. Keep in mind that no Type 2 LSAs exist because R4 is connected to R3 via a P2P link. Now, R1 will be configured as an ASBR by configuring a static route on the router and redistributing this information into OSPF. This configuration is implemented on R1 as follows:

```
R1(config)#ip route 150.100.0.0 255.255.0.0 Null0
R1(config)#router ospf 1
R1(config-router)#redistribute static subnets
R1(config-router)#exit
```

NOTE: Route redistribution is described in detail later in this guide.

Because R1 is injecting external information into the OSPF domain, it automatically becomes an ASBR, and a Type 4 LSA is generated by the ABR and flooded into their connected areas. Beginning with R3, the Type 4 LSA is generated by R2 (ABR) and advertised to this router. This entry is now present in the LSDB on R3 as illustrated in the following output:

```
R3#show ip ospf database

           OSPF Router with ID (3.3.3.3) (Process ID 3)
...

[Truncated Output]

           Summary ASB Link States (Area 0)

Link ID          ADV Router       Age        Seq#        Checksum
1.1.1.1          2.2.2.2          161        0x80000001 0x00935C

...

[Truncated Output]

           Summary ASB Link States (Area 2)

Link ID          ADV Router       Age        Seq#        Checksum
1.1.1.1          3.3.3.3          161        0x80000001 0x007F6B

...

[Truncated Output]
```

In the output above, the Type 4 LSA flooded in Area 0 contains the Link ID (router ID) of the ASBR, which is 1.1.1.1. This LSA is generated by R2, as specified in the ADV Router field. Because R3 is also an ASBR, it generates the Type 4 LSA for Area 4 and changes the ADV Router field to itself (3.3.3.3). Detailed information on the Type 4 LSA can be viewed by issuing the show ip ospf database asbr-summary [Link State ID] command as follows:

```
R3#show ip ospf database asbr-summary 1.1.1.1

           OSPF Router with ID (3.3.3.3) (Process ID 3)

           Summary ASB Link States (Area 0)
```

```
Routing Bit Set on this LSA
LS age: 426
Options: (No TOS-capability, DC, Upward)
LS Type: Summary Links(AS Boundary Router)
Link State ID: 1.1.1.1 (AS Boundary Router address)
Advertising Router: 2.2.2.2
LS Seq Number: 80000001
Checksum: 0x935C
Length: 28
Network Mask: /0
      TOS: 0  Metric: 64


            Summary ASB Link States (Area 2)


LS age: 425
Options: (No TOS-capability, DC, Upward)
LS Type: Summary Links(AS Boundary Router)
Link State ID: 1.1.1.1 (AS Boundary Router address)
Advertising Router: 3.3.3.3
LS Seq Number: 80000001
Checksum: 0x7F6B
Length: 28
Network Mask: /0
      TOS: 0  Metric: 65
```

On R4, the show ip ospf database asbr-summary command also lists the router ID of the ASBR (R1) but indicates that the LSA is generated by R3 (ABR) as illustrated below:

```
R4#show ip ospf database asbr-summary

          OSPF Router with ID (4.4.4.4) (Process ID 4)


            Summary ASB Link States (Area 2)


Routing Bit Set on this LSA
LS age: 1974
Options: (No TOS-capability, DC, Upward)
LS Type: Summary Links(AS Boundary Router)
Link State ID: 1.1.1.1 (AS Boundary Router address)
Advertising Router: 3.3.3.3
LS Seq Number: 80000001
Checksum: 0x7F6B
Length: 28
Network Mask: /0
      TOS: 0  Metric: 65
```

External Summary Link State Advertisements (Type 5)

The External Link State Advertisement is used to describe destinations that are external to the autonomous system. In other words, Type 5 LSAs provide the network information necessary to reach the external networks. In addition to external routes, the default route for an OSPF routing domain can also be injected as a Type 5 Link State Advertisement.

The External LSA has a domain-flooding scope. This means that the ABR no longer stops the flooding process but, instead, continues it into its respective areas. The only areas that External LSAs are not flooded to are Stub-type areas. Stub-type areas are special OSPF areas that will be described in detail in the following section. Before Type 5 LSAs are installed into the routing table, the following two conditions must be satisfied:
1. The router calculating the Type 5 LSA must have a Type 4 LSA for the ASBR
2. The router must know about the forwarding address contained in the Type 5 LSA

Without a Type 4 LSA in the LSDB, it is not possible for the router to calculate the route to the ASBR. As described in the previous section, the Type 4 LSA is generated by the ABR and advertises the route to the ASBR; however, it does not actually advertise the external routing information to the rest of the OSPF domain.

The Forwarding Address is a 4-byte field that is contained within the External Type 5 LSA. This field specifies the address to which data to the advertised external network should be forwarded. The default value contained in this field is 0.0.0.0, which means that traffic to the advertised external network should be forwarded to the ASBR. Continuing from the previous output, R4 received the Type 4 LSA from R3 when R1 was configured as an ASBR. The corresponding External Type 5 LSA for the external route is therefore also included in the Link State Database on R4 as illustrated in the following output:

```
R4#show ip ospf database

          OSPF Router with ID (4.4.4.4) (Process ID 4)
...
[Truncated Output]

          Summary ASB Link States (Area 2)

Link ID         ADV Router      Age         Seq#        Checksum
1.1.1.1         3.3.3.3         1391        0x80000002  0x007D6C

          Type-5 AS External Link States

Link ID         ADV Router      Age         Seq#        Checksum Tag
```

```
150.100.0.0    1.1.1.1              430          0x80000004 0x006935 0
...
[Truncated Output]
```

Detailed information regarding the Type 5 LSA can be viewed via the show ip ospf database external command. The output printed by this command is illustrated below:

```
R4#show ip ospf database external

             OSPF Router with ID (4.4.4.4) (Process ID 4)

             Type-5 AS External Link States

    Routing Bit Set on this LSA
    LS age: 483
    Options: (No TOS-capability, DC)
    LS Type: AS External Link
    Link State ID: 150.100.0.0 (External Network Number)
    Advertising Router: 1.1.1.1
    LS Seq Number: 80000004
    Checksum: 0x6935
    Length: 36
    Network Mask: /16
          Metric Type: 2 (Larger than any Link State path)
          TOS: 0
          Metric: 20
          Forward Address: 0.0.0.0
          External Route Tag: 0
```

Referencing the output shown above, the Link State type field indicates that this is an External Type 5 LSA. The Link State ID field contains the external network number. The Advertising Router field contains the router ID (RID) of the ASBR, which is R1. R4 is able to reach the ASBR because of the Type 4 LSA in the LSDB. The Network Mask field contains the mask of the external network.

OSPF uses two types of external metrics: Type 1 or Type 2. By default, Cisco IOS software will always specify external routes as Type 2 externals. The difference between Type 1 and Type 2 external metrics is that in a Type 1 metric, the OSPF metric and costs change at every hop in the network; however, with Type 2, the external metric does not change. External Type 1 routes consider both internal and external metrics (costs), whereas external Type 2 routes consider the external metric (costs). This will be described in detail again in the following chapter on route redistribution.

Finally, the Forward Address field contains all zeros, which means traffic to the external network should be forwarded to the ASBR. However, four situations in which this field will contain a non-zero value are as follows:

- The ASBR's next-hop interface network type is not P2P, or point-to-multipoint.
- OSPF is enabled on the ASBR's next-hop interface.
- The next-hop interface of the ASBR falls into a defined OSPF network range.
- The ASBR's next-hop interface is not a passive OSPF interface.

As an example of when a non-zero Forward Address would be shown, the static route that was previously configured on R1 is changed to point to the next-hop address 172.16.1.254 of the Ethernet0/0 interface of R1 instead of the Null0 interface as illustrated in the following output:

```
R1(config)#no ip route 150.100.0.0 255.255.0.0 Null0
R1(config)#ip route 150.100.0.0 255.255.0.0 Ethernet0/0 172.16.1.254
R1(config)#router ospf 1
R1(config-router)#redistribute static subnets
R1(config-router)#exit
```

Because the 172.16.1.0/24 subnet on R1 has already been advertised by OSPF, there is no need to configure a network statement for this subnet. However, based on this configuration change, and because the next-hop interface of the ASBR falls into a defined OSPF network range, the Forward Address on the Type 5 LSA contains the next-hop IP address and not the default all-zero value as illustrated below on R4:

```
R4#show ip ospf database external

        OSPF Router with ID (4.4.4.4) (Process ID 4)

        Type-5 AS External Link States

    Routing Bit Set on this LSA
    LS age: 322
    Options: (No TOS-capability, DC)
    LS Type: AS External Link
    Link State ID: 150.100.0.0 (External Network Number)
    Advertising Router: 1.1.1.1
    LS Seq Number: 80000001
    Checksum: 0x9A4A
    Length: 36
    Network Mask: /16
          Metric Type: 2 (Larger than any Link State path)
          TOS: 0
          Metric: 20
          Forward Address: 172.16.1.254
          External Route Tag: 0
```

Now that we have a solid understanding of the different types of LSAs, we will conclude this section by learning how to protect the Link State Database.

Protecting the Link State Database

In very large networks, the LSDB may become very, very large. This large number of LSAs requires more router resources, such as memory and processing cycles, to process. If these resources are heavily taxed, other router functions, such as the forwarding of data, may be affected. The size of the LSDB may be controlled by utilizing one of the following two methods:

Configuring Stub-type areas, restricting the propagation of certain LSAs to those areas
Restricting the number of non-self-originated LSAs the router will store in the LSDB

> **NOTE:** The operation and configuration of different Stub-type OSPF areas will be described in detail in the following section. This will not be included in this section.

Regarding the second point made above, the `max-lsa <maximum-number>` `[threshold-percentage]` `[warning-only]` `[ignore-time <minutes>]` `[ignore-count <count-number>]` `[reset-time <minutes>]` router configuration command can be used to specify the maximum number of LSAs generated by other routers that the local router will keep in the LSDB. The `threshold-percentage` allows you to specify a threshold, which, once exceeded, will cause the router to generate and log a warning message.

By default, the router will generate and log a warning message at 75% of the value specified in the `max-lsa <maximum-number>` configuration. The `warning-only` keyword configures the router to log a warning message and take no further action. The `ignore-time <minutes>` keyword configures the router to ignore all neighbors for the configured interval. The default value for this keyword is five minutes. The `ignore-count <count-number>` keyword specifies the number of times the OSPF process can be placed into the ignore state. The default for this keyword is five times. Finally, the `reset-time <minutes>` keyword specifies the time period after which the ignore count will be reset to zero. The default for this keyword is 10 times.

> **NOTE:** You are not expected to perform any advanced OSPF configurations using the `max-lsa` command. However, it is important that you have a basic understanding of its functionality and what it is used for. The following configuration example illustrates how to configure the router to store up to 100 LSAs from neighbors and generate a warning when received LSAs have reached 50% of this number:

```
R4(config)#router ospf 4
R4(config-router)#max-lsa 100 50
R4(config-router)#exit
```

This configuration is validated using the show ip ospf [process ID] command illustrated below:

```
R4#show ip ospf 4
 Routing Process "ospf 4" with ID 4.4.4.4
 Start time: 08:58:49.887, Time elapsed: 01:47:47.459
 Supports only single TOS(TOS0) routes
 Supports opaque LSA
 Supports Link-local Signaling (LLS)
 Supports area transit capability
 Maximum number of non-self-generated LSA allowed 100
    Threshold for warning message 50%
    Ignore-time 5 minutes, reset-time 10 minutes
    Ignore-count allowed 5, current ignore-count 0
 Router is not originating router-LSAs with maximum metric
 Initial SPF schedule delay 5000 msecs
 Minimum hold time between two consecutive SPFs 10000 msecs
 Maximum wait time between two consecutive SPFs 10000 msecs

...


[Truncated Output]
```

NOTE: The other variables that are configurable using the additional keywords supported by the max-lsa router configuration command are using their default values.

OSPF AREAS

In addition to the backbone (Area 0) and other non-backbone areas described and used in the examples in previous sections of this chapter, the OSPF specification also defines several 'special' types of areas. The configuration of these areas is used primarily to reduce the size of the Link State Database on routers residing within those areas by preventing the injection of different types of LSAs (primarily Type 5 LSAs) into certain areas, which include the following:

- Not-so-stubby Areas
- Totally Not-so-stubby Areas
- Stub Areas
- Totally Stubby Areas

Not-so-stubby Areas (NSSAs)

Not-so-stubby Areas (NSSAs) are a type of OSPF Stub area that allows the injection of external routing information by an ASBR using an NSSA External LSA (Type 7). As stated in the previous section, Type 4, Type 5, and Type 7 LSAs are used for external route calculation. Type 4 and Type 5

LSAs were described in the previous section. In this section, we will examine in detail Type 7 LSAs and how they are used in NSSAs.

The Type 7 LSA is used for external routing information from the ASBR within the NSSA. The external routing information within the LSA is converted by the ABR into a Type 5 LSA at the area boundary. The ABR then floods the Type 5 LSA into the OSPF domain, and other routers in the network are aware of the external networks. Type 7 LSAs have an area flooding scope, so only routers in the NSSA receive the Type 7 LSA. Figure 3-18 below illustrates the flooding and conversion of Type 7 LSAs to Type 5 LSAs:

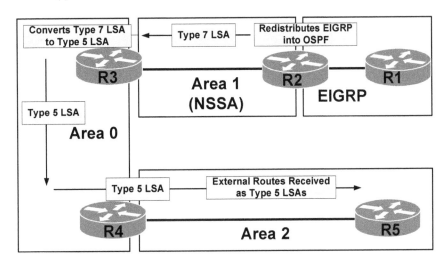

Fig. 3-18. Type 7 LSA to Type 5 LSA Conversion

Referencing Figure 3-18, R2, the ASBR, redistributes EIGRP routes into OSPF. R2 resides in an NSSA and generates Type 7 LSAs for the external routes. These LSAs are flooded only within the NSSA. The Type 7 LSAs are received by R3, the ABR. R3 converts the Type 7 LSAs to Type 5 LSAs and floods them to adjacent areas. These External LSAs are propagated to R4 and, ultimately, to R5. The Type 7 LSAs never leave Area 1. NSSAs have the following characteristics:

- They use Type 7 LSAs to carry external information within the NSSA
- The NSSA ABR converts Type 7 LSAs into Type 5 LSAs
- Type 4 and Type 5 LSAs are not allowed into Not-so-stubby Areas
- Network Summary LSAs are allowed into the NSSA

While Type 5 and Type 7 LSAs are used for external routes, there are some differences between the two types of LSAs with which you should be familiar. The first difference is that while both use a similar packet format, the Type field contains the value 7 instead of 5, indicating that this is a Type 7 LSA and not a Type 5 LSA.

The second important difference is that the Forwarding Address calculation is different for a Type 7 LSA. With Type 5 LSAs, the Forward Address field contains a value of 0, unless one of the following exceptions applies:

- The ASBR's next-hop interface network type is not P2P, or point-to-multipoint
- OSPF is enabled on the ASBR's next-hop interface
- The next-hop interface of the ASBR falls into a defined OSPF network range
- The ASBR's next-hop interface is not a passive OSPF interface

With Type 7 LSAs, if the route has a next-hop address (i.e., it is not a connected network), use the next-hop address in the Forward Address field. This holds true only if the route is an internal OSPF route. In other words, if the network between the NSSA boundary router and the adjacent AS is advertised into OSPF as an internal OSPF route, then the forwarding address should be the next-hop address.

However, if the network is not advertised into OSPF as an internal route, the Forward Address should be any of the active interfaces on the router. This means that if there is a Loopback interface enabled for OSPF routing in the area announcing the LSAs on the router, then use that interface. If there are no Loopback interfaces, then the address of the first operational interface in that area should be used.

The third difference also pertains to the LSA packet format. The Type 7 LSA Options field is slightly different for NSSAs. For Type 7 LSAs, the N/P bits must be used.

The N-bit describes the handling and support of NSSA LSAs as mentioned in RFC 1587. It is used in Hello packets and ensures NSSA configuration. When the N-bit is reset in the Hello packet sent out of a particular interface, it means that the router will neither send nor receive Type 7 LSAs on that interface. Two routers will not form an adjacency unless they agree on the state of the N-bit. In addition, it is imperative to know that if the N-bit is set in the options field, the E-bit must be reset.

As stated earlier in this chapter, the E-bit is used in External (Type 5) LSAs and specifies the type of external metric. NSSAs do not use E1 and E2 external routes but instead use N1 and N2 external routes. These routes are basically the same as those in External LSAs, but they pertain to NSSAs. N1 routes are comparable to E1 routes and N2 routes are comparable to E2 routes. By default, external NSSA routes are N2 in Cisco IOS software.

The P- (Propagation) bit is used for propagation control and tells the NSSA ABR whether to translate Type 7 LSAs into Type 5 LSAs. If the P-bit is set to 0, then no Type 7 to Type 5 LSA translation will occur. This typically occurs when the NSSA ASBR is also an NSSA ABR.

However, if the P-bit is set to 1, then Type 7 to Type 5 LSA translation will occur. In the event that multiple NSSA ABRs are present, the router with the lowest RID will perform the Type 7 to Type 5 LSA translation. NSSA configuration in Cisco IOS software is a straightforward process. The `area [area ID] nssa [default-information-originate [metric <value> | metric-type <type> | no-redistribution | no-summary | translate type7 suppress-fa]]` router configuration command is used to configure an area as an NSSA. The minimal required configuration would simply be the configuration `area [area ID] nssa` command on all routers within the NSSA.

The `default-information-originate [metric | metric-type]` keyword may be used on either the ABR or the NSSA ASBR. This keyword is used to generate a Type 7 default into the NSSA. The `metric` keyword is used to specific the metric for the default route, and the `metric-type` keyword is used to specify whether the default route should be N1 or N2. By default, external NSSA routes are N2 in Cisco IOS software.

The `no-redistribution` keyword is used on the NSSA ABR to prevent external routes into the NSSA, while allowing external routes into other (normal) OSPF areas. The `no-summary` keyword prevents Summary LSAs from being advertised into the NSSA.

Finally, the `translate type7 suppress-fa` keyword is used to configure OSPF Forwarding Address Suppression in Translated Type-5 LSAs. This configuration instructs the router to suppress the Forwarding Address in translated Type 5 LSAs. This configuration causes the router to be noncompliant with RFC 1587—The OSPF NSSA Option. This configuration is beyond the scope of the ROUTE exam requirements and is not illustrated in this chapter.

The topology shown in Figure 3-19 below will be used to illustrate NSSA configuration:

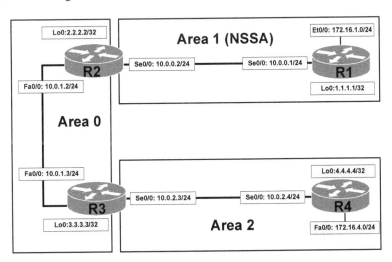

Fig. 3-19. Configuring NSSAs

Referencing the topology illustrated in Figure 3-19, Area 1 will be configured as an NSSA. R1 will also be configured as an ASBR and will redistribute the following static networks:

- 150.100.254.0/24—Next-hop 172.16.1.254
- 150.101.254.0/24—Next-hop 172.16.1.254
- 150.102.254.0/24—Next-hop 172.16.1.254
- 150.103.254.0/24—Next-hop 172.16.1.254

> **NOTE:** It should be assumed that basic OSPF configuration has already been implemented on the other routers in the network and all adjacencies are established. The basic configuration on R1 is performed as follows:

```
R1(config)#ip route 150.100.254.0 255.255.255.0 172.16.1.254
R1(config)#ip route 150.101.254.0 255.255.255.0 172.16.1.254
R1(config)#ip route 150.102.254.0 255.255.255.0 172.16.1.254
R1(config)#ip route 150.103.254.0 255.255.255.0 172.16.1.254
R1(config)#router ospf 1
R1(config-router)#redistribute static subnets
R1(config-router)#area 1 nssa
R1(config-router)#exit
```

Next, R2, the Area Border Router, is configured so that Area 1 is also an NSSA as follows:

```
R2(config)#router ospf 2
R2(config-router)#area 1 nssa
R2(config-router)#exit
```

On R1, the ASBR, the external routes are added to the LSDB as Type 7 External routes as illustrated in the following output:

```
R1#show ip ospf database | begin Type-7
                Type-7 AS External Link States (Area 1)

Link ID         ADV Router      Age        Seq#        Checksum Tag
150.100.254.0   1.1.1.1         78         0x80000001 0x00187C 0
150.101.254.0   1.1.1.1         78         0x80000001 0x000C87 0
150.102.254.0   1.1.1.1         78         0x80000001 0x00FF92 0
150.103.254.0   1.1.1.1         78         0x80000001 0x00F39D 0
```

On R2, the same routes are received as N2 external routes, which is the default. This is illustrated in the following output:

```
R2#show ip route ospf | include N2
O N2    150.102.254.0 [110/20] via 10.0.0.1, 00:05:06, Serial0/0
O N2    150.103.254.0 [110/20] via 10.0.0.1, 00:05:06, Serial0/0
```

```
O N2    150.100.254.0 [110/20] via 10.0.0.1, 00:05:06, Serial0/0
O N2    150.101.254.0 [110/20] via 10.0.0.1, 00:05:06, Serial0/0
```

As the ABR, R2 adds the Type 7 LSAs to the LSDB and generates Type 5 LSAs for each of the Type 7 LSAs. This is illustrated in the following output:

```
R2#show ip ospf database | begin Type-7
            Type-7 AS External Link States (Area 1)

Link ID         ADV Router      Age         Seq#       Checksum Tag
150.100.254.0   1.1.1.1         534         0x80000001 0x0011CA 0
150.101.254.0   1.1.1.1         534         0x80000001 0x0005D5 0
150.102.254.0   1.1.1.1         534         0x80000001 0x00F8E0 0
150.103.254.0   1.1.1.1         534         0x80000001 0x00ECEB 0


            Type-5 AS External Link States

Link ID         ADV Router      Age         Seq#       Checksum Tag
150.100.254.0   2.2.2.2         416         0x80000001 0x00875A 0
150.101.254.0   2.2.2.2         416         0x80000001 0x007B65 0
150.102.254.0   2.2.2.2         416         0x80000001 0x006F70 0
150.103.254.0   2.2.2.2         416         0x80000001 0x00637B 0
```

NOTE: The configuration of the NSSA results in a Type 4 LSA being generated for the ABR. In essence, the ABR becomes an ASBR because it is translating the Type 7 LSAs to Type 5 LSAs. The Type 4 LSA is flooded to all adjacent areas announcing the location of the ASBR. This can be verified on R3, for example, which floods the Type 4 LSA into Area 2. This is illustrated in the following output:

```
R3#show ip ospf database asbr-summary

        OSPF Router with ID (3.3.3.3) (Process ID 3)

        Summary ASB Link States (Area 2)


    LS age: 1121
    Options: (No TOS-capability, DC, Upward)
    LS Type: Summary Links(AS Boundary Router)
    Link State ID: 2.2.2.2 (AS Boundary Router address)
    Advertising Router: 3.3.3.3
    LS Seq Number: 80000006
    Checksum: 0xC45D
    Length: 28
```

```
Network Mask: /0
     TOS: 0  Metric: 1
```

Reverting back to NSSA configuration and validation, the show ip ospf database nssa-exter-nal [link state ID] command is used to view detailed information on the Type 7 LSAs. In the following output, the Forward Address field contains the IP address of the next-hop because the 172.16.1.0/24 network is advertised by OSPF on R1. This is illustrated below:

```
R2#show ip ospf database nssa-external 150.100.254.0

          OSPF Router with ID (2.2.2.2) (Process ID 2)

          Type-7 AS External Link States (Area 1)

  Routing Bit Set on this LSA
  LS age: 659
  Options: (No TOS-capability, Type 7/5 translation, DC)
  LS Type: AS External Link
  Link State ID: 150.100.254.0 (External Network Number)
  Advertising Router: 1.1.1.1
  LS Seq Number: 80000001
  Checksum: 0x11CA
  Length: 36
  Network Mask: /24
        Metric Type: 2 (Larger than any Link State path)
        TOS: 0
        Metric: 20
        Forward Address: 172.16.1.254
        External Route Tag: 0
```

The same Forward Address is also used in the Type 5 LSAs generated by R2 as illustrated below:

```
R4#show ip ospf database external 150.100.254.0

          OSPF Router with ID (4.4.4.4) (Process ID 4)

          Type-5 AS External Link States

  Routing Bit Set on this LSA
  LS age: 636
  Options: (No TOS-capability, DC)
  LS Type: AS External Link
  Link State ID: 150.100.254.0 (External Network Number)
  Advertising Router: 2.2.2.2
```

```
LS Seq Number: 80000001
Checksum: 0x875A
Length: 36
Network Mask: /24
        Metric Type: 2 (Larger than any Link State path)
        TOS: 0
        Metric: 20
        Forward Address: 172.16.1.254
        External Route Tag: 0
```

However, if the 172.16.1.0/24 subnet was not advertised by OSPF, the Forward Address field would default to the highest Loopback address of R1 for the Type 7 LSA. This value would also be included in the Type 5 LSAs generated by R2 and flooded to the rest of the OSPF domain as illustrated in the following output:

```
R2#show ip ospf database nssa-external 150.100.254.0

                OSPF Router with ID (2.2.2.2) (Process ID 2)

                Type-7 AS External Link States (Area 1)

    Routing Bit Set on this LSA
    LS age: 13
    Options: (No TOS-capability, Type 7/5 translation, DC)
    LS Type: AS External Link
    Link State ID: 150.100.254.0 (External Network Number)
    Advertising Router: 1.1.1.1
    LS Seq Number: 80000008
    Checksum: 0xA83
    Length: 36
    Network Mask: /24
        Metric Type: 2 (Larger than any Link State path)
        TOS: 0
        Metric: 20
        Forward Address: 1.1.1.1
        External Route Tag: 0
```

The same Forward Address is also used in the Type 5 LSAs generated by R2 as illustrated below:

```
R4#show ip ospf database external 150.100.254.0

                OSPF Router with ID (4.4.4.4) (Process ID 4)

                Type-5 AS External Link States
    Routing Bit Set on this LSA
```

```
LS age: 45
Options: (No TOS-capability, DC)
LS Type: AS External Link
Link State ID: 150.100.254.0 (External Network Number)
Advertising Router: 2.2.2.2
LS Seq Number: 80000008
Checksum: 0x8013
Length: 36
Network Mask: /24
        Metric Type: 2 (Larger than any Link State path)
        TOS: 0
        Metric: 20
        Forward Address: 1.1.1.1
        External Route Tag: 0
```

While the ABR translates Type 7 LSAs into Type 5 LSAs and floods the Type 5 LSAs to adjacent areas, because external routes (Type 5) are not permitted in NSSAs, the ABR will not translate Type 5 LSAs into Type 7 LSAs and flood them into the NSSA. For example, referencing the network topology illustrated in Figure 3-19, R4 is configured with an additional Loopback interface, which is then redistributed into OSPF to generate a Type 5 LSA. This is performed as illustrated in the following output:

```
R4(config)#interface loopback 144
R4(config-if)#ip address 144.144.144.4 255.255.255.255
R4(config-if)#exit
R4(config)#router ospf 4
R4(config-router)#redistribute connected subnets
R4(config-router)#exit
```

The Type 5 LSA is flooded throughout the OSPF domain and is present in the LSDB on R2 as illustrated in the following output:

```
R2#show ip ospf database | begin Type-7
            Type-7 AS External Link States (Area 1)

Link ID         ADV Router      Age         Seq#        Checksum Tag
150.100.254.0   1.1.1.1         583         0x80000003 0x00147E 0
150.101.254.0   1.1.1.1         583         0x80000003 0x000889 0
150.102.254.0   1.1.1.1         583         0x80000003 0x00FB94 0
150.103.254.0   1.1.1.1         583         0x80000003 0x00EF9F 0


            Type-5 AS External Link States
```

```
Link ID           ADV Router        Age       Seq#        Checksum Tag
144.144.144.4     4.4.4.4           15        0x80000001  0x00F2E7 0
150.100.254.0     2.2.2.2           411       0x80000003  0x008A0E 0
150.101.254.0     2.2.2.2           411       0x80000003  0x007E19 0
150.102.254.0     2.2.2.2           411       0x80000003  0x007224 0
150.103.254.0     2.2.2.2           411       0x80000003  0x00662F 0
```

However, while the ABR (R2) will flood Summary LSAs into the NSSA, R2 will not flood the Type 5 LSA into the NSSA. This is illustrated in the following output on R1:

```
R1#show ip ospf database

        OSPF Router with ID (1.1.1.1) (Process ID 1)

        Router Link States (Area 1)

Link ID           ADV Router        Age       Seq#        Checksum Link Count
1.1.1.1           1.1.1.1           1133      0x80000006  0x002E2F 3
2.2.2.2           2.2.2.2           962       0x80000008  0x00B9B0 2

        Summary Net Link States (Area 1)

Link ID           ADV Router        Age       Seq#        Checksum
2.2.2.2           2.2.2.2           1721      0x80000005  0x009889
3.3.3.3           2.2.2.2           1721      0x80000005  0x0074A8
4.4.4.4           2.2.2.2           1067      0x80000001  0x00D00C
10.0.1.0          2.2.2.2           1721      0x80000005  0x0067B7
10.0.2.0          2.2.2.2           1721      0x80000005  0x00DEFE
172.16.4.0        2.2.2.2           1721      0x80000005  0x00CF58

        Type-7 AS External Link States (Area 1)

Link ID           ADV Router        Age       Seq#        Checksum Tag
150.100.254.0     1.1.1.1           1133      0x80000003  0x00147E 0
150.101.254.0     1.1.1.1           1133      0x80000003  0x000889 0
150.102.254.0     1.1.1.1           1134      0x80000003  0x00FB94 0
150.103.254.0     1.1.1.1           1134      0x80000003  0x00EF9F 0
```

Based on the contents of the LSDB, R1 will not be able to reach the 144.144.144.4/32 address redistributed into OSPF on R4 for the following reasons:

- Because external routes are not advertised into an NSSA
- Because the ABR does not generate a default route for an NSSA by default

The first reason is based on the design of the protocol. This cannot be changed. However, the second reason is one that can be addressed by issuing the `area [area id] default-information-originate [metric | metric-type]` configuration command on the ABR. This configuration causes the ABR to generate a Type 7 default route into the NSSA. Referencing the network topology illustrated in Figure 3-19, this configuration would be implemented on R2 as follows:

```
R2(config)#router ospf 2
R2(config-router)#area 1 nssa default-information-originate
R2(config-router)#exit
```

The default route is added to the LSDB on R2 as a Type 7 LSA. This route will be generated as a Type 2 (N2) external route with a route metric of 1 and will be flooded only into the NSSA. In addition, the Forward Address will be 0.0.0.0, indicating that the traffic should be forwarded to R2. This is illustrated in the following output:

```
R2#show ip ospf database nssa-external 0.0.0.0

            OSPF Router with ID (2.2.2.2) (Process ID 2)

            Type-7 AS External Link States (Area 1)

  LS age: 64
  Options: (No TOS-capability, No Type 7/5 translation, DC)
  LS Type: AS External Link
  Link State ID: 0.0.0.0 (External Network Number)
  Advertising Router: 2.2.2.2
  LS Seq Number: 80000001
  Checksum: 0xD0D8
  Length: 36
  Network Mask: /0
        Metric Type: 2 (Larger than any Link State path)
        TOS: 0
        Metric: 1
        Forward Address: 0.0.0.0
        External Route Tag: 0
```

The same information is also reflected in the LSDB on R1 as illustrated in the following output:

```
R1#show ip ospf database nssa-external 0.0.0.0

            OSPF Router with ID (1.1.1.1) (Process ID 1)

            Type-7 AS External Link States (Area 1)
```

```
Routing Bit Set on this LSA
LS age: 509
Options: (No TOS-capability, No Type 7/5 translation, DC)
LS Type: AS External Link
Link State ID: 0.0.0.0 (External Network Number)
Advertising Router: 2.2.2.2
LS Seq Number: 80000001
Checksum: 0xD0D8
Length: 36
Network Mask: /0
      Metric Type: 2 (Larger than any Link State path)
      TOS: 0
      Metric: 1
      Forward Address: 0.0.0.0
      External Route Tag: 0
```

The default route is installed into the routing table and R1 is able to ping the external network that was redistributed into OSPF on R4 as illustrated below:

```
R1#show ip route 0.0.0.0
Routing entry for 0.0.0.0/0, supernet
  Known via "ospf 1", distance 110, metric 1, candidate default path, type
NSSA extern 2, forward metric 64
  Last update from 10.0.0.2 on Serial0/0, 00:05:56 ago
  Routing Descriptor Blocks:
  * 10.0.0.2, from 2.2.2.2, 00:05:56 ago, via Serial0/0
      Route metric is 1, traffic share count is 1
```

NOTE: The Forward Metric shown in the output above is the cost from R1 to R2. The actual route metric itself never changes for a Type 2 external route.

When the area [area ID] nssa default-information-originate router configuration command is issued on R2, it effectively becomes an ASBR and a Type 4 LSA is generated for this router. A Type 4 LSA would also be generated for R4 because it is redistributing external routes into OSPF. However, a Type 4 LSA will not be generated for the NSSA ASBR. Both Type 4 LSAs will be listed in the LSDB on R3 as illustrated in the following output:

```
R3#show ip ospf database

          OSPF Router with ID (3.3.3.3) (Process ID 3)

          Router Link States (Area 0)
```

```
Link ID          ADV Router      Age        Seq#        Checksum Link Count
2.2.2.2          2.2.2.2         186        0x8000000A  0x005A88 2
3.3.3.3          3.3.3.3         536        0x8000000D  0x003E96 2

                 Net Link States (Area 0)

Link ID          ADV Router      Age        Seq#        Checksum
10.0.1.3         3.3.3.3         536        0x80000007  0x0058AD

                 Summary Net Link States (Area 0)

Link ID          ADV Router      Age        Seq#        Checksum
1.1.1.1          2.2.2.2         1441       0x80000005  0x00A348
4.4.4.4          3.3.3.3         1769       0x80000003  0x00FEDE
10.0.0.0         2.2.2.2         186        0x80000007  0x0041A3
10.0.2.0         3.3.3.3         536        0x80000007  0x000DD1
172.16.4.0       3.3.3.3         281        0x80000007  0x00FD2B

                 Summary ASB Link States (Area 0)

Link ID          ADV Router      Age        Seq#        Checksum
4.4.4.4          3.3.3.3         1769       0x80000003  0x00E6F6

                 Router Link States (Area 2)

Link ID          ADV Router      Age        Seq#        Checksum Link Count
3.3.3.3          3.3.3.3         537        0x80000009  0x0078DF 2
4.4.4.4          4.4.4.4         1747       0x80000010  0x0071E6 4

                 Summary Net Link States (Area 2)

Link ID          ADV Router      Age        Seq#        Checksum
1.1.1.1          3.3.3.3         1523       0x80000005  0x008F57
2.2.2.2          3.3.3.3         537        0x80000007  0x00DA46
3.3.3.3          3.3.3.3         537        0x80000007  0x00A27B
10.0.0.0         3.3.3.3         537        0x80000007  0x002DB2
10.0.1.0         3.3.3.3         537        0x80000007  0x009F7F

                 Summary ASB Link States (Area 2)

Link ID          ADV Router      Age        Seq#        Checksum
2.2.2.2          3.3.3.3         537        0x80000006  0x00C45D

                 Type-5 AS External Link States

Link ID          ADV Router      Age        Seq#        Checksum Tag
```

144.144.144.4	4.4.4.4	1230	0x80000003 0x00EEE9 0
150.100.254.0	2.2.2.2	1448	0x80000005 0x008610 0
150.101.254.0	2.2.2.2	1448	0x80000005 0x007A1B 0
150.102.254.0	2.2.2.2	1448	0x80000005 0x006E26 0
150.103.254.0	2.2.2.2	1448	0x80000005 0x006231 0

Totally Not-so-stubby Areas (TNSSAs)

Totally Not-so-stubby Areas (TNSSAs) are an extension of NSSAs. Like NSSAs, Type 5 LSAs are not allowed into a TNSSA. However, unlike NSSAs, Summary LSAs are not allowed into a TNSSA. In addition, when a TNSSA is configured, the default route is injected into the area as a Type 7 LSA. TNSSAs have the following characteristics:

- Type 7 LSAs are converted into Type 5 LSAs at the NSSA ABR
- They do not allow Network Summary LSAs
- They do not allow External LSAs
- The default route is injected as a Summary LSA

The no-summary keyword is used to configure an NSSA. This configuration prevents Network Summary LSAs from being advertised into the area. By default, when an area is configured as an NSSA, Network Summary LSAs are still flooded into the area. Referencing the topology illustrated in Figure 3-19, assuming that Area 1 is still configured as an NSSA, the Type 3 LSAs will still be flooded by R2 (ABR) into this area and can be seen on R1 as follows:

```
R1#show ip ospf database

        OSPF Router with ID (1.1.1.1) (Process ID 1)

        Router Link States (Area 1)

Link ID         ADV Router      Age      Seq#       Checksum Link Count
1.1.1.1         1.1.1.1         555      0x8000000C 0x002235 3
2.2.2.2         2.2.2.2         791      0x8000000C 0x00B1B4 2

        Summary Net Link States (Area 1)

Link ID         ADV Router      Age      Seq#       Checksum
2.2.2.2         2.2.2.2         15       0x80000001 0x00A085
3.3.3.3         2.2.2.2         15       0x80000001 0x007CA4
4.4.4.4         2.2.2.2         15       0x80000001 0x00D00C
10.0.1.0        2.2.2.2         15       0x80000001 0x006FB3
10.0.2.0        2.2.2.2         15       0x80000001 0x00E6FA
172.16.4.0      2.2.2.2         15       0x80000001 0x00D754

        Type-7 AS External Link States (Area 1)
```

```
Link ID         ADV Router      Age       Seq#        Checksum Tag
150.100.254.0   1.1.1.1         555       0x80000009 0x000884 0
150.101.254.0   1.1.1.1         555       0x80000009 0x00FB8F 0
150.102.254.0   1.1.1.1         557       0x80000009 0x00EF9A 0
150.103.254.0   1.1.1.1         557       0x80000009 0x00E3A5 0
```

To configure Area 1 as a TNSSA and prevent Summary LSAs from being advertised into the area, R2 (ABR) would be configured as follows:

```
R2(config)#router ospf 2
R2(config-router)#area 1 nssa no-summary
R2(config-router)#exit
```

When this configuration is implemented, R2 generates and advertises a default route into the area as a Type 3 LSA. All other Summary LSAs are not flooded into the area. This can be validated by checking the LSDB on R1 as illustrated in the following output:

```
R1#show ip ospf database

         OSPF Router with ID (1.1.1.1) (Process ID 1)

         Router Link States (Area 1)

Link ID         ADV Router      Age       Seq#        Checksum Link Count
1.1.1.1         1.1.1.1         684       0x8000000C 0x002235 3
2.2.2.2         2.2.2.2         920       0x8000000C 0x00B1B4 2

         Summary Net Link States (Area 1)

Link ID         ADV Router      Age       Seq#        Checksum
0.0.0.0         2.2.2.2         12        0x80000001 0x00FC31

         Type-7 AS External Link States (Area 1)

Link ID         ADV Router      Age       Seq#        Checksum Tag
150.100.254.0   1.1.1.1         684       0x80000009 0x000884 0
150.101.254.0   1.1.1.1         684       0x80000009 0x00FB8F 0
150.102.254.0   1.1.1.1         684       0x80000009 0x00EF9A 0
150.103.254.0   1.1.1.1         684       0x80000009 0x00E3A5 0
```

The Link State ID for the default route will be set to 0.0.0.0. In addition, the route uses a default metric value of 1 as illustrated in the following output on R1:

```
R1#show ip ospf database summary 0.0.0.0

          OSPF Router with ID (1.1.1.1) (Process ID 1)

          Summary Net Link States (Area 1)

   Routing Bit Set on this LSA
   LS age: 115
   Options: (No TOS-capability, DC, Upward)
   LS Type: Summary Links(Network)
   Link State ID: 0.0.0.0 (summary Network Number)
   Advertising Router: 2.2.2.2
   LS Seq Number: 80000001
   Checksum: 0xFC31
   Length: 28
   Network Mask: /0
         TOS: 0  Metric: 1
```

NOTE: The same entry is also installed into the LSDB on R2 for Area 1. In addition, it is important to remember that while the default route generated when the `area [area ID] nssa default-information-originate` router configuration command is used in NSSA configuration will be a Type 2 External NSSA route, the default route flooded into the area when a TNSSA is configured will be marked as an inter-area route, not an external route as illustrated below on R1:

```
R1#show ip route 0.0.0.0
Routing entry for 0.0.0.0/0, supernet
  Known via "ospf 1", distance 110, metric 65, candidate default path, type
inter area
  Last update from 10.0.0.2 on Serial0/0, 00:05:57 ago
  Routing Descriptor Blocks:
  * 10.0.0.2, from 2.2.2.2, 00:05:57 ago, via Serial0/0
      Route metric is 65, traffic share count is 1
```

Notice that this time the route has a metric of 65. This metric is calculated by adding the metric advertised by R2 (1) and the cost of the link between R1 and R2 (64). To determine the default link cost, use the `show ip ospf interface [name]` command as follows:

```
R1#show ip ospf interface Serial0/0
Serial0/0 is up, line protocol is up
   Internet Address 10.0.0.1/24, Area 1
   Process ID 1, Router ID 1.1.1.1, Network Type POINT_TO_POINT, Cost: 64
   Transmit Delay is 1 sec, State POINT_TO_POINT,
```

```
Timer intervals configured, Hello 10, Dead 40, Wait 40, Retransmit 5
  oob-resync timeout 40
  Hello due in 00:00:06
Index 1/1, flood queue length 0
Next 0x0(0)/0x0(0)
Last flood scan length is 4, maximum is 4
Last flood scan time is 0 msec, maximum is 0 msec
Neighbor Count is 1, Adjacent neighbor count is 1
  Adjacent with neighbor 2.2.2.2
Suppress Hello for 0 neighbor(s)
```

NOTE: OSPF metrics are described in detail later in this chapter.

Stub Areas

Stub areas are somewhat similar to NSSAs with the major exception being that external routes (Type 5 or Type 7) are not allowed into Stub areas. It is important to understand that Stub functionality in OSPF and EIGRP is not at all similar. In OSPF, the configuration of an area as a Stub area reduces the size of the routing table and the OSPF database for the routers within the Stub area by preventing external LSAs from being advertised into such areas without any further configuration. Stub areas have the following characteristics:

- The default route is injected into the Stub area by the ABR as a Type 3 LSA
- Type 3 LSAs from other areas are permitted into these areas
- External route LSAs (i.e., Type 4 and Type 5 LSAs) are not allowed

NOTE: Because Type 5 LSAs are not allowed into Stub areas, this negates the need to advertise Type 4 LSAs, which advertise the ASBR. Therefore, Type 4 LSAs are essentially also filtered from Stub areas. While we know that Type 5 LSAs are used for external routes, Type 4 LSAs should also be implied, because, as was stated earlier in this chapter, Type 1, Type 2, and Type 3 LSAs are used for internal route calculation, while Type 4, Type 5, and Type 7 LSAs are used for external route calculation.

In Cisco IOS software, Stub areas are configured using the `area [area ID] stub [no-summary]` router configuration command. The `no-summary` keyword prevents Summary LSAs from being flooded into the area. If this keyword is used, the area becomes a Totally Stubby Area (TSA). TSAs are described in the following section.

The topology shown in Figure 3-20 below will be used to illustrate Stub area configuration:

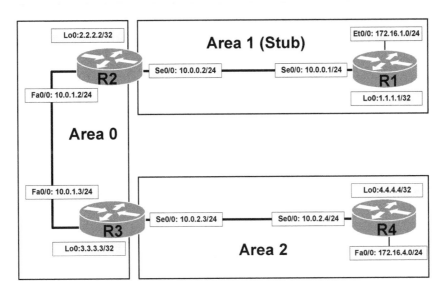

Fig. 3-20. Configuring Stub Areas

Referencing the topology illustrated in Figure 3-20, Area 1 is configured as a Stub area by issuing the `area 1 stub` router configuration commands on R1 and R2 as follows:

```
R1(config)#router ospf 1
R1(config-router)#area 1 stub
R1(config-router)#exit

R2(config)#router ospf 2
R2(config-router)#area 1 stub
R2(config-router)#exit
```

Following this configuration, the ABR (R2) generates a default route into the Stub area. This is generated as a Type 3 LSA and is flooded only into the Stub area as illustrated below:

```
R2#show ip ospf database summary 0.0.0.0

        OSPF Router with ID (2.2.2.2) (Process ID 2)

            Summary Net Link States (Area 1)

  LS age: 199
  Options: (No TOS-capability, DC, Upward)
  LS Type: Summary Links(Network)
  Link State ID: 0.0.0.0 (summary Network Number)
  Advertising Router: 2.2.2.2
  LS Seq Number: 80000004
  Checksum: 0x6FC3
```

```
Length: 28
Network Mask: /0
      TOS: 0  Metric: 1
```

By default, the route is assigned a metric of 1. In addition, the route is generated as an inter-area route as illustrated below in the output of the show ip route command on R1:

```
R1#show ip route 0.0.0.0
Routing entry for 0.0.0.0/0, supernet
  Known via "ospf 1", distance 110, metric 65, candidate default path, type
inter area
  Last update from 10.0.0.2 on Serial0/0, 00:04:47 ago
  Routing Descriptor Blocks:
  * 10.0.0.2, from 2.2.2.2, 00:04:47 ago, via Serial0/0
      Route metric is 65, traffic share count is 1
```

This external route is used by routers in the Stub area to reach external destinations because Type 5 LSAs are not flooded into Stub areas. However, Type 3 LSAs are still permitted. This can be validated by viewing the LSDB on R1 as illustrated in the following output:

```
R1#show ip ospf database

            OSPF Router with ID (1.1.1.1) (Process ID 1)

            Router Link States (Area 1)

Link ID         ADV Router      Age       Seq#        Checksum Link Count
1.1.1.1         1.1.1.1         1829      0x80000011  0x008AD1 3
2.2.2.2         2.2.2.2         85        0x80000012  0x001852 2

            Summary Net Link States (Area 1)

Link ID         ADV Router      Age       Seq#        Checksum
0.0.0.0         2.2.2.2         85        0x80000005  0x006DC4
2.2.2.2         2.2.2.2         85        0x80000003  0x001517
3.3.3.3         2.2.2.2         85        0x80000003  0x00F036
4.4.4.4         2.2.2.2         85        0x80000003  0x00459D
10.0.1.0        2.2.2.2         85        0x80000003  0x00E345
10.0.2.0        2.2.2.2         85        0x80000003  0x005B8C
172.16.4.0      2.2.2.2         85        0x80000003  0x004CE5
```

If, for example, router R4 was configured as an ASBR by redistributing routes into OSPF, while the Type 4 and Type 5 LSAs would be propagated to R2, neither would be flooded into the Stub area. The LSDB of R2 would show the following entries:

```
R2#show ip ospf database asbr-summary

            OSPF Router with ID (2.2.2.2) (Process ID 2)

            Summary ASB Link States (Area 0)

  Routing Bit Set on this LSA
  LS age: 763
  Options: (No TOS-capability, DC, Upward)
  LS Type: Summary Links(AS Boundary Router)
  Link State ID: 4.4.4.4 (AS Boundary Router address)
  Advertising Router: 3.3.3.3
  LS Seq Number: 80000008
  Checksum: 0xDCFB
  Length: 28
  Network Mask: /0
        TOS: 0  Metric: 64


R2#show ip ospf database external

            OSPF Router with ID (2.2.2.2) (Process ID 2)

            Type-5 AS External Link States

  Routing Bit Set on this LSA
  LS age: 189
  Options: (No TOS-capability, DC)
  LS Type: AS External Link
  Link State ID: 144.144.144.4 (External Network Number)
  Advertising Router: 4.4.4.4
  LS Seq Number: 80000008
  Checksum: 0xE4EE
  Length: 36
  Network Mask: /32
        Metric Type: 2 (Larger than any Link State path)
        TOS: 0
        Metric: 20
        Forward Address: 0.0.0.0
        External Route Tag: 0
```

However, neither would be flooded into Area 1 because of the following Stub configuration:

```
R1#show ip ospf database

            OSPF Router with ID (1.1.1.1) (Process ID 1)
```

```
                Router Link States (Area 1)

  Link ID          ADV Router      Age          Seq#         Checksum Link Count
  1.1.1.1          1.1.1.1         233          0x80000012 0x0088D2 3
  2.2.2.2          2.2.2.2         524          0x80000012 0x001852 2


                Summary Net Link States (Area 1)

  Link ID          ADV Router      Age          Seq#         Checksum
  0.0.0.0          2.2.2.2         524          0x80000005 0x006DC4
  2.2.2.2          2.2.2.2         524          0x80000003 0x001517
  3.3.3.3          2.2.2.2         524          0x80000003 0x00F036
  4.4.4.4          2.2.2.2         524          0x80000003 0x00459D
  10.0.1.0         2.2.2.2         524          0x80000003 0x00E345
  10.0.2.0         2.2.2.2         524          0x80000003 0x005B8C
                   2.2.2.2         524     0x80000003 0x004CE5
```

Totally Stubby Areas

Totally Stubby Areas (TSAs) are an extension of Stub areas. However, unlike Stub areas, TSAs further reduce the size of the LSDB on routers in the TSA by restricting Type 3 LSAs in addition to the external LSAs. TSAs are typically configured on routers that have a single ingress and egress point into the network, for example in a traditional hub-and-spoke network. The area routers forward all external traffic to the ABR. The ABR is also the exit point for all backbone and inter-area traffic to the TSA, which has the following characteristics:

- The default route is injected into Stub areas as a Type 3 Network Summary LSA
- Type 3, Type 4, and Type 5 LSAs from other areas are not permitted into these areas

Totally Stubby Areas are configured by issuing the area [area ID] stub no-summary command on the ABR. Referencing the topology illustrated in Figure 3-20, Area 1 would be configured as a TSA by configuring R2 (ABR) as follows:

```
R2(config)#router ospf 2
R2(config-router)#area 1 stub no-summary
R2(config-router)#exit
```

This configuration results in a single Type 3 LSA (default route) being flooded into Area 1; however, all other Type 3 LSAs are suppressed as illustrated in the following output:

```
R1#show ip ospf database

           OSPF Router with ID (1.1.1.1) (Process ID 1)
                Router Link States (Area 1)
```

```
Link ID          ADV Router      Age        Seq#        Checksum Link Count
1.1.1.1          1.1.1.1         1288       0x80000012 0x0088D2 3
2.2.2.2          2.2.2.2         1579       0x80000012 0x001852 2

                 Summary Net Link States (Area 1)

Link ID          ADV Router      Age        Seq#        Checksum
0.0.0.0          2.2.2.2         581        0x80000006 0x006BC5
```

The default route is advertised as an inter-area route with a default metric of 1. The cumulative metric is calculated on R1 by adding the default metric (1) to the cost of the link between R1 and R2 (64). This is illustrated in the following output:

```
R1#show ip route 0.0.0.0
Routing entry for 0.0.0.0/0, supernet
  Known via "ospf 1", distance 110, metric 65, candidate default path, type
inter area
  Last update from 10.0.0.2 on Serial0/0, 00:09:55 ago
  Routing Descriptor Blocks:
  * 10.0.0.2, from 2.2.2.2, 00:09:55 ago, via Serial0/0
      Route metric is 65, traffic share count is 1
```

Now that we have a solid understanding of the configuration of the different types of areas that are described in this section, it is important to understand where and when to use such configurations. NSSAs should be used on Stub routers (e.g., in the spoke routers in hub-and-spoke networks) when you want to import (redistribute) external routes into OSPF. These routes may be static routes, connected routes, or even routes from another routing protocol.

Because external routing information (Type 4 and Type 5) is not allowed into the NSSA, this reduces the size of the LSDB. In addition, the TNSSA prevents the flooding of Network Summary LSAs into the TNSSA, further reducing the size of the LSDB.

Stub areas should be configured when connecting to Stub routers. Unlike NSSAs, Stub areas do not allow any external routes. While Stub areas reduce the overall size of the LSDB for routers in those areas, they do have some limitations with which you are expected to be familiar. These limitations are as follows:

- You cannot include an ASBR in a Stub area because external routes are not allowed
- All routers in the Stub area must be configured as Stub routers
- You cannot configure a virtual link across a Stub area
- The OSPF backbone area (Area 0) cannot be configured as a Stub area

ROUTE METRICS AND BEST ROUTE SELECTION

In this section, we will learn about the OSPF metric and how it is calculated. We will also learn about inter-area and intra-area routes and how OSPF routers select the best route to the destination network. Finally, at the end of the section, we will look at the ways in which metric calculation can be influenced and the effects of such configurations.

Calculating the OSPF Metric

The OSPF metric is commonly referred to as the cost. The cost is derived from the bandwidth of a link using the formula 10^8/bandwidth (in bps). This means that different links are assigned different cost values, depending on their bandwidth. Using this formula, the OSPF cost of a 10Mbps Ethernet interface would be calculated as follows:

- Cost = 10^8/bandwidth (bps)
- Cost = 100 000 000/10 000 000
- Cost = 10

Using the same formula, the OSPF cost of a T1 link would be calculated as follows:

- Cost = 10^8/bandwidth (bps)
- Cost = 100 000 000/1 544 000
- Cost = 64.77

> **NOTE:** When calculating the OSPF metric, point math is not used. Therefore, any such values are always rounded down to the nearest integer. Regarding the previous example, the actual cost for a T1 link would be rounded down to 64.

The OSPF cost of an interface can be viewed using the show ip ospf interface [name] command as was illustrated in the previous section. The default reference bandwidth used in metric calculation can be viewed in the output of the show ip protocols command as is illustrated in the following output:

```
R4#show ip protocols
Routing Protocol is "ospf 4"
  Outgoing update filter list for all interfaces is not set
  Incoming update filter list for all interfaces is not set
  Router ID 4.4.4.4
  Number of areas in this router is 1. 1 normal 0 stub 0 nssa
  Maximum path: 4
  Routing for Networks:
    0.0.0.0 255.255.255.255 Area 2
  Reference bandwidth unit is 100 mbps
  Routing Information Sources:
```

```
Gateway          Distance      Last Update
3.3.3.3               110      00:00:03
Distance: (default is 110)
```

The default reference bandwidth used in OSPF cost calculation can be adjusted using the `auto-cost reference-bandwidth <1-4294967>` router configuration command and specifying the reference bandwidth value in Mbps. This is particularly important in networks that have links that have a bandwidth value over 100Mbps, for example, GigabitEthernet links. In such networks, the default value assigned to the GigabitEthernet link would be the same as that of a FastEthernet link. In most cases, this is certainly not desirable, especially if OSPF attempts to load-balance across both links.

To prevent this skewed calculation of cost value, the `auto-cost reference-bandwidth 1000` router configuration command should be issued on the router. This results in a recalculation of cost values on the router using the new reference bandwidth value. For example, following this configuration, the cost of a T1 link would be recalculated as follows:

- Cost = 10^9/bandwidth (bps)
- Cost = 1 000 000 000/1 544 000
- Cost = 647.66

NOTE: Again, because the OSPF metric does not support point values, this would be rounded down to a metric value of simply 647 as illustrated in the following output:

```
R4#show ip ospf interface Serial0/0
Serial0/0 is up, line protocol is up
  Internet Address 10.0.2.4/24, Area 2
  Process ID 4, Router ID 4.4.4.4, Network Type POINT_TO_POINT, Cost: 647
  Transmit Delay is 1 sec, State POINT_TO_POINT
  Timer intervals configured, Hello 10, Dead 60, Wait 60, Retransmit 5
    oob-resync timeout 60
    Hello due in 00:00:01
  Supports Link-local Signaling (LLS)
  Index 2/2, flood queue length 0
  Next 0x0(0)/0x0(0)
  Last flood scan length is 1, maximum is 1
  Last flood scan time is 0 msec, maximum is 0 msec
  Neighbor Count is 0, Adjacent neighbor count is 0
  Suppress Hello for 0 neighbor(s)
```

When the `auto-cost reference-bandwidth 1000` router configuration command is issued, Cisco IOS software prints the following message indicating that this same value should be applied to all routers within the OSPF domain. This is illustrated in the following output:

```
R4(config)#router ospf 4
R4(config-router)#auto-cost reference-bandwidth 1000
% OSPF: Reference bandwidth is changed.
        Please ensure reference bandwidth is consistent across all routers.
```

While this may seem like an important warning, keep in mind that the use of this command simply affects the local router. It is not mandatory to configure it on all routers; however, for exam purposes, ensure that a consistent configuration is implemented on all routers.

Intra-Area Route Metric Calculation

Intra-area routes (Type 1 and Type 2 LSAs) are routes within a single OSPF area. In Cisco IOS software, these routes are preceded by an O in the output of the show ip route command. This is illustrated in the following output:

```
R2#show ip route ospf
      1.0.0.0/32 is subnetted, 1 subnets
O        1.1.1.1 [110/65] via 10.0.0.1, 02:34:40, Serial0/0
      3.0.0.0/32 is subnetted, 1 subnets
O        3.3.3.3 [110/2] via 10.0.1.3, 02:34:40, FastEthernet0/0
      4.0.0.0/32 is subnetted, 1 subnets
```

The metric for intra-area routes is calculated by adding the cumulative cost of all links from the router to the destination network or link. To better understand this concept, refer to the network topology illustrated in Figure 3-21 below:

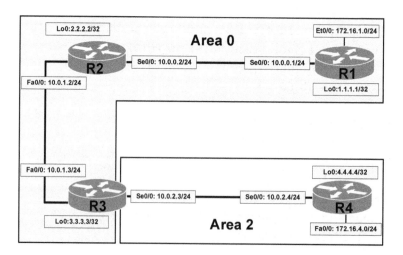

Fig. 3-21. Calculating Intra-Area Route Metrics

Referencing Figure 3-21, R1, R2, and R3 are all backbone routers and reside in Area 0. R1 and R2 are connected via a T1 Serial link (default cost = 64), while R2 and R3 are connected via a FastEthernet link (default cost = 1). To calculate the cost of the intra-area route from R1 to the Loopback interface of R3 (default cost = 1), you would simply add up the cumulative cost values as follows:

- Route Metric = [cost of R1-R2 link + cost of R2-R3 link + cost of Loopback interface]
- Route Metric = [64 + 1 + 1]
- Route Metric = 66

If you did not know the cost of the Loopback interface, or any of the links between R1 and R3, you could derive this value using one of the following two methods:

1. Using the show ip ospf interface [name] command
2. Adding up the metric (cost) values in the LSAs

The show ip ospf interface [name] command includes the OSPF cost for a particular link or interface. Once derived, this would then be added to the cost values of all other transit links between the router and the destination network or link to derive the route metric. The following illustrates the output printed by this command for a Loopback interface:

```
R3#show ip ospf interface Loopback0
Loopback0 is up, line protocol is up
  Internet Address 3.3.3.3/32, Area 0
  Process ID 3, Router ID 3.3.3.3, Network Type LOOPBACK, Cost: 1
  Loopback interface is treated as a stub Host
```

The second method involves a little more work and requires a greater understanding of both the overall network topology and LSDB. While there is no single standard method of using this method, as an example, we could first look at the Type 1 LSAs advertised by R2. This will provide us with all links on this router, which includes the P2P connection between R1 and R2 and the LAN (transit) link between R2 and R3. Both are highlighted in bold below:

```
R1#show ip ospf database router adv-router 2.2.2.2

            OSPF Router with ID (1.1.1.1) (Process ID 1)

            Router Link States (Area 0)

  LS age: 1209
  Options: (No TOS-capability, DC)
  LS Type: Router Links
  Link State ID: 2.2.2.2
```

```
Advertising Router: 2.2.2.2
LS Seq Number: 80000016
Checksum: 0x41DF
Length: 72
Number of Links: 4

  Link connected to: another Router (point-to-point)
   (Link ID) Neighboring Router ID: 1.1.1.1
   (Link Data) Router Interface address: 10.0.0.2
    Number of TOS metrics: 0
     TOS 0 Metrics: 64

  Link connected to: a Stub Network
   (Link ID) Network/subnet number: 10.0.0.0
   (Link Data) Network Mask: 255.255.255.0
    Number of TOS metrics: 0
     TOS 0 Metrics: 64

  Link connected to: a Stub Network
   (Link ID) Network/subnet number: 2.2.2.2
   (Link Data) Network Mask: 255.255.255.255
    Number of TOS metrics: 0
     TOS 0 Metrics: 1

  Link connected to: a Transit Network
   (Link ID) Designated Router address: 10.0.1.3
   (Link Data) Router Interface address: 10.0.1.2
    Number of TOS metrics: 0
     TOS 0 Metrics: 1
```

Noting the metric value of 64 for the P2P link between R1 and R2, and the metric value of 1 for the LAN (transit) link between R2 and R3, next, we can use the same command to view the metric (cost) for the Loopback interface on R3 as follows:

```
R1#show ip ospf database router 3.3.3.3

        OSPF Router with ID (1.1.1.1) (Process ID 1)

            Router Link States (Area 0)

  Routing Bit Set on this LSA
  LS age: 279
  Options: (No TOS-capability, DC)
  LS Type: Router Links
```

```
Link State ID: 3.3.3.3
Advertising Router: 3.3.3.3
LS Seq Number: 80000018
Checksum: 0x28A1
Length: 48
Area Border Router
Number of Links: 2

  Link connected to: a Stub Network
   (Link ID) Network/subnet number: 3.3.3.3
   (Link Data) Network Mask: 255.255.255.255
    Number of TOS metrics: 0
     TOS 0 Metrics: 1

  Link connected to: a Transit Network
   (Link ID) Designated Router address: 10.0.1.3
   (Link Data) Router Interface address: 10.0.1.3
    Number of TOS metrics: 0
     TOS 0 Metrics: 1
```

If we add up the metrics in the LSAs, we would get 64 + 1 + 1 = 66. This is a longer, alternate method of arriving at the metric derived using the simple addition in the first method. However, the second method's advantage is that the more you look at the LSDB, the more familiar you become with the output and the information contained therein, as well as the different commands that you can use to look up different things. Regardless of the method used, the route metric calculated is printed in the output of the show ip route command as follows:

```
R1#show ip route 3.3.3.3 255.255.255.255
Routing entry for 3.3.3.3/32
  Known via "ospf 1", distance 110, metric 66, type intra area
  Last update from 10.0.0.2 on Serial0/0, 00:08:15 ago
  Routing Descriptor Blocks:
  * 10.0.0.2, from 3.3.3.3, 00:08:15 ago, via Serial0/0
      Route metric is 66, traffic share count is 1
```

Inter-Area Route Metric Calculation

Inter-area routes (Type 3 LSAs) are for routes outside of the local area but within the routing domain. Inter-area routes are preceded by an O IA in the output of the show ip route command as illustrated in the following output:

```
R1#show ip route ospf
O IA    4.4.4.4 [110/130] via 10.0.0.2, 00:18:56, Serial0/0
      172.16.0.0/24 is subnetted, 2 subnets
```

```
O IA    172.16.4.0 [110/130] via 10.0.0.2, 00:18:56, Serial0/0
        144.144.0.0/32 is subnetted, 1 subnets
O IA    144.144.144.4 [110/130] via 10.0.0.2, 00:18:56, Serial0/0
        10.0.0.0/24 is subnetted, 3 subnets
O IA    10.0.2.0 [110/129] via 10.0.0.2, 00:18:56, Serial0/0
```

The same basic calculation used in the first method in intra-area route metric calculation can be used to calculate the inter-area cost. However, because Type 3 LSAs provide only a summary of the information contained in other areas, routers cannot use this same basic method. Instead, routers calculate the cost of inter-area routes by adding the cost (metric) included in the Type 3 LSA to the cost of reaching the ABR that originated the LSA. The route metric included in the Type 3 LSA is the ABRs best (lowest) metric to the destination network or host.

Referencing the topology illustrated in Figure 3-21, R1 would calculate the route metric for the 4.4.4.4/32 route on R4 by adding the metric in the Type 3 LSA to the cost of reaching R3 (ABR) from R1. The metric in the Type 3 LSA can be viewed using the show ip ospf database summary adv-router 3.3.3.3 or show ip ospf database summary 4.4.4.4 commands on R1. The output printed by the latter of the two commands is illustrated below:

```
R1#show ip ospf database summary 4.4.4.4

        OSPF Router with ID (1.1.1.1) (Process ID 1)

        Summary Net Link States (Area 0)

    Routing Bit Set on this LSA
    LS age: 1175
    Options: (No TOS-capability, DC, Upward)
    LS Type: Summary Links(Network)
    Link State ID: 4.4.4.4 (summary Network Number)
    Advertising Router: 3.3.3.3
    LS Seq Number: 80000004
    Checksum: 0xFCDF
    Length: 28
    Network Mask: /32
        TOS: 0  Metric: 65
```

In the output above, the LSA is originated by R3, which is listed as the Advertising Router. The metric of 65 is R3's metric to this address. This is derived simply by adding the cost of the connected link (default cost for the Loopback = 1) to the cost of the P2P connection between R3 and R4 (default cost for T1 Serial interface = 64): therefore, 64 + 1 = 65.

Using this information, R1 calculates the route to the same network by adding 65 to the cost of getting from itself to the ABR (R3). Using basic math, we can add the cost of the T1 Serial link between R1 and R2 to the cost of the FastEthernet link between R2 and R3 to 65 and calculate the metric for the 4.4.4.4/32 route on R1 as follows:

- Route Metric = [ABR cost + cost of reaching the ABR]
- Route Metric = [ABR cost + cost of R1-R2 link + cost of R2-R3 link]
- Route Metric = [65 + 64 + 1]
- Route Metric = 130

NOTE: The default cost of a FastEthernet link is 1, and it is 64 for a T1 Serial link

We can validate our calculation by looking at the route metric for this route as printed in the following output of the show ip route command on R1:

```
R1#show ip route 4.4.4.4 255.255.255.255
Routing entry for 4.4.4.4/32
  Known via "ospf 1", distance 110, metric 130, type inter area
  Last update from 10.0.0.2 on Serial0/0, 00:08:42 ago
  Routing Descriptor Blocks:
  * 10.0.0.2, from 3.3.3.3, 00:08:42 ago, via Serial0/0
      Route metric is 130, traffic share count is 1
```

The same logic would also be applicable to the calculation of the 172.16.1.0/24 network that is connected to the Ethernet0/0 interface of R1 from R4. First, R4 would look at the cost to this destination network as advertised by the ABR (R3) as illustrated below:

```
R4#show ip ospf database summary 172.16.1.0

            OSPF Router with ID (4.4.4.4) (Process ID 4)

            Summary Net Link States (Area 2)

  Routing Bit Set on this LSA
  LS age: 723
  Options: (No TOS-capability, DC, Upward)
  LS Type: Summary Links(Network)
  Link State ID: 172.16.1.0 (summary Network Number)
  Advertising Router: 3.3.3.3
  LS Seq Number: 80000001
  Checksum: 0x8F98
  Length: 28
  Network Mask: /24
        TOS: 0  Metric: 75
```

The metric included in the LSA is the ABR's (R3s) metric to this destination network. R4 would calculate its route metric to the same network by adding that metric to the cost of getting from R1 to R3. This calculation is performed as follows:

- Route Metric = [ABR cost + cost of reaching the ABR]
- Route Metric = [ABR cost + cost of R4-R3 link]
- Route Metric = [75 + 64]
- Route Metric = 139

Again, we can validate our calculation by viewing the route metric for this route as printed in the following output of the show ip route command on R4:

```
R4#show ip route 172.16.1.0 255.255.255.0
Routing entry for 172.16.1.0/24
  Known via "ospf 4", distance 110, metric 139, type inter area
  Last update from 10.0.2.3 on Serial0/0, 00:16:52 ago
  Routing Descriptor Blocks:
  * 10.0.2.3, from 3.3.3.3, 00:16:52 ago, via Serial0/0
      Route metric is 139, traffic share count is 1
```

Selecting the Best Routes

When determining the best route, the route with the best metric to the destination network will be selected. However, an important exception to this rule must be remembered. By default, ABRs will always select intra-area routes over inter-area routes, regardless of the metric of the intra-area route. To better understand this concept, consider the network topology illustrated in Figure 3-22 below:

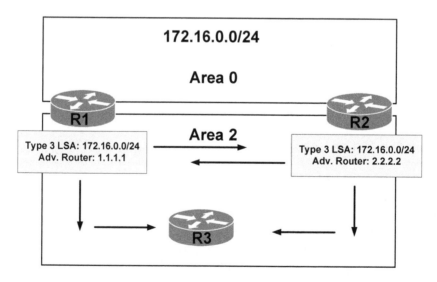

Fig. 3-22. Selecting the Best Route

Figure 3-22 shows a basic OSPF network with two ABRs. Both ABRs generate a Type 3 LSA for the 172.16.0.0/24 subnet in the backbone and flood it into Area 2. R3 receives both LSAs and, based on the route metric calculation, if both paths are equal, load-balances across them both.

Invariably, R1 and R2 also receive the Type 3 LSAs advertised by the opposite ABR. In addition to not flooding inter-area routes into the backbone as was described earlier in this chapter, ABRs will not consider these routes in their own route calculation if they have an intra-area route to the same destination. This happens regardless of the metric of the inter-area route.

Influencing OSPF Metric Calculation

The calculation of the OSPF metric can be directly influenced by performing the following:

- Adjusting the interface bandwidth using the bandwidth command
- Manually specifying a cost using the ip ospf cost command

The use of the bandwidth command was described in the previous chapter when we discussed EIGRP metric calculation. As stated earlier, the default OSPF cost is calculated by dividing the link bandwidth by a reference bandwidth of 10^8 or 100 Mbps. Either incrementing or decrementing the link bandwidth directly affects the OSPF cost for the particular link. This is typically a path control mechanism used to ensure that one path is preferred over another.

However, as was described in the previous chapter, the bandwidth command affects more than just the routing protocol. It is for this reason that the second method, manually specifying a cost value, is the recommended method for influencing OSPF metric calculation.

The ip ospf cost <1-65535> interface configuration command is used to manually specify the cost of a link. The lower the value, the greater the probability that the link will be preferred over other links to the same destination network but with higher cost values. The following example illustrates how to configure an OSPF cost of 5 for a Serial (T1) link:

```
R1(config)#interface Serial0/0
R1(config-if)#ip ospf cost 5
R1(config-if)#exit
```

This configuration can be validated using the show ip ospf interface [name] command as illustrated in the following output:

```
R1#show ip ospf interface Serial0/0
Serial0/0 is up, line protocol is up
  Internet Address 10.0.0.1/24, Area 0
  Process ID 1, Router ID 1.1.1.1, Network Type POINT_TO_POINT, Cost: 5
```

```
Transmit Delay is 1 sec, State POINT_TO_POINT,
Timer intervals configured, Hello 10, Dead 40, Wait 40, Retransmit 5
  oob-resync timeout 40
  Hello due in 00:00:04
Index 2/2, flood queue length 0
Next 0x0(0)/0x0(0)
Last flood scan length is 1, maximum is 4
Last flood scan time is 0 msec, maximum is 0 msec
Neighbor Count is 1, Adjacent neighbor count is 1
  Adjacent with neighbor 2.2.2.2
Suppress Hello for 0 neighbor(s)
```

While manually adjusting the link cost using the ip ospf cost command is a straightforward process, it is very important to understand the underlying operations that are affected by this configuration change. This is described in the following section.

As you may recall, in Chapter 1 we learned that the SPF algorithm creates a shortest-path tree to all hosts in an area or in the network backbone, with the router that is performing the calculation at the root of that tree. As the router goes through the SPF calculation, the node in the TENT set or list that is closest to the root is moved to the PATH or PATHS list or set. This process is repeated until all nodes are in the PATH set and the shortest-path tree is built. Once the tree has been completely built, routes are then derived from the tree.

The router calculates the cost to each node in the tree. This is performed by adding the cost to the PATH node and the cost from the PATH node to the TENT node. When the ip ospf cost command is issued, the change in the cost value requires that the router run the SPF algorithm again to determine the cost to all other nodes in that area. The show ip ospf process [process ID] command can be used to view the number of times the SPF algorithm has been run on a per-area basis as illustrated below:

```
R4#show ip ospf 4
 Routing Process "ospf 4" with ID 4.4.4.4

[Truncated Output]

 Number of areas in this router is 1. 1 normal 0 stub 0 nssa
 Number of areas transit capable is 0
 External flood list length 0
    Area 2
        Number of interfaces in this area is 4 (2 Loopback)
        Area has no authentication
```

```
SPF algorithm last executed 00:05:40.838 ago
SPF algorithm executed 7 times
Area ranges are
Number of LSA 8. Checksum Sum 0x089833
Number of opaque link LSA 0. Checksum Sum 0x000000
Number of DCbitless LSA 0
Number of indication LSA 0
Number of DoNotAge LSA 0
Flood list length 0
```

In the output above, the SPF algorithm has been run 7 times for Area 2 and it was last run almost 6 minutes ago. If we changed the cost of a link in Area 2 using the ip ospf cost interface configuration command, SPF would have to be run again to recalculate the Type 1 and Type 2 LSAs because of the configuration change. As an example, the link cost for Serial0/0 is adjusted using the ip ospf cost interface configuration command as follows:

```
R4(config)#interface Serial0/0
R4(config-if)#ip ospf cost 4
R4(config-if)#exit
```

Based on this change, the following output of the show ip ospf [process ID] command shows that the SPF algorithm has been run again in Area 2:

```
R4#show ip ospf 4
 Routing Process "ospf 4" with ID 4.4.4.4

[Truncated Output]

 Number of areas in this router is 1. 1 normal 0 stub 0 nssa
 Number of areas transit capable is 0
 External flood list length 0
    Area 2
        Number of interfaces in this area is 4 (2 Loopback)
        Area has no authentication
        SPF algorithm last executed 00:00:30.843 ago
        SPF algorithm executed 8 times
        Area ranges are
        Number of LSA 8. Checksum Sum 0x08F5D2
        Number of opaque link LSA 0. Checksum Sum 0x000000
        Number of DCbitless LSA 0
        Number of indication LSA 0
        Number of DoNotAge LSA 0
        Flood list length 0
```

In addition to running on the local router, the SPF algorithm also runs for all other routers in the same area. Depending on the size of the network, the router resource utilization, and other conditions, this can have an adverse impact on the forwarding of traffic in production networks. Ensure that you understand the network topology and potential impact before implementing this configuration command on a network-wide basis.

The show ip ospf statistics [detail] command can be used to view SPF calculation statistics on the local router. When used without the [detail] keyword, the command prints a summary of SPF calculations and the events that triggered the calculations. The information printed by this command is shown in the following output:

```
R4#show ip ospf statistics

               OSPF Router with ID (4.4.4.4) (Process ID 4)

  Area 2: SPF algorithm executed 4 times

  Summary OSPF SPF statistic

  SPF calculation time
Delta T    Intra D-Intra Summ   D-Summ  Ext     D-Ext    Total  Reason
01:42:35   0     0        0      0       0       0        0      X
01:27:08   0     0        0      0       0       0        0      X
01:24:50   0     0        0      0       0       0        0      X
01:24:35   0     0        0      0       0       0        0      X
01:24:25   0     0        0      0       0       0        0      X
01:24:15   0     0        0      0       0       0        0      X
01:19:23   0     0        0      0       0       0        0      X
01:19:13   0     0        0      0       0       0        0      X
00:16:11   0     0        0      0       0       0        0      R, SN,
00:16:01   0     0        0      0       0       0        0      R,

  RIB manipulation time during SPF (in msec):
Delta T     RIB Update    RIB Delete
01:42:35    0             0
01:27:10    0             0
01:24:52    0             0
01:24:37    0             0
01:24:27    0             0
01:24:17    0             0
01:19:25    0             0
01:19:15    0             0
00:16:13    0             0
00:16:03    0             0
```

In the output above, the Reason field lists the reason the SPF calculation was performed. The different values that may be found in this field are listed and described in Table 3-3 below:

Table 3-3. SPF Calculation Reason Codes

Reason Code	Description
R	A change in a Router LSA (Type 1) has occurred
N	A change in a Network LSA (Type 2) has occurred
SN	A change in a Summary Network LSA (Type 3) has occurred
SA	A change in a Summary ASBR LSA (Type 4) has occurred
X	A change in an External Type-7 (NSSA) LSA has occurred

In-depth information on SPF calculation can be viewed by appending the [detail] keyword to the end of the show ip ospf statistics command as illustrated below:

```
R4#show ip ospf statistics detail

        OSPF Router with ID (4.4.4.4) (Process ID 4)

  Area 2: SPF algorithm executed 4 times

SPF 1 executed 02:25:42 ago, SPF type Full
  SPF calculation time (in msec):
  SPT     Intra  D-Intr Summ   D-Summ Ext7   D-Ext7 Total
  0       0      0      0       0      0      0      0
  RIB manipulation time (in msec):
  RIB Update    RIB Delete
  0             0
  LSIDs processed R:1 N:0 Stub:2 SN:2 SA:0 X7:0
  Change record
  LSIDs changed 2
  Changed LSAs. Recorded is LS ID and LS type:
  3.3.3.3(R) 4.4.4.4(R)

SPF 2 executed 02:25:32 ago, SPF type Full
  SPF calculation time (in msec):
  SPT     Intra  D-Intr Summ   D-Summ Ext7   D-Ext7 Total
  0       0      0      0       0      0      0      0
  RIB manipulation time (in msec):
  RIB Update    RIB Delete
  1             0
  LSIDs processed R:2 N:0 Stub:4 SN:6 SA:0 X7:0
```

```
Change record
LSIDs changed 2
Changed LSAs. Recorded is LS ID and LS type:
3.3.3.3(R) 4.4.4.4(R)

SPF 3 executed 00:14:42 ago, SPF type Full
  SPF calculation time (in msec):
  SPT    Intra  D-Intr Summ   D-Summ Ext7   D-Ext7 Total
  0      0      0      0       0      0      0      0
  RIB manipulation time (in msec):
  RIB Update    RIB Delete
  0             0
  LSIDs processed R:2 N:0 Stub:4 SN:5 SA:0 X7:0
  Change record
  LSIDs changed 1
  Changed LSAs. Recorded is LS ID and LS type:
  4.4.4.4(R)
```

Keep in mind that this is not the TSHOOT exam. You are not expected to demonstrate advanced OSPF troubleshooting skills in the ROUTE exam.

OSPF DEFAULT ROUTING

Unlike EIGRP, which supports several different ways of generating and advertising the default route, OSPF uses only the default-information originate [always] [metric <value>] [metric-type <1|2>] [route-map <name>] router configuration command to advertise dynamically the default route.

The default-information originate command used by itself will configure the router to advertise a default route only if a default route is already present in the routing table. However, the always keyword can be appended to this command to force the router to generate a default route even when one does not exist in the routing table. This keyword should be used with caution as it may result in the black-holing of traffic within the OSPF domain or the forwarding of packets for all unknown destinations to the configured router.

The metric <value> keyword is used to specify the route metric for the generated default route. The metric-type <1|2> keyword can be used to change the metric type for the default route. Finally, the route-map <name> keyword configures the router to generate a default route only if the conditions specified in the named route map are met.

NOTE: The configuration of route maps is described in detail later in this guide.

The following configuration example illustrates how to configure an OSPF-enabled router to generate and advertise a default route if one already exists in the routing table. The existing default route can be a static route or even a default route from another routing protocol if multiple routing protocols have been configured on the router. The output below illustrates this configuration based on a configured static default route:

```
R4(config)#ip route 0.0.0.0 0.0.0.0 FastEthernet0/0 172.16.4.254
R4(config)#router ospf 4
R4(config-router)#network 172.16.4.0 0.0.0.255 Area 2
R4(config-router)#default-information originate
R4(config-router)#exit
```

By default, the default route is advertised as a Type 5 LSA. On the local router, the show ip ospf database external command can be used to view the default route parameters as illustrated below:

```
R4#show ip ospf database external 0.0.0.0

            OSPF Router with ID (4.4.4.4) (Process ID 4)

            Type-5 AS External Link States

    LS age: 513
    Options: (No TOS-capability, DC)
    LS Type: AS External Link
    Link State ID: 0.0.0.0 (External Network Number)
    Advertising Router: 4.4.4.4
    LS Seq Number: 80000003
    Checksum: 0x4796
    Length: 36
    Network Mask: /0
          Metric Type: 2 (Larger than any Link State path)
          TOS: 0
          Metric: 1
          Forward Address: 172.16.4.254
          External Route Tag: 4
```

Referencing the output above, the Link State ID for the default route will always be 0.0.0.0. The Advertising Router field will contain the RID of the router (ASBR) that generated the default route. A corresponding Type LSA will be generated for this router.

The Network Mask for the default route will also always be zero, as it represents the 0.0.0.0/0 network. The default metric type assigned to all external OSPF routes will always be 2. The metric is derived from the metric of the interface to which the default route is pointing. Based on the output above, the metric is derived from the cost of the FastEthernet interface, which is 1. The Forward Address field contains the value 172.16.4.254. This field contains a non-zero value because the 172.16.4.0/24 subnet is advertised via OSPF on R4. If the prefix was not advertised via OSPF on R4, this field would reflect a value of 0.0.0.0, which would mean traffic to this destination network should be forwarded to the ASBR.

Finally, the External Route Tag field contains the process ID of the OSPF process that generated this default route, which is 4. All of these values remain consistent as the LSA is propagated throughout the network. This is illustrated in the following output of the show ip ospf database external command on another router that resides within the same OSPF domain:

```
R1#show ip ospf database external 0.0.0.0

            OSPF Router with ID (1.1.1.1) (Process ID 1)

            Type-5 AS External Link States

Routing Bit Set on this LSA
LS age: 818
Options: (No TOS-capability, DC)
LS Type: AS External Link
Link State ID: 0.0.0.0 (External Network Number)
Advertising Router: 4.4.4.4
LS Seq Number: 80000003
Checksum: 0x4796
Length: 36
Network Mask: /0
      Metric Type: 2 (Larger than any Link State path)
      TOS: 0
      Metric: 1
      Forward Address: 172.16.4.254
      External Route Tag: 4
```

The following example illustrates how to generate a default route on a router when a default route does not exist in the routing table:

```
R4(config)#router ospf 4
R4(config-router)#default-information originate always
R4(config-router)#exit
```

Before we validate this configuration, we will ensure that a default route does not presently exist in the routing table. This is performed using the show ip route command as illustrated below:

```
R4#show ip route 0.0.0.0
% Network not in table
```

Using the show ip ospf database external command, we can validate that the router has indeed generated and is advertising a default route, even though none exists in the IP routing table. The output of this command is illustrated as follows:

```
R4#show ip ospf database external 0.0.0.0

            OSPF Router with ID (4.4.4.4) (Process ID 4)

            Type-5 AS External Link States

    LS age: 204
    Options: (No TOS-capability, DC)
    LS Type: AS External Link
    Link State ID: 0.0.0.0 (External Network Number)
    Advertising Router: 4.4.4.4
    LS Seq Number: 80000001
    Checksum: 0xF8A6
    Length: 36
    Network Mask: /0
          Metric Type: 2 (Larger than any Link State path)
          TOS: 0
          Metric: 1
          Forward Address: 0.0.0.0
          External Route Tag: 4
```

The information printed in this output is almost the same as that in the previous output, with the exception of the Forward Address field. This time, the field contains the all-zeros value, indicating that traffic to this destination network should be forwarded to the ASBR (R4). The same is reflected on another router within the same routing domain as illustrated in the following output:

```
R1#show ip ospf database external 0.0.0.0

            OSPF Router with ID (1.1.1.1) (Process ID 1)

            Type-5 AS External Link States

    Routing Bit Set on this LSA
    LS age: 407
    Options: (No TOS-capability, DC)
    LS Type: AS External Link
    Link State ID: 0.0.0.0 (External Network Number)
    Advertising Router: 4.4.4.4
    LS Seq Number: 80000001
```

```
Checksum: 0xF8A6
Length: 36
Network Mask: /0
        Metric Type: 2 (Larger than any Link State path)
        TOS: 0
        Metric: 1
        Forward Address: 0.0.0.0
        External Route Tag: 4
```

OSPF VIRTUAL LINKS

A virtual link is a logical extension of the OSPF backbone. As we learned earlier in this chapter, when implementing a multi-area OSPF network, one area must be designated as the backbone area and all non-backbone areas must be connected to the backbone area. In most cases, a physical link is used to connect the non-backbone area to the backbone area; however, this is not always possible or feasible. In addition to being used to connect areas that have no physical connection to the OSPF backbone, virtual links can also be used for redundancy as well as connecting a discontinuous or partitioned backbone.

Connecting to the Backbone

In multi-area OSPF networks, virtual links are primarily used to connect disconnected non-backbone areas to the backbone. Consider the topology illustrated in Figure 3-23 below:

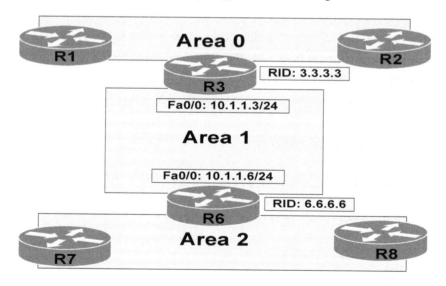

Fig. 3-23. Connecting to the Backbone

Figure 3-23 shows a multi-area OSPF network comprised of three areas, which are Area 0, Area 1, and Area 2. Area 1 is physically connected to the backbone; however, Area 2 is not. Given the OSPF requirement that all non-backbone areas must be connected to the backbone, a virtual link is required to logically connect Area 2 to the backbone. Two conditions must be met before the virtual link is configured, which are as follows:

1. One area must be connected to the backbone area before the virtual link can be created
2. The transit area must be a common area between the two endpoint routers

Because a virtual link is a logical extension of Area 0, the area across which the virtual link is configured must be connected to the backbone as well. If that area were not connected to the backbone, then it too would require a virtual link to connect it to the backbone. The second condition is that the area across which the virtual link traverses (the transit area) must be a common area between the two endpoints of the virtual link. In other words, if R3 and R6 resided in different areas, then the virtual link could not be configured between the two endpoints. This would apply even if R6 were in an area that was connected to the backbone.

The simplest way of remembering what a virtual link is is to think of it as a tunnel between two endpoints that joins disconnected areas to the backbone. In fact, virtual links do operate in a tunnel-like manner, as will be described shortly.

Referencing Figure 3-23, the virtual link across the transit area (Area 1) would be configured between R3 and R6. R3 is the ABR connected to the backbone and R6 is the router that is connected to the disconnected area (Area 2). It is important to understand that until the virtual link is established, R4 is not considered an ABR. Before we move on, it is important to take a moment to understand this statement.

Recall that, at the beginning of this chapter, we learned that an ABR is an OSPF router that connects one or more OSPF areas to the OSPF backbone. This means that it must have at least one interface in Area 0 and another interface, or interfaces, within a different OSPF area. Based on this definition, even though R6 is connected to both Area 1 and Area 2, it is not technically an ABR because it has no interfaces in the backbone area.

Because R6 is not an ABR, it cannot generate Type 3 LSAs for the intra-area (i.e., Type 1 and Type 2) routes in either area and flood those to the adjacent areas as inter-area (i.e., Type 3 LSAs) routes. Given this, Area 1 and Area 0 are oblivious of Area 2, and vice-versa, as Areas 1 and 0 have no inter-area routes for Area 2 and Area 2 has no inter-area routes for Areas 1 and 0. At this point, the OSPF network is considered broken and these different areas cannot communicate.

When the virtual link is established between R3 and R6, Area 0 is extended to R6. Once R6 has this logical connection to the backbone, it considers itself an ABR. R6 therefore generates Type 3 LSAs for all areas it is connected to and floods them to adjacent areas. Areas 0, 1, and 2 now have inter-area routes for all other areas and all subnets in all networks have full connectivity between each other. The network is no longer broken and connectivity is completely restored.

When a virtual link is established, OSPF uses Unicast, not Multicast, to send routing updates between the virtual link endpoints. For example, referencing Figure 3-23, routing updates across the virtual link from R3 to R6 would be tunneled across the virtual link and would be sourced from the FastEthernet0/0 interface of R3, which has the IP address 10.1.1.3, and would have a destination address of 10.1.1.6, which is the FastEthernet0/0 interface of R6.

 REAL WORLD IMPLEMENTATION

When configuring virtual links in production networks, if there is a firewall in the transit area, it is important to ensure that the firewall rules are configured to allow traffic between the two virtual link endpoints. In most cases, simply allowing IP protocol 89 (OSPF) between the two endpoint addresses will suffice; however, depending on the firewall type, more configuration may be required. Make sure you remember this, as it can save you a lot of troubleshooting and heartache in the real world.

While routing protocol updates are tunneled, it is important to know that normal traffic is not tunneled and is not subject to any tunneling overhead. This is the primary advantage of using virtual links. The configuration of virtual links in Cisco IOS software is a straightforward process. This is performed using the `area [transit area] virtual-link [router-id] [hello-interval <seconds>] [retransmit-interval <seconds>] [transmit-delay <seconds>] [dead-interval <seconds>] [ttl-security hops <hop-count>]` router configuration command on the ABR and the router connected to the disconnected area.

When using the `area...virtual-link` router configuration command, the `transit area` refers to the common transit area that the virtual link will traverse. Referencing the topology illustrated in Figure 3-23, the transit area would be Area 1.

The `router-id` specifies the router ID of the end of the virtual link. This address is the actual OSPF RID as seen in the output of the `show ip protocols` or any of the `show ip ospf` commands, not the interface address of the remote endpoint. The specified router ID does not have to be reachable, as the virtual link packets are tunneled using the physical interface addresses as source and destination addresses in the routing protocol updates. Because intra-area routes exist for these interfaces already, the router ID does not have to be reachable.

As an example, even if the router ID was configured using the `router-id <address>` router configuration command, the same value should be used when configuring the virtual link between the routers. If you use the interface address, the virtual link will not be established between the routers. This is often a point of confusion. Ensure that you remember this when you are configuring virtual links in Cisco IOS software.

The `hello-interval <seconds>` keyword can be used to specify a Hello interval for the virtual link endpoints. This value must match on both routers. If this keyword is not used, OSPF will send Hello packets across the virtual link every 10 seconds by default.

The `retransmit-interval <seconds>` keyword is used to specify the time between Link State Advertisement (LSA) retransmissions, and the `transmit-delay <seconds>` keyword specifies the estimated time (in seconds) required to send a link-state update packet on the interface. These advanced configurations are beyond the scope of the ROUTE exam requirements and are not illustrated in the following configuration examples.

The `dead-interval <seconds>` keyword specifies the time after which the neighbor is declared down if a Hello packet has not been received in the value specified. If this is configured, it must be the same on all routers. If not, it defaults to four times the Hello interval, which is 40 seconds. The timer automatically changes when the Hello time is changed.

The `ttl-security hops <hop-count>` keyword configures Time-to-Live (TTL) security on a virtual link. TTL security is used to configure a TTL value for incoming IP packets received from the neighbor. The implementation of this virtual link configuration is beyond the scope of the ROUTE exam requirements and is not illustrated in the following configuration examples.

To reinforce the virtual link fundamentals, the topology illustrated in Figure 3-24 below will be used to demonstrate both the configuration and the validation of virtual links:

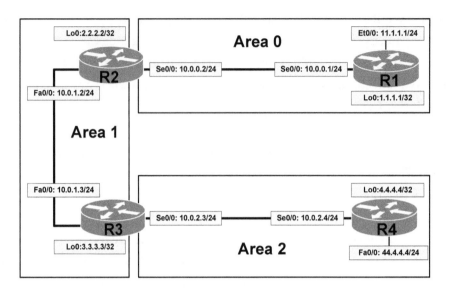

Fig. 3-24. Configuring Virtual Links

Assuming that OSPF has been configured correctly on all routers, we will begin by viewing the contents of the Link State Databases on all routers included in the topology. The LSDB on R1 shows the intra-area routes for Area 0 and the inter-area routes for Area 1, which were flooded into the area by the ABR (R2) as illustrated below:

```
R1#show ip ospf database

        OSPF Router with ID (1.1.1.1) (Process ID 1)

        Router Link States (Area 0)

Link ID         ADV Router      Age         Seq#        Checksum Link Count
1.1.1.1         1.1.1.1         384         0x80000001 0x0096AC 4
2.2.2.2         2.2.2.2         384         0x80000003 0x00185F 2

        Summary Net Link States (Area 0)

Link ID         ADV Router      Age         Seq#        Checksum
2.2.2.2         2.2.2.2         419         0x80000001 0x00FA31
3.3.3.3         2.2.2.2         370         0x80000001 0x00D650
10.0.1.0        2.2.2.2         374         0x80000003 0x00C561
```

The LSDB on R2 shows the intra-area routes for Area 0 as well as the inter-area routes, which R2 flooded into the area. We can also see the intra-area routes for Area 1, as well as the inter-area (Area 0) routes that R2 has flooded into Area 1 as illustrated below:

```
R2#show ip ospf database

          OSPF Router with ID (2.2.2.2) (Process ID 2)

             Router Link States (Area 0)

Link ID         ADV Router      Age        Seq#        Checksum Link Count
1.1.1.1         1.1.1.1         506        0x80000001  0x0096AC 4
2.2.2.2         2.2.2.2         505        0x80000003  0x00185F 2

             Summary Net Link States (Area 0)

Link ID         ADV Router      Age        Seq#        Checksum
2.2.2.2         2.2.2.2         540        0x80000001  0x00FA31
3.3.3.3         2.2.2.2         490        0x80000001  0x00D650
10.0.1.0        2.2.2.2         494        0x80000003  0x00C561

             Router Link States (Area 1)

Link ID         ADV Router      Age        Seq#        Checksum Link Count
2.2.2.2         2.2.2.2         500        0x80000002  0x006488 2
3.3.3.3         3.3.3.3         500        0x80000002  0x00518F 2

             Net Link States (Area 1)

Link ID         ADV Router      Age        Seq#        Checksum
10.0.1.3        3.3.3.3         501        0x80000001  0x0064A7

             Summary Net Link States (Area 1)

Link ID         ADV Router      Age        Seq#        Checksum
1.1.1.1         2.2.2.2         501        0x80000001  0x00AB44
10.0.0.0        2.2.2.2         547        0x80000001  0x004D9D
11.1.1.0        2.2.2.2         501        0x80000001  0x008D50
```

The LSDB on R3 shows the intra-area routes for Area 1 as well as the inter-area routes, which R2 flooded into the area. We can also see the intra-area routes for Area 1, as well as the inter-area (Area 0) routes that R2 has flooded into Area 1. In addition, the LSDB also shows the intra-area routes for Area 2.

However, because R3 is not an ABR (i.e., has no connection to the backbone) it does not generate Summary LSAs (inter-area) for these routes and flood them into Area 1, nor can it generate a Summary LSA for the intra-area routes in Area 2 and flood it into Area 1. This means that neither R2 nor R1 is aware of Area 2, and R4 is not aware of Area 1 or Area 0, as illustrated in the following output:

```
R3#show ip ospf database

            OSPF Router with ID (3.3.3.3) (Process ID 3)

            Router Link States (Area 1)

Link ID         ADV Router      Age         Seq#        Checksum Link Count
2.2.2.2         2.2.2.2         736         0x80000002 0x006488 2
3.3.3.3         3.3.3.3         735         0x80000002 0x00518F 2

            Net Link States (Area 1)

Link ID         ADV Router      Age         Seq#        Checksum
10.0.1.3        3.3.3.3         735         0x80000001 0x0064A7

            Summary Net Link States (Area 1)

Link ID         ADV Router      Age         Seq#        Checksum
1.1.1.1         2.2.2.2         735         0x80000001 0x00AB44
10.0.0.0        2.2.2.2         780         0x80000001 0x004D9D
11.1.1.0        2.2.2.2         735         0x80000001 0x008D50

            Router Link States (Area 2)

Link ID         ADV Router      Age         Seq#        Checksum Link Count
3.3.3.3         3.3.3.3         815         0x80000003 0x0081DD 2
4.4.4.4         4.4.4.4         866         0x80000003 0x00B043 4
```

Finally, The LSDB on R4 shows only the intra-area routes in Area 2 because there is no ABR to create and flood Summary LSAs into the area as illustrated below:

```
R4#show ip ospf database

            OSPF Router with ID (4.4.4.4) (Process ID 4)

            Router Link States (Area 2)

Link ID         ADV Router      Age         Seq#        Checksum Link Count
3.3.3.3         3.3.3.3         1135        0x80000003 0x0081DD 2
4.4.4.4         4.4.4.4         1183        0x80000003 0x00B043 4
```

The configuration of the virtual link connecting Area 2 to the backbone would be implemented on R2 and R3. This configuration would be performed as follows:

```
R2(config)#router ospf 2
R2(config-router)#area 1 virtual-link 3.3.3.3
R2(config-router)#exit

R3(config)#router ospf 3
R3(config-router)#area 1 virtual-link 2.2.2.2
R3(config-router)#exit
```

When the virtual link has been configured successfully, an adjacency is established between R2 and R3. This adjacency is similar to a typical OSPF adjacency and is included in the output of the show ip ospf neighbor command as illustrated below:

```
R3#show ip ospf neighbor

Neighbor ID     Pri    State        Dead Time    Address      Interface
2.2.2.2           0    FULL/  -         -         10.0.1.2     OSPF_VL0
2.2.2.2           1    FULL/BDR    00:00:39      10.0.1.2     FastEthernet0/0
4.4.4.4           0    FULL/  -     00:00:35      10.0.2.4     Serial0/0
```

Adding the detail keyword to the show ip ospf neighbor command prints detailed information about the virtual link as illustrated in the output below:

```
R3#show ip ospf neighbor detail
 Neighbor 2.2.2.2, interface address 10.0.1.2
    In the Area 0 via interface OSPF_VL0
    Neighbor priority is 0, State is FULL, 6 state changes
    DR is 0.0.0.0 BDR is 0.0.0.0
    Options is 0x32 in Hello (E-bit L-bit DC-bit )
    Options is 0x72 in DBD (E-bit L-bit DC-bit O-bit)
    LLS Options is 0x1 (LR)
    Neighbor is up for 00:03:19
    Index 1/3, retransmission queue length 0, number of retransmission 1
    First 0x0(0)/0x0(0) Next 0x0(0)/0x0(0)
    Last retransmission scan length is 1, maximum is 1
    Last retransmission scan time is 0 msec, maximum is 0 msec
```

Referencing the sections in bold above, the output of the show ip ospf neighbor detail command for the virtual link includes the neighbor router ID and the interface address that will be used to source routing protocol packets. The state of the neighbor is also included in this output. This state should always be FULL.

The command also includes options included in the Hello and DBD packets for the virtual link. The different options in Hello and DBD packets were described earlier in this chapter. The virtual link Hello and DBD packets include the following options:

- The DC bit, which indicates that it supports Demand Circuits mentioned in RFC 1793
- The L bit, which indicates that it supports Link Local Signaling (LLS)
- The E Bit, which indicates that it supports External LSAs
- The O Bit, which indicates that it supports Opaque LSAs mentioned in RFC 2370

Based on RFC 1793, Demand Circuits are defined as "network segments whose cost depends on either connect time and/or usage (expressed in terms of bytes or packets). Examples include ISDN circuits and X.25 SVCs." OSPF Demand Circuits have the following two characteristics:

1. Periodic Hellos are suppressed
2. Periodic LSA refreshes are suppressed

The original school of thought that resulted in virtual links being considered Demand Circuits was based on concern over the routing protocol overhead when virtual links were used across low-bandwidth links. The suppression of the periodic Hello packets and LSA refreshes was recommended to reduce this overhead.

When a link is configured as a demand circuit, periodic Hellos are suppressed only if it is a point-to-point or a point-to-multipoint network type. However, Hellos are not suppressed for other network types. As stated earlier in this chapter, by default, OSPF re-floods all LSAs every 30 minutes (1800 seconds). When the virtual link is established, if the DC bit is supported by routers, the DoNotAge (DNA) is set in the LSA age, effectively preventing LSAs received across the Demand Circuit from being aged out.

NOTE: The Link State Age field states the time (in seconds) since the Link State Advertisement was originated. Within this field, the DNA bit is the most significant bit. When this bit is set, the LSA stops aging and no periodic updates are sent. However, even for an OSPF, Demand Circuit periodic refresh will occur when there is a change to the network topology. This exception is used to ensure the accuracy of routing information when virtual links are used.

The L bit indicates Link Local Signaling support. This is beyond the scope of the ROUTE exam requirements and is not described further in this guide. The E bit indicates External (Type 5) LSA support. In other words, External LSAs can also be flooded across the virtual link. The O bit indicates Opaque LSA support. Types 9, 10, and 11 are Opaque LSAs.

Type 9 Opaque LSAs have a link-local flooding scope and are not flooded beyond the local link or local network. Type 10 Opaque LSAs have an area flooding scope and are not flooded beyond their area. Type 11 Opaque LSAs are similar to Type 5 LSAs in that they have a domain flooding scope. In addition, these LSAs are not flooded into Stub areas. Opaque LSAs allow for upgrades to OSPF for application-specific purposes and are included for the future extensibility of the protocol. Going into further detail on these LSAs is beyond the scope of the ROUTE exam requirements. These LSAs will not be described in any further detail in this guide.

The show ip ospf virtual-links command can be used to view additional information about the virtual link. The output printed by this command is shown below:

```
R3#show ip ospf virtual-links
Virtual Link OSPF_VL0 to router 2.2.2.2 is up
  Run as Demand Circuit
  DoNotAge LSA allowed.
  Transit Area 1, via interface FastEthernet0/0, Cost of using 1
  Transmit Delay is 1 sec, State POINT_TO_POINT,
  Timer intervals configured, Hello 10, Dead 40, Wait 40, Retransmit 5
    Hello due in 00:00:06
    Adjacency State FULL (Hello suppressed)
    Index 1/3, retransmission queue length 0, number of retransmission 1
    First 0x0(0)/0x0(0) Next 0x0(0)/0x0(0)
    Last retransmission scan length is 1, maximum is 1
    Last retransmission scan time is 0 msec, maximum is 0 msec
```

Referencing the sections in bold above, the output of the show ip ospf virtual-links command shows that the virtual link is configured as a Demand Circuit. This means periodic Hellos and LSA refreshes are suppressed across the virtual link and the DNA bit is set in the Link State Age field for all LSAs received across the virtual link. This can be validated by viewing the LSDB on the ABR (R3) as illustrated below:

```
R3#show ip ospf database

        OSPF Router with ID (3.3.3.3) (Process ID 3)

        Router Link States (Area 0)

Link ID       ADV Router    Age        Seq#        Checksum Link Count
1.1.1.1       1.1.1.1       1285 (DNA) 0x80000001 0x0096AC 4
2.2.2.2       2.2.2.2       1    (DNA) 0x80000004 0x00EF5B 3
3.3.3.3       3.3.3.3       1003       0x80000004 0x000CF2 1
```

Summary Net Link States (Area 0)

Link ID	ADV Router	Age		Seq#	Checksum
2.2.2.2	2.2.2.2	1320	(DNA)	0x80000001	0x00FA31
2.2.2.2	3.3.3.3	1003		0x80000003	0x00E242
3.3.3.3	2.2.2.2	1269	(DNA)	0x80000001	0x00D650
3.3.3.3	3.3.3.3	1003		0x80000003	0x00AA77
4.4.4.4	3.3.3.3	1003		0x80000003	0x00FEDE
10.0.1.0	2.2.2.2	1274	(DNA)	0x80000003	0x00C561
10.0.1.0	3.3.3.3	1003		0x80000003	0x00A77B
10.0.2.0	3.3.3.3	1003		0x80000003	0x0015CD
44.4.4.0	3.3.3.3	1003		0x80000003	0x001D9C

Router Link States (Area 1)

Link ID	ADV Router	Age	Seq#	Checksum	Link Count
2.2.2.2	2.2.2.2	188	0x80000005	0x005E8B	2
3.3.3.3	3.3.3.3	1005	0x80000006	0x00587F	2

Net Link States (Area 1)

Link ID	ADV Router	Age	Seq#	Checksum
10.0.1.3	3.3.3.3	249	0x80000004	0x005EAA

Summary Net Link States (Area 1)

Link ID	ADV Router	Age	Seq#	Checksum
1.1.1.1	2.2.2.2	190	0x80000004	0x00A547
4.4.4.4	2.2.2.2	951	0x80000003	0x0027B9
4.4.4.4	3.3.3.3	1005	0x80000003	0x00FEDE
10.0.0.0	2.2.2.2	190	0x80000004	0x0047A0
10.0.2.0	2.2.2.2	951	0x80000003	0x003DA8
10.0.2.0	3.3.3.3	1005	0x80000003	0x0015CD
11.1.1.0	2.2.2.2	190	0x80000004	0x008753
44.4.4.0	2.2.2.2	951	0x80000003	0x004577
44.4.4.0	3.3.3.3	1005	0x80000003	0x001D9C

Router Link States (Area 2)

Link ID	ADV Router	Age	Seq#	Checksum	Link Count
3.3.3.3	3.3.3.3	1005	0x80000006	0x007EDC	2
4.4.4.4	4.4.4.4	311	0x80000006	0x00AA46	4

Summary Net Link States (Area 2)

```
Link ID          ADV Router     Age        Seq#         Checksum
1.1.1.1          3.3.3.3        1008       0x80000003 0x009355
2.2.2.2          3.3.3.3        1008       0x80000003 0x00E242
3.3.3.3          3.3.3.3        1008       0x80000003 0x00AA77
10.0.0.0         3.3.3.3        1008       0x80000003 0x0035AE
10.0.1.0         3.3.3.3        1008       0x80000003 0x00A77B
11.1.1.0         3.3.3.3        1008       0x80000003 0x007561
```

In the output above, following the establishment of the virtual link, R3 now has intra-area and inter-area routes for Area 0. Only the LSAs received across the virtual link will have the DNA bit set. The LSAs generated and flooded to adjacent areas by R3 will not. This is illustrated in the output below:

```
R3#show ip ospf database summary 2.2.2.2

                OSPF Router with ID (3.3.3.3) (Process ID 3)

                Summary Net Link States (Area 0)

  LS age: 1320 (DoNotAge)
  Options: (No TOS-capability, DC, Upward)
  LS Type: Summary Links(Network)
  Link State ID: 2.2.2.2 (summary Network Number)
  Advertising Router: 2.2.2.2
  LS Seq Number: 80000001
  Checksum: 0xFA31
  Length: 28
  Network Mask: /32
        TOS: 0  Metric: 1

  LS age: 898
  Options: (No TOS-capability, DC, Upward)
  LS Type: Summary Links(Network)
  Link State ID: 2.2.2.2 (summary Network Number)
  Advertising Router: 3.3.3.3
  LS Seq Number: 80000003
  Checksum: 0xE242
  Length: 28
  Network Mask: /32
        TOS: 0  Metric: 2
```

Going back to the output of the show ip ospf virtual-links command, the transit area is also printed, including the interface used to reach the remote endpoint and the cost of the virtual link. This is the cumulative cost between the local router and the remote endpoint. In the topology illustrated in Figure 3-24, R2 and R3 are connected via a FastEthernet link. If additional routers were in the path between these two endpoints, the virtual link cost value would reflect the cumulative metric between the two endpoints.

Finally, the last bolded section in the output of the `show ip ospf virtual-links` command shows that the adjacency state is FULL and Hello packets are being suppressed, which is the default for demand circuits.

Going back to the topology used in the virtual link configuration example, R4 now has both intra-area and inter-area routes in its Link State Database. The inter-area (Type 3) routes are flooded into the area by the ABR (R3) as illustrated in the following output:

```
R4#show ip ospf database

          OSPF Router with ID (4.4.4.4) (Process ID 4)

          Router Link States (Area 2)

Link ID       ADV Router      Age       Seq#       Checksum Link Count
3.3.3.3       3.3.3.3         1633      0x80000006 0x007EDC 2
4.4.4.4       4.4.4.4         934       0x80000006 0x00AA46 4

          Summary Net Link States (Area 2)

Link ID       ADV Router      Age       Seq#       Checksum
1.1.1.1       3.3.3.3         1633      0x80000003 0x009355
2.2.2.2       3.3.3.3         1633      0x80000003 0x00E242
3.3.3.3       3.3.3.3         1633      0x80000003 0x00AA77
10.0.0.0      3.3.3.3         1633      0x80000003 0x0035AE
10.0.1.0      3.3.3.3         1633      0x80000003 0x00A77B
11.1.1.0      3.3.3.3         1633      0x80000003 0x007561
```

NOTE: Connectivity to other routers can be performed using a simple ping as follows:

```
R4#ping 1.1.1.1

Type escape sequence to abort.
Sending 5, 100-byte ICMP Echos to 1.1.1.1, timeout is 2 seconds:
!!!!!
Success rate is 100 percent (5/5), round-trip min/avg/max = 4/4/4 ms
```

While virtual links provide a flexible way of connecting disconnected areas to the backbone, the major disadvantage to using them is that they cannot be configured over Stub areas. If the transit area is configured as a Stub area, then a tunnel must be used instead of a virtual link. Again, referencing the topology illustrated in Figure 3-24, if Area 1 was a Stub area, then a tunnel must be configured between R2 and R3.

The tunnel is configured in a similar manner to a physical interface. This tunnel interface must then be placed into Area 0 using either the `ip ospf [process ID] area 0` interface configuration command or the `network x.x.x.x y.y.y.y area 0` router configuration command. Tunnel interface configuration is described in detail later in this guide.

Using Virtual Links for Redundancy

In addition to being used to connect disconnected areas to the backbone, virtual links may also be used to provide redundancy. Consider the network illustrated in Figure 3-25 below:

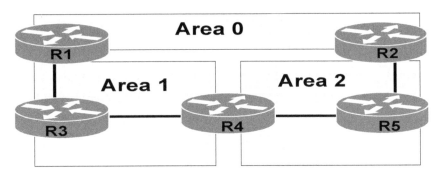

Fig. 3-25. Using Virtual Links for Redundancy

Figure 3-25 illustrates a basic multi-area OSPF network. R1 and R2 are connected to Area 0 and to routers R3 and R5 in Areas 1 and 2, respectively. R4 is connected to Area 1 and Area 2. Although virtual links would not be required in this implementation, they can be configured to provide redundancy in the event that Area 1 or Area 2 lost its connection to the backbone. Figure 3-26 below illustrates how the OSPF network would be broken if the connection between R3 and R1, for example, was removed due to a link or other failure:

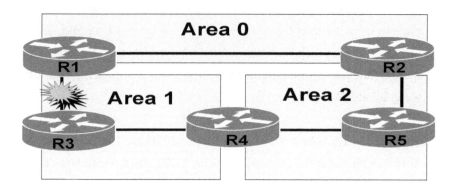

Fig. 3-26. Using Virtual Links for Redundancy

Following the failure of the link between R1 and R3, as illustrated in Figure 3-26, Area 1 will no longer be connected to the backbone. The same would be applicable to Area 2 if the connection between R2 and R5 failed. In this case, virtual links can be configured ahead of time to ensure that these areas have a connection to the backbone in the event of a link failure. The virtual link would be configured between R1 and R4 and between R2 and R4 for Areas 1 and 2, respectively.

In addition to being used for redundant connectivity for non-backbone areas, virtual links can also be configured to provide redundancy in the event of a link failure that would result in the backbone area being partitioned or disconnected. This is illustrated in Figure 3-27 below:

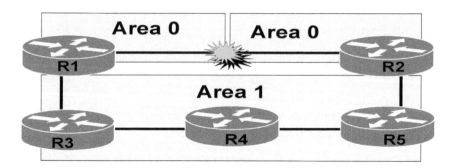

Fig. 3-27. Using Virtual Links for Redundancy

Referencing the network diagram in Figure 3-27, a link failure between R1 and R2 would result in the breakup or partitioning of the OSPF backbone. While a partitioned backbone is allowed when implementing multi-area OSPF, the two separate backbones must be connected using a virtual link. To avoid the partitioning of the backbone in the network in Figure 3-26, a virtual link would be configured between R1 and R2, using Area 1 as the transit area. This allows normal OSPF operation in the event of the failure of the link or connection between R1 and R2.

Connecting Partitioned Backbones

A partitioned backbone is an OSPF backbone that has been split in two. This is similar to what would happen in the event of a link failure between R1 and R2 as shown in Figure 3-27. Sometimes, a partitioned backbone is necessary to connect two different OSPF networks. These two OSPF networks may need to be joined together following an acquisition or merger, for example, as illustrated in Figure 3-28 below:

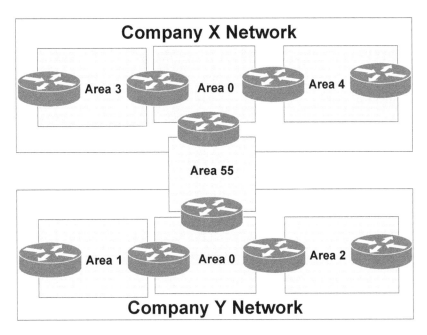

Fig. 3-28. Connecting Partitioned Backbones

In Figure 3-28, two companies have recently merged and are in the process of integrating their networks. The two companies are using OSPF as the IGP of choice. To merge the two OSPF networks, a common area would need to be configured between the two backbone areas belonging to each individual area. A virtual link would then be configured across this common area to join the two backbone areas.

Following virtual link implementation rules, the transit area between the two networks should not be configured as a Stub area. If it must be configured as a Stub area, a tunnel would need to be used instead of a virtual link. In addition to connecting the two backbones, general design verifications, such as ensuring there are no overlapping areas or IP address space, would also be undertaken. These issues cannot be resolved simply by implementing a virtual link.

There are some significant differences in the operation of virtual links and tunnels that you should remember in choosing when to use one over the other to connect disconnected areas to the backbone or to connect a partitioned backbone. These differences are listed in Table 3-4 below:

Table 3-4. Comparing Virtual Links and Tunnels

Characteristic	When Using a Tunnel	When Using a Virtual Link
OSPF Network Type	Defaults to point-to-point	Defaults to point-to-point
Demand Circuit	No	Yes
DoNotAge Bit Set	No	Yes
Hellos Suppressed	No	Yes
Routing Updates	Tunneled between endpoints	Tunneled between endpoints
Normal User Data	Tunneled between endpoints	Not tunneled; sent natively
Cost (Metric)	Based on tunnel bandwidth	Cumulative between endpoints
Able to Transit Stub Area	Yes	No

OSPF ROUTE SUMMARIZATION

By default, OSPF does not perform automatic route summarization. Instead, OSPF-enabled routers must be configured manually to summarize routes. In Cisco IOS software, different commands must be used to summarize internal and external routing information. The following sections describe both types of route summarization and delve into the specifics on each type of summary and how it is propagated throughout the OSPF domain.

Internal Route Summarization

In OSPF, ABRs are responsible for generating a single Type 3 Summary LSA for each intra-area route (i.e., Type 1 and Type 2 LSAs) within their area. These LSAs are then flooded to adjacent areas, allowing for reachability between subnets and hosts in different areas. In large networks, this typically increases the overall size of the LSDB and the IP routing table. In addition, router resources, such as memory and processor utilization, may become heavily taxed, resulting in poor overall network and device performance.

Assuming that a hierarchical IP addressing scheme is in place, internal route summarization can be implemented on the ABR, allowing it to generate a single Type 3 LSA to represent a collection of intra-area routes. This reduces the overall size of the LSDB and IP routing table for routers in adjacent areas, also effectively reducing resource utilization on those devices. In Cisco IOS software, internal route summarization is configured by using the `area [area ID] range [<address> <mask> [advertise | not-advertise]] [cost <cost>]` router configuration command on the Area Border Router (ABR).

The `area ID` is used to specify the OSPF area for which the summary route is being generated. The `<address>` and `<mask>` keywords are used to specify the aggregate (summary) address and its subnet mask. The `advertise` keyword allows the ABR to generate a Type 3 LSA for the summary route and flood it to adjacent areas. By default, this keyword is enabled when the `area...range` command is configured on the ABR.

The `not-advertise` keyword sets the DoNotAdvertise bit in the Type 3 LSA. This keyword configures the ABR to suppress both the aggregate Type 3 LSA as well as the Type 3 LSAs for the specific routes that are included in the summary. This is essentially a method of preventing Type 3 LSAs from being generated and flooded to adjacent areas. In other words, this keyword can be used to perform Type 3 LSA filtering in OSPF networks.

Finally, the `cost <cost>` keyword is used to manually specify the metric or cost for this summary route, which is used during OSPF SPF calculation to determine the shortest paths to the destination. The value can be 0 to 16777215. By default, the cost of the Type 3 LSA is derived from the lowest route metric of the specific routes contributing to the summary. The topology illustrated in Figure 3-29 below will be used to demonstrate the configuration and validation of OSPF internal route summarization:

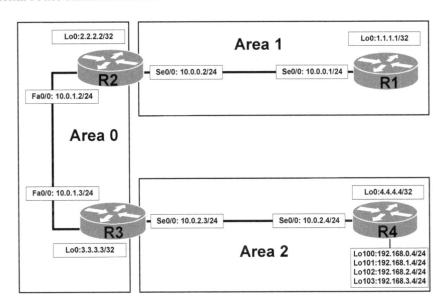

Fig. 3-29. OSPF Internal Route Summarization

Figure 3-29 shows a very basic multi-area OSPF network. R4 is advertising the 192.168.0.0/24, 192.168.1.0/24, 192.168.2.0/24, and 192.168.3.0/24 subnets to R3, the ABR. The respective Loopback interfaces on R4 have been assigned to Area 2 using the `ip ospf 4 area 2` interface configuration command. In addition, the Loopback interfaces have also been assigned different cost values using the `ip ospf cost` interface configuration command. This configuration is illustrated in the following output:

```
R4#show ip ospf interface brief | include Lo
Interface   PID   Area        IP Address/Mask    Cost  State  Nbrs F/C
Lo100       4     2           192.168.0.4/24     1     LOOP   0/0
Lo101       4     2           192.168.1.4/24     1     LOOP   0/0
Lo102       4     2           192.168.2.4/24     2     LOOP   0/0
Lo103       4     2           192.168.3.4/24     3     LOOP   0/0
```

These intra-area routes are flooded into Area 2 by R4 and R3, the ABR, generating a single Type 3 Summary LSA for each individual route, and then floods this Summary LSA into the backbone area as illustrated in the following output of the show ip ospf database summary command on R3:

```
R3#show ip ospf database summary

          OSPF Router with ID (3.3.3.3) (Process ID 3)

          Summary Net Link States (Area 0)

[Truncated Output]

LS age: 167
Options: (No TOS-capability, DC, Upward)
LS Type: Summary Links(Network)
Link State ID: 192.168.0.4 (summary Network Number)
Advertising Router: 3.3.3.3
LS Seq Number: 80000001
Checksum: 0xE1A0
Length: 28
Network Mask: /32
     TOS: 0  Metric: 65

LS age: 167
Options: (No TOS-capability, DC, Upward)
LS Type: Summary Links(Network)
Link State ID: 192.168.1.4 (summary Network Number)
Advertising Router: 3.3.3.3
LS Seq Number: 80000001
Checksum: 0xD6AA
Length: 28
Network Mask: /32
     TOS: 0  Metric: 65

LS age: 167
Options: (No TOS-capability, DC, Upward)
LS Type: Summary Links(Network)
```

```
Link State ID: 192.168.2.4 (summary Network Number)
Advertising Router: 3.3.3.3
LS Seq Number: 80000001
Checksum: 0xD5A9
Length: 28
Network Mask: /32
      TOS: 0  Metric: 66

LS age: 169
Options: (No TOS-capability, DC, Upward)
LS Type: Summary Links(Network)
Link State ID: 192.168.3.4 (summary Network Number)
Advertising Router: 3.3.3.3
LS Seq Number: 80000001
Checksum: 0xD4A8
Length: 28
Network Mask: /32
      TOS: 0  Metric: 67

...

[Truncated Output]
```

Using the `area...range` command, the ABR (R3) can be configured to suppress the more specific routes and advertises a single Type 3 LSA representing these subnets. This configuration would be implemented on R3 as follows:

```
R3(config)#router ospf 3
R3(config-router)#area 2 range 192.168.0.0 255.255.252.0
R3(config-router)#exit
```

After the configuration of the summary route on the ABR, the following happens:
- An intra-area route for the summary pointing to Null0 is installed into the routing table
- The specific Type 3 entries in the LSDB are replaced by the single Type 3 LSA

The first point can be validated using the `show ip route` command on R3 as illustrated below:

```
R3#show ip route 192.168.0.0 255.255.252.0
Routing entry for 192.168.0.0/22, supernet
  Known via "ospf 3", distance 110, metric 0, type intra area
  Routing Descriptor Blocks:
  * directly connected, via Null0
      Route metric is 0, traffic share count is 1
```

To view the specific routes included in the summary address, the `longer-prefixes` keyword can be appended to this command as illustrated in the following output:

```
R3#show ip route 192.168.0.0 255.255.252.0 longer-prefixes
Codes: C - connected, S - static, R - RIP, M - mobile, B - BGP
       D - EIGRP, EX - EIGRP external, O - OSPF, IA - OSPF inter area
       N1 - OSPF NSSA external type 1, N2 - OSPF NSSA external type 2
       E1 - OSPF external type 1, E2 - OSPF external type 2
       i - IS-IS, su - IS-IS summary, L1 - IS-IS level-1, L2 - IS-IS level-2
       ia - IS-IS inter area, * - candidate default, U - per-user static
route
       o - ODR, P - periodic downloaded static route

Gateway of last resort is not set

     192.168.0.0/32 is subnetted, 1 subnets
O       192.168.0.4 [110/65] via 10.0.2.4, 00:15:35, Serial0/0
     192.168.1.0/32 is subnetted, 1 subnets
O       192.168.1.4 [110/65] via 10.0.2.4, 00:15:35, Serial0/0
     192.168.2.0/32 is subnetted, 1 subnets
O       192.168.2.4 [110/66] via 10.0.2.4, 00:15:35, Serial0/0
     192.168.3.0/32 is subnetted, 1 subnets
O       192.168.3.4 [110/67] via 10.0.2.4, 00:15:35, Serial0/0
O    192.168.0.0/22 is a summary, 00:15:35, Null0
```

Regarding the second point, the show `ip ospf database` command can be issued on R3 to view the single aggregate entry in the LSDB as shown in the following output:

```
R3#show ip ospf database | begin Summary
                Summary Net Link States (Area 0)

Link ID         ADV Router      Age       Seq#       Checksum

[Truncated Output]

192.168.0.0    3.3.3.3          3         0x80000001 0x00FA8E
```

The show `ip ospf database summary 192.168.0.0` command prints more detailed information on the summary. This includes the network ID, the advertising router, the network mask, and the metric. The metric is derived by simply adding the cost of the link to the cost of reaching the network from R3 as illustrated in the following output:

```
R3#show ip ospf database summary 192.168.0.0

        OSPF Router with ID (3.3.3.3) (Process ID 3)
```

```
                Summary Net Link States (Area 0)

LS age: 185
Options: (No TOS-capability, DC, Upward)
LS Type: Summary Links(Network)
Link State ID: 192.168.0.0 (summary Network Number)
Advertising Router: 3.3.3.3
LS Seq Number: 80000001
Checksum: 0xFA8E
Length: 28
Network Mask: /22
      TOS: 0  Metric: 65
```

The cost of the link is the metric included in the LSA that is flooded by R2 to R3. This value can be viewed in the output of the show ip ospf database summary command on R3 prior to implementing the summarization configuration on the router. This is illustrated below:

```
R3#show ip ospf database summary

        OSPF Router with ID (3.3.3.3) (Process ID 3)

                Summary Net Link States (Area 0)

[Truncated Output]

LS age: 119
Options: (No TOS-capability, DC, Upward)
LS Type: Summary Links(Network)
Link State ID: 192.168.0.4 (summary Network Number)
Advertising Router: 3.3.3.3
LS Seq Number: 80000001
Checksum: 0xE1A0
Length: 28
Network Mask: /32
      TOS: 0  Metric: 65

LS age: 119
Options: (No TOS-capability, DC, Upward)
LS Type: Summary Links(Network)
Link State ID: 192.168.1.4 (summary Network Number)
Advertising Router: 3.3.3.3
LS Seq Number: 80000001
Checksum: 0xD6AA
Length: 28
Network Mask: /32
      TOS: 0  Metric: 65
```

```
LS age: 120
Options: (No TOS-capability, DC, Upward)
LS Type: Summary Links(Network)
Link State ID: 192.168.2.4 (summary Network Number)
Advertising Router: 3.3.3.3
LS Seq Number: 80000001
Checksum: 0xD5A9
Length: 28
Network Mask: /32
      TOS: 0  Metric: 66

LS age: 121
Options: (No TOS-capability, DC, Upward)
LS Type: Summary Links(Network)
Link State ID: 192.168.3.4 (summary Network Number)
Advertising Router: 3.3.3.3
LS Seq Number: 80000001
Checksum: 0xD4A8
Length: 28
Network Mask: /32
      TOS: 0  Metric: 67

...

[Truncated Output]
```

When the `not-advertise` keyword is configured, the ABR suppresses the specific route entries and does not advertise the summary route. The DoNotAdvertise bit is set in the LSA and the LSA is not flooded to adjacent areas.

> **NOTE:** Do not confuse the DoNotAdvertise bit with the DoNotAge bit in Demand Circuits. The two are not the same and they do not operate in the same manner.

Referencing the topology in Figure 3-29, and continuing with the same configuration examples, the following illustrates how to configure OSPF to suppress specific route entries that are included in the aggregate address by setting the DoNotAdvertise bit on the Type 3 LSA:

```
R3(config)#router ospf 3
R3(config-router)#area 2 range 192.168.0.0 255.255.252.0 not-advertise
R3(config-router)#exit
```

After this configuration has been implemented on the router, the following happens:

- The specific entries included in the summary address range are removed from the LSDB
- The router does not generate a route to Null0 for the summary address
- The Type 3 LSA for the summary address will not be present in the LSDB

To verify the above, first we will ensure that the routes are indeed still received by R3 from R4 as illustrated in the following output:

```
R3#show ip route ospf | include 192.168.
     192.168.0.0/32 is subnetted, 1 subnets
0       192.168.0.4 [110/65] via 10.0.2.4, 00:08:05, Serial0/0
     192.168.1.0/32 is subnetted, 1 subnets
0       192.168.1.4 [110/65] via 10.0.2.4, 00:08:05, Serial0/0
     192.168.2.0/32 is subnetted, 1 subnets
0       192.168.2.4 [110/66] via 10.0.2.4, 00:08:05, Serial0/0
     192.168.3.0/32 is subnetted, 1 subnets
0       192.168.3.4 [110/67] via 10.0.2.4, 00:08:05, Serial0/0
```

Next, view the contents of the LSDB on R3 to ensure that neither the specific entries nor the Type 3 LSA for the summary route is included as illustrated below:

```
R3#show ip ospf database

        OSPF Router with ID (3.3.3.3) (Process ID 3)

        Router Link States (Area 0)

Link ID         ADV Router      Age       Seq#        Checksum Link Count
2.2.2.2         2.2.2.2         1088      0x80000013 0x005F7D 2
3.3.3.3         3.3.3.3         1055      0x80000003 0x003CA3 2

        Net Link States (Area 0)

Link ID         ADV Router      Age       Seq#        Checksum
10.0.1.2        2.2.2.2         1088      0x80000003 0x009876
        Summary Net Link States (Area 0)

Link ID         ADV Router      Age       Seq#        Checksum
1.1.1.1         2.2.2.2         1088      0x80000005 0x00A348
4.4.4.4         3.3.3.3         1055      0x80000003 0x00FEDE
10.0.0.0        2.2.2.2         1088      0x80000005 0x0045A1
10.0.2.0        3.3.3.3         1055      0x80000003 0x0015CD

        Router Link States (Area 2)

Link ID         ADV Router      Age       Seq#        Checksum Link Count
3.3.3.3         3.3.3.3         1055      0x80000003 0x0084D9 2
```

```
4.4.4.4          4.4.4.4          882         0x80000016 0x00A87A 7

                 Summary Net Link States (Area 2)

Link ID          ADV Router       Age         Seq#       Checksum
1.1.1.1          3.3.3.3          1057        0x80000003 0x009355
2.2.2.2          3.3.3.3          1057        0x80000003 0x00E242
3.3.3.3          3.3.3.3          1057        0x80000003 0x00AA77
10.0.0.0         3.3.3.3          1057        0x80000003 0x0035AE
10.0.1.0         3.3.3.3          1057        0x80000003 0x00A77B
```

Finally, the cost keyword overrides the metric for the summary address and uses the value specified in the configuration of the summary. This configuration is illustrated below:

```
R3(config)#router ospf 3
R3(config-router)#area 2 range 192.168.0.0 255.255.252.0 cost 333
R3(config-router)#exit
```

Based on this configuration, the show ip ospf database summary 192.168.0.0 command reflects the manually configured cost value for the Type 3 LSA as illustrated below:

```
R3#show ip ospf database summary 192.168.0.0

          OSPF Router with ID (3.3.3.3) (Process ID 3)

          Summary Net Link States (Area 0)

    LS age: 36
    Options: (No TOS-capability, DC, Upward)
    LS Type: Summary Links(Network)
    Link State ID: 192.168.0.0 (summary Network Number)
    Advertising Router: 3.3.3.3
    LS Seq Number: 80000002
    Checksum: 0x7A01
    Length: 28
    Network Mask: /22
         TOS: 0  Metric: 333
```

This cost value will be included in the Type 3 LSAs flooded into adjacent areas. For example, R2 would reflect the same value in its LSDB and then increment that value by the cost of reaching R3 from itself before flooding it to adjacent areas (i.e., Area 1) as illustrated below:

```
R2#show ip ospf database summary 192.168.0.0

          OSPF Router with ID (2.2.2.2) (Process ID 2)
```

```
                    Summary Net Link States (Area 0)


Routing Bit Set on this LSA
LS age: 210
Options: (No TOS-capability, DC, Upward)
LS Type: Summary Links(Network)
Link State ID: 192.168.0.0 (summary Network Number)
Advertising Router: 3.3.3.3
LS Seq Number: 80000002
Checksum: 0x7A01
Length: 28
Network Mask: /22
      TOS: 0   Metric: 333




                    Summary Net Link States (Area 1)


LS age: 209
Options: (No TOS-capability, DC, Upward)
LS Type: Summary Links(Network)
Link State ID: 192.168.0.0 (summary Network Number)
Advertising Router: 2.2.2.2
LS Seq Number: 80000002
Checksum: 0xA2DB
Length: 28
Network Mask: /22
      TOS: 0   Metric: 334
```

R2 would calculate the route metric for the 192.168.0.0/22 network by adding the received metric value to the cost of reaching R2 from itself. Assuming the default OSPF reference bandwidth is used, the default cost for the FastEthernet link between R2 and R3 would be 1. R2 would simply add 1 to 333 to derive the route metric 334 for this subnet as illustrated below:

```
R2#show ip route 192.168.0.0 255.255.252.0
Routing entry for 192.168.0.0/22, supernet
  Known via "ospf 2", distance 110, metric 334, type inter area
  Last update from 10.0.1.3 on FastEthernet0/0, 00:06:57 ago
  Routing Descriptor Blocks:
  * 10.0.1.3, from 3.3.3.3, 00:06:57 ago, via FastEthernet0/0
      Route metric is 334, traffic share count is 1
```

External Route Summarization

When configuring OSPF route summarization, internal route summarization is configured on the ABR; however, external route summarization must be configured on the ASBR. External route summarization in OSPF is configured using the `summary-address [<address> <mask> | prefix] [not-advertise] [tag <tag>] [nssa-only]` router configuration command. The `<address> <mask>` keywords are used to specify the summary network address and its subnet mask.

The `prefix` keyword is used to specify a prefix mask length for the summary network address instead of a dotted-decimal subnet mask. The `not-advertise` keyword suppresses both the specific external entries and the summary route entry from being advertised. The `tag <tag>` keyword is used to specify the route tag for the summary address. By default, as was illustrated earlier in this chapter, this field will contain the process ID of the ASBR.

Finally, the `nssa-only` keyword is used on the NSSA ASBR to set the NSSA-only attribute for the summary route. This limits the summary to not-so-stubby-area (NSSA) areas.

Referencing the topology illustrated in Figure 3-29, the Loopback interfaces that are configured on R4 and previously advertised internal OSPF routes are now redistributed into OSPF on the same router using the `redistribute connected subnets` router configuration command, making R4 an ASBR. The LSDB of R4 is illustrated in the following output:

```
R4#show ip ospf database | begin External
            Type-5 AS External Link States

Link ID         ADV Router      Age      Seq#        Checksum Tag
192.168.0.0     4.4.4.4         21       0x8000000D 0x00A575 0
192.168.1.0     4.4.4.4         26       0x80000001 0x00B273 0
192.168.2.0     4.4.4.4         26       0x80000001 0x00A77D 0
192.168.3.0     4.4.4.4         26       0x80000001 0x009C87 0
```

These routes are then advertised to R3 as External Type 2 (default) routes as illustrated in the following output of the `show ip route` command on R3:

```
R3#show ip route ospf | include 192.168
O E2 192.168.0.0/24 [110/20] via 10.0.2.4, 00:00:48, Serial0/0
O E2 192.168.1.0/24 [110/20] via 10.0.2.4, 00:00:53, Serial0/0
O E2 192.168.2.0/24 [110/20] via 10.0.2.4, 00:00:53, Serial0/0
O E2 192.168.3.0/24 [110/20] via 10.0.2.4, 00:00:53, Serial0/0
```

Before summarizing on these routes on the ASBR, we will take a detailed look at one of the individual route entries in the LSDB using the `show ip ospf database external` command as illustrated in the following output:

```
R3#show ip ospf database external 192.168.1.0

            OSPF Router with ID (3.3.3.3) (Process ID 3)

            Type-5 AS External Link States

    Routing Bit Set on this LSA
    LS age: 76
    Options: (No TOS-capability, DC)
    LS Type: AS External Link
    Link State ID: 192.168.1.0 (External Network Number)
    Advertising Router: 4.4.4.4
    LS Seq Number: 80000001
    Checksum: 0xB273
    Length: 36
    Network Mask: /24
        Metric Type: 2 (Larger than any Link State path)
        TOS: 0
        Metric: 20
        Forward Address: 0.0.0.0
        External Route Tag: 0
```

In the output above, the section printed in bold, the Type 5 LSA for the 192.168.1.0/24 subnet, is advertised to R3 by R4. By default, OSPF routes are Type 2 External LSAs. The metric value assigned to the route is 20. This brings up two important points:

1. When routes are redistributed into OPSF from external routing sources (e.g., connected interfaces or routes received via EIGRP), if a metric is not specified during redistribution, then the routes are assigned a default metric value of 20 because the metric values of external protocols are incompatible with OSPF metric values. This same value will be applied to the summary.

2. When routes are redistributed into OSPF from another OSPF process, the metric values are carried over because they are compatible. In this case, the summary metric will be set to the lowest metric value of all contributing routes.

The output below illustrates the metric on routes redistributed from another OSPF process using the redistribute ospf [process ID] subnets router configuration command:

```
R3#show ip ospf database External 192.168.1.0

            OSPF Router with ID (3.3.3.3) (Process ID 3)

            Type-5 AS External Link States
```

```
Routing Bit Set on this LSA
LS age: 18
Options: (No TOS-capability, DC)
LS Type: AS External Link
Link State ID: 192.168.1.0 (External Network Number)
Advertising Router: 4.4.4.4
LS Seq Number: 80000001
Checksum: 0x58D6
Length: 36
Network Mask: /24
      Metric Type: 2 (Larger than any Link State path)
      TOS: 0
      Metric: 11
      Forward Address: 0.0.0.0
      External Route Tag: 0
```

The Forward Address will always be 0.0.0.0, indicating that traffic to this network should be forwarded to the ASBR. A corresponding Type 4 for the ASBR is automatically generated and flooded to adjacent areas. Finally, the Route Tag field contains a value of 0 for all redistributed routes, by default. However, Cisco IOS software allows all redistributed routes to be assigned a route tag during redistribution. The tag can then be used for route filtering.

NOTE: Route redistribution is described in detail later in this guide.

The following configuration example shows how to summarize the external routes that have been redistributed into OSPF on R4 and generate a single route entry:

```
R4(config)#router ospf 4
R4(config-router)#summary-address 192.168.0.0 255.255.252.0
R4(config-router)#exit
```

After this configuration has been implemented, the following is performed on the ASBR:
- An intra-area route for the summary pointing to Null0 is installed into the routing table
- The specific Type 5 entries in the LSDB are replaced by the single Type 5 LSA

The intra-area route representing the configuration summary address can be viewed by issuing the show ip route command as illustrated in the output below:

```
R4#show ip route 192.168.0.0 255.255.252.0
Routing entry for 192.168.0.0/22, supernet
  Known via "ospf 4", distance 110, metric 0, type intra area
```

```
Routing Descriptor Blocks:
* directly connected, via Null0
    Route metric is 0, traffic share count is 1
```

The second point can be validated by viewing the contents of the LSDB on R4 as illustrated in the following output:

```
R4#show ip ospf database External

            OSPF Router with ID (4.4.4.4) (Process ID 4)

            Type-5 AS External Link States

  LS age: 4
  Options: (No TOS-capability, DC)
  LS Type: AS External Link
  Link State ID: 192.168.0.0 (External Network Number)
  Advertising Router: 4.4.4.4
  LS Seq Number: 80000001
  Checksum: 0xAE7B
  Length: 36
  Network Mask: /22
        Metric Type: 2 (Larger than any Link State path)
        TOS: 0
        Metric: 20
        Forward Address: 0.0.0.0
        External Route Tag: 0
```

Alternatively, the show ip ospf summary command could be used to verify most of the parameters illustrated above. The output of this command is shown below:

```
R4#show ip ospf summary-address
OSPF Process 4, Summary-address
192.168.0.0/255.255.252.0 Metric 20, Type 2, Tag 0
```

Because the summary address is advertised as a Type 2 External LSA, the assigned route metric remains consistent throughout the network as illustrated below on R3:

```
R3#show ip route 192.168.0.0 255.255.252.0
Routing entry for 192.168.0.0/22, supernet
  Known via "ospf 3", distance 110, metric 20, type extern 2, forward metric
64
  Last update from 10.0.2.4 on Serial0/0, 00:04:39 ago
  Routing Descriptor Blocks:
```

```
* 10.0.2.4, from 4.4.4.4, 00:04:39 ago, via Serial0/0
    Route metric is 20, traffic share count is 1
```

We will conclude this section by listing the differences between the area...range and the summary-address router configuration commands. It is important to understand the differences between these two commands as they apply to the configuration of OSPF route summarization. The important aspects to remember regarding the area...range router configuration command are as follows:

- This command is issued on the Area Border Router (ABR)
- An intra-area route for the summary pointing to Null0 is installed into the routing table
- The specific Type 3 entries in the LSDB are replaced by the single Type 3 LSA
- The summary is not advertised if none of the contributing entries are in the routing table
- The summary address metric can be set directly using this command
- The summary metric is equal to the lowest metric of all contributing routes
- This command can be used for OSPF route filtering

The important aspects to remember regarding the summary-address router configuration command are as follows:

- This command is issued on the Autonomous System Border Router (ASBR)
- An intra-area route for the summary pointing to Null0 is installed into the routing table
- The specific Type 5 entries in the LSDB are replaced by the single Type 5 LSA
- The summary is not advertised if none of the contributing entries are in the routing table
- The summary metric defaults to 20 for non-OSPF external routes
- The summary metric uses the lowest contributing route metric for external OSPF routes
- This command can be used for OSPF route filtering
- The summary address metric cannot be set directly using this command

OSPF PASSIVE INTERFACES

In Chapter 2, passive interfaces were described as interfaces over which no routing updates are sent. In Cisco IOS software, an interface is configured as passive by using the passive-interface [name] router configuration command. If there are multiple interfaces on the router that need to be configured as passive, the passive-interface default router configuration command should be used. This command configures all interfaces that fall within the configured network range on the router to be passive. Interfaces on which adjacencies or neighbor relationships should be allowed can then be configured using the passive-interface [name] router configuration command.

Passive interface configuration works the same for both OSPF and EIGRP in that if an interface is marked as passive, all neighbor relationships via that interface will be torn down and Hello packets will not send or receive packets via that interface. However, the interface will continue to be advertised based on the configured `network` statement configuration on the router.

SECURING OSPF MESSAGES

In this section, we will learn about the different types of authentication supported by OSPF. Unlike EIGRP, OSPF supports plain text and MD5 authentication. The authentication method used by OSPF is specified in the OSPF packet header in the 16-bit Auth Type field. This field may contain one of the following three codes:

- Code 0—Used to indicate that there is Null or no authentication
- Code 1—Used to indicate plain text authentication
- Code 2—Used to indicate Message Digest 5 (MD5) authentication

By default, an OSPF-enabled router uses Null authentication (Code 0), which means that routing exchanges over a network are not authenticated and are therefore prone to security attacks.

In Cisco IOS software, OSPF authentication can be configured for the entire OSPF area or on a per-interface basis. Both methods are described in detail in the following sections.

Configuring Area Authentication

The `area [area ID] authentication [message-digest]` command is used to enable plain text or MD5 authentication for the specified OSPF area. This command must be accompanied by the `ip ospf authentication-key [password]` or the `ip ospf message-digest-key [key ID] md5 [password]` interface configuration commands on all interfaces within the specified OSPF area to enable either plain text authentication or MD5 authentication, respectively.

When configuring MD5 authentication, the key ID on both interfaces must match. The interfaces use the password configured in the lowest key ID when exchanging messages. Additionally, when configuring plain text authentication the password can be configured using any continuous string of characters that can be entered from the keyboard and can be up to 8 bytes in length. However, when configuring MD5 authentication, the password must be an alphanumeric password of up to 16 bytes in length.

When plain text authentication is enabled, the specified password is used as a key that is then inserted into the OSPF header when the router originates OSPF packets. A separate password can be assigned to each network on a per-interface basis. In other words, different subnets within the area can use different passwords. However, all neighboring routers on the same subnet must have the same password in order to be able to exchange OSPF routing information.

NOTE: By default, the configuration password will be shown in plain text in the router configuration unless the `service password-encryption` global command is issued.

Figure 3-30 below illustrates a basic multi-area OSPF network. R3 is connected to the backbone area in addition to Area 2. Both R4 and R6 reside in Area 2. Based on this topology, MD5 authentication will be enabled for Area 2:

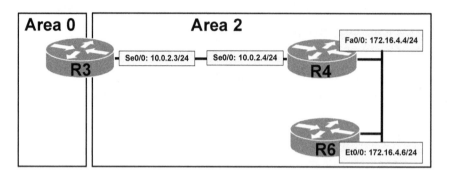

Fig. 3-30. OSPF Area Authentication

NOTE: It should be assumed that OSPF routing has been enabled correctly and the routers have established adjacencies with each other.

The first requirement when configuring area authentication is to enable the authentication type for the desired area. This is performed using the `area [area ID] authentication [message-digest]` router configuration command. This command must be enabled on all routers within the same area. This configuration is performed as follows:

```
R3(config)#router ospf 3
R3(config-router)#area 2 authentication message-digest
R3(config-router)#exit

R4(config)#router ospf 4
R4(config-router)#area 2 authentication message-digest
R4(config-router)#exit

R6(config)#router ospf 6
R6(config-router)#area 2 authentication message-digest
R6(config-router)#exit
```

The next required step is to configure authentication on all interfaces within Area 2 using the `ip ospf message-digest-key [key ID] md5 [password]` interface configuration command. The key ID configured on the routers must match, otherwise authentication will fail and the adjacency will not be established. To highlight the fact that the passwords can be different on different subnets, R3 and R4 will be configured to use the password ospf-md5-1 for MD5 authentication between the two routers. This is performed as follows:

```
R3(config)#interface Serial0/0
R3(config-if)#ip ospf message-digest-key 1 md5 ospf-md5-1
R3(config-if)#exit

R4(config)#interface Serial0/0
R4(config-if)#ip ospf message-digest-key 1 md5 ospf-md5-1
R4(config-if)#exit
```

Following this configuration, OSPF authentication can be verified using the show ip ospf and the show ip ospf interface [name] commands. The show ip ospf command simply indicates the type of authentication configured for the OSPF area as illustrated below:

```
R4#show ip ospf | begin Area 2
    Area 2
        Number of interfaces in this area is 3 (2 Loopback)
        Area has message digest authentication
        SPF algorithm last executed 00:08:50.465 ago
        SPF algorithm executed 16 times
        Area ranges are
        Number of LSA 10. Checksum Sum 0x0532CC
        Number of opaque link LSA 0. Checksum Sum 0x000000
        Number of DCbitless LSA 0
        Number of indication LSA 0
        Number of DoNotAge LSA 0
        Flood list length 0
```

The show ip ospf and the show ip ospf interface [name] command, on the other hand, indicates the type of authentication configured, as well as shows the key ID (MD5) used for authentication on the interface as illustrated in the following output:

```
R4#show ip ospf interface Serial0/0
Serial0/0 is up, line protocol is up
  Internet Address 10.0.2.4/24, Area 2
  Process ID 4, Router ID 4.4.4.4, Network Type POINT_TO_POINT, Cost: 64
  Enabled by interface config, including secondary ip addresses
  Transmit Delay is 1 sec, State POINT_TO_POINT
  Timer intervals configured, Hello 10, Dead 40, Wait 40, Retransmit 5
    oob-resync timeout 40
```

```
  Hello due in 00:00:04
 Supports Link-local Signaling (LLS)
 Index 3/3, flood queue length 0
 Next 0x0(0)/0x0(0)
 Last flood scan length is 1, maximum is 1
 Last flood scan time is 0 msec, maximum is 0 msec
 Neighbor Count is 1, Adjacent neighbor count is 1
  Adjacent with neighbor 3.3.3.3
 Suppress Hello for 0 neighbor(s)
 Message digest authentication enabled
  Youngest key id is 1
```

Finally, as previously stated, it is important to remember that the passwords are displayed in plain text in the router configuration unless the service password-encryption command is enabled. This is illustrated in the following output:

```
R4#show running-config interface Serial0/0
Building configuration...

Current configuration : 159 bytes
!
interface Serial0/0
 ip address 10.0.2.4 255.255.255.0
 ip ospf message-digest-key 1 md5 ospf-md5-1
 ip ospf 4 area 2
end
```

Continuing with the area authentication configuration example, R4 and R6 will be configured to use the password ospf-md5-2 for MD5 authentication between the two routers. These routers will also use a key ID of 2. This is performed as follows:

```
R4(config)#interface FastEthernet0/0
R4(config-if)#ip ospf message-digest-key 2 md5 ospf-md5-2
R4(config-if)#exit

R6(config)#interface Ethernet0/0
R6(config-if)#ip ospf message-digest-key 2 md5 ospf-md5-2
R6(config-if)#exit
```

Again, OSPF authentication configuration can be verified using the show ip ospf and the show ip ospf interface [name] commands. Following is the output of the show ip ospf interface command on R6:

```
R6#show ip ospf interface Ethernet0/0
Ethernet0/0 is up, line protocol is up
  Internet Address 172.16.4.6/24, Area 2
  Process ID 6, Router ID 6.6.6.6, Network Type BROADCAST, Cost: 10
  Transmit Delay is 1 sec, State DR, Priority 1
  Designated Router (ID) 6.6.6.6, Interface address 172.16.4.6
  Backup Designated router (ID) 4.4.4.4, Interface address 172.16.4.4
  Timer intervals configured, Hello 10, Dead 40, Wait 40, Retransmit 5
    oob-resync timeout 40
    Hello due in 00:00:08
  Index 1/1, flood queue length 0
  Next 0x0(0)/0x0(0)
  Last flood scan length is 0, maximum is 1
  Last flood scan time is 0 msec, maximum is 0 msec
  Neighbor Count is 1, Adjacent neighbor count is 1
    Adjacent with neighbor 4.4.4.4  (Backup Designated Router)
  Suppress Hello for 0 neighbor(s)
  Message digest authentication enabled
    Youngest key id is 2
```

NOTE: When configuring MD5 authentication and a key ID is specified, you cannot simply change the password by entering the ip ospf message-digest-key [key ID] md5 [password] interface configuration command with the desired new password. Instead, you must negate the original configuration and re-enter this command with the desired new password. If this is attempted, the router will print an error message similar to the following:

```
R4(config)#interface FastEthernet0/0
R4(config-if)#ip ospf message-digest-key 2 md5 my-new-password
OSPF: Key 2 already exists
```

NOTE: If an additional key is configured on an interface that is already configured for MD5 authentication, the router begins the rollover process and sends multiple copies of the same packet, each authenticated by the different configured keys. For example, assume that key 5 was configured on the Serial0/0 interface of R4 in addition to key 1, which is currently being used for authentication with R3. Based on this configuration, the show ip ospf interface [name] command shows the following for the Serial0/0 interface of R4:

```
R4#show ip ospf interface Serial0/0
Serial0/0 is up, line protocol is up
  Internet Address 10.0.2.4/24, Area 2
  Process ID 4, Router ID 4.4.4.4, Network Type POINT_TO_POINT, Cost: 64
  Enabled by interface config, including secondary ip addresses
  Transmit Delay is 1 sec, State POINT_TO_POINT
```

```
Timer intervals configured, Hello 10, Dead 40, Wait 40, Retransmit 5
  oob-resync timeout 40
  Hello due in 00:00:05
Supports Link-local Signaling (LLS)
Index 3/3, flood queue length 0
Next 0x0(0)/0x0(0)
Last flood scan length is 1, maximum is 1
Last flood scan time is 0 msec, maximum is 0 msec
Neighbor Count is 1, Adjacent neighbor count is 1
  Adjacent with neighbor 3.3.3.3
Suppress Hello for 0 neighbor(s)
Message digest authentication enabled
  Youngest key id is 5
  Rollover in progress, 1 neighbor(s) using the old key(s):
    key id 1
```

Using the debug ip ospf events command, we can validate that R4 is indeed sending multiple copies of the same packets to R3, each using a different key as illustrated below:

```
R4#debug ip ospf events
OSPF events debugging is on
R4#
*Mar  1 20:12:13.250: OSPF: Send with key 1
*Mar  1 20:12:13.250: OSPF: Send Hello to 224.0.0.5 Area 2 on Serial0/0 from
10.0.2.4
*Mar  1 20:12:13.250: OSPF: Send with key 5
*Mar  1 20:12:13.250: OSPF: Send Hello to 224.0.0.5 Area 2 on Serial0/0 from
10.0.2.4
```

R4 will continue to send multiple copies of the same OSPF packets with as many keys as are configured on the interface until R3 is configured with the new key (5). At this point, the old key ceases being used and both routers use the new key. Following is the output of the debug ip ospf events command after R5 has also been configured with the new key:

```
R4#debug ip ospf events
OSPF events debugging is on
R4#
*Mar  1 20:22:33.275: OSPF: Send with youngest Key 5
*Mar  1 20:22:33.275: OSPF: Send Hello to 224.0.0.5 Area 2 on Serial0/0 from
10.0.2.4

[Truncated Output]
```

```
*Mar  1 20:22:43.275: OSPF: Send with youngest Key 5
*Mar  1 20:22:43.275: OSPF: Send Hello to 224.0.0.5 Area 2 on Serial0/0 from
10.0.2.4
```

The old key is retained in the configuration until it is negated. However, the following output of the show ip ospf interface command shows only that the new key is being used:

```
R4#show ip ospf interface Serial0/0
Serial0/0 is up, line protocol is up
  Internet Address 10.0.2.4/24, Area 2
  Process ID 4, Router ID 4.4.4.4, Network Type POINT_TO_POINT, Cost: 64
  Enabled by interface config, including secondary ip addresses
  Transmit Delay is 1 sec, State POINT_TO_POINT
  Timer intervals configured, Hello 10, Dead 40, Wait 40, Retransmit 5
    oob-resync timeout 40
    Hello due in 00:00:09
  Supports Link-local Signaling (LLS)
  Index 3/3, flood queue length 0
  Next 0x0(0)/0x0(0)
  Last flood scan length is 1, maximum is 1
  Last flood scan time is 0 msec, maximum is 0 msec
  Neighbor Count is 1, Adjacent neighbor count is 1
    Adjacent with neighbor 3.3.3.3
  Suppress Hello for 0 neighbor(s)
  Message digest authentication enabled
    Youngest key id is 5
```

Configuring Interface Authentication

Interface authentication is enabled first by using the ip ospf authentication [message-digest|null] interface configuration command. Used without additional keywords, this command enables plain text authentication for the configured interface. The message-digest keyword configures the interface to use MD5 authentication. The null keyword is used to specify that no authentication will be used for this interface. This is the default.

Interface-based authentication provides flexibility in that authentication can be configured on some subnets and not others for routers residing in the same OSPF area. When area authentication is configured, all routers must be configured for authentication. Interface-based authentication negates the need to configure all routers in the area for authentication. For example, if the LAN link between R4 and R6 was secure, perhaps due to a firewall on the LAN, but the WAN link between R3 and R4 was not secure, interface-based authentication could be configured on that link only, securing routing protocol packets between R3 and R4.

After specifying the interface authentication type, the next step when configuring interface-based authentication is to use the `ip ospf authentication-key [password]` or the `ip ospf message-digest-key [key ID] md5 [password]` interface configuration commands, which must be used to configure the password depending on the type of authentication enabled at the interface level. Referencing the topology illustrated in Figure 3-30, plain text interface-based authentication will be configured for the connection between R3 and R4. This configuration is implemented as follows:

```
R3(config)#interface Serial0/0
R3(config-if)#ip ospf authentication-key secure
R3(config-if)#exit

R4(config)#interface Serial0/0
R4(config-if)#ip ospf authentication
R4(config-if)#ip ospf authentication-key secure
R4(config-if)#exit
```

NOTE: If the plain text password is longer than 8 bytes (8 characters), then the following warning message will be printed on the console:

```
R3(config)#interface Serial0/0
R3(config-if)#ip ospf authentication-key howtonetwork
%OSPF: Warning: The password/key will be truncated to 8 characters
```

When interface-based authentication is configured, the `show ip ospf` command correctly reflects that authentication for the area is not configured as illustrated below:

```
R4#show ip ospf | begin Area 2
    Area 2
        Number of interfaces in this area is 3 (2 Loopback)
        Area has no authentication
        SPF algorithm last executed 00:01:27.548 ago
        SPF algorithm executed 19 times
        Area ranges are
        Number of LSA 10. Checksum Sum 0x0541DD
        Number of opaque link LSA 0. Checksum Sum 0x000000
        Number of DCbitless LSA 0
        Number of indication LSA 0
        Number of DoNotAge LSA 0
        Flood list length 0
```

However, the `show ip ospf interface [name]` command can be used to validate the configured authentication type for the specified interface as illustrated below:

```
R4#show ip ospf interface Serial0/0
Serial0/0 is up, line protocol is up
  Internet Address 10.0.2.4/24, Area 2
  Process ID 4, Router ID 4.4.4.4, Network Type POINT_TO_POINT, Cost: 64
  Enabled by interface config, including secondary ip addresses
  Transmit Delay is 1 sec, State POINT_TO_POINT
  Timer intervals configured, Hello 10, Dead 40, Wait 40, Retransmit 5
    oob-resync timeout 40
    Hello due in 00:00:01
  Supports Link-local Signaling (LLS)
  Index 3/3, flood queue length 0
  Next 0x0(0)/0x0(0)
  Last flood scan length is 1, maximum is 1
  Last flood scan time is 0 msec, maximum is 4 msec
  Neighbor Count is 1, Adjacent neighbor count is 1
    Adjacent with neighbor 3.3.3.3
  Suppress Hello for 0 neighbor(s)
  Simple password authentication enabled
```

NOTE: Plain text authentication cannot be validated using the debug ip ospf events command as is the case for MD5 authentication.

CONFIGURING OSPF OVER NON-BROADCAST NETWORKS

A Non-Broadcast Multi-Access (NBMA) network is a network type that allows multiple hosts to connect to the same network; however, an NBMA does not natively support Broadcast and Multicast packets. One of the most commonly implemented NBMA technologies is Frame Relay. The implementation of OSPF on NBMA networks requires a great deal of thought and planning. OSPF can be implemented on NBMA networks in the following three modes:

1. Simulated Broadcast Mode
2. Point-to-Point Mode
3. Point-to-Multipoint Mode

Each mode has its advantages and disadvantages. It is therefore important to weigh them accordingly based on the network in which you want to implement OSPF. The following sections describe these three modes, their advantages, and their disadvantages.

Simulated Broadcast Mode

Simulated Broadcast mode simulates a traditional Broadcast model by electing a Designated Router and a Backup Designated Router on the NBMA network. There are two ways in which OSPF can be implemented in simulated Broadcast mode for NBMA network types:

1. Using the default network type and the `neighbor` router configuration command
2. By changing the default network type to the `broadcast` network type

When OSPF is enabled on a Frame Relay network, the default network type is Non-Broadcast. Unlike with Broadcast network types, Multicast Hello packets are not used for dynamic neighbor discovery on NBMA networks. Instead, because OSPF assumes that the underlying infrastructure is incapable of sending and receiving Broadcast and Multicast packets, static neighbor configuration is required to allow the routers on the NBMA network to communicate using Unicast packets instead of Multicast packets.

This requirement is mandatory even if the `broadcast` keyword has been added to the end of the `frame-relay map` command or if Inverse ARP has been used to map remote IP addresses dynamically to local DLCIs. In Cisco IOS software, static OSPF neighbors are defined using the `neighbor [address] [priority <number>] [poll-interval <seconds>] [cost <number>] [database-filter all]` router configuration command for each directly connected neighbor router.

The `[address]` keyword specifies the IP address of the neighbor router. It is important to remember that the specified address is the interface address connected to the non-Broadcast network, and not the router ID. If the router ID is specified, the adjacency will not be established.

NOTE: If the router ID and the interface IP address are the same, then adjacency will be established.

The `priority <number>` keyword specifies the router priority of the neighbor associated with the IP address specified. A router priority value between 0 and 255 can be specified for the neighbor. By default, the neighbor priority value is set to 1. Assigning a priority value of 0 indicates that the neighbor will not participate in DR/BDR election. The router with the lowest priority value will be elected DR. If the priority values are the same, the RID will be used.

The `poll-interval <seconds>` keyword is used to configure the poll interval time based on RFC 1247 recommendations. This is not the Hello interval. The poll interval can be any integer between 0 and 4294967295. The default value is 120 seconds.

The `cost <number>` keyword specifies the neighbor router cost. This keyword is applicable only to point-to-multipoint configuration.

Finally, the `database-filter all` keyword is used to filter all outgoing Link State Advertisements to the specified OSPF neighbor router(s). Figure 3-31 below illustrates a typical full mesh

Frame Relay network topology wherein all routers are connected to each other via a permanent virtual circuit (DLCI):

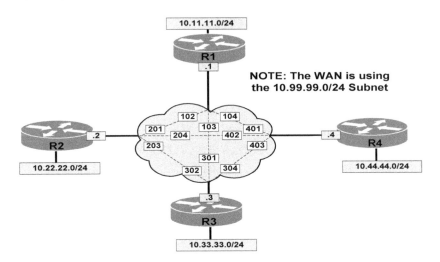

Fig. 3-31. A Full Mesh Frame Relay WAN

Referencing Figure 3-31, by default, when OSPF is enabled over Frame Relay, the interface defaults to a Non-Broadcast network type as illustrated in the output of the show ip ospf interface command below:

```
R1#show ip ospf interface Serial0/0
Serial0/0 is up, line protocol is up
  Internet Address 10.99.99.1/24, Area 0
  Process ID 1, Router ID 1.1.1.1, Network Type NON_BROADCAST, Cost: 64

...

[Truncated Output]
```

Because of the default network type, OSPF neighbors must be statically configured in Cisco IOS software in order for adjacencies to be established between the neighbor routers. Although the neighbors use Unicast packets to communicate, the election of the DR and BDR routers follows the same rules as are applicable in Broadcast network types.

Again, referencing Figure 3-31 above, OSPF would be configured and implemented as follows on the network topology illustrated in the diagram:

```
R1(config)#interface FastEthernet0/0
R1(config-if)#ip ospf 3 Area 0
R1(config-if)#exit
R1(config)#interface Serial0/0
```

```
R1(config-if)#ip ospf 3 Area 0
R1(config-if)#exit
R1(config)#router ospf 1
R1(config-router)#neighbor 10.99.99.2
R1(config-router)#neighbor 10.99.99.3
R1(config-router)#neighbor 10.99.99.4
R1(config-router)#exit

R2(config)#router ospf 2
R2(config-router)#router-id 2.2.2.2
R2(config-router)#network 10.22.22.0 0.0.0.255 Area 0
R2(config-router)#network 10.99.99.0 0.0.0.255 Area 0
R2(config-router)#neighbor 10.99.99.1
R2(config-router)#neighbor 10.99.99.3
R2(config-router)#neighbor 10.99.99.4
R2(config-router)#exit

R3(config)#interface FastEthernet0/0
R3(config-if)#ip ospf 3 Area 0
R3(config-if)#exit
R3(config)#interface Serial0/0
R3(config-if)#ip ospf 3 Area 0
R3(config-if)#exit
R3(config)#router ospf 3
R3(config-router)#neighbor 10.99.99.1
R3(config-router)#neighbor 10.99.99.2
R3(config-router)#neighbor 10.99.99.4
R3(config-router)#exit

R4(config)#router ospf 4
R4(config-router)#router-id 4.4.4.4
R4(config-router)#network 10.44.44.0 0.0.0.255 Area 0
R4(config-router)#network 10.99.99.0 0.0.0.255 Area 0
R4(config-router)#neighbor 10.99.99.1
R4(config-router)#neighbor 10.99.99.2
R4(config-router)#neighbor 10.99.99.3
R4(config-router)#exit
```

NOTE: The ip ospf and the network commands are used in the configurations above to reinforce the statement that either method of configuration is valid and acceptable.

Following the configuration of OSPF, the show ip ospf neighbor command is used to validate the configuration and verify the adjacencies and DR/BDR election as illustrated below:

```
R1#show ip ospf neighbor

Neighbor ID    Pri    State           Dead Time    Address       Interface
2.2.2.2          1    2WAY/DROTHER    00:01:31     10.99.99.2    Serial0/0
3.3.3.3          1    FULL/BDR        00:01:37     10.99.99.3    Serial0/0
4.4.4.4          1    FULL/DR         00:01:56     10.99.99.4    Serial0/0

R2#show ip ospf neighbor

Neighbor ID    Pri    State           Dead Time    Address       Interface
3.3.3.3          1    FULL/BDR        00:01:52     10.99.99.3    Serial0/0
1.1.1.1          1    2WAY/DROTHER    00:01:37     10.99.99.1    Serial0/0
4.4.4.4          1    FULL/DR         00:01:56     10.99.99.4    Serial0/0

R3#show ip ospf neighbor

Neighbor ID    Pri    State           Dead Time    Address       Interface
2.2.2.2          1    FULL/DROTHER    00:01:56     10.99.99.2    Serial0/0
1.1.1.1          1    FULL/DROTHER    00:01:32     10.99.99.1    Serial0/0
4.4.4.4          1    FULL/DR         00:01:50     10.99.99.4    Serial0/0

R4#show ip ospf neighbor

Neighbor ID    Pri    State           Dead Time    Address       Interface
2.2.2.2          1    FULL/DROTHER    00:01:50     10.99.99.2    Serial0/0
3.3.3.3          1    FULL/BDR        00:01:50     10.99.99.3    Serial0/0
1.1.1.1          1    FULL/DROTHER    00:01:48     10.99.99.1    Serial0/0
```

From the output above, R4 has been elected DR (based on the RID) and R3 has been elected BDR (also based on the RID). Routers R1 and R2 are DROther routers. These two routers establish an adjacency with the DR and BDR but not with each other. If the DR fails, the BDR assumes the role of DR and a new BDR would then be elected, as would be the case on a traditional Broadcast network. The second method of implementing OSPF in simulated Broadcast mode entails the changing of the default OSPF network type for the NBMA network using the ip ospf network broadcast interface configuration command on all routers. This configuration allows for DR/BDR election but negates the need to configure manually static neighbors. This is because a Broadcast network is one that natively supports both Broadcast and Multicast traffic. This lifts the restriction imposed by the Non-Broadcast network type and OSPF can use Multicast Hello packets to discover neighbors dynamically.

NOTE: When implementing OSPF in simulated Broadcast mode by changing the default OSPF network type, it is important to ensure that the Frame Relay network has been configured to support Broadcast and Multicast packets either via Inverse ARP (dynamic mappings) or by the addition of the broadcast keyword to frame-relay map statements.

Following the configuration of the ip ospf network broadcast interface configuration command on all WAN interfaces of R1, R2, R3, and R4, the show ip ospf neighbor command is used to validate the configuration and verify the adjacencies as shown for R3 below:

```
R3#show ip ospf neighbor

Neighbor ID      Pri   State          Dead Time   Address      Interface
2.2.2.2            1   FULL/DROTHER   00:00:32    10.99.99.2   Serial0/0
1.1.1.1            1   FULL/DROTHER   00:00:35    10.99.99.1   Serial0/0
4.4.4.4            1   FULL/DR        00:00:33    10.99.99.4   Serial0/0
```

The show ip ospf interface command is used to verify the non-default network type as illustrated in the following output:

```
R3#show ip ospf interface Serial0/0
Serial0/0 is up, line protocol is up
  Internet Address 10.99.99.3/24, Area 0
  Process ID 3, Router ID 3.3.3.3, Network Type BROADCAST, Cost: 64
  Enabled by interface config, including secondary ip addresses
  Transmit Delay is 1 sec, State BDR, Priority 1
  Designated Router (ID) 4.4.4.4, Interface address 10.99.99.4
  Backup Designated router (ID) 3.3.3.3, Interface address 10.99.99.3
  Timer intervals configured, Hello 10, Dead 40, Wait 40, Retransmit 5
    oob-resync timeout 40
    Hello due in 00:00:08
  Supports Link-local Signaling (LLS)
  Index 2/2, flood queue length 0
  Next 0x0(0)/0x0(0)
  Last flood scan length is 0, maximum is 1
  Last flood scan time is 0 msec, maximum is 4 msec
  Neighbor Count is 3, Adjacent neighbor count is 3
    Adjacent with neighbor 2.2.2.2
    Adjacent with neighbor 1.1.1.1
    Adjacent with neighbor 4.4.4.4  (Designated Router)
  Suppress Hello for 0 neighbor(s)
```

While the previous configuration examples have illustrated the implementation of OSPF in simulated Broadcast mode over a fully meshed Frame Relay network, it is important to understand that the same solution can also be applied to a partially meshed Frame Relay network. However, it is imperative to ensure the following when doing so:

- The DR must have a direct connection (virtual circuit) to every other router
- The DR must have a direct connection (virtual circuit) to the BDR
- The BDR must have a direct connection (virtual circuit) to every other router

Figure 3-32 below illustrates a topology that meets these specifications:

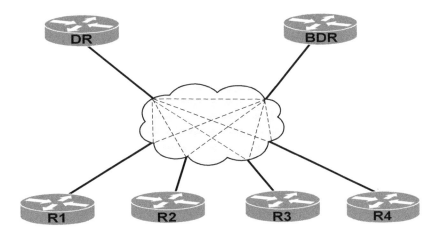

Fig. 3-32. A Redundant Partial Mesh Frame Relay WAN

Referencing Figure 3-32, both the DR and the BDR are connected to each other and all other routers connecting across the Frame Relay network. The spoke routers (R1, R2, R3, and R4) do not need to have a direct connection between them. When implementing OSPF in simulated Broadcast mode over such a topology, it is important to ensure that none of the spoke routers is ever elected DR or BDR inadvertently. The recommended solution in this network would be to issue the `ip ospf priority 0` interface configuration command on each of the spoke routers, or, alternatively, use a network type that does not require or elect a DR or a BDR router.

The primary advantage gained by using simulated Broadcast mode is the use of the Designated Router. The DR (and BDR) reduces the amount of traffic and updates required between individual routers by acting as a central point of contact for all routers connected to the multi-access network. In addition, the number of adjacencies required on the multi-access network is also reduced, as DROther routers establish adjacencies only with the DR and BDR routers. The disadvantages of using simulated Broadcast mode is that all routers must have a direct connection (full mesh) between them or additional configuration is required to ensure that spoke routers do not become the DR or BDR (partial mesh).

Point-to-Point Mode

Point-to-point mode is perhaps the simplest method of implementing OSPF on NBMA network types. By default, OSPF uses Multicast on point-to-point network types for dynamic neighbor discovery, even on Frame Relay subinterfaces. When configuring point-to-point Frame Relay subinterfaces, the `frame-relay interface-dlci` subinterface configuration command must be used instead of the `frame-relay map` command. The following configuration illustrates how to configure a point-to-point connection between two routers:

```
R1(config)#interface Serial0/0
R1(config-if)#no ip address
R1(config-if)#encapsulation frame-relay
R1(config-if)#exit
R1(config)#interface Serial0/0.1 point-to-point
R1(config-subif)#ip address 10.99.99.1 255.255.255.252
R1(config-subif)#frame-relay interface-dlci 102
R1(config-fr-dlci)#exit
R1(config-subif)#exit
R1(config)#router ospf 1
R1(config-router)#network 10.99.99.1 255.255.255.252 Area 0
R1(config-router)#exit

R2(config)#interface Serial0/0
R2(config-if)#no ip address
R2(config-if)#encapsulation frame-relay
R2(config-if)#exit
R2(config)#interface Serial0/0.2 point-to-point
R2(config-subif)#ip address 10.99.99.2 255.255.255.252
R2(config-subif)#ip ospf 2 Area 0
R2(config-subif)#frame-relay interface-dlci 201
R2(config-fr-dlci)#exit
```

Following this configuration, the `show ip ospf interface` command is used to validate the network type as well as adjacency formed with the remote router as illustrated below:

```
R2#show ip ospf interface Serial0/0.2
Serial0/0.2 is up, line protocol is up
  Internet Address 10.99.99.2/30, Area 0
  Process ID 2, Router ID 2.2.2.2, Network Type POINT_TO_POINT, Cost: 64
  Enabled by interface config, including secondary ip addresses
  Transmit Delay is 1 sec, State POINT_TO_POINT
  Timer intervals configured, Hello 10, Dead 40, Wait 40, Retransmit 5
    oob-resync timeout 40
    Hello due in 00:00:03
  Supports Link-local Signaling (LLS)
```

```
Index 2/2, flood queue length 0
Next 0x0(0)/0x0(0)
Last flood scan length is 1, maximum is 1
Last flood scan time is 0 msec, maximum is 0 msec
Neighbor Count is 1, Adjacent neighbor count is 1
  Adjacent with neighbor 1.1.1.1
Suppress Hello for 0 neighbor(s)
```

The primary advantage of using OSPF point-to-point mode is that it is easy to configure and implement. However, there are certain factors that should be taken into consideration. The first factor pertains to IP address space. If IP address space is plentiful, this is not an issue. However, if IP address space is scarce, or almost depleted, it may not be feasible to allocate a subnet for each individual point-to-point connection, especially in a large deployment.

Another factor that should be taken into consideration is the size of the Link State Database. Although Type 2 LSAs are not generated for the point-to-point subnets, a Type 3 LSA is still generated by the ABR for each one. In a large deployment, this will increase the size of the LSBD on routers in adjacent areas, which could lead to performance issues. However, if the IP address space is contiguous, the area...range command can be used to mitigate this.

Point-to-Multipoint Mode

Point-to-multipoint mode is a non-default OSPF mode. In Cisco IOS software, this configuration is used to treat the NBMA network as a collection of point-to-point connections or links. This mode allows all routers connected to each other to establish an adjacency without the need to elect a DR or a BDR. Point-to-point mode can be configured to allow OSPF to use either Multicast (default) or Unicast packets to establish adjacencies with other routers.

In Cisco IOS software, the ip ospf network point-to-multipoint [broadcast] interface configuration command is used to configure point-to-multipoint mode. When this command is issued, a host route is created for all routers that reside on the multi-access network. This negates the need to configure multiple frame-relay map statements for all of the routers connected to the Frame Relay network. Figure 3-33 below illustrates a typical hub-and-spoke network wherein the spoke routers, routers R2 and R3, have a single virtual circuit provisioned to the hub router (R1). All routers, however, are part of the same logical Layer 3 network 10.99.99.0/24 as shown in the following diagram:

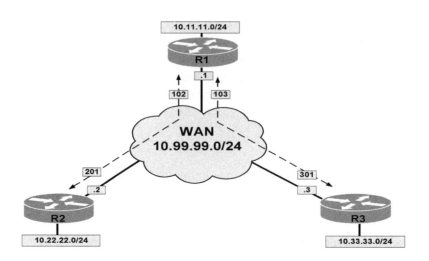

Fig. 3-33. A Traditional Hub-and-Spoke Network

Referencing Figure 3-33, the two spoke routers are connected to the hub router via a single virtual circuit (DLCI). While both simulated Broadcast and point-to-point mode could be implemented in the same network, the additional configuration required to implement both methods makes point-to-multipoint mode the best possible option, as it accommodates the current network design and requires the least amount of additional configuration. The following output illustrates how to implement OSPF point-to-multipoint mode on the three routers illustrated in Figure 3-33:

```
R1(config)#router ospf 1
R1(config-router)#router-id 1.1.1.1
R1(config-router)#network 10.99.99.0 255.255.255.0 Area 0
R1(config-router)#network 10.11.11.0 255.255.255.0 Area 0
R1(config-router)#exit
R1(config)#interface Serial0/0
R1(config-if)#ip ospf network point-to-multipoint
R1(config-if)#exit
R1(config)#

R2(config)#interface FastEthernet0/0
R2(config-if)#ip ospf 2 Area 0
R2(config-if)#exit
R2(config)#interface Serial0/0
R2(config-if)#ip ospf 2 Area 0
R2(config-if)#ip ospf network point-to-multipoint
R2(config-if)#exit
R2(config)#router ospf 2
R2(config-router)#router-id 2.2.2.2
R2(config-router)#exit
```

```
R3(config)#interface FastEthernet0/0
R3(config-if)#ip ospf 3 Area 0
R3(config-if)#exit
R3(config)#interface Serial0/0
R3(config-if)#ip ospf network point-to-multipoint
R3(config-if)#ip ospf 3 Area 0
R3(config-if)#exit
R3(config)#router ospf 3
R3(config-router)#router-id 3.3.3.3
R3(config-router)#exit
```

To validate this configuration, either the show ip ospf interface or the show ip ospf neighbor commands can be used. Following is the output of the show ip ospf interface command on R1, the hub router, and the output of the show ip ospf neighbor command on spoke routers R2 and R3:

```
R1#show ip ospf interface Serial0/0
Serial0/0 is up, line protocol is up
  Internet Address 10.99.99.1/24, Area 0
  Process ID 1, Router ID 1.1.1.1, Network Type POINT_TO_MULTIPOINT, Cost:
64
  Transmit Delay is 1 sec, State POINT_TO_MULTIPOINT,
  Timer intervals configured, Hello 30, Dead 120, Wait 120, Retransmit 5
    oob-resync timeout 120
    Hello due in 00:00:24
  Index 1/1, flood queue length 0
  Next 0x0(0)/0x0(0)
  Last flood scan length is 1, maximum is 2
  Last flood scan time is 0 msec, maximum is 4 msec
  Neighbor Count is 2, Adjacent neighbor count is 2
    Adjacent with neighbor 2.2.2.2
    Adjacent with neighbor 3.3.3.3
  Suppress Hello for 0 neighbor(s)

R2#show ip ospf neighbor

Neighbor ID     Pri   State           Dead Time   Address     Interface
1.1.1.1           0   FULL/  -        00:01:38    10.99.99.1  Serial0/0

R3#show ip ospf neighbor

Neighbor ID     Pri   State           Dead Time   Address     Interface
1.1.1.1           0   FULL/  -        00:01:51    10.99.99.1  Serial0/0
```

While the implementation of point-to-multipoint mode is very simple and straightforward, it is important to remember that a host route is generated for each of the interfaces connected to the NBMA network. This is illustrated on R1 below:

```
R1#show ip route ospf
     10.0.0.0/8 is variably subnetted, 6 subnets, 2 masks
O       10.99.99.2/32 [110/64] via 10.99.99.2, 00:08:35, Serial0/0
O       10.99.99.3/32 [110/64] via 10.99.99.3, 00:08:35, Serial0/0
O       10.33.33.0/24 [110/65] via 10.99.99.3, 00:08:35, Serial0/0
O       10.22.22.0/24 [110/65] via 10.99.99.2, 00:08:35, Serial0/0
```

In a small network such as the one illustrated in Figure 3-33, this is typically not even an issue. However, if, for example, R1 were connected to additional OSPF areas as the ABR, the router would also generate a Type 3 LSA for each host route and flood it to all of the adjacent areas as illustrated in the following output:

```
R1#show ip ospf database

            OSPF Router with ID (1.1.1.1) (Process ID 1)

            Router Link States (Area 0)

Link ID          ADV Router       Age         Seq#        Checksum Link Count
1.1.1.1          1.1.1.1          740         0x80000006 0x00CDFF 4
2.2.2.2          2.2.2.2          1016        0x80000003 0x00E9F7 3
3.3.3.3          3.3.3.3          1041        0x80000015 0x006B44 3

            Summary Net Link States (Area 0)

Link ID          ADV Router       Age         Seq#        Checksum
172.16.1.1       1.1.1.1          735         0x80000001 0x00DA9E

            Router Link States (Area 1)

Link ID          ADV Router       Age         Seq#        Checksum Link Count
1.1.1.1          1.1.1.1          740         0x80000002 0x00FB6D 1

            Summary Net Link States (Area 1)

Link ID          ADV Router       Age         Seq#        Checksum
10.11.11.0       1.1.1.1          740         0x80000001 0x00F423
10.22.22.0       1.1.1.1          741         0x80000001 0x007948
10.33.33.0       1.1.1.1          741         0x80000001 0x007B30
10.99.99.1       1.1.1.1          741         0x80000001 0x00F076
```

```
10.99.99.2      1.1.1.1         741        0x80000001 0x0069BC
10.99.99.3      1.1.1.1         741        0x80000001 0x005FC5
```

In the output above, R1 has been configured as an ABR by connecting it to Area 1. Following the expected operation of an ABR, R1 generates a Type 3 LSA for each of the individual hosts and floods it into Area 1. In large networks, this may result in a large number of LSAs being flooded into adjacent areas. Again, it is important to remember that one of the core principles when implementing OSPF is to attempt to keep the database as lean as possible, as this reduces OSPF convergence time and results in better protocol performance in the network.

OSPF Routing and Metric Calculation over Frame Relay Networks

One of the most common errors engineers make when implementing OSPF in Frame Relay networks is forgetting to look at the underlying technology. In most Frame Relay implementations, DLCIs typically have different Committed Information Rate (CIR) values, especially in situations where two routers are used to back each other up at the same site. Consider the topology illustrated in Figure 3-34 below:

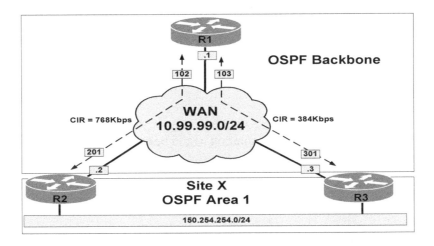

Fig. 3-34. A Basic Redundant Site

Figure 3-34 illustrates a basic network topology wherein two individual routers are connected to the 150.254.254.0/24 subnet and are redundantly connected across the Frame Relay WAN to the hub router (R1). The CIR for the DLCI provisioned between R1 and the primary router at the site (R2) is 768Kbps. The CIR for the DLCI provisioned between R1 and the secondary (backup) router at the site is 384Kbps.

From a network engineer's perspective, OSPF point-to-multipoint mode would arguably be the simplest solution when implementing OSPF in this network. The issue, however, arises with the way that OSPF calculates its metric. By default, OSPF will use the cost value assigned to the interface to determine the metric to the destination network. Assuming that both R2 and R3 are using similar cost interfaces, R1 calculates the cost to the 150.254.254.0/24 subnet as being the same for the paths between both R2 and R3 as illustrated in the following output:

```
R1#show ip route 150.254.254.0 255.255.255.0
Routing entry for 150.254.254.0/24
  Known via "ospf 1", distance 110, metric 65, type inter area
  Last update from 10.99.99.3 on Serial0/0, 00:00:28 ago
  Routing Descriptor Blocks:
  * 10.99.99.2, from 2.2.2.2, 00:00:28 ago, via Serial0/0
      Route metric is 65, traffic share count is 1
    10.99.99.3, from 3.3.3.3, 00:00:28 ago, via Serial0/0
      Route metric is 65, traffic share count is 1
```

Based on the output above, OSPF will perform equal cost load balancing to the 150.254.254.0/24 subnet using both R2 and R3. However, because the DLCIs are provisioned with different CIR values, it is therefore important to look at the underlying infrastructure before deciding on which OSPF mode to implement on the NBMA network.

Referencing the topology in Figure 3-34, while the first option that comes to mind would be the use of the ip ospf cost interface configuration command, it is important to understand that this would result only in a different equal cost metric for both paths and would not ensure that the path via R2 is preferred over the path via R3.

In Cisco IOS software, the recommended solution would be to use the neighbor [address] cost <value> router configuration command. This command allows administrators to specify manually a unique cost value for each OSPF neighbor and can be used only with point-to-multipoint (Non-Broadcast) mode. If you do not look at the overall picture, you will most likely find yourself having to reconfigure routers to accommodate such situations. The following configuration examples demonstrate how to use point-to-multipoint (Non-Broadcast) mode to ensure that R1 prefers the path via R2 to reach the 150.254.254.0/24 subnet:

```
R1(config)#interface Serial0/0
R1(config-if)#ip ospf network point-to-multipoint non-broadcast
R1(config-if)#exit
R1(config)#router ospf 1
R1(config-router)#neighbor 10.99.99.2 cost 1
R1(config-router)#neighbor 10.99.99.3 cost 2
R1(config-router)#exit

R2(config)#interface Serial0/0
R2(config-if)#ip ospf network point-to-multipoint non-broadcast
```

```
R2(config-if)#router ospf 2
R2(config-router)#neighbor 10.99.99.1
R2(config-router)#exit

R3(config)#interface Serial0/0
R3(config-if)#ip ospf network point-to-multipoint non-broadcast
R3(config-if)#exit
R3(config)#router ospf 3
R3(config-router)#neighbor 10.99.99.1
R3(config-router)#exit
```

This configuration is validated using the show ip ospf neighbor command as follows:

```
R1#show ip ospf interface Serial0/0
Serial0/0 is up, line protocol is up
  Internet Address 10.99.99.1/24, Area 0
  Process ID 1, Router ID 1.1.1.1, Network Type POINT_TO_MULTIPOINT, Cost:
64
  Transmit Delay is 1 sec, State POINT_TO_MULTIPOINT,
  Timer intervals configured, Hello 30, Dead 120, Wait 120, Retransmit 5
    oob-resync timeout 120
    Hello due in 00:00:11
  Index 1/1, flood queue length 0
  Next 0x0(0)/0x0(0)
  Last flood scan length is 1, maximum is 2
  Last flood scan time is 0 msec, maximum is 4 msec
  Neighbor Count is 2, Adjacent neighbor count is 2
    Adjacent with neighbor 3.3.3.3, cost is 2
    Adjacent with neighbor 2.2.2.2, cost is 1
  Suppress Hello for 0 neighbor(s)
```

After this change, the routing table on R1 for the 150.254.254.0/24 subnet is illustrated as follows:

```
R1#show ip route 150.254.254.0 255.255.255.0
Routing entry for 150.254.254.0/24
  Known via "ospf 1", distance 110, metric 2, type inter area
  Last update from 10.99.99.2 on Serial0/0, 00:02:41 ago
  Routing Descriptor Blocks:
  * 10.99.99.2, from 2.2.2.2, 00:02:41 ago, via Serial0/0
      Route metric is 2, traffic share count is 1
```

If you attempt to configure a cost value on the default network type (i.e., Non-Broadcast), the following error message will be printed on the console:

```
R1(config-if)#router ospf 1
R1(config-router)#neighbor 10.99.99.2 cost 1
OSPF: Cost and database-filter option are allowed only for point-to-
multipoint network
```

In summation, as has been demonstrated in this section, OSPF can be implemented in NBMA networks in numerous ways. It is important to plan and understand adequately the topology prior to deciding on the OSPF mode that will be best suited for implementation. By understanding the design of the Layer 2 Frame Relay network, you can accurately design the Layer 3 topology and avoid any pitfalls or redesigns at a later stage.

 REAL WORLD IMPLEMENTATION

While this section focuses exclusively on OSPF, when EIGRP is enabled across the Frame Relay WAN, it is important to remember that there are no cost configurations available in Cisco IOS software. Therefore, the `bandwidth` interface configuration command must be used. In topologies such as that illustrated in Figure 3-34, if EIGRP is the routing protocol being used, you must configure the bandwidth to represent the minimum CIR multiplied by the number of circuits. This approach may result in the higher CIR circuits not being fully utilized, but it ensures that the circuits with the lowest CIR are not oversubscribed. An alternative solution with EIGRP would be to use point-to-point subinterfaces instead and then configure the `bandwidth` statement to match the provided Frame Relay CIR.

Additionally, when EIGRP is used as the routing protocol across a Frame Relay WAN, Cisco IOS software automatically attempts to ensure that no single DLCI/PVC is oversubscribed, dividing the interface bandwidth with the number of DLCIs/PVCs provisioned and then limiting the rate per individual DLCI/PVC to approximately 50% of that value. For example, if you had a T1 interface (1.544Mbps) and four DLCIs/PVCs provisioned on it, Cisco IOS would divide 1.544Mbps by 4, resulting in approximately 384Kbps per DLCI/PVC, and then restrict traffic per DLCI/PVC to approximately 50% of that value, which would be approximately 193Kbps. This default behavior makes it somewhat easier to implement EIGRP over Frame Relay than is applicable when implementing OSPF over Frame Relay.

NOTE: The default behavior can be adjusted using the `ip bandwidth-percent eigrp [ASN]` `[percentage]` interface configuration command when using EIGRP as the IGP.

OSPF LOGGING AND REPORTING

In this final section, we will look at some of the OSPF logging and reporting configurations that are supported in Cisco IOS software. By default, the router will send a Syslog message when an OSPF neighbor goes up and down. This is enabled using the log-adjacency-changes router configuration command.

In addition to sending a Syslog message when a neighbor goes up and down, Cisco IOS software also allows the logging of each state change by appending the detail keyword to the log-adjacency-changes router configuration command. The following configuration illustrates how to configure the router to log each OSPF state change:

```
R2(config)#router ospf 2
R2(config-router)#log-adjacency-changes detail
R2(config-router)#exit
```

To verify this configuration, you can use the clear ip ospf process privileged EXEC command to reset the OSPF process and then view the contents of the log to validate that each state change is being logged as configured as illustrated below:

```
R2#clear logging
Clear logging buffer [confirm]
R2#
R2#clear ip ospf process
Reset ALL OSPF processes? [no]: y
R2#
R2#
R2#show logging
Syslog logging: enabled (11 messages dropped, 6 messages rate-limited,
                0 flushes, 0 overruns, xml disabled, filtering disabled)
    Console logging: disabled
    Monitor logging: level debugging, 0 messages logged, xml disabled,
                     filtering disabled
    Buffer logging: level debugging, 55 messages logged, xml disabled,
                    filtering disabled
    Logging Exception size (4096 bytes)
    Count and timestamp logging messages: disabled

No active filter modules.

    Trap logging: level informational, 77 message lines logged

Log Buffer (4096 bytes):

*Mar  1 23:05:29.535: %OSPF-5-ADJCHG: Process 2, Nbr 3.3.3.3 on Serial0/0
from FULL to DOWN, Neighbor Down: Interface down or detached
```

```
*Mar  1 23:05:29.535: %OSPF-5-ADJCHG: Process 2, Nbr 0.0.0.0 on Serial0/0
from DOWN to ATTEMPT, NBMA Start
*Mar  1 23:05:29.535: %OSPF-5-ADJCHG: Process 2, Nbr 0.0.0.0 on Serial0/0
from ATTEMPT to ATTEMPT, Start
*Mar  1 23:05:29.535: %OSPF-5-ADJCHG: Process 2, Nbr 1.1.1.1 on Serial0/0
from 2WAY to EXSTART, AdjOK?
*Mar  1 23:05:29.535: %OSPF-5-ADJCHG: Process 2, Nbr 1.1.1.1 on Serial0/0
from EXSTART to DOWN, Neighbor Down: Interface down or detached
*Mar  1 23:05:29.535: %OSPF-5-ADJCHG: Process 2, Nbr 0.0.0.0 on Serial0/0
from DOWN to ATTEMPT, NBMA Start
*Mar  1 23:05:29.539: %OSPF-5-ADJCHG: Process 2, Nbr 4.4.4.4 on Serial0/0
from FULL to DOWN, Neighbor Down: Interface down or detached
*Mar  1 23:05:29.539: %OSPF-5-ADJCHG: Process 2, Nbr 0.0.0.0 on Serial0/0
from DOWN to ATTEMPT, NBMA Start
*Mar  1 23:05:29.567: %OSPF-5-ADJCHG: Process 2, Nbr 0.0.0.0 on Serial0/0
from ATTEMPT to ATTEMPT, Start
*Mar  1 23:05:29.567: %OSPF-5-ADJCHG: Process 2, Nbr 0.0.0.0 on Serial0/0
from ATTEMPT to ATTEMPT, Start
*Mar  1 23:05:29.567: %OSPF-5-ADJCHG: Process 2, Nbr 0.0.0.0 on Serial0/0
from ATTEMPT to ATTEMPT, Start
*Mar  1 23:05:29.571: %OSPF-5-ADJCHG: Process 2, Nbr 0.0.0.0 on Serial0/0
from ATTEMPT to ATTEMPT, Start
*Mar  1 23:05:29.571: %OSPF-5-ADJCHG: Process 2, Nbr 0.0.0.0 on Serial0/0
from ATTEMPT to ATTEMPT, Start
*Mar  1 23:05:29.571: %OSPF-5-ADJCHG: Process 2, Nbr 0.0.0.0 on Serial0/0
from ATTEMPT to ATTEMPT, Start
*Mar  1 23:05:31.770: %OSPF-5-ADJCHG: Process 2, Nbr 1.1.1.1 on Serial0/0
from ATTEMPT to INIT, Received Hello
*Mar  1 23:05:31.770: %OSPF-5-ADJCHG: Process 2, Nbr 1.1.1.1 on Serial0/0
from INIT to 2WAY, 2-Way Received
*Mar  1 23:05:36.815: %OSPF-5-ADJCHG: Process 2, Nbr 3.3.3.3 on Serial0/0
from ATTEMPT to INIT, Received Hello
*Mar  1 23:05:36.815: %OSPF-5-ADJCHG: Process 2, Nbr 3.3.3.3 on Serial0/0
from INIT to 2WAY, 2-Way Received
*Mar  1 23:05:36.815: %OSPF-5-ADJCHG: Process 2, Nbr 3.3.3.3 on Serial0/0
from 2WAY to EXSTART, AdjOK?
*Mar  1 23:05:36.823: %OSPF-5-ADJCHG: Process 2, Nbr 3.3.3.3 on Serial0/0
from EXSTART to EXCHANGE, Negotiation Done
*Mar  1 23:05:36.831: %OSPF-5-ADJCHG: Process 2, Nbr 3.3.3.3 on Serial0/0
from EXCHANGE to LOADING, Exchange Done
*Mar  1 23:05:36.839: %OSPF-5-ADJCHG: Process 2, Nbr 3.3.3.3 on Serial0/0
from LOADING to FULL, Loading Done
*Mar  1 23:05:58.635: %OSPF-5-ADJCHG: Process 2, Nbr 4.4.4.4 on Serial0/0
from ATTEMPT to INIT, Received Hello
*Mar  1 23:05:58.635: %OSPF-5-ADJCHG: Process 2, Nbr 4.4.4.4 on Serial0/0
from INIT to 2WAY, 2-Way Received
*Mar  1 23:05:58.639: %OSPF-5-ADJCHG: Process 2, Nbr 4.4.4.4 on Serial0/0
from 2WAY to EXSTART, AdjOK?
```

```
*Mar  1 23:05:58.643: %OSPF-5-ADJCHG: Process 2, Nbr 4.4.4.4 on Serial0/0
from EXSTART to EXCHANGE, Negotiation Done
*Mar  1 23:05:58.655: %OSPF-5-ADJCHG: Process 2, Nbr 4.4.4.4 on Serial0/0
from EXCHANGE to LOADING, Exchange Done
*Mar  1 23:05:58.655: %OSPF-5-ADJCHG: Process 2, Nbr 4.4.4.4 on Serial0/0
from LOADING to FULL, Loading Done
```

As was stated earlier in this chapter, Cisco routers do not support Type 6 LSAs, which are used for Multicast OSPF (MOSPF) implementations. If a router receives a Type 6 LSA, the router will generate a Syslog message informing the administrators of the received OSPF Type 6 LSA. In multi-vendor environments, where some vendor routers do support Type 6 LSAs, this may result in a large number of Syslog messages being generated by the router. In order to avoid the large number of Syslog messages and to disable this default behavior, you can use the ignore lsa mospf router configuration command as illustrated below:

```
R2(config)#router ospf 2
R2(config-router)#ignore lsa mospf
R2(config-router)#exit
```

CHAPTER SUMMARY

The following section is a summary of the major points you should be aware of in this chapter.

OSPF Overview and Fundamentals

* RFC 1131 describes the first iteration of OSPF
* RFC 1584 provides extensions to OSPF for Multicast support. This is not supported by Cisco
* RFC 1587 describes the operation of an OSPF Not-So-Stubby Area (NSSA)
* RFC 1850 allows network management of OSPF using SNMP
* RFC 2328 details the latest update to OSPF version 2
* RFC 2740 describes the modifications to OSPF to support version 6 of the Internet Protocol
* The SPF algorithm is run following the database exchange
* After the SPF algorithm is run, routes are derived and the routing table is built
* OSPF only supports IP and supports both versions 4 and 6 of the IP protocol
* OSPF supports VLSM, authentication and sends routing updates using Multicast
* OSPF is a hierarchical routing protocol that logically divides the network into areas
* OSPF runs directly over Internet Protocol using IP protocol number 89
* Areas are used to limit the scope of LSA flooding throughout the OSPF domain
* The OSPF backbone is the logical center of the OSPF network
* All other non-backbone areas must be physically or logically connected to the backbone
* The hierarchical nature of OSPF allows for the following:

1. Reduces the scope of LSA flooding throughout the OSPF domain
2. Hides detailed topology information between areas
3. Allows for end-to-end connectivity within the OSPF domain
4. Creates logical boundaries within the OSPF domain

- OSPF uses different default network types for different media, which are the following:
    1. Non-Broadcast
    2. Point-to-Point
    3. Broadcast
    4. Point-to Multipoint

- Non-Broadcast network types do not support natively Broadcast or Multicast traffic
- A DR and/or BDR is elected on Non-Broadcast network types
- OSPF sends Hello packets every 30 seconds on Non-Broadcast network types
- The dead interval for Non-Broadcast network types is 120 seconds
- OSPF does not elect a DR or BDR on point-to-point network types
- OSPF sends Hello packet every 10 seconds on point-to-point network types
- The dead interval for point-to-point network types is 40 seconds
- Broadcast network types support Broadcast and Multicast traffic natively
- OSPF sends Hello packets every 10 seconds on Broadcast network types
- The dead interval for Broadcast network types is 40 seconds
- The point-to-multipoint network type is a non-default OSPF network type
- The point-to-multipoint network type can either be Broadcast (default) or non-Broadcast
- The point-to-multipoint non-Broadcast type requires static neighbor configuration
- OSPF sends Hello packets every 30 seconds for point-to-multipoint network types
- The dead interval for point-to-multipoint network types is 120 seconds
- OSPF can establish adjacencies using different network types if the timers are the same
- OSPF timers can also be adjusted to reduce protocol convergence time
- The BDR provides redundancy in case the DR fails. The BDR is not mandatory
- DROther routers sends updates to the AllDRRouter Multicast group 224.0.0.6
- The DR/BDR send updates to the AllSPFRouters Multicast group address 224.0.0.5
- The DR/BDR election is based on the following:
    1. The highest router priority value
    2. The highest router ID

- OSPF uses the DR and BDR routers as follows:
    1. To reduce the number of adjacencies required on the segment
    2. To advertise the routers on the multi-access segment
    3. To ensure that updates are sent to all routers on the segment

- The additional router types that are commonly found within the OSPF network include the following:
  1. Area Border Routers
  2. Autonomous System Boundary Routers
  3. Internal Routers
  4. Backbone Routers

- An ABR is an OSPF router that connects one or more OSPF areas to the OSPF backbone
- An ASBR, in the traditional sense, is resides at the edge of the routing domain
- An ASBR injects external routing information into the OSPF domain
- An ASBR defines the boundary between the internal and external networks
- Internal routers maintain all operational interfaces within a single area
- Backbone routers are routers that have an interface in the OSPF backbone
- OSPF routers can have multiple roles

OSPF Configuration Fundamentals
- The OSPF process ID is an integer between 1 and 65,535
- The OSPF process ID is locally significant
- Cisco IOS creates a PDB to allow a process to be created if no interfaces are configured
- Within the configuration the most specific network entries are listed first in the output
- The OSPF area ID may be configured as an integer or using dotted-decimal notation

OSPF Packet Types
- OSPF packets share a common 24-byte OSPF header
- These five packet types use by OSPF are as follows:
  1. Type 1 = Hello packet
  2. Type 2 = Database Description packet
  3. Type 3 = Link State Request packet
  4. Type 4 = Link State Update packet
  5. Type 5 = Link State Acknowledgement packet

- Hello packets are used for neighbor discovery and to establish OSPF neighbor adjacencies
- OSPF packets are sent with an IP TTL value of 1
- OSPF Hello packets are also used on Broadcast links to elect a DR and/or BDR router
- Database Description packets are used during the database exchange
- The first DBD packet is used for the master and slave election for database exchange
- The DBD packet also contains the initial sequence number selected by the master
- The master and slave election is performed on a per-neighbor basis

- The router with the highest RID is elected as the master; this router polls the slave
- The master and slave election is not the same as the DR/BDR election
- It is possible for the DR to be the slave during the master and slave election
- DBD packets summarize the local database by sending LSA headers to the remote router
- LSR packets are sent to request missing or out-of-date database information
- The different types of Link State packets that are used are:
- It may contain one of the following fields:
    1. Type 1 = Router Link State Advertisement
    2. Type 2 = Network Link State Advertisement
    3. Type 3 = Network Summary Link State Advertisement
    4. Type 4 = ASBR Summary Link State Advertisement
    5. Type 5 = AS External Link State Advertisement
    6. Type 6 = Multicast Link State Advertisement
    7. Type 7 = NSSA External Link State Advertisement
    8. Type 8 = External Attributes Link State Advertisement
    9. Type 9 = Opaque Link State Advertisement—Link Local
    10. Type 10 = Opaque Link State Advertisement—Area
    11. Type 11 = Opaque Link State Advertisement—Autonomous System

- Link State Update (LSU) packets are used by the router to advertise LSAs
- LSU packets may be Unicast to an OSPF neighbor in response to a received LSR
- The Link State Acknowledgement (LSAck) packet is used to acknowledge each LSA
- The LSAck contains the common OSPF header followed by a list of LSA headers

Establishing Adjacencies

- OSPF routers transition through several phases before they establish a neighbor adjacency
- The Down state is the starting state for all OSPF routers
- The Attempt state is valid only for OSPF neighbors on NBMA networks
- The Init state indicates a received Hello but the local RID is not in the Neighbor field
- The 2-Way state indicates bi-directional communication with the OSPF neighbor(s)
- The Exstart state is used for the initialization of the database synchronization process
- The Exchange state is where routers describe their databases using DBD packets
- In the Loading state OSPF routers build an LSR and Link State Retransmission list
- The Full state indicates that the OSPF neighbors have exchanged their entire databases
- The following neighbor parameters must match for an adjacency to be established:
    1. The interface MTU values
    2. The Hello and Dead Timers
    3. The Area ID

4. The Authentication Type and Password

5. The Stub Area flag

OSPF LSAs and the Link State Database (LSDB)

- Each LSA begins with a standard 20-byte LSA header. This header contains the following:

    1. Link State Age

    2. Options

    3. Link State Type

    4. Link State ID

    5. Advertising Router

    6. Link State Sequence Number

    7. Link State Checksum

    8. Length

- Type 1 LSAs or Router LSAs are generated by each router for each area the router belongs to
- The Router LSA lists the originating router's router ID (RID)
- The Type 1 LSA Link ID identifies the link itself. The following link types are supported:

    1. Point-to-point

    2. Link to Transit Network

    3. Link to Stub Network

    4. Virtual Link

- The Network LSA (Type 2 LSA) is used to advertise the routers on the multi-access segment
- The Network LSA is generated by the DR and is flooded only within the area
- The Network (Type 3) LSA summarizes destinations outside local area, but in the domain
- The Network LSA does not carry any topological information
- Type 3 LSAs are generated by the ABRs and are flooded to all adjacent OSPF areas
- Each Type 3 LSA matches a single Type 1 or 2 LSA on a one-for-one basis
- The Type 4 LSA describes information about an Autonomous System Boundary Router
- Like the Type 3 LSA, the Type 4 LSA is generated by the ABR
- The Type 4 LSA is created by the ABR for each ASBR reachable by a Router LSA
- The External (Type 5) LSA describes destinations that are external to the AS
- The External LSA has a domain-flooding scope
- The only areas that External LSAs are not flooded to are Stub-type Areas

OSPF Areas

- In addition to normal areas and the backbone, OSPF also supports the following are types:

    1. Not-so-stubby Areas

2. Totally Not-so-stubby Areas

3. Stub Areas

4. Totally Stubby Areas

- NSSAs are a type of OSPF Stub area that allows the injection of external routing information
- NSSAs have the following characteristics:
    1. They use Type 7 LSAs to carry external information within the NSSA
    2. The NSSA ABR converts Type 7 LSAs into Type 5 LSAs
    3. Type 4 and Type 5 LSAs are not allowed into Not-so-stubby Areas
    4. Network Summary LSAs are allowed into the NSSA

- Totally Not-so-stubby Areas (TNSSAs) are an extension of NSSAs
- TNSSAs have the following characteristics:
    1. Type 7 LSAs are converted into Type 5 LSAs at the NSSA ABR
    2. They do not allow Network Summary LSAs
    3. They do not allow External LSAs
    4. The default route is injected as a Summary LSA

- Stub areas are similar to NSSAs; however, they do not allow external routing information
- Stub areas have the following characteristics:
    1. The default route is injected into Stub area by the ABR as a Type 3 LSA
    2. Type 3 LSAs from other areas are permitted into these areas
    3. External route LSAs, i.e. Type 4 and Type 5 LSAs are not allowed

- Totally Stubby Areas (TSAs) are an extension of Stub areas
- TSAs have the following characteristics:
    1. The default route is injected into Stub areas as a Type 3 LSA
    2. Type 3, 4, and 5 LSAs from other areas are not permitted into these areas

- There are certain Stub area limitations you should know. These limitations are as follows:
    1. You cannot include an ASBR in a Stub area because external routes are not allowed
    2. All routers in the Stub Area must be configured as Stub routers
    3. You cannot configure a Virtual Link across a Stub area
    4. The OSPF backbone area (area 0) cannot be configured as a Stub area

Route Metrics and Best Route Selection

- The OSPF metric is commonly referred to as the OSPF cost
- The cost is derived from the bandwidth of a link using the formula 10^8/bandwidth (in bps)

- OSPF routes down to the nearest integer when calculating the metric
- Intra-area routes are preceded by an O in the IP routing table
- Inter-area routes are preceded by an O IA in the IP routing table
- In most cases, the route with the best metric will be used
- However, ABRs will always select intra-area routes over inter-area routes
- The calculation of the OSPF metric can be directly influenced by performing the following:
    1. Adjusting the interface bandwidth using the bandwidth command
    2. Manually specifying a cost using the ip ospf cost command

- Changing the OSPF cost value results in an SPF calculation

OSPF Default Routing
- The default-information originate command generates a default route for OSPF
- By default, the default route must exist in the routing table to be advertised
- The always keyword can generate a default route even when one does not exist

OSPF Virtual Links
- A virtual link is a logical extension of the OSPF backbone
- Virtual links can be used for the following:
    1. Connecting non-backbone areas to the OSPF backbone are
    2. Providing network redundancy
    3. Connecting a discontinuous or partitioned backbone

- Before a virtual link can be configured, the following requirements must be met:
    1. One area must be connected to the backbone area before the virtual link can be created
    2. The transit area must be a common area between the two endpoint routers

OSPF Route Summarization
- By default, OSPF does not perform automatic route summarization
- OSPF supports the following two types of route summarization:
    1. Summarizing internal routes
    2. Summarizing external routes

- Internal route summarization is configured on the ABR
- The ABR generates a Type 3 LSA for the summary and suppresses specific routes
- The ABR summary route points to the Null0 interface
- External router summarization is configured on the ASBR
- The ABR generates a Type 5 LSA for the summary and suppresses specific routes
- The ASBR summary route points to the Null0 interface

OSPF Passive Interfaces

- When any router interfaces are configured as passive, OSPF will not send routing updates
- OSPF will not establish adjacencies on interfaces that are passive
- OSPF will continue to advertise passive interfaces if the configuration includes the interfaces

Securing OSPF Messages

- The 16-bit Auth Type field may contain one of the following three codes:
  1. Code 0—Used to indicate that there is Null or no authentication
  2. Code 1—Used to indicate that the plain text authentication
  3. Code 2—Used to indicate Message Digest 5 (MD5) authentication

- OSPF authentication can be configured as follows:
  1. For all routers within the area (area authentication)
  2. For specific interfaces (interface authentication)

Configuring OSPF over Non-Broadcast Networks

- OSPF can be implemented in the following three modes on NBMA networks:
  1. Simulated Broadcast Mode
  2. Point-to-Point Mode
  3. Point-to-Multipoint Mode

- The simulated Broadcast model simulates a traditional Broadcast model
- A DR and BDR are elected in simulated Broadcast mode
- Simulated Broadcast mode is implemented using either of the following:
  1. Using the default network type and the `neighbor` router configuration command
  2. By changing the default network type to the `broadcast` network type

- For simulated Broadcast mode, the following routers should be connected as follows:
  1. The DR must have a direct connection (virtual circuit) to every other router
  2. The DR must have a direct connection (virtual circuit) to the BDR
  3. The BDR must have a direct connection (virtual circuit) to every other router

- Point-to-point mode requires no DR/BDR election
- Point-to-point mode allows OSPF to use Multicast packets to establish adjacencies
- Point-to-multipoint mode is a non-default OSPF mode
- Point-to-multipoint mode can use Multicast or Unicast to establish adjacencies

CHAPTER 4

IGP Route Filtering and Route Redistribution

In addition to planning, implementing, and supporting routing protocols, it is also important to have a solid understanding of the route filtering capabilities supported by each protocol in Cisco IOS software. Route filtering and route redistribution, which allows different protocols to exchange routing information, are core requirements of the ROUTE exam. Route filtering and route redistribution can be used separately or in conjunction with one another.

In addition to filtering routes or allowing different routing protocols to exchange routing information, both techniques can be used for path control. It is therefore important to understand the logic behind each of these techniques and how they should be applied in a given network scenario. The core ROUTE exam objective covered in this chapter is as follows:

- Implement an IPv4-based redistribution solution, given a network design and a set of requirements

This chapter contains the following sections:

- Access Lists and IP Prefix Lists Fundamentals
- Understanding Route Maps
- Filtering EIGRP Routes
- Filtering OSPF Routes
- Protocol Independent Route Filtering
- Route Redistribution Overview
- Configuring and Verifying Route Redistribution
- Route Redistribution Design Considerations

ACCESS LISTS AND IP PREFIX LISTS FUNDAMENTALS

Before we delve into the specifics of both route filtering and route redistribution, it is important to have a solid understanding of both Access Control Lists (ACLs) and IP prefix lists, as these are integral components of effective route filtering and route redistribution implementation. Although ACLs are described at a basic level in CCNA, it is important to go above and beyond basic Access Control List configuration, as a detailed understanding of ACLs can be used to simplify and reduce configuration commands that are required to perform route filtering and route redistribution.

Access Control Lists

In Cisco IOS software, Access Control Lists may be used for many different functions, such as for Network Address Translation, defining traffic to encrypt, and filtering IP traffic. Despite their many uses, this chapter focuses exclusively on how ACLs are used for both route filtering and route redistribution.

Cisco IOS software supports named and numbered standard and extended ACLs. Standard ACLs are used to filter based on the source address, while extended ACLs provide more granular filtering using source and destination addresses. It should be noted that while extended ACLs can also be used to filter based on protocol type (e.g., ICMP, TCP or UDP), this type of filtering is not relevant to route filtering or route redistribution and will not be illustrated or described in any further detail in this chapter. Instead, the core emphasis simply will be on ACLs as they pertain to IP address filtering.

ACL Wildcard Masks or Inverse Masks

Access Control Lists use wildcard masks or inverse masks to specify what networks should be permitted or denied. The simplest method of determining the wildcard or inverse mask is to subtract the actual subnet mask from 255.255.255.255. For example, the wildcard mask or the inverse mask to permit hosts on the 172.16.1.0 255.255.255.0 network would be calculated as follows:

```
255.255.255.255–255.255.255.0 = 0.0.0.255
```

> **NOTE:** While the terms wildcard mask and inverse mask are interchangeable, the remainder of this guide will use the former (i.e., wildcard masks) instead of the latter term.

It is important to understand the implications of the wildcard mask when using both standard and extended ACLs to perform route filtering and route redistribution. In most cases, it is highly recommended that an extended ACL be used when possible. For example, consider the following standard ACL configuration:

```
access-list 1 permit 172.16.1.0 0.0.0.255
```

When used in IP traffic filtering, this standard ACL would permit traffic from the 172.16.1.0/24 subnet, as well as any other subnets of that network. For example, the ACL would also permit traffic from the 172.16.1.0/25 subnet, the 172.16.1.128/25 subnet, etc. When used in route filtering or route redistribution, the same ACL would permit the same subnets. If the desired intention is to permit specifically only the 172.16.1.0/24 subnet, this configuration will produce unexpected results, as it denies other subnets that should otherwise be permitted.

In order to permit specifically only the 172.16.1.0/24 network, an extended ACL must be used. Extended ACLs can be configured to permit (or deny) a specific network or a range of networks, depending on the configuration of the wildcard mask. For example, the following extended ACL would be used to permit only the 172.16.1.0/24 subnet:

```
access-list 100 permit ip 172.16.1.0 0.0.0.0 255.255.255.0 0.0.0.0
```

NOTE: If you use the `any` keyword in the ACL, then any mask is matched.

Because the `host` keyword is a valid replacement for a wildcard mask of `0.0.0.0` in Cisco IOS software, this ACL can be further simplified and configured as :

```
access-list 100 permit ip host 172.16.1.0 host 255.255.255.0
```

If, for example, the same extended ACL were configured as `access-list 100 permit ip 172.16.1.0 0.0.0.255 255.255.255.0 0.0.0.255`, then the ACL would not only permit the 172.16.1.0/24 subnet, it would also permit any other subnets in the same network, which would include the subnets 172.16.1.0/25, 172.16.1.128/25, 172.16.1.0/26, etc.

It is important to ensure that you are absolutely clear about the requirements when performing route filtering or route redistribution. In addition, it is also important to have a solid understanding of the configuration of ACLs; otherwise, your implemented configuration may cause more problems than it resolves and may introduce other issues, such as suboptimal routing or even routing loops. Because the configuration of ACLs can become complicated quite easily, especially when attempting to filter ranges of networks, for example, Cisco IOS software supports IP prefix lists, which provide a simpler method of matching and filtering any specific network or even ranges of networks. IP prefix lists are described in the following section.

IP Prefix Lists

IP prefix lists are used to match specific prefixes based on number and length. IP prefix lists can also be used to match a range of networks that fall within the specified prefix, as is possible with extended ACLs. In Cisco IOS software, prefix lists are configured using the `ip prefix-list [list-name [seq <number>] [deny | permit] network/length [ge <ge-length>] [le <le-length>] | description <description> | sequence-number]]` global configuration command. Table 4-1 below lists and describes the keywords that are used within the configuration of prefix lists:

Table 4-1. IP Prefix List Configuration Keywords

Keyword	Description
list-name	This is used to define the prefix list name. All prefix lists must be configured with a unique name on the router.
seq <number>	This keyword is optional and is used to apply a sequence number to the configured prefix list entry.
deny	This keyword denies access for a match against the prefix list.
permit	This keyword permits access for a match against the prefix list.

network/ length	This keyword is used to configure the network address and the length of the network mask in bits. The network number can be any valid IP address or prefix, and the bit mask can be a number from 1 to 32.
ge <ge-length>	This keyword is optional and represents the greater than or equal to operator; it is used to specify the lesser value of a range. This represents the 'from' portion of the specified range based on the specified <ge-length> argument.
le <le-length>	This keyword is optional and represents the less than or equal to operator; it is used to specify the greater value of a range. This represents the 'to' portion of the specified range based on the specified <le-length> argument.
description <description>	This keyword is optional and is used to apply a description to the configured prefix list.
sequence- number	This keyword is optional and is used to enable or disable the use of sequence numbers for prefix lists.

While the configuration of prefix lists seems confusing at first glance, it becomes easier the more you practice, as is the case with anything else. IP prefix lists consume fewer CPU cycles than traditional ACLs. In addition, once you understand them, you will also find that the IP prefix lists simplify filtering configuration that would otherwise require complicated extended ACL implementation. For example, using the same 172.16.1.0/24 subnet used in previous examples, the extended ACL required to match that subnet would be configured as follows:

```
ip access-list extended MYACL
 permit ip host 172.16.1.0 host 255.255.255.0
```

However, when using prefix lists, the same task can be accomplished as follows:

```
ip prefix-list MYLIST seq 5 permit 172.16.1.0/24
```

While this is just a basic example of IP prefix list configuration, the simplified nature of prefix lists becomes more apparent when attempting to perform advanced route filtering. For example, assume that you want to permit all possible subnets in the 172.16.0.0/16 network. Using extended ACLs, the following configuration would be required to do this:

```
ip access-list extended MYACL
 permit ip 172.16.0.0 0.0.255.255 255.255.0.0 0.0.255.255
```

The same configuration would be applied as follows using a prefix list:

```
ip prefix-list MYLIST seq 5 permit 172.16.0.0/16 le 32
```

As yet another example, assume you wanted to filter all networks with a subnet mask greater than /25 within the 10.0.0.0/8 subnet. The equivalent ACL configuration would be as follows:

```
ip access-list extended MYACL
 deny ip 10.0.0.0 0.255.255.255 255.255.255.128 0.0.0.127
```

However, with a prefix list, the configuration can be simplified to the following statement:

```
ip prefix-list MYLIST seq 5 deny 10.0.0.0/8 ge 25
```

As a final example, assume you wanted to match only a portion of the major 10.0.0.0/8 network, such that only subnets with a mask between 25 bits and 31 bits long within this address space were permitted. Based on this requirement, if an extended ACL was to be used, the configuration required to accomplish this would be as follows:

```
ip access-list extended MYACL
 deny ip 10.0.0.0 0.255.255.255 255.255.255.128 0.0.0.126
```

However, using a prefix list, the same configuration can be simplified to the following:

```
ip prefix-list MYLIST seq 5 deny 10.0.0.0/8 ge 25 le 31
```

While far too many examples of different combinations could be used, it is clear from the examples above that the prefix list configuration is much less complicated than the extended ACL configuration. The key to understanding prefix lists is to understand the use of the ge and le operators that are used in conjunction with prefix lists.

When configuring a prefix list, the prefix length listed in the network/length configuration must be less than the specified greater than or equal to operator length specified in the ge-length configuration. The specified ge-length in turn must be less than the specified less than or equal to operator length specified in the le-length configuration.

NOTE: If the greater than or equal to operator is used and the less than or equal to operator is omitted, then the software assumes that the less than or equal to operator is 32.

In summation, keep in mind that as was the case when you first learned about ACLs, it will also take some time to understand thoroughly prefix lists. Table 4-2 below shows some prefix list configurations and the IP prefixes that will be matched based on these specific configurations:

Table 4-2. IP Prefix List Matching

Prefix List Statement	What This Will Match
0.0.0.0/0	Only the default route; i.e., network 0.0.0.0/0
0.0.0.0/0 le 32	Any and all prefixes, up to and including a 32-bit mask
0.0.0.0/0 ge 16	All prefixes with a 16-bit mask or longer, up to and including a 32-bit mask
0.0.0.0/0 le 27	All prefixes with a 27-bit mask or less
0.0.0.0/0 ge 24 le 30	All prefixes with a 24-bit mask or longer, up to and including a 30-bit mask
0.0.0.0/0 ge 24 le 24	All prefixes with a 24-bit mask, because the ge and le operators are the same

NOTE: It should be noted that IP prefix lists also have an implicit deny at the end.

UNDERSTANDING ROUTE MAPS

Like ACLs, route maps can also be applied in many different scenarios. Route maps and ACLs have common characteristics and they are as follows:

- Route maps and ACLs are an ordered sequence of individual statements. Each individual sequence is configured with either a permit or a deny result.
- The evaluation of route maps or ACLs is based on a list scan, in a predetermined order, and an evaluation of the criteria of each statement that matches. This list scan is aborted once the first statement match is found and an action associated with the statement match is performed.
- They are both generic mechanisms that can be used in multiple tasks. Criteria matches and match interpretation are dictated by the way they are applied. For example, the same route map applied to different tasks might be interpreted differently, as would be the case with an ACL applied to different tasks.

While route maps and ACLs do share common characteristics, there are some notable differences between these two mechanisms and they are as follows:

- Route maps can, and often do, use ACLs as matching criteria. However, ACLs do not and cannot use route maps as match criteria.
- While ACLs are used simply to permit or deny the matched criteria, route maps can be used to do the same and much more. For example, a route map could be configured to perform a certain action (e.g., set a route metric) following a successful match. Additionally, route maps can also be used to match on other criteria, such as route tags and a specified route source.
- By design, each individual ACL ends with an implicit deny statement. However, this is not true for route maps, and different actions will be taken depending on how the route map is

applied. However, when used in route filtering and route redistribution, route maps behave in the same manner as an ACL. For example, if a route is not permitted in the route-filtering configuration, then the route will not be permitted. Likewise, if a route is not permitted explicitly during route redistribution, then the route will not be redistributed.

In Cisco IOS software, route maps are configured using the route-map [name] [permit | deny] [sequence-number] global configuration command. The [name] keyword is the configured route map name. Each individual route map must have a unique name.

When the route map is used to perform basic route filtering, the [permit] keyword allows the matched criteria. When the route map is used for route redistribution, the [permit] keyword allows the route to be redistributed; however, if the specified criterion is not matched when this keyword is used, the next entry in the route map will be checked. If a route does not pass any of the match criteria for the set of route map entries, it is not redistributed.

The [deny] keyword simply denies the route, when using route filtering, or prevents the route from being redistributed, when used in route redistribution configuration.

Finally, the optional [sequence-number] keyword allows more than one permit or deny statement to be used in the same route map. The [sequence-number] keyword determines the position of the route map entry in relation to other entries within the same route map. You can use any integer you want. The maximum value supported will depend on the software version and platform. For example, to configure a route-map named MYMAP and assign the first permit statement a sequence number of 1, you would issue the command route-map MYMAP permit 1. This will then take you into route-map configuration mode, where you can configure match and set statements using the available options.

Once a route map has been configured in global configuration mode, one or more match or set clauses can be configured. The following section describes the functions of these statements.

Route Map Match Clauses

Match clauses are used to match against predefined criteria (i.e., the conditions that must be met). Match clauses are configured by using the match subcommand in route map configuration mode. Cisco IOS software provides very granular matching capabilities, ranging from ACLs and IP prefix lists to the type of route (e.g., internal or external) and even from a particular source protocol (e.g., OSPF, EIGRP, and BGP).

Following is a list of supported keywords that can be used in conjunction with route map match clauses:

```
R2(config)#route-map MYMAP permit 5
R2(config-route-map)#match ?
  as-path           Match BGP AS path list
  clns              CLNS information
  community         Match BGP community list
  extcommunity      Match BGP/VPN extended community list
  interface         Match first hop interface of route
  ip                IP-specific information
  ipv6              IPv6-specific information
  length            Packet length
  local-preference  Local preference for route
  metric            Match metric of route
  mpls-label        Match routes that have MPLS labels
  nlri              BGP NLRI type
  policy-list       Match IP policy list
  route-type        Match route-type of route
  source-protocol   Match source-protocol of route
  tag               Match tag of route
```

NOTE: Keep in mind that these options will vary across different versions of IOS software.

Route Map Set Clauses

Set clauses are used to determine what happens once a positive match has been made. Set clauses are configured using the set subcommand in route map configuration mode. Set clauses may be used to set route metrics, the type of route metric (e.g., External Type 1 or External Type 2), and even route tags that can be used to identify routes. Following is a list of supported keywords that can be used in conjunction with route map set clauses:

```
R2(config)#route-map MYMAP permit 5
R2(config-route-map)#set ?
  as-path           Prepend string for a BGP AS-path attribute
  automatic-tag     Automatically compute TAG value
  clns              OSI summary address
  comm-list         set BGP community list (for deletion)
  community         BGP community attribute
  dampening         Set BGP route flap dampening parameters
  default           Set default information
  extcommunity      BGP extended community attribute
  interface         Output interface
  ip                IP-specific information
  ipv6              IPv6-specific information
  level             Where to import route
  local-preference  BGP local preference path attribute
  metric            Metric value for destination routing protocol
  metric-type       Type of metric for destination routing protocol
  mpls-label        Set MPLS label for prefix
  nlri              BGP NLRI type
```

```
origin              BGP origin code
tag                 Tag value for destination routing protocol
traffic-index       BGP traffic classification number for accounting
vrf                 Define VRF name
weight              BGP weight for routing table
```

NOTE: Keep in mind that these options will vary across different versions of IOS software.

FILTERING EIGRP ROUTES

Cisco IOS software supports route filtering for both EIGRP and OSPF using distribute lists. Both protocols also support additional route filtering mechanisms that are exclusive to each individual protocol. While going into all filtering mechanisms is beyond the scope of the ROUTE exam requirements, you should be intimately familiar with distribute lists and their application when using either OSPF or EIGRP.

NOTE: Redistribution can also be used to filter routing information from external route sources. Redistribution is described in detail later in this chapter.

Filtering EIGRP Routes Using Distribute Lists

A distribute list can be used to filter incoming or outgoing EIGRP routing updates. Distribute lists can be used in conjunction with ACLs, IP prefix lists, or route maps. A distribute list calls upon an ACL, a prefix list, or a route map to perform the filtering functions in the inbound or outbound direction. In Cisco IOS software, distribute lists are configured using the distribute-list router configuration command. The options that are available for use with this command are illustrated below:

```
R2(config)#router eigrp 2
R2(config-router)#distribute-list ?
  <1-199>       IP access list number
  <1300-2699>   IP expanded access list number
  WORD          Access-list name
  gateway       Filtering incoming updates based on gateway
  prefix        Filter prefixes in routing updates
  route-map     Filter prefixes based on the route-map
```

As stated earlier in this section, distribute lists can call upon ACLs, which may be named and numbered standard or extended, and prefix lists and route maps. In addition, the gateway keyword can also be used to filter updates received from a specific gateway or router. Figure 4-1 below shows a basic EIGRP network that includes two routers: R2 and R3. R2 is advertising the 172.16.0.0/24, 172.16.1.0/24, 172.16.2.0/24, 172.16.3.0/24, and the 172.16.4.0/24 subnets to R3:

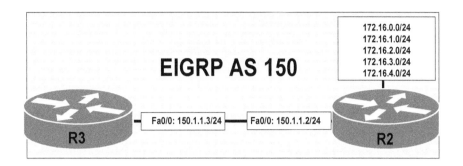

Fig. 4-1. EIGRP Distribute List Filtering

Assuming that basic EIGRP configuration has been implemented on both routers, the routing table on R3 shows that the following routes are being received from R2:

```
R3#show ip route eigrp
      172.16.0.0/16 is variably subnetted, 10 subnets, 2 masks
D        172.16.4.0/24 [90/156160] via 150.1.1.2, 00:00:19, FastEthernet0/0
D        172.16.0.0/24 [90/156160] via 150.1.1.2, 00:00:19, FastEthernet0/0
D        172.16.1.0/24 [90/156160] via 150.1.1.2, 00:00:19, FastEthernet0/0
D        172.16.2.0/24 [90/156160] via 150.1.1.2, 00:00:19, FastEthernet0/0
D        172.16.3.0/24 [90/156160] via 150.1.1.2, 00:00:19, FastEthernet0/0
```

Using a simple outbound distribute list, in conjunction with an ACL, it is possible to filter some of the routing updates sent by R2 to R3. The following configuration example illustrates how to filter the 172.16.0.0/24 through 172.16.3.0/24 subnets, while allowing the 172.16.4.0/24 subnet:

```
R2(config)#access-list 1 remark 'Deny 172.16.0.0 - 172.16.3.0'
R2(config)#access-list 1 deny 172.16.0.0 0.0.3.255
R2(config)#access-list 1 remark 'Permit 172.16.4.0'
R2(config)#access-list 1 permit 172.16.4.0
R2(config)#router eigrp 150
R2(config-router)#distribute-list 1 out FastEthernet0/0
R2(config-router)#exit
```

NOTE: Keep in mind that the same goal could be accomplished in many other ways.

The matches against the ACL can be validated using the show ip access-lists command. The show ip protocols command can also be used to validate that the distribute list has been applied successfully. The relevant output printed by this command is highlighted below:

```
R2#show ip protocols
Routing Protocol is "eigrp 150"
  Outgoing update filter list for all interfaces is not set
    FastEthernet0/0 filtered by 1, default is 1
```

```
Incoming update filter list for all interfaces is not set
Default networks flagged in outgoing updates

...

[Truncated Output]
```

Finally, based on the configuration implemented on R2, the routing table on R3 now shows only the 172.16.4.0/24 subnet as illustrated below:

```
R3#show ip route eigrp
      172.16.0.0/16 is variably subnetted, 6 subnets, 2 masks
D        172.16.4.0/24 [90/156160] via 150.1.1.2, 00:06:05, FastEthernet0/0
```

As another example of the use of distribute lists, consider the topology illustrated in Figure 4-2 below:

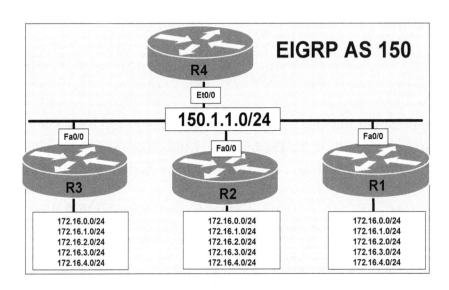

Fig. 4-2. EIGRP Distribute List Filtering

Referencing the topology illustrated in Figure 4-2, routers R1, R2, R3, and R4 are connected to the same multi-access network segment. All four routers are running EIGRP, using AS 150. Routers R1, R2, and R3 are advertising the 172.16.0.0/24, 172.16.1.0/24, 172.16.2.0/24, 172.16.3.0/24 and 172.16.4.0/24 subnets to R4. The current routing table on R4 displays the following entries:

```
R4#show ip route eigrp
      172.16.0.0/24 is subnetted, 5 subnets
D        172.16.4.0 [90/409600] via 150.1.1.1, 00:00:08, Ethernet0/0
                    [90/409600] via 150.1.1.3, 00:00:08, Ethernet0/0
                    [90/409600] via 150.1.1.2, 00:00:08, Ethernet0/0
D        172.16.0.0 [90/409600] via 150.1.1.1, 00:00:08, Ethernet0/0
```

```
                    [90/409600] via 150.1.1.3, 00:00:08, Ethernet0/0
                    [90/409600] via 150.1.1.2, 00:00:08, Ethernet0/0
D        172.16.1.0 [90/409600] via 150.1.1.1, 00:00:08, Ethernet0/0
                    [90/409600] via 150.1.1.3, 00:00:08, Ethernet0/0
                    [90/409600] via 150.1.1.2, 00:00:08, Ethernet0/0
D        172.16.2.0 [90/409600] via 150.1.1.1, 00:00:08, Ethernet0/0
                    [90/409600] via 150.1.1.3, 00:00:08, Ethernet0/0
                    [90/409600] via 150.1.1.2, 00:00:08, Ethernet0/0
D        172.16.3.0 [90/409600] via 150.1.1.1, 00:00:08, Ethernet0/0
                    [90/409600] via 150.1.1.3, 00:00:08, Ethernet0/0
                    [90/409600] via 150.1.1.2, 00:00:08, Ethernet0/0
```

Assume that management has requested that router R4 use only router R2 to reach any of the 172.16 subnets. A possible solution would be to configure outbound distribute lists on routers R1 and R3 filtering these subnets. However, this would effectively mean that these two routers would never advertise these subnets to any other router in the network. This would be an issue if, for example, another router were added to the network.

Configuring an inbound distribute list on R4 using either a prefix list or an ACL would deny all the prefixes from all advertising routers. This leaves two possible options, which can both be used to filter based on the source gateway: (1) using the distribute-list route-map router configuration command; or (2) using the distribute-list gateway router configuration command.

The distribute-list route-map command can be applied to R4 using a route map that filters incoming updates based on the route source (gateway). This is implemented as follows:

```
R4(config)#access-list 1 remark 'Permit Routes Only From R2'
R4(config)#access-list 1 permit 150.1.1.2
R4(config)#route-map MYMAP permit 10
R4(config-route-map)#description 'Match Only Routes From R2'
R4(config-route-map)#match ip route-source 1
R4(config-route-map)#exit
R4(config)#router eigrp 150
R4(config-router)#distribute-list route-map MYMAP in Ethernet0/0
R4(config-router)#exit
```

The configuration above configures an inbound distribute list on R4 that references a route map named MYMAP. This route map matches all routes sourced from the address specified in ACL 1. ACL 1, in this example, matches only host address 150.1.1.2 (R2). After the implementation of this configuration, the routing table on R4 displays the following:

```
R4#show ip route eigrp
     172.16.0.0/24 is subnetted, 5 subnets
D       172.16.4.0 [90/409600] via 150.1.1.2, 00:00:03, Ethernet0/0
D       172.16.0.0 [90/409600] via 150.1.1.2, 00:00:03, Ethernet0/0
D       172.16.1.0 [90/409600] via 150.1.1.2, 00:00:03, Ethernet0/0
```

```
D        172.16.2.0 [90/409600] via 150.1.1.2, 00:00:03, Ethernet0/0
D        172.16.3.0 [90/409600] via 150.1.1.2, 00:00:03, Ethernet0/0
```

The second option is to use the distribute-list gateway router configuration command. This configuration is performed as follows:

```
R4(config)#ip prefix-list MYLIST description 'Allow Only R2 Updates'
R4(config)#ip prefix-list MYLIST seq 5 permit 150.1.1.2/32
R4(config)#router eigrp 150
R4(config-router)#distribute-list gateway MYLIST in Ethernet0/0
R4(config-router)#exit
```

Following this configuration, the routing table on R4 displays the following entries:

```
R4#show ip route eigrp
     172.16.0.0/24 is subnetted, 5 subnets
D        172.16.4.0 [90/409600] via 150.1.1.2, 00:00:05, Ethernet0/0
D        172.16.0.0 [90/409600] via 150.1.1.2, 00:00:05, Ethernet0/0
D        172.16.1.0 [90/409600] via 150.1.1.2, 00:00:05, Ethernet0/0
D        172.16.2.0 [90/409600] via 150.1.1.2, 00:00:05, Ethernet0/0
D        172.16.3.0 [90/409600] via 150.1.1.2, 00:00:05, Ethernet0/0
```

NOTE: The same objective could also be accomplished by performing the following:

```
R4(config)#ip prefix-list R2ONLY description 'Allow Only R2 Updates'
R4(config)#ip prefix-list R2ONLY seq 5 permit 150.1.1.2/32
R4(config)#ip prefix-list ALLROUTES description 'Allow All Routes'
R4(config)#ip prefix-list ALLROUTES seq 5 permit 0.0.0.0/0 le 32
R4(config)#router eigrp 150
R4(config-router)#distribute-list prefix ALLROUTES gateway R2ONLY in Eth0/0
R4(config-router)#exit
```

The configuration above constructs a distribute list that allows all routes from R2 to be permitted. Because a prefix list has an implicit deny statement at the end, all routes from gateways not included in the prefix list R2ONLY will be rejected. The result of this configuration is as follows:

```
R4#show ip route eigrp
     172.16.0.0/24 is subnetted, 5 subnets
D        172.16.4.0 [90/409600] via 150.1.1.2, 00:00:53, Ethernet0/0
D        172.16.0.0 [90/409600] via 150.1.1.2, 00:00:53, Ethernet0/0
D        172.16.1.0 [90/409600] via 150.1.1.2, 00:00:53, Ethernet0/0
D        172.16.2.0 [90/409600] via 150.1.1.2, 00:00:53, Ethernet0/0
D        172.16.3.0 [90/409600] via 150.1.1.2, 00:00:53, Ethernet0/0
```

This configuration can be validated by viewing the router configuration or by using the show ip protocols command, the output of which is illustrated below:

```
R4#show ip protocols
Routing Protocol is "eigrp 150"
  Outgoing update filter list for all interfaces is not set
  Incoming update filter list for all interfaces is not set
    Ethernet0/0 filtered by (prefix-list) ALLROUTES gateway R2ONLY
  Default networks flagged in outgoing updates
  Default networks accepted from incoming updates
  EIGRP metric weight K1=1, K2=0, K3=1, K4=0, K5=0
  EIGRP maximum hopcount 100
  EIGRP maximum metric variance 1
  Redistributing: eigrp 150
  EIGRP NSF-aware route hold timer is 240s
  Automatic network summarization is not in effect
  Maximum path: 4
  Routing for Networks:
    150.1.1.0/24
    192.168.1.0
  Routing Information Sources:
    Gateway         Distance      Last Update
    150.1.1.2             90      00:05:09
    150.1.1.3             90      00:05:09
    150.1.1.1             90      00:05:10
  Distance: internal 90 external 170
```

To view statistics on matches against the configured prefix lists, use the show ip prefix-list detail command as illustrated in the following output:

```
R4#show ip prefix-list detail
Prefix-list with the last deletion/insertion: R2ONLY
ip prefix-list ALLROUTES:
   Description: 'Allow All Routes'
   count: 1, range entries: 1, sequences: 5 - 5, refcount: 3
   seq 5 permit 0.0.0.0/0 le 32 (hit count: 5, refcount: 1)
ip prefix-list R2ONLY:
   Description: 'Allow Only R2 Updates'
   count: 1, range entries: 0, sequences: 5 - 5, refcount: 4
   seq 5 permit 150.1.1.2/32 (hit count: 5, refcount: 1)
```

As has been illustrated in this section, many various configurations can be used to accomplish the same objective. It is therefore important to have a solid understanding of the current network topology as well as any future proposals or possibilities. A failure to understand the potential implications of your configuration may cause unexpected results and may require the (unnecessary) re-configuration of internetworking devices at a later stage.

Filtering Default Routing Information in EIGRP Networks

In Cisco IOS, the default-information allowed [in | out] router configuration command is used to configure EIGRP to permit or deny default routing information. By default, all EIGRP routers will always accept and pass default routing information between EIGRP processes. This default behavior can be validated in the output of the show ip protocols command as illustrated below:

```
R1#show ip protocols
Routing Protocol is "eigrp 150"
  Outgoing update filter list for all interfaces is not set
  Incoming update filter list for all interfaces is not set
  Default networks flagged in outgoing updates
  Default networks accepted from incoming updates
  EIGRP metric weight K1=1, K2=0, K3=1, K4=0, K5=0
  EIGRP maximum hopcount 100

...

[Truncated Output]
```

In some cases, it may be necessary to prevent the default route from being advertised into or out of the EIGRP autonomous system. To demonstrate where filtering the default route would be a recommended solution, consider the topology illustrated in Figure 4-3 below:

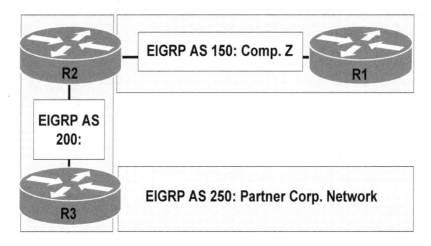

Fig. 4-3. EIGRP Default Route Filtering

Referencing the topology illustrated in Figure 4-3, routers R1 and R2 reside within the EIGRP domain belonging to Company Z. R2 has a connection to R3, which belongs to a partner of Company Z. Because both companies are using EIGRP within their interior networks, they decide to use a unique autonomous system between their two interconnect routers R2 and R3.

R2 is redistributing routing information received from the partner and advertising it to the rest of the EIGRP domain belonging to Company Z. R3 is redistributing routing information received from Company Z and advertising it into the rest of the EIGRP domain belonging to the partner. This allows for network connectivity between the two sites.

Now assume that Company Z's partner has flagged the 200.254.1.0/24 subnet as a network of last resort. This network is flagged as the default network and is received with all the routes received from the partner as illustrated below on R2:

```
R2#show ip route eigrp
D    200.254.4.0/24 [90/2297856] via 10.99.99.3, 00:00:12, Serial0/0
D    200.254.5.0/24 [90/2297856] via 10.99.99.3, 00:00:12, Serial0/0
D*   200.254.1.0/24 [90/2172416] via 10.99.99.3, 00:00:12, Serial0/0
D    200.254.2.0/24 [90/2297856] via 10.99.99.3, 00:00:12, Serial0/0
D    200.254.3.0/24 [90/2297856] via 10.99.99.3, 00:00:12, Serial0/0
```

Because R2 is redistributing the routes received from the partner network into Company Z's EIGRP domain, this network is also advertised to R1 as a candidate default path:

```
R1#show ip route 200.254.1.0 255.255.255.0
Routing entry for 200.254.1.0/24
  Known via "eigrp 150", distance 170, metric 2174976, candidate default
path, type external
  Redistributing via eigrp 150
  Last update from 150.1.1.2 on FastEthernet0/0, 00:00:55 ago
  Routing Descriptor Blocks:
  * 150.1.1.2, from 150.1.1.2, 00:00:55 ago, via FastEthernet0/0
      Route metric is 2174976, traffic share count is 1
      Total delay is 20200 microseconds, minimum bandwidth is 1544 Kbit
      Reliability 255/255, minimum MTU 1500 bytes
      Loading 1/255, Hops 2
```

Company Z does not want this default path in their network; however, they still want routing information for the 200.254.1.0/24 subnet. If a distribute list was used to filter this network, reachability to the 200.254.1.0/24 subnet would be lost, as R2 would not advertise this to the rest of the EIGRP domain belonging to Company Z. In this situation, the default-information allowed [in | out] router configuration command can be used to 'un-flag' the 200.254.1.0/24 subnet as a candidate default, while still allowing the subnet to be advertised throughout the EIGRP domain belonging to Company Z. This is performed as follows:

```
R2(config)#router eigrp 150
R2(config-router)#no default-information allowed out
R2(config-router)#exit
```

Again, this configuration can be validated using the show ip protocols command:

```
R2#show ip protocols
Routing Protocol is "eigrp 150"
  Outgoing update filter list for all interfaces is not set
  Incoming update filter list for all interfaces is not set
  Default networks not flagged in outgoing updates
  Default networks accepted from incoming updates
  EIGRP metric weight K1=1, K2=0, K3=1, K4=0, K5=0
  EIGRP maximum hopcount 100

...

[Truncated Output]
```

Following this configuration, R2 'un-flags' the 200.254.1.0/24 subnet as a candidate default but still advertises it to R1. On R1, the route now displays the following:

```
R1#show ip route 200.254.1.0 255.255.255.0
Routing entry for 200.254.1.0/24
  Known via "eigrp 150", distance 170, metric 2174976, type external
  Redistributing via eigrp 150
  Last update from 150.1.1.2 on FastEthernet0/0, 00:26:08 ago
  Routing Descriptor Blocks:
  * 150.1.1.2, from 150.1.1.2, 00:26:08 ago, via FastEthernet0/0
      Route metric is 2174976, traffic share count is 1
      Total delay is 20200 microseconds, minimum bandwidth is 1544 Kbit
      Reliability 255/255, minimum MTU 1500 bytes
      Loading 1/255, Hops 2
```

An alternate configuration would be to configure the default-information allowed in router configuration command on R1. However, if R2 has more than one EIGRP neighbor, this command would need to be applied to all neighbors. While the ultimate result is the same, applying the command to one router (R2) versus applying it to several routers makes more sense from a network design and implementation perspective. Additionally, it also validates your understanding of EIGRP and its capabilities in Cisco IOS software.

FILTERING OSPF ROUTES

Like EIGRP, OSPF also supports distribute lists. However, as will be described in the following section, distribute lists do not operate in the same manner when used in conjunction with OSPF as they would when used in conjunction with EIGRP. In addition to distribute lists, OSPF also supports additional route filtering tools that are unique to the protocol. These different tools are also described in detail in the following sections.

Filtering OSPF Routes Using Distribute Lists

The same options available with EIGRP are also supported when configuring OSPF distribute lists. Following is the list of supported keywords for the distribute-list command:

```
R2(config)#router ospf 2
R2(config-router)#distribute-list ?
  <1-199>      IP access list number
  <1300-2699>  IP expanded access list number
  WORD         Access-list name
  gateway      Filtering incoming updates based on gateway
  prefix       Filter prefixes in routing updates
  route-map    Filter prefixes based on the route-map
```

OSPF is a Link State routing protocol. OSPF routers build their LSDBs based on LSAs flooded into the area by other routers. This same information is ultimately used to build the SPF tree. For this reason, outbound distribute lists are not permitted by the CLI when using OSPF as the routing protocol. Although outbound distribute lists are not supported, OSPF does support inbound distribute lists. As is the case with EIGRP, inbound OSPF distribute lists can be used in conjunction with ACLs, prefix lists, and route-maps, and can also filter prefixes based on the specified gateway (router).

When filtering inbound prefixes, route maps provide the most flexibility. Route maps are used to filter inbound prefixes and can be configured to match prefixes using the following:
- Based on Route Tag
- Based on Next-Hop
- Based on Interface
- Based on Route Source
- Based on Route Type
- Based on Prefix List
- Based on Access List

A route tag can be assigned to a group of external prefixes during redistribution into OSPF. The distribute list can then be used in conjunction with a route map to filter prefixes based on the route tag. The following example shows how to configure a distribute list that permits only the routes that have been assigned the route tag 888:

```
R1(config)#route-map MATCH-TAG permit 10
R1(config-route-map)#match tag 888
R1(config-route-map)#exit
R1(config)#router ospf 1
R1(config-router)#distribute-list route-map MATCH-TAG in
R1(config-router)#exit
```

Route maps can be used to match the next-hop interface, which represents the next IP hop for the route that OSPF is attempting to install into the routing table. The following configuration example illustrates how to filter inbound prefixes and allow only those prefixes with a next-hop IP address of 150.1.1.1 to be installed into the routing table:

```
R1(config)#access-list 5 permit 150.1.1.1
R1(config)#route-map MATCH-NEXT-HOP permit 10
R1(config-route-map)#match ip next-hop 5
R1(config-route-map)#exit
R1(config)#router ospf 1
R1(config-router)#distribute-list route-map MATCH-NEXT-HOP in
```

Interface matching is based on the outgoing interface for the route that OSPF is attempting to install into the routing table (i.e., the interface toward the destination network). The following example illustrates how to filter inbound prefixes whose outgoing interface is Serial0/0. This configuration effectively filters all routes received via Serial0/0:

```
R1(config-router)#route-map FROM-INTERFACE-SERIAL-0/0 deny 10
R1(config-route-map)#match interface Serial0/0
R1(config-route-map)#exit
R1(config)#router ospf 1
R1(config-router)#distribute-list route-map FROM-INTERFACE-SERIAL-0/0 in
R1(config-router)#exit
```

A route map can also be used to filter routes based on the route source. The route source is the OSPF router ID of the LSA originator for the specified prefix(es). The following example illustrates how to filter all of the routes that were advertised by a router with the RID 1.1.1.1:

```
R2(config)#ip prefix-list R1-RID seq 5 permit 1.1.1.1/32
R2(config)#route-map R1-FILTER deny 10
R2(config-route-map)#match ip route-source prefix-list R1-RID
R2(config-route-map)#exit
R2(config)#router ospf 1
R2(config-router)#distribute-list route-map R1-FILTER in
```

The route type can also be used for route filtering when distribute lists are used in conjunction with route maps. Route maps can be used to match internal (intra-area and inter-area) routes and external (Type 1, Type 2, and NSSA External) routes. The following configuration illustrates how to configure the router to deny all Type 1 and Type 2 external routes but allow all others:

```
R2(config)#route-map EXTERNAL-ROUTES deny 10
R2(config-route-map)#match route-type external type-1 external type-2
R2(config-route-map)#exit
R2(config)#route-map EXTERNAL-ROUTES permit 20
R2(config-route-map)#exit
R2(config)#router ospf 2
```

```
R2(config-router)#distribute-list route-map EXTERNAL-ROUTES in
R2(config-router)#exit
```

NOTE: Because the second route map statement has no match clauses, it matches everything. In addition, because it is a permit statement, it allows all other routes.

Route maps can also filter based on matched prefix lists and ACLs. A prefix list is matched in a route map using the match ip address prefix [name] route map configuration command, while an ACL is matched using the match ip address [name | number] route map configuration command. The configuration of prefix lists and ACLs was illustrated in previous configuration examples.

It is important to remember that when filtering inbound prefixes, the denied (filtered) prefixes are not installed into the routing table; however, the LSAs for those prefixes will continue to exist in the Link State Database. In other words, inbound filtering with the distribute lists filters only the actual prefix itself and not the specific LSA. To both demonstrate and reinforce this statement, reference the OSPF network illustrated in Figure 4-4:

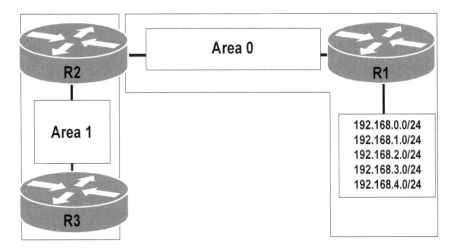

Fig. 4-4. OSPF Distribute List Filtering

Figure 4-4 illustrates a basic OSPF network. R1 and R2 are both ABRs and they are connected to the backbone and Area 1, respectively. R1 is advertising the 192.168 prefixes via OSPF. Assuming basic OSPF configuration, the routing table on R2 displays the following route entries:

```
R2#show ip route ospf
O    192.168.4.0/24 [110/2] via 150.254.1.1, 00:04:43, FastEthernet0/0
O    192.168.0.0/24 [110/2] via 150.254.1.1, 00:04:43, FastEthernet0/0
O    192.168.1.0/24 [110/2] via 150.254.1.1, 00:04:43, FastEthernet0/0
```

```
O     192.168.2.0/24 [110/2] via 150.254.1.1, 00:04:43, FastEthernet0/0
O     192.168.3.0/24 [110/2] via 150.254.1.1, 00:04:43, FastEthernet0/0
```

As an example, assume we wanted to filter odd subnets (i.e., 192.168.1.0/24 and 192.168.3.0/24). The following configuration would be implemented on R2:

```
R2(config)#ip access-list standard FILTER-ODD-SUBNETS
R2(config-std-nacl)#deny 0.0.1.0 255.255.254.255
R2(config-std-nacl)#permit any
R2(config-std-nacl)#exit
R2(config)#router ospf 2
R2(config-router)# distribute-list FILTER-ODD-SUBNETS in FastEthernet0/0
R2(config-router)#exit
```

NOTE: The logic in the ACL configured above is that it matches against any network that has an odd third octet. The 254 in the third octet of the wildcard mask matches any network with the value 1 as the last bit of the third octet. In Binary, the third octet for 192.168.1.0/24 would be 00000001. Likewise, in Binary, the third octet for 192.168.3.0 would be 00000011. The same ACL would match 192.168.5.0/24, 192.168.7.0/24, and so forth. Inversely, if we used the statement permit 0.0.0.0 0.0.254.255, this statement would allow only networks where the last bit in the third octet was an even number. For example, in Binary, the third octet for 192.168.2.0/24 would be written as 00000020 while that for 192.168.4.0/24 would be written as 00000400, and so forth, for networks such as 192.168.6.0/24, 192.168.8.0/24, etc. Keep in mind, however, that you are not expected to implement any such advanced ACL configurations in the ROUTE exam.

Based on this distribute list configuration, the routing table on R2 displays the following entries:

```
R2#show ip route ospf
O IA 192.168.4.0/24 [110/2] via 150.254.1.1, 00:00:41, FastEthernet0/0
O IA 192.168.0.0/24 [110/2] via 150.254.1.1, 00:00:41, FastEthernet0/0
O IA 192.168.2.0/24 [110/2] via 150.254.1.1, 00:00:41, FastEthernet0/0
```

As was stated earlier, although the odd prefixes have been filtered from the routing table, it is important to remember that the Type 3 LSAs for these prefixes are not filtered by the inbound distribute list. This can be validated by viewing the LSDB on R2 as follows:

```
R2#show ip ospf database

            OSPF Router with ID (2.2.2.2) (Process ID 2)

            Router Link States (Area 0)

  Link ID        ADV Router       Age         Seq#       Checksum Link Count
```

```
1.1.1.1          1.1.1.1         550        0x8000000D 0x00C3A6 7
2.2.2.2          2.2.2.2         1324       0x8000000E 0x00A031 2

                 Summary Net Link States (Area 0)

Link ID          ADV Router      Age        Seq#       Checksum
10.99.99.0       2.2.2.2         1324       0x80000008 0x0051CB

                 Router Link States (Area 1)

Link ID          ADV Router      Age        Seq#       Checksum Link Count
2.2.2.2          2.2.2.2         1328       0x8000000C 0x00E9EE 2
3.3.3.3          3.3.3.3         1511       0x80000006 0x009248 2

                 Summary Net Link States (Area 1)

Link ID          ADV Router      Age        Seq#       Checksum
150.254.1.0      2.2.2.2         1324       0x80000008 0x00A4F1
192.168.0.0      2.2.2.2         541        0x80000003 0x00AB1C
192.168.1.0      2.2.2.2         546        0x80000001 0x00A424
192.168.2.0      2.2.2.2         541        0x80000003 0x009530
192.168.3.0      2.2.2.2         546        0x80000001 0x008E38
192.168.4.0      2.2.2.2         541        0x80000003 0x007F44
```

Referencing the output above, although the prefixes have been filtered on R2, R1 will still flood LSAs for the 192.168.1.0/24 and 192.168.3.0/24 networks into Area 1. Because the LSAs have been flooded into Area 1, R3 still shows them in both its LSDB and its routing table. The routing table on R3 displays the following entries:

```
R3#show ip route ospf
O IA 192.168.4.0/24 [110/66] via 10.99.99.2, 00:12:31, Serial0/0
O IA 192.168.0.0/24 [110/66] via 10.99.99.2, 00:12:31, Serial0/0
O IA 192.168.1.0/24 [110/66] via 10.99.99.2, 00:12:35, Serial0/0
O IA 192.168.2.0/24 [110/66] via 10.99.99.2, 00:12:31, Serial0/0
     150.254.0.0/24 is subnetted, 1 subnets
O IA    150.254.1.0 [110/65] via 10.99.99.2, 00:25:31, Serial0/0
O IA 192.168.3.0/24 [110/66] via 10.99.99.2, 00:12:36, Serial0/0
```

This is misleading because it appears that R3 is able to reach the odd subnets even though they have been filtered on R2. However, confirmation that the subnets are not actually reachable is given by executing a simple ping to one of the subnet addresses as illustrated below:

```
R3#ping 192.168.1.1

Type escape sequence to abort.
Sending 5, 100-byte ICMP Echos to 192.168.1.1, timeout is 2 seconds:
U.U.U
Success rate is 0 percent (0/5)
```

Filtering Type 3 LSAs at the Area Border Router

Continuing with the previous example, the use of distribute lists presents a dilemma in that while the prefixes are filtered, the ABR still floods Summary LSAs to adjacent areas. Fortunately, in Cisco IOS software, the area [area ID] filter-list prefix [prefix-list-name][in | out] router configuration command can be used on the ABR to filter prefixes advertised in Network Summary LSAs between OSPF areas.

When applied inbound, the prefix list is applied to prefixes advertised to the specified area from other areas. When applied outbound, the prefix list is applied to prefixes advertised out of the specified area to other areas. Referencing the topology in Figure 4-4, R2, the ABR, can be configured to filter Type 3 LSAs for the odd subnets from the backbone from being advertised to other areas by applying the following configuration on the router:

```
R2(config)#ip prefix-list DENY-ODD-ONLY seq 5 deny 192.168.1.0/24
R2(config)#ip prefix-list DENY-ODD-ONLY seq 7 deny 192.168.3.0/24
R2(config)#ip prefix-list DENY-ODD-ONLY seq 9 permit 0.0.0.0/0 le 32
R2(config)#router ospf 2
R2(config-router)#area 0 filter-list prefix DENY-ODD-ONLY out
R2(config-router)#exit
```

This configuration can be validated using the show ip ospf command as illustrated below:

```
R2#show ip ospf 2 | section Area
    Area BACKBONE(0)
        Area has no authentication
        Area ranges are
        Area-filter DENY-ODD-ONLY out
    Area 1
        Area has no authentication
        Area ranges are
```

It is important to remember that unlike distribute lists, the area...filter-list command does not filter the prefixes R2 receives from R1 as can be seen in the following output:

```
R2#show ip route ospf
O    192.168.4.0/24 [110/2] via 150.254.1.1, 00:10:08, FastEthernet0/0
O    192.168.0.0/24 [110/2] via 150.254.1.1, 00:10:08, FastEthernet0/0
O    192.168.1.0/24 [110/2] via 150.254.1.1, 00:10:08, FastEthernet0/0
O    192.168.2.0/24 [110/2] via 150.254.1.1, 00:10:08, FastEthernet0/0
O    192.168.3.0/24 [110/2] via 150.254.1.1, 00:10:08, FastEthernet0/0
```

Instead, all the command does is prevent the ABR, which is R2, from flooding Summary LSAs for the prefixes that are filtered to other areas. This means that all Type 3 LSAs that are advertised by R2, based on information from Area 0, are filtered by the prefix list before they are flooded to adjacent areas. R2 will therefore not flood Type 3 LSAs for the 192.168.1.0/24 and the

192.168.3.0/24 prefixes to Area 1 as can be seen in the LSDB on R2 illustrated in the following output:

```
R2#show ip ospf database | begin Area 1
                Router Link States (Area 1)

Link ID         ADV Router      Age         Seq#        Checksum Link Count
2.2.2.2         2.2.2.2         579         0x8000000F 0x00E3F1 2
3.3.3.3         3.3.3.3         1099        0x80000008 0x008E4A 2


                Summary Net Link States (Area 1)

Link ID         ADV Router      Age         Seq#        Checksum
150.254.1.0     2.2.2.2         575         0x80000003 0x00AEEC
192.168.0.0     2.2.2.2         575         0x80000003 0x00AB1C
192.168.2.0     2.2.2.2         575         0x80000003 0x009530
192.168.4.0     2.2.2.2         575         0x80000003 0x007F44
```

Because the Type 3 LSAs are not flooded to Area 1, R3 will not receive these LSAs and they will not be stored in the LSDB as illustrated in the following output:

```
R3#show ip ospf database | begin Summary
                Summary Net Link States (Area 1)

Link ID         ADV Router      Age         Seq#        Checksum
150.254.1.0     2.2.2.2         1093        0x80000003 0x00AEEC
192.168.0.0     2.2.2.2         1093        0x80000003 0x00AB1C
192.168.2.0     2.2.2.2         1093        0x80000003 0x009530
192.168.4.0     2.2.2.2         1093        0x80000003 0x007F44
```

Finally, because the LSAs are not in the LSBD, they will also not be in the routing table on R3. This too is validated in the following output:

```
R3#show ip route ospf
O IA 192.168.4.0/24 [110/66] via 10.99.99.2, 00:19:03, Serial0/0
O IA 192.168.0.0/24 [110/66] via 10.99.99.2, 00:19:03, Serial0/0
O IA 192.168.2.0/24 [110/66] via 10.99.99.2, 00:19:03, Serial0/0
     150.254.0.0/24 is subnetted, 1 subnets
O IA    150.254.1.0 [110/65] via 10.99.99.2, 00:19:03, Serial0/0
```

Filtering Outgoing LSAs

In addition to distribute lists and Summary LSA filtering, OSPF also supports the filtering of all LSAs out of an outgoing interface, or for NBMA networks, to a specific neighbor. The ip ospf database-filter all out interface configuration command filters all outgoing LSAs on the interface on which it is implemented. For OSPF implementations in NBMA network environments, the neighbor [address] database-filter router configuration command performs the same function on a per-neighbor basis. Unlike distribute lists, these commands actually will filter LSAs and do prevent specified neighbors or neighbor routers discovered by the interface from having a full Link State Database, which ultimately means that those neighbors would not be able to build a complete routing table.

The filtering of LSAs is typically performed to reduce the effects of LSAs flooding over congested links. The assumption is that the specified neighbor router or routers known by that interface have another means of receiving LSAs (e.g., via a redundant link to another OSPF router). Because the filtering of LSAs can result in serious problems in the OSPF network, the recommended solution would be to use the `ip ospf flood-reduction` interface configuration command to suppress the unnecessary flooding of LSAs in stable topologies.

PROTOCOL INDEPENDENT ROUTE FILTERING

When most network engineers think of route filtering, they automatically assume that some kind of distribute list is required. However, it is important to think outside the box and consider all possible options before implementing a route filtering policy. Recall that in Cisco IOS software, administrative distance is used to determine the reliability of one source of routing information from another and it is a locally significant value.

Different route sources are assigned different administrative distance values. This default value is an integer between 0 and 255, with a value of 0 assigned to the most reliable source of information and a value of 255 being assigned to the least reliable source of information. Routes that are assigned an administrative distance value of 255 are considered untrusted and will not be placed into the routing table. This effectively means that if a route is assigned a default administrative distance value of 255, the route will not be installed into the routing table. With static routes, the administrative distance value can be specified using the `ip route` global configuration command. For dynamic routes, the `distance [admin distance] [address] [wildcard-mask] [ip-standard-acl | ip-extended-acl | access-list-name]` router configuration command can be used to adjust the default administrative distance value of dynamically received routes, effectively allowing routes to be filtered.

The `[admin distance]` keyword is used to specify the administrative distance for the route or routes. The `[address]` keyword specifies the network address the routes are learned from. This can be used with or without the `[wildcard-mask]` keyword. The command can also be used with named and numbered standard or extended ACLs for more granular filtering. To demonstrate the use of this command, consider the network illustrated in Figure 4-5 below:

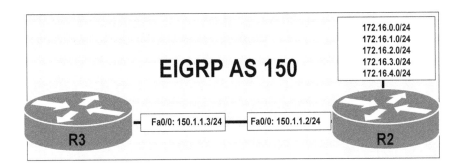

Fig. 4-5. Filtering Routes Using Administrative Distance

Figure 4-5 illustrates a basic EIGRP network. R2 is advertising several 172.16 prefixes to router R3. Assuming that EIGRP has been correctly configured between the two routers, the routing table on R3 displays the following route entries:

```
R3#show ip route eigrp
     172.16.0.0/24 is subnetted, 5 subnets
D       172.16.4.0 [90/156160] via 150.1.1.2, 00:00:06, FastEthernet0/0
D       172.16.0.0 [90/156160] via 150.1.1.2, 00:00:06, FastEthernet0/0
D       172.16.1.0 [90/156160] via 150.1.1.2, 00:00:06, FastEthernet0/0
D       172.16.2.0 [90/156160] via 150.1.1.2, 00:00:06, FastEthernet0/0
D       172.16.3.0 [90/156160] via 150.1.1.2, 00:00:06, FastEthernet0/0
```

If you wanted to filter all routes R3 is receiving from R2, you would perform the following:

```
R3(config)#router eigrp 150
R3(config-router)#distance 255 0.0.0.0 255.255.255.255
R3(config-router)#exit
```

Because routes with an administrative distance value of 255 will not be installed into the IP routing table, the routes are effectively filtered as illustrated in the following output:

```
R3#show ip route eigrp

R3#
```

In addition, the entries are also not present in the EIGRP Topology Table as illustrated below:

```
R3#show ip eigrp topology
IP-EIGRP Topology Table for AS(150)/ID(150.1.1.3)
Codes: P - Passive, A - Active, U - Update, Q - Query, R - Reply,
       r - reply Status, s - sia Status

P 150.1.1.0/24, 1 successors, FD is 28160
       via Connected, FastEthernet0/0
```

With OSPF, however, it is important to remember that even though the routes are not installed into the routing table, the LSAs are still received and are present in the LSDB. Assuming that OSPF was the routing protocol in Figure 4-5, R3 would display the route entries as follows:

```
R3#show ip route ospf
     172.16.0.0/24 is subnetted, 5 subnets
O IA    172.16.4.0 [110/2] via 150.1.1.2, 00:00:01, FastEthernet0/0
O IA    172.16.0.0 [110/2] via 150.1.1.2, 00:00:01, FastEthernet0/0
O IA    172.16.1.0 [110/2] via 150.1.1.2, 00:00:01, FastEthernet0/0
O IA    172.16.2.0 [110/2] via 150.1.1.2, 00:00:01, FastEthernet0/0
O IA    172.16.3.0 [110/2] via 150.1.1.2, 00:00:01, FastEthernet0/0
```

The same configuration could then be applied to filter all routes received from R2 as follows:

```
R3(config)#router ospf 3
R3(config-router)#distance 255 0.0.0.0 255.255.255.255
R3(config-router)#exit
```

Using the show ip route command, we can verify that the routes are no longer in the RIB as illustrated below:

```
R3#show ip route ospf
R3#
```

However, the Summary LSAs for the routes are still present in the LSDB as illustrated below:

```
R3#show ip ospf database

            OSPF Router with ID (3.3.3.3) (Process ID 3)

            Router Link States (Area 0)

Link ID         ADV Router      Age       Seq#         Checksum Link Count
2.2.2.2         2.2.2.2         34        0x80000004 0x003996 2
3.3.3.3         3.3.3.3         213       0x80000002 0x00D9F3 2

            Summary Net Link States (Area 0)

Link ID         ADV Router      Age       Seq#         Checksum
172.16.0.0      2.2.2.2         30        0x80000001 0x00D1A5
172.16.1.0      2.2.2.2         30        0x80000001 0x00C6AF
172.16.2.0      2.2.2.2         30        0x80000001 0x00BBB9
172.16.3.0      2.2.2.2         30        0x80000001 0x00B0C3
172.16.4.0      2.2.2.2         30        0x80000001 0x00A5CD
```

It is important to understand that the distance command provides far more granularity than has been illustrated in this section. For example, the command could be used to filter only specific routes from a specific router. As an example, assume that there were other routers on the LAN illustrated in Figure 4-5 and you were requested to filter the even subnets (i.e., 172.16.0.0/24, 172.16.2.0/24, and 172.16.4.0/24) advertised only by R2 to R3. To accomplish this task, the following configuration would be implemented on R3:

```
R3(config)#ip access-list standard EVEN-SUBNET-FILTER
R3(config-std-nacl)#remark 'Match Even Subnets'
R3(config-std-nacl)#permit 0.0.0.0 255.255.254.255
R3(config-std-nacl)#exit
R3(config)#router eigrp 150
R3(config-router)#distance 255 150.1.1.2 0.0.0.0 EVEN-SUBNET-FILTER
R3(config-router)#exit
```

After this configuration, the routing table on R3 would display the following route entries:

```
R3#show ip route eigrp
     172.16.0.0/24 is subnetted, 2 subnets
D       172.16.1.0 [90/156160] via 150.1.1.2, 00:00:01, FastEthernet0/0
D       172.16.3.0 [90/156160] via 150.1.1.2, 00:00:01, FastEthernet0/0
```

When filtering routes from OSPF, you must specify the router ID and not the interface address. For example, assume that the same configuration was applied to OSPF as illustrated below:

```
R3(config)#ip access-list standard EVEN-SUBNET-FILTER
R3(config-std-nacl)#remark 'Match Even Subnets'
R3(config-std-nacl)#permit 0.0.0.0 255.255.254.255
R3(config-std-nacl)#exit
R3(config)#router ospf 3
R3(config-router)#distance 255 150.1.1.2 0.0.0.0 EVEN-SUBNET-FILTER
R3(config-router)#exit
```

Even though the configuration above instructs the router to set the administrative distance of routes received from 150.1.1.2 to 255, the routing table would still reflect the following entries:

```
R3#show ip route ospf
     172.16.0.0/24 is subnetted, 5 subnets
O IA    172.16.4.0 [110/2] via 150.1.1.2, 00:05:31, FastEthernet0/0
O IA    172.16.0.0 [110/2] via 150.1.1.2, 00:05:31, FastEthernet0/0
O IA    172.16.1.0 [110/2] via 150.1.1.2, 00:05:31, FastEthernet0/0
O IA    172.16.2.0 [110/2] via 150.1.1.2, 00:05:31, FastEthernet0/0
O IA    172.16.3.0 [110/2] via 150.1.1.2, 00:05:31, FastEthernet0/0
```

Because the router ID has not been specified for OSPF, the routes are not filtered. In order to filter the routes, the router ID printed in the output of the show ip ospf neighbor command must be used. From R3, this command displays the following:

```
R3#show ip ospf neighbor

Neighbor ID     Pri   State    Dead Time   Address         Interface
2.2.2.2           1   FULL/BDR 00:00:32    150.1.1.2       FastEthernet0/0
```

The distance configuration must therefore be modified as follows:

```
R3(config)#router ospf 3
R3(config-router)#distance 255 2.2.2.2 0.0.0.0 EVEN-SUBNET-FILTER
R3(config-router)#exit
```

After implementing this configuration, the routing table on R3 displays the following entries:

```
R3#show ip route ospf
      172.16.0.0/24 is subnetted, 2 subnets
O IA    172.16.1.0 [110/2] via 150.1.1.2, 00:00:42, FastEthernet0/0
O IA    172.16.3.0 [110/2] via 150.1.1.2, 00:00:42, FastEthernet0/0
```

ROUTE REDISTRIBUTION OVERVIEW

Route redistribution allows routing protocols to exchange routing information about similar routed protocols. This means that, for example, you can redistribute between two different routing protocols for IP networks, but between IP and IPX. The router on which redistribution is implemented is referred to as the Autonomous System Boundary Router (ASBR).

How Route Redistribution Works

The fact that route redistribution allows dissimilar routing protocols to exchange similar routed protocol information often leads to the incorrect conclusion that by enabling or configuring route redistribution, the routing protocols begin to interact with each other to exchange this routing information. However, it is important to understand that this is not the case, as will be described in this section.

Routing information learned by a particular routing protocol is stored in the routing table, also referred to as the Routing Information Base (RIB). This is the central repository for all qualified routes (based on the route selection process), and the information stored in the RIB is used to forward packets to destination networks via the next-hop address(es) for each network.

Because routing protocols are different and employ different types of algorithms (e.g., EIGRP uses DUAL while OSPF uses SPF), the algorithms along with the metrics used by the routing protocols are incompatible, meaning that the routing protocols themselves cannot communicate directly with each other to exchange routing information. This means that there must be some kind of middleman, if you will, that allows this interaction when route redistribution is enabled on the router. This middleman is the RIB as shown in Figure 4-6 below:

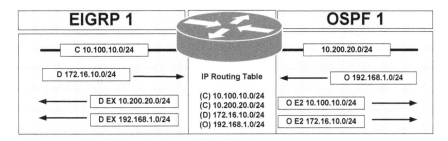

Fig. 4-6. Understanding Route Redistribution

Referencing Figure 4-6, mutual redistribution has been configured between EIGRP and OSPF. After running their respective algorithms, both routes have installed routes into the RIB. Following the redistribution configuration, EIGRP queries the RIB for OSPF routes, which include the connected 10.200.20.0/24 subnet, as well as the 192.168.1.0/24 subnet. These routes are then advertised by the router into the EIGRP domain as external EIGRP routes. OSPF performs the same actions and queries the routing table for EIGRP routes, which include the connected 10.100.10.0/24 subnet and the dynamically learned 172.16.10.0/24 subnets. These two subnets are advertised into the OSPF domain as external OSPF routes. The two routing protocols do not directly interact with each other at any time during the route redistribution.

CONFIGURING AND VERIFYING ROUTE REDISTRIBUTION

In Cisco IOS software, route redistribution is configured via the redistribute [protocol] [process ID] [autonomous-system-number] [metric <value>] [metric-type <type>] [match <internal | external 1 | external 2>] [tag <tag>] [route-map <name>] [subnets] [nssa-only] router configuration command. Table 4-3 below lists and describes the functions of these keywords:

Table 4-3. Route Redistribution Configuration Keywords

Keyword	Description
protocol	This specifies the protocol that is to be redistributed. Options include connected, static, EIGRP, OSPF, and BGP, for example.
process ID	This specifies the process ID of the external route source. This is applicable only if the protocol being redistributed is OSPF.
autonomous-system-number	This specifies the autonomous system number of the external route source. This is applicable with EIGRP and BGP.

`metric-type <type>`	This specifies the metric type and is applicable when redistributing into OSPF. A metric type of Type 1 or Type 2 can be specified with the default being Type 2 for external OSPF routes.
`match <internal | external 1 | external 2>`	This is used when redistributing OSPF into BGP. By default, only OSPF internal and external Type 1 routes are redistributed. EIGRP will redistribute all OSPF routes.
`tag <tag>`	This is used to specify a route tag for the redistributed routes. If a route tag is not specified, then the remote autonomous system number is used for routes from BGP. For other protocols, a value of zero is used.
`route-map <name>`	This is used to specify the route map that will be used during redistribution. If not specified, all routes are redistributed. If you specify that a route map should be used but do not specify the route map name, no routes will be imported.
`subnets`	This keyword is applicable only with OSPF. By default, OSPF will only redistribute Classful networks unless this keyword is included in the redistribution configuration.
`nssa-only`	This keyword is applicable only with OSPF. It sets the NSSA-only attribute for all routes redistributed into OSPF.

The sections that follow will describe the route redistribution configuration and verification tasks for both OSPF and EIGRP. These sections describe the following scenarios:

- EIGRP Redistribution Metrics
- Redistributing between Two EIGRP Autonomous Systems
- Redistributing OSPF Routes into EIGRP
- Redistributing Connected and Static Routes into EIGRP
- OSPF Redistribution Metrics
- Redistributing Classful and Classless Subnets into OSPF
- Redistributing between Two OSPF Processes
- Redistributing EIGRP Routes into OSPF
- Redistributing Connected and Static Routes into OSPF
- OSPF NSSA Type 1 and Type 2 External Routes
- Troubleshooting OSPF Route Redistribution Issues

EIGRP Redistribution Metrics

By default, when external routing information is redistributed into EIGRP, the external routes are assigned a default metric of infinity. The only three exceptions to this rule are the following:

- When redistributing between two EIGRP autonomous systems
- When redistributing static routes into EIGRP
- When redistributing connected interfaces (subnets) into EIGRP

EIGRP preserves all metrics when redistributing between the two EIGRP autonomous systems. When connected subnets (interfaces) and static routes are redistributed into EIGRP, the redistributed routes are assigned a default external metric value of 0. This default behavior will be illustrated in detail later in the following sections.

When redistributing any other external route source (e.g., OSPF or BGP), a metric must be specified manually for those external routes. In Cisco IOS software, this can be performed using one of the three following methods:

1. By specifying the seed (default) EIGRP metric for redistributed routes
2. By indirectly specifying the EIGRP metric during redistribution using a route map
3. By directly specifying the EIGRP metric during route redistribution

The seed metric is the metric value that will be assigned to all the redistributed routes. In other words, this is the initial metric that will be assigned to the external routing information when redistribution into EIGRP is configured. The seed metric is configured using the `default-metric [bandwidth] [delay] [reliability] [loading] [mtu]` router configuration command. The following configuration example illustrates how to configure the seed metric using a bandwidth value of 10000 Kbps, a delay value of 1000 microseconds, a reliability value of 255/255, a loading value of 1/255, and, finally, an MTU value of 1500 bytes:

```
R4(config)#router eigrp 4
R4(config-router)#default-metric 10000 100 255 1 1500
R4(config-router)#exit
```

NOTE: As was stated in Chapter 2, the delay value used in EIGRP metric calculation is in tens of microseconds. Therefore, the delay value in microseconds must be divided by 10 to compute the EIGRP metric.

This configuration can be verified using the `show ip protocols` command as follows:

```
R4#show ip protocols
Routing Protocol is "eigrp 4"
  Outgoing update filter list for all interfaces is not set
  Incoming update filter list for all interfaces is not set
  Default networks flagged in outgoing updates
  Default networks accepted from incoming updates
  EIGRP metric weight K1=1, K2=0, K3=1, K4=0, K5=0
  EIGRP maximum hopcount 100
  EIGRP maximum metric variance 1
  Default redistribution metric is 10000 100 255 1 1500
  Redistributing: eigrp 4
  EIGRP NSF-aware route hold timer is 240s
  Automatic network summarization is not in effect

...

[Truncated Output]
```

The second method of specifying the initial route metric for redistributed routes is to use a route map during route redistribution. This option provides greater flexibility in that different metrics can be assigned to different route sources. Within a route map, the EIGRP metric is specified using the `set metric [bandwidth] [delay] [reliability] [loading] [mtu]` route map configuration command. The following configuration example illustrates how to set the EIGRP metric for different external OSPF routes using a route map:

```
R4(config)#route-map OSPF-into-EIGRP permit 10
R4(config-route-map)#description 'Match OSPF Internal Routes Only'
R4(config-route-map)#match route-type internal
R4(config-route-map)#set metric 10000 100 255 1 1500
R4(config-route-map)#exit
R4(config)#route-map OSPF-into-EIGRP permit 20
R4(config-route-map)#description 'Match OSPF External Type 1 Routes Only'
R4(config-route-map)#set metric 100000 10 255 1 1500
R4(config-route-map)#exit
R4(config)#route-map OSPF-into-EIGRP permit 30
R4(config-route-map)#description 'Match OSPF External Type 2 Routes Only'
R4(config-route-map)#match route-type external type-2
R4(config-route-map)#set metric 1544 2000 255 1 1500
R4(config-route-map)#exit
R4(config)#router eigrp 4
R4(config-router)#redistribute ospf 4 route-map OSPF-into-EIGRP
R4(config-router)#exit
```

Referencing the configuration above, redistributed OSPF routes are assigned an initial metric based on the metric values specified for each route type in the route map configuration. This configuration can be validated by viewing any specific OSPF route simply by using the `show ip route` command as illustrated below:

```
R4#show ip route 10.11.11.0 255.255.255.0
Routing entry for 10.11.11.0/24
  Known via "ospf 4", distance 110, metric 65, type inter area
  Redistributing via eigrp 4
  Advertised by eigrp 150 route-map OSPF-into-EIGRP
  Last update from 10.99.99.1 on Serial0/0, 00:02:05 ago
  Routing Descriptor Blocks:
  * 10.99.99.1, from 1.1.1.1, 00:02:05 ago, via Serial0/0
      Route metric is 65, traffic share count is 1
```

The EIGRP values used for the metric assigned to the route, which is internal (inter-area) in this example, can then be validated using the `show ip eigrp topology` command as follows:

```
R4#show ip eigrp topology 10.11.11.0 255.255.255.0
IP-EIGRP (AS 4): Topology entry for 10.11.11.0/24
  State is Passive, Query origin flag is 1, 1 Successor(s), FD is 281600
  Routing Descriptor Blocks:
```

```
10.99.99.1, from Redistributed, Send flag is 0x0
    Composite metric is (281600/0), Route is External
    Vector metric:
      Minimum bandwidth is 10000 Kbit
      Total delay is 1000 microseconds
      Reliability is 255/255
      Load is 1/255
      Minimum MTU is 1500
      Hop count is 0
    External data:
      Originating router is 172.16.1.4 (this system)
      AS number of route is 4
      External protocol is OSPF, external metric is 65
      Administrator tag is 0 (0x00000000)
```

The values used to derive the initial metric are those specified for internal OSPF routes in the route map as can be seen in the output of the show route-map command below:

```
R4# show route-map OSPF-into-EIGRP
route-map OSPF-into-EIGRP, permit, sequence 10
  Match clauses:
    route-type internal
  Set clauses:
    metric 10000 100 255 1 1500
  Policy routing matches: 0 packets, 0 bytes

...

[Truncated Output]
```

Finally, the third method of specifying the initial EIGRP metric to be used for imported routes (redistributed routes) is directly during redistribution configuration using the redistribute [protocol] metric [bandwidth] [delay] [reliability] [loading] [mtu] router configuration command. Different values can be used for different route sources as illustrated in the following configuration example:

```
R4(config)#router eigrp 4
R4(config-router)#redistribute ospf 4 metric 10000 100 255 1 1500
R4(config-router)#redistribute bgp 4 metric 100000 10 255 1 1500
R4(config-router)#redistribute static metric 1544 2000 255 1 1500
R4(config-router)#exit
```

Redistributing between Two EIGRP Autonomous Systems

When redistributing between two EIGRP autonomous systems, EIGRP simply uses the metric value of the other EIGRP autonomous system and a metric does not have to be configured during the redistribution process. Consider the network topology illustrated in Figure 4-7 below, which shows a basic EIGRP network. R1 and R2 reside in Autonomous System 1, while R2 and R3 reside in Autonomous System 2. Because R2 resides in both autonomous systems, it is considered the ASBR. This is the router on which redistribution will be performed. Because one EIGRP process is being redistributed into another, the redistribution configuration will be straightforward, as there is no need to specify manually a metric for the redistributed routes.

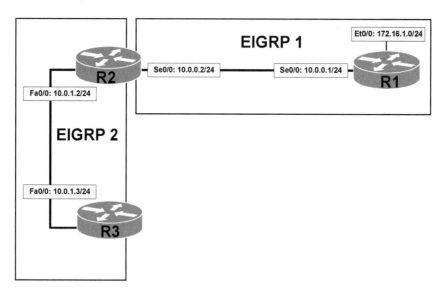

Fig. 4-7. Redistributing between Two EIGRP Autonomous Systems

The redistribution of EIGRP 1 into EIGRP 2 is performed as follows on R2:

```
R2(config)#router eigrp 2
R2(config-router)#redistribute eigrp 1
R2(config-router)#exit
```

The initial metric value assigned to the 172.16.1.0/24 subnet advertised via EIGRP Autonomous System 1 on R1 to R2 can be validated using the show ip eigrp topology command:

```
R2#show ip eigrp topology 1 172.16.1.0 255.255.255.0
IP-EIGRP (AS 1): Topology entry for 172.16.1.0/24
  State is Passive, Query origin flag is 1, 1 Successor(s), FD is 2172416
  Routing Descriptor Blocks:
  10.0.0.1 (Serial0/0), from 10.0.0.1, Send flag is 0x0
      Composite metric is (2172416/28160), Route is Internal
      Vector metric:
        Minimum bandwidth is 1544 Kbit
        Total delay is 20100 microseconds
        Reliability is 255/255
        Load is 1/255
        Minimum MTU is 1500
        Hop count is 1
```

Because no explicit metric was specified during the redistribution of EIGRP 1 into EIGRP 2, the same metric value is assigned to the external route under EIGRP Autonomous System 2 as illustrated below:

```
R2#show ip eigrp topology 2 172.16.1.0 255.255.255.0
IP-EIGRP (AS 2): Topology entry for 172.16.1.0/24
  State is Passive, Query origin flag is 1, 1 Successor(s), FD is 2172416
  Routing Descriptor Blocks:
  10.0.0.1, from Redistributed, Send flag is 0x0
      Composite metric is (2172416/0), Route is External
      Vector metric:
        Minimum bandwidth is 1544 Kbit
        Total delay is 20100 microseconds
        Reliability is 255/255
        Load is 1/255
        Minimum MTU is 1500
        Hop count is 1
      External data:
        Originating router is 10.0.1.2 (this system)
        AS number of route is 1
        External protocol is EIGRP, external metric is 2172416
        Administrator tag is 0 (0x00000000)
```

This routing information is propagated downstream to R3 as illustrated below:

```
R3#show ip eigrp topology 2 172.16.1.0 255.255.255.0
IP-EIGRP (AS 2): Topology entry for 172.16.1.0/24
  State is Passive, Query origin flag is 1, 1 Successor(s), FD is 2174976
  Routing Descriptor Blocks:
  10.0.1.2 (FastEthernet0/0), from 10.0.1.2, Send flag is 0x0
      Composite metric is (2174976/2172416), Route is External
      Vector metric:
        Minimum bandwidth is 1544 Kbit
        Total delay is 20200 microseconds
        Reliability is 255/255
        Load is 1/255
        Minimum MTU is 1500
        Hop count is 2
      External data:
        Originating router is 10.0.1.2
        AS number of route is 1
        External protocol is EIGRP, external metric is 2172416
        Administrator tag is 0 (0x00000000)
```

NOTE: Although the Topology Table on R3 shows the original metric of the external EIGRP route, the metric assigned during redistribution will change just as any EIGRP metric would, as EIGRP routes are propagated to downstream routers in the autonomous system. R3's metric includes the delay for the link between itself and R2.

Redistributing OSPF Routes into EIGRP

When redistributing OSPF routes into EIGRP, a metric must be specified manually because the two routing protocols use different metrics and EIGRP does not assign a default metric. In addition, while Cisco IOS software allows the configuration to be implemented, the routes will not be redistributed by the router. As an example, consider the topology illustrated in Figure 4-8 below, which shows a basic network running both EIGRP and OSPF:

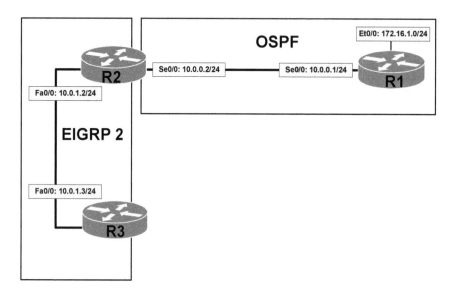

Fig. 4-8. Redistributing between Two EIGRP Autonomous Systems

Referencing Figure 4-8, R1 and R2 are both running OSPF, while R2 and R3 are both running EIGRP. Assuming that the network is correctly configured, R2 shows the following routes:

```
R2#show ip route ospf
     172.16.0.0/24 is subnetted, 1 subnets
O       172.16.1.0 [110/65] via 10.0.0.1, 00:05:04, Serial0/0
```

Next, router R2 is configured to redistribute the OSPF routes into EIGRP as follows:

```
R2(config)#router eigrp 2
R2(config-router)#redistribute ospf 2
R2(config-router)#exit
```

Following this configuration, the output of the show ip route command for the 172.16.1.0/24 subnet shows that the route is being redistributed via EIGRP as was configured. This is illustrated as follows:

```
R2#show ip route 172.16.1.0 255.255.255.0
Routing entry for 172.16.1.0/24
  Known via "ospf 2", distance 110, metric 65, type intra area
```

```
Redistributing via eigrp 2
Last update from 10.0.0.1 on Serial0/0, 00:00:01 ago
Routing Descriptor Blocks:
* 10.0.0.1, from 1.1.1.1, 00:00:01 ago, via Serial0/0
    Route metric is 65, traffic share count is 1
```

However, because no metric was specified, the route is actually not being redistributed and is not present in the EIGRP Topology Table; instead, only the connected subnet is present since this does not require a metric to be specified when being redistributed into EIGRP. This is illustrated as follows:

```
R2#show ip eigrp 2 topology
IP-EIGRP Topology Table for AS(2)/ID(10.0.1.2)
Codes: P - Passive, A - Active, U - Update, Q - Query, R - Reply,
       r - reply Status, s - sia Status

P 10.0.0.0/24, 1 successors, FD is 2169856
        via Redistributed (2169856/0)
```

In order to redistribute the 172.16.1.0/24 subnet into EIGRP, the metric must be specified using any one of the three methods described earlier in this section. The following illustrates how to set the metric directly using the redistribute router configuration command:

```
R2(config)#router eigrp 2
R2(config-router)#redistribute ospf 2 metric 1544 2000 255 1 1500
R2(config-router)#exit
```

Following this configuration, the route is now included in the EIGRP Topology Table as illustrated below:

```
R2#show ip eigrp 2 topology 172.16.1.0 255.255.255.0
IP-EIGRP (AS 2): Topology entry for 172.16.1.0/24
  State is Passive, Query origin flag is 1, 1 Successor(s), FD is 2169856
  Routing Descriptor Blocks:
  10.0.0.1, from Redistributed, Send flag is 0x0
      Composite metric is (2169856/0), Route is External
      Vector metric:
        Minimum bandwidth is 1544 Kbit
        Total delay is 20000 microseconds
        Reliability is 255/255
        Load is 1/255
        Minimum MTU is 1500
        Hop count is 0
      External data:
        Originating router is 10.0.1.2 (this system)
        AS number of route is 2
        External protocol is OSPF, external metric is 65
        Administrator tag is 0 (0x00000000)
```

Finally, the output of the show ip route command illustrates that the EIGRP is redistributing the subnet; however, this time, the metric used during redistribution is included as follows:

```
R2#show ip route 172.16.1.0 255.255.255.0
Routing entry for 172.16.1.0/24
  Known via "ospf 2", distance 110, metric 65, type intra area
  Redistributing via eigrp 2
  Advertised by eigrp 2 metric 1544 2000 255 1 1500
  Last update from 10.0.0.1 on Serial0/0, 00:00:01 ago
  Routing Descriptor Blocks:
  * 10.0.0.1, from 1.1.1.1, 00:00:01 ago, via Serial0/0
      Route metric is 65, traffic share count is 1
```

R2 advertises the route downstream to R3, which displays the following in the Topology Table:

```
R3#show ip eigrp 2 topology 172.16.1.0 255.255.255.0
IP-EIGRP (AS 2): Topology entry for 172.16.1.0/24
  State is Passive, Query origin flag is 1, 1 Successor(s), FD is 2172416
  Routing Descriptor Blocks:
  10.0.1.2 (FastEthernet0/0), from 10.0.1.2, Send flag is 0x0
      Composite metric is (2172416/2169856), Route is External
      Vector metric:
        Minimum bandwidth is 1544 Kbit
        Total delay is 20100 microseconds
        Reliability is 255/255
        Load is 1/255
        Minimum MTU is 1500
        Hop count is 1
      External data:
        Originating router is 10.0.1.2
        AS number of route is 2
        External protocol is OSPF, external metric is 65
        Administrator tag is 0 (0x00000000)
```

Redistributing Connected and Static Routes into EIGRP

As was stated earlier in this section, by default, EIGRP redistributes connected and static routes with a metric value of 0. Therefore, a metric does not have to be configured explicitly when redistributing connected routes into EIGRP.

Figure 4-9 below shows a basic EIGRP network comprised of two routers. R2 and R3 reside in EIGRP Autonomous System 2. R2 has two additional Loopback interfaces, Loopback 253, with the IP address 192.168.253.2/24 and Loopback 254, with the IP address 192.168.254.2/24. These subnets will be redistributed into EIGRP on R2. In addition, two static routes are also configured on R2. The two static routes for the 172.16.253.0/24 and 172.16.254.0/24 subnets both point to the Null0 interface. These static routes will also be redistributed into EIGRP.

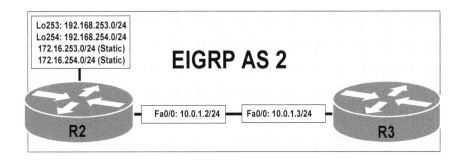

Fig. 4-9. Redistributing Connected and Static Routes into EIGRP

Assuming that EIGRP has been configured correctly between R2 and R3, the redistribution of the connected subnets is performed as follows:

```
R2(config)#router eigrp 2
R2(config-router)#redistribute connected
R2(config-router)#redistribute static
R2(config-router)#end
```

Following this configuration, the show ip eigrp topology command can be used to view the EIGRP metric values assigned to each of these routes that are derived from the interfaces. This is illustrated below:

```
R2#show ip eigrp 2 topology 192.168.253.0/24
IP-EIGRP (AS 2): Topology entry for 192.168.253.0/24
  State is Passive, Query origin flag is 1, 1 Successor(s), FD is 128256
  Routing Descriptor Blocks:
  0.0.0.0, from Rconnected, Send flag is 0x0
      Composite metric is (128256/0), Route is External
      Vector metric:
        Minimum bandwidth is 10000000 Kbit
        Total delay is 5000 microseconds
        Reliability is 255/255
        Load is 1/255
        Minimum MTU is 1514
        Hop count is 0
      External data:
        Originating router is 10.0.1.2 (this system)
        AS number of route is 0
        External protocol is Connected, external metric is 0
        Administrator tag is 0 (0x00000000)
```

The same command, when used for any one of the static routes, displays the following:

```
R2#show ip eigrp 2 topology 172.16.254.0/24
IP-EIGRP (AS 2): Topology entry for 172.16.254.0/24
  State is Passive, Query origin flag is 1, 1 Successor(s), FD is 256
```

```
Routing Descriptor Blocks:
0.0.0.0, from Rstatic, Send flag is 0x0
    Composite metric is (256/0), Route is External
    Vector metric:
      Minimum bandwidth is 10000000 Kbit
      Total delay is 0 microseconds
      Reliability is 0/255
      Load is 0/255
      Minimum MTU is 1500
      Hop count is 0
    External data:
      Originating router is 10.0.1.2 (this system)
      AS number of route is 0
      External protocol is Static, external metric is 0
      Administrator tag is 0 (0x00000000)
```

When redistributing connected and static routes, it always is considered good practice to use a route map to ensure that only the routes that should be imported are redistributed into EIGRP. For example, assume that only the 192.168.254.0/24 and the 172.16.254.0/24 prefixes should be redistributed into EIGRP. Based on the configuration implemented on R2 in the previous example, a distribute list could be used to filter these prefixes so that they would not be advertised to R3. However, this requires additional unnecessary configuration. The recommended solution, therefore, is to use a route map with route redistribution as follows:

```
R2(config)#route-map CONNECTED-into-EIGRP permit 10
R2(config-route-map)#description 'Only Loopback 254 Should Be Redistributed'
R2(config-route-map)#match interface Loopback 254
R2(config-route-map)#exit
R2(config)#route-map STATIC-into-EIGRP permit 10
R2(config-route-map)#description 'Only 172.16.254.0 Should Be Redistributed'
R2(config-route-map)#match ip address 1
R2(config-route-map)#exit
R2(config)#access-list 1 permit 172.16.254.0
R2(config)#router eigrp 2
R2(config-router)#redistribute connected route-map CONNECTED-into-EIGRP
R2(config-router)#redistribute static route-map STATIC-into-EIGRP
R2(config-router)#exit
```

Following this configuration, the EIGRP Topology Table on R2 shows the following:

```
R2#show ip eigrp 2 topology
IP-EIGRP Topology Table for AS(2)/ID(10.0.1.2)
Codes: P - Passive, A - Active, U - Update, Q - Query, R - Reply,
       r - reply Status, s - sia Status

P 10.0.1.0/24, 1 successors, FD is 28160
       via Connected, FastEthernet0/0
P 172.16.254.0/24, 1 successors, FD is 256
```

```
        via Rstatic (256/0)
P 192.168.254.0/24, 1 successors, FD is 128256
        via Rconnected (128256/0)
```

NOTE: An alternative approach when redistributing static routes is to assign each static route
a route tag. This can then be matched during redistribution. This negates the need to manually
add to the ACL used to match static subnets when redistributing routes. The use of route tags
is illustrated in the following configuration example:

```
R2(config)#ip route 172.16.250.0 255.255.255.0 Null0 tag 888
R2(config)#ip route 172.16.251.0 255.255.255.0 Null0 tag 999
R2(config)#ip route 172.16.252.0 255.255.255.0 Null0 tag 888
R2(config)#ip route 172.16.253.0 255.255.255.0 Null0 tag 999
R2(config)#ip route 172.16.254.0 255.255.255.0 Null0 tag 888
R2(config)#ip route 172.16.255.0 255.255.255.0 Null0 tag 999
R2(config)#route-map STATIC-into-EIGRP permit 10
R2(config-route-map)#match tag 888
R2(config-route-map)#exit
R2(config)#router eigrp 2
R2(config-router)#redistribute static route-map STATIC-into-EIGRP
R2(config-router)#exit
```

In the configuration above, six static routes have been configured on R2. The static routes with an
even third octet have been assigned a route tag of 888, while those with an odd third octet have
been assigned a route tag of 999. EIGRP has been configured to redistribute static routes based on
the specified route map. The route map, in turn, has been configured to match routes only with a
route tag of 888. Following this configuration, the EIGRP Topology Table on R2 shows the following
route entries:

```
R2#show ip eigrp 2 topology
IP-EIGRP Topology Table for AS(2)/ID(10.0.1.2)
Codes: P - Passive, A - Active, U - Update, Q - Query, R - Reply,
       r - reply Status, s - sia Status

P 172.16.252.0/24, 1 successors, FD is 256, tag is 888
        via Rstatic (256/0)
P 172.16.254.0/24, 1 successors, FD is 256, tag is 888
        via Rstatic (256/0)
P 172.16.250.0/24, 1 successors, FD is 256, tag is 888
        via Rstatic (256/0)
```

OSPF Redistribution Metrics

Unlike EIGRP, OSPF does not require that a metric be specified when redistribution from any route
source into OSPF is performed. OSPF assigns a default route metric based on the route source.
These default assignments are as follows:

- Redistributed routes from BGP are assigned a metric or cost of 1
- Redistributed routes from another OSPF process use the source route's cost
- All other redistributed routes are assigned a default metric of 20

As with EIGRP, the OSPF metric can be configured several ways during redistribution. The seed metric for all routes can be configured using the `default-metric <value>` router configuration command. The metric can also be configured directly during redistribution using the `redistribute [protocol] metric <value>` router configuration command. Finally, the OSPF metric can also be specified in a route map using the `redistribute [protocol] route-map <name>` router configuration command. The configuration of the OSPF metric using these three values is no different than was illustrated for EIGRP in the previous section, with the exception being that the metric will be the OSPF metric and not the EIGRP composite metric.

In addition to the metric, all OSPF external routes are designated as Type 2 external routes by default. However, this default behavior can be changed using the `redistribute [protocol] metric-type <1 | 2>` router configuration command or by setting the metric in a route map referenced during redistribution using the `set metric-type [type-1 | type-2]` route map configuration command. Before we delve into the specifics of external OSPF routes, it is important to have a solid understanding of the differences between Type 2 and Type 1 external OSPF routes. These are described in the following sections.

Understanding and Calculating Type 2 External Routes

If no metric is assigned during redistribution, external routes are assigned a default metric of 20. Also, by default, OSPF external routes are Type 2 external routes. However, both the metric and the metric type can be specified manually during redistribution into OSPF. Before we delve into the specifics of OSPF route redistribution, it is important to understand the difference between Type 1 and Type 2 external routes.

The primary difference between Type 1 and Type 2 external routes is the way in which the cost or metric is calculated. In Cisco IOS software, external OSPF routes are designated as Type 2 routes. When routes are redistributed into OSPF as Type 2, every router in the domain will see the same cost to reach the external networks. In other words, the cost of the External (Type 5) LSA that is generated for the Type 2 external route will never change and the same value will be seen on all routers in the network, regardless of how far away they are from the ASBR that injected the external route into the OSPF domain.

Because the metric for Type 2 external routes remains consistent as the LSA is flooded through the OSPF domain, routers need to be able to have some kind of method to use as a tiebreaker when more than one ASBR injects the same external LSA into the routing domain or when there is more than one path to the ASBR. The tiebreaker is calculated in a different manner, depending on whether the ASBR resides within the same area or in another area.

If the ASBR resides within the same area, routers look at the router ID listed in the Advertising Router field in the Type 5 LSA to determine the router ID of the ASBR. The routers then look at the intra-area Link State Advertisements to determine the best path to this router. The router then forwards traffic to the ASBR using the best intra-area route to the ASBR. To clarify this point further, consider the basic OSPF network topology that is illustrated in Figure 4-10 below, which shows fours routers in a single area:

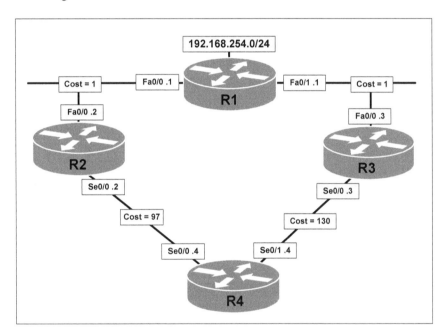

Fig. 4-10. Understanding OSPF Type 2 External Routes

Referencing Figure 4-10, R1 is redistributing the 192.168.254.0/24 subnet into OSPF. The router generates a Type 5 LSA, which is then flooded by R2 and R3 to R4. The cost of the respective links between R1 and R2 and between R2 and R3 is 1. However, the cost of the link between R2 and R4 is 97 and the cost of the link between R3 and R4 is 130.The Link State Database on R4 displays the following Type 5 LSA entries for this external route:

```
R4#show ip ospf database external 192.168.254.0

        OSPF Router with ID (4.4.4.4) (Process ID 4)

        Type-5 AS External Link States

    Routing Bit Set on this LSA
```

```
LS age: 1366
Options: (No TOS-capability, DC)
LS Type: AS External Link
Link State ID: 192.168.254.0 (External Network Number)
Advertising Router: 1.1.1.1
LS Seq Number: 80000001
Checksum: 0x2311
Length: 36
Network Mask: /24
      Metric Type: 2 (Larger than any Link State path)
      TOS: 0
      Metric: 20
      Forward Address: 0.0.0.0
      External Route Tag: 0
```

Because R1 receives this LSA from both R2 and R3, the router looks at the intra-area LSAs for both routers to determine the next-hop router and interface it will use to forward traffic to the destination network. The intra-area LSA for R2 displays the following:

```
R4#show ip ospf database router 2.2.2.2

            OSPF Router with ID (4.4.4.4) (Process ID 4)

            Router Link States (Area 0)

LS age: 886
Options: (No TOS-capability, DC)
LS Type: Router Links
Link State ID: 2.2.2.2
Advertising Router: 2.2.2.2
LS Seq Number: 80000004
Checksum: 0x2FBB
Length: 72
Number of Links: 4

  Link connected to: another Router (point-to-point)
   (Link ID) Neighboring Router ID: 4.4.4.4
   (Link Data) Router Interface address: 10.0.2.2
    Number of TOS metrics: 0
     TOS 0 Metrics: 97

  Link connected to: a Stub Network
   (Link ID) Network/subnet number: 10.0.2.0
   (Link Data) Network Mask: 255.255.255.0
    Number of TOS metrics: 0
     TOS 0 Metrics: 97

  Link connected to: another Router (point-to-point)
   (Link ID) Neighboring Router ID: 1.1.1.1
   (Link Data) Router Interface address: 10.0.0.2
    Number of TOS metrics: 0
     TOS 0 Metrics: 1
```

```
      Link connected to: a Stub Network
       (Link ID) Network/subnet number: 10.0.0.0
       (Link Data) Network Mask: 255.255.255.0
        Number of TOS metrics: 0
         TOS 0 Metrics: 1
```

Referencing the output above, the cost of the link between R4 and R2 is 97 while the cost of the link between R2 and R1 is 1. The total cost for this path is therefore 98. The router LSA for R3 displays the following information:

```
R4#show ip ospf database router 3.3.3.3

            OSPF Router with ID (4.4.4.4) (Process ID 4)

            Router Link States (Area 0)

  LS age: 1035
  Options: (No TOS-capability, DC)
  LS Type: Router Links
  Link State ID: 3.3.3.3
  Advertising Router: 3.3.3.3
  LS Seq Number: 80000004
  Checksum: 0xC1D8
  Length: 72
  Number of Links: 4

    Link connected to: another Router (point-to-point)
     (Link ID) Neighboring Router ID: 4.4.4.4
     (Link Data) Router Interface address: 10.0.3.3
      Number of TOS metrics: 0
       TOS 0 Metrics: 130

    Link connected to: a Stub Network
     (Link ID) Network/subnet number: 10.0.3.0
     (Link Data) Network Mask: 255.255.255.0
      Number of TOS metrics: 0
       TOS 0 Metrics: 130

    Link connected to: another Router (point-to-point)
     (Link ID) Neighboring Router ID: 1.1.1.1
     (Link Data) Router Interface address: 10.0.1.3
      Number of TOS metrics: 0
       TOS 0 Metrics: 1

    Link connected to: a Stub Network
     (Link ID) Network/subnet number: 10.0.1.0
     (Link Data) Network Mask: 255.255.255.0
      Number of TOS metrics: 0
       TOS 0 Metrics: 1
```

Referencing the output above, the cost of the link between R4 and R3 is 130, while the cost of the link between R3 and R1 is 1. The total cost for this path is therefore 131. Given that the path via R2 is the best intra-area path to R1, R4 forwards traffic to the 192.168.254.0/24 subnet via Serial0/0 and shows 98 as the forward metric (i.e., the internal metric to get to the ASBR). However, the actual route metric for a Type 2 external route will never change and will always be set to 20. This is validated using the show ip route command on R4 as follows:

```
R4#show ip route 192.168.254.0 255.255.255.0
Routing entry for 192.168.254.0/24
  Known via "ospf 4", distance 110, metric 20, type extern 2, forward metric
98
  Last update from 10.0.2.2 on Serial0/0, 00:28:02 ago
  Routing Descriptor Blocks:
  * 10.0.2.2, from 1.1.1.1, 00:28:02 ago, via Serial0/0
      Route metric is 20, traffic share count is 1
```

In the output above, because the route is a Type 2 external route, the actual route metric will always be consistent. However, the forward metric will vary depending on how far the router is from the ASBR. For example, if the link between R4 and R2 failed, R4 would use the path via router R3 to reach the ASBR. While the route would still show the default metric of 20, the forward metric would change to reflect the intra-area cost to reach the ASBR as illustrated below:

```
R4#show ip route 192.168.254.0 255.255.255.0
Routing entry for 192.168.254.0/24
  Known via "ospf 4", distance 110, metric 20, type extern 2, forward metric
131
  Last update from 10.0.3.3 on Serial0/1, 00:00:00 ago
  Routing Descriptor Blocks:
  * 10.0.3.3, from 1.1.1.1, 00:00:00 ago, via Serial0/1
      Route metric is 20, traffic share count is 1
```

For inter-area routes, the router calculates the forward metric to the ASBR (R1) by adding the cost to reach the ABR that flooded the Type 5 LSA into the area to the cost of reaching the ASBR from the ABR. To reinforce this point further, consider the basic multi-area OSPF network topology illustrated in Figure 4-11 below. R1, R2, and R3 are backbone routers. R4 resides in Area 1. R1 (ASBR) is redistributing the 192.168.254.0/24 subnet into the OSPF domain. R2 and R3 flood the Type 5 LSA for this external entry into Area 1 and it is received by router R4:

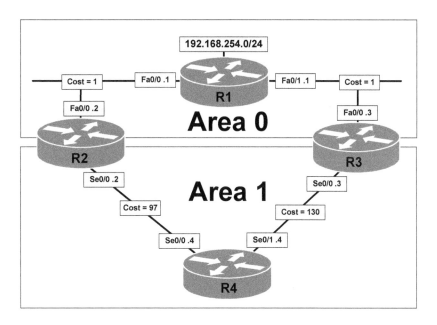

Fig. 4-11. Understanding OSPF Type 2 External Routes

Based on the topology illustrated in Figure 4-11, the LSDB on R4 displays the following entry:

```
R4#show ip ospf database external 192.168.254.0

          OSPF Router with ID (4.4.4.4) (Process ID 4)

          Type-5 AS External Link States

Routing Bit Set on this LSA
LS age: 690
Options: (No TOS-capability, DC)
LS Type: AS External Link
Link State ID: 192.168.254.0 (External Network Number)
Advertising Router: 1.1.1.1
LS Seq Number: 80000003
Checksum: 0x1F13
Length: 36
Network Mask: /24
      Metric Type: 2 (Larger than any Link State path)
      TOS: 0
      Metric: 20
      Forward Address: 0.0.0.0
      External Route Tag: 0
```

R4 calculates the cost of the metric of the external route by first looking at the cost to reach each individual ABR. This is performed by viewing the intra-area LSAs as was illustrated in the output of the show ip ospf database router command in the previous example. Because the values in Figure 4-10 are the same as those in Figure 4-11, there is no need to re-validate this step, as we already know that the cost from R4 and R2 is 97, while the cost from R4 to R3 is 130.

As we learned in Chapter 3, a Type 4 LSA is created by each ABR for every ASBR that is reachable via an intra-area LSA. Although the Type 4 LSA is flooded by the ABR, it contains information on the ASBR, which includes the ABR metric to the ASBR. Based on this topology, the LSDB on R4 shows the two Type 4 LSAs received from ABRs R2 and R3. This is illustrated as follows:

```
R4#show ip ospf database asbr-summary 1.1.1.1

            OSPF Router with ID (4.4.4.4) (Process ID 4)

            Summary ASB Link States (Area 1)

   Routing Bit Set on this LSA
   LS age: 1121
   Options: (No TOS-capability, DC, Upward)
   LS Type: Summary Links(AS Boundary Router)
   Link State ID: 1.1.1.1 (AS Boundary Router address)
   Advertising Router: 2.2.2.2
   LS Seq Number: 80000001
   Checksum: 0x1B14
   Length: 28
   Network Mask: /0
         TOS: 0  Metric: 1

   LS age: 1150
   Options: (No TOS-capability, DC, Upward)
   LS Type: Summary Links(AS Boundary Router)
   Link State ID: 1.1.1.1 (AS Boundary Router address)
   Advertising Router: 3.3.3.3
   LS Seq Number: 80000001
   Checksum: 0xFC2E
   Length: 28
   Network Mask: /0
         TOS: 0  Metric: 1
```

Both of the Type 4 LSAs received by R4 from routers R2 and R3 show a metric of 1, which is the cost of each ABR to the ASBR. R4 calculates the forward metric to the external route by adding up the cost to the ABR and the cost from the ABR to the ASBR. The cost of the path through R2 would be 97 + 1 = 98, while the cost of the path through R3 would be 130 + 1 = 131. R4 prefers the path through R2 and uses this router as the next-hop device to the 192.168.254.0/24 subnet. This is illustrated as follows:

```
R4#show ip route 192.168.254.0 255.255.255.0
Routing entry for 192.168.254.0/24
  Known via "ospf 4", distance 110, metric 20, type extern 2, forward metric 98
  Last update from 10.0.2.2 on Serial0/0, 00:15:31 ago
  Routing Descriptor Blocks:
  * 10.0.2.2, from 1.1.1.1, 00:15:31 ago, via Serial0/0
      Route metric is 20, traffic share count is 1
```

You can use the `show ip ospf border-routers` command to list all know ABRs and ASBRs and determine the best path to the ASBR. The output of this command displays the following on R4:

```
R4#show ip ospf border-routers

OSPF Process 4 internal Routing Table

Codes: i - Intra-area route, I - Inter-area route

I 1.1.1.1 [98] via 10.0.2.2, Serial0/0, ASBR, Area 1, SPF 3
i 2.2.2.2 [97] via 10.0.2.2, Serial0/0, ABR, Area 1, SPF 3
i 3.3.3.3 [130] via 10.0.3.3, Serial0/1, ABR, Area 1, SPF 3
```

From the output above, we can determine that from R4's perspective, the best path to the ASBR (R1) is via Serial0/0, which transits through R2 and has a total path cost of 98. This cost is the same value in the forward metric as seen in the output of the `show ip route` command. This command also includes the cost of reaching both ABRs from R4 itself. These cost values are the same as those shown in Figure 4-10 and Figure 4-11. Table 4-4 below lists and describes the information included in the output of the `show ip ospf border-routers` command:

Table 4-4. The `show ip ospf border-routers` **Command Fields**

Field	Description
I or i	The code may be one of two values that are used to indicate whether the route is intra-area (i) or inter-area (I).
1.1.1.1	This contains the router ID of the OSPF destination router.
[98]	This indicates the cost of the path to the destination router.
via 10.0.2.2	This indicates the next-hop address to the destination router.
Serial0/0	This indicates the outgoing interface to the destination router.
ASBR or ABR	The router type may be one of two values that are used to indicate whether the router is an ASBR or an ABR.
Area 1	This indicates the area via which the route has been learned, not the area in which the router resides.
SPF 3	This indicates the internal number of the SPF calculation that installs this route.

Understanding and Calculating Type 1 External Routes

Unlike for Type 2 external routes, the OSPF route metric for a Type 1 external route is calculated using the internal OSPF cost to the ASBR and the external redistribution cost. This means that unlike Type 2 external routes, if any routes are redistributed into OSPF as Type 1 external routes, the actual route metric will vary from router to router, depending on how far downstream the router is from the ASBR and based on the cumulative cost of the links from the router to the ASBR. Going back to the topology illustrated in Figure 4-10 wherein routers R1, R2, R3, and R4 reside within the same area, R1 is configured to redistribute the 192.168.254.0/24 subnet as a Type 1 external route. The corresponding Type 5 LSA on R4 displays the following:

```
R4#show ip ospf database external 192.168.254.0

            OSPF Router with ID (4.4.4.4) (Process ID 4)

          Type-5 AS External Link States

  Routing Bit Set on this LSA
  LS age: 6
  Options: (No TOS-capability, DC)
  LS Type: AS External Link
  Link State ID: 192.168.254.0 (External Network Number)
  Advertising Router: 1.1.1.1
  LS Seq Number: 80000005
  Checksum: 0x9719
  Length: 36
  Network Mask: /24
        Metric Type: 1 (Comparable directly to Link State metric)
        TOS: 0
        Metric: 20
        Forward Address: 0.0.0.0
        External Route Tag: 0
```

In the output above, the Type 5 LSA shows the default metric that has been assigned during redistribution, which is 20. R4 calculates the route metric to the 192.168.254.0/24 subnet by adding this value to the cost of reaching the ASBR. The cumulative cost of reaching the ASBR can be determined by viewing the intra-area LSAs as illustrated below:

```
R4#show ip ospf database router 2.2.2.2

            OSPF Router with ID (4.4.4.4) (Process ID 4)

           Router Link States (Area 0)

    LS age: 476
    Options: (No TOS-capability, DC)
    LS Type: Router Links
    Link State ID: 2.2.2.2
    Advertising Router: 2.2.2.2
    LS Seq Number: 8000000B
    Checksum: 0x21C2
    Length: 72
    Number of Links: 4

    Link connected to: another Router (point-to-point)
```

```
(Link ID) Neighboring Router ID: 4.4.4.4
(Link Data) Router Interface address: 10.0.2.2
 Number of TOS metrics: 0
  TOS 0 Metrics: 97

Link connected to: a Stub Network
 (Link ID) Network/subnet number: 10.0.2.0
 (Link Data) Network Mask: 255.255.255.0
 Number of TOS metrics: 0
  TOS 0 Metrics: 97

Link connected to: another Router (point-to-point)
 (Link ID) Neighboring Router ID: 1.1.1.1
 (Link Data) Router Interface address: 10.0.0.2
 Number of TOS metrics: 0
  TOS 0 Metrics: 1

Link connected to: a Stub Network
 (Link ID) Network/subnet number: 10.0.0.0
 (Link Data) Network Mask: 255.255.255.0
 Number of TOS metrics: 0
  TOS 0 Metrics: 1
```

In the output above, the cost of the link between R2 and R1 is 1, while the cost of the link between R2 and R4 is 97. The total path cost to the ASBR through R2 is 98. The same command will also provide the same information for the path cost through R3, as follows:

```
R4#show ip ospf database router 3.3.3.3

            OSPF Router with ID (4.4.4.4) (Process ID 4)

            Router Link States (Area 0)

  LS age: 653
  Options: (No TOS-capability, DC)
  LS Type: Router Links
  Link State ID: 3.3.3.3
  Advertising Router: 3.3.3.3
  LS Seq Number: 80000009
  Checksum: 0xB7DD
  Length: 72
  Number of Links: 4

    Link connected to: another Router (point-to-point)
     (Link ID) Neighboring Router ID: 4.4.4.4
     (Link Data) Router Interface address: 10.0.3.3
      Number of TOS metrics: 0
       TOS 0 Metrics: 130

    Link connected to: a Stub Network
     (Link ID) Network/subnet number: 10.0.3.0
```

```
(Link Data) Network Mask: 255.255.255.0
 Number of TOS metrics: 0
  TOS 0 Metrics: 130

Link connected to: another Router (point-to-point)
 (Link ID) Neighboring Router ID: 1.1.1.1
 (Link Data) Router Interface address: 10.0.1.3
 Number of TOS metrics: 0
  TOS 0 Metrics: 1

Link connected to: a Stub Network
 (Link ID) Network/subnet number: 10.0.1.0
 (Link Data) Network Mask: 255.255.255.0
 Number of TOS metrics: 0
  TOS 0 Metrics: 1
```

In this case, the path cost between R4 and R3 is 130, while the cost of the link between R3 and R1 is 1. The total path cost through R3 would be 131. After having derived this information, R4 calculates the route metric for the 192.168.254.0/24 subnet as follows:

- Total Cost to ASBR via R2 (98) + Redistribution Metric (20) = Route Metric of 118
- Total Cost to ASBR via R3 (131) + Redistribution Metric (20) = Route Metric of 151

The metric for the path via R2 is better. This route is placed into the RIB as follows:

```
R4#show ip route 192.168.254.0 255.255.255.0
Routing entry for 192.168.254.0/24
  Known via "ospf 4", distance 110, metric 118, type extern 1
  Last update from 10.0.2.2 on Serial0/0, 00:12:00 ago
  Routing Descriptor Blocks:
  * 10.0.2.2, from 1.1.1.1, 00:12:00 ago, via Serial0/0
      Route metric is 118, traffic share count is 1
```

If the link between R2 and R4 failed, then the path via R3 would be used. This would have a route metric of 151 as illustrated in the following output:

```
R4#show ip route 192.168.254.0 255.255.255.0
Routing entry for 192.168.254.0/24
  Known via "ospf 4", distance 110, metric 151, type extern 1
  Last update from 10.0.3.3 on Serial0/1, 00:00:04 ago
  Routing Descriptor Blocks:
  * 10.0.3.3, from 1.1.1.1, 00:00:04 ago, via Serial0/1
      Route metric is 151, traffic share count is 1
```

For inter-area Type 1 external routes, the router uses the total cost from itself to the ABR, which would include intra-area LSAs, the cost of the ABR to the ASBR (which is included in the Type 4 LSAs), and the external metric assigned during redistribution. The cost from the local router itself to the ABR and from the ABR to the ASBR represents the internal OSPF cost. Referencing the multi-area OSPF topology shown in Figure 4-11, R4 would calculate the best path to 192.168.254.0/24 as follows:

- Path via R2 = R4 cost to R2 (97) + R2 cost to R1 (1) + redistribution metric (20) = 118
- Path via R3 = R4 cost to R3 (130) + R3 cost to R1 (1) + redistribution metric (20) = 151

The route metric for the best path (via R2) is displayed in the following output:

```
R4#show ip route 192.168.254.0 255.255.255.0
Routing entry for 192.168.254.0/24
  Known via "ospf 4", distance 110, metric 118, type extern 1
  Last update from 10.0.2.2 on Serial0/0, 00:07:31 ago
  Routing Descriptor Blocks:
  * 10.0.2.2, from 1.1.1.1, 00:07:31 ago, via Serial0/0
      Route metric is 118, traffic share count is 1
```

A simpler way to calculate the metric manually would be to add the metric included to the ASBR illustrated in the output of the show ip ospf border-routers command to the redistribution metric as illustrated below:

```
R4#show ip ospf border-routers

OSPF Process 4 internal Routing Table

Codes: i - Intra-area route, I - Inter-area route

I 1.1.1.1 [98] via 10.0.2.2, Serial0/0, ASBR, Area 1, SPF 8
i 2.2.2.2 [97] via 10.0.2.2, Serial0/0, ABR, Area 1, SPF 8
i 3.3.3.3 [130] via 10.0.3.3, Serial0/1, ABR, Area 1, SPF 8
```

The route metric for the path via R3, which would be used only when the path via R2 was not available, is illustrated in the following output:

```
R4#show ip route 192.168.254.0 255.255.255.0
Routing entry for 192.168.254.0/24
  Known via "ospf 4", distance 110, metric 151, type extern 1
  Last update from 10.0.3.3 on Serial0/1, 00:00:00 ago
  Routing Descriptor Blocks:
  * 10.0.3.3, from 1.1.1.1, 00:00:00 ago, via Serial0/1
      Route metric is 151, traffic share count is 1
```

Again, this can be calculated simply by adding the metric in the output of the show ip ospf border-routers command to the redistribution metric as illustrated below:

```
R4#show ip ospf border-routers
OSPF Process 4 internal Routing Table
```

```
Codes: i - Intra-area route, I - Inter-area route

I 1.1.1.1 [131] via 10.0.3.3, Serial0/1, ASBR, Area 1, SPF 9
i 3.3.3.3 [130] via 10.0.3.3, Serial0/1, ABR, Area 1, SPF 9
```

In summation, it is important to remember that the metric of a Type 2 route is always the metric assigned during redistribution (i.e., the external cost). Routers will forward traffic to external subnets to the ASBR that advertises the lowest metric to the destination network, irrespective of the interior cost to reach that route. However, if the external route metrics are the same, then internal costs will be used to break the tie.

The Type 1 metric is derived from the external cost and the internal cost used to reach that route. By default, OSPF will always prefer a Type 1 route to a Type 2 route for the same destination network(s). This happens regardless of the internal cost. These concepts are described in further detail in the route redistribution configuration examples that follow.

Redistributing Classful and Classless Networks into OSPF

By default, when redistribution into OSPF is configured, OSPF will redistribute only Classful networks. This default behavior can be changed by including the subnets keyword when redistributing routes into OSPF. As an example, assume that a router is receiving the following routes via EIGRP in Autonomous System 1:

```
R2#show ip route eigrp
     10.0.0.0/24 is subnetted, 5 subnets
D       10.0.1.0 [90/30720] via 10.0.0.1, 00:00:08, FastEthernet0/0
D    192.168.254.0/24 [90/156160] via 10.0.0.1, 00:00:08, FastEthernet0/0
     192.168.253.0/29 is subnetted, 1 subnets
D       192.168.253.0 [90/156160] via 10.0.0.1, 00:00:08, FastEthernet0/0
```

It is required that these routes be redistributed into OSPF. To demonstrate the default behavior of OSPF when the subnets keyword is omitted, the redistribution is configured as follows:

```
R2(config)#router ospf 2
R2(config-router)#redistribute eigrp 1
% Only classful networks will be redistributed
R2(config-router)#exit
```

In the output above, following the redistribution of EIGRP into OSPF, Cisco IOS software prints a warning message that only Classful networks will be redistributed because the subnets keyword is omitted, which means that only the 192.168.254.0/24 network will be imported (redistributed) into OSPF. The 10.0.1.0/24 and 192.168.253.0/29 subnets will not be redistributed. This can be validated by viewing the Link State Database of R2 as illustrated below:

```
R2#show ip ospf database | begin Type-5
                Type-5 AS External Link States

Link ID          ADV Router     Age        Seq#        Checksum Tag
192.168.254.0    2.2.2.2        178        0x80000001 0x00052B 0
```

To include the subnetted networks, the subnet keyword must be used during redistribution as illustrated in the configuration below:

```
R2(config)#router ospf 2
R2(config-router)#redistribute eigrp 1 subnets
R2(config-router)#exit
```

Following this configuration modification, the Link State Database on R2 displays the following:

```
R2#show ip ospf database | begin Type-5
                Type-5 AS External Link States

Link ID          ADV Router     Age        Seq#        Checksum Tag
10.0.0.0         2.2.2.2        42         0x80000001 0x002965 0
10.0.1.0         2.2.2.2        42         0x80000001 0x001E6F 0
192.168.253.0    2.2.2.2        42         0x80000001 0x00E552 0
192.168.254.0    2.2.2.2        293        0x80000001 0x00052B 0
```

NOTE: The additional 10.0.0.0 Link ID is for the connection between R2 and the EIGRP router.

The subnets keyword is applicable when redistributing any protocol into OSPF and must also be used when redistributing another OSPF process into OSPF. If omitted, only Classful networks will be imported (redistributed) into OSPF. It always is considered good practice to include this keyword, regardless of the addressing scheme in use. When the subnets keyword is configured, the statement 'includes subnets in redistribution' will be included in the output of the show ip protocols command as illustrated below:

```
R2#show ip protocols
Routing Protocol is "ospf 2"
  Outgoing update filter list for all interfaces is not set
  Incoming update filter list for all interfaces is not set
  Router ID 2.2.2.2
  It is an autonomous system boundary router
  Redistributing External Routes from,
    eigrp 1, includes subnets in redistribution
  Number of areas in this router is 1. 1 normal 0 stub 0 nssa

...

[Truncated Output]
```

However, when not included, this statement will be omitted, as illustrated below:

```
R2#show ip protocols
Routing Protocol is "ospf 2"
  Outgoing update filter list for all interfaces is not set
  Incoming update filter list for all interfaces is not set
  Router ID 2.2.2.2
  It is an autonomous system boundary router
  Redistributing External Routes from,
    eigrp 1
  Number of areas in this router is 1. 1 normal 0 stub 0 nssa

...

[Truncated Output]
```

Redistributing between Two OSPF Processes

When redistributing between two OSPF processes, OSPF uses the metric of the route source as the metric of the generated Type 5 LSA. This is applicable for both Type 1 and Type 2 external routes. As an example, consider the basic network topology illustrated in Figure 4-12 below:

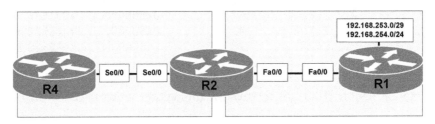

Fig. 4-12. Redistributing between Two OSPF Processes

Referencing Figure 4-12, R2 is running two OSPF processes: process ID 1 and process ID 2. R2 is using process ID 1 for the segment between itself and R1 and process ID 2 for the link between itself and R4. R2 is currently receiving the following routes from R1:

```
R2#show ip route ospf | include 192.168
O    192.168.254.0/24 [110/2] via 10.0.0.1, 00:00:10, FastEthernet0/0
     192.168.253.0/29 is subnetted, 1 subnets
O       192.168.253.0 [110/2] via 10.0.0.1, 00:00:10, FastEthernet0/0
```

As can be seen in the output above, both routes are received with a metric of 2. Next, process ID 1 is redistributed into process ID 2 as follows:

```
R2(config)#router ospf 2
R2(config-router)#redistribute ospf 1 subnets
R2(config-router)#exit
```

Even though no metric has been specified during redistribution, because the routes are being redistributed from another OSPF process, OSPF will simply use the metric of the other OSPF process. This is confirmed by viewing the entries in the LSDB on R2 as follows:

```
R2#show ip ospf database external

            OSPF Router with ID (2.2.2.2) (Process ID 2)

            Type-5 AS External Link States

LS age: 75
Options: (No TOS-capability, DC)
LS Type: AS External Link
Link State ID: 192.168.253.0 (External Network Number)
Advertising Router: 2.2.2.2
LS Seq Number: 80000001
Checksum: 0x3119
Length: 36
Network Mask: /29
      Metric Type: 2 (Larger than any Link State path)
      TOS: 0
      Metric: 2
      Forward Address: 0.0.0.0
      External Route Tag: 0

LS age: 79
Options: (No TOS-capability, DC)
LS Type: AS External Link
Link State ID: 192.168.254.0 (External Network Number)
Advertising Router: 2.2.2.2
LS Seq Number: 80000001
Checksum: 0x50F1
Length: 36
Network Mask: /24
      Metric Type: 2 (Larger than any Link State path)
      TOS: 0
      Metric: 2
      Forward Address: 0.0.0.0
      External Route Tag: 0
```

The three ways in which the metric for redistributed routes can be set are as follows:

1. Directly using the `default-metric` router configuration command
2. Indirectly by setting the metric value in a route map using the `set metric` command
3. Directly by using the `metric` command with the `redistribute` command

The use of the `default-metric` router configuration command sets the value specified as the metric for all external routes. This command works in the same manner for OSPF as was illustrated in the EIGRP configuration examples. If this command is specified and a route map is used or the metric value is specified in the redistribute command, then the metric values specified in the route map or using the redistribute command take precedence. This also applies to EIGRP. The set metric command allows individual metrics to be specified for matching prefixes based on the route map configuration. Finally, the metric command may be used with the redistribute command to set the metric for all routes from the route source.

Referencing the topology illustrated in Figure 4-12, the following example illustrates how to set a metric of 253 for the 192.168.253.0/29 subnet and a metric of 254 for the 192.168.254.0/24 subnet that R2 is receiving from R1 using a route map:

```
R2(config)#ip prefix-list NET-253 description 'Match 192.168.253.0/29 Only'
R2(config)#ip prefix-list NET-253 seq 5 permit 192.168.253.0/29
R2(config)#ip prefix-list NET-254 description 'Match 192.168.254.0/24 Only'
R2(config)#ip prefix-list NET-254 seq 5 permit 192.168.254.0/24
R2(config)#route-map OSPF-1-into-OSPF-2 permit 10
R2(config-route-map)#description 'Set Metric For 192.168.253.0/29'
R2(config-route-map)#match ip address prefix-list NET-253
R2(config-route-map)#set metric 253
R2(config-route-map)#exit
R2(config)#route-map OSPF-1-into-OSPF-2 permit 20
R2(config-route-map)#description 'Set Metric For 192.168.254.0/24'
R2(config-route-map)#match ip address prefix-list NET-254
R2(config-route-map)#set metric 254
R2(config-route-map)#exit
R2(config)#router ospf 2
R2(config-router)#redistribute ospf 1 subnets route-map OSPF-1-into-OSPF-2
R2(config-router)#exit
```

Following this configuration, the Link State Database on R2 displays the following:

```
R2#show ip ospf database external

            OSPF Router with ID (2.2.2.2) (Process ID 2)

            Type-5 AS External Link States

  LS age: 162
  Options: (No TOS-capability, DC)
  LS Type: AS External Link
  Link State ID: 192.168.253.0 (External Network Number)
  Advertising Router: 2.2.2.2
  LS Seq Number: 80000002
  Checksum: 0x746
  Length: 36
  Network Mask: /29
        Metric Type: 2 (Larger than any Link State path)
        TOS: 0
        Metric: 253
```

```
        Forward Address: 0.0.0.0
        External Route Tag: 0

    LS age: 162
    Options: (No TOS-capability, DC)
    LS Type: AS External Link
    Link State ID: 192.168.254.0 (External Network Number)
    Advertising Router: 2.2.2.2
    LS Seq Number: 80000002
    Checksum: 0x3014
    Length: 36
    Network Mask: /24
        Metric Type: 2 (Larger than any Link State path)
        TOS: 0
        Metric: 254
        Forward Address: 0.0.0.0
        External Route Tag: 0
```

Unlike the route metric, the metric type (i.e., Type 1 external or Type 2 external) can be set using only one of the following two methods:

1. Directly using the metric-type command with the redistribute command
2. Indirectly by setting the type in a route map using the set metric-type command

The following configuration illustrates how to redistribute all routes from OSPF 1 into OSPF 2 on R2 as Type 1 external routes using the redistribute command:

```
R2(config)#router ospf 2
R2(config-router)#redistribute ospf 1 subnets metric-type 1
R2(config-router)#exit
```

Following this configuration, the Link State Database on R2 displays the following:

```
R2#show ip ospf database external

        OSPF Router with ID (2.2.2.2) (Process ID 2)

        Type-5 AS External Link States

    LS age: 12
    Options: (No TOS-capability, DC)
    LS Type: AS External Link
    Link State ID: 192.168.253.0 (External Network Number)
    Advertising Router: 2.2.2.2
    LS Seq Number: 80000001
    Checksum: 0xAD1D
    Length: 36
    Network Mask: /29
```

```
        Metric Type: 1 (Comparable directly to Link State metric)
        TOS: 0
        Metric: 2
        Forward Address: 0.0.0.0
        External Route Tag: 0

  LS age: 12
  Options: (No TOS-capability, DC)
  LS Type: AS External Link
  Link State ID: 192.168.254.0 (External Network Number)
  Advertising Router: 2.2.2.2
  LS Seq Number: 80000006
  Checksum: 0xC2FA
  Length: 36
  Network Mask: /24
        Metric Type: 1 (Comparable directly to Link State metric)
        TOS: 0
        Metric: 2
        Forward Address: 0.0.0.0
        External Route Tag: 0
```

When redistributing into OSPF, it is important to know that you can use a combination of all the different commands at the same time. As an example, assume that R1 is now advertising the following networks to R2 via OSPF:

```
R2#show ip route ospf | include 192.168
      192.168.251.0/27 is subnetted, 1 subnets
O        192.168.251.0 [110/2] via 10.0.0.1, 00:00:05, FastEthernet0/0
O     192.168.254.0/24 [110/2] via 10.0.0.1, 00:00:05, FastEthernet0/0
      192.168.253.0/29 is subnetted, 1 subnets
O        192.168.253.0 [110/2] via 10.0.0.1, 00:00:05, FastEthernet0/0
      192.168.252.0/25 is subnetted, 1 subnets
O        192.168.252.0 [110/2] via 10.0.0.1, 00:00:05, FastEthernet0/0
```

Assume that you have been requested to change the default OSPF metrics and metric types for these received prefixes as illustrated in Table 4-5 below:

Table 4-5. Setting OSPF Metrics and Metric Types

Prefix	Metric	Metric Type
192.168.251.0/27	111	E1
192.168.252.0/25	222	E1
192.168.253.0/29	111	E1
192.168.254.0/24	333	E1

```
R2(config)#ip prefix-list NET-252 description 'Match 192.168.252.0/25 Only'
R2(config)#ip prefix-list NET-252 seq 5 permit 192.168.252.0/25
R2(config)#ip prefix-list NET-254 description 'Match 192.168.254.0/24 Only'
R2(config)#ip prefix-list NET-254 seq 5 permit 192.168.254.0/24
R2(config)#route-map OSPF-1-into-OSPF-2 permit 10
R2(config-route-map)#description 'Set Metric for 192.168.252.0/25 Only'
R2(config-route-map)#match ip address prefix-list NET-252
R2(config-route-map)#set metric 222
R2(config-route-map)#exit
R2(config)#route-map OSPF-1-into-OSPF-2 permit 20
R2(config-route-map)#description 'Set Metric for 192.168.254.0/24 Only'
R2(config-route-map)#match ip address prefix-list NET-254
R2(config-route-map)#set metric 333
R2(config-route-map)#exit
R2(config)#route-map OSPF-1-into-OSPF-2 permit 30
R2(config-route-map)#exit
R2(config)#route-map OSPF-1-into-OSPF-2 permit 30
R2(config-route-map)#description 'Allow All Other Prefixes'
R2(config-route-map)#exit
R2(config)#router ospf 2
R2(config-router)#redistribute ospf 1 metric 111 metric-type 1 subnets
route-map OSPF-1-into-OSPF-2
R2(config-router)#exit
```

This configuration can be verified by viewing the Link State Database of R2 as follows:

```
R2#show ip ospf database external

            OSPF Router with ID (2.2.2.2) (Process ID 2)

            Type-5 AS External Link States

   LS age: 125
   Options: (No TOS-capability, DC)
   LS Type: AS External Link
   Link State ID: 192.168.251.0 (External Network Number)
   Advertising Router: 2.2.2.2
   LS Seq Number: 80000002
   Checksum: 0x77FE
   Length: 36
   Network Mask: /27
        Metric Type: 1 (Comparable directly to Link State metric)
        TOS: 0
        Metric: 111
        Forward Address: 0.0.0.0
        External Route Tag: 0

   LS age: 126
   Options: (No TOS-capability, DC)
   LS Type: AS External Link
   Link State ID: 192.168.252.0 (External Network Number)
```

```
Advertising Router: 2.2.2.2
LS Seq Number: 80000002
Checksum: 0x84E1
Length: 36
Network Mask: /25
        Metric Type: 1 (Comparable directly to Link State metric)
        TOS: 0
        Metric: 222
        Forward Address: 0.0.0.0
        External Route Tag: 0

LS age: 126
Options: (No TOS-capability, DC)
LS Type: AS External Link
Link State ID: 192.168.253.0 (External Network Number)
Advertising Router: 2.2.2.2
LS Seq Number: 80000002
Checksum: 0xF16A
Length: 36
Network Mask: /29
        Metric Type: 1 (Comparable directly to Link State metric)
        TOS: 0
        Metric: 111
        Forward Address: 0.0.0.0
        External Route Tag: 0

LS age: 126
Options: (No TOS-capability, DC)
LS Type: AS External Link
Link State ID: 192.168.254.0 (External Network Number)
Advertising Router: 2.2.2.2
LS Seq Number: 80000007
Checksum: 0xBAB5
Length: 36
Network Mask: /24
        Metric Type: 1 (Comparable directly to Link State metric)
        TOS: 0
        Metric: 333
        Forward Address: 0.0.0.0
        External Route Tag: 0
```

Referencing the configuration above, the route map is used to set explicitly the route metric for the 192.168.252.0/25 and 192.168.254.0/24 prefixes. This metric value is assigned because the route map always takes precedence over the redistribute and default-metric commands. However, because no metric type is specified in the route map statements matching these two prefixes, the metric type defaults to the type specified in the redistribute command. The third route map permit statement allows all routes. No metric or metric type is specified in this statement and so all routes that match this statement are assigned the metric and metric type values configured using the redistribute command.

Keep in mind that this is one way of accomplishing the required task. Many different variations of the configuration can be used to do the same. The main purpose here is to demonstrate the flexibility of Cisco IOS software. While this example is based on OSPF redistribution, the same concept is applicable when redistributing routes into other routing protocols, such as EIGRP.

Redistributing EIGRP Routes into OSPF

When EIGRP is redistributed into OSPF, if the metric or the metric type values are not configured explicitly during redistribution, then the routes will be imported as Type 2 external routes with a default metric of 20. When redistributing EIGRP into OSPF, always ensure that you use the sub-nets keyword during your configuration. The following illustrates how to configure OSPF to import or redistribute EIGRP routes using default values but with a route tag of 222:

```
R2(config)#router ospf 2
R2(config-router)#redistribute eigrp 1 subnets tag 222
R2(config-router)#exit
```

The administrator-defined route tag can be viewed in the Link Stated Database as follows:

```
R2#show ip ospf database | begin Type-5
                Type-5 AS External Link States

Link ID         ADV Router      Age         Seq#        Checksum Tag
192.168.253.0   2.2.2.2         64          0x80000001 0x0091C7 222
192.168.254.0   2.2.2.2         64          0x80000001 0x00B0A0 222
```

NOTE: The use of route tags is described in detail later in this chapter.

Redistributing Connected and Static Routes into OSPF

Any directly connected interfaces (subnets) and static routes can be redistributed into an OSPF process using the redistribute connected subnets and redistribute static subnets commands, respectively. As is the case with dynamic route sources, the metric and metric types for these route sources can also be specified manually during redistribution.

Additionally, as was demonstrated in the EIGRP configuration examples, static routes can be tagged and then a route-map can be used to match the tagged routes. The following configuration demonstrates how to redistribute static routes into OSPF as Type 2 external routes with a default metric and a tag of 111, and connected subnets as Type 1 external routes with a metric of 111 and no administrator tag:

```
R1(config)#interface Loopback 254
R1(config-if)#ip address 192.168.254.1 255.255.255.0
R1(config-if)#exit
```

```
R1(config)#ip route 192.168.252.0 255.255.255.128 Null0
R1(config)#router ospf 1
R1(config-router)#redistribute static subnets tag 111
R1(config-router)#redistribute connected metric 111 metric-type 1 subnets
R1(config-router)#exit
```

In the output above, while the subnets keyword is not technically required to redistribute the 192.168.254.0/24 network, it always is considered good practice to include it in redistribution. Following this configuration, the Link State Database on R1 displays the following:

```
R1#show ip ospf database external

            OSPF Router with ID (1.1.1.1) (Process ID 1)

            Type-5 AS External Link States

  LS age: 354
   Options: (No TOS-capability, DC)
   LS Type: AS External Link
   Link State ID: 192.168.252.0 (External Network Number)
   Advertising Router: 1.1.1.1
   LS Seq Number: 80000001
   Checksum: 0x1234
   Length: 36
   Network Mask: /25
        Metric Type: 2 (Larger than any Link State path)
        TOS: 0
        Metric: 20
        Forward Address: 0.0.0.0
        External Route Tag: 111

  LS age: 4
   Options: (No TOS-capability, DC)
   LS Type: AS External Link
   Link State ID: 192.168.254.0 (External Network Number)
   Advertising Router: 1.1.1.1
   LS Seq Number: 80000001
   Checksum: 0x3128
   Length: 36
   Network Mask: /24
        Metric Type: 1 (Comparable directly to Link State metric)
        TOS: 0
        Metric: 111
        Forward Address: 0.0.0.0
        External Route Tag: 0
```

OSPF NSSA Type 1 and Type 2 External Routes

The Type 1 and Type 2 metric types for Type 5 LSAs are also comparable to Type 1 and Type 2 metric types for Type 7 LSAs generated by the NSSA ASBR. When routes are redistributed into the NSSA, the `show ip ospf database nssa-external` command can be used to view the corresponding Type 7 LSAs for these routes.

The Type 7 LSAs are then translated to Type 5 LSAs by the ABR and flooded into other adjacent areas. By default, all routes redistributed into the NSSA are Type 2 external routes, and the ABR generates a corresponding Type 5 LSA with a Type 2 metric type for these routes. If the routes are redistributed into the NSSA as Type 1, then a corresponding Type 5 LSA with a Type 1 external metric is generated by the ABR. To reinforce this point, the following output shows an ABR that is receiving a Type 2 external route from a neighbor in an NSSA:

```
R2#show ip route ospf
     10.0.0.0/24 is subnetted, 4 subnets
O       10.0.9.0 [110/128] via 10.0.2.4, 00:02:29, Serial0/0
O       10.0.3.0 [110/192] via 10.0.2.4, 00:02:29, Serial0/0
O N2 192.168.254.0/24 [110/20] via 10.0.0.1, 00:02:19, FastEthernet0/0
```

The `show ip ospf database nssa-external` command provides detailed information on the Type 7 LSA, including the route metric and the metric type as illustrated below:

```
R2#show ip ospf database nssa-external

          OSPF Router with ID (2.2.2.2) (Process ID 2)

            Type-7 AS External Link States (Area 1)

  Routing Bit Set on this LSA
  LS age: 286
  Options: (No TOS-capability, Type 7/5 translation, DC)
  LS Type: AS External Link
  Link State ID: 192.168.254.0 (External Network Number)
  Advertising Router: 192.168.254.1
  LS Seq Number: 80000001
  Checksum: 0x1E9B
  Length: 36
  Network Mask: /24
        Metric Type: 2 (Larger than any Link State path)
        TOS: 0
        Metric: 20
        Forward Address: 10.0.0.1
        External Route Tag: 0
```

When R2 generates the Type 5 LSA, all fields remain consistent, including the IP address that is specified in the Forward Address field as illustrated below:

```
R2#show ip ospf database external

            OSPF Router with ID (2.2.2.2) (Process ID 2)

            Type-5 AS External Link States

    LS age: 278
    Options: (No TOS-capability, DC)
    LS Type: AS External Link
    Link State ID: 192.168.254.0 (External Network Number)
    Advertising Router: 2.2.2.2
    LS Seq Number: 80000001
    Checksum: 0x81A3
    Length: 36
    Network Mask: /24
            Metric Type: 2 (Larger than any Link State path)
            TOS: 0
            Metric: 20
            Forward Address: 10.0.0.1
            External Route Tag: 0
```

If you recall, in Chapter 3 we learned that one of the primary differences between Type 5 and Type 7 LSAs is the Forwarding Address calculation. With Type 5 LSAs, the Forward Address field contains a value of 0, unless one of the following exceptions applies:

- The ASBR's next-hop interface network type is not P2P, or point-to-multipoint
- OSPF is enabled on the ASBR's next-hop interface
- The next-hop interface of the ASBR falls into a defined OSPF network range
- The ASBR's next-hop interface is not a passive OSPF interface

With Type 7 LSAs, if the route has a next-hop address (i.e., it is not a connected network), then use the next-hop address in the Forward Address field. This holds true only if the route is an internal OSPF route. In other words, if the network between the NSSA boundary router and the adjacent autonomous system is advertised into OSPF as an internal OSPF route, then the forwarding address should be the next-hop address.

However, if the network is not advertised into OSPF as an internal route, the Forward Address should be any of the active interfaces on the router. This means that if there is a Loopback interface enabled for OSPF routing in the area announcing the LSAs on the router, then use that interface. If there are no Loopback interfaces, then the address of the first operational interface in that area should be used.

Although the translate type7 suppress-fa keyword can be used in conjunction with the area [area ID] nssa router configuration command to configure OSPF Forwarding Address Suppression in Translated Type-5 LSAs, this configuration causes the router to be noncompliant with RFC 1587—The OSPF NSSA Option. The primary reason the Forward Address is included is to prevent suboptimal routing following the Type 7 to Type 5 translation.

Troubleshooting OSPF Route Redistribution Issues

In some instances, you may change the route redistribution configuration and notice that routes are not redistributed into OSPF. For example, you may be using a route map during redistribution that matches a specified prefix list and add permitted prefixes to this list but do not see them in the LSDB following the configuration change. In such situations, assuming that the correct configuration has been implemented, you can use the `clear ip ospf redistribution` privileged EXEC command to flush external LSAs (i.e., Type 5 or Type 7 LSAs) and force the router to scan the routing table for permitted redistributed routes.

When issued, the local router sets the delete flag for all external LSAs and flushes and renews the external LSAs. Because Type 5 LSAs have a domain flooding scope, all other routers in the network perform a partial SPF calculation so they can flush and renew these LSAs. The following output shows a Type 7 LSA marked to be flushed after issuing the `clear ip ospf redistribution` privileged EXEC command on a router:

```
R2#show ip ospf database nssa-external

            OSPF Router with ID (2.2.2.2) (Process ID 2)

            Type-7 AS External Link States (Area 1)

   Delete flag is set for this LSA
   LS age: MAXAGE(3601)
   Options: (No TOS-capability, No Type 7/5 translation, DC)
   LS Type: AS External Link
   Link State ID: 200.1.1.0 (External Network Number)
   Advertising Router: 2.2.2.2
   LS Seq Number: 80000001
   Checksum: 0x4685
   Length: 36
   Network Mask: /24
        Metric Type: 2 (Larger than any Link State path)
        TOS: 0
        Metric: 20
        Forward Address: 0.0.0.0
        External Route Tag: 0
```

This LSA would be flooded into the NSSA and cause all routers in the NSSA to perform a partial SPF calculation. The corresponding Type 5 LSA would also reflect the same as illustrated below:

```
R2#show ip ospf database external

            OSPF Router with ID (2.2.2.2) (Process ID 2)

            Type-5 AS External Link States

    Delete flag is set for this LSA
    LS age: MAXAGE(3600)
    Options: (No TOS-capability, DC)
    LS Type: AS External Link
    Link State ID: 200.1.1.0 (External Network Number)
    Advertising Router: 2.2.2.2
    LS Seq Number: 80000001
    Checksum: 0x626B
    Length: 36
    Network Mask: /24
          Metric Type: 2 (Larger than any Link State path)
          TOS: 0
          Metric: 20
          Forward Address: 0.0.0.0
          External Route Tag: 0
```

Because Type 5 LSAs are flooded throughout the domain, this would cause all other routers in the network, except routers in stubby-type areas because Type 5 LSAs are not flooded into stubby-type areas, to perform a partial SPF calculation, and then flush and renew the Type 5 LSA.

ROUTE REDISTRIBUTION DESIGN CONSIDERATIONS

Now that we understand how route redistribution works and how to configure and verify route redistribution, we will conclude this chapter by looking at the ways in which route redistribution can be implemented and at general design considerations that should be taken into account when implementing route redistribution in networks.

Route redistribution can be performed either one-way or two-way. In addition, one-way or two-way route redistribution can be implemented on a single router in the network, which is referred to as single-point redistribution, or on two or more routers, which is referred to as multipoint redistribution. Regardless of the method used, it is important to know that if poorly implemented, routed redistribution can cause suboptimal routing or even routing loops. The following sections describe these types of redistribution and look at some common issues that may result when either of these methods is implemented.

One-Way and Two-Way Route Redistribution

One-way route redistribution occurs when a single routing protocol imports external routing information from another routing protocol, but not vice versa. An example of one-way redistribution would be the redistribution of static routes into EIGRP using the `redistribute static metric 1544 2000 255 1 255` router configuration command when configuring EIGRP route redistribution on a router.

One-way redistribution is commonly implemented at the network edge. While the following diagram illustrates the configuration of one-way route redistribution between a static and a dynamic routing protocol, it is important to understand that one-way redistribution can also be performed between dynamic routing protocols. Consider the basic network topology that is illustrated in Figure 4-13 below:

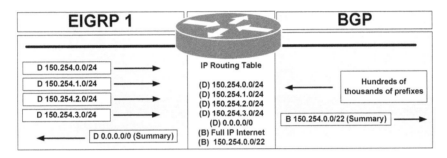

Fig. 4-13. One-Way Redistribution between Dynamic Route Sources

Referencing Figure 4-13, the router is connected to both an ISP and the interior network. BGP has been enabled between the router and the ISP, and the ISP is advertising the full Internet routing table to the router, which includes hundreds of thousands of prefixes. The customer owns the 150.254.0.0/22 address space. The specific EIGRP subnets advertised to the router can be redistributed into BGP and a single aggregate route advertised to the Internet.

However, because redistributing the complete Internet routing table into the interior network would very quickly overwhelm an Interior Gateway Protocol, a default route is configured instead and advertised to the interior network, allowing routers within the EIGRP domain to send packets to unknown destinations (e.g., the Internet) to this router.

Two-way route redistribution is also referred to as mutual redistribution. Mutual redistribution allows two routing protocols to exchange dynamic routing information as was illustrated in examples earlier in this chapter. When implementing route redistribution, it always is considered good practice to use some form of filtering mechanism (e.g., route maps) to ensure that only the correct subnets are redistributed into the domain.

Single-Point Route Redistribution

Single-point route redistribution occurs at a single point in the network. This is considered an easy and safe method of redistributing between different route sources because a single ingress and egress point resides between the route sources. However, it should be noted that single-point route redistribution could also result in suboptimal routing in some environments. Consider the network topology illustrated in Figure 4-14 below:

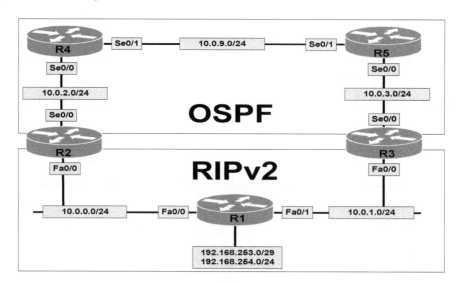

Fig. 4-14. Implementing Single-Point Redistribution

Figure 4-14 shows a basic multi-protocol network. R1, R2, and R3 are running RIP version 2. R2 and R3 are also running OSPF and reside in the same OSPF domain as R4 and R5. Based on this topology, the routing table of R2 currently displays the following RIP entries:

```
R2#show ip route rip
     10.0.0.0/24 is subnetted, 5 subnets
R       10.0.1.0 [120/1] via 10.0.0.1, 00:00:03, FastEthernet0/0
R    192.168.254.0/24 [120/1] via 10.0.0.1, 00:00:03, FastEthernet0/0
     192.168.253.0/29 is subnetted, 1 subnets
R       192.168.253.0 [120/1] via 10.0.0.1, 00:00:03, FastEthernet0/0
```

The routing table on R3 currently displays the following RIP route entries:

```
R3#show ip route rip
     10.0.0.0/24 is subnetted, 5 subnets
R       10.0.0.0 [120/1] via 10.0.1.1, 00:00:27, FastEthernet0/0
R    192.168.254.0/24 [120/1] via 10.0.1.1, 00:00:27, FastEthernet0/0
     192.168.253.0/29 is subnetted, 1 subnets
R       192.168.253.0 [120/1] via 10.0.1.1, 00:00:27, FastEthernet0/0
```

Next, mutual redistribution between RIP and OSPF is configured on R2 as follows:

```
R2(config)#router rip
R2(config-router)#redistribute ospf 2 metric 1
R2(config-router)#exit
R2(config)#router ospf 2
R2(config-router)#redistribute rip subnets
R2(config-router)#exit
```

After this configuration change, the routing table on R2 displays the following entries:

```
R2#show ip route rip
     10.0.0.0/24 is subnetted, 5 subnets
R       10.0.1.0 [120/1] via 10.0.0.1, 00:00:22, FastEthernet0/0
R    192.168.254.0/24 [120/1] via 10.0.0.1, 00:00:22, FastEthernet0/0
     192.168.253.0/29 is subnetted, 1 subnets
R       192.168.253.0 [120/1] via 10.0.0.1, 00:00:22, FastEthernet0/0
```

Although everything on R2 is in order, the issue actually resides on R3. After the mutual route redistribution between RIP and OSPF on R2, the routing table on R3 is illustrated as follows:

```
R3#show ip route | begin Gateway
Gateway of last resort is not set

     10.0.0.0/24 is subnetted, 5 subnets
O       10.0.9.0 [110/128] via 10.0.3.5, 00:04:31, Serial0/0
O       10.0.2.0 [110/192] via 10.0.3.5, 00:04:31, Serial0/0
C       10.0.3.0 is directly connected, Serial0/0
O E2    10.0.0.0 [110/111] via 10.0.3.5, 00:04:31, Serial0/0
C       10.0.1.0 is directly connected, FastEthernet0/0
O E2 192.168.254.0/24 [110/111] via 10.0.3.5, 00:04:31, Serial0/0
     192.168.253.0/29 is subnetted, 1 subnets
O E2    192.168.253.0 [110/111] via 10.0.3.5, 00:04:31, Serial0/0
```

Because of the redistribution performed on R2, R3 now prefers the external OSPF routes to all the RIP subnets because the administrative distance of 110 is lower than the default administrative distance of 120 used by RIP. This is a suboptimal path because the direct path from R3 to R1 is clearly the better path.

If you are thinking that implementing mutual redistribution on R3 will resolve the issue, you are incorrect. This goes back to the fundamentals of building the routing table, which are described in Chapter 1, as well as to the fundamentals of route redistribution, which are described earlier in this chapter. To reinforce this statement, mutual redistribution is configured on R3 as follows:

```
R3(config)#router ospf 3
R3(config-router)#redistribute rip subnets
R3(config-router)#exit
R3(config)#router rip
R3(config-router)#redistribute ospf 3 metric 1
R3(config-router)#exit
```

However, the routing table on R3 still displays the following route entries:

```
R3#show ip route | begin Gateway
Gateway of last resort is not set

     10.0.0.0/24 is subnetted, 5 subnets
O       10.0.9.0 [110/128] via 10.0.3.5, 00:15:41, Serial0/0
O       10.0.2.0 [110/192] via 10.0.3.5, 00:15:41, Serial0/0
C       10.0.3.0 is directly connected, Serial0/0
O E2    10.0.0.0 [110/111] via 10.0.3.5, 00:15:41, Serial0/0
C       10.0.1.0 is directly connected, FastEthernet0/0
O E2 192.168.254.0/24 [110/111] via 10.0.3.5, 00:15:41, Serial0/0
     192.168.253.0/29 is subnetted, 1 subnets
O E2    192.168.253.0 [110/111] via 10.0.3.5, 00:15:41, Serial0/0
```

As illustrated in the output above, even though mutual route redistribution has been configured between OSPF and RIP on R3, R3 still prefers the OSPF routes to the RIP routes. Why? Well, referencing the first point made, in Chapter 1, when we learned about how the routing table is built, the third step states the following:

1. If the route entry is the same as an existing one, but is received from a more preferred route source, then replace the old entry with the new entry.

So, originally, R3 preferred the RIP routes for the RIP networks because these routes were not known via OSPF. However, once the routes were redistributed into OSPF, because the same entries were received from a more preferred route source (i.e., because the administrative distance of OSPF is better than that of RIP), even though the routes are external OSPF routes, the RIP entries were replaced with the OSPF entries.

The second point ties into the first point. When redistribution is configured on the routers, the routing protocols communicate with the routing table. Since all the RIP subnets have been installed into the routing table as OSPF external routes, when the redistribute rip subnets command is configured on R3, OSPF queries the routing table for RIP routes.

However, no routes exist, since they are all known via OSPF following the redistribution on R2. R3 therefore does not import any RIP routes, as the routing table shows no entries. Three possible solutions may be used to ensure that R3 prefers the RIP routes for the RIP subnets and they are as follows:

1. Change the OSPF administrative distance for all RIP routes on R3
2. Change the administrative distance for external OSPF routes only on R3
3. Use EIGRP in place of OSPF as the routing protocol

The OSPF administrative distance for all RIP routes can be modified using the `distance` router configuration command. This command can be used in conjunction with an ACL to increment the administrative distance of the OSPF external routes for the RIP subnets so that R3 prefers the routes received via RIP from R1. This configuration is performed on R3 as illustrated below:

```
R3(config)#ip access-list standard RIP-ROUTES-ONLY
R3(config-std-nacl)#remark 'Change AD For RIP Routes Only'
R3(config-std-nacl)#permit 10.0.0.0
R3(config-std-nacl)#permit 192.168.253.0
R3(config-std-nacl)#permit 192.168.254.0
R3(config-std-nacl)#exit
R3(config)#router ospf 3
R3(config-router)#distance 130 2.2.2.2 0.0.0.0 RIP-ROUTES-ONLY
R3(config-router)#exit
```

By incrementing the OSPF administrative distance for the RIP subnets, the RIP routes are now preferred over the OSPF routes and the routing table on R3 displays the following:

```
R3#show ip route | begin Gateway
Gateway of last resort is not set

     10.0.0.0/24 is subnetted, 5 subnets
O       10.0.9.0 [110/128] via 10.0.3.5, 00:01:51, Serial0/0
O       10.0.2.0 [110/192] via 10.0.3.5, 00:01:51, Serial0/0
C       10.0.3.0 is directly connected, Serial0/0
R       10.0.0.0 [120/1] via 10.0.1.1, 00:00:20, FastEthernet0/0
C       10.0.1.0 is directly connected, FastEthernet0/0
R    192.168.254.0/24 [120/1] via 10.0.1.1, 00:00:20, FastEthernet0/0
     192.168.253.0/29 is subnetted, 1 subnets
R       192.168.253.0 [120/1] via 10.0.1.1, 00:00:20, FastEthernet0/0
```

The second solution would be to change the default administrative distance for all the external OSPF routes. This negates the need to modify constantly the Access Control List that was used in conjunction with the `distance` command in the previous section. For example, if R1 was advertising 50 additional RIP subnets, then it would become cumbersome and unnecessarily labor intensive to include every one of those subnets in the ACL.

Cisco IOS software allows administrators to change the default administrative distance for both internal and external OSPF routes using the `distance ospf [external | inter-area | intra-area]` router configuration command. Any administrative distance values between 1 and 255 can be specified for any of these different route types.

Referencing the topology in Figure 4-14, the following configuration illustrates how to modify the default administrative distance value of all OSPF external routes on R3 to 150, which ensures that whenever additional RIP subnets advertised by R1 are redistributed into OSPF on R3, the router will always prefer the same subnets received from R1, as they will have a lower administrative distance value and will therefore be installed into the routing table:

```
R3(config)#router ospf 3
R3(config-router)#distance ospf external 150
R3(config-router)#exit
```

Following this change, the routing table on R3 displays the following entries:

```
R3#show ip route | begin Gateway
Gateway of last resort is not set

     10.0.0.0/24 is subnetted, 5 subnets
O       10.0.9.0 [110/128] via 10.0.3.5, 00:00:22, Serial0/0
O       10.0.2.0 [110/192] via 10.0.3.5, 00:00:22, Serial0/0
C       10.0.3.0 is directly connected, Serial0/0
R       10.0.0.0 [120/1] via 10.0.1.1, 00:00:16, FastEthernet0/0
C       10.0.1.0 is directly connected, FastEthernet0/0
R    192.168.254.0/24 [120/1] via 10.0.1.1, 00:00:16, FastEthernet0/0
     192.168.253.0/29 is subnetted, 1 subnets
R       192.168.253.0 [120/1] via 10.0.1.1, 00:00:16, FastEthernet0/0
```

The third possible solution would be to use EIGRP. This solution would require no additional configuration other than enabling EIGRP on R3. This is because EIGRP uses a default administrative distance of 170 for all external routes. Therefore, when the RIP subnets that are advertised by R1 are redistributed into EIGRP on R2, they would be propagated as external EIGRP routes with an administrative distance of 170. Because R3 is receiving the same routes from RIP, with a default administrative distance value of 120, the RIP routes would be used.

NOTE: You are not required to perform any RIP redistribution in the ROUTE exam. RIP has been used in this example for simplicity. The same issue could be replicated using EIGRP on R1 instead, and redistributing the 192.168.253.0/29 and 192.168.254.0/24 subnets into EIGRP and advertising them to R2 and R3. Assuming this, the routing table on R2 would display the following initial route entries:

```
R2#show ip route eigrp
     10.0.0.0/24 is subnetted, 5 subnets
D       10.0.1.0 [90/30720] via 10.0.0.1, 00:00:36, FastEthernet0/0
D EX 192.168.254.0/24 [170/156160] via 10.0.0.1, 00:00:36, FastEthernet0/0
     192.168.253.0/29 is subnetted, 1 subnets
D EX    192.168.253.0 [170/156160] via 10.0.0.1, 00:00:36, FastEthernet0/0
```

Likewise, the routing table on R3 would display the following initial route entries:

```
R3#show ip route | begin Gateway
Gateway of last resort is not set

     10.0.0.0/24 is subnetted, 5 subnets
O       10.0.9.0 [110/128] via 10.0.3.5, 00:00:17, Serial0/0
O       10.0.2.0 [110/192] via 10.0.3.5, 00:00:17, Serial0/0
C       10.0.3.0 is directly connected, Serial0/0
D       10.0.0.0 [90/30720] via 10.0.1.1, 00:05:39, FastEthernet0/0
C       10.0.1.0 is directly connected, FastEthernet0/0
D EX 192.168.254.0/24 [170/156160] via 10.0.1.1, 00:00:17, FastEthernet0/0
     192.168.253.0/29 is subnetted, 1 subnets
D EX    192.168.253.0 [170/156160] via 10.0.1.1, 00:00:23, FastEthernet0/0
```

However, after mutual route redistribution is configured between OSPF and EIGRP on R2, the routing table on R3 would display the following route entries:

```
R3#show ip route | begin Gateway
Gateway of last resort is not set

     10.0.0.0/24 is subnetted, 5 subnets
O       10.0.9.0 [110/128] via 10.0.3.5, 00:00:09, Serial0/0
O       10.0.2.0 [110/192] via 10.0.3.5, 00:00:09, Serial0/0
C       10.0.3.0 is directly connected, Serial0/0
D       10.0.0.0 [90/30720] via 10.0.1.1, 00:03:14, FastEthernet0/0
C       10.0.1.0 is directly connected, FastEthernet0/0
O E2 192.168.254.0/24 [110/20] via 10.0.3.5, 00:00:09, Serial0/0
     192.168.253.0/29 is subnetted, 1 subnets
O E2    192.168.253.0 [110/20] via 10.0.3.5, 00:00:09, Serial0/0
```

The same three solutions used to address the suboptimal routing issue caused when mutual redistribution between RIP and OSPF was performed on R2 can also be used to resolve the suboptimal routing issue caused by the redistribution of EIGRP into OSPF on R2.

Multipoint Route Redistribution

When redistributing at multiple points in the network, the chances that either routing loops or suboptimal routing will occur are greatly increased. When implementing multipoint redistribution, a general rule of thumb is to always filter routes so that the same routes are not re-advertised back into the source protocol at another point of redistribution in the network as illustrated in Figure 4-15 below:

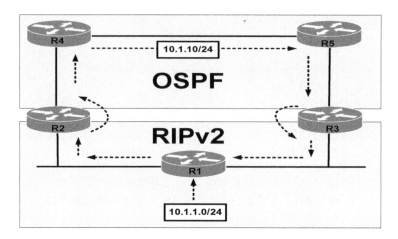

Fig. 4-15. Multipoint Redistribution Considerations

Referencing Figure 4-5, R1 is receiving the 10.1.1.0/24 prefix from a downstream RIP router. This prefix is then advertised to routers R2 and R3. RIP is redistributed into OSPF on R2 and the prefix is propagated as an external route to R4, which sends it to R5, which in turn sends it to R3. At this point, R3 removes the 10.1.1.0/24 prefix learned via RIP and replaces it with the 10.1.1.0/24 prefix learned via OSPF because OSPF is a more reliable route source.

Following the redistribution of RIP into OSPF on R2, R3 prefers the 10.1.1.0/24 prefix received via OSPF to the 10.1.1.0/24 prefix received via RIP. When mutual route redistribution is performed on R3, the 10.1.1.0/24 prefix, which has been installed into the routing table as an OSPF route, is imported into RIP and is then re-advertised back into the RIP domain. Depending on the route metrics used during redistribution, this may result in suboptimal routing or may cause a routing loop for packets destined to the 10.1.1.0/24 from routers within the OSPF network. Cisco IOS software supports several methods and techniques that can be used in conjunction with route redistribution to avoid such pitfalls. These methods include the following:

- Using distribute lists to filter routes
- Using route maps to filter routes
- Modifying administrative distance values

Distribute lists were described earlier in this chapter. Referencing the basic scenario illustrated in Figure 4-15, distribute lists could be configured for RIP on R2 and R3, denying the 10.1.1.0/24 subnet from these two gateways. This would prevent the re-advertising of this prefix into the RIP domain during route redistribution.

The second method would be to use route maps during redistribution. This is the recommended method. The route map can be used to filter routes by referencing an ACL, a prefix list, or route tags. The use of route maps will be illustrated in detail in the following configuration example.

The third method would be to manipulate the administrative distance of the 10.1.1.0/24 prefix for all OSPF external routes on R2 and R3. This would prevent the prefix from being redistributed back into the RIP domain at either one of these routers, as the RIP-learned route would always be preferred based on the administrative distance.

Because mutual redistribution is a core requirement of the ROUTE exam and is an often-confusing topic, we will use the topology illustrated in Figure 4-16 below to reinforce the considerations described in the previous section and to see how a poorly implemented mutual redistribution implementation can result in suboptimal routing and routing loops within the routed network:

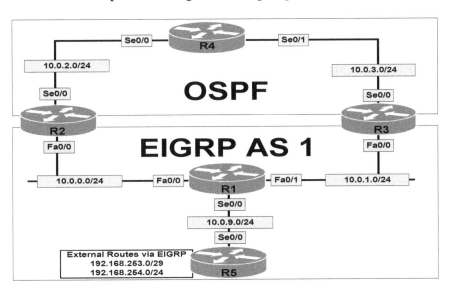

Fig. 4-16. Implementing Mutual Route Redistribution

Figure 4-16 shows a basic routed network using EIGRP and OSPF. R1, R2, and R3 are running EIGRP and reside in Autonomous System 1. R1 is receiving the 192.168.253.0/29 and 192.168.254.0/24 external EIGRP routes from a downstream neighbor and is advertising them to R2 and R3. R2 and R3 are also running OSPF, and these routers reside in the backbone area with R1. Assuming that both the OSPF and EIGRP routing protocols have been implemented correctly on all routers, the routing tables on all routers in the network display the following:

```
R1#show ip route | begin Gateway
Gateway of last resort is not set

     10.0.0.0/24 is subnetted, 3 subnets
C       10.0.9.0 is directly connected, Serial0/0
C       10.0.0.0 is directly connected, FastEthernet0/0
C       10.0.1.0 is directly connected, FastEthernet0/1
D EX 192.168.254.0/24 [170/18311936] via 10.0.9.5, 00:01:33, Serial0/0
     192.168.253.0/29 is subnetted, 1 subnets
D EX    192.168.253.0 [170/18311936] via 10.0.9.5, 00:01:33, Serial0/0
```

```
R2#show ip route | begin Gateway
Gateway of last resort is not set

      10.0.0.0/24 is subnetted, 5 subnets
D        10.0.9.0 [90/5514496] via 10.0.0.1, 01:06:53, FastEthernet0/0
C        10.0.2.0 is directly connected, Serial0/0
O        10.0.3.0 [110/128] via 10.0.2.4, 00:11:11, Serial0/0
C        10.0.0.0 is directly connected, FastEthernet0/0
D        10.0.1.0 [90/30720] via 10.0.0.1, 01:10:59, FastEthernet0/0
D EX 192.168.254.0/24 [170/18314496] via 10.0.0.1, 00:03:03, FastEthernet0/0
     192.168.253.0/29 is subnetted, 1 subnets
D EX    192.168.253.0 [170/18314496] via 10.0.0.1, 00:03:03, FastEthernet0/0

R3#show ip route | begin Gateway
Gateway of last resort is not set

      10.0.0.0/24 is subnetted, 5 subnets
D        10.0.9.0 [90/5514496] via 10.0.1.1, 01:07:16, FastEthernet0/0
O        10.0.2.0 [110/128] via 10.0.3.4, 00:11:33, Serial0/0
C        10.0.3.0 is directly connected, Serial0/0
D        10.0.0.0 [90/30720] via 10.0.1.1, 01:11:22, FastEthernet0/0
C        10.0.1.0 is directly connected, FastEthernet0/0
D EX 192.168.254.0/24 [170/18314496] via 10.0.1.1, 00:03:26, FastEthernet0/0
     192.168.253.0/29 is subnetted, 1 subnets
D EX    192.168.253.0 [170/18314496] via 10.0.1.1, 00:03:26, FastEthernet0/0

R4#show ip route | begin Gateway
Gateway of last resort is not set

      10.0.0.0/24 is subnetted, 2 subnets
C        10.0.2.0 is directly connected, Serial0/0
C        10.0.3.0 is directly connected, Serial0/1
```

After verifying the routes, mutual redistribution between EIGRP and OSPF is configured on the two ASBRs, R2 and R3. This is performed as follows:

```
R2(config)#router ospf 2
R2(config-router)#redistribute eigrp 1 subnets
R2(config-router)#exit
R2(config)#router eigrp 1
R2(config-router)#redistribute ospf 2 metric 100000 10 255 1 1500
R2(config-router)#exit

R3(config)#router ospf 3
R3(config-router)#redistribute eigrp 1 subnets
R3(config-router)#exit
R3(config)#router eigrp 1
R3(config-router)#redistribute ospf 3 metric 100000 10 255 1 1500
R3(config-router)#exit
```

After redistribution, we will revisit the routing tables on each of the routers, beginning with R2 as follows:

```
R2#show ip route | begin Gateway
Gateway of last resort is not set

     10.0.0.0/24 is subnetted, 5 subnets
D       10.0.9.0 [90/5514496] via 10.0.0.1, 01:22:55, FastEthernet0/0
C       10.0.2.0 is directly connected, Serial0/0
O       10.0.3.0 [110/128] via 10.0.2.4, 00:02:52, Serial0/0
C       10.0.0.0 is directly connected, FastEthernet0/0
D       10.0.1.0 [90/30720] via 10.0.0.1, 01:27:01, FastEthernet0/0
D EX 192.168.254.0/24 [170/33280] via 10.0.0.1, 00:02:43, FastEthernet0/0
     192.168.253.0/29 is subnetted, 1 subnets
D EX    192.168.253.0 [170/33280] via 10.0.0.1, 00:02:43, FastEthernet0/0
```

In the output above, R2 is showing the correct outbound interface for all the EIGRP and OSPF routes. This router will have no problems getting to the subnets in either domain. Moving on, the routing table on R4 displays the following entries:

```
R4#show ip route | begin Gateway
Gateway of last resort is not set

     10.0.0.0/24 is subnetted, 5 subnets
O E2    10.0.9.0 [110/20] via 10.0.2.2, 00:03:32, Serial0/0
                 [110/20] via 10.0.3.3, 00:03:32, Serial0/1
C       10.0.2.0 is directly connected, Serial0/0
C       10.0.3.0 is directly connected, Serial0/1
O E2    10.0.0.0 [110/20] via 10.0.2.2, 00:03:32, Serial0/0
                 [110/20] via 10.0.3.3, 00:03:32, Serial0/1
O E2    10.0.1.0 [110/20] via 10.0.2.2, 00:03:32, Serial0/0
                 [110/20] via 10.0.3.3, 00:03:32, Serial0/1
O E2 192.168.254.0/24 [110/20] via 10.0.2.2, 00:03:32, Serial0/0
     192.168.253.0/29 is subnetted, 1 subnets
O E2    192.168.253.0 [110/20] via 10.0.2.2, 00:03:32, Serial0/0
```

In the output above, R4 is learning about the 10.0.0.0, 10.0.1.0, and 10.0.9.0 EIGRP subnets from both R2 and R3, given that EIGRP routes were redistributed into OSPF on both routers using the same (default) metric. However, R4 is learning about the 192.168.253.0 and 192.168.254.0 routes only from R2. This is where the problems begin. The reason for this is that when EIGRP was redistributed into OSPF on R2, the routes we propagated throughout the OSPF domain to R3 were external routes. These routes were then installed into the routing table as OSPF routes, not EIGRP routes. Given this, the routing table on R3 displays the following entries:

```
R3#show ip route | begin Gateway
Gateway of last resort is not set

     10.0.0.0/24 is subnetted, 5 subnets
D       10.0.9.0 [90/5514496] via 10.0.1.1, 01:23:52, FastEthernet0/0
O       10.0.2.0 [110/128] via 10.0.3.4, 00:03:49, Serial0/0
```

```
C       10.0.3.0 is directly connected, Serial0/0
D       10.0.0.0 [90/30720] via 10.0.1.1, 01:27:58, FastEthernet0/0
C       10.0.1.0 is directly connected, FastEthernet0/0
O E2 192.168.254.0/24 [110/20] via 10.0.3.4, 00:03:49, Serial0/0
     192.168.253.0/29 is subnetted, 1 subnets
O E2    192.168.253.0 [110/20] via 10.0.3.4, 00:03:49, Serial0/0
```

In the output above, R3 is learning about the 10.0.0.0 and 10.0.9.0 subnets via EIGRP. These are internal EIGRP routes and are therefore preferred over the external routes redistributed into OSPF by router R2. The 10.0.2.0 route is learned for the subnet between R2 and R4. This is an internal OSPF route. However, unlike R2, R3 prefers the 192.168.253.0 and 192.168.254.0 routes advertised by OSPF instead of EIGRP because the routes redistributed into OSPF on R2 have a lower administrative distance than the external EIGRP routes advertised by R1.

Because R3 prefers the 192.168.253.0 and 192.168.254.0 routes received via OSPF, when mutual redistribution is configured between EIGRP and OSPF on R3, these same routes will be redistributed into EIGRP and re-advertised back into the EIGRP domain. Because of this behavior, the routing table on R1 displays the following network entries:

```
R1#show ip route | begin Gateway
Gateway of last resort is not set

     10.0.0.0/24 is subnetted, 5 subnets
C       10.0.9.0 is directly connected, Serial0/0
D EX    10.0.2.0 [170/30720] via 10.0.0.2, 00:34:02, FastEthernet0/0
                 [170/30720] via 10.0.1.3, 00:34:02, FastEthernet0/1
D EX    10.0.3.0 [170/30720] via 10.0.0.2, 00:34:02, FastEthernet0/0
                 [170/30720] via 10.0.1.3, 00:34:02, FastEthernet0/1
C       10.0.0.0 is directly connected, FastEthernet0/0
C       10.0.1.0 is directly connected, FastEthernet0/1
D EX 192.168.254.0/24 [170/30720] via 10.0.1.3, 00:34:02, FastEthernet0/1
     192.168.253.0/29 is subnetted, 1 subnets
D EX    192.168.253.0 [170/30720] via 10.0.1.3, 00:34:02, FastEthernet0/1
```

Based on the output of R1's routing table, a routing loop has been created. As an example, assume that a packet from R4 is sent to the 192.168.253.0 subnet. R4 will forward this to R2. R2 receives the packet and forwards it to R1. R1 receives the packet and forwards it to R3. R3 receives the same packet and forwards it to R4. The entire process is repeated continuously until the TTL field in the packet reaches zero, after which the packet is discarded. To validate this theory, we will perform a Traceroute from R4 to the 192.168.253.1 address as follows:

```
R4#traceroute ip 192.168.253.1

Type escape sequence to abort.
```

```
Tracing the route to 192.168.253.1

  1 R2-Se0-Interface (10.0.2.2) 4 msec 4 msec 4 msec
  2 R1-Fa0-Interface (10.0.0.1) 4 msec 4 msec 4 msec
  3 R3-Fa0-Interface (10.0.1.3) 4 msec 4 msec 0 msec
  4 R4-Se1-Interface (10.0.3.4) 4 msec 4 msec 4 msec
  5 R2-Se0-Interface (10.0.2.2) 4 msec 0 msec 0 msec
  6 R1-Fa0-Interface (10.0.0.1) 4 msec 4 msec 4 msec
  7 R3-Fa0-Interface (10.0.1.3) 0 msec 4 msec 4 msec
  8 R4-Se1-Interface (10.0.3.4) 4 msec 4 msec 4 msec
  9 R2-Se0-Interface (10.0.2.2) 0 msec 4 msec 4 msec
 10 R1-Fa0-Interface (10.0.0.1) 4 msec 8 msec 4 msec
 11 R3-Fa0-Interface (10.0.1.3) 4 msec 4 msec 4 msec
 12 R4-Se1-Interface (10.0.3.4) 8 msec 4 msec 4 msec
 13 R2-Se0-Interface (10.0.2.2) 4 msec 4 msec 4 msec
 14 R1-Fa0-Interface (10.0.0.1) 4 msec 8 msec 4 msec
 15 R3-Fa0-Interface (10.0.1.3) 4 msec 4 msec 4 msec
 16 R4-Se1-Interface (10.0.3.4) 8 msec 4 msec 4 msec
 17 R2-Se0-Interface (10.0.2.2) 4 msec 8 msec 4 msec
 18 R1-Fa0-Interface (10.0.0.1) 4 msec 4 msec 8 msec
 19 R3-Fa0-Interface (10.0.1.3) 4 msec 4 msec 8 msec
 20 R4-Se1-Interface (10.0.3.4) 4 msec 4 msec 4 msec
 21 R2-Se0-Interface (10.0.2.2) 4 msec 4 msec 8 msec
 22 R1-Fa0-Interface (10.0.0.1) 8 msec 8 msec 8 msec
 23 R3-Fa0-Interface (10.0.1.3) 4 msec 4 msec 4 msec
 24 R4-Se1-Interface (10.0.3.4) 4 msec 8 msec 8 msec
 25 R2-Se0-Interface (10.0.2.2) 8 msec 8 msec 8 msec
 26 R1-Fa0-Interface (10.0.0.1) 8 msec 8 msec 8 msec
 27 R3-Fa0-Interface (10.0.1.3) 8 msec 4 msec 4 msec
 28 R4-Se1-Interface (10.0.3.4) 8 msec 8 msec 8 msec
 29 R2-Se0-Interface (10.0.2.2) 4 msec 8 msec 8 msec
 30 R1-Fa0-Interface (10.0.0.1) 8 msec 8 msec 8 msec
```

NOTE: R4 is configured to query a DNS server for IP to hostname address resolution, which is why the router interface names appear in the output of the Traceroute.

In the Traceroute output above, we can confirm that a routing loop has indeed formed based on the implemented route redistribution configuration. The routing loop is caused primarily because of the redistribution metric applied when OSPF routes were redistributed into EIGRP on R2 and R3. The result of the configuration is that R1 prefers the external routes that are redistributed into EIGRP from R3 for the 192.168.253.0 and 192.168.254.0 subnets versus the external routes advertised to R1 by its downstream neighbor. The EIGRP Topology Table displays the following entries for the 192.168.253.0 subnet:

```
R1#show ip eigrp topology 192.168.253.0 255.255.255.248
IP-EIGRP (AS 1): Topology entry for 192.168.253.0/29
  State is Passive, Query origin flag is 1, 1 Successor(s), FD is 30720
```

```
Routing Descriptor Blocks:
10.0.1.3 (FastEthernet0/1), from 10.0.1.3, Send flag is 0x0
    Composite metric is (30720/28160), Route is External
    Vector metric:
      Minimum bandwidth is 100000 Kbit
      Total delay is 200 microseconds
      Reliability is 255/255
      Load is 1/255
      Minimum MTU is 1500
      Hop count is 1
    External data:
      Originating router is 10.0.3.3
      AS number of route is 3
      External protocol is OSPF, external metric is 20
      Administrator tag is 0 (0x00000000)
10.0.9.5 (Serial0/0), from 10.0.9.5, Send flag is 0x0
    Composite metric is (18311936/17799936), Route is External
    Vector metric:
      Minimum bandwidth is 512 Kbit
      Total delay is 520000 microseconds
      Reliability is 255/255
      Load is 1/255
      Minimum MTU is 1500
      Hop count is 1
    External data:
      Originating router is 192.168.254.1
      AS number of route is 0
      External protocol is Connected, external metric is 0
      Administrator tag is 0 (0x00000000)
```

Likewise, the EIGRP Topology Table displays the following entries for the 192.168.254.0 subnet:

```
R1#show ip eigrp topology 192.168.254.0 255.255.255.0
IP-EIGRP (AS 1): Topology entry for 192.168.254.0/24
  State is Passive, Query origin flag is 1, 1 Successor(s), FD is 30720
  Routing Descriptor Blocks:
  10.0.1.3 (FastEthernet0/1), from 10.0.1.3, Send flag is 0x0
      Composite metric is (30720/28160), Route is External
      Vector metric:
        Minimum bandwidth is 100000 Kbit
        Total delay is 200 microseconds
        Reliability is 255/255
        Load is 1/255
        Minimum MTU is 1500
        Hop count is 1
      External data:
        Originating router is 10.0.3.3
        AS number of route is 3
        External protocol is OSPF, external metric is 20
        Administrator tag is 0 (0x00000000)
  10.0.9.5 (Serial0/0), from 10.0.9.5, Send flag is 0x0
```

```
Composite metric is (18311936/17799936), Route is External
Vector metric:
  Minimum bandwidth is 512 Kbit
  Total delay is 520000 microseconds
  Reliability is 255/255
  Load is 1/255
  Minimum MTU is 1500
  Hop count is 1
External data:
  Originating router is 192.168.254.1
  AS number of route is 0
  External protocol is Connected, external metric is 0
  Administrator tag is 0 (0x00000000)
```

In both outputs, the route redistributed into EIGRP by R3 is preferred over the route advertised to R1 by its downstream neighbor. There are several methods that can be used to resolve this issue and they include the following:

- Redistributing OSPF routes with a worse (higher) metric
- Filtering routes using distribute lists
- Changing the default administrative distance values
- Using route map filtering during redistribution

The first method is simple. On both R2 and R3, OSPF routes are redistributed into the EIGRP domain using a higher metric than that for the external route received by R1 from its downstream neighbor. As an example, OSPF could be redistributed into EIGRP on both routers as follows:

```
R2(config)#router eigrp 1
R2(config-router)#redistribute ospf 2 metric 256 500000 255 1 1500
R2(config-router)#exit

R3(config)#router eigrp 1
R3(config-router)#redistribute ospf 3 metric 256 500000 255 1 1500
R3(config-router)#exit
```

After this configuration, R1 prefers the routes via its downstream neighbor (R5) to the 192.168.253.0 and 192.168.254.0 subnets as follows:

```
R1#show ip route eigrp | include 192.168
D EX 192.168.254.0/24 [170/18311936] via 10.0.9.5, 00:00:09, Serial0/0
     192.168.253.0/29 is subnetted, 1 subnets
D EX    192.168.253.0 [170/18311936] via 10.0.9.5, 00:00:09, Serial0/0
```

R4 is now able to reach the 192.168.253.1 address as illustrated in the following Traceroute:

```
R4#traceroute ip 192.168.253.1

Type escape sequence to abort.
Tracing the route to 192.168.253.1

  1 R2-Se0-Interface (10.0.2.2) 4 msec 4 msec 4 msec
  2 R1-Fa0-Interface (10.0.0.1) 4 msec 4 msec 4 msec
  3 R5-Se0-Interface (10.0.9.5) 0 msec *  4 msec
```

Keep in mind that this option addresses one of two issues, which is the routing loop. It does not, however, address the suboptimal routing to the 192.168.253.0 and 192.68.254.0 subnets on R3, which still prefers the OSPF routes to the external EIGRP routes. This is illustrated as follows:

```
R3#show ip route | include 192.168.
O E2 192.168.254.0/24 [110/20] via 10.0.3.4, 00:29:54, Serial0/0
      192.168.253.0/29 is subnetted, 1 subnets
O E2    192.168.253.0 [110/20] via 10.0.3.4, 00:29:54, Serial0/0
```

Using the second method, either OSPF or EIGRP distribute lists can be configured on R2 and R3 to resolve the routing loop. The following example illustrates how to configure inbound distribute lists on R2 and R3 filtering all external routes originated by either one of the routers:

```
R2(config)#route-map DENY-OSPF-EXTERNAL-FROM-R3 deny 10
R2(config-route-map)#match source-protocol ospf 3
R2(config-route-map)#match route-type external
R2(config-route-map)#exit
R2(config)#route-map DENY-OSPF-EXTERNAL-FROM-R3 permit 20
R2(config-route-map)#exit
R2(config)#router ospf 2
R2(config-router)#distribute-list route-map DENY-OSPF-EXTERNAL-FROM-R3 in
R2(config-router)#

R3(config)#route-map DENY-OSPF-EXTERNAL-FROM-R2 deny 10
R3(config-route-map)#match source-protocol ospf 2
R3(config-route-map)#match route-type external
R3(config-route-map)#exit
R3(config)#route-map DENY-OSPF-EXTERNAL-FROM-R2 permit 20
R3(config-route-map)#exit
R3(config)#router ospf 3
R3(config-router)#distribute-list route-map DENY-OSPF-EXTERNAL-FROM-R2 in
R3(config-router)#exit
```

This solution addresses both the suboptimal routing issue on R3 as well as the routing loop that was caused by the mutual redistribution. The routing tables on R2 and R3 display the following:

```
R2#show ip route | include 192.168
D EX 192.168.254.0/24 [170/18314496] via 10.0.0.1, 00:34:37, FastEthernet0/0
      192.168.253.0/29 is subnetted, 1 subnets
```

```
D EX    192.168.253.0 [170/18314496] via 10.0.0.1, 00:34:37, FastEthernet0/0

R3#show ip route | include 192.168
D EX 192.168.254.0/24 [170/18314496] via 10.0.1.1, 00:34:52, FastEthernet0/0
     192.168.253.0/29 is subnetted, 1 subnets
D EX    192.168.253.0 [170/18314496] via 10.0.1.1, 00:34:52, FastEthernet0/0
```

NOTE: When using distribute lists, it is important to understand the impact your filtering will have on downstream routers. For example, incorrect configuration on R2 and R3 would effectively prevent those two routers from learning about the 192.168.253.0 and 192.168.254.0 prefixes via OSPF; however, it may also result in these subnets not being advertised to R4. Because of the implementation of the distribute list, this potential pitfall is averted and the RIB on router R4 still contains all route entries as illustrated below:

```
R4#show ip route ospf
      10.0.0.0/24 is subnetted, 5 subnets
O E2    10.0.9.0 [110/20] via 10.0.2.2, 01:23:34, Serial0/0
                 [110/20] via 10.0.3.3, 01:23:34, Serial0/1
O E2    10.0.0.0 [110/20] via 10.0.2.2, 01:23:34, Serial0/0
                 [110/20] via 10.0.3.3, 01:23:34, Serial0/1
O E2    10.0.1.0 [110/20] via 10.0.3.3, 01:23:35, Serial0/1
                 [110/20] via 10.0.2.2, 01:23:35, Serial0/0
O E2 192.168.254.0/24 [110/20] via 10.0.3.3, 00:35:23, Serial0/1
                      [110/20] via 10.0.2.2, 00:35:23, Serial0/0
      192.168.253.0/29 is subnetted, 1 subnets
O E2    192.168.253.0 [110/20] via 10.0.3.3, 00:35:23, Serial0/1
                      [110/20] via 10.0.2.2, 00:35:23, Serial0/0
```

Again, to validate our configuration, a Traceroute from R4 to 192.168.253.1 is performed:

```
R4#traceroute ip 192.168.253.1

Type escape sequence to abort.
Tracing the route to 192.168.253.1

  1 R2-Se0-Interface (10.0.2.2) 0 msec
    R3-Se0-Interface (10.0.3.3) 4 msec
    R2-Se0-Interface (10.0.2.2) 4 msec
  2 R1-Fa1-Interface (10.0.1.1) 4 msec
    R1-Fa0-Interface (10.0.0.1) 0 msec
    R1-Fa1-Interface (10.0.1.1) 0 msec
  3 R5-Se0-Interface (10.0.9.5) 4 msec *  4 msec
```

NOTE: Because both the suboptimal routing and routing loop issues have been resolved, R4 is able to load-share between the paths via routers R2 and R3.

The third method that could be used would be to increment the administrative distance values for OSPF to a value higher than that assigned to external EIGRP routes as illustrated below:

```
R3(config)#router ospf 3
R3(config-router)#distance ospf external 175
R3(config-router)#exit

R2(config)#router ospf 2
R2(config-router)#distance ospf external 175
R2(config-router)#exit
```

Following this configuration, the routing tables on R2 and R3 display the following route entries:

```
R2#show ip route | include 192.168
D EX 192.168.254.0/24 [170/18314496] via 10.0.0.1, 00:00:20, FastEthernet0/0
     192.168.253.0/29 is subnetted, 1 subnets
D EX    192.168.253.0 [170/18314496] via 10.0.0.1, 00:00:20, FastEthernet0/0


R3#show ip route | include 192.168
D EX 192.168.254.0/24 [170/18314496] via 10.0.1.1, 00:01:30, FastEthernet0/0
     192.168.253.0/29 is subnetted, 1 subnets
D EX    192.168.253.0 [170/18314496] via 10.0.1.1, 00:01:30, FastEthernet0/0
```

Once again, we can use a Traceroute from R4 to the 192.168.253.1 address for verification as illustrated below:

```
R4#traceroute ip 192.168.253.1

Type escape sequence to abort.
Tracing the route to 192.168.253.1

  1 R3-Se0-Interface (10.0.3.3) 4 msec
    R2-Se0-Interface (10.0.2.2) 0 msec
    R3-Se0-Interface (10.0.3.3) 4 msec
  2 R1-Fa0-Interface (10.0.0.1) 4 msec
    R1-Fa1-Interface (10.0.1.1) 4 msec
    R1-Fa0-Interface (10.0.0.1) 4 msec
  3 R5-Se0-Interface (10.0.9.5) 4 msec *  4 msec
```

The final solution requires much more configuration but it is the recommended solution because of its scalability. This method uses a route map during redistribution to prevent routes learned from one route source from being advertised into another route source, and vice versa. While route maps can be used to match against many different criteria, when redistributing, the most scalable solution is to use route tag for filtering. This is implemented as follows on R2:

```
R2(config)#route-map EIGRP-into-OSPF deny 10
R2(config-route-map)#description 'Deny Routes With A Tag of 3'
R2(config-route-map)#match tag 3
R2(config-route-map)#exit
R2(config)#route-map EIGRP-into-OSPF permit 20
R2(config-route-map)#description 'Tag Routes With A Tag of 2'
```

```
R2(config-route-map)#set tag 2
R2(config-route-map)#exit
R2(config)#route-map OSPF-into-EIGRP deny 10
R2(config-route-map)#description 'Deny Routes With A Tag of 3'
R2(config-route-map)#match tag 3
R2(config-route-map)#exit
R2(config)#route-map OSPF-into-EIGRP permit 20
R2(config-route-map)#description 'Tag Routes With A Tag of 2'
R2(config-route-map)#set tag 2
R2(config-route-map)#exit
R2(config)#router ospf 2
R2(config-router)#redistribute eigrp 1 subnets route-map EIGRP-into-OSPF
R2(config-router)#exit
R2(config)#router eigrp 1
R2(config-router)#default-metric 100000 10 255 1 1500
R2(config-router)#redistribute ospf 2 route-map OSPF-into-EIGRP
R2(config-router)#exit
```

The inverse configuration is then implemented on R3 as follows:

```
R3(config)#route-map EIGRP-into-OSPF deny 10
R3(config-route-map)#description 'Deny Routes With A Tag of 2'
R3(config-route-map)#match tag 2
R3(config-route-map)#exit
R3(config)#route-map EIGRP-into-OSPF permit 20
R3(config-route-map)#description 'Tag Routes With A Tag of 3'
R3(config-route-map)#set tag 3
R3(config-route-map)#exit
R3(config)#route-map OSPF-into-EIGRP deny 10
R3(config-route-map)#description 'Deny Routes With A Tag of 2'
R3(config-route-map)#match tag 2
R3(config-route-map)#exit
R3(config)#route-map OSPF-into-EIGRP permit 20
R3(config-route-map)#description 'Tag Routes With A Tag of 3'
R3(config-route-map)#set tag 3
R3(config-route-map)#exit
R3(config)#router ospf 3
R3(config-router)#redistribute eigrp 1 subnets route-map EIGRP-into-OSPF
R3(config-router)#exit
R3(config)#router eigrp 1
R3(config-router)#default-metric 100000 10 255 1 1500
R3(config-router)#redistribute ospf 3 route-map OSPF-into-EIGRP
R3(config-router)#exit
```

While this configuration may appear intimidating and confusing at first glance, it is very simple to understand. The following sections describe the logic of the route map configurations:

On R2, the EIGRP-into-OSPF route map performs the following actions:

- The first deny statement denies all routes with a route tag of 3. These OSPF routes are redistributed into EIGRP on R3.

- The second permit statement allows all EIGRP routes and assigns an administrator tag value of 2 for those routes during redistribution into OSPF.

On R2, the OSPF-into-EIGRP route map performs the following actions:
- The first deny statement denies all routes with a route tag of 3. These EIGRP routes are redistributed into OSPF on R3.
- The second permit statement allows all OSPF routes and assigns an administrator tag value of 2 for those routes during redistribution into EIGRP.

On R3, the EIGRP-into-OSPF route map performs the following actions:
- The first deny statement denies all routes with a route tag of 2. These OSPF routes are redistributed into EIGRP on R2.
- The second permit statement allows all EIGRP routes and assigns an administrator tag value of 3 for those routes during redistribution into OSPF.

On R3, the OSPF-into-EIGRP route map performs the following actions:
- The first deny statement denies all routes with a route tag of 2. These EIGRP routes are redistributed into OSPF on R2.
- The second permit statement allows all EIGRP routes and assigns an administrator tag value of 3 for those routes during redistribution into OSPF.

By preventing EIGRP routes from being re-advertised back into the EIGRP domain, R1 will prefer the external EIGRP routes received from its downstream neighbor, as the same prefix is not being re-advertised back into EIGRP by either R2 or R3. This prevents routing loops from forming and can be validated by viewing the routing table of R1, which displays the following entries:

```
R1#show ip route | begin Gateway
Gateway of last resort is not set

     10.0.0.0/24 is subnetted, 5 subnets
C       10.0.9.0 is directly connected, Serial0/0
D EX    10.0.2.0 [170/30720] via 10.0.0.2, 00:02:23, FastEthernet0/0
                 [170/30720] via 10.0.1.3, 00:02:23, FastEthernet0/1
D EX    10.0.3.0 [170/30720] via 10.0.0.2, 00:02:23, FastEthernet0/0
                 [170/30720] via 10.0.1.3, 00:02:23, FastEthernet0/1
C       10.0.0.0 is directly connected, FastEthernet0/0
C       10.0.1.0 is directly connected, FastEthernet0/1
D EX 192.168.254.0/24 [170/18311936] via 10.0.9.5, 00:02:23, Serial0/0
     192.168.253.0/29 is subnetted, 1 subnets
D EX    192.168.253.0 [170/18311936] via 10.0.9.5, 00:02:23, Serial0/0
```

As a point of interest, it should be noted that using route map filtering with tags does not mean that there will be no suboptimal routing issues in the OSPF domain. For example, R3 continues to prefer the external OSPF route for the 192.168.253.0 and 192.168.254.0 subnets over the external EIGRP routes for the same destinations as can be seen in the routing table of R3 below:

```
R3#show ip route | begin Gateway
Gateway of last resort is not set

     10.0.0.0/24 is subnetted, 5 subnets
D       10.0.9.0 [90/5514496] via 10.0.1.1, 02:48:48, FastEthernet0/0
O       10.0.2.0 [110/128] via 10.0.3.4, 01:07:41, Serial0/0
C       10.0.3.0 is directly connected, Serial0/0
D       10.0.0.0 [90/30720] via 10.0.1.1, 02:48:48, FastEthernet0/0
C       10.0.1.0 is directly connected, FastEthernet0/0
O E2 192.168.254.0/24 [110/20] via 10.0.3.4, 00:05:31, Serial0/0
     192.168.253.0/29 is subnetted, 1 subnets
O E2    192.168.253.0 [110/20] via 10.0.3.4, 00:05:31, Serial0/0
```

The simplest way to resolve this issue would be to adjust the default administrative distance for external OSPF routes on R3. However, on the positive side, the routing loop has been averted and R4 is still able to reach either the 192.168.253.0/29 or the 192.168.254.0/24 subnets. This is illustrated below:

```
R4#traceroute ip 192.168.253.1

Type escape sequence to abort.
Tracing the route to 192.168.253.1

  1 R2-Se0-Interface (10.0.2.2) 0 msec 0 msec 0 msec
  2 R1-Fa0-Interface (10.0.0.1) 4 msec 0 msec 0 msec
  3 R5-Se0-Interface (10.0.9.5) 4 msec *   4 msec

R4#ping 192.168.253.1

Type escape sequence to abort.
Sending 5, 100-byte ICMP Echos to 192.168.253.1, timeout is 2 seconds:
!!!!!
Success rate is 100 percent (5/5), round-trip min/avg/max = 4/5/8 ms

R4#traceroute ip 192.168.254.1

Type escape sequence to abort.
Tracing the route to 192.168.254.1

  1 R2-Se0-Interface (10.0.2.2) 4 msec 0 msec 0 msec
  2 R1-Fa0-Interface (10.0.0.1) 0 msec 0 msec 4 msec
  3 R5-Se0-Interface (10.0.9.5) 4 msec *   4 msec
```

```
R4#ping 192.168.254.1

Type escape sequence to abort.
Sending 5, 100-byte ICMP Echos to 192.168.254.1, timeout is 2 seconds:
!!!!!
Success rate is 100 percent (5/5), round-trip min/avg/max = 4/4/4 ms
```

In summation, although much has been discussed in this chapter, make it a point to remember the following when implementing route redistribution:

- When possible, use a protocol that can use different administrative distance values for internal and external routes. Examples would be BGP, EIGRP, and OSPF, but not RIP.
- If possible, redistribute external routes with a higher administrative distance value than that of the route source. EIGRP does this automatically; OSPF and BGP do not.
- Use route tagging or other filters to ensure that only routes internal to the route source or prefixes that originate from the route source domain are redistributed.
- Redistribute external routes with a higher metric (worse), ensuring that if routes are redistributed back into the original domain, they are less preferred.

While route redistribution is sometimes the only solution to incorporating routes from one route source into another (e.g., when two companies merge), it is important to understand that you should always consider other alternatives before considering redistribution. For example, assume that a router is configured with the following static routes:

```
R1(config)#ip route 150.254.100.0 255.255.255.0 serial0/0
R1(config)#ip route 150.254.101.0 255.255.255.0 serial0/0
R1(config)#ip route 150.254.102.0 255.255.255.0 serial0/0
R1(config)#ip route 150.254.103.0 255.255.255.0 serial0/0
```

If you are running EIGRP as the IGP of choice, for example, rather than redistribute the static routes into EIGRP, consider using the network statement instead as illustrated below:

```
R1(config)#router eigrp 1
R1(config-router)#network 150.254.100.0 0.0.3.255
R1(config-router)#exit
```

With this configuration, the static routes are redistributed into EIGRP without having to use the redistribute command as illustrated in the EIGRP Topology Table below:

```
R1#show ip eigrp 1 topology | begin 150.254.100
P 150.254.100.0/24, 1 successors, FD is 5511936
        via Rstatic (5511936/0)
P 150.254.101.0/24, 1 successors, FD is 5511936
```

```
        via Rstatic (5511936/0)
P 150.254.102.0/24, 1 successors, FD is 5511936
        via Rstatic (5511936/0)
P 150.254.103.0/24, 1 successors, FD is 5511936
        via Rstatic (5511936/0)
```

The advantage of using this technique is that the routes are advertised to downstream routers as internal EIGRP routes and not as external routes as illustrated in the following output:

```
R2#show ip route eigrp | include 150.254
      150.254.0.0/24 is subnetted, 4 subnets
D        150.254.100.0 [90/5514496] via 10.0.0.1, 00:05:54, FastEthernet0/0
D        150.254.101.0 [90/5514496] via 10.0.0.1, 00:05:46, FastEthernet0/0
D        150.254.102.0 [90/5514496] via 10.0.0.1, 00:05:39, FastEthernet0/0
D        150.254.103.0 [90/5514496] via 10.0.0.1, 00:05:32, FastEthernet0/0
```

By advertising static routes within the autonomous system as internal routes, you can quickly identify external routes that are imported from dynamic routing protocols, for example. Additionally, it keeps the routing policy within the interior network consistent (i.e., all routes within the interior network are internal routes).

> **NOTE:** In order to use the network statement for static routes, the subnet for the interface via which the routes point should be included in EIGRP network statement configuration.

As another example, assume that a router running OSPF has 50 Loopback interfaces configured. While it is tempting to simply use the redistribute connected subnets command to redistribute the connected interfaces, this configuration will result in the generation of 50 Type 5 LSAs, which are then flooded to all routers in all areas. Instead, consider using the network command to advertise the subnets and then use the passive-interface command to prevent OSPF packets from being sent on these interfaces. This reduces the size of the LSDB for routers within the area. If possible, the ABR can then be configured to advertise a single summary LSA for the Type 5 routes, keeping the OSPF database for routers in other areas lean.

Finally, avoid mutual redistribution where possible; consider implementing one-way redistribution and using a default route for one of the route sources instead of performing mutual redistribution. Consider the network topology illustrated in Figure 4-17 below:

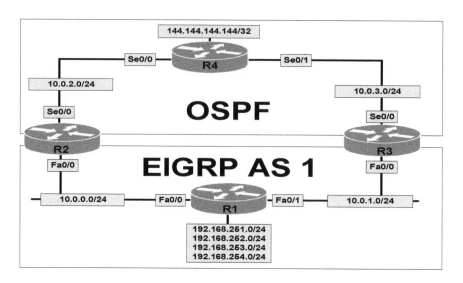

Fig. 4-17. One-Way Redistribution with a Default Route

Referencing Figure 4-17, instead of configuring mutual redistribution between OSPF and EIGRP on R2 and R3, along with the relevant route maps and administrative distance tweaking, the EIGRP routes simply could be redistributed into OSPF and a default route could be advertised into the EIGRP domain, allowing R1 to reach all OSPF subnets as follows:

```
R2(config)#router ospf 2
R2(config-router)#redistribute eigrp 1 subnets
R2(config-router)#exit
R2(config)#interface FastEthernet0/0
R2(config-if)#ip summary-address eigrp 1 0.0.0.0 0.0.0.0
R2(config-if)#exit

R3(config)#router ospf 3
R3(config-router)#redistribute eigrp 1 subnets
R3(config-router)#exit
R3(config)#interface FastEthernet0/0
R3(config-if)#ip summary-address eigrp 1 0.0.0.0 0.0.0.0
R3(config-if)#exit
```

Using this configuration, R1 and R4 still have end-to-end connectivity as illustrated below:

```
R1#ping  144.144.144.144 repeat 10 source 192.168.254.1

Type escape sequence to abort.
Sending 10, 100-byte ICMP Echos to 144.144.144.144, timeout is 2 seconds:
Packet sent with a source address of 192.168.254.1
!!!!!!!!!!
Success rate is 100 percent (10/10), round-trip min/avg/max = 1/3/4 ms
```

You can also perform a Traceroute to verify the path taken to R4 as follows:

```
R1#traceroute ip 144.144.144.144

Type escape sequence to abort.
Tracing the route to 144.144.144.144

  1 R3-Fa0-Interface (10.0.1.3) 0 msec
    R2-Fa0-Interface (10.0.0.2) 4 msec
    R3-Fa0-Interface (10.0.1.3) 0 msec
  2 R4-Se0-Interface (10.0.2.4) 0 msec
    R4-Se1-Interface (10.0.3.4) 0 msec *
```

CHAPTER SUMMARY

The following section is a summary of the major points you should be aware of in this chapter.

Access Lists and IP Prefix Lists Fundamentals

*   ACLs use wildcard masks to specify what networks should be permitted or denied
*   IP prefix lists are used to match specific prefixes based on number and length
*   IP prefix lists can also be used to match a range of networks that fall within a prefix
*   IP prefix lists consume fewer CPU cycles than traditional ACLs

Understanding Route Maps

*   Route maps and ACLs have common characteristics. These characteristics are as follows:
    1. Route maps and ACLs are an ordered sequence of individual statements
    2. The evaluation of route maps or ACLs is based on a list scan, in a predetermined order
    3. They are both generic mechanisms that can be used in multiple tasks

*   There are some differences between ACLs and route maps which are as follows:
    1. Route maps can, and often do, use ACLs as matching criteria
    2. Route maps can do more than simply permit or deny
    3. By design, each individual ACL ends with an implicit deny statement

*   Match clauses are used to match against predefined criteria
*   Set clauses are used to determine what happens a positive match has been made

Filtering EIGRP Routes

*   EIGRP supports the following route filtering mechanisms
    1. Distribute Lists
    2. Denying or permitting the default route

Filtering OSPF Routes

- OSPF supports the following route filtering mechanisms
  1. Distribute Lists
  2. Filtering Type 3 LSAs at the Area Border Router
  3. Filtering Outgoing LSAs

Protocol Independent Route Filtering

- The `distance` command can be used to filter routes if the distance is set to 255
- The `distance` command can be used in conjunction with any routing protocol

Route Redistribution Overview

- When redistribution is configured, different routes sources communicate with the RIB
- Different routing protocols or instances will never communicate directly
- Only route that have been installed into the RIB will actually be redistributed

Configuring and Verifying Route Redistribution

- The redistribute command is used to configure route redistribution between route sources
- By default, EIGRP assigns a metric of infinity during redistribution except:
  1. When redistributing between two EIGRP autonomous systems
  2. When redistributing static routes into EIGRP
  3. When redistributing connected interfaces (subnets) into EIGRP

- The EIGRP metric to be used for redistribution can be set in the following ways:
  1. By specifying the seed (default) EIGRP metric for redistributed routes
  2. By indirectly specifying the EIGRP metric during redistribution using a route map
  3. By directly specifying the EIGRP metric during route redistribution

- When redistributing routes into OSPF, the default metric assignments are as follows:
  1. Redistributed routes from BGP are assigned a metric or cost of 1
  2. Redistributed routes from another OSPF process use the source routes cost
  3. All other redistributed routes are assigned a default metric of 20

- OSPF external routes may either be Type 1 or Type 2. This is also applicable to NSSAs
- The difference between Type 1 and Type 2 external routes is metric calculation
- The metric for Type 2 external routes will never change
- The metric for Type 1 external routes will increment at every router (hop)
- By default, OSPF will only redistribute Classful networks
- To redistribute subnetted networks, the `subnets` keyword must be used

- For OSPF, there are three ways in which the metric for redistributed routes can be set:
  1. Directly using the `default-metric` router configuration command
  2. Indirectly by setting the metric value in a route map using the `set metric` command
  3. Directly by using the `metric` command with the `redistribute` command

- For OSPF, there are two ways the metric type, i.e. Type 1 or Type 2, can be set:
  1. Directly using the `metric-type` command with the `redistribute` command
  2. Indirectly by setting the type in a route map using the `set metric-type` command

Route Redistribution Design Considerations

- Route redistribution can be performed or implemented one-way or two-way
- Redistribution can also be performed on a single router or multiple router
- For redistribution, use the following to avoid routing loops and suboptimal routing

In summation, although a lot has been discussed in this chapter, make it a point to remember the following when implementing route redistribution:

- Use a protocol that can use different distance values for internal and external routes
- If possible, redistribute external routes with a higher administrative distance value
- Use route tagging or other filters to ensure that only internal routes are redistributed
- Redistribute external routes with a higher metric (worse)

CHAPTER 5

Path Control and Route Optimization

Path control allows administrators to control the path taken by traffic to an intended destination network. Path control can be implemented in various ways. Route optimization allows the traffic to take the best path out of the network. In Cisco IOS software, tools such as Performance Routing (PfR) provide automatic route optimization and load distribution for multiple connections between networks. These tools and more are described in detail in this chapter. The core ROUTE exam objective covered in this chapter is as follows:

*   Implement a Layer 3 path control solution

This chapter contains the following sections:
*   Cisco IOS IP Service Level Agreement
*   Cisco IOS Embedded Event Manager
*   Virtual Routing and Forwarding
*   Cisco Performance Routing
*   Path Control Using Route Redistribution
*   Cisco IOS Policy-Based Routing

CISCO IOS IP SERVICE LEVEL AGREEMENT

Cisco IOS IP Service Level Agreement (SLA) allows you to monitor, analyze, and verify IP service levels for IP applications and services, to increase productivity, to lower operational costs, and to reduce occurrences of network congestion or outages. IP SLA uses active traffic monitoring for measuring network performance. IP SLA was first integrated and introduced into Cisco IOS software as Response Time Reporter (RTR). Following some improvements, it was renamed Cisco Service Assurance Agent (SAA). In current IOS versions, the same tool is referred to as IP SLA.

IP SLA can measure and monitor network performance metrics such as jitter, latency (delay), and packet loss. IP SLA has evolved with advanced measurement features, such as application performance, MPLS awareness, and enhanced voice measurements. IP SLA uses active traffic monitoring, which is the generation of traffic in a continuous, reliable, and predictable manner, for measuring network performance edge-to-edge over a network. Given this, IP SLA operations are based on active probes because synthetic network traffic is generated strictly for the purpose of measuring a network performance characteristic of the defined operation.

> **NOTE:** A passive probe is one that captures actual network traffic flows for analysis. Examples would be a packet capture (e.g., Ethereal or Wireshark) and Cisco IOS NetFlow. Cisco IOS NetFlow is described in detail in the TSHOOT guide. It will not be described in this guide.

IP SLA has several uses and advantages, which include the following:

- IP SLA has visibility of the processing time on the device versus just the transit or on-the-wire time (passive probes), which gives a more granular and accurate measurement.
- IP SLA can differentiate among different measurements (e.g., UDP vs. ICMP or TCP statistics), so the measurement specifically reflects the current operation and not a generalized overview of the entire traffic.
- IP SLA can be used as a proactive tool since it allows traffic to be created in a controlled environment using different protocols and ports, which allows greater flexibility in terms of simulating future growth with expected traffic patterns or creating a baseline with existing benchmarks.
- IP SLA provides near-millisecond precision.
- IP SLA supports proactive notification using SNMP traps based on a defined threshold or trigger of another IP SLA operation.
- IP SLA allows for and provides historical data storage.
- IP SLA has comprehensive hardware support. Because it is integrated into Cisco IOS, it can be used on many different router and switch platforms, making this a cost-effective and scalable solution because it does not require dedicated probes.
- IP SLA can be used to monitor and measure Quality of Service (QoS) for Voice over IP (VoIP) and for videoconferencing applications.
- From a business perspective, IP SLA provides Service Level Agreement monitoring, measurements, and verification.
- IP SLA can be used to perform a network health assessment.
- Because of its flexibility, IP SLA is a very powerful network troubleshooting tool.

IP SLA Components

IP Service Level Agreement is comprised of the following two components:

1. Source
2. Target

The source, which is also sometimes referred to as the agent, is where IP SLA operations are defined. In other words, this is where the bulk of the configuration is implemented. Based on the configuration parameters, the source generates packets specific to the defined IP SLA operations, and analyzes the results and records them so they can be accessed through the Command-Line Interface (CLI) or using Simple Network Management Protocol (SNMP).

A source router can be any Cisco router or switch that can support the IP SLA operation being configured. A particular source or agent can have multiple IP SLA tests running to many remote responders. In addition, a particular router or switch can be both an agent and a responder for different IP SLA configurations.

The IP SLA target depends upon the type of IP SLA operation defined and may be a computer or an internetwork device, such as a router or a switch. For example, for IP SLA FTP or HTTP operations, the target would be an FTP or HTTP server. For Routing Table Protocol (RTP) and UDP jitter (VoIP), the target must be a Cisco device.

If the target is a Cisco device, the `ip sla responder` global configuration command must be configured on this device because both the source and the target participate in the performance measurement. The IP SLA responder has an added benefit of accuracy because it inserts in and out time-stamps into the packet payload and therefore measures the CPU time spent.

The IP SLA responder (target) is a Cisco IOS software component that is configured to respond to IP SLA request packets. The IP SLA source establishes a connection with the target using control packets before the configured IP SLA operation begins.

Following the acknowledgement of the control packets, the source then sends the responder test packets. The responder inserts a time-stamp when it receives a packet, and factors out the destination processing time and adds time-stamps to the sent packets. This allows for the calculation of unidirectional packet loss, latency, and jitter measurements with the kind of accuracy that is not possible using simple ping tests or other dedicated (passive) probe testing.

IP SLA Functional Areas

IP SLA operations can be broadly categorized into the following five functional areas:
1. Availability monitoring
2. Network monitoring
3. Application monitoring
4. Voice monitoring
5. Video monitoring

Availability monitoring can be used to monitor network-level availability and is performed primarily using ICMP and UDP packets. IP SLA availability monitoring operations are described in detail in the following section.

Network monitoring is used to monitor Layer 2 operations, such as Asynchronous Transfer Mode (ATM), Frame Relay, DLSw+, and Multiprotocol Label Switching (MPLS). ATM, Frame Relay, and DLSw+ are beyond the scope of the ROUTE exam requirements. MPLS is described later in this guide.

Application monitoring is used to monitor common network applications, which include HTTP, FTP, DHCP, and DNS. Voice monitoring is used to determine voice quality scores, Post Dial Delay

(PDD), Real Time Protocol (RTP), and gatekeeper registration delay. Video monitoring is used to monitor video traffic. No specific IP SLA tests for video monitoring exist; however, the UDP jitter operation can be used to simulate some video traffic.

IP SLA Availability Monitoring

IP SLA supports the following for availability monitoring:

- ICMP echo
- ICMP path echo
- ICMP jitter
- ICMP path jitter
- UDP echo
- UDP jitter

ICMP echo measures the end-to-end response time between a Cisco router or switch and any IP device by measuring the time between sending an ICMP echo request message to the destination and receiving an ICMP echo reply. This operation takes into account the processing time taken by the sender but cannot take into account any processing time in the target device. This is a good tool to measure availability but it does not give much indication of whether any underlying problems exist in the network or the destination host.

The ICMP path echo operation is different from the regular ICMP echo in that it first does a Traceroute to discover the path from a source to the destination and then measures the response time between the source router or switch and each of the intermittent hops in the path. It also has an option of using strict and loose source routing (LSR), which enables IP SLA to use a particular path instead of using the path discovered using Traceroute. This provides more detail on the IP addresses of the hops taken as well as any failures in the intermediate path.

The ICMP jitter operation is very similar to ICMP echo, but it also provides latency, jitter, and packet loss in addition to the round-trip measurement. Jitter, also known as IP Packet Delay Variation (IPDV), is a measurement of delay variation.

The ICMP path jitter operation is very similar to the ICMP path echo operation, but it also includes jitter operation statistics, such as latency, jitter, and packet loss on a per-hop basis. The operation first discovers the path using Traceroute, and then it sends an ICMP echo message to determine the response time, jitter, and packet loss for each of the hops.

The UDP echo operation is more useful than the ICMP echo operation because the target understands UDP echo packets; therefore, this operation accounts for the processing time taken by the target system, or responder, to generate a more accurate measurement.

The IP SLA UDP jitter operation was primarily designed to determine IP network suitability for traffic applications, such as VoIP, video over IP, or real-time conferencing. This is the only IP SLA operation that supports microsecond precision, which makes it ideal for monitoring voice, video, and other highly sensitive applications. One-way jitter accuracy depends on clock synchronization between the source and its destination. It is therefore recommended that Network Time Protocol (NTP) be used in conjunction with this for accuracy because The UDP jitter packets generated have sequencing information as well as time-stamps for both the sending and receiving sides. IP SLA UDP jitter operations are capable of measuring the following:

- Per-direction jitter (source to destination and destination to source)
- Per-direction packet loss
- Per-direction delay (one-way delay)
- Round-trip delay (average round-trip time)
- Out-of-sequence and corrupted packets

Reliable Static Routing Backup Using Object Tracking and IP SLA

While IP SLA is a monitoring tool, it can also be used for path control in conjunction with either static routes or Policy-Based Routing (PBR). PBR is described in detail later in this chapter. The Reliable Static Routing Backup Using Object Tracking feature uses Cisco IOS IP to generate ICMP pings to monitor the state of the connection to the primary gateway. Cisco IOS IP SLA is configured to ping a target, such as the link IP address of the ISP router (gateway).

A track object is then created to monitor the status of the IP SLA configuration. The track object tracks either the reachability or the state of the IP SLA operation. If reachability is lost or the state changes, a preconfigured floating static route will be installed into the IP routing table and will be used to forward packets. When the primary path is back up, the static route through the primary path is reinstalled into the routing table and is used to forward packets. This concept is illustrated in Figure 5-1 below, which shows a dual-homed Internet connection:

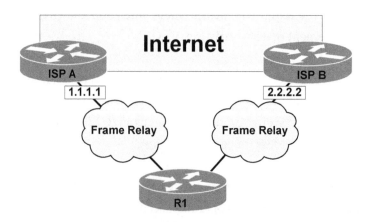

Fig. 5-1. IP SLA and Reliable Static Routing Backup Using Object Tracking

Figure 5-1 illustrates a basic network. R1 is dual-homed to ISP A and ISP B. The primary path is via ISP A. The path via ISP B should be used only in the event that the primary path is unavailable. In Frame Relay networks, it is actually possible for the link on the ISP side to fail while the local link remains up. When using dynamic routing protocols, the adjacency is destroyed and the routing table is cleared. This allows a backup floating static route to be used to send traffic across an alternate path.

However, with static routes, if the local link remains up, the static route is not removed from the routing table. This can result in a black-holing of traffic. Network monitoring with IP SLA for Reliable Static Routing Backup Using Object Tracking allows the router to determine the state of the primary connection without enabling a dynamic routing protocol.

Referencing Figure 5-1, R1 can be configured to ping the IP address of the router belonging to ISP A. If no response is received, the static route to the Internet is withdrawn from the routing table and the backup route is installed. Traffic is then forwarded using the alternate path. Following restoration of the connection between R1 and ISP A, the static route via ISP A is then installed back into the routing table and traffic flows through the primary path.

While network monitoring using IP SLA typically uses ICMP echo (ping) operations, the same can be accomplished using HTTP GET, User Datagram Protocol (UDP) echo, or any other protocol supported by IP SLA.

The Reliable Static Routing Backup Using Object Tracking and IP SLA feature is configured in the following three steps:
1. Configure the Cisco IOS IP SLA Operations
2. Configure Enhanced Object Tracking
3. Configure Floating Static Routes Using Tracked Objects

Configuring Cisco IOS IP SLA Operations

IP SLA operations are configured in global configuration mode. The configuration of the IP SLA feature depends on the software version running on the router.

In Cisco IOS software versions 12.3(14)T, 12.4, 12.4(2)T, and 12.2(33)SXH, IP SLA is configured using the `ip sla monitor [operation number]` global configuration command. In Cisco IOS 12.4(4)T and later, IP SLA is configured using the `ip sla [operation number]` global configuration command.

The `operation number` keyword used in all three variations of IP SLA configuration is an integer between 1 and 2147483647. This allows for the configuration of multiple IP SLA operations on the same device. Following IP SLA configuration in global configuration mode, the router transitions to IP SLA monitor configuration mode.

In Cisco IOS software versions 12.3(14)T, 12.4, 12.4(2)T, and 12.2(33)SXH, the IP SLA operation is configured using the `type` IP SLA monitor configuration command. Given that the most commonly used operation is to send ICMP echo packets, this would be configured using the `type echo protocol ipIcmpEcho [hostname | address] [source-ipaddr <address> | hostname]` IP SLA monitor configuration command.

In Cisco IOS 12.4T and later, the `icmp-echo [hostname | address] [source-ip <address> | hostname | source-interface <name>]` IP SLA monitor configuration command would be used to configure the same ICMP echo operation.

Three additional parameters that are commonly specified when configuring the IP SLA ICMP echo operation are timeout, frequency, and threshold. The timeout is used to specify the amount of time for which the Cisco IOS IP SLA's operation waits for a response from its request packet. This value is specified in milliseconds. The default timeout value varies depending on the type of IP SLA operation you are configuring.

The frequency is specified in seconds and is used to specify the rate at which a specified Cisco IOS IP SLA operation is sent into the network. For example, if you specify a frequency of 10 when using the ICMP echo operation, ping packets will be sent every 10 seconds.

The threshold sets the rising threshold used to generate a reaction event and stores the history information for the Cisco IOS IP SLA operation. The threshold is specified in milliseconds and the default is 5000 ms. The threshold commonly used in advanced IP SLA implementations will not be included in the configuration examples in this chapter.

After configuring the IP SLA operation and specifying additional parameters, the operation can then be enabled using the `ip sla monitor schedule [operation number]` global configuration command. While this command can be used with several parameters, parameters typically used when configuring IP SLA for use with the Reliable Static Routing Backup Using Object Tracking include the `life` keyword and the `start-time` keyword.

The `life` keyword is used to specify the length of time to execute the operation. The life can be specified in either seconds (up to 2147483647) or infinitely using the `forever` keyword. The `start-time` keyword is used to specify when the operation should begin. The most common implementation is to use the `now` keyword to begin the operation immediately. However, the operation can be configured to start at a specified time, after a specified amount of time, or on a specific date at a specific time, for example.

NOTE: After configuring and starting IP SLA operations, the results of the operations are then stored on the source device in the Cisco RTTMON MIB. This MIB can also be used to configure IP SLA operations using SNMP set commands. No explicit configuration is required to begin storing data in the Cisco RTTMOM MIB. You are not required to go into any further detail on either the Cisco RTTMON MIB or SNMP configuration for the current ROUTE exam.

Configuring Enhanced Object Tracking

Enhanced Object Tracking (EOT) allows network administrators to configure the router or the switch to track the following parameters:

- The IP routing state of an interface
- IP route reachability
- The threshold of IP-route metrics
- IP SLA operations

When EOT is configured, each tracked object is identified by a unique number that is specified on the tracking Command-Line Interface (CLI). Client processes use this number to track a specific object. The tracking process periodically polls the tracked objects and notes any change of value. The changes in the tracked object are communicated to interested client processes, either immediately or after a specified delay, depending on the tracking configuration. The object values are reported as either up or down. The advantages of EOT include the following:

- EOT increases the availability and speed of recovery of a router system
- EOT decreases outages and their duration
- EOT allows other processes to track objects or a list of objects

NOTE: EOT can also be used with HSRP, VRRP, and other processes, in addition to static routes.

EOT is configured using the Cisco IOS `track [tracked object] [parameter]` global configuration command. To track IP SLA operations, the `track [tracked object] ip sla [operation number][reachability | state]` command must be used in IOS version 12.4(4)T and later. In earlier versions, the `track [tracked object] rtr [operation number][reachability | state]` command should be issued instead.

When configuring EOT, you can specify a period of time, in seconds, to delay communicating state changes of a tracked object using the `delay [up <seconds> | down <seconds>]` track configuration mode subcommand. These subcommands configure the tracking process to send changes (as up and down values) following the specified delay values instead of sending them immediately. This is commonly used to prevent route flapping.

Configuring Floating Static Routes Using Tracked Objects

Floating static routes can be configured to track objects by appending the `track <object number>` keyword to the end of the `ip route` global configuration command. The `<object number>` is an integer between 1 and 500 that references the tracked object configured using the `track` configuration command in the previous configuration step.

> **NOTE**: Floating static routes are simply static routes that have been configured with an administrative distance that is greater than the administrative distance of dynamically learned routes. This configuration makes the static route less desirable than a dynamic route. The floating static route is not used when the dynamic route is available. However, if the dynamic route is lost, the static route is installed into the routing table and will be used to forward traffic to the destination network. When the dynamically learned route is available again, it is reinstalled into the routing table and the floating static route is no longer used.

Configuring and Verifying Reliable Static Routing Backup Using Object Tracking and IP Service Level Agreement Operations

The following configuration example shows how to implement the Cisco IOS software Reliable Static Routing Backup Using Object Tracking and the IP Service Level Agreement feature following the three steps that were described previously. In this example, the router is configured with two default routes to two ISPs. The first default route to 10.0.0.1 is the primary route. The second route, to 10.0.2.4, is the backup or alternate route.

Cisco IOS IP SLA ICMP echo operations are configured to monitor both routes and to ping the endpoint event every five seconds beginning immediately and going on for infinity. Enhanced Object Tracking is configured to track reachability for both operations. This configuration is implemented on the router as illustrated in the following configuration for Cisco IOS 12.4(4)T:

```
R2(config)#ip sla 1
R2(config-ip-sla)#icmp-echo 10.0.0.1
R2(config-ip-sla-echo)#frequency 5
R2(config-ip-sla-echo)#exit
R2(config)#ip sla 2
R2(config-ip-sla)#icmp-echo 10.0.2.4
R2(config-ip-sla-echo)#frequency 5
R2(config-ip-sla-echo)#exit
R2(config)#ip sla schedule 1 life forever start-time now
R2(config)#ip sla schedule 2 life forever start-time now
R2(config)#track 1 ip sla 1 reachability
R2(config-track)#exit
R2(config)#track 2 ip sla 2 reachability
```

```
R2(config-track)#exit
R2(config)#ip route 0.0.0.0 0.0.0.0 10.0.0.1 name PRIMARY track 1
R2(config)#ip route 0.0.0.0 0.0.0.0 10.0.2.4 5 name BACKUP track 2
```

This same configuration would be implemented in Cisco IOS versions 12.3(14)T, 12.4, 12.4(2)T, and 12.2(33)SXH as follows:

```
R2(config)#ip sla monitor 1
R2(config-sla-monitor)#type echo protocol ipIcmpEcho 10.0.0.1
R2(config-sla-monitor-echo)#frequency 5
R2(config-sla-monitor-echo)#exit
R2(config)#ip sla monitor 2
R2(config-sla-monitor)#type echo protocol ipIcmpEcho 10.0.2.4
R2(config-sla-monitor-echo)#frequency 5
R2(config-sla-monitor-echo)#exit
R2(config)#ip sla monitor schedule 1 life forever start-time now
R2(config)#ip sla monitor schedule 2 life forever start-time now
R2(config)#track 1 rtr 1 reachability
R2(config-track)#exit
R2(config)#track 2 rtr 2 reachability
R2(config-track)#exit
R2(config)#ip route 0.0.0.0 0.0.0.0 10.0.0.1 name PRIMARY track 1
R2(config)#ip route 0.0.0.0 0.0.0.0 10.0.2.4 5 name BACKUP track 2
```

Both configurations work in the same way. Referencing the two configurations, the IP SLA configuration can be validated using the show ip sla statistics [operation number] or the show ip sla monitor statistics [operation number] commands. The output of the show ip sla statistics [operation number] is illustrated as follows:

```
R2#show ip sla statistics 1
IPSLAs Latest Operations Statistics

IP SLAs operation id: 1
        Latest RTT: 1 ms
Latest operation start time: *18:23:10.708 CST Fri Mar 1 2002
Latest operation return code: OK
Number of successes: 102
Number of failures: 0
Operation time to live: Forever
```

The output of the show ip sla monitor statistics [operation number] command has a slightly different output but it includes all the same information as illustrated below:

```
R2#show ip sla monitor statistics 2
Round trip time (RTT)    Index 2
        Latest RTT: 1 ms
Latest operation start time: *18:23:14.181 CST Fri Mar 1 2002
```

```
Latest operation return code: OK
Number of successes: 134
Number of failures: 0
Operation time to live: Forever
```

The actual configuration parameters can be validated via the show ip sla configuration [operation number] or show ip sla monitor configuration [operation number] commands. The relevant key fields in both commands are the same. These key fields are highlighted in bold in the following output:

```
R2#show ip sla monitor configuration 1
IP SLA Monitor, Infrastructure Engine-II.
Entry number: 1
Owner:
Tag:
Type of operation to perform: echo
Target address: 10.0.0.1
Request size (ARR data portion): 28
Operation timeout (milliseconds): 5000
Type Of Service parameters: 0x0
Verify data: No
Operation frequency (seconds): 5
Next Scheduled Start Time: Start Time already passed
Group Scheduled : FALSE
Life (seconds): Forever
Entry Ageout (seconds): never
Recurring (Starting Everyday): FALSE
Status of entry (SNMP RowStatus): Active
Threshold (milliseconds): 5000
Number of statistic hours kept: 2
Number of statistic distribution buckets kept: 1
Statistic distribution interval (milliseconds): 20
Number of history Lives kept: 0
Number of history Buckets kept: 15
History Filter Type: None
Enhanced History:
```

To verify the EOT configuration, the show track [object number] command is used. The output of this command is similar for both IOS versions. 12.4(4)T prints the following:

```
R2#show track 1
Track 1
  IP SLA 1 reachability
  Reachability is Up
    9 changes, last change 00:05:13
  Latest operation return code: OK
  Latest RTT (millisecs) 1
  Tracked by:
    STATIC-IP-ROUTING 0
```

Cisco IOS versions 12.3(14)T, 12.4, 12.4(2)T, and 12.2(33)SXH print the following:

```
R2#show track 2
Track 2
  Response Time Reporter 2 reachability
  Reachability is Up
    1 change, last change 00:42:19
  Latest operation return code: OK
  Latest RTT (millisecs) 1
  Tracked by:
    STATIC-IP-ROUTING 0
```

To verify static route tracking, the show ip route track-table command can be used. The output of this command is illustrated below:

```
R2#show ip route track-table
 ip route 0.0.0.0 0.0.0.0 10.0.0.1 name PRIMARY track 1 state is [up]
 ip route 0.0.0.0 0.0.0.0 10.0.2.4 5 name BACKUP track 2 state is [up]
```

Based on the configuration implemented on the router, the default route to 10.0.0.1 is installed into the routing table as can be seen in the following output of the show ip route command:

```
R2#show ip route | begin Gateway
Gateway of last resort is 10.0.0.1 to network 0.0.0.0

     10.0.0.0/24 is subnetted, 2 subnets
C       10.0.2.0 is directly connected, Serial0/0
C       10.0.0.0 is directly connected, FastEthernet0/0
S*   0.0.0.0/0 [1/0] via 10.0.0.1
```

We can verify the dynamic failover by disabling the link between R2 and ISP A, which is the FastEthernet0/0 interface. This changes the state of IP SLA operation 1 to down as follows:

```
R2(config)#interface FastEthernet0/0
R2(config-if)#shutdown
R2(config-if)#
*Mar  2 01:03:37.790: %LINK-5-CHANGED: Interface FastEthernet0/0, changed
state to administratively down
*Mar  2 01:03:38.792: %LINEPROTO-5-UPDOWN: Line protocol on Interface
FastEthernet0/0, changed state to down
*Mar  2 01:03:41.657: %TRACKING-5-STATE: 1 IP SLA 1 reachability Up->Down
```

The tracking table now displays the following state for the primary route:

```
R2#show ip route track-table
 ip route 0.0.0.0 0.0.0.0 10.0.0.1 name PRIMARY track 1 state is [down]
 ip route 0.0.0.0 0.0.0.0 10.0.2.4 5 name BACKUP track 2 state is [up]
```

The backup route with the administrative distance of 5 is installed into the routing table as illustrated in the following output:

```
R2#show ip route | begin Gateway
Gateway of last resort is 10.0.2.4 to network 0.0.0.0

     10.0.0.0/24 is subnetted, 1 subnets
C       10.0.2.0 is directly connected, Serial0/0
S*   0.0.0.0/0 [5/0] via 10.0.2.4
```

When the primary path is restored and the IP SLA operation verifies reachability to the 10.0.0.1 address, the route is installed into the routing table and the backup path is withdrawn:

```
R2(config)#interface FastEthernet0/0
R2(config-if)#no shutdown
R2(config-if)#
*Mar  2 01:06:05.609: %LINK-3-UPDOWN: Interface FastEthernet0/0, changed
state to up
*Mar  2 01:06:07.608: %LINEPROTO-5-UPDOWN: Line protocol on Interface
FastEthernet0/0, changed state to up
*Mar  2 01:06:21.663: %TRACKING-5-STATE: 1 IP SLA 1 reachability Down->Up
```

The routing table reflects this change as illustrated in the following output:

```
R2#show ip route | begin Gateway
Gateway of last resort is 10.0.0.1 to network 0.0.0.0

     10.0.0.0/24 is subnetted, 2 subnets
C       10.0.2.0 is directly connected, Serial0/0
C       10.0.0.0 is directly connected, FastEthernet0/0
S*   0.0.0.0/0 [1/0] via 10.0.0.1
```

You can also configure the router to monitor the state of the route using the track [object number] [parameter] state command. State tracking is the default if the reachability keyword is not configured. Additionally, you can configure delay values instructing the tracking process to send changes (as up and down values) following the specified delay values instead of sending them immediately. For example, configure EOT to track the state of IP SLA Operation 1, wait 30 seconds before notifying that the state of this tracked object is down, and wait 60 seconds before notifying that the object state is now up as illustrated below:

```
R2(config)#track 1 ip sla 1
R2(config-track)#delay down 30 up 60
R2(config-track)#exit
```

This configuration can be validated using the show track [object number] command:

```
R2#show track 1
Track 1
  IP SLA 1 state
  State is Up
    11 changes, last change 00:14:17
  Delay up 60 secs, down 30 secs
  Latest operation return code: OK
  Latest RTT (millisecs) 1
  Tracked by:
    STATIC-IP-ROUTING 0
```

The same test performed in the previous examples can be used to verify the following configuration:

```
R2(config)#interface FastEthernet0/0
R2(config-if)#shutdown
R2(config-if)#
*Mar  2 01:22:02.321: %LINK-5-CHANGED: Interface FastEthernet0/0, changed
state to administratively down
*Mar  2 01:22:03.323: %LINEPROTO-5-UPDOWN: Line protocol on Interface
FastEthernet0/0, changed state to down
*Mar  2 01:22:36.701: %TRACKING-5-STATE: 1 IP SLA 1 state Up->Down
```

Referencing the timestamps in the output above, we can see that the link protocol for Fa0/0 was logged as being down at 01:22:03. The tracked object was logged as being down at 01:22:36, which is approximately 30 seconds later as specified by the delay down 30 track configuration commands. Again, the secondary path is installed into the routing table as illustrated below:

```
R2#show ip route 0.0.0.0 0.0.0.0
Routing entry for 0.0.0.0/0, supernet
  Known via "static", distance 5, metric 0, candidate default path
  Routing Descriptor Blocks:
  * 10.0.2.4
      Route metric is 0, traffic share count is 1
```

To verify the configuration of the delay up 60 track configuration command, the Fa0/0 interface is simply re-enabled as follows:

```
R2(config)#interface FastEthernet0/0
R2(config-if)#no shutdown
R2(config-if)#
*Mar  2 01:26:57.994: %LINK-3-UPDOWN: Interface FastEthernet0/0, changed
state to up
*Mar  2 01:26:59.376: %LINEPROTO-5-UPDOWN: Line protocol on Interface
FastEthernet0/0, changed state to up
*Mar  2 01:28:11.715: %TRACKING-5-STATE: 1 IP SLA 1 state Down->Up
```

Referencing the timestamps in bold font above, a little over a minute elapses following the line protocol state change on Fa0/0 before the object state transitions from down to up. It is important to remember that the configured times may, and often do, vary by a few seconds, depending on the additional tasks the router is performing, resource utilization, etc.

CISCO IOS EMBEDDED EVENT MANAGER

Cisco IOS Embedded Event Manager (EEM) is yet another tool that can be used for availability monitoring. EEM is a powerful and flexible subsystem that provides real-time network event detection and onboard automation. EEM also increases the intelligence of network devices, allowing them to act on and facilitate management actions for specific network events. A series of event detector processes designed to monitor explicit operational aspects of the switch are built into Cisco IOS Software. These can be primed to look for a specific event, and when that event occurs, they can act as a trigger to start up a user-loaded script. These scripts are programmed either using simple Command-Line Interface (CLI) commands or using a scripting language called Tool Command Language (Tcl).

> **NOTE:** You are not required to implement any IOS EEM configurations in the current ROUTE exam. The following section is included only to demonstrate the configuration and verification of a basic CLI EEM implementation using Cisco IOS software.

Configuring and Verifying Cisco IOS Embedded Event Manager

When using the CLI to configure EEM, you must first configure an EEM applet. The EEM applet is a simple form of policy that is defined within the CLI configuration using the `event manager applet [name]` global configuration command. After you have configured the EEM applet, the router then transitions to EEM applet configuration mode. This configuration mode supports three commands, which are `event`, `action`, and `set` commands.

The `event` commands are used to specify the event criteria that trigger the applet to run. The `action` commands are used to specify an action to perform when the EEM applet is triggered. Finally, the `set` command is used to set the value of an EEM applet variable. Following the configuration, the `show event manager policy registered` command can then be used to display a list of registered applets.

The following configuration example shows how to configure a basic EEM applet using the CLI. This applet will be triggered when the message "`Serial0/0, changed state to down`" is logged by the router. When triggered by this event, the applet will print a Syslog message that reads "`Switch To Backup`" and then configure a default route via Serial0/1. This configuration is implemented as follows:

```
R2(config)#event manager applet INSTALL-BACKUP-ROUTE
R2(config-applet)#event syslog pattern "Serial0/0, changed state to down"
R2(config-applet)#action 1.1 syslog msg "Switch To Backup"
R2(config-applet)#action 1.2 cli command "enable"
R2(config-applet)#action 1.3 cli command "configure terminal"
R2(config-applet)#action 1.4 cli command "ip route 0.0.0.0 0.0.0.0 Se0/1"
R2(config-applet)#exit
```

Next, another EEM applet is configured to monitor the router log for the message "Serial0/0, changed state to up". When this message is seen, the applet is triggered and prints the message "Switch To Primary". The applet is then configured to remove the previously configured static route via Serial0/1, allowing traffic to the Internet to flow through the Serial0/0 interface, which is the primary path to the Internet. This is implemented as follows:

```
R2(config)#event manager applet RESTORE-PRIMARY-ROUTE
R2(config-applet)#event syslog pattern "Serial0/0, changed state to up"
R2(config-applet)#action 1.1 syslog msg "Switch To Primary"
R2(config-applet)#action 1.2 cli command "enable"
R2(config-applet)#action 1.3 cli command "configure terminal"
R2(config-applet)#action 1.4 cli command "no ip route 0.0.0.0 0.0.0.0 se 0/1"
R2(config-applet)#exit
```

Before verifying the EEM configuration, the current state of the routing table is verified and shows the default route pointing out the Serial0/0 interface as illustrated below:

```
R2#show ip route | b Gateway
Gateway of last resort is 0.0.0.0 to network 0.0.0.0

     10.0.0.0/24 is subnetted, 2 subnets
C       10.0.2.0 is directly connected, Serial0/1
C       10.0.0.0 is directly connected, Serial0/0
S*   0.0.0.0/0 is directly connected, Serial0/0
```

To test this configuration, the Serial0/0 interface is disabled using the shutdown command:

```
R2(config)#interface Serial0/0
R2(config-if)#shutdown
R2(config-if)#
*Mar  2 02:00:55.630: %LINK-5-CHANGED: Interface Serial0/0, changed state to
administratively down
*Mar  2 02:00:56.632: %LINEPROTO-5-UPDOWN: Line protocol on Interface
Serial0/0, changed state to down
*Mar  2 02:00:56.648: %HA_EM-6-LOG: INSTALL-BACKUP-ROUTE: Switch To Backup
```

When the "Serial0/0, changed state to down" message is logged, Cisco IOS EEM prints the configured message, which states that the backup path is being used, and the router is then transparently configured using the commands specified for the applet configuration. The routing table on R2 now displays the following entries:

```
R2#show ip route | b Gateway
Gateway of last resort is 0.0.0.0 to network 0.0.0.0

     10.0.0.0/24 is subnetted, 1 subnets
C       10.0.2.0 is directly connected, Serial0/1
S*   0.0.0.0/0 is directly connected, Serial0/1
```

To verify the operation of the restoration configuration, Serial0/0 is enabled as follows:

```
R2(config)#interface Serial0/0
R2(config-if)#no shutdown
R2(config-if)#
*Mar  2 02:02:00: %LINK-3-UPDOWN: Interface Serial0/0, changed state to up
*Mar  2 02:02:00: %HA_EM-6-LOG: RESTORE-PRIMARY-ROUTE: Switching To Primary
```

The backup static route is removed and the routing table on R2 displays the following:

```
R2#show ip route | b Gateway
Gateway of last resort is 0.0.0.0 to network 0.0.0.0

     10.0.0.0/24 is subnetted, 2 subnets
C       10.0.2.0 is directly connected, Serial0/1
C       10.0.0.0 is directly connected, Serial0/0
S*   0.0.0.0/0 is directly connected, Serial0/0
```

While the example above is a very basic example of the capabilities of EEM, the flexibility that is afforded by EEM allows for advanced configurations. For example, EEM can be used in conjunction with IP SLA and SNMP notifications, and then implement the desired configuration or action on the router. The capabilities of EEM are limited only by your imagination.

VIRTUAL ROUTING AND FORWARDING

Virtual Routing and Forwarding (VRF) allows multiple routing table instances to co-exist on the same physical router at the same time by creating logical routing tables for each VRF. A VRF routing table is also referred to as a Virtual Private Network (VPN) routing table. The routing instances of each VPN routing table are independent of each other. This allows the same or overlapping IP address space to be used within the different VPNs.

While VRF is commonly implemented by Internet Service Providers using Multiprotocol Label Switching (MPLS) networks, a simpler form, referred to as VRF Lite or Multi-VRF, is also commonly used within enterprise networks to segregate Layer 3 traffic. Within the enterprise, VRF Lite can be used to perform Layer 3 segregation of network traffic for different departments within the same organization, for example. The same IP address space can be allocated to all departments, without creating any conflicts.

Another example might be separating the management network from the production network. Yet another example might be separating guest traffic from corporate traffic. The traffic belonging to the different VRFs can then be routed over different paths, some of which may even traverse the same physical devices. This concept is illustrated in Figure 5-2 below:

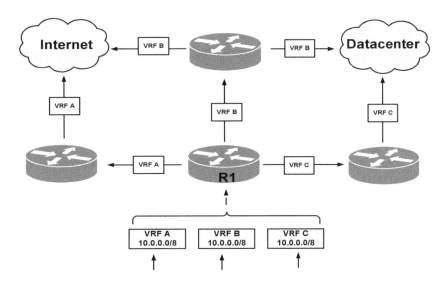

Fig. 5-2. Virtual Routing and Forwarding

In Figure 5-2, multiple VRFs have been configured on R1. All of the VRFs are using the 10.0.0.0/8 address space. Because the routing tables for each VRF are independent instances, this configuration is supported. In addition, given the illustrated VRF implementation, R1 forwards traffic in different VRFs through different paths as defined by the administrators. For example, users in VRF A will never have access to the datacenter. Similarly, based on the configuration, users in VRF C have no access to the Internet. However, users in VRF B have access to both the datacenter and the Internet.

NOTE: You are not required to implement any IOS VRF configurations in the current ROUTE exam. The following section is included only to demonstrate the configuration and verification of a basic VRF Lite implementation using Cisco IOS software.

Implementing Virtual Routing and Forwarding Lite

While the configuration of VRF is technically beyond the scope of the current ROUTE exam requirements, you should have a basic understanding of how to configure and verify VRF Lite in Cisco IOS software. VRF Lite implementation, configuration, and verification is described in this and the following sections.

In Cisco IOS software, the configuration of VRF Lite is a simple task. First, the VRF name must be defined using the `ip vrf [name]` global configuration command. Next, a route distinguisher is assigned to the VRF using the `rd [route distinguisher]` VRF configuration command. The route distinguisher is used to identify the VPN and is used to distinguish multiple VPN routes that have an identical prefix. The route distinguisher can be configured using either ASN:*nn* or IP-address:*nn* format.

NOTE: The *n* simply represents an integer. You can use and specify one integer or two integers.

Next, assign an interface to a particular VRF using the `ip vrf forwarding [name]` interface configuration command. Finally, configure either static routing or a dynamic routing protocol for VRF. In Cisco IOS software, supported dynamic IGP routing protocols include OSPF, EIGRP, and RIPv2. VRF Lite is not supported in IS-IS.

In Cisco IOS software, VRF Lite using OSPF is configured using the `router ospf [process ID] vrf [name]` global configuration command followed by the `capability vrf-lite` router configuration command. The remainder of the configuration (e.g., `network` statements) is performed in a similar manner to when VRF Lite is not being used.

For EIGRP and RIPv2, VRF configuration is implemented using the `address-family ipv4 vrf [name]` router configuration command. In addition, for EIGRP, the `autonomous-system [number]` VRF configuration subcommand must be used to specify the autonomous system number. Static routes for each VRF can be configured using the `ip route vrf [prefix] [mask] [interface | address]` global configuration command.

Configuring and Verifying Virtual Routing and Forwarding Lite

Figure 5-3 below shows a basic network. R1 is connected to router R2. R1 and R2 are running VRF Lite. The FastEthernet0/0-to-FastEthernet0/0 link between R1 and R2, respectively, is assigned to and is used for traffic in VRF-A. The FastEthernet0/1-to-FastEthernet0/1 link between R1 and R2, respectively, is assigned to and is used for traffic in VRF-B. Both VRFs are using the 10.10.0.0/16 address space. OSPF will be used on the FastEthernet0/0-to-FastEthernet0/0 link between R1 and R2, respectively, while EIGRP is used for the FastEthernet0/1-to-FastEthernet0/1 link that is between R1 and R2, respectively. The network topology is illustrated below:

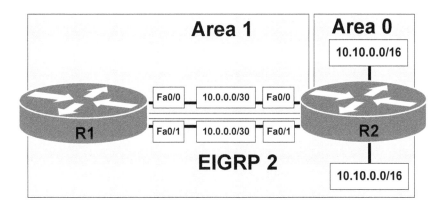

Fig. 5-3. Configuring and Verifying VRF Lite

The first task when configuring VRF Lite is to configure the VRF name and assign it a route distinguisher. This is implemented as follows on router R1:

```
R1(config)#ip vrf VRF-A
R1(config-vrf)#rd 1:1
R1(config-vrf)#exit
R1(config)#ip vrf VRF-B
R1(config-vrf)#rd 2:2
R1(config-vrf)#exit
```

A similar configuration is also implemented on router R2 as illustrated below:

```
R2(config)#ip vrf VRF-A
R2(config-vrf)#rd 1:1
R2(config-vrf)#exit
R2(config)#ip vrf VRF-B
R2(config-vrf)#rd 2:2
R2(config-vrf)#exit
```

Next, the interfaces are assigned to the configured VRFs on router R1 as illustrated below:

```
R1(config)#interface FastEthernet0/0
R1(config-if)#ip vrf forwarding VRF-A
R1(config-if)#ip address 10.0.0.1 255.255.255.252
R1(config-if)#exit
R1(config)#interface FastEthernet0/1
R1(config-if)#ip vrf forwarding VRF-B
R1(config-if)#ip address 10.0.0.1 255.255.255.252
R1(config-if)#exit
```

A similar configuration is also implemented on router R2 as illustrated in the following output:

```
R2(config)#interface Fastethernet0/0
R2(config-if)#ip vrf forwarding VRF-A
R2(config-if)#ip address 10.0.0.2 255.255.255.252
R2(config-if)#exit
R2(config)#interface FastEthernet0/1
R2(config-if)#ip vrf forwarding VRF-B
R2(config-if)#ip address 10.0.0.2 255.255.255.252
R2(config-if)#exit
```

NOTE: When an interface is assigned to or removed from a particular VRF, the interface IP address is removed by default. This is illustrated in the following output:

```
R1(config)#interface FastEthernet0/1
R1(config-if)#ip address 10.0.0.1 255.255.255.252
R1(config-if)#ip vrf forwarding VRF-B
% Interface FastEthernet0/1 IP address 10.0.0.1 removed due to enabling VRF
VRF-B
R1(config-if)#exit
R1(config)#interface FastEthernet0/1
R1(config-if)#no ip vrf forwarding VRF-B
% Interface FastEthernet0/1 IP address 10.0.0.1 removed due to disabling VRF
VRF-B
```

Therefore, when assigning an interface to a VRF, configure the VRF first, and then assign the IP address. It saves the additional step of having to re-specify the IP address again.

Continuing with the VRF Lite configuration example, this initial configuration can be validated using the show ip vrf [<name> | brief | detail | id <name> | interfaces <name>] command. On R1, the show ip vrf detail command prints out the following:

```
R1#show ip vrf detail
VRF VRF-A; default RD 1:1; default VPNID <not set>
  Interfaces:
    Fa0/0
  Connected addresses are not in global routing table
  No Export VPN route-target communities
  No Import VPN route-target communities
  No import route-map
  No export route-map
  VRF label distribution protocol: not configured
VRF VRF-B; default RD 2:2; default VPNID <not set>
  Interfaces:
    Fa0/1
  Connected addresses are not in global routing table
  No Export VPN route-target communities
  No Import VPN route-target communities
  No import route-map
  No export route-map
  VRF label distribution protocol: not configured
```

The third step is to configure the routing protocol. First, OSPF will be configured for the Partner 1 VRF. This configuration is implemented on R1 as follows:

```
R1(config)#router ospf 1 vrf VRF-A
R1(config-router)#router-id 1.1.1.1
R1(config-router)#network 10.0.0.0 0.0.0.3 Area 1
R1(config-router)#capability vrf-lite
R1(config-router)#exit
```

The OSPF VRF Lite configuration on R2 is implemented as follows:

```
R2(config)#router ospf 1 vrf VRF-A
R2(config-router)#router-id 2.2.2.2
R2(config-router)#network 10.10.0.0 0.0.255.255 Area 0
R2(config-router)#network 10.0.0.0 0.0.0.3 Area 1
R2(config-router)#capability vrf-lite
R2(config-router)#exit
```

Following this configuration, the `show ip ospf neighbor` command is used to verify that the adjacency between R1 and R2 has been established.

```
R1#show ip ospf neighbor

Neighbor ID     Pri   State       Dead Time   Address     Interface
2.2.2.2           0   FULL/  -    00:00:39    10.0.0.2    FastEthernet0/0
```

> **NOTE:** For simplicity, the LAN segment has been configured as a point-to-point network type, which is why there is no DR/BDR elected for this segment. This is not a requirement when configuring VRF Lite. However, it prevents the unnecessary Type 2 LSA for this LAN segment.

When VRF Lite is configured, the `show ip route vrf [name]` command must be used to view the routing table(s) for each VRF. If you do not specify the VRF name, the command will show the contents of the global IP routing table only, and not for any VRFs. The routing table for VRF-A displays the following entry on R1 based on the implemented configurations:

```
R1#show ip route vrf VRF-A | begin Gateway
Gateway of last resort is not set

     10.0.0.0/8 is variably subnetted, 2 subnets, 2 masks
O IA    10.10.0.0/16 [110/2] via 10.0.0.2, 00:03:49, FastEthernet0/0
C       10.0.0.0/30 is directly connected, FastEthernet0/0
```

Next, EIGRP will be configured for VRF-B. This configuration is implemented on R1 as follows:

```
R1(config)#router eigrp 1
```

```
R1(config-router)#no auto-summary
R1(config-router)#address-family ipv4 vrf VRF-B
R1(config-router-af)#autonomous-system 2
R1(config-router-af)#network 10.0.0.0 0.0.0.3
R1(config-router-af)#no auto-summary
R1(config-router-af)#exit
```

In the output above, EIGRP Autonomous System 1 is the global routing process for the business. The VRF configuration for Partner 2 is configured in address-family mode, and the autonomous system and any networks for the Partner 2 VRF are specified there.

The show ip eigrp vrf [name] neighbors command can be used to verify the EIGRP neighbor relationship(s) for the specified VRF as shown in the following output:

```
R1#show ip eigrp vrf VRF-B neighbors
IP-EIGRP neighbors for process 2
H   Address              Interface        Hold Uptime    SRTT   RTO   Q   Seq
                                          (sec)          (ms)         Cnt  Num
0   10.0.0.2             Fa0/1            13 00:00:13     4    200   0   3
```

Again, the show ip route vrf [name] command is used to view the routing table for the VRF configured for Partner 2. The output of this command displays the following:

```
R1#show ip route vrf VRF-B | begin Gateway
Gateway of last resort is not set

     10.0.0.0/8 is variably subnetted, 2 subnets, 2 masks
D       10.10.0.0/16 [90/156160] via 10.0.0.2, 00:11:28, FastEthernet0/1
C       10.0.0.0/30 is directly connected, FastEthernet0/1
```

To verify reachability to the 10.10.0.0/16 subnets of Partner 1 and Partner 2, a simple ping using the ping vrf [name] command is used as illustrated in the following output:

```
R1#ping vrf VRF-A 10.10.0.2

Type escape sequence to abort.
Sending 5, 100-byte ICMP Echos to 10.10.0.2, timeout is 2 seconds:
!!!!!
Success rate is 100 percent (5/5), round-trip min/avg/max = 1/2/4 ms

R1#ping vrf VRF-B 10.10.0.2

Type escape sequence to abort.
Sending 5, 100-byte ICMP Echos to 10.10.0.2, timeout is 2 seconds:
!!!!!
Success rate is 100 percent (5/5), round-trip min/avg/max = 1/2/4 ms
```

While simple to deploy and appropriate for small to medium-sized enterprises, as well as shared data center environments, VRF Lite does not scale to the size required by global enterprises or large carriers, as there is the need to implement each VRF instance on every router or Layer 3 switch within the network. Additional configuration is also required to leak routes between the different VRFs to allow connectivity to shared resources.

CISCO PERFORMANCE ROUTING

Cisco Performance Routing (PfR) leverages the intelligence that is integrated into Cisco IOS software to determine the optimal path based on network and application policies. PfR can be used to detect automatically the degradation of a path and respond accordingly to avoid any further degradation. Cisco PfR policies can be based on the following parameters:

- WAN outbound performance: Delay, loss, reachability, throughput, jitter, and MOS
- WAN inbound performance: Delay, loss, reachability, and throughput
- WAN and Internet path parameters: Reachability, throughput, load, and link usage cost

PfR routing is different from classic routing, which is based only on reachability, and does take into consideration traffic service needs, such as low loss or low delay. In addition, Cisco PfR allows a multi-homed enterprise to use all available WAN or Internet links by tracking throughput, link usage, and link cost, and automatically determines the best load balancing to optimize throughput, load, and cost. PfR consists of two elements, which are as follows:

1. Border routers
2. Master controller

The border routers connect enterprises to the WAN or the Internet. These routers gather traffic and path information that they then send to the master controller, which places all information received from the border routers into a database.

The master controller is a software entity supported by Cisco IOS software on a router platform. The master controller is configured with the requested service policies, so it is aware of everything that happens at the network edge and can automatically detect and take action when certain parameters are out-of-policy (OOP). Figure 5-4 below illustrates a typical PfR deployment:

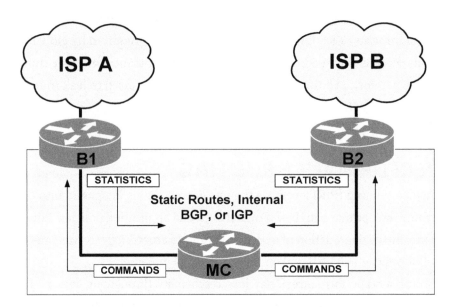

Fig. 5-4. Understanding Cisco Performance Routing (PfR)

Referencing Figure 5-4, border routers, B1 and B2, which are connected to two different Internet Service Providers (ISPs), send statistics to the master controller, router MC. The master controller sends relevant commands to the border routers, depending on policy configuration implemented on the router. For example, if the link between border router B1 and ISP A is congested, the master controller may send Internet-bound traffic via the link between border router B2 and ISP B instead by injecting routes on router B2 based on policy configuration.

This overall solution allows for routing based on network performance and is not dependent on NetFlow, Cisco IOS IP SLA, or other Cisco IOS software features explicitly on either the master controller or the border router. PfR is its own technology, although it may be used in conjunction with other Cisco IOS software technologies, as will be described later in this section.

Implementing Cisco Performance Routing

Cisco PfR is supported natively in Cisco IOS software and requires no additional licensing to enable this functionality, other than a supported IOS image. In order to run PfR, the border routers must be configured to run Cisco Express Forwarding (CEF). Additionally, the master controller must be able to communicate with and reach all border routers.

NOTE: Cisco Express Forwarding (CEF) operates at the data plane and is a topology-driven proprietary switching mechanism that creates a forwarding table that is tied to the routing table (i.e., the control plane). CEF will be described later in this chapter; however, more detailed information on CEF can be found in the SWITCH guide in the chapter on Multilayer Switching.

In Cisco IOS software, the initial implementation of Cisco PfR uses Cisco IOS Optimized Edge Routing (OER) techniques. In other words, PfR functions are enabled using OER CLI commands. OER was introduced in Cisco IOS version 12.3(8)T, with additional features added in Cisco IOS versions 12.3(11)T, 12.3(14)T, and 12.4(2)T.

When implementing PfR, the minimum design requirement is for at least one master controller function, one border router function, and two WAN links. However, both master controller and border router functions can be implemented on the same router. In addition, it is mandatory that the border router must be in the traffic forwarding path; that is, packets to the WAN or Internet must physically traverse the border router. However, this requirement is not mandatory for the master controller, which does not have to be in the forwarding path. As of the time of writing this text, the master controller can manage up to 10 border routers.

When implementing PfR, each border router must be configured as follows:
- The border router must have Cisco Express Forwarding (CEF) enabled
- The session between the border router and the master controller must be authenticated
- The local PfR interface must be able to communicate with the master controller
- The border router must be configured with the IP address of the master controller

When implementing PfR, the master controller must be configured as follows:
- The master controller must be configured with the IP addresses of all its border routers
- PfR policies must be configured on the master controller
- The session between the border router and the master controller must be authenticated

PfR Traffic Classes, Prefixes, and Monitoring

PfR monitors performance for selected prefixes or traffic classes. When implementing PfR, you must specify the prefixes or traffic classes to monitor, as well as what aspects of performance to monitor for those prefixes or traffic classes. A traffic class is a combination of prefix, protocol, port numbers, and Differentiated Services Code Point (DSCP) values.

NOTE: DSCP is described in detail in the SWITCH guide in the chapter on LAN Quality of Service. A basic overview of DSCP will be provided later in this chapter.

In Cisco IOS software, PfR can be instructed to learn these interesting elements through manual router configuration using dynamic learning based on Cisco IOS NetFlow technology. PfR monitors the set of prefixes or traffic classes using the following three methods of performance measurement, which are described in the following sections:

1. Passive monitoring
2. Active monitoring
3. Active and passive monitoring

Passive monitoring is used to measure the performance metrics of interesting prefixes while the traffic is flowing through the device using NetFlow. NetFlow data captures delay and throughput statistics. The delay measurements are based on TCP RTT. The data also records TCP packet loss and reachability.

Active monitoring is enabled via the generation of a stream of traffic replicating the interesting traffic classes as closely as possible in order to measure the performance metrics of this traffic. Active probing can be configured to use IP SLA operations, and metrics used include delay, reachability, MOS, and jitter, which can be measured using SLA ICMP echoes, TCP connections, and UDP echoes, as was described earlier in this chapter. Finally, active and passive monitoring uses both active and passive monitoring functions to generate a more complete picture of traffic flows within the network.

> **NOTE:** PfR configuration will not be illustrated in this chapter or in the remainder of this guide for the simple reason that there are far too many ways in which PfR can be implemented, meaning there is no 'one-size-fits-all' implementation. Additionally, the configuration of PfR exceeds the required level of knowledge for the current ROUTE exam.

PATH CONTROL USING ROUTE REDISTRIBUTION

Route redistribution, which was described in detail in the previous chapter, is another tool that can be used for path control. Path control can be implemented by redistributing the same or different routes with higher metrics at the ASBR, effectively ensuring that internal routers will prefer the path with the lowest metric to reach the external destination network.

When using different metrics during route redistribution, if only one protocol is configured to use different metrics, this will typically result in asymmetric routing as shown in Figure 5-5 below:

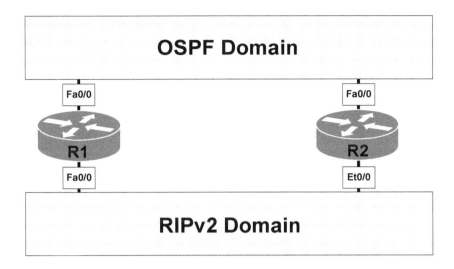

Fig. 5-5. Asymmetric Routing During Redistribution

Figure 5-5 shows a basic network running RIPv2 and OSPF. The RIPv2 domain is connected to R1 via a FastEthernet link and to R2 via an Ethernet link. Network administrators decide to ensure that the RIPv2 domain uses the path via R1 to reach subnets in the OSPF domain. The path through R2 will be used as a secondary path. In order to influence this path selection, the administrators configure RIPv2 to redistribute OSPF routes as follows on R1:

```
R1(config)#router rip
R1(config-router)#redistribute ospf 1 metric 1
R1(config-router)#exit
```

RIPv2 is configured to redistribute OSPF routes on R2 as follows:

```
R2(config)#router rip
R2(config-router)#redistribute ospf 2 metric 2
R2(config-router)#exit
```

Given the configuration above, RIP prefers the path to the OSPF domain via R1 because these routes have a lower metric (hop count). Because the OSPF domain is connected to R1 and R2 using FastEthernet links, administrators decide simply to redistribute RIP into OSPF using the default OSPF metrics. The redistribution configuration on R1 is implemented as follows:

```
R1(config)#router ospf 1
R1(config-router)#redistribute rip subnets
R1(config-router)#exit
```

The same configuration is also applied to R2 as illustrated in the following output:

```
R2(config)#router ospf 2
R2(config-router)#redistribute rip subnets
R2(config-router)#exit
```

Given this implementation, the RIPv2 domain has a single preferred path to the OSPF domain; however, the OSPF domain has two equal-cost paths to the RIPv2 domain, resulting in asymmetric routing. While typically not an issue in such a network, consideration should be given to implementing a symmetric routing solution when using stateful firewalls as is illustrated in the modified topology in Figure 5-6 below:

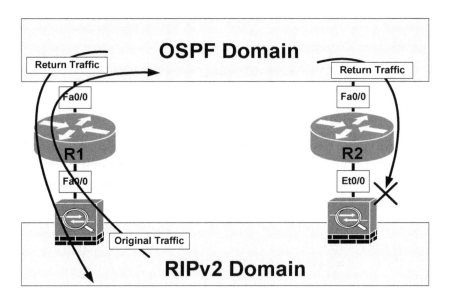

Fig. 5-6. Asymmetric Routing with Stateful Firewalls

Figure 5-6 shows the same basic network that is illustrated in Figure 5-5, with the addition of two stateful firewalls, such as the Cisco ASA firewalls. Based on the configurations implemented on R1 and R2 in the previous section, traffic from the RIPv2 domain to the OSPF domain flows through the firewall connected to R1 en route to its destination.

Traffic from the OSPF domain has two valid equal cost paths through R1 and R2. The return packets from the OSPF domain to the RIPv2 domain are therefore sent using both paths. Referencing the arrows in Figure 5-6, the return traffic through R1 will be permitted by the stateful firewall because the traffic originated inside the RIPv2 domain and the stateful firewall knows about this traffic. At this point, everything works well.

However, because no traffic from the RIPv2 domain was sent to the OSPF domain via router R2 due to the stateful firewall, the RIPv2 domain does not know about any internally originated sessions and therefore denies the return traffic. Such a situation may cause intermittent connectivity issues between the RIPv2 and OSPF domains. The recommended solution would therefore be to implement a symmetric routing solution. For example, the configuration on R1 could be modified as follows to ensure that the path through R1 is the preferred path to the RIP domain:

```
R1(config)#router ospf 1
R1(config-router)#redistribute rip subnets metric 10
R1(config-router)#exit
```

An alternative solution would be to redistribute the routes into OSPF on R2 with a higher metric as illustrated in the following configuration:

```
R2(config)#router ospf 2
R2(config-router)#redistribute rip subnets metric 30
R2(config-router)#exit
```

CISCO IOS POLICY-BASED ROUTING

In this section, we will learn about Policy-Based Routing (PBR) and the application of this tool in Cisco IOS software. However, before delving into the specifics of PBR, it is important to have a fundamental understanding of the forwarding process in Cisco IOS routers.

Routing or Forwarding Packets through Cisco Routers

To route or forward the packets that it has received, the router must perform the following:

- The router must make a routing decision using routing
- The router must forward packets to the next-hop destination using switching

The router makes a routing decision by determining whether the packet's destination is reachable by checking for a valid entry for the destination address in the routing table. Two processes are involved in the building and maintenance of the routing table in a router. These two processes are comprised of the routing processes and the routing table. The various routing processes are those processes that actually run a network routing protocol, such as EIGRP and OSPF. The routing table accepts information from the routing processes.

In order to forward packets to the next-hop destination, en route to the destination network, the router uses switching. While the routing process is used to determine the best path for moving traffic to the destination, it is the switching process that actually moves traffic from an input interface to one or more output interfaces. The switching process is used because it is faster and has lower latency than the routing process.

Using the switching process, the router must first determine the next-hop address toward that destination and the interface through which that next-hop is reachable. Next, the router must re-write the Media Access Control (MAC) header on the packet so the packet will be able to reach the next-hop successfully. It is important to remember that the routing table replies to requests for information from the switching or forwarding process, which requests this information from the routing table to make a packet forwarding or switching decision. In other words, the packet forwarding process relies on the information that is provided by the routing process to make packet forwarding decisions.

Cisco IOS software supports multiple switching paths, which include the following:
- Process switching
- Fast switching
- CEF switching

Process switching is supported in all Cisco IOS software versions and on all Cisco routing platforms. With process switching, the router first copies the received packet to the system buffer. Next, the router performs a routing lookup for the destination. This is performed to determine the next-hop and the output interface. The router then checks the ARP cache to determine the correct Layer 2 address for the next-hop. Once the address has been determined, the frame is rewritten with the destination address and sent to the outgoing interface that is connected to that destination. The same switching path is then used for any other subsequent packets for that same destination.

Unlike process switching, fast switching stores the forwarding information and MAC header re-write string using a binary tree. This allows for faster lookups and references than is possible with process switching. When packets are fast switched, the first packet is copied to the packet memory and the destination network is found in the fast-switching cache, which is derived from the binary tree structure. This negates the need to check the ARP cache to determine the correct Layer 2 address for the next-hop. The frame is then rewritten and sent to the outgoing interface that services the destination. The same switching path is then used for any other subsequent packets for that same destination.

Cisco Express Forwarding (CEF) switching uses a trie instead of a binary tree. This means that the actual information being searched for is not in the data structure; instead, the data is stored in a separate data structure, and the trie simply points to it. In other words, rather than storing the outbound interface and MAC header rewrite within the tree itself, CEF stores this information in a separate data structure. This separate data structure is called the Adjacency Table.

NOTE: A trie is simply an ordered multi-way tree structure used for storing information.

In addition to the Adjacency Table, which is created to contain all connected next-hops, CEF also uses another data structure referred to as the Forwarding Information Base (FIB). The FIB is used to make IP destination prefix-based switching decisions. The FIB is conceptually similar to a routing table or information base in that it maintains a mirror image of the forwarding information contained in the IP routing table.

NOTE: oth fast switching and CEF are classified as interrupt context switching processes. CEF is described in detail in the SWITCH guide in the chapter on Multilayer Switching.

Now that we have a solid understanding of how traditional routing and forwarding works, we can delve into the specifics of Policy-Based Routing so as to understand how it differs from traditional forwarding as described in the previous sections.

Understanding Policy-Based Routing

Regardless of the routing or switching process implemented on the router, traditional routers forward traffic based on the destination address. While different path control techniques and configurations can be applied by the administrator to influence the path taken to a specific destination network, it is almost possible to configure the path a single routing protocol will take to route traffic from a particular source network to a specific destination network. To accomplish such objectives, Policy-Based Routing (PBR) must be implemented.

PBR provides a flexible mechanism for network administrators to customize the operation of the routing table and the flow of traffic within their networks. When configured, PBR takes precedence over the traditional router forwarding process. In other words, all packets received on an interface with PBR routing enabled are considered for PBR routing before the normal routing process is considered. This means that if PBR is configured on the router, after the router receives a packet, it first looks at the PBR configuration to determine how to forward the packet based on the criteria specified in this configuration. If the packet does not match any of the configured PBR policies, then the packet will be routed using the normal forwarding process.

When implemented, PBR routing is applied either to incoming packets or for packets that are originated by the router itself, depending on the manner in which the configuration is applied to the router. Within Cisco IOS software, PBR is implemented using route maps, which are described in detail in the previous chapter. Leveraging the match and set capabilities of route maps, PBR can be implemented to influence the path taken to a destination based on the following:

- The identity of a particular host
- An application
- A specific protocol

- The packet size
- The source network

Route Map Match Clauses for Policy-Based Routing

Within the route map, PBR is configured to match on the specified criteria using match clauses that are configured by using the `match` subcommand. When configuring match clauses for PBR, Cisco IOS software supports matches against standard or extended named or numbered ACLs. Using extended ACLs provides greater granularity in that they can match based on application, protocol type, and Quality of Service (QoS) parameters, such as Type of Service (TOS), IP Precedence, and the Differentiated Services Code Point (DSCP) value.

> **NOTE**: Advanced QoS knowledge is beyond the scope of the ROUTE exam requirements. However, QoS is a core requirement of the SWITCH exam and is included in the chapter on LAN QoS. Refer to that guide for more information on TOS, IP Precedence, and DSCP.

The second match criterion that can be specified when configuring the route maps for PBR is the packet length. Cisco IOS software allows you to specify a minimum and a maximum packet length, which can be used to distinguish between interactive and bulk traffic. Interactive traffic typically has smaller packet sizes, whereas bulk traffic usually has larger packet sizes.

In most cases, a single match clause is used, for example, to reference an ACL that matches a particular source network. However, when configuring PBR, multiple match clauses may be used within the same route map statement. If multiple match clauses are used, the packet must meet all specified criteria before a positive match is made. When PBR is implemented, the policy routing process proceeds through the route map until a match is found. By default, there is an implicit deny at the end of the list of match statements. Therefore, if no match is found in the route map, or the route map entry is a deny statement instead of a permit statement, then normal destination-based routing of the traffic ensues.

When configuring matching against ACLs, the `match ip address [<1-199> | <1300-2699> | <name>]` subcommand is used within the route map to match against a named or numbered ACL. When matching against the packet length, the `match length <minimum length> <maximum length>` subcommand is used within the route map to match packets within the specified packet-size range.

Route Map Set Clauses for Policy-Based Routing

If the packet or packets satisfy the match clause(s) defined within the route map, the next action is to apply one or more set clauses before the packet is forwarded to the destination. Set clause configuration is specified using the `set` subcommand in route map configuration mode.

Although more than one set clause can be specified, set clauses specifying a next-hop IP address or egress interface are always evaluated in a specific order. These set statements are evaluated in the following order:

- The list of next-hop IP addresses
- The list of specified interfaces
- The list of default next-hop IP addresses
- The list of default interfaces

The list of next-hop IP addresses is specified using the set ip next-hop [<address> | verify-availability <address> <sequence> track <object number>] route map mode subcommand.

The <address> specifies the next-hop IP address. If this address is reachable, the router will send the packets that satisfy the match clause to this IP address. If the address is not reachable, the router will use the path to the destination network that is stored in the routing table. If the address is not reachable and there is no entry in the routing table for the destination network, then the packet is simply dropped.

The verify-availability [<address> <sequence> track <object number>] keywords are used when PBR is configured in conjunction with IP SLA operations. This configuration allows PBR to verify that the specified next-hop address is reachable based on IP SLA operations reporting for the tracked object. This will be described later in this chapter.

The list of specified interfaces is configured using the set interface [name] subcommand. This command is used to indicate the egress interface for packets that pass a match clause of the route map for policy routing. When more than one interface is specified, the router will forward packets using the first interface that is in an up state. The operation of PBR when the set interface command is specified is not as simple as it may appear. First, this command should be used for point-to-point interfaces unless a route-cache entry (e.g., in the Cisco Express Forwarding table that was described earlier in this section) exists using the same interface. If no cache entry exists and a FastEthernet interface is specified, for example, then the command is ignored and the normal forwarding process is used.

Additionally, when this command is specified, the router will also validate that it has an explicit route to the specified destination network in the routing table before it forwards the packets. If there is no explicit route, or if only a default route is present in the routing table, then the command will also be ignored. It is important to ensure these conditions are met prior to using this command.

The list of default next-hop IP addresses is specified using the set ip default next-hop [<address> | verify-availability] subcommand. When this command is specified, if the router has an explicit route to the specified destination network (i.e., via a routing protocol), then it will use that route first and ignore the PBR configuration. However, if only a default route exists in the routing table, the router will execute this command instead of using the default route to forward packets to the specified destination network.

The `verify-availability` keyword is used to force the router to check the Cisco Discovery Protocol (CDP) database to determine if an entry is available for the next-hop that is specified by the `set ip default next-hop` command. This command prevents traffic from being black-holed in situations where the specified next-hop IP address is not directly connected to the router, for example. In such cases, if the specified next-hop IP address does become unreachable, the router would never know and will continue sending packets to it, resulting in a black-holing of traffic. This keyword is applied using a separate line in the route map.

The list of default interfaces is specified using the `set default interface [name]` subcommand. As is the case with the `set ip default next-hop` command, if an explicit route entry for the destination is present in the routing table, this command is ignored. However, if no explicit route entry for the destination network exists, or the router only has a default route, then this command is applied.

Applying the Policy-Based Routing Configuration

Following the configuration of the desired route map permit and deny statements, along with the relevant match and set clauses, the PBR configuration can be applied to an interface for ingress traffic using the `ip policy route-map [name]` interface configuration command. Only one instance of this command can be specified per interface. If you configure another instance of this command, then the previous entry will be removed and replaced with the new entry.

By default, PBR configuration applied to the interface does not affect traffic originated by the router itself. To apply the PBR configuration to traffic originated by the router, local policy routing must be configured by using the `ip local policy route-map [name]` global configuration command. The following section contains several PBR configuration examples to reinforce the concepts described in the sections above.

Configuring and Verifying Policy-Based Routing in Cisco IOS Software

The PBR configuration examples in this section are based on the topology shown in Figure 5-7 below:

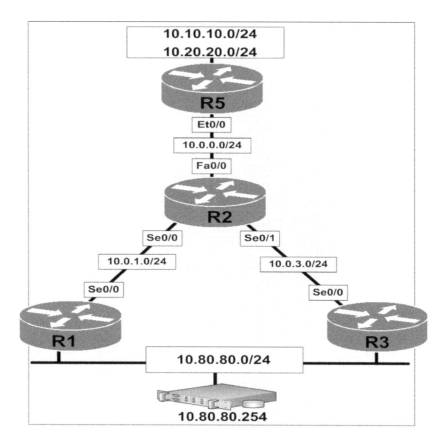

Fig. 5-7. Configuring and Verifying Policy-Based Routing

Figure 5-7 shows a basic network. R2 is connected to R1, R3, and R5. R1 and R3 are advertising the 10.80.80.0/24 subnet via EIGRP as an external route. Based on the redistribution configuration implemented on these routers, R2 prefers the path via R1 to this network, as it has the better metric. R2 is also receiving internal EIGRP routes from R5. Based on this implementation, the routing table on router R5 shows the following network entries:

```
R2#show ip route eigrp
      10.0.0.0/24 is subnetted, 6 subnets
D EX    10.80.80.0 [170/2172416] via 10.0.1.1, 00:08:14, Serial0/0
D       10.20.20.0 [90/156160] via 10.0.0.5, 00:01:20, FastEthernet0/0
D       10.10.10.0 [90/156160] via 10.0.0.5, 00:01:20, FastEthernet0/0
```

Management has requested that all traffic sourced from the 10.10.10.0/24 subnet use the path via R2 to reach only server 10.80.80.254, while all traffic sourced from the 10.20.20.0/24 subnet continue to use the primary path via R1. The current path taken by the 10.10.10.0/24 subnet to the 10.80.80.254 server is via R1 as illustrated in the following Traceroute issued from R5:

```
R5#traceroute ip

Target IP address: 10.80.80.254
```

```
Source address: 10.10.10.5
Numeric display [n]:
Timeout in seconds [3]:
Probe count [3]:
Minimum Time to Live [1]:
Maximum Time to Live [30]:
Port Number [33434]:
Loose, Strict, Record, Timestamp, Verbose[none]:
Type escape sequence to abort.
Tracing the route to 10.80.80.254

   1 R2-Fa0-Interface (10.0.0.2) 4 msec 4 msec 4 msec
   2 R1-Se0-Interface (10.0.1.1) 4 msec *  4 msec
```

To satisfy this requirement, the following PBR configuration would be implemented on R2:

```
R2(config)#ip access-list extended Net-10-To-Server-Only
R2(config-ext-nacl)#permit ip 10.10.10.0 0.0.0.255 host 10.80.80.254
R2(config-ext-nacl)#exit
R2(config)#route-map Policy-Route-Net-10-To-Server
R2(config-route-map)#match ip address Net-10-To-Server-Only
R2(config-route-map)#set ip next-hop 10.0.3.3
R2(config-route-map)#exit
R2(config)#interface FastEthernet0/0
R2(config-if)#ip policy route-map Policy-Route-Net-10-To-Server
R2(config-if)#exit
```

In the configuration above, an extended ACL is configured to match only traffic sourced from the 10.10.10.0/24 subnet destined to host 10.80.80.254. This ensures that all other traffic from the 10.10.10.0/24 subnet to any other destination is not policy routed. Next, the route map is configured to match the extended ACL. The set ip next-hop command is then used to forward packets that match this statement to 10.0.3.3, which is R3's Serial0/0 interface. Finally, the PBR configuration is applied to FastEthernet0/0 on R2. This is the ingress interface for packets sourced from the 10.10.10.0/24 subnet. Following this configuration, the Traceroute from R5 to the 10.80.80.254 address now displays the following:

```
R5#traceroute ip

Target IP address: 10.80.80.254
Source address: 10.10.10.5
Numeric display [n]:
Timeout in seconds [3]:
Probe count [3]:
Minimum Time to Live [1]:
Maximum Time to Live [30]:
Port Number [33434]:
Loose, Strict, Record, Timestamp, Verbose[none]:
```

```
Type escape sequence to abort.
Tracing the route to 10.80.80.254

  1 R2-Fa0-Interface (10.0.0.2) 4 msec 4 msec 4 msec
  2 R3-Se0-Interface (10.0.3.3) 4 msec 4 msec 4 msec
```

However, any other traffic sourced from the 10.10.10.0/24 subnet to any other address other than 10.80.80.254 will not be policy routed, as it will not satisfy the match clause in the route map and because there is an implicit deny at the end of the route map. This is validated by tracing the route from the 10.10.10.0/24 subnet to any other address as illustrated below:

```
R5#traceroute ip

Target IP address: 10.80.80.100
Source address: 10.10.10.5
Numeric display [n]:
Timeout in seconds [3]:
Probe count [3]:
Minimum Time to Live [1]:
Maximum Time to Live [30]:
Port Number [33434]:
Loose, Strict, Record, Timestamp, Verbose[none]:
Type escape sequence to abort.
Tracing the route to 10.80.80.100

  1 R2-Fa0-Interface (10.0.0.2) 4 msec 4 msec 0 msec
  2 R1-Se0-Interface (10.0.1.1) 4 msec 4 msec 4 msec
```

The show route-map [name] command can be used on the router on which the Policy-Based Routing configuration has been implemented to view matches against the configured policy. The output of this command is illustrated below:

```
R2#show route-map Policy-Route-Net-10-To-Server
route-map Policy-Route-Net-10-To-Server, permit, sequence 10
  Match clauses:
    ip address (access-lists): Net-10-To-Server-Only
  Set clauses:
    ip next-hop 10.0.3.3
  Policy routing matches: 6 packets, 360 bytes
```

To view real-time (debugging) information on policy routing decisions, you can use the debug ip policy command. When debugging PBR, keep in mind that as with any other debugging commands, you should exercise caution when enabling them in production networks. In the following output, PBR debugging is enabled on R2 to view real-time policy-routing operation:

```
R2#debug ip policy
Policy routing debugging is on
```

Next, a simple ping is initiated from R5, sourced from the 10.10.10.5 address, to the server with the address 10.80.80.254. This is performed as follows:

```
R5#ping 10.80.80.254 source 10.10.10.5

Type escape sequence to abort.
Sending 5, 100-byte ICMP Echos to 10.80.80.254, timeout is 2 seconds:
Packet sent with a source address of 10.10.10.5
!!!!!
Success rate is 100 percent (5/5), round-trip min/avg/max = 4/5/8 ms
```

Going back to R2, the debug output shows the following:

```
*Mar  2 00:08:36.635: IP: s=10.10.10.5 (FastEthernet0/0), d=10.80.80.254,
len 100, FIB policy match
*Mar  2 00:08:36.635: IP: s=10.10.10.5 (FastEthernet0/0), d=10.80.80.254,
g=10.0.3.3, len 100, FIB policy routed

...

[Truncated Output]
```

NOTE: The FIB is the Forwarding Information Base used with Cisco Express Forwarding. If CEF is not enabled on the router, the debug output would show the following instead:

```
*Mar  2 00:15:17.332: IP: s=10.10.10.5 (FastEthernet0/0), d=10.80.80.254,
len 100, policy match
*Mar  2 00:15:17.332: IP: route map Policy-Route-Net-10-To-Server, item 10,
permit
*Mar  2 00:15:17.332: IP: s=10.10.10.5 (FastEthernet0/0), d=10.80.80.254
(Serial0/1), len 100, policy routed
*Mar  2 00:15:17.336: IP: FastEthernet0/0 to Serial0/1 10.0.3.3

...

[Truncated Output]
```

If, for example, a ping was sourced from the 10.10.10.0/24 subnet to any other address, these packets would not satisfy the PBR match clause and would not be policy routed. The packets would be forwarded using the normal forwarding process. In that case, the debug output would display the following:

```
*Mar  2 00:08:04.911: IP: s=10.10.10.5 (FastEthernet0/0), d=10.80.80.100,
len 100, FIB policy rejected(no match) - normal forwarding
*Mar  2 00:08:04.915: IP: s=10.10.10.5 (FastEthernet0/0), d=10.80.80.100,
len 100, FIB policy rejected(no match) - normal forwarding
```

```
...

[Truncated Output]
```

If CEF is not enabled, the debugging output displays the following instead:

```
*Mar  2 00:20:59.741: IP: s=10.10.10.5 (FastEthernet0/0), d=10.80.80.100
(Serial0/0), len 100, policy rejected -- normal forwarding
*Mar  2 00:21:01.744: IP: s=10.10.10.5 (FastEthernet0/0), d=10.80.80.100
(Serial0/0), len 100, policy rejected -- normal forwarding

...

[Truncated Output]
```

Continuing with the PBR configuration examples, assume that management has now requested that all packets between 219 bytes and 1500 bytes from any subnet destined to the 10.80.80.254 address should be forwarded out of the Serial0/1 interface. All other packets to this host, or any other destination, should be forwarded using the normal forwarding process. The configuration would be implemented as follows on router R2:

```
R2(config)#ip access-list extended To-Match-Large-Packets-To-Host
R2(config-ext-nacl)#permit ip any host 10.80.80.254
R2(config-ext-nacl)#exit
R2(config)#route-map To-Policy-Route-Large-Packets
R2(config-route-map)#match ip address To-Match-Large-Packets-To-Host
R2(config-route-map)#match length 219 1500
R2(config-route-map)#set interface Serial0/1
R2(config-route-map)#exit
R2(config)#interface FastEthernet0/0
R2(config-if)#ip policy route-map To-Policy-Route-Large-Packets
R2(config-if)#exit
```

To validate this configuration, an 800 byte ping is sourced from the 10.20.20.0/25 subnet to the 10.80.80.254 host address. This ping is sourced from R5 as illustrated in the following output:

```
R5#ping 10.80.80.254 source 10.20.20.5 size 800

Type escape sequence to abort.
Sending 5, 800-byte ICMP Echos to 10.80.80.254, timeout is 2 seconds:
Packet sent with a source address of 10.20.20.5
!!!!!
Success rate is 100 percent (5/5), round-trip min/avg/max = 12/13/16 ms
```

We can then use the show route-map command to validate the policy-routing configuration:

```
R2#show route-map To-Policy-Route-Large-Packets
route-map Policy-Route-Large-Packets, permit, sequence 10
  Match clauses:
    ip address (access-lists): To-Match-Large-Packets-To-Host
    length 219 1500
  Set clauses:
    interface Serial0/1
  Policy routing matches: 5 packets, 4070 bytes
```

The output of the `debug ip policy` command confirms the same as illustrated below:

```
*Mar  2 01:57:00.376: IP: s=10.20.20.5 (FastEthernet0/0), d=10.80.80.254,
len 800, FIB policy match
*Mar  2 01:57:00.376: fibidb->namestring: Serial0/1
*Mar  2 01:57:00.380: ipfib_policy_set_interface_lookup: tag_ptr: 0x0
*Mar  2 01:57:00.380: adj 0x0, NULL
*Mar  2 01:57:00.380: IP: s=10.20.20.5 (FastEthernet0/0), d=10.80.80.254
(Serial0/1), len 800, FIB policy routed


...


[Truncated Output]
```

If Cisco Express Forwarding was not enabled, the debug output would display the following:

```
*Mar  2 01:59:23.227: IP: s=10.20.20.5 (FastEthernet0/0), d=10.80.80.254,
len 800, policy match
*Mar  2 01:59:23.227: IP: route map To-Policy-Route-Large-Packets, item 10,
permit
*Mar  2 01:59:23.227: IP: s=10.20.20.5 (FastEthernet0/0), d=10.80.80.254
(Serial0/1), len 800, policy routed
```

As a final configuration example, assume that you have been requested to ensure that all Telnet traffic from R2 to the 10.80.80.0/24 subnet is policy routed out of the Serial0/1 interface with an IP precedence value of 3. This configuration would be implemented as follows:

```
R2(config)#access-list 100 permit icmp any 10.80.80.0 0.0.0.255 echo
R2(config)#route-map Policy-Route-Locally-Originated-PINGs
R2(config-route-map)#match ip address 100
R2(config-route-map)#set interface Serial0/1
R2(config-route-map)#set ip precedence 3
R2(config-route-map)#exit
R2(config)#ip local policy route-map Policy-Route-Locally-Originated-PINGs
R2(config)#exit
```

This configuration can be validated by pinging from R2 to either R3 or R1 as illustrated below:

```
R2#ping 10.80.80.1 repeat 20
Type escape sequence to abort.
Sending 20, 100-byte ICMP Echos to 10.80.80.1, timeout is 2 seconds:
!!!!!!!!!!!!!!!!!!!!!!
Success rate is 100 percent (20/20), round-trip min/avg/max = 4/4/4 ms
```

The following output of the show route-map command shows that the traffic has been policy routed:

```
R2#show route-map Policy-Route-Locally-Originated-PINGs
route-map Policy-Route-Local-Telnet, permit, sequence 10
  Match clauses:
    ip address (access-lists): 100
  Set clauses:
    ip precedence flash
    interface Serial0/1
  Policy routing matches: 20 packets, 2000 bytes
```

The following output of the debug ip policy command also confirms the same:

```
*Mar  2 02:10:42.192: IP: s=10.0.1.2 (local), d=10.80.80.1, len 100, policy
match
*Mar  2 02:10:42.192: IP: route map Policy-Route-Locally-Originated-PINGs,
item 10, permit
*Mar  2 02:10:42.192: IP: s=10.0.1.2 (local), d=10.80.80.1 (Serial0/1), len
100, policy routed
*Mar  2 02:10:42.196: IP: local to Serial0/1 10.80.80.1

...

[Truncated Output]
```

While the debug output will not show the QoS implementation configured using the set ip precedence operation, this can be validated by checking configured QoS policies on the outbound router interface. For example, assuming that the Modular QoS CLI has been used to configure an outbound QoS policy for Serial0/1 that matches packets with an IP Precedence value of 5, 4, or 3, following the ping sourced from R1 to 10.80.80.1, the QoS policy would display the following matches:

```
R2#show policy-map interface Serial0/1 output
 Serial0/1

  Service-policy output: QoS-Outbound-Policy

    Class-map: Match-IP-Precedence-5 (match-all)
      0 packets, 0 bytes
```

```
      5 minute offered rate 0 bps, drop rate 0 bps
      Match: ip precedence 5
      Traffic Shaping
            Target/Average   Byte    Sustain    Excess     Interval   Increment
               Rate          Limit   bits/int   bits/int   (ms)       (bytes)
            512000/512000     3200   12800      12800      25         1600

      Adapt   Queue     Packets    Bytes      Packets    Bytes     Shaping
      Active  Depth                           Delayed    Delayed   Active
      -         0          0         0           0          0       no

   Class-map: Match-IP-Precedence-4 (match-all)
      0 packets, 0 bytes
      5 minute offered rate 0 bps, drop rate 0 bps
      Match: ip precedence 4
      Traffic Shaping
            Target/Average   Byte    Sustain    Excess     Interval   Increment
               Rate          Limit   bits/int   bits/int   (ms)       (bytes)
            384000/384000     2400   9600       9600       25         1200

      Adapt   Queue     Packets    Bytes      Packets    Bytes     Shaping
      Active  Depth                           Delayed    Delayed   Active
      -         0          0         0           0          0       no

   Class-map: Match-IP-Precedence-3 (match-all)
      20 packets, 2080 bytes
      5 minute offered rate 1000 bps, drop rate 0 bps
      Match: ip precedence 3
      Traffic Shaping
            Target/Average   Byte    Sustain    Excess     Interval   Increment
               Rate          Limit   bits/int   bits/int   (ms)       (bytes)
            256000/256000     1984   7936       7936       31         992

      Adapt   Queue     Packets    Bytes      Packets    Bytes     Shaping
      Active  Depth                           Delayed    Delayed   Active
      -         0          20        2080        0          0       no

...
```

[Truncated Output]

PBR Tracking with IP SLA Operations

As was stated earlier in this section, the verify-availability [<address> <sequence> track <object number>] keywords are used when PBR is configured in conjunction with IP SLA operations. This configuration allows PBR to verify that the specified next-hop address is reachable based on IP SLA operations reporting for the tracked object. The following sequence of steps is required to configure PBR tracking with Cisco IOS IP SLA Operations:

- Configure the Cisco IOS IP SLA operation
- Configure Enhanced Object Tracking
- Configure PBR to verify next-hop-reachability

NOTE: You will not be expected to implement any such advanced configurations in the current ROUTE exam; however, ensure that you are familiar with this capability when using PBR.

Referencing Figure 5-7, which was used in the previous PBR configuration examples, R2 is now configured to policy route all traffic via R2 if the IP SLA operation being tracked is reported as reachable. If not, then R2 will policy route all traffic via R1 as illustrated below:

NOTE: The following configuration is based on pre-12.4(4)T Cisco IOS software versions.

```
R2(config)#ip sla monitor 1
R2(config-sla-monitor)#type echo protocol ipIcmpEcho 10.0.3.3
R2(config-sla-monitor-echo)#frequency 5
R2(config-sla-monitor-echo)#exit
R2(config)#ip sla monitor 2
R2(config-sla-monitor)#type echo protocol ipIcmpEcho 10.0.1.1
R2(config-sla-monitor-echo)#frequency 5
R2(config-sla-monitor-echo)#exit
R2(config)#ip sla monitor schedule 1 life forever start-time now
R2(config)#ip sla monitor schedule 2 life forever start-time now
R2(config)#track 1 rtr 1 reachability
R2(config-track)#exit
R2(config)#track 2 rtr 2 reachability
R2(config-track)#exit
R2(config)#ip access-list extended Match-All-Traffic
R2(config-ext-nacl)#permit ip any any
R2(config-ext-nacl)#exit
R2(config)#route-map Policy-Route-All-Traffic permit 10
R2(config-route-map)#match ip address Match-All-Traffic
R2(config-route-map)#set ip next-hop verify-availability 10.0.3.3 1 track 1
R2(config-route-map)#set ip next-hop verify-availability 10.0.1.1 2 track 2
R2(config-route-map)#exit
R2(config)#interface FastEthernet0/0
R2(config-if)#ip policy route-map Policy-Route-All-Traffic
R2(config-if)#exit
```

The show track command can be used to verify the configuration by listing the IP SLA operation and the process that is tracking it as illustrated in the following output:

```
R2#show track
Track 1
  Response Time Reporter 1 reachability
  Reachability is Up
    4 changes, last change 00:11:18
  Latest operation return code: OK
  Latest RTT (millisecs) 1
  Tracked by:
    ROUTE-MAP 0
Track 2
```

```
Response Time Reporter 2 reachability
Reachability is Up
  4 changes, last change 00:11:18
Latest operation return code: OK
Latest RTT (millisecs) 1
Tracked by:
  ROUTE-MAP 0
```

To validate this configuration, a simple ping is initiated from R5 to server 10.80.80.254:

```
R5#ping 10.80.80.1 repeat 20

Type escape sequence to abort.
Sending 20, 100-byte ICMP Echos to 10.80.80.1, timeout is 2 seconds:
!!!!!!!!!!!!!!!!!!!!!
Success rate is 100 percent (20/20), round-trip min/avg/max = 4/4/4 ms
```

The following output of the show route-map command shows that the traffic is policy routed:

```
R2#show route-map Policy-Route-All-Traffic
route-map Policy-Route-All-Traffic, permit, sequence 10
  Match clauses:
    ip address (access-lists): Match-All-Traffic
  Set clauses:
    ip next-hop verify-availability 10.0.3.3 1 track 1  [up]
    ip next-hop verify-availability 10.0.1.1 2 track 2  [up]
  Policy routing matches: 20 packets, 2280 bytes
```

NOTE: In 12.4(4)T and above, the same configuration would be implemented as follows:

```
R2(config)#ip sla 1
R2(config-sla-monitor)#icmp-echo 10.0.3.3
R2(config-sla-monitor-echo)#frequency 5
R2(config-sla-monitor-echo)#exit
R2(config)#ip sla 2
R2(config-sla-monitor)#icmp-echo 10.0.1.1
R2(config-sla-monitor-echo)#frequency 5
R2(config-sla-monitor-echo)#exit
R2(config)#ip sla schedule 1 life forever start-time now
R2(config)#ip sla schedule 2 life forever start-time now
R2(config)#track 1 ip sla 1 reachability
R2(config-track)#exit
R2(config)#track 2 ip sla 2 reachability
R2(config-track)#exit
R2(config)#ip access-list extended Match-All-Traffic
R2(config-ext-nacl)#permit ip any any
R2(config-ext-nacl)#exit
R2(config)#route-map Policy-Route-All-Traffic permit 10
R2(config-route-map)#match ip address Match-All-Traffic
```

```
R2(config-route-map)#set ip next-hop verify-availability 10.0.3.3 1 track 1
R2(config-route-map)#set ip next-hop verify-availability 10.0.1.1 2 track 2
R2(config-route-map)#exit
R2(config)#interface FastEthernet0/0
R2(config-if)#ip policy route-map Policy-Route-All-Traffic
R2(config-if)#exit
```

The Advantages of Using Policy-Based Routing

We will conclude this section, and chapter, by discussing the following advantages of using Policy-Based Routing:

- Source-based transit provider selection
- Quality of Service (QoS)
- Cost savings via load sharing

Source-based transit provider selection means that PBR can be used to selectively route traffic from different source networks or hosts to different egress interfaces on the router. As was illustrated in the previous configuration examples, PBR can be used to route the traffic from a specific source network or host to a specific destination network or host. This is not possible using a routing protocol alone.

In addition to forwarding packets, PBR can also be used to apply QoS settings to packets. The QoS settings may be the Type of Service, IP Precedence, or a DSCP value. Setting the QoS bits allows traffic flows to be differentiated from one another. This allows certain classes of traffic to be prioritized over other classes of traffic.

Finally, PBR can be used to load-share traffic between different paths based on the traffic type. For example, PBR can be used to load-share interactive and bulk traffic between low-cost permanent paths and high-bandwidth, high-cost, switched paths. Routing protocols cannot load-balance depending on traffic types, so PBR offers added flexibility within the Cisco IOS software. This provides cost savings because the paths are utilized rather than sitting idle.

CHAPTER SUMMARY

The following section is a summary of the major points you should be aware of in this chapter.

Cisco IOS IP Service Level Agreement

- SLA allows you to monitor, analyze and verify service levels for IP applications and services
- IP SLA uses active traffic monitoring for measuring network performance
- IP SLA can measure and monitor performance metrics like jitter, latency and packet loss

- IP SLA generate synthetic traffic for monitoring network performance metrics
- The advantages of IP SLA include the following:
  1. IP SLA has visibility of the processing time on the device
  2. IP SLA can differentiate among different measurements
  3. IP SLA can be used as a proactive tool
  4. IP SLA supports proactive notification using SNMP traps
  5. IP SLA provides near millisecond precision
  6. IP SLA also allows for and provides historical data storage
  7. IP SLA has comprehensive hardware support
  8. IP SLA can be used for monitoring and measuring QoS
  9. IP SLA provides Service Level Agreement monitoring, measurements and verification
  10. IP SLA can also be used to perform a network health assessment
  11. IP SLA is a very powerful network troubleshooting tool

- IP Service Level Agreement is comprised of the following two components:
  1. Source
  2. Target

- IP SLA operations can be broadly categorized into the following five functional areas:
  1. Availability monitoring
  2. Network monitoring
  3. Application monitoring
  4. Voice monitoring
  5. Video monitoring

- Reliable static routing backup using EOT and IP SLA configuration requires the following three steps:
  1. Configuring the Cisco IOS IP SLA Operations
  2. Configuring Enhanced Object Tracking
  3. Configuring Floating Static Routes using Tracked Objects

Cisco Embedded Event Manager
- EEM is a powerful and flexible subsystem that provides real-time network event detection
- EEM also provides onboard automation on the router itself
- EEM also increases the intelligence of Cisco IOS network devices
- EEM can be configured using the CLI or via Tcl scripts
- EEM can be used in conjunction with IP SLA and SNMP notifications

Virtual Routing and Forwarding

- VRF allows multiple routing table instances to co-exist on the same physical router
- A VRF routing table is also referred to as a VPN routing table
- VRF Lite can be used to perform Layer 3 segregation of network the traffic

Cisco Performance Routing

- Cisco PfR leverages the intelligence that is integrated into the Cisco IOS software
- PfR determines the optimal path based upon network and application policies
- PfR is enabled using OER configurations
- PfR can be used to automatically detect the degradation of a path and respond accordingly
- Cisco PfR policies can be based on the following three parameters:
  1. WAN outbound performance: Delay, loss, reachability, throughput, jitter, and MOS
  2. WAN inbound performance: Delay, loss, reachability, and throughput
  3. WAN and Internet path parameters: Reachability, throughput, load, and link usage cost

- PfR consists of the following two elements:
  1. Border Routers
  2. Mater Controller

- When implementing PfR, each border router must be configured as follows:
  1. The border router must have Cisco Express Forwarding (CEF) enabled
  2. The session between the border router and the master controller must be authenticated
  3. The local PfR interface must be able to communicate with the master controller
  4. The border router must be configured with the IP address of the master controller

- When implementing PfR, the master controller must be configured as follows:
  1. The master controller must be configured with the IP addresses of all its border routers
  2. PfR policies must be configured on the master controller
  3. The session between the border router and the master controller must be authenticated

- PfR monitors the set of prefixes or traffic classes using the following three methods:
  1. Passive Monitoring
  2. Active Monitoring
  3. Active and Passive Monitoring

Path Control Using Route Redistribution

- Route redistribution can be used for path control by setting different metrics
- Route redistribution can result in asymmetric routing
- Symmetric configurations should be used to ensure effective path control

Cisco IOS Policy Based Routing

- To route or forward the packets that it has received, the router must perform the following two functions:
    1. The router must make a routing decision using routing
    2. The router must forward packets to the next-hop destination using switching

- Cisco IOS software supports multiple switching paths, which include the following:
    1. Process Switching
    2. Fast Switching
    3. CEF Switching

- PBR provides a flexible mechanism for network administrators to customize routing
- PBR is considered before the normal forwarding process is used
- PBR can be implemented to influence the path taken to a destination based on the following:
    1. The identity of a particular host
    2. An application
    3. A specific protocol
    4. The packet size
    5. The source network

- PBR route map match clauses match against IP ACLs or packet length
- PBR route map set statements can be used to specify a next-hop IP address or interface
- PBR route map set statements are evaluated in the following order:
    1. The list of next-hop IP addresses
    2. The list of specified interfaces
    3. The list of default next-hop IP addresses
    4. The list of default interfaces

- PBR can be used in conjunction with EOT and Cisco IOS IP SLA Operations
- PBR provides the following three advantages over routing protocols:
    1. Source-Based Transit Provider Selection
    2. Quality of Service (QoS)
    3. Cost Savings via load sharing

CHAPTER 6

Internal (iBGP) and External (eBGP) Fundamentals

order Gateway Protocol (BGP) is first and foremost a policy control tool. Unlike the traditional IP routing protocols that are used to exchange routing information within an autonomous system, BGP is traditionally used to exchange routing information between routing domains or autonomous systems. However, BGP can also be used to exchange routing information within a single routing domain. The core ROUTE exam objective covered in this chapter is as follows:

- Implement an eBGP-based solution, given a network design and a set of requirements

This chapter contains the following sections:

- An Introduction to Border Gateway Protocol
- Border Gateway Protocol Characteristics
- Border Gateway Protocol AS Numbering System
- Connecting to Internet Service Providers
- Receiving Routes from Internet Service Providers
- Border Gateway Protocol Messages
- Establishing Border Gateway Protocol Adjacencies
- Border Gateway Protocol Attributes
- Border Gateway Protocol Loop Prevention
- The BGP Path Selection Process
- Enabling BGP in Cisco IOS
- Configuring and Verifying External BGP
- Configuring and Verifying Internal BGP
- Advertising Routes with Border Gateway Protocol

AN INTRODUCTION TO BORDER GATEWAY PROTOCOL

Border Gateway Protocol is a Path Vector protocol that is used primarily to exchange Network Layer Reachability Information (NLRI) between routing domains or autonomous systems. In other words, BGP is used as an inter-domain or inter-autonomous system protocol. NLRI is exchanged between BGP routers, referred to as BGP speakers, using UPDATE messages. The NLRI is composed of a prefix and a length. The prefix refers to the network address for that subnet, and the length specifies the number of network bits and is simply a network mask in CIDR notation. Some NLRI examples include 10.0.0.0/8 or 150.1.1.0/24.

NOTE: The different BGP messages are described in detail later in this chapter.

Although BGP is a Path Vector protocol, it is important to understand and remember that BGP is first and foremost a policy control tool. IGPs, such as OSPF and EIGRP, are designed to provide reachability within a single autonomous system; however, BGP was designed with greater policy control and scalability considerations than traditional IGPs. The differences between BGP and IGPs will be described in greater detail as we progress through this chapter.

Unlike EIGRP and OSPF that run directly over IP, using ports 88 and 89, respectively, BGP runs directly over TCP, using port 179. Because BGP runs over TCP, BGP peers establish a connection-oriented and reliable stream of data between them and can rely on TCP for the following services:

- Acknowledgments
- Segmentation and reassembly
- Checksums
- Data sequencing
- Flow control
- Reliable operation

Acknowledgments ensure the integrity of data delivered and guarantee that data will not be lost or duplicated. This process is referred to as positive acknowledgement with retransmission. After sending a TCP segment, a retry timer starts decrementing until a receipt acknowledgment is received from the other end of the connection. When the timer reaches 0, the segment is retransmitted. The far-end acknowledgment is actually delayed up to one second to determine if any data should be sent along with the acknowledgment.

With segmentation and reassembly, the BGP data is segmented, if necessary, into smaller sizes for transmission across the network. If segmented, the data is reassembled at the destination. The checksum is maintained on both the TCP header and BGP data to ensure the transmission is error-free. If a received checksum is not the same as the advertised value, then the segment will be discarded. No acknowledgment is sent to the source and the segment is retransmitted.

Data sequencing involves the use of TCP sequence numbers, which allow the receiving peer to re-order the BGP data in the event of an out-of-sequence receipt. This ensures that data arrives at the end destination in sequential order.

With flow control, each BGP peer advertises its available buffer space to allow the far end of the session to send only a specific amount of data. This prevents a sending host from overflowing the buffers of a receiving host. Forms of flow control are buffering, windowing, and congestion avoidance. Finally, because TCP uses the three-way handshake to establish a virtual circuit between the sending and receiving hosts, a reliable connection is established between TCP hosts.

Cisco IOS Software Border Gateway Protocol Processes

While BGP is an industry standard that is supported by most vendors, it is important to have a basic understanding of the BGP processes in Cisco IOS software, which are as follows:

- The BGP Open process
- The BGP I/O process
- The BGP Scanner process
- The BGP Router process

Although going into detail on these processes is beyond the scope of the ROUTE exam requirements, it is still important to have a basic understanding of the functionality of each process. The following section includes a brief description of each of these processes.

The BGP Open process is used for peer establishment. This process runs at initialization, when establishing a TCP connection with a BGP peer.

The BGP I/O process handles the reading, writing, and execution of BGP messages, such as the UPDATE and KEEPALIVE messages. This process provides the interface between TCP and BGP and reads messages from the TCP socket, placing them into the BGP input queue so they can be processed by the BGP Router process, before moving messages. The I/O process also moves messages in the output queue (OutQ) to the TCP socket.

> **NOTE:** The different BGP messages are described in detail later in this chapter.

The BGP Scanner process periodically scans the BGP Routing Information Base (RIB) in order to determine whether prefixes and attributes should be deleted and whether route map or filter caches should be flushed. Additionally, the BGP Scanner walks the BGP table and confirms reachability of the next-hops; that is, it validates that next-hops are still valid. If the next-hop for a prefix is not reachable, all BGP entries that use that next-hop are removed from the BGP RIB. By default, the BGP Scanner runs every 60 seconds; however, this interval can be changed using CLI commands. These commands, however, are beyond the scope of the ROUTE exam requirements and will not be described in this chapter or in the remainder of this guide.

> **NOTE:** The different BGP path attributes are described in detail later in this chapter.

The BGP Router process sends and receives routes, establishes peers, and interacts with the RIB. This process is also used to calculate the BGP best path and receives commands entered via the CLI. The BGP Router process is the main process responsible for initiating the other BGP processes. The three major components of the BGP Router process are as follows:

1. The BGP Routing Information Base
2. The IP Routing Information Base for BGP-learned prefixes
3. The IP switching component for BGP-learned prefixes

The BGP RIB contains network entries, path entries, path attributes, and additional information, such as route map and BGP filter list cache entries.

The BGP-learned prefixes are stored in the IP RIB in two types of structures, which are Network Description Blocks (NDBs) and Routing Descriptor Blocks (RDBs). An NDB is a single entry in the routing table that represents a network prefix and contains information such as the network address, mask, and administrative distance. The NDB is stored in the routing table with an RDB, which is used to store the actual next-hop information.

Because each prefix in an NDB potentially can be reached through multiple paths, more than one RDB can be linked to each individual NDB. Each route in the RIB requires one NDB and one RDB for each individual path, if more than one path exists. While this may sound confusing, the concept is simple. Consider, for example, the output of the show ip route command that is illustrated below:

```
R1#show ip route 2.2.2.2 255.255.255.255
Routing entry for 2.2.2.2/32
  Known via "ospf 1", distance 110, metric 65, type intra area
  Last update from 10.0.0.2 on Serial0/0, 00:00:52 ago
  Routing Descriptor Blocks:
  * 10.0.1.2, from 10.0.1.2, 00:00:52 ago, via Serial0/1
      Route metric is 65, traffic share count is 1
    10.0.0.2, from 10.0.1.2, 00:00:52 ago, via Serial0/0
      Route metric is 65, traffic share count is 1
```

The output above shows the NDP for the 2.2.2.2/32 route installed in the RIB. Associated with the NDB are the network, mask, and administrative distance and information. This NBD has two RDBs, one for each path, since the prefix is learned via two paths—one via Serial0/0 and the other via Serial0/1. Each RDB is a single route. The asterisk (*) next to one of the block entries corresponds to the active route that is used for new traffic.

The IP switching component refers to structures such as the Forwarding Information Base (FIB), which is applicable when Cisco Express Forwarding (CEF) is enabled. The FIB and other switching paths are described in detail in the SWITCH guide. These technologies will not be described in any greater detail in this chapter or in the remainder of this guide. For any additional information, please refer to the current SWITCH guide.

In summation, keep in mind that this is not a BGP exam. You are not required to go into the level of detail on BGP as would be expected in the CCIP certification, for example. However, as a CCNP-level engineer, you are still expected to demonstrate a solid grasp of not only the theoretical aspects pertaining to BGP but also the implementation and operation of BGP in Cisco IOS software. Understanding the platform on which the protocol is running is as important as understanding the protocol itself when troubleshooting and supporting the network.

BORDER GATEWAY PROTOCOL CHARACTERISTICS

As stated earlier in this chapter, BGP is typically used for inter-domain routing, while IGP is used for intra-domain routing. As is the case with the different IGPs we learned about in previous chapters in this guide, it is important to have a solid understanding of BGP, not only as a Path Vector routing protocol but also as a policy control tool. BGP has the following characteristics:

- Reliability
- Stability
- Scalability
- Flexibility

These characteristics are described in detail in the following sections.

Reliability

Unlike OSPF and EIGRP that run directly over IP, BGP runs directly over TCP, using port 179. Because TCP is a reliable, connection-oriented protocol, BGP does not need to worry about update retransmissions, fragmentation, acknowledgements, and sequencing because these are all performed by the underlying protocol, TCP.

Additionally, BGP also establishes a session between BGP speakers. This connection-oriented session is maintained by regular keepalives. When a BGP speaker fails to receive keepalives within a specified interval, the session with the neighbor is closed and all of the BGP routing and forwarding information for that session is cleared by the local BGP speaker.

Unlike traditional IGPs, BGP also incorporates path attributes to ensure protocol reliability and routing information accuracy. In addition to being used to select the best path to a destination prefix, path attributes are also used to prevent routing loops and to ensure that the next-hop IP address for a specified BGP prefix is reachable before BGP uses the next-hop address to forward packets to that destination prefix.

Stability

As was stated in Chapter 1, one of the core objectives of routing protocols is stability. In essence, routing algorithms should be stable enough to accommodate unforeseen network events, such as hardware failures, incorrect implementations, or even flapping interfaces or routes. Following such network changes, routing protocols must be able to converge quickly in order to avoid the black-holing of traffic, or even to avoid routing loops.

Routing protocol convergence and stability is critical in large enterprise networks with a large number of prefixes, and even more so for Internet Service Providers whose routers typically contain a complete or full Internet routing table. BGP provides more features than traditional IGPs that can be used to ensure a stable topology. In addition to timers, BGP can also be configured to monitor routing information for signs of instability using route flap dampening. Route dampening is used to penalize route or prefix entries that are repeatedly transitioning between the up and down states. This is commonly referred to as bouncing or flapping. Route dampening will be described in detail in the following chapter.

BGP also allows for the soft reset of neighbor sessions when routing policy changes and updates need to be sent. Soft resets are used to change the BGP policy without resetting the BGP session. This capability prevents packet loss or even the black-holing of traffic if the session is reset and all routing information for that session was flushed.

Scalability

BGP is very scalable. An external BGP (eBGP) implementation does not require all the routers within an autonomous system to participate in the BGP protocol. Only the border routers that provide connectivity between the local autonomous system and its adjacent autonomous system(s) participate in BGP. This allows an eBGP implementation that can scale to support hundreds of peer sessions and well over one hundred thousand prefixes (full Internet table).

While there are some scalability issues for internal BGP (iBGP) implementations, wherein all routers within the autonomous system participate in the BGP protocol, several methods are available to address these scalability issues and implement large iBGP networks. These different methods are described in Chapter 7, Advanced BGP Design and Implementation.

Flexibility

BGP provides far greater flexibility than traditional IGPs. Flexibility is provided by the number of path attributes that can be used to define BGP policies. It is for this reason that BGP is considered first and foremost a policy tool and then a routing protocol. BGP path attributes can be used to define both routing policies, such as how traffic routes in and out of an administrative domain (autonomous system), and administrative policies, such as limiting the number of prefixes received from a specific autonomous system.

BORDER GATEWAY PROTOCOL AS NUMBERING SYSTEM

As was stated earlier in this chapter, BGP provides NLRI connectivity between different routing domains (autonomous systems) or within the same routing domain. Therefore, when BGP is enabled, the BGP speaker must be configured with an autonomous number using the `router bgp [autonomous system number]` global configuration command.

While EIGRP also uses autonomous system (AS) numbers, there are some significant differences in the use of AS numbers when implementing EIGRP and when implementing BGP. With EIGRP, routers establish a neighbor relationship only if they are part of the same autonomous system, although you should keep in mind that this is in addition to other EIGRP requirements, such as being on the same subnet, etc. With BGP, however, the peer relationship can be established between two BGP speakers in different autonomous systems, which is referred to as an external BGP (eBGP) relationship, or between BGP speakers within the same autonomous system, which is referred to as an internal (iBGP) relationship.

> **NOTE:** Both iBGP and eBGP similarities and differences are described later in this chapter.

Another significant difference between EIGRP AS numbers (ASNs) and those used by BGP is that BGP uses both public and private ASNs. The configuration AS range for BGP is 65,535, which is the same as that used by EIGRP; however, with BGP, the top 1,024 AS numbers (i.e., autonomous system numbers 64,512 through 65,535) are considered private autonomous system numbers and they cannot be used on the Internet. Private autonomous system numbers are used to conserve globally unique AS numbers in the same way that RFC 1918 address space is used to conserve publically routed global IPv4 address space.

Autonomous system numbers 1 through 64,511 are considered public AS numbers that can be used on the Internet. While any organization can use private AS numbers within their enterprise network, public AS numbers must be obtained from a regional registry. The allocated AS numbers cannot be used by any other organization. Public AS numbers are assigned in blocks by the Internet Assigned Numbers Authority (IANA) to Regional Internet Registries (RIRs). The appropriate RIR then assigns AS numbers to entities within its designated area from the block assigned by the IANA. Entities wishing to receive an ASN must complete the application process of their local RIR and be approved before being assigned an ASN. There are five Regional Internet Registries, which are as follows:

- Latin American and Caribbean Internet Addresses Registry (LACNIC)—www.lacnic.net
- African Network Information Centre (AfriNIC)—www.afrinic.net
- Réseaux IP Européens Network Coordination Centre (RIPE NCC)—www.ripe.net
- American Registry for Internet Numbers (ARIN)—www.arin.net
- Asia-Pacific Network Information Centre (APNIC)—www.apnic.net

NOTE: AfriNIC is for Africa, while ARIN serves Canada, several parts of the Caribbean region, and the United States. APNIC serves Asia, Australia, and neighboring countries. LACNIC serves Latin America and parts of the Caribbean region. Finally, RIPE NCC serves Europe, the Middle East, and Central Asia.

It is important to understand that an organization that does not have a publically assigned AS number can still use BGP to connect to an upstream provider, and then to the Internet. In such cases, the ISP or Service Provider BGP speaker simply removes the private AS number when it propagates network information to the Internet. This concept is illustrated below in Figure 6-1:

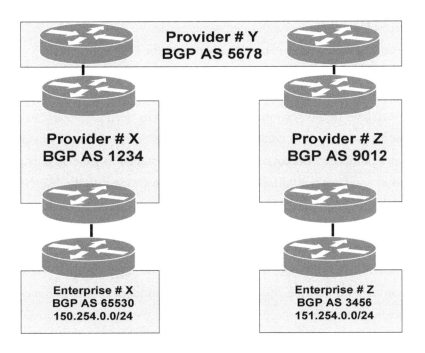

Fig. 6-1. Removing Private AS Numbers

Referencing the network topology that is illustrated in Figure 6-1, Provider X is connected to an enterprise network belonging to Enterprise X. Enterprise X does not have a publically assigned autonomous system number and is therefore using private AS number 65,530. Enterprise X is advertising the 150.254.0.0/24 subnet via eBGP to Provider X. Before propagating this prefix to upstream providers, the edge router belonging to Provider X that has the eBGP peering with the edge router belonging to Provider Y removes the private AS number used by Enterprise X. From the perspectives of Provider Y, Provider Z, and Enterprise Z, the 150.254.0.0/24 prefix that is originated by Enterprise X appears to originate in AS 1234, which is the AS of Provider X.

Now that we have a solid understanding of BGP AS numbers, the following section describes the different ways an enterprise can connect to an Internet Service Provider, and the AS numbers used in the different implementations and BGP deployments when connecting the enterprise network to an ISP.

CONNECTING TO INTERNET SERVICE PROVIDERS

Several factors should be taken into consideration when connecting the enterprise network to an ISP and they are as follows:

- Whether you want to use dynamic or static routing
- Whether you have a public AS number
- Whether you have your own registered public IP address space
- The acceptable or desired level of Internet redundancy
- What type(s) of link(s) you will need to connect to the ISP

It is important to understand that you do not need to enable BGP in order to connect to an ISP. As will be explained later in this section, static routing can be used to connect to an ISP. If you do want to use BGP for greater policy control, your implementation options will vary depending on whether you have a public autonomous system number assigned to your organization. Again, it is not mandatory that you have a publically assigned ASN to connect to the ISP; however, having a publically assigned ASN provides the most flexibility.

Consideration should be given to the acceptable level of Internet redundancy. For small enterprises, Internet connectivity may not be critical; however, for large enterprises that host their own Internet-facing servers, for example, both reliable and redundant Internet connectivity would be critical to the organization. The enterprise BGP implementation should therefore take this into consideration when connecting to ISPs.

The following three types of implementations or deployment models can be used when connecting to Internet Service Providers:

1. Single-homed implementations
2. Stub Multi-homed implementations
3. Multi-homed implementations

A single-homed implementation is one where the enterprise network has a single connection to the ISP. A multi-homed implementation is one where the enterprise network has more than one path to one or more ISPs. While single-homed implementations are the easiest method of connecting to an ISP, multi-homed implementations provide greater reliability and allow for optimal routing.

Multi-homing provides a greater level of redundancy by eliminating single points of failure. This allows for a much more reliable service than that afforded by single-homed implementations. In addition, multi-homing provides network engineers with greater routing policy control, allowing for optimal routing into and out of the enterprise network. These deployment models are described in the following sections.

Single-Homed (Stub) Implementations

A network is single-homed when it has a single connection to the ISP. This implementation is also commonly referred to as a Stub network. Figure 6-2 below illustrates a single-homed or Stub enterprise network that is connected to an Internet Service Provider:

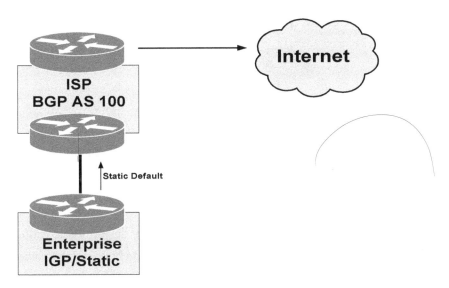

Fig. 6-2. Single-Homed (Stub) Network Implementation

Referencing Figure 6-2, the enterprise network is single-homed to an Internet Service Provider that may be either directly connected or indirectly connected to the Internet. Stub implementations are commonly used by small businesses for which Internet access is not critical, as they provide a low-cost solution for connecting the enterprise network to the Internet. The ISP advertises the Stub network subnet to the rest of the Internet community.

In addition to being a low-cost solution, single-homed or Stub implementations are also simple to deploy, as it is not necessary to implement Border Gateway Protocol on the customer edge router.

Instead, a single static default route to the ISP router for all Internet-bound traffic can be used. The provider then uses BGP to advertise the network to the Internet, and all policy control is solely in the hands of the provider. In other words, the enterprise cannot influence how the Stub network is advertised to the rest of the Internet community.

It is important to understand that while single-homed implementations offer little redundancy due to both the edge router and the circuit being single points of failure, an Internet outage due to a circuit failure can be mitigated against by provisioning multiple circuits between the enterprise (customer) edge router and the provider edge router, as illustrated in Figure 6-3 below:

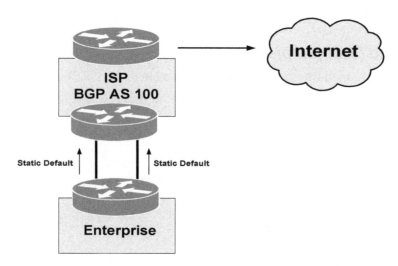

Fig. 6-3. Circuit Redundancy for a Single-Homed Connection to a Service Provider

Referencing Figure 6-3, multiple (two) circuits between the customer edge and provider edge routers reduce the likelihood of an outright Internet outage due to a single circuit failing. In implementations such as the one illustrated in Figure 6-3, multiple default static routes can be configured on the customer edge router, or the physical circuits can be bonded into a single logical link, using WAN technologies such as PPP Multilink, for example.

Stub Multi-Homed Implementations

A Stub multi-homed network is one that is connected to two or more edge routers that belong to the same Internet Service Provider. Stub multi-homed networks can have a single edge router or multiple edge routers for redundancy. Most Stub multi-homed implementations have the following characteristics:

- BGP is used to exchange routing information with the ISP
- A private BGP AS number (i.e., 64,512 to 65,535) is used
- The upstream ISP advertises the Stub network to the Internet
- BGP is used for greater routing policy control

Figure 6-4 below illustrates a Stub multi-homed network using a single edge router connected to two provider edge routers belonging to the same Internet Service Provider:

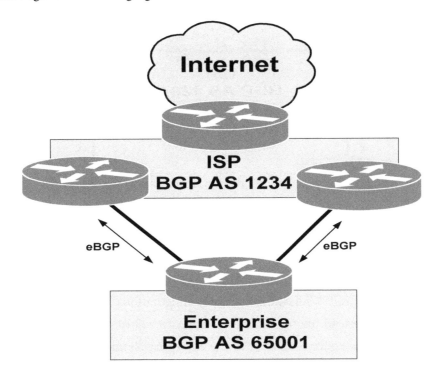

Fig. 6-4. Single Edge Stub Multi-Homed Networks

Referencing Figure 6-4, BGP is used to exchange routing information between the enterprise and the ISP. It should be noted that static routes can also be used between the enterprise edge router and the ISP edge router; however, static routes do not provide the flexibility provided by BGP and do not afford the enterprise the same granular routing and traffic flow controls.

Because the enterprise is connected to a single ISP, a private AS number can be used, negating the need for the enterprise to obtain a public AS number from a regional registry. As was described earlier in this chapter, the ISP simply removes the private AS number from routing updates to upstream autonomous systems or the Internet.

In order to eliminate the single enterprise edge router as a single point of failure, the Stub multi-homed implementations can also be deployed using multiple edge routers. Multi-edge Stub multi-homed networks are implemented by connecting more than one edge router to multiple provider edge routers (belonging to the same ISP) as illustrated in Figure 6-5 below:

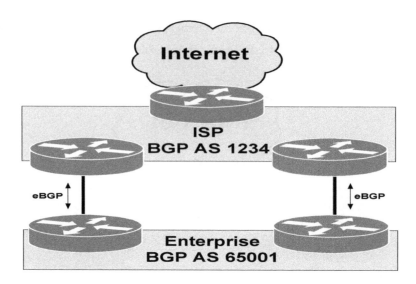

Fig. 6-5. Multi-Edge Stub Multi-Homed Networks

Figure 6-5 shows the same enterprise network depicted in Figure 6-4; however, this time two edge routers are being used instead. While the same basic configurations would be used when using two customer edge routers instead of one, if there are any Layer devices that will be providing transit service between the two edge routers, then the enterprise should implement an internal BGP (iBGP) mesh between these devices and the edge routers. This ensures that intermediate devices have routing information for the BGP networks being advertised between the edge routers, while negating the need to redistribute BGP routes into the IGP. It also prevents the black-holing of network traffic. Such an implementation is illustrated in Figure 6-6 below:

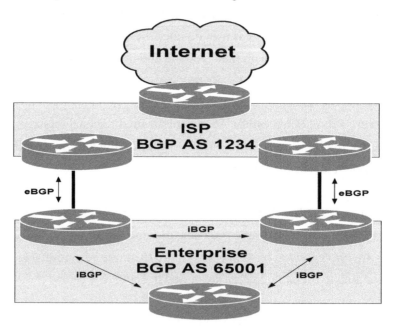

Fig. 6-6. Using iBGP in Multi-Edge Stub Multi-Homed Networks

Referencing the network topology illustrated in Figure 6-6, a full iBGP mesh is implemented in the enterprise (AS 65001), allowing the intermediate router providing transit services between the two edge routers to learn about the routes received by the edge routers from the ISP via BGP, versus through the redistribution of these routes into an IGP on either edge router. This is most commonly implemented when the ISP is advertising a partial or full Internet table, which can be well over a hundred thousand prefixes, to the enterprise. This large number of prefixes can quickly overwhelm an IGP. However, if the ISP is advertising only a single default route, this can be redistributed into the IGP and propagated downstream through the enterprise network.

> **NOTE:** The options that are available when receiving routes from the Internet Service Provider are described in detail in the following main section.

Multi-homed Implementations

Standard multi-homed implementations are commonly used by medium to large enterprise organizations. A standard multi-homed network is one that is connected to multiple upstream Internet Service Providers. Most standard multi-homed implementations have the following characteristics:

- BGP is used to exchange routing information with the ISP
- A public BGP AS number (i.e., 1 to 64,511) is used
- Public IP address space is used
- BGP is used for greater routing policy control

As with Stub multi-homed implementations, standard multi-homed implementations also use external BGP to exchange NLRI between enterprise and provider autonomous systems. However, unlike Stub multi-homed implementations, standard multi-homed implementations use a publically registered autonomous system number, as well as IP address space. Because they use publically registered ASNs and global addressing, standard multi-homed implementations can be used to peer to more than one Internet Service Provider. Figure 6-7 below illustrates a standard multi-homed implementation using a single edge router:

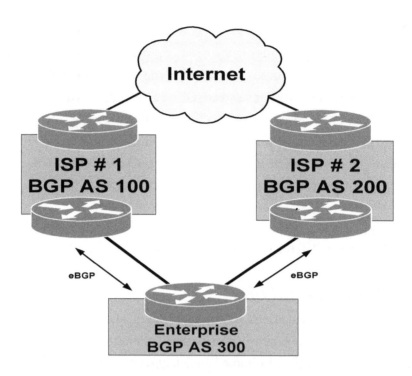

Fig. 6-7. Standard Single-Edge Multi-Homed Network

Referencing Figure 6-7, the enterprise network is multi-homed to two different ISPs using a single edge router. This solution provides the enterprise with redundancy against a single circuit or provider edge router failure. This implementation also allows BGP to be used for greater path control for packets originated from the enterprise network to the Internet, as well as for traffic from the Internet to the enterprise.

 While this implementation does provide circuit and provider edge redundancy, the single edge enterprise router still represents a single point of failure. A more commonly implemented solution, which shows multiple enterprise edge routers, is illustrated in the diagram in Figure 6-8 below:

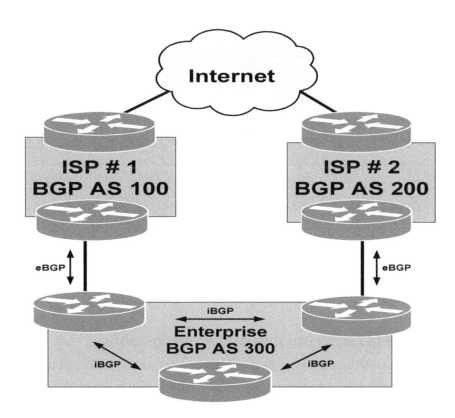

Fig. 6-8. Standard Multi-Edge Multi-Homed Network

Figure 6-8 shows a standard dual-homed network connected to two different ISPs. Within the enterprise network, iBGP may be used to ensure that any transit devices between the two enterprise edge routers know about the BGP routes received by the edge routers, as was also stated in the section on Stub multi-homed implementations.

RECEIVING ROUTES FROM INTERNET SERVICE PROVIDERS

Now that we are familiar with the options that are available when connecting to the Internet, the next step is to determine what routing information you want to receive from the Internet Service Provider(s). The following three options are available for receiving routes from the ISP:

1. Default route only
2. Default route plus a partial Internet routing table
3. Full Internet routing table

The following sections describe these three options.

Default Route Only

This option can be used with or without BGP. When BGP is used, the ISP simply advertises only a default route to the enterprise edge routers. This route is then redistributed into the IGP and propagated to downstream internetwork devices, allowing for connectivity to the Internet. When BGP is not used, the enterprise simply configures one or more static default routes that point to the provider edge router. This static default route can also be redistributed into the IGP and propagated to downstream internetwork devices.

The primary advantage of using a default route only is that it is not resource intensive (i.e., it does not greatly consume router resources such as memory). In addition, this is an easy solution to implement. However, when BGP is used and only a default route is received, no path manipulation is possible (i.e., there is a loss of BGP policy control). Additionally, this solution can also lead to suboptimal routing, as was described in previous chapters in this guide.

Default Route Plus a Partial Internet Routing Table

This is the most commonly implemented solution by enterprises connected to Internet Service Providers. This solution uses more bandwidth and router resources than the default route only solution but uses less bandwidth and router resources than the full Internet routing table solution, which is described in the following section.

The default route plus partial Internet routing table solution can be implemented in two ways. Using the first method, the enterprise can request the ISP to send full Internet routing tables and then use inbound route filtering to accept only certain prefixes and the default route, for example. With the second method, the ISP can advertise the enterprise prefixes for its local networks, as well as those for other customers of the same ISP, and then advertise the default route to allow reachability to networks belonging to upstream ISPs and the general Internet community.

Full Internet Routing Table

Receiving a full or complete Internet routing table is performed only by very large enterprise customers and service providers. With this solution, the complete Internet routing table is advertised to the customer edge routers. This solution consumes the most router and bandwidth resources. However, the advantage of this solution is that it provides specific information for all reachable prefixes and allows for the greatest amount of route optimization.

BORDER GATEWAY PROTOCOL MESSAGES

All Border Gateway Protocol messages share a common header that is 19-bytes long. The Border Gateway Protocol packet header contains three fields, which are illustrated in Figure 6-9 below:

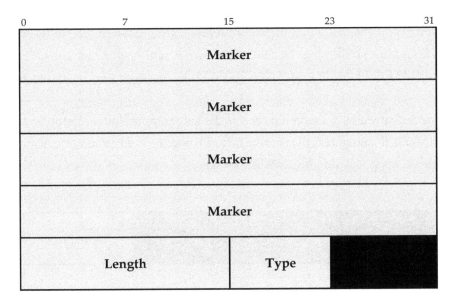

Fig. 6-9. The BGP Message Header

The 16-byte Marker field is used to detect a loss of synchronization between two BGP speakers, as well as to authentic incoming BGP messages. If the message is an OPEN message, or if the OPEN message has no authentication information, the Marker must be set to a value of all ones.

The 2-byte Length field contains the total length of the BGP message, including the header. This field can range from 19 to 4,096 bytes. Because no padding of extra data after the message is allowed, the Length field must have the smallest value required given the rest of the message.

The 1-byte Type field contains the type of BGP message. Only four BGP messages are available as follows:
1. The OPEN message
2. The UPDATE message
3. The NOTIFICATION message
4. The KEEPALIVE message

The following sections describe each of these messages, as well as their function and use.

The OPEN Message (Message Type 1)

The Open message, BGP message Type 1, is the first packet BGP sends to a peer after the TCP connection has been established. It allows the two peers to negotiate the parameters of the peer session. The different parameters include the BGP version, the hold time for the session, authentication data, refresh capabilities, and support for multiple NLRI. If the OPEN message is acceptable, a KEEPALIVE message confirming the OPEN message is sent back. Once the OPEN message is confirmed, UPDATE, KEEPALIVE, and NOTIFICATION messages may be exchanged.

The OPEN message includes parameters such as the autonomous system number; authentication information (MD5), if configured; the router ID (RID); and the hold-time value. Figure 6-10 below shows the fields contained within the OPEN message:

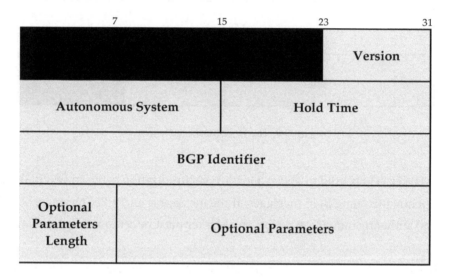

Fig. 6-10. The BGP OPEN Message Format

Within the BGP OPEN message, the 1-byte Version field specifies the current BGP version, which, by default, is set to 4. The 2-byte Autonomous System field specifies the local Autonomous System configured on the router.

The 2-byte Hold Time field indicates the sender's proposed hold-time value. The two BGP peers then negotiate this value to the lower of the two proposals. In other words, the lower of the two hold-time values specified on the two BGP peers will be used.

The 4-byte BGP Identifier field specifies the BGP router ID of the local router, while the 1-byte Optional Parameters Length field contains the total length of the Optional Parameters field. If this field contains a value of 0, then this indicates that no parameters are included in the message.

The final field, the Optional Parameters field, has a variable length that is determined by any optional parameters used by the local router. Possibilities include support for route refresh, authentication, and various NLRI. Each parameter is encoded in a TLV triplet. The parameter's Type and Length fields are 1 octet each and are followed by a variable-length Value field.

The Optional Parameters field may contain Authentication Information, which is Parameter Type 1; however, this is deprecated in RFC 5492 with the Capabilities Optional Parameter, which is Parameter Type 2.

The UPDATE Message (Message Type 2)

The BGP UPDATE message (Type 2) is used to send and withdraw BGP routing information or NLRI. Additionally, the UPDATE message also contains information previously advertised by the local router that is no longer valid, as well as new information that is being advertised to the remote peer. Each UPDATE message contains a single set of BGP attributes and all of the routes using those attributes. The format of this message reduces the total number of packets that routers must send between the BGP peers when exchanging NLRI. Figure 6-11 below illustrates the fields within the BGP UPDATE message:

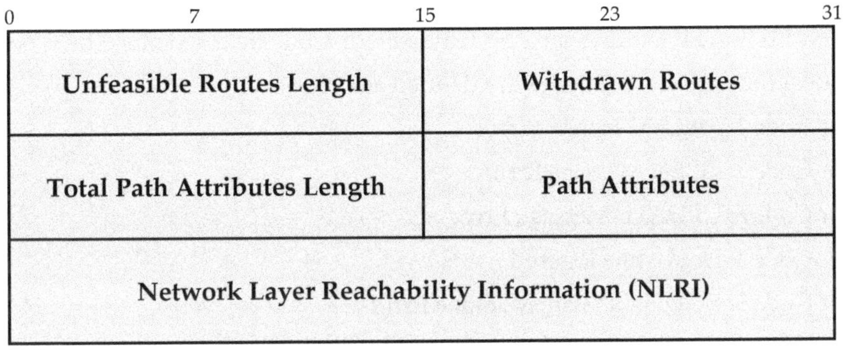

0	7	15	23	31
Unfeasible Routes Length		Withdrawn Routes		
Total Path Attributes Length		Path Attributes		
Network Layer Reachability Information (NLRI)				

Fig. 6-11. The BGP UPDATE Message Format

Within the UPDATE message, the 2-byte Unfeasible Routes Length field specifies the length of the Withdrawn Routes field that follows. A value of 0 designates that no routes are being withdrawn with this UPDATE message. The 2-byte Withdrawn Routes field lists the routes or the prefixes previously announced that are now being withdrawn. Each route is encoded as a Length/Prefix tuple, where the Length is the number of bits in the subnet mask and the Prefix is the IPv4 NLRI. This field is variable in length, depending on the routes withdrawn.

The 2-byte Total Path Attributes Length field is used to specify the length of the Path Attributes field that follows. A value of zero designates that no routes are being advertised with this message. BGP path attributes are a core ROUTE exam requirement and will be described in detail later in this chapter.

The variable length Path Attributes field contains the BGP attributes assigned to the path. Each attribute is encoded as a TLV triplet. Finally, the variable length NLRI field lists the routes advertised to the remote peer. Each route is encoded as a Length/Prefix tuple, where the Length is the number of bits in the subnet mask and the Prefix is the IPv4 route.

The NOTIFICATION Message (Message Type 3)

The BGP NOTIFICATION message (Type 3) is sent when an error condition is detected. When a BGP peer detects an error within the session, it sends a NOTIFICATION message to the remote router and immediately closes both the BGP and TCP sessions. The minimum length of the NOTIFICATION message is 21 bytes, including the header. Figure 6-12 below illustrates the fields that are contained within the BGP NOTIFICATION message:

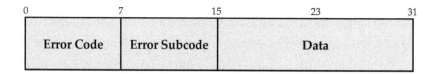

Fig. 6-12. The BGP NOTIFICATION Message Format

Within the NOTIFICATION message, the 1-byte Error Code field specifies the type of BGP error seen by the local router. Six error codes are defined as follows:

- Error Code 1: Message Header Error
- Error Code 2: OPEN Message Error
- Error Code 3: UPDATE Message Error
- Error Code 4: Hold Time Expired
- Error Code 5: BGP Finite State Machine Error
- Error Code 6: Cease

Keep in mind that this is not a BGP-specific exam; however, because BGP is a requirement of the ROUTE exam, it is important to familiarize yourself with the different error subcodes. Subcodes are listed and described in the following sections and tables.

The 1-byte Error Subcode field contains specific information about the error. Table 6-1 below lists the different Message Header Error subcodes:

Table 6-1. Message Header Error Subcodes

Subcode Value	Subcode Name
1	Connection Not Synchronized
2	Bad Message Length
3	Bad Message Type

Table 6-2 below lists the different OPEN Message Error subcodes:

Table 6-2. OPEN Message Error Subcodes

Subcode Value	Subcode Name
1	Unsupported Version Number
2	Bad Peer AS
3	Bad BGP Identifier
4	Unsupported Optional Parameter
5	Deprecated (i.e., obsolete)
6	Unacceptable Hold Time

Table 6-3 below lists the different UPDATE Message Error subcodes:

Table 6-3. UPDATE Message Error Subcodes

Subcode Value	Subcode Name
1	Malformed Attribute List
2	Unrecognized Well-known Attribute
3	Missing Well-known Attribute
4	Attribute Flags Error
5	Attribute Length Error
6	Invalid ORIGIN Attribute
7	Deprecated (i.e., obsolete)
8	Invalid NEXT_HOP Attribute
9	Optional Attribute Error
10	Invalid Network Field
11	Malformed AS_PATH

Table 6-4 below lists the different Cease subcodes:

Table 6-4. Cease Subcodes

Subcode Value	Subcode Name
1	Maximum Number of Prefixes Reached
2	Administrative Shutdown
3	Peer De-configured
4	Administrative Reset
5	Connection Rejected
6	Other Configuration Change
7	Connection Collision Resolution
8	Out of Resources

Finally, in the NOTIFICATION message, the variable length Data field is used to diagnose the reason for the NOTIFICATION. The contents of the Data field depend upon the Error Code and the Error Subcode. The length of the Data field can be determined from the Message Length field using the following formula:

Message Length = 21 + Data Length

The KEEPALIVE Message (Message Type 4)

The KEEPALIVE message (Type 4) is used to determine whether a host or a link has failed. This message type contains a single 19-byte header and no other data. By default, BGP peers exchange KEEPALIVE messages every 60 seconds. In addition, by default, the hold-time value used by BGP is three times the value of the keepalive interval. The values for these parameters are verified using the show ip bgp neighbors command as illustrated in the following output:

```
R2#show ip bgp neighbors
BGP neighbor is 10.0.0.1,  remote AS 1, external link
  BGP version 4, remote router ID 1.1.1.1
  BGP state = Established, up for 00:03:02
  Last read 00:00:02, last write 00:00:02, hold time is 180, keepalive
interval is 60 seconds

...

[Truncated Output]
```

The advertisement of an UPDATE message within the keepalive period resets the timer to 0. In other words, the KEEPALIVE message is sent only in the absence of other messages for a particular session. If the local router does not receive a KEEPALIVE or an UPDATE message within the hold-time period, a NOTIFICATION message of Hold Time Expired is generated and the session is torn down.

ESTABLISHING BORDER GATEWAY PROTOCOL ADJACENCIES

Now that we have a solid understanding of the different BGP packets, we will look at how and when these packets are exchanged during the establishment and maintenance of the BGP session. Like OSPF and EIGRP, BGP also transitions through several states before a neighbor relationship is established. However, unlike OSPF and EIGRP, BGP does not discover neighbors dynamically. Instead, BGP neighbors must be configured manually, as will be illustrated later in this chapter.

Because BGP is unique in that it uses TCP as the underlying protocol, the process of establishing a neighbor relationship is two-fold: the first phase is the establishment of the TCP session, and the second phase is the establishment of the BGP peer session. RFC 1771 includes a section on the BGP Finite State Machine (FSM). The FSM includes an overview of BGP operations by state. The six different states that BGP will go through before a neighbor relationship is established are as follows:

1. The Idle state
2. The Connect state
3. The Active state

4. The OpenSent state
5. The OpenConfirm state
6. The Established state

The first three states pertain to the establishment of the underlying TCP connection between the BGP speakers. The second three states pertain to the establishment of the actual BGP session. The `show ip bgp summary` or the `show ip bgp neighbors` commands can be used to view some, but not all, of these states in Cisco IOS software, as will be illustrated in the sections that follow. These six different states are described below.

The Idle State

The Idle state is the initial BGP state after BGP is enabled on a router, or when a router is reset. No BGP resources are allocated to the peer in this state. Additionally, when in this state, no incoming connections are allowed. Following is the output of the `show ip bgp neighbors` command immediately after BGP has been enabled and a neighbor has been defined.

```
R2#show ip bgp neighbors
BGP neighbor is 10.0.1.1,  remote AS 1, external link
  BGP version 4, remote router ID 0.0.0.0
  BGP state = Idle
  Last read 00:00:00, last write 00:00:00, hold time is 180, keepalive
interval is 60 seconds

  . . .

[Truncated Output]
```

The same state would be seen as follows if the `show ip bgp summary` command were used:

```
R2#show ip bgp summary
BGP router identifier 2.2.2.2, local AS number 2
BGP table version is 1, main routing table version 1

Neighbor     V   AS MsgRcvd MsgSent   TblVer  InQ OutQ Up/Down  State/PfxRcd
10.0.1.1     4    1       0       0        0    0    0 never    Idle
```

The Connect State

In this state, BGP waits for a TCP connection to be completed. If successful, the local router will send an OPEN message to the peer and the BGP state machine transitions to the OpenSent state. However, if the TCP connection attempt fails, the local router resets the ConnectRetry timer and transitions to the Active state. Additionally, depending on the failure condition, the local router could also revert back to the Idle state.

Additionally, if the ConnectRetry timer reaches 0 while the local router is in the Connect state, the timer is reset and another connection attempt is made. In this case, the local router remains in the Connect state.

The Active State

In the Active state, a TCP connection is initiated to establish a BGP neighbor relationship, also referred to as a BGP peer relationship. In plain English, the BGP routing process tries to establish a TCP session with the peer. If the session establishes successfully, then an OPEN message is sent to the peer, the Hold timer is set to a large value, and the local router transitions to the OpenSent state. However, if the TCP session fails to establish, then the local router initiates another session, sets the ConnectRetry timer to 0, and transitions back to the Connect state.

During this state, if the remote peer attempts to establish a connection to the local router using an unexpected IP address for the session, the local router will refuse the connection. The local router will remain in the Active state and reset the ConnectRetry timer. If any other failures occur, then the local router releases all BGP resources associated with the connection and transitions back to the Idle state. The output of the `show ip bgp neighbors` command following the completion of the Connect state is illustrated below:

```
R2#show ip bgp neighbors
BGP neighbor is 10.0.1.1,  remote AS 1, external link
  BGP version 4, remote router ID 0.0.0.0
  BGP state = Active
  Last read 00:00:01, last write 00:00:01, hold time is 180, keepalive
interval is 60 seconds

  ...

[Truncated Output]
```

The same state would be seen as follows if the `show ip bgp summary` command were used:

```
R2#show ip bgp summary
BGP router identifier 2.2.2.2, local AS number 2
BGP table version is 1, main routing table version 1

Neighbor     V    AS MsgRcvd MsgSent   TblVer  InQ OutQ Up/Down   State/PfxRcd
10.0.1.1     4     1     215     215        0    0    0 00:00:01  Active
```

The OpenSent State

After sending the OPEN message to the peer, BGP then transitions to the OpenSent state. In this state, the local router waits for a response to the sent OPEN message. When an OPEN message is received, all fields in the message are checked. If an error is detected, the local router will send the peer a NOTIFICATION message and transition back to the Idle state. However, if a successful (i.e., error-free response) is received, then the BGP state moves to OpenConfirm and BGP sends a KEEPALIVE message and sets a KeepAlive timer. Additionally, the previously large Hold timer set in the Active state is replaced with the new negotiated hold-time value as the BGP peers negotiate and agree on parameters for the session.

Finally, if a TCP disconnect is received while in this state, the local router terminates the BGP session, resets the ConnectRetry timer, and transitions back to the Active state.

The OpenConfirm State

The OpenConfirm state is the penultimate state before the final state, the Established state, is reached. In this state, BGP waits for a KEEPALIVE or a NOTIFICATION message. If the local router receives a KEEPALIVE message, then it transitions to the Established state. However, if a KEEPALIVE is not received before the negotiated Hold timer expires, then the local router will send a NOTIFICATION message to the peer with the error code 'Hold Timer Expired' and transition to the Idle state. Additionally, if the local router receives a NOTIFICATION message from its peer, it will also immediately transition to the Idle state.

In this state, if any other failure is detected, then the local router sends a NOTIFICATION message with the error code 'Finite State Machine Error' and transitions back to the Idle state. BGP goes through the same steps again to try to establish the connection.

The Established State

The Established state is reached when the initial KEEPALIVE message is received while BGP is in the OpenConfirm state. This is the final state of a peer relationship and designates a fully operational connection. Two BGP peers can exchange routing information only when the Established state is reached. In the Established state, BGP can exchange UPDATE, NOTIFICATION, and KEEPALIVE messages with its peer. The Established state can be validated using the show ip bgp neighbors command as illustrated in the output below:

```
R2#show ip bgp neighbors
BGP neighbor is 10.0.0.1,  remote AS 1, external link
  BGP version 4, remote router ID 1.1.1.1
  BGP state = Established, up for 00:12:17
  Last read 00:00:17, last write 00:00:17, hold time is 180, keepalive
interval is 60 seconds
```

Unlike the show ip bgp neighbors command, the show ip bgp summary command will not show the Established state. The state will not be listed but the number of prefixes received from the peer(s) will be listed instead. If no prefixes are received from the peers, then a value of 0 will be present. This is illustrated in the following output on a BGP speaker with multiple peers or neighbors in the Established state:

```
R2#show ip bgp summary
BGP router identifier 2.2.2.2, local AS number 2
BGP table version is 3, main routing table version 3
2 network entries using 234 bytes of memory
3 path entries using 156 bytes of memory
3/2 BGP path/bestpath attribute entries using 372 bytes of memory
1 BGP AS-PATH entries using 24 bytes of memory
0 BGP route-map cache entries using 0 bytes of memory
0 BGP filter-list cache entries using 0 bytes of memory
BGP using 786 total bytes of memory
BGP activity 3/1 prefixes, 4/1 paths, scan interval 60 secs

Neighbor     V    AS MsgRcvd MsgSent   TblVer  InQ OutQ Up/Down  State/PfxRcd
10.0.0.1     4     1      87      88        3    0    0 00:15:05           1
10.0.1.1     4     1      90      94        3    0    0 00:15:19           1
10.0.3.3     4     3      19      23        3    0    0 00:07:25           0
```

In the output above, R2 has three BGP peers in the Established state. Peers 10.0.0.1 and 10.0.1.1 are advertising a single prefix to R2, while peer 10.0.3.3 is not advertising any prefixes to R2.

NOTE: The remainder of the fields in the output of the show ip bgp summary command will be described later in this chapter.

BORDER GATEWAY PROTOCOL ATTRIBUTES

At the beginning of this chapter, we learned that BGP uses path attributes to ensure protocol reliability and routing information accuracy. In addition to being used to select the best path to a destination prefix, path attributes are also used to prevent BGP loops and ensure that the next-hop IP address for a specified BGP prefix is reachable before BGP uses the next-hop address to forward packets to that destination prefix.

Later in this chapter, we also learned that each BGP UPDATE message contains a single set of attributes and all of the routes using those attributes. Within the BGP UPDATE message, the variable length Path Attributes field contains the BGP attributes assigned to the path. Each BGP attribute is encoded as a TLV triplet, which includes the Attribute Type, the Attribute Length, and the Attribute Value. The Attribute Type portion of this TLV is a 2-byte field comprised of the Attribute Flags octet followed by the Attribute Type Code byte. Figure 6-13 below illustrates the format of the Attribute Type field:

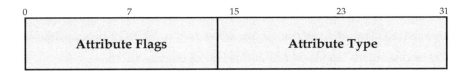

Fig. 6-13. The BGP Attribute Type Field

Bit 0 (the high-order bit) of the Attribute Flags field is the Optional bit. If this bit is set to 1, then the attribute is optional. If this bit is set to 0, then the attribute is well-known.

Bit 1 (the second high-order bit) of the Attribute Flags field is the Transitive bit. This bit is used to specify whether the optional attribute is transitive (set to 1) or non-transitive (set to 0). If the high-order bit is set to 0 (well-known attribute), then this field must be set to 1.

> **NOTE:** Transitive attributes are those that transit different autonomous systems, while non-transitive attributes are locally significant within an autonomous system.

Bit 2 (the third high-order bit) is the Partial bit. If this bit is set to 1, then it indicates that information in the optional transitive attribute is optional. It is therefore not mandatory for routers to understand or recognize this attribute. Additionally, a value of 1 also indicates that at least one BGP router along the path did not recognize the attribute. For well-know and optional non-transitive attributes, this bit must be set to 0. A value of 0 indicates that each BGP router along the path recognized this attribute.

Bit 3 is the Extended Length bit. This bit is used to set the size of the TLV Length portion to one byte, which is indicated by a value of 0, or two bytes, which is indicated by a value of 1. Bits 4 through 7 are unused and must be set to a value of 0.

The Attribute Type Code byte contains the Attribute Type Code. BGP path attributes fall into the following four categories:
1. Well-known mandatory
2. Well-known discretionary
3. Optional transitive
4. Optional non-transitive

All BGP speakers must recognize all of the well-known mandatory attributes, which must be included for all prefixes. However, discretionary attributes may or may not be included for a particular prefix. Discretionary attributes may be used based on the decision of the network administrator; however, their use is not mandatory.

BGP speakers do not have to understand optional attributes but must re-advertise them based on their transitive setting. Transitive attributes are advertised to all BGP peers, while non-transitive attributes may be discarded if the local router does not recognize them.

Because BGP is first and foremost a routing policy tool, BGP makes extensive use of these path attributes in selecting the best path to a destination. A solid understanding of these path attributes is required in order to both design and implement an effective BGP routing architecture. However, while Cisco IOS software supports many different BGP attributes, only those that are within the scope of the ROUTE exam are described in this section as follows:

- The ORIGIN attribute
- The AS_PATH attribute
- The NEXT_HOP attribute
- The MULTI_EXIT_DISC attribute
- The LOCAL_PREF attribute
- The ATOMIC_AGGREGATE and AGGREGATOR attributes
- The COMMUNITY attribute
- The ORIGINATOR_ID attribute
- The CLUSTER_LIST attribute
- The Cisco-proprietary WEIGHT attribute

These attributes are described in the following sections.

The ORIGIN Attribute (Type Code 1)

The ORIGIN attribute, defined as Attribute Type Code 1, is a well-known mandatory attribute. The ORIGIN attribute is generated by the autonomous system that originates the routing information. This attribute is automatically defined when a route or prefix is injected into BGP but may be modified using a route map in Cisco IOS software. The three possible Origin values are as follows:

1. IGP
2. EGP
3. INCOMPLETE

An ORIGIN of IGP indicates that the prefix was injected into BGP using the network command in Cisco IOS software. Prefixes with this ORIGIN code are displayed with the letter 'I' and are encoded as a value of 0. These routes are internal to the originating AS.

An ORIGIN code of EGP indicates that the prefix originated from the Exterior Gateway Protocol (EGP). Prefixes with this ORIGIN code are displayed with the letter 'E' and are encoded as a value of 1. EGP is beyond the scope of the ROUTE exam requirements and is not described within this guide.

Finally, an ORGIN code of INCOMPLETE indicates that the original source or the prefix is not known to the router injecting the route into BGP. This code is used for prefixes that are redistributed into BGP using the `redistribute` command. In Cisco IOS software, prefixes with the IN-COMPLETE attribute code are displayed with the symbol '?' and are encoded as a value of 2. Table 6-5 below summarizes the BGP ORIGIN attribute codes, the Cisco IOS software representation for prefixes using the specific code, and the description of the code:

Table 6-5. ORIGIN Attribute Codes

Attribute Code	Cisco IOS Representation	Description
0	I	The prefix is internal to the originating AS
1	E	The prefix is received from External Gateway Protocol
2	?	The prefix has been learned via another means—the most common being redistribution

The AS_PATH Attribute (Type Code 2)

The AS_PATH attribute, defined as Attribute Type Code 2, is a well-known mandatory attribute that contains a reverse-order sequenced list of AS numbers that represent the domains the prefix has transited. The first AS listed in the AS_PATH attribute list is the last AS traversed, while the last AS listed in the AS_PATH attribute list is the originating AS. For example, if the AS_PATH for a prefix is 10, 20, 30, 40, 50, then it means that the prefix originated in AS 50 and traversed ASs 40, 30, 20, and finally 10 before it was received by the local router. This is illustrated in Figure 6-14 below:

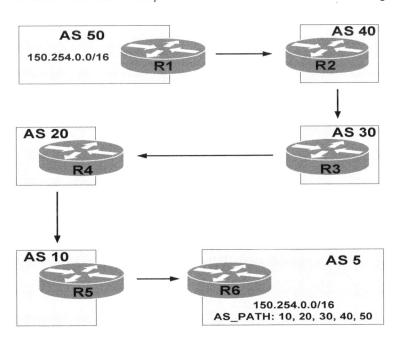

Fig. 6-14. The BGP AS_PATH List

It is extremely important to remember that the AS_PATH attribute is changed only when an UPDATE is sent to an eBGP neighbor, but never to an iBGP peer. In other words, an iBGP speaker will never change the AS_PATH attribute when advertising a prefix to another iBGP speaker; however, an eBGP speaker will change the AS_PATH attribute when advertising a prefix to another eBGP speaker. This concept is illustrated in Figure 6-15 below:

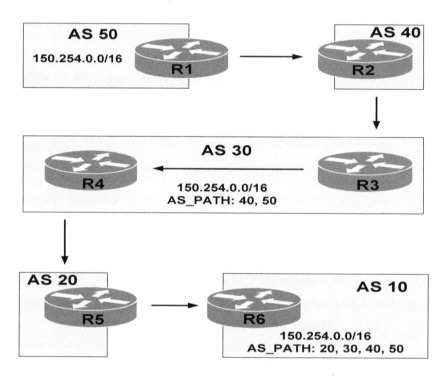

Fig. 6-15. External and Internal BGP AS_PATH Updates

Referencing Figure 6-15, R1 in AS 50 originates the 150.254.0.0/16 prefix. The prefix is advertised to R2, which is an eBGP neighbor. This attribute is changed from a Null value to 50 in the UPDATE message because R2 is an eBGP neighbor. The AS_PATH for this prefix from router R2's perspective is 50.

AS 40 is peered to AS 30 and R2 advertises this prefix to R3. Because router R3 is an eBGP peer, the AS_PATH attribute is changed in the UPDATE message sent by R2 to R3 to also include AS 40 (its own AS number). The AS_PATH for this prefix from router R3's perspective is 40, 50.

R3 is peered to R4, which is an iBGP peer. In this case, R3 does not add its own AS number to the UPDATE it sends to R4 for the 150.254.0.0/16 prefix. From the perspective of R4, the AS_PATH remains 40, 50 for the 150.254.0.0/16 prefix.

R4 is peered to R5, which is an eBGP peer. Because the neighbor is external to the AS, R4 adds its own AS, AS 30, to the list of ASs for the 150.254.0.0/16 prefix and includes that in the UPDATE message sent to R5. The AS_PATH for this prefix from R3's perspective is 30, 40, 50.

Finally, R5 is peered to R6, which is also an eBGP peer. Again, because the neighbor is external to the local AS, R5 adds its own AS number to the list of ASs for the 150.254.0.0/16 prefix and includes that in the UPDATE message sent to R6. The AS_PATH for this prefix from R6's perspective is 20, 30, 40, 50.

The AS_PATH segment is represented by a TLV triplet, which includes the Path Segment Type, the Path Segment Length, and the Path Segment Value. The Path Segment Type is a 1-byte field that can contain the following four AS segments, all of which are supported in Cisco IOS software:
1. AS_SET
2. AS_SEQUENCE
3. AS_CONFED_SEQUENCE
4. AS_CONFED_SET

The AS_SET segment is an unordered set of autonomous systems that a route in the UPDATE message has traversed. The AS_SEQUENCE segment is an ordered set of autonomous systems that a route in the UPDATE message has traversed. The AS_CONFED_SEQUENCE segment is an ordered set of member autonomous systems in the local Confederation that the UPDATE message has traversed. Finally, the AS_CONFED_SET segment is an unordered set of member autonomous systems in the local Confederation that the UPDATE message has traversed.

BGP Confederations will be described in detail in the following chapter; however, the primary emphasis in this section should be placed on remembering that the difference between the SET and SEQUENCE segments is that within the SET segments, the list of autonomous systems traversed is unordered, while within the SEQUENCE segments, the list of autonomous systems traversed is ordered.

The AS_PATH attribute serves the following two primary functions:
1. BGP path selection
2. Loop prevention

By default, BGP will always prefer the path that has the shortest AS_PATH list to a destination prefix when comparing two or more UPDATE messages for the same destination prefix. The use of the AS_PATH attribute in preventing loops will be described in detail in the following main section of this chapter, which delves into BGP loop prevention mechanisms.

The NEXT_HOP Attribute (Type Code 3)

The NEXT_HOP attribute, defined as Attribute Type Code 3, is a well-known mandatory attribute that is used to define the next-hop IP address to the destination prefix from the BGP perspective. Unlike with traditional IGPs, the next-hop for a BGP prefix does not have to be directly connected. In such cases, the local router performs a recursive lookup in the routing table to locate a route to the BGP next-hop. The result of this recursive lookup is the physical next-hop assigned to the BGP route in the routing and forwarding tables.

It is important to understand that there are variable ways in which the NEXT_HOP for a prefix is determined and set. These variable ways include the following:

- When the prefix is first injected into BGP
- When the prefix is advertised via eBGP
- When the next-hop is changed manually

When a prefix is first injected into BGP, then the BGP speaker on which the prefix is injected will be responsible for setting the NEXT_HOP attribute. The actual value (i.e., the actual IP address specified) depends on how the prefix is injected into BGP. If the prefix is injected into BGP using the network command and the prefix is a directly connected subnet, then the NEXT_HOP address will be 0.0.0.0 on the local BGP speaker. The BGP speaker will then use its own IP address before sending the UPDATE message to peers. As an example, a router (R2) has been configured with a Loopback interface on the 150.254.2.0/24 subnet. The show ip route command for this prefix shows the following entry:

```
R2#show ip route 150.254.2.0 255.255.255.0
Routing entry for 150.254.2.0/24
  Known via "connected", distance 0, metric 0 (connected, via interface)
  Routing Descriptor Blocks:
  * directly connected, via Loopback0
      Route metric is 0, traffic share count is 1
```

The same prefix is then advertised via BGP using the network command. Because the prefix is directly connected, the NEXT_HOP on the local router shows 0.0.0.0, which can be validated using the show ip bgp command as illustrated in the following output:

```
R2#show ip bgp
BGP table version is 4, local router ID is 2.2.2.2
Status codes: s suppressed, d damped, h history, * valid, > best, i -
internal,
            r RIB-failure, S Stale
Origin codes: i - IGP, e - EGP, ? - incomplete

   Network          Next Hop          Metric LocPrf Weight Path
*> 150.254.2.0/24   0.0.0.0                0         32768 i
```

However, if a prefix is injected into BGP using the `network` command and that prefix is known via an IGP, such as OSPF, then the NEXT_HOP contains the IP address of the IGP next-hop router. As another example, the same router used in the previous example is receiving routing information for the 153.254.0.0/16 via OSPF as illustrated in the following output:

```
R2#show ip route 153.254.0.0 255.255.0.0
Routing entry for 153.254.0.0/16
  Known via "ospf 2", distance 110, metric 65, type intra area
  Last update from 10.0.3.3 on Serial0/1, 00:09:05 ago
  Routing Descriptor Blocks:
  * 10.0.3.3, from 3.3.3.3, 00:09:05 ago, via Serial0/1
      Route metric is 65, traffic share count is 1
```

The next-hop address for this prefix is 10.3.3.3. If the same prefix were advertised via BGP using the network command, the NEXT_HOP would be set to the OSPF next-hop address by the local router on which the prefix is injected into BGP as illustrated in the following output:

```
R2#show ip bgp
BGP table version is 6, local router ID is 2.2.2.2
Status codes: s suppressed, d damped, h history, * valid, > best, i - internal,
              r RIB-failure, S Stale
Origin codes: i - IGP, e - EGP, ? - incomplete

   Network          Next Hop            Metric LocPrf Weight Path
*> 153.254.0.0      10.0.3.3                65          32768 i
```

NOTE: The configuration and advertisement of prefixes using BGP will be described in detail later in this chapter. Primary emphasis at this point should be placed on understanding the setting of the NEXT_HOP attribute.

Finally, when BGP route summarization is configured using the `aggregate-address` router configuration command, the NEXT_HOP is set to the address of the router that is performing the summarization when an UPDATE message is sent. BGP route summarization will be described in detail in the following chapter on advanced BGP implementation.

Regarding the second point made about how the NEXT_HOP attribute is determined, when the prefix is advertised via eBGP, the NEXT_HOP attribute will be set automatically to the IP address of the eBGP speaker that is sending the UPDATE message for the prefix. However, if more than two eBGP peers reside on the same multi-access segment, the BGP speaker that is advertising the prefix sets the NEXT_HOP address in the UPDATE message to the original BGP speaker on the same segment rather than to itself. To clarify this point further, we will use the BGP topology in Figure 6-16 below:

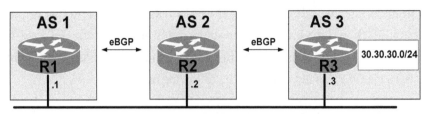

Multi-Access Ethernet Segment – 10.0.0.0/24

Fig. 6-16. External BGP NEXT_HOP on Multi-Access Segments

Referencing Figure 6-16, routers R1, R2, and R3 reside on the multi-access 10.0.0.0/24 segment. These three routers are all BGP speakers. R1 resides in AS 1 and has an eBGP neighbor relationship with R2 in AS 2. R2 is also peered with R3 in AS 3. R3 is advertising the 30.30.30.0/24 prefix via BGP. R1 and R3 are not directly peered with each other. Focusing only on the NEXT_HOP attribute at this point, R3 shows the following entry for the 30.30.30.0/24 prefix that is injected into BGP on this router using the `network` command:

```
R3#show ip bgp
BGP table version is 1, local router ID is 153.254.0.3
Status codes: s suppressed, d damped, h history, * valid, > best, i - internal,
              r RIB-failure, S Stale
Origin codes: i - IGP, e - EGP, ? - incomplete

   Network          Next Hop            Metric LocPrf Weight Path
*  30.30.30.0/24    0.0.0.0                  0          32768 i
```

Moving on to R2, this router shows the following entry for the 30.30.30.0/24 received from R1:

```
R2#show ip bgp
BGP table version is 2, local router ID is 2.2.2.2
Status codes: s suppressed, d damped, h history, * valid, > best, i - internal,
              r RIB-failure, S Stale
Origin codes: i - IGP, e - EGP, ? - incomplete

   Network          Next Hop            Metric LocPrf Weight Path
*> 30.30.30.0/24    10.0.0.3                 0              0 3 i
```

R2 in turn advertises this to eBGP neighbor R1. Under normal circumstances, R2 would set the NEXT_HOP address in the UPDATE message to its own IP address; however, because the routers reside on the same multi-access segment, this default method of operation is forgone. Instead, R2 simply retains the IP address of R3 in this field, as can be seen on R1 in the following output:

```
R1#show ip bgp
BGP table version is 2, local router ID is 1.1.1.1
Status codes: s suppressed, d damped, h history, * valid, > best, i - internal,
              r RIB-failure, S Stale
```

```
Origin codes: i - IGP, e - EGP, ? - incomplete

   Network          Next Hop            Metric LocPrf Weight Path
*> 30.30.30.0/24    10.0.0.3                            0 2 3 i
```

Finally, regarding the third point made on how the NEXT_HOP attribute is set, the next-hop can also be changed manually by using the `next-hop-self` neighbor configuration command for an iBGP peer or by using a route map to change the NEXT_HOP attribute for an eBGP peer. Because this is an important concept, we will take a moment to explain it further.

By default, the NEXT_HOP is not changed when a prefix is advertised by a BGP speaker to an iBGP peer. Consider the topology illustrated in Figure 6-17 below, for example:

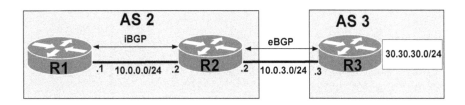

Fig. 6-17. Understanding iBGP Default NEXT_HOP Behavior

Figure 6-17 shows a basic routed network. R3 resides in AS 3 and is peered to R2 in AS 2. R2 is in turn also peered to R1, which is in the same AS. R3 is advertising the 30.30.30.0/24 prefix. Focusing exclusively on the NEXT_HOP attribute, the BGP Table on R2 displays the following:

```
R2#show ip bgp 30.30.30.0 255.255.255.0
BGP routing table entry for 30.30.30.0/24, version 6
Paths: (1 available, best #1, table Default-IP-Routing-Table)
  Advertised to update-groups:
     1
  3
    10.0.3.3 from 10.0.3.3 (3.3.3.3)
      Origin IGP, metric 0, localpref 100, valid, external, best
```

This prefix is advertised by R2 to iBGP peer R1. The BGP Table on R1 displays the following:

```
R1#show ip bgp 30.30.30.0 255.255.255.0
BGP routing table entry for 30.30.30.0/24, version 0
Paths: (1 available, no best path)
  Not advertised to any peer
  3
    10.0.3.3 (inaccessible) from 10.0.0.2 (2.2.2.2)
      Origin IGP, metric 0, localpref 100, valid, internal
```

In the output above, the prefix is marked as being inaccessible due to the following:
- The NEXT_HOP attribute was not changed when R2 advertised this prefix to R1
- R1 does not have a route to the 10.0.3.3 address specified in the NEXT_HOP

The recommended solution is to configure R2 to change the NEXT_HOP attribute and insert its IP address instead of that of the eBGP peer by using the next-hop-self command. This is implemented as follows on R2:

```
R2(config)#router bgp 2
R2(config-router)#neighbor 10.0.0.1 next-hop-self
R2(config-router)#exit
```

Following this configuration, the BGP Table on R1 now displays the following for the prefix:

```
R1#show ip bgp 30.30.30.0 255.255.255.0
BGP routing table entry for 30.30.30.0/24, version 2
Paths: (1 available, best #1, table Default-IP-Routing-Table)
  Not advertised to any peer
  3
    10.0.0.2 from 10.0.0.2 (2.2.2.2)
      Origin IGP, metric 0, localpref 100, valid, internal, best
```

The second solution would be to use an IGP to advertise dynamically the 10.0.3.0/24 subnet between R2 and R3 or to configure a static route to this address on R3. While both options are valid, the next-hop-self configuration is the recommended solution.

NOTE: BGP neighbor configuration is illustrated in detail later in this chapter.

For eBGP peers to set the NEXT_HOP IP address to a value other than that of the local BGP speaker, a route map must be used. This configuration is illustrated in the following chapter.

The MULTI_EXIT_DISC Attribute (Type Code 4)

The MULTI_EXIT_DISC (MED) attribute Discriminator attribute is a 32-bit positive integer that is defined as Attribute Type Code 4. In addition, MED is an optional non-transitive attribute. MED is typically used on inter-AS links and allows BGP to choose among multiple exit points to the same neighboring AS.

In other words, MED, which is expressed as a metric value, is used as a suggestion to the peer external AS regarding the preferred route into the local AS that is advertising the metric. The term 'suggestion' is used because it is not mandatory for the neighboring AS to adhere to the values specified using this attribute. Figure 6-18 below depicts the use of the MED attribute in BGP:

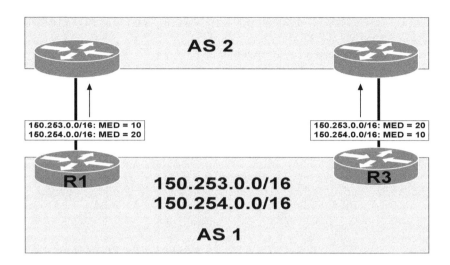

Fig. 6-18. Understanding the MULTI_EXIT_DISC Attribute

Referencing Figure 6-18, AS 1 is peered to AS 2. AS 1 is advertising the 150.253.0.0/16 as well as the 150.254.0.0/16 prefixes to AS 2. Leveraging the policy control capabilities of BGP, R1 has been configured to advertise the 150.253.0.0/16 prefix to AS 2 with a MED (metric) of 10, while advertising the 150.254.0.0/16 prefix with a MED (metric) of 20. R3 has been configured to advertise the 150.253.0.0/16 prefix to AS 2 with a MED (metric) of 20, while also advertising the 150.254.0.0/16 prefix, but with a MED (metric) of 10.

The result of this implementation is that the lower MED values influence AS 1 to forward traffic destined to the 150.253.0.0/16 prefix via R1 and the traffic destined to the 150.254.0.0/16 prefix via R3. The alternate paths will be used when the primary (preferred) paths are unavailable.

In addition to understanding the use of the MED attribute, it is also important to understand Cisco IOS software rules on MED setting and advertisement. These rules apply to the following:

1. Assigning a MED value to a prefix
2. Advertising prefixes to iBGP peers
3. Advertising prefixes to eBGP peers

The MED value for a prefix is determined by the manner in which that prefix has been injected into BGP on the local BGP speaker. If the prefix is for a directly connected network and the network or redistribute command is used to inject the prefix into BGP, then the BGP MED value is set to 0. As an example, assume that the local router has the 150.254.2.0/24 subnet directly connected as illustrated in the following output:

```
R2#show ip route 150.254.2.0 255.255.255.0
Routing entry for 150.254.2.0/24
```

```
Known via "connected", distance 0, metric 0 (connected, via interface)
Routing Descriptor Blocks:
* directly connected, via Loopback0
    Route metric is 0, traffic share count is 1
```

If this prefix is injected into BGP using the `network` or `redistribute` command, the MED value will be set to 0 as illustrated in the following output:

```
R2#show ip bgp
BGP table version is 4, local router ID is 2.2.2.2
Status codes: s suppressed, d damped, h history, * valid, > best, i - internal,
         r RIB-failure, S Stale
Origin codes: i - IGP, e - EGP, ? - incomplete

   Network          Next Hop          Metric LocPrf Weight Path
*> 150.254.2.0/24   0.0.0.0                0         32768 i
```

However, if the prefix is received from an IGP, such as OSPF or EIGRP, when it is injected into BGP using either the `network` or the `redistribute` command, then the MED value is set to the IGP metric. As an example, a router is receiving the 153.254.0.0/16 prefix via an OSPF as illustrated in the following output:

```
R2#show ip route 153.254.0.0 255.255.0.0
Routing entry for 153.254.0.0/16
  Known via "ospf 2", distance 110, metric 65, type intra area
  Last update from 10.0.3.3 on Serial0/1, 00:09:05 ago
  Routing Descriptor Blocks:
  * 10.0.3.3, from 3.3.3.3, 00:09:05 ago, via Serial0/1
      Route metric is 65, traffic share count is 1
```

In the output above, the prefix has an IGP route metric of 65. When the prefix is injected into R2 using either the `network` or the `redistribute` command, the MED value reflects the IGP metric. The next-hop address for this prefix is 10.3.3.3.

If the same prefix were advertised via BGP using the `network` command, the NEXT_HOP would be set to the OSPF next-hop address by the local router on which the prefix is injected into BGP as illustrated in the following output:

```
R2#show ip bgp
BGP table version is 6, local router ID is 2.2.2.2
Status codes: s suppressed, d damped, h history, * valid, > best, i -
internal,
          r RIB-failure, S Stale
Origin codes: i - IGP, e - EGP, ? - incomplete

   Network          Next Hop          Metric LocPrf Weight Path
*> 153.254.0.0      10.0.3.3               65         32768 i
```

Finally, if the prefix is injected into BGP using the aggregate-address command (i.e., it is a summary prefix), then the MED value is not set. As was stated earlier, BGP summarization will be described in detail in the following chapter.

Regarding the second rule, advertising prefixes to iBGP peers, a BGP speaker will advertise prefixes with the same metric to another iBGP peer. This is illustrated in Figure 6-19 below:

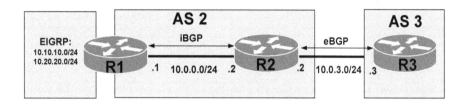

Fig. 6-19. Understanding iBGP Default NEXT_HOP Behavior

Referencing Figure 6-19, R1 and R2 reside within AS 2. R2 is receiving some routes via EIGRP as verified and illustrated in the following output:

```
R1#show ip route eigrp
     10.0.0.0/24 is subnetted, 5 subnets
D       10.20.20.0 [90/409600] via 192.168.1.5, 00:08:45, FastEthernet0/0
D       10.10.10.0 [90/409600] via 192.168.1.5, 00:08:45, FastEthernet0/0
```

Both EIGRP prefixes have a route metric of 409600. These prefixes are then injected into BGP on R2 using the redistribute eigrp command. Because the routes are received from an IGP, BGP retains the IGP metric and sets that as the MED value. R1 then advertises the prefixes to its iBGP peer, R2. Because this is an iBGP peer relationship, the MED value is unchanged as illustrated in the following output:

```
R2#show ip bgp
BGP table version is 10, local router ID is 2.2.2.2
Status codes: s suppressed, d damped, h history, * valid, > best, i - internal,
              r RIB-failure, S Stale
Origin codes: i - IGP, e - EGP, ? - incomplete

   Network          Next Hop            Metric LocPrf Weight Path
*>i10.10.10.0/24    192.168.1.5         409600    100      0 ?
*>i10.20.20.0/24    192.168.1.5         409600    100      0 ?
```

Continuing with this scenario and moving on to the third rule, which pertains to the advertising of prefixes to eBGP peers, R2 in turn advertises these received prefixes to eBGP peer R3. By default, if the prefix is learned from an iBGP peer, then the edge router (R2) will remove the MED value before advertising the prefix to an eBGP peer. Therefore, the same prefixes that R2 received from

R1 with the metric value of 409600, will be advertised to R3, the eBGP peer with no metric value, as illustrated in the following output on R3:

```
R3#show ip bgp
BGP table version is 6, local router ID is 3.3.3.3
Status codes: s suppressed, d damped, h history, * valid, > best, i - internal,
              r RIB-failure, S Stale
Origin codes: i - IGP, e - EGP, ? - incomplete

   Network          Next Hop            Metric LocPrf Weight Path
*> 10.10.10.0/24    10.0.3.2                              0 2 ?
*> 10.20.20.0/24    10.0.3.2                              0 2 ?
```

NOTE: While the MED value is compared only for prefixes received from the same AS, Cisco IOS software does allow MED values to be compared for prefixes received from different ASs using the `bgp always-compare-med` router configuration command. This is beyond the scope of the ROUTE exam requirements and will not be illustrated in this chapter or in this guide.

The LOCAL_PREF Attribute (Type Code 5)

The LOCAL_PREF attribute is a 32-bit positive integer that defines a preference over one exit point in an AS. This attribute is a well-known discretionary BGP attribute, defined as Attribute Type Code 5. The LOCAL_PREF attribute is used only within an AS for path selection manipulation. If an iBGP speaker receives an UPDATE for the same destination from multiple iBGP peers, it will prefer the path with the highest LOCAL_PREF value.

In Cisco IOS software, the default LOCAL_PREF value is 100; however, this value can be changed to any value between 0 and 4294967295. Influencing path selection using the LOCAL_PREF attribute will be illustrated and described in detail in the following chapter.

The ATOMIC_AGGREGATE and AGGREGATOR Attributes (Type Codes 6 and 7)

Both the ATOMIC_AGGREGATE and AGGREGATOR attributes are used when BGP routing information is summarized. The ATOMIC_AGGREGATE is Attribute Type Code 6 and is a well-known discretionary attribute. This attribute is used to alert other routers that some BGP attribute information has been lost as a result of route aggregation.

The AGGREGATOR attribute is defined as Attribute Type Code 7 and is an optional, transitive attribute. This attribute type identifies the BGP router that performed the route aggregation. Both attributes will be illustrated in the following chapter when we delve into BGP summarization.

The COMMUNITY Attribute (Type Code 8)

The COMMUNITY attribute, defined as Attribute Type Code 8, is an optional transitive attribute that is used to group destinations, called communities. Once the destination prefixes have been grouped, routing decisions, such as acceptance, preference, and redistribution, can be applied. Route maps are used in conjunction with BGP to set the COMMUNITY attribute.

The attribute is encoded as a four-octet value, where the first two octets represent an AS number and the remaining two octets represent a locally defined value. Two types of communities exist as follows:

1. Well-known communities
2. Private communities

Well-known communities are those that have predefined meanings. Cisco IOS software supports four well-known communities, which are as follows:

1. NO_EXPORT
2. NO_ADVERTISE
3. INTERNET
4. LOCAL_AS

The NO_EXPORT well-known community prevents BGP prefixes that are specifically assigned this predefined community attribute value from being advertised to any eBGP peers. The prefixes, however, will continue to be advertised to all other BGP speakers within the local AS. In other words, prefixes assigned this community value will remain local to the AS.

The NO_ADVERTISE community prevents any prefixes that are assigned this predefined community attribute from being advertised to any peer—internal or external.

The INTERNET community allows all prefixes assigned to this community to be advertised to any and all BGP peers (assuming no filtering, etc., is in place). In Cisco IOS software, all BGP prefixes belong to the INTERNET community by default.

Finally, the LOCAL_AS community is used in a somewhat similar manner to another of the previously described communities: the NO_EXPORT community. If used in a Confederation, the LOCAL_AS community prevents all prefixes assigned this community from being advertised out of the local sub-autonomous system. When Confederations are not implemented, the LOCAL_AS community is applied in the same manner as the NO_EXPORT community.

NOTE: BGP Confederations are described in detail in the following chapter.

Unlike the well-known communities, private communities must be defined manually by the network administrators, and actions for prefixes assigned those communities must also be defined explicitly. Private communities are typically configured using the AA:NN format, where AA represents the AS Number and NN is a randomly selected number. The following chapter on advanced BGP implementation includes community configuration examples.

The ORIGINATOR_ID Attribute (Type Code 9)

The ORIGINATOR_ID attribute, specified in RFC 4456 as Attribute Type Code 9, is 4 bytes in length and is used to prevent routing loops in iBGP implementations that are using Route Reflectors. A Route Reflector (RR) is a special type of BGP speaker that reflects routes received from client routers to other routers, negating the need to implement a fully meshed iBGP topology. Think of the RR as being somewhat similar to the designated router (DR) used in OSPF. Non-DR routers will establish an adjacency only with the DR (and BDR). The DR then updates all other non-DR routers, negating the need for the routers on the multi-access segment to establish an adjacency with every other router on the segment.

Likewise, when an RR is implemented in an iBGP deployment, all non-RR routers, referred to as RR Clients, are configured such that they peer only with the RR, or RRs if more than one exists for redundancy. The RR then reflects routing information received from one client to all other clients with which it has an adjacency. This negates the need for iBGP routers to be fully meshed. Route reflection is described further in the following chapter.

Continuing with the discussion on the ORIGINATOR_ID attribute, this attribute should be received only from iBGP peers. The ORIGINATOR_ID is created or set by the RR, either to the address of the iBGP speaker that originated the route within the local AS or to the address of the iBGP speaker that learned the route via eBGP (i.e., the edge router). The ORIGINATOR_ID is an optional, non-transitive BGP attribute.

The CLUSTER_LIST Attribute (Type Code 10)

The CLUSTER_LIST attribute is an optional, non-transitive BGP attribute defined as Attribute Type Code 10. The CLUSTER_LIST is a sequence of CLUSTER_ID values representing the reflection path that the prefix has traversed. In other words, this attribute is also used when RRs have been implemented.

When the RR reflects a route, it must prepend the local CLUSTER_ID to the CLUSTER_LIST. If the UPDATE message has an empty CLUSTER_LIST, then the RR must create a new one. Like the ORIGINATOR_ID attribute, the CLUSTER_LIST attribute is also used for preventing loops in iBGP implementations. BGP loop prevention is described in the following main section.

The Cisco-proprietary WEIGHT Attribute

The final BGP attribute we will learn about is the Cisco-proprietary WEIGHT attribute. Unlike all other attributes that have been described in the previous sections, the WEIGHT attribute is not an open-standard attribute but, rather, is a Cisco-proprietary attribute. In other words, this attribute cannot be used on non-Cisco devices.

The WEIGHT attribute is used in a manner similar to the LOCAL_PREF attribute. That is, this attribute is used to define a preference over one exit point in an AS over another. However, unlike the LOCAL_PREF attribute, which is propagated to other routers in the AS, the Cisco WEIGHT attribute is locally significant to the device on which it is configured—much like administrative distance values. This attribute, therefore, does not follow the routing policy of other neighbor routers, nor will it be sent to other routers.

The WEIGHT is a 4-byte integer between 0 and 65,535. While this attribute is proprietary, it has priority over all other attributes in the BGP path selection process, which is described later in this chapter. By default, all prefixes injected into BGP on the local BGP speaker are assigned a WEIGHT of 32,768. Because this attribute is locally significant, this default value is not set in the UPDATE messages sent to any other neighbors. In Cisco IOS software, the higher the WEIGHT, the more preferred the path. This is illustrated in detail in the following chapter.

In conclusion, Table 6-6 below summarizes the different attributes described in this section, their Type Codes, and their category:

Table 6-6. Summary of BGP Attributes

Attribute	Type Code	Category
ORIGIN	1	Well-known Mandatory
AS_PATH	2	Well-known Mandatory
NEXT_HOP	3	Well-known Mandatory
MULTI_EXIT_DISC	4	Optional, Non-Transitive
LOCAL_PREF	5	Well-known Discretionary
ATOMIC_AGGREGATE	6	Well-known Discretionary
AGGREGATOR	7	Optional, Transitive
COMMUNITY	8	Optional, Transitive
ORIGINATOR_ID	9	Optional, Non-Transitive
CLUSTER_LIST	10	Optional, Non-Transitive
WEIGHT	N/A	Proprietary

BORDER GATEWAY PROTOCOL LOOP PREVENTION

Two types of loops exist in routed networks. These loops are applicable to both IGPs and BGP. Given that IGP loop prevention mechanisms are described in detail in previous chapters, this chapter focuses exclusively on BGP loop prevention. The two types of loops are as follows:

1. Routing information loops
2. Routing loops

Routing information loops are loops that occur when routing information is both received and accepted by the router that advertised it. Figure 6-20 below illustrates a routing information loop:

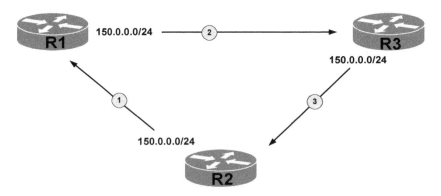

Fig. 6-20. Routing Information Loop

Referencing Figure 6-20, R2 is peered to both R1 and R3. R2 advertises the 150.0.0.0/24 prefix to R1, which in turn advertises the same prefix to R3. R3 re-advertises the same prefix back to R2. The same would be applicable to the route advertised to R3, which would turn around and advertise it to R1 and R1 would re-advertise it back to R2.

If R2 accepts these routes, a routing information loop will occur. The different routing protocols we learned about in the previous chapters have different means or methods for ensuring that routing information loops do not occur. For example, if this were an EIGRP network, the routes that R2 received from R1 and R3 would not meet the feasibility condition and would therefore not be placed into the EIGRP Topology Table and, ultimately, the RIB. This prevents the routing information loop from forming in the EIGRP domain.

A routing loop occurs when packets are sent back and forth between two or more routers, as was illustrated in Chapter 4, IGP Route Filtering and Route Redistribution. In this case, the packets loop back and forth between the devices until the IP TTL value reaches 0, after which they are discarded. In this section, we will learn about both routing information and routing loops as they pertain to BGP.

Preventing Routing Information Loops in BGP Implementations

Fortunately, like most routing protocols, BGP includes built-in mechanisms that are used to avoid routing information from being received and accepted by the router that originated it. With BGP, however, it is important to understand that different mechanisms are used for external BGP (eBGP) and internal BGP (iBGP) implementations. The following mechanism is used to prevent routing information loops for eBGP:

- The AS_PATH attribute

The following mechanisms are used to prevent routing information loops for iBGP:

- Preventing iBGP speakers from advertising iBGP routes to iBGP peers
- The ORIGINATOR_ID attribute
- The CLUSTER_LIST attribute

The AS_PATH Attribute

The AS_PATH attribute is used to prevent routing information loops in inter-AS BGP (i.e., eBGP) implementations. The AS_PATH attribute contains a reverse-order sequenced list of autonomous system numbers that represent the domains the prefix has transited. This attribute is changed only when an UPDATE is sent to an eBGP neighbor, but not when sent to an iBGP peer; hence, the reason that this attribute is applicable only for external BGP implementations.

When an eBGP speaker receives UPDATE messages, it looks at the AS_PATH list to determine the best (shortest) path to the destination prefix. However, if the eBGP speaker notices its autonomous system number in the AS_PATH list, it ignores this UPDATE message and does not take it into consideration in the path selection process. This prevents the router from receiving and accepting information that it originated, or was originated within its own autonomous system. To clarify this point further, consider the topology illustrated in Figure 6-21 below:

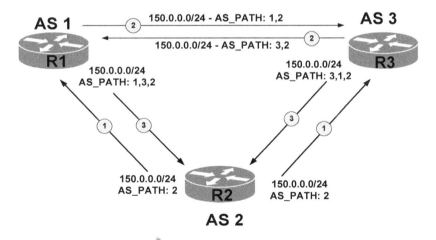

Fig. 6-21. Using the AS_PATH to Prevent Loops

Figure 6-21 shows a basic network comprised of three routers in three different ASs. All three routers are peered with each other and R2 is advertising the 150.0.0.0/24 prefix to R1 and R3. When R1 receives this UPDATE message, it includes its AS and advertises the prefix to R3. R3 also does the same and advertises the prefix received from R2 to R1.

R1 and R3 now have two paths for the same destination: the path via R2, which contains only a single AS, and the path via each other, which contains two AS numbers. By default, the path with the shortest AS_PATH list will be selected, and both R1 and R3 forward packets destined to the 150.0.0.0/24 prefix directly to R2. In addition, both R1 and R3 advertise the paths that they also received from each other to R2 after they have included their respective ASs.

When R2 receives these UPDATE messages, it notices that its own AS is included. Because AS 2 is included in the AS_PATH list, R2 ignores these paths and they are not placed into either the BGP table or the IP routing table. This default behavior prevents a routing information loop from being formed when prefixes are re-advertised back to the originating autonomous system.

Preventing iBGP Speakers from Advertising iBGP Routes to iBGP Peers

With iBGP implementations, the AS_PATH attribute cannot be used because the AS_PATH list is not updated when an UPDATE message is sent from one iBGP speaker to another iBGP speaker, as stated earlier in this chapter. This means that iBGP implementations cannot use the AS_PATH attribute to prevent routing information loops because this attribute is preserved within the same autonomous system. Therefore, iBGP implementations must use other techniques to prevent routing information loops within the domain.

To prevent routing information loops in an iBGP network, when iBGP speakers reside within an autonomous system that is not fully meshed, or is using Route Reflectors or Confederations, any prefix learned from an iBGP speaker will not be advertised to another iBGP peer. These prefixes will be advertised only to eBGP peers. This concept is illustrated in Figure 6-22 below:

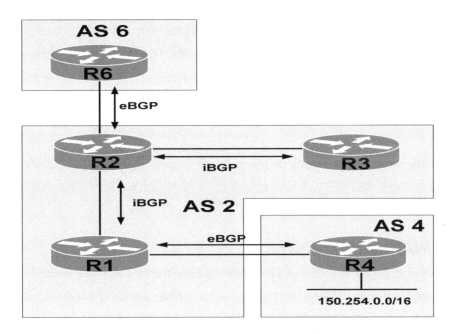

Fig. 6-22. iBGP Routing Information Loop Prevention

Referencing the topology illustrated in Figure 6-22, R1, R2, and R3 reside within AS 2. R1 has an eBGP neighbor relationship with R4 and an iBGP neighbor relationship with R2. R2 has an iBGP neighbor relationship with R3 and an eBGP neighbor relationship with R6. R3 has an iBGP neighbor relationship only with R2.

R4, in AS 4, advertises the 150.254.0.0/16 prefix to R1. R1, in turn, advertises the same prefix to its iBGP neighbor, R2. When R2 receives this UPDATE message, it advertises the prefix to R6 because this is an eBGP neighbor; however, it will not advertise a prefix received from another iBGP peer to another iBGP speaker. R2 therefore does not advertise the prefix to R3. The end result is that all routers illustrated in this topology, except for R3, have a valid routing entry for the 150.254.0.0/16 prefix. Therefore, while this default behavior does prevent routing information loops in iBGP networks, not all routers in the domain have routing information. This can be addressed using one of the three following methods:

1. Implement a full iBGP mesh
2. Use Route Reflectors
3. Implement Confederations

The first method is the most simple. Using this method, R1 and R3 can be configured as iBGP peers. Because BGP does not require that neighbors be directly connected to establish a neighbor relationship, as will be illustrated later in this chapter, this would be as simple as configuring R1 and R3 with neighbor commands for each other.

While this solution is easy to implement, it is not scalable. For example, if there were 10 iBGP speakers in the domain, N(N-1) neighbor statements would need to be configured in order to create a fully meshed iBGP network. This would result in a total of 90 adjacencies, with each iBGP speaker having 9 neighbor statements. This scalability limitation can be lifted by implementing the second and third solutions, which are more complex than the first solution.

NOTE: Route Reflectors and Confederations are described in detail in the following chapter. The emphasis in this section should be placed on remembering the methods used to prevent routing information loops in iBGP implementations.

The ORIGINATOR_ID Attribute

The ORIGINATOR_ID attribute is used in iBGP implementations that use Route Reflectors. This attribute is used to prevent routing information loops within the iBGP network. The RR sets the BGP Identifier of the client router that originated the route as the ORIGINATOR_ID. Therefore, when a client receives an UPDATE message from the RR and it recognizes the ORIGINATOR_ID as its BGP Identifier, the client will ignore it. This prevents the iBGP speaker from both receiving and accepting routes that it originated or injected into BGP.

The CLUSTER_LIST Attribute

The CLUSTER_LIST attribute is used in iBGP implementations that are using Route Reflectors. When the RR reflects a prefix, it must prepend the CLUSTER_ID to the CLUSTER_LIST. Using this attribute, an RR can identify whether the routing information has looped back to the same cluster. If the local CLUSTER_ID is found in the CLUSTER_LIST, then the received advertisement is ignored. This prevents the RR from accepting information that it advertised.

Preventing Routing Loops in BGP Implementations

Now that we are familiar with the mechanisms employed by both eBGP and iBGP speakers to prevent routing information loops, the following section focuses on the prevention of traditional routing loops when implementing BGP. As you will recall, earlier in this chapter when we learned about the different types of connectivity options to ISPs, we learned that if there are any Layer devices that will be providing transit service between the two edge routers, then the enterprise should implement an iBGP mesh between these devices and the edge routers.

This ensures that all intermediate devices have routing information for the BGP networks being advertised between the edge routers, while negating the need to redistribute BGP routes into the IGP. It also prevents the black-holing of network traffic. To expand on this concept, consider the topology illustrated in Figure 6-23 below:

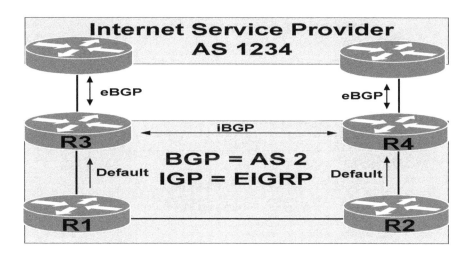

Fig. 6-23. Preventing Routing Loops in BGP Implementations

Figure 6-23 illustrates a basic network. Routers R1, R2, R3, and R4 reside within AS 2. Only R3 and R4 are BGP speakers. These two routers have an iBGP neighbor relationship between themselves and an eBGP neighbor relationship to the ISP in AS 1234. EIGRP has been enabled within AS 2, allowing for IP connectivity between all routers. However, BGP is not being redistributed into EIGRP. Instead, for simplicity's sake, assume that the `ip summary-address eigrp 2 0.0.0.0 0.0.0.0` command has been configured on the ASBR interfaces connected to the interior routers. Based on this configuration, interior routers R1 and R2 prefer the default received from their upstream ASBRs.

Assume that the link between R3 and the ISP fails. Despite this failure, R3 is still able to receive Internet routes from iBGP peer R4. However, the problem arises when R1 sends an Internet-bound packet to the 200.1.1.1 address to R3—its preferred default gateway. The routing loop is established based on the following sequence of events:

1. R1 forwards the packet to the 200.1.1.1 address to R3, its preferred Autonomous System Border Router (ASBR) based on the IGP configuration.

2. R3 has received routing information for this destination from R4, via iBGP, and so R3 performs a recursive lookup for the NEXT_HOP address in this UPDATE message. The NEXT_HOP address could be either the address of R4 or that of the ISP edge router. In this case, assume it is the address of R4. R3 then sends the packet to the next-hop address of the NEXT_HOP, which is R1.

3. R1 receives a packet destined to 200.1.1.1 from R3. Since this router does not know how to reach this destination, it forwards the packet using its default route—which points back to R3. A routing loop has formed. This is illustrated in Figure 6-24 below:

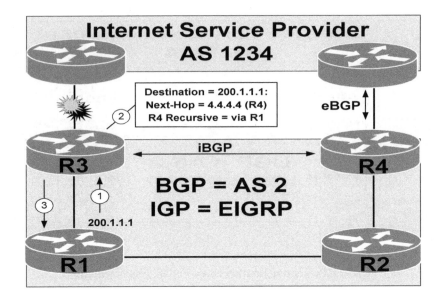

Fig. 6-24. Understanding Routing Loops in BGP Implementations

To resolve this issue, one of two solutions must be implemented as follows:
1. Enabling BGP on all transit or intermediate devices between the edge routers
2. Redistributing BGP into EIGRP, or any other IGP that may be running

The first solution is the recommended solution. With this option, an iBGP mesh is implemented within AS 2 and all routers are configured to peer with each other. This ensures that all routers have routing knowledge of all external destinations and prevents the formation of routing loops on transit devices that do not have BGP enabled.

The second solution is valid but is dangerous and is not recommended. A full Internet routing table contains upwards of 100,000 prefixes. While BGP was designed to carry a large number of prefixes, IGPs were not. This solution could cause serious issues within the network. While route filtering during redistribution could be used to reduce the number of prefixes injected into the IGP, determining which prefixes to import is a headache within itself. This solution should be avoided whenever possible.

THE BGP PATH SELECTION PROCESS

Unlike traditional IGPs, BGP uses a complex path selection process before electing a path that will be used to forward packets destined to each destination prefix. Understanding and being intimately familiar with the BGP path selection process is a mandatory requirement of the ROUTE exam. It is imperative that you take your time to ensure that you are very comfortable with the path selection process that is described in this section.

By default, a BGP speaker receiving UPDATE messages selects only a single best path from this set of multiple UPDATES and installs that into the IP routing table. Having stated this, it is very important to remember that multiple paths may be installed into the BGP Table; however, only one of those paths (by default) will be installed into the IP routing table.

The BGP best path selection process is performed based on attributes. Each received UPDATE message is compared against all others until one UPDATE message wins and is placed into the routing table. By default BGP assigns the first valid path received as the best path; however, as other UPDATE messages are received, this path is compared against those received UPDATES, and so forth, through the received list until all valid paths have been compared. The following section lists the sequence of steps in the BGP best path selection process:

1. If the path specifies a NEXT_HOP that is inaccessible, drop the UPDATE message. This means that the NEXT_HOP for each route must be reachable in the local routing table; otherwise, the local router discards the route.

2. Prefer the path with the largest WEIGHT. WEIGHT is a Cisco proprietary attribute that is locally significant to the BGP speaker on which it is configured.

3. If the WEIGHT values are the same, prefer the path with the largest LOCAL_PREF. Unlike WEIGHT, LOCAL_PREF is propagated throughout the AS; higher values are preferred.

4. If LOCAL_PREF values are the same, prefer the path that was originated by BGP running on this router. This could be via the use of the `network` or `aggregate-address` router configuration commands or through redistribution of another routing protocol into BGP via the `redistribute` command. Local paths sourced using the `network` or `redistribute` commands are preferred over those sourced using the `aggregate-address` command.

5. If no route was originated, prefer the route that has the shortest AS_PATH. However, if the `bgp bestpath as-path ignore` command is issued on the router, the AS_PATH attribute is not used in BGP best path selection. In addition, when comparing this attribute, an AS_SET is counted once, regardless of the number of autonomous systems in the set. Finally, the AS_CONFED_SEQUENCE is not included in the AS_PATH length.

6. If all paths have the same AS_PATH length, then prefer the path with the lowest ORIGIN. An ORIGIN of IGP (I) is more preferred (lower) than EGP (E) , which in turn is more preferred (lower) than Incomplete (?). In mathematical terms, IGP < EGP < Incomplete.

7. If the ORIGIN codes are the same, prefer the path with the lowest MED attribute. This step is executed, by default, only for routes from the same neighboring AS. MED values are not compared for routes received from different autonomous systems unless the `bgp always-compare-med` command is enabled on the router. Additionally, the `bgp deterministic-med` command can also be used to influence this step. This command is beyond the scope of the ROUTE exam requirements and is not illustrated in this guide.

8. If the paths have the same MED, prefer the external path to the internal path. In other words,

prefer the path known via eBGP versus the one known via iBGP.

9. If the paths are still the same, prefer the path through the closest IGP neighbor. In other words, prefer the path with the lowest IGP metric to the NEXT_HOP IP address.

10. Determine if multiple paths require installation into the routing table for BGP Multipath. Unlike other routing protocols that can load-balance up to four equal cost paths, by default, BGP installs only a single route into the routing table. However, BGP Multipath allows installation of multiple BGP paths to the same destination into the routing table.

11. When both paths are external, then prefer the path that was received first (i.e., the oldest one). This step minimizes route-flap because a newer path does not displace an older one, even if the newer path would be the preferred route based on the next decision criteria. This step can be omitted by issuing the `bgp bestpath compare-routerid` router subcommand.

12. Prefer the route that comes from the BGP router with the lowest router ID. The router ID is the highest IP address on the router, with preference given to Loopback addresses. You can use the `bgp router-id` command to set the RID manually. If a path contains Route Reflector (RR) attributes, then the ORIGINATOR_ID is substituted for the RID in the BGP path selection process. The ORIGINATOR_ID attribute was described earlier in this chapter.

13. If the ORIGINATOR_ID or the router ID is the same for multiple paths, then prefer the path with the minimum CLUSTER_LIST length. This is only applicable to Route Reflector environments. It allows clients to peer with RRs or clients in other clusters. In this scenario, the client must be aware of the RR-specific BGP attribute.

14. Prefer the path that comes from the lowest neighbor address. This address is the IP address that is used for BGP peering and not the RID of the BGP peer. The address corresponds to the remote peer that is used in the TCP connection with the local router.

Now that we have the BGP fundamentals covered, the following sections delve into the actual configuration of BGP in Cisco IOS software. We will begin by looking at how to enable BGP routing in Cisco IOS software, followed by the configuration and validation of eBGP peers and the configuration and validation of iBGP peers. We will conclude this chapter by learning how to advertise networks using BGP.

ENABLING BGP IN CISCO IOS

In Cisco IOS software, BGP routing is enabled using the `router bgp [autonomous system number]` global configuration command. The valid range of autonomous system numbers that can be configured is between 1 and 65,535. As was stated earlier in this chapter, BGP uses both private and public autonomous system numbers. If your enterprise does not have a public autonomous system number (i.e., a number between 1 and 64,511), then you must specify and use a private autonomous system number (i.e., a number between 64,512 and 65,535).

In addition to enabling BGP, it is also recommended that you manually specify or configure a unique RID on each BGP speaker. This is configured using the bgp router-id [address] router configuration command.

 REAL WORLD IMPLEMENTATION

When enabling BGP in live networks, it is important to know that two additional commands should also be specified when enabling BGP on the router, if it is running any IOS version older than 12.2(8)T. These commands are as follows:

- The no synchronization command
- The no auto-summary command

In pre-IOS 12.2(8)T versions, BGP synchronization was enabled by default. Synchronization forced BGP to synchronize with the IGP and prevented BGP from advertising prefixes to external neighbors unless those prefixes were local or were known via an IGP. In software versions after 12.2(8)T, this feature is disabled by default and BGP will advertise prefixes without having to ensure that they are local or are known by the IGP. In essence, BGP can advertise prefixes independent of whether the IGP is aware of them.

Also in pre-IOS 12.2(8)T versions, automatic summarization at the Classful boundary was enabled for BGP. This automatic summarization applies to connected, static, and redistributed routes. In IOS releases 12.2(8)T and later, this feature has also been disabled by default and BGP no longer performs automatic summarization at the Classful boundary.

The following output illustrates how to enable BGP using private AS 65001 and configure a BGP RID of 2.2.2.2 on the local BGP speaker:

```
R2(config)#router bgp 65001
R2(config-router)#bgp router-id 2.2.2.2
R2(config-router)#exit
```

As of the time of the writing of this guide, it is important to understand that only a single BGP instance can be configured in Cisco IOS software. If you already have BGP enabled using one autonomous system number and attempt to enable another instance using another autonomous system number, an error message similar to the following is printed on the console:

```
R2(config)#router bgp 65001
BGP is already running; AS is 2
R2(config)#
```

Following the configuration of BGP, the show ip protocols command can be used to view the default BGP parameters. The output of this command displays the following:

```
R2#show ip protocols
Routing Protocol is "bgp 65001"
  Outgoing update filter list for all interfaces is not set
  Incoming update filter list for all interfaces is not set
  IGP synchronization is disabled
  Automatic route summarization is disabled
  Maximum path: 1
  Routing Information Sources:
    Gateway         Distance        Last Update
  Distance: external 20 internal 200 local 200
```

Referencing the output above, we can determine that the local router has been configured as a BGP speaker in AS 65001. In addition, because synchronization and automatic summarization at Classful boundaries are disabled, the router is running at least Cisco IOS software 12.2(8)T. Moreover, the default maximum path of 1 is also shown as well as the default administrative distance values for external and internal BGP routes. Local BGP routes are beyond the scope of the ROUTE exam requirements and are not described in this guide.

NOTE: Although automatic summarization and synchronization are disabled by default, if you are unsure about the image running on the router, it is good practice to disable them explicitly.

CONFIGURING AND VERIFYING EXTERNAL BGP

An external BGP (eBGP) neighbor relationship is established between two routers that reside within different autonomous systems. There are two ways to configure eBGP neighbor relationships as follows:

1. Peer the routers using the physical interface IP addresses
2. Peer the routers using non-directly connected interfaces

The first method is the most commonly implemented method used when peering with another autonomous system. Using this method, the neighbor [address] command is used to specify the physical interface IP address of the eBGP peer.

Peering the BGP speakers using non-directly connected interfaces is commonly used in the Stub multi-homed implementations described earlier in this chapter when there are multiple physical circuits between the enterprise edge and provider edge routers. In such cases, rather than configuring multiple BGP peers using the physical interface IP addresses, an eBGP session can be established between the routers by peering to interfaces that are not directly connected, such as Loopback interfaces. This is illustrated in Figure 6-25 below:

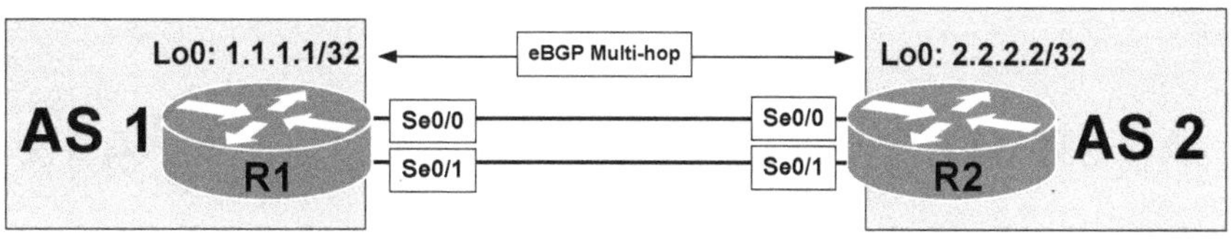

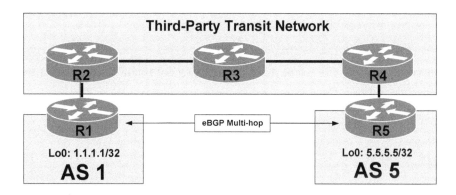

Fig. 6-25. External BGP Peering Using Multiple Circuits to the Same Router

In Figure 6-25, two physical links, which are Serial 0/0 and Serial 0/1, have been provisioned between R1 and R2. Instead of using the IP addresses on the physical interfaces to establish external BGP neighbor relationships, a single eBGP neighbor relationship can be configured using the IP addresses assigned to the Loopback interfaces for peering.

Another situation in which the eBGP peers might need to be established using interfaces that are not directly connected might be when a third-party device resides between the enterprise and the provider. Such a situation requires that eBGP multi-hop be used to establish peer relationships between the BGP speakers, as illustrated in Figure 6-26 below:

Fig. 6-26. External BGP Peering when Transiting another Network

Unlike the configuration of directly connected eBGP peers, the configuration of non-directly connected eBGP peers requires additional configuration in Cisco IOS software. This configuration is required due to the default operation of BGP, as will be explained in the following section describing the configuration of directly connected peers.

Configuring Directly Connected eBGP Neighbor Relationships

The configuration of directly connected eBGP neighbors is straightforward. After BGP has been enabled on the router, the neighbor [address] remote-as [autonomous system number] router configuration command must be configured manually for each desired neighbor using the IP address assigned to the physical interface and referencing the autonomous system that remote neighbor resides in. Figure 6-27 below illustrates a basic neighbor relationship, which shows two routers. R1 resides in AS 65001, while R2 resides in AS 2:

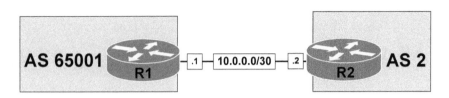

Fig. 6-27. External BGP Peering Using Physical Interface Addresses

The configuration of the eBGP peer on R1 is performed as follows:

```
R1(config)#router bgp 65001
R1(config-router)#bgp router-id 1.1.1.1
R1(config-router)#neighbor 10.0.0.2 remote-as 2
R1(config-router)#exit
```

The configuration of the eBGP peer on R2 is performed as follows:

```
R2(config)#router bgp 2
R2(config-router)#bgp router-id 2.2.2.2
R2(config-router)#neighbor 10.0.0.1 remote-as 65001
R2(config-router)#exit
```

Following this configuration, the show ip bgp summary command can be used to verify the state of the configured neighbors. The output of this command displays the following:

```
R1#show ip bgp summary
BGP router identifier 1.1.1.1, local AS number 65001
BGP table version is 1, main routing table version 1

Neighbor    V    AS MsgRcvd MsgSent   TblVer  InQ OutQ Up/Down   State/PfxRcd
10.0.0.2    4    2      3      3         1    0    0 00:00:41            0
```

Before we proceed any further, it is important to understand the information printed by this command. This information is listed and described in Table 6-7 below:

Table 6-7. Fields in the show ip bgp summary **Command**

Field	Description
Neighbor	Specifies the IP address of the neighbor as specified in the neighbor configuration command
V	Specifies the BGP version; the default is 4
AS	Specifies the AS of the BGP neighbor
MsgRcvd	Specifies the number of messages received from the neighbor
MsgSent	Specifies the number of messages sent to the neighbor
TblVer	Specifies the last version of the BGP database that was sent to the neighbor

InQ	Specifies the number of messages queued to be processed from the neighbor
OutQ	Specifies the number of messages queued to be sent to the neighbor
Up/Down	Specifies the length of time that the BGP session has been in the Established state, or the current status if not in the Established state
State/PfxRcd	Specifies the state of the BGP session and the number of prefixes that have been received from a neighbor or peer group. When the maximum number is reached, the string "PfxRcd" appears in the entry, the neighbor is shut down, and the connection is set to Idle. An (Admin) entry with Idle status indicates that the connection has been shut down using the neighbor shutdown command.

In addition to using the show ip bgp summary command, the show ip bgp neighbors command can be used to view detailed information for a specific neighbor or all configured neighbors. Keep in mind that this command produces a lot of output, which includes the neighbor address (as specified by the neighbor command), whether the neighbor is internal or external, the autonomous system the neighbor resides in, the BGP version, the neighbor RID, the state of the connection, and how long the connection has been up.

Additional information included in the output printed by this command includes the Hold timer and keepalive interval, the capabilities of the neighbor, the number of BGP messages sent and received, the number of prefixes sent and received, the default TTL of the BGP packets (this is explained in the following section), and the local and remote ports used to establish the session. These fields are printed in bold in the following output:

```
R1#show ip bgp neighbors
BGP neighbor is 10.0.0.2,  remote AS 2, external link
  BGP version 4, remote router ID 2.2.2.2
  BGP state = Established, up for 00:07:58
  Last read 00:00:58, last write 00:00:58, hold time is 180, keepalive
interval is 60 seconds
  Neighbor capabilities:
    Route refresh: advertised and received(old & new)
    Address family IPv4 Unicast: advertised and received
  Message statistics:
    InQ depth is 0
    OutQ depth is 0
                        Sent         Rcvd
    Opens:               1            1
    Notifications:       0            0
    Updates:             0            0
    Keepalives:          9            9
    Route Refresh:       0            0
    Total:              10           10
  Default minimum time between advertisement runs is 30 seconds
```

```
For address family: IPv4 Unicast
 BGP table version 1, neighbor version 1/0
Output queue size : 0
 Index 1, Offset 0, Mask 0x2
 1 update-group member
                                      Sent        Rcvd
  Prefix activity:                    ----        ----
    Prefixes Current:                  0           0
    Prefixes Total:                    0           0
    Implicit Withdraw:                 0           0
    Explicit Withdraw:                 0           0
    Used as bestpath:                 n/a          0
    Used as multipath:                n/a          0

                                    Outbound     Inbound
  Local Policy Denied Prefixes:     --------     -------
    Total:                              0           0
  Number of NLRIs in the update sent: max 0, min 0

  Connections established 1; dropped 0
  Last reset never
Connection state is ESTAB, I/O status: 1, unread input bytes: 0
Connection is ECN Disabled, Minimum incoming TTL 0, Outgoing TTL 1
Local host: 10.0.0.1, Local port: 24319
Foreign host: 10.0.0.2, Foreign port: 179


...


[Truncated Output]
```

Configuring Non-directly Connected eBGP Neighbor Relationships

The configuration of eBGP peers that are not directly connected requires the use of additional commands in Cisco IOS software. By default, eBGP packets are sent with a TTL value of 1, meaning that the specified neighbor can be only one hop away (i.e., directly connected). This default value can be validated by issuing the show ip bgp neighbors command for a directly connected neighbor and looking for the statement or line that reads: Outgoing TTL 1.

> **NOTE:** The Outgoing TTL 1 statement is printed in bold in the output of the show ip bgp neighbors command shown in the previous section.

In order to establish an eBGP session with a neighbor that is more than a single hop away, the neighbor [address] ebgp-multihop [1-255] router configuration must be used. The ebgp-multihop [1-255] configuration statement is used to specify the TTL of the BGP packet (i.e., how far away the peer is from the local router in terms of the number of hops). If the hop count is not specified, then this command sets a default hop count of 255, meaning that eBGP packets will be sent with an IP TTL of 255. For example, if the neighbor 2.2.2.2 ebgp-multihop configuration command was issued when configuring an indirectly connected eBGP peer, because no TTL value was specified, Cisco IOS software will set the TTL of packets to 255, allowing a neighbor relationship to be established with a router up to a maximum of 255 hops away. This default behavior can be validated using the show ip bgp neighbors command as illustrated in the following output:

```
R1#show ip bgp neighbors 2.2.2.2
BGP neighbor is 2.2.2.2,  remote AS 2, external link
  BGP version 4, remote router ID 0.0.0.0
  BGP state = Active
  Last read 00:00:04, last write 00:00:04, hold time is 180, keepalive
interval is 60 seconds

[Truncated Output]

  Connections established 0; dropped 0
  Last reset never
  External BGP neighbor may be up to 255 hops away.
  No active TCP connection
```

In addition to specifying the TTL, the neighbor [address] update-source [interface name] command must also be used when configuring indirectly connected eBGP peers. This command is used to allow BGP sessions to use any operational interface for TCP connections. The difference between the neighbor [address] ebgp-multihop [1-255] and the neighbor [address] update-source [interface name] command is that the neighbor [address] ebgp-multihop [1-255] command is used to provide IP reachability to the specified eBGP neighbor, while the neighbor [address] update-source [interface name] command is used to provide TCP reachability between the routers by specifying the interfaces that will be used for the establishment of the actual TCP session between the routers.

Figure 6-28 below shows a basic network with two routers. R1 resides in AS 65001 and R2 resides in AS 2. The two routers have two physical point-to-point links between them. An eBGP session will be established between the routers using the Loopback addresses for peering:

Fig. 6-28. External BGP Peering Using Physical Interface Addresses

Before configuring the eBGP session, it is important to verify IP connectivity between the two Loopback addresses. In most cases, static routes are configured on the edge routers, allowing connectivity between these two addresses. This would be implemented on R1 as follows:

```
R1(config)#ip route 2.2.2.2 255.255.255.255 Serial0/0
R1(config)#ip route 2.2.2.2 255.255.255.255 Serial0/1
```

Assuming a similar configuration has been implemented on R2, a simple ping test should be used to verify IP connectivity between the 1.1.1.1/32 and 2.2.2.2/32 addresses as follows:

```
R1#ping 2.2.2.2 source 1.1.1.1 repeat 10

Type escape sequence to abort.
Sending 10, 100-byte ICMP Echos to 2.2.2.2, timeout is 2 seconds:
Packet sent with a source address of 1.1.1.1
!!!!!!!!!!
Success rate is 100 percent (10/10), round-trip min/avg/max = 1/2/4 ms
```

Following the verification of IP connectivity between the two addresses, the eBGP session can now be configured. This is performed as follows on R1:

```
R1(config)#router bgp 65001
R1(config-router)#bgp router-id 1.1.1.1
R1(config-router)#neighbor 2.2.2.2 remote-as 2
R1(config-router)#neighbor 2.2.2.2 update-source Loopback0
R1(config-router)#neighbor 2.2.2.2 ebgp-multihop 2
R1(config-router)#exit
```

Referencing the configuration above, BGP is enabled on R1, specifying the autonomous system 65001. Next, the BGP RID of the router is configured manually. After configuring the peer, R2, using the desired peering address of 2.2.2.2, the neighbor 2.2.2.2 update-source loopback 0 command means that all BGP updates are sourced from the Loopback0 interface of R1. This is the same address that will be configured as the neighbor address on R2 when configuring BGP on that router. Finally, the neighbor 2.2.2.2 ebgp-multihop 2 command means that neighbor 2.2.2.2 can be up to two hops away from R1. This command also sets the TTL in the IP header of the BGP packet to 2.

Following the same sequence of steps, the eBGP multi-hop configuration on R2 would be implemented as illustrated in the following output:

```
R2(config)#router bgp 2
R2(config-router)#bgp router-id 2.2.2.2
R2(config-router)#neighbor 1.1.1.1 remote-as 65001
R2(config-router)#neighbor 1.1.1.1 ebgp-multihop 2
R2(config-router)#neighbor 1.1.1.1 update-source Loopback0
R2(config-router)#exit
```

The same logic is used, only that the peer being specified on R2 is 1.1.1.1. This is the IP address of the Loopback0 interface of R1—the same interface BGP packets are sourced from based on the configuration of R1. Following this configuration, the show ip bgp summary command can be used to verify the peer relationship between the routers as illustrated in the output below:

```
R1#show ip bgp summary
BGP router identifier 1.1.1.1, local AS number 65001
BGP table version is 1, main routing table version 1

Neighbor     V    AS MsgRcvd MsgSent   TblVer   InQ OutQ Up/Down  State/PfxRcd
2.2.2.2      4     2      5       5        1     0    0 00:01:22       0
```

The show ip bgp summary command would also show the peer relationship on R2 as illustrated below:

```
R2#show ip bgp summary
BGP router identifier 2.2.2.2, local AS number 2
BGP table version is 1, main routing table version 1

Neighbor     V    AS MsgRcvd MsgSent   TblVer   InQ OutQ Up/Down  State/PfxRcd
1.1.1.1      4 65001      5       5        1     0    0 00:01:01       0
```

CONFIGURING AND VERIFYING INTERNAL BGP

The configuration of iBGP peers in Cisco IOS follows the same basic sequence of steps that is used when configuring eBGP peers. The two ways to configure iBGP neighbor relationships, which also apply to external BGP peers, are as follows:

1. Peer the routers using the physical interface IP addresses
2. Peer the routers using indirectly connected interfaces

Configuring Directly Connected iBGP Neighbor Relationships

The configuration of directly connected iBGP neighbors is straightforward. After BGP has been enabled on the router, the neighbor [address] remote-as [autonomous system number] router configuration command must be configured manually for each desired neighbor using the IP address assigned to the physical interface and referencing the autonomous system that remote neighbor resides in. Figure 6-29 below illustrates a basic neighbor relationship, which shows two routers. Both R1 and R2 reside in AS 65001:

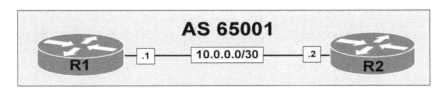

Fig. 6-29. Internal BGP Peering Using Physical Interface Addresses

The configuration of the iBGP peer on R1 is performed as follows:

```
R1(config)#router bgp 65001
R1(config-router)#bgp router-id 1.1.1.1
R1(config-router)#neighbor 10.0.0.2 remote-as 65001
R1(config-router)#exit
```

The configuration of the eBGP peer on R2 is performed as follows:

```
R2(config)#router bgp 65001
R2(config-router)#bgp router-id 2.2.2.2
R2(config-router)#neighbor 10.0.0.1 remote-as 65001
R2(config-router)#exit
```

Following this configuration, the show ip bgp summary command can be used to verify the state of the configured neighbors. The output of this command displays the following:

```
R1#show ip bgp summary
BGP router identifier 1.1.1.1, local AS number 65001
BGP table version is 1, main routing table version 1

Neighbor     V    AS MsgRcvd MsgSent   TblVer  InQ OutQ Up/Down  State/PfxRcd
10.0.0.2     4 65001       2       2        0    0    0 00:00:15            0
```

On R2, the output of the show ip bgp summary also displays the established peer relationship:

```
R2#show ip bgp summary
BGP router identifier 2.2.2.2, local AS number 65001
BGP table version is 1, main routing table version 1

Neighbor     V    AS MsgRcvd MsgSent   TblVer  InQ OutQ Up/Down  State/PfxRcd
10.0.0.1     4 65001       2       2        0    0    0 00:00:05            0
```

For iBGP peers, the output of the show ip bgp neighbors command is similar to that of the same command when eBGP peers have been configured on the router, with the primary difference being that the link type is internal versus external, as illustrated in the following output:

```
R1#show ip bgp neighbors 10.0.0.2
BGP neighbor is 10.0.0.2,  remote AS 65001, internal link
  BGP version 4, remote router ID 2.2.2.2
  BGP state = Established, up for 00:00:26
  Last read 00:00:26, last write 00:00:26, hold time is 180, keepalive
interval is 60 seconds

...

[Truncated Output]
```

Configuring Non-directly Connected eBGP Neighbor Relationships

The configuration of iBGP peers that are not directly connected requires additional commands in Cisco IOS software, as is the case when configuring eBGP peers that are not directly connected. While the `neighbor [address] update-source [interface name]` command is still required for TCP connectivity, the `multihop` command is not required when configuring iBGP peers that are not directly connected.

The reason the `multihop` command is not required is that Cisco IOS software sets the IP TTL to 255 because it is assumed that iBGP peers are not always directly connected. There is currently no command in Cisco IOS software to modify this default behavior (i.e., to change the IP TTL of these packets when configuring iBGP peers that are not directly connected). The primary advantage of setting the TTL to 255 is that it allows iBGP peers to use alternate paths to maintain the adjacency in case some physical interfaces within the interior network fail.

Unlike with eBGP peers, where the preferred peer configuration uses the physical interface IP addresses, with iBGP, the preferred peer configuration is to use Loopback interfaces. These interfaces are the most resilient interfaces in Cisco IOS routers. In addition, because most interior networks have multiple paths between devices for redundancy, this peering implementation allows iBGP sessions to stay up even when some of the physical links in the interior network fail. This also allows for greater stability within the autonomous system.

Figure 6-30 below shows a basic network comprised of two routers. Both routers reside in autonomous system 65001. The Loopback0 interface of R1 is 1.1.1.1/32, while the Loopback0 interface of R2 is 2.2.2.2/32. Two physical links are provisioned between the routers for redundancy.

The network is running OSPF as the IGP of choice. OSPF is used primarily to provide router Loopback-to-Loopback connectivity between the two routers. The logical topology is illustrated below:

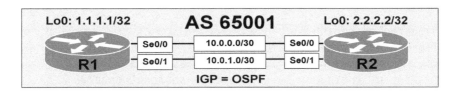

Fig. 6-30. External BGP Peering Using Physical Interface Addresses

Prior to configuring the non-directly connected peer relationship, it is always prudent to verify IP connectivity or reachability between the two routers. Following is the output of the `show ip route` command on R1 for the 2.2.2.2/32 address, which is the address of R2's Loopback0:

```
R1#show ip route 2.2.2.2 255.255.255.255
Routing entry for 2.2.2.2/32
  Known via "ospf 1", distance 110, metric 65, type intra area
  Last update from 10.0.0.2 on Serial0/0, 00:00:52 ago
  Routing Descriptor Blocks:
  * 10.0.1.2, from 10.0.1.2, 00:00:52 ago, via Serial0/1
      Route metric is 65, traffic share count is 1
    10.0.0.2, from 10.0.1.2, 00:00:52 ago, via Serial0/0
      Route metric is 65, traffic share count is 1
```

However, as we learned in previous chapters, just because a route is in the routing table does not mean that it is reachable. It is therefore always good practice to verify Loopback-to-Loopback connectivity using a simple ping, for example, as illustrated in the following output:

```
R1#ping 2.2.2.2 source 1.1.1.1 repeat 10

Type escape sequence to abort.
Sending 10, 100-byte ICMP Echos to 2.2.2.2, timeout is 2 seconds:
Packet sent with a source address of 1.1.1.1
!!!!!!!!!!
Success rate is 100 percent (10/10), round-trip min/avg/max = 1/2/4 ms
```

Once connectivity has been confirmed, the non-directly connected iBGP peers are configured following the same sequence of steps used when configuring non-directly connected eBGP peers; however, the neighbor [address] ebgp-multihop command is omitted. This is implemented on R1as follows:

```
R1(config)#router bgp 65001
R1(config-router)#bgp router-id 1.1.1.1
R1(config-router)#neighbor 2.2.2.2 remote-as 65001
R1(config-router)#neighbor 2.2.2.2 update-source Loopback0
R1(config-router)#exit
```

Similar configuration is also implemented on R2 as illustrated in the following output:

```
R2(config)#router bgp 65001
R2(config-router)#bgp router-id 2.2.2.2
R2(config-router)#neighbor 1.1.1.1 remote-as 65001
R2(config-router)#neighbor 1.1.1.1 update-source Loopback0
R2(config-router)#exit
```

Again, the show ip bgp summary should be used to verify that the peer relationship has been established. This is confirmed on R1 as follows:

```
R1#show ip bgp summary
BGP router identifier 1.1.1.1, local AS number 65001
BGP table version is 1, main routing table version 1
```

```
Neighbor   V    AS MsgRcvd MsgSent   TblVer  InQ OutQ Up/Down  State/PfxRcd
2.2.2.2    4 65001      4       4        1    0    0 00:00:28            0
```

Now that we have a solid understanding of how to enable iBGP and eBGP using both directly connected interfaces and non-directly connected interfaces, we will conclude this chapter by learning about the different methods that can be used to advertise networks when running BGP.

ADVERTISING ROUTES WITH BORDER GATEWAY PROTOCOL

When advertising routes with BGP, a BGP speaker will advertise or receive updates only from a peer only when the local BGP speaker and the peer relationship is in the Established state. If the peer relationship is in any other state, no routes will be advertised or received.

Additionally, when in the Established state, it is important to remember that, by default, a BGP speaker will advertise the best path in the BGP RIB only to its peer(s). In other words, the prefix must exist and must be installed into the routing table before BGP will advertise it to any other peers.

As was stated earlier in this chapter, Border Gateway Protocol is a Path Vector protocol. A Path Vector protocol is a variant of a Distance Vector protocol and employs techniques similar to those used by Distance Vector protocols. BGP uses a split-horizon-like behavior when advertising prefixes and will not re-advertise a prefix learned from a peer back to that neighbor if that prefix is the best path to the specified destination network.

In Cisco IOS software, three methods can be used to advertise networks when using Border Gateway Protocol and they are as follows:

1. Using the `network` command
2. Using the `aggregate-address` command
3. Using the `redistribute` command

The `network` command is the recommended method for advertising the specified network when running BGP. This command, when used with BGP, does not enable BGP for the specified network, as would be the case if it were used when configuring an IGP, for example.

Instead, the `network` command is used to flag the network as being local to the autonomous system as well as to instruct BGP to advertise the specified network. The complete syntax for this command is `network [network] [mask <mask>] [route-map <name>]`.

The [network] keyword specifies the network that BGP should advertise. The specified network must be present in the routing table before it will be advertised by BGP. The [mask <mask>] keyword is optional and is required only when BGP is required to advertise either subnets or supernets. For example, to advertise the 10.0.0.0/30 subnet, the mask keyword would be required. Excluding the mask keyword and simply entering the network 10.0.0.0 command would not result in this subnet being advertised. However, the mask keyword would not be required to advertise the 10.0.0.0/8 network, as long as there was a matching route for this prefix in the routing table.

The [route-map <name>] keyword allows the configuration applied in the named route map to be referenced for the specified network. This route map could be used to manipulate BGP attributes, such as the MED, or metric, for that specific network. BGP path attribute manipulation is a core ROUTE exam requirement and is described in the following chapter.

The aggregate-address command is used to summarize BGP routes. Before this command can be used, the subnets being summarized must exist in the routing table. Additionally, when this command is issued, a route pointing to the Null0 interface is generated by the router. Summarization for BGP is described in detail in the following chapter. The options that are available with this command are also described in the same chapter.

Finally, the redistribute command is used to inject external routes into BGP. These may be static, connected, or dynamically learned routes. As is the case with route summarization, route redistribution between BGP and the different IGPs is described in the following chapter.

Advertising Routes Using the network Command

As previously stated, the network command is the recommended and preferred method for advertising networks when running BGP. The following output shows how to advertise a directly connected network using this command:

```
R1(config)#interface Loopback254
R1(config-if)#ip address 10.254.254.1 255.255.255.0
R1(config-if)#exit
R1(config)#router bgp 65001
R1(config-router)#network 10.254.254.0 mask 255.255.255.0
R1(config-router)#exit
```

To verify that the network has been installed into the BGP RIB, you should use the show ip bgp command as illustrated in the following output:

```
R1#show ip bgp
BGP table version is 2, local router ID is 1.1.1.1
Status codes: s suppressed, d damped, h history, * valid, > best, i - internal,
```

```
                      r RIB-failure, S Stale
   Origin codes: i - IGP, e - EGP, ? - incomplete

     Network          Next Hop            Metric LocPrf Weight Path
   *> 10.254.254.0/24  0.0.0.0                 0         32768 i
```

Regarding the output above, the asterisk (*) indicates that the path is valid (i.e., the path has a valid next-hop). The caret (>) indicates that this is the best path to the destination network. If there are multiple entries in the BGP RIB, the path selection is used to select the best path. Only this path will have the caret symbol assigned to it. All other valid paths will simply have the asterisk beside them, indicating that they can be used in the event that the current best path is removed or withdrawn from the BGP table.

For directly connected subnets, the next-hop address will always be 0.0.0.0, indicating that the next-hop is the local BGP speaker. Additionally, the route metric of the prefix will also be shown. Because connected routes have a metric of 0, the same metric will be used by BGP. By default, the prefix will be assigned a default LOCAL_PREF of 100. By default, the prefix is assigned a WEIGHT value of 32,768. Finally, because the network was injected into BGP using the network command, the ORIGIN code of I is used. Detailed information on the network can be viewed using the show ip bgp [prefix] command as illustrated below:

```
R1#show ip bgp 10.254.254.0/24
BGP routing table entry for 10.254.254.0/24, version 3
Paths: (1 available, best #1, table Default-IP-Routing-Table)
Flag: 0x4820
  Advertised to update-groups:
     1
  Local
    0.0.0.0 from 0.0.0.0 (1.1.1.1)
      Origin IGP, metric 111, localpref 100, weight 32768, valid, sourced,
local, best
```

One additional important observation from the output above is the section stating Advertised to update-groups, followed by the number 1 directly below it. Cisco IOS software uses the BGP Update Group to create dynamically Update Groups that contain BGP neighbors that can share UPDATE messages. No explicit administrator configuration is required, as members are added dynamically to the Update Group based on shared outbound policies. In other words, all members are neighbors that have similar outbound BGP policies. The show ip bgp update-group command can be used to view the members assigned to each Update Group. This command prints the following output when issued on R1:

```
R1#show ip bgp update-group
BGP version 4 update-group 1, external, Address Family: IPv4 Unicast
```

```
BGP Update version : 2/0, messages 0
Update messages formatted 1, replicated 0
Number of NLRIs in the update sent: max 1, min 1
Minimum time between advertisement runs is 30 seconds
Has 1 member (* indicates the members currently being sent updates):
 2.2.2.2
```

From the output above, Update Group 1 is for peers that are external to the local autonomous system configured on R1. The second bolded section shows that a single NLRI has been advertised to the member(s) within this Update Group. Finally, the last bolded section shows that this Update Group contains only a single member, which is router 2.2.2.2. Subsequent peers that share the same outbound policies as this peer will be included in the same Update Group.

If internal peers (i.e., iBGP peers) were also configured, then a separate Update Group for those types of peers, assuming they share the same outbound policies, would be dynamically created. This feature allows for optimal UPDATE message generation.

If a prefix is advertised using the network command and the prefix is known via an IGP, then BGP will use the next-hop IP address of the IGP versus a next-hop address of 0.0.0.0. For example, R2 is receiving the 150.254.0.0/16 prefix from OSPF as illustrated in the output below:

```
R2#show ip route 150.254.0.0 255.255.0.0
Routing entry for 150.254.0.0/16
  Known via "ospf 2", distance 110, metric 65, type intra area
  Last update from 10.0.3.3 on Serial0/1, 00:09:05 ago
  Routing Descriptor Blocks:
  * 10.0.3.3, from 3.3.3.3, 00:09:05 ago, via Serial0/1
      Route metric is 65, traffic share count is 1
```

The prefix is then injected into BGP using the network statement as follows:

```
R2(config)#router bgp 65002
R2(config-router)#network 150.254.0.0
R2(config-router)#exit
```

NOTE: The mask is not required in this case because this is a Classful network and the same Classful network exists in the routing table. Remember, the mask is only required for advertising either subnets or supernets. It is not required for advertising Classful networks.

```
R2#show ip bgp
BGP table version is 6, local router ID is 2.2.2.2
Status codes: s suppressed, d damped, h history, * valid, > best, i - internal,
              r RIB-failure, S Stale
```

```
Origin codes: i - IGP, e - EGP, ? - incomplete

   Network          Next Hop          Metric LocPrf Weight Path
*> 150.254.0.0      10.0.3.3              65           32768 i
```

In addition to the next-hop address, BGP also assigns the prefix the same metric that is used by the IGP, which is 65 in this example. The WEIGHT, LOCAL_PREF, and ORIGIN attributes, however, do not change and all remain the same.

CHAPTER SUMMARY

The following section is a summary of the major points you should be aware of in this chapter.

An Introduction to Border Gateway Protocol

• Border Gateway Protocol is a Path Vector protocol, a derivative of Distance Vector protocols

• BGP is primarily used to exchange NLRI between autonomous systems

• NLRI is exchanged between BGP routers or speakers using UPDATE messages

• NLRI is composed of a prefix and a length

• BGP is first and foremost a policy control tool, and then a routing protocol

• BGP runs directly over TCP, using port 179

• BGP can rely on the connection-oriented nature of TCP for the following services:
  1. Acknowledgments
  2. Segmentation and Reassembly
  3. Checksums
  4. Data sequencing
  5. Flow control
  6. Reliable Operation

• There are several BGP processes in Cisco IOS software, which are as follows:
  1. The BGP Open process
  2. The BGP I/O process
  3. The BGP Scanner process
  4. The BGP Router process

• The BGP Open process is started during initialization and is used for peer establishment

• The BGP I/O process reads, writes, and executes BGP messages

• The BGP Scanner performs housekeeping services, such as verifying next-hops

• The BGP Router process is responsible for initiating the other BGP processes

Border Gateway Protocol Characteristics

- BGP has the following characteristics:
    1. Reliability
    2. Stability
    3. Scalability
    4. Flexibility

Border Gateway Protocol AS Numbering System

- Unlike EIGRP which also uses AS numbers, BGP AS numbers can be public or private
- Public autonomous system numbers range from 1 to 64,511
- Public autonomous system numbers are assigned by IANA to RIRs
- The RIR assigns AS numbers to entities in its designated area
- Private autonomous system numbers range from 64,512 to 65,535
- There are five Regional Internet Registries, which are as follows:
    1. Latin American and Caribbean Internet Addresses Registry (LACNIC) - www.lacnic.net
    2. African Network Information Centre (AfriNIC) - www.afrinic.net
    3. Réseaux IP Européens Network Coordination Centre (RIPE NCC) - www.ripe.net
    4. American Registry for Internet Numbers (ARIN) - www.arin.net
    5. Asia-Pacific Network Information Centre (APNIC) - www.apnic.net

Connecting to Internet Service Providers

- Several factors should be taken into consideration when connecting to ISPs. These include the following:
    1. Whether or not you want to use dynamic or static routing
    2. Whether or not you have a public AS number
    3. Whether or not you have your own registered public IP address space
    4. The acceptable or desired level of Internet redundancy
    5. What type(s) of link(s) you will need to connect to the ISP

- The three types of implementations that can be used to connect to ISPs are as follows:
    1. Single-homed implementations
    2. Stub Multi-homed implementations
    3. Multi-homed implementations

Receiving Routes from Internet Service Providers

- The three options available for receiving routes from the ISP are as follows:
    1. Default Route Only
    2. Default Route plus a Partial Internet Routing Table
    3. Full Internet Routing Table

Border Gateway Protocol Messages

- All Border Gateway Protocol messages all share a common header which is 19-bytes long
- There are only four BGP messages available, which are as follows:
    1. The OPEN Message
    2. The UPDATE Message
    3. The NOTIFICATION Message
    4. The KEEPALIVE Message

- The Open message is the first packet sent to a peer after the TCP connection is established
- The BGP UPDATE message is used to send and withdraw BGP routing information
- The BGP NOTIFICATION message is sent when an error condition is detected
- The KEEPALIVE message is used to determine whether or not a host or a link has failed

Establishing Border Gateway Protocol Adjacencies

- The adjacency is established in two phases which are TCP and BGP session establishment
- The different states BGP will go through before a neighbor relationship is established are as follows:
    1. The Idle State
    2. The Connect State
    3. The Active State
    4. The OpenSent State
    5. The OpenConfirm State
    6. The Established State

Border Gateway Protocol Attributes

- BGP uses path attributes to ensure protocol reliability and routing information accuracy
- Path attributes are also used to prevent BGP loops
- Each BGP UPDATE message contains a single set of attributes for routes
- BGP path attributes fall into four separate categories, which are as follows:
    1. Well-known mandatory
    2. Well-known discretionary
    3. Optional transitive
    4. Optional non-transitive

- The following table summarizes the BGP attributes within the ROUTE exam requirements:

Attribute	Type Code	Category
ORIGIN	1	Well-known Mandatory
AS_PATH	2	Well-known Mandatory
NEXT_HOP	3	Well-known Mandatory
MULTI_EXIT_DISC	4	Optional, Non-Transitive
LOCAL_PREF	5	Well-known Discretionary
ATOMIC_AGGREGATE	6	Well-known Discretionary
AGGREGATOR	7	Optional, Transitive
COMMUNITY	8	Optional, Transitive
ORIGINATOR_ID	9	Optional, Non-Transitive
CLUSTER_LIST	10	Optional, Non-Transitive
WEIGHT	N/A	Proprietary

Border Gateway Protocol Loop Prevention

- The two types of loops that exist in routed networks are as follows:
    1. Routing Information Loops
    2. Routing Loops

- The following mechanism is used to prevent routing information loops for eBGP:
    1. The AS_PATH attribute

- The following mechanisms are used to prevent routing information loops for iBGP:
    1. Preventing iBGP speakers from advertising iBGP routes to iBGP peers
    2. The ORIGINATOR_ID attribute
    3. The CLUSTER_LIST attribute

- BGP routing loops can be avoided by implementing one of the following solutions:
    1. Enabling BGP on all transit or intermediate devices between the edge routers
    2. Redistributing BGP into EIGRP, or any other IGP that may be running

The BGP Path Selection Process

- BGP uses a complex path selection process before electing the best path
- By default, a BGP speaker receiving UPDATES selects only a single best path
- The BGP best path selection process is performed based on attributes

CHAPTER 7

Advanced BGP Design and Implementation

In the previous chapter, Chapter 6, we learned about the basics pertaining to Border Gateway Protocol, which included design considerations, protocol characteristics, and attributes, and then concluded the chapter by learning how to establish both internal and external BGP neighbor adjacencies and advertise routes using BGP.

This chapter expands on the fundamentals described in the previous chapter and, taking this one step further, delves into detail on path control using BGP and other advanced BGP implementations, such as Route Reflectors and Confederations. The core ROUTE exam objective covered in this chapter is as follows:

- Implement an eBGP-based solution, given a network design and a set of requirements

This chapter contains the following sections:
- Border Gateway Protocol Path Control Overview
- Influencing Inbound Path Selection
- Influencing Outbound Path Selection
- Basic BGP Load Balancing and Load Sharing
- Border Gateway Protocol Peer Groups
- Border Gateway Protocol Route Filtering
- Border Gateway Protocol Aggregation
- BGP and IGP Route Redistribution
- BGP Route Reflectors and Confederations
- Border Gateway Protocol Dampening
- Border Gateway Protocol Authentication

BORDER GATEWAY PROTOCOL PATH CONTROL OVERVIEW

As was stated in the previous chapter, BGP is first and foremost a policy control tool. In order to understand how to leverage the routing policy control capabilities of BGP, it is important to understand the different BGP attributes, which are described in the previous chapter, and how these attributes can be used to influence both inbound and outbound routing.

Border Gateway Protocol attributes can be used not only to influence the path routers within the autonomous system take out of the autonomous system but also to influence the path that neighboring autonomous systems take into the local autonomous system. This granular control provides BGP with capabilities that are otherwise not possible when using traditional IGPs, such as EIGRP and OSPF.

In Cisco IOS software, the BGP path control policies are implemented using route maps, which are then applied to neighbors using the `neighbor [address] route-map [name] [in|out]` router configuration command. When configuring route maps, only a single route map can be applied to any given neighbor in the inbound or outbound direction. Because the same route map can also be used for additional functions, such as route filtering, it is very important to plan thoroughly what you want to do with BGP prior to configuring and implementing the route maps in an ad hoc manner. The importance of planning cannot be stressed enough. More often than not, BGP-related issues are not related to the protocol itself but to the configurations implemented by the engineers implementing BGP.

When BGP policies are implemented or changed, it is important to understand that they do not take effect immediately. If you recall, at the beginning of Chapter 6, when learning about the different BGP processes in Cisco IOS software, we learned that the BGP Scanner process periodically scans the BGP RIB in order to determine whether prefixes and attributes should be deleted and whether route map or filter caches should be flushed. By default, the BGP Scanner runs every 60 seconds. Instead of waiting for the BGP Scanner process to run, Cisco IOS software allows administrators to use the `clear ip bgp` command to apply the configuration changes immediately. The complete syntax of this command is as follows:

```
clear ip bgp [* | all | <autonomous-system-number> | <address> | peer-group
<name>] [in [prefix-filter] | out | slow | soft [in [prefix-filter] | out | slow]]
```

While not all keywords are applicable to, or are even within the scope of, the current ROUTE exam requirements, Table 7-1 below lists and describes the keywords that can be used with this command:

Table 7-1. Cisco IOS `clear ip bgp` **Command Keywords**

Keyword	Function
*	The asterisk (*) resets all BGP peers (i.e., it tears down and resets all BGP sessions). This should be used with extreme caution.
all	This optional keyword specifies the reset of all address family (AF) sessions (e.g., ipv4 [IPv4 AF] and ipv6 [IPv6 AF]).
autonomous-system-number	This specifies the number of the autonomous system in which all BGP peer sessions will be reset.
address	This specifies that only the identified BGP neighbor will be reset. The value for this argument can be either an IPv4 or anIPv6 address.
peer-group <name>	This specifies that only the identified BGP peer group will be reset.
in	This optional keyword initiates inbound reconfiguration. If neither the in nor the out keywords are specified, both inbound and outbound sessions are reset.

prefix-filter	This optional keyword clears the existing Outbound Route Filter (ORF) prefix list to trigger a new route refresh or soft reconfiguration, which updates the ORF prefix list.
out	This optional keyword initiates outbound reconfiguration. If neither the in nor the out keywords are specified, both inbound and outbound sessions are reset.
slow	This optional keyword clears slow-peer status forcefully and moves it to the original update group.
soft	This optional keyword initiates a soft reset. In other words, using this keyword does not tear down the BGP session.

NOTE: Regarding the keywords specified above, BGP peer groups are described in detail later in this chapter. However, the Outbound Route Filter (ORF) is beyond the scope of the ROUTE exam requirements and will not be described in this chapter or in the remainder of this guide.

INFLUENCING INBOUND PATH SELECTION

As previously stated, BGP allows administrators to influence the path that traffic destined into the enterprise network takes. In other words, BGP can be used to influence which path traffic from a neighboring autonomous system takes back into the address space that is advertised out by the enterprise. When using BGP attributes to influence inbound path selection, the configuration must be implemented in the outbound direction. In other words, the attributes used to influence the path a neighboring autonomous system uses to take back into the originating autonomous system are advertised in UPDATE messages sent to that neighboring autonomous system. The following two BGP attributes are used to influence the inbound path:

1. The MULTI_EXIT_DISC (MED) attribute
2. The AS_PATH attribute

Influencing Inbound Path Selection Using the MED Attribute

Before we delve into the specific configuration of these policies in Cisco IOS software, it is very important to understand when either of these attributes may be used. As was stated in the previous chapter, the MED attribute is used on inter-autonomous system links. This attribute allows BGP to choose among multiple exit points to the same neighboring autonomous system. The following section describes how and when to use the MED attribute to influence the BGP path selection process. This example is based on the topology in Figure 7-1 below:

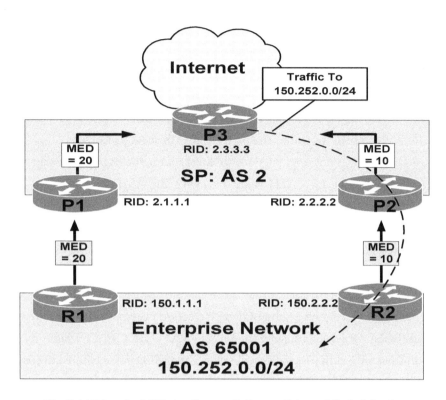

Fig. 7-1. Using the MED Attribute to Influence Inbound Path Selection

Referencing Figure 7-1, AS 65001, the enterprise, is peered to AS 2, the service provider in a Stub multi-homed Border Gateway Protocol implementation. The enterprise owns the 150.252.0.0/24 address space. The enterprise has two paths to the service provider. The primary path, via R2, has two T1 links (approximately 3Mbps). The backup path, via R1, has a single T1 link (1.544Mbps). The enterprise would like the service provider to send all traffic destined to their subnet via the primary path. The secondary path should be used only in the event that the primary path is not available (i.e., its physical circuits are down or the BGP neighbor relationship is not established).

Because the enterprise has no control over the configuration of the service provider routers, the solution must be implemented on the enterprise border routers. By advertising the 150.252.0.0/24 prefix with a higher metric (MED) out of R1 (toward the service provider), the enterprise is effectively suggesting that the service provider use the path with the lower metric instead. This is the preferred path (i.e., the path via P2 and R2). The following steps illustrate the path selection process on R3, which is receiving two paths for the 150.252.0.0/24 prefix—one from router P1 and the other from router P2. The path selected will be the one that this router uses to forward packets received from the Internet destined to this prefix:

- The first step in the path selection process is validating the NEXT_HOP address. Assuming that the NEXT_HOP address in the UPDATE messages received from P1 and P2 is valid, the BGP process on R3 continues with the path selection process...

- Next, the BGP process on R3 considers the WEIGHT value. Assuming default configuration in the service provider BGP implementation, both UPDATE messages received by P3 from P1 and P2 have the same WEIGHT value. The path selection process continues...

- Next, the BGP process on R3 considers the LOCAL_PREF value for both received UPDATE messages. Again, as the service provider is using default BGP parameters, the LOCAL_PREF value for both paths is the same. The path election process continues...

- Because the path was not originated on the local router, the BGP process on R3 will skip this step and consider the AS_PATH value. However, the AS_PATH value for both UPDATE messages is the same. In order to break the tie, the path election process continues...

- Next, the ORIGIN value is considered. We will assume that the 150.252.0.0/24 prefix has been injected into BGP using the `network` command on both routers R1 and R2. Based on this configuration, and assuming basic default BGP configuration within the service provider network, the UDPATE messages that P3 receives from P1 and P3 have the same ORIGIN value. In order to break the tie, the BGP path election process on R3 continues...

- Next, the BGP process will consider the MULTI_EXIT_DISC (MED) value. By default, as was stated in Chapter 6, a BGP speaker will remove the MED value before advertising the prefix to an eBGP peer. However, by setting the MED values on the enterprise edge routers, these values will be advertised to routers P1 and P2. P1 and P2 will include the MED value in the UPDATE messages sent to P3, their iBGP peer. This effectively means that P3 will select the path with the lowest MED value and use that to forward packets received from the Internet destined to the 150.252.0.0/24 prefix as shown in Figure 7-1.

Setting the MULTI_EXIT_DISC (MED) Value in Cisco IOS Software

In Cisco IOS software, the MED value is set within a route map using the `set metric [metric]` route map configuration command. When configuring the metric, lower values are preferred. Following the configuration of the route map, the `neighbor [address] route-map [name] out` command must be issued to apply the configured route map. Referencing the topology illustrated in Figure 7-1, the following output shows the state of the BGP RIB on router P3 prior to any attribute manipulation (i.e., following basic default configuration parameters):

```
P3#show ip bgp 150.252.0.0/24
BGP routing table entry for 150.252.0.0/24, version 5
Paths: (2 available, best #2, table Default-IP-Routing-Table)
  Not advertised to any peer
  65001
    10.0.4.1 from 10.0.4.1 (2.2.2.2)
      Origin IGP, metric 0, localpref 100, valid, internal
  65001
    10.0.3.1 from 10.0.3.1 (2.1.1.1)
      Origin IGP, metric 0, localpref 100, valid, internal, best
```

In the output above, router P3 has selected the path via 2.1.1.1 (P1) as the best path because, all else being equal, this path was received from a router with a lower router ID. In order to influence the path that AS 2 takes to the 150.252.0.0/24 prefix, R1 must be configured to send UPDATE messages for this prefix with a higher MED value than the value advertised by R2 to router P2. This configuration is implemented as follows on R1:

```
R1(config)#ip prefix-list NET-150 seq 5 permit 150.252.0.0/24
R1(config)#route-map SET-MED permit 10
R1(config-route-map)#match ip address prefix-list NET-150
R1(config-route-map)#set metric 20
R1(config-route-map)#exit
R1(config)#router bgp 65001
R1(config-router)#neighbor 10.0.0.2 route-map SET-MED out
R1(config-router)#exit
R1(config)#exit
R1#clear ip bgp * soft out
```

Before we move on to the configuration implemented on R2, we will first discuss the sequence of commands illustrated in the configuration above. First, a prefix list is configured to match the 150.252.0.0/24 prefix. Because the enterprise is advertising a single prefix to the service provider, it is not necessary to configure a prefix list; however, it is a recommended practice.

Next, a route map is configured. This route map matches the configured prefix list and then sets a metric (MED) value of 20 to this prefix. In the third step, the route map is applied in the outbound direction for UPDATE messages sent to P1. In the final step, rather than waiting for the BGP Scanner process to run, the `clear ip bgp * soft out` command is issued to ensure that these changes take effect immediately. Following these steps, the BGP RIB on router P3 now shows that the path through router P2 is the best (preferred) path as illustrated in the output below:

```
P3#show ip bgp 150.252.0.0/24
BGP routing table entry for 150.252.0.0/24, version 7
Paths: (2 available, best #1, table Default-IP-Routing-Table)
Flag: 0x800
  Not advertised to any peer
  65001
    10.0.4.1 from 10.0.4.1 (2.2.2.2)
      Origin IGP, metric 10, localpref 100, valid, internal, best
  65001
    10.0.3.1 from 10.0.3.1 (2.1.1.1)
      Origin IGP, metric 20, localpref 100, valid, internal
```

Influencing Inbound Path Selection Using the AS_PATH Attribute

While the MED attribute works well when dual-homed to the same provider, as illustrated in Figure 7-1, the same attribute cannot be used when dual-homed to multiple providers. As an example, consider the topology illustrated in Figure 7-2 below:

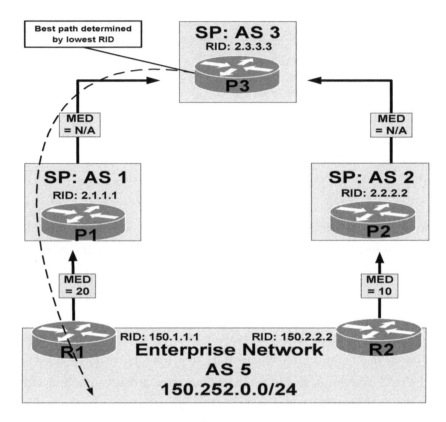

Fig. 7-2. Understanding When Not to Use the MED Attribute

Referencing Figure 7-2, route maps setting different MED values are configured on routers R1 and R2. These route maps match the 150.252.0.0/24 prefix. The MED value is set to 20 for UPDATE messages sent from R1 to P1, while it is set to 10 for UPDATE messages sent from R2 to P2. While both AS 1 and AS 2 receive the different MED values for the 150.252.0.0/24 prefix, these same values are not included in UPDATE messages sent to AS 3 because MED is a non-transitive attribute.

> **NOTE:** Even if the MED values received from the enterprise were sent in the UPDATE messages from AS 1 and AS 2 to AS 3, by default, router P3 would not consider the MED values, as Cisco IOS software does not allow MED values to be compared for prefixes received from two different autonomous systems, unless the `bgp always-compare-med` router configuration command was issued on router P3. In most cases, service providers will not implement this command.

Given these two limitations, the AS_PATH attribute should be used in such situations to influence the path into the network. In Cisco IOS software, this is performed by prepending the AS_PATH attribute using a route map, which is then applied in the outbound direction for the specified BGP peer. This is illustrated in Figure 7-3 below:

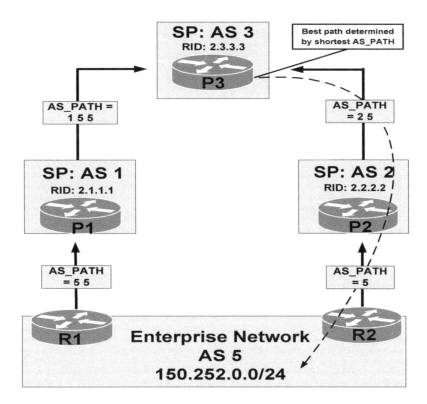

Fig. 7-3. Using the AS_PATH Attribute to Influence Inbound Path Selection

Referencing Figure 7-3, AS 5 is prepended only once in UPDATE messages sent by R1 to P1. The result of this configuration is that when P3 receives the UPDATE messages for the 150.252.0.0/24 prefix from P1 and P2, the path via P2 is selected because the AS_PATH length in the UPDATE messages is shorter than that in the UPDATE messages received from P1.

By prepending the AS_PATH attribute once on R1, UPDATE messages that are sent to P1 show that the 150.252.0.0/24 prefix is two autonomous systems away. This includes the originating autonomous system and the single prepended autonomous system. When P1 sends UPDATE messages to P3 for the 150.252.0.0/24 prefix, it includes its own autonomous system number. The AS_PATH attribute for this prefix on router P3 now reflects three autonomous systems. Because no AS_PATH prepending was performed on R2, the AS_PATH attribute in UPDATE messages sent to router P2 shows only a single autonomous system. When router P2 advertises this to P3, the AS_PATH shows that 150.252.0.0/24 is only two autonomous system hops away. This path is the shorter path and is therefore elected the best path, assuming all else is equal.

Prepending the AS_PATH Attribute in Cisco IOS Software

In Cisco IOS software, AS_PATH prepending is performed by configuring route maps, which are then applied to BGP peers in the outbound direction. Within the route map, the set as-path prepend [as 1] [as 2] ... set clause is used to prepend AS numbers. When prepending autonomous systems, keep the following in mind:

- Prepend using only your assigned or registered AS number. Do not use an AS number that is registered to another entity.

- Always prepend one AS at a time and continue in increments of one until the desired objective has been attained.

- Cisco IOS software supports a default of 255 AS_PATH segments in received inbound UPDATE messages. If a route is received with an AS_PATH segment that exceeds the limit, the BGP routing process will discard the route.

It is extremely important to remember and adhere to these rules, especially when prepending the AS_PATH attribute in production environments. Failure to do so can result in unexpected and undesirable BGP and routing operation. Before we delve into the specifics on prepending the AS_PATH attribute in Cisco IOS software, the following output illustrates the BGP RIB on router P3 for the 150.252.0.0/24 prefix prior to any attribute manipulation on any of the routers in Figure 7-2:

```
P3#show ip bgp 150.252.0.0 255.255.255.0
BGP routing table entry for 150.252.0.0/24, version 4
Paths: (2 available, best #2, table Default-IP-Routing-Table)
  Not advertised to any peer
  2 5
    10.0.4.1 from 10.0.4.1 (2.2.2.2)
      Origin IGP, localpref 100, valid, external
  1 5
    10.0.3.1 from 10.0.3.1 (2.1.1.1)
      Origin IGP, localpref 100, valid, external, best
```

In the output above, router P3 prefers the path via router P1 because, all else being equal, this path was received by the router with the lower RID. Assuming the enterprise wants traffic destined to the 150.252.0.0/24 prefix to ingress their network via router R2, the following AS_PATH prepending configuration would be implemented for outbound UPDATE messages on R1:

```
R1(config)#ip prefix-list NET-150 seq 5 permit 150.252.0.0/24
R1(config)#route-map SET-AS-PATH permit 10
R1(config-route-map)#match ip address prefix-list NET-150
R1(config-route-map)#set as-path prepend 5
R1(config-route-map)#exit
R1(config)#router bgp 5
R1(config-router)#neighbor 10.0.0.2 route-map SET-AS-PATH out
R1(config-router)#exit
```

```
R1(config)#exit
R1#
R1#clear ip bgp * soft out
```

In the configuration above, the prefix list is configured to match the 150.252.0.0/24 prefix. This prefix list is then matched in the route map named SET-AS-PATH. Following the match clause, the set clause in the route map prepends AS 5 to the AS_PATH attribute for that prefix. This additional autonomous system number is included in UPDATE messages to router P1 and increases the length of the AS_PATH segment from one to two autonomous systems.

P1 then adds its own autonomous system in UPDATE messages sent to neighbor P3. When P3 receives these UPDATE message, the AS_PATH attribute shows three autonomous system hops for the 150.252.0.0/24 prefix. However, the AS_PATH attribute for the UPDATE messages received from P2 shows only two autonomous system hops. This path is selected because of the shorter AS_PATH segment:

```
P3#show ip bgp 150.252.0.0 255.255.255.0
BGP routing table entry for 150.252.0.0/24, version 5
Paths: (2 available, best #1, table Default-IP-Routing-Table)
  Not advertised to any peer
  2 5
    10.0.4.1 from 10.0.4.1 (2.2.2.2)
      Origin IGP, localpref 100, valid, external, best
  1 5 5
    10.0.3.1 from 10.0.3.1 (2.1.1.1)
      Origin IGP, localpref 100, valid, external
```

In the output above, the path via P2 (2.2.2.2) is selected as the best path because the AS_PATH segment of 2,5 is shorter than that included in the UPDATE message from P1 (2.1.1.1), which is 1,5,5. All traffic from AS 3 (and its upstream neighbors) will therefore use the path through AS 2 when sending packets to the 150.252.0.0/24 prefix. The path via AS 1 will be used when the primary path is unavailable or if the AS_PATH configuration in AS 5 is changed or updated.

Influencing Inbound Path Selection Using Multiple Attributes

While the previous sections illustrate two distinct instances in which both the MED and AS_PATH attributes can be used, it is imperative to understand that some implementations require that both of these attributes be used at the same time to influence inbound path selection. To clarify this statement further, consider the topology illustrated in Figure 7-4 below:

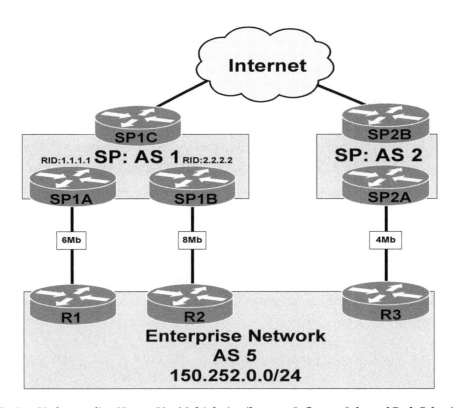

Fig. 7-4. Understanding How to Use Multiple Attributes to Influence Inbound Path Selection

Figure 7-4 shows an enterprise network that has three edge or border routers. Border routers R1 and R2 are connected to the same ISP, while border router R3 is connected to another ISP. The enterprise would like all traffic destined to the 150.252.0.0/24 prefix to ingress the network through the SP1B-R2 path. In the event that this path is not available, the second most preferred path should be the SP1A-R1 path. Finally, if neither the SP1A-R1 nor the SP2B-R2 paths are available, the traffic should ingress the network using the SP2A-R3 path.

In order to satisfy these requirements, the first configuration task would be to configure a route map on R3 and prepend the AS_PATH attribute so that the AS_PATH segment in the UPDATE messages sent by AS 2 to the Internet is longer than the AS_PATH segment in the UPDATE messages sent by AS 1 to the Internet. In other words, the Internet routers will prefer the path via AS 1 to reach the 150.252.0.0/24 prefix.

Now that we have influenced which of the providers the traffic comes in through, the next task is to influence the specific path within AS 1 that is used to forward packets destined to this subnet. All else being equal, router SP1C in AS 1 would prefer the path via R1 because this router has the lower RID. Therefore, to ensure that the SP1B-R2 path is preferred, a route map would be configured on R1 with a higher MED (metric) for the 150.252.0.0/24 prefix than that advertised by R2. The end result is that SP 1 uses the SP1B-R2 path as the primary path to send packets destined to the

150.252.0.0/24 prefix. The SP1A-R1 will be used in the event that the primary path is unavailable. Finally, if neither of the paths via SP 1 are available, then the routers in the Internet community will prefer the path via SP 2, as this will be the remaining valid path to the 150.252.0.0/24 prefix. This attribute manipulation is shown in Figure 7-5 below:

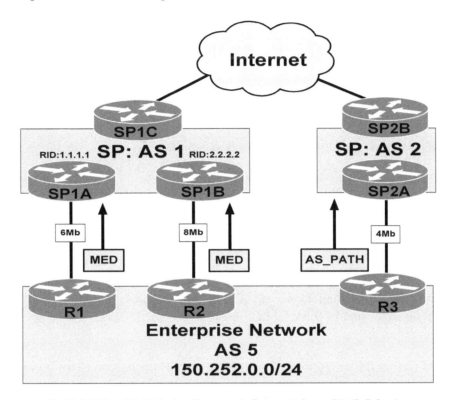

Fig. 7-5. Using Multiple Attributes to Influence Inbound Path Selection

Now that we have a solid understanding of the two attributes that can be used to influence the path that an upstream autonomous system or multiple upstream autonomous systems take back into the enterprise network, the following section takes a look at the BGP attributes that can be used to influence the path that routers will take to exit the enterprise network.

INFLUENCING OUTBOUND PATH SELECTION

Two attributes are used to influence the path that BGP speakers within the same autonomous system will take to exit the autonomous system. Unlike the attributes used to influence inbound path selection, the attributes used to influence outbound path selection are applied in the inbound direction, but they also use route maps. These two attributes are as follows:

1. The LOCAL_PREF attribute
2. The WEIGHT attribute

The use of these two attributes and how they are applied when configuring BGP in Cisco IOS software is described in detail in the following sections.

Influencing Outbound Path Selection Using the LOCAL_PREF Attribute

The LOCAL_PREF attribute is used for path selection only within an autonomous system. That is, this attribute is not passed on between autonomous systems; however, the attribute is propagated within a single autonomous system. If an iBGP speaker receives an UPDATE message for the same destination from multiple iBGP peers, it will prefer the path with the highest LOCAL_PREF value. However, if a BGP speaker receives an UPDATE message that includes the LOCAL_PREF value and this message is received from another BGP speaker that is not in the same autonomous system (i.e., an eBGP peer), then the LOCAL_PREF value is ignored.

By default, Cisco IOS software assigns a LOCAL_PREF value of 100 for all prefixes. This value can be changed administratively to influence path selection using either route maps or the `bgp default local-preference [value]` command.

> **NOTE:** The `bgp default local-preference [value]` command defaults to a value of 100. If this command is issued, then the default LOCAL_PREF value is set to the specified value for all UPDATE messages sent by the local BGP speaker.

To understand further the application of the LOCAL_PREF attribute in Cisco IOS software, consider the basic BGP network topology that is illustrated in Figure 7-6 below:

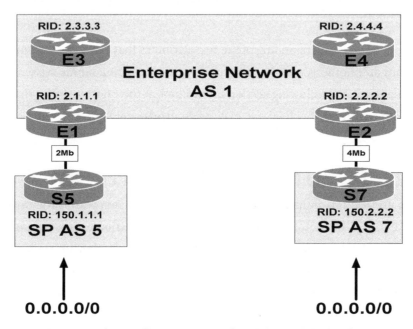

Fig. 7-6. Understanding How to Use the LOCAL_PREF Attribute

Figure 7-6 shows a basic enterprise network that has four BGP speakers. For simplicity, assume that all routers have an iBGP peer relationship with all other routers. In other words, assume that a fully meshed iBGP implementation has been deployed. Within AS 1, edge routers E1 and E2 are peered to two different service providers. The link between E1 and S5 is 2Mb, while the link between E2 and S7 is 4Mb. The service providers, in AS 5 and AS 7, are advertising a single default route to the enterprise network.

Assuming a basic BGP implementation in AS 1 (i.e., no attribute manipulation), the routers in AS 1 select the best path for the default route as follows:

- Router E1 receives the default route from external neighbor 150.1.1.1 (AS 5), as well as from internal neighbor 2.2.2.2 (E2). Assuming all else is equal, this router prefers the external path over the internal path and selects the router via S5 as the best path. This path is installed into the routing table on router E1.

- Router E2 receives the default route from external neighbor 150.2.2.2 (AS 7), as well as from internal neighbor 2.1.1.1 (E1). Assuming all else is equal, this router prefers the external path over the internal path and selects the router via S7 as the best path. This path is installed into the routing table on router E2.

- Router E3 receives the default route from internal neighbors 2.1.1.1 (E1) and 2.2.2.2 (E2). Assuming all else is equal, E3 selects the path received from the router with the lowest RID as the best path and installs the path received from E1 into the routing table.

- Router E4 receives the default route from internal neighbors 2.1.1.1 (E1) and 2.2.2.2 (E2). Assuming all else is equal, E4 selects the path received from the router with the lowest RID as the best path and installs the path received from E1 into the routing table.

Based on the best path calculations, routers E1, E3, and E4 all prefer the default route received from AS 5, while only router E2 prefers the default route received from AS 7. Given that the path via AS 7 should be the preferred path, because of the higher bandwidth link between E2 and S7, the LOCAL_PREF attribute can be used to influence the path routers within AS 1 will take when forwarding packets using the default route.

In Cisco IOS software, this configuration is implemented by using route maps, which are then applied in the inbound direction on a per-neighbor basis. Within the route map, the set local-preference [value] command is used to set the LOCAL_PREF value. This is illustrated and verified in the following section.

Setting the LOCAL_PREF Value in Cisco IOS Software

As was stated in the previous section, the LOCAL_PREF value is set using a route map, which is then applied in the inbound direction. UPDATE messages propagated by the local BGP speaker to any other iBGP peers include the configured LOCAL_PREF value, which is then used to select the best path out of the autonomous system by the other routers. To ensure that all routers within AS 1 prefer the default route via AS 7, the following configuration would be implemented on E2:

```
E2(config)#route-map SET-LOCAL-PREF permit 10
E2(config-route-map)#set local-preference 123
E2(config-route-map)#exit
E2(config)#router bgp 1
E2(config-router)#neighbor 77.7.7.2 route-map SET-LOCAL-PREF in
E2(config-router)#exit
E2(config)#exit
E2#clear ip bgp * soft in
```

Before viewing the contents of the BGP RIB on the routers in AS 1, we will first go through the commands executed in the output above. The first configuration command configures a route map that sets the LOCAL_PREF value to 123 for all routes. Next, this route map is applied inbound on router E2 for its external BGP session with router S7 in AS 7. Finally, a soft reset is executed to ensure that this policy becomes effective immediately. After implementing the configuration on E2, the BGP RIB on router E3 displays the following:

```
E3#show ip bgp 0.0.0.0/0
BGP routing table entry for 0.0.0.0/0, version 6
Paths: (2 available, best #2, table Default-IP-Routing-Table)
  Not advertised to any peer
  5
    10.0.4.1 from 10.0.4.1 (2.1.1.1)
      Origin IGP, metric 0, localpref 100, valid, internal
  7
    10.0.4.2 from 10.0.4.2 (2.2.2.2)
      Origin IGP, metric 0, localpref 123, valid, internal, best
```

NOTE: A similar output will also be displayed by E4 and E1. This output is omitted for brevity.

In essence, by simply configuring a higher LOCAL_PREF value on E2, iBGP speakers within AS 1 prefer the default route that E2 is advertising into the autonomous system, and all traffic destined to external networks is forwarded across the E2-S7 link, which is the preferred egress.

Now that we have a solid understanding of how to use the LOCAL_PREF attribute to influence the path routers within an autonomous system used to exit the autonomous system, the following section describes the use of the Cisco-proprietary WEIGHT attribute, how it also can be used to influence the path routers within an autonomous system used to exit the autonomous system, and the differences between the LOCAL_PREF and WEIGHT attributes.

Influencing Outbound Path Selection Using the WEIGHT Attribute

Several differences between the WEIGHT attribute and the LOCAL_PREF attribute exist and they are as follows:

- WEIGHT is a Cisco-proprietary attribute; LOCAL_PREF is a standard BGP attribute.
- WEIGHT is locally significant; LOCAL_PREF is significant within the AS.
- WEIGHT is not included in UPDATE messages; LOCAL_PREF is included in UPDATE messages.

Despite their differences, these two attributes do have some similarities. For example, Cisco IOS software assigns a default LOCAL_PREF (100) and WEIGHT (32,768) to prefixes. However, keep in mind that the default WEIGHT is only locally significant and is for prefixes injected into BGP on the local BGP speaker, and not for received prefixes.

Another similarity is that the higher the value, the more preferred the path. In other words, prefixes with higher WEIGHT and LOCAL_PREF values are preferred over those with lower values during best path selection.

One of the most commonly asked question regarding the use of these attributes is that if the LO-CAL_PREF attribute can be used to influence outbound path selection within the autonomous system, why does Cisco use the WEIGHT attribute? To answer that question, consider the basic topology shown in Figure 7-7 below:

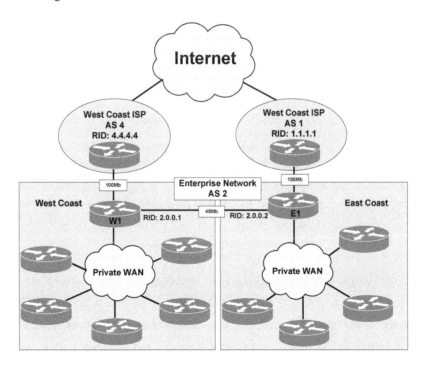

Fig. 7-7. Understanding How to Use the WEIGHT Attribute

Figure 7-7 illustrates an enterprise network that has been separated into two regions: the West Coast and the East Coast. Within each region, remote site routers are connected to each other and the Internet-facing routers (W1 and E1). These Internet-facing routers have a 45Mbps link between them that allows remote offices in either region to communicate with each other.

The enterprise prefers that this link be used only for Internet traffic from either region when the Interface-facing routers lose their BGP peering to their respective ISPs. The Internet-facing routers are receiving a full Internet routing table from their respective upstream ISPs. These two routers also have an iBGP peer relationship, which allows Internet routes to be advertised to either region in the event that one of the regions loses connectivity to its upstream ISP. Finally, in addition to the site prefixes the Internet-facing routers advertise to their respective regional remote offices, these two routers are also advertising a default route that allows regional sites to forward Internet-bound packets to them.

While the topology seems simple enough, if we understand the BGP path selection process, we can determine that the default implementation alone will result in the 45Mbps link between the routers being used for Internet traffic, even when both Internet-facing routers have established BGP sessions with their respective ISP peer routers. Let's expand on this by going through an example.

Assume that within the complete Internet routing tables, both the West Coast and the East Coast Internet-facing routers receive the 150.254.254.0/24 prefix from their respective upstream peers. The prefix W1 receives from the West Coast ISP has the following AS_PATH segment:

- 150.254.254.0/24: AS_PATH = 4, 10, 30

The prefix E1 received from the West Coast ISP has the following AS_PATH segment:

- 150.254.254.0/24: AS_PATH = 1, 30

NOTE: The WEIGHT is a non-factor at this point, as this is a locally significant attribute that is not carried in UPDATE messages. The LOCAL_PREF attribute is also a non-factor because both routers are receiving this prefix from an eBGP peer. Any LOCAL_PREF values set by the eBGP peer are ignored when included in UPDATE messages. The first valid attribute that is therefore used for best path selection is the AS_PATH attribute.

Given the AS_PATH lengths for the 150.254.254.0/24 prefix, the West Coast Internet-facing router, W1, will prefer the path via its iBGP peer E1 because that path has the shorter AS_PATH length. This means that all traffic from remote West Coast sites destined to any address in the 150.254.254.0/24 prefix will be forwarded by W1 to E1 and then to the Internet. The same logic would apply to all other prefixes received by either router. This is undesirable.

If, for example, you attempted to influence the path to the Internet that router W1 took by using the LOCAL_PREF attribute, this configuration would affect Internet-bound traffic on router E1, as this router would now prefer the path via W1, its iBGP peer, instead of via the East Coast ISP because the UPDATE messages for all prefixes received from W1 would have a higher LOCAL_PREF value. Again, this solution is also undesirable and does not resolve the issue.

To resolve this issue, the Cisco WEIGHT attribute should be used to influence the path selection process. By configuring both the W1 and E1 routers with a higher WEIGHT value for all prefixes that are received via their eBGP peers, both routers prefer those routes, as the WEIGHT is the second attribute (after validating the NEXT_HOP address) that is used in the BGP path selection process in Cisco IOS software. Because the WEIGHT is locally significant, this configuration has no effect on either router.

As with all other attributes described in the previous sections, the WEIGHT is specified within a route map using the set weight [value] command. Once configured, the route map would then be applied in the inbound direction on routers W1 and E1. Prior to using the WEIGHT attribute to influence outbound path selection, referencing the topology illustrated in Figure 7-7, the BGP RIB on router W1 shows the following for the 150.254.254.0/24 prefix:

```
W1#show ip bgp 150.254.254.0/24
BGP routing table entry for 150.254.254.0/24, version 3
Paths: (2 available, best #2, table Default-IP-Routing-Table)
Flag: 0x820
  Advertised to update-groups:
    1
  4 10 30
    10.0.0.2 from 10.0.0.2 (4.4.4.4)
      Origin IGP, metric 0, localpref 100, valid, external
  1 30
    10.0.9.2 from 10.0.9.2 (2.0.0.2)
      Origin IGP, metric 0, localpref 100, valid, internal, best
```

In the output above, we can see that W1 prefers the path via E1 when sending packets to the 150.254.254.0/24 prefix. This means that instead of using the West Coast ISP, the traffic is forwarded via the private 45Mbps link between the East and West Coast regions. The same would apply to any other prefixes with the same basic attributes. As previously stated, the enterprise prefers that all Internet-bound traffic within each region use the regional Internet Service Provider. This can be accomplished using the WEIGHT attribute.

Following is the configuration that would be applied to router W1 to ensure that this router preferred the West Coast ISP for all Internet prefixes received:

```
W1(config)#route-map PREFER-WEST-COAST-ISP permit 10
W1(config-route-map)#set weight 100
W1(config-route-map)#exit
W1(config)#router bgp 2
W1(config-router)#neighbor 10.0.0.2 route-map PREFER-WEST-COAST-ISP in
W1(config-router)#exit
W1(config)#exit
W1#clear ip bgp * soft in
```

After this change, the BGP RIB on router W1 now displays the following:

```
W1#show ip bgp 150.254.254.0/24
BGP routing table entry for 150.254.254.0/24, version 4
Paths: (2 available, best #1, table Default-IP-Routing-Table)
Flag: 0x820
  Advertised to update-groups:
     2
  4 10 30
    10.0.0.2 from 10.0.0.2 (4.4.4.4)
      Origin IGP, metric 0, localpref 100, weight 100, valid, external, best
  1 30
    10.0.9.2 from 10.0.9.2 (2.0.0.2)
      Origin IGP, metric 0, localpref 100, valid, internal
```

Even though the path via the West Coast ISP has a longer AS_PATH segment, because the WEIGHT attribute is used prior to the AS_PATH attribute in the path selection, that path is the preferred path because of the higher WEIGHT value of 100. For consistency, the same must also be applied network-wide (i.e., on router E1). While a route map is the most common way of setting the WEIGHT, Cisco IOS software allows you to configure a default weight for all prefixes received from a peer using the neighbor [address] weight [value] router configuration command. The following configuration illustrates how to use this command to configure a WEIGHT of 100 for all prefixes that router E1 receives from the East Coast ISP:

```
E1(config)#router bgp 2
E1(config-router)#neighbor 10.0.1.2 weight 100
E1(config-router)#exit
E1(config)#exit
E1#clear ip bgp * soft in
```

After this configuration, the BGP RIB on router E1 displays the following:

```
E1#show ip bgp 150.254.254.0 255.255.255.0
BGP routing table entry for 150.254.254.0/24, version 3
Paths: (2 available, best #2, table Default-IP-Routing-Table)
Flag: 0x800
  Advertised to update-groups:
     2
  4 10 30
```

```
   10.0.9.1 from 10.0.9.1 (2.0.0.1)
     Origin IGP, metric 0, localpref 100, valid, internal
 1 30
   10.0.1.2 from 10.0.1.2 (1.1.1.1)
     Origin IGP, metric 0, localpref 100, weight 100, valid, external, best
```

Comparing the output of the show ip bgp command on routers W1 and E1, we can see that both routers prefer the path via their respective ISP. However, both routers also have a secondary path via their respective iBGP peer. This path will be used when the primary path is not available.

Because the WEIGHT and LOCAL_PREF attributes are somewhat similar, they are very often used incorrectly. It is very important to take the time to understand when to use one or the other. For example, assume that the same route map configured on router W1 specified the LOCAL_PREF instead of the WEIGHT as illustrated in the following output:

```
W1(config)#route-map PREFER-WEST-COAST-ISP permit 10
W1(config-route-map)#set local-preference 200
W1(config-route-map)#exit
W1(config)#router bgp 2
W1(config-router)#neighbor 10.0.0.2 route-map PREFER-WEST-COAST-ISP in
W1(config-router)#exit
W1(config)#exit
W1#clear ip bgp * soft in
```

The result of this configuration is that W1 prefers the West Coast ISP for the 150.254.254.0/24 prefix. This can be validated by viewing the BGP RIB as follows:

```
W1#show ip bgp 150.254.254.0/24
BGP routing table entry for 150.254.254.0/24, version 5
Paths: (1 available, best #1, table Default-IP-Routing-Table)
Flag: 0x800
  Advertised to update-groups:
    2
 4 10 30
   10.0.0.2 from 10.0.0.2 (4.4.4.4)
     Origin IGP, metric 0, localpref 200, valid, external, best
```

However, because the LOCAL_PREF value is included in UPDATE messages sent within an AS, this configuration would also mean that E1 prefers the same path as illustrated below:

```
E1#show ip bgp 150.254.254.0
BGP routing table entry for 150.254.254.0/24, version 5
Paths: (2 available, best #1, table Default-IP-Routing-Table)
Flag: 0x820
  Advertised to update-groups:
    1
```

```
 4 10 30
    10.0.9.1 from 10.0.9.1 (2.0.0.1)
      Origin IGP, metric 0, localpref 200, valid, internal, best
 1 30
    10.0.1.2 from 10.0.1.2 (1.1.1.1)
      Origin IGP, metric 0, localpref 100, valid, external
```

From the output above, we can see that using the LOCAL_PREF attribute in this case produces undesirable results based on the requirements that the 45Mbps private link between the East and West Coast be used primarily for inter-coast enterprise traffic, while each region should use its own ISP for Internet-bound traffic.

In conclusion, much has been described in this section and it will probably take some time to grasp all of it. Therefore, we will conclude this section by including Table 7-2 below, which lists the attributes described in this section, as well as what they are used for and how to apply them:

Table 7-2. BGP Attributes for Inbound and Outbound Path Manipulation

BGP Attribute	Influences BGP Path Selection in Which Direction	Direction in Which This Attribute Is Applied	Most Preferred Value for This Attribute
MULTI_EXIT_DISC	Inbound	Outbound	Lowest MED
AS_PATH	Inbound	Outbound	Shortest AS_PATH
LOCAL_PREF	Outbound	Inbound	Highest LOCAL_PREF
WEIGHT	Outbound	Inbound	Highest WEIGHT

BASIC BGP LOAD BALANCING AND LOAD SHARING

BGP supports both load balancing and load sharing implementations. However, before delving into the specifics on the techniques that are within the scope of the ROUTE exam requirements, it is imperative to have a good understanding of the differences between the two similar terms.

Load Balancing

Load balancing is used to split the load to the same destination across multiple paths. This may be to a destination network or even to a destination host. With load balancing, the traffic is distributed in an even manner across the multiple links to the same destination network. Load balancing is therefore unidirectional because it does not necessarily mean that the same multiple paths will be used by return traffic from that same destination network or host. Cisco IOS software supports different types of load-balancing algorithms, such as per-packet, per-destination, and round-robin load balancing.

It is important to understand that not all load-balancing algorithms are the same. Even though the router might have multiple equal cost paths to the same destination, the switching algorithm that is used to actually forward the packets might only support a single path due to algorithm limitations or operation. Load balancing is supported at Layers 2, 3, and 4 and is unidirectional. In other words, load balancing is performed in a single direction. Just because the local router is load balancing across multiple links does not necessarily mean the same links will also be used for load balancing in the return direction. This too must be configured.

Load Sharing

Like load balancing, load sharing is also used to split the load to the same destination across multiple paths. However, unlike load balancing, load sharing does not distribute the traffic evenly across the multiple paths; instead it just sends packets over multiple paths.

While load balancing is used only to distribute outgoing traffic, load sharing can be used to distribute both incoming and outgoing traffic. This solution provides greater flexibility in implementations with unequal cost links to the same destination. For example, EIGRP can be used to load-share across multiple unequal cost links. The same can be done with BGP.

Now that we have a solid understanding of the differences between load balancing and load sharing, the following sections describe basic BGP techniques that can be used for load balancing as well as for load sharing. As previously stated, while Cisco IOS software supports multiple options, the majority of those are beyond the scope of the current ROUTE exam requirements and are not included in this chapter or in the remainder of this guide.

Border Gateway Protocol Inbound Load Balancing and Load Sharing

As was previously stated, there are numerous ways in which load balancing and load sharing can be implemented when using BGP. The most load balancing and load sharing options are available in Stub multi-homed implementations. If, for example, two links are provisioned between the enterprise edge and provider edge routers, load balancing can be performed by peering the routers using the eBGP multi-hop solution as shown in Figure 7-8 below:

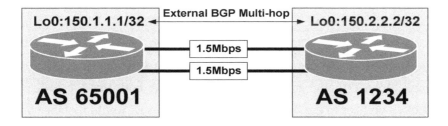

Fig. 7-8. BGP Multi-hop Load Balancing

Referencing Figure 7-8, the BGP multi-hop feature can be used to load-balance inbound, as well as outbound, traffic. While BGP is not configured explicitly to load-balance, the static routes configured on both the ISP and enterprise routers are equal cost paths and, assuming the router switching mechanism supports using more than one equal cost path (e.g., Cisco Express Forwarding [CEF]), packets are sent on a one-for-one basis across both of the physical links as the NEXT_HOP for the BGP prefixes in the Loopback0 interface.

When connected to the same ISP using two routers, it is also possible to implement an inbound load-sharing policy by splitting the subnet in half and then advertising it to the ISP. For example, assume that an enterprise owns the 150.254.254.0/24 address space. The enterprise is dual-homed to the same ISP using two physical routers. In order to utilize both links, the enterprise could split the address space in half and have one edge router advertise the 150.254.254.0/25 prefix to its upstream ISP peer, while the other edge router advertises the 150.254.254.128/25 prefix to its upstream ISP peer. For redundancy, both routers would also still advertise the 150.254.254.0/24. This implementation is illustrated in Figure 7-9 below:

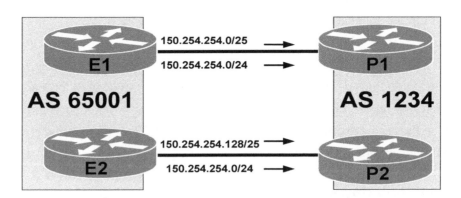

Fig. 7-9. BGP Inbound Load Sharing Using the Same ISP

Referencing Figure 7-9, AS 1234 (the ISP) uses the E1-P1 link to send traffic destined to the 150.254.254.0/25 prefix and the E2-P2 link to send traffic destined to the 150.254.254.128/25 prefix. If either of the links between the enterprise and the ISP is unavailable, the 150.254.254.0/24 prefix is used to forward packets to the portion of the subnet that is no longer being advertised. This provides redundancy for the inbound load-sharing implementation.

An alternative solution would be to use BGP attributes to influence the inbound load sharing. For example, AS 65001 (the enterprise) could advertise both the 150.254.254.0/25 and the 150.254.254.128/25 prefixes to the ISP. Enterprise edge router E1 would then be configured to advertise the 150.254.254.128/25 prefix with a higher MED value to the ISP, while enterprise edge router E2 would be configured to advertise the 150.254.254.0/25 prefix with a higher MED value to the ISP. The result is that AS 1234 prefers the E1-P1 link for all of the traffic destined to the 150.254.254.0/25 prefix, and prefers the E2-P2 link for all traffic destined to the 150.254.254.128/25 prefix. If either one of the links fails, this implementation still allows for redundancy using the remaining individual path.

> **NOTE:** It is important to know that splitting the subnet in half does not automatically mean that load balancing is being performed. It is quite possible that the bulk of the traffic may be destined to hosts in only one half of the subnet, meaning that one of the links is more utilized than the other. Do not confuse this solution with load balancing.

The final scenario we will discuss in this section is how to implement load sharing when peered to more than one Internet Service Provider. This is performed using the AS_PATH attribute, specifically AS_PATH prepending in Cisco IOS software. Continuing from the previous example, AS_PATH prepending could be used to advertise one prefix with a longer AS_PATH segment to one ISP, while advertising the second prefix to the second ISP with a longer AS_PATH segment. This type of implementation is illustrated in Figure 7-10 below:

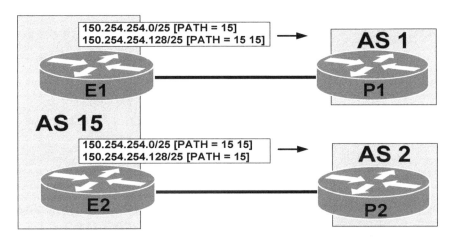

Fig. 7-10. BGP Inbound Load Sharing Using Two Different ISPs

Figure 7-10 illustrates the use of the AS_PATH attribute and how it can be used to implement inbound load sharing—not load balancing—when multi-homed to more than a single ISP. By prepending an additional autonomous system to the AS_PATH list for the 150.254.254.128/25 prefix, the path advertised by router E1 to the ISP in AS 1 will be longer than the path advertised by router E2 to the ISP in AS 2 when propagated to upstream autonomous systems and the general Internet community. This means that the path via router AS 2 is preferred for inbound traffic from autonomous systems upstream of AS 2, including other Internet communities. The same concept is also applicable to the 150.254.254.0/25 prefix, with the exception that the preferred inbound path is via the ISP using AS 1.

Border Gateway Protocol Outbound Load Balancing and Load Sharing

As was stated in the previous section, the multi-hop feature can be used for both inbound and out-bound load balancing—assuming equal cost links are provisioned between the enterprise edge and service provider edge routers. In addition, BGP also supports additional configurations that can be used to perform outbound load balancing. A commonly used eBGP command is the `maximum-paths <1-6>` router configuration command.

As we learned in the previous chapter, BGP selects only one best path and installs that path into the routing table. However, in implementations where a single enterprise edge router is dual-homed to the same ISP, the `maximum-paths <1-6>` command can be used to load-balance between the equal cost paths. The implementation of this command is illustrated in Figure 7-11 below:

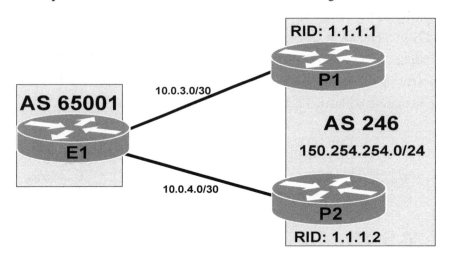

Fig. 7-11. External BGP Outbound Load Balancing

Prior to using the `maximum-paths <1-6>` router configuration command, assuming default BGP configuration, router E1 prefers the route received from P1 as illustrated below:

```
E1#show ip bgp 150.254.254.0
BGP routing table entry for 150.254.254.0/24, version 7
Paths: (2 available, best #2, table Default-IP-Routing-Table)
  Advertised to non peer-group peers:
  10.0.4.1
  246
    10.0.4.1 from 10.0.4.1 (1.1.1.2)
      Origin IGP, metric 0, localpref 100, valid, external
  246
    10.0.3.1 from 10.0.3.1 (1.1.1.1)
      Origin IGP, metric 0, localpref 100, valid, external, best
```

This same path is installed into the IP RIB and is used to forward packets to 150.254.254.0/24 as illustrated in the following output:

```
E1#show ip route 150.254.254.0
Routing entry for 150.254.254.0/24
  Known via "bgp 65001", distance 20, metric 0
  Tag 246, type external
  Last update from 10.0.3.1 00:01:43 ago
  Routing Descriptor Blocks:
  * 10.0.3.1, from 10.0.3.1, 00:01:43 ago
      Route metric is 0, traffic share count is 1
      AS Hops 1
```

Assuming that both links are similar (e.g., they are both T1 links), the maximum-paths <1-6> router configuration command can be used to configure router E1 to perform outbound load balancing using both links. This configuration is implemented as follows:

```
E1(config)#router bgp 65001
E1(config-router)#maximum-paths 2
E1(config-router)#exit
```

Following this configuration, the BGP RIB on router E1 shows that eBGP Multipath has been configured as illustrated in the following output:

```
E1#show ip bgp 150.254.254.0
BGP routing table entry for 150.254.254.0/24, version 2
Paths: (2 available, best #2, table Default-IP-Routing-Table)
Multipath: eBGP
Flag: 0x820
  Advertised to non peer-group peers:
  10.0.4.1
  246
    10.0.4.1 from 10.0.4.1 (1.1.1.2)
      Origin IGP, metric 0, localpref 100, valid, external, multipath
  246
    10.0.3.1 from 10.0.3.1 (1.1.1.1)
      Origin IGP, metric 0, localpref 100, valid, external, multipath, best
```

Referencing the output above, it is important to remember that the eBGP Multipath feature does affect the path selection process. As can be seen, router E1 still shows that the best path to the destination network is via router P1 (1.1.1.1). Although this is the best path, the eBGP Multipath feature allows the router to install up to the maximum number of specified equal cost paths into the routing table. This can be validated using the show ip route command as shown below:

```
E1#show ip route 150.254.254.0 255.255.255.0
Routing entry for 150.254.254.0/24
  Known via "bgp 65001", distance 20, metric 0
  Tag 246, type external
  Last update from 10.0.3.1 00:03:08 ago
  Routing Descriptor Blocks:
```

```
*  10.0.4.1, from 10.0.4.1, 00:03:08 ago
      Route metric is 0, traffic share count is 1
      AS Hops 1
    10.0.3.1, from 10.0.3.1, 00:03:08 ago
      Route metric is 0, traffic share count is 1
      AS Hops 1
```

While the maximum-paths <1-6> command is used to configure eBGP Multipath, the same command cannot be used for iBGP Multipath. Instead, the maximum-paths ibgp <number> command must be used. Unlike the maximum-paths <1-6> command, with the maximum-paths ibgp <number> command, the supported number of paths is dependent on the version of Cisco IOS software that the router is running. Table 7-3 below lists the maximum supported number of paths for various Cisco IOS software versions:

Table 7-3. Supported Number of Paths for iBGP Load Balancing

Cisco IOS Software Version	Maximum Paths Supported
12.0S	8 paths
12.3T, 12.4, 12.4T, and 15.0	16 paths
12.2S	32 paths

NOTE: You are not required to memorize the IOS versions and maximum supported paths in Table 7-3. The ROUTE exam is based on IOS 12.4, which has a maximum number of 16 paths.

The use of the command is illustrated referencing the iBGP topology illustrated in Figure 7-12 below:

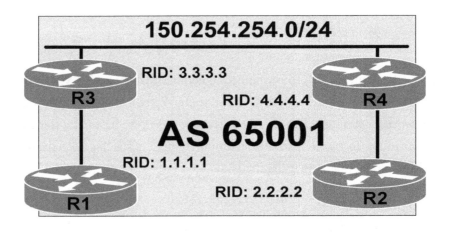

Fig. 7-12. Internal BGP Outbound Load Balancing

Figure 7-12 shows a basic network that includes four routers. All routers reside within AS 65001 and all routers have an iBGP peer relationship with every other router. In other words, this is a full mesh iBGP implementation. Routers R3 and R4 are connected to external subnet 150.254.254.0/24. These routers are advertising this prefix to the other iBGP peers, R1 and R2. Assuming a basic iBGP implementation, the BGP RIB on R1 displays the following:

```
R1#show ip bgp 150.254.254.0 255.255.255.0
BGP routing table entry for 150.254.254.0/24, version 4
Paths: (2 available, best #1, table Default-IP-Routing-Table)
Flag: 0x900
  Not advertised to any peer
  Local
    3.3.3.3 (metric 2) from 3.3.3.3 (3.3.3.3)
      Origin IGP, metric 0, localpref 100, valid, internal, best
  Local
    4.4.4.4 (metric 66) from 4.4.4.4 (4.4.4.4)
      Origin IGP, metric 0, localpref 100, valid, internal
```

The single entry (best path) is then installed into the routing table, which displays the following:

```
R1#show ip route 150.254.254.0 255.255.255.0
Routing entry for 150.254.254.0/24
  Known via "bgp 65001", distance 200, metric 0, type internal
  Last update from 3.3.3.3 00:01:12 ago
  Routing Descriptor Blocks:
  * 3.3.3.3, from 3.3.3.3, 00:01:12 ago
      Route metric is 0, traffic share count is 1
      AS Hops 0
```

To configure iBGP Multipath, allowing both routes to be installed into the routing table, the following configuration must be implemented on R1:

```
R1(config)#router bgp 65001
R1(config-router)#maximum-paths ibgp 2
R1(config-router)#exit
```

After this configuration, the BGP RIB on router R1 displays the following:

```
R1#show ip bgp 150.254.254.0 255.255.255.0
BGP routing table entry for 150.254.254.0/24, version 5
Paths: (2 available, best #1, table Default-IP-Routing-Table)
Multipath: iBGP
Flag: 0x900
  Not advertised to any peer
  Local
    3.3.3.3 (metric 3) from 3.3.3.3 (3.3.3.3)
```

```
       Origin IGP, metric 0, localpref 100, valid, internal, multipath, best
   Local
      4.4.4.4 (metric 3) from 4.4.4.4 (4.4.4.4)
       Origin IGP, metric 0, localpref 100, valid, internal, multipath
```

As is the case with eBGP Multipath, the BGP path selection process is not affected by the actual Multipath configuration because we can see in the output above that R1 still shows the path from R3 (3.3.3.3) as the best path since R3 has a lower RID than R4. However, the Multipath configuration allows the local router to install both paths into the RIB as follows:

```
R1#show ip route 150.254.254.0 255.255.255.0
Routing entry for 150.254.254.0/24
  Known via "bgp 65001", distance 200, metric 0, type internal
  Last update from 4.4.4.4 00:02:37 ago
  Routing Descriptor Blocks:
    4.4.4.4, from 4.4.4.4, 00:02:37 ago
      Route metric is 0, traffic share count is 1
      AS Hops 0
  * 3.3.3.3, from 3.3.3.3, 00:09:29 ago
      Route metric is 0, traffic share count is 1
      AS Hops 0
```

NOTE: When implementing iBGP Multipath, the NEXT_HOP values must have the same IGP route metric. If not, then iBGP Multipath will not work, even if configured on the router. Given Loopback interfaces are used for peering in this example, it is important to ensure that the IGP route metric for 3.3.3.3/32 and 4.4.4.4/32 is the same on R1 and R2 as shown for 3.3.3.3/32 on R1 in the following output:

```
R1#show ip route 3.3.3.3 255.255.255.255
Routing entry for 3.3.3.3/32
  Known via "ospf 1", distance 110, metric 3, type intra area
  Last update from 10.0.0.2 on FastEthernet0/0, 00:06:11 ago
  Routing Descriptor Blocks:
  * 10.0.0.2, from 3.3.3.3, 00:06:11 ago, via FastEthernet0/0
      Route metric is 3, traffic share count is 1
```

The IGP metric for 4.4.4.4/32 is also the same as illustrated in the following output:

```
R1#show ip route 4.4.4.4 255.255.255.255
Routing entry for 4.4.4.4/32
  Known via "ospf 1", distance 110, metric 3, type intra area
  Last update from 10.0.9.2 on Serial0/0, 00:07:33 ago
  Routing Descriptor Blocks:
  * 10.0.9.2, from 4.4.4.4, 00:07:33 ago, via FastEthernet0/0
      Route metric is 3, traffic share count is 1
```

NOTE: In addition to using default IGP metric calculation, you can also adjust the route metric manually using supported commands for the specific IGP; however, this is not recommended and should be avoided when implementing the iBGP Multipath feature.

In addition to using the `maximum-paths` commands for load balancing, BGP also supports a plethora of other options that can also be used to implement outbound load sharing. Common implementations make use of route filtering, either by filtering or by using AS_PATH filtering, as well as the manipulation of other BGP attributes, such as LOCAL_PREF and WEIGHT attributes.

The options that will be available to you for outbound load sharing or load balancing depends on the number of prefixes received from the upstream ISP(s). For example, if only a default route is received, then the options are minimal. However, if a complete Internet routing table is received, many more options can be used to implement load sharing in the outbound direction.

BORDER GATEWAY PROTOCOL PEER GROUPS

Peer groups are used to simplify the BGP configuration for internal and external peers with the same characteristics. The peer group feature not only is used to simplify and reduce BGP configuration on the router but also is used to optimize BGP by improving convergence time. The primary advantages provided by using BGP peer groups are configuration reduction and the ability to replicate updates between BGP peers, with the former being the most common reason administrators choose to implement and use peer groups.

Without peer groups, for example, if a BGP speaker is configured with multiple iBGP peers and knows about 100,000 prefixes via BGP, the router has to go through the entire BGP Table for each peer independently and send UPDATE messages to each peer independently. However, when peer groups are used for peers with the same outbound policy, the BGP UPDATE message is generated only once for the peer group and is reused for all of the neighbors in the peer group. To clarify further the use of peer groups, consider the topology illustrated in Figure 7-13 below:

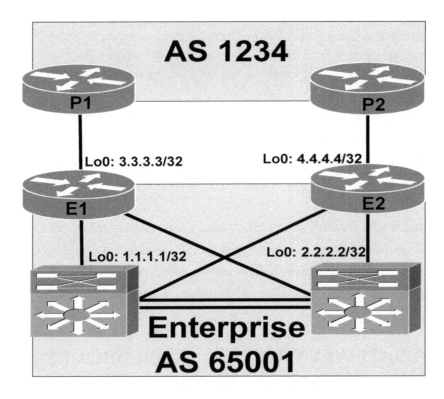

Fig. 7-13. Understanding BGP Peer Groups

Figure 7-13 shows a basic network. AS 65001 belongs to the enterprise and has two routers and two Multilayer switches. The enterprise network is connected to an ISP in AS 1234. Within the enterprise network, all devices have Loopback interfaces configured and an IGP provides reachability between these Loopback interfaces. Assuming a full-mesh iBGP implementation using Loopback interfaces, each individual Layer 3 device within AS 65001 will require three BGP peer statements and three neighbor [address] update-source [interface] commands as illustrated below on R1:

```
R1(config)#router bgp 65001
R1(config-router)#bgp router-id 1.1.1.1
R1(config-router)#neighbor 2.2.2.2 remote-as 65001
R1(config-router)#neighbor 2.2.2.2 update-source Loopback0
R1(config-router)#neighbor 3.3.3.3 remote-as 65001
R1(config-router)#neighbor 3.3.3.3 update-source Loopback0
R1(config-router)#neighbor 4.4.4.4 remote-as 65001
R1(config-router)#neighbor 4.4.4.4 update-source Loopback0
R1(config-router)#exit
```

Assume, for example, that R1 is also configured with both inbound and outbound route maps for each individual peer for BGP policy control. Given this requirement, the following configuration would need to be applied to router R1:

```
R1(config)#router bgp 65001
R1(config-router)#neighbor 2.2.2.2 route-map INBOUND in
R1(config-router)#neighbor 2.2.2.2 route-map OUTBOUND out
R1(config-router)#neighbor 3.3.3.3 route-map INBOUND in
R1(config-router)#neighbor 3.3.3.3 route-map OUTBOUND out
R1(config-router)#neighbor 4.4.4.4 route-map INBOUND in
R1(config-router)#neighbor 4.4.4.4 route-map OUTBOUND out
R1(config-router)#exit
```

Even with just three peers, we can quickly see that this configuration becomes rather cumbersome. In addition, it requires BGP to implement routing policy logic using multiple UPDATE messages to each individual peer. To optimize BGP and improve convergence times, BGP peer groups should be implemented in such a scenario.

In Cisco IOS software, a peer group is configured using the `neighbor [name] peer-group` router configuration command. Common configuration settings that apply to all routers are configured using the peer group name versus the individual router peer addresses. Finally, individual routers that share common policies are then added to the peer group using the `neighbor [address] peer-group [name]` command. Continuing from the previous example, the following output illustrates how to configure a peer group on R1 and apply the same common configuration settings for the iBGP peers. Prior to the peer group configuration, the running configuration on router R1 is as follows:

```
R1#show running-config | section bgp
router bgp 65001
 no synchronization
 bgp router-id 1.1.1.1
 bgp log-neighbor-changes
 neighbor 2.2.2.2 remote-as 65001
 neighbor 2.2.2.2 update-source Loopback0
 neighbor 2.2.2.2 route-map INBOUND in
 neighbor 2.2.2.2 route-map OUTBOUND out
 neighbor 3.3.3.3 remote-as 65001
 neighbor 3.3.3.3 update-source Loopback0
 neighbor 3.3.3.3 route-map INBOUND in
 neighbor 3.3.3.3 route-map OUTBOUND out
 neighbor 4.4.4.4 remote-as 65001
 neighbor 4.4.4.4 update-source Loopback0
 neighbor 4.4.4.4 route-map INBOUND in
 neighbor 4.4.4.4 route-map OUTBOUND out
 no auto-summary
```

To reduce the configuration and optimize convergence, a peer group is implemented as follows:

```
R1(config)#router bgp 65001
R1(config-router)#bgp router-id 1.1.1.1
R1(config-router)#neighbor INTERNAL-PEERS peer-group
```

```
R1(config-router)#neighbor INTERNAL-PEERS remote-as 65001
R1(config-router)#neighbor INTERNAL-PEERS update-source Loopback0
R1(config-router)#neighbor INTERNAL-PEERS route-map INBOUND in
R1(config-router)#neighbor INTERNAL-PEERS route-map OUTBOUND out
R1(config-router)#neighbor 2.2.2.2 peer-group INTERNAL-PEERS
R1(config-router)#neighbor 3.3.3.3 peer-group INTERNAL-PEERS
R1(config-router)#neighbor 4.4.4.4 peer-group INTERNAL-PEERS
R1(config-router)#exit
```

From the output above, it is clear that significantly fewer commands have been implemented on R1 to mirror the previous configuration. The running configuration displays the following:

```
R1#show running-config | section bgp
router bgp 65001
 no synchronization
 bgp router-id 1.1.1.1
 bgp log-neighbor-changes
 neighbor INTERNAL-PEERS peer-group
 neighbor INTERNAL-PEERS remote-as 65001
 neighbor INTERNAL-PEERS update-source Loopback0
 neighbor INTERNAL-PEERS route-map INBOUND in
 neighbor INTERNAL-PEERS route-map OUTBOUND out
 neighbor 2.2.2.2 peer-group INTERNAL-PEERS
 neighbor 3.3.3.3 peer-group INTERNAL-PEERS
 neighbor 4.4.4.4 peer-group INTERNAL-PEERS
 no auto-summary
```

In addition to reducing the router configuration, the BGP peer group configuration results in the implementation of routing policy logic using a single UPDATE message for all peers in the group versus individually for each peer. This can be validated using the show ip bgp peer-group [name] command as illustrated in the following output on R1:

```
R1#show ip bgp peer-group
BGP peer-group is INTERNAL-PEERS,  remote AS 65001
  BGP version 4
  Default minimum time between advertisement runs is 0 seconds

 For address family: IPv4 Unicast
  BGP neighbor is INTERNAL-PEERS, peer-group internal, members:
  2.2.2.2 3.3.3.3 4.4.4.4
  Index 0, Offset 0, Mask 0x0
  Route map for incoming advertisements is INBOUND
  Route map for outgoing advertisements is OUTBOUND
  Update messages formatted 0, replicated 0
  Number of NLRIs in the update sent: max 0, min 0
```

The show ip bgp neighbors [address] command can also be used to view the BGP peer group each individual neighbor has been assigned to as illustrated below on R1 for neighbor R2:

```
R1#show ip bgp neighbors 2.2.2.2
BGP neighbor is 2.2.2.2,  remote AS 65001, internal link
 Member of peer-group INTERNAL-PEERS for session parameters
  BGP version 4, remote router ID 2.2.2.2
  BGP state = Established, up for 00:07:18
  Last read 00:00:17, last write 00:00:17, hold time is 180, keepalive
interval is 60 seconds
  Neighbor capabilities:
    Route refresh: advertised and received(old & new)
    Address family IPv4 Unicast: advertised and received

[Truncated Output]

 For address family: IPv4 Unicast
  BGP table version 6, neighbor version 6/0
 Output queue size : 0
  Index 1, Offset 0, Mask 0x2
  1 update-group member
  INTERNAL-PEERS peer-group member
  Inbound path policy configured
  Outbound path policy configured
  Route map for incoming advertisements is INBOUND
  Route map for outgoing advertisements is OUTBOUND

 ...

[Truncated Output]
```

Within each peer group, a peer group leader is elected based on the lowest router ID. The local BGP speaker on which the peer group configuration has been implemented then creates an UPDATE message for the peer group leader. This message is then replicated for all other members of the peer group. This negates the need for BGP to scan the BGP RIB and create an UPDATE message for each of the individual peers, which, depending on the number of peers configured, significantly reduces both memory and processor utilization on the local BGP speaker. BGP processor and memory utilization can be viewed using the show processes cpu and show memory commands and filtering to include only BGP information. The following illustrates the output of the show processes cpu to include only BGP information:

```
R1#show processes cpu | include BGP
 119         56      3229        17  0.00%  0.00%  0.00%  0 BGP Router
 148        136       198       686  0.00%  0.00%  0.00%  0 BGP I/O
 150        757       102      7421  0.57%  0.06%  0.01%  0 BGP Scanner
```

BORDER GATEWAY PROTOCOL ROUTE FILTERING

In Cisco IOS software, many techniques can be used to implement a route filtering policy when using BGP. As previously stated, BGP is first and foremost a policy control tool. Given this, it is important to understand not only basic BGP implementation, as described earlier in previous sections of this chapter, but also how to implement an effective policy control solution when using BGP. The following route filtering policy control tools are described in this section:

- Effective policy control using IP prefix lists
- Effective policy control with communities
- Effective policy control using AS-path filters

Effective Policy Control Using IP Prefix Lists

Prefix lists, which were described in detail earlier in this guide, can be used for inbound and outbound filtering policies. For BGP, prefix lists can be applied in the following two ways:

- Using the `neighbor [address] prefix-list [name] <in|out>` command
- Using the `neighbor [address] route-map [name] <in|out>` command

The `neighbor [address] prefix-list [name] <in|out>` command applies prefix-list filtering in the inbound or outbound direction for the specified neighbor or peer group. As an example, the following output shows the BGP RIB of an iBGP speaker that is receiving prefixes from another iBGP speaker:

```
R2#show ip bgp
BGP table version is 7, local router ID is 2.2.2.2
Status codes: s suppressed, d damped, h history, * valid, > best, i - internal,
              r RIB-failure, S Stale
Origin codes: i - IGP, e - EGP, ? - incomplete

   Network          Next Hop            Metric LocPrf Weight Path
*>i172.16.0.0/24    1.1.1.1                  0    100      0 i
*>i172.16.1.0/24    1.1.1.1                  0    100      0 i
*>i172.16.2.0/24    1.1.1.1                  0    100      0 i
*>i172.16.3.0/24    1.1.1.1                  0    100      0 i
```

If, for example, we wanted this router to accept only the 172.16.0.0/24 and the 172.16.2.0/24 prefixes, the following configuration would be implemented on the local router:

```
R2(config)#ip prefix-list FILTER-PREFIXES seq 5 permit 172.16.0.0/24
R2(config)#ip prefix-list FILTER-PREFIXES seq 7 permit 172.16.2.0/24
R2(config)#router bgp 65001
R2(config-router)#neighbor 1.1.1.1 prefix-list FILTER-PREFIXES in
R2(config-router)#exit
R2(config)#exit
R2#clear ip bgp * soft in
```

After this configuration, the BGP RIB on the same router now displays the following:

```
R2#show ip bgp
BGP table version is 9, local router ID is 2.2.2.2
Status codes: s suppressed, d damped, h history, * valid, > best, i - internal,
              r RIB-failure, S Stale
Origin codes: i - IGP, e - EGP, ? - incomplete

   Network          Next Hop            Metric LocPrf Weight Path
*>i172.16.0.0/24    1.1.1.1                  0    100      0 i
*>i172.16.2.0/24    1.1.1.1                  0    100      0 i
```

Following the configuration of inbound or outbound prefix-list filters, you can use the show ip bgp neighbors [address] command to verify the filter applied to the neighbor as follows:

```
R2#show ip bgp neighbors 1.1.1.1
BGP neighbor is 1.1.1.1,  remote AS 65001, internal link
  BGP version 4, remote router ID 1.1.1.1
  BGP state = Established, up for 01:49:02

[Truncated Output]

  Incoming update prefix filter list is FILTER-PREFIXES
                            Sent       Rcvd
  Prefix activity:          ----       ----
    Prefixes Current:          0          2 (Consumes 104 bytes)
    Prefixes Total:            0         10
    Implicit Withdraw:         0          8
    Explicit Withdraw:         0          0
    Used as bestpath:        n/a          2
    Used as multipath:       n/a          0

                          Outbound    Inbound
  Local Policy Denied Prefixes:  --------   -------
    prefix-list                  0          2
    Suppressed duplicate:        0          6
    Bestpath from this peer:     4        n/a
    Bestpath from iBGP peer:     1        n/a
    Total:                       5          8

  ...

[Truncated Output]
```

In addition to showing the prefix list used for inbound filtering, this command also shows the current number of received prefixes, as well as the count of prefixes denied by the prefix-list filtering configuration and whether those prefixes are in the inbound or the outbound direction. These two sections are printed in bold font in the previous output.

In Cisco IOS software, the `show ip bgp prefix-list [name]` command can also be used to validate inbound or outbound prefix-list filtering. This command filters the BGP RIB output based on the configuration in the specified prefix list. The following example illustrates how to use this command to filter BGP RIB output based on the named prefix list:

```
R2#show ip bgp prefix-list FILTER-PREFIXES
BGP table version is 9, local router ID is 2.2.2.2
Status codes: s suppressed, d damped, h history, * valid, > best, i - internal,
              r RIB-failure, S Stale
Origin codes: i - IGP, e - EGP, ? - incomplete

   Network          Next Hop            Metric LocPrf Weight Path
*>i172.16.0.0/24    1.1.1.1                  0    100      0 i
*>i172.16.2.0/24    1.1.1.1                  0    100      0 i
```

NOTE: Keep in mind that the same configuration could also have been applied in the outbound direction on the router advertising these prefixes.

The `neighbor [address] route-map [name] <in|out>` command can also be used to perform prefix-list filtering. The primary advantage of using route maps is their flexibility, as has been demonstrated in previous chapters. For example, in addition to matching a specified prefix list, the same route map could also be used to perform other functions, such as path attribute manipulation, within the same configuration. The following example illustrates how to use a route map to perform the same filtering illustrated in the previous example:

```
R2(config)#ip prefix-list FILTER-PREFIXES seq 5 permit 172.16.0.0/24
R2(config)#ip prefix-list FILTER-PREFIXES seq 7 permit 172.16.2.0/24
R2(config)#route-map INBOUND-FILTER permit 10
R2(config-route-map)#match ip address prefix-list FILTER-PREFIXES
R2(config-route-map)#exit
R2(config)#router bgp 65001
R2(config-router)#neighbor 1.1.1.1 route-map INBOUND-FILTER in
R2(config-router)#exit
R2(config)#exit
R2#clear ip bgp * soft in
```

As with direct prefix-list configuration, the `show ip bgp neighbors` command can be used to validate the applied route map and view information on the number of prefixes as illustrated below:

```
R2#show ip bgp neighbors 1.1.1.1
BGP neighbor is 1.1.1.1,  remote AS 65001, internal link
  BGP version 4, remote router ID 1.1.1.1
  BGP state = Established, up for 02:05:24

[Truncated Output]
```

```
Inbound path policy configured
Route map for incoming advertisements is INBOUND-FILTER
                                    Sent        Rcvd
Prefix activity:                    ----        ----
   Prefixes Current:                   0           2 (Consumes 104 bytes)
   Prefixes Total:                     0          16
   Implicit Withdraw:                  0          14
   Explicit Withdraw:                  0           0
   Used as bestpath:                 n/a           2
   Used as multipath:                n/a           0

                                 Outbound     Inbound
Local Policy Denied Prefixes:    --------     -------
   route-map:                          0           2
   prefix-list                         0           2
   Suppressed duplicate:               0          10
   Bestpath from this peer:            6         n/a
   Bestpath from iBGP peer:            1         n/a
   Total:                              7          14

...
```

[Truncated Output]

Finally, the show ip bgp route-map [name] command can be used to filter the contents of the
BGP RIB, showing only those matched by the specified route map as illustrated below:

```
R2#show ip bgp route-map INBOUND-FILTER
BGP table version is 13, local router ID is 2.2.2.2
Status codes: s suppressed, d damped, h history, * valid, > best, i - internal,
              r RIB-failure, S Stale
Origin codes: i - IGP, e - EGP, ? - incomplete

   Network          Next Hop        Metric LocPrf Weight Path
*>i172.16.0.0/24    1.1.1.1              0    100      0 i
*>i172.16.2.0/24    1.1.1.1              0    100      0 i
```

NOTE: The same policy could also be implemented in the outbound direction on R1 and the
same commands could be used to validate this configuration.

In enterprise networks, one of the most common (and recommended) uses for prefix lists is to filter
Martian addresses. Martians are networks that should not be routed on the Internet. In essence,
these addresses are illegal on the Internet, although they may be used within private enterprise
networks. When implementing an inbound route filtering policy for BGP, the following Martian
addresses should be filtered in UPDATE messages received from the ISP:

- Network 0.0.0.0/8 Addresses—0.0.0.0/8 (this does not include the default 0.0.0.0/0)
- RFC 1918 Address Space—10.0.0.0/8, 172.16.0.0/12, and 192.168.0.0/16

- System Local Address Space—127.0.0.0/8
- Autoconfiguration Address Space—169.254.0.0/16
- Test Network Address Space—192.0.2.0/24
- Class D and Class E Address Space—224.0.0.0/3

The following configuration illustrates how to configure a local BGP speaker peered to an ISP BGP speaker in AS 456 to filter Martian addresses and allow all other prefixes:

```
R3(config)#ip prefix-list NO-MARTIANS seq 1 deny 0.0.0.0/8 le 32
R3(config)#ip prefix-list NO-MARTIANS seq 2 deny 10.0.0.0/8 le 32
R3(config)#ip prefix-list NO-MARTIANS seq 3 deny 172.16.0.0/12 le 32
R3(config)#ip prefix-list NO-MARTIANS seq 4 deny 192.168.0.0/16 le 32
R3(config)#ip prefix-list NO-MARTIANS seq 5 deny 127.0.0.0/8 le 32
R3(config)#ip prefix-list NO-MARTIANS seq 6 deny 169.254.0.0/16 le 32
R3(config)#ip prefix-list NO-MARTIANS seq 7 deny 192.0.2.0/24 le 32
R3(config)#ip prefix-list NO-MARTIANS seq 8 deny 224.0.0.0/3 le 32
R3(config)#ip prefix-list NO-MARTIANS seq 9 permit 0.0.0.0/0 le 32
R3(config)#router bgp 123
R3(config-router)#neighbor 150.1.1.2 remote-as 456
R3(config-router)#neighbor 150.1.1.2 description ISP Internet Router
R3(config-router)#neighbor 150.1.1.2 prefix-list NO-MARTIANS in
R3(config-router)#exit
```

The same configuration can also be used with a route map that matches the specified prefix list.

Effective Policy Control with Communities

In the previous chapter, regarding the different BGP attributes, we learned that the COMMUNITY attribute provides a way of grouping destinations, called communities, to which routing decisions (such as acceptance, preference, and redistribution) can be applied.

The attribute is encoded as a four-octet value, where the first two octets represent an AS number and the remaining two octets represent a locally defined value. Two types of communities exist and they are as follows:

- Well-known communities
- Private communities

The well-know communities are those that have predefined meanings, such as the following:

1. NO_EXPORT
2. NO_ADVERTISE
3. INTERNET
4. LOCAL_AS

Unlike the well-known communities, private communities must be defined manually by the network administrators, and actions for prefixes assigned those communities must also be defined explicitly. Private communities are typically configured using the AA:NN format, where AA represents the AS number and NN is a randomly selected number.

> **NOTE:** The implementation, use, and configuration of private communities are beyond the scope of the current ROUTE exam requirements and will not be illustrated in this chapter. Instead, this chapter will focus exclusively on the use of well-known communities.

To better understand the use of well-known communities, consider the topology in Figure 7-14 below:

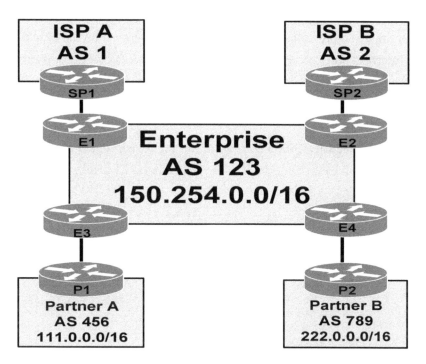

Fig. 7-14. Understanding BGP Communities

Figure 7-14 shows an enterprise that is multi-homed to two ISPs as well as two partners. This enterprise is receiving full Internet tables from both ISPs and routes for the prefixes owned by the two partners. Without any type of route filtering, the Internet prefixes received from the ISPs will be advertised to the partners. In addition, the prefixes that are also received from the partners will be advertised to the ISPs. This is not desirable.

The first reason for this is that if the enterprise advertises the Internet routes to the partners, these two routing domains might prefer the path via the enterprise to reach prefixes in AS 1 and AS 2, in addition to any other Internet-based prefixes that have a shorter AS_PATH segment via the enterprise network. The second reason is that AS 1 and AS 2 might also prefer the path through AS 123 for prefixes originated in AS 456 and AS 789. The third reason is that the partner ASs could also now prefer the path via AS 123 to reach each other. Regardless of the way you look at it, the enterprise becomes a transit autonomous system for both the partner networks and the ISPs.

Instead of using prefix lists to filter prefixes in the inbound and outbound directions, AS 123 could simply route filtering by using communities. For example, using a simple policy, the enterprise edge routers could be configured to set the NO_EXPORT well-known community on all of the prefixes received from the ISPs and the partners.

The NO_EXPORT well-known community prevents BGP prefixes that are specifically assigned this predefined community attribute value from being advertised to any eBGP peers. The prefixes, however, will continue to be advertised to all other iBGP speakers within the local AS. This solution means that the Internet routes received from the ISPs will not be advertised to either partner. Additionally, the prefixes received from both partners will not be advertised to the ISPs or the other partner. Only AS 123 maintains full reachability to all other ASs.

Referencing the topology illustrated in Figure 7-14, the enterprise edge router is receiving a partial routing table plus a default route from the ISP. The BGP RIB on E1 displays the following routes:

```
E1#show ip bgp
BGP table version is 54, local router ID is 3.3.3.3
Status codes: s suppressed, d damped, h history, * valid, > best, i - internal,
              r RIB-failure, S Stale
Origin codes: i - IGP, e - EGP, ? - incomplete
```

	Network	Next Hop	Metric	LocPrf	Weight	Path
*>	0.0.0.0	10.0.3.2			0	1 i
*>	120.0.0.0/16	10.0.3.2	0		0	1 10 20 i
*>	121.0.0.0/16	10.0.3.2	0		0	1 10 20 i
*>	122.0.0.0/16	10.0.3.2	0		0	1 10 20 i
*>	123.0.0.0/16	10.0.3.2	0		0	1 10 20 i
*>	145.0.0.0	10.0.3.2	0		0	1 10 20 i
*>	145.1.0.0	10.0.3.2	0		0	1 15 30 45 i
*>	155.2.0.0	10.0.3.2	0		0	1 15 30 45 i
*>	155.3.0.0	10.0.3.2	0		0	1 15 30 45 i
*>	160.0.0.0	10.0.3.2	0		0	1 15 30 45 i
*>	161.0.0.0	10.0.3.2	0		0	1 15 30 45 i
*>	162.0.0.0	10.0.3.2	0		0	1 15 30 45 i
*>	163.0.0.0	10.0.3.2	0		0	1 15 30 45 i
*>	175.0.0.0	10.0.3.2	0		0	1 88 i
*>	175.1.0.0	10.0.3.2	0		0	1 88 i
*>	175.2.0.0	10.0.3.2	0		0	1 88 i
*>	175.3.0.0	10.0.3.2	0		0	1 88 i
	Network	Next Hop	Metric	LocPrf	Weight	Path

```
*> 180.0.0.0         10.0.3.2                 0                  0 1 88 i
*> 181.0.0.0         10.0.3.2                 0                  0 1 88 i
*> 182.0.0.0         10.0.3.2                 0                  0 1 88 i
*> 183.0.0.0         10.0.3.2                 0                  0 1 2 4 6 8 i
*> 184.0.0.0         10.0.3.2                 0                  0 1 2 4 6 8 i
*> 185.0.0.0         10.0.3.2                 0                  0 1 2 4 6 8 i
*> 190.0.0.0         10.0.3.2                 0                  0 1 2 4 6 8 i
*> 191.0.0.0         10.0.3.2                 0                  0 1 2 4 6 8 i
*> 202.0.0.0/16      10.0.3.2                 0                  0 1 i
*> 203.0.0.0/16      10.0.3.2                 0                  0 1 i
*> 204.0.0.0/16      10.0.3.2                 0                  0 1 i
*> 205.0.0.0/16      10.0.3.2                 0                  0 1 i
```

The received prefixes are advertised to peers E2, E3, and E4. Taking router E2, for example, the same prefixes are then advertised to the partner router, along with the 150.254.0.0/16 prefix, which is owned by the enterprise. In addition, the prefix that router E4 receives from Partner B is also included in the advertised prefixes. The prefixes that are advertised to router P1 can be validated using the show ip bgp neighbors [address] advertised-routes command. The output of this command on E3 displays the following advertisements:

```
E3#show ip bgp neighbors 10.0.9.2 advertised-routes
BGP table version is 70, local router ID is 1.1.1.1
Status codes: s suppressed, d damped, h history, * valid, > best, i - internal,
              r RIB-failure, S Stale
Origin codes: i - IGP, e - EGP, ? - incomplete

   Network          Next Hop              Metric LocPrf Weight Path
*>i0.0.0.0          10.0.0.2                 0    100      0 1 i
*>i120.0.0.0/16     10.0.0.2                 0    100      0 1 10 20 i
*>i121.0.0.0/16     10.0.0.2                 0    100      0 1 10 20 i
*>i122.0.0.0/16     10.0.0.2                 0    100      0 1 10 20 i
*>i123.0.0.0/16     10.0.0.2                 0    100      0 1 10 20 i
*>i145.0.0.0        10.0.0.2                 0    100      0 1 10 20 i
*>i145.1.0.0        10.0.0.2                 0    100      0 1 15 30 45 i
*> 150.254.0.0      0.0.0.0                  0         32768 i
*>i155.2.0.0        10.0.0.2                 0    100      0 1 15 30 45 i
*>i155.3.0.0        10.0.0.2                 0    100      0 1 15 30 45 i
*>i160.0.0.0        10.0.0.2                 0    100      0 1 15 30 45 i
*>i161.0.0.0        10.0.0.2                 0    100      0 1 15 30 45 i
*>i162.0.0.0        10.0.0.2                 0    100      0 1 15 30 45 i
*>i163.0.0.0        10.0.0.2                 0    100      0 1 15 30 45 i
*>i175.0.0.0        10.0.0.2                 0    100      0 1 88 i
*>i175.1.0.0        10.0.0.2                 0    100      0 1 88 i
*>i175.2.0.0        10.0.0.2                 0    100      0 1 88 i
   Network          Next Hop              Metric LocPrf Weight Path
*>i175.3.0.0        10.0.0.2                 0    100      0 1 88 i
*>i180.0.0.0        10.0.0.2                 0    100      0 1 88 i
*>i181.0.0.0        10.0.0.2                 0    100      0 1 88 i
*>i182.0.0.0        10.0.0.2                 0    100      0 1 88 i
```

```
*>i183.0.0.0          10.0.0.2                    0    100      0 1 2 4 6 8 i
*>i184.0.0.0          10.0.0.2                    0    100      0 1 2 4 6 8 i
*>i185.0.0.0          10.0.0.2                    0    100      0 1 2 4 6 8 i
*>i190.0.0.0          10.0.0.2                    0    100      0 1 2 4 6 8 i
*>i191.0.0.0          10.0.0.2                    0    100      0 1 2 4 6 8 i
*>i202.0.0.0/16       10.0.0.2                    0    100      0 1 i
*>i203.0.0.0/16       10.0.0.2                    0    100      0 1 i
*>i204.0.0.0/16       10.0.0.2                    0    100      0 1 i
*>i205.0.0.0/16       10.0.0.2                    0    100      0 1 i
*>i222.0.0.0/16       10.0.1.2                    0    100      0 789 i

Total number of prefixes 31
```

As previously stated, the NO_EXPORT well-known community can be used to prevent the local routers within AS 123 from advertising Partner and Internet prefixes to external peers. Continuing with this example, router E1 would be configured with a route map that set the community to NO_EXPORT for all prefixes received from ISP A. A similar route map would also be configured on router E4 to set the same community for the single prefix that is also received from Partner B. These community values would be included in the UPDATE messages sent to the other BGP speakers within AS 123.

In Cisco IOS software, basic community configuration using communities is implemented using route maps. Within the route map, the set community [type] set clause is used to specify the type of community to set for prefixes matching the match clause. Following the configuration of the route map, the neighbor [address] send-community command is required to configure Cisco IOS software to allow the sending of community attributes for BGP peers. If this command is not configured, the community policy will not take effect for the peer.

The following configuration illustrates how to configure a route map on router E1 so that the NO_EXPORT community is set for all prefixes received from the ISP. Assuming peer-group configuration for the other iBGP peers (i.e., E2, E3, and E4), the router is configured to send the community attribute to these peers using the peer group configuration as follows:

```
E1(config)#route-map NO_EXPORT_COMMUNITY permit 10
E1(config-route-map)#set community no-export
E1(config-route-map)#exit
E1(config)#router bgp 123
E1(config-router)#neighbor INTERNAL_PEERS send-community
E1(config-router)#neighbor INTERNAL_PEERS route-map NO_EXPORT_COMMUNITY out
E1(config-router)#exit
E1(config)#exit
E3#clear ip bgp * soft out
```

On router E4, which is peered to Partner B, a similar configuration would be implemented for the 222.0.0.0/16 prefix received from Partner B. Following this configuration, router E3 will continue to receive all Internet prefixes from router E1, as well as the Partner B prefix from router E4 as shown in the following output:

```
E3#show ip bgp
BGP table version is 100, local router ID is 1.1.1.1
Status codes: s suppressed, d damped, h history, * valid, > best, i - internal,
              r RIB-failure, S Stale
Origin codes: i - IGP, e - EGP, ? - incomplete

   Network          Next Hop           Metric LocPrf Weight Path
*>i0.0.0.0          10.0.0.2                0    100      0 1 i
*>i120.0.0.0/16     10.0.0.2                0    100      0 1 10 20 i
*>i121.0.0.0/16     10.0.0.2                0    100      0 1 10 20 i
*>i122.0.0.0/16     10.0.0.2                0    100      0 1 10 20 i
*>i123.0.0.0/16     10.0.0.2                0    100      0 1 10 20 i
*>i145.0.0.0        10.0.0.2                0    100      0 1 10 20 i
*>i145.1.0.0        10.0.0.2                0    100      0 1 15 30 45 i
*> 150.254.0.0      0.0.0.0                 0          32768 i
*>i155.2.0.0        10.0.0.2                0    100      0 1 15 30 45 i
*>i155.3.0.0        10.0.0.2                0    100      0 1 15 30 45 i
*>i160.0.0.0        10.0.0.2                0    100      0 1 15 30 45 i
*>i161.0.0.0        10.0.0.2                0    100      0 1 15 30 45 i
*>i162.0.0.0        10.0.0.2                0    100      0 1 15 30 45 i
*>i163.0.0.0        10.0.0.2                0    100      0 1 15 30 45 i
*>i175.0.0.0        10.0.0.2                0    100      0 1 88 i
*>i175.1.0.0        10.0.0.2                0    100      0 1 88 i
*>i175.2.0.0        10.0.0.2                0    100      0 1 88 i
   Network          Next Hop           Metric LocPrf Weight Path
*>i175.3.0.0        10.0.0.2                0    100      0 1 88 i
*>i180.0.0.0        10.0.0.2                0    100      0 1 88 i
*>i181.0.0.0        10.0.0.2                0    100      0 1 88 i
*>i182.0.0.0        10.0.0.2                0    100      0 1 88 i
*>i183.0.0.0        10.0.0.2                0    100      0 1 2 4 6 8 i
*>i184.0.0.0        10.0.0.2                0    100      0 1 2 4 6 8 i
*>i185.0.0.0        10.0.0.2                0    100      0 1 2 4 6 8 i
*>i190.0.0.0        10.0.0.2                0    100      0 1 2 4 6 8 i
*>i191.0.0.0        10.0.0.2                0    100      0 1 2 4 6 8 i
*>i202.0.0.0/16     10.0.0.2                0    100      0 1 i
*>i203.0.0.0/16     10.0.0.2                0    100      0 1 i
*>i204.0.0.0/16     10.0.0.2                0    100      0 1 i
*>i205.0.0.0/16     10.0.0.2                0    100      0 1 i
*>i222.0.0.0/16     10.0.1.2                0    100      0 i
```

A detailed view of any of the Internet prefixes received from router E1 shows that the prefix has the NO_EXPORT community assigned to it as can be seen in the following output:

```
E1#show ip bgp 155.3.0.0 255.255.0.0
BGP routing table entry for 155.3.0.0/16, version 88
Paths: (1 available, best #1, table Default-IP-Routing-Table, not advertised
```

```
to EBGP peer)
   Not advertised to any peer
   1 15 30 45
     10.0.0.2 from 10.0.0.2 (3.3.3.3)
       Origin IGP, metric 0, localpref 100, valid, internal, best
       Community: no-export
```

The same is also applicable to the Partner B prefix received from router E4:

```
E3#show ip bgp 222.0.0.0 255.255.0.0
BGP routing table entry for 222.0.0.0/16, version 100
Paths: (1 available, best #1, table Default-IP-Routing-Table, not advertised
to EBGP peer)
   Not advertised to any peer
   789
     10.0.1.2 (metric 2) from 10.0.1.2 (4.4.4.4)
       Origin IGP, metric 0, localpref 100, valid, internal, best
       Community: no-export
```

As seen in the output above, the prefixes are marked so that they are not advertised to an eBGP peer. The result of this configuration is that only the local address space is advertised to Partner B. This is validated using the show ip bgp neighbors [address] advertised-routes command on router E3. The output of this command displays the following on router E3:

```
E3#show ip bgp neighbors 10.0.9.2 advertised-routes
BGP table version is 100, local router ID is 1.1.1.1
Status codes: s suppressed, d damped, h history, * valid, > best, i - internal,
              r RIB-failure, S Stale
Origin codes: i - IGP, e - EGP, ? - incomplete

   Network          Next Hop           Metric LocPrf Weight Path
*> 150.254.0.0      0.0.0.0                 0         32768 i

Total number of prefixes 1
```

Effective Policy Control Using AS-Path Filters

In Cisco IOS software, AS-path filters are used to perform BGP filtering policy control based on the AS_PATH attribute. The AS_PATH attribute pattern used in these filters is defined by a regular expression string that is configured using the ip as-path access-list [number] [permit | deny] <regexp> global configuration command. The configured filter list may then be applied directly on a per-neighbor basis using the neighbor [address] filter-list <as_path_acl_number> router configuration command or indirectly on a per-neighbor basis by referencing a route map that matches one or more AS-path filters using the match as-path <as_path_acl_number> route map match clause.

Before we delve into the configuration and implementation of AS-path filters, it is important to have a solid understanding of regular expressions as they are used in Cisco IOS software. A regular expression is a pattern to match against an input string. When you build a regular expression, you specify a string that an input must match. In the case of BGP, you specify a string that consists of path information that an input must match. A regular expression is comprised of the following four parts, which are described in the following sections:

- A range
- An atom
- A piece
- A branch

A range is a sequence of characters within left and right square brackets. Examples of ranges are [abcd] or [1-9] or [0,4-7]. An atom is a single character. Table 7-4 below lists common atoms and their functions and descriptions:

Table 7-4. Regular Expression Atoms

Atom	Function / Description
.	The period (.) matches a single character
$	The dollar sign ($) matches the end of the input string
\	The back slash (\) matches the character immediately following it and turns it into a regular expression
^	The caret (^) matches the start of the input string
_	The underscore (_) matches a comma (,), left brace ({), right brace (}), the start of the input string, the end of the input string, or a space
|	The pipe (|) matches either of two strings; this is an OR, when used in regular expression configurations

A piece or multiplier is a symbol that follows an atom. Common pieces are listed in Table 7-5 below:

Table 7-5. Regular Expression Pieces

Piece	Function / Description
*	The star (*) matches 0 or more sequences of the atom
+	The plus sign (+) matches 1 or more sequences of the atom
?	The question mark (?) matches the atom or the null string

Finally, a branch is 0 or more concatenated pieces (i.e., 0 or more pieces used together in a regular expression), for example ^[0-9]+ [0-9]+?$. Understandably, regular expressions seem intimidating at first; however, with practice, you will find that they are not as complicated as initially presented. In addition, you are not required to demonstrate any advanced regular expression knowledge or configuration in the current ROUTE exam. These complex configurations are currently applicable only to the CCIE-level exams. Table 7-6 below shows basic regular expression configuration and their matches:

Table 7-6. Regular Expression Pieces

Regular Expression	Matches
.*	This regular expression is used to match all prefixes
^$	This regular expression matches only prefixes local to the AS
_254$	This regular expression matches only prefixes that originate in AS 254
^254_ [0-9]*$	This regular expression matches prefixes received from directly connected AS 254 and any ASs directly attached to AS 254
_254_	This regular expression matches prefixes that have traversed AS 254
^254$	This regular expression matches only prefixes originated from directly connected AS 254

Prior to the configuration and implementation of BGP policy control using regular expressions, you can verify that the pattern that you want to configure will match what you are trying to allow or deny. This is performed using the show ip bgp regexp [expression] command. For example, if you were trying to match all prefixes originated in AS 88, then you would issue the following command on the router:

```
R3#show ip bgp regexp _88$
BGP table version is 84, local router ID is 3.3.3.3
Status codes: s suppressed, d damped, h history, * valid, > best, i - internal,
              r RIB-failure, S Stale
Origin codes: i - IGP, e - EGP, ? - incomplete

   Network          Next Hop          Metric LocPrf Weight Path
*> 175.0.0.0        10.0.3.2               0             0 1 88 i
*> 175.1.0.0        10.0.3.2               0             0 1 88 i
*> 175.2.0.0        10.0.3.2               0             0 1 88 i
*> 175.3.0.0        10.0.3.2               0             0 1 88 i
*> 180.0.0.0        10.0.3.2               0             0 1 88 i
*> 181.0.0.0        10.0.3.2               0             0 1 88 i
*> 182.0.0.0        10.0.3.2               0             0 1 88 i
```

As another example, assume that you wanted to allow only prefixes from AS 1. In this case, you should issue the following command on the router to validate the proposed regular expression:

```
R3#show ip bgp regexp ^1$
BGP table version is 84, local router ID is 3.3.3.3
Status codes: s suppressed, d damped, h history, * valid, > best, i - internal,
              r RIB-failure, S Stale
```

```
Origin codes: i - IGP, e - EGP, ? - incomplete

    Network           Next Hop          Metric LocPrf Weight Path
*> 0.0.0.0           10.0.3.2                            0 1 i
*> 202.0.0.0/16      10.0.3.2               0            0 1 i
*> 203.0.0.0/16      10.0.3.2               0            0 1 i
*> 204.0.0.0/16      10.0.3.2               0            0 1 i
*> 205.0.0.0/16      10.0.3.2               0            0 1 i
```

And yet another example, assume that you wanted to filter all prefixes that transited AS 30. In this case, you would issue the following command on the router to view all prefixes that have traversed through AS 30:

```
R3#show ip bgp regexp _30_
BGP table version is 84, local router ID is 3.3.3.3
Status codes: s suppressed, d damped, h history, * valid, > best, i - internal,
              r RIB-failure, S Stale
Origin codes: i - IGP, e - EGP, ? - incomplete

    Network           Next Hop          Metric LocPrf Weight Path
*> 145.1.0.0         10.0.3.2               0            0 1 15 30 45 i
*> 155.2.0.0         10.0.3.2               0            0 1 15 30 45 i
*> 155.3.0.0         10.0.3.2               0            0 1 15 30 45 i
*> 160.0.0.0         10.0.3.2               0            0 1 15 30 45 i
*> 161.0.0.0         10.0.3.2               0            0 1 15 30 45 i
*> 162.0.0.0         10.0.3.2               0            0 1 15 30 45 i
*> 163.0.0.0         10.0.3.2               0            0 1 15 30 45 i
```

As a final example, assume that you wanted to view all prefixes that are local to the AS. In this case, the AS_PATH attribute will be empty, since it is not included in UPDATE messages for the locally originated prefixes. The corresponding regular expression would therefore be as follows:

```
R3#show ip bgp regexp ^$
BGP table version is 84, local router ID is 3.3.3.3
Status codes: s suppressed, d damped, h history, * valid, > best, i - internal,
              r RIB-failure, S Stale
Origin codes: i - IGP, e - EGP, ? - incomplete

    Network           Next Hop          Metric LocPrf Weight Path
*>i150.254.0.0       10.0.0.1               0    100      0 i
```

In the output above, because the AS_PATH is a null string in the regular expression, the show ip bgp regexp ^$ command will match only prefixes that are locally originated within the AS. The following example illustrates how to configure and apply an AS-path filter that denies all prefixes originated in AS 88, while permitting all others:

```
R3(config)#ip as-path access-list 1 deny _88$
R3(config)#ip as-path access-list 1 permit .*
R3(config)#router bgp 123
R3(config-router)#neighbor 10.0.3.2 filter-list 1 in
R3(config-router)#exit
R3(config)#exit
R3#clear ip bgp * soft in
```

Because these prefixes are filtered, the show ip bgp regexp _88$ command shows no matches
for any prefixes originated in AS 88 as can be seen in the following output:

```
R3#show ip bgp regexp _88$

R3#
```

The router, however, continues to accept UPDATE messages for all other prefixes as illustrated
below:

```
R3#show ip bgp regexp .*
BGP table version is 113, local router ID is 3.3.3.3
Status codes: s suppressed, d damped, h history, * valid, > best, i - internal,
              r RIB-failure, S Stale
Origin codes: i - IGP, e - EGP, ? - incomplete

     Network          Next Hop         Metric LocPrf Weight Path
*>  0.0.0.0           10.0.3.2                        0 1 i
*>  120.0.0.0/16      10.0.3.2              0          0 1 10 20 i
*>  121.0.0.0/16      10.0.3.2              0          0 1 10 20 i
*>  122.0.0.0/16      10.0.3.2              0          0 1 10 20 i
*>  123.0.0.0/16      10.0.3.2              0          0 1 10 20 i
*>  145.0.0.0         10.0.3.2              0          0 1 10 20 i
*>  145.1.0.0         10.0.3.2              0          0 1 15 30 45 i
*>i150.254.0.0        10.0.0.1              0    100   0 i
*>  155.2.0.0         10.0.3.2              0          0 1 15 30 45 i
*>  155.3.0.0         10.0.3.2              0          0 1 15 30 45 i
*>  160.0.0.0         10.0.3.2              0          0 1 15 30 45 i
*>  161.0.0.0         10.0.3.2              0          0 1 15 30 45 i
*>  162.0.0.0         10.0.3.2              0          0 1 15 30 45 i
*>  163.0.0.0         10.0.3.2              0          0 1 15 30 45 i
*>  183.0.0.0         10.0.3.2              0          0 1 2 4 6 8 i
*>  184.0.0.0         10.0.3.2              0          0 1 2 4 6 8 i
*>  185.0.0.0         10.0.3.2              0          0 1 2 4 6 8 i
     Network          Next Hop         Metric LocPrf Weight Path
*>  190.0.0.0         10.0.3.2              0          0 1 2 4 6 8 i
*>  191.0.0.0         10.0.3.2              0          0 1 2 4 6 8 i
*>  202.0.0.0/16      10.0.3.2              0          0 1 i
*>  203.0.0.0/16      10.0.3.2              0          0 1 i
*>  204.0.0.0/16      10.0.3.2              0          0 1 i
*>  205.0.0.0/16      10.0.3.2              0          0 1 i
```

The policy configuration can be validated on a per-neighbor basis using the `show ip bgp neighbors [address]` command as illustrated in the following output on R3:

```
R3#show ip bgp neighbors 10.0.3.2
BGP neighbor is 10.0.3.2,  remote AS 1, external link
  BGP version 4, remote router ID 10.0.10.2
  BGP state = Established, up for 02:08:05

[Truncated Output]

  Inbound path policy configured
  Incoming update AS path filter list is 1
                              Sent        Rcvd
  Prefix activity:            ----        ----
    Prefixes Current:            1          22 (Consumes 1056 bytes)
    Prefixes Total:              3         193
    Implicit Withdraw:           2         171
    Explicit Withdraw:           0           0
    Used as bestpath:          n/a          22
    Used as multipath:         n/a           0

                            Outbound    Inbound
  Local Policy Denied Prefixes:  --------    -------
    filter-list:                    0          7
    Suppressed duplicate:           0         89
    Well-known Community:          59        n/a
    Bestpath from this peer:       89        n/a
    Total:                        148         96
  Number of NLRIs in the update sent: max 1, min 0

  ...

[Truncated Output]
```

Finally, to view the configured AS-path filter, use the `show ip as-path-access-list [number]` command as illustrated in the output below:

```
R3#show ip as-path-access-list 1
AS path access list 1
    deny _88$
    permit .*
```

In addition to using the `neighbor [address] filter-list` configuration command, route maps, as previously stated, can also be used to implement policy control by referencing an AS-path filter. The primary advantage of using route maps is that additional attributes can also be manipulated in the same configuration. The following configuration illustrates how to configure an AS-path filter that allows prefixes originated in AS 45 and assigns them a BGP WEIGHT of 1000. Additionally, the policy allows prefixes that transit AS 4 and assigns them a LOCAL_PREF value of 500. All other prefixes are denied:

```
R3(config)#ip as-path access-list 1 permit _4_
R3(config)#ip as-path access-list 2 permit _45$
R3(config)#ip as-path access-list 3 permit .*
R3(config)#route-map INBOUND-FILTER permit 10
R3(config-route-map)#match as-path 1
R3(config-route-map)#set local-preference 500
R3(config-route-map)#exit
R3(config)#route-map INBOUND-FILTER permit 20
R3(config-route-map)#match as-path 2
R3(config-route-map)#set weight 1000
R3(config-route-map)#exit
R3(config)#route-map INBOUND-FILTER permit 30
R3(config-route-map)#match as-path 3
R3(config-route-map)#exit
R3(config)#router bgp 123
R3(config-router)#neighbor 10.0.3.2 route-map INBOUND-FILTER in
R3(config-router)#exit
R3(config)#exit
R3#clear ip bgp * soft in
```

After this configuration, the BGP RIB on R3 displays the following path entries:

```
R3#show ip bgp
BGP table version is 142, local router ID is 3.3.3.3
Status codes: s suppressed, d damped, h history, * valid, > best, i - internal,
              r RIB-failure, S Stale
Origin codes: i - IGP, e - EGP, ? - incomplete

     Network          Next Hop          Metric LocPrf Weight Path
*>  145.1.0.0         10.0.3.2               0         1000 1 15 30 45 i
*>  155.2.0.0         10.0.3.2               0         1000 1 15 30 45 i
*>  155.3.0.0         10.0.3.2               0         1000 1 15 30 45 i
*>  160.0.0.0         10.0.3.2               0         1000 1 15 30 45 i
*>  161.0.0.0         10.0.3.2               0         1000 1 15 30 45 i
*>  162.0.0.0         10.0.3.2               0         1000 1 15 30 45 i
*>  163.0.0.0         10.0.3.2               0         1000 1 15 30 45 i
*>  183.0.0.0         10.0.3.2               0    500     0 1 2 4 6 8 i
*>  184.0.0.0         10.0.3.2               0    500     0 1 2 4 6 8 i
*>  185.0.0.0         10.0.3.2               0    500     0 1 2 4 6 8 i
*>  190.0.0.0         10.0.3.2               0    500     0 1 2 4 6 8 i
*>  191.0.0.0         10.0.3.2               0    500     0 1 2 4 6 8 i
```

In addition to inbound filtering, AS-path filters are also commonly used to ensure that only the internal address space is advertised to external peers. For example, assume that an enterprise was multi-homed to two ISPs and also had external BGP peer sessions with multiple partners. Instead

```
   Advertised to update-groups:
      1          2
   Local, (aggregated by 123 1.1.1.1)
      0.0.0.0 from 0.0.0.0 (1.1.1.1)
         Origin IGP, localpref 100, weight 32768, valid, aggregated, local,
atomic-aggregate, best
```

Like the network command, the aggregate-address command used without any options will advertise both the aggregate and the more specific route entries. For example, using the same networks used in the previous example, an aggregate is configured as follows:

```
R1(config)#router bgp 123
R1(config-router)#aggregate-address 12.0.0.0 255.255.252.0
R1(config-router)#exit
R1(config)#exit
```

Following this configuration, the aggregate is entered into the BGP RIB on the local router. The output of the show ip bgp command (filtered) displays the following:

```
R1#show ip bgp regexp ^$
BGP table version is 222, local router ID is 1.1.1.1
Status codes: s suppressed, d damped, h history, * valid, > best, i - internal,
              r RIB-failure, S Stale
Origin codes: i - IGP, e - EGP, ? - incomplete

   Network          Next Hop         Metric LocPrf Weight Path
*> 12.0.0.0/24      0.0.0.0               0         32768 i
*> 12.0.0.0/22      0.0.0.0                         32768 i
*> 12.0.1.0/24      0.0.0.0               0         32768 i
*> 12.0.2.0/24      0.0.0.0               0         32768 i
*> 12.0.3.0/24      0.0.0.0               0         32768 i
```

The same command, if issued on either an internal or an external peer, shows that the aggregate, as well as the more specific entries, are still being received from the router on which aggregation was performed. This is illustrated in the following output on an iBGP peer:

```
R3#show ip bgp regexp ^$
BGP table version is 24, local router ID is 3.3.3.3
Status codes: s suppressed, d damped, h history, * valid, > best, i - internal,
              r RIB-failure, S Stale
Origin codes: i - IGP, e - EGP, ? - incomplete

   Network          Next Hop         Metric LocPrf Weight Path
*>i12.0.0.0/24      10.0.0.1              0    100      0 i
*>i12.0.0.0/22      10.0.0.1              0    100      0 i
*>i12.0.1.0/24      10.0.0.1              0    100      0 i
*>i12.0.2.0/24      10.0.0.1              0    100      0 i
*>i12.0.3.0/24      10.0.0.1              0    100      0 i
```

The `summary-only` keyword configures the local BGP speaker to advertise only the summary address and to suppress the more specific entries included in the specified range. This configuration is implemented on router R1 as follows:

```
R1(config)#router bgp 123
R1(config-router)#aggregate-address 12.0.0.0 255.255.252.0 summary-only
R1(config-router)#exit
R1(config)#exit
R1#clear ip bgp * soft out
```

After this configuration change, the BGP RIB on R1 now displays the following:

```
R1#show ip bgp regexp ^$
BGP table version is 226, local router ID is 1.1.1.1
Status codes: s suppressed, d damped, h history, * valid, > best, i - internal,
              r RIB-failure, S Stale
Origin codes: i - IGP, e - EGP, ? - incomplete

   Network          Next Hop          Metric LocPrf Weight Path
s> 12.0.0.0/24      0.0.0.0                0         32768 i
*> 12.0.0.0/22      0.0.0.0                          32768 i
s> 12.0.1.0/24      0.0.0.0                0         32768 i
s> 12.0.2.0/24      0.0.0.0                0         32768 i
s> 12.0.3.0/24      0.0.0.0                0         32768 i
```

If you compare the output prior to the use of the `summary-only` keyword with the one above, you will notice that all the specific prefixes now have an 's' preceding them. This indicates that the entries are suppressed and are not advertised to any peer as shown in the following output:

```
R1#show ip bgp 12.0.0.0/24
BGP routing table entry for 12.0.0.0/24, version 223
Paths: (1 available, best #1, table Default-IP-Routing-Table, Advertisements
suppressed by an aggregate.)
  Not advertised to any peer
  Local
    0.0.0.0 from 0.0.0.0 (1.1.1.1)
      Origin IGP, metric 0, localpref 100, weight 32768, valid, sourced,
local, best
```

This behavior can be validated by viewing the RIB of any peer of R1 as shown below:

```
R3#show ip bgp regexp ^$
BGP table version is 28, local router ID is 3.3.3.3
Status codes: s suppressed, d damped, h history, * valid, > best, i - internal,
              r RIB-failure, S Stale
Origin codes: i - IGP, e - EGP, ? - incomplete

   Network          Next Hop          Metric LocPrf Weight Path
*>i12.0.0.0/22      10.0.0.1               0    100     0 i
```

BGP AND IGP ROUTE REDISTRIBUTION

In Chapter 5, pertaining to path control, we learned about route redistribution as it applies to the various IGPs that are within the scope of the ROUTE exam requirements. This section focuses on redistribution between BGP and EIGRP or OSPF.

Redistributing EIGRP Routes into BGP

EIGRP-learned routes are redistributed into BGP by using the `redistribute eigrp [AS] [metric <MED>] [route-map <name>]` router configuration command. The `[metric <MED>]` keyword specifies the MED metric that will be assigned to the prefixes when they are redistributed into BGP. If this keyword is omitted, then the IGP metric will be used instead. The `[route-map <name>]`keyword is used to specify a route map that will be used for policy control. For example, the referenced route map may be used to set attributes, such as the BGP LOCAL_PREF or WEIGHT attributes for the redistributed prefixes. The following output shows the routing table entry for the 192.168.1.0/24 prefix, which is learned by R1 via EIGRP:

```
R1#show ip route 192.168.1.0 255.255.255.0
Routing entry for 192.168.1.0/24
  Known via "eigrp 1", distance 90, metric 2297856, type internal
  Redistributing via eigrp 1
  Last update from 10.0.9.2 on Serial0/0, 00:00:14 ago
  Routing Descriptor Blocks:
  * 10.0.9.2, from 10.0.9.2, 00:00:14 ago, via Serial0/0
      Route metric is 2297856, traffic share count is 1
        Total delay is 25000 microseconds, minimum bandwidth is 1544 Kbit
        Reliability 255/255, minimum MTU 1500 bytes
        Loading 1/255, Hops 1
```

To redistribute this, and only this, prefix into BGP on R1, the following must be performed:

```
R1(config)#ip prefix-list NET-192-ONLY seq 5 permit 192.168.1.0/24
R1(config)#route-map EIGRP-INTO-BGP permit 10
R1(config-route-map)#match ip address prefix-list NET-192-ONLY
R1(config-route-map)#exit
R1(config)#route-map EIGRP-INTO-BGP deny 20
R1(config-route-map)#exit
R1(config)#router bgp 123
R1(config-router)#redistribute eigrp 1 route-map EIGRP-INTO-BGP
R1(config-router)#exit
R1(config)#exit
R1#clear ip bgp * soft out
```

In the output above, notice that although a route map was used for policy control, ensuring that only the 192.168.1.0/24 prefix was redistributed into BGP, no metric was set. By default, the prefix will therefore be assigned a metric that is equal to the IGP metric. In addition, when routes are redistributed into BGP from an IGP, the NEXT_HOP address is set to the next hop IP address of the IGP. In this example, the NEXT_HOP attribute for this prefix will be 10.0.9.2. Additionally, the ORIGIN will be set to INCOMPLETE; however, all other attributes (e.g., LOCAL_PREF and WEIGHT) will use default BGP values. These default parameters can be validated using the `show ip bgp` command as follows:

```
R1#show ip bgp 192.168.1.0/24
BGP routing table entry for 192.168.1.0/24, version 227
Paths: (1 available, best #1, table Default-IP-Routing-Table)
  Advertised to update-groups:
     1         2
  Local
    10.0.9.2 from 0.0.0.0 (1.1.1.1)
      Origin incomplete, metric 2297856, localpref 100, weight 32768, valid,
sourced, best
```

NOTE: If the NEXT_HOP address is not known to other iBGP peers, then the prefix will be marked as inaccessible. To resolve this, the subnet running EIGRP must be advertised into the interior network or the local BGP speaker must be configured with the `neighbor [address] next-hop-self` route configuration command for all internal peers.

Redistributing OSPF Routes into BGP

While the redistribution of EIGRP routes into BGP is a straightforward process, redistributing OSPF routes into BGP entails a little more thought. By default, when OSPF routes are redistributed into BGP, only internal OSPF and external Type 1 routes will be redistributed. To clarify this point further, router R1 is receiving the following routes via OSPF:

```
R1#show ip route ospf
O    192.168.1.0/24 [110/2] via 10.0.9.2, 00:02:08, Serial0/0
O E2 192.168.2.0/24 [110/20] via 10.0.9.2, 00:00:17, Serial0/0
```

OSPF is then redistributed into BGP using the `redistribute ospf [process]` router configuration command on R1 as illustrated in the following output:

```
R1(config)#router bgp 123
R1(config-router)#redistribute ospf 1
R1(config-router)#exit
R1(config)#exit
R1#clear ip bgp * soft out
```

Following this configuration, the BGP RIB on R1 shows that only the internal OSPF route (i.e., the 192.168.1.0/24 prefix) has been redistributed. This is illustrated below:

```
R1#show ip bgp regexp ^$
BGP table version is 240, local router ID is 1.1.1.1
Status codes: s suppressed, d damped, h history, * valid, > best, i - internal,
              r RIB-failure, S Stale
Origin codes: i - IGP, e - EGP, ? - incomplete

   Network          Next Hop          Metric LocPrf Weight Path
*> 192.168.1.0      10.0.9.2               2          32768 ?
```

Because the default OSPF external route type is a Type 2 external route, the redistribution of these prefixes into BGP can be facilitated by performing one of the following two actions:

- Changing the default OSPF external route type to a Type 1 external route
- Using the redistribute ospf [process] match [type] command

The first action was described in detail in OSPF redistribution earlier in this guide. To avoid being repetitive, and for brevity, this will not be described again in this chapter. Refer to Chapter 5 on path control if you are unable to recall how to configure Type 1 external routes during redistribution into OSPF. The second option is the preferred option, as it negates the need to change your OSPF redistribution configuration, assuming you used the default parameters, which results in a Type 2 external route for all redistributed routes. When OSPF routes are redistributed into BGP, the router can be configured to match the following:

- Internal
- NSSA External 1
- NSSA External 2
- External 1
- External 2

The match internal configuration command configures BGP to redistribute routes that are local to the autonomous system (i.e., internal OSPF routes). By default, these routes are redistributed. The match external 1 configuration command configures BGP to redistribute external Type 1 OSPF routes. By default, these routes are redistributed. The match external 2 configuration command configures BGP to redistribute external Type 2 OSPF routes. While Cisco IOS software defaults to Type 2 external routes when external routing information is injected into OSPF on the ASBR, these routes are not redistributed into BGP by default and the router must be configured manually to redistribute these prefixes.

The match nssa-external 1 configuration command configures BGP to redistribute NSSA external Type 1 OSPF routes. By default, these routes are not redistributed. The match nssa-external 2 configuration command configures BGP to redistribute NSSA external Type 2 OSPF routes. By default, these routes are also not redistributed.

Continuing with the example used in the previous section that showed the internal and external OSPF routes being received on R1, BGP is now configured to redistribute Type 2 external routes in addition to the internal route received. This is performed as follows:

```
R1(config)#router bgp 123
R1(config-router)#redistribute ospf 1 match internal external 2
R1(config-router)#exit
R1(config)#exit
R1#clear ip bgp * soft out
```

Following this configuration, both prefixes are now present in the BGP RIB on R1. The internal prefix, 192.168.1.0/24 has the same MED metric as the OSPF route. The second prefix, which was redistributed into OSPF using default parameters, has the default OSPF metric of 20 assigned to it. The NEXT_HOP value for both prefixes is the IGP next-hop value. All other attributes use the default values. These values can all be validated using the show ip bgp command as illustrated below:

```
R1#show ip bgp regexp ^$
BGP table version is 241, local router ID is 1.1.1.1
Status codes: s suppressed, d damped, h history, * valid, > best, i - internal,
              r RIB-failure, S Stale
Origin codes: i - IGP, e - EGP, ? - incomplete

   Network          Next Hop            Metric LocPrf Weight Path
*> 192.168.1.0      10.0.9.2                 2          32768 ?
*> 192.168.2.0      10.0.9.2                20          32768 ?
```

Redistributing BGP Routes into IGPs

NOTE: While this section illustrates how to redistribute BGP routes into IGPs, it is important to remember that this is never recommended, unless absolutely necessary. In situations where you must redistribute BGP into any IGP, it is highly recommended that you use route maps during redistribution to ensure that you redistribute only those prefixes that you want. NEVER redistribute BGP into any IGP without using route maps or any other IOS filtering mechanisms.

When redistributing BGP routes into IGPs, by default, iBGP routes will not be redistributed into the IGP. Instead, only eBGP routes will be redistributed. The primary reason for this default behavior is to avoid routing loops within the interior network. In most cases, iBGP routes are already known by the IGP that is running in the interior network. It therefore goes without saying that these routes should not be redistributed back into the IGP; hence, the default Cisco IOS software behavior. The redistribution of BGP routes into an IGP follows the same basic logic used when redistributing any other routes into the particular Interior Gateway Protocol.

When redistributing BGP routes into EIGRP, the metric must be specified during redistribution by issuing the `redistribute bgp [AS] metric` router configuration command. Alternatively, the default (seed) metric for the redistributed routes can also be specified using the `default-metric` router configuration command in EIGRP configuration mode. The following configuration illustrates how to redistribute the default route from BGP into EIGRP:

```
R3(config)#ip prefix-list DEFAULT-ONLY description 'Only The Default Route'
R3(config)#ip prefix-list DEFAULT-ONLY seq 5 permit 0.0.0.0/0
R3(config)#route-map BGP-INTO-EIGRP permit 10
R3(config-route-map)#description 'Redistribute Only The Default Route'
R3(config-route-map)#match ip address prefix-list DEFAULT-ONLY
R3(config-route-map)#exit
R3(config)#route-map BGP-INTO-EIGRP deny 20
R3(config-route-map)#description 'Explicitly Deny All Other Routes'
R3(config-route-map)#exit
R3(config)#router eigrp 1
R3(config-router)#default-metric 10000 100 255 1 1500
R3(config-router)#redistribute bgp 123 route-map BGP-INTO-EIGRP
R3(config-router)#exit
```

Following this configuration, use the `show ip route` command to verify that the default route is known via BGP and is being redistributed into EIGRP using the specified route map. The output of this command displays the following for the default route:

```
R3#show ip route 0.0.0.0 0.0.0.0
Routing entry for 0.0.0.0/0, supernet
  Known via "bgp 123", distance 20, metric 0, candidate default path
  Tag 1, type external
  Redistributing via eigrp 1
  Advertised by eigrp 1 route-map BGP-INTO-EIGRP
  Last update from 10.0.3.2 00:06:12 ago
  Routing Descriptor Blocks:
  * 10.0.3.2, from 10.0.3.2, 00:06:12 ago
      Route metric is 0, traffic share count is 1
      AS Hops 1
```

The same can also be confirmed by viewing the EIGRP Topology Table as illustrated below:

```
R3#show ip eigrp topology 0.0.0.0 0.0.0.0
IP-EIGRP (AS 1): Topology entry for 0.0.0.0/0
  State is Passive, Query origin flag is 1, 1 Successor(s), FD is 281600
  Routing Descriptor Blocks:
  10.0.3.2, from Redistributed, Send flag is 0x0
      Composite metric is (281600/0), Route is External
      Vector metric:
        Minimum bandwidth is 10000 Kbit
        Total delay is 1000 microseconds
        Reliability is 255/255
```

```
        Load is 1/255
        Minimum MTU is 1500
        Hop count is 0
      External data:
        Originating router is 3.3.3.3 (this system)
        AS number of route is 123
        External protocol is BGP, external metric is 0
        Administrator tag is 1 (0x00000001)
        Exterior flag is set
```

When redistributing routes into OSPF, a route metric does not have to be specified during the re-distribution. If not specified, then OSPF uses the following default values:

- Redistributed routes from BGP are assigned a metric or cost of 1
- Redistributed routes from another OSPF process use the source route's cost
- All other redistributed routes are assigned a default metric of 20

As is the case with EIGRP, it is imperative to implement filtering when redistributing any BGP routes into OSPF. In addition, it is important to remember to use the subnets keyword when redistributing routes into OSPF. If this keyword is omitted, only Classful subnets will be redistributed. The following configuration example illustrates how to configure OSPF to redistribute only the default route from BGP:

```
R3(config)#ip prefix-list DEFAULT-ONLY description 'Only The Default Route'
R3(config)#ip prefix-list DEFAULT-ONLY seq 5 permit 0.0.0.0/0
R3(config)#route-map BGP-INTO-OSPF permit 10
R3(config-route-map)#description 'Redistribute Only The Default Route'
R3(config-route-map)#match ip address prefix-list DEFAULT-ONLY
R3(config-route-map)#exit
R3(config)#route-map BGP-INTO-OSPF deny 20
R3(config-route-map)#description 'Explicitly Deny All Other Routes'
R3(config-route-map)#exit
R3(config)#router ospf 3
R3(config-router)#default-information originate
R3(config-router)#redistribute bgp 123 subnets route-map BGP-INTO-OSPF
R3(config-router)#exit
```

NOTE: Regarding the output above, by default, the default route will not be installed into the LSDB unless the default-information originate command is issued under the OSPF process. After this configuration, the LSDB on router R3 displays the following Type 5 LSA:

```
R3#show ip ospf database external 0.0.0.0

          OSPF Router with ID (3.3.3.3) (Process ID 3)

          Type-5 AS External Link States
```

```
LS age: 50
Options: (No TOS-capability, DC)
LS Type: AS External Link
Link State ID: 0.0.0.0 (External Network Number)
Advertising Router: 3.3.3.3
LS Seq Number: 80000001
Checksum: 0x59F
Length: 36
Network Mask: /0
        Metric Type: 2 (Larger than any Link State path)
        TOS: 0
        Metric: 1
        Forward Address: 0.0.0.0
        External Route Tag: 3
```

NOTE: When redistributing into OSPF, keep in mind that you may need to issue the `clear ip ospf redistribution` command following the configuration change.

Finally, to conclude this section, the `bgp redistribute-internal` command must be used when redistributing iBGP routes into an IGP. By default, this behavior is disabled. The following configuration illustrates how to configure a local BGP speaker to redistribute iBGP-learned prefixes into an Interior Gateway Protocol:

```
R3(config)#router bgp 123
R3(config-router)#bgp redistribute-internal
R3(config-router)#exit
```

BGP ROUTE REFLECTORS AND CONFEDERATIONS

Earlier in this guide, we learned that, by default, a BGP speaker will not advertise any routes received from an iBGP peer to another iBGP peer. While this default behavior is designed to prevent loops in iBGP implementations, it also imposes scalability issues. If, for example, a network has four routers running BGP, then all routers must be peered to each other in order for all routers to learn about the iBGP prefixes. This means that each BGP speaker must have three neighbor statements—one for every other router—resulting in twelve neighbor relationships for BGP. As the number of routers increases, so does the number of neighbor relationships. The two ways to scale iBGP implementations without having to employ a full-mesh implementation is via Route Reflectors (RR) and Confederations.

Route Reflectors

Route reflection works via the use of a Route Reflector (RR) or Route Reflector routers within an iBGP network. By implementing RRs in iBGP networks, iBGP routers are classified into the following three router groups:

1. Route Reflectors
2. Regular iBGP speakers (non-clients)
3. Route Reflector clients

Route Reflectors are BGP speakers that reflect routes between the following BGP speakers:
- Between clients and non-clients
- Between clients and clients (called client-to-client reflection)
- Between non-clients and clients

To clarify this point further, consider the network topology illustrated in Figure 7-15 below:

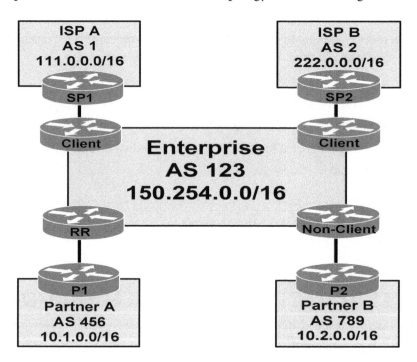

Fig. 7-15. Understanding BGP Route Reflectors

Figure 7-15 illustrates a basic BGP network. The RR is peered to Partner A in AS 456. The RR is also peered to two clients (connected to the ISP) and a non-client (connected to Partner B). In order to avoid loops due to this implementation, the route follows certain rules pertaining to prefix advertisement. These rules include the following:
- The RR reflects only the best path. For example, if the RR received two paths for an Internet prefix from the two clients, it would reflect the best path to any other client or non-client routers. It would not advertise both paths.
- By default, the RR will always advertise received prefixes to any eBGP peer. Referencing Figure 7-15, any prefixes received by the RR would be advertised to the external peer in AS 456 (i.e. Partner A).

- By default, the RR will advertise all prefixes learned from an external peer to all client and non-client peers. Referencing Figure 7-15, the RR will advertise the prefix learned from AS 456 (Partner A) to the two client and one non-client routers.

- If the RR receives a prefix from a non-client peer, it will reflect the prefix to all client peers. For example, the RR will reflect the Partner B prefix received from the non-client to the client peers connected to the ISPs (as well as to the external peer in AS 456).

- Finally, when the RR receives prefixes from a client, it will advertise them to all client and non-client peers, including external peers as well.

In Cisco IOS software, the configuration of Route Reflectors is straightforward and there is no special configuration required on the client or non-client routers. On the RR itself, the `neighbor [address] route-reflector-client` command is required for all clients of the RR. These clients peer only with the RR. For non-clients and external peers, the standard BGP peering configuration is also used. The configuration of RRs will be illustrated in the following section based on the topology in Figure 7-16 below:

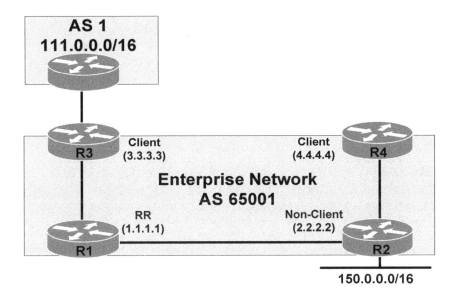

Fig. 7-16. Configuring Route Reflectors in Cisco IOS Software

Before configuring the RR, the following illustrates the configuration on routers R2, R3, and R4, beginning with the configuration on router R2:

```
R2(config)#router bgp 65001
R2(config-router)#bgp router-id 2.2.2.2
R2(config-router)#neighbor 1.1.1.1 remote-as 65001
R2(config-router)#neighbor 1.1.1.1 update-source Loopback0
R2(config-router)#network 150.0.0.0 mask 255.255.0.0
R2(config-router)#exit
```

The base configuration on router R3 is as follows:

```
R3(config)#router bgp 65001
R3(config-router)#bgp router-id 3.3.3.3
R3(config-router)#neighbor 1.1.1.1 next-hop-self
R3(config-router)#neighbor 1.1.1.1 remote-as 65001
R3(config-router)#neighbor 1.1.1.1 update-source Loopback0
R3(config-router)#neighbor 10.0.3.2 remote-as 1
R3(config-router)#exit
```

NOTE: R3 is also configured with the `neighbor [address] next-hop-self` command because it will be peered to an external BGP speaker. If this command is not used and the subnet between R3 and the ISP is not advertised into the interior network, the NEXT_HOP for the prefix received from the ISP will be inaccessible to the iBGP speakers in AS 65001.

The base configuration on router R4 is as follows:

```
R4(config)#router bgp 65001
R4(config-router)#bgp router-id 4.4.4.4
R4(config-router)#neighbor 1.1.1.1 remote-as 65001
R4(config-router)#neighbor 1.1.1.1 update-source Loopback0
R4(config-router)#exit
```

Assuming the base configuration, the only peer relationship that will be in the Established state is R3 and the ISP in AS 1. This is validated as follows:

```
R3#show ip bgp summary
BGP router identifier 3.3.3.3, local AS number 65001
BGP table version is 2, main routing table version 2
1 network entries using 101 bytes of memory
1 path entries using 48 bytes of memory
1 BGP path attribute entries using 60 bytes of memory
1 BGP AS-PATH entries using 24 bytes of memory
0 BGP route-map cache entries using 0 bytes of memory
0 BGP filter-list cache entries using 0 bytes of memory
BGP using 233 total bytes of memory
BGP activity 1/0 prefixes, 1/0 paths, scan interval 60 secs

Neighbor     V     AS MsgRcvd MsgSent   TblVer  InQ OutQ Up/Down   State/PfxRcd
1.1.1.1      4 65001       0       0        0    0    0 never     Active
10.0.3.2     4     1      23      22        2    0    0 00:00:47          1
```

In the output above, the neighbor relationship between R3 and the ISP router is established. R3 is receiving a single prefix from the ISP, which can be viewed by looking at the BGP RIB in the following output:

```
R3#show ip bgp
BGP table version is 2, local router ID is 3.3.3.3
Status codes: s suppressed, d damped, h history, * valid, > best, i - internal,
              r RIB-failure, S Stale
Origin codes: i - IGP, e - EGP, ? - incomplete

   Network          Next Hop          Metric LocPrf Weight Path
*> 111.0.0.0/16     10.0.3.2              0             0 1 i
```

Following the configuration of the client and non-client routers, we will now configure the RR. As previously stated, the configuration remains the same, with the exception that the neighbor [address] route-reflector-client command must be specified for all client routers. This command is not required for external peers or non-client routers. Referencing the topology in Figure 7-16, R3 and R4 are clients, but R2 is not. The configuration on R1 (RR) is therefore implemented as follows:

```
R1(config)#router bgp 65001
R1(config-router)#bgp router-id 1.1.1.1
R1(config-router)#neighbor RR-CLIENTS peer-group
R1(config-router)#neighbor RR-CLIENTS remote-as 65001
R1(config-router)#neighbor RR-CLIENTS update-source Loopback0
R1(config-router)#neighbor RR-CLIENTS route-reflector-client
R1(config-router)#neighbor 3.3.3.3 peer-group RR-CLIENTS
R1(config-router)#neighbor 4.4.4.4 peer-group RR-CLIENTS
R1(config-router)#neighbor 2.2.2.2 remote-as 65001
R1(config-router)#neighbor 2.2.2.2 update-source Loopback0
R1(config-router)#exit
```

In the configuration above, a peer group has been used to simplify the configuration of the RR clients. Routers R3 and R4 are assigned to this peer group. R2, which is a non-client, is not assigned to a peer group; however, if there were more non-clients, a peer group could also be created for those routers in order to simplify BGP configuration and improve convergence. Following the configuration on router R3, the show ip bgp summary command should be used to verify neighbor relationships. The output of this command displays the following:

```
R1#show ip bgp summary
BGP router identifier 1.1.1.1, local AS number 65001
BGP table version is 4, main routing table version 4
2 network entries using 234 bytes of memory
2 path entries using 104 bytes of memory
3/2 BGP path/bestpath attribute entries using 372 bytes of memory
1 BGP AS-PATH entries using 24 bytes of memory
0 BGP route-map cache entries using 0 bytes of memory
0 BGP filter-list cache entries using 0 bytes of memory
BGP using 734 total bytes of memory
BGP activity 2/0 prefixes, 2/0 paths, scan interval 60 secs
```

```
Neighbor      V     AS MsgRcvd MsgSent    TblVer   InQ OutQ Up/Down   State/PfxRcd
2.2.2.2       4 65001       8       8         4     0    0 00:03:29             1
3.3.3.3       4 65001       7       8         4     0    0 00:02:11             1
4.4.4.4       4 65001       6       8         4     0    0 00:02:18             0
```

The show ip bgp neighbors command can be used to determine whether a specific peer is a client or a non-client. For example, if this command were used to view the detailed neighbor information for router R3, the output of the command would display the following:

```
R1#show ip bgp neighbors 3.3.3.3
BGP neighbor is 3.3.3.3,  remote AS 65001, internal link
 Member of peer-group RR-CLIENTS for session parameters
  BGP version 4, remote router ID 3.3.3.3
  BGP state = Established, up for 00:03:18

[Truncated Output]

 For address family: IPv4 Unicast
  BGP table version 4, neighbor version 4/0
 Output queue size : 0
  Index 2, Offset 0, Mask 0x4
  Route-Reflector Client
  2 update-group member
  RR-CLIENTS peer-group member
                                   Sent       Rcvd
 Prefix activity:                  ----       ----
    Prefixes Current:                2          1 (Consumes 52 bytes)
    Prefixes Total:                  2          1
    Implicit Withdraw:               1          0
    Explicit Withdraw:               0          0
    Used as bestpath:              n/a          1
    Used as multipath:             n/a          0

                                Outbound    Inbound
 Local Policy Denied Prefixes:   --------    -------
    Total:                              0          0
 Number of NLRIs in the update sent: max 1, min 1

 Connections established 1; dropped 0

...

[Truncated Output]
```

A similar output would also be shown for router R4, but not for router R2, which is not a client. Having verified basic neighbor status, we will move on to prefix validation. First, we will take a detailed look at the prefix that the RR receives from client R3. The show ip bgp command shows the following for the 111.0.0.0/16 prefix:

```
R1#show ip bgp 111.0.0.0 255.255.0.0
BGP routing table entry for 111.0.0.0/16, version 6
Paths: (1 available, best #1, table Default-IP-Routing-Table)
Flag: 0x820
  Advertised to update-groups:
     1        2
  1, (Received from a RR-client)
    3.3.3.3 (metric 3) from 3.3.3.3 (3.3.3.3)
      Origin IGP, metric 0, localpref 100, valid, internal, best
```

In the output above, the prefix is marked as being received from the RR client, which validates the configuration implemented in AS 65001. The prefix is sent to two update groups, group 1 and group 2. A single group will be created for the peers in the peer group, while another group will be created for the non-peer-group peer, R2. Detailed information on the two update groups can be viewed using the show ip bgp update-group command as shown below:

```
R1#show ip bgp update-group
BGP version 4 update-group 1, internal, Address Family: IPv4 Unicast
  BGP Update version : 7/0, messages 0
  Update messages formatted 3, replicated 0
  Number of NLRIs in the update sent: max 1, min 0
  Minimum time between advertisement runs is 0 seconds
  Has 1 member (* indicates the members currently being sent updates):
   2.2.2.2

BGP version 4 update-group 2, internal, Address Family: IPv4 Unicast
  BGP Update version : 7/0, messages 0
  Route-Reflector Client
  Update messages formatted 7, replicated 4
  Number of NLRIs in the update sent: max 1, min 0
  Minimum time between advertisement runs is 0 seconds
  Has 2 members (* indicates the members currently being sent updates):
   3.3.3.3         4.4.4.4
```

As was stated in the prefix advertisement rules, when the RR receives prefixes from a client, it will advertise them to all client and non-client peers, including external peers as well. From the output above, R1 (RR) is advertising the received prefix from client R3 to client R4 and non-client R2. On router R3, the BGP RIB shows the following entry for this prefix:

```
R3#show ip bgp 111.0.0.0
BGP routing table entry for 111.0.0.0/16, version 6
Paths: (1 available, best #1, table Default-IP-Routing-Table)
  Not advertised to any peer
  1
    3.3.3.3 (metric 77) from 1.1.1.1 (1.1.1.1)
      Origin IGP, metric 0, localpref 100, valid, internal, best
      Originator: 3.3.3.3, Cluster list: 1.1.1.1
```

In Chapter 6, when we learned about preventing routing information loops, we learned about the AS_PATH attribute, which is used for external peers, and the following two attributes that are used exclusively in internal BGP implementations:

- The ORIGINATOR_ID attribute
- The CLUSTER_LIST attribute

In the output of the show ip bgp command on router R2 in the following example, we can see that these two attributes are included in the output. The ORIGINATOR_ID attribute is set by the RR (R1) with a value equal to the BGP ID of the client router that originated the route. We know that the route was advertised to the RR by R3; therefore, the ORIGINATOR_ID is set to 3.3.3.3 before this is reflected to other client and non-client peers.

The second attribute, the CLUSTER_LIST attribute, is used by the RR itself to prevent it from receiving and accepting information that it has advertised. If R1 receives the same UPDATE message from another router, for example, it will ignore the UPDATE message because the local CLUSTER_ID, which it set, is found in the CLUSTER_LIST attribute.

The same information is also included for the advertisement sent to non-client router R2 as illustrated below:

```
R2#show ip bgp 111.0.0.0 255.255.0.0
BGP routing table entry for 111.0.0.0/16, version 5
Paths: (1 available, best #1, table Default-IP-Routing-Table)
  Not advertised to any peer
  1
    3.3.3.3 (metric 67) from 1.1.1.1 (1.1.1.1)
      Origin IGP, metric 0, localpref 100, valid, internal, best
      Originator: 3.3.3.3, Cluster List: 1.1.1.1
```

Next, we will look at the prefix received from non-client R2 as seen on the RR as follows:

```
R1#show ip bgp 150.0.0.0
BGP routing table entry for 150.0.0.0/16, version 7
Paths: (1 available, best #1, table Default-IP-Routing-Table)
  Advertised to update-groups:
    2
  Local
    2.2.2.2 (metric 2) from 2.2.2.2 (2.2.2.2)
      Origin IGP, metric 0, localpref 100, valid, internal, best
```

In the output above, because R2 is a non-client, the prefix is not marked as being received from a client—further validating our configuration. The received prefix is reflected to peers in update group 2—which are the internal RR client peers, as was validated earlier in this section. If we viewed the same prefix on either of the client routers, then we would see the following:

```
R3#show ip bgp 150.0.0.0/16
BGP routing table entry for 150.0.0.0/16, version 9
Paths: (1 available, best #1, table Default-IP-Routing-Table)
  Advertised to non peer-group peers:
  10.0.3.2
  Local
    2.2.2.2 (metric 3) from 1.1.1.1 (1.1.1.1)
      Origin IGP, metric 0, localpref 100, valid, internal, best
      Originator: 2.2.2.2, Cluster list: 1.1.1.1
```

In the output above, R3 receives and advertises this prefix to its external peer, the ISP in AS 1. The UPDATE message includes both the ORIGINATOR_ID and CLUSTER_LIST attributes; however, these attributes are not advertised out of the local autonomous system. This is because both attributes are optional, non-transitive attributes. If you recall, in Chapter 6 we learned that transitive attributes are those that transit different autonomous systems, while non-transitive attributes are locally significant within an autonomous system. This can be validated by viewing the prefix that the ISP in AS 1 receives from router R3:

```
R3#show ip bgp 150.0.0.0/16
BGP routing table entry for 150.0.0.0/16, version 5
Paths: (1 available, best #1, table Default-IP-Routing-Table)
  Not advertised to any peer
  65001
    10.0.3.1 from 10.0.3.1 (3.3.3.3)
      Origin IGP, localpref 100, valid, external, best
```

Confederations

The second method that is used to mitigate the iBGP scalability issues is to use Confederations, which are used to split the autonomous system into member autonomous systems or sub-autonomous systems using different private AS numbers. This essentially means that within the global autonomous system, you have multiple external sub-autonomous systems. Because BGP speakers will advertise prefixes to all external peers, the use of these sub-autonomous systems negates the need to implement a full-mesh iBGP network. Figure 7-17 below illustrates a BGP confederation:

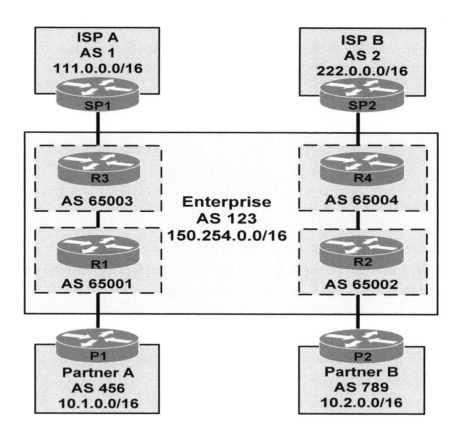

Fig. 7-17. Understanding BGP Confederations

Referencing Figure 7-17, the enterprise network has been split up into four sub-autonomous or member autonomous systems: AS 65001, AS 65002, AS 65003, and AS 65004. Because the sub-autonomous systems use different AS numbers, external BGP sessions can be established between them. This negates the need to implement a fully meshed iBGP solution. Assume, for example, that the sub-autonomous systems are peered in the following manner:

• AS 65003 < > AS 65001 < > AS 65002 < > AS 65004

Because the sessions between the sub-autonomous systems are external, if R3 in sub-AS 65003 receives an UPDATE from ISP A, then it will advertise this to AS 65001 (R1). R1, in turn, will advertise this to external sub-AS peer R2 (AS 65002). R2 will then advertise the prefix to external sub-AS peer R4 (AS 65004).

While the sub-autonomous systems follow the same prefix advertisement rules as external BGP speakers, they are not the same as external BGP speakers. These sub-autonomous systems are external only within AS 123, which belongs to the enterprise. To the outside world, both the ISP and the partner routers would peer with routers R1, R2, R3, and R4 using AS 123, not the sub-autonomous system numbers.

While the sub-autonomous system establishes external iBGP (eiBGP) sessions, commonly referred to as intra-Confederation BGP sessions, to negate the need for a full-mesh iBGP implementation within the core autonomous system, it is important to understand that within each Confederation, normal iBGP rules are still applicable. For example, if there are 10 routers in a particular sub-AS, then either these 10 routers must be fully meshed or a Route Reflector must be used to negate this need.

The configuration of Confederations is a little more complex than that required to configure and implement Route Reflectors. In Cisco IOS software, the following sequence of steps is required to configure and implement BGP Confederations:

- Configure the local BGP speaker with the desired private AS number using the `router bgp [private AS number]` global configuration command.
- Configure the local BGP speaker with the public AS number using the `bgp confederation identifier [public AS number]` router configuration command.
- Specify one or more sub-AS peers that this local BGP speaker will peer to using the `bgp confederation peers [sub-AS]` router configuration command. If the local BGP speaker will not peer to any other sub-AS, this command must be omitted.
- Configure the BGP neighbor relationships following the standard steps. However, if a local BGP speaker will be peered to another BGP speaker in a different sub-AS, then you must use the `neighbor [address] ebgp-multihop` command if you will be using Loopback interfaces for the BGP session.

Figure 7-18 below illustrates a basic BGP network that is using Confederations. The enterprise owns and has registered AS 123. The enterprise has decided to use Confederations to negate implementing a full-mesh iBGP solution. The three routers in the AS—R1, R2, and R3—will use sub-AS 65001, 65002, and 65003, respectively. R3 will be peered to R1. R1 will be peered to R2 and R3. R2 will be peered to R1 and R4. R4 will be peered only to R2. All of the routers in the topology will use their Loopback interfaces for peering.

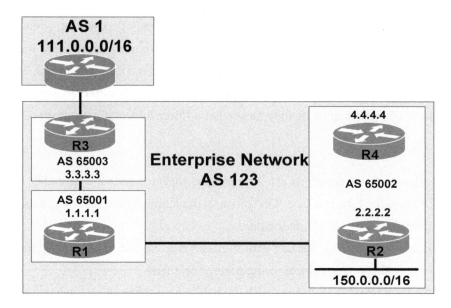

Fig. 7-18. Configuring Confederations in Cisco IOS Software

Following the configuration steps in the previous section, R3 is configured as follows:

```
R3(config)#router bgp 65003
R3(config-router)#bgp router-id 3.3.3.3
R3(config-router)#bgp confederation identifier 123
R3(config-router)#bgp confederation peers 65001
R3(config-router)#neighbor 10.0.3.2 remote-as 1
R3(config-router)#neighbor 1.1.1.1 remote-as 65001
R3(config-router)#neighbor 1.1.1.1 update-source Loopback0
R3(config-router)#neighbor 1.1.1.1 next-hop-self
R3(config-router)#neighbor 1.1.1.1 ebgp-multihop 2
R3(config-router)#exit
```

Prior to continuing with the configuration on routers R1 and R2, we will first verify the BGP neighbor relationship between R3 and the ISP in AS 1. The show ip bgp summary command on R3 shows that the neighbor relationship is established and the router is receiving a single prefix from the ISP edge router as illustrated below:

```
R3#show ip bgp summary
BGP router identifier 3.3.3.3, local AS number 65003
BGP table version is 2, main routing table version 2
1 network entries using 101 bytes of memory
1 path entries using 48 bytes of memory
1 BGP path attribute entries using 60 bytes of memory
1 BGP AS-PATH entries using 24 bytes of memory
0 BGP route-map cache entries using 0 bytes of memory
0 BGP filter-list cache entries using 0 bytes of memory
BGP using 233 total bytes of memory
BGP activity 1/0 prefixes, 1/0 paths, scan interval 60 secs
```

```
Neighbor      V      AS MsgRcvd MsgSent   TblVer  InQ OutQ Up/Down  State/PfxRcd
1.1.1.1       4 65001      12      12        0    0    0 never    Active
10.0.3.2      4     1       8       7        2    0    0 00:01:44           1
```

Continuing with the Confederation configuration, R1 is configured as follows:

```
R1(config)#router bgp 65001
R1(config-router)#bgp router-id 1.1.1.1
R1(config-router)#bgp confederation identifier 123
R1(config-router)#bgp confederation peers 65002 65003
R1(config-router)#neighbor EXT-IBGP-PEERS peer-group
R1(config-router)#neighbor EXT-IBGP-PEERS ebgp-multihop 2
R1(config-router)#neighbor EXT-IBGP-PEERS update-source Loopback0
R1(config-router)#neighbor 2.2.2.2 remote-as 65002
R1(config-router)#neighbor 2.2.2.2 peer-group EXT-IBGP-PEERS
R1(config-router)#neighbor 3.3.3.3 remote-as 65003
R1(config-router)#neighbor 3.3.3.3 peer-group EXT-IBGP-PEERS
R1(config-router)#exit
```

In the output above, a peer group has been used for neighbors R2 and R3, which both require the `ebgp-multihop` and `update-source` commands for their peer sessions. Separate commands are used to define the remote ASs for each peer, as they reside in different ASs. Continuing with the Confederation configuration, router R2 is configured as follows:

```
R2(config)#router bgp 65002
R2(config-router)#bgp router-id 2.2.2.2
R2(config-router)#bgp confederation identifier 123
R2(config-router)#bgp confederation peers 65001
R2(config-router)#neighbor 1.1.1.1 remote-as 65001
R2(config-router)#neighbor 1.1.1.1 update-source Loopback0
R2(config-router)#neighbor 1.1.1.1 ebgp-multihop 2
R2(config-router)#neighbor 4.4.4.4 remote-as 65002
R2(config-router)#neighbor 4.4.4.4 update-source Loopback0
R2(config-router)#network 150.0.0.0 mask 255.255.0.0
R2(config-router)#exit
```

Finally, the last router in the topology, router R4, is configured as follows:

```
R4(config)#router bgp 65002
R4(config-router)#bgp router-id 4.4.4.4
R4(config-router)#bgp confederation identifier 123
R4(config-router)#neighbor 2.2.2.2 remote-as 65002
R4(config-router)#neighbor 2.2.2.2 update-source Loopback0
R4(config-router)#exit
```

NOTE: In the final configuration on router R4, notice that the `bgp confederation peers` command has been omitted because this router is internal to the Confederation and has no external Confederation peers. This command is therefore not required when configuring R4.

Following this configuration, the `show ip bgp summary` command should be used to verify the peer relationships between all routers. Referencing the topology used in the configuration examples, this command will be issued on R1, which is the central router in the Confederation implementation. The output of this command displays the following:

```
R1#show ip bgp summary
BGP router identifier 1.1.1.1, local AS number 65001
BGP table version is 3, main routing table version 3
2 network entries using 234 bytes of memory
2 path entries using 104 bytes of memory
3/2 BGP path/bestpath attribute entries using 372 bytes of memory
2 BGP AS-PATH entries using 48 bytes of memory
0 BGP route-map cache entries using 0 bytes of memory
0 BGP filter-list cache entries using 0 bytes of memory
BGP using 758 total bytes of memory
BGP activity 4/2 prefixes, 4/2 paths, scan interval 60 secs

Neighbor     V    AS MsgRcvd MsgSent   TblVer  InQ OutQ Up/Down  State/PfxRcd
2.2.2.2      4 65002      19      19        3    0    0 00:00:11            1
3.3.3.3      4 65003      23      23        3    0    0 00:00:10            1
```

In the output above, both neighbor relationships with R2 and R3 are established. R1 is receiving a single prefix from both routers. The prefix received from R3 is that from AS 1, while the prefix received from R2 is that which was injected locally into BGP on that router. From this output, it is not possible to determine that Confederations are being used. Therefore, the `show ip bgp neighbors` command must be used to validate the Confederation implementation. The output of this command displays the following for neighbor 2.2.2.2:

```
R1#show ip bgp neighbors 2.2.2.2
BGP neighbor is 2.2.2.2,  remote AS 65002, external link
 Member of peer-group EXT-IBGP-PEERS for session parameters
  BGP version 4, remote router ID 2.2.2.2
  Neighbor under common administration
  BGP state = Established, up for 00:03:11

[Truncated Output]

  For address family: IPv4 Unicast
  BGP table version 3, neighbor version 3/0
 Output queue size : 0
  Index 1, Offset 0, Mask 0x2
  1 update-group member
  EXT-IBGP-PEERS peer-group member
                              Sent       Rcvd
  Prefix activity:           ----       ----
    Prefixes Current:           1          1 (Consumes 52 bytes)
    Prefixes Total:             1          1
```

```
Implicit Withdraw:                   0          0
Explicit Withdraw:                   0          0
Used as bestpath:                  n/a          1
Used as multipath:                 n/a          0


...

[Truncated Output]
```

In the output of the show ip bgp neighbors command, the neighbor is listed as an external neighbor—because it resides in a different autonomous system. However, the next line in bold font, which reads Neighbor under common administration, indicates that this neighbor is part of the same Confederation. There is no explicit message indicating Confederation implementation in Cisco IOS software. Look for this line when determining whether BGP Confederations have been implemented within the autonomous system.

Having validated the neighbor relationships, we will look at prefix advertisement and BGP RIB entries following the implementation of the Confederation. First, we will look at the BGP RIB entry for the prefix that router R2 receives from R1. The BGP RIB on R2 displays the following:

```
R2#show ip bgp 111.0.0.0/16
BGP routing table entry for 111.0.0.0/16, version 3
Paths: (1 available, best #1, table Default-IP-Routing-Table)
Flag: 0x820
  Not advertised to any peer
  (65001 65003) 1
    3.3.3.3 (metric 67) from 1.1.1.1 (1.1.1.1)
      Origin IGP, metric 0, localpref 100, valid, confed-external, best
```

The output above is slightly different from what we are accustomed to seeing. The first notable difference is the inclusion of the private member autonomous systems in parenthesis (brackets). These are in parenthesis to indicate the sub-autonomous systems the prefix has traversed before being received by the local router. The last AS in the list, AS 1, is the external, public AS where this prefix originated. Reading this output, R2 can determine that the prefix traversed sub-AS 65001 (R1) and sub-AS 65003 (R3), and originated in AS 1 (ISP).

In the last line of the output above, the prefix shows the default attributes but also includes the confed-external statement, indicating that it was received from an eiBGP peer. On router R4, the same command illustrates the following:

```
R4#show ip bgp 111.0.0.0/16
BGP routing table entry for 111.0.0.0/16, version 3
Paths: (1 available, best #1, table Default-IP-Routing-Table)
```

```
  Not advertised to any peer
  (65001 65003) 1
    3.3.3.3 (metric 77) from 2.2.2.2 (2.2.2.2)
      Origin IGP, metric 0, localpref 100, valid, confed-internal, best
```

In the output above, the traversed sub-ASs remain the same because iBGP peers do not update the AS_PATH attribute when advertising a prefix to another iBGP peer. However, because the prefix is received from an iBGP peer within the Confederation, it is flagged as confed-internal instead of confed-external. Make sure to remember this subtle difference.

Next, we will view the 150.0.0.0/16 prefix advertised by R2. From the perspective of R4, this will also be a confed-internal prefix. Because the prefix is received from an iBGP neighbor, the AS_PATH attribute will contain a null value, as the route is local to sub-AS 65002. This can be validated using the show ip bgp command as illustrated in the following output:

```
R4#show ip bgp 150.0.0.0
BGP routing table entry for 150.0.0.0/16, version 2
Paths: (1 available, best #1, table Default-IP-Routing-Table)
  Not advertised to any peer
  Local
    2.2.2.2 (metric 11) from 2.2.2.2 (2.2.2.2)
      Origin IGP, metric 0, localpref 100, valid, confed-internal, best
```

On routers R1 and R3, however, the same prefix will be a confed-external prefix because it was originated in an external sub-AS. The BGP RIB on R3 displays the following information:

```
R3#show ip bgp 150.0.0.0 255.255.0.0
BGP routing table entry for 150.0.0.0/16, version 5
Paths: (1 available, best #1, table Default-IP-Routing-Table)
  Advertised to non peer-group peers:
  10.0.3.2
  (65001 65002)
    2.2.2.2 (metric 3) from 1.1.1.1 (1.1.1.1)
      Origin IGP, metric 0, localpref 100, valid, confed-external, best
```

Again, the sub-ASs traversed are included in the output of the show ip bgp command. And, as expected, the prefix is a confed-external prefix originated in sub-AS 65002. This same prefix is advertised by R3 to the ISP in AS 1. Because Confederations reside within the global AS, this information is not included in UPDATE messages sent to external, non-Confederation peers. Instead, the AS_PATH segment includes only the global autonomous system in which the prefix was originated. In essence, there is no way for external, non-Confederation peers to know that Confederations are being used inside the global AS. This is validated by viewing the BGP RIB on the ISP router:

```
R3#show ip bgp 150.0.0.0 255.255.0.0
BGP routing table entry for 150.0.0.0/16, version 9
Paths: (1 available, best #1, table Default-IP-Routing-Table)
  Not advertised to any peer
  123
    10.0.3.1 from 10.0.3.1 (3.3.3.3)
      Origin IGP, localpref 100, valid, external, best
```

As can be seen in the output above, from the ISP's perspective, the prefix is originated in AS 123. There is no indication that Confederations are being used within that autonomous system. In conclusion, when going through this chapter, keep in mind that you will not be expected to implement or configure either Route Reflectors or Confederations. The configuration examples included in this section are there to reinforce the theoretical fundaments of these iBGP implementation methodologies. Focus on understanding the basic functionality and differences as they pertain to both Route Reflectors and Confederations.

BORDER GATEWAY PROTOCOL DAMPENING

Because BGP speakers often carry thousands of prefixes, convergence can, and will, be affected as some of these prefixes transition between the up and down states. This in turn leads to instability and can result in packet loss and poor performance. To mitigate flapping prefixes, RFC 2439 defined route-flap dampening, which includes the following three goals:

1. It provides a mechanism to reduce router-processing load caused by unstable routes.
2. It prevents sustained route fluctuations (i.e., routes from going up and down).
3. It provides stability without sacrificing convergence time for well-behaved routes.

Route dampening is used to penalize route or prefix entries that are repeatedly transitioning between the up and down states. This is commonly referred to as bouncing or flapping. Flapping is commonly caused by unstable links or routing issues. The BGP dampening algorithm has several parameters as follows:

- History state
- Penalty
- Suppress limit
- Damp state
- Half life
- Reuse limit
- Maximum suppress limit

Following the order of the parameters listed above, when dampening is enabled, if a prefix or a route flaps, it is assigned a penalty and the dampening state for that prefix is set to History. Next, with each subsequent flap, the penalty increases. By default, in Cisco IOS software, the penalty increments by a value of 1000. However, if the only change pertaining to the prefix is the attributes associated with it, then the penalty increments only by 500.

Once the prefix exceeds the suppress limit, the route is dampened (suppressed). The route state is changed from History to Damp. By default, the suppress limit is 2000. This means that in order for a prefix to be suppressed, the penalty must exceed the suppress limit value of 2000. If the penalty is 2000 or less, then the prefix will not be suppressed. Given that the penalty increments by a value of 1000, the prefix must flap at least three times before it is suppressed.

When a prefix is in the Damp state, the router will not forward traffic via that path, nor will it advertise the prefix to its peers. After a route is penalized, the penalty value assigned is decreased based on the half-life period, which is 15 minutes by default. The penalty on a prefix is reduced every 5 seconds.

When the penalty for a prefix that has been suppressed falls below the reuse limit value, the prefix is unsuppressed. By default, the reuse limit value is 750. The router checks for suppressed prefixes to unsuppress every 10 seconds. However, if a prefix continues to flap, the penalty increases to the maximum possible value. Further flaps result in the prefix penalty value remaining at the maximum limit, which keeps the route dampened. By default, the maximum suppress limit (i.e., time the route will be dampened [suppressed]) is 60 minutes.

While technically beyond the scope of the ROUTE exam requirements, BGP dampening is configured using the bgp dampening router configuration command. While the default parameters for this command may be changed, this configuration is beyond the scope of the ROUTE exam requirements. Additionally, advanced dampening configuration, such as using route maps, is also beyond the scope of the ROUTE exam requirements. The following example shows how to enable dampening:

```
R3(config)#router bgp 65003
R3(config-router)#bgp dampening
R3(config-router)#exit
```

To verify the default dampening parameters, which should be left as is unless you or someone with advanced knowledge of dampening requests changes to these default values, issue the show ip bgp dampening parameters command, the output of which is illustrated below:

```
R3#show ip bgp dampening parameters
 dampening 15 750 2000 60 (DEFAULT)
  Half-life time       : 15 mins      Decay Time        : 2320 secs
  Max suppress penalty: 12000         Max suppress time: 60 mins
  Suppress penalty    : 2000          Reuse penalty     : 750
```

Following the configuration of route dampening, the show ip bgp dampening flap-statistics command can be used to view information on prefixes that are flapping as illustrated below:

```
R3#show ip bgp dampening flap-statistics
BGP table version is 8, local router ID is 3.3.3.3
Status codes: s suppressed, d damped, h history, * valid, > best, i - internal,
              r RIB-failure, S Stale
Origin codes: i - IGP, e - EGP, ? - incomplete

   Network          From            Flaps Duration Reuse    Path
 h 111.0.0.0/16     10.0.3.2        2     00:01:40          1
*d 112.0.0.0/16     10.0.3.2        3     00:03:56 00:05:49 1
```

In the output above, the 111.0.0.0/16 prefix has flapped twice and is set to History. However, the 112.0.0.0/16 prefix has flapped three times and is now dampened, or suppressed. All prefixes in the dampened stated can be viewed using the show ip bgp dampening dampened-paths command. The output of this command is illustrated below:

```
R3#show ip bgp dampening dampened-paths
BGP table version is 10, local router ID is 3.3.3.3
Status codes: s suppressed, d damped, h history, * valid, > best, i - internal,
              r RIB-failure, S Stale
Origin codes: i - IGP, e - EGP, ? - incomplete

   Network          From            Reuse    Path
*d 112.0.0.0/16     10.0.3.2        00:03:19 1 i
```

When dampened, the prefix will not be advertised to any other peers—internal or external. The BGP RIB entry for the 112.0.0.0/16 prefix will display the following output for this prefix:

```
R3#show ip bgp 112.0.0.0/16
BGP routing table entry for 111.0.0.0/16, version 10
Paths: (1 available, no best path)
  Not advertised to any peer
  1, (suppressed due to dampening)
    10.0.3.2 from 10.0.3.2 (10.0.10.2)
      Origin IGP, metric 0, localpref 100, valid, external
      Dampinfo: penalty 2280, flapped 3 times in 00:07:33, reuse in 00:02:09
```

From the output above, we can determine that the 112.0.0.0/16 prefix has been suppressed, as it flapped three times—exceeding the suppress limit of 2000 (assigned as 1000 for each flap). Given this, the prefix is not advertised to any peers until the reuse limit is reset. This prevents instability within the BGP network and allows for faster protocol convergence.

BORDER GATEWAY PROTOCOL AUTHENTICATION

In the final section in this chapter, we will learn about securing the messages that are exchanged between BGP peers. As we already know, BGP uses TCP as the underlying protocol. Attacks on BGP are typically implemented by attacking the underlying TCP protocol.

To mitigate these attacks, BGP supports Message Digest 5 (MD5) authentication, which is used to secure or verify the security of the TCP segments between two BGP peers. When the BGP TCP MD5 shared password is configured between two peers, Cisco IOS software checks the MD5 signature of every segment sent on the TCP connection. If MD5 authentication is invoked and a segment fails authentication, then an error message will be displayed in the console. The error message that will be printed on the console will be similar to the following:

```
*Mar  2 22:15:37.606: %TCP-6-BADAUTH: Invalid MD5 digest from 2.2.2.2(57322)
to 1.1.1.1(179)
*Mar  2 22:15:45.607: %TCP-6-BADAUTH: Invalid MD5 digest from 2.2.2.2(57322)
to 1.1.1.1(179)
```

The 18-byte TCP MD5 signature is based on packet data as well as the shared password that is configured between the two BGP speakers. In Cisco IOS software, the shared password is configured using the neighbor [address] password [password] router configuration command. This command must be issued on both of the BGP peers. If only one of the BGP speakers is configured with the shared password, the following error is printed on the console:

```
*Mar  2 22:19:35.977: %TCP-6-BADAUTH: No MD5 digest from 2.2.2.2(179) to
1.1.1.1(28906)
*Mar  2 22:19:40.456: %TCP-6-BADAUTH: No MD5 digest from 2.2.2.2(54666) to
1.1.1.1(179)
```

The following section illustrates how to configure a shared password to be used for the TCP MD5 signature on two BGP peers. The configuration on the first BGP speaker is as follows:

```
R1(config)#router bgp 65001
R1(config-router)#neighbor 2.2.2.2 password *H2N-CCNP#1
R1(config-router)#exit
```

A mirrored configuration on the peer is implemented as follows:

```
R2(config)#router bgp 65002
R2(config-router)#neighbor 1.1.1.1 password *H2N-CCNP#1
R2(config-router)#exit
```

As of the time of the writing of this guide, other than verifying the router configuration, there is no explicit show command that will indicate that the password has been configured. Following is the output of the current configuration on router R1:

```
R1#show running-config | section bgp
router bgp 65001
 no synchronization
 bgp router-id 1.1.1.1
 bgp log-neighbor-changes
 neighbor 2.2.2.2 remote-as 65002
 neighbor 2.2.2.2 update-source Loopback0
 neighbor 2.2.2.2 password *H2N-CCNP#1
 no auto-summary
```

When configuring the shared password, the following should be taken into consideration:

- The password is a case-sensitive string that may be up to 25 characters in length
- The string can contain any alphanumeric characters, including spaces
- A password cannot be configured with a leading number, followed by a space

CHAPTER SUMMARY

The following section is a summary of the major points you should be aware of in this chapter.

Border Gateway Protocol Path Control Overview

- It is important to remember that BGP is first and foremost a routing policy control tool
- BGP attributes can be used to influence both inbound and outbound routing
- In Cisco IOS software, the BGP path control policies are implemented using route maps
- When BGP policies are implemented or changed they do not take effect immediately
- Use the `clear ip bgp` command to immediately apply the configuration changes

Influencing Inbound Path Selection

- There are BGP two attributes that are used to influence the inbound path as follows:
  1. The MULTI_EXIT_DISC attribute
  2. The AS_PATH attribute

- The MED should be used when multihomed to the same neighboring AS
- The MED is not compared for routes from different ASes
- The received MED is not re-advertised to external peers
- The AS_PATH should be used when multihomed to more than a single AS

Influencing Outbound Path Selection

- The two attributes that are used to influence the outbound path are as follows:
  1. The LOCAL_PREF Attribute
  2. The WEIGHT Attribute

- The LOCAL_PREF is ignored in UPDATE messages received from external peers
- The LOCAL_PREF is included in UPDATE messages sent to internal peers
- The WEIGHT is a Cisco-proprietary attribute
- The WEIGHT is a locally significant attribute that affects only the local BGP speaker

Basic BGP Load Balancing and Load Sharing

- Load balancing is used to split the load to the same destination across multiple paths
- Load balancing distributes traffic evenly across multiple links
- Load balancing is unidirectional
- Load balancing is supported at Layers 2, 3 and 4
- Load sharing is also used to split the load to the same destination across multiple paths
- Load sharing does not distribute the traffic evenly across the multiple paths
- Load sharing can be used to distribute both incoming and outgoing network traffic

Border Gateway Protocol Peer Groups

- Peers groups are used to simplify the BGP configuration for internal and external peers
- Members in the peer group must have common characteristics
- Peer groups are also used to optimize BGP by reducing the convergence time
- All peer groups have a peer group leader
- The members in the peer group must be synched to the leader
- The local BGP speaker generates an UPDATE for the leader and replicates it to members

Border Gateway Protocol Route Filtering

- Cisco IOS software supports many options that can be used for BGP routing policy control
- BGP routing policy control tools include the following:
  1. IP Prefix Lists
  2. BGP Communities
  3. AS_PATH Filters

- For BGP, prefix lists can be applied in the following two ways:
  1. Using the `neighbor [address] prefix-list [name] <in|out>` command
  2. Using the `neighbor [address] route-map [name] <in|out>` command

- For BGP, the well-known communities can be assigned to prefixes using route maps
- To include communities, the `neighbor send-community` command must be used
- AS path filters are based on regular expressions and match on the AS_PATH
- A regular expression is a pattern to match against an input string
- A regular expression comprises the following four main parts:
  1. A Range
  2. An Atom
  3. A Piece
  4. A Branch

Border Gateway Protocol Aggregation

- The two ways BGP can be configured to perform route summarization are as follows:
  1. Using the `network [network] mask [mask]` command
  2. Using the `aggregate-address [network][mask]` command

- The `aggregate-address` command allows specific entries to be advertised by default
- The `summary-only` keyword suppresses specific entries when aggregating

BGP and IGP Route Redistribution

- There is no special configuration when redistributing EIGRP routes into BGP
- Special considerations for redistributing OSPF into BGP include the following:
  1. By default, all of the internal OSPF routes, i.e. routes marked O and IA, are redistributed
  2. By default, external Type 1 OSPF routes, i.e. routes marked E1, are redistributed
  3. By default, external Type 2 OSPF routes, i.e. routes marked E2, are NOT redistributed

- To redistribute external Type 2 routes, you must use the `match external` command
- BGP routes should NEVER be redistributed into an IGP without filtering
- By default, only external BGP routes are imported into the IGP during redistribution
- The `bgp redistribute-internal` command is used to redistribute iBGP routes

BGP Route Reflectors and Confederations

- By default, an iBGP peer will not advertised iBGP-received routes to another iBGP peer
- The default iBGP behavior means a full mesh is required to allow route connectivity
- The two features that can be used to negate the full mesh internal BGP requirement are as follows:
  1. Route Reflectors
  2. Confederations

- Route reflection works via the use of a Route Reflector or Route Reflector routers

- With RRs, iBGP routers are classified into the following three different router groups:
  1. Route Reflectors (RR)
  2. Regular iBGP speakers (non-clients)
  3. Route Reflector Clients

- Route Reflectors are BGP speakers that reflect routes between the following BGP speakers:
  1. Between clients and non-clients
  2. Between clients and clients (called client-to-client reflection)
  3. Between non-clients and clients

- UPDATES received from the RR include the ORIGINATOR_ID and CLUSTER_LIST
- The ORIGINATOR_ID contains the RID of the router that generated the UPDATE
- The CLUSTER_LIST contains the CLUSTER_ID set by the local RR
- These two additional attributes are not included in UPDATES sent to external peers
- Confederations are used to split the AS into sub-ASes
- Peers in different sub-ASes establish external iBGP (eiBGP) peer sessions
- UPDATES for prefixes from a router in an external sub-AS are CONFED-EXTERNAL
- UPDATES for prefixes from a router in the same sub-AS are CONFED-INTERNAL
- The sub-ASes traversed are printed in parenthesis (brackets)
- The sub-ASes are not included in UPDATES to external, non-confederation peers

Border Gateway Protocol Dampening
- BGP route flap dampening, as defined in RFC 2439 has three major goals, which are as follows:
  1. It provides a mechanism to reduce router processing load caused by unstable routes
  2. It prevents sustained route fluctuations, i.e. routes going up and down
  3. It provides stability without sacrificing convergence time for well-behaved routes

- Route dampening is used to penalize route or prefix entries that are repeatedly flapping
- The `bgp dampening` router command is used to enable route flap dampening

Border Gateway Protocol Authentication
- MD5 authentication is used to secure or verify the security of the TCP segments
- MD5 authentication requires the use of a shared password between peers
- The shared password is configured using the `neighbor...password` command
- When configuring the shared password, the following should be taken into consideration:
  1. The password is a case-sensitive string that may be up to 25 characters in length
  2. The string can contain any alphanumeric characters, including spaces
  3. A password cannot be configured with a leading number, followed by a space

CHAPTER 8

IPv6 Fundamentals and Routing

In previous chapters in this guide, all references to the Internet Protocol (IP) have applied to version 4 (IPv4). In this chapter, we will learn about version 6 of the Internet Protocol (IPv6). In addition to understanding the routed protocol itself, as well as the fundamental differences between IPv4 and IPv6, the current ROUTE exam also requires a solid understanding of routing protocols that support IPv6 routing. The core ROUTE exam objective covered in this chapter is as follows:

* Implement an IPv6-based solution, given a network design and a set of requirements

This chapter contains the following sections:

* The History of Internet Protocol version 6
* IPv6 Packet Formats
* Reasons for Migrating to IPv6
* IPv6 Addressing
* IPv6 Address Representation
* The Different IPv6 Address Types
* IPv6 Protocols and Mechanisms
* Enabling IPv6 in Cisco IOS Software
* Configuring Static IPv6 Routes
* RIPng for IPv6
* EIGRP for IPv6
* OSPF version 3
* BGP4+ or MP-BGP for IPv6
* IPv6 Redistribution

THE HISTORY OF INTERNET PROTOCOL VERSION 6

As mentioned in the introduction for this chapter, in previous chapters, all references to the Internet Protocol referred to version 4—the de facto standard used in modern-day networks. Internet Protocol version 6 is the recommended replacement for Internet Protocol version 4. The fact that the standard jumped from version 4 (IPv4) to version 6 (IPv6) often results in the following question: What happened to version 5? The omission of IPv5 and the resultant standardization of IPv6 are described in the following section.

IPv5 is an experimental reservation protocol designed to provide Quality of Service (QoS) and is defined as the Stream Protocol (ST). IPv5 provides real-time transport of multimedia, such as voice and video across the Internet, as defined in IETF Experimental Note 199. IPv5 is comprised of two distinct protocols: Stream Protocol (ST) and Stream Control Message Protocol (SCMP). ST is used for traditional data transport, while SCMP is used for control messages. SCMP is defined in RFCs 1819 and 1190.

Version 2 of the Stream Protocol (ST2) was designed to coexist with IPv4 and was named IPv5 because it uses the same link-layer framing as IPv4. This allows both IPv4 and IPv5 to be used at the same time; that is, IPv4 can be used to transport data and control information, such as TCP/UDP packets, while IPv5 can be used to transport real-time traffic, such as voice and video.

The Stream Protocol uses the same addressing schemes as IPv4 to identity and address network hosts. Other traditional protocols, such as the Resource Reservation Protocol (RSVP), are used to provide resource reservation within the network. A host uses RSVP to request a specific QoS level from the network, on behalf of an application data stream. RSVP carries the request through the network, visiting each node the network uses to carry the stream. At each node, RSVP attempts to make a resource reservation for the stream. Depending on the capabilities of the routers between the source and destination, the requested reservation may or may not be made. Detailed information of RSVP is beyond the scope of the ROUTE exam requirements and will not be included in this chapter or in the remainder of this guide.

Because IPv5 offered no real solution to the rapidly depleting IPv4 address space, numerous other versions of IP were proposed to replace IPv4. However, Simple Internet Protocol Plus (SIPP) was eventually chosen as the official assignment for the successor IPv4 and was subsequently standardized as IPv6. IP protocol number 41 was reserved for its use.

NOTE: IPv5 is not supported in Cisco IOS software, as it was never standardized or deployed on production networks. It is simply an experimental protocol.

IPV6 PACKET FORMATS

Internet Protocol version 6 uses different packets for different functions. While delving into the details on all of these packets is beyond the scope of the ROUTE exam requirements, it is important to have some basic understanding of the packet formats and what these packets are used for. In this section, the following IPv6 packets will be described:

- The IPv6 Packet Header
- The Hop-by-Hop Options Header
- The Routing Header
- The Fragment Header
- The Destination Options Header

The IPv6 Packet Header

Each IPv6 packet contains a standard 40-byte header, which allows for basic addressing, traffic flows, Class of Service (CoS), and routing loop prevention. The fields contained within the IPv6

Packet header are slightly different from those contained in the IPv4 Packet header. Figure 8-1 below displays the fields that are contained within the IPv6 Packet header:

```
Internet Protocol Version 6
 0110 .... = Version: 6
 [0110 .... = This field makes the filter "ip.version == 6" possible: 6]
 .... 0000 0000 .... .... .... .... .... = Traffic class: 0x00000000
 .... .... .... 0000 0000 0000 0000 0000 = Flowlabel: 0x00000000
 Payload length: 60
 Next header: ICMPv6 (0x3a)
 Hop limit: 64
 Source: 2001::20c:ceff:fea7:f3a0 (2001::20c:ceff:fea7:f3a0)
 Destination: 2001::213:19ff:fe86:a20 (2001::213:19ff:fe86:a20)
```

Fig. 8-1. The IPv6 Packet Header

Referencing the fields illustrated in Figure 8-1, the 4-bit Version field displays the version of IP contained in the packet. For IPv4, this field would contain a value of 4, and for IPv6, this field contains a value of 6. The next field within the IPv6 Packet header is the Traffic Class, or simply Class, field. This 1-byte field encodes bit values used for Class of Service within the network. Because all 8 bits are defined for this purpose, up to 255 separate CoS settings are supported.

Following the Class field, the 20-bit Flow Label field is used to maintain a flow of traffic through the network. The sending host places a unique value in this field that allows the network devices to treat these packets in a specific method. Routers that do not support the concept of a flow label can either ignore the value or reset it to 0x00000. The flow label will be described later in this chapter.

The 2-byte Payload Length field contains the length, in bytes, of the IPv6 headers and packet data after the standard 40-byte IPv6 header. The size of this field limits IPv6 packets to a maximum length of 65,575 bytes. This value is calculated by adding the 65,535 bytes in the packet data to the 40 bytes in the header.

The 1-byte Next Header field is used to encode the value of the header following the standard IPv6 header. It replaces the Protocol field in an IPv4 packet and uses those same values. Referencing Figure 8-1, we can see that the packet is an ICMP version 6 (ICMPv6) packet. This field allows for easy extensibility and the addition of optional header fields.

The 1-byte Hop Limit field contains the maximum number of hops a packet may traverse before being dropped by the network. The hop limit is set by the sending host and is used to prevent packets from endlessly circulating on an IPv6 internetwork. Each internetwork device that forwards the packet decrements the value in this field by 1. The Hop Limit field replaces the Time-to-Live field in an IPv4 packet and more accurately depicts its purpose.

Finally, the Source and Destination Address fields contain the 16-byte (128-bit) source and destination IPv6 addresses. Unlike IPv4, which uses 32-bit addresses, IPv6 uses 128-bit addresses. IPv6 addressing and address formats will be described in detail later in this chapter.

NOTE: When the IPv6 header is followed by packet data, the Next Header field contains a value of 6 for TCP or a value of 17 for UDP.

In addition to the IPv6 Packet header, the remainder of this section also describes the optional IPv6 Packet header, which has been defined to allow for different transmitting options, fragmentation, and source routing. These include the Hop-by-Hop Options header (protocol 0), the Routing header (protocol 43), the Fragment header (protocol 44), and the Destination Options header (protocol 60). It is important to remember that these optional headers always follow the IPv6 header and precede either the TCP header or the UDP header.

NOTE: You are not required to demonstrate detailed knowledge of these optional headers for the current ROUTE exam. They are described only briefly in the following sections.

The Hop-by-Hop Options Header (Protocol Number 0)
The Hop-by-Hop Options header is designed to notify routers along the path about any special handling requirements of the packet. Additionally, this header is used for padding the entire packet to a 64-bit boundary, for indicating an oversized payload, and for carrying a router alert option that allows the protocol to interoperate with RSVP.

The Routing Header (Protocol Number 43)
The implementation of source routing in IPv6 is accomplished with the inclusion of the Routing header. Source routing is a technique whereby the sender of a packet can specify the route that a packet should take through the network. The Routing header contains a list of node addresses through which the packet must pass on its way to the destination.

The Fragment Header (Protocol Number 44)
In an IPv6 network, fragmentation is accomplished only by the sending nodes. Fragmentation is used to break up a datagram into a number of pieces that can be reassembled later. In IPv6, it is expected that each node in the network will determine the path MTU from itself to the destination. If the packet is larger than the path MTU, the source node fragments the packet data and places it into multiple smaller packets, each containing the Fragment header.

The Destination Options Header (Protocol Number 60)
The IPv6 Destination Options header is designed as a way for the sending host to communicate

packet-handling requests to the destination host. As of the time of the writing of this chapter, the only option defined is a padding option for ending the entire packet on a 64-bit boundary.

REASONS FOR MIGRATING TO IPV6

Now that we have a fundamental understanding of IP version 6, it is important to understand the advantages offered by IPv6 and the reasons for migrating to this version of the Internet Protocol. There are several advantages that can be gained by transitioning from IPv4 to IPv6, and they include, but are not limited to, the following:

- The simplified IPv6 Packet header
- Larger address space
- IPv6 addressing hierarchy
- IPv6 extensibility
- IPv6 broadcast elimination
- Stateless autoconfiguration
- Integrated mobility
- Integrated enhanced security

The Simplified IPv6 Packet Header

The header fields in an IPv4 packet are very detailed and complete. However, not all fields in the IPv4 Packet header are used or are required—for example, the Type of Service field. Other headers, such as the Checksum header, are no longer a necessity, nor are they used because transmission link quality has greatly improved over the years. In contrast, the header fields of an IPv6 packet are much simpler and contain the bare minimum of information required to route the packet. This allows for greater routing efficiency with IPv6 than is afforded by IPv4.

Larger Address Space

As was stated in the previous section, in contrast to the 32-bit addresses used in IPv4, the IPv6 addresses are 128-bits in length. This extended address length allows for billions of host addresses. This sheer amount of address space eliminates the need to perform Network Address Translation (NAT) in IPv6 because a global address can be assigned to each individual host. Furthermore, because IP global addresses can be assigned to each individual device (e.g., computers, laptops, and phones), the Internet reverts to a true end-to-end model when using IPv6.

IPv6 Addressing Hierarchy

Because of the much larger address space provided by IPv6, multiple levels of hierarchy can be used within the IPv6 address space. This allows providers and other organizations to use this hierarchy to better manage the IPv6 address space based on bit-boundaries. The use of an addressing hierarchy allows route summarization in IPv6 to be performed in a more organized manner than is currently performed using the IPv4 address space. IPv6 addressing is described in detail later in this chapter.

IPv6 Extensibility

When using IPv4, because all of the fields of the IPv4 Packet header are currently defined, new extensions to the protocol must rely on the variable-length Options field. However, the use of this field makes the IPv4 header size vary from packet to packet. If IP options are specified within an IPv4 packet, internetwork devices must read all the options and decide whether they will support them and, if so, whether they will act upon them. If the options are not supported on the router, then it simply forwards the packet. Given that millions of packets may be transiting the router, looking at each packet to determine whether any options in the Options field are supported and must be acted upon can cause serious performance degradation on the router.

Unlike IPv4, IPv6 has a fixed-size header field and additional header extensions are included to support new features. These additional headers are outside the standard IPv6 header and are referenced in such a way that all individual internetwork devices can skip the extension if they do not support it. This reduces the processing overhead of routers routing IPv6 packets.

IPv6 Broadcast Elimination

In IPv6, ARP Broadcasts are replaced by Multicast packets on the local network segment. This prevents devices that do not need to receive these packets from receiving them and avoids the problems that Broadcasts can cause (e.g., wasting host resources and network performance degradation). The mechanisms employed by IPv6 to eliminate Broadcasts on network segments are described in detail later in this chapter.

Stateless Autoconfiguration

Both IPv4 and IPv6 support stateful autoconfiguration, which allows network hosts to receive their addressing information from a network server (i.e., via DHCP). In addition to supporting stateful autoconfiguration, IPv6 also supports stateless autoconfiguration. Stateless autoconfiguration allows hosts to configure their IPv6 Unicast addresses by themselves based on prefix advertisements from routers on the local network segment. IPv6 autoconfiguration will be described in detail later in this chapter.

Integrated Mobility

While Mobile IP is available for both IPv4 and IPv6, it is built into IPv6, whereas it is an added function in IPv4. IPv6 mobility allows IPv6-capable devices, such as PDAs, cell phones, and wireless laptops, to roam between the IPv6 networks of wireless or cellular providers by using the Mobile IP protocol. This allows any IPv6 host to use Mobile IP as needed, while only IPv4 hosts that have this added functionality can use Mobile IP.

Integrated Enhanced Security

IPv6 uses the inbuilt security mechanisms afforded by the IP Security (IPSec) protocol. The key difference between IPSec in IPv4 and IPv6 is that it is optional in IPv4 but is mandatory in IPv6. As defined in RFC 2460, IPv6 includes the use of the Authentication Header (AH) and Encapsulating Security Payload (ESP) extension headers in a complete implementation. The use of IPSec allows routers to provide security for the following:

+ OSPF version 3
+ Mobile IPv6
+ Tunnels
+ Network management

NOTE: While a detailed understanding of IPSec is beyond the scope of the current ROUTE exam requirements, you are required to demonstrate a basic understanding of this protocol. Additional information on IPSec is included in Chapter 10, which covers branch office networking and connectivity.

IPV6 ADDRESSING

As we already know, IPv6 uses 128-bit addresses. Because the address format is different from the IPv4 address format that we are all accustomed to, it is often confusing at first glance. However, once understood, the logic and structure is all very simple. The 128-bit IPv6 addresses use Hexadecimal values. The Hexadecimal numbering system uses the numbers 0 through 9 and the letters A through F. While in IPv4 the subnet mask can be represented in either CIDR notation (e.g., /16 or /32) or in dotted-decimal notation (e.g., 255.255.0.0 or 255.255.255.255), IPv6 subnet masks are represented only in CIDR notation due to the length of the IPv6 address. Global 128-bit IPv6 addresses are divided into the following three sections:

1. The provider-assigned prefix
2. The site prefix
3. The interface or host ID

The provider-assigned prefix, which is also referred to as the Global Address Space, is a 48-bit prefix that is divided into the following three distinct parts:

1. The 16-bit reserved IPv6 global prefix
2. The 16-bit provider-owned prefix
3. The 16-bit provider-assigned prefix

The IPv6 global prefix is the prefix that is used to represent the IPv6 global address space. All IPv6 global Internet addresses fall within the 2000::/16—3FFF::/16 range. The 16-bit provider-owned

IPv6 prefix is the prefix that is assigned to and owned by the provider. The assignment of these prefixes follows the same rules as prefix assignment in IPv4. The provider-owned prefix falls within the 0000::/32—FFFF::/32 range.

The next 16-bits represent an IPv6 prefix assigned to an organization by the actual provider from within the provider-assigned prefix address space. This prefix falls within the 0000::/48—FFFF::/48 range. Collectively, these first 48-bits are referred to as the provider-assigned prefix, which is illustrated in Figure 8-2 below:

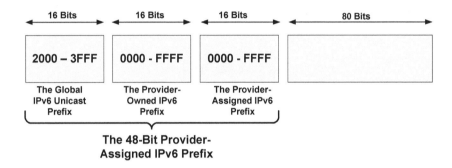

Fig. 8-2. The Provider-Assigned 48-Bit IPv6 Prefix

The site prefix is the next 16-bits following the provider-assigned 48-bit prefix. The subnet mask length for a site prefix is /64, which includes the 48-bit provider-assigned prefix. This prefix length allows for 2^{64} addresses within each site prefix. Figure 8-3 below illustrates the 16-bit site prefix:

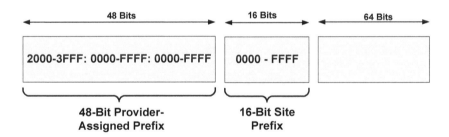

Fig. 8-3. The 16-Bit IPv6 Site Prefix

Following the site prefix, the next 64 bits are used for interface or host addressing. The interface or host ID portion of an IPv6 address represents the network device or host on the IPv6 subnet. The different ways in which the interface or host address is determined will be described in detail later in this chapter. To reinforce what we have learned in this section, Figure 8-4 below illustrates how IPv6 prefixes are assigned:

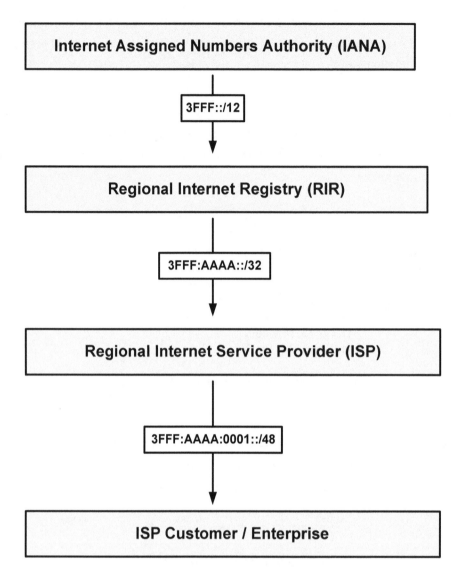

Fig. 8-4. Assigning IPv6 Prefixes

Referencing Figure 8-4, once customers have been assigned the /48 prefix by the ISP, they are then free to assign and use whatever site prefixes and host or interface addresses they want within that 48-bit provider-assigned prefix. The sheer amount of address space available makes it impossible for any single enterprise customer to require more than a single provider-assigned prefix, while still allowing all devices within the enterprise network to be allocated a unique IPv6 global address. NAT, therefore, will never be required for IPv6.

IPV6 ADDRESS REPRESENTATION

The three ways in which IPv6 addresses can be represented are as follows:

1. The preferred or complete address representation or form
2. Compressed representation
3. IPv6 addresses with an embedded IPv4 address

While the preferred form or representation is the most commonly used method for representing the 128-bit IPv6 address in text format, it is also important to be familiar with the other two methods of IPv6 address representation. These methods are described in the following sections.

The Preferred Form

The preferred representation for an IPv6 address is the longest format, also referred to as the complete form of an IPv6 address. This format represents all 32 Hexadecimal characters that are used to form an IPv6 address. This is performed by writing the address as a series of eight 16-bit Hexadecimal fields, separated by a colon (e.g., 3FFF:1234:ABCD:5678:020C:CEFF:FEA7:F3A0).

Each 16-bit field is represented by four Hexadecimal characters, with each of the Hexadecimal character representing 4-bits. Each 16-bit Hexadecimal field can have a value of between 0x0000 and 0xFFFF, although, as will be described later in this chapter, different values have been reserved for use in the first 16 bits and all possible values are not used. When writing IPv6 addresses, each Hexadecimal character is not case sensitive. In other words 2001:ABCD:0000 and 2001:abcd:0000 are the exact same thing. The complete form for IPv6 address representation is illustrated in Figure 8-5 below:

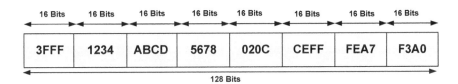

Fig. 8-5. The Preferred Form for IPv6 Address Representation

The following IPv6 addresses are examples of valid IPv6 addresses in the preferred form:

- 0000:0000:0000:0000:0000:0000:0000:0001
- 2001:0000:0000:1234:0000:5678:af23:bcd5
- 3FFF:0000:0000:1010:1A2B:5000:0B00:DE0F
- fec0:2004:ab10:00cd:1234: 0000:0000:6789
- 0000:0000:0000:0000:0000:0000:0000:0000

Compressed Representation

Compressed representation allows for IPv6 addresses to be compressed in one of two ways. The first method allows a double colon (::) to be used to compress consecutive zero values in a valid IPv6 address for successive 16-bit fields comprised of zeros or for leading zeros in the IPv6 address. When using this method, it is important to remember that the double colon can be used only once in an IPv6 address.

When the compressed format is used, each node and router is responsible for counting the number of bits on either side of the double colon to determine the exact number of zeros it represents. Table 8-1 below shows IPv6 addresses in the preferred form and the compressed representation of those addresses:

Table 8-1. Representing Complete IPv6 Addresses in the Preferred Compressed Form

Complete IPv6 Address Representation	Compressed IPv6 Address Representation
0000:0000:0000:0000:0000:0000:0000:0001	::0001
2001:0000:0000:1234:0000:5678:af23:bcd5	2001::1234:0000:5678:af23:bcd5
3FFF:0000:0000:1010:1A2B:5000:0B00:DE0F	3FFF::1010:1A2B:5000:0B00:DE0F
FEC0:2004:AB10:00CD:1234:0000:0000:6789	FEC0:2004:AB10:00CD:1234::6789
0000:0000:0000:0000:0000:FFFF: 172.16.255.1	::FFFF: 172.16.255.1
0000:0000:0000:0000:0000:0000:172.16.255.1	::172.16.255.1
0000:0000:0000:0000:0000:0000:0000:0000	::

As previously stated, the double colon cannot be used more than once in a single IPv6 address. If, for example, you wanted to represent the complete IPv6 address 2001:0000:0000:1234:0000:0000:af23:bcd5 in compressed form, you could use the double colon only once, even though there are two consecutive strings of zeros within the address. Therefore, attempting to compress the address to 2001::1234::af23:bcd5 would be considered illegal; however, the same IPv6 address could be compressed to either 2001::1234:0000:0000:af23:bcd5 or 2001:0000:0000:1234::af23:bcd5, depending on preference.

The second method of IPv6 compressed address representation is applicable to each 16-bit field and allows leading zeros to be omitted from the IPv6 address. When using this method, if every bit in the 16-bit field is set to 0, then one zero must be used to represent this field. In this case, not all of the zero values can be omitted. Table 8-2 below shows IPv6 addresses in the preferred form and how they can be compressed using the second method of IPv6 compressed form representation.

Table 8-2. Representing Complete IPv6 Addresses in the Alternative Compressed Form

Complete IPv6 Address Representation	Compressed IPv6 Address Representation
0000:0123:0abc:0000:04b0:0678:f000:0001	0:123:abc:0:4b0:678:f000:1
2001:0000:0000:1234:0000:5678:af23:bcd5	2001:0:0:1234:0:5678:af23:bcd5
3FFF:0000:0000:1010:1A2B:5000:0B00:DE0F	3FFF:0:0:1010:1A2B:5000:B00:DE0F
fec0:2004:ab10:00cd:1234:0000:0000:6789	fec0:2004:ab10:cd:1234:0:0:6789
0000:0000:0000:0000:0000:FFFF: 172.16.255.1	0:0:0:0:0:FFFF: 172.16.255.1
0000:0000:0000:0000:0000:0000:172.16.255.1	0:0:0:0:0:0:172.16.255.1
0000:0000:0000:0000:0000:0000:0000:0000	0:0:0:0:0:0:0:0

While there are two methods of representing the complete IPv6 address in compressed form, it is important to remember that both methods are not mutually exclusive. In other words, these methods can be used at the same time to represent the same IPv6 address. This is commonly used when the complete IPv6 address contains both consecutive strings of zeros as well as leading zeros in other fields within the address. Table 8-3 below shows IPv6 addresses in the complete form that include both consecutive strings of zeros and leading zeros and how these addresses are represented in the compressed form:

Table 8-3. Representing Complete IPv6 Addresses Using Both Compressed Form Methods

Complete IPv6 Address Representation	Compressed IPv6 Address Representation
0000:0000:0000:0000:01a2b:000c:f123:456	::1a2b:c:f123:456
FEC0:0004:AB10:00CD:1234:0000:0000:6789	FEC0:4:AB10:CD:1234::6789
3FFF:0c00:0000:1010:1A2B:0000:0000:DE0F	3FFF:c00:0:1010:1A2B::DE0F
2001:0000:0000:1234:0000:5678:af23:00d5	2001::1234:0:5678:af23:d5

IPv6 Addresses with an Embedded IPv4 Address

The third representation of an IPv6 address is to use an embedded IPv4 address within the IPv6 address. While valid, it is important to keep in mind that this method is being deprecated and is considered obsolete because it is applicable only in the transition of IPv4 to IPv6.

When an IPv6 address is embedded with an IPv4 address, the first part of the IPv6 address uses the Hexadecimal notation and the remainder of the address is in the traditional dotted-decimal notation used by IPv4 addresses. However, it is permissible to convert the 32-bit dotted-decimal IPv4 address into Hexadecimal notation and embed that into the IPv6 address instead. The IPv6 address with an embedded IPv4 address is comprised of six fields of 16-bit Hexadecimal characters and four fields of 8-bit decimal characters. The two kinds of IPv6 addresses that contain an embedded IPv4 address are as follows:

1. IPv4-compatible IPv6 addresses
2. IPv4-mapped IPv6 addresses

While these terms sound similar, you should be familiar with some of the significant differences in these addresses. First, IPv4-compatible IPv6 addresses are used in the transition from IPv4 to IPv6. These addresses are used to establish automatic tunnels for IPv6 packets over native IPv4 networks. IPv4-compatible IPv6 addresses have the first 96 bits set to 0 and are then followed by the 32-bit IPv4 address as illustrated in Figure 8-6 below:

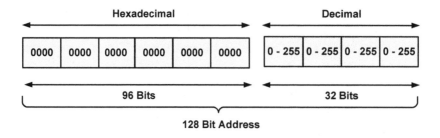

Fig. 8-6. IPv4-Compatible IPv6 Addresses

Referencing Figure 8-6, it is important to understand that the compressed form can also be used to represent IPv4-compatible IPv6 addresses. For example, the IPv4-compatible IPv6 addresses for a Loopback interface with the IPv4 address 172.16.255.1/32 would be represented as 0000:0000:0000:0000:0000:0000:172.16.255.1. This same address can then be compressed as 0:0:0:0:0:0:172.16.255.1/32 or simply as ::172.16.255.1/32. Additionally, it is also important to remember that the decimal IPv4 address could be converted to Hexadecimal notation and used to create the IPv4-compatible IPv6 address 0:0:0:0:0:0: AC10:FF01/128 or simply ::AC10:FF01/128.

Unlike the IPv4-compatible IPv6 addresses, the IPv4-mapped IPv6 addresses are used locally on devices that are running both IPv4 and IPv6. IPv4-mapped IPv6 addresses are never advertised as IPv6 addresses. These addresses have the first 80 bits set to 0; the next 16 bits are set to a value of all 1s, which is FFFF in Hexadecimal notation, and are then followed by the IPv4 dotted-decimal address. Figure 8-7 below illustrates the IPv4-mapped IPv6 address format:

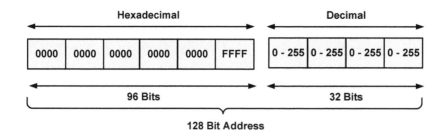

Fig. 8-7. IPv4-Mapped IPv6 Addresses

Using IP address 172.16.255.1/32 as an example, this address could be represented in the IPv4-mapped IPv6 address format as 0000:0000:0000:0000:0000:FFFF:172.16.255.1/128. Because it is perfectly legal to represent the address in the compressed form, the same address could also be written as either 0:0:0:0:0:FFFF:172.16.255.1/128 or ::FFFF:172.16.255.1/128. Additionally, the IPv4 address could also be converted to Hexadecimal notation producing the IPv4-mapped IPv6 address 0:0:0:0:0: FFFF:AC10:FF01/128 or simply ::FFFF:AC10:FF0/128.

THE DIFFERENT IPV6 ADDRESS TYPES

IPv4 supports four different classes of addresses, which are Anycast, Broadcast, Multicast, and Unicast. While the term Anycast has not been used in previous chapters in this guide, it is important to remember that Anycast addresses are not special types of addresses. Instead, an Anycast address is simply an IP address that is assigned to multiple interfaces. Common examples of technologies that use Anycast addressing include IP Multicast implementations, and 6to4 relay implementation.

> **NOTE:** 6to4 is a transition mechanism for migrating from IPv4 to IPv6. 6to4 will be described in detail later in this chapter.

With Anycast addressing, devices use the common address that is closest to them based on the routing protocol metric. The next closest address is then used in the event that the primary address is no longer reachable. This concept is illustrated in Figure 8-8 below:

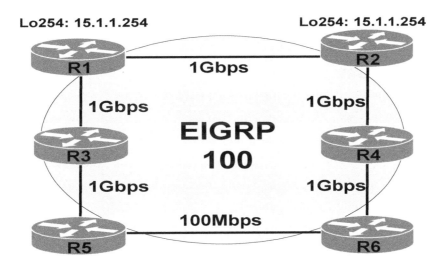

Fig. 8-8. Understanding Anycast Addressing

Referencing Figure 8-8, both R1 and R2 have a Loopback 254 interface that is configured using a common address: 15.1.1.254/32. This prefix is then advertised dynamically via EIGRP. By default, both R1 and R2 will prefer the 15.1.1.254/32 prefix via their respective Loopback interfaces, as that is a directly connected subnet. Therefore, the common address used will never result in a conflict on either router.

Assuming normal EIGRP metric calculation, routers R3 and R5 will prefer the Anycast address advertised by router R1 due to the lower IGP metric. Similarly, R4 and R6 will prefer the Anycast address advertised by router R2 due to the lower IGP metric. In the event that either router R1 or R2 fails, the remaining routers in the network will use the Anycast address advertised by the remaining router. When using Anycast addressing, organizations can use a Unicast address either in the RFC 1918 address space or within their public block.

> **NOTE:** You are not expected to implement any Anycast addressing or solutions in the current ROUTE exam. However, it is important to be familiar with the concept.

At this level, IPv4 Broadcast, Multicast, and Unicast addresses require no further explanation and will not be described in any additional detail in this chapter or in the remainder of this guide. While IPv4 supports these four different types of addresses, IPv6 does away with the Broadcast addresses and instead supports only the following types of addresses:

- Link-Local Addresses
- Site-Local Addresses
- Aggregate Global Unicast Addresses
- Multicast Addresses
- Anycast Addresses
- Loopback Addresses
- Unspecified Addresses

Link-Local Addresses

IPv6 Link-Local addresses can be used only on the local link (i.e., a shared segment between devices) and are automatically assigned to each interface when IPv6 is enabled on that interface. These addresses are assigned from the Link-Local prefix FE80::/10. Keep in mind that FE80::/10 is the equivalent of FE80:0:0:0:0:0:0:0/10, which can also be represented as FE80:0000:0000:0000:0000:0000:0000:0000/10. To complete the address, bits 11 through 64 are set to 0 and the interface Extended Unique Identifier 64 (EUI-64) is appended to the Link-Local address as the low-order 64-bits. The EUI-64 is comprised of the 24-bit manufacturer ID assigned by the IEEE and the 40-bit value assigned by that manufacturer to its products. EUI-64 addressing is described in greater detail later in this chapter when we learn about configuring IPv6 addresses. The format of a Link-Local address is illustrated in Figure 8-9 below:

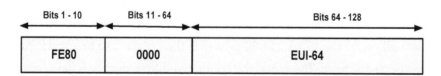

Fig. 8-9. IPv6 Link-Local Addressing

Link-Local addresses are unique in that they do not change once assigned to an interface. This means that if an interface is assigned a public IPv6 address (e.g., 2001:1000::1/64) and the public IPv6 prefix was changed (i.e., 2001:2000::1/64), the Link-Local address would not change. This allows the host or router to remain reachable while IPv6 global Internet addresses change.

Site-Local Addresses

Site-Local addresses are Unicast addresses that are used only within a site. Unlike Link-Local addresses, Site-Local addresses must be configured manually on network devices. These addresses are the IPv6 equivalent of the private IPv4 address space defined in RFC 1918 and can be used by organizations that do not have globally routable IPv6 address space. These addresses are not routable on the IPv6 Internet.

While it is possible to perform NAT for IPv6, it is not recommended; hence, the reason for the much larger IPv6 addresses. Site-Local addresses are comprised of the FEC0::/10 prefix, a 54-bit Subnet ID, and an interface identifier in the EUI-64 format used by Link-Local addresses. While the 54-bits in a Link-Local address are set to a value of 0, the same 54-bits in Site-Local addresses are used to create different IPv6 prefixes (up to 2^{54}). The format of the Site-Local address is illustrated in Figure 8-10 below:

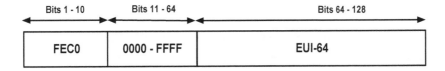

Fig. 8-10. IPv6 Site-Local Addressing

While IPv6 Site-Local Addresses are described in this section and are still supported in Cisco IOS software, it is important to know that these addresses are deprecated by RFC 4193, which describes Unique-Local Addresses (ULAs), which serve the same function as Site-Local addresses and are not routable on the IPv6 global Internet.

Unique-Local Addresses are assigned from the `FC00::/7`, IPv6 address block, `which is then also further` divided into two /8 address groups referred to as the assigned and random groups. These two groups are the FC00::/8 and the FD00::/8 IPv6 address blocks. The FC00::/8 block is to be managed by an allocation authority for /48s in use, while the FD00::/8 block is formed by appending a randomly-generated 40-bit string to derive a valid /48 block.

Aggregate Global Unicast Addresses

Aggregate Global Unicast addresses are the IPv6 addresses used for generic IPv6 traffic as well as for the IPv6 Internet. These are similar to the public addresses used in IPv4. From a network addressing point of view, each IPv6 Global Unicast address is comprised of three main sections: the prefix received from the provider (48-bit in length), the site prefix (16-bit in length), and the host portion (64-bit in length). This makes up the 128-bit address used in IPv6.

As we learned earlier in this chapter, the provider-assigned prefix is assigned to an organization by an IPv6 provider. By default, these prefixes use /48 prefix lengths. In addition, these prefixes are assigned from the IPv6 address spaces (i.e., the /32 prefix lengths) that are owned by the provider. Each provider will own its own IPv6 address space, and the IPv6 prefix assigned by one provider cannot be used on the network of another provider.

Within a site, administrators can then subnet the provider-assigned 48-bit prefix into 64-bit site prefixes by using bits 49-64 for subnetting, allowing for 65,535 different subnets for use within their network. The host portion of an IPv6 address represents the network device or host on the IPv6 subnet. This is represented by the low-order 64-bits of the IPv6 address.

Aggregate Global Unicast addresses for IPv6 are assigned by the Internet Assigned Numbers Authority (IANA) and fall within the IPv6 prefix 2000::/3. This allows for a range of Aggregate Global Unicast addresses from 2000 to 3FFF as illustrated in Table 8-4 below:

Table 8-4. IPv6 Aggregate Global Unicast Addresses

Description	Address
First Address in Range	2000:0000:0000:0000:0000:0000:0000:0000
Last Address in Range	3FFF:FFFF:FFFF:FFFF:FFFF:FFFF:FFFF:FFFF
Binary Notation	The three high-order bits are set to 001

From the 2000::/3 IPv6 block, only three subnets have been allocated for use as of the time of the writing of this chapter. These allocations are illustrated in Table 8-5 below:

Table 8-5. Assigned IPv6 Aggregate Global Unicast Addresses

IPv6 Global Prefix	Binary Representation	Description
2001::/16	0010 0000 0000 0001	Global IPv6 Internet (Unicast)
2002::/16	0010 0000 0000 0010	6to4 Transition Prefix
3FFE::/16	0010 1111 1111 1110	6bone Prefix

NOTE: The 6to4 transition addresses and the 6bone prefix are described later in this guide.

Within the range of IPv6 Global Aggregate Unicast addresses, a special experimental range is reserved. This range is the ORCHID address range. ORCHID addresses are non-routed IPv6 addresses used for Cryptographic Hash Identifiers. These addresses use the IPv6 prefix 2001:10::/28. ORCHID is an acronym for Overlay Routable Cryptographic Hash Identifiers and is defined in RFC 4843. Going into detail on ORCHID addresses is beyond the scope of the current ROUTE exam requirements and will not be included in this chapter or in the remainder of this guide.

Multicast Addresses

The Multicast addresses used in IPv6 are derived from the FF00::/8 IPv6 prefix. In IPv6, Multicast operates in a different manner than that of Multicast in IPv4. IP Multicast is used extensively in IPv6 and replaces IPv4 protocols, such as the Address Resolution Protocol (ARP). In addition, Multicast is used in IPv6 for prefix advertisements and renumbering, as well as for Duplicate Address Detection (DAD). These concepts are all described later in this chapter.

Multicast packets in IPv6 do not use the TTL value to restrict such packets to the local network segment. Instead, the scoping is defined within the Multicast address itself via the use of the Scope field. IPv6 nodes on a network segment listen to Multicast and may even send Multicast packets to exchange information. This allows all nodes on an IPv6 segment to know about all other neighbors on that same segment. The format of Multicast addresses used in IPv6 networks is illustrated in Figure 8-11 below:

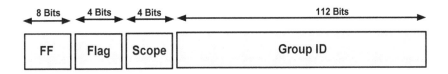

Fig. 8-11. IPv6 Multicast Addressing

As illustrated in Figure 8-11, the format of the IPv6 Multicast address is slightly different from the formats of the other IPv6 addresses we have learned about up until this point. The first 8 bits of the IPv6 Multicast address represent the Multicast prefix FF::/8. The Flag field in the IPv6 Multicast address is used to indicate the type of Multicast address, either permanent or temporary.

Permanent IPv6 Multicast addresses are assigned by IANA, while temporary IPv6 Multicast addresses can be used in pre-deployment Multicast testing. The Flag field may contain one of the two possible values as illustrated and described in Table 8-6 below:

Table 8-6. IPv6 Permanent and Temporary Multicast Addresses

Type of Multicast Address	Binary Representation	Hexadecimal Value
Permanent	0000	0
Temporary	0001	1

The next 4 bits in the Multicast address represent the scope. In IPv6 Multicasting, this field is a mandatory field that restricts Multicast packets from being sent to other areas in the network. This field essentially provides the same function as the TTL field that is used in IPv4. However, with IPv6, there are several types of scopes, which are listed in Table 8-7 below:

Table 8-7. IPv6 Multicast Address Scopes

Scope Type	Binary Representation	Hexadecimal Value
Interface-Local	0001	1
Link-Local	0010	2
Subnet-Local	0011	3
Admin-Local	0100	4
Site-Local	0101	5
Organization	1000	8
Global	1110	E

Within the IPv6 Multicast prefix, certain addresses are reserved. These reserved addresses are referred to as Multicast Assigned addresses, which are presented and described in Table 8-8 below:

Table 8-8. IPv6 Reserved Multicast Addresses

Address	Scope	Description
FF01::1	Hosts	All hosts on the Interface-Local scope
FF01::2	Hosts	All routers on the Interface-Local scope
FF02::1	Link-Local	All hosts on the Link-Local scope
FF02::2	Link-Local	All routers on the Link-Local scope
FF05::2	Site	All routers on the Site scope

In addition to these addresses, a Solicited-Node Multicast address is enabled automatically for each Unicast and Anycast address configured on a router interface or network host. This address has a Link-Local scope, which means that it will never traverse farther than the local network segment. Solicited-Node Multicast addresses are used for the following two reasons: the replacement of IPv4 ARP and Duplicate Address Detection (DAD).

Because IPv6 does not use ARP, Solicited-Node Multicast addresses are used by network hosts and routers to learn the Data Link addresses of neighboring devices. This allows for the conversion and sending of IPv6 packets to IPv6 hosts and routers as frames. DAD is a part of the IPv6 Neighbor Discovery Protocol (NDP), which is described in detail later in this chapter. DAD simply allows a device to validate whether an IPv6 address is already in use on the local segment before it configures the address as its own using autoconfiguration. In essence, it provides a similar function to Gratuitous ARP used in IPv4. Solicited-Node Multicast addresses are defined by the IPv6 prefix FF02::1:FF00:0000/104. These addresses are comprised of the FF02::1:FF00:0000/104 prefix in conjunction with the low-order 24-bits of the Unicast or Anycast address. Figure 8-12 below illustrates the format of these IPv6 addresses:

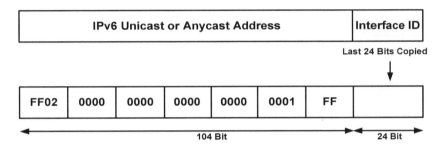

Fig. 8-12. IPv6 Solicited-Node Multicast Addresses

In a manner similar to IPv4 Multicast mapping for Ethernet, IPv6 also uses a unique means to map Layer 3 IPv6 Multicast addresses to Layer 2 Multicast addresses. Multicast mapping in IPv6 is enabled by appending the low-order 32-bits of a Multicast address to the 16-bit prefix 33:33, which is the defined Multicast Ethernet prefix for IPv6 networks. This is illustrated in Figure 8-13 below for all the routers on the Interface-Local scope prefix FF01::2:

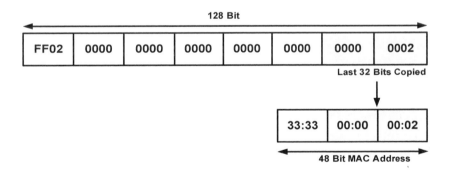

Fig. 8-13. IPv6 Multicast Addresses

NOTE: While IPv6 Multicast addresses have been included in this chapter, keep in mind that you are not required to implement any Multicast solutions in the current ROUTE exam. In fact, IP Multicast, for both IPv4 and IPv6, is excluded from the scope of the current ROUTE exam.

Anycast Addresses

Anycast, which was described earlier in this section, can be described simply as one-to-nearest communication because the nearest common address, based on routing protocol metrics, will always be preferred by the local device. In IPv6, Anycast addresses use Global Unicast, Site-Local, or even Link-Local addresses. However, there is an Anycast address reserved for special use. This special address is referred to as the Subnet-Router Anycast address and is formed with the subnets 64-bit Unicast prefix, with the remaining 64-bits set to zero (e.g., 2001:1a2b:1111:d 7e5:0000:0000:000:0000). These addresses are typically used by protocols such as Mobile IPv6, which was described earlier in this chapter.

Loopback Addresses

Loopback addresses used in IPv6 are used in the same manner as in IPv4. Each device has one IPv6 Loopback address, which is comparable to the 127.0.0.1 Loopback address used in IPv4, and this address is used by the device itself. IPv6 Loopback addresses use the prefix ::1, which can be represented as 0000:0000:0000:0000:0000:0000:0000:0001 in the preferred address format. This means that in Loopback addresses, all bits are set to 0 except for the last bit, which is always set to 1. These addresses are always assigned automatically when IPv6 is enabled on a device and they can never be changed.

Unspecified Addresses

In IPv6 addressing, unspecified addresses are simply Unicast addresses that are not assigned to any interface. These addresses indicate the absence of an IPv6 address and are used for special purposes that include IPv6 DHCP and DAD. Unspecified addresses are represented by all 0 values in the IPv6 address and can be written using the :: prefix. In the preferred format, these addresses are represented as 0000:0000:0000:0000:0000:0000:0000:0000.

IPV6 PROTOCOLS AND MECHANISMS

While version 6 of the Internet Protocol is similar to version 4, there are significant differences in the operation of the former as compared to the latter. While the primary emphasis of the current ROUTE exam is centered on routing for IPv6 networks, it is still important to have a fundamental understanding of the different protocols and mechanisms used by IPv6. The following IPv6 protocols and mechanisms are described in this section:
- ICMP for IPv6
- The IPv6 Neighbor Discovery Protocol (NDP)
- IPv6 stateful autoconfiguration
- IPv6 stateless autoconfiguration

NOTE: As previously stated, the current ROUTE exam is centered on IPv6 routing; therefore, while additional IPv6 protocols and mechanisms are described in this section, configurations pertaining to these protocols and mechanisms will not be included, as they are beyond the scope of the current ROUTE exam requirements.

ICMP for IPv6

ICMP is used to report errors and other information to the source hosts regarding the delivery of IP packets to the intended destination. ICMPv6, which is defined in RFC 2463 as protocol number 58, supports messages for ICMPv4 and includes additional messages for ICMPv6. ICMPv6 is used in the Next Header field of the basic IPv6 packet header. Unlike in IPv4, IPv6 views ICMPv6 as an upper-layer protocol, such as TCP, for example, which means that ICMPv6 is placed after all possible extension headers in the IPv6 packet. The fields that are contained within the ICMPv6 packet are illustrated in Figure 8-14 below:

```
Internet Protocol Version 6
Internet Control Message Protocol v6
Type: 128 (Echo request)
Code: 0
Checksum: 0xdbe0 [correct]
ID: 0x1afa
Sequence: 0x0000
Data (52 bytes)
 Data: 000102030405060708090A0B0C0D0E0F1011121314151617...
```

Fig. 8-14. The ICMPv6 Packet Header

Within the ICMPv6 packet header, the 8-bit Type field is used to indicate or identify the type of ICMPv6 message. This field is used to provide both error and informational messages. Table 8-9 below lists and describes some common values that can be found within this field:

Table 8-9. ICMPv6 Message Types

ICMPv6 Type	Description
1	Destination Unreachable
2	Packet Too Big
3	Time Exceeded
128	Echo Request
129	Echo Reply

NOTE: It should be noted that these same message types are also used in ICMPv4.

Following the Type field, the 8-bit Code field provides details pertaining to the type of message sent. Table 8-10 below illustrates common values for this field, which are also shared by ICMPv4:

Table 8-10. ICMPv6 Codes

ICMPv6 Code	Description
0	Echo Reply
3	Destination Unreachable
8	Echo
11	Time Exceeded

Following the Code field, the 16-bit Checksum field contains a computed value used to detect data corruption in ICMPv6. Finally, the Message or Data field is an optional, variable-length field that contains the data specific to the message type indicated by the Type and Code fields. When used, this field provides information to the destination host. ICMPv6 is a core component of IPv6. Within IPv6, ICMPv6 is used for the following:

- Duplicate Address Detection (DAD)
- The replacement of ARP
- IPv6 stateless autoconfiguration
- IPv6 prefix renumbering
- Path MTU Discovery (PMTUD)

NOTE: Of the options printed above, DAD and stateless autoconfiguration will be described later in this section. PMTUD is beyond the scope of the current ROUTE exam requirements and will not be described in any additional detail in this chapter or in the remainder of this guide.

The IPv6 Neighbor Discovery Protocol (NDP)

The IPv6 Neighbor Discovery Protocol (NDP) is defined in RFC 2461 and is an integral part of IPv6. NDP operates in the Link Layer and is responsible for discovery of other nodes on the link, determining the Link Layer addresses of other nodes, finding available routers, and maintaining reachability information about the paths to other active neighbor nodes. NDP performs functions for IPv6 similar to the way ARP and ICMP Router Discovery and Router Redirect protocols do for IPv4. However, it is important to remember that NDP provides greater functionality than the mechanisms used in IPv4. Used in conjunction with ICMPv6, NDP allows for the following:

- Dynamic neighbor and router discovery
- The replacement of ARP
- IPv6 stateless autoconfiguration
- Router redirection
- Host parameter discovery
- IPv6 address resolution
- Next-hop router determination

- • Neighbor Unreachability Detection (NUD)
- • Duplicate Address Detection (DAD)

NOTE: You are not required to delve into specifics on each of the advantages listed above.

Neighbor Discovery Protocol defines five types of ICMPv6 packets, which are listed and described in Table 8-11 below:

Table 8-11. ICMPv6 NDP Message Types

ICMPv6 Type	Message Type Description and IPv6 Usage
133	Used for Router Solicitation (RS) messages
134	Used for Router Advertisement (RA) messages
135	Used for Neighbor Solicitation (NS) messages
136	Used for Neighbor Advertisement (NA) messages
137	Used for Router Redirect messages

Router Solicitation messages are sent by hosts when interfaces are enabled for IPv6. These messages are used to request that routers on the local segment generate RA messages immediately, rather than at the next scheduled RA interval. Figure 8-15 below illustrates a wire capture of an RS message:

```
Internet Protocol Version 6
Internet Control Message Protocol v6
 Type: 133 (Router solicitation)
 Code: 0
 Checksum: 0x6e61 [correct]
 ICMPv6 Option (Source link-layer address)
 Type: Source link-layer address (1)
 Length: 8
 Link-layer address: 00:24:e8:f5:7e:a2
```

Fig. 8-15. IPv6 Router Solicitation Messages

Upon receiving the RS message, advertise their presence using RA messages, which typically include prefix information for the local link as well as any additional configuration, such as suggested hop limits. The information contained within the RA is illustrated in Figure 8-16 below:

```
Internet Protocol Version 6
Internet Control Message Protocol v6
 Type: 134 (Router advertisement)
 Code: 0
 Checksum: 0x17ed [correct]
 Cur hop limit: 64
 Flags: 0x00
 Router lifetime: 1800
 Reachable time: 0
 Retrans timer: 0
 ICMPv6 Option (Source link-layer address)
 ICMPv6 Option (MTU)
 ICMPv6 Option (Prefix information)
 ICMPv6 Option (Prefix information)
```

Fig. 8-16. IPv6 Router Advertisement Messages

IPv6 NS messages are Multicast by IPv6 routers on the local network segment and are used to determine the Data-Link address of a neighbor or to verify that a neighbor is still reachable. These messages are also used for Duplicate Address Detection. While delving into detail on NS messages is beyond the scope of the ROUTE exam requirements, Figure 8-17 below illustrates a wire capture of an IPv6 Neighbor Solicitation message:

```
Internet Control Message Protocol v6
 Type: 135 (Neighbor solicitation)
 Code: 0
 Checksum: 0x3f71 [correct]
 Target: fe80::213:19ff:fe86:a20
 ICMPv6 Option (Source link-layer address)
  Type: Source link-layer address (1)
  Length: 8
  Link-layer address: 00:24:e8:f5:7e:a2
```

Fig. 8-17. IPv6 Neighbor Solicitation Messages

Neighbor Advertisement messages are typically sent by routers on the local network segment in response to received NS messages. However, if, for example, an IPv6 prefix changes, then routers may also send out unsolicited NS messages advising other devices on the local network segment of the change. As is the case with NA messages, while going into detail on the format or fields contained within the NA message is beyond the scope of the ROUTE exam requirements, Figure 8-18 below illustrates a wire capture of the Neighbor Advertisement message, which is also sent via IPv6 Multicast:

```
Internet Control Message Protocol v6
 Type: 136 (Neighbor advertisement)
 Code: 0
 Checksum: 0x909f [correct]
 Flags: 0xa0000000
  1... .... .... .... .... .... .... .... = Router
  .0.. .... .... .... .... .... .... .... = Not adverted
  ..1. .... .... .... .... .... .... .... = Override
 Target: fe80::20c:ceff:fea7:f3a0
 ICMPv6 Option (Target link-layer address)
  Type: Target link-layer address (2)
  Length: 8
  Link-layer address: 00:0c:ce:a7:f3:a0
```

Fig. 8-18. IPv6 Neighbor Advertisement Messages

Finally, router redirection uses ICMPv6 Redirect messages, which are defined as message type 137. Router redirection is used to inform network hosts that a router with a better path to the intended destination exists on the network. It works in the same manner as ICMPv4 redirects used in current IPv4 networks.

IPv6 Stateful Autoconfiguration

As previously stated in this chapter, stateful autoconfiguration allows network hosts to receive their addressing information from a network server (e.g., via DHCP). This method of autoconfiguration is supported by both IPv4 and IPv6. In IPv6 networks, DHCPv6 is used to provide stateful auto-configuration services for IPv6 hosts. In IPv6 implementations, when an IPv6 host receives RA messages from routers on the local network segment, the host examines these packets to determine whether DHCPv6 can be used. The RA messages provide this information by setting either the M or the O bits to 1.

The M bit in Router Advertisement messages is the Managed Address Configuration Flag bit. When this bit is set (i.e., contains a value of 1), it instructs the IPv6 host to obtain a stateful address, which is provided by DHCPv6 servers. The O bit in Router Advertisement messages is the Other Stateful Configuration Flag bit. When this bit is set (i.e., contains a value of 1), it instructs the IPv6 host to use DHCPv6 to obtain more configuration settings, such as DNS and WINS servers, for example. While one of the advantages of IPv6 is stateless autoconfiguration capability, stateful autoconfiguration still provides several advantages, which include the following:

- Greater controls than those provided by stateless autoconfiguration
- Can be used on networks when stateless autoconfiguration is available
- Provides addressing to network hosts in the absence of routers
- Can be used for network renumbering by assigning new prefixes to hosts
- Can be used to issue entire subnets to customer premise equipment

IPv6 Stateless Autoconfiguration

In IPv6, stateless autoconfiguration allows hosts to configure their Unicast IPv6 addresses by themselves based on prefix advertisements from routers on the local network segment. The three mechanisms that allow for stateless autoconfiguration in IPv6 are as follows:

1. Prefix advertisement
2. Duplicate Address Detection (DAD)
3. Prefix renumbering

IPv6 prefix advertisement uses ICMPv6 Router Advertisement messages, which are sent to the all-hosts-on-the-local-link IPv6 Multicast address FF02::1. By design, only routers are allowed to advertise prefixes on the local link. When stateless autoconfiguration is employed, it is imperative to remember that the prefix length used must be 64-bits (e.g., 2001:1a2b::/64).

Following the configuration of the prefix, RA messages used for IPv6 stateless autoconfiguration include the following information:

- The IPv6 prefix
- The lifetime
- Default router information
- Flags and/or Options

As previously stated, the IPv6 prefix must be 64-bits. In addition, multiple IPv6 prefixes may be advertised on the local segment. When hosts on the network segment receive the IPv6 prefix, they append their MAC address to the prefix in EUI-64 format, which was described earlier in this chapter, and automatically configure their IPv6 Unicast address. This provides a unique 128-bit IPv6 address to each host on the network segment.

The lifetime value for each advertised prefix is also provided to the nodes and may contain a value from 0 to infinite. When nodes receive the prefix, they validate the lifetime value and cease using the prefix when the lifetime value reaches 0. Alternatively, if a value of infinite is received for a particular prefix, the network hosts will never cease using that prefix. Each advertised prefix contains two lifetime values: the valid lifetime value and the preferred lifetime value.

The valid lifetime value is used to determine how long the host address will remain valid. When this value expires (i.e., reaches a value of 0), the host address becomes invalid. The preferred lifetime value is used to determine the duration for how long an address configured via stateless autoconfiguration will remain valid. This value must be less than or equal to the value specified in the valid lifetime and is typically used for prefix renumbering.

The default router provides information about the existence and lifetime of the default router's IPv6 address. By default, the default IPv6 address used for default routers is the Link-Local address (FE80::/10). This allows the global Unicast address to be changed without interrupting network services, as would be the case in IPv4 if a network were renumbered. Finally, the Flags and Options fields can be used to instruct network hosts to use stateless autoconfiguration or stateful autoconfiguration. These fields are included in the wire capture of the Router Advertisement shown in Figure 8-16.

Duplicate Address Detection is an NDP mechanism used in stateless autoconfiguration when a host on the network segment is booting up. DAD mandates that before a network host permanently configures its own IPv6 during boot up, it should validate that another network host is not already using the IPv6 address it wants to use.

Duplicate Address Detection performs this by using Neighbor Solicitation (ICMPv6 Type 135) and Solicited-Node Multicast addresses. The host sends a Neighbor Solicitation on the local network segment using an unspecified IPv6 address (i.e., the :: address) as its source address and the Solicited-Node Multicast address of the IPv6 Unicast address it wants to use as the destination address. If no other host is using this same address, the host will not automatically configure itself with this address; however, if no other device is using the same address, the host automatically configures itself and begins to use this IPv6 address.

Finally, prefix renumbering allows for the transparent renumbering of network prefixes in IPv6 when changing from one prefix to another. Unlike in IPv4, where the same global IP address can be advertised by multiple providers, the strict aggregation of the IPv6 address space prevents providers from advertising prefixes that do not belong to their organization.

In cases where a transition is made from one IPv6 Internet provider to another, the IPv6 prefix renumbering mechanism provides a smooth and transparent transition from one prefix to another. Prefix renumbering uses the same ICMPv6 messages and Multicast address used in prefix advertisement. Prefix renumbering is made possible by using the time parameters contained within the Router Advertisement messages.

In Cisco IOS software, routers can be configured to advertise current prefixes with the valid and preferred lifetime values decreased to a value closer to zero, which allows those prefixes to become invalid faster. The routers are then configured to advertise the new prefixes on the local network segments. This allows the old and new prefixes to exist on the same network segment.

During this transition period, hosts on the local network segment use two Unicast addresses: one from the old prefix and one from the new prefix. Any current connections using the old prefix are still handled; however, any new connections from these hosts are made using the new prefix. When the old prefix expires, only the new prefix is used.

ENABLING IPV6 ROUTING IN CISCO IOS SOFTWARE

Now that we have a solid understanding of IPv6 fundamentals, the remainder of the chapter will focus on the configuration of IPv6 in Cisco IOS software. By default, IPv6 routing functionality is disabled in Cisco IOS software. Therefore, IPv6 routing functionality must be enabled manually using the `ipv6 unicast-routing` global configuration command.

After enabling IPv6 routing globally, the `ipv6 address [ipv6-address/prefix-length | prefix-name sub-bits/prefix-length | anycast | autoconfig <default> | dhcp | eui-64 | link-local]` interface configuration command can be used to configure interface IPv6 addressing. The `ipv6-address/prefix-length` keyword is used to specify the IPv6 prefix and prefix length assigned to the interface. The following configuration illustrates how to configure a router interface with the first address on the 3FFF:1234:ABCD:5678::/64 subnet:

```
R1(config)#ipv6 unicast-routing
R1(config)#interface FastEthernet0/0
R1(config-if)#ipv6 address 3FFF:1234:ABCD:5678::1/64
R1(config-if)#exit
```

Following this configuration, the show ipv6 interface [name] command can be used to validate the configured IPv6 address subnet as illustrated below:

```
R1#show ipv6 interface FastEthernet0/0
FastEthernet0/0 is up, line protocol is up
  IPv6 is enabled, link-local address is FE80::20C:CEFF:FEA7:F3A0
  Global unicast address(es):
    3FFF:1234:ABCD:5678::1, subnet is 3FFF:1234:ABCD:5678::/64
  Joined group address(es):
    FF02::1
    FF02::2
    FF02::1:FF00:1
    FF02::1:FFA7:F3A0

...

[Truncated Output]
```

As was stated earlier in this chapter, IPv6 allows multiple prefixes to be configured on the same interface. If multiple prefixes have been configured on the same interface, the show ipv6 interface [name] prefix command can be used to view all assigned prefixes as well as their valid and preferred lifetime values. The following output displays the information that is printed by this command for a router interface with multiple IPv6 subnets configured:

```
R1#show ipv6 interface FastEthernet0/0 prefix
IPv6 Prefix Advertisements FastEthernet0/0
Codes: A - Address, P - Prefix-Advertisement, O - Pool
       U - Per-user prefix, D - Default
       N - Not advertised, C - Calendar

    default [LA] Valid lifetime 2592000, preferred lifetime 604800
AD   3FFF:1234:ABCD:3456::/64 [LA] Valid lifetime 2592000, preferred
lifetime 604800
AD   3FFF:1234:ABCD:5678::/64 [LA] Valid lifetime 2592000, preferred
lifetime 604800
AD   3FFF:1234:ABCD:7890::/64 [LA] Valid lifetime 2592000, preferred
lifetime 604800
AD   3FFF:1234:ABCD:9012::/64 [LA] Valid lifetime 2592000, preferred
lifetime 604800
```

NOTE: As was stated earlier in this chapter, the valid and preferred lifetime values can be adjusted from default values allowing for a smooth transition when implementing prefix renumbering. This configuration, however, is beyond the scope of the ROUTE exam requirements and will not be illustrated in this chapter.

Continuing with the use of the `ipv6 prefix` interface configuration command, the `prefix-name sub-bits/prefix-length` keyword is used to configure a general prefix, which specifies the leading bits of the subnet to be configured on the interface. This configuration is beyond the scope of the current ROUTE exam requirements and will not be illustrated in this chapter.

The `anycast` keyword is used to configure an IPv6 Anycast address. As was stated earlier in this chapter, Anycast addressing simply allows the same common address to be assigned to multiple router interfaces. Hosts use the Anycast address that is closest to them based on routing protocol metrics. Anycast configuration is beyond the scope of the ROUTE exam requirements and will not be illustrated in this chapter.

The `autoconfig <default>` keywords enable stateless autoconfiguration. If used, then the router will dynamically learn prefixes on the link and then add EUI-64 addresses for all the learned prefixes. The `<default>` keyword is an optional keyword that allows a default route to be installed. The following configuration example illustrates how to enable stateless autoconfiguration on a router interface and additionally allow the default route to be installed.

```
R2(config)#ipv6 unicast-routing
R2(config)#interface FastEthernet0/0
R2(config-if)#ipv6 address autoconfig default
R2(config-if)#exit
```

Following this configuration, router R2 will listen to Router Advertisement messages on the local segment on which the FastEthernet0/0 interface resides. The router will configure dynamically an EUI-64 address for each learned prefix and then install the default route pointing to the Link-Local address of the advertising router. The dynamic address configuration is validated using the `show ipv6 interface [name]` command as illustrated below:

```
R2#show ipv6 interface FastEthernet0/0
FastEthernet0/0 is up, line protocol is up
  IPv6 is enabled, link-local address is FE80::213:19FF:FE86:A20
  Global unicast address(es):
    3FFF:1234:ABCD:3456:213:19FF:FE86:A20, subnet is
3FFF:1234:ABCD:3456::/64 [PRE]
      valid lifetime 2591967 preferred lifetime 604767
    3FFF:1234:ABCD:5678:213:19FF:FE86:A20, subnet is
```

```
3FFF:1234:ABCD:5678::/64 [PRE]
     valid lifetime 2591967 preferred lifetime 604767
   3FFF:1234:ABCD:7890:213:19FF:FE86:A20, subnet is
3FFF:1234:ABCD:7890::/64 [PRE]
     valid lifetime 2591967 preferred lifetime 604767
   3FFF:1234:ABCD:9012:213:19FF:FE86:A20, subnet is
3FFF:1234:ABCD:9012::/64 [PRE]
     valid lifetime 2591967 preferred lifetime 604767
   FEC0:1111:1111:E000:213:19FF:FE86:A20, subnet is
FEC0:1111:1111:E000::/64 [PRE]
     valid lifetime 2591967 preferred lifetime 604767
  Joined group address(es):
   FF02::1
   FF02::2
   FF02::1:FF86:A20
  MTU is 1500 bytes


...

[Truncated Output]
```

In the output above, notice that while no explicit IPv6 addresses were configured on the interface, an EUI-64 address was configured dynamically for the subnet the router discovered by listening to Router Advertisement messages. The timers for each of these prefixes are derived from the router advertising the RA messages. In addition to verifying the stateless autoconfiguration, the show ipv6 route command can be used to validate the default route to the Link-Local address of the preferred advertising router as illustrated below:

```
R2#show ipv6 route ::/0
IPv6 Routing Table - 13 entries
Codes: C - Connected, L - Local, S - Static, R - RIP, B - BGP
       U - Per-user Static route
       I1 - ISIS L1, I2 - ISIS L2, IA - ISIS interarea, IS - ISIS summary
       O - OSPF intra, OI - OSPF inter, OE1 - OSPF ext 1, OE2 - OSPF ext 2
       ON1 - OSPF NSSA ext 1, ON2 - OSPF NSSA ext 2
S    ::/0 [1/0]
     via FE80::20C:CEFF:FEA7:F3A0, FastEthernet0/0
```

Continuing with the ipv6 address command, the dhcp keyword is used to configure the router interface to use stateful autoconfiguration (i.e., DHCPv6) to acquire the interface addressing configuration. With this configuration, an additional keyword, the rapid-commit keyword, can also be appended to the end of this command to allow the two-message exchange method for address assignment and other configuration information.

NOTE: The `ipv6 address dhcp rapid-commit` interface configuration command is used to configure the router as a DHCPv6 client that will use a two-message exchange instead of the traditional four-message exchange to acquire addressing and configuration information. Figure 8-19 below illustrates the traditional four-way message exchange between DHCPv6 servers and clients:

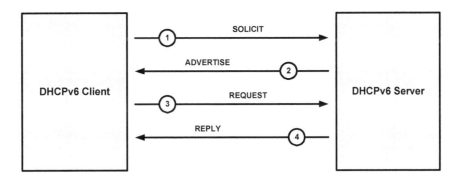

Fig. 8-19. DHCPv6 Four-Way Exchange

Referencing Figure 8-19, in step 1, the IPv6 client sends a Multicast Solicit message to the All-DHCPv6-Agent's address FF00::1:2 using its Link-Local address as the source. This message is Multicast to find a DHCPv6 server and ask for a lease. In step 2, any server that can fulfill the client's request responds to it with an Advertise message. In step 3, the client then chooses one of the servers and sends a Request message to it, asking to confirm the offered address and other parameters. Finally, in step 4, the DHCPv6 server responds to the DHCPv6 client with a Reply message finalizing the process. The Rapid Commit feature shortens this traditional process by using only two messages.

The DHCPv6 client first sends a Solicit message and indicates that a DHCPv6 server should respond back immediately with a Reply message. If the client has already received addressing information via stateless autoconfiguration but is seeking only additional information (e.g., DNS), then the client sends an Information-Request message via Multicast and a DHCPv6 server with configuration information for the client sends back a Reply message.

NOTE: You are not required to go into detail on DHCPv6 in the current ROUTE exam.

Reverting back to the topic of discussion, the `ipv6 address` command, the `eui-64` keyword is used to configure an IPv6 address for an interface and enables IPv6 processing on the interface using an EUI-64 interface ID in the low-order 64-bits of the address. By default, Link-Local, Site-Local, and IPv6 stateless autoconfiguration all use the EUI-64 format to make their IPv6 addresses. EUI-64 addressing expands the 48-bit MAC address into a 64-bit address. This is performed in two steps, both of which are described in the following section.

In the first step of creating the EUI-64 address, the value FFEE is inserted into the middle of the MAC address, thereby expanding the MAC address from 48-bits, which is 12 Hexadecimal characters, to 64-bits, which is 16 Hexadecimal characters. The conversion of the 48-bit MAC address into the 64-bit EUI address is illustrated in Figure 8-20 below:

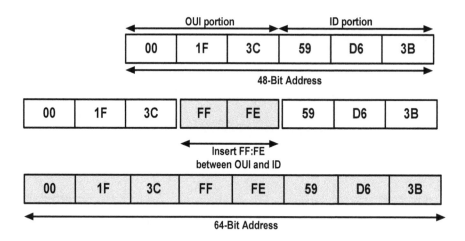

Fig. 8-20. Creating the EUI-64 Address

The second step of EUI-64 addressing entails the setting of the 7th bit of the 64-bit address. This 7th bit is used to identify whether the MAC address is unique. If this bit is set to 1, this indicates that the MAC address is a globally-managed MAC address—which means that the MAC address has been assigned by a vendor. If this bit is set to 0, this indicates that the MAC address is locally assigned—which means that the MAC address has been added by the administrator, for example. To clarify this statement further, as an example, MAC address 02:1F:3C:59:D6:3B would be considered a globally-assigned MAC address, while MAC address 00:1F:3C:59:D6:3B would be considered a local address. This is illustrated in Figure 8-21 below:

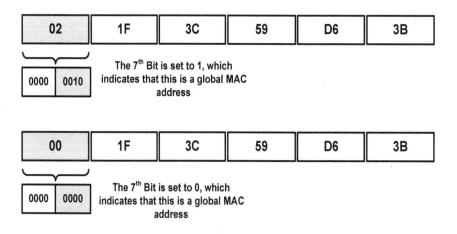

Fig. 8-21. Determining Local and Global MAC Addresses

The following configuration example illustrates how to assign an IPv6 prefix to an interface and configure the router to create the interface ID automatically using EUI-64 addressing:

```
R2(config)#interface FastEthernet0/0
R2(config-if)#ipv6 address 3fff:1a2b:3c4d:5e6f::/64 eui-64
R2(config-if)#exit
```

Following this configuration, the show ipv6 interface command can be used to validate the IPv6 interface ID assigned to the FastEthernet0/0 interface as illustrated below:

```
R2#show ipv6 interface FastEthernet0/0
FastEthernet0/0 is up, line protocol is up
  IPv6 is enabled, link-local address is FE80::213:19FF:FE86:A20
  Global unicast address(es):
    3FFF:1A2B:3C4D:5E6F:213:19FF:FE86:A20, subnet is
3FFF:1A2B:3C4D:5E6F::/64 [EUI]
  Joined group address(es):
    FF02::1
    FF02::2
    FF02::1:FF86:A20
  MTU is 1500 bytes

...

[Truncated Output]
```

To validate the creation of the EUI-64 address, you can verify the complete IPv6 address by also viewing the MAC address for the specified interface using the show interface command:

```
R2#show interface FastEthernet0/0
FastEthernet0/0 is up, line protocol is up
  Hardware is AmdFE, address is 0013.1986.0a20 (bia 0013.1986.0a20)
   Internet address is 10.0.1.1/30
```

From the output above, we can determine that the EUI-64 address is indeed valid and is based on the MAC address of the interface. In addition, the address is global, as the 7th bit has been enabled (i.e., contains a non-zero value).

Finally, the link-local keyword is used to assign a Link-Local address to the interface. By default, it is important to remember that an IPv6 prefix does not have to be enabled on the interface in order for a Link-Local address to be created dynamically. Instead, if the ipv6 enable interface configuration command is issued under an interface, a Link-Local address is created automatically for that interface using EUI-64 addressing.

To configure a Link-Local address manually, you must assign an address within the FE80::/10 Link-Local address block. The following configuration example illustrates how to configure a Link-Local address on an interface:

```
R3(config)#interface FastEthernet0/0
R3(config-if)# ipv6 address fe80:1234:abcd:1::3 link-local
R3(config-if)#exit
```

Following this configuration, the show ipv6 interface [name] command can be used to validate the manual configuration of the Link-Local address as shown in the output below:

```
R3#show ipv6 interface FastEthernet0/0
FastEthernet0/0 is up, line protocol is up
  IPv6 is enabled, link-local address is FE80:1234:ABCD:1::3
  Global unicast address(es):
    2001::1, subnet is 2001::/64
  Joined group address(es):
    FF02::1
    FF02::2
    FF02::1:FF00:1
    FF02::1:FF00:1111
  MTU is 1500 bytes

...

[Truncated Output]
```

> **NOTE:** When configuring Link-Local addresses manually, if Cisco IOS software detects another host using one of its IPv6 addresses, an error message will be printed on the console and the command will be rejected. Be very careful when configuring Link-Local addressing manually.

CONFIGURING STATIC IPV6 ROUTES

The configuration of static IPv6 routes follows similar logic to that of static IPv4 routes. In Cisco IOS software, the ipv6 route [ipv6-prefix/prefix-length] [next-hop-address | interface] [distance <1-254> | multicast | tag | unicast] global configuration command is used to configure static IPv6 routes. While the other keywords are familiar, because they are also applicable to IPv4 static routes, the multicast keyword is exclusive to IPv6 and is used to configure an IPv6 static Multicast route. If this keyword is used, the route will not be entered into the Unicast routing table and will never be used to forward Unicast traffic. To ensure that the route is never installed into the Unicast RIB, Cisco IOS software sets the administrative distance value for the route to 255.

Inversely, the `unicast` keyword is used to configure an IPv6 static Unicast route. If this keyword is used, the route will not be entered into the Multicast routing table and will be used only to forward Unicast traffic. If neither the `multicast` keyword nor the `unicast` keyword is used, by default, the route will be used for both Unicast and Multicast packets.

The following configuration example illustrates how to configure three static IPv6 routes. The first route, to subnet 3FFF:1234:ABCD:0001::/64, will forward traffic out of the FastEthernet0/0 interface. This route will be used only for Unicast traffic. The second route, to subnet 3FFF:1234:ABCD:0002::/64, will forward packets to that subnet out of Serial0/0 using the Link-Local address of the next-hop router as the IPv6 next-hop address. This route will be used only for Multicast traffic. Finally, a default route pointing out of interface Serial0/1 is also configured. This default route will forward packets to unknown IPv6 destinations via Serial0/1 using the Link-Local address of the next-hop router as the IPv6 next-hop address. These routes are illustrated below:

```
R1(config)#ipv6 route 3FFF:1234:ABCD:0001::/64 Fa0/0 unicast
R1(config)#ipv6 route 3FFF:1234:ABCD:0002::/64 Se0/0 FE80::2222 multicast
R1(config)#ipv6 route ::/0 Serial0/1 FE80::3333
```

Following this configuration, the `show ipv6 route` command can be used to verify the static route configuration implemented on the local router as illustrated below:

```
R1#show ipv6 route static
IPv6 Routing Table - 13 entries
Codes: C - Connected, L - Local, S - Static, R - RIP, B - BGP
       U - Per-user Static route
       I1 - ISIS L1, I2 - ISIS L2, IA - ISIS interarea, IS - ISIS summary
       O - OSPF intra, OI - OSPF inter, OE1 - OSPF ext 1, OE2 - OSPF ext 2
       ON1 - OSPF NSSA ext 1, ON2 - OSPF NSSA ext 2
S   ::/0 [1/0]
     via FE80::3333, Serial0/1
S   3FFF:1234:ABCD:1::/64 [1/0]
     via ::, FastEthernet0/0
S   3FFF:1234:ABCD:2::/64 [1/0]
     via FE80::2222, Serial0/0
```

In addition to using the `show ipv6 route` command, the `show ipv6 static [prefix] [detail]` command can also be used to view detailed information about all or just specified static routes. The following output illustrates how to use this command:

```
R1#show ipv6 static 3FFF:1234:ABCD:1::/64 detail
IPv6 Static routes
Code: * - installed in RIB
* 3FFF:1234:ABCD:1::/64 via interface FastEthernet0/0, distance 1
```

When configuring static routes, the `tag` keyword performs the same function as when used in the configuration of static IPv4 routes. Using this keyword, static IPv6 routes can be assigned administrator-defined tags, which can then be matched in route maps when configuring IPv6 route redistribution and route filtering. The following configuration illustrates how to assign a route tag to a static IPv6 route:

```
R1(config)#ipv6 route 3FFF:1234:ABCD:0002::/64 Serial0/0 FE80::2222 tag 44
```

Again, the `show ipv6 route` command can be used to validate this configuration as follows:

```
R1#show ipv6 route 3FFF:1234:ABCD:0002::/64
IPv6 Routing Table - 13 entries
Codes: C - Connected, L - Local, S - Static, R - RIP, B - BGP
       U - Per-user Static route
       I1 - ISIS L1, I2 - ISIS L2, IA - ISIS interarea, IS - ISIS summary
       O - OSPF intra, OI - OSPF inter, OE1 - OSPF ext 1, OE2 - OSPF ext 2
       ON1 - OSPF NSSA ext 1, ON2 - OSPF NSSA ext 2
S   3FFF:1234:ABCD:2::/64 [1/0], tag 44
     via FE80::2222, Serial0/0
```

From the output printed above, we can see the administrator-defined tag in the output of the `show ipv6 route` command. This specified tag can then be matched using the `match tag` route map match clause when redistributing the static IPv6 route into a dynamic routing protocol, for example, in the same way that would also be performed for static IPv4 routes.

Now that we have a solid understanding of how to configure and validate static IPv6 routes, the following sections pertain to dynamic routing protocols and how they have been modified to allow for the routing of IPv6 prefixes. All of the major IP routing protocols have been either modified or updated in order to support both IPv6 addressing and routing. New versions of the Routing Information Protocol (RIP) and Open Shortest Path First (OSPF) have been standardized by the Internet community. The existing implementations of Intermediate System to Intermediate System (IS-IS) and Border Gateway Protocol (BGP) are now extended and usable by IPv6 routers. In addition, the Cisco-proprietary EIGRP routing protocol has also been updated and is now capable of IPv6 routing. While IS-IS is beyond the scope of the current ROUTE exam requirements, the other mentioned routing protocols are not. These are described in the following sections.

RIPNG FOR IPV6

Interestingly, while Routing Information Protocol is beyond the scope of the ROUTE exam requirements as it is covered in the current CCNA exam, Routing Information Protocol next generation (RIPng), which evolved from RIPv2 and is updated specifically to support IPv6, is a requirement of the current ROUTE exam. For the most part, RIPng is very similar to the RIPv2 specification. The similarities between RIPng and RIPv2 are listed in Table 8-12 below:

Table 8-12. RIPv2 and RIPng Similarities

Protocol Characteristic	RIPv2	RIPng
Protocol Classification	Distance Vector	Distance Vector
Hop Limitation	15	15
Split Horizon	Yes	Yes
Poison Reverse	Yes	Yes
Transport Layer Protocol	UDP	UDP
Multicast Updates	Yes (224.0.0.9)	Yes (FF02::9)
Administrative Distance	120	120
Hold-down Timers	Yes	Yes

However, while there are many similarities between RIPv2 and RIPng, it is also important to be familiar with the notable differences between the two protocols. The first notable difference is the supported routed protocol. While both the protocols support IP, RIPv2 supports IPv4, while RIPng supports IPv6. Given the differences in routed protocol support, the next difference between the two routing protocols is that with RIPv2, destination prefixes are 32-bits, while with RIPng, destination prefixes are 128-bits due to the longer length of IPv6 addressing.

The different routed protocol also means that the next-hop address used in RIPng is longer than that used in RIPv2, with the former being 128-bits and the latter being 32-bits. While both RIPv2 and RIPng still send the same types of messages (i.e., requests and replies), RIPv2 messages are sent over IPv4 packets, while RIPng messages are sent over IPv6 packets. In addition, while both protocols still use UDP as the Transport Layer protocol, RIPv2 has a standard UDP port number of 520, while RIPng uses UDP port 521.

While RIPv2 does support authentication, it must be configured manually by the administrator. RIPng does not require manual authentication configuration, as IPSec is built into the IPv6 protocol. Instead, IPSec is used to ensure the integrity of RIPng messages. Finally, a significant difference between RIPv2 and RIPng is that RIPng updates are sent to adjacent routers using the Link-Local address as the source address, meaning that received RIPng routes will always have a Link-Local next-hop address. While going into the details of RIPng packets is beyond the scope of the ROUTE exam requirements, Figure 8-22 below displays the RIPng reply (response) packet, which shows the differences described in the previous section:

```
Frame 1 (206 bytes on wire, 206 bytes captured)
Ethernet II, Src: Cisco_a7:f3:a0 (00:0c:ce:a7:f3:a0), Dst: IPv6mcast_00:00:00:09 (33:33:00:00:00:09)
Internet Protocol Version 6
User Datagram Protocol, Src Port: ripng (521), Dst Port: ripng (521)
RIPng
 Command: Response (2)
 Version: 1
 IP Address: 3fff:1234:abcd:5678::/64, Metric: 1
 IP Address: 3fff:1234:abcd:9012::/64, Metric: 1
 IP Address: 3fff:1234:abcd:3456::/64, Metric: 1
 IP Address: 3fff:1234:abcd:7890::/64, Metric: 1
 IP Address: 2001::/64, Metric: 1
 IP Address: 2002::/64, Metric: 1
 IP Address: 2003::/64, Metric: 1
```

Fig. 8-22. RIPng Reply (Response) Packet

To reinforce what we learned pertaining to the differences between RIPv2 and RIPng, Table 8-13 below summarizes the differences described in the previous section, as well as other notable differences between these two routing protocols:

Table 8-13. RIPv2 and RIPng Differences

Protocol Characteristic	RIPv2	RIPng
Destination Prefix Length	32-bit	128-bit
Next-Hop Length	32-bit	128-bit
Next-Hop Address	Primary Interface Address	Link-Local Address
Transport	IPv4	IPv6
UDP Port Number	520	521
Authentication	Text and MD5	Inbuilt into IPv6 (IPSec)
Automatic Summarization	Yes (enabled by default)	Not Applicable
Can Broadcast Updates	Yes	Not Applicable

Cisco IOS Software RIPv2 and RIPng Configuration Differences

There are several significant differences between the configuration of RIPng and RIPv2, such as the omission of the `network` command when configuring RIPng, among many others. This section describes the fundamental differences between configuring and enabling RIPv2 and RIPng routing in Cisco IOS software.

The first difference between the configuration of RIPv2 and RIPng in Cisco IOS software is how the routing protocol is enabled. For RIPv2, the `router rip` global configuration command is required, followed by the `version 2` router configuration subcommand. Based on this configuration scheme, by default, only a single instance of RIP can be configured on the router. When enabling RIPng, the `router rip` command has been replaced by the `ipv6 router rip [tag]` global configuration command. The use of the tag allows multiple instances of RIPng to be enabled on the same physical router. Each instance is uniquely identified by the tag that is specified when the RIPng process is enabled by the administrator.

NOTE: The administrator-defined tag is somewhat similar to the OSPF process ID in that while a unique tag must be specified for each individual instance, the tag is locally significant to the router on which it is configured and need not be the same on adjacent RIPng routers. It is often a commonly misunderstood concept when enabling RIPng in Cisco IOS software.

The second notable difference between the configuration of RIPv2 and RIPng is the omission of the standard `network` router configuration subcommand that is used when enabling RIPv2. Instead, with RIPng, RIP routing is enabled on a per-interface basis using the `ipv6 rip [tag] enable` interface configuration command, with the tag referencing the administrator-specified tag for the unique RIPng process. The `ipv6 rip [tag] enable` interface configuration command allows multiple RIPng instances to be assigned to the same interface.

Additional RIP configuration, while slightly different for RIPng and RIPv2, follows the same basic configuration logic in Cisco IOS software. Table 8-14 below lists some common configuration commands and how they are applied in RIPv2 and RIPng, respectively:

Table 8-14. RIPv2 and RIPng Cisco IOS Software Configuration Differences

Command Function	RIPv2 Command	RIPng Command
Enable RIP routing	Use the `router rip` global configuration command	Use the `ipv6 router rip [tag]` global configuration command
Advertise networks or prefixes using RIP	Use the `network` router configuration command	Use the `ipv6 rip [tag] enable` interface configuration command
Generate a RIP default route	Use the `default-information originate` router configuration command	Use the `ipv6 rip [tag] default-information originate` interface configuration command
Enable or disable Split Horizon	Use the `[no] ip split-horizon` interface configuration command	Use the `[no] split-horizon` router configuration command
Verify received RIP routing information	Use the `show ip route [rip]` command	Use the `show ipv6 route [rip]` command
Verify the RIP database	Use the `show ip rip database` command	Use the `show ipv6 rip [tag] database` command

Configuring and Verifying RIPng in Cisco IOS Software

The actual configuration of RIPng in Cisco IOS software is a fairly straightforward process once you are comfortable with the fundamental configuration differences between RIP and RIPng. The following sequence of steps should be taken to enable RIPng routing in Cisco IOS software:

- Globally enable IPv6 routing using the `ipv6 unicast-routing` global configuration command. By default, IPv6 routing is disabled in Cisco IOS software.
- Configure one or more RIPng processes using the `ipv6 router rip [tag]` global configuration command.
- Enable IPv6 on the desired interfaces using the `ipv6 address` and `ipv6 enable` interface configuration commands.
- Enable one or more RIPng processes under the interface using the `ipv6 rip [tag] enable` interface configuration command.

Because automatic summarization is not applicable to RIPng, there is no need, and no command used, to disable this behavior. To solidify the configuration of RIPng, consider the topology illustrated in Figure 8-23 below, which illustrates a network comprised of two routers. Both routers will be running RIPng. Additionally, router R3 will be advertising two additional prefixes via RIPng:

Fig. 8-23. Configuring RIPng in Cisco IOS Software

Following the sequence of configuration steps described in the previous section, RIPng will be configured on router R1 as follows:

```
R1(config)#ipv6 unicast-routing
R1(config)#ipv6 router rip R1-RIP-NG
R1(config-rtr)#exit
R1(config)#interface Serial0/1
R1(config-if)#ipv6 address 3fff:1234:abcd:1::1/64
R1(config-if)#ipv6 enable
R1(config-if)#ipv6 rip R1-RIP-NG enable
R1(config-if)#exit
```

Following the same sequence of steps, RIPng routing is configured on router R3 as follows:

```
R3(config)#ipv6 unicast-routing
R3(config)#ipv6 router rip R2-RIP-NG
```

```
R3(config-rtr)#exit
R3(config)#interface Serial1/0
R3(config-if)#ipv6 address 3fff:1234:abcd:1::3/64
R3(config-if)#ipv6 enable
R3(config-if)#ipv6 rip R2-RIP-NG enable
R3(config-if)#exit
R3(config)#interface FastEthernet0/0
R3(config-if)#ipv6 address 3fff:1234:abcd:2::3/64
R3(config-if)#ipv6 address 3fff:1234:abcd:3::3/64
R3(config-if)#ipv6 enable
R3(config-if)#ipv6 rip R2-RIP-NG enable
R3(config-if)#exit
```

Following the configuration of RIPng on both routers, basic show commands should be used to validate both the configuration and the routing information. For example, to view basic RIPng protocol status (e.g., timers), the show ipv6 rip command would be used. This command prints the same basic information as the show ip protocols command used to verify RIPv2. The output of this command displays the following on R1:

```
R1#show ipv6 rip
RIP process "R1-RIP-NG", port 521, multicast-group FF02::9, pid 150
     Administrative distance is 120. Maximum paths is 16
     Updates every 30 seconds, expire after 180
     Holddown lasts 0 seconds, garbage collect after 120
     Split horizon is on; poison reverse is off
     Default routes are not generated
     Periodic updates 20, trigger updates 3
   Interfaces:
     Serial0/1
   Redistribution:
     None
```

From the output printed above, we can determine that the local RIPng instance has been named R1-RIP-NG. The default UDP port used by RIPng (521), as well as the default IPv6 Multicast group FF02::9, is also included in the output of this command. Additional information includes the default administrative distance of 120, the default RIP timer values, and the interfaces under which the process has been enabled.

In addition to validating base protocol configuration parameters, it is also important to verify that routing updates are being received. When running RIPng, this is performed using the show ipv6 route [rip] command. The output of this command displays the following on R1:

```
R1#show ipv6 route rip
IPv6 Routing Table - 6 entries
Codes: C - Connected, L - Local, S - Static, R - RIP, B - BGP
       U - Per-user Static route
```

```
      I1 - ISIS L1, I2 - ISIS L2, IA - ISIS interarea, IS - ISIS summary
      O - OSPF intra, OI - OSPF inter, OE1 - OSPF ext 1, OE2 - OSPF ext 2
      ON1 - OSPF NSSA ext 1, ON2 - OSPF NSSA ext 2
R    3FFF:1234:ABCD:2::/64 [120/2]
      via FE80::213:7FFF:FEAF:3E00, Serial0/1
R    3FFF:1234:ABCD:3::/64 [120/2]
      via FE80::213:7FFF:FEAF:3E00, Serial0/1
```

From the output above, router R1 is receiving both the prefixes that were configured on R3 and are advertised via RIPng. In addition, notice that the next-hop address for both prefixes is not the global IPv6 Unicast address 3FFF:1234:ABCD:1::3 but rather the Link-Local address of router R3. As was previously stated, the Link-Local address will always be used in updates sent to any adjacent RIPng routers. The use of the Link-Local address allows for seamless prefix renumbering when using IPv6. In other words, it is possible to migrate from one global prefix to another without losing connectivity because the Link-Local address will never change.

Finally, as any prudent network engineer would do, you should also verify reachability to the prefixes advertised by router R3. This can be performed using a simple ping test as follows:

```
R1#ping 3FFF:1234:ABCD:2::3 repeat 10

Type escape sequence to abort.
Sending 10, 100-byte ICMP Echos to 3FFF:1234:ABCD:2::3, timeout is 2 seconds:
!!!!!!!!!!!
Success rate is 100 percent (10/10), round-trip min/avg/max = 12/13/16 ms
```

EIGRP FOR IPV6

In addition to open standard protocols, the Cisco-proprietary EIGRP routing protocol has also been modified to support IPv6. This modified version of EIGRP is sometimes referred to as EIGRPv6 because of its support for IPv6 and not because it is revision 6 of the EIGRP routing protocol. Similarly, EIGRP for IPv4 is also sometimes referred to as EIGRPv4 to differentiate between the routed protocol versions supported by either version.

For the most part, just as is the case with RIPng and RIPv2, EIGRPv6 retains the same basic core functions as EIGRPv4. For example, both versions still use DUAL to ensure loop-free paths, and both protocols use Multicast packets to send updates—although EIGRPv6 uses IPv6 Multicast address FF02::A instead of the 224.0.0.10 group address used by EIGRPv4. While the same core fundamentals are retained, there are some differences between these versions. Table 8-15 below lists the differences between EIGRPv4 and EIGRPv6, or simply and more commonly between EIGRP for IPv4 and EIGRP for IPv6:

Table 8-15. EIGRPv4 and EIGRPv6 Differences

Protocol Characteristic	EIGRP for IPv4	EIGRP for IPv6
Automatic Summarization	Yes	Not Applicable
Authentication or Security	MD5	Built into IPv6
Common Subnet for Peers	Yes	No
Advertisement Contents	Subnet/Mask	Prefix/Length
Packet Encapsulation	IPv4	IPv6

NOTE: Because EIGRPv6 uses the Link-Local address of the neighbor as the next-hop address, the global IPv6 Unicast subnets do not need to be the same for a neighbor relationship to be established between two routers that reside within the same autonomous system and are on a common network segment. This is one of the most significant differences between EIGRPv4, which requires neighbors to be on a common subnet, and EIGRPv6, which negates this need by using the Link-Local addresses for neighbor relationships instead.

Cisco IOS Software EIGRPv4 and EIGRPv6 Configuration Differences

As is the case with RIPv2 and RIPng, there are some notable differences in the configuration of EIGRPv4 and EIGRPv6 in Cisco IOS software. The first notable difference is the way in which the routing protocol is enabled. For EIGRPv4, the `router eigrp [ASN]` global configuration command is required to enable EIGRPv4 routing and to specify the EIGRPv4 autonomous system number. When configuring EIGRPv6, the `ipv6 router eigrp [ASN]` global configuration command is used instead to enable EIGRPv6 and to specify the local router autonomous system number.

While enabling EIGRPv4 and EIGRPv6 is somewhat similar, there is a very notable significant difference in the protocol states once the routing process has been enabled. By default, when EIGRPv4 is enabled, the protocol automatically starts and, assuming correct configuration, begins sending Hello packets on all specified operational interfaces. When enabling EIGRPv6 in Cisco IOS software, by default, after the protocol has been enabled, it remains in the shutdown state. This means that even if enabled under specified interfaces, the EIGRP process will not be operational until the `no shutdown` router configuration command is issued.

Yet another configuration difference between EIGRPv4 and EIGRPv6 is that with EIGRPv6, the router ID is mandatory and must be specified in IPv4 dotted-decimal notation. When assigning the RID, keep in mind that the address does not have to be a routable or reachable address.

NOTE: If there are any interfaces with IPv4 addresses configured on the local router, then the router will select the router ID from these interfaces—preferring Loopback interfaces, and then using physical interfaces if no Loopback interfaces are configured or operational on the router. The highest IP address of the Loopback interface(s), if up, will be selected. If not, the RID will be selected from the highest IP address of the physical interfaces, if up. If neither is configured on the router, the `eigrp router-id [IPv4 Address]` command must be used.

657

Configuring and Verifying EIGRPv6 in Cisco IOS Software

Continuing from the previous section, which highlighted the configuration differences between EIGRPv4 and EIGRPv6, this section goes through the steps required to enable and verify EIGRPv6 functionality and routing in Cisco IOS software. The following sequence of steps should be taken to enable EIGRPv6 routing in Cisco IOS software:

- Globally enable IPv6 routing using the `ipv6 unicast-routing` global configuration command. By default, IPv6 routing is disabled in Cisco IOS software.
- Configure one or more EIGRPv6 processes using the `ipv6 router eigrp [ASN]` global configuration command.
- If there are no operational interfaces with an IPv4 address configured on the router, then configure the EIGRPv6 RID manually using the `eigrp router-id [IPv4 Address]` router configuration command.
- Enable the EIGRPv6 process(es) using the `no shutdown` router configuration command.
- Enable IPv6 on the desired interfaces using the `ipv6 address` and `ipv6 enable` interface configuration commands.
- Enable one or more EIGRPv6 processes under the interface using the `ipv6 eigrp [ASN]` interface configuration command.

Because automatic summarization is not applicable to EIGRPv6, there is no need to disable this behavior. To solidify the configuration of EIGRPv6, consider the topology illustrated in Figure 8-24 below, which illustrates a network comprised of two routers. Both routers will be running EIGRPv6 using AS 1.Router R3 will be advertising two additional prefixes via EIGRPv6:

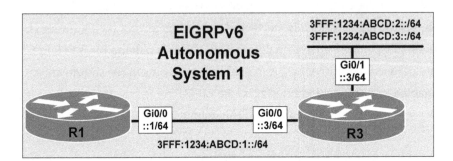

Fig. 8-24. Configuring EIGRPv6 in Cisco IOS Software

Following the sequence of configuration steps described in the previous section, EIGRPv6 will be configured on router R1 as follows:

```
R1(config)#ipv6 unicast-routing
R1(config)#ipv6 router eigrp 1
R1(config-rtr)#eigrp router-id 1.1.1.1
R1(config-rtr)#no shutdown
```

```
R1(config-rtr)#exit
R1(config)#interface GigabitEthernet0/0
R1(config-if)#ipv6 address 3fff:1234:abcd:1::1/64
R1(config-if)#ipv6 enable
R1(config-if)#ipv6 eigrp 1
R1(config-if)#exit
```

Following the same sequence of steps, EIGRPv6 routing is configured on router R3 as follows:

```
R3(config)#ipv6 unicast-routing
R3(config)#ipv6 router eigrp 1
R3(config-rtr)#eigrp router-id 3.3.3.3
R3(config-rtr)#no shutdown
R3(config-rtr)#exit
R3(config)#interface GigabitEthernet0/0
R3(config-if)#ipv6 address 3fff:1234:abcd:1::3/64
R3(config-if)#ipv6 enable
R3(config-if)#ipv6 eigrp 1
R3(config-if)#exit
R3(config)#interface GigabitEthernet0/1
R3(config-if)#ipv6 address 3fff:1234:abcd:2::3/64
R3(config-if)#ipv6 address 3fff:1234:abcd:3::3/64
R3(config-if)#ipv6 enable
R3(config-if)#ipv6 eigrp 1
R3(config-if)#exit
```

The verification process for EIGRPv6 follows the same as that for EIGRPv4. First, verify that the EIGRP neighbor relationships have been established successfully. For EIGRPv6, this is performed using the `show ipv6 eigrp neighbors` command as illustrated below:

```
R1#show ipv6 eigrp neighbors
EIGRP-IPv6 Neighbors for AS(1)
H   Address                  Interface      Hold Uptime    SRTT   RTO  Q  Seq
                                            (sec)          (ms)        Cnt Num
0   Link-local address:      Gi0/0          13 00:01:37      1    200  0  3
    FE80::1AEF:63FF:FE63:1B00
```

As was stated earlier, notice that the next-hop address (EIGRP neighbor address) is specified as the Link-Local address, rather than the global Unicast address. All of the other information printed by this command is the same as that printed for the `show ip eigrp neighbors` command. To view detailed neighbor information, you can simply append the `detail` keyword to the end of the `show ipv6 eigrp neighbors` command. Using this option prints information on the EIGRP version, as well as the number of prefixes received from that particular EIGRP neighbor, as illustrated below:

```
R1#show ipv6 eigrp neighbors detail
EIGRP-IPv6 Neighbors for AS(1)
H   Address                  Interface      Hold Uptime    SRTT   RTO  Q  Seq
                                            (sec)          (ms)        Cnt Num
```

```
0   Link-local address:      Gi0/0           12 00:01:52   1   200   0   3
    FE80::1AEF:63FF:FE63:1B00
    Version 5.0/3.0, Retrans: 1, Retries: 0, Prefixes: 3
    Topology-ids from peer - 0
```

Following the verification of the EIGRPv6 neighbor relationships, you can then verify routing information. For example, to view the IPv6 prefixes received from EIGRPv6 neighbors, you would use
the show ipv6 route command as illustrated in the following output:

```
R1#show ipv6 route eigrp
IPv6 Routing Table - default - 6 entries
Codes: C - Connected, L - Local, S - Static, U - Per-user Static route
       B - BGP, HA - Home Agent, MR - Mobile Router, R - RIP
       I1 - ISIS L1, I2 - ISIS L2, IA - ISIS interarea, IS - ISIS summary
       D - EIGRP, EX - EIGRP external, ND - Neighbor Discovery
D   3FFF:1234:ABCD:2::/64 [90/3072]
     via FE80::1AEF:63FF:FE63:1B00, GigabitEthernet0/0
D   3FFF:1234:ABCD:3::/64 [90/3072]
     via FE80::1AEF:63FF:FE63:1B00, GigabitEthernet0/0
```

Again, notice that the received prefixes all contain the Link-Local address of the neighbor as the
next-hop IPv6 address for all received prefixes. To view the EIGRPv6 Topology Table, the show
ipv6 eigrp topology command should be used. This command supports the same options as
are available with the show ip eigrp topology command used to view the EIGRPv4 Topology
Table. Based on the implemented configuration, the Topology Table on R1 displays the following
IPv6 prefix information:

```
R1#show ipv6 eigrp topology
EIGRP-IPv6 Topology Table for AS(1)/ID(1.1.1.1)
Codes: P - Passive, A - Active, U - Update, Q - Query, R - Reply,
       r - reply Status, s - sia Status

P 3FFF:1234:ABCD:2::/64, 1 successors, FD is 3072
       via FE80::1AEF:63FF:FE63:1B00 (3072/2816), GigabitEthernet0/0
P 3FFF:1234:ABCD:1::/64, 1 successors, FD is 2816
       via Connected, GigabitEthernet0/0
P 3FFF:1234:ABCD:3::/64, 1 successors, FD is 3072
       via FE80::1AEF:63FF:FE63:1B00 (3072/2816), GigabitEthernet0/0
```

As is the case with EIGRPv4, you can append a prefix to the end of this command in order to view
the detailed information on that prefix or subnet. For example, to view detailed information on
the 3FFF:1234:ABCD:2::/64 subnet, you would simply enter the show ipv6 eigrp topology
3FFF:1234:ABCD:2::/64 command as illustrated below:

```
R1#show ipv6 eigrp topology 3FFF:1234:ABCD:2::/64
EIGRP-IPv6 Topology Entry for AS(1)/ID(1.1.1.1) for 3FFF:1234:ABCD:2::/64
```

```
    State is Passive, Query origin flag is 1, 1 Successor(s), FD is 3072
    Descriptor Blocks:
    FE80::1AEF:63FF:FE63:1B00 (GigabitEthernet0/0), from
    FE80::1AEF:63FF:FE63:1B00, Send flag is 0x0
        Composite metric is (3072/2816), route is Internal
        Vector metric:
          Minimum bandwidth is 1000000 Kbit
          Total delay is 20 microseconds
          Reliability is 255/255
          Load is 1/255
          Minimum MTU is 1500
          Hop count is 1
          Originating router is 3.3.3.3
```

Finally, a simple ping can and should be used to verify connectivity between subnets. The following is a ping from R1 to the 3FFF:1234:ABCD:2::3 address on R3:

```
R1#ping 3FFF:1234:ABCD:2::3 repeat 10

Type escape sequence to abort.
Sending 10, 100-byte ICMP Echos to 3FFF:1234:ABCD:2::3, timeout is 2 seconds:
!!!!!!!!!!
Success rate is 100 percent (10/10), round-trip min/avg/max = 0/0/4 ms
```

As is the case with EIGRPv4, the default protocol values for EIGRPv6 can be validated using the show ipv6 protocols command, the output of which is printed below. This command includes the interfaces enabled for the EIGRP instance, route redistribution information (if applicable), and the manually specified or configured dotted-decimal EIGRPv6 router ID.

```
R1#show ipv6 protocols
IPv6 Routing Protocol is "eigrp 1"
EIGRP-IPv6 Protocol for AS(1)
  Metric weight K1=1, K2=0, K3=1, K4=0, K5=0
  NSF-aware route hold timer is 240
  Router-ID: 1.1.1.1
  Topology : 0 (base)
    Active Timer: 3 min
    Distance: internal 90 external 170
    Maximum path: 16
    Maximum hopcount 100
    Maximum metric variance 1

  Interfaces:
    GigabitEthernet0/0
  Redistribution:
```

OSPF VERSION 3

OSPFv3 is defined in RFC 2740 and is the counterpart of OSPFv2, but is designed explicitly for the IPv6 routed protocol. The version is derived from the Version field in the OSPF packet, which has been updated to a value of 3. The OSPFv3 specification is based mainly on OSPFv2 but contains additional enhancements because of the added support for IPv6.

Both OSPFv2 and OSPFv3 can run on the same router. In other words, the same physical router can route for both IPv4 and IPv6 because each address family has a different SPF process. This does not mean that the SPF algorithm itself is different for OSPFv2 and OSPFv3; the statement simply means that a separate instance of the same SPF algorithm is run for OSPFv2 and OSPFv3. The similarities shared by OSPFv2 and OSPFv3 are as follows:

- OSPFv3 continues to use the same packets that are also used by OSPFv2. These packets include Database Description (DBD), Link State Requests (LSR), Link State Updates (LSU), and Link State Advertisements (LSA) packets.
- The mechanisms for dynamic neighbor discovery and the adjacency formation process (i.e., the different neighbor states that OSPF transitions through from the INIT or ATTEMPT state through to the FULL state) remain the same in OSPFv3 as in OSPFv2.
- OSPFv3 still maintains RFC-compliant on different technologies. For example, if OSPFv3 is enabled over a PPP link, the network type is still specified as point-to-point. In a similar manner, if OSPFv3 is enabled over Frame Relay, the default network type is still specified as non-Broadcast. In addition, the default network type can still be changed manually using the different interface-specific commands in Cisco IOS software.
- Both OSPFv2 and OSPFv3 use the same LSA flooding and aging mechanisms.
- Like OSPFv2, the OSPFv3 router ID still requires the use of a 32-bit IPv4 address. When OSPFv3 is enabled on a router running dual-stack (i.e., both IPv4 and IPv6), the same RID selection process used by Cisco IOS routers for OSPFv2 is used to determine the router ID to be used. However, when OSPFv3 is enabled on a router that has no operational IPv4 interfaces, then it is mandatory that the OSPFv3 router ID be configured manually using the `router-id` router configuration command.
- The OSPFv3 Link ID indicates that the links are not IPv6-specific and is still based on a 32-bit IPv4 address, as is the case in OSPFv2.

While there are similarities between OSPFv2 and OSPFv3, it is important to understand that some significant differences exist with which you must be familiar. These include the following:

- In a manner similar to EIGRP for IPv6 and RIPng, OSPFv3 runs over a link. This negates the need to have a `network` statement for OSPFv3. Instead, the link is configured as part of an OSPF process by using the `ipv6 router ospf [process ID] area [area ID]` interface configuration command. However, like OSPFv2, the OSPF process ID is still specified in global configuration mode using the `ipv6 router ospf [process ID]` global configuration command.

- OSPFv3 uses Link-Local addresses to identify the OSPFv3 adjacencies. Like RIPng and EIGRPv6, the next-hop IPv6 address for OSPFv3 routes will reflect the Link-Local address of the adjacent or neighboring router(s).

- OSPFv3 introduces two new OSPF LSA types. These are the Link-LSA, defined as LSA Type 0x0008, or LSA Type 8, and the Intra-Area-Prefix LSA, defined as LSA Type 0x2009, or LSA Type 9. The Link-LSA provides the router's Link-Local address and provides all the IPv6 prefixes attached to the link. There is one Link-LSA per link. There can be multiple Intra-Area-Prefix LSAs with different Link-State IDs. The Area flooding scope can therefore be an associated prefix with the transit network referencing a Network LSA or it can be an associated prefix with a router or Stub referencing a Router LSA.

- The transport used by OSPFv2 and OSPFv3 is different in that OSPFv3 messages are sent over (encapsulated in) IPv6 packets.

- OSPFv3 uses two standard IPv6 Multicast addresses. The Multicast address FF02::5 is the equivalent of the AllSPFRouters Multicast address 224.0.0.5 used in OSPFv2, while the Multicast address FF02::6 address is the AllDRRouters Multicast address and is the equivalent of the 224.0.0.6 group address used in OSPFv2.

- OSPFv3 leverages the inbuilt capabilities of IPSec and uses the AH and ESP extension headers as an authentication mechanism instead of the numerous authentication mechanisms configurable in OSPFv2. Therefore, the Authentication and AuType fields have been removed from the OSPF packet header in OSPFv3.

- The Options field in Hello packets and Database Description packets has been expanded to 24-bits and includes two option bits, which are the R-bit and the V6-bit. The R-bit indicates whether the originator is an active router and the V6-bit is used to determine whether the router or link should be included or excluded from IPv6 routing calculations. These bits have been added to the Options field for processing Router LSAs during the SPF calculation. The functions of these bits are as follows:
  - If the R-bit is clear, then the router can participate in OSPF topology distribution without being used to forward transit traffic.
  - If the V6-bit is clear, then the router can participate in OSPF topology distribution without being used to forward IPv6 datagrams.
  - If the R-bit is set and theV6-bit is clear, then IPv6 datagrams are not forwarded, but datagrams belonging to another protocol family (e.g., IPv4) may be forwarded.

- Finally, the last significant difference is that the OSPFv3 Hello packet now contains no address information at all but includes an Interface ID, which the originating router has assigned to uniquely identify its interface to the link. This Interface ID becomes the Network LSA's Link-State ID, should the router become the Designated-Router on the link.

Cisco IOS Software OSPFv2 and OSPFv3 Configuration Differences

As is the case with the other routing protocols described in the previous sections, there are some configuration differences in Cisco IOS software when configuring OSPFv2 versus OSPFv3. However, it should be noted that these differences are not as significant as those between other versions of IPv4 routing protocols and their IPv6 counterparts.

In Cisco IOS software, OSPFv3 routing is enabled using the `ipv6 router ospf [process ID]` global configuration command. As is the case with OSPFv2, the OSPF process ID is locally significant to the router and does not need to be the same on adjacent routers in order for an adjacency to be established.

As is required for EIGRPv6, the router ID for OSPFv3 either must be specified manually or must be configured as an operational interface with an IPv4 address (e.g., a Loopback interface). Similar to both RIPng and EIGRPv6, there are no `network` commands used when enabling OSPFv3. Instead, OSPFv3 is enabled on a per-interface basis and multiple instances may be enabled on the same interface.

Finally, when configuring OSPFv3 over NBMA networks, such as Frame Relay and ATM, the neighbor statements are specified under the specific interface using the `ipv6 ospf neighbor [link local address]` interface configuration command. In OSPFv2, these would be configured in router configuration mode.

> **NOTE:** When configuring OSPFv3 over NBMA technologies, you should create static Frame Relay map statements using Link-Local addresses. This is because the Link-Local address is used to establish adjacencies and not the global Unicast address. For example, to create a static Frame Relay map statement and specify an OSPF neighbor for a Frame Relay implementation, the following configuration would be implemented on the router:

```
R1(config)#ipv6 unicast-routing
R1(config)#ipv6 router ospf 1
R1(config-rtr)#router-id 1.1.1.1
R1(config-rtr)#exit
R1(config)#interface Serial0/0
R1(config-if)#frame-relay map ipv6 FE80::205:5EFF:FE6E:5C80 111 broadcast
R1(config-if)#ipv6 ospf neighbor FE80::205:5EFF:FE6E:5C80
R1(config-if)#exit
```

Configuring and Verifying OSPFv3 in Cisco IOS Software

Continuing from the previous section, which highlighted the configuration differences between OSPFv2 and OSPFv3, this section goes through the steps required to enable and verify OSPFv3 functionality and routing in Cisco IOS software. The following sequence of steps should be taken to enable OSPFv3 routing in Cisco IOS software:

- Globally enable IPv6 routing using the `ipv6 unicast-routing` global configuration command. By default, IPv6 routing is disabled in Cisco IOS software.
- Configure one or more OSPFv3 processes using the `ipv6 router ospf [process ID]` global configuration command.
- If there are no operational interfaces with an IPv4 address configured on the router, then configure the OSPFv3 RID manually using the `router-id [IPv4 Address]` router configuration command.
- Enable IPv6 on the desired interfaces using the `ipv6 address` and `ipv6 enable` interface configuration commands.
- Enable one or more OSPFv3 processes under the interface using the `ipv6 ospf [process ID] area [area ID]` interface configuration command.

The same topology used in the previous configuration examples will also be used to illustrate the configuration of OSPFv3 in Cisco IOS software. However, because the implementation of OSPF in general is more complex than the implementation of either RIP or EIGRP, this section will include several configuration examples, using the same physical topology but also illustrating the configuration of unique OSPF aspects, such as non-normal areas, as well as OSPF virtual links when running OSPFv3. The first basic multi-area OSPFv3 configuration example is based on the topology that is illustrated in Figure 8-25 below:

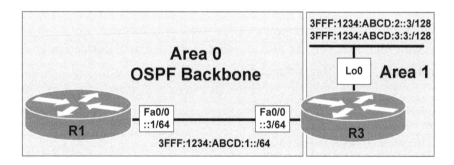

Fig. 8-25. Configuring Basic Multi-Area OSPFv3 in Cisco IOS Software

Following the sequence of configuration steps described in the previous section, OSPFv3 will be configured on router R1 as follows:

```
R1(config)#ipv6 unicast-routing
R1(config)#ipv6 router ospf 1
R1(config-rtr)#router-id 1.1.1.1
R1(config-rtr)#exit
R1(config)#interface FastEthernet0/0
R1(config-if)#ipv6 address 3fff:1234:abcd:1::1/64
R1(config-if)#ipv6 enable
R1(config-if)#ipv6 ospf 1 Area 0
R1(config-if)#exit
```

Following the same sequence of steps, OSPFv3 routing is configured on router R3 as follows:

```
R3(config)#ipv6 unicast-routing
R3(config)#ipv6 router ospf 3
R3(config-rtr)#router-id 3.3.3.3
R3(config-rtr)#exit
R3(config)#interface FastEthernet0/0
R3(config-if)#ipv6 address 3fff:1234:abcd:1::3/64
R3(config-if)#ipv6 enable
R3(config-if)#ipv6 ospf 3 Area 0
R3(config-if)#exit
R3(config)#interface Loopback0
R3(config-if)#ipv6 address 3fff:1234:abcd:2::3/128
R3(config-if)#ipv6 address 3fff:1234:abcd:3::3/128
R3(config-if)#ipv6 enable
R3(config-if)#ipv6 ospf 3 Area 1
R3(config-if)#exit
```

Following the configuration of OSPFv3 on both routers, you can use the show ipv6 ospf neighbors command to verify the state of the OSPFv3 adjacency as illustrated below on R1:

```
R1#show ipv6 ospf neighbor

Neighbor   ID Pri  State     Dead Time   Interface ID   Interface
3.3.3.3        1   FULL/BDR  00:00:36    4              FastEthernet0/0
```

As is the case with EIGRPv6, you can also view detailed neighbor information by appending the detail keyword to the end of this command:

```
R1#show ipv6 ospf neighbor detail
 Neighbor 3.3.3.3
    In the area 0 via interface FastEthernet0/0
    Neighbor: interface-id 4, link-local address FE80::213:19FF:FE86:A20
    Neighbor priority is 1, State is FULL, 6 state changes
    DR is 1.1.1.1 BDR is 3.3.3.3
    Options is 0x000013 in Hello (V6-Bit E-Bit R-bit )
    Options is 0x000013 in DBD (V6-Bit E-Bit R-bit )
    Dead timer due in 00:00:39
    Neighbor is up for 00:06:40
    Index 1/1/1, retransmission queue length 0, number of retransmission 0
    First 0x0(0)/0x0(0)/0x0(0) Next 0x0(0)/0x0(0)/0x0(0)
    Last retransmission scan length is 0, maximum is 0
    Last retransmission scan time is 0 msec, maximum is 0 msec
```

In the output above, notice that the actual neighbor interface address is the Link-Local address and not the configured global IPv6 Unicast address. Additionally, notice the different bits, which were described earlier in this section, set for OSPFv3 Hello and DBD packets. An additional bit, the E-bit, is set only if the interface attaches to a non-Stub area, which is the case based on the configuration implemented on the routers.

In addition, as was stated earlier in this section, OSPFv3 introduces two new types of LSAs, which are the Type 8 and Type 9 LSAs. These LSAs are present in the LSDB and can be viewed, along with all other OSPF LSAs in the LSDB, using the show ipv6 ospf database command. Referencing the configuration implemented on R1, the LSDB of this router displays the following:

```
R1#show ipv6 ospf database

           OSPFv3 Router with ID (1.1.1.1) (Process ID 1)

           Router Link States (Area 0)

ADV Router      Age        Seq#          Fragment ID  Link count  Bits
1.1.1.1         275        0x80000004    0            1           None
3.3.3.3         81         0x80000003    0            1           B

           Net Link States (Area 0)

ADV Router      Age        Seq#          Link ID      Rtr count
1.1.1.1         275        0x80000002    4            2

           Inter-Area-Prefix Link States (Area 0)

ADV Router      Age        Seq#          Prefix
3.3.3.3         82         0x80000002    3FFF:1234:ABCD:2::3/128
3.3.3.3         82         0x80000002    3FFF:1234:ABCD:3::3/128

           Link (Type-8) Link States (Area 0)

ADV Router      Age        Seq#          Link ID      Interface
1.1.1.1         275        0x80000002    4            Fa0/0
3.3.3.3         85         0x80000002    4            Fa0/0

           Intra-Area-Prefix Link States (Area 0)

ADV Router      Age        Seq#          Link ID      Ref-lstype   Ref-LSID
1.1.1.1         279        0x80000002    4096         0x2002       4
```

You can view detailed information on the Link and Intra-Area LSAs by appending the link or the prefix keywords to the end of the show ipv6 ospf database, respectively. Therefore, to view detailed information on the Link LSA, which provides the router's Link-Local address and provides all the IPv6 prefixes attached to the link, you would issue the show ipv6 ospf database link command as illustrated in the following output:

```
R1#show ipv6 ospf database link

           OSPFv3 Router with ID (1.1.1.1) (Process ID 1)
```

```
                    Link (Type-8) Link States (Area 0)

LS age: 459
Options: (V6-Bit E-Bit R-bit DC-Bit)
LS Type: Link-LSA (Interface: FastEthernet0/0)
Link State ID: 4 (Interface ID)
Advertising Router: 1.1.1.1
LS Seq Number: 80000002
Checksum: 0x34F3
Length: 56
Router Priority: 1
Link Local Address: FE80::20C:CEFF:FEA7:F3A0
Number of Prefixes: 1
Prefix Address: 3FFF:1234:ABCD:1::
Prefix Length: 64, Options: None

LS age: 265
Options: (V6-Bit E-Bit R-bit DC-Bit)
LS Type: Link-LSA (Interface: FastEthernet0/0)
Link State ID: 4 (Interface ID)
Advertising Router: 3.3.3.3
LS Seq Number: 80000002
Checksum: 0x85D4
Length: 56
Router Priority: 1
Link Local Address: FE80::213:19FF:FE86:A20
Number of Prefixes: 1
Prefix Address: 3FFF:1234:ABCD:1::
Prefix Length: 64, Options: None
```

Similarly, to view detailed information on the Intra-Area-Prefix LSA, you can use the show ipv6
ospf database prefix command as illustrated in the following output:

```
R1#show ipv6 ospf database prefix

            OSPFv3 Router with ID (1.1.1.1) (Process ID 1)

            Intra-Area-Prefix Link States (Area 0)

Routing Bit Set on this LSA
LS age: 492
LS Type: Intra-Area-Prefix LSA
Link State ID: 4096
Advertising Router: 1.1.1.1
LS Seq Number: 80000002
Checksum: 0xECBB
Length: 44
Referenced LSA Type: 2002
Referenced Link State ID: 4
Referenced Advertising Router: 1.1.1.1
Number of Prefixes: 1
```

```
Prefix Address: 3FFF:1234:ABCD:1::
Prefix Length: 64, Options: None, Metric: 0
```

The OSPFv3 Intra-Area-Prefix LSA contains the same information that is contained in OSPFv2 Router and Network LSAs. It is originated by each router and is used to describe the prefix assigned to each router. It is also generated by each router to advertise prefixes associated with Stub or transit networks. This means that there can be multiple Intra-Area-Prefix LSAs with different Link-State IDs. The Area flooding scope can therefore be an associated prefix with the transit network referencing a Network LSA or it an associated prefix with a router or Stub referencing a Router LSA. The same command, if issued on R3, would also display the following:

```
R3#show ipv6 ospf database prefix

          OSPFv3 Router with ID (3.3.3.3) (Process ID 3)

          Intra-Area-Prefix Link States (Area 0)

  Routing Bit Set on this LSA
  LS age: 1578
  LS Type: Intra-Area-Prefix LSA
  Link State ID: 4096
  Advertising Router: 1.1.1.1
  LS Seq Number: 80000002
  Checksum: 0xECBB
  Length: 44
  Referenced LSA Type: 2002
  Referenced Link State ID: 4
  Referenced Advertising Router: 1.1.1.1
  Number of Prefixes: 1
  Prefix Address: 3FFF:1234:ABCD:1::
  Prefix Length: 64, Options: None, Metric: 0


          Intra-Area-Prefix Link States (Area 1)

  Routing Bit Set on this LSA
  LS age: 1382
  LS Type: Intra-Area-Prefix LSA
  Link State ID: 0
  Advertising Router: 3.3.3.3
  LS Seq Number: 80000002
  Checksum: 0x8C36
  Length: 72
  Referenced LSA Type: 2001
  Referenced Link State ID: 0
  Referenced Advertising Router: 3.3.3.3
  Number of Prefixes: 2
  Prefix Address: 3FFF:1234:ABCD:2::3
  Prefix Length: 128, Options: LA , Metric: 0
  Prefix Address: 3FFF:1234:ABCD:3::3
  Prefix Length: 128, Options: LA , Metric: 0
```

Continuing with the OSPFv3 implementation validation, you can use the show ipv6 route command to view OSPFv3 prefixes received from different OSPFv3 neighbors. As is the case with the other IPv6 routing protocols, these prefixes will all have the Link-Local address of the neighbor as the next-hop address as illustrated in the following output:

```
R1#show ipv6 route
IPv6 Routing Table - 6 entries
Codes: C - Connected, L - Local, S - Static, R - RIP, B - BGP
       U - Per-user Static route
       I1 - ISIS L1, I2 - ISIS L2, IA - ISIS interarea, IS - ISIS summary
       O - OSPF intra, OI - OSPF inter, OE1 - OSPF ext 1, OE2 - OSPF ext 2
       ON1 - OSPF NSSA ext 1, ON2 - OSPF NSSA ext 2
C   3FFF:1234:ABCD:1::/64 [0/0]
     via ::, FastEthernet0/0
L   3FFF:1234:ABCD:1::1/128 [0/0]
     via ::, FastEthernet0/0
OI  3FFF:1234:ABCD:2::3/128 [110/1]
     via FE80::213:19FF:FE86:A20, FastEthernet0/0
OI  3FFF:1234:ABCD:3::3/128 [110/1]
     via FE80::213:19FF:FE86:A20, FastEthernet0/0
L   FE80::/10 [0/0]
     via ::, Null0
L   FF00::/8 [0/0]
     via ::, Null0
```

The second basic OSPFv3 configuration example demonstrates the configuration of non-normal OSPF areas (e.g., Stub and NSSA areas). This example is based on the topology in Figure 8-26 below:

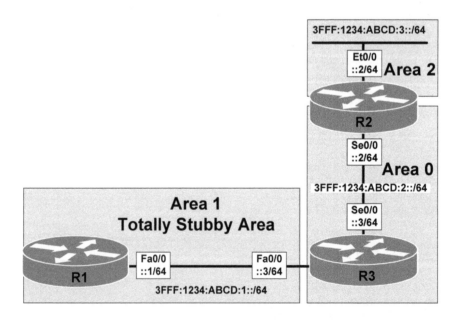

Fig. 8-26. Configuring Non-Normal OSPFv3 Areas in Cisco IOS Software

Following the sequence of configuration steps described in the previous section, OSPFv3 will be configured on router R1 as follows:

```
R1(config)#ipv6 unicast-routing
R1(config)#ipv6 router ospf 1
R1(config-rtr)#router-id 1.1.1.1
R1(config-rtr)#area 1 stub
R1(config-rtr)#exit
R1(config)#interface FastEthernet0/0
R1(config-if)#ipv6 address 3fff:1234:abcd:1::1/64
R1(config-if)#ipv6 enable
R1(config-if)#ipv6 ospf 1 Area 1
R1(config-if)#exit
```

Following the same sequence of steps, router R3 is configured as follows:

```
R3(config)#ipv6 unicast-routing
R3(config)#ipv6 router ospf 3
R3(config-rtr)#router-id 3.3.3.3
R3(config-rtr)#area 1 stub no-summary
R3(config-rtr)#exit
R3(config)#interface FastEthernet0/0
R3(config-if)#ipv6 address 3fff:1234:abcd:1::3/64
R3(config-if)#ipv6 enable
R3(config-if)#ipv6 ospf 3 Area 1
R3(config-if)#exit
R3(config)#interface Serial0/0
R3(config-if)#ipv6 address 3fff:1234:abcd:2::3/64
R3(config-if)#ipv6 enable
R3(config-if)#ipv6 ospf 3 Area 0
R3(config-if)#exit
```

Finally, referencing the topology in Figure 8-26, router R2 would be configured as follows:

```
R2(config)#ipv6 unicast-routing
R2(config)#ipv6 router ospf 2
R2(config-rtr)#router-id 2.2.2.2
R2(config-rtr)#exit
R2(config)#interface Serial0/0
R2(config-if)#ipv6 address 3fff:1234:abcd:2::2/64
R2(config-if)#ipv6 enable
R2(config-if)#ipv6 ospf 2 Area 0
R2(config-if)#exit
R2(config)#interface Ethernet0/0
R2(config-if)#ipv6 address 3fff:1234:abcd:3::2/64
R2(config-if)#ipv6 enable
R2(config-if)#ipv6 ospf 2 Area 2
R2(config-if)#exit
```

Assuming that all OSPF neighbor adjacencies are up, we will begin our OSPFv3 validation tasks by viewing the OSPFv3 process implemented on R3, the central router in the topology. This is performed using the show ipv6 ospf [process ID] command as follows:

```
R3#show ipv6 ospf 3
 Routing Process "ospfv3 3" with ID 3.3.3.3
 It is an area border router
 SPF schedule delay 5 secs, Hold time between two SPFs 10 secs
 Minimum LSA interval 5 secs. Minimum LSA arrival 1 secs
 LSA group pacing timer 240 secs
 Interface flood pacing timer 33 msecs
 Retransmission pacing timer 66 msecs
 Number of external LSA 0. Checksum Sum 0x000000
 Number of areas in this router is 2. 1 normal 1 stub 0 nssa
 Reference bandwidth unit is 100 mbps
    Area BACKBONE(0)
        Number of interfaces in this area is 1
        SPF algorithm executed 11 times
        Number of LSA 7. Checksum Sum 0x035FE0
        Number of DCbitless LSA 0
        Number of indication LSA 0
        Number of DoNotAge LSA 0
        Flood list length 0
    Area 1
        Number of interfaces in this area is 1
        It is a stub area, no summary LSA in this area
          generates stub default route with cost 1
        SPF algorithm executed 8 times
```

The output above validates the configuration implemented on all three routers. Router R3 is an ABR because it has interfaces in both Area 0 and Area 1. Additionally, we can also see that Area 1 is a Totally Stubby Area (as configured) and no summary LSAs are injected into this area except for a single default route. This means that the prefix advertised by router R2 will not be advertised into this area. This can be validated by viewing the LSDB on router R3 as illustrated below:

```
R3#show ipv6 ospf database

            OSPFv3 Router with ID (3.3.3.3) (Process ID 3)

            Router Link States (Area 0)

ADV Router      Age         Seq#            Fragment ID  Link count  Bits
2.2.2.2         46          0x80000006      0            1           B
3.3.3.3         362         0x80000009      0            1           B

            Inter-Area-Prefix Link States (Area 0)

ADV Router      Age         Seq#         Prefix
2.2.2.2         36          0x80000001   3FFF:1234:ABCD:3::/64
```

```
3.3.3.3            362          0x80000001  3FFF:1234:ABCD:1::/64

                   Link (Type-8) Link States (Area 0)

ADV Router         Age          Seq#         Link ID    Interface
2.2.2.2            630          0x80000001   3          Se0/0
3.3.3.3            362          0x80000001   5          Se0/0

                   Intra-Area-Prefix Link States (Area 0)

ADV Router         Age          Seq#         Link ID    Ref-lstype  Ref-LSID
2.2.2.2            46           0x80000003   0          0x2001      0
3.3.3.3            365          0x80000001   0          0x2001      0

                   Router Link States (Area 1)

ADV Router         Age          Seq#         Fragment ID Link count  Bits
3.3.3.3            361          0x80000006   0           0           B

                   Inter-Area-Prefix Link States (Area 1)

ADV Router         Age          Seq#         Prefix
3.3.3.3            365          0x80000001   ::/0

                   Link (Type-8) Link States (Area 1)

ADV Router         Age          Seq#         Link ID    Interface
3.3.3.3            1451         0x80000003   4          Fa0/0

                   Intra-Area-Prefix Link States (Area 1)

ADV Router         Age          Seq#         Link ID    Ref-lstype  Ref-LSID
3.3.3.3            361          0x80000004   0          0x2001      0
```

The same can also be determined by viewing the Inter-Area-Prefix LSAs in the LSDB on router R1 as illustrated in the following output:

```
R1#show ipv6 ospf database inter-area prefix

            OSPFv3 Router with ID (1.1.1.1) (Process ID 1)

            Inter-Area-Prefix Link States (Area 1)

  Routing Bit Set on this LSA
  LS age: 669
  LS Type: Inter-Area-Prefix Links
  Link State ID: 3
  Advertising Router: 3.3.3.3
  LS Seq Number: 80000001
  Checksum: 0x35F9
  Length: 28
```

```
Metric: 1
Prefix Address: ::
Prefix Length: 0, Options: None
```

The same can also be confirmed further by simply viewing the routing table on router R1 as illustrated below:

```
R1#show ipv6 route
IPv6 Routing Table - 5 entries
Codes: C - Connected, L - Local, S - Static, R - RIP, B - BGP
       U - Per-user Static route
       I1 - ISIS L1, I2 - ISIS L2, IA - ISIS interarea, IS - ISIS summary
       O - OSPF intra, OI - OSPF inter, OE1 - OSPF ext 1, OE2 - OSPF ext 2
       ON1 - OSPF NSSA ext 1, ON2 - OSPF NSSA ext 2
OI  ::/0 [110/2]
     via FE80::213:19FF:FE86:A20, FastEthernet0/0
C   3FFF:1234:ABCD:1::/64 [0/0]
     via ::, FastEthernet0/0
L   3FFF:1234:ABCD:1::1/128 [0/0]
     via ::, FastEthernet0/0
L   FE80::/10 [0/0]
     via ::, Null0
L   FF00::/8 [0/0]
     via ::, Null0
```

The third basic OSPFv3 configuration example demonstrates the configuration of virtual links when running OSPFv3. This example is based on the topology in Figure 8-27 below:

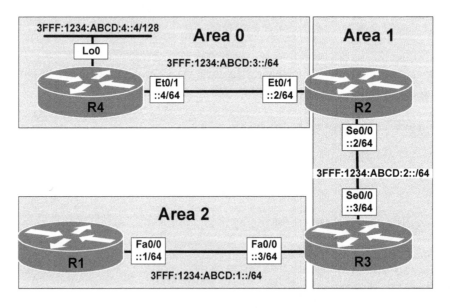

Fig. 8-27. Configuring OSPFv3 Virtual Links in Cisco IOS Software

Assuming basic OSPFv3 configuration on all routers illustrated in the topology, the LSDB on R1 displays the following entries and LSAs:

```
R1#show ipv6 ospf database

            OSPFv3 Router with ID (1.1.1.1) (Process ID 1)

            Router Link States (Area 2)

ADV Router      Age         Seq#            Fragment ID Link count  Bits
1.1.1.1         9           0x80000004      0           1           None
3.3.3.3         15          0x80000004      0           1           None

            Net Link States (Area 2)

ADV Router      Age         Seq#            Link ID     Rtr count
3.3.3.3         17          0x80000001      4           2

            Link (Type-8) Link States (Area 2)

ADV Router      Age         Seq#            Link ID     Interface
1.1.1.1         59          0x80000001      4           Fa0/0
3.3.3.3         91          0x80000001      4           Fa0/0

            Intra-Area-Prefix Link States (Area 2)

ADV Router      Age         Seq#            Link ID     Ref-lstype  Ref-LSID
3.3.3.3         17          0x80000001      4096        0x2002      4
```

The routing table on router R1 also reflects no inter-area LSAs and displays the following entries:

```
R1#show ipv6 route
IPv6 Routing Table - 4 entries
Codes: C - Connected, L - Local, S - Static, R - RIP, B - BGP
       U - Per-user Static route
       I1 - ISIS L1, I2 - ISIS L2, IA - ISIS interarea, IS - ISIS summary
       O - OSPF intra, OI - OSPF inter, OE1 - OSPF ext 1, OE2 - OSPF ext 2
       ON1 - OSPF NSSA ext 1, ON2 - OSPF NSSA ext 2
C   3FFF:1234:ABCD:1::/64 [0/0]
     via ::, FastEthernet0/0
L   3FFF:1234:ABCD:1::1/128 [0/0]
     via ::, FastEthernet0/0
L   FE80::/10 [0/0]
     via ::, Null0
L   FF00::/8 [0/0]
     via ::, Null0
```

As we already know, based on what we learned in the chapter on OSPFv2, by default, an ABR will not advertise routes received from a non-backbone area into another non-backbone area. Given this default protocol behavior, R3 will never advertise the prefixes received from R2 to R1. In order for Area 2 to receive inter-area routes, this area must be connected either logically or physically to the OSPF backbone. Because no physical connection exists, a virtual link must be configured between routers R2 and R3, using Area 1 as the transit area. The configuration on router R2 is implemented as follows:

```
R2(config)#ipv6 router ospf 2
R2(config-rtr)#area 1 virtual-link 3.3.3.3
R2(config-rtr)#exit
```

In a similar manner, the virtual link on router R3 will be configured as follows:

```
R3(config)#ipv6 router ospf 3
R3(config-rtr)#area 1 virtual-link 2.2.2.2
R3(config-rtr)#exit
```

Following the configuration of the virtual-link, the show ipv6 ospf virtual-links command should be used to validate that the virtual link is established as illustrated in the output below:

```
R3#show ipv6 ospf virtual-links
Virtual Link OSPFv3_VL1 to router 2.2.2.2 is up
  Interface ID 11, IPv6 address 3FFF:1234:ABCD:2::2
  Run as demand circuit
  DoNotAge LSA allowed.
  Transit Area 1, via interface Serial0/0, Cost of using 64
  Transmit Delay is 1 sec, State POINT_TO_POINT,
  Timer intervals configured, Hello 10, Dead 40, Wait 40, Retransmit 5
    Adjacency State FULL (Hello suppressed)
    Index 1/1/3, retransmission queue length 0, number of retransmission 2
    First 0x0(0)/0x0(0)/0x0(0) Next 0x0(0)/0x0(0)/0x0(0)
    Last retransmission scan length is 1, maximum is 1
    Last retransmission scan time is 0 msec, maximum is 0 msec
```

In the output above, notice that the IPv6 address used for the virtual link is the global Unicast IPv6 address and not the Link-Local address that used to establish non-virtual link adjacencies. This difference can be viewed by looking at detailed neighbor information as follows:

```
R3#show ipv6 ospf neighbor detail
 Neighbor 2.2.2.2
    In Area 0 via interface OSPFv3_VL1
    Neighbor: interface-id 8, IPv6 address 3FFF:1234:ABCD:2::2
    Neighbor priority is 1, State is FULL, 12 state changes
    Options is 0x000033 in Hello (V6-Bit E-Bit R-bit DC-Bit)
    Options is 0x000033 in DBD (V6-Bit E-Bit R-bit DC-Bit)
    Neighbor is up for 00:02:32
    Index 1/1/3, retransmission queue length 0, number of retransmission 2
    First 0x0(0)/0x0(0)/0x0(0) Next 0x0(0)/0x0(0)/0x0(0)
```

```
            Last retransmission scan length is 1, maximum is 1
            Last retransmission scan time is 0 msec, maximum is 0 msec
        Neighbor 2.2.2.2
            In Area 1 via interface Serial0/0
            Neighbor: interface-id 3, link-local address FE80::204:C1FF:FE6F:8741
            Neighbor priority is 1, State is FULL, 6 state changes
            Options is 0x000013 in Hello (V6-Bit E-Bit R-bit )
            Options is 0x000013 in DBD (V6-Bit E-Bit R-bit )
            Dead timer due in 00:00:34
            Neighbor is up for 00:29:45
            Index 1/1/1, retransmission queue length 0, number of retransmission 1
            First 0x0(0)/0x0(0)/0x0(0) Next 0x0(0)/0x0(0)/0x0(0)
            Last retransmission scan length is 2, maximum is 2
            Last retransmission scan time is 0 msec, maximum is 0 msec
        Neighbor 1.1.1.1
            In Area 2 via interface FastEthernet0/0
            Neighbor: interface-id 4, link-local address FE80::20C:CEFF:FEA7:F3A0
            Neighbor priority is 1, State is FULL, 6 state changes
            DR is 3.3.3.3 BDR is 1.1.1.1
            Options is 0x000013 in Hello (V6-Bit E-Bit R-bit )
            Options is 0x000013 in DBD (V6-Bit E-Bit R-bit )
            Dead timer due in 00:00:30
            Neighbor is up for 00:29:00
            Index 1/1/2, retransmission queue length 0, number of retransmission 0
            First 0x0(0)/0x0(0)/0x0(0) Next 0x0(0)/0x0(0)/0x0(0)
            Last retransmission scan length is 0, maximum is 0
            Last retransmission scan time is 0 msec, maximum is 0 msec
```

Finally, after the virtual link has been configured and established successfully, the LSDB on router R1 now displays the following:

```
R1#show ipv6 ospf database

            OSPFv3 Router with ID (1.1.1.1) (Process ID 1)

[Truncated Output]


            Inter-Area-Prefix Link States (Area 2)

ADV Router       Age        Seq#          Prefix
3.3.3.3          531        0x80000001    3FFF:1234:ABCD:2::/64
3.3.3.3          531        0x80000001    3FFF:1234:ABCD:2::2/128
3.3.3.3          521        0x80000001    3FFF:1234:ABCD:2::3/128
3.3.3.3          501        0x80000001    3FFF:1234:ABCD:3::/64
3.3.3.3          6          0x80000001    3FFF:1234:ABCD:4::4/128


...


[Truncated Output]
```

The same information is also now reflected in the routing table on router R1 as illustrated below:

```
R1#show ipv6 route ospf | section OI
      O - OSPF intra, OI - OSPF inter, OE1 - OSPF ext 1, OE2 - OSPF ext 2
OI  3FFF:1234:ABCD:2::/64 [110/65]
     via FE80::213:19FF:FE86:A20, FastEthernet0/0
OI  3FFF:1234:ABCD:2::2/128 [110/65]
     via FE80::213:19FF:FE86:A20, FastEthernet0/0
OI  3FFF:1234:ABCD:2::3/128 [110/1]
     via FE80::213:19FF:FE86:A20, FastEthernet0/0
OI  3FFF:1234:ABCD:3::/64 [110/75]
     via FE80::213:19FF:FE86:A20, FastEthernet0/0
OI  3FFF:1234:ABCD:4::4/128 [110/75]
     via FE80::213:19FF:FE86:A20, FastEthernet0/0
```

Finally, to complete the validation exercise, a simple ping test is used to verify connectivity between router R1 and the Loopback interface on router R4 as follows:

```
R1#ping 3FFF:1234:ABCD:4::4 repeat 10

Type escape sequence to abort.
Sending 10, 100-byte ICMP Echos to 3FFF:1234:ABCD:4::4, timeout is 2 seconds:
!!!!!!!!!!
Success rate is 100 percent (10/10), round-trip min/avg/max = 4/6/8 ms
```

BGP4+ OR MP-BGP FOR IPV6

An enhanced version to BGP, called BGP4+ or Multi-Protocol BGP (MP-BGP), extends the default BGPv4 specification to include multiple protocol extensions for address families such as IPv6. RFC 2858 and RFC 2545 define the attributes that were updated to handle IPv6 addresses with MP-BGP. These attributes are the NEXT_HOP attribute and the NLRI attribute.

The NEXT_HOP attribute in MP-BGP is defined as an IPv6 address. This attribute can contain either a global Unicast IPv6 address alone or both a global Unicast IPv6 address and the Link-Local address of the next-hop router. The use of Link-Local addresses for BGP4+ peering requires that the neighbor [address] update-source [interface] configuration command be used for BGP peering, even for routers that share a common network segment. This is because Link-Local addresses are tied to a specific interface, so the router must specify the interface in order to prevent any ambiguity.

The NLRI attribute defines a set of destinations, which are simply BGP prefixes. This attribute has now been updated so that it can be expressed as an IPv6 prefix when BGP4+ is enabled.

Unlike the previously described routing protocols, BGP still uses the same basic configuration commands to enable MP-BGP functionality. Figure 8-28 below highlights this information by showing a wire capture of an MP-BGP UPDATE message:

```
Border Gateway Protocol
 UPDATE Message
  Marker: 16 bytes
  Length: 88 bytes
  Type: UPDATE Message (2)
  Unfeasible routes length: 0 bytes
  Total path attribute length: 65 bytes
 Path attributes
  ORIGIN: IGP (4 bytes)
  AS_PATH: 3 (7 bytes)
  MULTI_EXIT_DISC: 0 (7 bytes)
  MP_REACH_NLRI (47 bytes)
   Flags: 0x80 (Optional, Non-transitive, Complete)
   Type code: MP_REACH_NLRI (14)
   Length: 44 bytes
   Address family: IPv6 (2)
   Subsequent address family identifier: Unicast (1)
   Next hop network address (32 bytes)
    Next hop: 3fff:1234:abcd:1::3 (16)
    Next hop: fe80::213:19ff:fe86:a20 (16)
   Subnetwork points of attachment: 0
   Network layer reachability information (7 bytes)
    3fff:1234:efab::/48
     MP Reach NLRI prefix length: 48
     MP Reach NLRI prefix: 3fff:1234:efab::
```

Fig. 8-28. MP-BGP UPDATE Format

In Cisco IOS software, MP-BGP is enabled using the `router bgp [ASN]` global configuration command. IPv6 prefixes are advertised via the use of the `network` router configuration command and MP-BGP neighbors are still configured using the `neighbor` router configuration command, although these two options now provide the capability to use IPv6 addresses instead of just IPv4 address, as was described and illustrated earlier in this guide.

In addition, all other BGP attributes, such as LOCAL_PREF, WEIGHT, ORIGIN, etc., are still applicable to IPv6 prefixes and are manipulated using route maps, as is the case in IPv4 routing. However, there is one significant aspect pertaining to MP-BGP that you must take into consideration: if MP-BGP is enabled in an IPv6-only environment, then the `no bgp default ipv4-unicast` router configuration command should be issued to disable the IPv4 address family. However, as is the case with EIGRPv6 and OSPFv3, MP-BGP still requires an IPv4 address to use as the BGP RID. This means that on an IPv6-only router with no IPv4 interfaces, the `bgp router-id` command must be used to specify an IPv4 RID. You cannot use an IPv6 address as the RID for BGP4+.

While the basic MP-BGP configuration commands remain the same, Cisco IOS software now introduces a new set of commands to view MP-BGP information. For example, the `show bgp [ipv6] summary` command is now used to view summary MP-BGP information, including neighbors and received prefixes, in the same manner that the `show ip bgp summary` command is used in IPv4 routing. The only significant notable difference is that the neighbors will be using IPv6 addresses instead of IPv4 addresses.

Cisco IOS Software BGP4+ and MP-BGP Configuration Differences

As previously stated, there are not that many significant configuration differences between the configuration of BGP4+ and MP-BGP. However, when configuring MP-BGP, although the configuration of `neighbor` statements uses the same commands as those used when configuring BGP4+, with the exception that IPv6 addresses are used instead of the IPv4 addresses and prefixes we are accustomed to, it is important to remember that neighbors must be activated manually under the IPv6 Unicast address family mode. This is performed using the `neighbor [address] active` IPv6 address family sub-command. If the MP-BGP neighbor or neighbors are not active, then the session will not be established. In addition to this, any `network` statements used to advertise prefixes must be issued under the IPv6 address family.

> **NOTE:** By default, in Cisco IOS software, routing information for the IPv4 address family will be advertised for each BGP routing session configured with the `neighbor remote-as` command and no further configuration is required. However, IPv6 address prefixes are not enabled and each individual neighbor must be activated.

Configuring and Verifying MP-BGP in Cisco IOS Software

While delving into advanced MP-BGP configuration is beyond the scope of the current ROUTE exam requirements, it is still important to have a basic understanding of how to enable both external and internal MP-BGP sessions. This section describes the configuration and validation tasks for enabling external MP-BGP sessions and advertising IPv6 prefixes referencing the basic network topology illustrated in Figure 8-29 below. Internal MP-BGP is addressed in the following section.

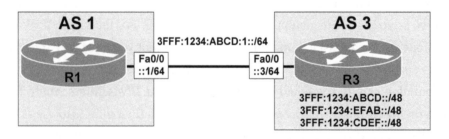

Fig. 8-29. Configuring and Verifying MP-BGP Using IPv6 Global Addresses

Referencing Figure 8-29, MP-BGP will be configured on R1 and R3. Router R1 resides in AS 1, while R3 resides in AS 3. Router R3 will be advertising three prefixes to R1 using MP-BGP. Assuming basic IPv6 addressing configuration on both routers, MP-BGP is implemented as follows on R1:

```
R1(config)#router bgp 1
R1(config-router)#bgp router-id 1.1.1.1
R1(config-router)#no bgp default ipv4-unicast
R1(config-router)#neighbor 3FFF:1234:ABCD:1::3 remote-as 3
R1(config-router)#address-family ipv6 unicast
R1(config-router-af)#neighbor 3FFF:1234:ABCD:1::3 activate
R1(config-router-af)#exit
R1(config-router)#exit
```

NOTE: The `no bgp default ipv4-unicast` command in the configuration above is used to disable the IPv4 Unicast address family. This should be performed only on a router that is running only IPv6. If there are IPv4 neighbors, this command should be omitted. The configuration above is based on the assumption that there are no IPv4 neighbors or prefixes being advertised by MP-BGP. In other words, it assumes this is an IPv6-only BGP speaker.

NOTE: The `unicast` keyword used at the end of the `address-family ipv6` command is optional. This is the default keyword used if no other keywords are issued. Additional supported keywords include `multicast` (for IPv6 Multicast) and `vpnv6` (for VPN version 6). Both IPv6 Multicast and VPN version 6 are beyond the scope of the current ROUTE exam requirements and will not be described in any further detail in this chapter or in the remainder of this guide.

Continuing with the configuration example, MP-BGP is configured on router R3 as follows:

```
R3(config)#router bgp 3
R3(config-router)#bgp router-id 3.3.3.3
R3(config-router)#no bgp default ipv4-unicast
R3(config-router)#neighbor 3fff:1234:abcd:1::1 remote-as 1
R3(config-router)#address-family ipv6
R3(config-router-af)#neighbor 3fff:1234:abcd:1::1 activate
R3(config-router-af)#network 3fff:1234:abcd::/48
R3(config-router-af)#network 3fff:1234:efab::/48
R3(config-router-af)#network 3fff:1234:cdef::/48
R3(config-router-af)#exit
R3(config-router)#exit
```

In the configuration above, notice that the `unicast` keyword has been omitted from the end of the `address-family ipv6` command simply to reinforce that this is an optional command. Additionally, take heed to the fact that the network statements are configured under the IPv6 address family and not in router configuration mode, as would be the case when using IPv4.

Following the configuration of MP-BGP, the first verification task is to validate that the external BGP session has been established. This is performed using the `show bgp ipv6 unicast summary` command as illustrated below on router R1:

```
R1#show bgp ipv6 unicast summary
BGP router identifier 1.1.1.1, local AS number 1
```

```
BGP table version is 6, main routing table version 6
3 network entries using 447 bytes of memory
3 path entries using 228 bytes of memory
2/1 BGP path/bestpath attribute entries using 248 bytes of memory
1 BGP AS-PATH entries using 24 bytes of memory
0 BGP route-map cache entries using 0 bytes of memory
0 BGP filter-list cache entries using 0 bytes of memory
BGP using 947 total bytes of memory
BGP activity 9/6 prefixes, 10/7 paths, scan interval 60 secs

Neighbor      V    AS MsgRcvd MsgSent   TblVer  InQ OutQ Up/Down   State/PfxRcd
3FFF:1234:ABCD:1::3
              4    3      43      37        6    0    0 00:14:08             3
```

Notice that the primary difference between the output of this command and that printed by the show ip bgp summary command is the IPv6 address that is used for the neighbor. To view the contents of the MP-BGP RIB, you can use the show bgp ipv6 unicast command. The output of this command displays the following entries on R1:

```
R1#show bgp ipv6 unicast
BGP table version is 6, local router ID is 1.1.1.1
Status codes: s suppressed, d damped, h history, * valid, > best, i - internal,
              r RIB-failure, S Stale
Origin codes: i - IGP, e - EGP, ? - incomplete

   Network          Next-Hop          Metric LocPrf Weight Path
*> 3FFF:1234:ABCD::/48
                    3FFF:1234:ABCD:1::3
                                           0           0 3 i
*> 3FFF:1234:CDEF::/48
                    3FFF:1234:ABCD:1::3
                                           0           0 3 i
*> 3FFF:1234:EFAB::/48
                    3FFF:1234:ABCD:1::3
                                           0           0 3 i
```

Again, the output printed by this command is the same as that which is printed by the show ip bgp command, with the difference being that IPv6 prefixes and next-hop addresses are used instead of IPv4 prefixes and addresses.

While using the global Unicast addresses to establish the external MP-BGP session works just fine, IPv6 provides flexibility that allows for prefix renumbering by allowing the Link-Local addresses to be used to establish the peer session instead. However, when implementing this solution, the following must be performed:

- You must use the neighbor [address] update-source [interface] command to ensure that the session will be established because Link-Local addresses are specific to interfaces. This is required only when using Link-Local addresses for peering.

- You must use a route map to specify the global Unicast address as the next-hop address for the UPDATE messages sent by the local router.

NOTE: When configuring MP-BGP, it is preferred that you use the IPv6 global Unicast address instead of the Link-Local address. Using Link-Local addresses requires additional configuration in the form of a route map that is required to set an IPv6 global next-hop.

While technically beyond the scope of the current ROUTE exam requirements, the following section describes how to configure MP-BGP peering using Link-Local addresses and to use a route map to ensure that the NEXT_HOP attribute contains the Link-Local and IPv6 global Unicast addresses. This configuration is based on the topology illustrated in Figure 8-30 below:

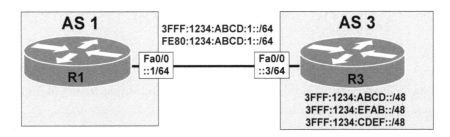

Fig. 8-30. Configuring and Verifying MP-BGP Using Link-Local Addresses

Referencing the topology illustrated in Figure 8-30, router R3 is configured as follows:

```
R3(config)#ipv6 unicast-routing
R3(config)#interface FastEthernet0/0
R3(config-if)#ipv6 address fe80:1234:abcd:1::3 link-local
R3(config-if)#ipv6 address 3fff:1234:abcd:1::3/64
R3(config-if)#ipv6 enable
R3(config-if)#exit
R3(config)#ipv6 prefix-list MATCH-PREFIXES seq 5 permit 3fff:1234:abcd::/48
R3(config)#ipv6 prefix-list MATCH-PREFIXES seq 7 permit 3fff:1234:efab::/48
R3(config)#ipv6 prefix-list MATCH-PREFIXES seq 9 permit 3fff:1234:cdef::/48
R3(config)#route-map NEXT-HOP permit 10
R3(config-route-map)#match ipv6 address prefix-list MATCH-PREFIXES
R3(config-route-map)#set ipv6 next-hop 3fff:1234:abcd:1::3
R3(config-route-map)#exit
R3(config)#router bgp 3
R3(config-router)#bgp router-id 3.3.3.3
R3(config-router)#no bgp default ipv4-unicast
R3(config-router)#neighbor fe80:1234:abcd:1::1 remote-as 1
R3(config-router)#neighbor fe80:1234:abcd:1::1 update-source Fa0/0
R3(config-router)#address-family ipv6 unicast
R3(config-router-af)#neighbor fe80:1234:abcd:1::1 activate
R3(config-router-af)#neighbor fe80:1234:abcd:1::1 route-map NEXT-HOP out
R3(config-router-af)#network 3fff:1234:abcd::/48
```

```
R3(config-router-af)#network 3fff:1234:efab::/48
R3(config-router-af)#network 3fff:1234:cdef::/48
R3(config-router-af)#exit
R3(config-router)#exit
```

Before we move on, take a moment to understand the configuration that is implemented on router R3 section by section. The first section, which is illustrated below, is straightforward. IPv6 routing is enabled globally on the router and then the FastEthernet0/0 interface is configured with the specified IPv6 global Unicast and Link-Local addresses. Finally, IPv6 is enabled on the FastEthernet0/0 interface.

```
R3(config)#ipv6 unicast-routing
R3(config)#interface FastEthernet0/0
R3(config-if)#ipv6 address fe80:1234:abcd:1::3 link-local
R3(config-if)#ipv6 address 3fff:1234:abcd:1::3/64
R3(config-if)#ipv6 enable
R3(config-if)#exit
```

While the following configuration section might appear rather complicated at first glance, it too is also very straightforward. The first three lines configure an IPv6 prefix list that matches the prefixes that will be advertised by router R3. Following that configuration, a route map is created. The match clause in the route map matches the configured IPv6 prefix list and the set clause in the route map sets an IPv6 next-hop address of 3FFF:1234:ABCD:1::3. This is the IPv6 global Unicast address of the local BGP speaker (i.e., router R3). This is the address that will be included in the NEXT_HOP attribute for UPDATE messages sent by this router to other peers.

```
R3(config)#ipv6 prefix-list MATCH-PREFIXES seq 5 permit 3fff:1234:abcd::/48
R3(config)#ipv6 prefix-list MATCH-PREFIXES seq 7 permit 3fff:1234:efab::/48
R3(config)#ipv6 prefix-list MATCH-PREFIXES seq 9 permit 3fff:1234:cdef::/48
R3(config)#route-map NEXT-HOP permit 10
R3(config-route-map)#match ipv6 address prefix-list MATCH-PREFIXES
R3(config-route-map)#set ipv6 next-hop 3fff:1234:abcd:1::3
R3(config-route-map)#exit
```

Finally, the last section of this configuration enables MP-BGP on the local router, specifying an autonomous system number of 3. Because there will be no IPv4 prefixes or neighbors, the IPv4 address family is disabled using the `no bgp default ipv4-unicast` router configuration command. Next, an external MP-BGP peer is configured using the Link-Local address, which is illustrated in Figure 8-30. To ensure that UPDATE messages sent to this peer also include the IPv6 global Unicast address in the NEXT_HOP attribute, the route map is applied in the outbound direction for the MP-BGP peer. Finally, the neighbor is activated in the IPv6 address family and the three prefixes are advertised via MP-BGP.

```
R3(config)#router bgp 3
R3(config-router)#bgp router-id 3.3.3.3
R3(config-router)#no bgp default ipv4-unicast
R3(config-router)#neighbor fe80:1234:abcd:1::1 remote-as 1
R3(config-router)#neighbor fe80:1234:abcd:1::1 update-source Fa0/0
R3(config-router)#address-family ipv6 unicast
R3(config-router-af)#neighbor fe80:1234:abcd:1::1 activate
R3(config-router-af)#neighbor fe80:1234:abcd:1::1 route-map NEXT-HOP out
R3(config-router-af)#network 3fff:1234:abcd::/48
R3(config-router-af)#network 3fff:1234:efab::/48
R3(config-router-af)#network 3fff:1234:cdef::/48
R3(config-router-af)#exit
R3(config-router)#exit
```

Assuming basic MP-BGP configuration on R1, the show bgp ipv6 unicast summary command
is used to verify that the MP-BGP session has been established as follows:

```
R1#show bgp ipv6 unicast summary
BGP router identifier 1.1.1.1, local AS number 1
BGP table version is 4, main routing table version 4
3 network entries using 447 bytes of memory
3 path entries using 228 bytes of memory
2/1 BGP path/bestpath attribute entries using 248 bytes of memory
1 BGP AS-PATH entries using 24 bytes of memory
0 BGP route-map cache entries using 0 bytes of memory
0 BGP filter-list cache entries using 0 bytes of memory
BGP using 947 total bytes of memory
BGP activity 3/0 prefixes, 3/0 paths, scan interval 60 secs

Neighbor      V    AS MsgRcvd MsgSent   TblVer  InQ OutQ Up/Down   State/PfxRcd
FE80:1234:ABCD:1::3
              4    3     5       4        4     0   0 00:00:01        3
```

Following the verification of the MP-BGP session between the two routers, use the show bgp ipv6
unicast command to view the contents of the MP-BGP RIB as follows:

```
R1#show bgp ipv6 unicast
BGP table version is 7, local router ID is 1.1.1.1
Status codes: s suppressed, d damped, h history, * valid, > best, i - internal,
              r RIB-failure, S Stale
Origin codes: i - IGP, e - EGP, ? - incomplete

   Network          Next-Hop          Metric LocPrf Weight Path
*> 3FFF:1234:ABCD::/48
                    3FFF:1234:ABCD:1::3
                                           0           0 3 i
*> 3FFF:1234:CDEF::/48
                    3FFF:1234:ABCD:1::3
                                           0           0 3 i
```

685

```
*> 3FFF:1234:EFAB::/48
                 3FFF:1234:ABCD:1::3
                                                0            0 3 i
```

In the output above, notice that the MP-BGP RIB reflects the IPv6 global Unicast address as the IPv6 NEXT_HOP attribute for all prefixes received from router R3, although the MP-BGP peering configuration specified Link-Local addresses. This is because of the outbound route map that was used to change the NEXT_HOP attribute in UPDATE messages sent by R3 to R1 to the IPv6 global Unicast address. This allows the NEXT_HOP attribute to contain both the Link-Local and the IPv6 global Unicast addresses as shown below:

```
R1#show bgp ipv6 unicast 3FFF:1234:ABCD::/48
BGP routing table entry for 3FFF:1234:ABCD::/48, version 7
Paths: (1 available, best #1, table Global-IPv6-Table)
  Not advertised to any peer
  3
    3FFF:1234:ABCD:1::3 (FE80:1234:ABCD:1::3) from FE80:1234:ABCD:1::3 (3.3.3.3)
      Origin IGP, metric 0, localpref 100, valid, external, best
```

IPV6 REDISTRIBUTION

In the final section of this chapter, we will learn about the differences between IPv6 and IPv4 redistribution. However, it should be noted that the fundamental redistribution principles described earlier in this guide are applicable as much to IPv4 routing protocols as they are to IPv6 routing protocols. Those same principles (e.g., using appropriate filters) are still very much applicable when implementing route redistribution in IPv6 networks. While the general rules and configuration for IPv6 and IPv4 redistribution are similar, there are some notable differences that you should be familiar with, which include the following:

- With RIPng, if multiple instances are configured on the same router, by default, these instances will share routing information with each other (i.e., with no explicit redistribution configuration) if they use the same default Multicast group and UDP port. This default behavior can be changed by specifying different UDP port numbers for RIPng instances using the port [number] multicast-group [address] router configuration command when configuring the RIPng instances.

- By default, when redistributing between dynamic routing protocols, connected routes are not automatically included in redistribution for IPv6. Instead, the include-connected router configuration command must be appended to the end of the redistribute [protocol] router configuration command.

- When redistributing between IPv6 routing protocols, any route filtering implemented during redistribution (i.e., distribute lists and route maps) must reference either IPv6 ACLs or IPv6 prefix lists.

- When redistributing IPv6 prefixes into OSPFv3, the subnets keyword is not required, as IPv6 does not use Classful networks as IPv4 does.
- By default, all local routes (i.e., routes marked with an 'L' in the RIB) are not included in the route redistribution for any IPv6 routing protocol.
- Only IPv6 global addresses are redistributed. Link-Local addresses, which are used as the next-hop address for IPv6 IGPs, cannot be redistributed.

Configuring and Verifying RIPng Route Redistribution

The redistribution of prefixes into RIPng is a straightforward process that is performed using the redistribute [protocol] metric [hop count] router configuration command. The following configuration example illustrates how to redistribute a connected prefix matched in a specified route map into RIPng and to specify a route metric of 5 during redistribution:

```
R4(config)#ipv6 router rip ROUTE-CLASS
R4(config-rtr)#redistribute connected route-map LOOPBACK metric 5
R4(config-rtr)#exit
R4(config)#route-map LOOPBACK permit 10
R4(config-route-map)#match interface Loopback0
R4(config-route-map)#exit
```

Following this, the prefix would appear in the routing table of an adjacent router as illustrated below:

```
R2#show ipv6 route rip
IPv6 Routing Table - 7 entries
Codes: C - Connected, L - Local, S - Static, R - RIP, B - BGP
       U - Per-user Static route
       I1 - ISIS L1, I2 - ISIS L2, IA - ISIS interarea, IS - ISIS summary
       O - OSPF intra, OI - OSPF inter, OE1 - OSPF ext 1, OE2 - OSPF ext 2
       ON1 - OSPF NSSA ext 1, ON2 - OSPF NSSA ext 2
R    3FFF:1234:ABCD:4::4/128 [120/6]
     via FE80::230:80FF:FE3F:EA82, Ethernet0/1
```

The same could also be validated by viewing the local RIPng database on the adjacent router as illustrated in the following output:

```
R2#show ipv6 rip database
RIP process "INS-1", local RIB
  3FFF:1234:ABCD:4::4/128, metric 6, installed
     Ethernet0/1/FE80::230:80FF:FE3F:EA82, expires in 159 secs
RIP process "INS-2", local RIB
 3FFF:1234:ABCD:2::/64, metric 2
     Serial0/0/FE80::213:19FF:FE86:A20, expires in 179 secs
```

NOTE: You are not expected to perform any advanced RIPng configurations in the ROUTE exam. However, be familiar with the redistribution concepts described in the IPv4 route redistribution chapter, such as using distribute lists and route maps during the redistribution.

Configuring and Verifying EIGRPv6 Route Redistribution

The redistribution of external routing information into EIGRPv6 follows the same logic as that used when redistributing external routing information into EIGRPv4. The following configuration example illustrates how to redistribute connected prefixes into EIGRPv6 without implementing any type of route filtering:

```
R3(config)#ipv6 router eigrp 1
R3(config-rtr)#default-metric 1000000 100 255 1 1500
R3(config-rtr)#redistribute connected
R3(config-rtr)#exit
```

NOTE: While the seed metric is used for redistribution, you can also specify the metric that is used by appending it to the end of the redistribute command.

Assuming two prefixes are matched by this redistribution configuration, the following would be seen from an EIGRPv6 neighbor router:

```
R1#show ipv6 route eigrp
IPv6 Routing Table - default - 6 entries
Codes: C - Connected, L - Local, S - Static, U - Per-user Static route
       B - BGP, HA - Home Agent, MR - Mobile Router, R - RIP
       I1 - ISIS L1, I2 - ISIS L2, IA - ISIS interarea, IS - ISIS summary
       D - EIGRP, EX - EIGRP external, ND - Neighbor Discovery
EX  3FFF:1234:ABCD:2::/64 [170/28416]
     via FE80::1AEF:63FF:FE63:1B00, GigabitEthernet0/0
EX  3FFF:1234:ABCD:3::/64 [170/28416]
     via FE80::1AEF:63FF:FE63:1B00, GigabitEthernet0/0
```

Finally, the EIGRPv6 Topology Table would also provide the same basic information on the external route as that included in the EIGRPv4 Topology Table:

```
R1#show ipv6 eigrp topology 3FFF:1234:ABCD:3::/64
EIGRP-IPv6 Topology Entry for AS(1)/ID(1.1.1.1) for 3FFF:1234:ABCD:3::/64
  State is Passive, Query origin flag is 1, 1 Successor(s), FD is 28416
  Descriptor Blocks:
  FE80::1AEF:63FF:FE63:1B00 (GigabitEthernet0/0), from
FE80::1AEF:63FF:FE63:1B00, Send flag is 0x0
      Composite metric is (28416/28160), route is External
      Vector metric:
        Minimum bandwidth is 1000000 Kbit
        Total delay is 1010 microseconds
        Reliability is 255/255
        Load is 1/255
        Minimum MTU is 1500
        Hop count is 1
      External data:
```

```
Originating router is 3.3.3.3
AS number of route is 0
External protocol is Connected, external metric is 0
Administrator tag is 0 (0x00000000)
```

Configuring and Verifying OSPFv3 Route Redistribution

As was previously stated, the redistribution of routes into OSPFv3 is similar to that of OSPFv2, with the major difference being the exclusion of the `subnets` keyword, as IPv6 does not use Classful boundaries. The following section illustrates how to configure OSPFv3 redistribution. Router R3 is receiving two prefixes via RIP as illustrated in the following output:

```
R3#show ipv6 route rip
IPv6 Routing Table - 11 entries
Codes: C - Connected, L - Local, S - Static, R - RIP, B - BGP
       U - Per-user Static route
       I1 - ISIS L1, I2 - ISIS L2, IA - ISIS interarea, IS - ISIS summary
       O - OSPF intra, OI - OSPF inter, OE1 - OSPF ext 1, OE2 - OSPF ext 2
       ON1 - OSPF NSSA ext 1, ON2 - OSPF NSSA ext 2
R    3FFF:1234:ABCD:3::/64 [120/2]
       via FE80::204:C1FF:FE6F:8741, Serial0/0
R    3FFF:1234:ABCD:4::4/128 [120/7]
       via FE80::204:C1FF:FE6F:8741, Serial0/0
```

The RIP database shows three subnets, the two that are received via Serial0/0 and the connected subnet configured under Serial0/0 as illustrated in the following output:

```
R3#show ipv6 rip database
RIP process "INS-2", local RIB
 3FFF:1234:ABCD:2::/64, metric 2
     Serial0/0/FE80::204:C1FF:FE6F:8741, expires in 163 secs
 3FFF:1234:ABCD:3::/64, metric 2, installed
     Serial0/0/FE80::204:C1FF:FE6F:8741, expires in 163 secs
 3FFF:1234:ABCD:4::/64, metric 7, installed
     Serial0/0/FE80::204:C1FF:FE6F:8741, expires in 163 secs
```

As previously stated, by default, IPv6 routing protocols will not redistribute directly connected subnets unless the `include-connected` keyword is issued when configuring route redistribution. Having stated that, the following configuration example illustrates how to redistribute the RIPng subnets into OSPF as follows:

- The connected subnet will be redistributed using the default OSPF parameters. This will be performed using the `include-connected` keyword.
- The 3FFF:1234:ABCD:3::/64 subnet will be redistributed into OSPFv3 as an external Type 2 LSA (default) with a metric of 15.
- The 3FFF:1234:ABCD:4::4/128 host route will be redistributed into OSPFv3 as an external Type 1 LSA with a metric of 5.

Adhering to these requirements, the redistribution configuration on R3 is performed as follows:

```
R3(config)#ipv6 prefix-list SUBNET-3 seq 5 permit 3FFF:1234:ABCD:3::/64
R3(config)#ipv6 prefix-list SUBNET-4 seq 5 permit 3FFF:1234:ABCD:4::/64
R3(config)#route-map RIP permit 10
R3(config-route-map)#description 'Allow Subnet 3 Only'
R3(config-route-map)#match ipv6 address prefix-list SUBNET-3
R3(config-route-map)#set metric 15
R3(config-route-map)#exit
R3(config)#route-map RIP permit 20
R3(config-route-map)#description 'Allow Subnet 4 Only'
R3(config-route-map)#match ipv6 address prefix-list SUBNET-4
R3(config-route-map)#set metric-type type-1
R3(config-route-map)#set metric 5
R3(config-route-map)#exit
R3(config)#route-map RIP permit 30
R3(config-route-map)#description 'Allow All Other Subnets'
R3(config-route-map)#exit
R3(config)#ipv6 router ospf 3
R3(config-rtr)#redistribute rip INS-2 route-map RIP include-connected
R3(config-rtr)#exit
```

Following this configuration, the LSDB on router R3 displays the external LSA entries below:

```
R3#show ipv6 ospf database

          OSPFv3 Router with ID (3.3.3.3) (Process ID 3)

          Router Link States (Area 0)

ADV Router      Age        Seq#          Fragment ID  Link Count  Bits
1.1.1.1         1014       0x80000004    0            1           None
3.3.3.3         305        0x8000000E    0            1           E

          Net Link States (Area 0)

ADV Router      Age        Seq#          Link ID    Rtr Count
1.1.1.1         1014       0x80000002    4          2

          Link (Type-8) Link States (Area 0)

ADV Router      Age        Seq#          Link ID    Interface
1.1.1.1         1014       0x80000002    4          Fa0/0
3.3.3.3         976        0x80000002    4          Fa0/0

          Intra-Area-Prefix Link States (Area 0)

ADV Router      Age        Seq#          Link ID    Ref-lstype  Ref-LSID
1.1.1.1         1014       0x80000002    4096       0x2002      4

          Type-5 AS External Link States
```

```
ADV Router       Age        Seq#          Prefix
3.3.3.3          534        0x80000002    3FFF:1234:ABCD:3::/64
3.3.3.3          501        0x80000003    3FFF:1234:ABCD:4::/64
3.3.3.3          491        0x80000001    3FFF:1234:ABCD:2::/64
```

To view detailed information, such as the metric and metric types, for the individual Type 5 LSAs, you would simply add the external keyword to the end of the show ipv6 ospf database command as illustrated in the following output:

```
R3#show ipv6 ospf database external

            OSPFv3 Router with ID (3.3.3.3) (Process ID 3)

            Type-5 AS External Link States

  LS age: 349
  LS Type: AS External Link
  Link State ID: 1
  Advertising Router: 3.3.3.3
  LS Seq Number: 80000002
  Checksum: 0x1B96
  Length: 36
  Prefix Address: 3FFF:1234:ABCD:3::
  Prefix Length: 64, Options: None
  Metric Type: 2 (Larger than any Link State path)
  Metric: 15

  LS age: 315
  LS Type: AS External Link
  Link State ID: 3
  Advertising Router: 3.3.3.3
  LS Seq Number: 80000003
  Checksum: 0x966
  Length: 44
  Prefix Address: 3FFF:1234:ABCD:4::
  Prefix Length: 64, Options: None
  Metric Type: 1 (Comparable directly to Link State metric)
  Metric: 5

  LS age: 306
  LS Type: AS External Link
  Link State ID: 4
  Advertising Router: 3.3.3.3
  LS Seq Number: 80000001
  Checksum: 0xBA0
  Length: 36
  Prefix Address: 3FFF:1234:ABCD:2::
  Prefix Length: 64, Options: None
  Metric Type: 2 (Larger than any Link State path)
  Metric: 20
```

Configuring and Verifying MP-BGP Route Redistribution

The configuration of redistribution into MP-BGP follows the same basic concepts as those used with BGP4+, with the exception that for IPv6 the `include-connected` keyword is required to redistribute connected routes and the redistribution configuration must be implemented in the IPv6 address family. To demonstrate the redistribution of external routing information into MP-BGP, consider router R3, which is receiving the following RIPng and OSPFv3 prefixes:

```
R3#show ipv6 route
IPv6 Routing Table - 15 entries
Codes: C - Connected, L - Local, S - Static, R - RIP, B - BGP
       U - Per-user Static route
       I1 - ISIS L1, I2 - ISIS L2, IA - ISIS interarea, IS - ISIS summary
       O - OSPF intra, OI - OSPF inter, OE1 - OSPF ext 1, OE2 - OSPF ext 2
       ON1 - OSPF NSSA ext 1, ON2 - OSPF NSSA ext 2
OE2  2001:1234:ABCD:1::/64 [110/20]
     via FE80:1234:ABCD:1::1, FastEthernet0/0
OE2  2001:1234:ABCD:2::/64 [110/20]
     via FE80:1234:ABCD:1::1, FastEthernet0/0
OE1  2001:1234:ABCD:3::/64 [110/21]
     via FE80:1234:ABCD:1::1, FastEthernet0/0
OE1  2001:1234:ABCD:4::/64 [110/21]
     via FE80:1234:ABCD:1::1, FastEthernet0/0
S    3FFF:1234:ABCD::/48 [1/0]
     via ::, Null0
C    3FFF:1234:ABCD:1::/64 [0/0]
     via ::, FastEthernet0/0
L    3FFF:1234:ABCD:1::3/128 [0/0]
     via ::, FastEthernet0/0
C    3FFF:1234:ABCD:2::/64 [0/0]
     via ::, Serial0/0
L    3FFF:1234:ABCD:2::3/128 [0/0]
     via ::, Serial0/0
R    3FFF:1234:ABCD:3::/64 [120/2]
     via FE80::204:C1FF:FE6F:8741, Serial0/0
R    3FFF:1234:ABCD:4::/64 [120/7]
     via FE80::204:C1FF:FE6F:8741, Serial0/0
S    3FFF:1234:CDEF::/48 [1/0]
     via ::, Null0
S    3FFF:1234:EFAB::/48 [1/0]
     via ::, Null0
L    FE80::/10 [0/0]
     via ::, Null0
L    FF00::/8 [0/0]
     via ::, Null0
```

The following example illustrates how to configure MP-BGP to redistribute all connected RIPng routes for an instance named INS-2, as well as all internal and external OSPFv3 routes into MP-BGP without using any route maps for route filtering:

```
R3(config)#router bgp 3
R3(config-router)#address-family ipv6 unicast
R3(config-router-af)#redistribute rip INS-2 include-connected
R3(config-router-af)#redistribute ospf 3 match internal include-
connected
R3(config-router-af)#redistribute ospf 3 match external 1 external 2
R3(config-router-af)#exit
R3(config-router)#exit
```

NOTE: Keep in mind that the OSPF redistribution configuration can be implemented on a single line. Two different lines have been used to avoid text wrapping in the output above. In the router configuration, the same configuration will be printed as follows:

```
R3#show running-config | section bgp
router bgp 3
 no synchronization
 bgp router-id 3.3.3.3
 bgp log-neighbor-changes
 no auto-summary
 !
 address-family ipv6
  redistribute rip INS-2 include-connected
  redistribute ospf 3 match internal external 1 external 2 include-connected
  no synchronization
 exit-address-family
```

Finally, following this configuration, the MP-BGP RIB on R3 displays the following entries:

```
R3#show bgp ipv6 unicast
BGP table version is 9, local router ID is 3.3.3.3
Status codes: s suppressed, d damped, h history, * valid, > best, i - internal,
              r RIB-failure, S Stale
Origin codes: i - IGP, e - EGP, ? - incomplete

   Network          Next-Hop          Metric LocPrf Weight Path
*> 2001:1234:ABCD:1::/64
                    ::                    20          32768 ?
*> 2001:1234:ABCD:2::/64
                    ::                    20          32768 ?
*> 2001:1234:ABCD:3::/64
                    ::                    21          32768 ?
*> 2001:1234:ABCD:4::/64
                    ::                    21          32768 ?
*> 3FFF:1234:ABCD:1::/64
                    ::                     0          32768 ?
*> 3FFF:1234:ABCD:2::/64
                    ::                     0          32768 ?
*> 3FFF:1234:ABCD:3::/64
                    ::                     2          32768 ?
*> 3FFF:1234:ABCD:4::/64
                    ::                     7          32768 ?
```

NOTE: In the output above, notice that the NEXT_HOP attribute for the redistributed prefixes is no longer the IGP next-hop address (Link-Local) but is, rather, the local BGP speaker itself. This is different from when external IPv4 routing information is redistributed into BGP. However, all other attributes from the IGP (i.e., the route metric) are redistributed into MP-BGP as received.

CHAPTER SUMMARY

The following section is a summary of the major points you should be aware of in this chapter.

The History of Internet Protocol version 6

- IPv5 is an experimental reservation protocol designed to provide Quality of Service
- IPv5 is defined as the Stream Protocol (ST)
- IPv5 provides real-time transport of multimedia such as voice and video data
- IPv5 is comprised of two distinct protocols: ST and SCMP
- ST is used for traditional data transport while SCMP is used for control messages
- IPv5 was never standardized
- Simple Internet Protocol Plus (SIPP) was eventually chosen as the successor of IPv4
- SIPP was subsequently standardized as IPv6 and uses protocol number 41

IPv6 Packet Formats

- Internet Protocol version 6 uses different packets for different functions
- Each IPv6 packet contains a standard 40-byte header
- The Hop-by-Hop Options header notifies routers about any special handling requirements
- The Routing Header allows for source routing in IPv6
- The Fragment Header allows for IPv6 packet or datagram fragmentation
- The Destination Options Header allows sending hosts to state packet-handling requests

Reasons for Migrating to IPv6

- There are several advantages that can be gained by transitioning from IPv4 to IPv6
- The advantages of IPv6 include, but are not limited to, the following:
  1. The Simplified IPv6 Packet Header
  2. Larger Address Space
  3. IPv6 Addressing Hierarchy
  4. IPv6 Extendibility
  5. IPv6 Broadcast Elimination
  6. Stateless Autoconfiguration
  7. Integrated Mobility
  8. Integrated Enhanced Security

IPv6 Addressing

- Unlike IPv4, IPv6 uses 128-bit addresses that are expressed in Hexadecimal notation
- Global 128-bit IPv6 addresses are divided into the following three sections:
  1. The Provider Assigned Prefix
  2. The Site Prefix
  3. The Interface or Host ID

- The provider assigned prefix, which is also referred to as the Global Address Space, is a 48-bit prefix that is divided into three distinct parts, which are as follows:
  1. The 16-bit reserved IPv6 global prefix
  2. The 16-bit provider owned prefix
  3. The 16-bit provider assigned prefix

- The IPv6 global prefix is the prefix that is used to represent the global IPv6 address space
- The 16-bit provider owned prefix is the prefix that is assigned to and owned by the provider
- The site prefix is the next 16-bits following the provider assigned 48-bit prefix
- Following the site prefix, the next 64 bits are used for interface or host addressing

IPv6 Address Representation

- The three ways in which IPv6 addresses can be represented are as follows:
  1. The Preferred or Complete Address Representation or Form
  2. The Compressed Representation
  3. The IPv6 Addresses with an Embedded IPv4 Address

- The preferred or complete representation for an IPv6 address is the longest format used
- The compressed form allows for IPv6 addresses to be compressed in one of the following two ways:
  1. By using the double-colon (::)
  2. By dropping leading zeros

- The IPv6 address with an embedded IPv4 address integrates IPv6 and IPv4 addresses

The Different IPv6 Address Types

- IPv4 supports four different classes of addresses: Anycast, Broadcast, Multicast, and Unicast
- The specific types of addresses used in IPv6 include the following:
  1. Link-Local Addresses
  2. Site-Local Addresses
  3. Aggregate Global Unicast Addresses
  4. Multicast Addresses

5. Anycast Addresses
6. Loopback Addresses
7. Unspecified Addresses

- IPv6 Link-Local can only be used on the local link and are assigned from the FE80::/10 prefix
- Site-Local addresses are Unicast addresses that are used only within a site
- Site-Local addresses are assigned from the FECO::/10 prefix
- Aggregate Global Unicast Addresses are the IPv6 addresses used for generic IPv6 traffic
- Aggregate Global Unicast Addresses for IPv6 are assigned by IANA
- Aggregate Global Unicast Addresses for IPv6 fall within the IPv6 prefix 2000::/3
- The Multicast addresses used in IPv6 are derived from the FF00::/8 IPv6 prefix
- Multicast packets in IPv6 do not use the TTL value to restrict them to the local network
- In IPv6, Anycast addresses use Global Unicast, Site-Local or even Link-Local addresses
- Loopback addresses used in IPv6 are used in the same manner as in IPv4
- Unspecified addresses are simply Unicast addresses that are not assigned to any interface

IPv6 Protocols and Mechanisms
- The IPv6 standard includes different protocols and mechanisms exclusively for IPv6
- These different protocols and mechanisms include the following:
  1. ICMP for IPv6
  2. The IPv6 Neighbor Discovery Protocol
  3. IPv6 Stateful Autoconfiguration
  4. IPv6 Stateless Autoconfiguration

- Unlike in IPv4, IPv6 views ICMPv6 as an upper-layer protocol like TCP, for example
- ICMPv6 supports ICMPv4 messages and includes addition messages specifically for IPv6
- Within IPv6, ICMPv6 is used for the following:
  1. Duplicate Address Detection (DAD)
  2. The replacement of ARP
  3. IPv6 Stateless Autoconfiguration
  4. IPv6 Prefix Renumbering
  5. Path MTU Discovery (PMTUD)

- NDP operates in the Link Layer and is responsible for several IPv6 functions, which include the following:
  1. Discovery of other nodes on the link
  2. Determining the link layer addresses of other nodes
  3. Finding available routers

4. Maintaining reachability information about the paths to other active neighbor nodes

- NDP performs functions for IPv6 similar to IPv4 ARP, IRDP and Router Redirect protocols
- NDP provides greater functionality than the mechanisms used in IPv4
- Used in conjunction with ICMPv6, NDP allows for the following:
    1. Dynamic Neighbor and Router Discovery
    2. The replacement of ARP
    3. IPv6 Stateless Autoconfiguration
    4. Router Redirection
    5. Host Parameter Discovery
    6. IPv6 Address Resolution
    7. Next-Hop Router Determination
    8. Neighbor Unreachability Detection (NUD)
    9. Duplicate Address Detection

- Stateful Autoconfiguration allows IPv6 hosts to receive addressing from a network server
- This method of Autoconfiguration is supported by both IPv4 and IPv6
- In IPv6, DHCPv6 is used to provide stateful Autoconfiguration services for IPv6 hosts
- Stateful Autoconfiguration provides several advantages, which include the following:
    1. Greater controls than those provided by Stateless Autoconfiguration
    2. It can be used on networks when Stateless Autoconfiguration is available
    3. It provides addressing to network hosts in the absence of routers
    4. It can be used for network renumbering by assigning new prefixes to hosts
    5. It can be used to issue entire subnets to customer premise equipment

- Stateless Autoconfiguration allows hosts to configure their own Unicast IPv6 addresses
- This is based on prefix advertisements from routers on the local network segment
- The three main mechanisms that allow for stateless Autoconfiguration in IPv6 are as follows:
    1. Prefix Advertisement
    2. Duplicate Address Detection
    3. Prefix Renumbering

Enabling IPv6 Routing in Cisco IOS Software
- By default, IPv6 routing is disabled in Cisco IOS software and must be manually enabled
- The `ipv6 unicast-routing` global configuration command enables IPv6 routing
- The `ipv6 address` command is used to configure IPv6 interface addressing on routers

Configuring Static IPv6 Routes

- IPv6 static routes are configured using the `ipv6 route` global configuration command
- The configuration of IPv6 static routes follows the same logic as for IPv4 static routes

RIPng for IPv6

- RIP next generation (RIPng) is the successor of RIPv2 but is exclusively for the IPv6 protocol
- RIPng is very similar to RIPv2; however, there are some differences listed in the table below:

Protocol Characteristic	RIPv2	RIPng
Destination Prefix Length	32-bit	128-bit
Next Hop Length	32-bit	128-bit
Next Hop Address	Primary Interface Address	Link-Local Address
Transport	IPv4	IPv6
UDP Port Number	520	521
Authentication	Text and MD5	Inbuilt into IPv6 (IPsec)
Automatic Summarization	Yes (enabled by default)	Not Applicable
Can Broadcast Updates	Yes	Not Applicable

EIGRP for IPv6

- EIGRP for IPv6, also called EIGRPv6, is very similar to EIGRP for IPv4 or EIGRPv4
- The same core routing protocol operation is applicable to both versions, e.g. DUAL
- The differences between EIGRPv4 and EIGRPv6 are listed in the following table:

Protocol Characteristic	EIGRP For IPv4	EIGRP For IPv6
Automatic Summarization	Yes	Not Applicable
Authentication or Security	MD5	Built into IPv6
Common Subnet for Peers	Yes	No
Advertisement Contents	Subnet/Mask	Prefix/Length
Packet Encapsulation	IPv4	IPv6

OSPF version 3

- OSPFv3 is the latest OSPF version, designed and updated explicitly to support IPv6 routing
- Both OSPFv2 and OSPFv3 can run on the same router
- While similar in many ways, OSPFv2 and OSPFv3 have many differences which include:
    1. Unlike OSPFv2, OSPFv3 runs over a link, negating the need to use `network` commands
    2. OSPFv3 uses Link-Local addresses to identify the OSPFv3 adjacencies
    3. OSPFv3 introduces two new OSPF LSA types, which are the Type 8 and Type 9 LSAs
    4. OSPFv3 encapsulates messages (transport) using IPv6 datagrams

5. OSPFv3 uses IPv6 Multicast groups FF02::5 and FF02::6 and not IPv4 Multicast groups

6. OSPFv3 leverages the inbuilt capabilities of IPSec for security

7. The Options field in Hello Packets and DBD packets has been expanded to 24-bits

8. The OSPFv3 Hello packet contains no address information, but includes an Interface ID

BGP4+ or MP-BGP for IPv6

- BGP4+ or MP-BGP extends the BGP4 specification to include multiple protocol extensions
- These multiple protocol extensions allow for address families such as IPv6
- The NEXT_HOP and NLRI attributes have been updated to support protocols like IPv6
- The NEXT_HOP attribute in MP-BGP is defined as an IPv6 address
- This NEXT_HOP attribute can contain the following types of IPv6 addresses:
    1. A global Unicast IPv6 address
    2. A global Unicast IPv6 address and the Link-Local address of the next hop router

- The NLRI attribute defines a set of destinations, which are simply the BGP prefixes
- The NLRI attributes has been updated so that it can be expressed as an IPv6 prefix

IPv6 Redistribution

- For the most part, IPv6 route redistribution follows the same logic as IPv4 redistribution
- However, there are some notable differences between the two, which include the following:
    1. With RIPng, instances using the same port and Multicast group will share information
    2. By default, connected routes are not automatically included in redistribution for IPv6
    3. Route filtering must reference either IPv6 ACLs or IPv6 prefix lists
    4. When redistributing IPv6 prefixes into OSPFv3, the `subnets` keyword is not required
    5. By default, all local routes, are not included in the route redistribution
    6. Only global IPv6 addresses are redistributed; Link-Local prefixes are not redistributed

CHAPTER 9

IPv4 and IPv6 Integration and Coexistence

In the previous chapter on IPv6, we focused exclusively on a pure-IPv6 environment and learned about how IPv6 operates, as well as how the different routing protocols that support IPv6 routing are configured and validated in Cisco IOS software. While it is important to have a solid understanding of IPv6 on its own, the reality of the situation is that IPv4 is still the most predominately used version of the IP protocol. For this reason, it is important to understand how to integrate the two different protocol stacks en route to migrating to a pure-IPv6 environment. The core ROUTE exam objective covered in this chapter is as follows:

- Implement an IPv6-based solution, given a network design and a set of requirements

This chapter contains the following sections:

- Integrating IPv4 and IPv6 Network Environments
- IPv4 and IPv6 Dual-Stack Implementation
- Tunneling IPv6 Datagrams across IPv4 Networks
- Translating between IPv4 and IPv6 Domains
- Additional IPv4 and IPv6 Integration Mechanisms

INTEGRATING IPV4 AND IPV6 NETWORK ENVIRONMENTS

As we learned in the previous chapter, numerous advantages can be gained by migrating from IPv4 to IPv6. To recap, these advantages include the following:

- The simplified IPv6 packet header
- Larger address space
- IPv6 addressing hierarchy
- IPv6 extensibility
- IPv6 Broadcast elimination
- Stateless autoconfiguration
- Integrated mobility
- Integrated enhanced security

NOTE: Because these advantages are described in detail in the previous chapter, they will not be described again in this chapter.

While migrating to an IPv6 environment would offer these advantages, the reality of the present situation is that not all addressable devices support IPv6, and therefore IPv4 and IPv6 must coexist within the same network to devices running the different protocol stacks in order to use the same network infrastructure. IPv4 and IPv6 integration and coexistence strategies are divided into three broad classes as follows:

1. Dual-stack implementations
2. Tunneling
3. Protocol Translation

Dual-stack implementations are those where internetwork devices and hosts use both protocol stacks (i.e., IPv4 and IPv6) at the same time. Dual-stack implementation allows the hosts to use either IPv4 or IPv6 to establish end-to-end IP sessions with other hosts.

NOTE: Dual-stack implementation does not mean that the IPv4-only and IPv6-only hosts have the ability to communicate with each other. To do so, additional protocols and mechanisms are needed. Dual-stack simply means that the hosts (and infrastructure) are able to support both the IPv4 protocol stack and the IPv6 protocol stack.

In situations where dual-stack implementations cannot be used, it is possible to tunnel the IPv6 packets over IPv4 networks. In these implementations, tunnels are used to encapsulate IPv6 packets in IPv4 packets, allowing them to be sent across portions of the network that have not or do not yet natively support IPv6. This allows the IPv6 'islands' to communicate over the underlying IPv4 infrastructure.

NOTE: Tunneling requires that nodes or internetwork devices support dual-stack in order to tunnel the IPv6 packets over the IPv4 infrastructure.

Finally, in some cases, it is possible that IPv4-only environments will need to communicate with IPv6-only environments, and vice-versa. In these situations, neither dual-stack nor tunneling implementations can be used so Protocol Translation between IPv4 and IPv6 must be enabled. While supported, this is the least desirable method of integrating IPv4 and IPv6 networks. However, because it is supported, it is important to understand how to do this.

The remainder of this chapter describes, in detail, these three methods of integrating IPv4 and IPv6 networks. Included are configuration examples specific to Cisco IOS software. We will conclude this chapter by also describing some other techniques that may be used to integrate IPv4 and IPv6 networked environments.

IPV4 AND IPV6 DUAL-STACK IMPLEMENTATIONS

With dual-stack implementations, while some hosts have the capability to use both the IPv4 and the IPv6 protocol stacks, they still require some help in deciding when to use the IPv6 protocol stack instead of the IPv4 protocol stack. Fortunately, this is possible using one of two methods, which are described as follows:

- The first method requires manual configuration by the user. If users know the IPv6 address of the destination IPv6 host, they can use that to establish an IPv6 session manually to that host from their dual-stack host. Although this method works well, it can become quite cumbersome to remember IPv4 and IPv6 addresses for multiple hosts.

- The second method entails using a naming service, such as DNS. With this method, the Fully Qualified Domain Names (FQDN), such as www.howtonetwork.net, are configured using both IPv4 and IPv6 addresses. The FQDN is represented by an A record for the IPv4 protocol stack and an AAAA record for the IPv6 protocol stack, which allows the DNS server to be queried using either IPv4 or IPv6.

Implementing Dual-Stack Support in Cisco IOS Software

While delving into the different ways in which different types of hosts by different vendors can support dual-stack implementations is beyond the scope of the ROUTE exam requirements, as a future network engineer, it is imperative to understand how to implement dual-stack solutions in Cisco IOS software. In Cisco IOS routers, dual-stack operation is enabled by simply configuring both an IPv4 address and an IPv6 address on the router interface.

Multiple IPv4 addresses can be specified by appending the `secondary` keyword to the end of the `ip address [address] [mask]` interface configuration command. For IPv6, however, the secondary keyword is not required, as multiple prefixes can be configured per interface using the `ipv6 address` interface configuration command, which was described in detail in the previous chapter. The following configuration example illustrates how to configure multiple IPv4 and IPv6 addresses and prefixes on a single router interface:

```
R3(config)#ipv6 unicast-routing
R3(config)#interface FastEthernet0/0
R3(config-if)#ip address 10.0.0.3 255.255.255.0
R3(config-if)#ip address 10.0.1.3 255.255.255.0 secondary
R3(config-if)#ip address 10.0.2.3 255.255.255.0 secondary
R3(config-if)#ipv6 address 3fff:1234:abcd:1::3/64
R3(config-if)#ipv6 address 3fff:1234:abcd:2::3/64
R3(config-if)#ipv6 address 3fff:1234:abcd:3::3/64
R3(config-if)#ipv6 enable
R3(config-if)#exit
```

NOTE: While IPv4 routing is enabled by default in Cisco IOS software, IPv6 routing is disabled by default and must be explicitly enabled.

Following the configuration of the IPv4 and IPv6 addresses, you can simply view the router configuration to validate your configuration as illustrated in the following output:

```
R3#show running-config interface FastEthernet0/0
Building configuration...

Current configuration : 395 bytes
!
interface FastEthernet0/0
 ip address 10.0.1.3 255.255.255.0 secondary
 ip address 10.0.2.3 255.255.255.0 secondary
 ip address 10.0.0.3 255.255.255.0
 ipv6 address 3FFF:1234:ABCD:1::3/64
 ipv6 address 3FFF:1234:ABCD:2::3/64
 ipv6 address 3FFF:1234:ABCD:3::3/64
 ipv6 enable
end
```

To view specific IPv4 and IPv6 interface parameters, simply use the Cisco IOS software `show ip interface [name]` or the `show ipv6 interface [name]` commands. Following is the output of the `show ip interface` command for the FastEthernet0/0 interface:

```
R3#show ip interface FastEthernet0/0 | section address
  Internet address is 10.0.0.3/24
  Broadcast address is 255.255.255.255
  Helper address is not set
  Secondary address 10.0.1.3/24
  Secondary address 10.0.2.3/24
  Network address translation is disabled
```

The following output illustrates the information printed by the `show ipv6 interface` command for the same FastEthernet0/0 interface used in the previous example:

```
R3#show ipv6 interface FastEthernet0/0 | section address
  IPv6 is enabled, link-local address is FE80::213:19FF:FE86:A20
  Global unicast address(es):
    3FFF:1234:ABCD:1::3, subnet is 3FFF:1234:ABCD:1::/64
    3FFF:1234:ABCD:2::3, subnet is 3FFF:1234:ABCD:2::/64
    3FFF:1234:ABCD:3::3, subnet is 3FFF:1234:ABCD:3::/64
  Joined group address(es):
    FF02::1
    FF02::2
    FF02::5
    FF02::6
    FF02::9
    FF02::1:FF00:3
  Hosts use stateless autoconfig for addresses.
```

Configuring Static IPv4 and IPv6 Host Addresses in Cisco IOS Software

Cisco IOS software supports the configuration of both static IPv4 and IPv6 host addresses using the `ip host [name] [v4-address]` and `ipv6 host [name] [v6-address]` global configuration commands, respectively. The following example illustrates how to configure static IPv4 and IPv6 host names and addresses in Cisco IOS software:

```
R1(config)#ip host TEST-HOST 10.0.0.3
R1(config)#ipv6 host TEST-HOST 3FFF:1234:ABCD:1::3
```

The static IPv4 and IPv6 host configuration can be validated using the show hosts command, the output of which is printed below:

```
R1#show hosts

[Truncated Output]

Host               Port  Flags       Age Type  Address(es)
TEST-HOST          None  (perm, OK)  0   IP    10.0.0.3
TEST-HOST          None  (perm, OK)  0   IPv6  3FFF:1234:ABCD:1::3
```

When the same host is configured with both a static IPv4 and IPv6 address, Cisco IOS software will use the IPv6 address. If DNS is used, the dual-stack host will first search AAAA (IPv6) records and then fall back to the A records (IPv4) when configured with both IPv6 and IPv4 DNS servers. This default behavior can be validated by performing a simple ping to the previously configured static host 'TEST-HOST' as follows:

```
R1#ping test-host repeat 10

Type escape sequence to abort.
Sending 10, 100-byte ICMP Echos to 3FFF:1234:ABCD:1::3, timeout is 2 seconds:
!!!!!!!!!!
Success rate is 100 percent (10/10), round-trip min/avg/max = 0/1/4 ms
```

Configuring IPv4 and IPv6 DNS Servers in Cisco IOS Software

The configuration of both IPv4 and IPv6 servers in Cisco IOS still uses the ip name-server [address] global configuration command. This same command has now been modified to allow the DNS server IP address to be specified as either an IPv4 or an IPv6 address. The following example illustrates how to configure a router to use both an IPv4 and an IPv6 DNS server:

```
R1(config)#ip name-server ?
  A.B.C.D     Domain server IP address (maximum of 6)
  X:X:X:X::X  Domain server IP address (maximum of 6)
R1(config)#ip name-server 3FFF:1234:ABCD:1::2
R1(config)#ip name-server 192.168.1.2
```

NOTE: As was previously mentioned, when IPv6 and IPv4 DNS servers are configured on the same router, the router will look for the AAAA records first (i.e., IPv6). However, if AAAA records are not found, the host looks for an A record to communicate with the hostname.

Cisco IOS Software IPv6 Application, Tool, and Protocol Support

In addition to DNS and the ping utility, Cisco IOS software provides dual-stack support for several applications, tools, and protocols, which include, but are not limited to, the following:

- Telnet
- SSH
- TFTP
- Traceroute
- HTTP
- Frame Relay
- FHRP

NOTE: While IPv6 support for the applications, protocols, and tools that are listed above will be described briefly in the following sections, keep in mind that going into specific detail and configuration requirements is beyond the scope of the current ROUTE exam requirements and will not be described or illustrated in this chapter.

Cisco IOS supports Telnet use of either IPv4 or IPv6 addresses on dual-stack internetwork devices. The `telnet <address>` command is still used to establish a Telnet session from the local router to the specified destination host, with the exception that in current Cisco IOS software versions the specified address can be either an IPv4 address or an IPv6 address. The following example illustrates how to configure Telnet on an IPv6 device:

```
R3#telnet 3fff:1234:abcd:1::1
Trying 3FFF:1234:ABCD:1::1 ... Open


User Access Verification

Password:
R1#
```

Given that SSH is much more secure than Telnet and should be the preferred method used for the remotely accessing devices, Cisco IOS software supports the use of either IPv4 or IPv6 addresses to establish SSH sessions. The following example illustrates how to configure SSH from one router to another router as user ROUTE while using an IPv6 address:

```
R1#ssh -l ROUTE 3FFF:1234:ABCD:1::3

Password:

R3#
```

Cisco IOS software also allows users to specify either IPv4 or IPv6 addresses when using the Trivial File Transfer Protocol (TFTP), which is commonly used to copy configuration or software images to internetwork devices.

Support for IPv6 addresses when using Traceroute is also integrated into the current Cisco IOS software versions. When using Traceroute, you can directly specify the IPv6 address using the `traceroute <v6-address>` command or using the `traceroute ipv6 <v6-address>` commands. The following is an example of Traceroute using IPv6 addresses:

```
R1#traceroute 3FFF:1234:ABCD:4::4

Type escape sequence to abort.
Tracing the route to 3FFF:1234:ABCD:4::4

  1 3FFF:1234:ABCD:1::3 0 msec 0 msec 4 msec
  2 3FFF:1234:ABCD:2::2 4 msec 4 msec 4 msec
  3 3FFF:1234:ABCD:4::4 8 msec 8 msec 8 msec
```

In current versions of Cisco IOS software, internetwork devices accept incoming HTTP sessions over both IPv4 and IPv6. There is no explicit configuration to enable or disable one protocol while using another. Cisco IOS software HTTP server functionality is still enabled using the `ip http server` global configuration command.

Frame Relay, in addition to other Layer 2 protocols, such as PPP and HDLC, also supports the IPv6 protocol. In Cisco IOS software, static Frame Relay maps are configured to use IPv6 addresses via the `frame-relay map ipv6 [address] [dlci]` interface configuration command. When enabling dynamic IPv6 IGPs over Frame Relay, the Link-Local address should be specified in the static Frame Relay configuration, as these are the addresses that are used to establish adjacencies and neighbor relationships, and as the next-hop addresses. With MP-BGP, global Unicast addresses should be specified if they are used for peering over Frame Relay. The following example illustrates how to configure a static IPv6 Frame Relay map:

```
R2(config)#interface Serial0/0
R2(config-if)#frame-relay map ipv6 FE80::205:5EFF:FE6E:5C80 111 broadcast
```

Finally, in later versions of Cisco IOS software, 12.4T and later, IPv6 support has now been extended to First Hop Redundancy Protocols (FHRP), such as the Hot Standby Router Protocol (HSRP) and the Gateway Load Balancing Protocol (GLBP). HSRP and GLBP are Cisco protocols that are used to allow for a transparent failover of the first-hop IP router.

NOTE: Keep in mind that the different applications, tools, and protocols described in this section are only a subset of the entire suite that is supported in Cisco IOS software.

TUNNELING IPV6 DATAGRAMS ACROSS IPV4 NETWORKS

Tunneling, the second method of integrating IPv6 and IPv4 networks, entails encapsulating the IPv6 packets or datagrams and sending them over IPv4 networks. In order to support the different tunneling mechanisms that will be described in this section, edge Cisco IOS routers must have a dual-stack implementation that allows the IPv6 packets to be encapsulated in IPv4 packets and then de-encapsulated at the terminating router. It should be noted that intermediate routers do not need to run IPv6. In other words, these routers would simply be IPv4-only routers. Figure 9-1 below illustrates a typical tunneling implementation:

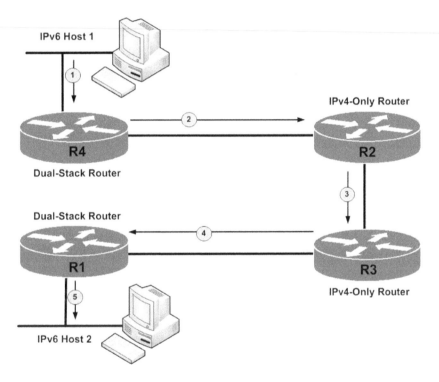

Fig. 9-1. Tunneling IPv6 Packets over IPv4 Networks

Referencing Figure 9-1, assuming that IPv6 Host 1 is sending datagrams to IPv6 Host 2, the following sequence of events occurs as those packets transit the network:

1. IPv6 Host 1 sends the IPv6 packets destined to IPv6 Host 2 to its default gateway, which is router R4. These are native IPv6 packets, with IPv6 source and destination addresses included in the header.

2. Router R4 is a dual-stack router. The LAN interface has been enabled for IPv6, while the WAN interface has been enabled for IPv4. R4 has a tunnel configured between its WAN

interface and the WAN interface of router R1, which is also a dual-stack router. Upon receiving the IPv6 packets, R4 encapsulates them in IPv4 packets and forwards them to R2. The destination address for these packets is sent to router R1 and the router sets the value of the IPv4 header to 41 to indicate encapsulation of IPv6 packets in IPv4 packets.

3. R2 receives the IPv4 packets and simply routes or forwards those toward their final destination using the destination address specified in the IPv4 header.

4. R3 receives the IPv4 packets from R2 and simply forwards those toward their final destination using the destination address specified in the IPv4 packet header.

5. Router R5, the terminating router and exit point for the tunnel, receives the native IPv4 packets and de-encapsulates them, leaving only the IPv6 datagrams. The router then forwards the IPv6 packets to Host 2.

The encapsulation and de-encapsulation process is transparent to the two hosts, as well as to the intermediate routers between the tunnel endpoints. Several methods can be used to tunnel IPv6 packets in IPv4 packets. These, which will be described in detail in the following sections, include the following:

• Static (manually configured) IPv6 tunneling
• 6to4 tunneling
• Automatic IPv4-compatible tunneling
• ISATAP tunneling
• Generic Routing Encapsulation tunneling

Static (Manually Configured) IPv6 Tunneling

Static IPv6-in-IPv4 tunneling requires the static configuration of tunnels on dual-stack devices in order to allow IPv6 packets to be tunneled across the IPv4 network. While the tunnel is assigned an IPv6 address, the tunnel source and destination addresses are configured using the IPv4 addresses of the two end-point routers. The tunnel destination address is the address that in included in the IPv4 packet header, which allows other intermediate devices that are only running IPv4 to know where to send these packets.

Following the configuration of static tunnels, static or dynamic routing protocols can be used to provide reachability to remote IPv6 subnets across the tunnel(s). All the routing protocols described in the previous chapter can be enabled on Tunnel interfaces. Similarly, static IPv6 routes can also be configured to point out of Tunnel interfaces.

The configuration of static tunnels in Cisco IOS software is a straightforward process. The following section goes through the configuration steps required to create static, or manually configured, tunnels for encapsulating IPv6 packets within IPv4 packets:

1. Configure a static Tunnel interface using the `interface tunnel [number]` global configuration command. The number range will vary depending on the version of Cisco IOS software that the router on which the tunnel is being configured is running.

2. Assign the static Tunnel interface an IPv6 address using the `ipv6 address` interface configuration command. You can use site local or global Unicast address ranges.

3. Configure a tunnel source for the static tunnel using the `tunnel source [IPv4 address | interface]` interface configuration command. This is used as the tunnel source address. All packets sent across this tunnel will have this IPv4 address as the source address included in the IPv4 packet header. This is typically a Loopback interface but can be any interface with a globally routable IP address.

4. Configure a tunnel destination for the static tunnel using the `tunnel destination [IPv4 address]` interface configuration command. This is the IPv4 address of the tunnel endpoint (i.e., the far-end side of the tunnel). This address should be the same as the tunnel source address for the tunnel endpoint.

5. Specify IPv6 as the passenger protocol and IPv4 as both the encapsulation and transport protocol for the manual IPv6 tunnel using the `tunnel mode ipv6ip` interface configuration command.

6. Configure either static routes to remote IPv6 subnets across the Tunnel interface using the `ipv6 route <prefix/length> tunnel <number>` global configuration command or enable a dynamic IPv6-capable routing protocol across the static tunnel.

The network topology in Figure 9-2 below will be used to illustrate the configuration of the different tunneling mechanisms that will be described in this section.

NOTE: The IP addresses of the intermediate routers in this topology are irrelevant. All that is required is IP connectivity between the Loopback0 interfaces of routers R1 and R4.

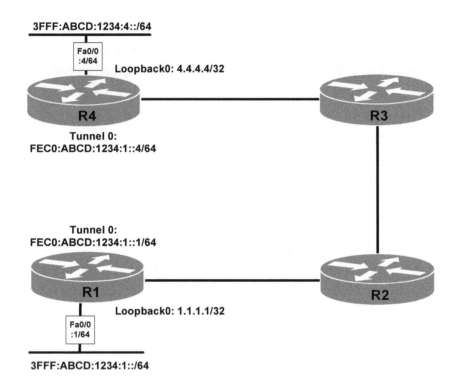

3FFF:ABCD:1234:4::/64

Fa0/0
:4/64

Loopback0: 4.4.4.4/32

R4

R3

Tunnel 0:
FEC0:ABCD:1234:1::4/64

Tunnel 0:
FEC0:ABCD:1234:1::1/64

R1

R2

Loopback0: 1.1.1.1/32

Fa0/0
:1/64

3FFF:ABCD:1234:1::/64

Fig. 9-2. Static Tunneling of IPv6 Packets over IPv4 Networks

NOTE: Prior to beginning the implementation of manually configured tunnels, a simple ping test should be used to validate Loopback-to-Loopback connectivity between R1 and R4. The ping test, initiated from R1, verifies end-to-end connectivity between the two Loopback interfaces:

```
R1#ping 4.4.4.4 source 1.1.1.1 repeat 10

Type escape sequence to abort.
Sending 10, 100-byte ICMP Echos to 4.4.4.4, timeout is 2 seconds:
Packet sent with a source address of 1.1.1.1
!!!!!!!!!!!
Success rate is 100 percent (10/10), round-trip min/avg/max = 4/4/8 ms
```

Continuing with the configuration of static, or manually, configured IPv6 tunneling, and going through the steps described previously, router R1 is configured as follows (you can configure the Loopback interfaces yourself):

```
R1(config)#ipv6 unicast-routing
R1(config)#interface Tunnel0
R1(config-if)#ipv6 address fec0:abcd:1234:1::1/64
R1(config-if)#ipv6 enable
R1(config-if)#tunnel source Loopback0
R1(config-if)#tunnel destination 4.4.4.4
R1(config-if)#tunnel mode ipv6ip
```

```
R1(config-if)#exit
R1(config)#interface FastEthernet0/0
R1(config-if)#ipv6 address 3fff:abcd:1234:1::1/64
R1(config-if)#ipv6 enable
R1(config-if)#exit
R1(config)#ipv6 route 3fff:abcd:1234:4::/64 Tunnel0
```

Following the same sequence of steps, router R4 is configured as follows:

```
R4(config)#ipv6 unicast-routing
R4(config)#interface Tunnel0
R4(config-if)#ipv6 address fec0:abcd:1234:1::4/64
R4(config-if)#ipv6 enable
R4(config-if)#tunnel source Loopback0
R4(config-if)#tunnel destination 1.1.1.1
R4(config-if)#tunnel mode ipv6ip
R4(config-if)#exit
R4(config)#interface FastEthernet0/0
R4(config-if)#ipv6 address 3fff:abcd:1234:4::1/64
R4(config-if)#ipv6 enable
R4(config-if)#exit
R4(config)#ipv6 route 3fff:abcd:1234:1::/64 Tunnel0
```

Following the configuration of the tunnels, the show interfaces command can be used to verify the status of the tunnel. The output of this command displays the following on R4:

```
R4#show interfaces Tunnel0
Tunnel0 is up, line protocol is up
  Hardware is Tunnel
  MTU 1514 bytes, BW 9 Kbit/sec, DLY 500000 usec,
     reliability 255/255, txload 1/255, rxload 1/255
  Encapsulation TUNNEL, Loopback not set
  Keepalive not set
  Tunnel source 4.4.4.4 (Loopback0), destination 1.1.1.1
  Tunnel protocol/transport IPv6/IP
  Tunnel TTL 255
  Fast tunneling enabled
  Tunnel transmit bandwidth 8000 (kbps)
  Tunnel receive bandwidth 8000 (kbps)

...

[Truncated Output]
```

The output of the show interfaces command prints out the configured tunnel parameters, which include the tunnel source and destination IPv4 addresses as well as encapsulation mode. Additional information, such as tunnel bandwidth and MTU, is also provided. However, it should be noted that while a value of 1514 is shown for the tunnel MTU, the default MTU value for manually configured tunnels in Cisco IOS software is 1480 bytes. This can be validated using the show ip interfaces command for tunnels configured with an IPv4 address or the show ipv6 interfaces command for those with an IPv6 address. Given that only an IPv6 address is configured on the Tunnel interfaces in this example, the show ipv6 interfaces command is used and it displays the following information:

```
R4#show ipv6 interface Tunnel0
Tunnel0 is up, line protocol is up
  IPv6 is enabled, link-local address is FE80::404:404
  Global unicast address(es):
    FEC0:ABCD:1234:1::4, subnet is FEC0:ABCD:1234:1::/64
  Joined group address(es):
    FF02::1
    FF02::2
    FF02::1:FF00:4
    FF02::1:FF04:404
  MTU is 1480 bytes

...


[Truncated Output]
```

To verify the operation of the tunnel, you can use a simple ping sourced from the LAN subnet of either router to the LAN subnet of the other router as illustrated in the following output:

```
R4#ping 3fff:abcd:1234:1::1 source 3fff:abcd:1234:4::4 repeat 10

Type escape sequence to abort.
Sending 10, 100-byte ICMP Echos to 3FFF:ABCD:1234:1::1, timeout is 2 seconds:
Packet sent with a source address of 3FFF:ABCD:1234:4::4
!!!!!!!!!!
Success rate is 100 percent (10/10), round-trip min/avg/max = 4/4/8 ms
```

6to4 Tunneling

6to4 tunnels are defined in RFC 3056 and are designed to allow IPv6 end sites to access the IPv6 backbone, commonly referred to as the 6bone, by tunneling across the IPv4 Internet. The 6bone is simply a worldwide information collaborative IPv6 test bed that is an outgrowth of the IETF IP Next Generation (IPng) project. The IPng designed and created the IPv6 protocol. Unlike static tunnel configuration, 6to4 tunneling has three main characteristics, which make it unique from static tunnel implementation. These characteristics include the following:

- Automatic or dynamic tunneling
- Automatic prefix assignment
- There is no IPv6 route propagation

6to4 automatic tunneling provides a dynamic method to deploy tunnels between IPv6 sites over IPv4 networks. Unlike with manually configured tunnels, there is no need to configure tunnel source and destination addresses manually in order to establish the tunnels. Instead, the tunneling of IPv6 packets between 6to4 sites is performed dynamically based on the destination IPv6 address of the packets originated by IPv6 hosts. These packets are then encapsulated in IPv4, and IPv4 routing protocols are used to transport the packets between the source and destination hosts.

Automatic prefix assignment provides a global aggregatable IPv6 prefix to each 6to4 site. This prefix is based on the 2002::/16 prefix assigned by IANA for 6to4 sites. As stated earlier in this section, the tunnel endpoint, or destination, is determined by the globally unique IPv4 address embedded in a 6to4 address. This address must be one that is globally routable. In other words, RFC 191 (private IP addresses) cannot be used for 6to4 tunnels because they are not unique. This 32-bit IPv4 address is converted to Hexadecimal characters and the final representation is a 48-bit prefix. For example, if the IP address 1.1.1.1 was embedded into the IPv6 6to4 prefix, the final representation would be 2002:0101:0101::/48.

Finally, 6to4 tunneling uses special addresses that are a combination of the unique IPv6 routing prefix 2002::/16 and a globally unique 32-bit IPv4 address. With 6to4 tunneling, the tunnel endpoint (destination) is determined by the globally unique IPv4 address embedded in the 6to4 address. Because 6to4 prefixes are based on the globally unique IPv4 address, the 48-bit IPv6 routes do not need to be propagated between 6to4 sites.

> **NOTE:** It is important to note that these special addresses used in 6to4 tunneling are not the same as the IPv4-compatible IPv6 addresses described in the previous chapter. The IPv4-compatible IPv6 addresses cannot be used for automatic 6to4 tunnels.

Because 6to4 tunneling may seem somewhat confusing at first glance, Figure 9-3 below will be used to illustrate how this tunneling mechanism works:

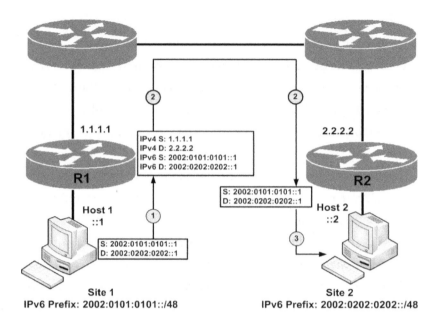

Fig. 9-3. Understanding 6to4 Tunneling

Referencing Figure 9-3, and assuming that Host 1 in Site 1 is sending packets to Host 2 in Site 2, the 6to4 tunneling mechanism works in the following manner:

1. Host 1 sends an IPv6 packet to Host 2 using an IPv6 source address of 2002:0101.0101::1 and an IPv6 destination address of 2002:0202.0202::2.

2. The packet is received by router R1, which is the default gateway for Host 1. R1 looks at the packet and extracts the embedded IPv4 address of 02.02.02.02, or simply 2.2.2.2. By doing this, router R1 knows that this packet should be forwarded to router R2. R1 then encapsulates the IPv6 packet(s) in IPv4 packets that contain a source address of 1.1.1.1, which is router R1's unique IPv4 global address and a destination address of 2.2.2.2, which is router R2's unique IPv4 global address. During this process, it is important to know that the source and destination fields in the IPv6 packet(s) remain unchanged. The packet is forwarded to router R2 by intermediate routers.

3. R2 receives the packet and de-encapsulates it. The IPv6 packet shows a destination address of 2002:0202.0202::2, and so R2 forwards the native IPv6 packet to Host 2.

The entire process is transparent to Host 1 and Host 2 and allows the two hosts to establish an end-to-end IPv6 session. Before we discuss the sequence of configuration steps required to implement 6to4 tunneling in Cisco IOS software, it is important to know first the restrictions and considerations to be mindful of when implementing 6to4 tunneling. These include the following:

• Using private IP addresses
• Prefix renumbering
• Traffic and protocol filtering

Because 6to4 tunneling uses globally unique IPv4 addresses, you cannot use RFC 1918 address space or any other subnets (e.g., Martians) that are not permitted on the Internet. Given that the site prefix for 6to4 tunneling is based on the unique IPv4 global address of the edge router, if the edge router IP address is changed, then the entire site must be renumbered using the new unique edge router IP global address. Finally, prior to enabling 6to4 tunneling, make sure that protocol and traffic filtering allows protocol 41. Additionally, it should be noted that filtering on inbound source addresses can also break 6to4 tunneling. Consideration should therefore be given to alternative methods of network security, if traffic and protocol filtering are not implemented, so that 6to4 tunneling works.

The configuration of 6to4 tunneling in Cisco IOS software is somewhat similar to that of static tunnels with the exception that no static tunnel destinations are configured. The following sequence of configuration steps is required to implement 6to4 tunneling in Cisco IOS software:

1. Configure an IPv6 address on the internal (inside) 6to4 site interface. This is typically the LAN interface to which IPv6 hosts are connected. This is configured using the `ipv6 address [address/prefix-length]` interface configuration command. When you configure the site prefix, it must come from the 2002::/16 range.

2. Configure a static Tunnel interface using the `interface tunnel [number]` global configuration command. The number range will vary depending on the version of Cisco IOS software that the router on which the tunnel is being configured is running.

3. Configure a tunnel source for the static tunnel using the `tunnel source [IPv4 address | interface]` interface configuration command. This is used as the tunnel source address. All packets sent across this tunnel will have this IPv4 address as the source address included in the IPv4 packet header. This is typically a Loopback interface but can be any interface with a globally routable IPv4 address.

4. Configure the Tunnel interface as an unnumbered interface that will use the IPv6 address of the inside (internal) 6to4 site interface using the `ipv6 unnumbered [interface name]` interface configuration command.

5. Specify IPv6 as the passenger protocol and IPv4 as both the encapsulation and transport protocol for the dynamic IPv6 tunnel and specify 6to4 operation using the `tunnel mode ipv6ip 6to4` interface configuration command.

6. Configure a static route to remote 6to4 IPv6 subnets across the Tunnel interface using the `ipv6 route <prefix/length> tunnel <number>` global configuration command.

The same topology used in Figure 9-2, which is shown again below in Figure 9-4 for ease of reading, will be used to illustrate the configuration of 6to4 tunneling in Cisco IOS software between Site 1 (R1) and Site 4 (R4):

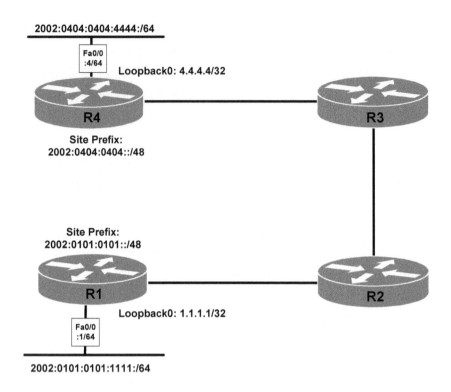

Fig. 9-4. Implementing 6to4 Tunneling in Cisco IOS Software

Following the sequence of steps described in the previous section, R1 is configured as follows:

```
R1(config)#ipv6 unicast-routing
R1(config)#interface Loopback0
R1(config-if)#ip address 1.1.1.1 255.255.255.255
R1(config-if)#exit
R1(config)#interface FastEthernet0/0
R1(config-if)#ipv6 address 2002:0101:0101:1111::1/64
R1(config-if)#ipv6 enable
R1(config-if)#exit
R1(config)#interface Tunnel0
R1(config-if)#ipv6 unnumbered FastEthernet0/0
R1(config-if)#tunnel source Loopback0
R1(config-if)#tunnel mode ipv6ip 6to4
R1(config-if)#exit
R1(config)#ipv6 route 2002::/16 Tunnel0
```

Following the same sequence of commands, router R4 is configured as follows:

```
R4(config)#ipv6 unicast-routing
R4(config)#interface Loopback0
R4(config-if)#ip address 4.4.4.4 255.255.255.255
R4(config-if)#exit
R4(config)#interface FastEthernet0/0
R4(config-if)#ipv6 address 2002:0404:0404:4444::4/64
```

```
R4(config-if)#ipv6 enable
R4(config-if)#exit
R4(config)#interface Tunnel0
R4(config-if)#ipv6 unnumbered FastEthernet0/0
R4(config-if)#tunnel source Loopback0
R4(config-if)#tunnel mode ipv6ip 6to4
R4(config-if)#exit
R4(config)#ipv6 route 2002::/16 Tunnel0
```

Again, following this configuration, it would be prudent to validate the tunnel state using the show interfaces command as was illustrated in the previous configuration example. Additionally, the show ipv6 interfaces command can also be used to verify IPv6 address configuration and other default interface parameters, such as the 1480-byte MTU. However, because the output will be similar to that in the previous example, this verification will be omitted in this section. To verify the operation of the 6to4 tunnel, a simple ping can be used to send LAN-to-LAN packets between the two routers as illustrated in the following output:

```
R4#ping 2002:0101:0101:1111::1 source 2002:0404:0404:4444::4 repeat 10

Type escape sequence to abort.
Sending 10, 100-byte ICMP Echos to 2002:101:101:1111::1, timeout is 2 seconds:
Packet sent with a source address of 2002:404:404:4444::4
!!!!!!!!!!
Success rate is 100 percent (10/10), round-trip min/avg/max = 4/4/8 ms
```

Automatic IPv4-compatible Tunneling

Automatic IPv4-compatible tunnels enable IPv6 hosts to enable tunnels automatically to other IPv6 hosts across an IPv4 network infrastructure. Unlike 6to4 tunneling, automatic IPv4-compatible tunneling does use the IPv4-compatible IPv6 addresses. Automatic IPv4-compatible tunnels use the IPv6 prefix ::/96. To complete the 128-bit IPv6 address, the low-order 32-bits are derived from the IPv4 address. These low-order 32-bits of the source and destination IPv6 addresses represent the source and destination IPv4 addresses of the tunnel endpoints in the same manner as the 6to4 tunnels, which were described in the previous section. Therefore, with automatic IPv4-compatible tunneling, the host or router at each end of an IPv4-compatible tunnel must support both the IPv4 and the IPv6 protocol stacks.

IPv4-compatible tunnels can be configured between border routers or between a border router and a host. While using IPv4-compatible tunnels is an easy method to create tunnels for IPv6 over IPv4, the technique does not scale well for large networks. Automatic IPv4-compatible tunnels are similar to manual IPv6 tunnels, with the exception that there is no destination address for the configured Tunnel interface. Instead, the Tunnel interface destination address is assigned dynamically from the IPv6 next-hop address of the IPv6 route. This functionality is enabled by using the tunnel mode `ipv6ip auto-tunnel` interface configuration command on the Tunnel interface, as will be illustrated later in this section.

In addition, in order to use automatic IPv4-compatible tunneling, you need to specify the next-hop of the IPv6 address by using either an explicit BGP neighbor address for MP-BGP or an IPv6 static route. While static routes are supported, the recommended method when implementing this tunneling mechanism is to use MP-BGP, which was described in the previous chapter and will be used in the following configuration example.

Automatic IPv4-compatible tunneling is considered obsolete and, while still supported in Cisco IOS software, is being deprecated. For this reason, while the explicit tasks required to implement this type of tunneling are excluded from this chapter, the following example illustrates configurations on two routers that are configured for automatic IPv4-compatible tunneling:

```
R1(config-if)#interface FastEthernet0/0
R1(config-if)#ipv6 address 3fff:abcd:1234:1::1/64
R1(config-if)#ipv6 enable
R1(config-if)#exit
R1(config-if)#interface Serial0/0
R1(config-if)#ip address 111.1.1.1 255.255.255.0
R1(config-if)#exit
R1(config)#interface Tunnel0
R1(config-if)#tunnel source Serial0/0
R1(config-if)#tunnel mode ipv6ip auto-tunnel
R1(config-if)#exit
R1(config)#router bgp 1
R1(config-router)#bgp router-id 1.1.1.1
R1(config-router)#no bgp default ipv4-unicast
R1(config-router)#neighbor ::222.2.2.2 remote-as 2
R1(config-router)#address-family ipv6 unicast
R1(config-router-af)#neighbor ::222.2.2.2 activate
R1(config-router-af)#neighbor ::222.2.2.2 next-hop-self
R1(config-router-af)#network 3ffe:abcd:1234:1::/64
R1(config-router-af)#exit
R1(config-router)#exit
R1(config)#exit
```

In a similar manner, the automatic IPv4-compatible tunnel configuration is implemented on router R4 in the following manner:

```
R2(config)#interface FastEthernet0/0
R2(config-if)#ipv6 address 3fff:abcd:5678:1::2/64
R2(config-if)#ipv6 enable
R2(config-if)#exit
R2(config)#interface Serial0/0
R2(config-if)#ip address 222.2.2.2 255.255.255.0
```

```
R2(config-if)#ipv6 enable
R2(config-if)#exit
R2(config)#interface Tunnel0
R2(config-if)#tunnel source Serial0/0
R2(config-if)#tunnel mode ipv6ip auto-tunnel
R2(config-if)#exit
R2(config)#router bgp 2
R2(config-router)#bgp router-id 2.2.2.2
R2(config-router)#no bgp default ipv4-unicast
R2(config-router)#neighbor ::111.1.1.1 remote-as 1
R2(config-router)#address-family ipv6
R2(config-router-af)#neighbor ::111.1.1.1 activate
R2(config-router-af)#neighbor ::111.1.1.1 next-hop-self
R2(config-router-af)#network 3fff:abcd:5678:1::/64
R2(config-router-af)#exit
R2(config-router)#exit
R2(config)#exit
```

Following the configuration, you can verify the received MP-BGP prefixes by viewing the BGP RIB on the local router using the show bgp ipv6 unicast command as follows:

```
R1#show bgp ipv6 unicast 3fff:abcd:5678:1::/64
BGP routing table entry for 3FFF:ABCD:5678:1::/64, version 6
Paths: (1 available, best #1, table Global-IPv6-Table)
  Not advertised to any peer
  2
    ::222.2.2.2 from ::222.2.2.2 (2.2.2.2)
      Origin IGP, metric 0, localpref 100, valid, external, best
```

Finally, this configuration can be validated using a simple LAN-to-LAN ping as follows:

```
R1#ping 3fff:abcd:5678:1::2 source 3fff:abcd:1234:1::1 repeat 10

Type escape sequence to abort.
Sending 10, 100-byte ICMP Echos to 3FFF:ABCD:5678:1::2, timeout is 2
seconds:
Packet sent with a source address of 3FFF:ABCD:1234:1::1
!!!!!!!!!!
Success rate is 100 percent (10/10), round-trip min/avg/max = 4/4/8 ms
```

ISATAP Tunneling

Intra-Site Automatic Tunnel Addressing Protocol (ISATAP) is an automatic overlay tunneling mechanism that uses the underlying IPv4 network as an NBMA Link Layer for IPv6. As the name suggests, ISATAP is designed for transporting IPv6 packets within a site where a native IPv6 infrastructure is not yet available. ISATAP tunnels allow individual IPv4 or IPv6 dual-stack hosts within a site to communicate with other such hosts on the same virtual link, creating a virtual IPv6 network using the IPv4 infrastructure. The main functionalities and components of ISATAP are automatic tunneling, the ISATAP address format, prefixes, the interface ID, and ISATAP prefix advertisement.

ISATAP tunnels are established between ISATAP hosts or between an ISATAP host and an ISA-TAP router. These tunnels are created automatically because there is no need to apply any manual configuration on hosts when ISATAP support is enabled. However, for ISATAP tunnels between ISATAP hosts and ISATAP routers, the ISATAP host must initially find the IP address of an ISA-TAP router from the Potential Router List, which is simply a list that contains the IPv4 addresses of all the ISATAP routers within a site.

ISATAP addresses assigned to ISATAP routers and hosts are created using the concatenation of an IPv6 global Unicast address dedicated to the ISATAP operation and the special format of the inter-face ID. The ISATAP prefix represents the high-order 64-bits of the IPv6 address. A single ISATAP address is enabled on the ISATAP host using the Link-Local prefix FE80::/10 and another global, or Site-Local 64-bit, prefix is assigned for ISATAP operation within the site. This prefix is then re-ceived by ISATAP hosts from router advertisement messages sent by ISATAP routers through the ISATAP tunnels established over the IPv4 infrastructure.

The interface ID used in ISATAP represents the low-order 64-bits of the IPv6 address assigned to the ISATAP host. ISATAP embeds IPv4 addresses in IPv6 addresses, in the same manner used in 6to4 tunneling. This interface ID is created by appending the 32-bit IPv4 address to the high-order 32-bit value 0000:5EFE. This value has been reserved by IANA exclusively for ISATAP use. Un-doubtedly, this all sounds very confusing. Therefore, to simplify the ISATAP addressing concept, Figure 9-5 below illustrates ISATAP address assignment for an ISATAP host and router:

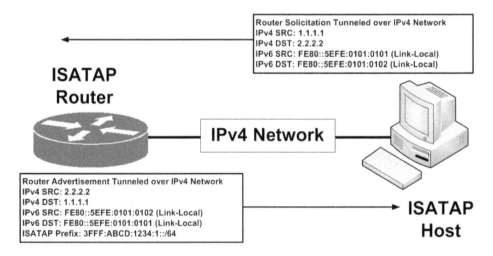

Fig. 9-5. Understanding Host-to-Router ISATAP Tunneling

Referencing Figure 9-5, after being enabled, the ISATAP host with the IPv4 address 1.1.1.1 will derive its Link-Local address by appending the 32-bit IPv4 address to the high-order 32-bit value 0000:5EFE, resulting in the Link-Local address FE80:: 5EFE:0101:0101. Once the Link-Local address has been derived, the host sends out a Route Solicitation message to the ISATAP router using an ISATAP tunnel. The ISATAP router responds with a Router Advertisement message specifying the prefix defined within the site, which is 3FFF:ABCD:1234:1::/64. Once the ISATAP host receives this prefix, it will automatically configure an IPv6 global address using ISATAP format based on this prefix. This global address is derived by appending the same low-order 64-bits that is used in the Link-Local address. The global address would therefore be 3FFF:ABCD:1234:1:0:5E FE:0101:0101. The ISATAP host then configures the Link-Local address of the router as its default gateway. Finally, when the ISATAP host has to send IPv6 packets to the ISATAP router, the host's interface will automatically encapsulate the IPv6 packets in IPv4 packets and send them across the IPv4 infrastructure. These IPv4 packets will use 1.1.1.1 as the source address and 2.2.2.2 as the destination address within the IPv4 header.

ISATAP router functionality is supported in Cisco IOS software; however, there is no support for ISATAP host functionality. Therefore, while understanding ISATAP host-to-router operation helps with the general understanding of the standard, greater emphasis should be placed on understanding router-to-router communication when ISATAP tunnels are implemented. As an example, consider the topology illustrated in Figure 9-6 below:

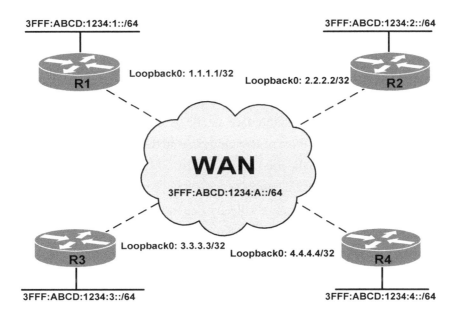

Fig. 9-6. Understanding Router-to-Router ISATAP Tunneling

In the topology illustrated in Figure 9-6, four routers are connected across a WAN. Each router has an IPv6 subnet assigned to its local LAN interface, to which IPv6 hosts are connected. ISATAP tunnels are configured on all routers. The global prefix used for these addresses is 3FFF:ABCD:1234:A::/64.

The tunnel source for these tunnels is the local Loopback0 interface on each router. From this address, each router derives the IPv6 address by appending the 32-bit IPv4 address to the high-order 32-bit value 0000:5EFE. For example, the address for the Tunnel interface on router R1 would be 3FFF:ABCD:1234:A:0:5EFE:0101:0101, while for router R2 it would be 3FFF:ABCD:1234:A:0:5EFE:0202:0202, and so forth for the remaining two routers. Each router would then be configured with static routes to the remote subnets that point to the ISATAP address of the remote router. Alternatively, BGP could also be used to advertise prefixes dynamically.

Given this, and assuming static route configuration, if, for example, router R1 received a packet from host 3FFF:ABCD:1234:1::1 that was destined to host 3FFF:ABCD:1234:4::1, then the packets would match the static route to the 3FFF:ABCD:1234:4::/64 subnet that pointed to the next-hop IPv6 address of 3FFF:ABCD:1234:A:0:5EFE:0404:0404. From this address, the router would use the low-order 32-bits to determine the tunnel's destination IPv4 address, which would be 4.4.4.4. The router would subsequently encapsulate the IPv6 packets and send them to router R4.

The configuration of ISATAP tunnels in Cisco IOS software is somewhat similar to configuring other automatic tunneling mechanisms in that you do not specify a tunnel destination. However, some differences are unique to the configuration of ISATAP tunneling. The following section describes the sequence of steps required to implement ISATAP tunnels:

1. Configure an interface and assign it an IPv4 address using the `ip address` interface configuration command. While any interface can be used, it is recommended that a Loopback interface be used, as it is the most resilient interface on the router. You should also ensure that this address is advertised to the rest of the network.

2. Configure a Tunnel interface using the `interface tunnel [number]` global configuration command. The number range will vary depending on the version of Cisco IOS software that the router on which the tunnel is being configured is running.

3. Configure a tunnel source for the static tunnel using the `tunnel source [IPv4 address | interface]` interface configuration command. This is used as the tunnel source address. All packets sent across this tunnel will have this IPv4 address as the source address included in the IPv4 packet header.

4. Specify IPv6 as the passenger protocol and IPv4 as both the encapsulation and transport protocol, and specify that this is an ISATAP tunnel using the `tunnel mode ipv6ip isatap` interface configuration command.

5. Assign the Tunnel interface an IPv6 address using the `ipv6 address [prefix / length]` `eui-64` interface configuration command. You can use site local or global Unicast address ranges.

6. Enable ICMP Router Advertisement messages on the Tunnel interface using the `no ipv6 nd suppress-ra` interface configuration command.

7. Configure static IPv6 routes to one or more remote destinations using the `ipv6 route` global configuration command. Alternatively, you can also use MP-BGP to advertise the subnets dynamically.

To reinforce what has been described in this section, the topology illustrated in Figure 9-7 below will be used to illustrate the configuration and verification of ISATAP tunnels:

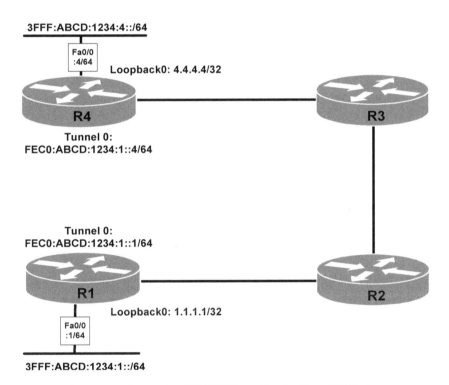

Fig. 9-7. Implementing ISATAP Tunneling in Cisco IOS Software

Following the sequence of configuration steps described previously, R1 is configured as follows:

```
R1(config)#ipv6 unicast-routing
R1(config)#interface FastEthernet0/0
R1(config-if)#ipv6 address 3fff:abcd:1234:1::1/64
R1(config-if)#ipv6 enable
R1(config-if)#exit
R1(config)#interface Loopback0
R1(config-if)#ip address 1.1.1.1 255.255.255.255
R1(config-if)#exit
```

```
R1(config)#interface Tunnel0
R1(config-if)#tunnel source Loopback0
R1(config-if)#tunnel mode ipv6ip isatap
R1(config-if)#ipv6 address fec0:abcd:1234:1::/64 eui-64
R1(config-if)#no ipv6 nd suppress-ra
R1(config-if)#exit
R1(config)#ipv rout 3fff:abcd:1234:4::/64 fec0:abcd:1234:1:0:5efe:0404:0404
R1(config)#exit
```

If you are wondering how I was able to determine the IPv6 next-hop address for the subnet that is connected to R4 before even configuring the router, I simply followed the logic of ISATAP addressing. Given the prefix, the last 64-bits of the address would be 5EFE:0404:0404 based on the IP address that will be configured as specified in the topology. The same logic is applicable to R1 and can be validated using the show ipv6 interface command as follows:

```
R1#show ipv6 interface Tunnel0
Tunnel0 is up, line protocol is up
  IPv6 is enabled, link-local address is FE80::5EFE:101:101
  Global unicast address(es):
    FEC0:ABCD:1234:1:0:5EFE:101:101, subnet is FEC0:ABCD:1234:1::/64 [EUI]
  Joined group address(es):
    FF02::1
    FF02::2
    FF02::1:FF01:101
  MTU is 1480 bytes
  ICMP error messages limited to one every 100 milliseconds
  ICMP redirects are enabled
  ND DAD is not supported
  ND reachable time is 30000 milliseconds
  ND advertised reachable time is 0 milliseconds
  ND advertised retransmit interval is 0 milliseconds
  ND router advertisements live for 1800 seconds
  Hosts use stateless autoconfig for addresses.
```

Continuing with the configuration example, router R4 is configured as follows:

```
R4(config)#ipv6 unicast-routing
R4(config)#interface FastEthernet0/0
R4(config-if)#ipv6 address 3fff:abcd:1234:4::4/64
R4(config-if)#ipv6 enable
R4(config-if)#exit
R4(config)#interface Loopback0
R4(config-if)#ip address 4.4.4.4 255.255.255.255
R4(config-if)#exit
R4(config)#interface Tunnel0
R4(config-if)#tunnel source Loopback0
R4(config-if)#tunnel mode ipv6ip isatap
R4(config-if)#ipv6 address fec0:abcd:1234:1::/64 eui-64
```

```
R4(config-if)#no ipv6 nd suppress-ra
R4(config-if)#exit
R4(config)#ipv rout 3fff:abcd:1234:1::/64 fec0:abcd:1234:1:0:5efe:0101:0101
R4(config)#exit
```

Again, the show ipv6 interface command can be used to validate ISATAP addressing for the Tunnel interface configured on R4 as follows:

```
R4#show ipv6 interface Tunnel0
Tunnel0 is up, line protocol is up
  IPv6 is enabled, link-local address is FE80::5EFE:404:404
  Global unicast address(es):
    FEC0:ABCD:1234:1:0:5EFE:404:404, subnet is FEC0:ABCD:1234:1::/64 [EUI]
  Joined group address(es):
    FF02::1
    FF02::2
    FF02::1:FF04:404
  MTU is 1480 bytes
  ICMP error messages limited to one every 100 milliseconds
  ICMP redirects are enabled
  ND DAD is not supported
  ND reachable time is 30000 milliseconds
  ND advertised reachable time is 0 milliseconds
  ND advertised retransmit interval is 0 milliseconds
  ND router advertisements live for 1800 seconds
  Hosts use stateless autoconfig for addresses.
```

As in previous examples, the show interfaces command can be used to verify the tunnel encapsulation, default tunnel values, and the state of the Tunnel interface as follows:

```
R4#show interfaces Tunnel0
Tunnel0 is up, line protocol is up
  Hardware is Tunnel
  MTU 1514 bytes, BW 9 Kbit/sec, DLY 500000 usec,
     reliability 255/255, txload 1/255, rxload 1/255
  Encapsulation TUNNEL, Loopback not set
  Keepalive not set
  Tunnel source 4.4.4.4 (Loopback0), destination UNKNOWN
  Tunnel protocol/transport IPv6 ISATAP

  Fast tunneling enabled
  Tunnel transmit bandwidth 8000 (kbps)
  Tunnel receive bandwidth 8000 (kbps)

...

[Truncated Output]
```

Finally, as in the previous examples, a simple LAN-to-LAN ping can be used to validate the ISA-TAP configuration as follows:

```
R4#ping 3fff:abcd:1234:1::1 source 3fff:abcd:1234:4::4 repeat 10

Type escape sequence to abort.
Sending 10, 100-byte ICMP Echos to 3FFF:ABCD:1234:1::1, timeout is 2
seconds:
Packet sent with a source address of 3FFF:ABCD:1234:4::4
!!!!!!!!!!
Success rate is 100 percent (10/10), round-trip min/avg/max = 4/5/8 ms
```

Generic Routing Encapsulation Tunneling

Generic Routing Encapsulation (GRE) is a tunnel encapsulation protocol that is used to tunnel protocols over an internetwork. GRE is the default encapsulation protocol used on Tunnel interfaces in Cisco IOS software if one is not explicitly configured. GRE supports multiple protocols and can be used to encapsulate and transport protocols such as IPX, AppleTalk, and IPv6 in IPv4 packets. This capability allows GRE to provide greater flexibility than other tunneling mechanisms.

In a manner similar to manually (i.e., statically) configured IPv6-in-IPv4 tunnels, GRE tunnels are configured statically between two routers to allow for the transport of IPv6 packets over an IPv4 infrastructure. The only notable difference is that while IPv6-in-IPv4 tunnels use a tunnel mode of ipv6ip, GRE tunnels use a tunnel mode of gre ip to tunnel IPv6 packets over the IPv4 infrastructure using GRE encapsulation.

> **NOTE:** If you configure a tunnel with IPv6 source and destination addresses, the tunnel mode gre ipv6 command would be used to specify IPv6 as the transport protocol. An example of when this might be used would be when encapsulating IPv4 packets in IPv6.

Given that the configuration steps required to configure GRE tunnels for IPv6 are the same as those used to configure IPv6-in-IPv4 tunnels, with the only difference being the tunnel mode, we will not be going into detail on this configuration of GRE. However, the following configuration example shows the use of the different tunnel mode when GRE for IPv6 is used. This configuration example is based on the same topology used in previous examples:

```
R4(config)#ipv6 unicast-routing
R4(config)#interface FastEthernet0/0
R4(config-if)#ipv6 address 3fff:abcd:1234:4::4/64
R4(config-if)#ipv6 enable
R4(config-if)#exit
R4(config)#interface Loopback0
R4(config-if)#ip address 4.4.4.4 255.255.255.255
R4(config-if)#exit
R4(config)#interface Tunnel0
R4(config-if)#ipv6 address 2001:abcd:1234:1::4/64
R4(config-if)#tunnel source Loopback0
```

```
R4(config-if)#tunnel destination 1.1.1.1
R4(config-if)#tunnel mode gre
R4(config-if)#exit
R4(config)#ipv6 route 3fff:abcd:1234:1::/64 Tunnel0
R4(config)#exit
```

Following the same sequence of steps, the remote router, R1, is configured as follows:

```
R1(config)#ipv6 unicast-routing
R1(config)#interface FastEthernet0/0
R1(config-if)#ipv6 address 3fff:abcd:1234:1::1/64
R1(config-if)#ipv6 enable
R1(config-if)#exit
R1(config)#interface Loopback0
R1(config-if)#ip address 1.1.1.1 255.255.255.255
R1(config-if)#exit
R1(config)#interface Tunnel0
R1(config-if)#ipv6 address 2001:abcd:1234:1::1/64
R1(config-if)#tunnel source Loopback0
R1(config-if)#tunnel destination 4.4.4.4
R1(config-if)#tunnel mode gre ipv6
R1(config-if)#exit
R1(config)#ipv6 route 3fff:abcd:1234:4::/64 Tunnel0
R1(config)#exit
```

Following this configuration, a simple LAN-to-LAN ping can be used to verify connectivity:

```
R1#ping 3fff:abcd:1234:4::4 source 3fff:abcd:1234:1::1 repeat 10

Type escape sequence to abort.
Sending 10, 100-byte ICMP Echos to 3FFF:ABCD:1234:4::4, timeout is 2 seconds:
Packet sent with a source address of 3FFF:ABCD:1234:1::1
!!!!!!!!!!
Success rate is 100 percent (10/10), round-trip min/avg/max = 4/6/8 ms
```

While GRE and manual (i.e., static) IPv6 tunnels are similar in many ways, you should be aware of a few differences between the two methods of statically configured tunnels as follows:

- The first difference between GRE and statically configured IPv6-in-IPv4 tunnels is the MTU value for the Tunnel interface. GRE tunnels have a default MTU value of 1476 bytes, while static IPv6-in-IPv4 tunnels have a default MTU value of 1480 bytes.
- The second difference between GRE and statically configured IPv6-in-IPv4 tunnels is the formation of the Link-Local address. For GRE tunnels, the Link-Local address is derived via the EIU-64 method using the lowest numbered MAC address of all operational interfaces. For the other tunneling mechanisms, the Link-Local address for static IPv6-in-IPv4 tunnels is derived from the FE80::/96 prefix plus the 32-bit address of the tunnel source.

To validate these statements, the following output shows the default MTU and Link-Local address for a GRE tunnel:

```
R1#show ipv6 interface Tunnel0
Tunnel0 is up, line protocol is up
  IPv6 is enabled, link-local address is FE80::20C:CEFF:FEA7:F3A0
  Global unicast address(es):
    2001:ABCD:1234:1::1, subnet is 2001:ABCD:1234:1::/64
  Joined group address(es):
    FF02::1
    FF02::2
    FF02::1:FF00:1
    FF02::1:FFA7:F3A0
  MTU is 1476 bytes
  ICMP error messages limited to one every 100 milliseconds
  ICMP redirects are enabled
  ND DAD is enabled, number of DAD attempts: 1
  ND reachable time is 30000 milliseconds
  Hosts use stateless autoconfig for addresses.
```

Next, the following output illustrates the default MTU and Link-Local address for a static IPv6-in-IPv4 tunnel:

```
R1#show ipv6 interface Tunnel0
Tunnel0 is up, line protocol is up
  IPv6 is enabled, link-local address is FE80::101:101
  Global unicast address(es):
    2001:ABCD:1234:1::1, subnet is 2001:ABCD:1234:1::/64
  Joined group address(es):
    FF02::1
    FF02::2
    FF02::1:FF00:1
    FF02::1:FF01:101
  MTU is 1480 bytes
  ICMP error messages limited to one every 100 milliseconds
  ICMP redirects are enabled
  ND DAD is enabled, number of DAD attempts: 1
  ND reachable time is 30000 milliseconds
  Hosts use stateless autoconfig for addresses.
```

NOTE: From the output above, we can determine that the tunnel source is an interface with the IPv4 address 1.1.1.1 based on the last 32-bits included in the Link-Local address.

- Finally, as was described earlier in this section, the third difference between the two tunneling mechanisms is that while GRE supports multiple protocols, static IPv6-in-IPv4 tunnels only support the encapsulation of IPv6 in IPv4 packets. GRE is therefore a more flexible option if the same tunnel will be used to support additional protocols.

Having gone through the various tunneling mechanisms supported in Cisco IOS software, it is also important to understand the implications of using these tunneling mechanisms. Although tunneling is one of the most common methods used to transport IPv6 packets over IPv4 networks, there are some factors that should be taken into consideration when implementing tunneling, which include the following:

- Maximum Transmission Unit issues
- ICMPv4 error messages
- Protocol filtering
- Network Address Translation

Maximum Transmission Unit (MTU) refers to the size (in bytes) of the largest protocol data unit that a given layer of a communications protocol can pass onwards. MTU has been described in great detail in previous chapters in this guide. When IPv6 packets are tunneled over IPv4 networks, the 20-byte IPv4 header is inserted before the IPv6 packet. This means that the IPv6 packet size is effectively reduced by 20 bytes.

The minimum MTU for any link in IPv6 networks is 1280 bytes. While the MTU on Tunnel interfaces is sufficient to allow most IP packets, the size of the packet when IPv6 is encapsulated in IPv4 may exceed this value, which means that the packets will need to be fragmented by IPv4. This will lead to additional processing on routers, as packets must be reassembled at the other end, which may adversely affect router and network performance.

In many older IPv4 routers, only 8 bytes of data beyond the packet's IPv4 header are returned in the event of an error during the transmission of the packet. This presents a potential issue in that if there is a problem, then the IPv6 host (which is sending the packets being tunneled in IPv4) will not know the address fields of the IPv6 packet that is in error.

In typical IPv4 networks, protocol 41 (IPv6) is filtered or blocked by firewalls, given that there is no need for it. While this is good practice, it does affect the deployment of IPv6-over-IPv4 tunnels. Consideration for IPv6 must be given when ACLs and firewalls are implemented.

As is the case with any other tunneling protocol, it is not possible to establish IPv6-over-IPv4 tunnels when dynamic Network Address Translation (NAT) or port redirection using NAT is configured within the network. However, if static NAT is used, then it is possible to establish IPv6-over-IPv4 tunnels.

TRANSLATING BETWEEN IPV4 AND IPV6 DOMAINS

Having gone through the two most common methods of integrating IPv4 and IPv6 domains, the following section describes the third, and least recommended, method that can also be used to integrate IPv4 and IPv6 domains: Protocol Translation (PT).

> **IMPORTANT NOTE:** Due to numerous problems, Network Address Translation-Protocol Translation (NAT-PT) has been made obsolete by RFC 4966 and has been deprecated to historic status. This means that we will not be going into detail regarding NAT-PT. However, because the configuration commands are still available within the Cisco IOS software suite, and because it may still be an option worth considering, it is important that you have an understanding of NAT-PT and its basic application in Cisco IOS software. Therefore, consider this section a history lesson on NAT-PT, which you may very likely be called upon to remember in the ROUTE certification exam

Before delving into the details pertaining to Network Address Translation-Protocol Translation (NAT-PT), it is important to understand why this is the least recommended method for integrating IPv4 and IPv6 environments. It should be noted that the reason is not specific to NAT-PT but rather to NAT in general. While NAT does have several advantages, such as allowing private networks to communicate, it also has several limitations, which include the following:

- Breaking the end-to-end IP model
- The need to maintain connection state issues
- The inhabitation of end-to-end security
- Applications that are not NAT-friendly
- Address space collision
- Ratio of internal and reachable IP addresses

The Internet Protocol was designed so that only network endpoints, such as hosts and servers, handle the connection. However, with the rapid depletion of IPv4 address space, NAT is typically used to connect network endpoints. While this allows hosts residing on the different private networks to communicate with each other, it also breaks the end-to-end IP session between these hosts because one or more intermediate NAT devices must terminate and then re-originate the session. While NAT works well for general data transfers, there are some applications that are adversely affected by the translations, such as Voice over IP protocols.

Network Address Translation requires that the device(s) performing the translation maintain the state of the translations and connections. If this service is not provided, then network reachability is lost. Depending on the number of hosts or translations required, such devices could be required to maintain very large state tables. Large state tables consume tremendous amounts of memory, which could affect router performance. In addition, because all packets must be processed, NAT can hinder network and router performance by introducing latency due to router processing delays. This results in longer round-trip times between source and destination hosts, which could cause severe performance problems for real-time traffic, such as voice and video applications.

Network Address Translation can also cause security headaches in identifying the sources of network breaches when traffic is coming from a NAT location. This is because NAT masks the true identity of the intruder. For example, when using Port Address Translation (PAT), hundreds of hosts could be hidden behind the same single IP address, making it impossible to determine which host is actually originating packets or is responsible for the security breach. Another inhibition to end-to-end security is the incompatibility of NAT with cryptography and encryption. When some security algorithms, such as IP Security (IPSec) are employed, they cannot be used in conjunction with NAT because NAT changes the source address of packets before they are forwarded to their destination. This change causes the cryptography method to fail because it thinks that the packet has been tampered with along the way.

Not all applications work in the same manner. This means that some applications, for example, applications that use proprietary protocols, etc., are not compatible with NAT. The two most common issues experienced with NAT are on applications that use embedded IP addresses or port numbers. When NAT changes these port numbers or IP addresses, as is the case with IPSec, the applications do not function as expected or, in some instances, cease functioning completely. This means that while NAT can be used to provide privately addressed devices access to public networks, it cannot be used in all instances.

Address space collision typically occurs when two or more organizations merge. Because RFC 1918 address space is commonly used internally in different organizations, with NAT enabling these privately addressed networks to communicate with the outside world, it is not uncommon for two organizations that merge to discover that they have the same address space. In such cases, if re-addressing the network is not an option, and it usually is not because of the complexity involved, then double-NAT is typically used to allow organizations with overlapping address space to communicate with each other. NATing more than once introduces additional complexity and amplifies the NAT issues described in the previous sections.

Finally, Network Address Translation works well when there are a few internal hosts that must be accessed from external networks, such as the Internet. However, NAT can become an issue, and a limitation when multiple hosts using private address space need to be accessed from the Internet. Given the rapidly depleted IPv4 global address space, it is not always possible to secure a public IP address range to accommodate all hosts that need to be accessed by external networks. Because this is not always possible, it highlights another limitation of IPv4, more so than a NAT limitation. However, since NAT is designed for IPv4, the responsibility and limitation is jointly shared.

IPv6 NAT Protocol Translation Overview

Network Address Translation-Protocol Translation (NAT-PT) is an IPv6-to-IPv4 translation mechanism (defined in RFC 2765 and RFC 2766) that allows IPv6-only devices to communicate with IPv4-only devices, and vice versa. NAT-PT is based on the Stateless IP/ICMP Translator (SIIT) algorithm defined in RFC 2765. This algorithm is used to translate between IPv4 and IPv6 packet headers, including ICMP headers.

Network Address Translation-Protocol Translation is a stateful mechanism (i.e., it keeps track of all connection states). In order to operate, NAT-PT requires a specific routing configuration within the network in which all IPv6 packets addressed to a predefined /96 prefix must be routed toward the NAT-PT device. This /96 prefix must be reserved within the IPv6 domain for NAT-PT use. The NAT-PT device can then translate destination IPv6 prefixes into IPv4 addresses according to configured mapping rules. Several different types of operations are defined for NAT-PT as follows:

- Static NAT-PT
- Dynamic NAT-PT
- NAPT-PT
- NAT-PT DNS ALG

These different NAT-PT operations are described in the following sections.

Static NAT-PT

Static NAT-PT is used to provide a one-to-one mapping between an IPv6 address and an IPv4 address. Each IPv4-address that should be reachable from the IPv6-only network must be configured with a static NAT translation statement in the NAT-PT device. Although this works well for smaller networks, static NAT-PT is not scalable in larger networks that may contain hundreds of, or more, IPv4-only devices that need to be reached by IPv6-only hosts. The configuration login behind static NAT-PT is similar to that of static NAT used in IPv4 networks, which was described in detail in the CCNA study guide available online.

Dynamic NAT-PT

Dynamic NAT-PT provides one-to-one mapping; however, unlike static NAT-PT, this method uses a pool of addresses. Dynamic NAT-PT is used to allow IPv6-only hosts to access IPv4-only hosts or, inversely, allow IPv4-only hosts to access IPv6-only hosts. This method uses a similar concept to that used by dynamic NAT in IPv4 networks.

Dynamic NAT-PT translation operation requires at least one static mapping for the IPv4 DNS server. After the IPv6-to-IPv4 connection is established, the reply packets from IPv4 to IPv6 take advantage of the previously established dynamic mapping to translate back from IPv4 to IPv6. If the connection is initiated by an IPv4-only host, then the explanation is reversed.

NAPT-PT

Network Address Port Translation-Protocol Translation provides one-to-many dynamic mapping entries between multiple IPv6 addresses in the NAT-PT prefix and a single IPv4 address. NAPT-PT operates in the same manner as Port Address Translation (PAT) in IPv4. The translation is performed simultaneously at Layer 3 (i.e., IPv4 and IPv6) and at Layer 4 (i.e., TCP and UDP). In a manner similar to PAT, NAPT-PT can translate only TCP, UDP, and ICMP.

NAT-PT DNS ALG

Dynamic NAT-PT mapping can be combined with the DNS Application Layer Gateway (ALG) to translate the DNS transactions and automatically build the translated addresses of the destination hosts. NAT-PT can intercept the DNS requests originating from the IPv6 network destined toward the IPv4 network; however, a DNS server, or simply a host in the IPv6 network, must first send a DNS query to the IPv4 DNS server through the NAT-PT device. Following that, NAT-PT then automatically translates the IPv4 DNS response into an IPv6 address. Going into detail on NAT-PT DNS ALG is beyond the scope of the ROUTE exam requirements.

Configuring Static NAT-PT

As was stated earlier in this section, NAT-PT is considered obsolete. While this may be the case, it should be noted that NAT-PT is still supported and configurable in the Cisco IOS software. Having stated that, this section describes how to configure and verify static NAT-PT in Cisco IOS software and thus allow the IPv6-only and IPv4-only hosts to communicate transparently.

When configuring static NAT-PT, Cisco IOS software provides two options for configuring the address translation. The `ipv6 nat v6v4 source [ipv6 address] [ipv4 address]` global configuration command is used to translate statically an IPv6 address to an IPv4 address. This configuration is used to allow the specified IPv6 host to be reachable to IPv4 hosts.

The `ipv6 nat v4v6 source [ipv4 address] [ipv6 address]` global configuration command is used to map statically an IPv4 address to an IPv6 address. This allows the IPv4 address to be reachable to IPv6 hosts.

One notable difference between NAT-PT and traditional NAT, as we know it, is that with NAT-PT, there is no concept of inside and outside interfaces. Instead, the `ipv6 nat` interface configuration command is applied to the IPv4 and IPv6 interfaces from which addresses would be NATed. To further clarify and reinforce the configuration of static NAT-PT in Cisco IOS software, the topology illustrated in Figure 9-8 below will be used to illustrate its configuration and verification:

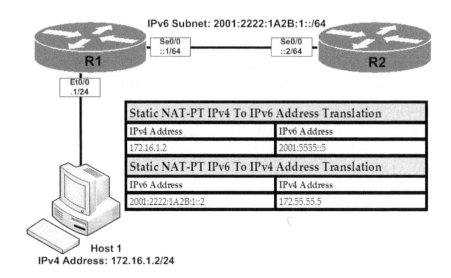

Static NAT-PT IPv4 To IPv6 Address Translation	
IPv4 Address	IPv6 Address
172.16.1.2	2001:5555::5
Static NAT-PT IPv6 To IPv4 Address Translation	
IPv6 Address	IPv4 Address
2001:2222:1A2B:1::2	172.55.55.5

Fig. 9-8. Implementing Static NAT-PT in Cisco IOS Software

Figure 9-8 illustrates a basic network comprised of two routers and a single host. Included in the diagram is a translation table, on which the configuration will be implemented as follows:

- The IPv4 address of Host 1 will be translated to the IPv6 address 2001:5555::5
- The IPv6 address of R2 will be translated to the IPv4 address 172.55.55.5

The result of this configuration will mean that if Host 1 connects to 172.55.55.5, then it will be in fact connecting to R2 because that IPv4 address will be mapped (translated) directly to the IPv6 address 2001:2222:1A2B:1::2, which is the IPv6 address of the Serial0/0 interface on R2. Inversely, if R2 connects to the IPv6 address 2001:5555::5, then it will be connecting to Host 1. This is because that IPv6 address will be mapped (translated) directly to the IPv4 address 172.16.1.2, which is the IPv4 address of Host 1.

NOTE: In order for this to work, both Host 1 and R2 must have an IPv4 and an IPv6 default route (respectively) to R1, which is the NAT-PT device.

The first step in configuring NAT-PT is to enable IPv6 NAT on all applicable router interfaces using the ipv6 nat interface configuration command. Referencing the topology that is illustrated in Figure 9-8, NAT-PT will be configured on both the Ethernet0/0 and Serial0/0 interfaces of R1. This configuration is implemented as follows:

```
R1(config)#ipv6 unicast-routing
R1(config)#interface Ethernet0/0
R1(config-if)#ip address 172.16.1.1 255.255.255.0
R1(config-if)#ipv6 nat
```

```
R1(config-if)#exit
R1(config)#interface Serial0/0
R1(config-if)#ipv6 address 2001:2222:1A2B:1::1/64
R1(config-if)#ipv6 nat
R1(config-if)#exit
```

The second step is to configure addressing on Host 1 and R2 and ensure that both devices are configured with a default route to R1. Host 1 is a Windows-based machine, so that configuration is omitted; however, you can use the `ipconfig` command at the Command prompt to validate that the host has been configured with the correct IP address of 172.16.1.2, the default gateway of 172.16.1.1. Router R2 is configured as follows:

```
R2(config)#ipv6 unicast-routing
R2(config)#interface Serial0/0
R2(config-if)#ipv6 address 2001:2222:1A2B:1::2/64
R2(config-if)#exit
R2(config)#ipv6 route ::/0 2001:2222:1A2B:1::1
```

NOTE: While the IPv6 global Unicast address has been used in the configuration of the default route, the best practice is to use Link-Local addresses, as these will never change.

The third step in static NAT-PT configuration is to configure the NAT-PT prefix that will be used for translations. It is mandatory that this prefix is 96-bits (i.e., uses a /96 prefix). This is performed via the `ipv6 nat prefix` global configuration command. In this example, we will allocate the 2001:5555::/96 prefix for NAT-PT. This configuration is applied to R1 as follows:

```
R1(config)# ipv6 nat prefix 2001:5555::/96
```

The fourth step in static NAT-PT configuration is to configure the static translations. The `ipv6 nat v6v4 source [ipv6 address] [ipv4 address]` command will be used to translate the IPv6 address of the Serial0/0 interface of R2 to the IPv4 address 172.55.55.5. In addition, the `ipv6 nat v4v6 source [ipv4 address] [ipv6 address]` command will be used to translate the IPv4 address of Host 1 to the IPv6 address 2001:5555::5. This configuration is implemented on router R1 as follows:

```
R1(config)# ipv6 nat v6v4 source 2001:2222:1A2B:1::2 172.55.55.5
R1(config)# ipv6 nat v4v6 source 172.16.1.2 2001:5555::5
```

Following the static NAT-PT translation configurations, the `show ipv6 nat translations` command can be used to view the configured NAT-PT translations. This command shows active NAT-PT translations for dynamic NAT-PT and any static NAT-PT translations for static NAT-PT.

Because dynamic NAT-PT has not been implemented, this command will print only persistent (static) NAT-PT translations as illustrated in the following output:

```
R1#show ipv6 nat translations
Prot  IPv4 source            IPv6 source
      IPv4 destination       IPv6 destination
---   ---                    ---
      172.16.1.2             2001:5555::5

---   172.55.55.5            2001:2222:1A2B:1::2
      ---                    ---
```

As can be seen, the output above validates the configuration that was implemented on R1. The output shows the static translations between the 172.16.1.2 and 2001:5555::5 addresses, as well as between the 172.55.55.5 and 2001:2222:1A2B:1::2 addresses as was configured on the router.

Following this verification, simple ping tests can be used to validate the configuration. Below is the output of a ping from R2 to IPv6 address 2001:5555::5, which is statically mapped to Host 1:

```
R2#ping 2001:5555::5

Type escape sequence to abort.
Sending 5, 100-byte ICMP Echos to 2001:5555::5, timeout is 2 seconds:
!!!!!
Success rate is 100 percent (5/5), round-trip min/avg/max = 4/5/8 ms
```

To complete the verification tests, Figure 9-9 below shows a ping test from Host 1 to the 172.55.55.5 address, which is statically mapped to the IPv6 address 2001:2222:1A2B:1::2 and is assigned to the Serial0/0 interface of router R2:

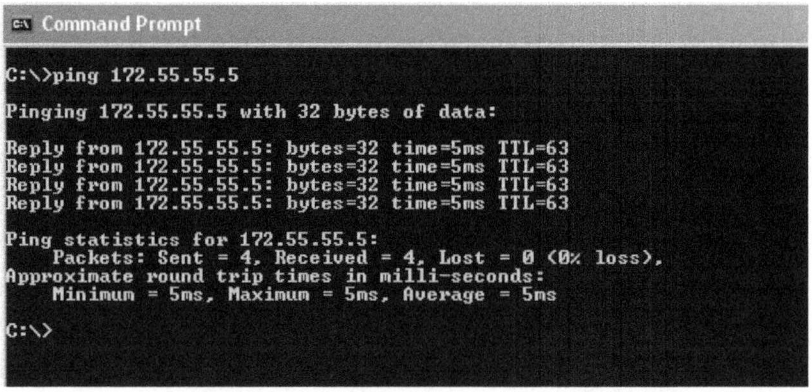

Fig. 9-9. Verifying Static NAT-PT Configuration

You can view the NAT-PT state table using the show ipv6 nat translations command. This command can be used to view only ICMP, TCP, or UDP translations by appending the icmp, tcp, and udp keywords to the end of the command. Alternatively, you can also append the verbose keyword to view detailed NAT-PT state information for all protocol types. As an example, Host 1 initiates a Telnet (TCP) connection to R2. Using the show ipv6 nat translations tcp command, you can view information specific to that session as shown in the following output:

```
R1#show ipv6 nat translations tcp
Prot  IPv4 source           IPv6 source
      IPv4 destination      IPv6 destination
tcp   172.55.55.5,23        2001:2222:1A2B:1::2,23
      172.16.1.2,4552       2001:5555::5,4552
```

Finally, as is the case with traditional NAT, you can also enable debugging for NAT-PT to see real-time translations and perform troubleshooting using the debug ipv6 nat [detailed] command. Following is the output of the debug ipv6 nat detailed command as Host 1 is pinging the IPv4 address 172.55.55.5, which is statically mapped to the IPv6 address 2001:2222:1A2B:1::2:

```
R1#debug ipv6 nat detailed
IPv6 NAT-PT detailed debugging is on
R1#
R1#
R1#
R1#
*Mar  1 15:00:59.173: IPv6 NAT: icmp src (172.16.1.2) -> (2001:5555::5), dst
(172.55.55.5) -> (2001:2222:1A2B:1::2)
*Mar  1 15:00:59.182: IPv6 NAT: icmp src (2001:2222:1A2B:1::2) ->
(172.55.55.5), dst (2001:5555::5) -> (172.16.1.2)

*Mar  1 15:01:00.183: IPv6 NAT: icmp src (172.16.1.2) -> (2001:5555::5), dst
(172.55.55.5) -> (2001:2222:1A2B:1::2)
*Mar  1 15:01:00.187: IPv6 NAT: icmp src (2001:2222:1A2B:1::2) ->
(172.55.55.5), dst (2001:5555::5) -> (172.16.1.2)

*Mar  1 15:01:01.181: IPv6 NAT: icmp src (172.16.1.2) -> (2001:5555::5), dst
(172.55.55.5) -> (2001:2222:1A2B:1::2)
*Mar  1 15:01:01.185: IPv6 NAT: icmp src (2001:2222:1A2B:1::2) ->
(172.55.55.5), dst (2001:5555::5) -> (172.16.1.2)

*Mar  1 15:01:02.182: IPv6 NAT: icmp src (172.16.1.2) -> (2001:5555::5), dst
(172.55.55.5) -> (2001:2222:1A2B:1::2)
*Mar  1 15:01:02.186: IPv6 NAT: icmp src (2001:2222:1A2B:1::2) ->
(172.55.55.5), dst (2001:5555::5) -> (172.16.1.2)
```

In the output above, each sequence shows the ICMP echo sent from Host 1(IPv4) to R2 (IPv6) and the ICMP echo-reply sent by R2 (IPv6) to Host 1 (IPv4).

While it will not be illustrated in this chapter, the configuration of dynamic NAT-PT follows the same logic as that of dynamic IPv4 NAT. As is the case with static NAT-PT configuration, different commands are used to configure IPv4-to-IPv6 translations and IPv6-to-IPv4 translations. The following section describes the commands required to perform translations:

- To translate IPv4 addresses to IPv6 addresses, use the `ipv6 nat v4v6 pool [name] <start-ipv6 end-ipv6> prefix-length <length>` and `ipv6 nat v4v6 source list [access-list | name] pool <name>` global configuration commands. Ensure that the `ipv6 nat` command is enabled on all applicable interfaces.
- To translate IPv6 addresses to IPv4 addresses, use the `ipv6 nat v6v4 pool [name] <start-ipv4 end-ipv4> prefix-length <length>` and `ipv6 nat v6v4 source list [access-list| route-map <name>] pool <name>` global configuration commands. Again, ensure that the `ipv6 nat` command is enabled on all applicable interfaces.
- Specify the prefix that will be used for NAT-PT translations using the `ipv6 nat prefix [prefix/length]` global configuration command.

Following the configuration, the verification of dynamic NAT-PT follows the same logic as that used for static NAT-PT. Now that we have a good understanding of NAT-PT, it is important to understand why this is the least preferred method for integrating IPv4 and IPv6 networks. While the limitations of NAT, in general, were listed and described earlier in this section, it is also important to have a fundamental understanding of the limitations pertaining to NAT-PT that must be taken into consideration before implementation. The limitations and NAT-PT considerations are described in the following section.

NAT-PT Limitations and Implementation Considerations

In a manner similar to NAT used in IPv4, NAT-PT also has several limitations, which must be considered before it is deployed. These limitations are as follows:

- Introduces a single point of failure
- Inhibition of end-to-end security
- Applications that are not NAT-friendly
- PMTUD
- IPv4 Options
- Multicast
- DNS

Given that NAT-PT is performed on a single device, this introduces a single point of failure for the network. In other words, if the NAT-PT device fails, all of the translated sessions between the IPv4-only and IPv6-only domains are lost, as well as connectivity between the two domains.

NAT-PT inhibits end-to-end security because of the termination of local sessions on the NAT-PT device. Additionally, it should also be noted that NAT-PT does not have complete knowledge of applications that use random dynamically allocated ports and rendezvous ports with embedded IP addresses. This means that the same problems in NAT in this regard are inherited in NAT-PT. While NAT-PT can be upgraded each time a new non-NAT-friendly application is available, this is not always feasible.

While Path MTU Discovery (PMTUD) is performed in different manners in IPv4 and IPv6, it is important to know that NAT-PT does not support PMTUD. In addition, NAT-PT does not support any IP Options specified in the IPv4 packet headers, such as Router Alert. Additionally, NAT-PT does not support Multicast, meaning that NAT-PT cannot be used for Multicast traffic between IPv4-only and IPv6-only networks. Finally, DNS Security (DNSSEC), which is defined in RFC 2535, is also not supported by NAT Protocol Translation.

ADDITIONAL IPV4 AND IPV6 INTEGRATION MECHANISMS

In the final section of this chapter, we will discuss additional mechanisms that can be used to integrate IPv4 and IPv6 environments. Given that these additional mechanisms are not implemented in Cisco IOS software, they will be described only briefly in the sections that follow. While going through this section, keep in mind that these additional methods are included only to present a complete picture of the suite of mechanisms and solutions available for integrating IPv4 and IPv6 environments.

Therefore, while you should make an effort to have a basic understanding of these mechanisms, your primary focus, as it applies to the ROUTE exam, is to focus on the different mechanisms and protocols described in the previous sections. The additional integration mechanisms that will be described in this section include the following:

- Application Layer Gateways
- Tunnel brokers
- Tunnel servers
- Teredo tunneling
- Bump in the Stack
- TCP-UDP Relay
- Dual-Stack Transition Mechanism
- SOCK-based IPv6/IPv4 gateway

Application Layer Gateways

Application Layer Gateways (ALGs) are used to allow the IPv6-only hosts to communicate with IPv4-only hosts. ALGs are implemented in between IPv6 and IPv4 networks. These devices provide communication between IPv6-only devices and IPv4-only devices. This means that these devices must be configured with both protocol stacks (i.e., dual-stack). However, because no other devices in the network run dual-stack, no tunneling mechanisms are used.

ALGs are used for the transition of Internet-based applications, such as e-mail and web traffic. For example, in an IPv6-only environment, hosts can send their e-mail messages using SMTP over IPv6 to their local SMTP server. After receiving the message, the SMTP server, which must have dual-stack support, acts as an ALG for SMTP and sends these messages out to their intended recipients, which could be IPv4-only hosts. However, because the messages are received via IPv6, it is important to know that the SMTP server will first attempt to send the messages via IPv6, and if this fails, then fall back to IPv4 to send the messages.

In a similar manner, web browsers on IPv6-only hosts also can be configured to use proxy web servers over IPv6 to reach any IPv4 website. The local proxy server, which must also have dual-stack support, provides ALG function for HTTP traffic in such cases. If the local proxy server receives the HTTP requests via IPv6, then it will attempt to reach the intended web destination via IPv6, and if this fails, then it will fall back to IPv4.

Tunnel brokers

Although manually configuring tunnels is a straightforward process, as was illustrated in the example above, this solution is not very scalable. For example, in a network with 100 routers, attempting to configure tunnels manually between all these routers in order to allow IPv6 packets to be tunneled over the IPv4 network would quickly become a very time-consuming, monotonous, and labor-intensive process.

Tunnel brokers are defined in RFC 3053. Tunnel brokers allow for the deployment of configured tunnels for IPv6 packets over IPv4 networks. Tunnel brokers are external systems (not routers) that act as servers on the IPv4 networks that receive tunneling requests from dual-stack hosts via HTTP. End-users can then use a web browser to request a configured tunnel for their dual-stack hosts, which allows them to communicate with IPv6 networks over an IPv4 infrastructure.

The tunnel broker service uses 6-over-4 tunnels to connect the end systems automatically to the 6bone, or IPv6 backbone. The service also manages tunnel requests and configuration for the enterprise, rather than forcing the network administrator to configure tunnels manually, which allows for a more scalable solution than manually configured tunnels.

The tunnel brokers send back information to the dual-stack nodes via HTTP, which allows these hosts to apply for the establishment of a tunnel to a dual-stack router. This information may include IPv4 and IPv6 addresses and default gateways, or even custom scripts, to allow the tunnel configuration on the operating system of the dual-stack host.

The tunnel broker then remotely applies configuration commands on a dual-stack router, which allows it to enable a tunnel for the dual-stack host. While the dual-stack router must be connected to an IPv-6 domain, the tunnel broker and dual-stack router communicate using IPv4 addresses. Tunnel broker functionality is not supported in Cisco IOS software.

Tunnel servers

Tunnel servers are simplified versions of tunnel brokers. These devices combine the functions of the dual-stack router and tunnel broker into the same device, rather than having two devices perform these functions. The same exchange of messages used when tunnel brokers and dual-stack routers are used is applicable in situations where tunnel servers are deployed, with the only exception being that a separate dual-stack router is not automatically configured because this functionality resides on the tunnel server. As is the case with tunnel broker implementations, tunnel server functionality is not supported in Cisco IOS software.

Teredo Tunneling

The main goal of Teredo is to deliver IPv6 packets to dual-stack nodes that are behind NAT devices in IPv4-only domains because, by default, protocol 41 (IPv6) does not work through NAT. However, using Teredo, the delivery of IPv6 connectivity through NAT devices is possible via the tunneling of IPv6 packets over IPv4 UDP packets. By using the combination of a single IPv4 address and the UDP mappings of a NAT device, Teredo can deliver IPv6 packets over IPv4 UDP to several hosts that reside behind the same NAT.

Teredo is comprised of three main components. These are the Teredo server, the Teredo relay, and the Teredo client. The Teredo server is connected to the IPv4 Internet and is reachable via an IPv4 global address. This device manages signaling traffic with the Teredo clients. The Teredo relay is the device acting as the IPv6 router. This device is connected to the IPv6 Internet and provides IPv6 connectivity over IPv4 UDP packets to Teredo clients that are behind NAT.

Teredo clients are located in an IPv4 domain behind the NAT device. These clients must initiate a request to the Teredo server to get IPv6 connectivity over IPv4 UDP packets from the Teredo relay. In order for these devices to communicate with the Teredo server, it must be configured with the IPv4 address of the server. Teredo clients are assigned an IPv6 address that starts with the Teredo prefix (2001:0000::/32).

Additionally, Teredo host-specific relays can also be utilized. These are dual-stack devices that can communicate directly with Teredo clients over the IPv4 Internet, without the need for an intermediate Teredo relay. The connectivity to the IPv4 Internet can be through a public IPv4 address or through a private IPv4 address and a neighboring NAT. The connectivity to the IPv6 Internet can be through a direct connection to the IPv6 Internet or through an IPv6 transition technology, such as 6to4, where IPv6 packets are tunneled across the IPv4 Internet. The Teredo host-specific relay listens on UDP port 3544 for Teredo traffic.

As is the case with tunnel broker and tunnel server functionality, Teredo tunneling functionality is not supported in Cisco IOS software.

Bump in the Stack

Bump in the Stack (BIS) is defined in RFC 2767. While other transition mechanisms are designed to work for IPv6-only and IPv4-only devices, BIS is designed to work only on dual-stack hosts. BIS translates between IPv4 and IPv6 by using the SIIT algorithm. The reason BIS was designed is to address the probability that during the transition from IPv4 to IPv6, it will be difficult for organizations to get IPv6 versions of all of their current applications—especially those that are customized. Therefore, BIS operates on dual-stack hosts, via software, by intercepting and then translating packets between the Application and Network layers. For example, if a dual-stack host receives IPv4 packets from an IPv4-only application, then BIS intercepts and translates these packets into IPv6 packets.

TCP-UDP Relay

TCP-UDP Relay is defined in RFC 3142. This mechanism is similar to NAT-PT in that it must be located between the IPv6-only and IPv4-only domains. However, unlike NAT-PT, TCP-UDP Relay performs translation only at the Transport Layer (i.e., for TCP and UDP), rather than at the Network Layer, as is performed by NAT-PT.

Dual-Stack Transition Mechanism

Dual-Stack Transition Mechanism (DSTM) is used to allow IPv6-only devices to communicate with IPv4-only devices by defining a method for establishing IPv4-over-IPv6 tunnels and the temporary allocation of IPv4 addresses to hosts in the IPv6-only domain. These IPv4-over-IPv6 tunnels are established between the DSTM server and DSTM hosts.

SOCKS-Based IPv6/IPv4 Gateway

SOCKS-based IPv6/IPv4 gateway is based on the SOCKS protocol. SOCKS is a proxy protocol for TCP/IP applications. It is comprised of SOCKS servers and SOCKS clients. In IPv6, SOCKS can be used to allow IPv4-only hosts (SOCKS clients) to communicate with IPv6-only servers, and vice-versa, through a SOCKS server that has dual-stack support. The SOCKS-based IPv6/IPv4 gateway is defined in RFC 3089.

CHAPTER SUMMARY

The following section is a summary of the major points you should be aware of in this chapter.

Integrating IPv4 and IPv6 Network Environments

- The advantages of migrating from IPv4 to IPv6 include the following:
    1. The Simplified IPv6 Packet Header
    2. Larger Address Space
    3. IPv6 Addressing Hierarchy
    4. IPv6 Extendibility
    5. IPv6 Broadcast Elimination
    6. Stateless Autoconfiguration
    7. Integrated Mobility
    8. Integrated Enhanced Security

- However, it is not always possible or actually feasible to migrate directly from IPv4 to IPv6
- In most cases, IPv4 and IPv6 environment must be integrated so they can co-exist
- IPv4 and IPv6 integration and co-existence strategies are divided into three broad classes as follows:
    1. Dual-Stack Implementations
    2. Tunneling
    3. Protocol Translation

- With dual-stack implementations, hosts and network devices run both IPv6 and IPv4
- With tunneling mechanisms, IPv6 packets are tunneled in IPv4 packets
- With protocol translation, IPv6-to-IPv4, and vice-versa, translation is implemented

IPv4 and IPv6 Dual-Stack Implementations

- There are two main methods for integrating IPv4 and IPv6 environments using dual-stack
- The first method requires manual configuration by the user
- The second method entails using a naming service, such as DNS
- In Cisco IOS software, dual-stack is implemented by configuring IPv4 and IPv6 addresses
- When dual-stack is implemented, IPv6 is preferred over IPv4
- Applications, tools and protocols that have dual-stack support in IOS software include the following:
    1. DNS

2. Ping
3. Telnet
4. SSH
5. TFTP
6. Traceroute
7. HTTP
8. Frame Relay
9. FHRPs, such as HSRP and GLBP

Tunneling IPv6 Datagrams across IPv4 Networks

- Tunneling allows IPv6 packets to be encapsulated and sent over native IPv4 internetworks
- The following tunneling mechanisms are supported in Cisco IOS software:
    1. Static (Manually Configured) IPv6 Tunneling
    2. 6to4 Tunneling
    3. Automatic IPv4-compatible Tunneling
    4. ISATAP Tunneling
    5. Generic Routing Encapsulation Tunneling

- Static tunneling requires the static configuration of tunnels on dual-stack devices
- Static tunneling requires tunnel source and destination addresses to be specified
- Static tunneling is enabled using the tunnel mode `ipv6ip` interface configuration command
- 6to4 tunneling allows tunnels to be dynamically created
- 6to4 tunneling requires no explicit tunnel destination to be configured
- 6to4 tunneling has the following characteristics:
    1. Automatic or Dynamic Tunneling
    2. Automatic Prefix Assignment
    3. There is no IPv6 Route Propagation

- 6to4 tunneling uses the IPv6 2002::/16 prefix which was assigned by IANA for 6to4 sites
- The `tunnel mode ipv6ip 6to4` command is used to enable 6to4 tunneling
- Automatic IPv4-compatible tunneling is also a dynamic tunneling mechanism
- Automatic IPv4-compatible tunnels use the IPv6 prefix ::/96
- The `tunnel mode ipv6ip auto-tunnel` enables automatic IPv4-compatible tunneling
- ISATAP is an automatic overlay tunneling mechanism
- ISATAP uses the underlying IPv4 network as an NBMA Link Layer for IPv6
- ISATAP addressing includes the 0000:5EFE high-order 32-bit value
- The `tunnel mode ipv6ip isatap` command is used to enable ISATAP tunneling
- GRE is a tunnel encapsulation protocol that is used to tunnel protocols over an internetwork

- GRE is the default encapsulation protocol used on Tunnel interfaces
- GRE provides much greater flexibility than the other different tunneling mechanisms
- GRE tunnels use a tunnel mode of `gre ip` to tunnel IPv6 packets over IPv4
- While GRE and manual tunnels have similar configurations, there are some differences as follows:
  1. Generic Routing Encapsulation tunnels have a default MTU value of 1476 bytes
  2. Static IPv6-in-IPv4 tunnels have a default MTU value of 1480 bytes
  3. For GRE tunnels, the Link-Local address is derived via the EIU-64 method
  4. For static IPv6-in-IPv4 tunnels, the Link-Local address is derived from the FE80::/96 prefix
  5. GRE supports multiple protocols
  6. Static IPv6-in-IPv4 tunnels only support the encapsulation of IPv6 in IPv4 packets

- Before implementing tunneling, the following factors should be taken into consideration:
  1. Maximum Transmission Unit issues
  2. ICMPv4 Error Messages
  3. Protocol Filtering
  4. Network Address Translation

Translating between IPv4 and IPv6 Domains

- NAT-Protocol Translation is used to translate between IPv4 and IPv6 and vice-versa
- NAT-PT has been made obsolete by RFC 4966 and deprecated to historic status
- NAT, in general, has the following limitations, which should be considered before deploying:
  1. Breaking the end-to-end IP model
  2. The need to maintain connection state issues
  3. The inhabitation of end-to-end security
  4. Applications that are not NAT-friendly
  5. Address space collision
  6. Ratio of internal and reachable IP addresses

- NAT-PT is a Stateful mechanism. In other words, NAT-PT keeps track of connection states
- NAT-PT requires that a predefined /96 prefix must be routed toward the NAT-PT device
- The different types of operations defined for NAT-PT include the following:
  1. Static NAT-PT
  2. Dynamic NAT-PT
  3. NAPT-PT
  4. NAT-PT DNS ALG

- Static NAT-PT is used to provide a one-to-one mapping between an IPv6 and IPv4 address
- Dynamic NAT-PT provides one-to-one mapping using a pool of addresses

- NAPT-PT provides one-to-many mappings for multiple IPv6 addresses & an IPv4 address
- NAT-PT DLS ALG uses a DNS ALG to translate the DNS transactions
- Specially, NAT-PT has the following limitations that should be considered before deploying:
    1. It introduces a single point of failure
    2. Inhibition of end-to-end security
    3. Applications that are not NAT-friendly
    4. PMTUD
    5. IPv4 Options
    6. Multicast
    7. DNS

Additional IPv4 and IPv6 Integration Mechanisms

- The following additional mechanisms can be used for IPv4 and IPv6 integrations
- The following mechanisms, while valid, are not supported in Cisco IOS software:
    1. Application Layer Gateways
    2. Tunnel Brokers
    3. Tunnel Servers
    4. Teredo Tunneling
    5. Bump in the Stack
    6. TCP-UDP Relay
    7. Dual-Stack Transition Mechanism
    8. SOCK-based IPv6/IPv4 gateway

CHAPTER 10

Branch Office and Teleworker Technologies

While previous chapters in this guide have centered on core site routing implementations, this chapter focuses on branch office and teleworker (mobile worker) technologies. In addition to understanding how to implement effective routing policy within the core or hub sites, it is also important to understand how to integrate remote or branch offices into the overall enterprise network. In addition, given that it is becoming more and more commonplace to find home-based and mobile workers, it is important to understand the available technologies that can be used to allow these workers access into the enterprise network. The core ROUTE exam objective covered in this chapter is as follows:

- Implement a Layer 3 path control solution

Within the core ROUTE exam objective, this chapter covers the following topics:

- Implement basic teleworker and branch services
- Describe broadband technologies
- Configure basic broadband connections
- Describe basic VPN technologies
- Configure GRE
- Describe branch access technologies

This chapter contains the following sections:

- Remote Site and Branch Office Considerations
- Branch Office Classification
- Data Transmission Basics
- Cable Access Technologies
- DSL Access Technologies
- Teleworker Connectivity Considerations
- Understanding VPN Technologies
- IP Security (IPSec)
- Site-to-Site VPN Technologies
- Remote Access VPN Technologies
- Branch Office Routing Solutions

REMOTE SITE AND BRANCH OFFICE CONSIDERATIONS

Branch offices are sometimes referred to as remote offices because they are located somewhere other than the company's main or campus enterprise network. Branch offices are implemented to serve certain geographic or demographic areas, as well as to expand the access of customer services and other services available to beyond the home office. These offices allow the company to have a presence in more communities than just the one location where the main or headquarters branch is located.

It is becoming commonplace that most enterprises have more employees in their branch offices than at their corporate headquarters. This 'distributed model,' if you will, means that these offices need a network infrastructure that performs as well as in the headquarters location. In addition, because most services (e.g., corporate application server) are commonly housed at either the headquarters or datacenters, these branch offices also require secure and reliable connectivity to such resources. Several factors should be taken into consideration when implementing branch office solutions as follows:

- Connectivity
- Security
- High Availability
- Routing
- IP Services
- Mobility
- Optimization

These considerations are described in the following sections.

Connectivity

One of the core considerations that should be taken into account when implementing branch office solutions is the connectivity technologies that will be used to connect the branch office back to the headquarters or main office. These Physical Layer technologies may include digital circuits, such as T1 and E1 lines, or broadband technologies, such as cable and Digital Subscriber Line (DSL). Because any one of these technologies is a viable option, it is important to have a solid understanding of how to provision each one of these in Cisco IOS software. These technologies and their configurations are described and illustrated later in this chapter.

Security

Security is another major factor that should be taken into consideration when implementing branch office solutions. The level and amount of security will typically depend on the type of business and the compliance requirements for that industry. For example, the financial industry would have more compliance and regulatory requirements than most other industries. In most cases, some type of Virtual Private Network (VPN) will be implemented. This could be either a trusted VPN solution, such as a Multiprotocol Label Switching (MPLS) VPN, or a secure VPN, such as an IP Security (IPSec) VPN. Consideration should also be given to how that VPN solution will affect routing to and from the branch offices. Both VPN types will be described in detail later in this chapter.

High Availability

High Availability (HA) or resiliency is another factor that should be taken into consideration when implementing branch office solutions. It is imperative to ask how much downtime a certain branch office or site can tolerate and then incorporate that into your design and implementation. For example, a remote site that houses a critical manufacturing operation might have higher uptime requirements than a sales office. Such considerations will affect the site design, including factors such as any alternate and backup paths in the event of primary path failure, as well as physical device redundancy.

Routing

Routing is a core consideration when implementing branch office solutions. Consideration must be given to whether the proposed WAN solution will support routing. Following that, further consideration should be given to the type of routing protocol that will be implemented. The routing solution will depend on the solution implemented and may range from static to dynamic routing protocols, such as Border Gateway Protocol. When implementing the routing solution, it is important ensure that the design is scalable and allows for growth.

IP Services

Consideration should also be given to the types of IP services required at the site. For example, if a remote site has a few users and an Internet-based DSL connection to the corporate network, then it is important to determine what IP services will be required for such a solution. These services may include Network Address Translation (NAT) and Dynamic Host Configuration Protocol (DHCP) services. For larger remote sites that may have a direct connection to the private corporate WAN, for example, consideration should be given to Quality of Service, especially if multimedia traffic (e.g., voice and video) is a requirement, and WAN optimization solutions.

Mobility

In some implementations, remote offices may offer VPN services for teleworkers who work out of that region or office rather than having such a user access the VPN from the main corporate network. This typically requires that these offices have their own Internet connection, which introduces a new set of security, performance, connectivity, and reliability challenges.

Optimization

Gone are the days when simply adding bandwidth was the primary solution used to address all network performance issues. In the cost-conscious business environment of today, there is a general trend toward doing more with less. Depending on the branch office solution implemented, you should also take WAN optimization and acceleration tools and solutions into consideration, as these can assist in better WAN utilization and overall network performance.

BRANCH OFFICE CLASSIFICATION

Branch offices are typically classified as small, medium, or large. These classifications typically drive the design for that specific branch office, including factors such as the type of connectivity, security, and the level of resiliency required for the particular site. The following sections describe general characteristics of these types of branch offices.

Small Branch Offices

Small branch offices typically connect directly to headquarters via either a private WAN link or a VPN over the Internet, or, in some cases, a VPN over the private WAN link. Because the Internet is typically used for small branch office connectivity, the considerations for these offices are typically broken up into two main categories: access technologies and VPN options. Small branch offices typically use broadband connections to access the main corporate network. These technologies include DSL and cable, both of which are described later in this chapter.

Additional IP services, such as DHCP and NAT, are typically performed by the router, which also provides the WAN and PSTN connectivity. The VPN solutions, used to ensure data integrity over public networks such as the Internet, will depend on the business and regulatory requirements of the industry. Figure 10-1 below illustrates typical branch office connectivity to the enterprise network:

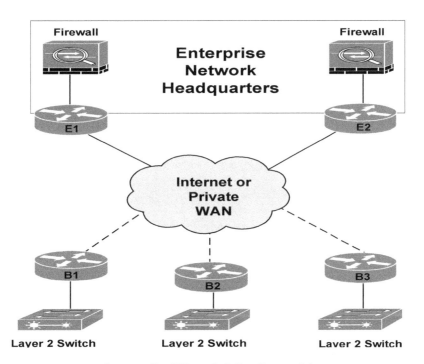

Fig. 10-1. Small Branch Office Connectivity

Figure 10-1 illustrates a typical small branch office implementation. Within the small branch offices themselves, users are typically connected to Layer 2 switches. Depending on the technologies implemented at these remote sites, for example, IP Telephony, these Layer 2 switches may provide Power over Ethernet (PoE) capability to provide power to IP phones. However, the core functionality at the remote site is provided by the branch office router, which is responsible for PSTN connectivity for phone service, NAT, DHCP, and VPN connectivity to the enterprise network. Depending on the VPN solution implemented, static or dynamic routing may be used to provide connectivity between the remote sites and the enterprise network.

Medium-Sized Branch Offices

Medium-sized branch offices typically require more resiliency than small branch offices. These types of offices typically have either redundant WAN routers connected to a private WAN or are using MPLS service in addition to an Internet-based backup solution. Because of the additional redundancy requirements, medium-sized branch offices may use either Layer 2 or Layer 3 switches and employ First Hop Redundancy Protocols (FHRPs), such as Hot Standby Router Protocol (HSRP), to ensure high availability.

In most cases, medium-sized branch offices will have their own DHCP server onsite to provide dynamic addressing and address resolution services for users. However, in other cases, the branch office routers may still be required to provide addressing services to local hosts that are connected to the LAN. Figure 10-2 below illustrates a typical medium-sized branch office implementation that has a primary connection through a private network and then a backup connection via the public network or Internet:

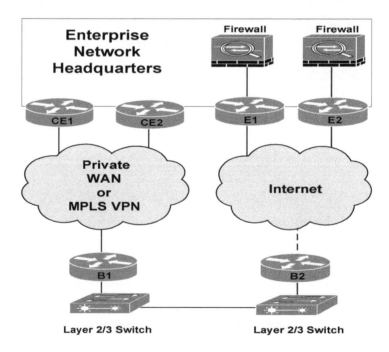

Fig. 10-2. Medium-Sized Branch Office Connectivity Using Multiple Routers

Referencing Figure 10-2, the medium-sized branch office has two connections for redundancy. The primary connection, via the private WAN or MPLS VPN, is backed up by an Internet VPN solution using router B2. FHRPs, such as HSRP, are typically employed on the LAN, allowing traffic at the site to use the primary connection and then, in the event that it fails or is unavailable, use the backup solution. Layer 2 or Layer 3 switches may be employed to connect both users and hosts, including any servers, if applicable.

While the design provides more resiliency than that of the small office, it also introduces some additional complexity, such as routing and route summarization. With such designs, consideration should also be given to traffic flows through the primary and backup connections to ensure complete reachability and functionality across both.

In some instances, the redundancy requirements for a basic medium-sized branch office may be satisfied using a single router that has both a connection to the private WAN or MPLS VPN and a connection to the Internet for backup purposes. While the solution is viable, it is important to remember that while the solution does provide connectivity redundancy, the router itself becomes a single point of failure. It is therefore important to understand the acceptable downtime for such offices in the event that the router itself fails. Additional preparation, such as having a similarly configured router on standby, may be used; however, if the hardware is available, it makes sense to integrate it and use it when the primary hardware is unavailable, instead of using it to replace the primary hardware in the event of failure. Figure 10-3 below illustrates a medium-sized branch office solution that uses a single router connected to both a private network, or MPLS VPN, and the Internet for redundancy:

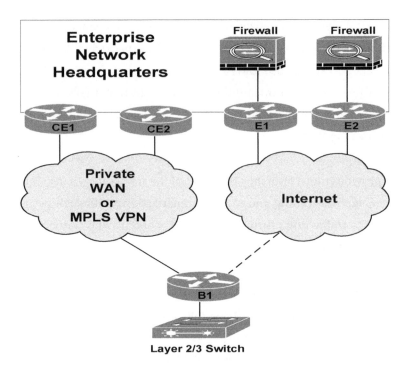

Fig. 10-3. Medium-Sized Branch Office Connectivity Using a Single Router

Referencing Figure 10-3, instead of using FHRPs for LAN redundancy, the single router is configured with floating static routes that forward traffic out of the backup Internet-based connection when the primary path is unavailable. A floating static route is simply one with a higher administrative distance that routes learned via a dynamic routing protocol or other configured static routes. The implementation of floating static routes will be illustrated later in this chapter.

Large Branch Offices

Large branch office designs commonly mirror campus or enterprise networks regarding their redundancy and resiliency requirements. Like medium-sized branch offices, these offices typically have redundant WAN connections. While large branch offices typically have redundant routers connected to the private WAN or MPLS VPN, they can also employ Internet-based backup connectivity in a similar manner to medium-sized branch offices.

Large branch offices typically include both Layer 2 and Layer 3 switches, allowing for site LAN redundancy similar to that provided at the enterprise network, although the level of Access Layer redundancy at such an office may not necessarily mirror that of the enterprise network. The following diagram, Figure 10-4, illustrates a redundant large branch office implementation that is dual-homed to either a private WAN or an MPLS VPN:

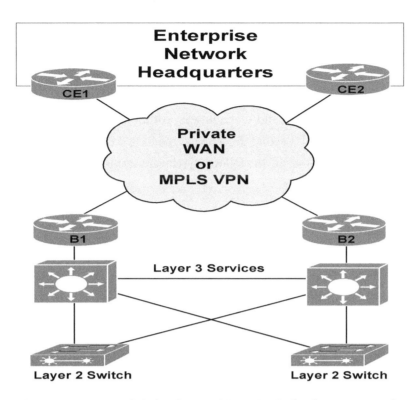

Fig. 10-4. Large Branch Office Connectivity Using Redundant Private Links

Referencing the topology illustrated in Figure 10-4, the large branch office is dual-homed to the private WAN or MPLS VPN, providing WAN connectivity. Layer 3 switches provide routing functionality within the branch office. These switches also provide gateway and first-hop redundancy for the LAN. Dynamic or static routing is used to ensure symmetric routing to and from the site. However, in some cases, load sharing or load balancing may also be used.

Layer 2 switches are used for user connectivity. If the site is using IP Telephony solutions, then these switches may also provide PoE for the IP phones that are connected to them. Although this design closely mirrors that of the enterprise network, there is typically a single Access Layer switch, such as a Catalyst 4500R series switch, to which all users and devices are connected per floor. Within the enterprise network, it is common for multiple Access Layer switches to be implemented, providing Access Layer redundancy in addition to redundancy at the other layers.

As was previously stated, it is also possible for the dual-WAN design for the large office to include an Internet-based backup connection and mirror a WAN design somewhat similar to that of the medium-sized office with multiple routers, as depicted in Figure 10-2. When that is the case, because the data will be traversing a public network, it is important to ensure that industry compliance and regulatory requirements are also taken into consideration.

DATA TRANSMISSION BASICS

Data transmission refers to the process of sending data or the progress of the sent data signals after they have been transmitted. It is imperative to have a solid understanding of some of the different technologies and principles pertaining to data transmission in order to understand completely cable and DSL transmission broadband technologies. Although going into detail on all specifics pertaining to data transmission is beyond the scope of the ROUTE exam requirements, the following sections cover and briefly describe the following relevant terms and technologies:

- Analog and digital signaling
- Data modulation
- Multiplexing
- Baseband and broadband
- Noise (interference)
- Attenuation
- Coaxial cable
- Twisted pair cable

Analog and Digital Signaling

On data networks, information can be transmitted using either analog signaling or digital signaling. Computers generate and interpret digital signals as electric current, which is measured in volts. The stronger the electrical signal, the higher the voltage. After the signal has been generated, it travels over copper cabling as electrical current, over fiber optic cabling as light pulses (waves), or through the atmosphere as electromagnetic (radio) waves.

Analog data signals are also generated as voltage. However, unlike digital signals, the voltage varies in analog signals and is represented as a wavy line when plotted on a graph. All analog signals are characterized by the following four characteristics:

- Amplitude
- Frequency
- Wavelength
- Pulse

The amplitude is a measure of the signal's (wave's) strength at any given time. The frequency is the number of times the wave's amplitude cycles from its starting point, through its highest amplitude and its lowest amplitude, and back to its starting point over a fixed period of time. Frequency is expressed in cycles per seconds, or hertz (Hz). Wavelength is the difference between the corresponding points on a wave's cycle, for example, between one peak and the next peak. Wavelengths are expressed in meters or feet. The wavelength is inversely proportional to the frequency, meaning that the higher the frequency, the shorter the wavelength, and vice versa.

Finally, the term 'phase' refers to the progress of a wave over time in relationship to a fixed point. If, for example, two waves start at the same time, with both being at their highest amplitude, the two waves would be in phase. However, if both waves started at the same time, with the first wave starting at its lowest amplitude and the second wave starting at its highest amplitude, the waves would be 180 degrees out of phase. These analog characteristics are illustrated in Figure 10-5 below:

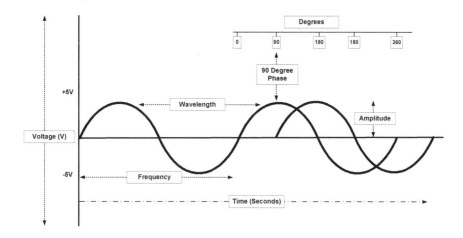

Fig. 10-5. Analog Signal Characteristics

Data Modulation

Given the advances in technology, data is primarily sent using digital transmission. However, there are still some network technologies, such as telephone lines, that use only analog transmission. The issue arises in the fact that the digital signals must be able to communicate over analog transmission networks, and vice versa. For example, when using dial-up Internet access, the computer uses digital transmission, even though it is connected to an analog transmission network (i.e., the telephone line). In such situations, a modem is required to modulate digital signals into analog signals at the transmitting end, and then demodulate analog signals into digital signals at the receiving end. The word modem actually stands for modulator and demodulator, which is a reflection of the functions performed by these devices, which include dial-up modems, cable modems, and DSL modems, for example.

Data modulation is a technology used to modify analog signals to make them more suitable for carrying data over a communication path. In modulation, a simple wave called a carrier wave is combined with the information or data wave to produce a unique signal that is transmitted from one node to another. The carrier wave contains preset properties, such as the frequency, amplitude, and phase, and when combined with the information wave, any one of the carrier wave properties is then modified, resulting in a new blended signal that contains the properties of both the carrier wave and the data wave. When the signal reaches its destination, the receiver separates the data (information) from the carrier wave via demodulation.

Multiplexing

Multiplexing is a form of transmission that allows multiple signals to travel simultaneously over a single medium. In order to carry multiple signals, the physical media is separated logically or segmented into smaller channels, also commonly referred to as sub-channels.

In order to combine and transmit multiple signals over a single medium, a multiplexer (mux) is required at the transmitting end of the channel. At the receiving end, a demultiplexer (demux) is required to separate the combined signals and regenerate them in their original form. Multiplexing allows networks to increase the amount of data that can be transmitted in a given amount of time over a given bandwidth.

There are many different types of multiplexing available, and the type that is used depends on the media, transmission, and reception that the equipment can handle. While going into all the different types of multiplexing is beyond the requirements of the ROUTE exam, we will describe Frequency Division Multiplexing because of its relevance in cable and DSL networks.

Frequency Division Multiplexing (FDM) assigns a unique frequency band to each individual communications sub-channel. Signals are modulated with different carrier frequencies and are then multiplexed to simultaneously travel over a single channel. Each signal is then demultiplexed at the receiving end. FDM was first used by telephone companies when they discovered that it allowed them to send multiple voice signals over a single cable. That meant that rather than running separate lines for each residence they could send as many as 24 multiplexed signals over a single neighborhood line. Each signal was then demultiplexed before being brought into the home.

With recent technological advances, telephone companies can use FDM to multiplex signals on the phone line that enters a home. Voice communications use the frequency band of 300 Hz to 3300 Hz, although the most common representation of this range is 300 Hz to 3KHz. Because everything above the 3 KHz range was simply unused space, telephone companies used FDM to allow them to send data signals in this space without interrupting voice communications, allowing for DSL service over existing telephone lines. In a similar manner to telephone companies, cable operators also use FDM to multiplex signals over a single channel to provide television, voice, and data services over cable networks.

Baseband and Broadband

Baseband is a transmission form in which signals are sent through direct current (DC) applied to the wire. Because DC requires the exclusive use of the wire, baseband systems can transmit only one signal, or channel, at a time and every device on the baseband system shares the same channel. When one node on a baseband system is transmitting data, all other nodes must wait for that transmission to end before they can send any data that they may need to send. A common example of baseband systems is half-duplex Ethernet.

Broadband is a form of transmission in which signals are modulated as radio frequency (RF) analog waves that use different frequency ranges. Unlike baseband, broadband technology does not encode information as digital pulses. Broadband systems handle a relatively wide range (band) of frequencies, which may be divided into channels or frequency bins. While broadband is generally more expensive than baseband, it can carry more data and span greater distances than baseband systems. An example of a broadband system is cable television.

Noise (Interference)

Noise is an undesirable influence that may distort or degrade a signal. While there are many different types of noise, one of the most common is electromagnetic interference (EMI), which is caused by waves that emanate from electrical devices, such as televisions, motors, power lines, and fluorescent lights, for example. While EMI greatly affects analog transmissions, it does not affect digital transmissions as much. Additionally, fiber optic cabling (which will be described last in this section) is completely unaffected by electromagnetic interference.

Attenuation

Attenuation is the loss of the strength of a signal as it travels away from its source. This is one of the most common transmission flaws. Fortunately, however, there are solutions that can be used to rectify this problem.

In order to boost the strength of analog signals, an amplifier is used. An amplifier is simply an electronic device that increases the voltage or strength of the signals. Cable operators use amplifiers to boost the strength of signals. It is important to know that amplifiers also increase the strength of any noise that is associated with the signal. In other words, when an analog signal is amplified, the noise that it has accumulated is also amplified, which may actually cause the analog signal to worsen significantly. This is especially observed after several amplifications.

Digital transmission does not use amplifiers to boost the signal strength. Instead, devices called repeaters are used. In addition, when digital signals are repeated, they are transmitted in their original form—without any accumulated noise—in a process called regeneration. Both amplifiers and repeaters operate at Layer 1 of the OSI Model.

Coaxial Cable

Coaxial cable, commonly referred to as coax, consists of a central metal core, often made of copper, surrounded by an insulator, a braided metal shielding called braiding or shield, and an outer cover, referred to as the sheath or jacket. The coax core may be constructed of one solid metal wire or several thin strands of metal wire.

The coax core carries the electromagnetic signal and the braided metal shielding acts as a shield against noise, as well as a ground for the signal. The insulator layer consists of a plastic material such as Polyvinyl Chloride (PVC) or Teflon. The insulation protects the core from the metal shielding because if the two made contact, the wire would short-circuit. The sheath, which protects the cable from physical damage, may also be made of PVC or other materials. Because of its shielding, most coax cable has a high resistance to noise. Additionally, coax also has the ability to carry signals further than twisted pair cabling, for example, before the signal needs to be amplified. Twisted pair cabling is described in the following section.

Twisted Pair Cable

Twisted pair cable consists of color-coded pairs of insulated copper wires, with each having a diameter of between 0.4 mm and 0.8 mm. Two wires are twisted around each other to form a pair and all the pairs are encased in a plastic sheath. The number of pairs in a cable varies depending on the type of cable. Twisted pair cable is relatively inexpensive, flexible, and easy to install. Additionally, it can travel significant differences before a repeater is needed; however, it cannot span greater distances than coaxial cable or fiber optic cable. All twisted pair cable falls into one of two categories: Shielded Twisted Pair (STP) and Unshielded Twisted Pair (UTP).

STP consists of twisted wire pairs that not only are individually insulated but also are surrounded by a shielding made of a metallic substance, such as foil, although some STP cabling uses a braided copper shielding. This shielding serves two purposes. The first is that it acts as a barrier to electromagnetic forces, and the second is that it is used to contain the electrical energy of the signals inside the cable.

UTP cabling consists of one or more insulated wire pairs encased in a plastic sheath. Unlike STP, UTP does not contain additional shielding for the twisted pairs, which makes it both less expensive and less resistant to interference than STP.

CABLE ACCESS TECHNOLOGIES

Having gone through the basics pertaining to branch offices, as well as data transmission basics, this section describes broadband cable access technologies, the components used within cable networks, and the configuration of Cisco routers when connected to cable access technologies.

Cable modems are network bridge devices that operate at Layer 1 and Layer 2 of the OSI Model and that connect home or branch office networks to the Internet through the cable television system. On the network side, cable modems support Ethernet, and on the cable side, cable modems support DOCSIS. However, it should be noted that although cable modems generally follow the DOCSIS standard, implementations commonly can and do vary by provider. DOCSIS is beyond the scope of the current ROUTE exam requirements and will not be described in any further detail in this chapter.

Cable companies use Hybrid Fiber Coaxial cable (HFC) networks to provide fiber and coaxial connections to the customer. The coaxial portion is used to carry the television service and the fiber optical cable is used for the data connection. HFC networks will be described in detail later in this section. Typical cable throughput varies anywhere between 1Mbps and 6Mbps for downloads and between 128Kbps and 768Kbps for uploads. In theory, however, cable modems have the ability to support up to 30Mbps download speeds. Cable networks are a shared multipoint circuit, which means that the actual download and upload speeds depend on the level of activity on the network at any given point in time.

While cable technology and functionality is not a core ROUTE exam requirement, it is still very important to have a basic understanding of cable network components. These components, which are described in the following sections, include the following:

- Cable Modems
- Cable Modem Termination Systems
- Hybrid Fiber Coaxial Networks
- Local Headend

Cable modems (CMs) communicate with routers, called Cable Modem Termination Systems (CMTSs), over the HFC plant using the DOCSIS standard. Cable modems are considered CPE, or Customer Premise Equipment, and they perform the modulation and demodulation of signals received from the computer, etc., to and from the CMTS.

The CMTS is a piece of equipment commonly located in a cable company's Local Headend (LE). The CMTS provides high-speed data services, such as cable Internet or Voice over IP, to cable subscribers. The CMTS receives analog data from the CM and modulates it back into a digital format before forwarding it on to the Internet.

Hybrid Fiber Coaxial (HFC) is used to describe a telecommunications industry term for a broadband network that combines both optical fiber and coaxial cable. The HFC network resides between the CM and the CMTS. Within the HFC, one or more fiber nodes are used to convert digital signals from the LE into analog signals, which are then sent to the CM at the premise, and vice-versa.

The Local Headend (LE) is the cable operator facility where the received signals are processed, formatted, and distributed over to the cable network. The CMTS resides at the LE. Understandably, these terms may be new and even confusing. Therefore, for additional clarity, Figure 10-6 below illustrates these components and how they are integrated in data cable networks:

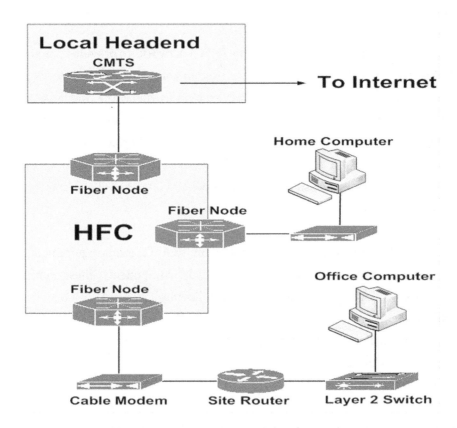

Fig. 10-6. Cable Access Data Network Components

The cable network components that were described in the previous section are illustrated in Figure 10-6. The diagram illustrates broadband connectivity for Small-Office Home-Office (SOHO) users, as well as for remote branch offices that connect using broadband technology. For the remote office, the site router will need to be configured to provide additional IP services, such as DHCP, NAT, and VPN connectivity to the enterprise network.

In most cases, when connecting to the Internet using cable, the cable typically provides the cable modem to which the router may then be connected. In some cases, however, your company may select to use their own brand of cable modems based on vendor preference and other factors, such as security, manageability, and control. It is therefore important to have a fundamental understanding of the tasks involved so that you are able to perform some basic troubleshooting. The following section describes the sequence of steps that a typical cable modem will transition through before it becomes operational. These seven steps are as follows:

1. The cable modem (CM) scans for the downstream (DS) frequency. By default, 53 MHz is the starting frequency for Cisco CMs. The CM locks on to the digital carrier center frequency and looks for the Hexadecimal 1FFE MPEG-2 packet identifier (PID), which signifies the DOCSIS standard.

2. The CM waits for all upstream channel descriptors (UCDs) used for frequency, modulation profile, channel width, and other information. If the CM receives the wrong UCD, it times out and it tries the next UCD until it finally connects. Some modems might actually listen to an upstream channel change (UCC) command sent by the CMTS on the DS frequency, which is used to advise the CM of the UCD it should be using. Current versions of Cisco CMs have the following three scanning algorithms:
   - Scan National Television System Committee (NTSC)
   - Scan select European (EuroDOCSIS) frequencies
   - Scan for a DOCSIS DS at every frequency divisible by 250 kHz or 1 MHz

3. The Layer 1 and Layer 2 connection between the CM and the CMTS is established. This allows the CM and the CMTS to become synchronized.

4. After the modem and the CMTS are synchronized with levels and timing, the modem obtains its IP address through DHCP. Most CM systems set up a non-routable address space for the modems, such as the 192.168.0.0/24 subnet, which can be allocated to clients, and use a public addressing network for CPE, to allow Internet access.

5. The modem obtains the DOCSIS configuration via TFTP. The DOCSIS configuration file is a binary file that contains the parameters required for the modem to come online. This configuration file will vary by provider. The DOCSIS file contains important information, such as maximum upstream and downstream speeds, radio frequency information, SNMP management information, and authentication information, among other things.

6. The modem registers Quality of Service (QoS) with the CMTS. QoS for networks is an industry-wide set of standards and mechanisms for ensuring high-quality performance for critical applications. QoS is very important, especially if the cable provider is also providing the subscriber with Voice over IP (VoIP) services.

7. The modem initializes IP services and downloads the configuration file, and configures routing and other IP services, such as NAT, so that one or many subscriber devices can access the Internet at the same time. The modem receives the following information from the provider DHCP server:
   - The IP address and subnet mask
   - The default gateway
   - The address of the TFTP server
   - The name of the DOCSIS configuration file
   - The address of the Time of Day (ToD) server

- The address of the Syslog server
- The DNS domain information

For easier reference, this sequence of steps is summarized and illustrated in Figure 10-7 below:

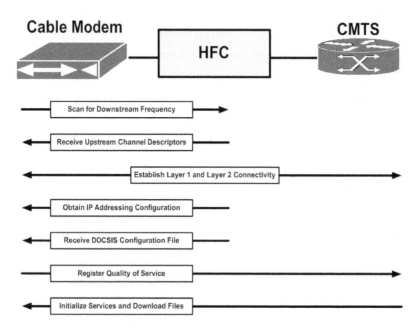

Fig. 10-7. Understanding Basic Cable Modem Initialization

Cisco IOS Router Configuration for Cable Internet Connectivity

Given that cable modems have an Ethernet handoff, the configuration of Cisco IOS routers for cable Internet connectivity requires no special configuration on the router itself. Instead, a selected LAN interface on the router is simply connected to the cable modem physically and is then configured to receive addressing configuration information via DHCP. Following this, additional standard configuration, such as DHCP and NAT, should be implemented to allow users connected to the internal network access to the Internet. The steps for configuring a router for cable Internet connectivity are as follows:

1. Configure the router Ethernet interface that is connected to the cable modem to receive addressing information via DHCP using the `ip address dhcp` interface configuration command. This allows the router to receive the default route and other addressing information (e.g., DNS servers) dynamically from the cable provider.

NOTE: In some instances, cable vendors may provide static addressing information for their business-class cable customers. If you are assigned static IP addresses, simply configure them on the router interface connected to the modem using the `ip address [address] [mask]` interface configuration command, followed by the `ip route 0.0.0.0 0.0.0.0 [next-hop-address]` global configuration command to specify the default route. Because cable is a shared medium, you should avoid configuring a default static route that points out of an interface (e.g., `ip route 0.0.0.0 0.0.0.0 FastEthernet0/0`). This eliminates extensive use of Address Resolution Protocol (ARP) and helps avoid intermittent connectivity issues due to ARP timeouts.

2. Configure IP addressing for the LAN interface that will be connected to the internal network using the `ip address [address] [mask]` interface configuration command. This interface typically uses networks within the private RFC 1918 range.

3. Configure Cisco IOS DHCP server functionality on the router. This allows hosts that are connected to the LAN to receive IP addressing information. This is implemented using the `ip dhcp pool [name]` global configuration command. When configuring Cisco IOS DHCP server functionality, you can either manually specify DNS servers or use the `import all` DHCP pool configuration command to allow the information the router will receive from the cable provider (e.g., DNS servers) to be provided to the LAN hosts.

4. Configure Network Address Translation/Port Address Translation on the router so that the privately-addressed hosts can access the Internet. Designate inside and outside interfaces using the `ip nat inside` and `ip nat outside` interface configuration commands on the internal and external interfaces, respectively.

The following configuration example shows how to configure a router for basic cable Internet connectivity, assuming that the router is receiving addressing information via DHCP. The configuration also configures the router to import all received DHCP parameters, which will include DNS, WINS server information, and the domain prefix. The router is configured to prevent the allocation of the 10.0.0.1 and 10.0.0.2 addresses, which are configured on the router itself and the connected LAN switch. Finally, NAT is also configured on the router, allowing hosts on the internal network to access the Internet.

```
Site-Router(config)#ip dhcp excluded-address 10.0.0.1 10.0.0.2
Site-Router(config)#interface FastEthernet0/0
Site-Router(config-if)#description 'Connected To Cable Modem'
Site-Router(config-if)#ip address dhcp
Site-Router(config-if)#no shutdown
Site-Router(config-if)#ip nat outside
Site-Router(config-if)#exit
Site-Router(config)#interface FastEthernet0/1
Site-Router(config-if)#description 'Connected To Internal LAN'
Site-Router(config-if)#ip address 10.0.0.1 255.255.255.0
Site-Router(config-if)#ip nat inside
```

```
Site-Router(config-if)#no shutdown
Site-Router(config-if)#exit
Site-Router(config)#ip dhcp pool LAN-POOL
Site-Router(dhcp-config)#network 10.0.0.0 255.255.255.0
Site-Router(dhcp-config)#import all
Site-Router(dhcp-config)#default-router 10.0.0.1
Site-Router(dhcp-config)#exit
Site-Router(config)#access-list 100 permit ip 10.0.0.0 0.0.0.255 any
Site-Router(config)#ip nat inside source list 100 interface Fa0/0 overload
```

As illustrated above, the configuration itself is very simple and straightforward. However, keep in mind that in some cases, corporate policy dictates that users use corporate DNS servers and domain prefixes. In that event, the import all command should not be used when configuring the DHCP pool, and those parameters should be entered manually as illustrated in the following configuration example, which shows the modified site router DHCP configuration:

```
Site-Router(config)#ip dhcp excluded-address 10.0.0.1 10.0.0.2
Site-Router(config)#ip dhcp pool LAN-POOL
Site-Router(dhcp-config)#network 10.0.0.0 255.255.255.0
Site-Router(dhcp-config)#dns-server 172.16.1.254 172.17.1.254
Site-Router(dhcp-config)#netbios-name-server 172.18.1.254
Site-Router(dhcp-config)#domain-name howtonetwork.net
Site-Router(dhcp-config)#default-router 10.0.0.1
Site-Router(dhcp-config)#exit
```

NOTE: If the import all command is included, by default, any explicit configuration commands take precedence. Imported options will be used only if no explicit option configuration is included in the Cisco IOS DHCP server functionality configuration. This is often a commonly confused topic when it comes to implementing Cisco IOS DHCP.

DSL ACCESS TECHNOLOGIES

Digital Subscriber Line (DSL) is an increasingly popular method used for branch office connectivity. A family of DSL types has been developed to provide high-speed Internet services over the existing telephone line infrastructure. The idea behind DSL technologies is to use a wider frequency band for communicating data over the existing twisted pair lines (telephone lines) at the same time as voiceband. This means that a second frequency band, above the voiceband, must be defined to perform data modulation. The two different frequency bands for voice and data are illustrated in Figure 10-8 below:

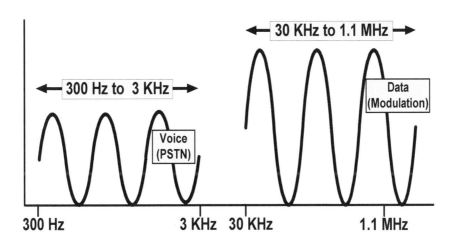

Fig. 10-8. Voice and Data Frequency Bands

Referencing Figure 10-8, the frequency range used for voice is from 300 Hz to 3 KHz, while the frequency range used for data ranges from 30 KHz to 1.1 MHz. The frequency band used for data is further segmented into two more bands, depending on the modulation technique implemented; however, this is beyond the scope of the ROUTE exam requirements and will not be described in any further detail in this chapter.

As with cable technologies, while you are not required to go into detail on the components used in different broadband technologies, it is important to have a basic understanding of the components in DSL networks, and how they interact and how they are used. The following sections describe the following DSL components:

- Digital Subscriber Line Modem
- POTS Splitter
- Digital Subscriber Line Access Multiplexer
- Asynchronous Transfer Mode

DSL modems contain receptacles to connect to the telephone line of the subscriber as well as to the computer. Current DSL modems also provide wireless connectivity. In DSL terminology, a DSL modem at the Customer Premise Equipment (CPE) end of the local loop (i.e., at the subscriber's house) is referred to as an *x*DSL Transmission Unit-Remote (*x*TU-R). The acronym *x*TU-R is used to refer to either a DSL modem or a DSL-capable router. The *x* in *x*TU-R is replaced by the actual DSL variant. For example, for Asymmetric DSL (ADSL), which is the most common type of DSL service, the modem would be referred to as an ATU-R, with the A standing for Asymmetric. DSL variants are described in detail later in this section.

The primary function of the DSL modem or ATU-R is to modulate outgoing signals from the telephone and computer and demodulate incoming DSL signals from the telephone provider network.

When the DSL modem or ATU-R receives the outgoing signal, it forwards the modulated signal across the local loop toward the central office (CO). Within the CO, a plain old telephone service (POTS) splitter is used to separate the data signal from any voice signals that are also carried on the line.

Once the signals have been separated, the data request is then sent to a Digital Subscriber Line Access Multiplexer (DSLAM), which exists for the sole purpose of terminating the CO side of the DSL link. A DSLAM is a single chassis that contains multiple subscriber-facing DSL modems, which are referred to as xTU-C devices. xTU-C stands for Transmission Unit-Central, which indicates that this is a DSL modem in the telephone provider's CO. As is the case with xTU-R devices, the x in xTU-C is replaced by the DSL variant. As an example, an ATU-C would be used for Asymmetric DSL (ADSL) service.

Once the DSLAM has received the data, it uses an integrated Asynchronous Transfer Mode (ATM) switch to send the data across the provider ATM network until it ends up on an aggregation router on the provider's network that connects to the Internet. ATM is standard for cell relay wherein information for multiple service types, such as voice, video, and data, are transmitted in small, fixed-size 53-byte cells via connection-oriented Virtual Circuits. ATM will be described in detail later in this chapter. Figure 10-9 below illustrates the DSL network components:

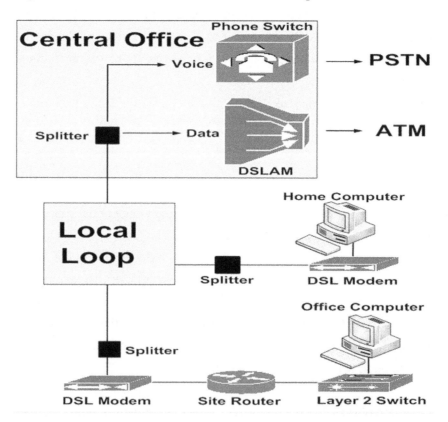

Fig. 10-9. Digital Subscriber Line Network Components

NOTE: In the DSL networks of today, microfilters replace splitters at the customer premise. A microfilter is a passive low-pass filter that is connected to the subscriber's telephone wall jack. Microfilters allow only frequencies in the 0 to 4 KHz range to pass through to connected analog devices, such as analog telephones, modems, and fax machines. Microfilters maintain voice quality on analog devices when DSL and voice are coexistent on the same telephone line.

DSL types can be divided into two broad categories, which are Symmetric DSL (SDSL) and Asymmetric DSL (ADSL). Although both are part of the DSL family of technologies, these types of DSL have different characteristics. It is therefore important to understand the differences between the two. These two flavors and their respective characteristics are both described in the following sections.

Symmetric Digital Subscriber Line

Symmetric Digital Subscriber Lines provide equal capacity for data traveling both upstream and downstream. Symmetrical transmission is most suited to users who both upload and download significant amounts of data. The following section describes SDSL variants.

Symmetric DSL is a DSL variant that runs over one pair of copper wires and supports data only. SDSL does not support analog calls because of the fact that it takes over the entire bandwidth of the line. SDSL is a proprietary technology that was never standardized. SDSL provides up to T1 and E1 downstream and upstream throughput. SDSL has a distance limit of 10,000 feet. SDSL is also typically offered in the speeds shown in Table 10-1 below:

Table 10-1. Symmetric DSL Variant Speeds

SDSL Variant	Upstream Speed	Downstream Speed
SDSL-192	192 Kbps	192 Kbps
SDSL-384	384 Kbps	384 Kbps
SDSL-768	768 Kbps	768 Kbps
SDSL-1.1	1.1 Mbps	1.1 Mbps

Single-Pair High-Speed DSL or Single-Line High bit-rate DSL (SHDSL) is an industry standard for SHDSL defined in ITU-T recommendation G.991.2. SHDSL is also referred to as G.SHDSL. SHDSL uses frequencies that overlap with those used by traditional POTS to provide symmetric data rates, which means SHDSL does not support analog calls. SHDSL provides symmetric throughput of 2.3 Mbps; however, an optional extended SHDSL mode makes it possible to allow even greater symmetric throughput speeds. SHDSL has a distance limitation of 26,000 feet.

High bit-rate DSL (HDSL) is the most mature of the xDSL approaches. HDSL can be used at either the T1 or the E1 rates. This DSL variant is commonly used in place of traditional T1 circuits. As is the case with SHDSL and SDSL, HDSL does not allow for standard telephone service over copper lines. HDSL has a distance limitation of 12,000 feet.

HDSL2 is the 2nd generation of HDSL, with a 6dB Noise Margin. HDLS2 provides symmetric service at T1 speeds using a single-wire pair rather than the two pairs of HDSL service. HDSL2 also was developed as a standard, allowing for interoperability between different vendors' equipment. HDSL2 employs a line coding technique known as trellis-coded pulse amplitude modulation (TC-PAM), also known as trellis-coded modulation (TCM), and has a distance limitation of 22,000 feet.

ISDN DSL (IDSL) uses ISDN-based technology to provide a data communication channel across existing copper telephone lines at a rate of 1.44 Kbps. IDSL uses a single-wire pair for symmetric speeds. While IDSL has a distance limitation of 18,000 feet, local telephone providers can increase this limitation to 45,000 feet using repeaters. Repeaters, which were described earlier in this chapter, are used to boost digital signals in the same manner that amplifiers are used to boost analog signals.

Asymmetric Digital Subscriber Line

ADSL is the most common type of DSL service. Unlike SDSL, which provides symmetric (same) upstream and downstream speeds, Asymmetric DSL provides different downstream and upstream speeds. In asymmetrical connections, the downstream throughput is higher than the downstream throughput. Additionally, it is important to know that unlike SDSL variants, ADSL variants allow for voice and data to be sent simultaneously over the existing telephone line. This is because ADSL operates at higher frequencies than PSTN/POTS so they can coexist on the same media. The following section describes ADSL variants.

Asymmetric DSL (ADSL) supports speeds of 1.5 to 8 Mbps, depending on line quality, distance, and wire gauge. Upstream rates range between 16 Kbps and 1 Mbps. Table 10-2 below lists the distance limitations for ADSL based on wire gauge and data rate:

Table 10-2. Asymmetric DSL Speeds and Distance Limitations

Data Rate (Mbps)	Wire Gauge (AWG)	Wire Size (mm)	Distance (feet)	Distance (kilometers)
1.5 or 2	24	0.5	18,000	5.5
1.5 or 2	26	0.4	15,000	4.6
6.1	24	0.5	12,000	3.7
6.1	26	0.4	9,000	2.7

G.Lite ADSL is also referred to as splitterless ADSL because it allows voice and data to coexist on the existing telephone line without using a splitter. The idea was to trade the potential for bandwidth greater than T1 speeds in order to enable 'splitterless' installation, meaning that if the functionality of splitting off the analog voice could be built into the ADSL modem, then it wouldn't be necessary to dispatch a technician for installation.

> **NOTE:** Although now standardized in ITU G.992.2, it is unclear if it will be widely deployed, since service providers are currently holding trials with another splitterless variation on ADSL that is faster (ADSL2). G.Lite ADSL has a distance limitation of up to 25,000 feet.

ADSL2 extends the capability of basic ADSL in data rates to 12 Mbps downstream and 3.5 Mbps upstream, with a mandatory capability of ADSL2 transceivers of 8 Mbps downstream and 800 Kbps upstream. However, actual speeds may be reduced, depending on line quality and the distance from the subscriber to the CO. ADSL2 is standardized in ITU G.992.3 and is referred to as G.DMT.bis. Splitterless ADSL2, on the other hand, is standardized in ITU G.992.4 and has the data rate mandatory capability reduced to 1.536 Mbps downstream and 512 Kbps upstream. It is also referred to as G.lite.bis. ADSL2 has a distance limitation of about 20,000 feet.

ADSL2Plus, or ADSL2+, is standardized in ITU G.992.5. ADSL2+ extends the capability of basic ADSL by doubling the number of downstream bits. The data rates can be as high as 24 Mbps downstream and 1.4 Mbps upstream, depending on the distance from the CO to the subscriber's home. ADSL2+ also allows port bonding, where multiple ports are provisioned physically to the subscriber and the total bandwidth is equal to the sum of all provisioned ports. For example, if two lines capable of 24 Mbps were bonded, then the end result would be a connection capable of 48 Mbps. ADSL2+ port bonding is also known as G.998.x or G.Bond. Not all vendor DSLAMs support port bonding, and it is important to know that speeds vary depending on distance. ADSL2+ has a distance limitation of about 20,000 feet.

Rate-adaptive DSL (RADSL) has the same transmission limits as ADSL but it automatically adjusts transmission speed according to the length and quality of the local line. While this is considered the defining characteristic of RADSL, it should be noted that standard ADSL also allows the DSL modem to adapt speeds of data transfer. With Rate-adaptive DSL, connection speed is established when the line syncs up, and varies between 600 Kbps and 7 Mbps downstream and between 128 Kbps and 1 Mbps upstream. RADSL has a distance limitation of 18,000 feet.

Very High bit-rate DSL (VDSL or VHDSL) is the fastest DSL technology, with downstream rates of 13 to 52 Mbps and upstream rates of 1.5 to 2.3 Mbps over a single wire pair. VDSL can also operate in symmetric mode at 26 Mbps. VDSL is standardized in ITU G.993.1 and has a distance limitation of only 4,500 feet, which is considered a very short local loop. VDSL was principally developed for the transport of ATM at high speed over a short distance.

Very High bit-rate DSL 2 (VDSL2 or VHDSL2) is an enhancement of VDSL and is standardized in ITU-T G.993.2. VDSL2 also allows for the transmission of asymmetric and symmetric aggregate data rates up to 200 Mbps on twisted pairs using a bandwidth up to 30 MHz. ADSL-like long reach performance is one of the key advantages of VDSL2. Long Reach VDSL2 (LR-VDSL2)-enabled systems are capable of supporting speeds of around 1 to 4 Mbps downstream over distances of 16,000 feet, increasing the bit-rate up to symmetric 100 Mbps, as the loop is shortened.

Because ADSL is the most common DSL implementation, the remainder of this chapter will be restricted to ADSL operation and configuration. DSL provides Layer 1 connectivity to the provider's network. This connectivity is established between the xTU-R and the xTU-C. As previously stated, the ATU-C and ATU-R are the main endpoint components in an ADSL data service network. On the DSL provider side, the DSLAM has connectivity to the provider network via an ATM network—with ATM being the Layer 2 technology used. On the subscriber side, several methods can be used and include the following:
- Long Range Ethernet
- Routed Bridged Encapsulation
- Multiprotocol Encapsulation over ATM
- Service Selection Gateway
- PPP over ATM
- PPP over Ethernet

The Cisco Long Range Ethernet (LRE) solution leverages VDSL technology to extend Ethernet services over existing Category 1, 2, or 3 twisted pair cabling at speeds from 5 to 15 Mbps and distances up to 5,000 feet. The Cisco LRE technology delivers broadband service on the same lines as POTS, digital telephone, and Integrated Services Digital Network (ISDN) traffic. In addition, Cisco LRE supports modes compatible with ADSL technologies, allowing providers to provision LRE to buildings where broadband services already exist. Cisco LRE configuration is beyond the scope of the ROUTE exam requirements and will not be described in this chapter.

Routed Bridged Encapsulation (RBE) is the process by which a Stub-bridged segment is terminated on a point-to-point routed interface. The router routes on an Ethernet header carried over a point-to-point protocol, such as PPP, RFC 1483 ATM, or RFC 1490 Frame Relay. RBE was developed to address the known RFC1483 bridging issues, including Broadcast storms and security. Except for the fact that it operates exclusively over ATM, the RBE feature functions identically to half-bridging. Additional scalability, performance, and security can be achieved by using the unique characteristics of xDSL subscribers. As is the case with LRE, RBE configuration is also beyond the scope of the ROUTE exam requirements and will not be described in any further detail in this chapter.

Multiprotocol Encapsulation over ATM was originally standardized in RFC 1483, which was then rendered obsolete by RFC 2684. Multiprotocol Encapsulation over ATM describes two different methods for carrying connectionless network interconnect traffic over an ATM network, which are routed protocol data units (PDUs) and bridged PDUs. Routing allows multiplexing of multiple protocols over a single ATM Virtual Circuit (VC). The protocol of a carried PDU is identified by prefixing the PDU with an IEEE 802.2 Logical Link Control (LLC) header. Bridging performs higher-layer protocol multiplexing implicitly by ATM VCs. The configuration of Multiprotocol Encapsulation over ATM is beyond the scope of the ROUTE exam requirements and will not be illustrated or described in the remainder of this chapter.

The Cisco Service Selection Gateway (SSG) is a switching solution for service providers who offer Intranet, Extranet, and Internet connections to subscribers using broadband access technology, such as DSL, cable modems, or wireless LAN. SSG works in conjunction with the Cisco Subscriber Edge Services Manager (SESM), a software toolkit that can reside on Windows, UNIX, and Linux servers. Together with the SESM, SSG provides subscriber authentication, service selection, service connection, and accounting capabilities to subscribers of Internet services. The SSG-SESM solution, which is collectively known as Subscriber Access and Management (SAM), also provides account self-care portals for subscribers and branding advertisement abilities for service providers. Subscribers interact with a SESM-based Web application using a standard Internet browser. Current deployments include DSL, Public Wireless LAN (PWLAN), and Mobile Wireless solutions.

PPP over ATM and PPP over Ethernet are core ROUTE exam requirements that are described in detail later in this chapter. However, prior to delving into the specifics on those technologies, the following section describes Asynchronous Transfer Mode (ATM), which is used in PPP over ATM implementations. PPP is a core CCNA requirement and is not described in this chapter.

Asynchronous Transfer Mode Basics

ATM is an ITU-T standard for cell relay wherein information for multiple service types, such as voice, video, or data, is conveyed in small, fixed-size 53-byte cells via connection-oriented Virtual Circuits (VCs). ATM provides two kinds of virtual connection services: permanent and switched. Permanent Virtual Circuits (PVCs) are set up manually and remain up indefinitely until manually torn down. Switched Virtual Circuits (SVCs) are established dynamically when data needs to be transferred. SVCs are beyond the scope of this topic. The two main types of ATM Permanent Virtual Circuits are as follows:

- Permanent Virtual Channel Connections (PVCCs), which are specified by a Virtual Path Identifier (VPI) and a Virtual Channel Identifier (VCI)
- Permanent Virtual Path Connections (PVPCs), which are specified by a VPI only

Both PVCCs and PVPCs can support point-to-point and point-to-multipoint connections. A VCI is a unique identifier that indicates a particular Virtual Circuit on a network. It is a 16-bit field in the header of an ATM cell. VPI refers to an 8-bit user-to-network packet or 12-bit network-to-network packet field within the header of an ATM packet. The VPI, together with the VCI, is used to identify the next destination of a cell as it passes through a series of ATM switches on its way to its destination.

The use of ATM technology and services creates the need for an Adaptation Layer in order to support information transfer protocols, which are not based on ATM. The ATM Adaptation Layer defines how to segment and reassemble higher-layer packets into ATM cells, and how to handle various transmission aspects in the ATM Layer. Several ATM Adaptation Layer protocols (AALs) have been defined by the ITU-T. These protocols include the following:

- AAL 1
- AAL 2
- AAL 3/4
- AAL 5

Of these protocols, only AAL 5 is relevant to DSL technology. ATM AAL 5 was introduced to provide the following services and functions:

- Reduce protocol processing overhead
- Reduce transmission overhead
- Ensure adaptability to existing transport protocols

AAL 5 is used to send variable-length packets up to 65,535 bytes in size across an ATM network. Each AAL 5 packet is divided into a number of ATM cells and is reassembled into a packet before delivery to the receiving host in a process known as Segmentation and Reassembly (SAR). By default, AAL 5 SNAP encapsulation is used for ATM PVCs.

In AAL 5 SNAP (Subnetwork Access Protocol)-encapsulated PVCs, LLC (Logical Link Control) SNAP encapsulation is used to identify the protocol of packets transmitted across the ATM PVC. However, this encapsulation method adds bandwidth usage with the transmission of frames, which can affect voice quality. To address this issue, ATM AAL 5 MUX encapsulation can be used. AAL 5 MUX reduces SNAP encapsulation bandwidth usage by using multiplexed encapsulation to reduce the number of ATM cells needed to carry voice packets. ATM AAL 5 MUX in a VoIP environment results in improved throughput and bandwidth usage.

Point-to-Point Protocol over Ethernet

Point-to-Point Protocol over Ethernet (PPPoE) provides the ability to connect a network of hosts over a simple bridging access device to a remote access concentrator or aggregation concentrator. Each host uses its own PPP stack, thus presenting the user with a familiar user interface. Access control, billing, and type of service can be done on a per-user, rather than a per-site, basis. By default, PPPoE runs on top of ATM AAL 5 SNAP; however, PPPoE can also be configured to use ATM AAL 5 MUX encapsulation.

As specified in RFC 2516, PPPoE has two distinct stages: a discovery stage and a PPP session stage. When a host initiates a PPPoE session, it must first perform discovery to identify which server can meet the client's request, and then identify the Ethernet MAC address of the peer and establish a PPPoE session ID. While PPP defines a peer-to-peer relationship, discovery is inherently a client-server relationship.

At a very high level, during the discovery process, a host (referred to as the client) discovers one or more access concentrators and selects one. When discovery completes successfully, both the host and the selected access concentrator have the information to build their point-to-point connection over Ethernet. After a PPP session is established, both the host and the access concentrator must allocate the resources for a PPP virtual interface, although it should be noted that this is probably not the case for all implementations. The discovery phase has four steps as illustrated in Figure 10-10 below:

NOTE: For simplicity, only the relevant devices are depicted in this diagram.

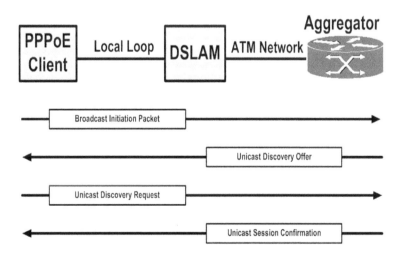

Fig. 10-10. Establishing a PPPoE Session

Referencing Figure 10-10, the following sequence of steps is undertaken before a PPPoE session is established between the PPPoE client and the aggregator. The aggregator is simply a router within the DSL network that is used to establish the PPPoE session with clients, among other things. Beginning with the client Broadcast initiation packet, the steps are as follows:

1. In the first step of the discovery phase, the PPPoE client broadcasts a PPPoE Active Discovery Initiating (PADI) packet. The PADI consists of one tag that indicates what service type it requests.

2. In the second step, one or more aggregators respond to the PADI packet via a PPPoE Active Discovery Offer (PADO) packet. The PADO packet is Unicast to the PPPoE client. If the access concentrator or aggregator cannot serve the PADI, it must not respond with a PADO. Because the PADI was broadcast, the host can receive more than one PADO, in the same manner that a DHCP client can receive a response from more than one DHCP server. It is up to the client to decide which concentrator it will use.

3. In the third step of the discovery phase, the PPPoE client looks through the PADO packets it receives (if more than one is received) and chooses one. The choice is based on the services offered by each access concentrator. The PPPoE client then sends a PPPoE Active Discovery Request (PADR) packet to the access concentrator it chooses. The destination address field is set to the Unicast Ethernet address of the access concentrator or aggregator that sends the PADO. At this stage, the request moves to the session phase.

4. In the fourth and final step of the discovery phase, the selected aggregator sends a confirmation packet. As previously stated, when the access concentrator receives a PADR packet, it prepares to begin a PPP session and generates a unique session ID for the PPPoE session, and then replies to the host with a PPPoE Active Discovery Session-confirmation (PADS) packet. The destination address of the PADS packet is the Unicast Ethernet address of the host that sends the PADR.

Once the PPPoE session begins, PPP data is sent as in any other PPP encapsulation. A PPPoE Active Discovery Terminate packet can be sent by either the PPPoE client or the access concentrator any time after a session is established to indicate that a PPP over Ethernet session has been terminated. The conversation between the PPPoE client and the aggregator takes place using Ethernet frames. PPP frames are encapsulated in PPPoE session frames, which have Ethernet frame type 0x8864. Once the session phase begins, PPP data may be sent. At this stage, all Ethernet packets are Unicast between the aggregation router and the PPPoE client.

PPPoE introduces an interesting and unique problem. The maximum Ethernet frame is 1518 bytes long. The header consumes 14 bytes and the Frame Checksum (FCS) consumes 4bytes, leaving 1500 bytes for the payload. For this reason, the Maximum Transmission Unit (MTU) of an Ethernet interface is usually 1500 bytes. This is the largest IP datagram that can be transmitted over the interface without fragmentation. PPPoE, however, adds another 6 bytes of overhead, and the PPP protocol field consumes 2 bytes, leaving 1492 bytes for the IP datagram. Because of this, RFC 2516 specifies the Maximum-Receive-Unit (MRU) option for PPPoE must not be negotiated to a size larger than 1492 bytes. The MTU of PPPoE interfaces must therefore be set to 1492 bytes.

While PPPoE is typically implemented using Ethernet interfaces, allowing the PPP packets to be encapsulated in the Ethernet frames, it can also be implemented using Asynchronous Transfer Mode (ATM) interfaces. In such cases, the PPPoE packets are encapsulated in ATM cells.

The PPPoE over ATM (PPPoEoA) AAL 5 MUX feature enables PPPoE over AAL 5-multiplexed (AAL 5 MUX) PVCs, which reduces LLC and SNAP encapsulation bandwidth usage, thereby improving bandwidth usage for the PVC. While going into detail on ATM cell formats is beyond the scope of the ROUTE exam requirements, ensure that you have a basic understanding of this concept and how the encapsulation is different from that applicable with Ethernet interfaces. PPPoEoA is standardized in RFC 1483/2648. PPPoE has numerous advantages, which are as follows:

1. Per session authentication based on Password Authentication Protocol (PAP) or Challenge Handshake Authentication Protocol (CHAP). This is the greatest advantage of PPPoE, as authentication overcomes the security hole in a bridging architecture.

2. Per-session accounting is possible, which allows the service provider to charge the subscriber for various services offered based on session time. The service provider can also require a minimal access charge.

3. You can use PPPoE on current CPE installations that cannot be upgraded to PPP or that do not have the ability to run PPPoA, which extends the PPP session over the bridged Ethernet LAN to the PC.

4. PPPoE preserves the point-to-point session used by Internet Service Providers (ISPs) in the current dialup model. PPPoE is the only protocol capable of running PPP over Ethernet without the requirement of an intermediate IP stack.

5. The Network Access Provider (NAP) or Network Service Provider (NSP) can provide secure access to a corporate gateway without the management of end-to-end Permanent Virtual Circuits (PVCs) and without the use of Layer 3 routing and/or Layer 2 Tunneling Protocol (L2TP) tunnels. This makes the business model of the sale of wholesale services and Virtual Private Networks (VPNs) scalable. L2TP is beyond the scope of this guide.

6. PPPoE can provide a host (PC) access to multiple destinations at a given time. In other words, PPPoE allows you to have multiple PPPoE sessions per PVC.

7. The NSP can oversubscribe by the deployment of idle and session time-outs with the help of an industry standard Remote Authentication Dial-In User Service (RADIUS) server for each subscriber. RADIUS is beyond the scope of the ROUTE exam requirements.

8. You can use PPP with the Service Selection Gateway (SSG) feature.

In contrast, however, Point-to-Point Protocol over Ethernet has the following disadvantages:
1. You must install PPPoE client software on all hosts (computers) that connect to the Ethernet segment. This means that the access provider must maintain the CPE and the client software on these hosts.
2. Since PPPoE implementation uses RFC 1483 bridging, it is susceptible to Broadcast storms and possible denial-of-service attacks.

Point-to-Point Protocol over Asynchronous Transfer Mode

Point-to-Point Protocol over Asynchronous Transfer Mode (PPPoA) is specified in RFC 2364. Though PPPoE is used in most countries, the UK and some parts of the U.S. use PPPoA to provide ADSL service. PPPoA is a network protocol for encapsulating PPP frames in ATM Adaptation Layer 5 (AAL 5). While PPPoA uses AAL 5 SNAP for encapsulation, by default, the most common encapsulation type used is AAL 5 MUX.

The network architecture of PPPoA is similar to that of PPPoE. However, the process for establishing connectivity is slightly different. For PPPoA, when the CPE (ATU-R) is first powered on, it starts sending PPP Link Control Protocol (PPP LCP) configuration requests to the aggregation router. The aggregation server, with the PVCs configured, also sends out the PPP LCP configuration request on a Virtual Access Interface that associated with the PVC. When the CPE and aggregation server (router) see each other's configuration requests, they both acknowledge the configuration requests and the PPP LCP state is opened.

For the authentication stage, the CPE sends the authentication request to the aggregation router or server. The router, depending on its configuration, authenticates either the user based on the domain name (if supplied) or the username using its local database or RADIUS servers. If the request from the subscriber is in the form of 'username@domainname', then the aggregation server will try to create a tunnel to the destination, if one is not already there.

After the tunnel is created, the aggregation router forwards the PPP requests from the subscriber to the destination. The destination, in turn, authenticates the user and assigns an IP address. If the request from the subscriber does not include the domain name, the user is authenticated by the local database. If SSG is configured on the aggregation router, the user can access the default network as specified and can get an option to select different services.

Point-to-Point Protocol over ATM has several advantages, which include the following:
1. Per-session authentication based on PAP or CHAP. This is the greatest advantage of PPPoA, as authentication overcomes the security hole in a bridging architecture.
2. Per-session accounting is possible, which allows the service provider to charge the subscriber

for various services offered based on session time. Per-session accounting enables a service provider to offer a minimum access level for minimal charge and then charge subscribers for additional services used.

3.   IP address conservation at the CPE. This allows the service provider to assign only one IP address for a CPE, with the CPE configured for NAT. All users behind one CPE can use a single IP address to reach different destinations. IP management overhead for the Network Access Provider/Network Services Provider (NAP/NSP) for each individual user is reduced while conserving IP addresses. Additionally, the service provider can provide a small subnet of IP addresses to overcome the limitations of PAT and NAT.

4.   NAPs and NSPs provide secure access to corporate gateways without managing end-to-end PVCs and using Layer 3 Routing or Layer 2 Forwarding (L2F) and Layer 2 Tunneling Protocol (L2TP) tunnels. Hence, these entities can scale their business models for selling wholesale services.

5.   Troubleshooting individual subscribers. The NSP can easily identify which subscribers are on or off based on active PPP sessions, rather than troubleshooting entire groups as is the case with bridging architecture.

6.   The NSP can oversubscribe by deploying idle and session timeouts using an industry standard RADIUS server for each subscriber.

7.   Highly scalable, as providers can terminate a very high number of PPP sessions on an aggregation router. Authentication, authorization, and accounting can be handled for each user using external RADIUS servers.

8.   It allows for the optimal use of features on the Service Selection Gateway (SSG).

On the downside, Point-to-Point Protocol over ATM has the following disadvantages:

1.   Only a single session per CPE on one VC. Since the username and password are configured on the CPE, all users behind the CPE for that particular VC can access only one set of services. Users cannot select different sets of services, although using multiple VCs and establishing different PPP sessions on different VCs is possible.

2.   Increased complexity of the CPE setup. Help desk personnel at the service provider need to be more knowledgeable. Since the username and password are configured on the CPE, the subscriber or the CPE vendor will need to make setup changes. Using multiple VCs increases configuration complexity.

3.   The service provider needs to maintain a database of usernames and passwords for all subscribers. If tunnels or proxy services are used, then the authentication can be done on the basis of the domain name and the user authentication is done at the corporate gateway. This reduces the size of the database that the service provider has to maintain.

4.   If a single IP address is provided to the CPE, and NAT or PAT is implemented, then certain applications, such as IPTV, which embed IP information in the payload, will not work. In addition, if an IP subnet feature is used, then an IP address has to be reserved for the CPE.

Now that we have a fundamental understanding of PPPoE and PPPoA, the following sections describe how to configure and enable these technologies in Cisco IOS software.

Configuring Point-to-Point Protocol over Ethernet (PPPoE) Connectivity

The PPPoE configuration and validation tasks in this section will be based on Figure 10-11 below, which illustrates the PPPoE client (Cisco IOS router) and the DSL provider aggregator router:

NOTE: You are not expected to perform any configuration tasks or troubleshooting on the DSLAM or aggregator. Assume that the necessary configuration in place is operational.

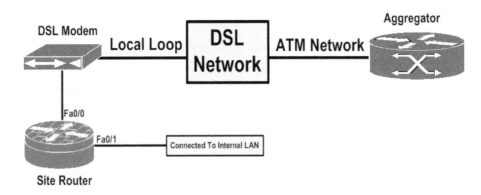

Fig. 10-11. Configuring PPPoE in Cisco IOS Software

Referencing the topology illustrated in Figure 10-11, following is the sequence of configuration steps required to configure PPPoE on the site router:

1. Enable PPPoE on the desired interface using the `pppoe enable` interface configuration command. This command effectively enables PPPoE on the specified interface.

2. Configure a PPPoE client and specify Dial-On-Demand Routing functionality using the `pppoe-client dial-pool-number [number]` interface configuration command. Dial-On-Demand Routing is a technique whereby a router can automatically initiate and close a circuit-switched session as transmitting stations demand. The `[number]` specified at the end of this command binds the interface to a logical Dialer interface, which must be configured manually, which will then have the PVC automatically provisioned across it.

3. Configure the Dialer interface, which is simply a logical DDR interface, by issuing the `interface dialer [number]` global configuration command. The `[number]` at the end of this command should be the same as that configured using the `pppoe-client dial-pool-number [number]` command in the previous step.

4. The interface must be configured to receive IP addressing dynamically via the `ip address negotiated` interface configuration command. However, in the rare case that the provider assigns you with a static IP address, the `ip address [address] [mask]` command can be

issued on the interface with the assigned IP address.

5. Because PPPoE must comply with RFC 2516, the Dialer interface MTU must be set to 1492 bytes using the `ip mtu 1492` interface configuration command.

6. In order to bind the Dialer interface to the Ethernet interface, the `dialer pool [number]` interface configuration command must be issued. The `[number]` should match the Dialer interface number, as well as the number specified in the `pppoe-client dial-pool-number [number]` command.

7. Assign the interface to a dialer access group using the `dialer-group <number>` interface configuration command. The dialer access group binds the interface to the dialer list, which defines the 'interesting' traffic that will trigger the DDR call.

8. Next, PPP encapsulation must be specified on the Dialer interface. This is performed by issuing the `encapsulation ppp` interface configuration command.

9. Enable PPP PAP or CHAP authentication under the interface for inbound calls using the `ppp authentication <pap | chap> callin` interface configuration command. The method used will be provided to you by your ISP. In some cases, both methods are used. For example, CHAP might be preferred, but if this failed, then they would permit PAP to be used for authentication instead.

10. Configure the CHAP or PAP username and password pair using either the `ppp chap hostname <username>` and `ppp chap password <password>` commands for CHAP or the `ppp pap sent-username <username> password <password>` command for PAP. If both methods are used, issue both sets of commands.

11. Configure the router to add a default route to the routing table using the `ppp ipcp route default` interface configuration command. It should be noted that this command is not supported in older Cisco IOS images. Therefore, you will need to upgrade the IOS image or use the next method specified, which entails configuring a static default route, instead. The static default route is most commonly used.

12. Configure a static default route point out of the configured Dialer interface by issuing the `ip route 0.0.0.0 0.0.0.0 dialer [number]` global configuration command. This command should be used only if you did not use the `ppp ipcp route default` interface configuration command under the Dialer interface. Do NOT issue both commands at the same time; select one or the other.

13. Define the DDR dialer list, which specifies the 'interesting' traffic that will trigger the DDR call. In most cases, this 'interesting' is simply IP traffic; therefore, configure the dialer list using the `dialer-list <number> protocol ip permit` global configuration command. The `<number>` should match the `<number>` specified in the `dialer-group <number>` interface configuration command configured in step 7.

14. Configure additional features, such as NAT/PAT and DHCP functionality, on the router to allow users residing on the internal network to access the Internet.

The following example illustrates a basic sample configuration of PPPoE in Cisco IOS software. The configuration below illustrates the use of the static default route instead of using the `ppp ipcp route default` interface configuration command under the Dialer interface. This configuration also includes basic PAT and Cisco IOS DHCP server configuration, in addition to PPP CHAP authentication configuration. PAP authentication configuration is not illustrated in this configuration example:

```
R1(config)#ip dhcp excluded-address 10.0.0.1 10.1.1.9
R1(config)#ip dhcp pool DEFAULT-LAN-DHCP-POOL
R1(dhcp-config)#network 10.0.0.0 /24
R1(dhcp-config)#default-router 10.0.0.1
R1(dhcp-config)#import all
R1(dhcp-config)#lease 8 0 0
R1(dhcp-config)#exit
R1(config)#interface FastEthernet0/0
R1(config-if)#description 'Connected To Private LAN'
R1(config-if)#ip nat inside
R1(config-if)#ip address 10.0.0.1 255.255.255.0
R1(config-if)#exit
R1(config)#interface FastEthernet0/1
R1(config-if)#description 'Connected To DSL'
R1(config-if)#pppoe enable
R1(config-if)#pppoe-client dial-pool-number 1
R1(config-if)#exit
R1(config)#interface Dialer1
R1(config-if)#ip address negotiated
R1(config-if)#ip mtu 1492
R1(config-if)#dialer pool 1
R1(config-if)#dialer-group 1
R1(config-if)#encapsulation ppp
R1(config-if)# ppp authentication chap callin
R1(config-if)#ppp chap hostname route@howtonetwork.net
R1(config-if)#ppp chap password pp03!23
R1(config-if)#ip nat outside
R1(config-if)#exit
R1(config)#ip route 0.0.0.0 0.0.0.0 Dialer1
R1(config)#ip nat inside source list 100 interface Dialer1 overload
R1(config)#access-list 100 permit ip 10.0.0.0 0.0.0.255 any
R1(config)#dialer-list 1 protocol ip permit
```

As can be seen above, the configuration itself is quite detailed. If, for example, the ISP required you to use PAP authentication instead, the configuration would be modified as follows:

```
[Remaining Configuration Remains The Same]

R1(config)#interface Dialer1
R1(config-if)#ppp authentication pap callin
R1(config-if)#ppp pap sent-username route@howtonetwork.net password pp03!23

[Remaining Configuration Remains The Same]
```

Configuring PPPoE over Asynchronous Transfer Mode

As stated earlier in this chapter, by default, PPPoE runs on top of AAL 5 SNAP. This means that when configuring ATM PVCs, no explicit encapsulation commands are required. This follows the same logic as when configuring Serial interfaces; because HDLC is the default encapsulation type, there is no need to configure explicitly the `encapsulation hdlc` interface configuration command. Similarly, with PPPoE on ATM interfaces, there is no need to configure explicitly the `encapsulation aal5snap` configuration command for the PVC.

The PPPoE configuration and validation tasks in this section will be based on the network topology diagram in Figure 10-12 below, which illustrates the PPPoE client and the aggregator:

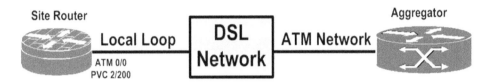

Fig. 10-12. Configuring and Verifying PPPoE in Cisco IOS Software

The following section describes the sequence of steps required to configure PPPoE over ATM:

1. Configure the ATM interface to use the proper modulation method by issuing the `dsl operating-mode {adsl2 [annex a | annex m] | adsl2+ [annex a | annex m] | ansi-dmt | auto | itu-dmt}` interface configuration command. The different options available with this command are described in Table 10-3 below:

Table 10-3. ATM Interface DSL Modulation Options

Keyword	Description
adsl2	Configures operation in ADSL2 operating mode—ITU G.992.3 Annex A, Annex L, and Annex M. If an Annex operating mode is not chosen, then Annex A, Annex L, and Annex M will all be enabled. The final mode will be decided by negotiation with the DSL access multiplexer (DSLAM).
adsl2+	Configures operation in ADSL2+ mode—ITU G.992.5 Annex A and Annex M. If an Annex A operating mode is not chosen, then both Annex A and Annex M will be enabled. The final mode will be decided by negotiation with DSLAM.
annex a | annex m	(Optional) If the annex option is not specified, then both Annex A and Annex M will be enabled. The final mode will be decided by negotiation with DSLAM.
ansi-dmt	Configures a router to operate in ANSI full-rate mode—ANSI T1.413.
auto	Default setting. Configures the router so that the DSLAM automatically picks the DSL operating mode. All supported modes are enabled.
itu-dmt	Configures operation in ITU G.992.1 Annex A full-rate mode.

NOTE: In most cases, you will not know what DSL modulation is actually being used. Given this, Cisco recommends that you use the `dsl operating-mode auto` command. This command allows the router to detect automatically the correct modulation method to use.

2. Configure a point-to-point ATM subinterface. The ATM PVC information must be configured on this subinterface using the `pvc [vpi/vci]` interface configuration command. Additionally, the `pppoe-client dial-pool-number [number]` command must be configured to bind the ATM PVC to a Dialer interface. Because the default encapsulation for PPPoE is AAL 5 SNAP, the encapsulation does not need to be configured manually under the PVC. These steps are illustrated in the output below on R1.

NOTE: In some implementations, the entire configuration (i.e., the PVC configuration) is performed on the physical ATM interface. Ensure that you remember that using a subinterface is simply another way of accomplishing the same task.

3. Configure the Dialer interface. The same steps performed when configuring PPPoE using Ethernet interfaces are applicable for PPPoE using ATM interfaces.
4. Configure a default route for the DSL router. However, again, keep in mind that this should be done only if you did not use the `ppp ipcp route default` interface configuration command under the Dialer interface. Do NOT issue both commands at the same time; select one or the other.
5. Configure additional IP services, such as NAT/PAT and DHCP, on the local router.

Following these configuration steps, and referencing the topology illustrated in Figure 10-12, the site router is configured for PPPoEoA service as follows:

```
R1(config)#interface atm0/0
R1(config-if)#dsl operating-mode auto
R1(config-if)#no shutdown
R1(config-if)#exit
R1(config)#exit
R1(config)#interface atm0/0.55 point-to-point
R1(config-subif)#pvc 2/200
R1(config-if-atm-vc)# pppoe-client dial-pool-number 55
R1(config-if-atm-vc)#exit
R1(config-subif)# exit
R1(config-if)#exit
R1(config)#interface Dialer 55
R1(config-if)#ip address negotiated
R1(config-if)#ip mtu 1492
R1(config-if)#dialer pool 55
R1(config-if)#encapsulation ppp
R1(config-if)#ppp authentication pap callin
```

```
R1(config-if)#ppp pap sent-username route@howtonetwork.net password p@p123
R1(config-if)#ppp ipcp route default
R1(config-if)#dialer group 1
R1(config-if)#no shutdown
R1(config-if)#ppp ipcp route default
R1(config-if)#exit
R1(config)#dialer-list 1 protocol ip permit
```

NOTE: Notice that the configuration above uses the ppp ipcp route default interface configuration command; therefore, a static default route is not configured on the router.

Configuring PPPoE over ATM—PPPoEoA Using AAL 5 MUX

The configuration steps for PPPoEoA using AAL 5 MUX encapsulation are the same as the steps followed when configuring PPPoEoA using the default AAL 5 SNAP encapsulation, with the primary difference being the inclusion of the additional encapsulation aal5mux ppp dialer PVC configuration command. To avoid being redundant, the same configuration steps will not be repeated again; however, the following output highlights this subtle difference when configuring PPPoEoA using AAL 5 MUX encapsulation:

```
R1(config)#interface atm0/0
R1(config-if)#dsl operating-mode auto
R1(config-if)#no shutdown
R1(config-if)#exit
R1(config)#exit
R1(config)#interface atm0/0.55 point-to-point
R1(config-subif)#pvc 2/200
R1(config-if-atm-vc)#encapsulation aal5mux ppp dialer
R1(config-if-atm-vc)# pppoe-client dial-pool-number 55
R1(config-if-atm-vc)#exit
R1(config-subif)# exit
R1(config-if)#exit
R1(config)#interface Dialer 55
R1(config-if)#ip address negotiated
R1(config-if)#ip mtu 1492
R1(config-if)#dialer pool 55
R1(config-if)#encapsulation ppp
R1(config-if)#ppp authentication chap pap callin
R1(config-if)#ppp chap hostname route@howtonetwork.net
R1(config-if)#ppp chap password ppp0@1
R1(config-if)#ppp pap sent-username route@howtonetwork.net password
ppp0@1
R1(config-if)#dialer-group 1
R1(config-if)#no shutdown
R1(config-if)#exit
R1(config)#ip route 0.0.0.0 0.0.0.0 Dialer 55
R1(config)#dialer-list 1 protocol ip permit
```

Configuring PPPoA Using Dialer Profiles: AAL 5 MUX Encapsulation

Unlike PPPoE, PPPoA is supported only on ATM interfaces. The PPPoA configuration in this section will be based on the same basic topology illustrated in Figure 10-12. Following is the sequence of steps required to configure PPPoA using dialer profiles and AAL 5 MUX:

1. Provision the ATM interface for the proper modulation method by issuing the `dsl operating-mode {adsl2 [annex a | annex m] | adsl2+ [annex a | annex m] | ansi-dmt | auto | itu-dmt}` interface configuration command. Cisco recommends using the `dsl operating-mode auto` command.

2. Configure the assigned PVC on the ATM interface using the `pvc [vpi/vci]` interface configuration command.

3. Enable AAL 5 MUX encapsulation for the PVC using the `encapsulation aal5mux ppp dialer` PVC configuration command.

4. Bind the PVC to the Dialer interface by using the `dialer pool-member [number]` PVC configuration command. The `[number]` specified in this command must be the same as the Dialer interface that will be configured for the ADSL service.

5. Configure the Dialer interface. The same configuration commands as those used for PPPoE are used; however, it is imperative to remember that the `ip mtu 1492` command is not used for PPP over ATM; it is only applicable to PPPoE implementations.

6. Configure a default route for the DSL router. However, again, keep in mind that this should be done only if you did not use the `ppp ipcp route default` interface configuration command under the Dialer interface. Do NOT issue both commands at the same time; select one or the other.

Following this sequence of steps, the DSL site router is configured in the following manner:

```
R1(config)#interface atm0/0
R1(config-if)#dsl operating-mode auto
R1(config-if)#pvc 2/200
R1(config-if-atm-vc)#encapsulation aal5mux ppp dialer
R1(config-if-atm-vc)#dialer pool-member 55
R1config-if-atm-vc)#no shut
R1config-if-atm-vc)#exit
R1(config-if)#no shutdown
R1(config-if)#exit
R1(config)#interface Dialer 55
R1(config-if)#ip address negotiated
R1(config-if)#dialer pool 55
R1(config-if)#encapsulation ppp
R1(config-if)#ppp authentication chap pap callin
R1(config-if)#ppp chap hostname route@howtonetwork.net
R1(config-if)#ppp chap password ppp0@1
R1(config-if)#ppp pap sent-username route@howtonetwork.net password ppp0@1
R1(config-if)#ppp ipcp route default
```

```
R1(config-if)#dialer-group 1
R1(config-if)#no shutdown
R1(config-if)#exit
R1(config)#dialer-list 1 protocol ip permit
```

NOTE: Notice that the configuration above uses the ppp ipcp route default interface configuration command; therefore, the static default route is not configured on the router.

Configuring PPPoA Using Dialer Profiles: AAL 5 SNAP Encapsulation

The configuration of PPPoA using dialer profiles and AAL 5 SNAP encapsulation is similar to the configuration of PPPoA using dialer profiles and AAL 5 MUX encapsulation, with the only difference being the encapsulation type under the PVC, which changes to encapsulation aal5snap ppp dialer. Therefore, to avoid being redundant, the same sequence of steps will not be repeated again. Instead, the following configuration highlights this subtle difference:

```
R1(config)#interface atm0/0
R1(config-if)#pvc 2/200
R1(config-if)#dsl operating-mode auto
R1(config-if-atm-vc)#encapsulation aal5snap ppp dialer
R1(config-if-atm-vc)#dialer pool-member 55
R1config-if-atm-vc)#no shut
R1config-if-atm-vc)#exit
R1(config-if)#no shutdown
R1(config-if)#exit
R1(config)#interface Dialer 55
R1(config-if)#ip address negotiated
R1(config-if)#dialer pool 55
R1(config-if)#encapsulation ppp
R1(config-if)#ppp authentication chap pap callin
R1(config-if)#ppp chap hostname route@howtonetwork.net
R1(config-if)#ppp chap password ppp0@1
R1(config-if)#ppp pap sent-username route@howtonetwork.net password ppp0@1
R1(config-if)#dialer-group 1
R1(config-if)#no shutdown
R1(config-if)#exit
R1(config)#ip route 0.0.0.0 0.0.0.0 Dialer 55
R1(config)#dialer-list 1 protocol ip permit
```

Configuring PPPoA Using Virtual Templates: AAL 5 SNAP Encapsulation

A virtual template is a logical interface (similar to a Dialer interface) that may also be used when configuring PPPoA. In a manner similar to Dialer interfaces, PPP authentication commands can be used on the virtual template, using credentials provided by the ISP. The configuration in this section is based on the topology in Figure 10-12:

1. Provision the router ATM interface for the proper modulation method by using the `dsl operating-mode {adsl2 [annex a | annex m] | adsl2+ [annex a | annex m] | ansi-dmt | auto | itu-dmt}` interface configuration command. However, as stated in the previous section, Cisco recommends using the `dsl operating-mode auto` command.

2. Configure the virtual template. This is performed via the `interface virtual-template [number]` global configuration command. It is important to configure the virtual template before it is applied to the PVC.

NOTE: By default, there is no need to enter the `encapsulation ppp` interface configuration command, as the virtual template interface uses PPP encapsulation by default.

3. Configure the PPP authentication credentials on the virtual template interface if these are required. The `ppp authentication` command must never be issued on the virtual template. Instead, the only PPP authentication commands that must be issued are the `ppp chap hostname [name]` and `ppp chap password [password]` commands to provide CHAP credentials or the `ppp pap sent-username [name] password [password]` command to provide PAP credentials.

4. Configure the PVC on the interface using the `pvc [vpi/vci]` interface configuration command.

5. Next, specify a VC class on the ATM interface. This class is used to set the circuit characteristics. The VC class is configured via the `class-int [name]` interface configuration command.

6. Configure the characteristics of the VC class configured in the fourth configuration task. This is performed by using the `vc-class atm [name]` global configuration command. The `[name]` used in the `vc-class atm [name]` global configuration command must be the same name used in the `class-int [name]` interface configuration command under the ATM interface.

7. Configure a static default route on the DSL router. This step now presents an interesting problem. In Cisco IOS, a static route cannot be configured to point to a virtual template. Therefore, the static route must be configured to point to the IP address of the aggregator router. Because of default PPP operation, a host route for this IP address will be installed into the IP routing table as soon as R1 connects to the aggregator. The static default route will then be placed into the routing table.

8. Configure additional IP services, such as DHCP and NAT, on the local DSL router.

Following these configuration steps, a Cisco IOS router would be configured for PPPoA via virtual templates using AAL 5 SNAP encapsulation as follows:

```
R1(config)#interface virtual-template 55
R1(config-if)#ip address negotiated
R1(config-if)#ppp authentication chap callin
R1(config-if)#ppp chap hostname route@howtonetwork.net
R1(config-if)#ppp chap password ch@p!23
R1(config-if)#exit
R1(config-if)#no shutdown
R1(config)#interface atm0/0
R1(config-if)#dsl operating-mode auto
R1(config-if)#pvc 2/200
R1(config-if-atm-vc)#exit
R1(config-if)#class-int PPPOA-CLASS
R1(config-if)#no shutdown
R1(config-if)#exit
R1(config)#vc-class atm PPOA-CLASS
R1(config-vc-class)#encapsulation aal5snap
R1(config-vc-class)#protocol ppp virtual-template 55
R1(config-vc-class)#exit
R1(config)#ip route 0.0.0.0 0.0.0.0 150.1.1.254
```

Configuring PPPoA Using Virtual Templates: AAL 5 MUX Encapsulation

While almost similar in nature, the configuration of PPPoA using virtual templates and AAL 5 MUX encapsulation follows the same steps as the configuration of PPPoA using virtual templates and AAL 5 SNAP encapsulation. To avoid being redundant, these steps will not be repeated again. Following this sequence of configuration steps, PPPoA using virtual templates and AAL 5 MUX encapsulation configuration is implemented on the site router as follows:

```
R1(config)#interface virtual-template 55
R1(config-if)#ip address negotiated
R1(config-if)#ppp authentication pap callin
R1(config-if)#ppp pap sent-username route&howtonetwork.net password p@p!23
R1(config-if)#no shutdown
R1(config-if)#exit
R1(config)#interface atm0/0
R1(config-if)#dsl operating-mode auto
R1(config-if)#pvc 2/200
R1(config-if-atm-vc)#encapsulation aal5mux ppp virtual-template 55
R1(config-if-atm-vc)#exit
R1(config-if)#no shutdown
R1(config-if)#exit
R1(config)#ip route 0.0.0.0 0.0.0.0 150.1.1.254
```

Alternatively, this configuration can also be performed using a VC class as illustrated below:

```
R1(config)#interface virtual-template 55
R1(config-if)#ip address negotiated
R1(config-if)#ppp authentication chap pap callin
R1(config-if)#ppp chap hostname route@howtonetwork.net
```

```
R1(config-if)#ppp chap password ppp0@123
R1(config-if)#ppp pap sent-username route@howtonetwork.net password ppp0@123
R1(config-if)#exit
R1(config-if)#no shutdown
R1(config)#interface atm0/0
R1(config-if)#dsl operating-mode auto
R1(config-if)#pvc 2/200
R1(config-if-atm-vc)#exit
R1(config-if)#class-int PPPOA-CLASS
R1(config-if)#no shutdown
R1(config-if)#exit
R1(config)#vc-class PPOA-CLASS
R1(config-vc-class)#encapsulation aal5ciscoppp virtual-template 55
R1(config-vc-class)#exit
R1(config)#ip route 0.0.0.0 0.0.0.0 150.1.1.254
```

Understandably, remembering all these various configuration steps seems like a daunting task. However, with time and repetition, you will become familiar with the configuration requirements for different scenarios and will remember how to implement them in their various ways in Cisco IOS software.

TELEWORKER CONNECTIVITY CONSIDERATIONS

Teleworkers, or mobile workers, are employees who work from a home office or from remote office centers. These workers typically have a broadband Internet connection that allows them to connect to the corporate network via VPN. The number of mobile workers has increased dramatically in recent years. This introduces new challenges for corporations that must allow these workers access to the corporate network, sometimes using personal computing devices, such as laptops, while still ensuring that network security standards are adhered to. Several factors should be taken into consideration when implementing teleworker or mobile worker solutions as follows:

- Bandwidth requirements
- Security considerations
- Simplified user experience
- Quality of Service
- Troubleshooting and support

Bandwidth Requirements

Teleworkers typically use the same applications as users in the enterprise network. However, unlike users in the enterprise network, bandwidth is not unlimited. For example, bandwidth-intensive applications may work well for users connected to the enterprise LAN due to the availability of high-speed links (e.g., GigabitEthernet link) between hosts and servers. Teleworkers, however, use remote access technologies, such as cable, DSL, and wireless service, that do not have the same bandwidth capacity as that found in the enterprise LAN. It is therefore important to understand the bandwidth requirements of the applications that the mobile workers will need to access when considering mobile worker implementations.

Security Considerations

As stated previously, mobile workers introduce new security risks. While it is common practice to issue mobile workers company-sanctioned and provided laptops, some technologies, such as SSL VPN, allow independent devices and connections from personal machines. In addition to adding security to remote devices in order to comply with certain regulations and requirements, organizations typically need to implement additional security mechanisms, such as Intrusion Prevention Systems (IPS) and URL Filtering, to protect the corporate network from remote users, while still allowing these users access to the enterprise network.

In addition to protecting the corporate network from teleworkers, additional challenges that should be taken into consideration include ensuring that host machines used by these employees have up-to-date software patches. While it is fairly easy to 'push' updates to the machines that are connected to the corporate network, the same is not as easy for teleworkers.

Simplified User Experience

One of the primary advantages of remote or mobile working is that it provides employees with flexible working locations. In other words, employees can work from almost anywhere as long as they have an Internet connection that allows them access to the VPN of the enterprise network. Despite this additional flexibility, mobile workers still expect the same user experience as the employees who work from within the office. For example, mobile workers might want to connect to devices in remote offices without performing additional administrative tasks, which may include multiple logins, etc. Increasing the administrative burden of mobile workers may lead to decreased satisfaction, and workers may prefer to work in the office instead of remotely simply because the user experience is much better.

Quality of Service

One of the main challenges of mobile working is ensuring an acceptable Quality of Service level for user applications. While applications such as e-mail may tolerate some delay, real-time data, such as voice and video, is very intolerant of delay. Consideration should therefore be given to the various prioritization and queuing mechanisms, as well as how to address QoS for different broadband access technologies, such as cable and DSL. The ultimate objective is to reduce the impact of data applications on voice services for mobile workers.

Troubleshooting and Support

One of the most challenging aspects regarding mobile workers is the management and support of these users. Within the enterprise network, it is easy for support personnel to both assist and troubleshoot issues for those users who are connected to the network. However, the same visibility is lost when it comes to mobile workers, as the corporate network has no control over their home networks. Troubleshooting complexity is increased because most mobile users are not trained to troubleshoot and resolve technical issues arising on their home network. This may significantly increase the amount of time and monetary cost of supporting such users.

UNDERSTANDING VPN TECHNOLOGIES

Having gone through remote office design considerations, access technologies, which are used to connect remote offices and teleworkers to the corporate network, and then teleworker consider-ations, the following sections will discuss the VPN technologies that can be used to connect remote offices and teleworkers to the corporate network.

The term Virtual Private Network (VPN) means different things to different people, depending on the industry they are in or the solutions they have implemented. A VPN is a network that provides remote offices or individual users with secure access to their organization's network. Contrary to the popular belief that a VPN provides secure connectivity across as public network such as the In-ternet, a VPN can also be used on a privately-owned network. The three types of VPN technologies that will be described in this section are as follows:

- Trusted VPNs
- Secure VPNs
- Hybrid VPNs

Trusted VPNs

Trusted VPNs are non-cryptographic VPNs. In other words, trusted VPNs do not employ the same cryptographic mechanisms used to encrypt data as those used in secure VPN. Unlike secure VPNs, the security and integrity of trusted VPN traffic relies on the fact that the circuit is not shared because each circuit is dedicated to a single site. An example of a trusted VPN implementation is Multiprotocol Label Switching (MPLS) VPN. While MPLS configuration is beyond the scope of the current ROUTE exam requirements, it is important that you have a basic understanding of MPLS VPN concepts. An MPLS VPN solution is illustrated in Figure 10-13 below:

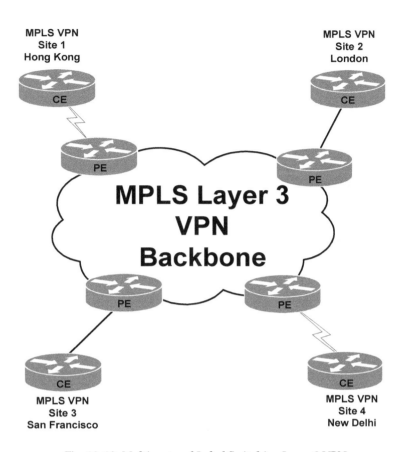

Fig. 10-13. Multiprotocol Label Switching Layer 3 VPN

Referencing Figure 10-13, the provider MPLS VPN allows multiple customer sites in different locations to connect to the same trusted VPN, allowing for secure LAN-to-LAN connectivity between these sites. While the MPLS VPN backbone is shared by multiple customers, VRFs (which were described earlier in this chapter) are used to prevent the different customer routing tables from becoming logically segregated. This also allows multiple customers to use the same IP address ranges without any issues.

Within the MPLS VPN architecture, providers install one or more managed routers at each one of the different customer locations or sites. These routers, referred to as Customer Edge (CE) routers, have a LAN interface to which the site internal network is connected. The configuration of these routers is strictly controlled by the provider, although in some instances the provider will provide read-only access to these routers for the customer. From your standpoint as a network engineer, your responsibility ends at the CE router. For this reason, the configuration of MPLS VPNs is beyond the scope of the current ROUTE exam requirements.

The CE routers are then connected to Provider Edge (PE) routers. The routers are then typically connected to multiple CE routers for multiple customers. They are, in essence, the portal into, and out of, the MPLS VPN backbone. While BGP is typically configured between PE and CE routers, any of the other routing protocols described in this guide can be used. Routes received from the site internal network are then redistributed into the PE-CE routing protocol and advertised to the PE router. From there, the prefixes are advertised to other sites within the customer VPN, allowing for connectivity between all of the customer sites.

Finally, within the MPLS VPN, core routers, referred to as Provider (P) routers, allow traffic to be switched between the different PE routers.

While the most common deployed trusted VPNs are Layer 3 VPNs, some service providers also provide Layer 2 VPN service for their customers using either Virtual Private LAN Service (VPLS) or Virtual Private Wire Service (VPWS) technologies. These technologies allow for the encapsulation of Layer 2 frames (e.g., Ethernet and Frame Relay) over MPLS or pure-IP networks. The primary difference between VPLS and VPWS is that VPLS provides point-to-multipoint connectivity, while VPWS provides only point-to-point connectivity. A Layer 2 (VPLS) VPN is illustrated in Figure 10-14 below:

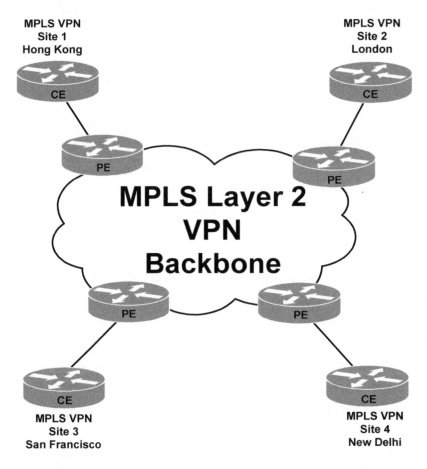

Fig. 10-14. Multiprotocol Label Switching Layer 2 (VPLS) VPN

Referencing Figure 10-14, the same basic components used in Layer 3 VPNs are used in the Layer 2 VPN implementations. However, there is a significant difference between Layer 2 and Layer 3 VPNs. Instead of configuring PE-CE routing protocols, Layer 2 VPNs allow the connected devices to appear as though they reside on the same LAN, even though all the sites may be, and typically are, geographically dispersed.

Because the sites are on the same logical LAN, the different CE routers are assigned an address on the same subnet. Any routing protocol of choice is then configured on these devices following the same logic as described in previous chapters within this guide. As is the case with Layer 3 VPNs, the configuration and implementation of Layer 2 VPNs is beyond the scope of the ROUTE exam requirements and will not be illustrated or described in any further detail in this chapter. You are not expected to implement this configuration.

Secure VPNs

Unlike trusted VPNs, secure VPNs are used to transport data across public data networks, such as the Internet. These VPN technologies use different cryptographic mechanisms to ensure data confidentiality, integrity, and authenticity as datagrams are carried across these unsecured networks. These VPN types are commonly used to replace or augment existing point-to-point networks that utilize dedicated leased lines or even WAN networks over common technologies, such as Frame Relay. Secure VPN technologies include the following:

- IP Security (IPSec)
- Layer 2 Tunneling Protocol version 3 (L2TPv3) over IPSec
- Point-to-Point Tunneling Protocol (PPTP)
- SSL Encryption (SSL VPN)

NOTE: Of the secure VPN types described, only IPSec and SSL VPNs will be described in detail later in this chapter. Both L2TPv3 and PPTP are described briefly in the following section.

Layer 2 Tunneling Protocol version 3 (L2TPv3) allows data to be tunneled across native core IP networks. Used alone, L2TPv3 does not provide any data encryption or confidentiality. To provide this additional level of security, L2TPv2 is commonly implemented with IP Security (IPSec). Point-to-Point Tunneling Protocol (PPTP) is also used to tunnel data across IP networks. Like L2TPv3, PPTP does not provide any data encryption or confidentiality and requires implementation with other protocols to provide authentication and encryption. The configuration of L2TPv3 and PPTP is beyond the scope of the ROUTE exam requirements. These protocols will not be described in any further detail in this chapter.

Continuing with secure VPN technologies, there are three types of secure VPN implementations. These common implementations are as follows:

- Intranet-based VPNs
- Internet-based VPNs
- Extranet-based VPNs

An Intranet-based VPN provides data security within an enterprise or organization that may or may not involve traffic traversing a WAN. An Intranet-based VPN connection takes advantage of IP connectivity in an organization Intranet and is implemented within the same organization's internal network.

Internet-based VPNs are the most common types of VPNs. These VPNs are used to protect the organization's data as it traverses the Internet. Internet-based VPNs can take several forms; however, only those that are applicable to the ROUTE exam will be described in this chapter. Examples of Internet-based VPNs include site-to-site or LAN-to-LAN IPSec VPNs and remote access VPNs, which are used to allow mobile workers to establish secure connections to the enterprise network. Both VPN types are described in detail later in this chapter.

Finally, Extranet-based VPNs provide private communications between two or more separate entities. For example, a company can deploy an Extranet VPN between its headquarters and certain business partner networks. The business partner is given access only to the headquarters public server to perform various IP-based network tasks, such as placing and managing product orders.

Hybrid Virtual Private Networks

A hybrid VPN is a combination of both a trusted VPN and a secure VPN. Hybrid VPNs are an emerging technology that are gaining momentum quickly. These VPNs allow providers that offer trusted VPNs to secure customer data in locations where such providers have no point-of-presence. Customer offices in these remote locations can then establish secured sessions to provider VPN Headend devices and from there access resources in other locations that are tied into the provider-trusted (MPLS) VPN, allowing for LAN-to-LAN security between customer sites on the trusted and secure VPNs. Figure 10-15 below illustrates a hybrid VPN implementation:

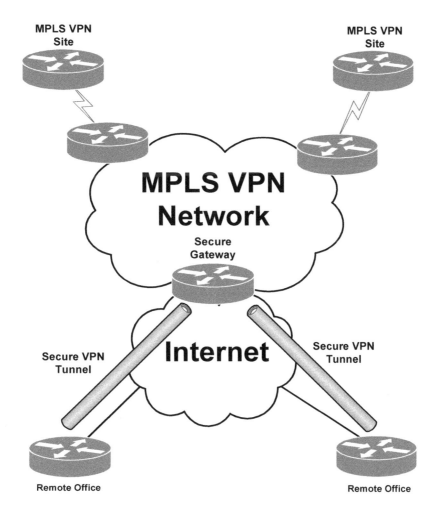

Fig. 10-15. Understanding Hybrid VPNs

NOTE: While you should be familiar with the hybrid VPN concept, the actual configuration of hybrid VPN components is beyond the scope of the ROUTE exam requirements and will not be illustrated or described in any additional detail in this chapter.

As stated in the previous section, the configuration of trusted VPNs is beyond the scope of the ROUTE exam requirements and will not be described in this guide. However, you are required to demonstrate both theoretical and configuration-level knowledge of Cisco-supported secure VPN technologies. Therefore, before we delve into detail on the site-to-site VPN solutions, it is important to have a solid fundamental understanding of the protocol that all these VPN solutions use to ensure data confidentiality, integrity, and authenticity. This protocol, which is described in detail in the following section, is IP Security (IPSec).

IP SECURITY (IPSEC)

IP Security (IPSec) is defined and standardized in RFC 2401. Following is an excerpt from that RFC, which defines the IPSec framework:

> IPSec provides security services at the IP layer by enabling a system to select required security protocols, determine the algorithm(s) to use for the service(s), and put in place any cryptographic keys required to provide the requested services. IPSec can be used to protect one or more "paths" between a pair of hosts, between a pair of security gateways, or between a security gateway and a host. The term "security gateway" is used throughout the IPSec documents to refer to an intermediate system that implements IPSec protocols. For example, a router or a firewall implementing IPSec is a security gateway.

The IPSec framework is a set of open standards developed by the Internet Engineering Task Force (IETF). IPSec is implemented by a set of cryptographic protocols for securing IP datagrams. The IPSec framework secures IP traffic operating at the Network Layer of the OSI Model, thus securing all network applications and communications that use the IP network.

While IPSec is defined in a number of RFCs, it is not a mandatory requirement for IP version 4. However, IPSec is a mandatory requirement for IP version 6. Using a combination of hashing, symmetric key, and asymmetric key cryptographic algorithms, the IPSec framework offers the following security services:

- Peer authentication
- Data confidentiality
- Data integrity
- Data origin authentication
- Replay detection
- Access control
- Traffic flow confidentiality

NOTE: A hash, also referred to as a message digest, is a unique number from a sequence of text that is generated by applying a mathematical formula. The basic function of a hash is to take a random-length block of data and return a fixed-size bit string, which is then referred to as the hash value or message digest. Hashing is used to provide data integrity. Symmetric key cryptography uses a single key for the encryption and decryption process and is commonly referred to as secret key or pre-shared key cryptography. Asymmetric key cryptography uses two keys for the encryption and decryption process (i.e., one key for encryption and another key for decryption). Asymmetric key cryptography is also referred to as public key cryptography.

IPSec uses Security Association (SA) to provide security to a given IP connection. IPSec SAs are unidirectional, which means that two SAs are required for bidirectional data communications sessions. Internet Security Association and Key Management Protocol (ISAKMP) describes the framework for key management and defines the procedure and packet format necessary to establish, negotiate, modify, and delete Security Association. ISAKMP offers the identification of the peers only; it does not offer a key exchange mechanism. ISAKAMP is documented in RFC 2408 but was made obsolete by RFC 4306, which standardized Internet Key Exchange (IKE) version 2.

Internet Key Exchange is a hybrid protocol. It is basically a combination of ISAKMP, Oakley key exchange, and the SKEME protocol. Oakley key exchange describes a series of key exchanges, called modes, and details the services provided by each. These services include perfect forward secrecy for keys, identity protection, and authentication. The SKEME protocol describes a versatile key exchange technique that provides anonymity, non-repudiation, and quick key refreshment.

Internet Key Exchange defines the mechanism for exchanging keys. IKE derives authenticated keying material and negotiates SAs that are used for the Encapsulating Security Payload (ESP) and Authentication Header (AH) protocols. IKE uses UDP port 500 and is documented in RFC 2409, and updated in RFC 4306, which is IKEv2 (the current IKE standard).

> **NOTE:** The terms ISAKMP and IKE are often used interchangeably in many texts because the protocols are almost the same. Therefore, while the remainder of this chapter will include references to IKE, you should be aware of this fact in case you encounter a question using either one of these terms on the ROUTE certification exam.

IKE is a two-phase, multimode protocol that offers the following three methods of authenticating a remote peer:

- Public key signature
- Pre-shared key
- Public key encryption

The public key signature method, also referred to as the RSA-Signature method, is the most secure method and requires Public Key Infrastructure (PKI). The pre-shared key method uses statically defined keys and is the most common method because of its ease of deployment; however, this method is not scalable or secure. Finally, public key encryption, commonly referred to as the RSA-Nonce, is similar to public key signature but requires prior knowledge of the peer's public key. However, it is important to know that this method has limited support and is not as widely implemented or used as the other two methods.

Internet Key Exchange phase 1 verifies the identity of a remote peer and the two peers establish a secure authentication communications channel. This phase is primarily concerned with the protection suite for IKE messages. IKE phase 1 also protects the negotiation of phase 2 communication. IKE phase 2 is used to protect data and establish SA for IPSec. IKE phase 2 is used to negotiate the protection suite (i.e., ESP and AH), the algorithms that will be used within the protection suite (e.g., DES, 3DES, AES, and SHA-1), the networks or traffic that is being encrypted (which is sometimes referred to as proxy identities or phase 2 identities), and any optional keying material for negotiated protocols.

NOTE: ESP and AH are IPSec headers that are used to protect data. These are described later in this section. DES, 3DES, AES, and SHA-1 are symmetric key cryptography standards that are used to encrypt the contents of a message in order to provide data confidentiality. Because you are not required to demonstrate any advanced security knowledge, this guide will not be going into any further detail on these standards in this chapter.

IPSec Modes

IPSec can use two different modes to secure data communications using one of two modes. The two modes that are used to secure a given IP connection are as follows:

- Transport mode
- Tunnel mode

Transport mode protects the payload (data) of the original IP datagram. This mode is typically used for host-to-host and end-to-end sessions. Tunnel mode, on the other hand, is used to protect data in network-to-network (i.e., between networks). This is the mode used to secure data traversing between two routers in site-to-site VPN implementations in Cisco IOS software.

In transport mode, the original IP header is retained while the IPSec header is inserted between the original IP header and the payload as illustrated in Figure 10-16 below:

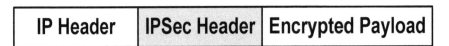

Fig. 10-16. IPSec Transport Mode

Unlike transport mode, tunnel mode allows IPSec to encapsulate the entire IP packet (i.e., the header as well as the payload) in a new IP packet. Tunnel mode is illustrated in Figure 10-17 below:

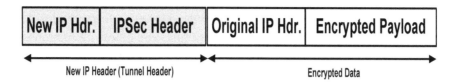

Fig. 10-17. IPSec Tunnel Mode

In both transport and tunnel mode, IPSec adds a new header to all the IP packets to provide the required information for securing the data within the original IP datagram. This header may be either an Encapsulating Security Payload (ESP) header or an Authentication Header (AH) header. ESP is an IP-based protocol that uses IP port 50 for communication between IPSec peers. ESP is documented in RFC 4303 and is used to provide confidentiality, integrity, and authenticity of the data. Additionally, ESP also provides anti-replay protection services. ESP does not provide any kind of protection for the outer IP header.

Authentication Header (AH) is an IP-based protocol that uses IP port 51 for communication between IPSec peers. AH is used to protect the integrity and authenticity of data, and also offers anti-replay protection; however, AH does not provide confidentiality protection. Unlike ESP, AH provides protection to the IP header; however, not all fields in the IP header are encrypted. For example, the TTL field is not encrypted. AH is described in RFC 2402.

NOTE: This is not a security-centric exam. Therefore, do not worry about understanding these concepts as would be required if this were a CCSP exam, for example. The objective here is to have a fundamental understanding of the IPSec framework and the components of which it is comprised. Core emphasis should center on the different site-to-site VPN technologies that will be described in the following sections, as those are core ROUTE exam requirements.

SITE-TO-SITE VPN TECHNOLOGIES

Site-to-site VPNs are established between dedicated VPN devices, allowing the users residing on the LAN on either side to communicate securely. The advantage of site-to-site VPNs is that they negate the need to install VPN client software on the hosts that reside on either LAN. Instead, the secure connection between the VPN gateways is transparent to the end users. Cisco IOS software supports several site-to-site VPN solutions. These solutions, which are described in subsequent sections, include the following:

- Traditional IPSec (IP Security) VPN
- Cisco Easy VPN
- DMVPN
- Group Encrypted Transport VPN

NOTE: As previously stated, this is not a security exam. However, you should still have a basic understanding of the different site-to-site VPN solutions. The following sections simply provide a brief overview of each of these solutions. With the exception of the IPSec VPN, which is the most common and most popular solution, the configuration of the other VPN solutions is beyond the scope of the ROUTE exam requirements and will not be included in this chapter.

Traditional IPSec (IP Security) VPN

IPSec VPN solutions are very popular and are one or the most commonly implemented VPN solutions. For site-to-site VPN implementations, IPSec VPNs can be implemented simply between two sites, in a full-mesh deployment, or even in a partial-mesh deployment. In all implementations, the IPSec VPN solution is used to secure communications between locations (e.g., remote and branch offices and the enterprise network) when data is sent across public networks, such as the Internet.

In Cisco IOS software, a traditional site-to-site IPSec VPN is implemented between two routers. This allows traffic that resides on the LAN (internal) interface of each router to be secured before it is sent to a remote network across the Internet, for example. As was previously stated, while the actual configuration of IPSec VPNs is beyond the scope of the ROUTE exam requirements, the following section describes how to implement a basic site-to-site VPN based on the topology that is illustrated in Figure 10-18 below:

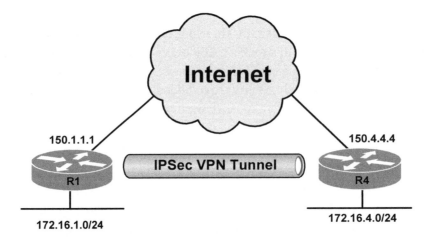

Fig. 10-18. Implementing Traditional IPSec Site-to-Site VPNs

In Cisco IOS software, a basic site-to-site IPSec VPN is configured using crypto configuration commands. These crypto commands are used to specify IPSec parameters, such as the encryption algorithm to be used, the Diffie Hellman group, and the shared secret to be used by the peer routers, among other things. In addition to the crypto commands, you must also configure an extended ACL specifying the traffic that will (or will not) be encrypted. Referencing the topology in Figure 10-18, the following configuration is implemented on R1:

```
R1(config)#crypto isakmp policy 1
R1(config-isakmp)#encr 3des
R1(config-isakmp)#authentication pre-share
R1(config-isakmp)#group 2
R1(config-isakmp)#exit
R1(config)#crypto isakmp key SECURE address 150.4.4.4
R1(config)#crypto ipsec transform-set ESP-3DES-SHA esp-3des esp-sha-hmac
R1(cfg-crypto-trans)#exit
R1(config)#crypto map VPN-EXAMPLE 1 ipsec-isakmp
% NOTE: This new crypto map will remain disabled until a peer
        and a valid access list have been configured.
R1(config-crypto-map)#description 'Secure VPN Tunnel To 150.4.4.4 (R4)'
R1(config-crypto-map)#set peer 150.4.4.4
R1(config-crypto-map)#set transform-set ESP-3DES-SHA
R1(config-crypto-map)#match address 100
R1(config-crypto-map)#exit
R1(config)#access-l 100 permit ip 172.16.1.0 0.0.0.255 172.16.4.0 0.0.0.255
R1(config)#interface Serial0/0
R1(config-if)#description 'Connected To Internet'
R1(config-if)#crypto map VPN-EXAMPLE
R1(config-if)#exit
R1(config)#ip route 0.0.0.0 0.0.0.0 Serial0/0
```

Before proceeding with the configuration on R4, the following section describes the commands used in the configuration of R1. The first section, illustrated below, is used to specify the IKE (ISAKMP) phase 1 parameters for SA. This includes the encryption algorithm, which is Triple DES in this example, as well as the Diffie Hellman group, which is group 2 in this example.

```
R1(config)#crypto isakmp policy 1
R1(config-isakmp)#encr 3des
R1(config-isakmp)#authentication pre-share
R1(config-isakmp)#group 2
R1(config-isakmp)#exit
```

NOTE: Diffie Hellman, or simply DH, allows two parties to establish a shared secret over some insecure communications channels, such as the Internet. Diffie-Hellman is a public-key distributing system, also known as key-exchange protocol, that uses asymmetric key cryptography. Cisco IOS supports three Diffie Hellman groups, which are listed in Table 10-4 below:

Table 10-4. Cisco IOS Diffie Hellman Group Support

DH Group Number	Description
1	This specifies the 768-bit Diffie-Hellman group
2	This specifies the 1024-bit Diffie-Hellman group
5	This specifies the 1536-bit Diffie-Hellman group

The following section, which is illustrated below, is used to define the pre-shared key for the two peers, as well as to specify IPSec encryption and authentication algorithms to be used.

```
R1(config)#crypto isakmp key SECURE address 150.4.4.4
R1(config)#crypto ipsec transform-set ESP-3DES-SHA esp-3des esp-sha-hmac
```

The following section is used to define IKE phase 2 SA parameters. The final configuration then defines the ACL, referenced in the crypto map configuration, which defines interesting traffic. Traffic that matches this ACL will be encrypted. Finally, the crypto map configuration is applied to the Internet-facing Serial 0/0 interface.

```
R1(config)#crypto map VPN-EXAMPLE 1 ipsec-isakmp
% NOTE: This new crypto map will remain disabled until a peer
        and a valid access list have been configured.
R1(config-crypto-map)#description 'Secure VPN Tunnel To 150.4.4.4 (R4)'
R1(config-crypto-map)#set peer 150.4.4.4
R1(config-crypto-map)#set transform-set ESP-3DES-SHA
R1(config-crypto-map)#match address 100
R1(config-crypto-map)#exit
R1(config)#access-l 100 permit ip 172.16.1.0 0.0.0.255 172.16.4.0 0.0.0.255
R1(config)#interface Serial0/0
R1(config-if)#description 'Connected To Internet'
R1(config-if)#crypto map VPN-EXAMPLE
```

Following the same logic, the same configuration is mirrored on peer router R4 as follows:

```
R4(config)#crypto isakmp policy 1
R4(config-isakmp)#encr 3des
R4(config-isakmp)#authentication pre-share
R4(config-isakmp)#group 2
R4(config-isakmp)#exit
R4(config)#crypto isakmp key SECURE address 150.1.1.1
R4(config)#crypto ipsec transform-set ESP-3DES-SHA esp-3des esp-sha-hmac
R4(cfg-crypto-trans)#exit
R4(config)#crypto map VPN-EXAMPLE 1 ipsec-isakmp
% NOTE: This new crypto map will remain disabled until a peer
        and a valid access list have been configured.
R4(config-crypto-map)#description 'Secure VPN Tunnel To 150.1.1.1 (R1)'
R4(config-crypto-map)#set peer 150.1.1.1
R4(config-crypto-map)#set transform-set ESP-3DES-SHA
R4(config-crypto-map)#match address 100
R4(config-crypto-map)#exit
R4(config)#access-l 100 permit ip 172.16.4.0 0.0.0.255 172.16.1.0 0.0.0.255
R4(config)#interface Serial0/0
R4(config-if)#description 'Connected To Internet'
R4(config-if)#crypto map VPN-EXAMPLE
R4(config-if)#exit
R4(config)#ip route 0.0.0.0 0.0.0.0 Serial0/0
```

As can be seen in the configuration above, the configuration that is implemented on R4 mirrors the configuration implemented on R1. Following this, use the show crypto map command to validate the crypto map configuration, including peers and interfaces to which the configuration has been applied. The output of this command displays the following on router R4:

```
R4#show crypto map
Crypto Map "VPN-EXAMPLE" 1 ipsec-isakmp
        Description: 'Secure VPN Tunnel To 150.1.1.1 (R1)'
        Peer = 150.1.1.1
        Extended IP access list 100
            access-list 100 permit ip 172.16.4.0 0.0.0.255 172.16.1.0 0.0.0.255
        Current peer: 150.1.1.1
        Security association lifetime: 4608000 kilobytes/3600 seconds
        PFS (Y/N): N
        Transform sets={
                ESP-3DES-SHA,
        }
        Interfaces using crypto map VPN-EXAMPLE:
                Serial0/0
```

Following this, a simple ping test between the two LAN interfaces of the routers can be used to verify the configuration as follows:

```
R4#ping 172.16.1.1 source 172.16.4.4

Type escape sequence to abort.
Sending 5, 100-byte ICMP Echos to 172.16.1.1, timeout is 2 seconds:
Packet sent with a source address of 172.16.4.4
.!!!!
Success rate is 80 percent (4/5), round-trip min/avg/max = 8/10/12 ms
```

NOTE: The first ping packet will time out, as the SA is not established. Subsequent ping packets will be successful after this initial timeout. This is normal behavior.

To validate your IPSec configuration further, use the show crypto isakmp sa [detail] command to show information about the SA. When using this command, remember that SA is unidirectional. Following is the output printed by this command after the ping from the LAN interface of R4 to the LAN interface of R1:

```
R4#show crypto isakmp sa
dst             src             state           conn-id slot status
150.1.1.1       150.4.4.4       QM_IDLE               1     0 ACTIVE
```

On the remote end, R1, the same command displays the following:

```
R1#show crypto isakmp sa
dst              src              state           conn-id slot status
150.1.1.1        150.4.4.4        QM_IDLE               1    0 ACTIVE
```

From both routers, a single SA has been established, allowing for bidirectional communication between the two routers (i.e., ICMP echo and echo-reply packets). Finally, you can use the show crypto ipsec sa command to view SA status, peer information, and tunnel settings, as well as to see the packet count for encrypted packets, in addition to the other information that is also printed by this command:

```
R4#show crypto ipsec sa

interface: Serial0/0
    Crypto map tag: VPN-EXAMPLE, local addr 150.4.4.4

   protected vrf: (none)
   local  ident (addr/mask/prot/port): (172.16.4.0/255.255.255.0/0/0)
   remote ident (addr/mask/prot/port): (172.16.1.0/255.255.255.0/0/0)
   current_peer 150.1.1.1 port 500
     PERMIT, flags={origin_is_acl,}
    #pkts encaps: 4, #pkts encrypt: 4, #pkts digest: 4
    #pkts decaps: 4, #pkts decrypt: 4, #pkts verify: 4
    #pkts compressed: 0, #pkts decompressed: 0
    #pkts not compressed: 0, #pkts compr. failed: 0
    #pkts not decompressed: 0, #pkts decompress failed: 0
    #send errors 1, #recv errors 0

     local crypto endpt.: 150.4.4.4, remote crypto endpt.: 150.1.1.1
     path mtu 1500, ip mtu 1500, ip mtu idb Serial0/0
     current outbound spi: 0xB423BDCB(3022241227)

     inbound esp sas:
      spi: 0xA53289A5(2771552677)
        transform: esp-3des esp-sha-hmac ,
        in use settings ={Tunnel, }
        conn id: 2001, flow_id: SW:1, crypto map: VPN-EXAMPLE
        sa timing: remaining key lifetime (k/sec): (4447497/3557)
        IV size: 8 bytes
        replay detection support: Y
        Status: ACTIVE

     inbound ah sas:

     inbound pcp sas:

     outbound esp sas:
      spi: 0xB423BDCB(3022241227)
        transform: esp-3des esp-sha-hmac ,
        in use settings ={Tunnel, }
        conn id: 2002, flow_id: SW:2, crypto map: VPN-EXAMPLE
```

```
sa timing: remaining key lifetime (k/sec): (4447497/3555)
IV size: 8 bytes
replay detection support: Y
Status: ACTIVE

outbound ah sas:

outbound pcp sas:
```

Cisco Easy VPN

The Cisco Easy VPN (EzVPN) solution can be used for both remote sites and remote or mobile workers. This solution, which is based on the Cisco Unified Client Framework, allows for centralized VPN management, dynamic policy distribution, and configuration simplicity. The EzVPN solution is comprised of the following two components:

- The Easy VPN Server
- The Easy VPN Remote

The EzVPN Server feature allows routers, Cisco Adaptive Security Appliances (ASAs), and the legacy Cisco PIX Appliances to act as Headend VPN devices in site-to-site or remote-access VPNs. This feature pushes security policies defined at the central site to the remote device so that it has up-to-date policies in place before a secure connection is established. It can also terminate VPN tunnels initiated by remote workers running the Cisco VPN Client software on computers, which allows mobile and remote workers to access critical data and applications on their corporate Intranet.

The EzVPN Remote feature, which is also referred to as the EzVPN Client feature, minimizes the configuration requirements at remote locations by allowing routers, Cisco ASA 5505 Adaptive Security Appliances, Cisco PIX Security Appliances, and the Cisco VPN Client to receive security policies upon a VPN tunnel connection from a Cisco Easy VPN Server. This solution is ideal for remote offices with little IT support or for large deployments where it is impractical to configure multiple remote devices individually. This feature makes VPN configuration as easy as entering a password, which minimizes local IT support, increases productivity, and lowers costs.

Dynamic Multipoint VPN

Dynamic Multipoint VPN (DMVPN) is a Cisco IOS solution that allows network engineers to build and implement scalable IPSec VPNs. DMVPN allows IPSec VPNs to scale better than traditional hub-and-spoke or spoke-to-spoke VPN solution. With traditional IPSec VPNs, all endpoints must be specified when implementing the crypto configuration. This becomes cumbersome and labor-intensive as the number of sites that need to communicate securely grows. DMVPN allows for such large implementations with relative ease by allowing dynamic hub-to-spoke and spoke-to-spoke (remote branch) IPSec tunnels with minimal configuration.

While both traditional IPSec VPN and DMVPN solutions use standards-based IPSec encryption protocols, DMVPN is different from the traditional IPSec VPN in many ways and offers more advantages for large-scale IPSec VPN implementations. The differences between traditional IPSec VPN and DMVPN implementation include the following:

- Generic Routing Encapsulation Tunneling
- Dynamic Address Resolution
- Dynamic Tunnel Creation
- Dynamic Routing Protocol Support

Unlike traditional IPSec VPNs, DMVPN uses the Cisco Generic Routing Encapsulation (GRE) protocol to encapsulate packets. GRE uses IP protocol number 47 and was described earlier in this chapter. The Cisco IOS DMVPN solution uses the Next Hop Resolution Protocol (NHRP) to allow routers to learn dynamically the addresses of other routers with which they wish to send data. This negates the need to implement the static peer configuration commands used when configuring traditional IPSec VPNs, which ultimately allows for greater scalability.

With traditional IPSec VPN implementation, all point-to-point IPSec tunnels must be configured on all the routers, even if some of these tunnels are not running or are not needed at all times, following the sequence of steps illustrated in the previous configuration example. This is applicable to both hub-and-spoke and spoke-to-spoke implementations and communication. With DMVPN, however, only the tunnel between the hub router and different spoke routers is continuously up. When data needs to be exchanged securely between spoke sites, the spokes use NHRP to determine dynamically the required destination address of the destination spoke. A tunnel is then established to the destination spoke router, allowing for secure data exchange. After the data transfer, the tunnel is dynamically torn down after a period of inactivity.

Because the DMVPN solution is based on GRE tunnels, which support the tunneling of Unicast, Multicast, and Broadcast packets, it also supports dynamic routing protocols, versus the traditional IPSec VPN solution. Routing protocol adjacencies are established between the hub and spoke routers, while NHRP is used for spoke-to-spoke routing logic.

Group Encrypted Transport VPN

The Cisco IOS Group Encrypted Transport VPN (GET VPN) solution allows for VPN service without tunnels by retaining the original IP packet header and encrypting only the payload or data. The GET VPN solution does this by copying the original IP packet header and placing it before the IPSec header. The advantage of retaining the IP header is that policy implementation, such as QoS markings, can be maintained, as this information is not lost or encapsulated. Additional advantages of using the GET VPN solution include, but are not limited to, the following:

- A single SA and key pair is used for entire any-to-any group communication
- It allows for any-to-any group communication
- It uses no overlay (e.g., tunneling)
- It allows the IP header, and information contained therein (e.g., QoS), to be retained
- It allows for the use of native routing

As previously stated, this is not a security exam. The ultimate objective here is simply to have a basic understanding of the different site-to-site VPN solutions supported in Cisco IOS software. Table 10-5 below summarizes the different site-to-site VPN solutions described above:

Table 10-5. Summarizing Site-to-Site VPN Solutions

VPN Solution	Characteristics
Traditional IPSec VPN	Permanent VPN connections Used for small- to medium-sized VPN implementations No dynamic routing support
Cisco Easy VPN	Permanent VPN connections Used for small- to medium-sized VPN implementations No dynamic routing support
DMVPN	Permanent VPN connections between hub and spokes Dynamic VPN connections between spokes Used for large VPN implementations Dynamic routing protocol support Best solution for secure data communication over the Internet
GET VPN	No VPN tunnel connections; uses native IP Supports dynamic routing protocols Best solution for secure data communication over a private WAN

REMOTE ACCESS VPN TECHNOLOGIES

Remote access VPNs are used to provide secure access to the corporate network by establishing an encrypted tunnel across the Internet. These connections are available any time and can be established using any access technology, for example, DSL or cable broadband connections. Depending on the remote access technology, users can be assigned different rights based on parameters such as function and group, for example. The two primary methods of implementing remote access VPN solutions, which are described in the following sections, are IPSec remote access VPNs and SSL remote access VPNs.

NOTE: Although these two VPN solutions are different, as will be described in the following section, it is important to remember that while some vendors require you to select one or the other, Cisco IOS software allows both VPN solutions to be implemented on the same physical router, providing greater flexibility in VPN implementation and deployment for enterprises.

IPSec VPN

IPSec VPNs are the most commonly used and implemented remote access VPN solutions. These solutions require the installation of some type of VPN client software on the user device from which the VPN itself is established. This limits the use of such VPN access to devices on which this software has been installed, providing greater security and protecting the corporate network from unprotected or unsanctioned devices.

As was stated in the previous section on different site-to-site VPN solutions, the Cisco EzVPN solution can also be used for remote access VPN solutions. Cisco EzVPN client software is available for Windows®, Macintosh®, Linux®, and Solaris® platforms. The current ROUTE exam does not require you to go into any further detail on remote access IPSec VPNs.

SSL VPN

Unlike IPSec VPNs, SSL remote access VPNs provide secure access to the corporate network from any device that has a Web browser and is connected to the Internet. SSL VPNs provide two different types of access, which are as follows:

- The clientless access method
- The full network access method

The clientless access method is the most flexible SSL remote access VPN solution. This access method does not require any specialized VPN software to be installed on the client machine or desktop. Instead, traffic is transmitted and received through a standard Web browser. The limitation with this method, however, is that because applications and network resources are accessed through a Web browser, only Web-enabled and some client-server applications, such as Intranets, applications with Web interfaces, e-mail, calendaring, and file servers, can be accessed using a clientless connection. However, this may be acceptable for some businesses.

Unlike the clientless access method, full network access SSL remote access VPN solutions install a lightweight VPN client package (software) onto the user machine or desktop when the user connects to the SSL VPN gateway. The use of this method allows clients access to applications that cannot be delivered across a Web-based clientless connection. Like clientless access SSL VPN solutions, full network access SSL VPN solutions also allow for customizable access privileges on a per-user basis.

As with site-to-site VPN configuration, the configuration of SSL VPN solutions is beyond the scope of the ROUTE exam requirements and will not be described in this chapter. In conclusion, Table 10-6 below summarizes the differences between IPSec and SSL remote access VPN solutions:

Table 10-6. Differences between IPSec and SSL Remote Access VPNs

IPSec Remote Access VPN	SSL Remote Access VPN
Allows access from company-owned devices	Allows access from any Web-enabled device
Requires pre-installed client device software	No pre-installed client device software
Requires that software be installed manually	In full access, software is installed dynamically
Provides no Web-port application access	Provides Web-port application access
Allows for VPN client customization	There is no VPN client customization
Does not allow for business partner access	Allows access for anyone the company wants

BRANCH OFFICE ROUTING SOLUTIONS

In the final section of this chapter, we will look at branch office routing solutions, specifically across floating static routes and Generic Routing Encapsulation (GRE) tunnels.

Floating Static Routes

Floating static routes are commonly used for backup connections in medium-sized branch office implementations, although they can also be used in full-sized branch office implementations. Floating static routes are simply static routes that are configured with a higher administrative distance than the primary route, which can be either statically configured or learned dynamically using a routing protocol. To demonstrate the use of floating static routes, consider the topology illustrated in Figure 10-19 below:

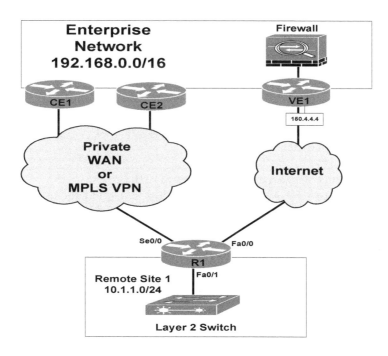

Fig. 10-19. Implementing Floating Static Routes

Referencing Figure 10-19, a remote site router, R1, is connected to the MPLS network as well as to the Internet. The primary connection should be the MPLS connection. The Internet connection should be used only in the event that the MPLS connection is unavailable. It should be assumed that the Ethernet interface is connected to a cable modem and the provider has assigned the customer a globally routable subnet, as they are a business-class customer. For the sake of simplicity, only static default routes are used. Taking into consideration all we have learned in this chapter, the site router, R1, would be configured as follows:

NOTE: For clarity, the floating static route is highlighted in the following configuration.

```
R1(config)#crypto isakmp policy 1
R1(config-isakmp)#encr 3des
R1(config-isakmp)#authentication pre-share
R1(config-isakmp)#group 2
R1(config-isakmp)#exit
R1(config)#crypto isakmp key SECURE address 150.4.4.4
R1(config)#crypto ipsec transform-set ESP-3DES-SHA esp-3des esp-sha-hmac
R1(cfg-crypto-trans)#exit
R1(config)#crypto map VPN-EXAMPLE 1 ipsec-isakmp
% NOTE: This new crypto map will remain disabled until a peer
        and a valid access list have been configured.
R1(config-crypto-map)#description 'Secure VPN Tunnel To 150.4.4.4 (R4)'
R1(config-crypto-map)#set peer 150.4.4.4
R1(config-crypto-map)#set transform-set ESP-3DES-SHA
R1(config-crypto-map)#match address 100
R1(config-crypto-map)#exit
R1(config)#access-l 100 permit ip 10.1.1.0 0.0.0.255 192.168.0.0 0.0.255.255
R1(config)#interface Serial0/0
R1(config-if)#description 'Primary Link Connected To MPLS WAN'
R1(config-if)#ip address 172.16.1.1 255.255.255.252
R1(config-if)#exit
R1(config)#interface FastEthernet0/0
R1(config-if)#description 'Connected To Cable Internet'
R1(config-if)#ip address 150.1.1.1 255.255.255.248
R1(config-if)#crypto map VPN-EXAMPLE
R1(config-if)#exit
R1(config)#ip route 0.0.0.0 0.0.0.0 Serial0/0
R1(config)#ip route 150.4.4.4 255.255.255.255 FastEthernet0/0 150.1.1.2
R1(config)#ip route 0.0.0.0 0.0.0.0 FastEthernet0/0 150.4.4.4 5
```

Based on the configuration implemented on R1, the MPLS connection will be used to forward all packets to the corporate and unknown networks. In the event that the MPLS connection is unavailable, the site-to-site VPN tunnel between R1 and the VPN Headend device VE1 is used to allow access securely to the enterprise network across the Internet. When the primary path is restored, the static route pointing out of the Serial0/0 interface is reinstalled into the RIB and is used to forward all packets via the MPLS VPN.

Generic Routing Encapsulation (GRE) Tunnels

Generic Routing Encapsulation tunnels, which were described in detail in Chapter 9, IPv4 and IPv6 Integration and Coexistence, support multiple protocols in addition to Unicast, Multicast, and Broadcast traffic, which allow dynamic routing protocols to be configured across them.

The configuration of static tunnels in Cisco IOS software is a straightforward process. The following section goes through the configuration steps required to create static, or manually configured, tunnels for encapsulating IPv6 packets within IPv4 packets:

1. Configure a static tunnel interface using the `interface tunnel [number]` global configuration command. The number range will vary depending on the version of Cisco IOS software that the router on which the tunnel is being configured is running.

2. Assign the static tunnel interface an IP address using the `ip address` interface configuration command.

3. Configure a tunnel source for the static tunnel using the `tunnel source [address | interface]` interface configuration command. This is used as the tunnel source address. All packets sent across this tunnel will have this IPv4 address as the source address included in the IPv4 packet header. This is typically a Loopback interface but can be any interface with a globally routable IP address.

4. Configure a tunnel destination for the static tunnel using the `tunnel destination [IPv4 address]` interface configuration command. This is the IPv4 address of the tunnel endpoint (i.e., the far-end side of the tunnel). This address should be the same as the tunnel source address for the tunnel endpoint

5. Because GRE is the default encapsulation protocol for Tunnel interfaces, you do not need to issue the `tunnel mode gre ip` command; however, issuing this command does not affect the implementation.

Referencing the topology in Figure 10-19, which was used to demonstrate the configuration of floating static routes, the following example illustrates how to configure a GRE tunnel to be used as a backup in the event that the primary tunnel via the MPLS WAN is unavailable or the routing protocol adjacency is down. The VPN Headend router is configured as follows:

```
VE1(config)#interface Loopback 15
VE1(config-if)#description 'Globally Routed Loopback Address'
VE1(config-if)#ip address 150.44.44.44 255.255.255.255
VE1(config-if)#exit
VE1(config)#interface Tunnel 15
VE1(config-if)#description 'Private Tunnel Headened Address'
VE1(config-if)#ip address 10.254.1.2 255.255.255.252
VE1(config-if)#tunnel source 150.44.44.44
VE1(config-if)#tunnel destination 150.11.11.11
VE1(config-if)#exit
```

```
VE1(config)#router eigrp 2
VE1(config-router)#network 10.254.1.2 0.0.0.0
VE1(config-router)#no auto-summary
VE1(config-router)#exit
```

Following the same logic, the remote site router, R1, is configured in a similar way as follows:

```
R1(config)#interface Loopback 15
R1(config-if)#description 'Globally Routed Loopback Address'
R1(config-if)#ip address 150.11.11.11 255.255.255.255
R1(config-if)#exit
R1(config)#interface Tunnel 15
R1(config-if)#description 'Private Tunnel Tailend Address'
R1(config-if)#ip address 10.254.1.1 255.255.255.252
R1(config-if)#tunnel source 150.11.11.11
R1(config-if)#tunnel destination 150.44.44.44
R1(config-if)#exit
R1(config)#router eigrp 2
R1(config-router)#network 10.254.1.1 0.0.0.0
R1(config-router)#no auto-summary
R1(config-router)#exit
```

Following this configuration, the `show ip eigrp neighbors` command is used to verify that the EIGRP neighbor relationship across the tunnel has been established as follows:

```
R1#show ip eigrp neighbors detail
IP-EIGRP neighbors for process 2
H   Address                 Interface       Hold Uptime   SRTT   RTO  Q  Seq
                                            (sec)         (ms)        Cnt Num
0   10.254.1.2              Tu15             14 00:10:05     6   5000  0  3
    Version 12.4/1.2, Retrans: 0, Retries: 0
```

> **NOTE:** Due to default tunnel bandwidth and delay values, in most cases the path via a Tunnel interface will always be less preferred than one via other interface types (e.g., Serial or Ethernet). Keep in mind that if you use a routing protocol such as EIGRP, then you can use the `variance` command to load-share traffic between the primary and backup connections, which allows for better utilization of resources. Consideration, however, should be given to the actual topology on which this implementation is being deployed. For example, this may not work in an environment that uses stateful firewalls. It is therefore important to consider the whole picture.

While GRE tunnels do allow routing protocols to be implemented across them, it is important to know that GRE tunnels by themselves do not provide any additional security. Therefore, the packets sent across the GRE tunnel over the Internet are still legible (i.e., are not in cryptographic form) and therefore can be intercepted and read. If security is a requirement, then IPSec can be used in conjunction with GRE tunnels, similar to DMVPN operation, to ensure and provide data confidentiality, integrity, and authenticity.

CHAPTER SUMMARY

The following section is a summary of the major points you should be aware of in this chapter.

Remote Site and Branch Office Considerations

- Branch offices are referred to as remote offices because they are located in different locations
- Branch offices are implemented to serve certain geographic or demographic areas
- Several factors should be taken into consideration when implementing branch office as follows:
    1. Connectivity
    2. Security
    3. High Availability
    4. Routing
    5. IP Services
    6. Mobility
    7. Optimization

Branch Office Classification

- Branch offices or remote offices are typically classified as being small, medium or large
- Small branch offices typically connect directly to headquarters using the following:
    1. Via a private WAN link
    2. Via a VPN over the private WAN link
    3. Via a VPN over the Internet

- Medium-sized branch offices typically require more resiliency than small branch offices
- Medium-sized branch offices typically have redundant WAN routers
- Medium-sized branch offices may use either Layer 2 or Layer 3 switches
- Medium-sized branch offices use FHRPs to provide LAN redundancy
- Large branch office designs commonly mirror campus or enterprise networks
- Large branch offices typically have redundant WAN connections
- Large branch offices typically include both Layer 2 and Layer 3 switches

Data Transmission Basics

- Analog and digital signals are generated as voltage or electric current
- The four core characteristics of analog signals are as follows:
    1. Amplitude
    2. Frequency
    3. Wavelength
    4. Pulse

- Data modulation is a technology used that is used to modify analog signals
- Data modulation makes analog signals more suitable for carrying data
- Multiplexing allows multiple signals to travel simultaneously over a single medium
- Baseband is a transmission form in which signals are sent through direct current
- Broadband is a form of transmission in which signals are modulated as radio frequency
- Noise is an undesirable influence that may distort or degrade a signal
- Attenuation is the loss of the strength of a signal as it travels away from its source
- In order to boost the strength of analog signals, an amplifier is used
- In order to boost the strength of digital signals, a repeater is used

Cable Access Technologies

- Cable modems are network bridge devices that operate at Layer 1 and 2 of the OSI Model
- On the network side, cable modems support Ethernet and on the cable side, DOCSIS
- Cable companies use HFC networks to provide fiber and coaxial connections to customers
- The core components of a data cable network are as follows:
    1. Cable Modems
    2. Cable Modem Termination Systems
    3. Hybrid Fiber Coaxial Networks
    4. Local Headend

DSL Access Technologies

- A DSL modem at the premise is referred to as an xDSL Transmission Unit-Remote (xTU-R)
- A DSL modem at the CO is referred to as an xDSL Transmission Unit-Central (xTU-C)
- ATM is standard for cell relay that transmits data in small, fixed-size 53-byte cells
- Symmetric DSL provides equal capacity for data traveling both upstream and downstream
- SDSL is a DSL variant that runs over one pair of copper wires and supports data only
- ADSL is the most common type of DSL service
- Unlike SDSL, Asymmetric DSL provides different downstream and upstream speeds
- Cisco IOS software supports the following methods for connecting to DSL networks:
    1. Long Range Ethernet
    2. Routed Bridged Encapsulation
    3. Multiprotocol Encapsulation over ATM
    4. Service Selection Gateway
    5. PPP over ATM
    6. PPP over Ethernet

Teleworker Connectivity Considerations

- Teleworkers or mobile workers are employees who work from home or from a remote office
- These workers typically have a broadband Internet connection
- Teleworker implementations should take the following factors into consideration:
  1. Bandwidth Requirements
  2. Security Considerations
  3. Simplified User Experience
  4. Quality of Service
  5. Troubleshooting and Support

Understanding VPN Technologies

- A VPN allows remote users or offices to gain secure access to enterprise network resources
- The three broad classifications of VPN are as follows:
  1. Trusted VPNs
  2. Secure VPNs
  3. Hybrid VPNs

- Trusted VPNs are non-cryptographic VPN, i.e. do not employ cryptographic mechanisms
- Examples of trusted VPNs include MPLS VPNs
- Secure VPNs are used to transport data across public data networks, such as the Internet
- Secure VPNs use cryptography to ensure data confidentiality, integrity and authenticity
- Secure VPN technologies include the following:
  1. IP Security (IPSec)
  2. Layer 2 Tunneling Protocol version 3 (L2TPv3) over IPSec
  3. Point-to-Point Tunneling Protocol (PPTP)
  4. SSL Encryption (SSL VPN)

- Secure VPN solutions use IP Security to ensure confidentiality, integrity and authenticity
- The IPSec framework offers the following security services:
  1. Peer Authentication
  2. Data Confidentiality
  3. Data Integrity
  4. Data Origin Authentication
  5. Replay Detection
  6. Access Control
  7. Traffic Flow Confidentiality

- IPSec uses security association (SA) to provide security to a given IP connection

- IPSec SAs are unidirectional; so SAs are required for bidirectional communications sessions
- IPSec uses ISAKMP/IKE for secure key exchange
- IPSec can use two different modes to secure data: transport mode and tunnel mode

Site-to-Site VPN Technologies

- Site-to-site VPNs are VPNs that are established between dedicated VPN devices
- Site-to-site VPNs do not require that clients be installed with VPN client software
- Cisco IOS software supports the following site-to-site VPN solutions:
    1. Traditional IPSec (IP Security) VPN
    2. Cisco Easy VPN
    3. DMVPN
    4. Group Encrypted Transport VPN

Remote Access VPN Technologies

- Remote access VPNs provide secure access to the corporate network via encrypted tunnels
- There are two methods of implementing remote access VPNs: IPSec and SSL
- IPSec VPNs are the most commonly used and implemented remote access VPN solutions
- IPSec VPNs require the installation of some type of VPN client software on the user device
- SSL remote access VPNs provide secure access to the corporate network via a Web browser
- SSL VPNs provide two different types of access, which are as follows:
    1. The Full Network Access Method
    2. The Clientless Access Method

Branch Office Routing Solutions

- The two commonly implemented solutions for branch office routing are as follows:
    1. Floating static routes
    2. GRE Tunnels

- Floating static routes are commonly used for backup connections or links for branch offices
- GRE tunnels allow dynamic routing protocol implementation
- GRE tunnels by themselves provide no data security; IPSec must also be used for security

PART 2

Labs

LAB 1

BGP Path Selection and Manipulation

Lab Objective:

The objective of this lab exercise is for you to learn and understand how to implement and verify BGP path selection and manipulation solutions in Cisco IOS software.

Lab Topology:

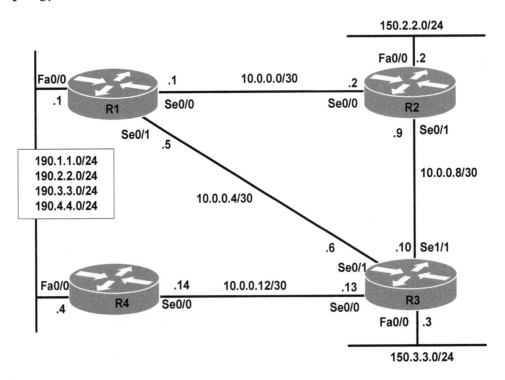

IMPORTANT NOTE:

If you are using the www.howtonetwork.net racks, please bring up the LAN interfaces connected to the routers by issuing the no shutdown command on the connected switches. If you are using a home lab with no switches, you can bring up the LAN interfaces using the following configurations on your routers:

```
interface fastethernet 0/0
 no keepalive
 loopback
 no shutdown
```

Alternately, you can simply connect the interfaces to a hub if you have one.

Task 1

Configure IP addressing on all routers as illustrated in the topology. For the LAN segment between R1 and R4, the 190.1.1.0/24 subnet should be the primary subnet for the LAN. Additionally, also configure the following the following Loopback interfaces on all routers:

Router	Loopback	Loopback Interface Address/Mask
R1	0	1.1.1.1/32
R2	0	2.2.2.2/32
R3	0	3.3.3.3/32
R4	0	4.4.4.4/32

Task 2

Configure OSPF on the LAN segment between R1 and R4. Ensure that R1 is the only router on the segment that will ever originate Type 2 LSAs. Advertise the Loopback 0 subnets on both routers using OSPF. Do not advertise the secondary subnets using OSPF. Additionally, do NOT configure OSPF using the `network [address] [mask] area [area ID]` command.

Task 3

Configure EIGRP on the 10.0.0.8/30 segment between R2 and R3. Advertise the Loopback 0 subnets on both routers using EIGRP. Use autonomous system number 1 for EIGRP.

Task 4

Configure an internal BGP peering between R1 and R4 using the Loopback 0 interfaces for the peer session. These routers reside in AS 254. Advertise the 190.2.2.0/24, 190.3.3.0/24 and 190.4.4.0/24 subnets only via BGP as follows:

- Do NOT use the network statement under BGP to inject these routes into BGP
- All routes should still have an ORIGIN of IGP
- The 190.2.2.0/24 should have a LOCAL_PREF of 222
- The 190.3.3.0/24 should have a LOCAL_PREF of 333
- The 190.4.4.0/24 should have a LOCAL_PREF of 444

Task 5

Configure internal BGP peering between R3 and R2 using their Loopback 0 interfaces. Advertise the 150.x.x.x subnets via BGP. These routers reside in AS 5

Task 6

Configure external BGP peering between R1 and R2 and R3. Use the directly connected subnets for the external BGP peer sessions

Task 7

Configure external BGP peering between R3 and R4. Use the directly connected subnets for the external BGP peer sessions

Task 8

Configure AS 254 to advertise the 190.x.x.x prefixes to AS 5 as follows:
- The 190.2.2.0/24 prefix should appear to originate from AS 222
- The 190.3.3.0/24 prefix should appear to originate from AS 333
- The 190.3.3.0/24 prefix should appear to originate from AS 444

Verify your configuration using the appropriate commands

Task 9

Without using either prefix lists or IP access lists, configure AS 5 outbound routing policy for R2 and R3 as is described in the following section:
- All traffic to the AS 222 subnets should prefer the R3-R4 link (path)
- All traffic to the AS 333 subnets should prefer the R3-R1 link (path)
- All traffic to the AS 444 subnets should prefer the R2-R1 link (path)

Verify your configuration using the appropriate commands

Task 10

Configure your network so that routers R2 and R3 in AS 5 can ping the 190.x.x.x subnets from their respective 150.x.x.x subnets, i.e. using an extended ping. Verify your configuration

LAB VALIDATION

Task 1

```
R2#show ip interface brief
Interface         IP-Address      OK? Method Status                Protocol
FastEthernet0/0   150.2.2.2       YES NVRAM  up                    up
Serial0/0         10.0.0.2        YES NVRAM  up                    up
Serial0/1         10.0.0.9        YES NVRAM  up                    up
Loopback0         2.2.2.2         YES NVRAM  up                    up
```

```
R3#show ip interface brief
Interface          IP-Address      OK? Method Status            Protocol
FastEthernet0/0    150.3.3.3       YES NVRAM  up                up
Serial0/0          10.0.0.13       YES NVRAM  up                up
Serial0/1          10.0.0.6        YES NVRAM  up                up
Serial1/1          10.0.0.10       YES NVRAM  up                up
Loopback0          3.3.3.3         YES NVRAM  up                up
```

For routers R1 and R4, you will need to configure the additional 190.x.x.x subnets as secondary IP addresses on the FastEthernet0/0 interfaces as follows:

```
R1(config)#interface fastethernet 0/0
R1(config-if)#ip address 190.1.1.1 255.255.255.0
R1(config-if)#ip address 190.2.2.1 255.255.255.0 secondary
R1(config-if)#ip address 190.3.3.1 255.255.255.0 secondary
R1(config-if)#ip address 190.4.4.1 255.255.255.0 secondary

R4(config)#interface fastethernet 0/0
R4(config-if)#ip address 190.1.1.2 255.255.255.0
R4(config-if)#ip address 190.1.1.2 255.255.255.0
R4(config-if)#ip address 190.1.1.4 255.255.255.0
R4(config-if)#ip address 190.2.2.4 255.255.255.0 secondary
R4(config-if)#ip address 190.3.3.4 255.255.255.0 secondary
R4(config-if)#ip address 190.4.4.4 255.255.255.0 secondary
R4(config-if)#end
```

NOTE: Secondary IP addresses do NOT show up in the output of the `show ip interfaces brief` command. Instead, you must use the `show interfaces` or `show run` commands.

```
R1#show ip int brief
Interface          IP-Address      OK? Method Status            Protocol
FastEthernet0/0    190.1.1.1       YES manual up                up
Serial0/0          10.0.0.1        YES NVRAM  up                up
Serial0/1          10.0.0.5        YES NVRAM  up                up
Loopback0          1.1.1.1         YES NVRAM  up                up

R4#show ip interface brief
Interface          IP-Address      OK? Method Status            Protocol
FastEthernet0/0    190.1.1.4       YES manual up                up
Serial0/0          10.0.0.14       YES NVRAM  up                up
Serial0/1          unassigned      YES NVRAM  administratively down down
Serial0/2          unassigned      YES NVRAM  administratively down down
Loopback0          4.4.4.4         YES NVRAM  up                up
```

Task 2

By default, only the DR will generate Type 2 LSAs on multi-access segments (transit networks). In the event that the DR is removed, the BDR assumes this role. Therefore, to ensure that R4 never generate Type 2 LSAs, it must be configured so that it will never be either the DR or BDR:

```
R1(config)#router ospf 1
R1(config-router)#router-id 1.1.1.1
R1(config-router)#exit
R1(config)#interface loopback 0
R1(config-if)#ip ospf 1 area 0
R1(config-if)#exit
R1(config)#interface fastethernet 0/0
R1(config-if)#ip ospf 1 area 0 secondaries none


R4(config)#router ospf 4
R4(config-router)#router-id 4.4.4.4
R4(config-router)#exit
R4(config)#interface loopback 0
R4(config-if)#ip ospf 4 area 0
R4(config-if)#exit
R4(config)#interface fastethernet 0/0
R4(config-if)#ip ospf priority 0
R4(config-if)#ip ospf 4 area 0 secondaries none
R4(config-if)#end
```

Following this configuration, first verify that the secondary subnets on the FastEthernet links on R1 and R4 are not advertised via OSPF using the show ip ospf interface command:

```
R1#show ip ospf interface fastethernet 0/0
FastEthernet0/0 is up, line protocol is up
  Internet Address 190.1.1.1/24, Area 0
  Process ID 1, Router ID 1.1.1.1, Network Type BROADCAST, Cost: 1
  Enabled by interface config, excluding secondary ip addresses
  Transmit Delay is 1 sec, State DR, Priority 1
  Designated Router (ID) 1.1.1.1, Interface address 190.1.1.1
  No backup designated router on this network
  Timer intervals configured, Hello 10, Dead 40, Wait 40, Retransmit 5
    oob-resync timeout 40
    Hello due in 00:00:07
  Supports Link-local Signaling (LLS)
  Index 1/1, flood queue length 0
  Next 0x0(0)/0x0(0)
  Last flood scan length is 1, maximum is 1
  Last flood scan time is 0 msec, maximum is 0 msec
  Neighbor Count is 1, Adjacent neighbor count is 1
    Adjacent with neighbor 4.4.4.4
  Suppress hello for 0 neighbor(s)


R4#show ip ospf interface fastethernet 0/0
FastEthernet0/0 is up, line protocol is up
  Internet Address 190.1.1.4/24, Area 0
  Process ID 4, Router ID 4.4.4.4, Network Type BROADCAST, Cost: 1
  Enabled by interface config, excluding secondary ip addresses
  Transmit Delay is 1 sec, State DROTHER, Priority 0
  Designated Router (ID) 1.1.1.1, Interface address 190.1.1.1
```

```
No backup designated router on this network
Timer intervals configured, Hello 10, Dead 40, Wait 40, Retransmit 5
  oob-resync timeout 40
  Hello due in 00:00:08
Supports Link-local Signaling (LLS)
Index 1/1, flood queue length 0
Next 0x0(0)/0x0(0)
Last flood scan length is 1, maximum is 1
Last flood scan time is 0 msec, maximum is 0 msec
Neighbor Count is 1, Adjacent neighbor count is 1
  Adjacent with neighbor 1.1.1.1  (Designated Router)
Suppress hello for 0 neighbor(s)
```

Task 3

```
R3(config)#router eigrp 1
R3(config-router)#network 3.3.3.3 0.0.0.0
R3(config-router)#network 10.0.0.8 0.0.0.3
R3(config-router)#no auto-summary
R3(config-router)#end

R2(config)#router eigrp 1
R2(config-router)#network 2.2.2.2 0.0.0.0
R2(config-router)#network 10.0.0.8 0.0.0.3
R2(config-router)#no auto-summary
R2(config-router)#end
```

Verify your configuration using the show ip eigrp interfaces command as follows:

```
R2#show ip eigrp interfaces detail
IP-EIGRP interfaces for process 1
                        Xmit Queue  Mean   Pacing Time  Multicast    Pending
Interface     Peers  Un/Reliable  SRTT  Un/Reliable  Flow Timer   Routes
Lo0             0       0/0         0       0/1           0           0
  Hello interval is 5 sec
  Next xmit serial <none>
  Un/reliable mcasts: 0/0  Un/reliable ucasts: 0/0
  Mcast exceptions: 0  CR packets: 0  ACKs suppressed: 0
  Retransmissions sent: 0  Out-of-sequence rcvd: 0
  Authentication mode is not set
  Use multicast
Se0/1           1       0/0         5       0/15         50           0
  Hello interval is 5 sec
  Next xmit serial <none>
  Un/reliable mcasts: 0/0  Un/reliable ucasts: 3/6
  Mcast exceptions: 0  CR packets: 0  ACKs suppressed: 3
  Retransmissions sent: 0  Out-of-sequence rcvd: 0
  Authentication mode is not set
  Use unicast
```

Task 4

This task is straightforward which requires a route map. The task is completed as follows:

```
R1(config)#ip prefix-list NET-2 seq 5 permit 190.2.2.0/24
R1(config)#ip prefix-list NET-3 seq 5 permit 190.3.3.0/24
R1(config)#ip prefix-list NET-4 seq 5 permit 190.4.4.0/24
R1(config)#route-map CONNECTED permit 10
R1(config-route-map)#match ip address prefix-list NET-2
R1(config-route-map)#set origin igp
R1(config-route-map)#set local-preference 222
R1(config-route-map)#exit
R1(config)#route-map CONNECTED permit 20
R1(config-route-map)#match ip address prefix-list NET-3
R1(config-route-map)#set origin igp
R1(config-route-map)# set local-preference 333
R1(config-route-map)#exit
R1(config)#route-map CONNECTED permit 30
R1(config-route-map)#match ip address prefix-list NET-4
R1(config-route-map)#set origin igp
R1(config-route-map)# set local-preference 444
R1(config-route-map)#exit
R1(config)#router bgp 254
R1(config-router)#bgp router-id 1.1.1.1
R1(config-router)#redistribute connected route-map CONNECTED
R1(config-router)#neighbor 4.4.4.4 remote-as 254
R1(config-router)#neighbor 4.4.4.4 update-source loopback 0
R1(config-router)#end

R4(config)#ip prefix-list NET-2 seq 5 permit 190.2.2.0/24
R4(config)#ip prefix-list NET-3 seq 5 permit 190.3.3.0/24
R4(config)#ip prefix-list NET-4 seq 5 permit 190.4.4.0/24
R4(config)#route-map CONNECTED permit 10
R4(config-route-map)#match ip address prefix-list NET-2
R4(config-route-map)#set origin igp
R4(config-route-map)#set local-preference 222
R4(config-route-map)#exit
R4(config)#route-map CONNECTED permit 20
R4(config-route-map)#match ip address prefix-list NET-3
R4(config-route-map)#set origin igp
R4(config-route-map)#set local-preference 333
R4(config-route-map)#exit
R4(config)#route-map CONNECTED permit 30
R4(config-route-map)#match ip address prefix-list NET-4
R4(config-route-map)#set origin igp
R4(config-route-map)#set local-preference 444
R4(config-route-map)#exit
R4(config)#router bgp 254
R4(config-router)#bgp router-id 4.4.4.4
R4(config-router)#redistribute connected route-map CONNECTED
R4(config-router)#neighbor 1.1.1.1 remote-as 254
R4(config-router)#neighbor 1.1.1.1 update-source loopback 0
R4(config-router)#end
```

Following this configuration, use the show ip bgp summary and show ip bgp commands to verify your implementation

```
R1#show ip bgp summary
BGP router identifier 1.1.1.1, local AS number 254
BGP table version is 10, main routing table version 10
3 network entries using 351 bytes of memory
6 path entries using 312 bytes of memory
4/3 BGP path/bestpath attribute entries using 496 bytes of memory
0 BGP route-map cache entries using 0 bytes of memory
0 BGP filter-list cache entries using 0 bytes of memory
BGP using 1159 total bytes of memory
BGP activity 3/0 prefixes, 6/0 paths, scan interval 60 secs

Neighbor      V    AS MsgRcvd MsgSent   TblVer  InQ OutQ Up/Down  State/PfxRcd
4.4.4.4       4   254       9       9       10    0    0 00:02:23            3


R1#show ip bgp
BGP table version is 10, local router ID is 1.1.1.1
Status codes: s suppressed, d damped, h history, * valid, > best, i - internal,
              r RIB-failure, S Stale
Origin codes: i - IGP, e - EGP, ? - incomplete

   Network          Next Hop          Metric LocPrf Weight Path
 * i190.2.2.0/24    4.4.4.4               0    222      0 i
 *>                 0.0.0.0               0    222  32768 i
 * i190.3.3.0/24    4.4.4.4               0    333      0 i
 *>                 0.0.0.0               0    333  32768 i
 * i190.4.4.0/24    4.4.4.4               0    444      0 i
 *>                 0.0.0.0               0    444  32768 i


R4#show ip bgp summary
BGP router identifier 4.4.4.4, local AS number 254
BGP table version is 7, main routing table version 7
3 network entries using 351 bytes of memory
6 path entries using 312 bytes of memory
4/3 BGP path/bestpath attribute entries using 496 bytes of memory
0 BGP route-map cache entries using 0 bytes of memory
0 BGP filter-list cache entries using 0 bytes of memory
BGP using 1159 total bytes of memory
BGP activity 3/0 prefixes, 6/0 paths, scan interval 60 secs

Neighbor      V    AS MsgRcvd MsgSent   TblVer  InQ OutQ Up/Down  State/PfxRcd
1.1.1.1       4   254       8       8        7    0    0 00:01:47            3


R4#show ip bgp
BGP table version is 7, local router ID is 4.4.4.4
Status codes: s suppressed, d damped, h history, * valid, > best, i - internal,
```

```
            r RIB-failure, S Stale
Origin codes: i - IGP, e - EGP, ? - incomplete

   Network          Next Hop        Metric LocPrf Weight Path
 * i190.2.2.0/24    1.1.1.1              0    222      0 i
 *>                 0.0.0.0              0    222  32768 i
 * i190.3.3.0/24    1.1.1.1              0    333      0 i
 *>                 0.0.0.0              0    333  32768 i
 * i190.4.4.0/24    1.1.1.1              0    444      0 i
 *>                 0.0.0.0              0    444  32768 i
```

Task 5

```
R3(config)#router bgp 5
R3(config-router)#bgp router-id 3.3.3.3
R3(config-router)#network 150.3.3.0 mask 255.255.255.0
R3(config-router)#neighbor 2.2.2.2 remote-as 5
R3(config-router)#neighbor 2.2.2.2 update-source loopback 0
R3(config-router)#end

R2(config)#router bgp 5
R2(config-router)#bgp router-id 2.2.2.2
R2(config-router)#network 150.2.2.0 mask 255.255.255.0
R2(config-router)#neighbor 3.3.3.3 remote-as 5
R2(config-router)#neighbor 3.3.3.3 update-source loopback 0
R2(config-router)#end
```

Following this configuration, use the show ip bgp summary and show ip bgp commands to verify your implementation

```
R3#show ip bgp summary
BGP router identifier 3.3.3.3, local AS number 5
BGP table version is 5, main routing table version 5
2 network entries using 234 bytes of memory
2 path entries using 104 bytes of memory
3/2 BGP path/bestpath attribute entries using 372 bytes of memory
0 BGP route-map cache entries using 0 bytes of memory
0 BGP filter-list cache entries using 0 bytes of memory
BGP using 710 total bytes of memory
BGP activity 2/0 prefixes, 2/0 paths, scan interval 60 secs

Neighbor     V    AS MsgRcvd MsgSent   TblVer  InQ OutQ Up/Down  State/PfxRcd
2.2.2.2      4     5       4       4        5    0    0 00:00:35            1


R3#show ip bgp
BGP table version is 5, local router ID is 3.3.3.3
Status codes: s suppressed, d damped, h history, * valid, > best, i - internal,
              r RIB-failure, S Stale
```

```
Origin codes: i - IGP, e - EGP, ? - incomplete

   Network          Next Hop           Metric LocPrf Weight Path
*>i150.2.2.0/24     2.2.2.2                 0    100      0 i
*> 150.3.3.0/24     0.0.0.0                 0          32768 i


R2#show ip bgp summary
BGP router identifier 2.2.2.2, local AS number 5
BGP table version is 4, main routing table version 4
2 network entries using 234 bytes of memory
2 path entries using 104 bytes of memory
3/2 BGP path/bestpath attribute entries using 372 bytes of memory
0 BGP route-map cache entries using 0 bytes of memory
0 BGP filter-list cache entries using 0 bytes of memory
BGP using 710 total bytes of memory
BGP activity 2/0 prefixes, 2/0 paths, scan interval 60 secs

Neighbor      V     AS MsgRcvd MsgSent   TblVer  InQ OutQ Up/Down  State/PfxRcd
3.3.3.3       4      5       5       5        4    0    0 00:01:08            1


R2#show ip bgp
BGP table version is 4, local router ID is 2.2.2.2
Status codes: s suppressed, d damped, h history, * valid, > best, i - internal,
              r RIB-failure, S Stale
Origin codes: i - IGP, e - EGP, ? - incomplete

   Network          Next Hop           Metric LocPrf Weight Path
*> 150.2.2.0/24     0.0.0.0                 0          32768 i
*>i150.3.3.0/24     3.3.3.3                 0    100      0 i
```

Task 6

```
R1(config)#router bgp 254
R1(config-router)#neighbor 10.0.0.2 remote-as 5
R1(config-router)#neighbor 10.0.0.6 remote-as 5
R1(config-router)#end


R2(config)#router bgp 5
R2(config-router)#neighbor 10.0.0.1 remote-as 254
R2(config-router)#end


R3(config)#router bgp 5
R3(config-router)#neighbor 10.0.0.5 remote-as 254
R3(config-router)#end
```

Following this configuration task, use the show ip bgp summary command to verify your implementation. Following is the output of this command on R1:

```
R1#show ip bgp summary
BGP router identifier 1.1.1.1, local AS number 254
BGP table version is 12, main routing table version 12
5 network entries using 585 bytes of memory
10 path entries using 520 bytes of memory
6/5 BGP path/bestpath attribute entries using 744 bytes of memory
1 BGP AS-PATH entries using 24 bytes of memory
0 BGP route-map cache entries using 0 bytes of memory
0 BGP filter-list cache entries using 0 bytes of memory
BGP using 1873 total bytes of memory
BGP activity 5/0 prefixes, 10/0 paths, scan interval 60 secs

Neighbor      V     AS MsgRcvd MsgSent   TblVer  InQ OutQ Up/Down  State/PfxRcd
4.4.4.4       4    254      19      21       12    0    0 00:12:52        3
10.0.0.2      4      5       7      10       12    0    0 00:01:14        2
10.0.0.6      4      5       7      10       12    0    0 00:01:25        2
```

Task 7

```
R3(config)#router bgp 5
R3(config-router)#neighbor 10.0.0.14 remote-as 254
R3(config-router)#end

R4(config)#router bgp 254
R4(config-router)#neighbor 10.0.0.13 remote-as 5
R4(config-router)#end
```

Following this configuration task, use the show ip bgp summary command to verify your implementation. Following is the output of this command on R3:

```
R3#show ip bgp summary
BGP router identifier 3.3.3.3, local AS number 5
BGP table version is 8, main routing table version 8
5 network entries using 585 bytes of memory
11 path entries using 572 bytes of memory
5/3 BGP path/bestpath attribute entries using 620 bytes of memory
1 BGP AS-PATH entries using 24 bytes of memory
0 BGP route-map cache entries using 0 bytes of memory
0 BGP filter-list cache entries using 0 bytes of memory
BGP using 1801 total bytes of memory
BGP activity 5/0 prefixes, 11/0 paths, scan interval 60 secs

Neighbor      V     AS MsgRcvd MsgSent   TblVer  InQ OutQ Up/Down  State/PfxRcd
2.2.2.2       4      5      39      39        8    0    0 00:34:27        4
10.0.0.5      4    254      40      37        8    0    0 00:31:31        3
10.0.0.14     4    254      33      33        8    0    0 00:26:04        3
```

Task 8

This task requires AS_PATH prepending on R1 and R4. Using the same prefix lists that were configured on these two routers, this is completed as follows:

```
R1(config)#route-map AS-PATH-PREPEND permit 10
R1(config-route-map)#match ip address prefix-list NET-2
R1(config-route-map)#set as-path prepend 222
R1(config-route-map)#exit
R1(config)#route-map AS-PATH-PREPEND permit 20
R1(config-route-map)#match ip address prefix-list NET-3
R1(config-route-map)#set as-path prepend 333
R1(config-route-map)#exit
R1(config)#route-map AS-PATH-PREPEND permit 30
R1(config-route-map)#match ip address prefix-list NET-4
R1(config-route-map)#set as-path prepend 444
R1(config-route-map)#exit
R1(config)#router bgp 254
R1(config-router)#neighbor 10.0.0.2 route-map AS-PATH-PREPEND out
R1(config-router)#neighbor 10.0.0.6 route-map AS-PATH-PREPEND out
R1(config-router)#end
R1#clear ip bgp * soft out

R4(config)#route-map AS-PATH-PREPEND permit 10
R4(config-route-map)#match ip address prefix-list NET-2
R4(config-route-map)#set as-path prepend 222
R4(config-route-map)#exit
R4(config)#route-map AS-PATH-PREPEND permit 20
R4(config-route-map)#match ip address prefix-list NET-3
R4(config-route-map)#set as-path prepend 333
R4(config-route-map)#exit
R4(config)#route-map AS-PATH-PREPEND permit 30
R4(config-route-map)#match ip address prefix-list NET-4
R4(config-route-map)#set as-path prepend 444
R4(config-route-map)#exit
R4(config)#router bgp 254
R4(config-router)#neighbor 10.0.0.13 route-map AS-PATH-PREPEND out
R4(config-router)#end
R4#
R4#clear ip bgp * soft out
```

Following this configuration, use the show ip bgp command on R2 and R3 to validate:

```
R2#show ip bgp
BGP table version is 10, local router ID is 2.2.2.2
Status codes: s suppressed, d damped, h history, * valid, > best, i - internal,
              r RIB-failure, S Stale
Origin codes: i - IGP, e - EGP, ? - incomplete

   Network          Next Hop            Metric LocPrf Weight Path
*> 150.2.2.0/24     0.0.0.0                  0         32768 i
```

```
*>i150.3.3.0/24      3.3.3.3                   0    100        0 i
*> 190.2.2.0/24      10.0.0.1                  0               0 254 222 i
*  i                 10.0.0.14                 0    100        0 254 222 i
*> 190.3.3.0/24      10.0.0.1                  0               0 254 333 i
*  i                 10.0.0.14                 0    100        0 254 333 i
*> 190.4.4.0/24      10.0.0.1                  0               0 254 444 i
*  i                 10.0.0.14                 0    100        0 254 444 i


R3#show ip bgp
BGP table version is 14, local router ID is 3.3.3.3
Status codes: s suppressed, d damped, h history, * valid, > best, i - internal,
              r RIB-failure, S Stale
Origin codes: i - IGP, e - EGP, ? - incomplete

    Network           Next Hop              Metric LocPrf Weight Path
*>i150.2.2.0/24      2.2.2.2                   0    100        0 i
*> 150.3.3.0/24      0.0.0.0                   0           32768 i
*> 190.2.2.0/24      10.0.0.14                 0               0 254 222 i
*  i                 10.0.0.1                  0    100        0 254 222 i
*                    10.0.0.5                  0               0 254 222 i
*> 190.3.3.0/24      10.0.0.14                 0               0 254 333 i
*  i                 10.0.0.1                  0    100        0 254 333 i
*                    10.0.0.5                  0               0 254 333 i
*> 190.4.4.0/24      10.0.0.14                 0               0 254 444 i
*  i                 10.0.0.1                  0    100        0 254 444 i
*                    10.0.0.5                  0               0 254 444 i
```

Task 9

This task requires the use of AS_PATH ACLs in conjunction with the LOCAL_PREF attribute.

This task is completed as follows:

```
R3(config)#ip as-path access-list 1 permit _222$
R3(config)#ip as-path access-list 2 permit _333$
R3(config)#route-map AS-222-INBOUND permit 10
R3(config-route-map)#match as-path 1
R3(config-route-map)#set local-preference 200
R3(config-route-map)#exit
R3(config)#route-map AS-333-INBOUND permit 10
R3(config-route-map)#match as-path 2
R3(config-route-map)#set local-preference 200
R3(config-route-map)#exit
R3(config)#router bgp 5
R3(config-router)#neighbor 10.0.0.14 route-map AS-222-INBOUND in
R3(config-router)#neighbor 10.0.0.5 route-map AS-333-INBOUND in
R3(config-router)#end
R3#clear ip bgp * soft in


R2(config)#ip as-path access-list 1 permit _444$
```

```
R2(config)#route-map AS-444-INBOUND permit 10
R2(config-route-map)#match as-path 1
R2(config-route-map)#set local-preference 1
R2(config-route-map)#exit
R2(config)#router bgp 5
R2(config-router)#neighbor 10.0.0.1 route-map AS-444-INBOUND in
R2(config-router)#end
R2#clear ip bgp * soft in
```

Following this configuration, use the show ip bgp command to verify your configuration:

```
R3#show ip bgp
BGP table version is 17, local router ID is 3.3.3.3
Status codes: s suppressed, d damped, h history, * valid, > best, i - internal,
              r RIB-failure, S Stale
Origin codes: i - IGP, e - EGP, ? - incomplete

   Network          Next Hop          Metric LocPrf Weight Path
*>i150.2.2.0/24     2.2.2.2                0    100      0 i
*> 150.3.3.0/24     0.0.0.0                0         32768 i
*> 190.2.2.0/24     10.0.0.14              0    200      0 254 222 i
*> 190.3.3.0/24     10.0.0.5               0    200      0 254 333 i
*  i190.4.4.0/24    10.0.0.1               0      1      0 254 444 i


R2#show ip bgp
BGP table version is 13, local router ID is 2.2.2.2
Status codes: s suppressed, d damped, h history, * valid, > best, i - internal,
              r RIB-failure, S Stale
Origin codes: i - IGP, e - EGP, ? - incomplete

   Network          Next Hop          Metric LocPrf Weight Path
*> 150.2.2.0/24     0.0.0.0                0         32768 i
*>i150.3.3.0/24     3.3.3.3                0    100      0 i
*  i190.2.2.0/24    10.0.0.14              0    200      0 254 222 i
*  i190.3.3.0/24    10.0.0.5               0    200      0 254 333 i
*> 190.4.4.0/24     10.0.0.1               0      1      0 254 444 i
```

Task 10

Because by default iBGP peers will never change the NEXT_HOP when advertising routes to another iBGP peer, each router in AS 5 shows the NEXT_HOP for external routes as inaccessible. For example, R3 shows the following for the 192.4.4.0/24 subnet it gets from R2:

```
R3#show ip bgp 190.4.4.0/24
BGP routing table entry for 190.4.4.0/24, version 16
Paths: (1 available, no best path)
Flag: 0x820
  Not advertised to any peer
```

```
254 444
   10.0.0.1 (inaccessible) from 2.2.2.2 (2.2.2.2)
      Origin IGP, metric 0, localpref 1, valid, internal
```

To resolve this issue, the NEXT_HOP attribute for external routes must be changed as follows:

```
R3(config)#router bgp 5
R3(config-router)#neighbor 2.2.2.2 next-hop-self
R3(config-router)#end
R3#clear ip bgp * soft out


R2(config)#router bgp 5
R2(config-router)#neighbor 3.3.3.3 next-hop-self
R2(config-router)#end
R2#clear ip bgp * soft out
```

Following this configuration, R3 now shows the following entry:

```
R3#show ip bgp 190.4.4.0/24
BGP routing table entry for 190.4.4.0/24, version 18
Paths: (1 available, best #1, table Default-IP-Routing-Table)
  Advertised to update-groups:
     2
  254 444
    2.2.2.2 (metric 2297856) from 2.2.2.2 (2.2.2.2)
       Origin IGP, metric 0, localpref 1, valid, internal, best
```

Following this configuration, the two routers can ping the 190.x.x.x subnets from their 150.x.x.x LAN subnets as follows:

```
R3#ping 190.4.4.1 source 150.3.3.3

Type escape sequence to abort.
Sending 5, 100-byte ICMP Echos to 190.4.4.1, timeout is 2 seconds:
Packet sent with a source address of 150.3.3.3
!!!!!
Success rate is 100 percent (5/5), round-trip min/avg/max = 4/4/4 ms

R3#ping 190.4.4.4 source 150.3.3.3

Type escape sequence to abort.
Sending 5, 100-byte ICMP Echos to 190.4.4.4, timeout is 2 seconds:
Packet sent with a source address of 150.3.3.3
!!!!!
Success rate is 100 percent (5/5), round-trip min/avg/max = 4/4/4 ms
```

```
R2#ping 190.2.2.1 source 150.2.2.2

Type escape sequence to abort.
Sending 5, 100-byte ICMP Echos to 190.2.2.1, timeout is 2 seconds:
Packet sent with a source address of 150.2.2.2
!!!!!
Success rate is 100 percent (5/5), round-trip min/avg/max = 4/4/4 ms

R2#ping 190.2.2.4 source 150.2.2.2

Type escape sequence to abort.
Sending 5, 100-byte ICMP Echos to 190.2.2.4, timeout is 2 seconds:
Packet sent with a source address of 150.2.2.2
!!!!!
Success rate is 100 percent (5/5), round-trip min/avg/max = 4/4/4 ms

R2#ping 190.3.3.1 source 150.2.2.2

Type escape sequence to abort.
Sending 5, 100-byte ICMP Echos to 190.3.3.1, timeout is 2 seconds:
Packet sent with a source address of 150.2.2.2
!!!!!
Success rate is 100 percent (5/5), round-trip min/avg/max = 4/4/4 ms

R2#ping 190.3.3.4 source 150.2.2.2

Type escape sequence to abort.
Sending 5, 100-byte ICMP Echos to 190.3.3.4, timeout is 2 seconds:
Packet sent with a source address of 150.2.2.2
!!!!!
Success rate is 100 percent (5/5), round-trip min/avg/max = 4/4/8 ms
```

DEVICE CONFIGURATIONS

```
R1#show running-config
Building configuration...

Current configuration : 2458 bytes
!
version 12.4
service timestamps debug datetime msec
service timestamps log datetime msec
no service password-encryption
!
hostname R1
!
boot-start-marker
boot-end-marker
!
```

```
no logging console
enable secret 5 $1$ZHZP$BfOgaK4Ei7zfUol9D8zpV/
!
no aaa new-model
no network-clock-participate slot 1
no network-clock-participate wic 0
ip cef
!
no ip domain lookup
ip auth-proxy max-nodata-conns 3
ip admission max-nodata-conns 3
!
ipv6 unicast-routing
!
interface Loopback0
 ip address 1.1.1.1 255.255.255.255
 ip ospf 1 area 0
!
interface FastEthernet0/0
 ip address 190.2.2.1 255.255.255.0 secondary
 ip address 190.3.3.1 255.255.255.0 secondary
 ip address 190.4.4.1 255.255.255.0 secondary
 ip address 190.1.1.1 255.255.255.0
 ip ospf 1 area 0 secondaries none
 duplex auto
 speed auto
!
interface Serial0/0
 ip address 10.0.0.1 255.255.255.252
 no fair-queue
!
interface Serial0/1
 ip address 10.0.0.5 255.255.255.252
!
router ospf 1
 router-id 1.1.1.1
 log-adjacency-changes
!
router bgp 254
 no synchronization
 bgp router-id 1.1.1.1
 bgp log-neighbor-changes
 redistribute connected route-map CONNECTED
 neighbor 4.4.4.4 remote-as 254
 neighbor 4.4.4.4 update-source Loopback0
 neighbor 10.0.0.2 remote-as 5
 neighbor 10.0.0.2 route-map AS-PATH-PREPEND out
 neighbor 10.0.0.6 remote-as 5
 neighbor 10.0.0.6 route-map AS-PATH-PREPEND out
 no auto-summary
!
ip forward-protocol nd
```

```
!
ip http server
no ip http secure-server
!
ip prefix-list NET-2 seq 5 permit 190.2.2.0/24
!
ip prefix-list NET-3 seq 5 permit 190.3.3.0/24
!
ip prefix-list NET-4 seq 5 permit 190.4.4.0/24
!
route-map AS-PATH-PREPEND permit 10
 match ip address prefix-list NET-2
 set as-path prepend 222
!
route-map AS-PATH-PREPEND permit 20
 match ip address prefix-list NET-3
 set as-path prepend 333
!
route-map AS-PATH-PREPEND permit 30
 match ip address prefix-list NET-4
 set as-path prepend 444
!
route-map CONNECTED permit 10
 match ip address prefix-list NET-2
 set local-preference 222
 set origin igp
!
route-map CONNECTED permit 20
 match ip address prefix-list NET-3
 set local-preference 333
 set origin igp
!
route-map CONNECTED permit 30
 match ip address prefix-list NET-4
 set local-preference 444
 set origin igp
!
control-plane
!
voice-port 1/0/0
!
voice-port 1/0/1
!
voice-port 1/1/0
!
voice-port 1/1/1
!
line con 0
line aux 0
line vty 0 4
 privilege level 15
 password cisco
```

```
 login
 !

end

R1#


R2#show running-config
Building configuration...

Current configuration : 1511 bytes
!
version 12.4
service timestamps debug datetime msec
service timestamps log datetime msec
no service password-encryption
!
hostname R2
!
boot-start-marker
boot-end-marker
!
no logging console
enable secret 5 $1$FsT/$/viPNrSsewWFUCy/QbD5lO
!
no aaa new-model
!
ip cef
no ip domain lookup
!
ipv6 unicast-routing
!
interface Loopback0
 ip address 2.2.2.2 255.255.255.0
!
interface FastEthernet0/0
 ip address 150.2.2.2 255.255.255.0
 loopback
 half-duplex
 no keepalive
!
interface Serial0/0
 ip address 10.0.0.2 255.255.255.252
 clock rate 2000000
 no fair-queue
!
interface FastEthernet0/1
 no ip address
 shutdown
 half-duplex
!
```

```
interface Serial0/1
 ip address 10.0.0.9 255.255.255.252
 clock rate 2000000
!
router eigrp 1
 network 2.2.2.2 0.0.0.0
 network 10.0.0.8 0.0.0.3
 no auto-summary
!
router bgp 5
 no synchronization
 bgp router-id 2.2.2.2
 bgp log-neighbor-changes
 network 150.2.2.0 mask 255.255.255.0
 neighbor 3.3.3.3 remote-as 5
 neighbor 3.3.3.3 update-source Loopback0
 neighbor 3.3.3.3 next-hop-self
 neighbor 10.0.0.1 remote-as 254
 neighbor 10.0.0.1 route-map AS-444-INBOUND in
 no auto-summary
!
ip http server
ip forward-protocol nd
!
ip as-path access-list 1 permit _444$
!


route-map AS-444-INBOUND permit 10
 match as-path 1
 set local-preference 1
!


control-plane
!
mgcp behavior g729-variants static-pt
!
gatekeeper
 shutdown
!
!
line con 0
line aux 0
line vty 0 4
 privilege level 15
 password cisco
 login
!
end

R2#
```

```
R3#show running-config
Building configuration...

Current configuration : 1926 bytes
!
version 12.4
service timestamps debug datetime msec
service timestamps log datetime msec
no service password-encryption
!
hostname R3
!
boot-start-marker
boot-end-marker
!
no logging console
enable secret 5 $1$mOsw$hNy9.KzOvGX2XmLabNBOT/
!
no aaa new-model
!
ip cef
no ip domain lookup
!
ipv6 unicast-routing
!
interface Loopback0
 ip address 3.3.3.3 255.255.255.255
!
interface FastEthernet0/0
 ip address 150.3.3.3 255.255.255.0
 loopback
 half-duplex
 no keepalive
!
interface Serial0/0
 ip address 10.0.0.13 255.255.255.252
 no fair-queue
!
interface FastEthernet0/1
 no ip address
 shutdown
 half-duplex
!
interface Serial0/1
 ip address 10.0.0.6 255.255.255.252
 clock rate 2000000
!
interface Ethernet1/0
 no ip address
 shutdown
 half-duplex
!
```

```
interface Serial1/0
 no ip address
 shutdown
!
interface Serial1/1
 ip address 10.0.0.10 255.255.255.252
!
router eigrp 1
 network 3.3.3.3 0.0.0.0
 network 10.0.0.8 0.0.0.3
 no auto-summary
!
router bgp 5
 no synchronization
 bgp router-id 3.3.3.3
 bgp log-neighbor-changes
 network 150.3.3.0 mask 255.255.255.0
 neighbor 2.2.2.2 remote-as 5
 neighbor 2.2.2.2 update-source Loopback0
 neighbor 2.2.2.2 next-hop-self
 neighbor 10.0.0.5 remote-as 254
 neighbor 10.0.0.5 route-map AS-333-INBOUND in
 neighbor 10.0.0.14 remote-as 254
 neighbor 10.0.0.14 route-map AS-222-INBOUND in
 no auto-summary
!
ip http server
ip forward-protocol nd
!
ip as-path access-list 1 permit _222$
ip as-path access-list 2 permit _333$
!
route-map AS-333-INBOUND permit 10
 match as-path 2
 set local-preference 200
!
route-map AS-222-INBOUND permit 10
 match as-path 1
 set local-preference 200
!

control-plane
!
mgcp behavior g729-variants static-pt
!
gatekeeper
 shutdown
!
line con 0
line aux 0
line vty 0 4
 privilege level 15
```

```
 password cisco
 login
!
end

R3#


R4#show running-config
Building configuration...

Current configuration : 2436 bytes
!
version 12.4
service timestamps debug datetime msec
service timestamps log datetime msec
no service password-encryption
!
hostname R4
!
boot-start-marker
boot-end-marker
!
no logging console
enable secret 5 $1$M/kd$Eb360Ygk4rDpv7JtJeRbP.
!
no aaa new-model
no network-clock-participate slot 1
no network-clock-participate wic 0
ip cef
!
ip auth-proxy max-nodata-conns 3
ip admission max-nodata-conns 3
!
ipv6 unicast-routing
!
interface Loopback0
 ip address 4.4.4.4 255.255.255.255
 ip ospf 4 area 0
!
interface FastEthernet0/0
 ip address 190.2.2.4 255.255.255.0 secondary
 ip address 190.3.3.4 255.255.255.0 secondary
 ip address 190.4.4.4 255.255.255.0 secondary
 ip address 190.1.1.4 255.255.255.0
 ip ospf priority 0
 ip ospf 4 area 0 secondaries none
 duplex auto
 speed auto
!
interface Serial0/0
 ip address 10.0.0.14 255.255.255.252
```

```
 no fair-queue
 clock rate 2000000
!
interface Serial0/1
 no ip address
 shutdown
!
interface Serial0/2
 no ip address
 shutdown
!
router ospf 4
 router-id 4.4.4.4
 log-adjacency-changes
!
router bgp 254
 no synchronization
 bgp router-id 4.4.4.4
 bgp log-neighbor-changes
 redistribute connected route-map CONNECTED
 neighbor 1.1.1.1 remote-as 254
 neighbor 1.1.1.1 update-source Loopback0
 neighbor 10.0.0.13 remote-as 5
 neighbor 10.0.0.13 route-map AS-PATH-PREPEND out
 no auto-summary
!
ip forward-protocol nd
!
ip http server
no ip http secure-server
!
ip prefix-list NET-2 seq 5 permit 190.2.2.0/24
!
ip prefix-list NET-3 seq 5 permit 190.3.3.0/24
!
ip prefix-list NET-4 seq 5 permit 190.4.4.0/24
!
route-map AS-PATH-PREPEND permit 10
 match ip address prefix-list NET-2
 set as-path prepend 222
!
route-map AS-PATH-PREPEND permit 20
 match ip address prefix-list NET-3
 set as-path prepend 333
!
route-map AS-PATH-PREPEND permit 30
 match ip address prefix-list NET-4
 set as-path prepend 444
!
route-map CONNECTED permit 10
 match ip address prefix-list NET-2
 set local-preference 222
```

```
 set origin igp
!
route-map CONNECTED permit 20
 match ip address prefix-list NET-3
 set local-preference 333
 set origin igp
!
route-map CONNECTED permit 30
 match ip address prefix-list NET-4
 set local-preference 444
 set origin igp
!
control-plane
!

voice-port 1/0/0
!
voice-port 1/0/1
!
voice-port 1/1/0
!
voice-port 1/1/1
!
line con 0
line aux 0
line vty 0 4
 privilege level 15
 password cisco
 login
!
end

R4#
```

LAB 2

BGP Peering and Prefix Advertisement

Lab Objective:

The objective of this lab exercise is for you to learn and understand how to implement and verify internal and external BGP peering solutions in Cisco IOS software.

Lab Topology:

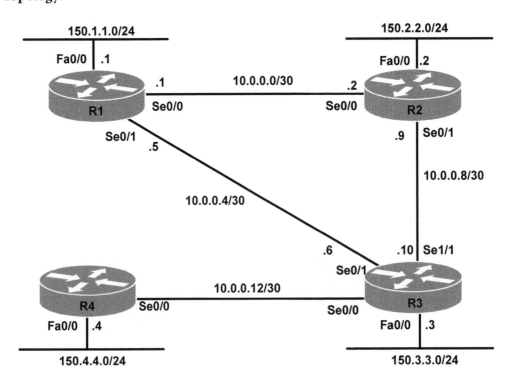

IMPORTANT NOTE:

If you are using the www.howtonetwork.net racks, please bring up the LAN interfaces connected to the routers by issuing the no shutdown command on the connected switches. If you are using a home lab with no switches, you can bring up the LAN interfaces using the following configurations on your routers:

```
interface fastethernet 0/0
 no keepalive
 loopback
 no shutdown
```

Alternately, you can simply connect the interfaces to a hub if you have one.

Task 1

Configure IP addressing on all routers as illustrated in the topology. Additionally, configure the following the following Loopback interfaces on all routers:

Router	Loopback	Loopback Interface Address/Mask
R1	0	1.1.1.1/32
R1	1	190.1.1.1/24
R2	0	2.2.2.2/32
R2	1	190.2.2.2/24
R3	0	3.3.3.3/32
R4	0	4.4.4.4/32

Task 2

Configure BGP on routers R1 and R2 as follows:
- R1 should reside in AS 111 while R2 should reside in AS 222
- The routers should peer with each other using their 10.0.0.0/30 addresses
- Statically configure the router ID using the Loopback 0 address
- Both routers should advertise their respective 150.x.x.x subnets via BGP
- Both routers should also advertise the 190.x.x.x subnets via BGP

Task 3

Configure BGP on routers R3 as follows:
- The router should reside in AS 333
- USE PEER GROUPS FOR YOUR BGP CONFIGURATION ON R3
- The router should peer with both R1 and R2 using their Loopback addresses
- Statically configure the RID using the Loopback 0 interface address
- Advertise the 150.3.3.0/24 subnet via BGP
- Verify that R3 can ping the 150.x.x.x and 190.x.x.x subnets
- Verify that R1 and R2 can ping the 150.3.3.0/24 subnet

Task 4

Configure OSPF between R3 and R4 as follows:
- Enable OSPF for the 10.0.0.12/30 subnet between the two routers
- Advertise the Loopback interfaces via OSPF
- Both routers should reside in OSPF area 0 (the backbone)
- Redistribute the 150.4.4.0/24 subnet into OSPF on R4

Task 5

Configure your network so that R4 has routes to the 150.x.x.x and 190.x.x.x subnets that are advertised by AS 111 and AS 222. Also configure your network so that R4 has a route to the 150.3.3.0/24 that is advertised by R3.

Task 6

Advertise the 150.4.4.0/24 subnet received by R3 from R4 to external BGP peers R1 and R2. This prefix should be redistributed into BGP on R3.

Task 7

Configure your network so that R4 can ping the 150.x.x.x and 190.x.x.x subnets advertised by R1 and R2. Also ensure that R1 and R2 can ping the 150.4.4.0/24 subnet. You are allowed to use only ONE static route in your configuration to complete this task. In addition to this, do NOT configure any additional route redistribution to complete this task.

LAB VALIDATION

Task 1

```
R1#show ip interface brief
Interface          IP-Address      OK? Method Status          Protocol
FastEthernet0/0    150.1.1.1       YES NVRAM  up              up
Serial0/0          10.0.0.1        YES NVRAM  up              up
Serial0/1          10.0.0.5        YES NVRAM  up              up
Loopback0          1.1.1.1         YES NVRAM  up              up
Loopback1          190.1.1.1       YES manual up              up


R2#show ip interface brief
Interface          IP-Address      OK? Method Status          Protocol
FastEthernet0/0    150.2.2.2       YES NVRAM  up              up
Serial0/0          10.0.0.2        YES NVRAM  up              up
Serial0/1          10.0.0.9        YES NVRAM  up              up
Loopback0          2.2.2.2         YES NVRAM  up              up
Loopback1          190.2.2.2       YES manual up              up


R3#show ip interface brief
Interface          IP-Address      OK? Method Status          Protocol
FastEthernet0/0    150.3.3.3       YES NVRAM  up              up
Serial0/0          10.0.0.13       YES NVRAM  up              up
Serial0/1          10.0.0.6        YES NVRAM  up              up
Serial1/1          10.0.0.10       YES NVRAM  up              up
Loopback0          3.3.3.3         YES NVRAM  up              up
```

```
R4#show ip interface brief
Interface          IP-Address      OK? Method Status              Protocol
FastEthernet0/0    150.4.4.4       YES NVRAM  up                  up
Serial0/0          10.0.0.14       YES NVRAM  up                  up
Loopback0          4.4.4.4         YES NVRAM  up                  up
```

Task 2

```
R1(config)#router bgp 111
R1(config-router)#bgp router-id 1.1.1.1
R1(config-router)#neighbor 10.0.0.2 remote-as 222
R1(config-router)#network 150.1.1.0 mask 255.255.255.0
R1(config-router)#network 190.1.1.0 mask 255.255.255.0
R1(config-router)#end
```

```
R2(config)#router bgp 222
R2(config-router)#bgp router-id 2.2.2.2
R2(config-router)#neighbor 10.0.0.1 remote-as 111
R2(config-router)#network 150.2.2.0 mask 255.255.255.0
R2(config-router)#network 190.2.2.0 mask 255.255.255.0
R2(config-router)#end
```

Following the completion of this task, use the show ip bgp summary command to verify that
the adjacency between R1 and R2 has been established:

```
R1#show ip bgp summary
BGP router identifier 1.1.1.1, local AS number 111
BGP table version is 5, main routing table version 5
4 network entries using 468 bytes of memory
4 path entries using 208 bytes of memory
3/2 BGP path/bestpath attribute entries using 372 bytes of memory
1 BGP AS-PATH entries using 24 bytes of memory
0 BGP route-map cache entries using 0 bytes of memory
0 BGP filter-list cache entries using 0 bytes of memory
BGP using 1072 total bytes of memory
BGP activity 4/0 prefixes, 4/0 paths, scan interval 60 secs

Neighbor     V    AS MsgRcvd MsgSent   TblVer  InQ OutQ Up/Down  State/PfxRcd
10.0.0.2     4    222       5       5        5    0    0 00:01:14            2
```

```
R2#show ip bgp summary
BGP router identifier 2.2.2.2, local AS number 222
BGP table version is 5, main routing table version 5
4 network entries using 468 bytes of memory
4 path entries using 208 bytes of memory
3/2 BGP path/bestpath attribute entries using 372 bytes of memory
1 BGP AS-PATH entries using 24 bytes of memory
0 BGP route-map cache entries using 0 bytes of memory
```

```
O BGP filter-list cache entries using O bytes of memory
BGP using 1072 total bytes of memory
BGP activity 4/0 prefixes, 4/0 paths, scan interval 60 secs

Neighbor     V    AS MsgRcvd MsgSent   TblVer  InQ OutQ Up/Down   State/PfxRcd
10.0.0.1     4   111       5       5        5    0    0 00:01:03             2
```

Task 3

This task requires configuration on routers R1, R2 and R3 as follows:

```
R1(config)#router bgp 111
R1(config-router)#neighbor 3.3.3.3 remote-as 333
R1(config-router)#neighbor 3.3.3.3 update-source loopback 0
R1(config-router)#neighbor 3.3.3.3 ebgp-multihop 2
R1(config-router)#exit
R1(config)#ip route 3.3.3.3 255.255.255.255 serial 0/1

R2(config)#router bgp 222
R2(config-router)#neighbor 3.3.3.3 remote-as 333
R2(config-router)#neighbor 3.3.3.3 update-source loopback 0
R2(config-router)#neighbor 3.3.3.3 ebgp-multihop 2
R2(config-router)#exit
R2(config)#ip route 3.3.3.3 255.255.255.255 serial 0/1

R3(config)#router bgp 333
R3(config-router)#bgp router-id 3.3.3.3
R3(config-router)#neighbor EXTERNAL peer-group
R3(config-router)#neighbor EXTERNAL update-source loopback 0
R3(config-router)#neighbor EXTERNAL ebgp-multihop 2
R3(config-router)#neighbor 1.1.1.1 remote-as 111
R3(config-router)#neighbor 1.1.1.1 peer-group EXTERNAL
R3(config-router)#neighbor 2.2.2.2 remote-as 222
R3(config-router)#neighbor 2.2.2.2 peer-group EXTERNAL
R3(config-router)#network 150.3.3.0 mask 255.255.255.0
R3(config-router)#exit
R3(config)#ip route 1.1.1.1 255.255.255.255 serial 0/1
R3(config)#ip route 2.2.2.2 255.255.255.255 serial 1/1
```

Again, following the configuration, use the show ip bgp summary command to verify that the BGP peer relationships have been established:

```
R3#show ip bgp summary
BGP router identifier 3.3.3.3, local AS number 333
BGP table version is 8, main routing table version 8
5 network entries using 585 bytes of memory
9 path entries using 468 bytes of memory
6/3 BGP path/bestpath attribute entries using 744 bytes of memory
4 BGP AS-PATH entries using 96 bytes of memory
```

```
0 BGP route-map cache entries using 0 bytes of memory
0 BGP filter-list cache entries using 0 bytes of memory
BGP using 1893 total bytes of memory
BGP activity 5/0 prefixes, 9/0 paths, scan interval 60 secs

Neighbor     V    AS MsgRcvd MsgSent   TblVer  InQ OutQ Up/Down  State/PfxRcd
1.1.1.1      4   111       7       8        8    0    0 00:00:43            4
2.2.2.2      4   222       8       8        8    0    0 00:00:19            4
```

Next, complete the second requirement of this task by performing simple pings from R3:

```
R3#ping 150.1.1.1

Type escape sequence to abort.
Sending 5, 100-byte ICMP Echos to 150.1.1.1, timeout is 2 seconds:
!!!!!
Success rate is 100 percent (5/5), round-trip min/avg/max = 1/3/4 ms

R3#ping 150.2.2.2

Type escape sequence to abort.
Sending 5, 100-byte ICMP Echos to 150.2.2.2, timeout is 2 seconds:
!!!!!
Success rate is 100 percent (5/5), round-trip min/avg/max = 4/4/4 ms

R3#ping 190.1.1.1

Type escape sequence to abort.
Sending 5, 100-byte ICMP Echos to 190.1.1.1, timeout is 2 seconds:
!!!!!
Success rate is 100 percent (5/5), round-trip min/avg/max = 1/3/4 ms
R3#ping 190.2.2.2

Type escape sequence to abort.
Sending 5, 100-byte ICMP Echos to 190.2.2.2, timeout is 2 seconds:
!!!!!
Success rate is 100 percent (5/5), round-trip min/avg/max = 4/4/4 ms
```

For the final verification, ping the 150.3.3.0/24 subnet from routers R1 and R2:

```
R1#ping 150.3.3.3

Type escape sequence to abort.
Sending 5, 100-byte ICMP Echos to 150.3.3.3, timeout is 2 seconds:
!!!!!
Success rate is 100 percent (5/5), round-trip min/avg/max = 1/1/4 ms
```

```
R2#ping 150.3.3.3

Type escape sequence to abort.
Sending 5, 100-byte ICMP Echos to 150.3.3.3, timeout is 2 seconds:
!!!!!
Success rate is 100 percent (5/5), round-trip min/avg/max = 4/4/4 ms
```

Task 4

```
R3(config)#router ospf 3
R3(config-router)#router-id 3.3.3.3
R3(config-router)#exit
R3(config)#interface serial 0/0
R3(config-if)#ip ospf 3 area 0
R3(config-if)#exit
R3(config)#interface loopback 0
R3(config-if)#ip ospf 3 area 0
R3(config-if)#end


R4(config)#router ospf 4
R4(config-router)#router-id 4.4.4.4
R4(config-router)#redistribute connected subnets
R4(config-router)#exit
R4(config)#interface serial 0/0
R4(config-if)#ip ospf 4 area 0
R4(config-if)#exit
R4(config)#interface loopback 0
R4(config-if)#ip ospf 4 area 0
R4(config-if)#exit
```

Next, verify your configuration using the show ip ospf interfaces and the show ip ospf neighbor commands as follows:

```
R4#show ip ospf interface brief
Interface   PID   Area        IP Address/Mask    Cost   State  Nbrs F/C
Lo0         4     0           4.4.4.4/32         1      LOOP   0/0
Fa0/0       4     0           150.4.4.4/24       1      DR     0/0
Se0/0       4     0           10.0.0.14/30       64     P2P    1/1


R4#show ip ospf neighbor

Neighbor ID    Pri   State      Dead Time   Address      Interface
3.3.3.3         0    FULL/ -    00:00:35    10.0.0.13    Serial0/0
```

And finally, verify that the 150.4.4.0/24 subnet exists in the LSDB of R3 as a Type 2 external LSA:

```
R3#show ip ospf database external 150.4.4.0

            OSPF Router with ID (3.3.3.3) (Process ID 3)

            Type-5 AS External Link States

  Routing Bit Set on this LSA
  LS age: 65
  Options: (No TOS-capability, DC)
  LS Type: AS External Link
  Link State ID: 150.4.4.0 (External Network Number )
  Advertising Router: 4.4.4.4
  LS Seq Number: 80000001
  Checksum: 0x6D84
  Length: 36
  Network Mask: /24
        Metric Type: 2 (Larger than any link state path)
        TOS: 0
        Metric: 20
        Forward Address: 0.0.0.0
        External Route Tag: 0
```

Task 5

This task calls for the redistribution of both internal and external BGP routes into OSPF on R3. This is completed as follows:

```
R3(config)#router bgp 333
R3(config-router)#bgp redistribute-internal
R3(config-router)#exit
R3(config)#router ospf 3
R3(config-router)#redistribute bgp 333 subnets
R3(config-router)#end
```

Next, verify your configuration by looking at the LSDB on R3. The LSDB should now contain the Type 5 LSAs for all BGP prefixes as follows:

```
R3#show ip ospf database | begin Type-5
            Type-5 AS External Link States

Link ID        ADV Router      Age       Seq#        Checksum Tag
150.1.1.0      3.3.3.3         837       0x80000001  0x00E7B7 111
150.2.2.0      3.3.3.3         837       0x80000001  0x00A687 222
150.3.3.0      3.3.3.3         837       0x80000001  0x00E327 0
150.4.4.0      4.4.4.4         249       0x80000001  0x006D84 0
190.1.1.0      3.3.3.3         837       0x80000001  0x00DD99 111
190.2.2.0      3.3.3.3         837       0x80000001  0x009C69 222
```

Next, verify the routing table on R4 using the show ip route command as follows:

```
R4#show ip route ospf | include O E2
O E2     190.1.1.0 [110/1] via 10.0.0.13, 00:03:14, Serial0/0
O E2     190.2.2.0 [110/1] via 10.0.0.13, 00:03:14, Serial0/0
O E2     150.1.1.0 [110/1] via 10.0.0.13, 00:03:14, Serial0/0
O E2     150.2.2.0 [110/1] via 10.0.0.13, 00:03:14, Serial0/0
O E2     150.3.3.0 [110/1] via 10.0.0.13, 00:03:14, Serial0/0
```

Task 6

Remember that by default BGP will only redistribute internal OSPF routes and Type 1 external routes. You must explicitly allow Type 2 external routes to be redistributed into BGP.

```
R3(config)#router bgp 333
R3(config-router)#redistribute ospf 3 match external 2
R3(config-router)#end
```

Verify this configuration by looking at the BGP RIB on R3 following the configuration:

```
R3#show ip bgp 150.4.4.0 255.255.255.0
BGP routing table entry for 150.4.4.0/24, version 9
Paths: (1 available, best #1, table Default-IP-Routing-Table)
Flag: 0x820
  Advertised to update-groups:
     1
  Local
    10.0.0.14 from 0.0.0.0 (3.3.3.3)
      Origin incomplete, metric 20, localpref 100, weight 32768, valid, sourced, best
```

Additionally, also verify that the prefix is received by routers R1 and R2:

```
R1#show ip bgp 150.4.4.0 255.255.255.0
BGP routing table entry for 150.4.4.0/24, version 7
Paths: (2 available, best #2, table Default-IP-Routing-Table)
Flag: 0x820
  Advertised to update-groups:
     1
  222 333
    10.0.0.2 from 10.0.0.2 (2.2.2.2)
      Origin incomplete, localpref 100, valid, external
  333
    3.3.3.3 from 3.3.3.3 (3.3.3.3)
      Origin incomplete, metric 20, localpref 100, valid, external, best
```

```
R2#show ip bgp 150.4.4.0 255.255.255.0
BGP routing table entry for 150.4.4.0/24, version 8
Paths: (2 available, best #2, table Default-IP-Routing-Table)
```

```
    Advertised to update-groups:
      1
  111 333
    10.0.0.1 from 10.0.0.1 (1.1.1.1)
      Origin incomplete, localpref 100, valid, external
  333
    3.3.3.3 from 3.3.3.3 (3.3.3.3)
      Origin incomplete, metric 20, localpref 100, valid, external, best
```

At this point, neither R1 nor R2 should be able to ping the 150.4.4.0/24 subnet:

```
R1#ping 150.4.4.4

Type escape sequence to abort.
Sending 5, 100-byte ICMP Echos to 150.4.4.4, timeout is 2 seconds:
.....
Success rate is 0 percent (0/5)


R2#ping 150.4.4.4

Type escape sequence to abort.
Sending 5, 100-byte ICMP Echos to 150.4.4.4, timeout is 2 seconds:
.....
Success rate is 0 percent (0/5)
```

Task 7

This task requires you to think outside the box. The first restriction is that only a single static route can be used to complete this task. The second is that you are not allowed to configure additional redistribution to complete this task.

The first step is therefore to ensure that R1 and R2 can reach R4. Given that we can only use a single static route, we can configure a default route pointing to Null0 and configure R3 to advertise this to R1 and R2 via BGP. This is performed as follows:

```
R3(config)#ip route 0.0.0.0 0.0.0.0 null 0
R3(config)#router bgp 333
R3(config-router)#default-information originate
R3(config-router)#network 0.0.0.0 mask 0.0.0.0
R3(config-router)#end
```

Following this configuration, R3 shows the following entry for the default route:

```
R3#show ip bgp 0.0.0.0
BGP routing table entry for 0.0.0.0/0, version 10
Paths: (1 available, best #1, table Default-IP-Routing-Table)
```

```
Flag: 0x820
  Advertised to update-groups:
     1
  Local
    0.0.0.0 from 0.0.0.0 (3.3.3.3)
      Origin IGP, metric 0, localpref 100, weight 32768, valid, sourced, local, best
```

Next, routers R1 and R2 receive this default route via BGP as follows:

```
R1#show ip bgp 0.0.0.0
BGP routing table entry for 0.0.0.0/0, version 8
Paths: (2 available, best #2, table Default-IP-Routing-Table)
  Advertised to update-groups:
     1
  222 333
    10.0.0.2 from 10.0.0.2 (2.2.2.2)
      Origin IGP, localpref 100, valid, external
  333
    3.3.3.3 from 3.3.3.3 (3.3.3.3)
      Origin IGP, metric 0, localpref 100, valid, external, best

R2#show ip bgp 0.0.0.0
BGP routing table entry for 0.0.0.0/0, version 9
Paths: (2 available, best #2, table Default-IP-Routing-Table)
Flag: 0x820
  Advertised to update-groups:
     1
  111 333
    10.0.0.1 from 10.0.0.1 (1.1.1.1)
      Origin IGP, localpref 100, valid, external
  333
    3.3.3.3 from 3.3.3.3 (3.3.3.3)
      Origin IGP, metric 0, localpref 100, valid, external, best
```

Next, because we have a default route in the routing table, the default-information origi-nate command can be issued under OSPF to advertise this to R4 as follows:

```
R3(config)#router ospf 3
R3(config-router)#default-information originate
R3(config-router)#end
```

NOTE: The always keyword is not required if a default route exists in the routing table.

```
R3#show ip ospf database external 0.0.0.0

          OSPF Router with ID (3.3.3.3) (Process ID 3)

             Type-5 AS External Link States

   LS age: 936
   Options: (No TOS-capability, DC)
   LS Type: AS External Link
   Link State ID: 0.0.0.0 (External Network Number )
   Advertising Router: 3.3.3.3
   LS Seq Number: 80000001
   Checksum: 0x59F
   Length: 36
   Network Mask: /0
        Metric Type: 2 (Larger than any link state path)
        TOS: 0
        Metric: 1
        Forward Address: 0.0.0.0
        External Route Tag: 3
```

The default route is now included in the routing table on R4:

```
R4#show ip route ospf | include O*E2
O E2    190.1.1.0 [110/1] via 10.0.0.13, 00:41:41, Serial0/0
O E2    190.2.2.0 [110/1] via 10.0.0.13, 00:41:41, Serial0/0
O E2    150.1.1.0 [110/1] via 10.0.0.13, 00:41:41, Serial0/0
O E2    150.2.2.0 [110/1] via 10.0.0.13, 00:41:41, Serial0/0
O E2    150.3.3.0 [110/1] via 10.0.0.13, 00:41:41, Serial0/0
O*E2 0.0.0.0/0 [110/1] via 10.0.0.13, 00:16:47, Serial0/0
```

And finally, use basic pings to validate your configuration as follows:

```
R4#ping 150.1.1.1

Type escape sequence to abort.
Sending 5, 100-byte ICMP Echos to 150.1.1.1, timeout is 2 seconds:
!!!!!
Success rate is 100 percent (5/5), round-trip min/avg/max = 1/3/4 ms

R4#ping 190.1.1.1

Type escape sequence to abort.
Sending 5, 100-byte ICMP Echos to 190.1.1.1, timeout is 2 seconds:
!!!!!
Success rate is 100 percent (5/5), round-trip min/avg/max = 4/4/4 ms

R4#ping 150.2.2.2
```

```
Type escape sequence to abort.
Sending 5, 100-byte ICMP Echos to 150.2.2.2, timeout is 2 seconds:
!!!!!
Success rate is 100 percent (5/5), round-trip min/avg/max = 4/4/4 ms

R4#ping 190.2.2.2

Type escape sequence to abort.
Sending 5, 100-byte ICMP Echos to 190.2.2.2, timeout is 2 seconds:
!!!!!
Success rate is 100 percent (5/5), round-trip min/avg/max = 4/4/4 ms

R1#ping 150.4.4.4

Type escape sequence to abort.
Sending 5, 100-byte ICMP Echos to 150.4.4.4, timeout is 2 seconds:
!!!!!
Success rate is 100 percent (5/5), round-trip min/avg/max = 4/4/4 ms

R2#ping 150.4.4.4

Type escape sequence to abort.
Sending 5, 100-byte ICMP Echos to 150.4.4.4, timeout is 2 seconds:
!!!!!
Success rate is 100 percent (5/5), round-trip min/avg/max = 4/4/4 ms
```

DEVICE CONFIGURATIONS

```
R1#show running-config
Building configuration...

Current configuration : 1499 bytes
!
version 12.4
service timestamps debug datetime msec
service timestamps log datetime msec
no service password-encryption
!
hostname R1
!
boot-start-marker
boot-end-marker
!
no logging console
enable secret 5 $1$ZHZP$BfOgaK4Ei7zfUol9D8zpV/
!
no aaa new-model
no network-clock-participate slot 1
no network-clock-participate wic 0
```

```
ip cef
!
no ip domain lookup
ip auth-proxy max-nodata-conns 3
ip admission max-nodata-conns 3
!
ipv6 unicast-routing
!
interface Loopback0
 ip address 1.1.1.1 255.255.255.255
!
interface Loopback1
 ip address 190.1.1.1 255.255.255.0
!
interface FastEthernet0/0
 ip address 150.1.1.1 255.255.255.0
 loopback
 duplex auto
 speed auto
 no keepalive
!
interface Serial0/0
 ip address 10.0.0.1 255.255.255.252
 no fair-queue
!
interface Serial0/1
 ip address 10.0.0.5 255.255.255.252
!
router bgp 111
 no synchronization
 bgp router-id 1.1.1.1
 bgp log-neighbor-changes
 network 150.1.1.0 mask 255.255.255.0
 network 190.1.1.0 mask 255.255.255.0
 neighbor 3.3.3.3 remote-as 333
 neighbor 3.3.3.3 ebgp-multihop 2
 neighbor 3.3.3.3 update-source Loopback0
 neighbor 10.0.0.2 remote-as 222
 no auto-summary
!
ip forward-protocol nd
ip route 3.3.3.3 255.255.255.255 Serial0/1
!
ip http server
no ip http secure-server
!

control-plane
!

voice-port 1/0/0
!
```

```
voice-port 1/0/1
!
voice-port 1/1/0
!
voice-port 1/1/1
!
line con 0
line aux 0
line vty 0 4
 privilege level 15
 password cisco
 login
!
end

R1#


R2#show running-config
Building configuration...

Current configuration : 1408 bytes
!
version 12.4
service timestamps debug datetime msec
service timestamps log datetime msec
no service password-encryption
!
hostname R2
!
boot-start-marker
boot-end-marker
!
no logging console
enable secret 5 $1$FsT/$/viPNrSsewWFUCy/QbD510
!
no aaa new-model
!
ip cef
no ip domain lookup
!
ipv6 unicast-routing
!
interface Loopback0
 ip address 2.2.2.2 255.255.255.0
!
interface Loopback1
 ip address 190.2.2.2 255.255.255.0
!
interface FastEthernet0/0
 ip address 150.2.2.2 255.255.255.0
 loopback
```

```
 half-duplex
 no keepalive
!
interface Serial0/0
 ip address 10.0.0.2 255.255.255.252
 clock rate 2000000
 no fair-queue
!
interface FastEthernet0/1
 no ip address
 shutdown
 half-duplex
!
interface Serial0/1
 ip address 10.0.0.9 255.255.255.252
 clock rate 2000000
!
router bgp 222
 no synchronization
 bgp router-id 2.2.2.2
 bgp log-neighbor-changes
 network 150.2.2.0 mask 255.255.255.0
 network 190.2.2.0 mask 255.255.255.0
 neighbor 3.3.3.3 remote-as 333
 neighbor 3.3.3.3 ebgp-multihop 2
 neighbor 3.3.3.3 update-source Loopback0
 neighbor 10.0.0.1 remote-as 111
 no auto-summary
!
ip http server
ip forward-protocol nd
ip route 3.3.3.3 255.255.255.255 Serial0/1
!
control-plane
!
mgcp behavior g729-variants static-pt
!
gatekeeper
 shutdown
!
line con 0
line aux 0
line vty 0 4
 privilege level 15
 password cisco
 login
!
end

R2#
```

```
R3#show running-config
Building configuration...

Current configuration : 1913 bytes
!
version 12.4
service timestamps debug datetime msec
service timestamps log datetime msec
no service password-encryption
!
hostname R3
!
boot-start-marker
boot-end-marker
!
no logging console
enable secret 5 $1$mOsw$hNy9.KzOvGX2XmLabNBOT/
!
no aaa new-model
!
ip cef
no ip domain lookup
!
ipv6 unicast-routing
!
interface Loopback0
 ip address 3.3.3.3 255.255.255.255
 ip ospf 3 area 0
!
interface Ethernet0/0
 bandwidth 100000
 ip address 150.3.3.3 255.255.255.0
 loopback
 half-duplex
 no keepalive
!
interface Serial0/0
 ip address 10.0.0.13 255.255.255.252
 ip ospf 3 area 0
 no fair-queue
!
interface Ethernet0/1
 no ip address
 shutdown
 half-duplex
!
interface Serial0/1
 ip address 10.0.0.6 255.255.255.252
 clock rate 2000000
!
interface Ethernet1/0
 no ip address
```

```
 shutdown
 half-duplex
!
interface Serial1/0
 no ip address
 shutdown
!
interface Serial1/1
 ip address 10.0.0.10 255.255.255.252
!
router ospf 3
 router-id 3.3.3.3
 log-adjacency-changes
 redistribute bgp 333 subnets
 default-information originate
!
router bgp 333
 no synchronization
 bgp router-id 3.3.3.3
 bgp log-neighbor-changes
 bgp redistribute-internal
 network 0.0.0.0
 network 150.3.3.0 mask 255.255.255.0
 redistribute ospf 3 match external 2
 neighbor EXTERNAL peer-group
 neighbor EXTERNAL ebgp-multihop 2
 neighbor EXTERNAL update-source Loopback0
 neighbor 1.1.1.1 remote-as 111
 neighbor 1.1.1.1 peer-group EXTERNAL
 neighbor 2.2.2.2 remote-as 222
 neighbor 2.2.2.2 peer-group EXTERNAL
 default-information originate
 no auto-summary
!
ip http server
ip forward-protocol nd
ip route 0.0.0.0 0.0.0.0 Null0
ip route 1.1.1.1 255.255.255.255 Serial0/1
ip route 2.2.2.2 255.255.255.255 Serial1/1
!
control-plane
!
mgcp behavior g729-variants static-pt
!
gatekeeper
 shutdown
!
line con 0
line aux 0
line vty 0 4
 privilege level 15
 password cisco
```

```
 login
 !
 end

R3#


R4#show running-config
Building configuration...

Current configuration : 1240 bytes
!
version 12.4
service timestamps debug datetime msec
service timestamps log datetime msec
no service password-encryption
!
hostname R4
!
boot-start-marker
boot-end-marker
!
no logging console
enable secret 5 $1$M/kd$Eb360Ygk4rDpv7JtJeRbP.
!
no aaa new-model
no network-clock-participate slot 1
no network-clock-participate wic 0
ip cef
!
ip auth-proxy max-nodata-conns 3
ip admission max-nodata-conns 3
!
ipv6 unicast-routing
!
interface Loopback0
 ip address 4.4.4.4 255.255.255.255
 ip ospf 4 area 0
!
interface FastEthernet0/0
 ip address 150.4.4.4 255.255.255.0
 loopback
 duplex auto
 speed auto
 no keepalive
!
interface Serial0/0
 ip address 10.0.0.14 255.255.255.252
 ip ospf 4 area 0
 no fair-queue
 clock rate 2000000
!
```

```
interface Serial0/1
 no ip address
 shutdown
!
interface Serial0/2
 no ip address
 shutdown
!
router ospf 4
 router-id 4.4.4.4
 log-adjacency-changes
 redistribute connected subnets
!
ip forward-protocol nd
!
ip http server
no ip http secure-server
!
control-plane
!

voice-port 1/0/0
!
voice-port 1/0/1
!
voice-port 1/1/0
!
voice-port 1/1/1
!
line con 0
line aux 0
line vty 0 4
 privilege level 15
 password cisco
 login
!
end

R4#
```

LAB 3

Branch and Remote Office Redundancy

Lab Objective:

The objective of this lab exercise is for you to learn and understand how to implement and verify branch and remote office redundancy solutions in Cisco IOS software.

Lab Topology:

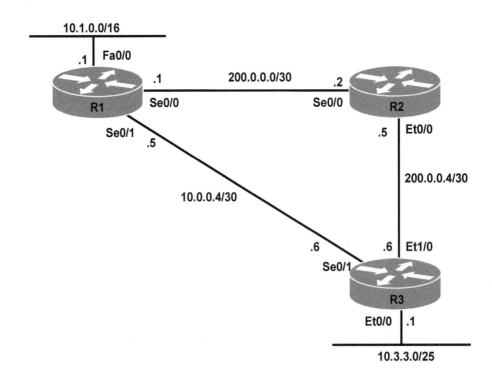

IMPORTANT NOTE:

If you are using the www.howtonetwork.net racks, please bring up the LAN interfaces connected to the routers by issuing the no shutdown command on the connected switches. If you are using a home lab with no switches, you can bring up the LAN interfaces using the following configurations on your routers:

```
interface fastethernet 0/0
 no keepalive
 loopback
 no shutdown
```

Alternately, you can simply connect the interfaces to a hub if you have one.

Task 1

Configure IP addressing on all routers as illustrated in the topology. Additionally, also configure the following the following Loopback interface on R2:

Router	Loopback	Loopback Interface Address/Mask
R2	0	192.0.2.254/32

Task 2

Configure a static default route on R1 pointing out of the Serial0/0 interface to R2. Verify that R1 can ping the 192.0.2.254 and 200.0.0.5 addresses following this configuration

Task 3

Configure BGP on R1 as R3 as follows:
- The routers should reside in AS 65001
- The routers should peer using their 10.0.0.4/30 interface addresses
- The routers should advertise their 10.x.x.x LAN subnets
- The routers should exchange Hello packets every 2 seconds
- The adjacency should be torn down after 6 seconds

Verify that both routers can ping the LAN subnet of the other

Task 4

Configure R3 to provide dynamic addressing information to LAN hosts as follows:
- Use a default gateway of 10.3.3.1
- Reserve addresses 10.3.3.1 – 10.3.3.5 for network and other devices, e.g. servers
- Use a domain name of howtonetwork.net
- DNS servers 10.1.0.253 and 10.1.0.254
- WINS server 10.1.0.254
- The client DHCP lease should expire after 8 days

Task 5

Assume that R2 belongs to an ISP. This link, however, will also be used as a backup link for access to the corporate LAN - 10.1.0.0/16 on R1, when the primary BGP connection is down. Based on these assumptions, configure R3 as follows:
- All Internet-bound traffic from the 10.3.3.0/128 subnet should be sent directly to R2
- All hosts on the 10.3.3.0/128 subnet to access the Internet
- Configure the backup Internet link to use OSPF to advertise the R1 and R3 LAN subnets
- Do NOT configure any static routes on R2 and do NOT configure OSPF on R2

Task 6

Ensure that BGP is used as the primary path; OSPF should be used only for backup

Task 7

With the primary and backup links up, verify your configuration as follows:
- Perform a LAN-to-LAN ping from R3 to 10.0.1.1 to verify connectivity to the hub site
- Perform a LAN-to-Internet ping from R3 to 192.0.2.254 to verify Internet connectivity

Task 8

With the primary link down, verify your backup link configuration as follows:
- Shut down the Serial0/1 link on R3. This will disable the primary link
- Perform a LAN-to-LAN ping from R3 to 10.0.1.1 to verify connectivity to the hub site
- Perform a LAN-to-Internet ping from R3 to 192.0.2.254 to verify Internet connectivity

LAB VALIDATION

Task 1

```
R1#show ip interface brief
Interface          IP-Address     OK? Method Status          Protocol
FastEthernet0/0    10.1.0.1       YES manual up              up
Serial0/0          200.0.0.1      YES manual up              up
Serial0/1          10.0.0.5       YES NVRAM  up              up


R2#show ip interface brief
Interface          IP-Address     OK? Method Status          Protocol
Ethernet0/0        200.0.0.5      YES manual up              up
Serial0/0          200.0.0.2      YES manual up              up
Loopback0          192.0.2.254    YES manual up              up


R3#show ip interface brief
Interface          IP-Address     OK? Method Status          Protocol
Ethernet0/0        10.3.3.1       YES manual up              up
Serial0/1          10.0.0.6       YES NVRAM  up              up
Ethernet1/0        200.0.0.6      YES manual up              up
```

Task 2

```
R1(config)#ip route 0.0.0.0 0.0.0.0 serial 0/0
```

```
R1#ping 192.0.2.254

Type escape sequence to abort.
Sending 5, 100-byte ICMP Echos to 192.0.2.254, timeout is 2 seconds:
!!!!!
Success rate is 100 percent (5/5), round-trip min/avg/max = 1/2/4 ms

R1#ping 200.0.0.5

Type escape sequence to abort.
Sending 5, 100-byte ICMP Echos to 200.0.0.5, timeout is 2 seconds:
!!!!!
Success rate is 100 percent (5/5), round-trip min/avg/max = 1/2/4 ms
```

Task 3

```
R1(config)#router bgp 65001
R1(config-router)#bgp router-id 1.1.1.1
R1(config-router)#network 10.1.0.0 mask 255.255.0.0
R1(config-router)#neighbor 10.0.0.6 remote-as 65001
R3(config-router)#neighbor 10.0.0.5 timers 2 6
R1(config-router)#end


R3(config)#router bgp 65001
R3(config-router)#bgp router-id 3.3.3.3
R3(config-router)#neighbor 10.0.0.5 remote-as 65001
R3(config-router)#network 10.3.3.0 mask 255.255.255.128
R1(config-router)#neighbor 10.0.0.6 timers 2 6
R3(config-router)#end
```

Following your configuration, use the show ip bgp summary and show ip bgp commands to verify your implementation. Following is the output of these commands on R3:

```
R3#show ip bgp summary
BGP router identifier 3.3.3.3, local AS number 65001
BGP table version is 4, main routing table version 4
2 network entries using 234 bytes of memory
2 path entries using 104 bytes of memory
3/2 BGP path/bestpath attribute entries using 372 bytes of memory
0 BGP route-map cache entries using 0 bytes of memory
0 BGP filter-list cache entries using 0 bytes of memory
BGP using 710 total bytes of memory
BGP activity 2/0 prefixes, 2/0 paths, scan interval 60 secs

Neighbor     V    AS MsgRcvd MsgSent   TblVer  InQ OutQ Up/Down  State/PfxRcd
10.0.0.5     4 65001       4       4        4    0    0 00:00:51            1
```

```
R3#show ip bgp
BGP table version is 4, local router ID is 3.3.3.3
Status codes: s suppressed, d damped, h history, * valid, > best, i - internal,
              r RIB-failure, S Stale
Origin codes: i - IGP, e - EGP, ? - incomplete

   Network          Next Hop            Metric LocPrf Weight Path
*>i10.1.0.0/16      10.0.0.5                 0    100      0 i
*> 10.3.3.0/25      0.0.0.0                  0           32768 i
```

To verify the configured BGP Hello and Hold timer values, you must use the show ip bgp neighbors command as follows:

```
R3#show ip bgp neighbors 10.0.0.5
BGP neighbor is 10.0.0.5,  remote AS 65001, internal link
  BGP version 4, remote router ID 1.1.1.1
  BGP state = Established, up for 00:01:30
  Last read 00:00:00, last write 00:00:00, hold time is 6, keepalive interval is
2 seconds
  Configured hold time is 6,keepalive interval is 2 seconds  Minimum holdtime
from neighbor is 0 seconds
  Neighbor capabilities:
    Route refresh: advertised and received(old & new)
    Address family IPv4 Unicast: advertised and received

[Truncated Output]
```

The final verification for this task is to perform a LAN-to-LAN ping between R1 and R3:

```
R1#ping 10.3.3.1 source 10.1.0.1

Type escape sequence to abort.
Sending 5, 100-byte ICMP Echos to 10.3.3.1, timeout is 2 seconds:
Packet sent with a source address of 10.1.0.1
!!!!!
Success rate is 100 percent (5/5), round-trip min/avg/max = 4/4/4 ms

R3#ping 10.1.0.1 source 10.3.3.1

Type escape sequence to abort.
Sending 5, 100-byte ICMP Echos to 10.1.0.1, timeout is 2 seconds:
Packet sent with a source address of 10.3.3.1
!!!!!
Success rate is 100 percent (5/5), round-trip min/avg/max = 1/3/4 ms
```

Task 4

This task calls for the configuration of Cisco IOS DHCP server and is completed as follows:

```
R3(config)#ip dhcp excluded-address 10.3.3.1 10.3.3.5
R3(config)#ip dhcp pool LAN-POOL
R3(dhcp-config)#network 10.3.3.0 /25
R3(dhcp-config)#default-router 10.3.3.1
R3(dhcp-config)#dns-server 10.1.0.253 10.1.0.254
R3(dhcp-config)#netbios-name-server 10.1.0.254
R3(dhcp-config)#domain-name howtonetwork.net
R3(dhcp-config)#lease 8
R3(dhcp-config)#end
```

Following this configuration, use the `show ip dhcp pool` command to verify the Cisco IOS DHCP server configuration settings. If you have actual hosts on the LAN, you can use the `show ip dhcp binding` command to see address allocations from the pool.

```
R3#show ip dhcp pool LAN-POOL

Pool LAN-POOL :
 Utilization mark (high/low)    : 100 / 0
 Subnet size (first/next)       : 0 / 0
 Total addresses                : 126
 Leased addresses               : 0
 Pending event                  : none
 1 subnet is currently in the pool :
 Current index       IP address range                     Leased addresses
 10.3.3.1            10.3.3.1          - 10.3.3.126        0
```

Alternatively, you can validate your configuration by looking at the router configuration:

```
R3#show running-config | section dhcp
ip dhcp excluded-address 10.3.3.1 10.3.3.5
ip dhcp pool LAN-POOL
   network 10.3.3.0 255.255.255.128
   default-router 10.3.3.1
   domain-name howtonetwork.net
   netbios-name-server 10.1.0.254
   dns-server 10.1.0.253 10.1.0.254
   lease 8
```

Task 5

This task requires a little thought but overall is a simple task. First, a default route pointing to R2 can be used to forward all Internet-bound traffic to this router. Because Ethernet is being used, specify a next hop IP address (and optionally interface). Specifying only an interface can result in intermittent connectivity. Additionally, since the 10.3.3.0/128 subnet is an RFC 1918 subnet, Network Address Translation (NAT) is required to allow the hosts on this subnet Internet access. This step is completed as follows:

```
R3(config)#ip route 0.0.0.0 0.0.0.0 ethernet 1/0 200.0.0.5
R3(config)#ip access-list extended NAT-ACL
R3(config-ext-nacl)#deny ip 10.3.3.0 0.0.0.127 10.1.0.0 0.0.255.255
R3(config-ext-nacl)#permit ip 10.3.3.0 0.0.0.127 any
R3(config-ext-nacl)#exit
R3(config)#interface ethernet 1/0
R3(config-if)#ip nat outside
R3(config-if)#exit
R3(config)#interface ethernet 0/0
R3(config-if)#ip nat inside
R3(config-if)#exit
R3(config)#ip nat inside source list NAT-ACL interface ethernet 1/0 overload
R3(config)#exit
```

Next, the backup link across the Internet should be enabled for OSPF; however, OSPF cannot be enabled on R2. Additionally, we are not allowed to configure any additional static routes. This requires a GRE tunnel between R1 and R3 (using R2 as transit) as follows:

```
R1(config)#router ospf 1
R1(config-router)#router-id 1.1.1.1
R1(config-router)#exit
R1(config)#interface fastethernet 0/0
R1(config-if)#ip ospf 1 area 0
R1(config-if)#exit
R1(config)#interface tunnel 0
R1(config-if)#ip address 192.168.1.1 255.255.255.252
R1(config-if)#tunnel source serial 0/0
R1(config-if)#tunnel destination 200.0.0.6
R1(config-if)#ip ospf 1 area 0
R1(config-if)#end
```

```
R3(config)#router ospf 3
R3(config-router)#router-id 3.3.3.3
R3(config-router)#exit
R3(config)#interface ethernet 0/0
R3(config-if)#ip ospf 3 area 0
R3(config-if)#exit
R3(config)#interface tunnel 0
R3(config-if)#ip address 192.168.1.2 255.255.255.252
R3(config-if)#tunnel source ethernet 1/0
R3(config-if)#tunnel destination 200.0.0.1
R3(config-if)#ip ospf 3 area 0
R3(config-if)#exit
```

Following this configuration, use the show interfaces command to verify the status of the tunnel then verify the OSPF adjacency using the show ip ospf neighbor command:

```
R3#show interfaces tunnel 0
Tunnel0 is up, line protocol is up
  Hardware is Tunnel
  Internet address is 192.168.1.2/30
  MTU 1514 bytes, BW 9 Kbit/sec, DLY 500000 usec,
     reliability 255/255, txload 1/255, rxload 1/255
  Encapsulation TUNNEL, loopback not set
  Keepalive not set
  Tunnel source 200.0.0.6 (Ethernet1/0), destination 200.0.0.1
  Tunnel protocol/transport GRE/IP
   Key disabled, sequencing disabled
   Checksumming of packets disabled

[Truncated Output]


R1#show interfaces tunnel 0
Tunnel0 is up, line protocol is up
  Hardware is Tunnel
  Internet address is 192.168.1.1/30
  MTU 1514 bytes, BW 9 Kbit/sec, DLY 500000 usec,
     reliability 255/255, txload 1/255, rxload 1/255
  Encapsulation TUNNEL, loopback not set
  Keepalive not set
  Tunnel source 200.0.0.1 (Serial0/0), destination 200.0.0.6
  Tunnel protocol/transport GRE/IP
   Key disabled, sequencing disabled
   Checksumming of packets disabled

[Truncated Output]
```

Continue and verify the OSPF adjacencies as follows:

```
R1#show ip ospf neighbor

Neighbor ID     Pri   State        Dead Time   Address        Interface
3.3.3.3           0   FULL/  -     00:00:35    192.168.1.2    Tunnel0


R3#show ip ospf neighbor

Neighbor ID     Pri   State        Dead Time   Address        Interface
1.1.1.1           0   FULL/  -     00:00:31    192.168.1.1    Tunnel0
```

Task 6

By default, following the configuration on R1 and R3, the OSPF routes will be preferred over the iBGP routes because of the lower administrative distance of OSPF as shown below:

```
R3#show ip route
Codes: C - connected, S - static, R - RIP, M - mobile, B - BGP
       D - EIGRP, EX - EIGRP external, O - OSPF, IA - OSPF inter area
       N1 - OSPF NSSA external type 1, N2 - OSPF NSSA external type 2
       E1 - OSPF external type 1, E2 - OSPF external type 2
       i - IS-IS, su - IS-IS summary, L1 - IS-IS level-1, L2 - IS-IS level-2
       ia - IS-IS inter area, * - candidate default, U - per-user static route
       o - ODR, P - periodic downloaded static route

Gateway of last resort is 200.0.0.5 to network 0.0.0.0

     200.0.0.0/30 is subnetted, 1 subnets
C       200.0.0.4 is directly connected, Ethernet1/0
     10.0.0.0/8 is variably subnetted, 3 subnets, 3 masks
C       10.3.3.0/25 is directly connected, Ethernet0/0
O       10.1.0.0/16 [110/11112] via 192.168.1.1, 00:21:51, Tunnel0
C       10.0.0.4/30 is directly connected, Serial0/1
     192.168.1.0/30 is subnetted, 1 subnets
C       192.168.1.0 is directly connected, Tunnel0
S*   0.0.0.0/0 [1/0] via 200.0.0.5, Ethernet1/0


R1#show ip route
Codes: C - connected, S - static, R - RIP, M - mobile, B - BGP
       D - EIGRP, EX - EIGRP external, O - OSPF, IA - OSPF inter area
       N1 - OSPF NSSA external type 1, N2 - OSPF NSSA external type 2
       E1 - OSPF external type 1, E2 - OSPF external type 2
       i - IS-IS, su - IS-IS summary, L1 - IS-IS level-1, L2 - IS-IS level-2
       ia - IS-IS inter area, * - candidate default, U - per-user static route
       o - ODR, P - periodic downloaded static route

Gateway of last resort is 0.0.0.0 to network 0.0.0.0

     1.0.0.0/32 is subnetted, 1 subnets
C       1.1.1.1 is directly connected, Loopback0
     200.0.0.0/30 is subnetted, 1 subnets
C       200.0.0.0 is directly connected, Serial0/0
     10.0.0.0/8 is variably subnetted, 3 subnets, 3 masks
O       10.3.3.0/25 [110/11112] via 192.168.1.2, 00:22:10, Tunnel0
C       10.1.0.0/16 is directly connected, FastEthernet0/0
C       10.0.0.4/30 is directly connected, Serial0/1
     192.168.1.0/30 is subnetted, 1 subnets
C       192.168.1.0 is directly connected, Tunnel0
S*   0.0.0.0/0 is directly connected, Serial0/0
```

In order to complete this task and ensure that the private link between R1 and R3 which is also running BGP is used as the preferred path, we need to adjust the default administrative distance of the better protocol (OSPF) allowing the iBGP routes, with a default administrative distance of 200, to be more preferred. This task is completed as follows:

```
R1(config)#router ospf 1
R1(config-router)#distance ospf intra-area 201 inter-area 201 external 201
R1(config-router)#end

R3(config)#router ospf 3
R3(config-router)#distance ospf intra-area 201 inter-area 201 external 201
R3(config-router)#end
```

The configuration can be validated using the show ip protocols command as follows:

```
R3#show ip protocols | section ospf
Routing Protocol is "ospf 3"
  Outgoing update filter list for all interfaces is not set
  Incoming update filter list for all interfaces is not set
  Router ID 3.3.3.3
  Number of areas in this router is 2. 2 normal 0 stub 0 nssa
  Maximum path: 4
  Routing for Networks:
  Routing on Interfaces Configured Explicitly (Area 0):
    Tunnel0
    Ethernet0/0
 Reference bandwidth unit is 100 mbps
  Routing Information Sources:
    Gateway         Distance      Last Update
    1.1.1.1              110      00:01:04
  Distance: (default is 201)
```

Following these configuration changes, the routing tables on R1 and R3 show the following:

```
R3#show ip route
Codes: C - connected, S - static, R - RIP, M - mobile, B - BGP
       D - EIGRP, EX - EIGRP external, O - OSPF, IA - OSPF inter area
       N1 - OSPF NSSA external type 1, N2 - OSPF NSSA external type 2
       E1 - OSPF external type 1, E2 - OSPF external type 2
       i - IS-IS, su - IS-IS summary, L1 - IS-IS level-1, L2 - IS-IS level-2
       ia - IS-IS inter area, * - candidate default, U - per-user static route
       o - ODR, P - periodic downloaded static route

Gateway of last resort is 200.0.0.5 to network 0.0.0.0

     200.0.0.0/30 is subnetted, 1 subnets
C       200.0.0.4 is directly connected, Ethernet1/0
     10.0.0.0/8 is variably subnetted, 3 subnets, 3 masks
```

```
C       10.3.3.0/25 is directly connected, Ethernet0/0
B       10.1.0.0/16 [200/0] via 10.0.0.5, 00:01:30
C       10.0.0.4/30 is directly connected, Serial0/1
     192.168.1.0/30 is subnetted, 1 subnets
C        192.168.1.0 is directly connected, Tunnel0
S*   0.0.0.0/0 [1/0] via 200.0.0.5, Ethernet1/0


R1#show ip route
Codes: C - connected, S - static, R - RIP, M - mobile, B - BGP
       D - EIGRP, EX - EIGRP external, O - OSPF, IA - OSPF inter area
       N1 - OSPF NSSA external type 1, N2 - OSPF NSSA external type 2
       E1 - OSPF external type 1, E2 - OSPF external type 2
       i - IS-IS, su - IS-IS summary, L1 - IS-IS level-1, L2 - IS-IS level-2
       ia - IS-IS inter area, * - candidate default, U - per-user static route
       o - ODR, P - periodic downloaded static route

Gateway of last resort is 0.0.0.0 to network 0.0.0.0

     1.0.0.0/32 is subnetted, 1 subnets
C        1.1.1.1 is directly connected, Loopback0
     200.0.0.0/30 is subnetted, 1 subnets
C        200.0.0.0 is directly connected, Serial0/0
     10.0.0.0/8 is variably subnetted, 3 subnets, 3 masks
B       10.3.3.0/25 [200/0] via 10.0.0.6, 00:02:45
C        10.1.0.0/16 is directly connected, FastEthernet0/0
C        10.0.0.4/30 is directly connected, Serial0/1
     192.168.1.0/30 is subnetted, 1 subnets
C        192.168.1.0 is directly connected, Tunnel0
S*   0.0.0.0/0 is directly connected, Serial0/0
```

Task 7

Perform the LAN-to-LAN ping between R3 and R1 as follows:

```
R3#ping 10.1.0.1 source 10.3.3.1 repeat 100

Type escape sequence to abort.
Sending 100, 100-byte ICMP Echos to 10.1.0.1, timeout is 2 seconds:
Packet sent with a source address of 10.3.3.1
!!!!!!!!!!!!!!!!!!!!!!!!!!!!!!!!!!!!!!!!!!!!!!!!!!!!!!!!!!!!!!!!!!!!!!!!!!
!!!!!!!!!!!!!!!!!!!!!!!!!!!!!!!!
Success rate is 100 percent (100/100), round-trip min/avg/max = 1/3/4 ms
```

Next, verify Internet access as follows:

```
R3#ping 192.0.2.254 source 10.3.3.1 repeat 100

Type escape sequence to abort.
Sending 100, 100-byte ICMP Echos to 192.0.2.254, timeout is 2 seconds:
```

```
Packet sent with a source address of 10.3.3.1
!!!!!!!!!!!!!!!!!!!!!!!!!!!!!!!!!!!!!!!!!!!!!!!!!!!!!!!!!!!!!!!!!!!!!!!!
!!!!!!!!!!!!!!!!!!!!!!!!!!!!!!!
Success rate is 100 percent (100/100), round-trip min/avg/max = 1/3/4 ms
```

Following this ping, you can use the show ip nat translations command to verify NAT:

```
R3#show ip nat translations
Pro Inside global      Inside local      Outside local      Outside global
icmp 200.0.0.6:16      10.3.3.1:16       192.0.2.254:16     192.0.2.254:16
```

Task 8

Disable the Serial0/1 interface as follows:

```
R3(config)#interface serial 0/1
R3(config-if)#shutdown
R3(config-if)#end
R3#
*Mar  1 14:50:11.991: %SYS-5-CONFIG_I: Configured from console by console
*Mar  1 14:50:12.959: %LINK-5-CHANGED: Interface Serial0/1, changed state to
administratively down
*Mar  1 14:50:13.959: %LINEPROTO-5-UPDOWN: Line protocol on Interface Serial0/1,
changed state to down
*Mar  1 14:50:15.963: %BGP-5-ADJCHANGE: neighbor 10.0.0.5 Down BGP Notification
sent
*Mar  1 14:50:15.963: %BGP-3-NOTIFICATION: sent to neighbor 10.0.0.5 4/0 (hold
time expired) 0 bytes
```

Next, verify the routing table using the show ip route command as follows:

```
R3#show ip route
Codes: C - connected, S - static, R - RIP, M - mobile, B - BGP
       D - EIGRP, EX - EIGRP external, O - OSPF, IA - OSPF inter area
       N1 - OSPF NSSA external type 1, N2 - OSPF NSSA external type 2
       E1 - OSPF external type 1, E2 - OSPF external type 2
       i - IS-IS, su - IS-IS summary, L1 - IS-IS level-1, L2 - IS-IS level-2
       ia - IS-IS inter area, * - candidate default, U - per-user static route
       o - ODR, P - periodic downloaded static route

Gateway of last resort is 200.0.0.5 to network 0.0.0.0

     200.0.0.0/30 is subnetted, 1 subnets
C       200.0.0.4 is directly connected, Ethernet1/0
     10.0.0.0/8 is variably subnetted, 2 subnets, 2 masks
C       10.3.3.0/25 is directly connected, Ethernet0/0
O       10.1.0.0/16 [201/11112] via 192.168.1.1, 00:01:11, Tunnel0
     192.168.1.0/30 is subnetted, 1 subnets
```

```
C       192.168.1.0 is directly connected, Tunnel0
S*   0.0.0.0/0 [1/0] via 200.0.0.5, Ethernet1/0
```

Continuing with task validation, perform a LAN-to-LAN ping from R3 to R1 as follows:

```
R3#ping 10.1.0.1 source 10.3.3.1 repeat 100

Type escape sequence to abort.
Sending 100, 100-byte ICMP Echos to 10.1.0.1, timeout is 2 seconds:
Packet sent with a source address of 10.3.3.1
!!!!!!!!!!!!!!!!!!!!!!!!!!!!!!!!!!!!!!!!!!!!!!!!!!!!!!!!!!!!!!!!!!!!!!!!!
!!!!!!!!!!!!!!!!!!!!!!!!!!!!!!!!
Success rate is 100 percent (100/100), round-trip min/avg/max = 4/4/8 ms
```

And finally, verify Internet access by pinging 192.0.2.254 from R3s LAN subnet as follows:

```
R3#ping 192.0.2.254 source 10.3.3.1 repeat 100

Type escape sequence to abort.
Sending 100, 100-byte ICMP Echos to 192.0.2.254, timeout is 2 seconds:
Packet sent with a source address of 10.3.3.1
!!!!!!!!!!!!!!!!!!!!!!!!!!!!!!!!!!!!!!!!!!!!!!!!!!!!!!!!!!!!!!!!!!!!!!!!!
!!!!!!!!!!!!!!!!!!!!!!!!!!!!!!!!
Success rate is 100 percent (100/100), round-trip min/avg/max = 1/3/4 ms
```

Again, the show ip nat translations command can be used to verify NAT configuration:

```
R3#show ip nat translations
Pro Inside global     Inside local      Outside local      Outside global
icmp 200.0.0.6:22     10.3.3.1:22       192.0.2.254:22     192.0.2.254:22
```

DEVICE CONFIGURATIONS

```
R1#show running-config
Building configuration...

Current configuration : 1539 bytes
!
version 12.4
service timestamps debug datetime msec
service timestamps log datetime msec
no service password-encryption
!
hostname R1
!
```

```
boot-start-marker
boot-end-marker
!
no logging console
enable secret 5 $1$ZHZP$BfOgaK4Ei7zfUol9D8zpV/
!
no aaa new-model
no network-clock-participate slot 1
no network-clock-participate wic 0
ip cef
!
no ip domain lookup
ip auth-proxy max-nodata-conns 3
ip admission max-nodata-conns 3
!
ipv6 unicast-routing
!
interface Loopback0
 ip address 1.1.1.1 255.255.255.255
!
interface Tunnel0
 ip address 192.168.1.1 255.255.255.252
 ip ospf 1 area 0
 tunnel source Serial0/0
 tunnel destination 200.0.0.6
!
interface FastEthernet0/0
 ip address 10.1.0.1 255.255.0.0
 ip ospf 1 area 0
 loopback
 duplex auto
 speed auto
 no keepalive
!
interface Serial0/0
 ip address 200.0.0.1 255.255.255.252
 no fair-queue
!
interface Serial0/1
 ip address 10.0.0.5 255.255.255.252
!
router ospf 1
 router-id 1.1.1.1
 log-adjacency-changes
 distance 201
!
router bgp 65001
 no synchronization
 bgp router-id 1.1.1.1
 bgp log-neighbor-changes
 network 10.1.0.0 mask 255.255.0.0
 neighbor 10.0.0.6 remote-as 65001
```

```
 neighbor 10.0.0.6 timers 2 6
 no auto-summary
!
ip forward-protocol nd
ip route 0.0.0.0 0.0.0.0 Serial0/0
!
ip http server
no ip http secure-server
!
control-plane
!
ce-port 1/0/0
!
voice-port 1/0/1
!
voice-port 1/1/0
!
voice-port 1/1/1
!
line con 0
line aux 0
line vty 0 4
 privilege level 15
 password cisco
 login
!
end

R1#


R2#show running-config
Building configuration...

Current configuration : 960 bytes
!
version 12.4
service timestamps debug datetime msec
service timestamps log datetime msec
no service password-encryption
!
hostname R2
!
boot-start-marker
boot-end-marker
!
no logging console
enable secret 5 $1$FsT/$/viPNrSsewWFUCy/QbD5lO
!
no aaa new-model
!
ip cef
```

```
no ip domain lookup
!
ipv6 unicast-routing
!
interface Loopback0
 ip address 192.0.2.254 255.255.255.255
!
interface Ethernet0/0
 bandwidth 100000
 ip address 200.0.0.5 255.255.255.252
 full-duplex
!
interface Serial0/0
 ip address 200.0.0.2 255.255.255.252
 clock rate 2000000
 no fair-queue
!
interface Ethernet0/1
 no ip address
 shutdown
 half-duplex
!
interface Serial0/1
 no ip address
 shutdown
 clock rate 2000000
!
ip http server
ip forward-protocol nd
!
control-plane
!
mgcp behavior g729-variants static-pt
!
gatekeeper
 shutdown
!
line con 0
line aux 0
line vty 0 4
 privilege level 15
 password cisco
 login
!
end

R2#
```

```
R3#show running-config
Building configuration...

Current configuration : 2147 bytes
!
version 12.4
service timestamps debug datetime msec
service timestamps log datetime msec
no service password-encryption
!
hostname R3
!
boot-start-marker
boot-end-marker
!
no logging console
enable secret 5 $1$mOsw$hNy9.KzOvGX2XmLabNBOT/
!
no aaa new-model
!
ip cef
no ip domain lookup
no ip dhcp use vrf connected
ip dhcp excluded-address 10.3.3.1 10.3.3.5
!
ip dhcp pool LAN-POOL
   network 10.3.3.0 255.255.255.128
   default-router 10.3.3.1
   domain-name howtonetwork.net
   netbios-name-server 10.1.0.254
   dns-server 10.1.0.253 10.1.0.254
   lease 8
!
ipv6 unicast-routing
!
interface Tunnel0
 ip address 192.168.1.2 255.255.255.252
 ip ospf 3 area 0
 tunnel source Ethernet1/0
 tunnel destination 200.0.0.1
!
interface Ethernet0/0
 bandwidth 100000
 ip address 10.3.3.1 255.255.255.128
 ip nat inside
 ip virtual-reassembly
 ip ospf 3 area 0
 loopback
 half-duplex
 no keepalive
!
interface Serial0/0
```

```
 no ip address
 shutdown
 no fair-queue
!
interface Ethernet0/1
 no ip address
 shutdown
 half-duplex
!
interface Serial0/1
 ip address 10.0.0.6 255.255.255.252
 clock rate 2000000
!
interface Ethernet1/0
 ip address 200.0.0.6 255.255.255.252
 ip nat outside
 ip virtual-reassembly
 full-duplex
!
interface Serial1/0
 no ip address
 shutdown
!
interface Serial1/1
 no ip address
 shutdown
!
router ospf 3
 router-id 3.3.3.3
 log-adjacency-changes
 distance 201
!
router bgp 65001
 no synchronization
 bgp router-id 3.3.3.3
 bgp log-neighbor-changes
 network 10.3.3.0 mask 255.255.255.128
 neighbor 10.0.0.5 remote-as 65001
 neighbor 10.0.0.5 timers 2 6
 no auto-summary
!
ip http server
ip forward-protocol nd
ip route 0.0.0.0 0.0.0.0 Ethernet1/0 200.0.0.5
!
ip nat inside source list NAT-ACL interface Ethernet1/0 overload
!
ip access-list extended NAT-ACL
 deny   ip 10.3.3.0 0.0.0.127 10.1.0.0 0.0.255.255
 permit ip 10.3.3.0 0.0.0.127 any
!
control-plane
```

```
!
mgcp behavior g729-variants static-pt
!
gatekeeper
 shutdown
!
line con 0
line aux 0
line vty 0 4
 privilege level 15
 password cisco
 login
!
end

R3#
```

LAB 4

EIGRP Multi-Technology Lab

Lab Objective:

The objective of this lab exercise is for you to learn and understand how to implement advanced EIGRP routing configurations in Cisco IOS software.

Lab Topology:

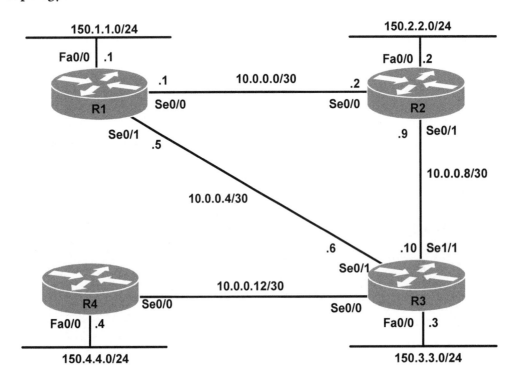

IMPORTANT NOTE:

If you are using the www.howtonetwork.net racks, please bring up the LAN interfaces connected to the routers by issuing the no shutdown command on the connected switches. If you are using a home lab with no switches, you can bring up the LAN interfaces using the following configurations on your routers:

```
interface fastethernet 0/0
 no keepalive
 loopback
 no shutdown
```

Alternately, you can simply connect the interfaces to a hub if you have one.

Task 1

Configure IP addressing on all routers as illustrated in the topology. Additionally, configure the following Loopback interfaces on all routers:

Router	Loopback	Loopback Interface Address/Mask
R1	0	1.1.1.1/32
R1	1	172.1.1.1/32
R1	2	172.2.2.2/32
R1	3	172.3.3.3/32
R1	4	172.4.4.4/32
R2	0	2.2.2.2/32
R3	0	3.3.3.3/32
R4	0	4.4.4.4/32

Task 2

Configure EIGRP 1 on R1 as follows:
- Enable EIGRP for the 10.x.x.x subnets belonging to the Serial interfaces
- Enable EIGRP for the 150.x.x.x subnet on FastEthernet0/0
- Enable EIGRP for the Loopback 0 subnet
- Inject the 172.x.x.x into EIGRP without using any `network` statements
- EIGRP should not automatically summarize at Classful boundaries

Task 3

Configure EIGRP 1 on R2 as follows:
- Enable EIGRP for the 10.x.x.x subnets belonging to the Serial interfaces
- Enable EIGRP for the 150.x.x.x subnet on FastEthernet0/0
- Enable EIGRP for the Loopback 0 subnet
- EIGRP should not automatically summarize at Classful boundaries

Task 4

Configure EIGRP 1 on R3 as follows:
- Enable EIGRP for the 10.x.x.x subnets belonging to the Serial interfaces
- Enable EIGRP for the 150.x.x.x subnet on FastEthernet0/0
- Enable EIGRP for the Loopback 0 subnet
- EIGRP should not automatically summarize at Classful boundaries

Task 5

Configure EIGRP 1 on R4 as follows:

- Enable EIGRP for the 10.x.x.x subnets belonging to the Serial interfaces
- Enable EIGRP for the 150.x.x.x subnet on FastEthernet0/0
- EIGRP should not summarize at Classful boundaries
- Configure this router such that it will never be queried by R3

Task 6

Configure EIGRP filtering on R3 as follows:

- The router should only accept the 172.1.1.1/32 and 172.3.3.3/32 prefixes via Se0/1
- The router should only accept the 172.2.2.2/32 and 172.4.4.4/32 prefixes via Se1/1
- The router should accept the 150.x.x.x subnets
- No other prefixes or subnets should be accepted by the router via these interfaces
- USE ONLY THREE LINES IN YOUR PREFIX LIST CONFIGRUATION

Task 7

Configure EIGRP filtering on R3 as follows:

- The router should only advertise a single default route to R4
- Verify that R4 is only receiving a default route from R3
- R4 should be able to ping all the 172.x.x.x prefixes
- R4 should be able to ping all the other 150.x.x.x prefixes

Task 8

Configure load balancing on router R3 as follows:

- R3 should load balance traffic to the 150.1.1.0/24 and 150.2.2.0/24 prefixes
- The route metric for both paths should be the same

Task 9

Authenticate EIGRP between R3 and R4 as follows:

- Use a password/secret of ROUTE for authentication
- Use any key chain name
- Use a key with an ID/number of your choosing

Task 10

Configure EIGRP on R1 to filter all the Loopback 0 subnets. Do **NOT** use distribute-lists.

LAB VALIDATION

Task 1

```
R1#show ip interface brief
Interface          IP-Address      OK? Method Status              Protocol
FastEthernet0/0    150.1.1.1       YES NVRAM  up                  up
Serial0/0          10.0.0.1        YES NVRAM  up                  up
Serial0/1          10.0.0.5        YES NVRAM  up                  up
Loopback0          1.1.1.1         YES NVRAM  up                  up
Loopback1          172.1.1.1       YES manual up                  up
Loopback2          172.2.2.2       YES manual up                  up
Loopback3          172.3.3.3       YES manual up                  up
Loopback4          172.4.4.4       YES manual up                  up

R2#show ip interface brief
Interface          IP-Address      OK? Method Status              Protocol
FastEthernet0/0    150.2.2.2       YES NVRAM  up                  up
Serial0/0          10.0.0.2        YES NVRAM  up                  up
Serial0/1          10.0.0.9        YES NVRAM  up                  up
Loopback0          2.2.2.2         YES NVRAM  up                  up

R3#show ip interface brief
Interface          IP-Address      OK? Method Status              Protocol
FastEthernet0/0    150.3.3.3       YES NVRAM  up                  up
Serial0/0          10.0.0.13       YES NVRAM  up                  up
Serial0/1          10.0.0.6        YES NVRAM  up                  up
Serial1/1          10.0.0.10       YES NVRAM  up                  up
Loopback0          3.3.3.3         YES NVRAM  up                  up

R4#show ip interface brief
Interface          IP-Address      OK? Method Status              Protocol
FastEthernet0/0    150.4.4.4       YES NVRAM  up                  up
Serial0/0          10.0.0.14       YES NVRAM  up                  up
Loopback0          4.4.4.4         YES NVRAM  up                  up
```

Task 2

```
R1(config)#router eigrp 1
R1(config-router)#network 10.0.0.0
R1(config-router)#network 1.0.0.0
R1(config-router)#network 150.1.0.0
R1(config-router)#redistribute connected
R1(config-router)#no auto-summary
R1(config-router)#exit
```

Verify your configuration using the `show ip eigrp topology` command or using the `show ip eigrp interfaces` command:

```
R1#show ip eigrp interfaces
IP-EIGRP interfaces for process 1
                         Xmit Queue   Mean   Pacing Time   Multicast    Pending
Interface      Peers   Un/Reliable   SRTT   Un/Reliable   Flow Timer   Routes
Se0/0            0         0/0         0        0/15           50          0
Se0/1            0         0/0         0        0/15           50          0
Lo0              0         0/0         0        0/1             0          0
Fa0/0            0         0/0         0        0/1             0          0
```

To view the redistributed 172.x.x.x subnets, you must use the `show ip eigrp topology` command as these are not included in the `show ip eigrp interfaces` output.

```
R1#show ip eigrp topology
IP-EIGRP Topology Table for AS(1)/ID(172.4.4.4)
Codes: P - Passive, A - Active, U - Update, Q - Query, R - Reply,
       r - reply Status, s - sia Status

P 1.1.1.1/32, 1 successors, FD is 128256
        via Connected, Loopback0
P 150.1.1.0/24, 1 successors, FD is 28160
        via Connected, FastEthernet0/0
P 172.4.4.4/32, 1 successors, FD is 128256
        via Rconnected (128256/0)
P 172.1.1.1/32, 1 successors, FD is 128256
        via Rconnected (128256/0)
P 172.2.2.2/32, 1 successors, FD is 128256
        via Rconnected (128256/0)
P 172.3.3.3/32, 1 successors, FD is 128256
        via Rconnected (128256/0)
```

Task 3

```
R2(config)#router eigrp 1
R2(config-router)#network 10.0.0.0
R2(config-router)#network 2.0.0.0
R2(config-router)#network 150.2.0.0
R2(config-router)#no auto-summary
R2(config-router)#exit
```

Verify your configuration using the `show ip eigrp topology` command or using the `show ip eigrp interfaces` command:

```
R2#show ip eigrp interfaces
IP-EIGRP interfaces for process 1
```

```
                        Xmit Queue   Mean   Pacing Time   Multicast    Pending
Interface        Peers  Un/Reliable  SRTT   Un/Reliable   Flow Timer   Routes
Se0/0            1      0/0          4      0/15          50           0
Se0/1            0      0/0          0      0/1           0            0
Lo0              0      0/0          0      0/1           0            0
Fa0/0            0      0/0          0      0/1           0            0
```

Task 4

```
R3(config)#router eigrp 1
R3(config-router)#network 10.0.0.0
R3(config-router)#network 3.0.0.0
R3(config-router)#network 150.3.0.0
R3(config-router)#no auto-summary
R3(config-router)#exit
```

Verify your configuration using the show ip eigrp topology command or using the show ip eigrp interfaces command:

```
R3#show ip eigrp interfaces
IP-EIGRP interfaces for process 1
                        Xmit Queue   Mean   Pacing Time   Multicast    Pending
Interface        Peers  Un/Reliable  SRTT   Un/Reliable   Flow Timer   Routes
Se0/0            0      0/0          0      0/1           0            0
Se0/1            1      0/0          5      0/15          50           0
Se1/1            1      0/0          10     0/15          55           0
Lo0              0      0/0          0      0/1           0            0
Fa0/0            0      0/0          0      0/1           0            0
```

Task 5

```
R4(config)#router eigrp 1
R4(config-router)#network 10.0.0.0
R4(config-router)#network 4.0.0.0
R4(config-router)#network 150.4.0.0
R4(config-router)#eigrp stub
R4(config-router)#no auto-summary
R4(config-router)#exit
```

Verify your configuration using the show ip eigrp topology command or using the show ip eigrp interfaces command:

```
R4#show ip eigrp interfaces
IP-EIGRP interfaces for process 1
                        Xmit Queue   Mean   Pacing Time   Multicast    Pending
Interface        Peers  Un/Reliable  SRTT   Un/Reliable   Flow Timer   Routes
```

```
Se0/0               1           0/0         2           0/15        50          0
Lo0                 0           0/0         0           0/1         0           0
Fa0/0               0           0/0         0           0/1         0           0
```

Use the `show ip protocols` command to verify the stub configuration on R4. By default, a stub router will advertise connected and summary routes:

```
R4#show ip protocols
Routing Protocol is "eigrp 1"
  Outgoing update filter list for all interfaces is not set
  Incoming update filter list for all interfaces is not set
  Default networks flagged in outgoing updates
  Default networks accepted from incoming updates
  EIGRP metric weight K1=1, K2=0, K3=1, K4=0, K5=0
  EIGRP maximum hopcount 100
  EIGRP maximum metric variance 1
  EIGRP stub, connected, summary
  Redistributing: eigrp 1
  EIGRP NSF-aware route hold timer is 240s
  Automatic network summarization is not in effect
  Maximum path: 4
  Routing for Networks:
    4.0.0.0
    10.0.0.0
    150.4.0.0
  Routing Information Sources:
    Gateway         Distance      Last Update
    (this router)         90      00:16:00
    10.0.0.13             90      00:01:28
  Distance: internal 90 external 170
```

On the stub neighbor router, R3, use the `show ip eigrp neighbors detail` command to validate the stub peer status for R4:

```
R3#show ip eigrp neighbors detail
IP-EIGRP neighbors for process 1
H   Address                 Interface         Hold Uptime   SRTT   RTO   Q  Seq
                                              (sec)         (ms)         Cnt Num
0   10.0.0.5                Se0/1             14 00:09:24    4     200   0  63
    Version 12.4/1.2, Retrans: 0, Retries: 0, Prefixes: 9
1   10.0.0.9                Se1/1             12 00:19:21    4     200   0  61
    Restart time 00:19:13
    Version 12.4/1.2, Retrans: 0, Retries: 0, Prefixes: 9
2   10.0.0.14               Se0/0             13 00:02:25    4     200   0  28
    Version 12.4/1.2, Retrans: 0, Retries: 0, Prefixes: 2
    Stub Peer Advertising ( CONNECTED SUMMARY ) Routes
    Suppressing queries
```

Task 6

Given the requirements, this configuration requires the use of two distribute lists for the EIGRP route filtering. This configuration is implemented on R3 as follows:

```
R3(config)#ip prefix-list FROM-R1 seq 1 permit 172.1.1.1/32
R3(config)#ip prefix-list FROM-R1 seq 2 permit 172.3.3.3/32
R3(config)#ip prefix-list FROM-R1 seq 3 permit 150.0.0.0/8 ge 24
!
R3(config)#ip prefix-list FROM-R2 seq 1 permit 172.2.2.2/32
R3(config)#ip prefix-list FROM-R2 seq 2 permit 172.4.4.4/32
R3(config)#ip prefix-list FROM-R2 seq 3 permit 150.0.0.0/8 ge 24
!
R3(config)#router eigrp 1
R3(config-router)#distribute-list prefix FROM-R1 in serial 0/1
R3(config-router)#distribute-list prefix FROM-R2 in serial 1/1
R3(config-router)#exit
```

Verify your configuration using the `show ip route eigrp` command. If your configuration is correct, the following entries should be reflected in the routing table on R3:

```
R3#show ip route eigrp | include 172|150
      172.1.0.0/32 is subnetted, 1 subnets
D EX    172.1.1.1 [170/2297856] via 10.0.0.5, 00:00:37, Serial0/1
      172.2.0.0/32 is subnetted, 1 subnets
D EX    172.2.2.2 [170/2809856] via 10.0.0.9, 00:01:50, Serial1/1
      172.3.0.0/32 is subnetted, 1 subnets
D EX    172.3.3.3 [170/2297856] via 10.0.0.5, 00:00:37, Serial0/1
      172.4.0.0/32 is subnetted, 1 subnets
D EX    172.4.4.4 [170/2809856] via 10.0.0.9, 00:01:50, Serial1/1
      150.1.0.0/24 is subnetted, 1 subnets
D       150.1.1.0 [90/2172416] via 10.0.0.5, 00:00:21, Serial0/1
      150.2.0.0/24 is subnetted, 1 subnets
D       150.2.2.0 [90/2195456] via 10.0.0.9, 00:00:21, Serial1/1
```

Task 7

Given the requirements, this configuration requires the use of a distribute list for the R3 EIGRP route filtering plus the use of the `ip summary-address` command to generate and advertise the default route to R4. This configuration is implemented on R3 as follows:

```
R3(config)#ip prefix-list TO-R4 seq 1 permit 0.0.0.0/0
R3(config)#router eigrp 1
R3(config-router)#distribute-list prefix TO-R4 out serial 0/0
R3(config-router)#exit
R3(config)#interface serial 0/0
R3(config-if)#ip summary-address eigrp 1 0.0.0.0 0.0.0.0
R3(config-if)#exit
```

Use the show ip route command on R4 to verify that only the default route is received:

```
R4#show ip route eigrp
D*   0.0.0.0/0 [90/2195456] via 10.0.0.13, 00:00:39, Serial0/0
```

Use simple ping tests to verify that R4 can ping the 172.x.x.x and 150.x.x.x subnets:

```
R4#ping 172.1.1.1

Type escape sequence to abort.
Sending 5, 100-byte ICMP Echos to 172.1.1.1, timeout is 2 seconds:
!!!!!
Success rate is 100 percent (5/5), round-trip min/avg/max = 4/4/4 ms

R4#ping 172.2.2.2

Type escape sequence to abort.
Sending 5, 100-byte ICMP Echos to 172.2.2.2, timeout is 2 seconds:
!!!!!
Success rate is 100 percent (5/5), round-trip min/avg/max = 4/4/4 ms

R4#ping 172.3.3.3

Type escape sequence to abort.
Sending 5, 100-byte ICMP Echos to 172.3.3.3, timeout is 2 seconds:
!!!!!
Success rate is 100 percent (5/5), round-trip min/avg/max = 1/3/4 ms

R4#ping 172.4.4.4

Type escape sequence to abort.
Sending 5, 100-byte ICMP Echos to 172.4.4.4, timeout is 2 seconds:
!!!!!
Success rate is 100 percent (5/5), round-trip min/avg/max = 4/4/4 ms

R4#ping 150.1.1.1

Type escape sequence to abort.
Sending 5, 100-byte ICMP Echos to 150.1.1.1, timeout is 2 seconds:
!!!!!
Success rate is 100 percent (5/5), round-trip min/avg/max = 1/3/4 ms

R4#ping 150.2.2.2

Type escape sequence to abort.
Sending 5, 100-byte ICMP Echos to 150.2.2.2, timeout is 2 seconds:
!!!!!
Success rate is 100 percent (5/5), round-trip min/avg/max = 4/4/4 ms

R4#ping 150.3.3.3
```

```
Type escape sequence to abort.
Sending 5, 100-byte ICMP Echos to 150.3.3.3, timeout is 2 seconds:
!!!!!
Success rate is 100 percent (5/5), round-trip min/avg/max = 4/4/4 ms
```

Task 8

This task requires some thought. First, the task calls for load balancing and not for load sharing. Therefore, the variance command cannot be used. In order to ensure that the metrics are the same, EIGRP offset lists will need to be used. The simplest method will be to offset the route metric of the best route such that it is equal to that of the worst (second) route. This will ensure that both routes have the same metric and EIGRP will automatically load balance. To complete this task, first use the show ip eigrp topology command to determine the route metrics:

```
R3#show ip eigrp topology 150.1.1.0/24
IP-EIGRP (AS 1): Topology entry for 150.1.1.0/24
  State is Passive, Query origin flag is 1, 1 Successor(s), FD is 2172416
  Routing Descriptor Blocks:
  10.0.0.5 (Serial0/1), from 10.0.0.5, Send flag is 0x0
      Composite metric is (2172416/28160), Route is Internal
      Vector metric:
        Minimum bandwidth is 1544 Kbit
        Total delay is 20100 microseconds
        Reliability is 255/255
        Load is 1/255
        Minimum MTU is 1500
        Hop count is 1
  10.0.0.9 (Serial1/1), from 10.0.0.9, Send flag is 0x0
      Composite metric is (2684416/2172416), Route is Internal
      Vector metric:
        Minimum bandwidth is 1544 Kbit
        Total delay is 40100 microseconds
        Reliability is 255/255
        Load is 1/255
        Minimum MTU is 1500
        Hop count is 2
```

Next, subtract the lowest (best) metric from the highest (worst) metric. Using the output above, we subtract 2172416 from 2684416 leaving us with a balance of 512000. The same logic is also applicable to the 150.2.2.0/24 prefix:

```
R3#show ip eigrp topology 150.2.2.0/24
IP-EIGRP (AS 1): Topology entry for 150.2.2.0/24
  State is Passive, Query origin flag is 1, 1 Successor(s), FD is 2195456
  Routing Descriptor Blocks:
  10.0.0.9 (Serial1/1), from 10.0.0.9, Send flag is 0x0
      Composite metric is (2195456/51200), Route is Internal
      Vector metric:
```

```
     Minimum bandwidth is 1544 Kbit
     Total delay is 21000 microseconds
     Reliability is 128/255
     Load is 1/255
     Minimum MTU is 1500
     Hop count is 1
  10.0.0.5 (Serial0/1), from 10.0.0.5, Send flag is 0x0
     Composite metric is (2707456/2195456), Route is Internal
     Vector metric:
     Minimum bandwidth is 1544 Kbit
     Total delay is 41000 microseconds
     Reliability is 128/255
     Load is 1/255
     Minimum MTU is 1500
     Hop count is 2
```

Following the same logic, if we subtract 2195456 from 2707456 the remaining balance is 512000. Following this, the offset lists are configured on R3 as follows:

```
R3(config)#ip access-list standard R1-LAN
R3(config-std-nacl)#permit host 150.1.1.0
R3(config-std-nacl)#exit
R3(config)#ip access-list standard R2-LAN
R3(config-std-nacl)#permit host 150.2.2.0
R3(config-std-nacl)#exit
R3(config)#router eigrp 1
R3(config-router)#offset-list R1-LAN in 512000 serial 0/1
R3(config-router)#offset-list R2-LAN in 512000 serial 1/1
R3(config-router)#end
```

Next, verify the load balancing using the show ip route command for both prefixes. R3 will now show the following for the 150.1.1.0/24 prefix:

```
R3#show ip route 150.1.1.0 255.255.255.0
Routing entry for 150.1.1.0/24
  Known via "eigrp 1", distance 90, metric 2684416, type internal
  Redistributing via eigrp 1
  Last update from 10.0.0.9 on Serial1/1, 00:02:18 ago
  Routing Descriptor Blocks:
    10.0.0.9, from 10.0.0.9, 00:02:18 ago, via Serial1/1
      Route metric is 2684416, traffic share count is 1
      Total delay is 40100 microseconds, minimum bandwidth is 1544 Kbit
      Reliability 255/255, minimum MTU 1500 bytes
      Loading 1/255, Hops 2
  * 10.0.0.5, from 10.0.0.5, 00:02:18 ago, via Serial0/1
      Route metric is 2684416, traffic share count is 1
      Total delay is 40100 microseconds, minimum bandwidth is 1544 Kbit
      Reliability 255/255, minimum MTU 1500 bytes
      Loading 1/255, Hops 1
```

R3 will now show the following for the 150.2.2.0/24 prefix:

```
R3#show ip route 150.2.2.0 255.255.255.0
Routing entry for 150.2.2.0/24
  Known via "eigrp 1", distance 90, metric 2707456, type internal
  Redistributing via eigrp 1
  Last update from 10.0.0.5 on Serial0/1, 00:02:08 ago
  Routing Descriptor Blocks:
  * 10.0.0.9, from 10.0.0.9, 00:02:08 ago, via Serial1/1
      Route metric is 2707456, traffic share count is 1
      Total delay is 41000 microseconds, minimum bandwidth is 1544 Kbit
      Reliability 128/255, minimum MTU 1500 bytes
      Loading 1/255, Hops 1
    10.0.0.5, from 10.0.0.5, 00:02:08 ago, via Serial0/1
      Route metric is 2707456, traffic share count is 1
      Total delay is 41000 microseconds, minimum bandwidth is 1544 Kbit
      Reliability 128/255, minimum MTU 1500 bytes
      Loading 1/255, Hops 2
```

Task 9

Remember that when configuring EIGRP authentication, the key chain name does NOT need to be the same; however, the key number used for authentication must be the same.

```
R3(config)#key chain R3-AUTH
R3(config-keychain)#key 1
R3(config-keychain-key)#key-string ROUTE
R3(config-keychain-key)#exit
R3(config-keychain)#exit
R3(config)#interface serial 0/0
R3(config-if)#ip authentication mode eigrp 1 md5
R3(config-if)#ip authentication key-chain eigrp 1 R3-AUTH
R3(config-if)#end

R4(config)#key chain R4-AUTH
R4(config-keychain)#key 1
R4(config-keychain-key)#key-string ROUTE
R4(config-keychain-key)#exit
R4(config-keychain)#exit
R4(config)#interface serial 0/0
R4(config-if)#ip authentication mode eigrp 1 md5
R4(config-if)#ip authentication key-chain eigrp 1 R4-AUTH
R4(config-if)#end
```

Next, use the show ip eigrp interfaces detail command to validate the configuration:

```
R4#show ip eigrp interfaces detail serial 0/0
IP-EIGRP interfaces for process 1
                          Xmit Queue   Mean   Pacing Time   Multicast   Pending
```

```
Interface       Peers  Un/Reliable  SRTT  Un/Reliable  Flow Timer  Routes
Se0/0               1      0/0          4     0/15          50         0
  Hello interval is 5 sec
  Next xmit serial <none>
  Un/reliable mcasts: 0/0  Un/reliable ucasts: 64/41
  Mcast exceptions: 0  CR packets: 0  ACKs suppressed: 6
  Retransmissions sent: 1  Out-of-sequence rcvd: 1
  Authentication mode is md5,  key-chain is "R4-AUTH"
  Use unicast
```

Task 10

As described in the ROUTE guide, an alternative method that can be used for route filtering is to use the distance command. Before implementing this configuration, R1 shows the following Loopback 0 subnet entries in the routing table:

```
R1#show ip route eigrp | include /32
     2.0.0.0/32 is subnetted, 1 subnets
     3.0.0.0/32 is subnetted, 1 subnets
     4.0.0.0/32 is subnetted, 1 subnets
```

The configuration required to complete this task is implemented as follows:

```
R1(config)#ip access-list standard LOOPBACK-SUBNETS
R1(config-std-nacl)#permit host 2.2.2.2
R1(config-std-nacl)#permit host 3.3.3.3
R1(config-std-nacl)#permit host 4.4.4.4
R1(config-std-nacl)#exit
R1(config)#router eigrp 1
R1(config-router)#distance 255 0.0.0.0 255.255.255.255 LOOPBACK-SUBNETS
R1(config-router)#end
```

Following this configuration, the Loopback0 subnets are no longer present in the routing table:

```
R1#show ip route eigrp | include /32
R1#
```

You can also use the show ip access-lists command to see matches against the ACL:

```
R1#show ip access-lists
Standard IP access list LOOPBACK-SUBNETS
    10 permit 2.2.2.2 (2 matches)
    20 permit 3.3.3.3 (3 matches)
    30 permit 4.4.4.4 (3 matches)
```

FINAL DEVICE CONFIGURATIONS

```
R1#show running-config
Building configuration...

Current configuration : 1576 bytes
!
version 12.4
service timestamps debug datetime msec
service timestamps log datetime msec
no service password-encryption
!
hostname R1
!
boot-start-marker
boot-end-marker
!
no logging console
enable secret 5 $1$ZHZP$BfOgaK4Ei7zfUol9D8zpV/
!
no aaa new-model
no network-clock-participate slot 1
no network-clock-participate wic 0
ip cef
!
no ip domain lookup
ip auth-proxy max-nodata-conns 3
ip admission max-nodata-conns 3
!
ipv6 unicast-routing
!
interface Loopback0
 ip address 1.1.1.1 255.255.255.255
!
interface Loopback1
 ip address 172.1.1.1 255.255.255.255
!
interface Loopback2
 ip address 172.2.2.2 255.255.255.255
!
interface Loopback3
 ip address 172.3.3.3 255.255.255.255
!
interface Loopback4
 ip address 172.4.4.4 255.255.255.255
!
interface FastEthernet0/0
 ip address 150.1.1.1 255.255.255.0
 loopback
 duplex auto
 speed auto
```

```
 no keepalive
!
interface Serial0/0
 ip address 10.0.0.1 255.255.255.252
 no fair-queue
!
interface Serial0/1
 ip address 10.0.0.5 255.255.255.252
!
router eigrp 1
 redistribute connected
 network 1.0.0.0
 network 10.0.0.0
 network 150.1.0.0
 distance 255 0.0.0.0 255.255.255.255 LOOPBACK-SUBNETS
 no auto-summary
!
ip forward-protocol nd
!
ip http server
no ip http secure-server
!
ip access-list standard LOOPBACK-SUBNETS
 permit 2.2.2.2
 permit 3.3.3.3
 permit 4.4.4.4
!
control-plane
!
voice-port 1/0/0
!
voice-port 1/0/1
!
voice-port 1/1/0
!
voice-port 1/1/1
!
line con 0
line aux 0
line vty 0 4
 privilege level 15
 password cisco
 login
!
end

R1#
```

```
R2#show running-config
Building configuration...

Current configuration : 1077 bytes
!
version 12.4
service timestamps debug datetime msec
service timestamps log datetime msec
no service password-encryption
!
hostname R2
!
boot-start-marker
boot-end-marker
!
no logging console
enable secret 5 $1$FsT/$/viPNrSsewWFUCy/QbD5lO
!
no aaa new-model
!
ip cef
no ip domain lookup
!
ipv6 unicast-routing
!
interface Loopback0
 ip address 2.2.2.2 255.255.255.255
!
interface FastEthernet0/0
 ip address 150.2.2.2 255.255.255.0
 loopback
 half-duplex
 no keepalive
!
interface Serial0/0
 ip address 10.0.0.2 255.255.255.252
 clock rate 2000000
 no fair-queue
!
interface FastEthernet0/1
 no ip address
 shutdown
 half-duplex
!
interface Serial0/1
 ip address 10.0.0.9 255.255.255.252
 clock rate 2000000
!
router eigrp 1
 network 2.0.0.0
 network 10.0.0.0
 network 150.2.0.0
```

```
 no auto-summary
!
ip http server
ip forward-protocol nd
!
control-plane
!
mgcp behavior g729-variants static-pt
!
gatekeeper
 shutdown
!
line con 0
line aux 0
line vty 0 4
 privilege level 15
 password cisco
 login
!
end

R2#


R3#show running-config
Building configuration...

Current configuration : 2069 bytes
!
version 12.4
service timestamps debug datetime msec
service timestamps log datetime msec
no service password-encryption
!
hostname R3
!
boot-start-marker
boot-end-marker
!
no logging console
enable secret 5 $1$mOsw$hNy9.KzOvGX2XmLabNBOT/
!
no aaa new-model
!
ip cef
no ip domain lookup
!
ipv6 unicast-routing
!
key chain R1-AUTH
 key 1
   key-string ROUTE
```

```
!
interface Loopback0
 ip address 3.3.3.3 255.255.255.255
!
interface FastEthernet0/0
 ip address 150.3.3.3 255.255.255.0
 loopback
 no keepalive
!
interface Serial0/0
 ip address 10.0.0.13 255.255.255.252
 ip authentication mode eigrp 1 md5
 ip authentication key-chain eigrp 1 R1-AUTH
 ip summary-address eigrp 1 0.0.0.0 0.0.0.0 5
 no fair-queue
!
interface FastEthernet0/1
 no ip address
 shutdown
!
interface Serial0/1
 ip address 10.0.0.6 255.255.255.252
 clock rate 2000000
!
interface FastEthernet1/0
 no ip address
 shutdown
!
interface Serial1/0
 no ip address
 shutdown
!
interface Serial1/1
 ip address 10.0.0.10 255.255.255.252
!
router eigrp 1
 offset-list R1-LAN in 512000 Serial0/1
 offset-list R2-LAN in 512000 Serial1/1
 network 3.0.0.0
 network 10.0.0.0
 network 150.3.0.0
 distribute-list prefix TO-R4 out Serial0/0
 distribute-list prefix FROM-R1 in Serial0/1
 distribute-list prefix FROM-R2 in Serial1/1
 no auto-summary
!
ip http server
ip forward-protocol nd
!
ip prefix-list FROM-R1 seq 1 permit 172.1.1.1/32
ip prefix-list FROM-R1 seq 2 permit 172.3.3.3/32
ip prefix-list FROM-R1 seq 3 permit 150.0.0.0/8 ge 24
```

```
!
ip prefix-list FROM-R2 seq 1 permit 172.2.2.2/32
ip prefix-list FROM-R2 seq 2 permit 172.4.4.4/32
ip prefix-list FROM-R2 seq 3 permit 150.0.0.0/8 ge 24
!
ip prefix-list TO-R4 seq 1 permit 0.0.0.0/0
!
ip access-list standard R1-LAN
 permit 150.1.1.0
ip access-list standard R2-LAN
 permit 150.2.2.0
!

control-plane
!
mgcp behavior g729-variants static-pt
!
gatekeeper
 shutdown
!
line con 0
line aux 0
line vty 0 4
 privilege level 15
 password cisco
 login
!
end

R3#


R4#show running-config
Building configuration...

Current configuration : 1360 bytes
!
version 12.4
service timestamps debug datetime msec
service timestamps log datetime msec
no service password-encryption
!
hostname R4
!
boot-start-marker
boot-end-marker
!
no logging console
enable secret 5 $1$M/kd$Eb360Ygk4rDpv7JtJeRbP.
!
no aaa new-model
no network-clock-participate slot 1
```

```
no network-clock-participate wic 0
ip cef
!
ip auth-proxy max-nodata-conns 3
ip admission max-nodata-conns 3
!
ipv6 unicast-routing
!
key chain R4-AUTH
 key 1
   key-string ROUTE
!
interface Loopback0
 ip address 4.4.4.4 255.255.255.255
!
interface FastEthernet0/0
 ip address 150.4.4.4 255.255.255.0
 loopback
 duplex auto
 speed auto
 no keepalive
!
interface Serial0/0
 ip address 10.0.0.14 255.255.255.252
 ip authentication mode eigrp 1 md5
 ip authentication key-chain eigrp 1 R4-AUTH
 no fair-queue
 clock rate 2000000
!
interface Serial0/1
 no ip address
 shutdown
!
interface Serial0/2
 no ip address
 shutdown
!
router eigrp 1
 network 4.0.0.0
 network 10.0.0.0
 network 150.4.0.0
 no auto-summary
 eigrp stub connected summary
!
ip forward-protocol nd
!
ip http server
no ip http secure-server
!
control-plane
!
voice-port 1/0/0
```

```
!
voice-port 1/0/1
!
voice-port 1/1/0
!
voice-port 1/1/1
!
line con 0
line aux 0
line vty 0 4
 privilege level 15
 password cisco
 login
!
end

R4#
```

LAB 5

Implementing Advanced Route Redistribution

Lab Objective:

The objective of this lab exercise is for you to learn and understand how to implement and verify advanced route redistribution solutions in Cisco IOS software.

Lab Topology:

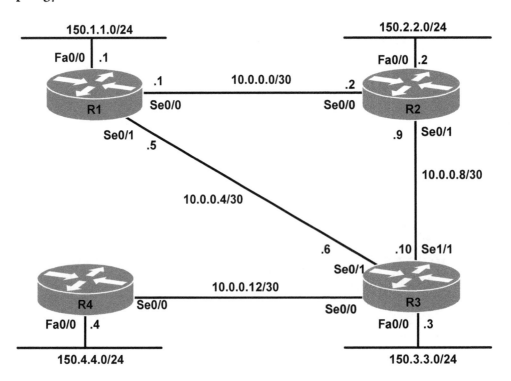

Task 1

Configure IP addressing on all routers as illustrated in the topology. Additionally, configure the following the following Loopback interfaces on all routers:

Router	Loopback	Loopback Interface Address/Mask
R1	0	1.1.1.1/32
R2	0	2.2.2.2/32
R3	0	3.3.3.3/32
R4	0	4.4.4.4/32

Task 2

Configure EIGRP AS 1 between R1 and R2. Do NOT advertise the 150.x.x.s subnets via EIGRP; also do NOT advertise the Loopback 0 subnets via EIGRP. Verify your configuration using the appropriate commands

Task 3

Configure EIGRP AS 2 between R2 and R3. Do NOT advertise any other networks via EIGRP 2. Verify your configuration using the appropriate commands

Task 4

Configure OSPF between R1 and R3. Statically configure the router ID using the IP address of the Loopback 0 interface. Do NOT advertise any other networks via OSPF. Configure both routers in area 0. Verify your configuration using the appropriate commands

Task 5

Configure OSPF between R3 and R4. Use the different process than the one already configured on R3. R4 should advertise all routes subnets via OSPF to R3. Both routers should reside in OSPF area 0. Verify your configuration using the appropriate commands

Task 6

Configure route redistribution in your network and verify the following:
- R1 should prefer the direct path via R3 to the 150.3.3.0/24 subnet
- R1 should prefer the direct path via R3 to the 150.4.4.0/24 subnet
- R1 should prefer the direct path via R2 to the 150.2.2.0/24 subnet

- R2 should prefer the direct path via R3 to the 150.3.3.0/24 subnet
- R2 should prefer the direct path via R1 to the 150.1.1.0/24 subnet
- R2 should prefer the direct path via R3 to the 150.4.4.0/24 subnet

- R3 should prefer the direct path via R2 to the 150.2.2.0/24 subnet
- R3 should prefer the direct path via R1 to the 150.1.1.0/24 subnet
- R3 should prefer the direct path via R4 to the 150.4.4.0/24 subnet

Task 7

Verify that all of the router routers can ping the Loopback 0 interfaces of all other routers. If you are unable to do so, you will need to correct your configuration

LAB VALIDATION

Task 1

```
R1#show ip interface brief
Interface          IP-Address     OK? Method Status          Protocol
FastEthernet0/0    150.1.1.1      YES NVRAM  up              up
Serial0/0          10.0.0.1       YES NVRAM  up              up
Serial0/1          10.0.0.5       YES NVRAM  up              up
Loopback0          1.1.1.1        YES NVRAM  up              up
Loopback1          190.1.1.1      YES manual up              up


R2#show ip interface brief
Interface          IP-Address     OK? Method Status          Protocol
FastEthernet0/0    150.2.2.2      YES NVRAM  up              up
Serial0/0          10.0.0.2       YES NVRAM  up              up
Serial0/1          10.0.0.9       YES NVRAM  up              up
Loopback0          2.2.2.2        YES NVRAM  up              up


R3#show ip interface brief
Interface          IP-Address     OK? Method Status          Protocol
FastEthernet0/0    150.3.3.3      YES NVRAM  up              up
Serial0/0          10.0.0.13      YES NVRAM  up              up
Serial0/1          10.0.0.6       YES NVRAM  up              up
Serial1/1          10.0.0.10      YES NVRAM  up              up
Loopback0          3.3.3.3        YES NVRAM  up              up


R4#show ip interface brief
Interface          IP-Address     OK? Method Status          Protocol
FastEthernet0/0    150.4.4.4      YES NVRAM  up              up
Serial0/0          10.0.0.14      YES NVRAM  up              up
Loopback0          4.4.4.4        YES NVRAM  up              up
```

Task 2

```
R1(config)#router eigrp 1
R1(config-router)#network 10.0.0.0 0.0.0.3
R1(config-router)#no auto-summary
R1(config-router)#end


R2(config)#router eigrp 1
R2(config-router)#network 10.0.0.0 0.0.0.3
R2(config-router)#no auto-summary
R2(config-router)#end
```

Verify your configuration using the show ip eigrp neighbors command on R1 and R2:

```
R1#show ip eigrp neighbors
IP-EIGRP neighbors for process 1
H   Address               Interface     Hold Uptime   SRTT  RTO  Q   Seq
                                        (sec)         (ms)       Cnt Num
0   10.0.0.2              Se0/0          13 00:02:10    3   200  0   8


R2#show ip eigrp neighbors
IP-EIGRP neighbors for process 1
H   Address               Interface     Hold Uptime   SRTT  RTO  Q   Seq
                                        (sec)         (ms)       Cnt Num
0   10.0.0.1              Se0/0          14 00:01:27    2   200  0   10
```

Task 3

```
R2(config)#router eigrp 2
R2(config-router)#network 10.0.0.8 0.0.0.3
R2(config-router)#no auto-summary
R2(config-router)#end


R3(config)#router eigrp 2
R3(config-router)#network 10.0.0.8 0.0.0.3
R3(config-router)#no auto-summary
R3(config-router)#end
```

Verify your configuration using the show ip eigrp neighbors command on R2 and R3:

```
R3#show ip eigrp neighbors
IP-EIGRP neighbors for process 2
H   Address               Interface     Hold Uptime   SRTT  RTO  Q   Seq
                                        (sec)         (ms)       Cnt Num
0   10.0.0.9              Se1/1          14 00:00:14    7   300  0   3


R2#show ip eigrp neighbors
IP-EIGRP neighbors for process 1
H   Address               Interface     Hold Uptime   SRTT  RTO  Q   Seq
                                        (sec)         (ms)       Cnt Num
0   10.0.0.1              Se0/0          14 00:05:01    2   200  0   10
IP-EIGRP neighbors for process 2
H   Address               Interface     Hold Uptime   SRTT  RTO  Q   Seq
                                        (sec)         (ms)       Cnt Num
0   10.0.0.10             Se0/1          11 00:00:31    6   200  0   3
```

Task 4

```
R1(config)#router ospf 1
R1(config-router)#router-id 1.1.1.1
R1(config-router)#exit
R1(config)#interface serial 0/1
R1(config-if)#ip ospf 1 area 0
R1(config-if)#end


R3(config)#router ospf 3
R3(config-router)#router-id 3.3.3.3
R3(config-router)#exit
R3(config)#interface serial 0/1
R3(config-if)#ip ospf 3 area 0
R3(config-if)#end
```

Use the show ip ospf neighbor command on R1 and R3 for verification:

```
R1#show ip ospf neighbor

Neighbor ID     Pri   State           Dead Time   Address     Interface
3.3.3.3           0   FULL/   -       00:00:39    10.0.0.6    Serial0/1


R3#show ip ospf neighbor

Neighbor ID     Pri   State           Dead Time   Address     Interface
1.1.1.1           0   FULL/   -       00:00:34    10.0.0.5    Serial0/1
```

Task 5

```
R3(config)#router ospf 33
R3(config-router)#router-id 33.33.33.33
R3(config-router)#exit
R3(config)#interface serial 0/0
R3(config-if)#ip ospf 33 area 0
R3(config-if)#end

R4(config)#router ospf 4
R4(config-router)#router-id 4.4.4.4
R4(config-router)#exit
R4(config)#interface serial 0/0
R4(config-if)#ip ospf 4 area 0
R4(config-if)#exit
R4(config)#interface fastethernet 0/0
R4(config-if)#ip ospf 4 area 0
R4(config-if)#end
```

Next, verify your configuration using the show ip ospf neighbor and show ip route commands on both routers as follows:

```
R4#show ip ospf neighbor

Neighbor ID      Pri   State            Dead Time   Address       Interface
33.33.33.33        0   FULL/  -         00:00:33    10.0.0.13     Serial0/0


R3#show ip ospf neighbor

Neighbor ID      Pri   State            Dead Time   Address       Interface
4.4.4.4            0   FULL/  -         00:00:35    10.0.0.14     Serial0/0
1.1.1.1            0   FULL/  -         00:00:37    10.0.0.5      Serial0/1


R3#show ip route ospf
     4.0.0.0/32 is subnetted, 1 subnets
O       4.4.4.4 [110/65] via 10.0.0.14, 00:02:52, Serial0/0
     150.4.0.0/24 is subnetted, 1 subnets
O       150.4.4.0 [110/65] via 10.0.0.14, 00:02:52, Serial0/0
```

Task 6

Although the redistribution looks complex, you do not necessarily need to implement route filtering when redistributing between the various routing protocols. Consideration, however, should be given to the different administrative distance values of the routing protocols:

```
R1(config)#access-list 1 permit host 150.2.2.0
R1(config)#router ospf 1
R1(config-router)#redistribute eigrp 1 subnets
R1(config-router)#redistribute connected subnets
R1(config-router)#distance 180 3.3.3.3 0.0.0.0 1
R1(config-router)#exit
R1(config)#router eigrp 1
R1(config-router)#default-metric 10000 100 255 1 1500
R1(config-router)#redistribute ospf 1
R1(config-router)#redistribute connected
R1(config-router)#end


R2(config)#access-list 1 permit host 150.3.3.0
R2(config)#access-list 1 permit host 150.4.4.0
R2(config)#router eigrp 1
R2(config-router)#redistribute connected
R2(config-router)#redistribute eigrp 2
R2(config-router)#offset-list 1 in 1000 serial 0/0
R2(config-router)#exit
R2(config)#router eigrp 2
R2(config-router)#redistribute eigrp 1
```

```
R2(config-router)#redistribute connected
R2(config-router)#end


R3(config)#access-list 1 permit host 150.2.2.0
R3(config)#router eigrp 2
R3(config-router)#default-metric 10000 100 255 1 1500
R3(config-router)#redistribute connected
R3(config-router)#redistribute ospf 3
R3(config-router)#redistribute ospf 33
R3(config-router)#exit
R3(config)#router ospf 3
R3(config-router)#redistribute connected subnets
R3(config-router)#redistribute eigrp 2 subnets
R3(config-router)#redistribute ospf 33 subnets
R3(config-router)#distance 180 1.1.1.1 0.0.0.0 1
R3(config-router)#exit
R3(config)#router ospf 33
R3(config-router)#redistribute connected subnets
R3(config-router)#redistribute eigrp 2 subnets
R3(config-router)#redistribute ospf 3 subnets
R3(config-router)#end
```

The following section verifies the requirements of this task and includes the configurations
required to adhere to the task requirements:

Requirement # 1: R1 should prefer the direct path via R3 to the 150.3.3.0/24 subnet

```
R1#show ip route 150.3.3.0 255.255.255.0
Routing entry for 150.3.3.0/24
Known via "ospf 1", distance 110, metric 20, type extern 2, forward metric 64
  Redistributing via eigrp 1
  Advertised by eigrp 1
  Last update from 10.0.0.6 on Serial0/1, 00:05:04 ago
  Routing Descriptor Blocks:
  * 10.0.0.6, from 3.3.3.3, 00:05:04 ago, via Serial0/1
      Route metric is 20, traffic share count is 1
```

Requirement # 2: R1 should prefer the direct path via R3 to the 150.4.4.0/24 subnet

```
R1#show ip route 150.4.4.0 255.255.255.0
Routing entry for 150.4.4.0/24
  Known via "ospf 1", distance 110, metric 129, type intra area
  Redistributing via eigrp 1
  Advertised by eigrp 1
  Last update from 10.0.0.6 on Serial0/1, 00:05:45 ago
  Routing Descriptor Blocks:
  * 10.0.0.6, from 4.4.4.4, 00:05:45 ago, via Serial0/1
      Route metric is 129, traffic share count is 1
```

Requirement # 3: R1 should prefer the direct path via R2 to the 150.2.2.0/24 subnet

Without the distance command configured on R1, R1 would prefer the OSPF route because of the lower administrative distance as illustrated below:

```
R1#show ip route 150.2.2.0 255.255.255.0
Routing entry for 150.2.2.0/24
Known via "ospf 1", distance 110, metric 20, type extern 2, forward metric 64
  Redistributing via eigrp 1
  Advertised by eigrp 1
  Last update from 10.0.0.6 on Serial0/1, 00:00:11 ago
  Routing Descriptor Blocks:
  * 10.0.0.6, from 3.3.3.3, 00:00:11 ago, via Serial0/1
      Route metric is 20, traffic share count is 1
```

However, by using the distance command, we can ensure that the EIGRP route is preferred:

```
R1(config-if)#router ospf 1
R1(config-router)#distance 180 3.3.3.3 0.0.0.0 1
R1(config-router)#end
```

The result of this configuration is that the direct path via EIGRP is preferred instead of OSPF:

```
R1#show ip route 150.2.2.0 255.255.255.0
Routing entry for 150.2.2.0/24
  Known via "eigrp 1", distance 170, metric 2195456, type external
  Redistributing via eigrp 1, ospf 1
  Advertised by ospf 1 subnets
  Last update from 10.0.0.2 on Serial0/0, 00:03:06 ago
  Routing Descriptor Blocks:
  * 10.0.0.2, from 10.0.0.2, 00:03:06 ago, via Serial0/0
      Route metric is 2195456, traffic share count is 1
      Total delay is 21000 microseconds, minimum bandwidth is 1544 Kbit
      Reliability 226/255, minimum MTU 1500 bytes
      Loading 1/255, Hops 1
```

Requirement # 4: R2 should prefer the direct path via R3 to the 150.3.3.0/24 subnet

```
R2#show ip route 150.3.3.0 255.255.255.0
Routing entry for 150.3.3.0/24
  Known via "eigrp 1", distance 170, metric 2195456, type external
  Redistributing via eigrp 1, eigrp 2
  Advertised by eigrp 2
  Last update from 10.0.0.1 on Serial0/0, 00:05:05 ago
  Routing Descriptor Blocks:
  * 10.0.0.1, from 10.0.0.1, 00:05:05 ago, via Serial0/0
```

```
Route metric is 2195456, traffic share count is 1
Total delay is 21000 microseconds, minimum bandwidth is 1544 Kbit
Reliability 255/255, minimum MTU 1500 bytes
Loading 1/255, Hops 1
```

In the output above, the router prefers the route from the router with the lowest router ID. This was included specifically as a real world example. In Cisco IOS software, when two EIGRP processes learn about the same path and the metric is the same, EIGRP will only install the path learned via the LOWER autonomous system number into the routing table, regardless of the administrative distance. From the output of the EIGRP Topology Table, we can see that the metrics for the path via R1 and R3 are the same for the 150.3.3.0/24 prefix as follows:

```
R2#show ip eigrp top 150.3.3.0/24
IP-EIGRP (AS 1): Topology entry for 150.3.3.0/24
  State is Passive, Query origin flag is 1, 1 Successor(s), FD is 2195456
  Routing Descriptor Blocks:
  10.0.0.1 (Serial0/0), from 10.0.0.1, Send flag is 0x0
      Composite metric is (2195456/281600), Route is External
      Vector metric:
        Minimum bandwidth is 1544 Kbit
        Total delay is 21000 microseconds
        Reliability is 253/255
        Load is 1/255
        Minimum MTU is 1500
        Hop count is 1
      External data:
        Originating router is 1.1.1.1
        AS number of route is 1
        External protocol is OSPF, external metric is 20
        Administrator tag is 0 (0x00000000)
IP-EIGRP (AS 2): Topology entry for 150.3.3.0/24
  State is Passive, Query origin flag is 1, 1 Successor(s), FD is 2195456
  Routing Descriptor Blocks:
  10.0.0.1, from Redistributed, Send flag is 0x0
      Composite metric is (2195456/0), Route is External
      Vector metric:
        Minimum bandwidth is 1544 Kbit
        Total delay is 21000 microseconds
        Reliability is 253/255
        Load is 1/255
        Minimum MTU is 1500
        Hop count is 1
      External data:
        Originating router is 2.2.2.2 (this system)
        AS number of route is 1
        External protocol is EIGRP, external metric is 2195456
        Administrator tag is 0 (0x00000000)
  10.0.0.10 (Serial0/1), from 10.0.0.10, Send flag is 0x0
      Composite metric is (2195456/51200), Route is External
```

```
Vector metric:
  Minimum bandwidth is 1544 Kbit
  Total delay is 21000 microseconds
  Reliability is 255/255
  Load is 1/255
  Minimum MTU is 1500
  Hop count is 1
External data:
  Originating router is 3.3.3.3
  AS number of route is 0
  External protocol is Connected, external metric is 0
  Administrator tag is 0 (0x00000000)
```

In the output above, the path via R1 is preferred because it is learned using the EIGRP process with the LOWER autonomous system number. This default behavior cannot be changed. However, you can use offset-lists to influence this behavior. This is implemented as follows:

```
R2(config)#access-list 1 permit host 150.3.3.0
R2(config)#router eigrp 1
R2(config-router)#offset-list 1 in 1000 serial 0/0
R2(config-router)#end
```

Following this configuration, the routing table on R2 now shows the following:

```
R2#show ip route 150.3.3.0 255.255.255.0
Routing entry for 150.3.3.0/24
  Known via "eigrp 2", distance 170, metric 2195456, type external
  Redistributing via eigrp 1, eigrp 2
  Advertised by eigrp 1
  Last update from 10.0.0.10 on Serial0/1, 00:08:24 ago
  Routing Descriptor Blocks:
  * 10.0.0.10, from 10.0.0.10, 00:08:24 ago, via Serial0/1
      Route metric is 2195456, traffic share count is 1
      Total delay is 21000 microseconds, minimum bandwidth is 1544 Kbit
      Reliability 255/255, minimum MTU 1500 bytes
      Loading 1/255, Hops 1
```

Requirement # 5: R2 should prefer the direct path via R1 to the 150.1.1.0/24 subnet

```
R2#show ip route 150.1.1.0 255.255.255.0
Routing entry for 150.1.1.0/24
  Known via "eigrp 1", distance 170, metric 2172416, type external
  Redistributing via eigrp 1, eigrp 2
  Advertised by eigrp 2
  Last update from 10.0.0.1 on Serial0/0, 00:04:46 ago
  Routing Descriptor Blocks:
  * 10.0.0.1, from 10.0.0.1, 00:04:46 ago, via Serial0/0
```

```
Route metric is 2172416, traffic share count is 1
Total delay is 20100 microseconds, minimum bandwidth is 1544 Kbit
Reliability 255/255, minimum MTU 1500 bytes
Loading 1/255, Hops 1
```

Requirement # 6: R2 should prefer the direct path via R3 to the 150.4.4.0/24 subnet

This prefix suffers the same fate as the 150.3.3.0/24 without intervention. That it, EIGRP will only install the path learned via the LOWER autonomous system into the routing table if the route is learned by two different processes and has the same route metric. The routing table shows the following entry for this prefix:

```
R2#show ip route 150.4.4.0 255.255.255.0
Routing entry for 150.4.4.0/24
  Known via "eigrp 1", distance 170, metric 2195456, type external
  Redistributing via eigrp 1, eigrp 2
  Advertised by eigrp 2
  Last update from 10.0.0.1 on Serial0/0, 00:00:03 ago
  Routing Descriptor Blocks:
  * 10.0.0.1, from 10.0.0.1, 00:00:03 ago, via Serial0/0
      Route metric is 2195456, traffic share count is 1
      Total delay is 21000 microseconds, minimum bandwidth is 1544 Kbit
      Reliability 255/255, minimum MTU 1500 bytes
      Loading 1/255, Hops 1
```

This is simply resolved by including this network in the offset-list configured previously:

```
R2(config)#access-list 1 permit host 150.3.3.0
R2(config)#access-list 1 permit host 150.4.4.0
R2(config)#router eigrp 1
R2(config-router)#offset-list 1 in 1000 serial 0/0
R2(config-router)#end
```

Following this change, the routing table now shows the following for this prefix:

```
R2#show ip route 150.4.4.0 255.255.255.0
Routing entry for 150.4.4.0/24
  Known via "eigrp 2", distance 170, metric 2195456, type external
  Redistributing via eigrp 1, eigrp 2
  Advertised by eigrp 1
  Last update from 10.0.0.10 on Serial0/1, 00:02:55 ago
  Routing Descriptor Blocks:
  * 10.0.0.10, from 10.0.0.10, 00:02:55 ago, via Serial0/1
      Route metric is 2195456, traffic share count is 1
      Total delay is 21000 microseconds, minimum bandwidth is 1544 Kbit
      Reliability 255/255, minimum MTU 1500 bytes
      Loading 1/255, Hops 1
```

Requirement # 7: R3 should prefer the direct path via R2 to the 150.2.2.0/24 subnet

```
R3#show ip route 150.2.2.0 255.255.255.0
Routing entry for 150.2.2.0/24
Known via "ospf 3", distance 110, metric 20, type extern 2, forward metric 64
  Redistributing via eigrp 2, ospf 33
  Advertised by eigrp 2
               ospf 33 subnets
  Last update from 10.0.0.5 on Serial0/1, 00:10:31 ago
  Routing Descriptor Blocks:
  * 10.0.0.5, from 1.1.1.1, 00:10:31 ago, via Serial0/1
      Route metric is 20, traffic share count is 1
```

Again, the OSPF route is preferred because of the lower administrative distance. This can be resolved using the distance command as follows:

```
R3(config)#access-list 1 permit host 150.2.2.0
R3(config)#router ospf 3
R3(config-router)#distance 180 1.1.1.1 0.0.0.0 1
R3(config-router)#end
```

Following this change, the routing table on R3 now shows the following:

```
R3#show ip route 150.2.2.0 255.255.255.0
Routing entry for 150.2.2.0/24
  Known via "eigrp 2", distance 170, metric 2195456, type external
  Redistributing via eigrp 2, ospf 3, ospf 33
  Advertised by ospf 3 subnets
               ospf 33 subnets
  Last update from 10.0.0.9 on Serial1/1, 00:00:50 ago
  Routing Descriptor Blocks:
  * 10.0.0.9, from 10.0.0.9, 00:00:50 ago, via Serial1/1
      Route metric is 2195456, traffic share count is 1
      Total delay is 21000 microseconds, minimum bandwidth is 1544 Kbit
      Reliability 183/255, minimum MTU 1500 bytes
      Loading 1/255, Hops 1
```

Requirement # 8: R3 should prefer the direct path via R1 to the 150.1.1.0/24 subnet

```
R3#show ip route 150.1.1.0 255.255.255.0
Routing entry for 150.1.1.0/24
Known via "ospf 3", distance 110, metric 20, type extern 2, forward metric 64
  Redistributing via eigrp 2, ospf 33
  Advertised by eigrp 2
               ospf 33 subnets
  Last update from 10.0.0.5 on Serial0/1, 00:02:06 ago
  Routing Descriptor Blocks:
  * 10.0.0.5, from 1.1.1.1, 00:02:06 ago, via Serial0/1
      Route metric is 20, traffic share count is 1
```

Requirement # 8: R3 should prefer the direct path via R1 to the 150.1.1.0/24 subnet

```
R3#show ip route 150.4.4.0 255.255.255.0
Routing entry for 150.4.4.0/24
  Known via "ospf 33", distance 110, metric 65, type intra area
  Redistributing via eigrp 2, ospf 3
  Advertised by eigrp 2
               ospf 3 subnets
  Last update from 10.0.0.14 on Serial0/0, 01:08:27 ago
  Routing Descriptor Blocks:
  * 10.0.0.14, from 4.4.4.4, 01:08:27 ago, via Serial0/0
      Route metric is 65, traffic share count is 1
```

Task 7

```
R1#ping 2.2.2.2

Type escape sequence to abort.
Sending 5, 100-byte ICMP Echos to 2.2.2.2, timeout is 2 seconds:
!!!!!
Success rate is 100 percent (5/5), round-trip min/avg/max = 4/4/4 ms

R1#ping 3.3.3.3

Type escape sequence to abort.
Sending 5, 100-byte ICMP Echos to 3.3.3.3, timeout is 2 seconds:
!!!!!
Success rate is 100 percent (5/5), round-trip min/avg/max = 1/1/1 ms

R1#ping 4.4.4.4

Type escape sequence to abort.
Sending 5, 100-byte ICMP Echos to 4.4.4.4, timeout is 2 seconds:
!!!!!
Success rate is 100 percent (5/5), round-trip min/avg/max = 1/3/4 ms


R2#ping 1.1.1.1

Type escape sequence to abort.
Sending 5, 100-byte ICMP Echos to 1.1.1.1, timeout is 2 seconds:
!!!!!
Success rate is 100 percent (5/5), round-trip min/avg/max = 4/4/4 ms

R2#ping 3.3.3.3

Type escape sequence to abort.
Sending 5, 100-byte ICMP Echos to 3.3.3.3, timeout is 2 seconds:
!!!!!
Success rate is 100 percent (5/5), round-trip min/avg/max = 4/5/8 ms
```

```
R2#ping 4.4.4.4

Type escape sequence to abort.
Sending 5, 100-byte ICMP Echos to 4.4.4.4, timeout is 2 seconds:
!!!!!
Success rate is 100 percent (5/5), round-trip min/avg/max = 4/4/8 ms


R3#ping 1.1.1.1

Type escape sequence to abort.
Sending 5, 100-byte ICMP Echos to 1.1.1.1, timeout is 2 seconds:
!!!!!
Success rate is 100 percent (5/5), round-trip min/avg/max = 1/2/4 ms

R3#ping 2.2.2.2

Type escape sequence to abort.
Sending 5, 100-byte ICMP Echos to 2.2.2.2, timeout is 2 seconds:
!!!!!
Success rate is 100 percent (5/5), round-trip min/avg/max = 1/2/4 ms

R3#ping 4.4.4.4

Type escape sequence to abort.
Sending 5, 100-byte ICMP Echos to 4.4.4.4, timeout is 2 seconds:
!!!!!
Success rate is 100 percent (5/5), round-trip min/avg/max = 1/3/4 ms


R4#ping 1.1.1.1

Type escape sequence to abort.
Sending 5, 100-byte ICMP Echos to 1.1.1.1, timeout is 2 seconds:
!!!!!
Success rate is 100 percent (5/5), round-trip min/avg/max = 4/4/4 ms

R4#ping 2.2.2.2

Type escape sequence to abort.
Sending 5, 100-byte ICMP Echos to 2.2.2.2, timeout is 2 seconds:
!!!!!
Success rate is 100 percent (5/5), round-trip min/avg/max = 4/4/8 ms

R4#ping 3.3.3.3

Type escape sequence to abort.
Sending 5, 100-byte ICMP Echos to 3.3.3.3, timeout is 2 seconds:
!!!!!
Success rate is 100 percent (5/5), round-trip min/avg/max = 1/3/4 ms
```

DEVICE CONFIGURATIONS

```
R1#show running-config
Building configuration...

Current configuration : 1421 bytes
!
version 12.4
service timestamps debug datetime msec
service timestamps log datetime msec
no service password-encryption
!
hostname R1
!
boot-start-marker
boot-end-marker
!
no logging console
enable secret 5 $1$ZHZP$BfOgaK4Ei7zfUol9D8zpV/
!
no aaa new-model
no network-clock-participate slot 1
no network-clock-participate wic 0
ip cef
!
no ip domain lookup
ip auth-proxy max-nodata-conns 3
ip admission max-nodata-conns 3
!
ipv6 unicast-routing
!
interface Loopback0
 ip address 1.1.1.1 255.255.255.255
!
interface FastEthernet0/0
 ip address 150.1.1.1 255.255.255.0
 loopback
 duplex auto
 speed auto
 no keepalive
!
interface Serial0/0
 ip address 10.0.0.1 255.255.255.252
 no fair-queue
!
interface Serial0/1
 ip address 10.0.0.5 255.255.255.252
 ip ospf 1 area 0
!
router eigrp 1
 redistribute connected
```

```
 redistribute ospf 1
 network 10.0.0.0 0.0.0.3
 default-metric 10000 100 255 1 1500
 no auto-summary
!
router ospf 1
 router-id 1.1.1.1
 log-adjacency-changes
 redistribute connected subnets
 redistribute eigrp 1 subnets
 distance 180 3.3.3.3 0.0.0.0 1
!
ip forward-protocol nd
!
ip http server
no ip http secure-server
!
access-list 1 permit 150.2.2.0
!
control-plane
!
voice-port 1/0/0
!
voice-port 1/0/1
!
voice-port 1/1/0
!
voice-port 1/1/1
!
line con 0
line aux 0
line vty 0 4
 privilege level 15
 password cisco
 login
!
end

R1#



R2#show running-config
Building configuration...

Current configuration : 1294 bytes
!
version 12.4
service timestamps debug datetime msec
service timestamps log datetime msec
no service password-encryption
!
hostname R2
```

```
!
boot-start-marker
boot-end-marker
!
no logging console
enable secret 5 $1$FsT/$/viPNrSsewWFUCy/QbD5l0
!
no aaa new-model
!
ip cef
no ip domain lookup
!
ipv6 unicast-routing
!
interface Loopback0
 ip address 2.2.2.2 255.255.255.0
!
interface FastEthernet0/0
 ip address 150.2.2.2 255.255.255.0
 loopback
 half-duplex
 no keepalive
!
interface Serial0/0
 ip address 10.0.0.2 255.255.255.252
 clock rate 2000000
 no fair-queue
!
interface FastEthernet0/1
 no ip address
 shutdown
 half-duplex
!
interface Serial0/1
 ip address 10.0.0.9 255.255.255.252
 clock rate 2000000
!
router eigrp 1
 redistribute connected
 redistribute eigrp 2
 offset-list 1 in 1000 Serial0/0
 network 10.0.0.0 0.0.0.3
 no auto-summary
!
router eigrp 2
 redistribute connected
 redistribute eigrp 1
 network 10.0.0.8 0.0.0.3
 no auto-summary
!
ip http server
ip forward-protocol nd
```

```
!
access-list 1 permit 150.3.3.0
access-list 1 permit 150.4.4.0
!
control-plane
!
mgcp behavior g729-variants static-pt
!
gatekeeper
 shutdown
!
line con 0
line aux 0
line vty 0 4
 privilege level 15
 password cisco
 login
!
end

R2#


R3#show running-config
Building configuration...

Current configuration : 1744 bytes
!
version 12.4
service timestamps debug datetime msec
service timestamps log datetime msec
no service password-encryption
!
hostname R3
!
boot-start-marker
boot-end-marker
!
no logging console
enable secret 5 $1$mOsw$hNy9.KzOvGX2XmLabNBOT/
!
no aaa new-model
!
ip cef
no ip domain lookup
!
ipv6 unicast-routing
!
interface Loopback0
 ip address 3.3.3.3 255.255.255.255
!
interface FastEthernet0/0
```

```
 ip address 150.3.3.3 255.255.255.0
 full-duplex
!
interface Serial0/0
 ip address 10.0.0.13 255.255.255.252
 ip ospf 33 area 0
 no fair-queue
!
interface FastEthernet0/1
 no ip address
 shutdown
 half-duplex
!
interface Serial0/1
 ip address 10.0.0.6 255.255.255.252
 ip ospf 3 area 0
 clock rate 2000000
!
interface FastEthernet1/0
 no ip address
 shutdown
 half-duplex
!
interface Serial1/0
 no ip address
 shutdown
!
interface Serial1/1
 ip address 10.0.0.10 255.255.255.252
!
router eigrp 2
 redistribute connected
 redistribute ospf 3
 redistribute ospf 33
 network 10.0.0.8 0.0.0.3
 default-metric 10000 100 255 1 1500
 no auto-summary
!
router ospf 3
 router-id 3.3.3.3
 log-adjacency-changes
 redistribute connected subnets
 redistribute eigrp 2 subnets
 redistribute ospf 33 subnets
 distance 180 1.1.1.1 0.0.0.0 1
!
router ospf 33
 router-id 33.33.33.33
 log-adjacency-changes
 redistribute connected subnets
 redistribute eigrp 2 subnets
 redistribute ospf 3 subnets
```

```
!
ip http server
ip forward-protocol nd
!
access-list 1 permit 150.2.2.0
!
control-plane
!
mgcp behavior g729-variants static-pt
!
gatekeeper
 shutdown
!
line con 0
line aux 0
line vty 0 4
 privilege level 15
 password cisco
 login
!
end


R3#


R4#show running-config
Building configuration...

Current configuration : 1226 bytes
!
version 12.4
service timestamps debug datetime msec
service timestamps log datetime msec
no service password-encryption
!
hostname R4
!
boot-start-marker
boot-end-marker
!
no logging console
enable secret 5 $1$M/kd$Eb36OYgk4rDpv7JtJeRbP.
!
no aaa new-model
no network-clock-participate slot 1
no network-clock-participate wic 0
ip cef
!
ip auth-proxy max-nodata-conns 3
ip admission max-nodata-conns 3
!
ipv6 unicast-routing
!
interface Loopback0
```

```
 ip address 4.4.4.4 255.255.255.255
 ip ospf 4 area 0
!
interface FastEthernet0/0
 ip address 150.4.4.4 255.255.255.0
 ip ospf 4 area 0
 loopback
 duplex auto
 speed auto
 no keepalive
!
interface Serial0/0
 ip address 10.0.0.14 255.255.255.252
 ip ospf 4 area 0
 no fair-queue
 clock rate 2000000
!
interface Serial0/1
 no ip address
 shutdown
!
interface Serial0/2
 no ip address
 shutdown
!
router ospf 4
 router-id 4.4.4.4
 log-adjacency-changes
!
ip forward-protocol nd
!
ip http server
no ip http secure-server
!
control-plane
!
voice-port 1/0/0
!
voice-port 1/0/1
!
voice-port 1/1/0
!
voice-port 1/1/1
!
line con 0
line aux 0
line vty 0 4
 privilege level 15
 password cisco
 login
!
end

R4#
```

LAB 6

Implementing IPv6 Routing Protocols

Lab Objective:

The objective of this lab exercise is for you to learn and understand how to implement and verify IPv6 routing solutions in Cisco IOS software.

Lab Topology:

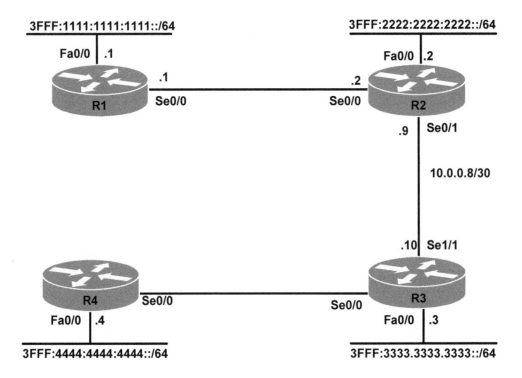

Task 1

Configure IP addressing on all routers as illustrated in the topology. Additionally, configure the following the following Loopback interfaces on all routers:

Router	Loopback	Loopback Interface Address/Mask
R2	0	2.2.2.2/32
R3	0	3.3.3.3/32

Task 2

Configure RIPng between R1 and R2. Do NOT configure a global IPv6 Unicast subnet between the two routers. Use a RIPng process of R1-RIP on R1 and a process of R2-RIP on R2. Advertise the LAN subnets via RIPng and verify your configuration.

Task 3

Configure a static IPv6 tunnel between R2 and R3. Use the FEC0::ABCD::/64 subnet for this tunnel. Verify that you can ping between R2 and R3 across this tunnel. Do not configure any IPv4 dynamic routing protocols. Use static routes instead.

Task 4

Configure MP-BGP between R2 and R3 using Link-Local addresses. Advertise the LAN subnet on R3 via MP-BGP. Use AS 5. Make sure that R2 can ping the LAN subnet configured on R3.

Task 5

Configure OSPFv3 between R3 and R4. Again, do NOT configure a global IPv6 Unicast subnet between the two routers. Both routers should reside in area 0. Advertise the LAN subnet on R4 via OSPFv3. This subnet should reside in area 1. Verify your configuration

Task 6

Redistribute between the IPv6 routing protocols. Make sure that R4 and R1 can ping each other end to end following your configuration

LAB VALIDATION

Task 1

```
R1#show ipv6 interface brief
FastEthernet0/0          [up/up]
    FE80::213:19FF:FE86:A20
    3FFF:1111:1111:1111::1
Serial0/0                [up/up]
Serial0/1                [up/up]
Loopback0                [up/up]

R2#show ipv6 interface brief
FastEthernet0/0          up/up]
    FE80::204:C1FF:FE6F:8741
    3FFF:2222:2222:2222::2
Serial0/0                [up/up]
FastEthernet0/1          [administratively down/down]
Serial0/1                [up/up]
Loopback0                [up/up]

R2#show ip interface brief
Interface      IP-Address    OK? Method Status            Protocol
Loopback0      2.2.2.2       YES NVRAM  up                up
Serial0/1      10.0.0.9      YES NVRAM  up                up
```

```
R3#show ipv6 interface brief
FastEthernet0/0              [up/up]
    FE80::230:80FF:FE3F:EA81
    3FFF:3333:3333:3333::3
Serial0/0                    [up/up]
FastEthernet0/1              [administratively down/down]
Serial0/1                    [up/up]
FastEthernet1/0              [administratively down/down]
Serial1/0                    [administratively down/down]
Serial1/1                    [up/up]
Loopback0                    [up/up]

R3#show ip interface brief
Interface       IP-Address      OK? Method Status              Protocol
Loopback0       3.3.3.3         YES NVRAM  up                  up

R4#show ipv6 interface brief
FastEthernet0/0              [up/up]
    FE80::20C:CEFF:FEA7:F3A0
    3FFF:4444:4444:4444::4
Serial0/0                    [up/up]
Serial0/1                    [administratively down/down]
Serial0/2                    [administratively down/down]
Loopback0                    [up/up]
```

Task 2

> **NOTE:** It is assumed that the ipv6 unicast-routing command was already enabled when you first configured IPv6 addressing on the routers.

```
R1(config)#ipv6 router rip R1-RIP
R1(config-rtr)#exit
R1(config)#interface fastethernet 0/0
R1(config-if)#ipv6 rip R1-RIP enable
R1(config-if)#ipv6 enable
R1(config-if)#exit
R1(config)#interface serial 0/0
R1(config-if)#ipv6 enable
R1(config-if)#ipv6 rip R1-RIP enable
R1(config-if)#end

R2(config)#ipv6 router rip R2-RIP
R2(config-rtr)#exit
R2(config)#interface fastethernet 0/0
R2(config-if)#ipv6 rip R2-RIP enable
R2(config-if)#ipv6 enable
R2(config-if)#exit
R2(config)#interface serial 0/0
R2(config-if)#ipv6 enable
R2(config-if)#ipv6 rip R2-RIP enable
R2(config-if)#end
```

Verify using the show ipv6 route and show ipv6 rip database commands as follows:

```
R1#show ipv6 rip database
RIP process "R1-RIP", local RIB
 3FFF:2222:2222:2222::/64, metric 2, installed
      Serial0/0/FE80::204:C1FF:FE6F:8741, expires in 158 secs


R1#show ipv6 route
IPv6 Routing Table - 5 entries
Codes: C - Connected, L - Local, S - Static, R - RIP, B - BGP
       U - Per-user Static route
       I1 - ISIS L1, I2 - ISIS L2, IA - ISIS interarea, IS - ISIS summary
       O - OSPF intra, OI - OSPF inter, OE1 - OSPF ext 1, OE2 - OSPF ext 2
       ON1 - OSPF NSSA ext 1, ON2 - OSPF NSSA ext 2
C   3FFF:1111:1111:1111::/64 [0/0]
     via ::, FastEthernet0/0
L   3FFF:1111:1111:1111::1/128 [0/0]
     via ::, FastEthernet0/0
R   3FFF:2222:2222:2222::/64 [120/2]
     via FE80::204:C1FF:FE6F:8741, Serial0/0
L   FE80::/10 [0/0]
     via ::, Null0
L   FF00::/8 [0/0]
     via ::, Null0


R2#show ipv6 rip database
RIP process "R2-RIP", local RIB
 3FFF:1111:1111:1111::/64, metric 2, installed
      Serial0/0/FE80::213:19FF:FE86:A20, expires in 173 secs


R2#show ipv6 route
IPv6 Routing Table - 5 entries
Codes: C - Connected, L - Local, S - Static, R - RIP, B - BGP
       U - Per-user Static route
       I1 - ISIS L1, I2 - ISIS L2, IA - ISIS interarea, IS - ISIS summary
       O - OSPF intra, OI - OSPF inter, OE1 - OSPF ext 1, OE2 - OSPF ext 2
       ON1 - OSPF NSSA ext 1, ON2 - OSPF NSSA ext 2
R   3FFF:1111:1111:1111::/64 [120/2]
     via FE80::213:19FF:FE86:A20, Serial0/0
C   3FFF:2222:2222:2222::/64 [0/0]
     via ::, Ethernet0/0
L   3FFF:2222:2222:2222::2/128 [0/0]
     via ::, Ethernet0/0
L   FE80::/10 [0/0]
     via ::, Null0
L   FF00::/8 [0/0]
     via ::, Null0
```

Task 3

```
R2(config)#ip route 3.3.3.3 255.255.255.255 serial 0/1
R2(config)#interface tunnel 0
R2(config-if)#ipv6 address fec0:abcd::2/64
R2(config-if)#tunnel source loopback 0
R2(config-if)#tunnel destination 3.3.3.3
R2(config-if)#tunnel mode ipv6ip
R2(config-if)#end


R3(config)#ip route 2.2.2.2 255.255.255.255 serial 1/1
R3(config)#interface tunnel 0
R3(config-if)#ipv6 address fec0:abcd::3/64
R3(config-if)#tunnel source loopback 0
R3(config-if)#tunnel destination 2.2.2.2
R3(config-if)#tunnel mode ipv6ip
R3(config-if)#end
```

Following your configuration, first verify the tunnel using the `show interfaces` command:

```
R3#show interfaces tunnel 0
Tunnel0 is up, line protocol is up
  Hardware is Tunnel
  MTU 1514 bytes, BW 9 Kbit/sec, DLY 500000 usec,
     reliability 255/255, txload 1/255, rxload 1/255
  Encapsulation TUNNEL, loopback not set
  Keepalive not set
  Tunnel source 3.3.3.3 (Loopback0), destination 2.2.2.2
  Tunnel protocol/transport IPv6/IP
  Tunnel TTL 255
  Fast tunneling enabled

[Truncated Output]


R2#show interfaces tunnel 0
Tunnel0 is up, line protocol is up
  Hardware is Tunnel
  MTU 1514 bytes, BW 9 Kbit/sec, DLY 500000 usec,
     reliability 255/255, txload 1/255, rxload 1/255
  Encapsulation TUNNEL, loopback not set
  Keepalive not set
  Tunnel source 2.2.2.2 (Loopback0), destination 3.3.3.3
  Tunnel protocol/transport IPv6/IP
  Tunnel TTL 255
[Truncated Output]
```

Next, use a simple ping to verify connectivity across the tunnel:

```
R3#ping fec0:abcd::2 repeat 100

Type escape sequence to abort.
Sending 100, 100-byte ICMP Echos to FEC0:ABCD::2, timeout is 2 seconds:
!!!!!!!!!!!!!!!!!!!!!!!!!!!!!!!!!!!!!!!!!!!!!!!!!!!!!!!!!!!!!!!!!!!!!!!!!
!!!!!!!!!!!!!!!!!!!!!!!!!!!!!!!!!
Success rate is 100 percent (100/100), round-trip min/avg/max = 4/4/4 ms
```

Task 4

When configuring MP-BGP, you must specify the router ID using an IPv4 address. In addition, when using Link-Local addresses for peering, you must use the neighbor [address] update-source [interface] command, even for directly connected neighbors. This task is completed as follows:

```
R2(config)#router bgp 5
R2(config-router)#bgp router-id 2.2.2.2
R2(config-router)#no bgp default ipv4-unicast
R2(config-router)#neighbor fe80::303:303 remote-as 5
R2(config-router)#neighbor fe80::303:303 update-source tunnel 0
R2(config-router)#address-family ipv6 unicast
R2(config-router-af)#neighbor fe80::303:303 activate
R2(config-router-af)#end

R3(config)#router bgp 5
R3(config-router)#bgp router-id 3.3.3.3
R3(config-router)#no bgp default ipv4-unicast
R3(config-router)#neighbor fe80::202:202 remote-as 5
R3(config-router)#neighbor fe80::202:202 update-source tunnel 0
R3(config-router)#address-family ipv6 unicast
R3(config-router-af)#network 3fff:3333:3333:3333::/64
R3(config-router-af)#neighbor fe80::202:202 activate
R3(config-router-af)#end
```

Following this configuration, use the show bgp ipv6 unicast summary and show bgp ipv6 unicast commands to verify your implementation:

```
R2#show bgp ipv6 unicast summary
BGP router identifier 2.2.2.2, local AS number 5
BGP table version is 2, main routing table version 2
1 network entries using 149 bytes of memory
1 path entries using 76 bytes of memory
2/1 BGP path/bestpath attribute entries using 248 bytes of memory
0 BGP route-map cache entries using 0 bytes of memory
0 BGP filter-list cache entries using 0 bytes of memory
BGP using 473 total bytes of memory
BGP activity 1/0 prefixes, 1/0 paths, scan interval 60 secs

Neighbor       V    AS MsgRcvd MsgSent   TblVer  InQ OutQ Up/Down   State/PfxRcd
FE80::303:303  4     5       5       5        2    0    0 00:00:05             1
```

```
R2#show bgp ipv6 unicast
BGP table version is 2, local router ID is 2.2.2.2
Status codes: s suppressed, d damped, h history, * valid, > best, i - internal,
              r RIB-failure, S Stale
Origin codes: i - IGP, e - EGP, ? - incomplete

   Network          Next Hop            Metric LocPrf Weight Path
*>i3FFF:3333:3333:3333::/64
                    FE80::303:303            0    100      0 i


R3#show bgp ipv6 unicast summary
BGP router identifier 3.3.3.3, local AS number 5
BGP table version is 3, main routing table version 3
1 network entries using 149 bytes of memory
1 path entries using 76 bytes of memory
2/1 BGP path/bestpath attribute entries using 248 bytes of memory
0 BGP route-map cache entries using 0 bytes of memory
0 BGP filter-list cache entries using 0 bytes of memory
BGP using 473 total bytes of memory
BGP activity 1/0 prefixes, 1/0 paths, scan interval 60 secs

Neighbor      V    AS MsgRcvd MsgSent   TblVer  InQ OutQ Up/Down  State/PfxRcd
FE80::202:202 4     5       5       6        3    0    0 00:01:30            0


R3#show bgp ipv6 unicast
BGP table version is 3, local router ID is 3.3.3.3
Status codes: s suppressed, d damped, h history, * valid, > best, i - internal,
              r RIB-failure, S Stale
Origin codes: i - IGP, e - EGP, ? - incomplete

   Network          Next Hop            Metric LocPrf Weight Path
*> 3FFF:3333:3333:3333::/64
                    ::                       0          32768 i
```

And finally, complete this task by pinging the R3 LAN subnet from R2 as follows:

```
R2#ping 3FFF:3333:3333:3333::3 repeat 100

Type escape sequence to abort.
Sending 100, 100-byte ICMP Echos to 3FFF:3333:3333:3333::3, timeout is 2
seconds:
!!!!!!!!!!!!!!!!!!!!!!!!!!!!!!!!!!!!!!!!!!!!!!!!!!!!!!!!!!!!!!!!!!!!!!!!!!!!
!!!!!!!!!!!!!!!!!!!!!!!!!!!!!!!
Success rate is 100 percent (100/100), round-trip min/avg/max = 0/1/4 ms
```

Task 5

```
R3(config)#ipv6 router ospf 3
R3(config-rtr)#router-id 3.3.3.3
R3(config-rtr)#exit
R3(config)#interface serial 0/0
R3(config-if)#ipv6 enable
R3(config-if)#ipv6 ospf 3 area 0
R3(config-if)#end


R4(config)#ipv6 router ospf 4
R4(config-rtr)#router-id 4.4.4.4
R4(config-rtr)#exit
R4(config)#interface serial 0/0
R4(config-if)#ipv6 enable
R4(config-if)#ipv6 ospf 4 area 0
R4(config-if)#exit
R4(config)#interface fastethernet 0/0
R4(config-if)#ipv6 ospf 4 area 1
R4(config-if)#end
```

Following this configuration, use the `show ipv6 ospf neighbor`, `show ipv6 ospf` and `show ipv6 route` commands to validate your implementation.

```
R4#show ipv6 ospf neighbor

Neighbor ID     Pri   State         Dead Time   Interface ID   Interface
3.3.3.3           1   FULL/  -      00:00:35    3              Serial0/0


R4#show ipv6 ospf
 Routing Process "ospfv3 4" with ID 4.4.4.4
 It is an area border router
 SPF schedule delay 5 secs, Hold time between two SPFs 10 secs
 Minimum LSA interval 5 secs. Minimum LSA arrival 1 secs
 LSA group pacing timer 240 secs
 Interface flood pacing timer 33 msecs
 Retransmission pacing timer 66 msecs
 Number of external LSA 0. Checksum Sum 0x000000
 Number of areas in this router is 2. 2 normal 0 stub 0 nssa
 Reference bandwidth unit is 100 mbps
    Area BACKBONE(0)
        Number of interfaces in this area is 1
        SPF algorithm executed 3 times
        Number of LSA 5. Checksum Sum 0x019342
        Number of DCbitless LSA 0
        Number of indication LSA 0
        Number of DoNotAge LSA 0
        Flood list length 0
    Area 1
```

```
        Number of interfaces in this area is 1
        SPF algorithm executed 2 times
        Number of LSA 3. Checksum Sum 0x01DC33
        Number of DCbitless LSA 0
        Number of indication LSA 0
        Number of DoNotAge LSA 0
        Flood list length 0

R3#show ipv6 route
IPv6 Routing Table - 7 entries
Codes: C - Connected, L - Local, S - Static, R - RIP, B - BGP
       U - Per-user Static route
       I1 - ISIS L1, I2 - ISIS L2, IA - ISIS interarea, IS - ISIS summary
       O - OSPF intra, OI - OSPF inter, OE1 - OSPF ext 1, OE2 - OSPF ext 2
       ON1 - OSPF NSSA ext 1, ON2 - OSPF NSSA ext 2
C   3FFF:3333:3333:3333::/64 [0/0]
     via ::, Ethernet0/0
L   3FFF:3333:3333:3333::3/128 [0/0]
     via ::, Ethernet0/0
OI  3FFF:4444:4444:4444::/64 [110/65]
     via FE80::20C:CEFF:FEA7:F3A0, Serial0/0
L   FE80::/10 [0/0]
     via ::, Null0
C   FEC0:ABCD::/64 [0/0]
     via ::, Tunnel0
L   FEC0:ABCD::3/128 [0/0]
     via ::, Tunnel0
L   FF00::/8 [0/0]
     via ::, Null0
```

Task 6

By default, when redistributing between IPv6 protocols, connected subnets are not included. It is important to remember to explicitly redistribute them. First redistribute between RIPng and MP-BGP on R2 as follows:

```
R2(config)#route-map CONNECTED-TO-BGP permit 10
R2(config-route-map)#match interface serial 0/0
R2(config-route-map)#exit
R2(config)#ipv6 router rip R2-RIP
R2(config-rtr)#redistribute connected metric 1
R2(config-rtr)#redistribute bgp 5 metric 2
R2(config-rtr)#exit
R2(config)#router bgp 5
R2(config-router)#address-family ipv6 unicast
R2(config-router-af)#redistribute connected route-map CONNECTED-TO-BGP
R2(config-router-af)#redistribute rip R2-RIP
R2(config-router-af)#bgp redistribute-internal
R2(config-router-af)#end
```

Next, verify your RIPng redistribution by looking at the routing table on R1 as follows:

```
R1#show ipv6 route
IPv6 Routing Table - 7 entries
Codes: C - Connected, L - Local, S - Static, R - RIP, B - BGP
       U - Per-user Static route
       I1 - ISIS L1, I2 - ISIS L2, IA - ISIS interarea, IS - ISIS summary
       O - OSPF intra, OI - OSPF inter, OE1 - OSPF ext 1, OE2 - OSPF ext 2
       ON1 - OSPF NSSA ext 1, ON2 - OSPF NSSA ext 2
C   3FFF:1111:1111:1111::/64 [0/0]
     via ::, FastEthernet0/0
L   3FFF:1111:1111:1111::1/128 [0/0]
     via ::, FastEthernet0/0
R   3FFF:2222:2222:2222::/64 [120/2]
     via FE80::204:C1FF:FE6F:8741, Serial0/0
R   3FFF:3333:3333:3333::/64 [120/2]
     via FE80::204:C1FF:FE6F:8741, Serial0/0
L   FE80::/10 [0/0]
     via ::, Null0
R   FEC0:ABCD::/64 [120/2]
     via FE80::204:C1FF:FE6F:8741, Serial0/0
L   FF00::/8 [0/0]
     via ::, Null0
```

Additionally, verify MP-BGP redistribution by looking at the MP-BGP RIB on R2 as follows:

```
R2#show bgp ipv6 unicast
BGP table version is 7, local router ID is 2.2.2.2
Status codes: s suppressed, d damped, h history, * valid, > best, i - internal,
              r RIB-failure, S Stale
Origin codes: i - IGP, e - EGP, ? - incomplete

   Network          Next Hop            Metric LocPrf Weight Path
*> 3FFF:1111:1111:1111::/64
                    ::                       2         32768 ?
*>i3FFF:3333:3333:3333::/64
                    FE80::303:303            0    100      0 i
```

Next, redistribute between MP-BGP and OSPFv3 on R3 as follows:

```
R3(config)#route-map CONNECTED-TO-BGP permit 10
R3(config-route-map)#match interface serial 0/0
R3(config-route-map)#exit
R3(config)#ipv6 router ospf 3
R3(config-rtr)#redistribute connected
R3(config-rtr)#redistribute bgp 5
R3(config-rtr)#exit
R3(config)#router bgp 5
R3(config-router)#address-family ipv6 unicast
```

```
R3(config-router-af)#redistribute connected route-map CONNECTED-TO-BGP
R3(config-router-af)#redistribute ospf 3
R3(config-router-af)#bgp redistribute-internal
R3(config-router-af)#end
```

Verify your configuration by looking at the LSDB and MP-BGP RIB on R3 as follows:

```
R3#show ipv6 ospf database

            OSPFv3 Router with ID (3.3.3.3) (Process ID 3)

            Router Link States (Area 0)

ADV Router      Age         Seq#        Fragment ID  Link count  Bits
3.3.3.3         15          0x80000004  0            1           E
4.4.4.4         1460        0x80000002  0            1           B

            Inter Area Prefix Link States (Area 0)

ADV Router      Age         Seq#        Prefix
4.4.4.4         1450        0x80000001  3FFF:4444:4444:4444::/64

            Link (Type-8) Link States (Area 0)

ADV Router      Age         Seq#        Link ID   Interface
3.3.3.3         1512        0x80000001  3         Se0/0
4.4.4.4         1468        0x80000001  5         Se0/0

            Type-5 AS External Link States

ADV Router      Age         Seq#        Prefix
3.3.3.3         146         0x80000001  3FFF:1111:1111:1111::/64
3.3.3.3         16          0x80000001  3FFF:3333:3333:3333::/64
3.3.3.3         16          0x80000001  FEC0:ABCD::/64


R3#show bgp ipv6 unicast
BGP table version is 9, local router ID is 3.3.3.3
Status codes: s suppressed, d damped, h history, * valid, > best, i - internal,
              r RIB-failure, S Stale
Origin codes: i - IGP, e - EGP, ? - incomplete

   Network          Next Hop            Metric LocPrf Weight Path
*>i3FFF:1111:1111:1111::/64
                 FE80::202:202            2    100      0 ?
*> 3FFF:3333:3333:3333::/64
                 ::                       0          32768 i
*> 3FFF:4444:4444:4444::/64
                 ::                      65          32768 ?
```

And finally, complete the task by performing a LAN-to-LAN ping between R1 and R4:

```
R4#ping 3FFF:1111:1111:1111::1 source 3FFF:4444:4444:4444::4 repeat 100

Type escape sequence to abort.
Sending 100, 100-byte ICMP Echos to 3FFF:1111:1111:1111::1, timeout is 2
seconds:
Packet sent with a source address of 3FFF:4444:4444:4444::4
!!!!!!!!!!!!!!!!!!!!!!!!!!!!!!!!!!!!!!!!!!!!!!!!!!!!!!!!!!!!!!!!!!!!!!!!!!!
!!!!!!!!!!!!!!!!!!!!!!!!!!!!!!!
Success rate is 100 percent (100/100), round-trip min/avg/max = 0/2/4 ms
```

DEVICE CONFIGURATIONS

```
R1#show running-config
Building configuration...

Current configuration : 1217 bytes
!
version 12.4
service timestamps debug datetime msec
service timestamps log datetime msec
no service password-encryption
!
hostname R1
!
boot-start-marker
boot-end-marker
!
no logging console
enable secret 5 $1$ZHZP$BfOgaK4Ei7zfUol9D8zpV/
!
no aaa new-model
no network-clock-participate slot 1
no network-clock-participate wic 0
ip cef
!
no ip domain lookup
ip auth-proxy max-nodata-conns 3
ip admission max-nodata-conns 3
!
ipv6 unicast-routing
!
interface FastEthernet0/0
 no ip address
 loopback
 duplex auto
 speed auto
```

```
 ipv6 address 3FFF:1111:1111:1111::1/64
 ipv6 enable
 ipv6 rip R1-RIP enable
 no keepalive
!
interface Serial0/0
 no ip address
 ipv6 enable
 ipv6 rip R1-RIP enable
 no fair-queue
!
interface Serial0/1
 no ip address
!
ip forward-protocol nd
!
ip http server
no ip http secure-server
!
ipv6 router rip R1-RIP
!
control-plane
!
voice-port 1/0/0
!
voice-port 1/0/1
!
voice-port 1/1/0
!
voice-port 1/1/1
!
line con 0
line aux 0
line vty 0 4
 privilege level 15
 password cisco
 login
!
end

R1#



R2#show running-config
Building configuration...

Current configuration : 1816 bytes
!
version 12.4
service timestamps debug datetime msec
service timestamps log datetime msec
```

```
no service password-encryption
!
hostname R2
!
boot-start-marker
boot-end-marker
!
no logging console
enable secret 5 $1$FsT/$/viPNrSsewWFUCy/QbD5l0
!
no aaa new-model
!
ip cef
no ip domain lookup
!
ipv6 unicast-routing
!
interface Loopback0
 ip address 2.2.2.2 255.255.255.0
!
interface Tunnel0
 no ip address
 ipv6 address FEC0:ABCD::2/64
 tunnel source Loopback0
 tunnel destination 3.3.3.3
 tunnel mode ipv6ip
!
interface FastEthernet0/0
 no ip address
 loopback
 half-duplex
 ipv6 address 3FFF:2222:2222:2222::2/64
 ipv6 enable
 ipv6 rip R2-RIP enable
 no keepalive
!
interface Serial0/0
 no ip address
 ipv6 enable
 ipv6 rip R2-RIP enable
 clock rate 2000000
 no fair-queue
!
interface FastEthernet0/1
 no ip address
 shutdown
 half-duplex
!
interface Serial0/1
 no ip address
 clock rate 2000000
!
```

```
router bgp 5
 bgp router-id 2.2.2.2
 no bgp default ipv4-unicast
 bgp log-neighbor-changes
 neighbor FE80::303:303 remote-as 5
 neighbor FE80::303:303 update-source Tunnel0
 !
 address-family ipv6
  neighbor FE80::303:303 activate
  bgp redistribute-internal
  redistribute connected route-map CONNECTED-TO-BGP
  redistribute rip R2-RIP
  no synchronization
 exit-address-family
!
ip http server
ip forward-protocol nd
ip route 3.3.3.3 255.255.255.255 Serial0/1
!
ipv6 router rip R2-RIP
 redistribute connected metric 1
 redistribute bgp 5 metric 1
!
route-map CONNECTED-TO-BGP permit 10
 match interface Serial0/0
!

control-plane
!
mgcp behavior g729-variants static-pt
!
gatekeeper
 shutdown
!
line con 0
line aux 0
line vty 0 4
 privilege level 15
 password cisco
 login
!
end

R2#


R3#show running-config
Building configuration...

Current configuration : 2039 bytes
!
version 12.4
```

```
service timestamps debug datetime msec
service timestamps log datetime msec
no service password-encryption
!
hostname R3
!
boot-start-marker
boot-end-marker
!
no logging console
enable secret 5 $1$mOsw$hNy9.KzOvGX2XmLabNBOT/
!
no aaa new-model
!
ip cef
no ip domain lookup
!
ipv6 unicast-routing
!
interface Loopback0
 ip address 3.3.3.3 255.255.255.255
!
interface Tunnel0
 no ip address
 ipv6 address FECO:ABCD::3/64
 tunnel source Loopback0
 tunnel destination 2.2.2.2
 tunnel mode ipv6ip
!
interface FastEthernet0/0
 no ip address
 loopback
 half-duplex
 ipv6 address 3FFF:3333:3333:3333::3/64
 no keepalive
!
interface Serial0/0
 no ip address
 ipv6 enable
 ipv6 ospf 3 area 0
 no fair-queue
!
interface Ethernet0/1
 no ip address
 shutdown
 half-duplex
!
interface Serial0/1
 no ip address
 clock rate 2000000
!
interface Ethernet1/0
 no ip address
 shutdown
```

```
  half-duplex
 !
 interface Serial1/0
  no ip address
  shutdown
 !
 interface Serial1/1
  no ip address
 !
 router bgp 5
  bgp router-id 3.3.3.3
  no bgp default ipv4-unicast
  bgp log-neighbor-changes
  neighbor FE80::202:202 remote-as 5
  neighbor FE80::202:202 update-source Tunnel0
  !
  address-family ipv6
   neighbor FE80::202:202 activate
   bgp redistribute-internal
   network 3FFF:3333:3333:3333::/64
   redistribute connected route-map CONNECTED-TO-BGP
   redistribute ospf 3
   no synchronization
  exit-address-family
 !
 ip http server
 ip forward-protocol nd
 ip route 2.2.2.2 255.255.255.255 Serial1/1
 !
 ipv6 router ospf 3
  router-id 3.3.3.3
  log-adjacency-changes
  redistribute connected
  redistribute bgp 5
 !
 route-map CONNECTED-TO-BGP permit 10
  match interface Serial0/0
 !
 control-plane
 !
 mgcp behavior g729-variants static-pt
 !
 gatekeeper
  shutdown
 !
 line con 0
 line aux 0
 line vty 0 4
  privilege level 15
  password cisco
  login
 !
 end
 R3#
```

```
R4#show running-config
Building configuration...

Current configuration : 1283 bytes
!
version 12.4
service timestamps debug datetime msec
service timestamps log datetime msec
no service password-encryption
!
hostname R4
!
boot-start-marker
boot-end-marker
!
no logging console
enable secret 5 $1$M/kd$Eb360Ygk4rDpv7JtJeRbP.
!
no aaa new-model
no network-clock-participate slot 1
no network-clock-participate wic 0
ip cef
!
ip auth-proxy max-nodata-conns 3
ip admission max-nodata-conns 3
!
ipv6 unicast-routing
!
interface FastEthernet0/0
 no ip address
 loopback
 duplex auto
 speed auto
 ipv6 address 3FFF:4444:4444:4444::4/64
 ipv6 enable
 ipv6 ospf 4 area 1
 no keepalive
!
interface Serial0/0
 no ip address
 ipv6 enable
 ipv6 ospf 4 area 0
 no fair-queue
 clock rate 2000000
!
interface Serial0/1
 no ip address
 shutdown
!
interface Serial0/2
 no ip address
 shutdown
```

```
!
ip forward-protocol nd
!
ip http server
no ip http secure-server
!
ipv6 router ospf 4
 router-id 4.4.4.4
 log-adjacency-changes
!
control-plane
!
voice-port 1/0/0
!
voice-port 1/0/1
!
voice-port 1/1/0
!
voice-port 1/1/1
!
line con 0
line aux 0
line vty 0 4
 privilege level 15
 password cisco
 login
!
end

R4#
```

LAB 7

IP SLA Operations and PBR Implementation

Lab Objective:

The objective of this lab exercise is for you to learn and understand how to implement and verify Cisco IP SLA operations and Policy Based Routing solutions in Cisco IOS software.

Lab Topology:

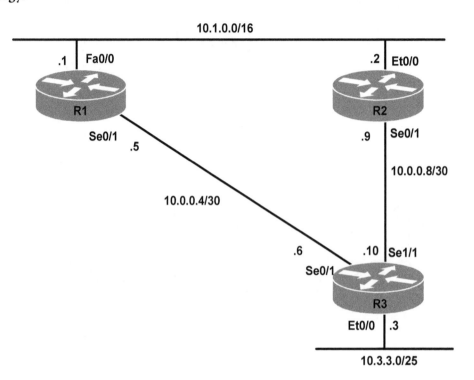

IMPORTANT NOTE:

If you are using the www.howtonetwork.net racks, please bring up the LAN interfaces connected to the routers by issuing the no shutdown command on the connected switches. If you are using a home lab with no switches, you can bring up the LAN interfaces using the following configurations on your routers:

```
interface fastethernet 0/0
 no keepalive
 loopback
 no shutdown
```

Alternately, you can simply connect the interfaces to a hub if you have one.

Task 1

Configure IP addressing on all routers as illustrated in the topology

Task 2

Configure IP SLA operation 1 on R3 to ping address 10.0.0.5 every 5 seconds. Configure IP SLA operation 2 to ping address 10.0.0.9 every 5 seconds. Verify your configuration

Task 3

Configure a default route on both R1 and R2 pointing to R3

Task 4

Configure two default routes on R3 as follows:
- The primary route should forward traffic via R1
- The primary route should be removed from the RIB if IP SLA operation 1 fails
- The secondary route should forward traffic via R2
- The secondary route should be removed from the RIB if IP SLA operation 2 fails

Task 5

Configure Cisco IOS Policy Based Routing on R3 as follows:
- Forward all 100-byte packets from R3s LAN to 10.1.0.0/16 via R1
- Forward all 200-byte packets from R3s LAN to 10.1.0.0/16 via R2

Task 6

Configure Cisco IOS Policy Based Routing so that all Telnet traffic originated on the local router to any destination is forwarded via R2. IP SLA operation 2 should be used to check for the status of this next hop. If this path is unavailable, only then should R1 be used. IP SLA operation 1 should be used to check for the status of this next hop. Verify your configuration using the appropriate commands

LAB VALIDATION

Task 1

```
R1#show ip interface brief
Interface        IP-Address    OK? Method Status        Protocol
FastEthernet0/0  10.1.0.1      YES manual up            up
Serial0/1        10.0.0.5      YES NVRAM  up            up
```

```
R2#show ip interface brief
Interface         IP-Address    OK? Method Status          Protocol
Ethernet0/0       10.1.0.2      YES manual up              up
Serial0/0         10.0.0.9      YES manual up              up

R3#show ip interface brief
Interface         IP-Address    OK? Method Status          Protocol
Ethernet0/0       10.3.3.3      YES manual up              up
Serial0/1         10.0.0.6      YES NVRAM  up              up
Serial1/1         10.0.0.10     YES NVRAM  up              up
```

Task 2

```
R3(config)#ip sla monitor 1
R3(config-sla-monitor)#type echo protocol ipIcmpEcho 10.0.0.5
R3(config-sla-monitor-echo)#frequency 5
R3(config-sla-monitor-echo)#exit
R3(config)#ip sla monitor 2
R3(config-sla-monitor)#type echo protocol ipIcmpEcho 10.0.0.9
R3(config-sla-monitor-echo)#frequency 5 ·
R3(config-sla-monitor-echo)#exit
R3(config)#ip sla monitor schedule 1 start-time now life forever
R3(config)#ip sla monitor schedule 2 start-time now life forever
```

Following this configuration, verify your implementation using the show ip sla monitor configuration command as follows:

```
R3#show ip sla monitor configuration
SA Agent, Infrastructure Engine-II
Entry number: 1
Owner:
Tag:
Type of operation to perform: echo
Target address: 10.0.0.5
Request size (ARR data portion): 28
Operation timeout (milliseconds): 5000
Type Of Service parameters: 0x0
Verify data: No
Operation frequency (seconds): 5
Next Scheduled Start Time: Start Time already passed
Group Scheduled : FALSE
Life (seconds): Forever
Entry Ageout (seconds): never
Recurring (Starting Everyday): FALSE
Status of entry (SNMP RowStatus): Active
Threshold (milliseconds): 5000
Number of statistic hours kept: 2
Number of statistic distribution buckets kept: 1
Statistic distribution interval (milliseconds): 20
```

```
Number of history Lives kept: 0
Number of history Buckets kept: 15
History Filter Type: None
Enhanced History:

Entry number: 2
Owner:
Tag:
Type of operation to perform: echo
Target address: 10.0.0.9
Request size (ARR data portion): 28
Operation timeout (milliseconds): 5000
Type Of Service parameters: 0x0
Verify data: No
Operation frequency (seconds): 5
Next Scheduled Start Time: Start Time already passed
Group Scheduled : FALSE
Life (seconds): Forever
Entry Ageout (seconds): never
Recurring (Starting Everyday): FALSE
Status of entry (SNMP RowStatus): Active
Threshold (milliseconds): 5000
Number of statistic hours kept: 2
Number of statistic distribution buckets kept: 1
Statistic distribution interval (milliseconds): 20
Number of history Lives kept: 0
Number of history Buckets kept: 15
History Filter Type: None
Enhanced History:
```

Additionally, use the show ip sla monitor statistics command to view the current status (statistics) of the operation as follows:

```
R3#show ip sla monitor statistics
Round trip time (RTT)    Index 1
        Latest RTT: 1 ms
Latest operation start time: *13:22:45.631 UTC Fri Mar 1 2002
Latest operation return code: OK
Number of successes: 53
Number of failures: 0
Operation time to live: Forever

Round trip time (RTT)    Index 2
        Latest RTT: 1 ms
Latest operation start time: *13:22:48.923 UTC Fri Mar 1 2002
Latest operation return code: OK
Number of successes: 53
Number of failures: 0
Operation time to live: Forever
```

Task 3

```
R1(config)#ip route 0.0.0.0 0.0.0.0 serial 0/1


R2(config)#ip route 0.0.0.0 0.0.0.0 serial 0/1
```

Task 4

```
R3(config)#track 1 rtr 1
R3(config-track)#exit
R3(config)#track 2 rtr 2
R3(config-track)#exit
R3(config)#ip route 0.0.0.0 0.0.0.0 10.0.0.5 track 1
R3(config)#ip route 0.0.0.0 0.0.0.0 10.0.0.9 2 track 2
```

Verify your tracking configuration using the show track command as follows:

```
R3#show track
Track 1
  Response Time Reporter 1 state
  State is Up
    1 change, last change 00:00:27
  Latest operation return code: OK
  Latest RTT (millisecs) 1
  Tracked by:
    STATIC-IP-ROUTING 0
Track 2
  Response Time Reporter 2 state
  State is Up
    1 change, last change 00:00:19
  Latest operation return code: OK
  Latest RTT (millisecs) 1
  Tracked by:
    STATIC-IP-ROUTING 0
```

Additionally, also verify the tracked static routes using the show ip route track-table command as follows:

```
R3#show ip route track-table
 ip route 0.0.0.0 0.0.0.0 10.0.0.5 track 1 state is [up]
 ip route 0.0.0.0 0.0.0.0 10.0.0.9 2 track 2 state is [up]
```

Because both routes are up, only the primary route should be installed in the RIB:

```
R3#show ip route
Codes: C - connected, S - static, R - RIP, M - mobile, B - BGP
       D - EIGRP, EX - EIGRP external, O - OSPF, IA - OSPF inter area
```

```
       N1 - OSPF NSSA external type 1, N2 - OSPF NSSA external type 2
       E1 - OSPF external type 1, E2 - OSPF external type 2
       i - IS-IS, su - IS-IS summary, L1 - IS-IS level-1, L2 - IS-IS level-2
       ia - IS-IS inter area, * - candidate default, U - per-user static route
       o - ODR, P - periodic downloaded static route

Gateway of last resort is 10.0.0.5 to network 0.0.0.0

     10.0.0.0/8 is variably subnetted, 3 subnets, 2 masks
C       10.0.0.8/30 is directly connected, Serial1/1
C       10.3.3.0/24 is directly connected, Ethernet0/0
C       10.0.0.4/30 is directly connected, Serial0/1
S*    0.0.0.0/0 [1/0] via 10.0.0.5
```

To verify the dynamic redundancy, simply shut the Serial0/1 interface on R3:

```
R3(config)#interface serial 0/1
R3(config-if)#shutdown
R3(config-if)#end
```

Following this change, R3 shows the following RIB entry for the default route:

```
R3#show ip route
Codes: C - connected, S - static, R - RIP, M - mobile, B - BGP
       D - EIGRP, EX - EIGRP external, O - OSPF, IA - OSPF inter area
       N1 - OSPF NSSA external type 1, N2 - OSPF NSSA external type 2
       E1 - OSPF external type 1, E2 - OSPF external type 2
       i - IS-IS, su - IS-IS summary, L1 - IS-IS level-1, L2 - IS-IS level-2
       ia - IS-IS inter area, * - candidate default, U - per-user static route
       o - ODR, P - periodic downloaded static route

Gateway of last resort is 10.0.0.9 to network 0.0.0.0

     10.0.0.0/8 is variably subnetted, 2 subnets, 2 masks
C       10.0.0.8/30 is directly connected, Serial1/1
C       10.3.3.0/24 is directly connected, Ethernet0/0
S*    0.0.0.0/0 [2/0] via 10.0.0.9
```

Again, you can use the show ip route track-table command to validate as follows:

```
R3#show ip route track-table
 ip route 0.0.0.0 0.0.0.0 10.0.0.5 track 1 state is [down]
 ip route 0.0.0.0 0.0.0.0 10.0.0.9 2 track 2 state is [up]
```

Task 5

When implementing PBR, keep in mind that the same ACL can be referenced in multiple route map match statements, or even in multiple route maps as follows:

```
R3(config)#access-list 100 permit ip 10.3.3.0 0.0.0.127 10.1.0.0 0.0.255.255
R3(config)#route-map ROUTE-PBR permit 10
R3(config-route-map)#match ip address 100
R3(config-route-map)#match length 100 100
R3(config-route-map)#set ip next-hop 10.0.0.5
R3(config-route-map)#exit
R3(config)#route-map ROUTE-PBR permit 20
R3(config-route-map)#match ip address 100
R3(config-route-map)#match length 200 200
R3(config-route-map)#set ip next-hop 10.0.0.9
R3(config-route-map)#exit
R3(config)#interface ethernet 0/0
R3(config-if)#ip policy route-map ROUTE-PBR
R3(config-if)#end
```

Following this configuration, verify your PBR configuration using the `show route-map` command as illustrated below:

```
R3#show route-map
route-map ROUTE-PBR, permit, sequence 10
  Match clauses:
    ip address (access-lists): 100
    length 100 100
  Set clauses:
    ip next-hop 10.0.0.5
  Policy routing matches: 0 packets, 0 bytes
route-map ROUTE-PBR, permit, sequence 20
  Match clauses:
    ip address (access-lists): 100
    length 200 200
  Set clauses:
    ip next-hop 10.0.0.9
  Policy routing matches: 0 packets, 0 bytes
```

For further validation, use the `ping` command to send traffic to the 10.1.0.0/16 subnet using 100-bye (default) pings and then 200-byte pings. Enable PBR debugging using the `debug ip policy` command while doing so.

Task 6

```
R3(config)#access-list 101 permit tcp any any eq telnet
R3(config)#route-map TELNET-POLICY permit 10
R3(config-route-map)#match ip address 101
```

```
R3(config-route-map)#set ip next-hop verify-availability 10.0.0.9 1 track 2
R3(config-route-map)#set ip next-hop verify-availability 10.0.0.5 2 track 1
R3(config-route-map)#exit
R3(config)#ip local policy route-map TELNET-POLICY
R3(config)#end
```

Next, use the show route-map command to verify your configuration as follows:

```
R3#show route-map
route-map TELNET-POLICY, permit, sequence 10
  Match clauses:
    ip address (access-lists): 101
  Set clauses:
    ip next-hop verify-availability 10.0.0.9 1 track 2  [up]
    ip next-hop verify-availability 10.0.0.5 2 track 1  [up]
  Policy routing matches: 22 packets, 1268 bytes
```

And finally, for further validation, you can enable PBR debugging via the debug ip policy command and then initiating a Telnet session from R3 to either R1 or R2 as follows:

```
R3#debug ip policy
Policy routing debugging is on
R3#
R3#
R3#telnet 10.1.0.1
Trying 10.1.0.1 ...
*Mar 1 13:58:02.903: IP: s=10.0.0.6 (local), d=10.1.0.1, len 44, policy match
*Mar 1 13:58:02.907: IP: route map TELNET-POLICY, item 10, permit
*Mar 1 13:58:02.907: IP: s=10.0.0.6 (local), d=10.1.0.1 (Serial1/1), len 44,
 policy routed
*Mar 1 13:58:02.907: IP: local to Serial1/1 10.0.0.9
```

DEVICE CONFIGURATIONS

```
R1#show running-config
Building configuration...

Current configuration : 1016 bytes
!
version 12.4
service timestamps debug datetime msec
service timestamps log datetime msec
no service password-encryption
!
hostname R1
!
boot-start-marker
```

```
boot-end-marker
!
no logging console
enable secret 5 $1$ZHZP$BfOgaK4Ei7zfUol9D8zpV/
!
no aaa new-model
no network-clock-participate slot 1
no network-clock-participate wic 0
ip cef
!
no ip domain lookup
ip auth-proxy max-nodata-conns 3
ip admission max-nodata-conns 3
!
ipv6 unicast-routing
!
interface FastEthernet0/0
 ip address 10.1.0.1 255.255.0.0
 duplex auto
 speed auto
!
interface Serial0/0
 no ip address
 shutdown
 no fair-queue
!
interface Serial0/1
 ip address 10.0.0.5 255.255.255.252
!
ip forward-protocol nd
ip route 0.0.0.0 0.0.0.0 Serial0/1
!
ip http server
no ip http secure-server
!
control-plane
!
voice-port 1/0/0
!
voice-port 1/0/1
!
voice-port 1/1/0
!
voice-port 1/1/1
!
line con 0
line aux 0
line vty 0 4
 privilege level 15
 password cisco
 login
!
end
R1#
```

```
R2#show running-config
Building configuration...

Current configuration : 927 bytes
!
version 12.4
service timestamps debug datetime msec
service timestamps log datetime msec
no service password-encryption
!
hostname R2
!
boot-start-marker
boot-end-marker
!
no logging console
enable secret 5 $1$FsT/$/viPNrSsewWFUCy/QbD5lO
!
no aaa new-model
!
ip cef
no ip domain lookup
!
ipv6 unicast-routing
!
interface Ethernet0/0
 bandwidth 100000
 ip address 10.1.0.2 255.255.0.0
 full-duplex
!
interface Serial0/0
 no ip address
 shutdown
 clock rate 2000000
 no fair-queue
!
interface Ethernet0/1
 no ip address
 shutdown
 half-duplex
!
interface Serial0/1
 ip address 10.0.0.9 255.255.255.252
 clock rate 2000000
!
ip http server
ip forward-protocol nd
ip route 0.0.0.0 0.0.0.0 Serial0/1
!
control-plane
!
mgcp behavior g729-variants static-pt
```

```
!
gatekeeper
 shutdown
!
!
line con 0
line aux 0
line vty 0 4
 privilege level 15
 password cisco
 login
!
end

R2#


R3#show running-config
Building configuration...

Current configuration : 2058 bytes
!
version 12.4
service timestamps debug datetime msec
service timestamps log datetime msec
no service password-encryption
!
hostname R3
!
boot-start-marker
boot-end-marker
!
logging buffered 4096 debugging
no logging console
enable secret 5 $1$mOsw$hNy9.KzOvGX2XmLabNBOT/
!
no aaa new-model
!
ip cef
no ip domain lookup
ip host R1 10.0.0.5
ip host R2 10.0.0.9
ip host R4 10.0.0.14
!
ip sla monitor 1
 type echo protocol ipIcmpEcho 10.0.0.5
 frequency 5
ip sla monitor schedule 1 life forever start-time now
ip sla monitor 2
 type echo protocol ipIcmpEcho 10.0.0.9
 frequency 5
ip sla monitor schedule 2 life forever start-time now
```

```
ipv6 unicast-routing
!
track 1 rtr 1
!
track 2 rtr 2
!
interface Ethernet0/0
 bandwidth 100000
 ip address 10.3.3.3 255.255.255.0
 ip policy route-map ROUTE-PBR
 full-duplex
!
interface Serial0/0
 no ip address
 shutdown
 no fair-queue
!
interface Ethernet0/1
 no ip address
 shutdown
 half-duplex
!
interface Serial0/1
 ip address 10.0.0.6 255.255.255.252
 clock rate 2000000
!
interface Ethernet1/0
 no ip address
 shutdown
 half-duplex
!
interface Serial1/0
 no ip address
 shutdown
!
interface Serial1/1
 ip address 10.0.0.10 255.255.255.252
!
ip local policy route-map TELNET-POLICY
ip http server
ip forward-protocol nd
ip route 0.0.0.0 0.0.0.0 10.0.0.5 track 1
ip route 0.0.0.0 0.0.0.0 10.0.0.9 2 track 2
!
access-list 100 permit ip 10.3.3.0 0.0.0.127 10.1.0.0 0.0.255.255
access-list 101 permit tcp any any eq telnet
!
route-map TELNET-POLICY permit 10
 match ip address 101
 set ip next-hop verify-availability 10.0.0.9 1 track 2
 set ip next-hop verify-availability 10.0.0.5 2 track 1
!
```

```
route-map ROUTE-PBR permit 10
 match ip address 100
 match length 100 100
 set ip next-hop 10.0.0.5
!
route-map ROUTE-PBR permit 20
 match ip address 100
 match length 200 200
 set ip next-hop 10.0.0.9
!
control-plane
!
mgcp behavior g729-variants static-pt
!
!
gatekeeper
 shutdown
!
line con 0
line aux 0
line vty 0 4
 privilege level 15
 password cisco
 login
!
end

R3#
```

LAB 8

OSPF Multi-Technology Lab

Lab Objective:

The objective of this lab exercise is for you to learn and understand how to implement advanced OSPF routing configurations in Cisco IOS software.

Lab Topology:

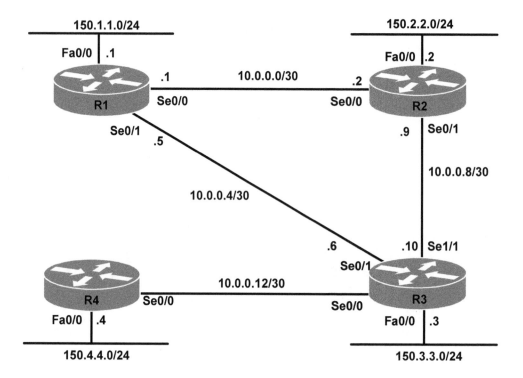

IMPORTANT NOTE:

If you are using the www.howtonetwork.net racks, please bring up the LAN interfaces connected to the routers by issuing the no shutdown command on the connected switches. If you are using a home lab with no switches, you can bring up the LAN interfaces using the following configurations on your routers:

```
interface fastethernet 0/0
 no keepalive
 loopback
 no shutdown
```

Alternately, you can simply connect the interfaces to a hub if you have one.

Task 1

Configure IP addressing on all routers as illustrated in the topology. Additionally, configure the following the following Loopback interfaces on all routers:

Router	Loopback	Loopback Interface Address/Mask
R1	0	1.1.1.1/32
R2	0	2.2.2.2/32
R3	0	3.3.3.3/32
R4	0	4.4.4.4/32

Task 2

Configure OSPF area 0 between R1 and R2 for the 10.0.0.0/30 subnet. Advertise the Loopback 0 subnets of both routers in area 0. Additionally, advertise the 150.2.2.0/24 subnet on R2 in area 0. Do NOT advertise the 150.1.1.0/24 subnet via OSPF. Use the Loopback 0 IP address as the router ID for all OSPF processes.

Task 3

Configure OSPF area 1 between R1 and R3 for the 10.0.0.4/30 subnet. Advertise the Loopback 0 interface of R3 in area 1. Use the Loopback 0 IP address as the router ID for all OSPF processes.

Task 4

Configure OSPF area 2 between R2 and R3 for the 10.0.0.8/30 subnet. This area should also be configured as a totally stubby OSPF area. R2 should advertise a default route into this area. Use the Loopback 0 IP address as the router ID for all OSPF processes.

Task 5

Configure OSPF area 4 between R3 and R1. Advertise the Loopback 0 subnet of R1 in area 4. Additionally, advertise the 150.1.1.0/24 and 150.2.2.0/24 subnets via OSPF; however, do NOT use any network commands when doing so. These prefixes should be advertised as Type 1 external OSPF routes and should have a route tag of 333. Verify your configuration using the appropriate commands. Use the Loopback 0 IP address as the router ID for all OSPF processes.

Task 6

Based on the current configuration, R3 has two connections to the OSPF backbone. Configure a redundant solution that will allow area 4 connectivity to the OSPF backbone in the event that either the Serial0/1 or Serial1/1 interfaces on R3 fails. Verify your solution by disabling each of these interfaces and ensuring that R4 is still reachable from all other routers in the domain.

Task 7

Configure R1 so that all routers can reach the 150.1.1.0/24 subnet. Do NOT advertise this subnet via OSPF. Consider alternative solutions instead.

Task 8

Configure interface-based plain text authentication for area 4. Use a password of your choosing. Verify your configuration.

Task 9

Configure MD5 authentication for area 0. Verify that all routers are still reachable from each other following this configuration. Use a password of your choosing.

Task 10

Protect the Link State Database on all routers in the network by preventing them from accepting more than 100 Link State Advertisements (LSAs)

LAB VALIDATION

Task 1

```
R1#show ip interface brief
Interface          IP-Address      OK? Method Status          Protocol
FastEthernet0/0    150.1.1.1       YES NVRAM  up              up
Serial0/0          10.0.0.1        YES NVRAM  up              up
Serial0/1          10.0.0.5        YES NVRAM  up              up
Loopback0          1.1.1.1         YES NVRAM  up              up

R2#show ip interface brief
Interface          IP-Address      OK? Method Status          Protocol
FastEthernet0/0    150.2.2.2       YES NVRAM  up              up
Serial0/0          10.0.0.2        YES NVRAM  up              up
Serial0/1          10.0.0.9        YES NVRAM  up              up
Loopback0          2.2.2.2         YES NVRAM  up              up
```

```
R3#show ip interface brief
Interface         IP-Address     OK? Method Status         Protocol
FastEthernet0/0   150.3.3.3      YES NVRAM  up             up
Serial0/0         10.0.0.13      YES NVRAM  up             up
Serial0/1         10.0.0.6       YES NVRAM  up             up
Serial1/1         10.0.0.10      YES NVRAM  up             up
Loopback0         3.3.3.3        YES NVRAM  up             up

R4#show ip interface brief
Interface         IP-Address     OK? Method Status         Protocol
FastEthernet0/0   150.4.4.4      YES NVRAM  up             up
Serial0/0         10.0.0.14      YES NVRAM  up             up
Loopback0         4.4.4.4        YES NVRAM  up             up
```

Task 2

```
R1(config)#router ospf 1
R1(config-router)#router-id 1.1.1.1
R1(config-router)#exit
R1(config)#interface serial 0/0
R1(config-if)#ip ospf 1 area 0
R1(config-if)#exit
R1(config)#interface loopback 0
R1(config-if)#ip ospf 1 area 0
R1(config-if)#exit

R2(config)#router ospf 2
R2(config-router)#network 10.0.0.0 0.0.0.3 area 0
R2(config-router)#network 2.2.2.2 0.0.0.0 area 0
R2(config-router)#network 150.2.2.0 0.0.0.255 area 0
R2(config-router)#router-id 2.2.2.2
R2(config-router)#exit
```

Following this configuration, use the show ip ospf interface and the show ip ospf neighbors commands to validate your configuration:

```
R2#show ip ospf interface brief
Interface    PID   Area      IP Address/Mask     Cost   State Nbrs F/C
Lo0          2     0         2.2.2.2/24          1      LOOP  0/0
Fa0/0        2     0         150.2.2.2/24        1      WAIT  0/0
Se0/0        2     0         10.0.0.2/30         64     P2P   1/1

R2#show ip ospf neighbor

Neighbor ID    Pri   State        Dead Time   Address      Interface
1.1.1.1          0   FULL/  -     00:00:30    10.0.0.1     Serial0/0
```

NOTE: The same commands would also be used on R1.

Task 3

```
R1(config)#interface s0/1
R1(config-if)#ip ospf 1 area 1
R1(config-if)#end

R3(config)#router ospf 3
R3(config-router)#router-id 3.3.3.3
R3(config-router)#exit
R3(config)#interface serial 0/1
R3(config-if)#ip ospf 3 area 1
R3(config-if)#exit
R3(config)#interface loopback 0
R3(config-if)#ip ospf 3 area 1
R3(config-if)#exit
```

Again, following this configuration, use the show ip ospf interface and the show ip ospf neighbors commands to validate your configuration:

```
R3#show ip ospf interface | section Serial0/1
Serial0/1 is up, line protocol is up
  Internet Address 10.0.0.6/30, Area 1
  Process ID 3, Router ID 3.3.3.3, Network Type POINT_TO_POINT, Cost: 64
  Enabled by interface config, including secondary ip addresses
  Transmit Delay is 1 sec, State POINT_TO_POINT
  Timer intervals configured, Hello 10, Dead 40, Wait 40, Retransmit 5
    oob-resync timeout 40
    Hello due in 00:00:09
  Supports Link-local Signaling (LLS)
  Index 1/1, flood queue length 0
  Next 0x0(0)/0x0(0)
  Last flood scan length is 1, maximum is 1
  Last flood scan time is 0 msec, maximum is 0 msec
  Neighbor Count is 1, Adjacent neighbor count is 1
    Adjacent with neighbor 1.1.1.1
  Suppress hello for 0 neighbor(s)
```

Task 4

```
R2(config)#router ospf 2
R2(config-router)#network 10.0.0.8 0.0.0.3 area 2
R2(config-router)#area 2 stub no-summary
R2(config-router)#exit

R3(config)#router ospf 3
R3(config-router)#area 2 stub
R3(config-router)#exit
R3(config)#interface serial 1/1
R3(config-if)#ip ospf 3 area 2
R3(config-if)#end
```

Following this configuration, use the show ip ospf command to verify that the areas are indeed configured correctly:

```
R2#show ip ospf
 Routing Process "ospf 2" with ID 2.2.2.2
 Start time: 01:04:07.968, Time elapsed: 00:12:11.920
 Supports only single TOS(TOS0) routes
 Supports opaque LSA
 Supports Link-local Signaling (LLS)
 Supports area transit capability
 It is an area border router
 Router is not originating router-LSAs with maximum metric
 Initial SPF schedule delay 5000 msecs
 Minimum hold time between two consecutive SPFs 10000 msecs
 Maximum wait time between two consecutive SPFs 10000 msecs
 Incremental-SPF disabled
 Minimum LSA interval 5 secs
 Minimum LSA arrival 1000 msecs
 LSA group pacing timer 240 secs
 Interface flood pacing timer 33 msecs
 Retransmission pacing timer 66 msecs
 Number of external LSA 0. Checksum Sum 0x000000
 Number of opaque AS LSA 0. Checksum Sum 0x000000
 Number of DCbitless external and opaque AS LSA 0
 Number of DoNotAge external and opaque AS LSA 0
 Number of areas in this router is 2. 1 normal 1 stub 0 nssa
 Number of areas transit capable is 0
 External flood list length 0
    Area BACKBONE(0)
        Number of interfaces in this area is 3 (1 loopback)
        Area has no authentication
        SPF algorithm last executed 00:01:27.060 ago
        SPF algorithm executed 7 times
        Area ranges are
        Number of LSA 5. Checksum Sum 0x01AF2D
        Number of opaque link LSA 0. Checksum Sum 0x000000
        Number of DCbitless LSA 0
        Number of indication LSA 0
        Number of DoNotAge LSA 0
        Flood list length 0
    Area 2
        Number of interfaces in this area is 1
        It is a stub area, no summary LSA in this area
          generates stub default route with cost 1
        Area has no authentication
        SPF algorithm last executed 00:01:27.060 ago
        SPF algorithm executed 3 times
        Area ranges are
        Number of LSA 2. Checksum Sum 0x00BA4E
        Number of opaque link LSA 0. Checksum Sum 0x000000
        Number of DCbitless LSA 0
```

```
Number of indication LSA 0
Number of DoNotAge LSA 0
Flood list length 0
```

At this point, the routing table on router R3 should show the following dynamic route entries:

```
R3#show ip route
Codes: C - connected, S - static, R - RIP, M - mobile, B - BGP
       D - EIGRP, EX - EIGRP external, O - OSPF, IA - OSPF inter area
       N1 - OSPF NSSA external type 1, N2 - OSPF NSSA external type 2
       E1 - OSPF external type 1, E2 - OSPF external type 2
       i - IS-IS, su - IS-IS summary, L1 - IS-IS level-1, L2 - IS-IS level-2
       ia - IS-IS inter area, * - candidate default, U - per-user static route
       o - ODR, P - periodic downloaded static route

Gateway of last resort is 10.0.0.9 to network 0.0.0.0

     1.0.0.0/32 is subnetted, 1 subnets
O IA    1.1.1.1 [110/65] via 10.0.0.5, 00:00:21, Serial0/1
     2.0.0.0/32 is subnetted, 1 subnets
O IA    2.2.2.2 [110/129] via 10.0.0.5, 00:00:21, Serial0/1
     3.0.0.0/32 is subnetted, 1 subnets
C       3.3.3.3 is directly connected, Loopback0
     10.0.0.0/30 is subnetted, 4 subnets
C       10.0.0.8 is directly connected, Serial1/1
C       10.0.0.12 is directly connected, Serial0/0
O IA    10.0.0.0 [110/128] via 10.0.0.5, 00:00:21, Serial0/1
C       10.0.0.4 is directly connected, Serial0/1
     150.2.0.0/24 is subnetted, 1 subnets
O IA    150.2.2.0 [110/129] via 10.0.0.5, 00:00:22, Serial0/1
     150.3.0.0/24 is subnetted, 1 subnets
C       150.3.3.0 is directly connected, Ethernet0/0
O*IA 0.0.0.0/0 [110/65] via 10.0.0.9, 00:00:23, Serial1/1
```

Task 5

```
R3(config)#interface serial 0/0
R3(config-if)#ip ospf 3 area 4
R3(config-if)#exit
R3(config)#route-map LAN-SUBNET permit 10
R3(config-route-map)#match interface fastethernet 0/0
R3(config-route-map)#set metric-type type-1
R3(config-route-map)#set tag 333
R3(config-route-map)#exit
R3(config)#router ospf 3
R3(config-router)#redistribute connected subnets route-map LAN-SUBNET
R3(config-router)#end
```

```
R4(config)#router ospf 4
R4(config-router)#router-id 4.4.4.4
R4(config-router)#network 10.0.0.12 0.0.0.3 area 4
R4(config-router)#network 4.4.4.4 0.0.0.0 area 4
R4(config-router)#redistribute connected subnets metric-type 1 tag 333
R4(config-router)#end
```

NOTE: The two variant configurations are used to illustrate how the metric type and route tag can be specified in more than one way when using OSPF.

Following this configuration, use the show ip ospf database external command to verify that the metric type and route tag have been set as configured.

```
R4#show ip ospf database external 150.4.4.0

            OSPF Router with ID (4.4.4.4) (Process ID 4)

            Type-5 AS External Link States

  LS age: 166
  Options: (No TOS-capability, DC)
  LS Type: AS External Link
  Link State ID: 150.4.4.0 (External Network Number )
  Advertising Router: 4.4.4.4
  LS Seq Number: 80000001
  Checksum: 0x6AB9
  Length: 36
  Network Mask: /24
        Metric Type: 1 (Comparable directly to link state metric)
        TOS: 0
        Metric: 20
        Forward Address: 0.0.0.0
        External Route Tag: 333
```

The same command on R3 would also reflect the same:

```
R3#show ip ospf database external 150.3.3.0

            OSPF Router with ID (3.3.3.3) (Process ID 3)

            Type-5 AS External Link States

  LS age: 381
  Options: (No TOS-capability, DC)
  LS Type: AS External Link
  Link State ID: 150.3.3.0 (External Network Number )
  Advertising Router: 3.3.3.3
```

```
LS Seq Number: 80000001
Checksum: 0x9F8A
Length: 36
Network Mask: /24
      Metric Type: 1 (Comparable directly to link state metric)
      TOS: 0
      Metric: 20
      Forward Address: 0.0.0.0
      External Route Tag: 333
```

Task 6

This task requires both a Virtual Link and a Tunnel. The Virtual Link can only be configured across a normal area (area 1). However, because area 2 is a stub area, a Virtual Link cannot be configured. Therefore, a simple GRE tunnel must be configured across this area and placed in OSPF area 0 (the backbone). This is implemented as follows:

```
R1(config)#router ospf 1
R1(config-router)#area 1 virtual-link 3.3.3.3
R1(config-router)#exit

R2(config)#interface tunnel 0
R2(config-if)#description 'Backbone Tunnel Across Stub Area'
R2(config-if)#tunnel source serial 0/1
R2(config-if)#tunnel destination 10.0.0.10
R2(config-if)#ip address 172.16.1.2 255.255.255.0
R2(config-if)#exit
R2(config)#router ospf 2
R2(config-router)#network 172.16.1.0 0.0.0.255 area 0
R2(config-router)#exit


R3(config)#router ospf 3
R3(config-router)#area 1 virtual-link 1.1.1.1
R3(config-router)#exit
R3(config)#interface tunnel 0
R3(config-if)#description 'Backbone Tunnel Across Stub Area'
R3(config-if)#tunnel source serial 1/1
R3(config-if)#tunnel destination 10.0.0.9
R3(config-if)#ip address 172.16.1.3 255.255.255.0
R3(config-if)#ip ospf 3 area 0
R3(config-if)#exit
```

NOTE: If you use Loopback interfaces for the tunnel, this will result in recursive routing.

Following this configuration, first verify OSPF adjacencies across the both the Virtual Link and the tunnel interfaces using the show ip ospf neighbor, show ip ospf virtual-links, and show interfaces tunnel 0 commands

```
R3#show ip ospf neighbor

Neighbor ID     Pri   State       Dead Time   Address       Interface
2.2.2.2          0    FULL/  -    00:00:37    172.16.1.2    Tunnel0
1.1.1.1          0    FULL/  -    -           10.0.0.5      OSPF_VL0
1.1.1.1          0    FULL/  -    00:00:38    10.0.0.5      Serial0/1
2.2.2.2          0    FULL/  -    00:00:36    10.0.0.9      Serial1/1
4.4.4.4          0    FULL/  -    00:00:31    10.0.0.14     Serial0/0


R3#show ip ospf virtual-links
Virtual Link OSPF_VL0 to router 1.1.1.1 is up
  Run as demand circuit
  DoNotAge LSA allowed.
  Transit area 1, via interface Serial0/1, Cost of using 64
  Transmit Delay is 1 sec, State POINT_TO_POINT,
  Timer intervals configured, Hello 10, Dead 40, Wait 40, Retransmit 5
    Hello due in 00:00:02
    Adjacency State FULL (Hello suppressed)
    Index 1/4, retransmission queue length 0, number of retransmission 0
    First 0x0(0)/0x0(0) Next 0x0(0)/0x0(0)
    Last retransmission scan length is 0, maximum is 0
    Last retransmission scan time is 0 msec, maximum is 0 msec


R3#show ip ospf interface tunnel 0
Tunnel0 is up, line protocol is up
  Internet Address 172.16.1.3/24, Area 0
  Process ID 3, Router ID 3.3.3.3, Network Type POINT_TO_POINT, Cost: 11111
  Enabled by interface config, including secondary ip addresses
  Transmit Delay is 1 sec, State POINT_TO_POINT
  Timer intervals configured, Hello 10, Dead 40, Wait 40, Retransmit 5
    oob-resync timeout 40
    Hello due in 00:00:05
  Supports Link-local Signaling (LLS)
  Index 2/6, flood queue length 0
  Next 0x0(0)/0x0(0)
  Last flood scan length is 1, maximum is 1
  Last flood scan time is 0 msec, maximum is 0 msec
  Neighbor Count is 1, Adjacent neighbor count is 1
    Adjacent with neighbor 2.2.2.2
  Suppress hello for 0 neighbor(s)
```

The next step is to verify the configured redundancy. First, verify the route for the 150.4.4.0/24 subnet from R1. This should be received via the Virtual Link because of the better OSPF metric over that of the tunnel interface. The show ip route command shows the following:

```
R1#show ip route 150.4.4.0 255.255.255.0
Routing entry for 150.4.4.0/24
  Known via "ospf 1", distance 110, metric 148
  Tag 333, type extern 1
```

```
Last update from 10.0.0.6 on Serial0/1, 00:15:32 ago
Routing Descriptor Blocks:
* 10.0.0.6, from 4.4.4.4, 00:15:32 ago, via Serial0/1
    Route metric is 148, traffic share count is 1
    Route tag 333
```

Next, a simple ping can be used to verify connectivity. Additionally, you can also use Traceroute to see the path R1 will take to this subnet:

```
R1#traceroute 150.4.4.4

Type escape sequence to abort.
Tracing the route to 150.4.4.4

  1 10.0.0.6 4 msec 0 msec 0 msec
  2 10.0.0.14 0 msec *  0 msec
```

Next, test your redundant configuration by shutting down the Serial link between R3 and R1:

```
R3(config)#interface serial 0/1
R3(config-if)#shutdown
R3(config-if)#
*Mar  1 15:00:30.711: %OSPF-5-ADJCHG: Process 3, Nbr 1.1.1.1 on Serial0/1 from
FULL to DOWN, Neighbor Down: Interface down or detached
*Mar  1 15:00:32.711: %LINK-5-CHANGED: Interface Serial0/1, changed state to
administratively down
*Mar  1 15:00:33.711: %LINEPROTO-5-UPDOWN: Line protocol on Interface Serial0/1,
changed state to down
*Mar  1 15:00:35.787: %OSPF-5-ADJCHG: Process 3, Nbr 1.1.1.1 on OSPF_VL0 from
FULL to DOWN, Neighbor Down: Interface down or detached
```

Next, verify that the tunnel between R3 and R2 is still up using the show ip ospf neighbor command on either router:

```
R3#show ip ospf neighbor

Neighbor ID     Pri   State           Dead Time   Address         Interface
2.2.2.2           0   FULL/ -         00:00:34    172.16.1.2      Tunnel0
2.2.2.2           0   FULL/ -         00:00:31    10.0.0.9        Serial1/1
4.4.4.4           0   FULL/ -         00:00:36    10.0.0.14       Serial0/0
```

And finally, on R1, use the show ip route command again to verify that the 150.4.4.0/24 route is now received via R2:

```
R1#show ip route 150.4.4.0 255.255.255.0
Routing entry for 150.4.4.0/24
  Known via "ospf 1", distance 110, metric 11259
```

```
Tag 333, type extern 1
Last update from 10.0.0.2 on Serial0/0, 00:01:58 ago
Routing Descriptor Blocks:
* 10.0.0.2, from 4.4.4.4, 00:01:58 ago, via Serial0/0
    Route metric is 11259, traffic share count is 1
    Route tag 333
```

And finally, a Traceroute can be used to verify the path to the 150.4.4.0/24 subnet. Following this, a simple ping is used to verify IP connectivity:

```
R1#traceroute 150.4.4.4

Type escape sequence to abort.
Tracing the route to 150.4.4.4

  1 10.0.0.2 0 msec 0 msec 4 msec
  2 172.16.1.3 4 msec 4 msec 4 msec
  3 10.0.0.14 4 msec *  4 msec


R1#ping 150.4.4.4

Type escape sequence to abort.
Sending 5, 100-byte ICMP Echos to 150.4.4.4, timeout is 2 seconds:
!!!!!
Success rate is 100 percent (5/5), round-trip min/avg/max = 4/6/8 ms
```

Task 7

To complete this task, you need to force OSPF on R1 to advertise a default route, which will allow the other routers in the domain to reach the 150.1.1.0/24 subnet without explicitly advertising it using OSPF. This is performed using the default-information originate always command on R1 as follows:

```
R1(config)#router ospf 1
R1(config-router)#default-information originate always
R1(config-router)#end
```

Verify your solution by testing for connectivity from R4 to R1. First, use the show ip route command to verify that the specific entry is NOT in the routing table. Instead, R4 should only be receiving a default route, which it would use to reach that subnet:

```
R4#show ip route 150.1.1.0 255.255.255.0 longer-prefixes
Codes: C - connected, S - static, R - RIP, M - mobile, B - BGP
       D - EIGRP, EX - EIGRP external, O - OSPF, IA - OSPF inter area
       N1 - OSPF NSSA external type 1, N2 - OSPF NSSA external type 2
```

```
E1 - OSPF external type 1, E2 - OSPF external type 2
i - IS-IS, su - IS-IS summary, L1 - IS-IS level-1, L2 - IS-IS level-2
ia - IS-IS inter area, * - candidate default, U - per-user static route
o - ODR, P - periodic downloaded static route

Gateway of last resort is 10.0.0.13 to network 0.0.0.0
```

Following this, use a simple ping to verify connectivity to the 150.1.1.0/24 subnet from R4:

```
R4#ping 150.1.1.1

Type escape sequence to abort.
Sending 5, 100-byte ICMP Echos to 150.1.1.1, timeout is 2 seconds:
!!!!!
Success rate is 100 percent (5/5), round-trip min/avg/max = 4/4/4 ms
```

Task 8

```
R3(config)#interface serial 0/0
R3(config-if)#ip ospf authentication
R3(config-if)#ip ospf authentication-key ROUTE
R3(config-if)#end


R4(config)#interface serial 0/0
R4(config-if)#ip ospf authentication
R4(config-if)#ip ospf authentication-key ROUTE
R4(config-if)#end
```

Following this configuration, use the show ip ospf interface command for verification:

```
R3#show ip ospf interface serial 0/0
Serial0/0 is up, line protocol is up
  Internet Address 10.0.0.13/30, Area 4
  Process ID 3, Router ID 3.3.3.3, Network Type POINT_TO_POINT, Cost: 64
  Enabled by interface config, including secondary ip addresses
  Transmit Delay is 1 sec, State POINT_TO_POINT
  Timer intervals configured, Hello 10, Dead 40, Wait 40, Retransmit 5
    oob-resync timeout 40
    Hello due in 00:00:05
  Supports Link-local Signaling (LLS)
  Index 1/4, flood queue length 0
  Next 0x0(0)/0x0(0)
  Last flood scan length is 1, maximum is 7
  Last flood scan time is 0 msec, maximum is 4 msec
  Neighbor Count is 1, Adjacent neighbor count is 1
    Adjacent with neighbor 4.4.4.4
  Suppress hello for 0 neighbor(s)
  Simple password authentication enabled
```

Task 9

This task requires a little more configuration than the previous task. MD5 authentication must be enabled on all interfaces in area 0, include the Virtual Link:

```
R1(config)#router ospf 1
R1(config-router)#area 0 authentication message-digest
R1(config-router)#area 1 virtual-link 3.3.3.3 message-digest-key 1 md5 ROUTE
R1(config-router)#exit
R1(config)#interface serial 0/0
R1(config-if)#ip ospf message-digest-key 1 md5 ROUTE
R1(config-if)#exit
R1(config)#interface serial 0/1
R1(config-if)#ip ospf message-digest-key 1 md5 ROUTE
R1(config-if)#end

R2(config)#router ospf 2
R2(config-router)#area 0 authentication message-digest
R2(config-router)#exit
R2(config)#interface serial 0/0
R2(config-if)#ip ospf message-digest-key 1 md5 ROUTE
R2(config-if)#exit
R2(config)#interface tunnel 0
R2(config-if)#ip ospf message-digest-key 1 md5 ROUTE
R2(config-if)#end

R3(config)#router ospf 3
R3(config-router)#area 0 authentication message-digest
R3(config-router)#area 1 virtual-link 1.1.1.1 message-digest-key 1 md5 ROUTE
R3(config-router)#exit
R3(config)#interface serial 0/1
R3(config-if)#ip ospf message-digest-key 1 md5 ROUTE
R3(config-if)#exit
R3(config)#interface tunnel 0
R3(config-if)#ip ospf message-digest-key 1 md5 ROUTE
R3(config-if)#end
```

Following this configuration, use the show ip ospf neighbor command to ensure that all OSPF adjacencies are up

```
R1#show ip ospf neighbor

Neighbor ID     Pri   State         Dead Time    Address       Interface
3.3.3.3          0    FULL/  -       -            10.0.0.6      OSPF_VL0
2.2.2.2          0    FULL/  -      00:00:36      10.0.0.2      Serial0/0
3.3.3.3          0    FULL/  -      00:00:34      10.0.0.6      Serial0/1

R2#show ip ospf neighbor

Neighbor ID     Pri   State         Dead Time    Address       Interface
3.3.3.3          0    FULL/  -      00:00:35      172.16.1.3    Tunnel0
```

```
1.1.1.1          0   FULL/  -      00:00:32   10.0.0.1     Serial0/0
3.3.3.3          0   FULL/  -      00:00:32   10.0.0.10    Serial0/1


R3#show ip ospf neighbor

Neighbor ID    Pri  State        Dead Time  Address      Interface
2.2.2.2          0   FULL/  -      00:00:32   172.16.1.2   Tunnel0
1.1.1.1          0   FULL/  -         -       10.0.0.5     OSPF_VL0
1.1.1.1          0   FULL/  -      00:00:32   10.0.0.5     Serial0/1
2.2.2.2          0   FULL/  -      00:00:39   10.0.0.9     Serial1/1
4.4.4.4          0   FULL/  -      00:00:35   10.0.0.14    Serial0/0
```

Additionally, you can also use the show ip ospf command to view area authentication types:

```
R3#show ip ospf
 Routing Process "ospf 3" with ID 3.3.3.3
 Start time: 01:08:09.448, Time elapsed: 01:48:45.536
 Supports only single TOS(TOS0) routes
 Supports opaque LSA
 Supports Link-local Signaling (LLS)
 Supports area transit capability
 It is an area border and autonomous system boundary router
 Redistributing External Routes from,
    connected, includes subnets in redistribution
 Router is not originating router-LSAs with maximum metric
 Initial SPF schedule delay 5000 msecs
 Minimum hold time between two consecutive SPFs 10000 msecs
 Maximum wait time between two consecutive SPFs 10000 msecs
 Incremental-SPF disabled
 Minimum LSA interval 5 secs
 Minimum LSA arrival 1000 msecs
 LSA group pacing timer 240 secs
 Interface flood pacing timer 33 msecs
 Retransmission pacing timer 66 msecs
 Number of external LSA 3. Checksum Sum 0x0123D6
 Number of opaque AS LSA 0. Checksum Sum 0x000000
 Number of DCbitless external and opaque AS LSA 0
 Number of DoNotAge external and opaque AS LSA 0
 Number of areas in this router is 4. 3 normal 1 stub 0 nssa
 Number of areas transit capable is 1
 External flood list length 0
    Area BACKBONE(0)
        Number of interfaces in this area is 2
        Area has message digest authentication
        SPF algorithm last executed 00:00:35.112 ago
        SPF algorithm executed 23 times
        Area ranges are
        Number of LSA 14. Checksum Sum 0x07C202
        Number of opaque link LSA 0. Checksum Sum 0x000000
        Number of DCbitless LSA 0
```

```
         Number of indication LSA 0
         Number of DoNotAge LSA 2
         Flood list length 0
     Area 1
         Number of interfaces in this area is 2 (1 loopback)
         This area has transit capability: Virtual Link Endpoint
         Area has no authentication
         SPF algorithm last executed 00:00:35.116 ago
         SPF algorithm executed 22 times
         Area ranges are
         Number of LSA 13. Checksum Sum 0x05E94A
         Number of opaque link LSA 0. Checksum Sum 0x000000
         Number of DCbitless LSA 0
         Number of indication LSA 0
         Number of DoNotAge LSA 0
         Flood list length 0
     Area 2
         Number of interfaces in this area is 1
         It is a stub area
           generates stub default route with cost 1
         Area has no authentication
         SPF algorithm last executed 00:00:36.588 ago
         SPF algorithm executed 10 times
         Area ranges are
         Number of LSA 13. Checksum Sum 0x06D454
         Number of opaque link LSA 0. Checksum Sum 0x000000
         Number of DCbitless LSA 0
         Number of indication LSA 0
         Number of DoNotAge LSA 0
         Flood list length 0
     Area 4
         Number of interfaces in this area is 1
         Area has no authentication
         SPF algorithm last executed 00:00:36.592 ago
         SPF algorithm executed 16 times
         Area ranges are
         Number of LSA 11. Checksum Sum 0x06D395
         Number of opaque link LSA 0. Checksum Sum 0x000000
         Number of DCbitless LSA 0
         Number of indication LSA 0
         Number of DoNotAge LSA 0
         Flood list length 0
```

Task 10

```
R1(config)#router ospf 1
R1(config-router)#max-lsa 100
R1(config-router)#end

R2(config)#router ospf 2
R2(config-router)#max-lsa 100
R2(config-router)#end
```

```
R3(config)#router ospf 3
R3(config-router)#max-lsa 100
R3(config-router)#end


R4(config)#router ospf 4
R4(config-router)#max-lsa 100
R4(config-router)#end
```

Finally, verify your configuration using the show ip ospf command as follows:

```
R1#show ip ospf
 Routing Process "ospf 1" with ID 1.1.1.1
 Start time: 01:00:47.683, Time elapsed: 02:02:55.696
 Supports only single TOS(TOS0) routes
 Supports opaque LSA
 Supports Link-local Signaling (LLS)
 Supports area transit capability
 Maximum number of non self-generated LSA allowed 100
    Threshold for warning message 75%
    Ignore-time 5 minutes, reset-time 10 minutes
    Ignore-count allowed 5, current ignore-count 0
 It is an area border and autonomous system boundary router
 Redistributing External Routes from,
 Router is not originating router-LSAs with maximum metric
 Initial SPF schedule delay 5000 msecs
 Minimum hold time between two consecutive SPFs 10000 msecs
 Maximum wait time between two consecutive SPFs 10000 msecs
 Incremental-SPF disabled
 Minimum LSA interval 5 secs
 Minimum LSA arrival 1000 msecs
 LSA group pacing timer 240 secs
 Interface flood pacing timer 33 msecs
 Retransmission pacing timer 66 msecs
 Number of external LSA 3. Checksum Sum 0x022020
 Number of opaque AS LSA 0. Checksum Sum 0x000000
 Number of DCbitless external and opaque AS LSA 0
 Number of DoNotAge external and opaque AS LSA 0
 Number of areas in this router is 2. 2 normal 0 stub 0 nssa
 Number of areas transit capable is 1
 External flood list length 0
    Area BACKBONE(0)
        Number of interfaces in this area is 3 (1 loopback)
        Area has message digest authentication
        SPF algorithm last executed 00:00:28.819 ago
        SPF algorithm executed 4 times
        Area ranges are
        Number of LSA 14. Checksum Sum 0x0DAB1F
        Number of opaque link LSA 0. Checksum Sum 0x000000
        Number of DCbitless LSA 0
        Number of indication LSA 0
```

```
        Number of DoNotAge LSA 5
        Flood list length 0
    Area 1
        Number of interfaces in this area is 1
        This area has transit capability: Virtual Link Endpoint
        Area has no authentication
        SPF algorithm last executed 00:00:28.823 ago
        SPF algorithm executed 4 times
        Area ranges are
        Number of LSA 13. Checksum Sum 0x094577
        Number of opaque link LSA 0. Checksum Sum 0x000000
        Number of DCbitless LSA 0
        Number of indication LSA 0
        Number of DoNotAge LSA 0
        Flood list length 0
```

DEVICE CONFIGURATIONS

```
R1#show running-config
Building configuration...

Current configuration : 1419 bytes
!
version 12.4
service timestamps debug datetime msec
service timestamps log datetime msec
no service password-encryption
!
hostname R1
!
boot-start-marker
boot-end-marker
!
no logging console
enable secret 5 $1$ZHZP$BfOgaK4Ei7zfUol9D8zpV/
!
no aaa new-model
no network-clock-participate slot 1
no network-clock-participate wic 0
ip cef
!
no ip domain lookup
ip auth-proxy max-nodata-conns 3
ip admission max-nodata-conns 3
!
ipv6 unicast-routing
!
interface Loopback0
 ip address 1.1.1.1 255.255.255.255
```

```
 ip ospf 1 area 0
!
interface FastEthernet0/0
 ip address 150.1.1.1 255.255.255.0
 loopback
 duplex auto
 speed auto
 no keepalive
!
interface Serial0/0
 ip address 10.0.0.1 255.255.255.252
 ip ospf message-digest-key 1 md5 ROUTE
 ip ospf 1 area 0
 no fair-queue
!
interface Serial0/1
 ip address 10.0.0.5 255.255.255.252
 ip ospf message-digest-key 1 md5 ROUTE
 ip ospf 1 area 1
!
router ospf 1
 router-id 1.1.1.1
 log-adjacency-changes
 max-lsa 100
 area 0 authentication message-digest
 area 1 virtual-link 3.3.3.3 message-digest-key 1 md5 ROUTE
 default-information originate always
!
ip forward-protocol nd
!
ip http server
no ip http secure-server
!
control-plane
!
voice-port 1/0/0
!
voice-port 1/0/1
!
voice-port 1/1/0
!
voice-port 1/1/1
!
line con 0
line aux 0
line vty 0 4
 privilege level 15
 password cisco
 login
!
end
R1#
```

```
R2#show running-config
Building configuration...

Current configuration : 1531 bytes
!
version 12.4
service timestamps debug datetime msec
service timestamps log datetime msec
no service password-encryption
!
hostname R2
!
boot-start-marker
boot-end-marker
!
no logging console
enable secret 5 $1$FsT/$/viPNrSsewWFUCy/QbD5lO
!
no aaa new-model
!
ip cef
no ip domain lookup
!
ipv6 unicast-routing
!
interface Loopback0
 ip address 2.2.2.2 255.255.255.0
!
interface Tunnel0
 description 'Backbone Tunnel Across Stub Area'
 ip address 172.16.1.2 255.255.255.0
 ip ospf message-digest-key 1 md5 ROUTE
 tunnel source Serial0/1
 tunnel destination 10.0.0.10
!
interface FastEthernet0/0
 ip address 150.2.2.2 255.255.255.0
 loopback
 half-duplex
 no keepalive
!
interface Serial0/0
 ip address 10.0.0.2 255.255.255.252
 ip ospf message-digest-key 1 md5 ROUTE
 clock rate 2000000
 no fair-queue
!
interface FastEthernet0/1
 no ip address
 shutdown
 half-duplex
!
```

```
interface Serial0/1
 ip address 10.0.0.9 255.255.255.252
 clock rate 2000000
!
router ospf 2
 router-id 2.2.2.2
 log-adjacency-changes
 max-lsa 100
 area 0 authentication message-digest
 area 2 stub no-summary
 network 2.2.2.2 0.0.0.0 area 0
 network 10.0.0.0 0.0.0.3 area 0
 network 10.0.0.8 0.0.0.3 area 2
 network 150.2.2.0 0.0.0.255 area 0
 network 172.16.1.0 0.0.0.255 area 0
!
ip http server
ip forward-protocol nd
!
control-plane
!
mgcp behavior g729-variants static-pt
!
gatekeeper
 shutdown
!
line con 0
line aux 0
line vty 0 4
 privilege level 15
 password cisco
 login
!
end

R2#



R3#show running-config
Building configuration...

Current configuration : 1860 bytes
!
version 12.4
service timestamps debug datetime msec
service timestamps log datetime msec
no service password-encryption
!
hostname R3
!
boot-start-marker
boot-end-marker
```

```
!
no logging console
enable secret 5 $1$mOsw$hNy9.KzOvGX2XmLabNBOT/
!
no aaa new-model
!
ip cef
no ip domain lookup
!
ipv6 unicast-routing
!
interface Loopback0
 ip address 3.3.3.3 255.255.255.255
 ip ospf 3 area 1
!
interface Tunnel0
 description 'Backbone Tunnel Across Stub Area'
 ip address 172.16.1.3 255.255.255.0
 ip ospf message-digest-key 1 md5 ROUTE
 ip ospf 3 area 0
 tunnel source Serial1/1
 tunnel destination 10.0.0.9
!
interface FastEthernet0/0
 ip address 150.3.3.3 255.255.255.0
 loopback
 half-duplex
 no keepalive
!
interface Serial0/0
 ip address 10.0.0.13 255.255.255.252
 ip ospf authentication
 ip ospf authentication-key ROUTE
 ip ospf 3 area 4
 no fair-queue
!
interface Ethernet0/1
 no ip address
 shutdown
 half-duplex
!
interface Serial0/1
 ip address 10.0.0.6 255.255.255.252
 ip ospf message-digest-key 1 md5 ROUTE
 ip ospf 3 area 1
 clock rate 2000000
!
interface FastEthernet1/0
 no ip address
 shutdown
 half-duplex
!
```

```
interface Serial1/0
 no ip address
 shutdown
!
interface Serial1/1
 ip address 10.0.0.10 255.255.255.252
 ip ospf 3 area 2
!
router ospf 3
 router-id 3.3.3.3
 log-adjacency-changes
 max-lsa 100
 area 0 authentication message-digest
 area 1 virtual-link 1.1.1.1 message-digest-key 1 md5 ROUTE
 area 2 stub
 redistribute connected subnets route-map LAN-SUBNET
!
ip http server
ip forward-protocol nd
!
route-map LAN-SUBNET permit 10
 match interface Ethernet0/0
 set metric-type type-1
 set tag 333
!
control-plane
!
mgcp behavior g729-variants static-pt
!
gatekeeper
 shutdown
!
line con 0
line aux 0
line vty 0 4
 privilege level 15
 password cisco
 login
!
end

R3#


R4#show running-config
Building configuration...

Current configuration : 1363 bytes
!
version 12.4
service timestamps debug datetime msec
service timestamps log datetime msec
```

```
no service password-encryption
!
hostname R4
!
boot-start-marker
boot-end-marker
!
no logging console
enable secret 5 $1$M/kd$Eb360Ygk4rDpv7JtJeRbP.
!
no aaa new-model
no network-clock-participate slot 1
no network-clock-participate wic 0
ip cef
!
ip auth-proxy max-nodata-conns 3
ip admission max-nodata-conns 3
!
ipv6 unicast-routing
!
interface Loopback0
 ip address 4.4.4.4 255.255.255.255
!
interface FastEthernet0/0
 ip address 150.4.4.4 255.255.255.0
 loopback
 duplex auto
 speed auto
 no keepalive
!
interface Serial0/0
 ip address 10.0.0.14 255.255.255.252
 ip ospf authentication
 ip ospf authentication-key ROUTE
 no fair-queue
 clock rate 2000000
!
interface Serial0/1
 no ip address
 shutdown
!
interface Serial0/2
 no ip address
 shutdown
!
router ospf 4
 router-id 4.4.4.4
 log-adjacency-changes
 max-lsa 100
 redistribute connected metric-type 1 subnets tag 333
 network 4.4.4.4 0.0.0.0 area 4
 network 10.0.0.12 0.0.0.3 area 4
```

```
!
ip forward-protocol nd
!
ip http server
no ip http secure-server
!
control-plane
!
voice-port 1/0/0
!
voice-port 1/0/1
!
voice-port 1/1/0
!
voice-port 1/1/1
!
line con 0
line aux 0
line vty 0 4
 privilege level 15
 password cisco
 login
!
end

R4#
```

Lightning Source UK Ltd.
Milton Keynes UK
UKHW052007010721
386492UK00003B/40